# The World Book Atlas

# The World Book Atlas

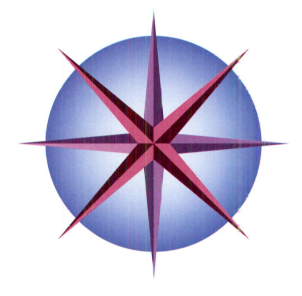

**World Book, Inc.**

a Scott Fetzer company

Chicago London Sydney Toronto

# Staff

**Publisher emeritus**    *William H. Nault*

**President**    *John E. Frere*

## Editorial

**Vice president, editor in chief**
*Robert J. Janus*

**Managing editor**
*Maureen Mostyn Liebenson*

**Associate editors**
*Sharon Nowakowski*
*Patricia Ohlenroth*

**Senior editor**
*Melissa Tucker*

**Permissions editor**
*Janet T. Peterson*

## Art

**Executive director**
*Roberta Dimmer*

**Art director**
*Wilma Stevens*

**Senior photographs editor**
*Sandra Dyrlund*

## Product production

**Vice president, production and technology**
*Daniel N. Bach*

**Director, manufacturing/pre-press**
*Sandra Van den Broucke*

**Manufacturing manager**
*Barbara Podczerwinski*

**Senior production manager**
*Randi Park*

World Book, Inc.
525 W. Monroe
Chicago, IL 60661

**Visit our Web site at**
**http://www.worldbook.com**

Maps of the world © Rand McNally & Company

Some illustrative material on pages vi–xxvi from *Goode's World Atlas*, © Rand McNally & Company

ISBN 0-7166-2699-3

Library of Congress Catalog Card Number 97-60892

Printed in the United States of America

1 2 3 4 5 6 7 8 9 10 02 01 00 99 98 97

## Acknowledgments

Illustration credits read from top to bottom and from left to right on each page. Illustrations that extend over two pages are credited to the lefthand page.

**vi,** *Artwork* © Mitchell Beazley Pub. Ltd. 1973 as *The Good Earth.* **vii,** © John Eastcott/Yva Momatiuk, Woodfin Camp, Inc.; © Marty Snyderman; © Jeff Foott, Bruce Coleman Ltd. **viii,** © Leo Touchet, Woodfin Camp, Inc.; Henry Ausloss, World Wildlife Fund from Bruce Coleman Ltd. **ix,** World Book *diagrams;* Terraphotographics/ BPS; Carlos Elmer, Shostal; Robert Glaze; © Loren McIntyre. **x,** *Artwork* Brian Delf. **xi,** Ronald Thompson/Frank W. Lane, Bruce Coleman Ltd.; © Jim Brandenburg Woodfin Camp, Inc.; Charlie Ott, Bruce Coleman Ltd. **xii,** © David Muench; World Book *artwork.* **xiii,** © Dwight Kuhn; *Artwork* © Mitchell Beazley Pub. Ltd. 1973 as *The Good Earth.* **xiv,** Norman Tomalin, Bruce Coleman Ltd.

**xv,** © David Muench; © Jeff Foott. **xvi,** *Animals* Coral Mula; *trees* Donald Myall. **xvii,** E. R. Degginger; Mike Price, Bruce Coleman Ltd. **xviii,** Hutchison Library; *Artwork* Bob Bampton/ The Garden Studio. **xix,** G. R. Plage, Bruce Coleman Ltd. **xx,** © Jodi Cobb, Woodfin Camp, Inc.; *Artwork* Jim Robins. **xxii,** © Dwight R. Kuhn; © J. Alsop, Bruce Coleman Inc.; © Dwight R. Kuhn. **xxiii,** E. R. Degginger; *Artwork* Donald Myall. **xxiv,** W. E. Ruth, Bruce Coleman Inc. **xxv,** Phil Degginger from E. R. Degginger; © Jim Brandenburg, Woodfin Camp, Inc.; *Wolf* Jean Hellmer for World Book; *other animals* Coral Mula. **xxvi,** World Book *artwork;* © B. and C. Alexander. **xxvii,** TSW/Chicago Ltd.; U.S. Naval Photographic Center; *Artwork* Jim Robins.

Locator maps on pages xvi, xviii, xxi, xxiii xxiv, xxvii were created exclusively for *The World Book Atlas.*

# Contents

The Ocean   vi
Mountains   viii
Rivers and Streams   x
Lakes and Ponds   xii
Swamps, Marshes, and Bogs   xiv
Tropical Forests   xvi
Deserts   xviii
Grasslands   xx
Midlatitude Forests   xxii
Subarctic Cold Lands   xxiv
Polar Caps   xxvi

World Time Zones   xxviii

Using the Atlas   xxx

**REFERENCE MAPS**
Map Symbols and Index Map   1
World   2-3

**EUROPE**   4-5
Northern Europe   6-7
British Isles   8-9
Central Europe   10-11
Belgium, Netherlands, and
    Luxembourg   12
Switzerland   13
France and the Alps   14-15
Spain and Portugal   16-17
Italy   18-19
Southeastern Europe   20-21
Baltic and Moscow Regions   22-23

**ASIA**   24-25
Northwest Asia   26-27
Northeast Asia   28-29
China, Japan, and Korea   30-31
Northeastern China and Korea   32-33
Eastern and Southeastern
    China   34-35
Japan   36-37
Southeastern Asia   38-39
Myanmar, Thailand, and
    Indochina   40-41
India, Pakistan, and Southwestern
    Asia   42-43
Northern India and Pakistan   44-45
Southern India and Sri Lanka   46
Southern Arabian Peninsula   47
The Middle East   48-49
Israel and Southern Lebanon   50-51

**AFRICA**   52-53
Western North Africa   54-55
Eastern North Africa   56-57
Southern Africa   58-59
Egypt and Sudan   60-61
Northern Africa   62-63
West Africa   64-65
Southern Africa and
    Madagascar   66-67

**AUSTRALIA**   68-69
Eastern Australia   70-71
New Zealand   72

**ANTARCTICA**   73

**SOUTH AMERICA**   74-75
Northern South America   76-77
Southern South America   78
Southeastern Brazil   79
Central Argentina and Chile   80-81
Peru, Bolivia, and Western
    Brazil   82-83
Colombia, Ecuador, Venezuela, and
    Guyana   84-85

**NORTH AMERICA**   86-87
Middle America and Caribbean   88-89
Mexico   90-91
Central America   92-93
Caribbean Region   94-95
Canada   96-97
United States of America   98-99
Alaska and the Yukon   100-101
Southwestern Canada   102-103
South-Central Canada   104-105
Southeastern Canada   106-107
Northeastern United States   108-109
Great Lakes Region   110-111
Southeastern United States   112-113
Mississippi Valley   114-115
Southern Great Plains   116-117
Northern Great Plains   118-119
Southern Rocky Mountains   120-121
Northwestern United States   122-123
California, Nevada, and
    Hawaii   124-125

**PACIFIC AND INDIAN
    OCEANS**   126-127

**ATLANTIC OCEAN**   128

Index   129-192

# The Ocean

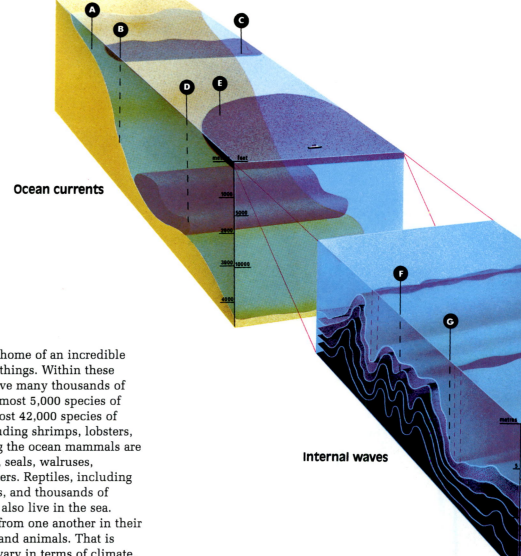

**Ocean currents**

**Internal waves**

More than 70 percent of the world's surface is covered by oceans. Oceans have been given different names, such as Atlantic and Pacific, but they are actually all one large, interconnected body of water, swept by winds that create waves, and moved by tides caused by the tug of the moon.

Oceans, often known as seas, are deep as well as vast. The bottoms of some seas lie more than 6 miles (10 kilometers) below their surfaces. Great mountains can rise from their floors and stick out above the water as islands.

Oceans are very important parts of the earth. The action of the sun's heat pouring down on an ocean turns enormous amounts of its surface into water vapor. This vapor rises into the air, cools, and forms clouds, which are carried by wind. When clouds are cooled even more, much of the water vapor forming them turns back into water and falls as rain or snow. This moisture creates the fresh water of rivers and lakes. It also provides the ground water that helps plants to grow, and thus animal life to exist.

Ocean water moves constantly in streams called currents. Currents are caused by a combination of the wind, the sun's heat, the salinity of the water, and the earth's rotation. The temperature of a current affects the temperature of the air above it. Therefore, warm currents bring warm air and water to some places, and cool currents bring cool air and water to other places. Without the help of the Equatorial Current, the Gulf Stream, and other currents, the air around the planet would be hotter both day and night near the equator and cooler both day and night at high latitudes.

Ocean water is salty. There is enough salt in the sea to cover every bit of dry land with a layer of salt 150 feet (45 meters) high. Actually, much of this salt originally came from the land. For countless millions of years, rivers that were supplied by rainfall runoff moved down mountainsides and across rolling lands. These rivers washed millions of tons of minerals out of the channels through which they flowed. The minerals, mainly various kinds of salts, were carried along by the rivers. Eventually, the rivers flowed into the ocean and released their cargoes of mud and salt. This accumulation of salt in its water keeps the ocean salty. Only pure water evaporates from its surface when water vapor forms.

Oceans are the home of an incredible number of living things. Within these bodies of water live many thousands of species of fish; almost 5,000 species of sponges; and almost 42,000 species of crustaceans, including shrimps, lobsters, and crabs. Among the ocean mammals are whales, dolphins, seals, walruses, manatees, and otters. Reptiles, including turtles and snakes, and thousands of species of worms also live in the sea. Oceans do differ from one another in their species of plants and animals. That is because the seas vary in terms of climate.

All these animals, together with ocean plants, are members of complex ecological systems. The ocean food chain begins with microscopic plantlike organisms. These organisms, called phytoplankton, drift in masses near the sunlit surfaces and give the water a greenish tint. Like green plants, they use sunlight to manufacture food for themselves. As a by-product of this process, the phytoplankton produce tiny amounts of oxygen. This oxygen is used by sea animals and plants. It also helps replenish the oxygen in the earth's air.

Floating among the phytoplankton are trillions of microscopic animals called zooplankton. These creatures cannot make their own food. Instead they feed on phytoplankton. Zooplankton themselves are eaten by small fish and crustaceans, which are eaten by bigger fish and other creatures. They, in turn, are food for still larger animals, such as 60-foot-long (18-meter-long) sperm whales. But without the tiny phytoplankton, the earth's oceans could not support this complex food chain.

**A continental shelf** is the land around a continent that slopes deeply underwater (**A**). Farther offshore, the continental slope (**B**) plunges to the ocean bottom. Ocean characteristics vary greatly. Below the warm Gulf Stream (**C**) off the United States east coast, moves a cold current (**D**). Near its source, the Gulf Stream borders the Sargasso Sea (**E**), a region of slow ocean currents surrounded by a boundary of fast-moving currents. Waves beneath the ocean surface (**F**) are caused by differences in salt content, density, and temperature. These internal waves move up and down like surface waves (**G**). Sometimes a dark band (**H**) on the surface marks an internal wave. The internal wave motion (**I**) shows how deep water is held back while surface waves lunge forward. A beach's breakpoint and foreshore determine where waves break. For example, a breakpoint at position (**J**) and foreshore at position (**K**) would cause waves to break at position (**L**). When the moon is full or new, incoming tides are at their highest and outgoing tides are at their lowest. These tides are called spring tides. In the diagram, (**M-M**) shows the spring tidal range. At the quarters of the moon, tides are neither high nor low. Such tides are called neap tides. The neap tidal range is shown at (**N-N**). Location (**O**) shows the average tide level. Strong ocean waves wear away shoreline rocks, producing sand. Sand can be dry (**P**) or permanently wet (**Q**). Surface sand often has ripple marks (**R**) created when water recedes after each wave.

**Wind action** on the water produces surface waves. Waves travel forward in the direction of the wind.

**In the ocean,** fish often travel in schools—large groups of the same species. Here a school of grunts passes by coral formations. Grunts are known for making grunting sounds when taken from the water.

**Waves on a beach**

**The sea otter swims,** often on its back, in the North Pacific Ocean and near the shores of western North America and Siberia. This brown, furry animal floats in masses of seaweed called kelp.

# Mountains

About one-fifth of the earth's land surface is made up of mountains. Mountains are composed of rock formations that rise 2,000 feet (610 meters) or more above the surrounding land. There are also mountains underwater. Those rock formations, called submarine mountains, form islands or are part of the ocean floor.

On land, mountains may be rocky and barren, or they may be green with vegetation. They may have high pointed peaks and narrow ridges. Their sides, or slopes, are long, broad, or slanting. Often mountains are cut by deep, wide indentations called canyons or valleys. Due to the decrease in temperature as elevation increases, mountainsides are made up of a number of different environments.

Mountains are formed over enormous amounts of time by movements of the earth's rocky crust. In some places, sideways shifts of the crust make huge wavelike wrinkles or folds. These movements result in fold mountains such as the Jura Mountains of Europe and the Appalachian Mountains of eastern North America. In other places, the crust is broken into gigantic blocks that are pushed upward along a fracture line called a fault to form fault-block mountains. The Sierra Nevada of California is an example of fault-block mountains. Dome mountains such as the Harlech Dome in Wales are created when molten rock called magma is forced upward under the surface rock to form a blisterlike swelling. The volcanic mountains of Washington and Oregon were created by volcanic activity.

The top of a very high mountain is generally covered with ice and snow. But a little farther down the slope, melted

**Mount Saint Elias, Alaska,** is one of the highest peaks in North America. It stands in the Saint Elias Mountains, a rugged series of the highest coastal mountains in the world.

**An ibex** climbs a rocky slope in the Italian Alps. The thinness of the forest shows that the animal is nearing the timber line.

snow can provide moisture for lichens, mosses, and low-growing flowering plants that flourish where soil develops. This region is called the alpine zone. A number of species of insects, particularly springtails and bristletails, thrive in this region. Brightly colored butterflies flit among the flowers. The American Rocky Mountain goat and the European ibex live here too. Small animals such as conies, chipmunks, and mountain ground hogs also make their homes near a mountain's top.

The animals of the high mountain regions are especially fitted for their environment. Many have enlarged hearts and lungs, and their blood contains extra oxygen-bearing red corpuscles. These features help the animals survive in a mountaintop's thin air. When winter comes, most of the smaller creatures take shelter in burrows and live on seeds and hay stored during summer. Larger animals and even some birds simply move a short way down the mountainside. There the temperature is not as cold and food is still available.

A little below the alpine region is the timber line. This is the highest point at which a tree can survive without freezing. The tallest trees in this region are often bush-size dwarf willows, birches, aspens, spruces, firs, and pines. Each winter they are mostly covered by snow, which actually protects them from the terrible freezing wind of the mountaintop. These trees may, however, have some shoots that reach above the snow. At lower levels of mountains, the same kinds of trees can reach full size and form forests. Birds, squirrels, deer, and bears are at home in openings in these wooded areas.

The lower the elevation, the higher the temperature. If a mountain is in a place that gets plenty of rainfall, there will generally be a forest growing on its lower slopes. But if the mountain is in a dry region, its lower slopes will be covered with grassy meadow or maybe even desert. The animals that live here are not true "mountain animals." The same kinds of creatures may be found in other environments that feature similar conditions.

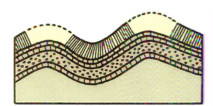

**Fold mountains** include the European Alps, *right*. The valleys and ridges that are characteristic of fold mountains are shown in the diagram above.

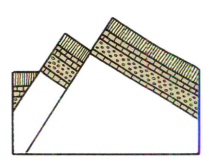

**Fault-block mountains** are found in the desert land near Las Vegas, Nevada, *right*. The diagram above shows the layers of cleanly broken sedimentary rock that are characteristic of fault-block mountains.

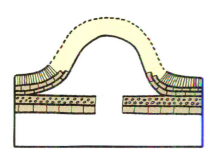

**Dome mountains,** such as Harlech Dome in Wales, *right*, are formed when the earth's crust rises into domes. The diagram above indicates that a dome's softer rock is eventually eroded.

**Volcanic mountains** include the Cascade Mountains of Washington and Oregon, *right*. Such mountains form when molten rock, or lava, from deep within the earth erupts and piles up on the surface. The diagram above shows the vents through which the lava moves.

# Rivers and Streams

Rivers and streams are bodies of water that flow through land in long passages called channels. They flow downhill and are fed by other waters that enrich them and increase their size. Eventually, they flow into another body of water, such as a larger river, a lake, or the ocean.

A river or stream channel is formed by the wearing away, or erosion, of the land by flowing water. The bottom of a channel is called the bed, and the sides are known as the banks. The channel of a small stream can be a few feet wide and less than a mile long. The channel of a large river, however, can be miles wide and can extend for thousands of miles.

A river often begins high on a mountain. It can start as trickles of water from melting snow, as a spring bubbling out of rocks, or as a stream flowing from a mountain lake. As the water flows along, it is fed by streams and smaller rivers. It becomes deeper and wider, and its size is increased further by rainfall.

A river or stream is a habitat for plant and animal life. The character of that life depends upon the temperature, depth, and speed of the water. A swift-moving, shallow mountain stream does not have much plant life. The exception is the jellylike algae that coat the rocky bottom. Black fly larvae inhabit the swift-moving stream. They use their tiny hooks to anchor themselves to rocks. These creatures have their food—microscopic

plants and animals—delivered to them by the swift-flowing water. The larvae, in turn, are a source of nourishment for such species of birds as dippers, or water ouzels, of western North America. These birds spend much of their time wading in streams and feeding on the insects there.

A larger, slow-moving river that is far from its mountain beginnings is a very different environment. Unlike a swift-flowing stream that sweeps its floor clean, the bed of a slow-moving river is filled with mud and silt. These materials form soil for plant life. "Forests" of algae or eel-grass often cover a sluggish river's bottom. Cattails and bulrushes grow thickly along the banks. Water lilies and similar plants float on the surface. Fish such as pike and bass lurk among the bottom greenery and dart out to snap up frogs and smaller fishes. Muskrats use cattails and other plants both as food and to line the insides of riverbank burrows. Frogs attach their eggs to plants and rocks. Insects rely on the river plants as resting places.

Many kinds of insects burrow in the mud below the water. They are food for such fish as carp. Predatory swimming insects, including dragonfly nymphs and diving beetles, often thrive in surface waters where light is more plentiful. Small fish, frogs, otters, and such birds as kingfishers are also among the creatures

that make these waters their regular hunting place. And in parts of Africa, warm, slow rivers are the natural habitat of hippopotamuses. Sometimes, a river changes its course to take a more direct path to the sea. The river may deposit earth in such a way that a river channel is cut off from the main stream. When this happens, an oxbow lake may form. Oxbow lakes are crescent-shaped, shallow, and often filled with sediment.

The place where a river empties into the sea is called the mouth. A low plain made up of clay, gravel, sand, and other sediments at a river's mouth is known as a delta, and a deep, broad mouth is called an estuary.

In an estuary, there is a mingling of fresh water and saltwater. This mixing creates a different kind of environment for life. The most common kind of estuary animal is the oyster. Hundreds of thousands of oysters may cover an estuary's bottom. Shrimps, crabs, and such fish as flounder are typical dwellers of this environment. Such sea plants as turtle grass and sea lettuce can also thrive in the quiet shallow, salty environment where a river and the ocean meet.

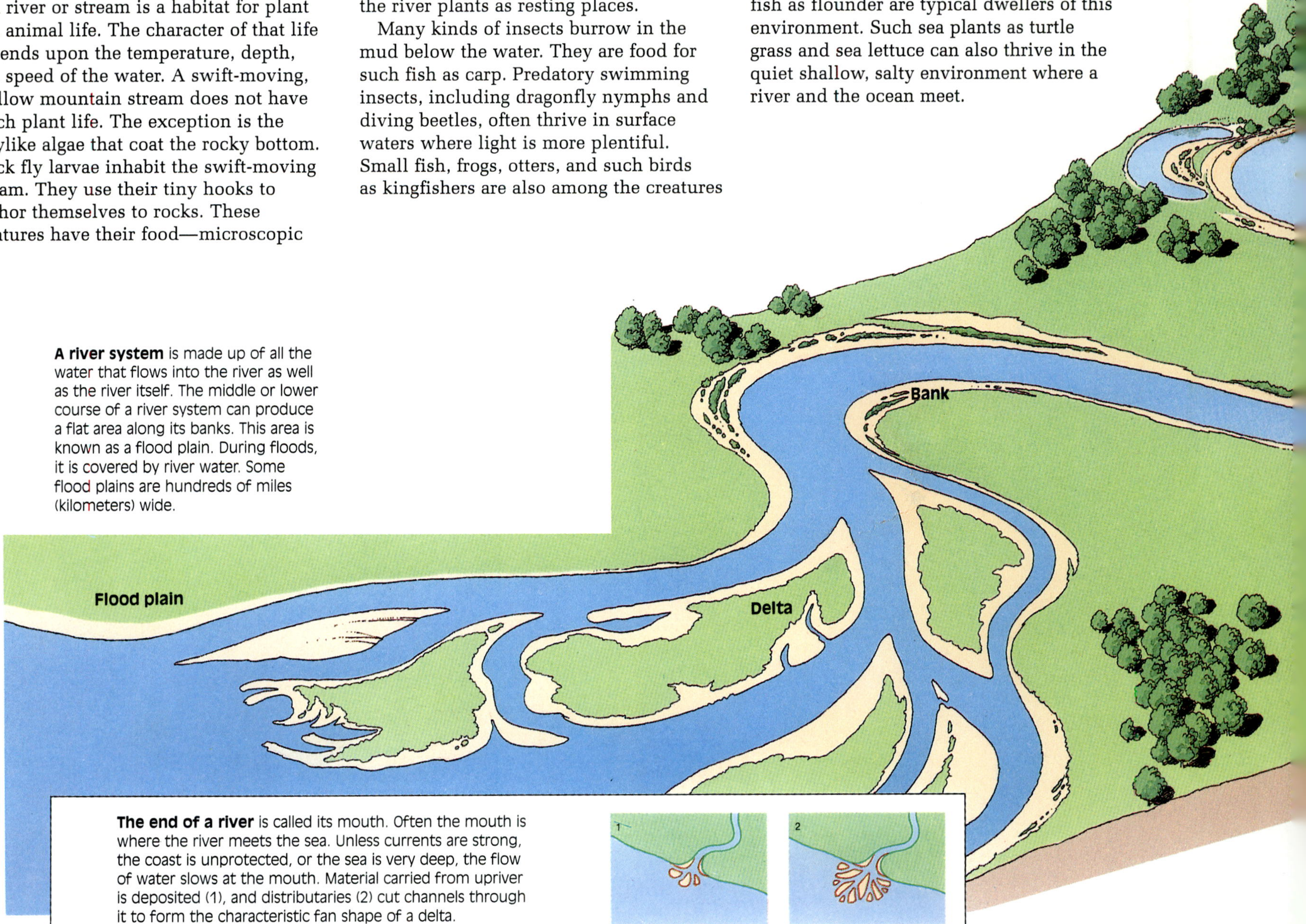

**A river system** is made up of all the water that flows into the river as well as the river itself. The middle or lower course of a river system can produce a flat area along its banks. This area is known as a flood plain. During floods, it is covered by river water. Some flood plains are hundreds of miles (kilometers) wide.

**Flood plain**

**Bank**

**Delta**

**The end of a river** is called its mouth. Often the mouth is where the river meets the sea. Unless currents are strong, the coast is unprotected, or the sea is very deep, the flow of water slows at the mouth. Material carried from upriver is deposited (1), and distributaries (2) cut channels through it to form the characteristic fan shape of a delta.

Oxbow lake

**The flow of water** in most rivers is fastest in the upper courses. Salmon have to fight to reach their upstream spawning grounds.

**A river's slope** tends to flatten near the mouth, and the water slows down. Painted turtles are at home in this environment.

**The muddy Klamath River** enters the clean, blue water of the Pacific Ocean north of Redwood National Park in northern California.

# Lakes and Ponds

Lakes and ponds are bodies of standing water that are surrounded by land. Lakes, which are larger than ponds, may be formed in many ways. Some lakes are made by stranded blocks of ice and blocked rivers that result when glaciers melt. Others are formed by the slow accumulation of rain water in volcanic craters. Still others are caused by the gradual filling in of sink holes with ground water. Sinkholes are depressions in the earth caused by the collapse of underground rock.

Lakes can be fed in many ways. Some are fed by rivers and mountain streams. Others are supplied by underground springs or streams, as well as ground water replenishment. Some lakes have inlets but no outlets. The excess waters of these kinds of lakes do not drain away. Instead, they slowly evaporate.

The presence of a large lake can affect weather conditions for the land around it. In summer, a lake does not get as warm as the surrounding land. Cool winds blowing off the water help hold down the temperature of the land. In winter, a lake does not cool off as fast as the land. This helps keep the nearby land warmer, at least until the lake freezes. Then, the lake acts the same way as a cold land surface.

**Crater Lake** is located in an inactive volcano in the Cascade Mountains of Oregon. It is the deepest lake in the United States, measuring 1,932 feet (589 meters).

Lake waters are divided into distinct layers, which are determined by the amount of penetrating sunlight. Each descending layer receives less sunlight than the one above it, unless the water is very clear. Therefore, the deeper a layer is, the colder and darker its waters.

The different layers of a lake are inhabited by distinct communities of animal and plant life. These communities depend on one another for food. For example, microscopic plants that drift in a lake's upper waters are eaten by microscopic animals. Both the tiny plants and the tiny animals are called plankton. Plankton is eaten by fish that live near a lake's surface.

Many kinds of insects live in the upper water of a lake. Whirligig beetles swim in this region. Their divided eyes look both above and below the water. Backswimmers, another type of insect, reside just at the surface, and they swim faceup. Water striders actually walk *upon* the water, which for them is like solid ground. All these insects feed on other insects that fall or alight upon the quiet surface water.

Many of a lake's plants and animals live near the shore, in what is called the littoral zone. Here, snails and worms creep on plant stems, and predatory fish lurk among bulrushes and other water plants. In the shallows near the shore, water birds often hunt and use bits of plants as nesting material.

Few of the littoral zone animals or water animals are found on the lake bottom. There is also little, if any, plant life there. The main inhabitants include snails and shrimplike crustaceans. These creatures eat the remains of dead plants and animals that drift down from the upper regions of the lake.

A pond is basically a miniature lake that is shallow enough for sunlight to reach the bottom and enable plants to grow there. Many ponds are formed naturally, but a great many are made by people. Most of the same creatures that are found in lakes are also found in ponds. Such creatures include fish, frogs, and water insects. In many cases, eggs and larvae of these animals are brought from one lake or pond to another by water birds. The birds carry the transported material on their feet or in their feathers. The wind is another transporter. It carries plant seeds from one water home to another. The seeds of water plants can also float to new locations.

Many ponds and small, shallow lakes are temporary features. Over time, the build-up of material on the water's floor and the spread of vegetation will fill in a small pond. Eventually, it will become a marsh or swamp. Over many hundreds or many thousands of years, climate change, sediment accumulation, and vegetation growth will turn even a large, shallow lake into a wetland.

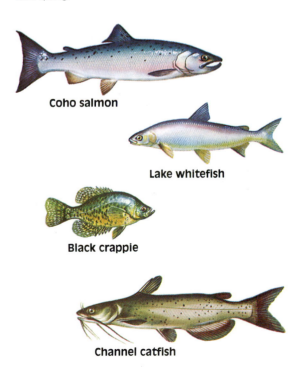

**Many species** of fish are found in lakes. If a lake freezes over in winter, the fish that live there can swim down to warmer water near the bottom until spring.

**Coho salmon**

**Lake whitefish**

**Black crappie**

**Channel catfish**

## Pond animal and plant life

In a pond, the primary food producers are microscopic plants that use sunlight to make food for primary consumers, such as tadpoles. A fish (secondary consumer) may eat the tadpole. Decomposers complete the food chain by cleaning up the waste and producing chemicals that primary producers use to make food.

### The pond environment

**The pond environment**
1  Common frog (male, x 0.5)
2  Starwort (x 0.5)
3  Water crowfoot (x 0.25)
4  Aplecta hypnorum (x 2)
5  Wandering snail (x 0.75)
6  Keeled ramshorn snail (x 0.5)
7  Curled pondweed (x 0.25)
8  Bithynia (x 1)
9  Ramshorn snail (x 0.3)
10  Water lily root (x 0.25)
11  Great pond snail (x 0.8)

**Near the surface**
12  Pond skater (x 0.5)
13  Whirligig beetle (x 0.25)
14  Water boatman (x 1)
15  Nonbiting midge (x 5)
16  Mosquito pupa (x 5)
17  Dragonfly (male, x 0.65)
18  China-marks moth (x 0.75)
19  Mayfly (female, x 0.2)

**Middle depths**
20  Water flea (Daphnia, x 2.5)
21  Smooth newt (male, x 0.5)
22  Cyclops (typical of species, x 8)
23  Flagellate (x 650)
24  Great diving beetle (male, x 1)
25  Hydra (x 4)
26  Stickleback (male, x 0.5)
27  Common frog tadpole (x 1.5)
28  Flagellate (Euglena, x 180)
29  Water mite (x 5)

**The bottom**
30  Caddis-fly larva in case
31  Chaetonotus (x 150)
32  Horny-orb shell (x 1)
33  Tubifex worms (x 0.2)
34  Midge larva (x 3.5)
35  Pond sponge (x 0.2)
36  Leech (Helobdella sp., x 4)
37  Water hog-louse (x 2.5)
38  Flatworm (x 2)

### Near the surface

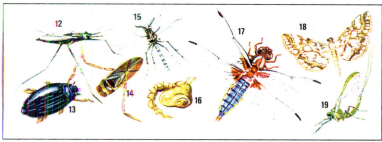

### Middle depths

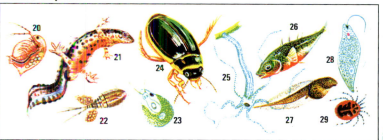

### The bottom

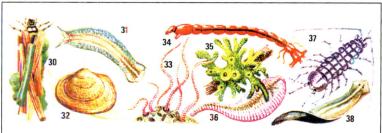

# Swamps, Marshes, and Bogs

**Okefenokee Swamp,** in southeastern Georgia and northeastern Florida, is the home of many animals, including deer, bears, wildcats, otters, raccoons, opossums, and alligators. About two-thirds of the swamp is a government wildlife preserve.

Swamps, marshes, and bogs are known as the earth's wetlands. A wetland is a land area where the water level remains near or above the surface of the ground for most of the year.

Swamps, the first type of wetland, are areas of muddy, watery land covered by trees and bushes. The major kinds of swamps are deepwater, shallow-water, and mangrove.

Deepwater swamps are near large, slow-flowing rivers that flood regularly. These floods spread water over adjoining land. Bald cypress and black gum trees, which thrive in muddy soil, grow easily in such areas. The thick foliage of these trees blocks out much of the sunlight. Thus, only certain kinds of plants can grow on the muddy ground.

Shallow-water swamps are usually found in areas where soil stays moist or water-covered for only part of the year. Bushes and trees, such as willows, oaks, and maples, flourish there. Water lilies and similar plants cover the surface of the standing water in springtime.

Unlike the other deepwater and shallow-water swamps that have fresh water, mangrove swamps have saltwater. These swamps lie along tropical seacoasts and are named for the mangrove shrubs that grow there.

Swamp water swarms with insects, frogs, and fish. These creatures are food for such long-legged birds as herons and egrets. The birds wade in the water and use their beaks to spear prey. In the tropics and subtropics, swamps are home to alligators, crocodiles, turtles, and snakes. Such animals prefer the combination of hot weather and watery conditions.

Many animals are equally at home in swamps and in inland marshes. Marshes, the second kind of wetland, are flat, treeless areas covered with water. There are, however, such animals as American redwinged blackbirds and muskrats that prefer marshes. Blackbirds nest among the cattails, bulrushes, and other water plants that grow thickly in this environment. Those same plants are food for muskrats and also nesting places for many kinds of waterfowl. Like muskrats, these birds are prey for mink, which live on marshland edges.

An inland marsh is also a major source of food for animals that do not actually inhabit it. Raccoons visit marshes to hunt fish and crayfish in the shallow water. Raccoons also dig up nests of turtle eggs and search for the egg-filled nests of ducks

and other waterfowl. Deer also visit marshes. There, they browse on water lilies, marsh marigolds, grasses, and grasslike plants called sedges.

In addition to inland marshes, there are also saltwater marshes. This type of marsh forms where river deltas empty into the sea. Fish, crabs, oysters, and mussels flourish in salt marshes where salt grasses are abundant. Such diving birds as ospreys are salt marsh dwellers, and gulls are frequent visitors.

Bogs, the third type of wetland, are wet, spongy areas. They are filled with mosses and large amounts of partly decayed plant matter called peat. These environments are usually found in the colder, northern parts of the world. Bogs generally evolve from deep lakes that have become filled with dead, compacted plant material. Sphagnum moss and sedges form a thick mat on the surface of the water. There, wild cranberries, other berry bushes, and a few dwarf trees may grow. Other species of plants that thrive in and around bogs are carnivorous plants such as the sundew, pitcher plant, and Venus's-flytrap. Aside from insects and frogs, few animals live permanently in this type of wetland. But many animals, among them moose and bear, visit bogs in search of food.

In addition to supporting plant and animal communities, wetlands are ecologically valuable in other ways. They can store large amounts of water for long periods of time. And because they hold back water, they help prevent floods.

**Bogs,** with their acidic soil and water, favor the growth of mosses—especially sphagnum moss, which absorbs water like a sponge.

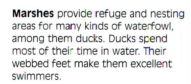

**Marshes** provide refuge and nesting areas for many kinds of waterfowl, among them ducks. Ducks spend most of their time in water. Their webbed feet make them excellent swimmers.

# Tropical Forests

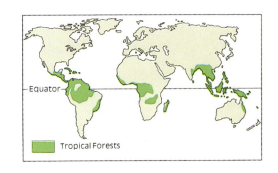

Equator

Tropical Forests

A broad band around the middle of the earth receives the planet's greatest amount of sunlight. This zone, known as the tropics, generally features year-round summer conditions. Humidity and temperatures are constantly high. Days are long and sunny, and many tropical regions are frequently rainy. In this climate, huge forests flourish. They are called tropical rain forests, and they almost always lie near the equator. These forests cover parts of the tropical portions of Africa, Asia, Australia, Central and South America, and the Pacific Islands.

Unlike a midlatitude forest, a tropical rain forest has few seasonal temperature changes. Because of the unending summer conditions, most trees in a tropical forest stay green all year. Such trees gradually lose old leaves as they grow new ones. However, there are some deciduous trees in tropical forests that shed all their leaves briefly during the dry season.

Generally, all the trees in a tropical rain forest have tall, straight trunks with branches only at the very top. The tops of the trees are called the crowns, and they merge to form a covering of leaves high in the air. This covering is known as the upper canopy. Its thickness blocks most of the sunlight from reaching the forest floor. Because the floor is so dim, few plants can grow there. Mushrooms and other fungi that need little light flourish in this environment.

Orchids, wild pineapples, other flowering plants, and ferns grow high up on the trunks of tropical trees. These plants begin as seeds that are carried by the wind. The seeds lodge within crevices in the tree bark and are warmed by sunlight. For water, the seeds soak up moisture from the air and rain that runs down the tree trunks.

Forest vines are rooted in the ground. Often, they wind up tree trunks and other vines until they reach the treetops. There they can spread out among the leafy branches of the upper canopy. Extremely tall trees called emergents thrust through the upper canopy's vines and branches.

Many kinds of insects and insect-eating birds live in the emergents. Large, predatory birds live there too. Such birds include harpy eagles, which prey on the monkeys that live below in the upper canopy.

Monkeys and many other creatures are attracted by the upper canopy's abundance of fruit and nuts. Fruit-eating birds, such as toucans, and leaf-eating mammals, such as sloths, also thrive in the crowns of tall trees. Hummingbirds and brilliantly colored butterflies flutter between the canopy's leaves and flowers. Tree frogs and lizards creep through the upper canopy branches, hunting insects. Snakes lurk among the leaves to capture these creatures. Other residents of the upper canopy include such gliding animals as the large bat called the flying fox and the flying dragon, a type of lizard.

Not all trees are tall enough to reach the upper canopy. Some full-grown trees can thrive at lower levels in the forest because they do not require an abundance of light. The crowns of these trees form one or two lower canopies that are generally quite sturdy. The lower canopies are inhabited by larger forest animals such as apes and leopards. These animals live both in trees and on the forest floor.

In many parts of tropical rain forest, tree trunks are spread far apart and few plants grow on the ground. But in places where abundant sunlight is able to reach the ground, there is a thick, tangled growth of bushes and low plants. Such areas are called jungles, and they grow frequently in former clearings and along the banks of wide rivers in the tropical regions of the world.

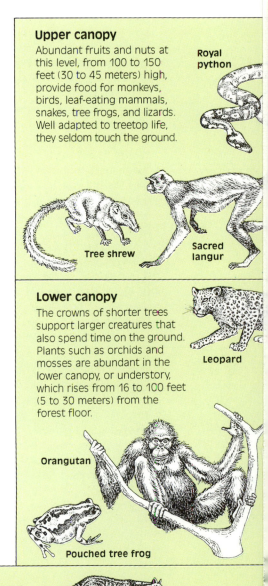

## Upper canopy
Abundant fruits and nuts at this level, from 100 to 150 feet (30 to 45 meters) high, provide food for monkeys, birds, leaf-eating mammals, snakes, tree frogs, and lizards. Well adapted to treetop life, they seldom touch the ground.

Royal python

Tree shrew

Sacred langur

## Lower canopy
The crowns of shorter trees support larger creatures that also spend time on the ground. Plants such as orchids and mosses are abundant in the lower canopy, or understory, which rises from 16 to 100 feet (5 to 30 meters) from the forest floor.

Leopard

Orangutan

Pouched tree frog

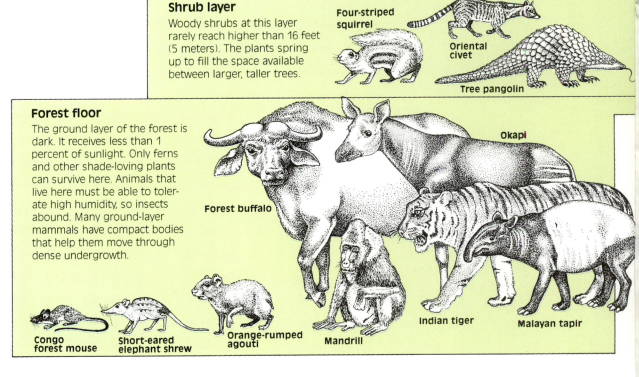

## Shrub layer
Woody shrubs at this layer rarely reach higher than 16 feet (5 meters). The plants spring up to fill the space available between larger, taller trees.

Four-striped squirrel

Oriental civet

Tree pangolin

## Forest floor
The ground layer of the forest is dark. It receives less than 1 percent of sunlight. Only ferns and other shade-loving plants can survive here. Animals that live here must be able to tolerate high humidity, so insects abound. Many ground-layer mammals have compact bodies that help them move through dense undergrowth.

Okapi

Forest buffalo

Congo forest mouse

Short-eared elephant shrew

Orange-rumped agouti

Mandrill

Indian tiger

Malayan tapir

## Emergent layer

The tallest trees in a tropical forest form the emergent layer, up to 200 feet (61 meters) high. Animal life at this level is mostly birds and insects.

Demidoff's bushbaby

Flying fox

Gray parrot

Flying squirrel

Gold Coast turaco

Chameleon

Chimpanzee

## Layers of the forest

Living conditions at different heights determine what creatures inhabit different layers of the forest. The topmost layers are so high up that only birds and insects are found there. To survive in the dense canopy and middle layer, animals must be streamlined and adapted for climbing. In the high humidity and gloom of the ground layer, insects and fungi break down rotting fruit and leaves from above. These decomposers enrich the soil that feeds the forest.

**Orchids,** which thrive in humid conditions, abound in tropical forests. They range in size from small flowers to huge vines as long as 100 feet (30 meters).

**In the dim** light near the edge of a Sumatra rain forest, the forest floor is relatively free of plant life.

# Deserts

About one-fifth of the earth's land is covered by deserts. In general, deserts are any areas that have little rainfall, dry soil, and a limited amount of very special kinds of plants. But there is no "typical" desert. Some, such as parts of the Sahara, consist mainly of lifeless, rocky surfaces and smaller areas of shifting piles of sand called dunes. Others are limited to rocky, dry areas full of plant and animal life. Those deserts, located in the subtropics, remain searingly hot throughout the year. But others such as the Great Basin and the Gobi Desert are bitterly cold in winter and very hot in summer.

Often a desert will gradually merge with a fertile grassland. But unlike the neighboring grasses, desert plants must cope with a minimal supply of water. Some of these plants have long roots that probe far underground to find water. Others have shallow, widespread roots that absorb the tiniest amounts of dew and rain that soak down from the surface. The leaves of these plants are small, and they often fall off during the dry season.

Many types of desert vegetation flourish only when there is a little rain. After a rainfall, previously inactive seeds quickly germinate and grow into plants. These plants—known as annuals—flower, form more seeds, then die. The new seeds lie dormant until it rains again. The next rainfall, however, may be years away.

Desert plants vary in form from the prickly pear cactus to giant cacti. Many shrub and low tree species also grow in deserts. Such desert plants enable wildlife to live among them. They do this by providing animals with food and moisture. Some desert plants also provide animals with shelter. For example, North American Gila woodpeckers drill holes in giant cacti. In these hollows, the birds raise their families. When they leave, the holes are taken over by other kinds of birds or by lizards, rats, or mice.

Extreme heat can kill an animal. That is why desert creatures must be able to keep their bodies from becoming too hot. There are various ways animals can control their body temperatures. Small creatures, among them insects, snakes, and tiny mammals, hide from the heat. They dig down into the sand and stay there. Or they keep cool in underground burrows or dark crevices in the rocks. Some creatures pant to cool themselves. Others escape the heat by going into a kind of hibernation for days or weeks. During this time, their bodies stay cool. Some desert animals have special body features that help them lose heat. The big ears of a desert fox or jack rabbit are examples of these features. Blood carries body heat up into the thin skin of these animals' ears. From the ears, heat radiates into the dry, hot air of the desert. Thus, the body temperature of the animals is lowered.

In addition to surviving the heat, desert animals must be adapted for an environment that has very little water. Desert larks of the Sahara, for example, can thrive for weeks without a drink. Camels and little furry dassies of South Africa can often live without drinking for months. These birds and mammals get moisture from the food they eat. They are also able to store this moisture in their bodies for a long time. There are also desert creatures, among them the kangaroo rat, that never need to drink. Their food gives them all the moisture they require.

Some desert dwellers, however, must find water each day. One such animal is the red kangaroo of the Australian Desert. This large mammal is known for grazing in the dry grasslands that border the desert. Each day, in search of water, the kangaroo must travel from the grasslands to one of the few watering holes in the almost waterless environment of the desert.

**Long-nosed bat**

**Different deserts** are home to different species of plants and animals. All desert creatures and vegetation, however, share the need to obtain and conserve water.

**Scattered throughout** the world's largest desert, the Sahara, are fertile areas known as oases. The water for Saharan oases comes mainly from springs or underground streams.

**Agave**

**Esparto grass**

**Monument Valley, Utah,** gets bitterly cold in winter. Red sandstone formations rise 1,000 feet (300 meters) from the desert floor.

Elf owl

Great horned owl

Gila monster

Fennec fox

Desert hedgehog

Roadrunner

Kangaroo rat

Fat sand rat

Saguaro cactus

Desert tortoise

Dorcas gazelle

Welwitschia

Addax antelope

# Grasslands

Between humid forests and arid deserts lie the earth's sun-filled grasslands. These areas, which may be flat or hilly, are literally seas of grasses.

The three types of grasslands are steppes, prairies, and savannas. A grassland is classified into one of these three types according to the average height of the grass that grows there. Plant height depends upon the amount of rainfall received.

Steppes, which are the driest grassland, are covered mainly by short grasses. Most plants in a steppe do not grow over 1 foot (30 centimeters) high. Steppes cover large areas of the interior of North America and Europe, and also extend into central Asia.

Prairies, which receive moderate rainfall, are blanketed chiefly by tall grasses. In moist prairies, grass may grow 6 feet (1.8 meters) high or even taller. The North American prairie reaches from central Texas to southern Saskatchewan. Saskatchewan, Alberta, and Manitoba are called Canada's "Prairie Provinces." Other prairies include the Pampa of Argentina.

Savannas are grasslands with widely scattered trees and shrubs. Most savannas are in the tropics, but some are in temperate regions. This type of grassland covers more than two-fifths of Africa and large parts of Australia, South America, and India.

One of the main types of grassland animals is the grazer, or grass-eater. The larger grazers are generally animals that live in herds, such as the American bison and antelope and the African gnu and zebra. In many places, however, wild grazers have been replaced by domesticated grazers such as sheep and cattle. The herds of grass-eaters roam across a grassland, eating as they go. The area they move across looks like a mowed lawn for a time, but the grass quickly grows again unless it is the dry season.

Actually, there are many more small grazers than big ones. Small grazers include many kinds of grasshoppers, ants, aphids, leaf hoppers, and other insects. Just as large predators prey on large grazers, such small predators as birds and mice prey on small grazers.

Many kinds of flowering plants such as sunflowers, prairie clover, and cornflowers grow in grasslands. They produce seeds and leaves that are eaten by the region's wildlife, which includes jack rabbits and colonies of prairie dogs. There are many predators of these seed- and leaf-eaters. All grasslands contain snakes, which hunt for prey among the grass stems. But in addition to being the hunter, snakes are also the hunted. The sky over a grassland is the natural range for hawks and other birds of prey that will swoop down to seize snakes, as well as rabbits.

In tropical savannas, the temperature stays hot all year, so life goes on unchanged, except for alternating rainy and dry seasons. But the steppes and prairies have warm summers and cool to cold winters. In most of these regions the grassland life is curtailed by cold weather. The ground freezes and the grass stops growing. Much of the insect life dies or burrows underground. The insect-eating birds migrate to other regions. Most of the smaller animals hibernate or remain in burrows through the cold season, living on stored food. But the coming of spring and the thawing of the ground, the grasslands quickly return to life.

Much of the world's grasslands have been turned into farmland where wheat and corn, which are actually grasses, are grown. Even in farmlands, however, much of the same life which may be found in a natural grassland exists. Insects, birds, small mammals, and other creatures thrive among the cultivated grasses.

**American buffalo,** or bison, live in herds and graze on the grasses and small plants found on American prairies.

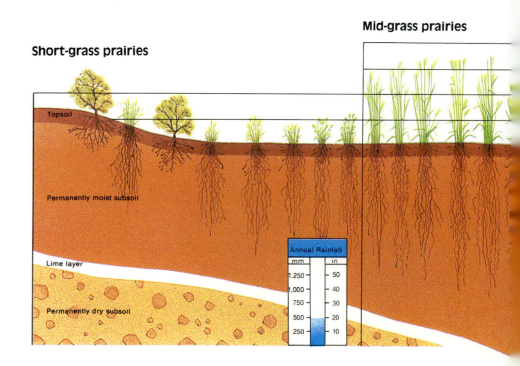

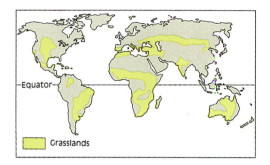

Equator

Grasslands

**Grassland creatures** solve the problem of survival by adapting to the environment in various ways. Many, such as small burrowing animals and certain invertebrates, seek protection underground. The marsupial mole lives almost entirely underground, while the prairie dog surfaces to eat. Snakes, of course, are well adapted for the pursuit of burrowing creatures. Small carnivores like the pampas cat often surprise their victims. Certain grassland predators rely on speed for catching prey—as do some of the creatures they hunt in the race for survival. The sharp-eyed hawk rides thermal winds in search of food, while the meadowlark adapts to a mostly treeless environment by singing to declare its territory. Camouflage protects many insects.

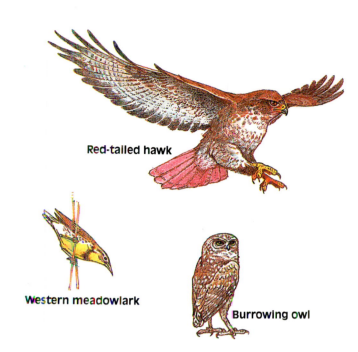

Red-tailed hawk

Western meadowlark

Burrowing owl

**Rainfall determines** what grasses grow where on the North American prairies. In general, the drier the climate, the shorter the grasses. In regions where annual rainfall is no more than 20 inches (500 millimeters), only short grass—with short root systems—can survive in the relatively narrow layer of permanently moist subsoil. As the depth of the subsoil increases, it can support the longer root systems of mid-grass and tall-grass prairies. Tall bluestem and Indian grass predominate in the regions where annual rainfall measures 40 inches (1,000 millimeters). The North American prairie includes most of Oklahoma, Kansas, Nebraska, Iowa, Illinois, South Dakota, and North Dakota, and parts of neighboring states and provinces. Alberta, Saskatchewan, and Manitoba are the "Prairie Provinces" of Canada.

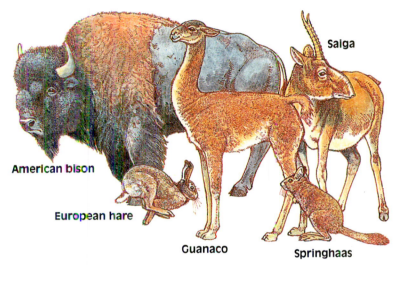

American bison

Saiga

European hare

Guanaco

Springhaas

**Tall-grass prairies**

| cm | ft |
|---|---|
| 215 | 7 |
| 180 | 6 |
| 150 | 5 |
| 120 | 4 |
| 90 | 3 |
| 60 | 2 |
| 30 | 1 |
| 0 | 0 |

| Annual Rainfall | |
|---|---|
| mm | in |
| 1,250 | 50 |
| 1,000 | 40 |
| 750 | 30 |
| 500 | 20 |
| 250 | 10 |

| Annual Rainfall | |
|---|---|
| mm | in |
| 1,250 | 50 |
| 1,000 | 40 |
| 750 | 30 |
| 500 | 20 |
| 250 | 10 |

Marbled polecat

Pampas cat

Gopher snake

Marsupial mole

Prairie dog

European souslik

Viscacha

Lubber grasshopper

Tumble bug

Praying mantis

# Midlatitude Forests

The earth's midlatitude regions lie between the polar circles and the tropics. Here, the seasonal climate ranges from warm summers to cold winters and, in some places, offers distinct dry and rainy seasons.

Deciduous trees, those with broad leaves that are shed annually, grow best in midlatitude regions where it is warm and moist at least four to five months a year. They are the main trees of most midlatitude forests, but many kinds of needle-leaved or broad-leaved evergreens also thrive in such a climate.

Midlatitude forests once covered eastern North America, western Europe, and eastern Asia. Changes in climate, together with activities such as forestry and farming, have reduced these forests to small areas.

Ground water generally freezes in midlatitude regions during winter. Thus, deciduous trees cannot draw up water into their leaves, and the leaves cannot tolerate freezing. This is why trees shed their leaves in autumn and stand bare during winter. However, evergreens can hold water in their needles throughout wintertime. This is how they can remain green all year.

In spring, when the ground begins to thaw, small flowers of the forest floor are first to bloom. Buds soon appear on trees and bushes and burst into pastel-colored flowers and tiny, pale-green leaves. Hibernating creatures stir. Birds return from the warm lands where they spent the winter. Insect and spider eggs, produced in autumn, now hatch by the millions.

Summer days are long and filled with sunshine and frequent rain. During this season, the tree leaves grow and become dark green with the substance called chlorophyll. Leaves are a tree's foodmakers. Using sunlight for power, their chlorophyll turns water absorbed by the roots and carbon dioxide from the air into sugars.

To get at this food in the leaves, leaf-eating insects, such as aphids, grasshoppers, and caterpillars, swarm among the upper branches of the trees. Many predatory insects and spiders live there too, preying on the leaf-eaters. And such a plentiful supply of insects and spiders attracts a variety of insect-eating birds.

The tops of the taller deciduous trees form the roof, or canopy, of the forest. The canopy is the home of insects, spiders, songbirds, squirrels, and nocturnal flying squirrels. Beneath the canopy is a second "layer" of trees called the understory. Some young trees in this layer must grow into the sunlight or they will die. Others are low-growing trees that do not need as much sunlight.

Beneath the understory is a layer of shrubs. These shrubs produce berries and seeds that are a source of food for mice and chipmunks. Under the bushes, upon the forest floor, are low-growing flowering plants, ferns, and mosses, which do not need much sunlight to make their food. Mushrooms also grow there. They need little sunlight, for they take their food from the rotting, decaying things on which they grow. Grouse, woodcocks, and pheasants feed on this vegetation. Deer also browse on the forest floor, and insects swarm there and are hunted by mice, frogs, and toads. They in turn are preyed upon by snakes, foxes, and raccoons.

In late summer, deciduous trees begin to prepare for winter. A layer of corklike substance grows where each leaf stem is attached to the branch. No more water can reach the leaves. Their green color fades and their true color, generally yellow or orange, is seen. After chlorophyll breaks down, red or purple pigments form in a dying leaf.

With no water, the leaves die, turn brown, and wither. Autumn wind and rains tear them loose to swirl to the ground. There, they become food for mushrooms, other fungi, and tiny animals. These will help turn the leaves into the soil of the forest floor. The seasonal cycle is now complete, and winter is approaching.

**Seasonal climate** is an important feature of midlatitude forests. Deciduous trees, which lose their leaves each autumn, flourish in such an environment.

**Mushrooms** get their nourishment from dead matter, such as decaying bark.

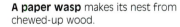

**A paper wasp** makes its nest from chewed-up wood.

**A flying squirrel** can spread its legs and glide through the air from tree to tree.

Equator

Midlatitude Forests

**Midlatitude forests** provide food and shelter for many animals and for a variety of plants.

**Hazel mouse**

**American black bear**

**Acorn woodpecker**

**Bluebell**

**European woodcock**

**Stag beetle**

**Hepatica**

# Subarctic Cold Lands

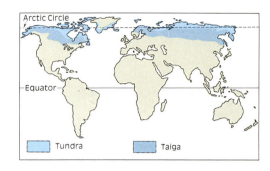

Tundra    Taiga

**The transitional area** between tundra and taiga is marked by shrubs, grasses, and the shoots of deciduous trees.

The dry, treeless, subarctic cold lands that lie near the Arctic Ocean are called arctic tundras. They include the northern parts of North America, Europe, and Asia. For three to four months a year, the sky over arctic tundras is dark both day and night. Beneath the darkened sky, snow blankets the frozen ground.

Change occurs on the tundra in spring, when the northern part of the earth is tilted toward the sun. This causes the tundra sky to lighten. Sunlight melts the snow and thaws the land's upper layer of soil, which is about 1-foot (30 centimeters) deep. Below this layer is the perpetually frozen ground known as permafrost.

Plants that have been dormant through the months of darkness abruptly burst into bloom in springtime. These plants are tough, low-growing, and ground-hugging. They include mosses, lichens, grasses, and small flowering plants such as bilberries and bearberries. The very cold winters with strong winds prevent plants from growing higher than the depth of the protective snow. Therefore, no full-size trees can survive on the tundra. Some willow shrubs, however, grow 3 to 10 feet (91 to 305 centimeters) high on slopes and valleys where winter snows are deep.

In spring and summer, the many flowering plants of the tundra turn the region into a sea of color. Arctic foxes, ermines, and snowy owls prey on the little mouselike lemming and arctic hare that search the tundra for tender leaves. Birds such as the willow ptarmigan nest and raise their young among the flowers. Mosquitoes, midges, and black flies are everywhere. Polar bears may leave the icepack and come on land to find food. Caribou, reindeer, and musk oxen browse on plants and are hunted by packs of wolves.

When earth tilts away from the sun, winter returns suddenly. In late August or early September, the ground freezes and snow begins to fall. Most birds and animals migrate southward during winter, but some live year-round on the tundra. Lemmings spend the winter in nests of leaves and feed on the green shoots of flowering plants and mosses. In winter, herds of shaggy musk oxen use their broad hoofs to search for grasses buried beneath the snow in patches.

The tundra regions spread southward for hundreds of miles until they reach regions that are slightly warmer. There, where the ground thaws more in summer, short trees

grow far apart from one another. A little farther south, taller trees grow closer and closer together until they form vast, thick stretches of forest. This is the northern boreal forest, or taiga. It covers much of Canada and the northern parts of the Scandinavian countries and Russia.

The trees of the taiga are mainly needle-leaf evergreens, such as the white spruce. A few species of hardy deciduous trees, among them birches, are also present. Mosses, lichens, and very few flowering plants cover the forest floor.

Throughout winter, trees in the taiga stand heaped with snow. Elk, caribou, reindeer, and moose graze through the forests. As they go, they eat shrubs, grasses, and shoots of deciduous trees. Snowshoe hare, squirrels, and ptarmigan are abundant and preyed on by lynxes, martins, and wolves. Bears spend their winters in the taiga in long periods of sleep or in complete hibernation.

In spring, the snow melts, soaking into the ground. This provides the taiga with a new supply of water for all the trees. Mosquitoes and horseflies swarm. Birds arrive. Hibernating animals become active. Like the tundra, the taiga teems with life through the short, warm summer.

**With the spring thaws,** bears emerge from their winter hibernation to forage along the banks of the McNeil River in Alaska.

Musk ox

Brant goose

Raven

**Seasonal changes** have tremendous effect on the animals of subarctic cold lands. Rock ptarmigans and arctic hares turn white in winter for warmth and camouflage. In spring, brant geese and 30 other species of birds migrate to the Arctic. Capercaillies move southward from the taiga each summer.

Wolf

**Flowers, mosses, and lichens** carpet the tundra when springtime relieves the long months of darkness. To survive, they must reproduce before the first snows come in September.

Snowy owl

Arctic hare

Capercaillie

Brown lemming

Rock ptarmigan

# Polar Caps

The polar caps are regions of permanent ice and snow located at earth's North and South Poles. These regions are the parts of the planet that receive the least sunlight. During four months of winter, no sunlight touches either pole. In summer, much of the continuous light that does reach the poles is reflected into space by the glare of snow.

The two polar caps are very different from one another. The North Pole lies on a frozen sea, the Arctic Ocean. The South Pole sits upon the continent of Antarctica, which is covered by a layer of ice and snow at least a mile (1.6 kilometers) deep. The ice at the North Pole is frozen salty seawater, but the ice covering Antarctica is frozen fresh water—the largest concentration of fresh water in the world.

These frozen regions are deserts for plants. Animal life, however, does exist in the seas at both polar caps. Many kinds of fish, including the 8- to 14-foot (2.4 to 4.2-meter) long polar shark, live beneath the ice in the Arctic Ocean waters. Seals and walruses are also at home in the sea, and it is there that they find their food. Seals eat mainly fish, while walruses dive to the ocean floor to scoop up clams and other shellfish. Even in the coldest waters, these large mammals are kept warm by their

extremely thick skin and layer of blubber. Of course, seals and walruses are air breathers. Thus, they must find or make openings in the ice so they can put their noses above water and breathe.

At the north polar cap, polar bears roam over the ice hunting for seals and other animals. These bears are excellent swimmers, and their thick, dense fur keeps them warm in freezing water. The fur's white color helps the animals blend in with the environment. Thus camouflaged, a bear can wait on ice near a seal's breathing hole and seize an unsuspecting victim when it comes up for air.

Several kinds of whales also make the Arctic Ocean their home. Such whales include the beluga, or white whale, and the narwhal. The narwhal is a small whale that has a maximum length of 18 feet (5.4 meters). The male narwhal has a long, spiral tusk that juts out from its upper jaw. The much larger bowhead whale is also an inhabitant of the Arctic Ocean.

The sea around Antarctica is the summer home of several species of whales that feed on small, shrimplike creatures called krill. These include blue, fin, humpback, and right whales. Southern bottlenose and southern fourtooth whales, which feed on squid and fish, are also Antarctic residents. Killer whales swim all year around in the cold Antarctic waters, preying on penguins, seals, and smaller whales in addition to fish and

squid. A number of seal species, including krill-eating Antarctic fur seals and crabeater seals, aggressive leopard seals, and massive southern elephant seals, nest on the Antarctic coastline or on nearby islands.

The main creature found on land at the southern pole cap is the penguin, a flightless bird that walks with a clumsy waddle. One species of penguin, the emperor penguin, lays eggs and rears its young on the snow-covered slopes of Antarctica during winter. The birds' feathers and layers of fat keep them warm. To keep their eggs warm, the male birds hold them on their feet and cover them with their bellies.

Although they are at home on land for several months of the year, penguins are primarily sea creatures. Emperor penguins are superb swimmers that live on fish, and the birds spend months at a time in cold, polar waters.

**A mother polar bear** usually has twin cubs. Most cubs stay with their mother for about two years.

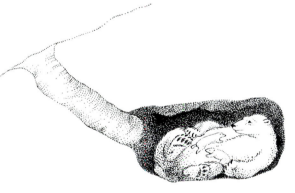

**Polar bears** live in underground shelters called dens during the colder months. Bears usually dig their dens in deep snowbanks.

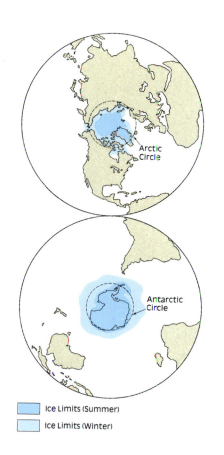

Arctic
Circle

Antarctic
Circle

Ice Limits (Summer)
Ice Limits (Winter)

**Penguins have adapted** to Antarctic conditions with short, dense feathers, thick layers of fat, webbed feet, and wings that serve as flippers.

**The Antarctic landscape** is made up of mountains, glaciers, and dry valleys, like those shown at the left. A dry valley is an ice-free rocky area carved out by a glacier that has retreated. Wind sweeps away most of the snow that falls in dry valleys.

**Blue whales** and crabeater seals eat millions of tons of krill, the Antarctic's chief food source. Leopard seals and killer whales prey on penguins.

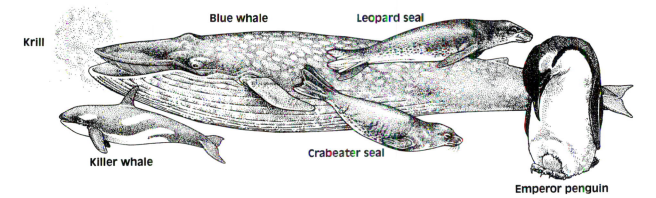

Krill

Blue whale

Leopard seal

Killer whale

Crabeater seal

Emperor penguin

# World Time Zones

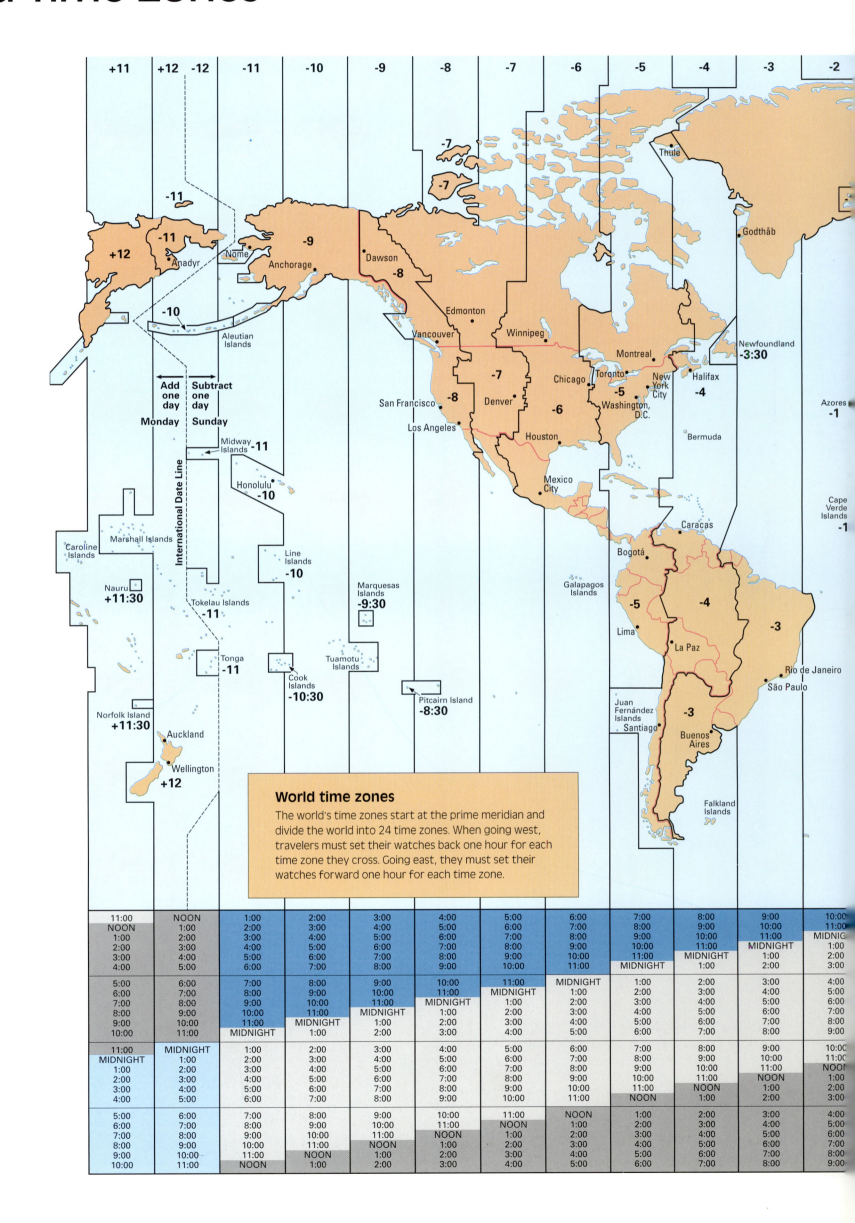

**World time zones**

The world's time zones start at the prime meridian and divide the world into 24 time zones. When going west, travelers must set their watches back one hour for each time zone they cross. Going east, they must set their watches forward one hour for each time zone.

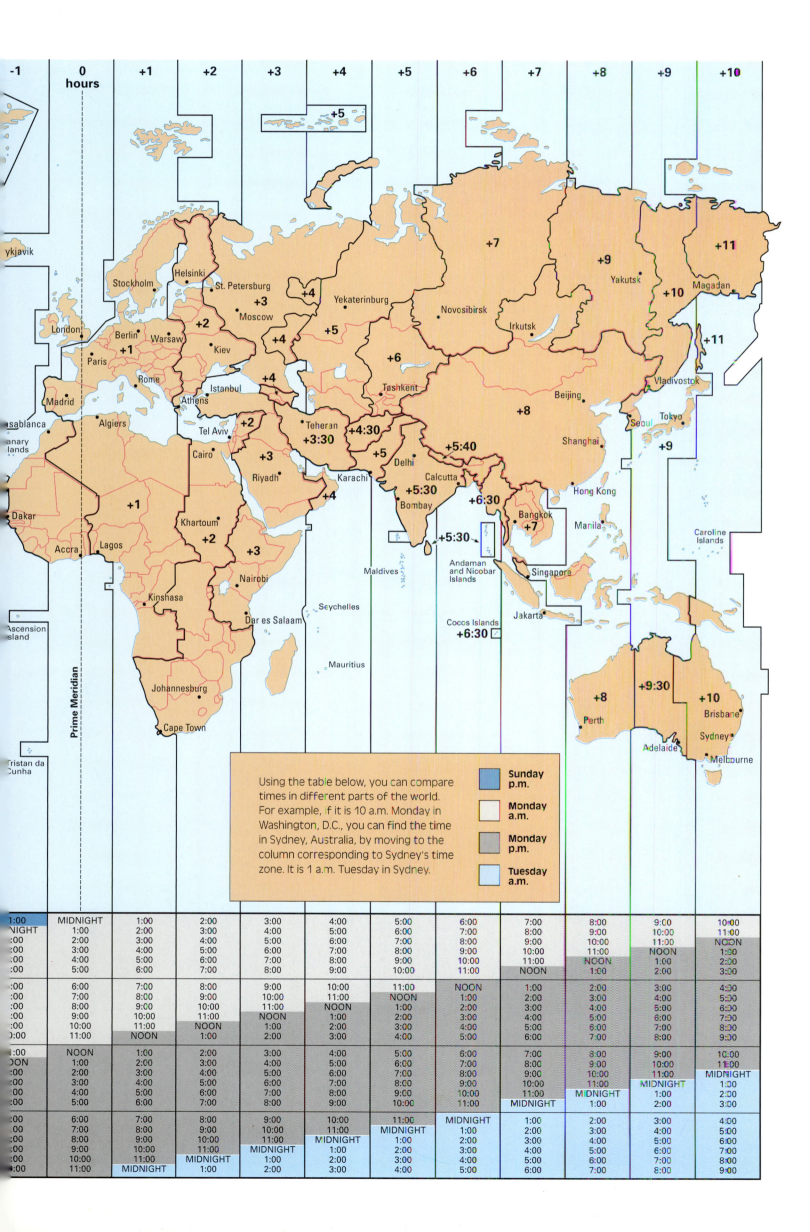

# Using the Atlas

**MAPS AND ATLASES**

Satellite images of the world (figure 1) constantly give us views of the shape and size of the earth. It is hard, therefore, to imagine how difficult it once was to determine the look of our planet. Yet from early history, we have evidence of humans trying to figure out what the world actually looked like.

Twenty-five hundred years ago, on a tiny clay tablet the size of a hand, the Babylonians drew a picture of the earth as a flat disk (figure 2) with Babylon at the center. And a section of the Cantino map of 1502 (figure 3) shows a chart used by mariners to chart the newly discovered Americas. Handsome and useful maps have been produced by many cultures. The beautiful Mexican map drawn in 1583 marks hills with wavy lines and roads with footprints between parallel lines (figure 4). The methods and materials used to create these maps were dependent upon the technology available. And because the technology was primitive, the accuracy of these maps was poor. A modern topographic map (figure 5), as well as those in this atlas, shows the detail and accuracy that cartographers are now able to achieve. They benefit from our ever-improving technology, including satellite imagery and computer-assisted cartography.

In 1589, Gerardus Mercator used the word *atlas* to describe a collection of maps. The word today is also used to describe an assortment of tables and other reference material. Atlases have become a unique and indispensable reference for graphically defining the world and answering the question where. Only on a map can the countries, cities, roads, rivers, and lakes covering a vast area be simultaneously viewed in their relative locations. Routes between places can be traced, trips planned, boundaries of neighboring states and countries examined, distances between places measured, the meandering of rivers and streams and the sizes of lakes visualized—and remote places imagined.

Figure 1

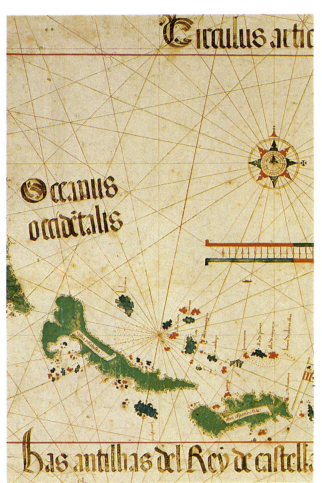

Figure 4

Figure 2

Figure 3

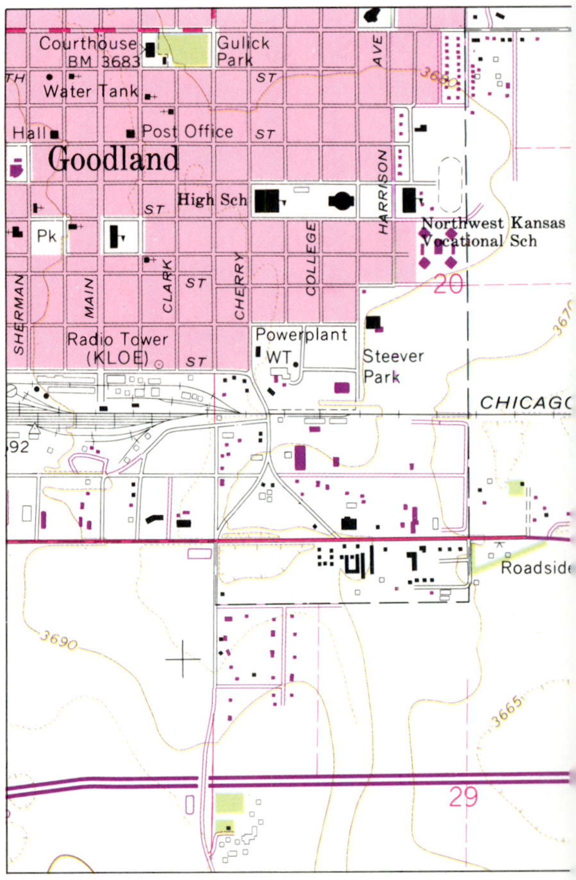

Figure 5

## SEQUENCE OF THE MAPS

The world is made up of seven major landmasses: the continents of Europe, Asia, Africa, Antarctica, Australia, South America, and North America (figure 6). The maps in this atlas follow this continental sequence. To allow for the inclusion of detail, each continent is broken down into a series of maps, and this grouping is arranged so that consecutive pages show continuous successive parts of the continent. Larger-scale maps are used for regions of greater detail (having many cities, for example) or for areas of global significance.

Figure 6

## GETTING THE INFORMATION

An atlas can be used for many purposes, from planning a trip to finding hot spots in the news. To realize the potential of an atlas the user must be able to:

1. Find places on the maps
2. Measure distances
3. Determine directions
4. Understand map symbols

## FINDING PLACES

One of the most important purposes of an atlas is to provide the location of a place in the world. A river's name in a book, a city mentioned in the news, or a desired vacation spot may prompt your need to know where a place is located. The illustrations and text below explain how to use the atlas. The example used here is the city Yangon (Rangoon) in the country Myanmar (Burma).

1. Look up the place-name in the index at the back of the atlas. Yangon, Myanmar, can be found on the map on page 38, and it can be located on the map by the letter-

| | | |
|---|---|---|
| Yangguanpu, China | C4 | 34 |
| Yangjia, China | I7 | 32 |
| Yangjiang, China | G9 | 30 |
| Yangkoushi, China | G7 | 34 |
| Yangliuqing, China | D5 | 32 |
| Yanglousi, China | F2 | 34 |
| Yangon (Rangoon), Mya. | B2 | 38 |
| Yangp'yong, S. Kor. | F15 | 32 |
| Yangquan, China | F1 | 32 |
| Yangsan, S. Kor. | H17 | 32 |
| Yangshuling, China | B6 | 32 |
| Yangtze see Chang, stm., China | E10 | 30 |
| Yangxiaodian, China | D5 | 34 |
| Yangyang, S. Kor. | E16 | 32 |
| Yangzhou, China | C8 | 34 |
| Yanheying, China | C7 | 32 |
| Yanji, China | A17 | 32 |
| Yankdök, N. Kor. | D14 | 32 |

Figure 7

Figure 8

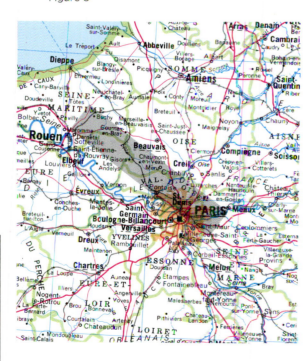

Figure 9

number key B2 (figure 7).

2. Turn to the map of Southeastern Asia found on page 38. Note that the letters A through H and the numbers 1 through 11 appear in the margins around the map.

3. To find Yangon on the map, place your left index finger on B and your right index finger on 2. Move your left finger across the map and your right finger down the map. Your fingers will meet at the area in which Yangon is located (figure 8).

## MEASURING DISTANCES

In planning trips, determining the distance between two places is essential, and an atlas can help in travel preparation. For instance, to determine the approximate distance between Paris and Rouen, France, follow these three steps:

1. Lay a slip of paper on the map on page 14 so that its edge touches the two cities. Adjust the paper so one corner touches Rouen. Mark the paper directly at the spot where Paris is located (figure 9).

2. Place the paper along the scale of miles beneath the map. Position the corner at 0 and line up the edge of the paper along the scale. The pencil mark on the paper indicates Rouen is between 50 and 100 miles from Paris (figure 10).

3. To find the exact distance, move the paper to the right so that the pencil mark is at 100 on the scale. The end of the paper hits the 30-mile mark on the scale. This means that the two towns are 100 minus 30, or 70 miles apart (figure 11).

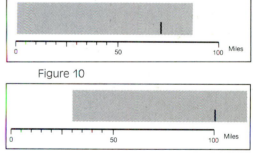

Figure 10

Figure 11

## DETERMINING DIRECTION

Most of the maps in the atlas are drawn so that when oriented for normal reading, north is at the top of the map, south is at the bottom, west is at the left, and east is at the right. Most maps have a series of lines drawn across them—the lines of latitude and longitude. Lines of latitude, or parallels of latitude, are drawn east and west. Lines of longitude, or meridians of longitude, are drawn north and south (figure 12).

Parallels and meridians appear as either curved or straight lines. For example, in the section of the map of Europe shown in figure 13, the parallels of latitude appear as curved lines. The meridians of longitude are straight lines that come together toward the top of the map. Latitude and longitude lines help locate places on maps. Parallels of latitude are numbered in degrees north and south of the equator. Meridians of longitude are numbered in degrees east and west of a line called the Prime Meridian, running through Greenwich, England, near London. Any place on earth can be located by the latitude and longitude lines running through it.

To determine directions or locations on the map, you must use the parallels and meridians. For example, suppose you want to know which is farther north, Bergen, Norway, or Stockholm, Sweden. The map in figure 13 shows that Stockholm is south of the 60° parallel of latitude and Bergen is north of it. Bergen is farther north than Stockholm. By looking at the meridians of longitude, you can determine which city is farther east. Bergen is approximately 5° east of the 0° meridian (Prime Meridian), and Stockholm is almost 20° east of it. Stockholm is farther east than Bergen.

## UNDERSTANDING MAP SYMBOLS

The world map is a kind of symbol that represents the world or a part of it. Each of the world's features—cities, rivers, etc.—is in turn represented on the map by a symbol. Map symbols may take the form of points, such as dots or squares (often used for cities, capital cities, or points of interest), or lines (roads, railroads, rivers). Symbols may also mark such areas as terrain, forests, and deserts and show the extent of their coverage. They seldom look like the feature they represent and therefore must be identified and interpreted. For instance, the maps in this atlas define political units by a colored line depicting their boundaries. Neither the colors nor the boundary lines are actually found on the surface of the earth, but because countries and states are such important political components of the world, strong symbols are used to represent them. The Map Symbols page in this atlas identifies the symbols used on the maps.

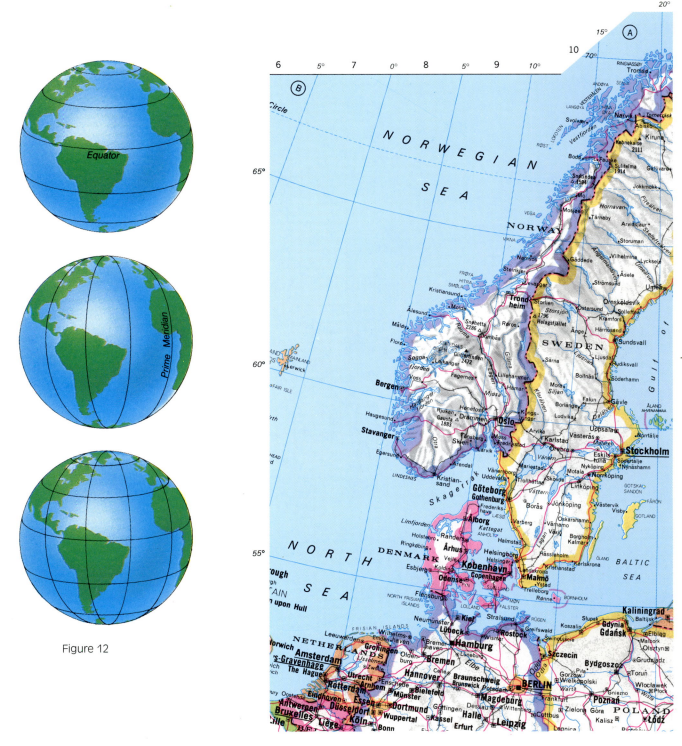

Figure 12

Figure 13

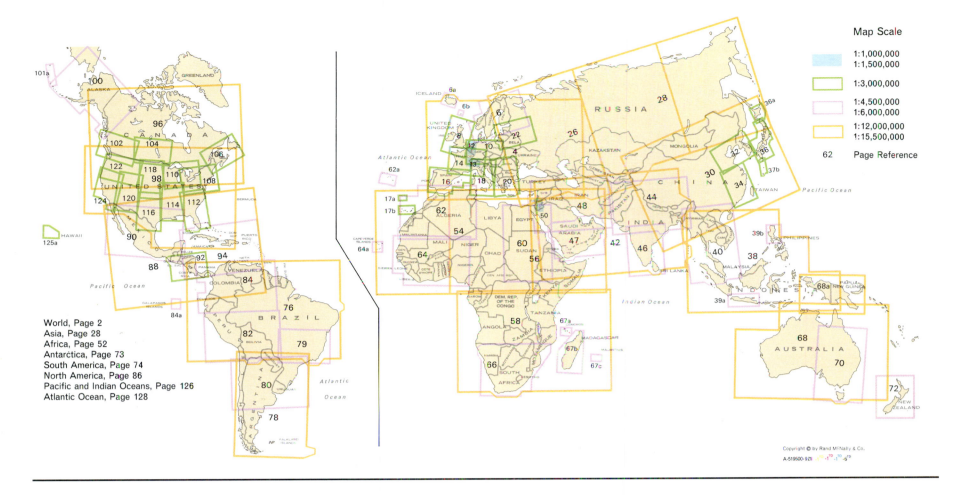

World, Page 2
Asia, Page 28
Africa, Page 52
Antarctica, Page 73
South America, Page 74
North America, Page 86
Pacific and Indian Oceans, Page 126
Atlantic Ocean, Page 128

**Map Scale**

| | |
|---|---|
| | 1:1,000,000 |
| | 1:1,500,000 |
| | 1:3,000,000 |
| | 1:4,500,000 |
| | 1:6,000,000 |
| | 1:12,000,000 |
| | 1:15,500,000 |
| 62 | Page Reference |

Copyright © by Rand McNally & Co.
A-519500-923

---

# World Maps Symbols

## Inhabited Localities

The size of type indicates the relative economic and political importance of the locality

| | | |
|---|---|---|
| Écommoy | Lisieux | **Rouen** |
| Trouville | **Orléans** | **PARIS** |
| Bi'r Safājah ° | Oasis | |

The symbol represents the population of the locality

| 1:1,000,000–1:6,000,000 | 1:12,000,000–1:15,500,000 | 1:24,000,000–1:48,000,000 |
|---|---|---|
| · 0—10,000 | · 0—50,000 | · 0—100,000 |
| ○ 10,000—25,000 | ⊙ 50,000—100,000 | ⊙ 100,000—1,500,000 |
| ⊙ 25,000—100,000 | ⊡ 100,000—250,000 | ■ >1,500,000 |
| ⊡ 100,000—250,000 | ⊞ 250,000—1,000,000 | |
| ▣ 250,000—1,000,000 | ☐ >1,000,000 | |
| ■ >1,000,000 | | |

English or second official language names are shown in reduced size lettering. Historical or other alternate names in the local language are shown in parentheses.

 Urban Area (Area of continuous industrial, commercial, and residential development)

### Capitals of Political Units

| | |
|---|---|
| BUDAPEST | Independent Nation |
| Cayenne | Dependency (Colony, protectorate, etc.) |
| Recife | State, Province, County, Oblast, etc. |

## Political Boundaries

### International (First-order political unit)

| | |
|---|---|
| | Demarcated and Undemarcated |
| | Disputed de jure |
| | Indefinite or Undefined |
| | Demarcation Line |

### Internal

| | |
|---|---|
| | State, Province, etc. (Second-order political unit) |
| MURCIA | Historical Region (No boundaries indicated) |
| GALAPAGOS (Ecuador) | Administering Country |

## Transportation

| | |
|---|---|
| | Primary Road |
| | Secondary Road |
| | Minor Road, Trail |
| | Railway |
| Canal du Midi | Navigable Canal |
| | Bridge |
| | Tunnel |
| TO MALMÖ | Ferry |

## Hydrographic Features

| | |
|---|---|
| | Shoreline |
| | Undefined or Fluctuating Shoreline |
| Amur | River, Stream |
| | Intermittent Stream |
| | Rapids, Falls |
| | Irrigation or Drainage Canal |
| | Reef |
| The Everglades | Swamp |
| RIMO GLACIER | Glacier |
| L. Victoria | Lake, Reservoir |
| Tuz Gölü | Salt Lake |
| | Intermittent Lake, Reservoir |
| | Dry Lake Bed |
| (395) | Lake Surface Elevation |

## Topographic Features

| | |
|---|---|
| Matterhorn △ 4478 | Elevation Above Sea Level |
| 76 ▽ | Elevation Below Sea Level |
| Mount Cook ▲ 3764 | Highest Elevation in Country |
| 133 ▼ | Lowest Elevation in Country |
| Khyber Pass ⊐⊏ 1067 | Mountain Pass |

Elevations are given in meters.
The highest and lowest elevations in a continent are underlined

| | |
|---|---|
| | Sand Area |
| | Lava |
| | Salt Flat |

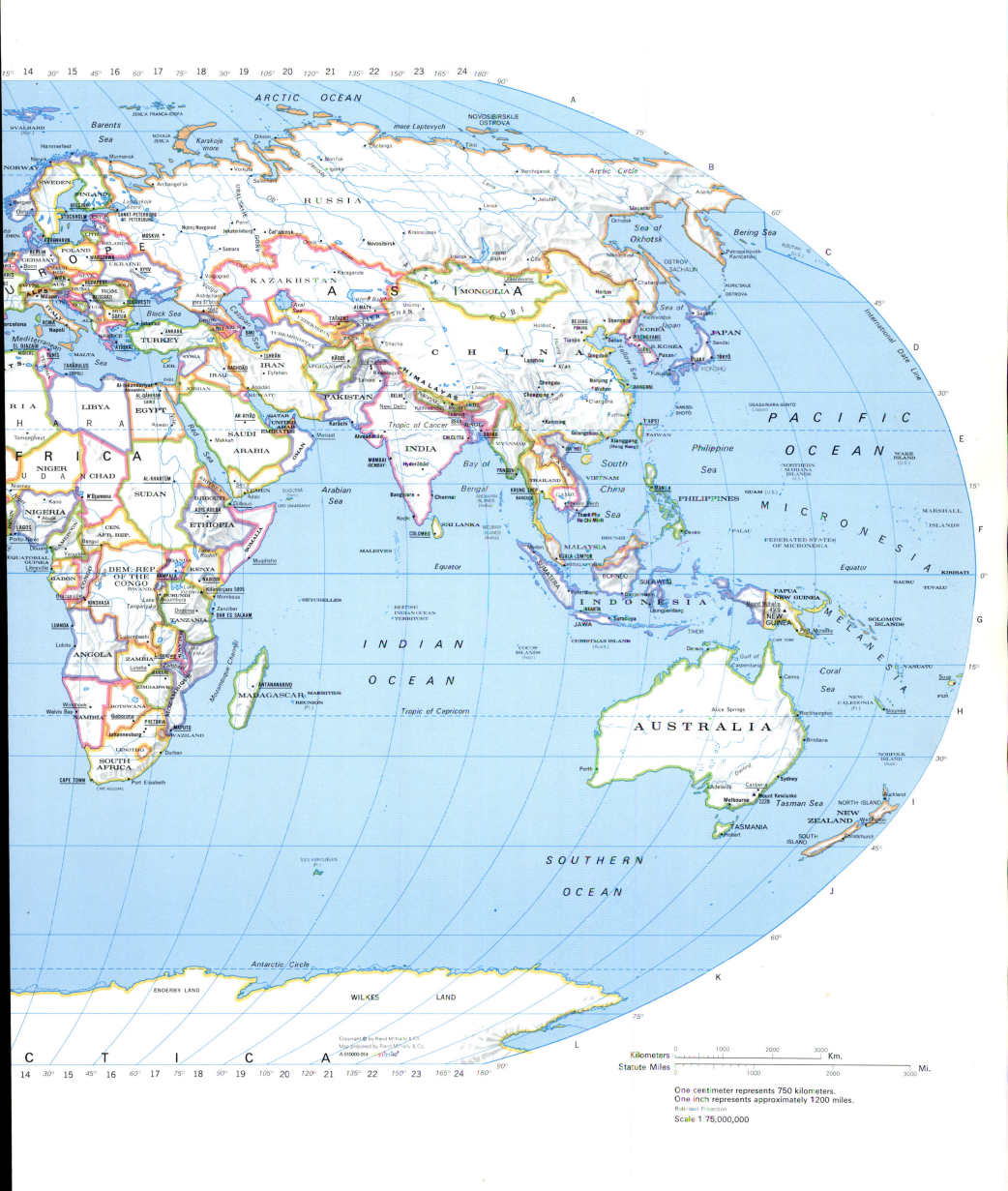

One centimeter represents 750 kilometers.
One inch represents approximately 1200 miles.
Robinson Projection
Scale 1:75,000,000

# Europe

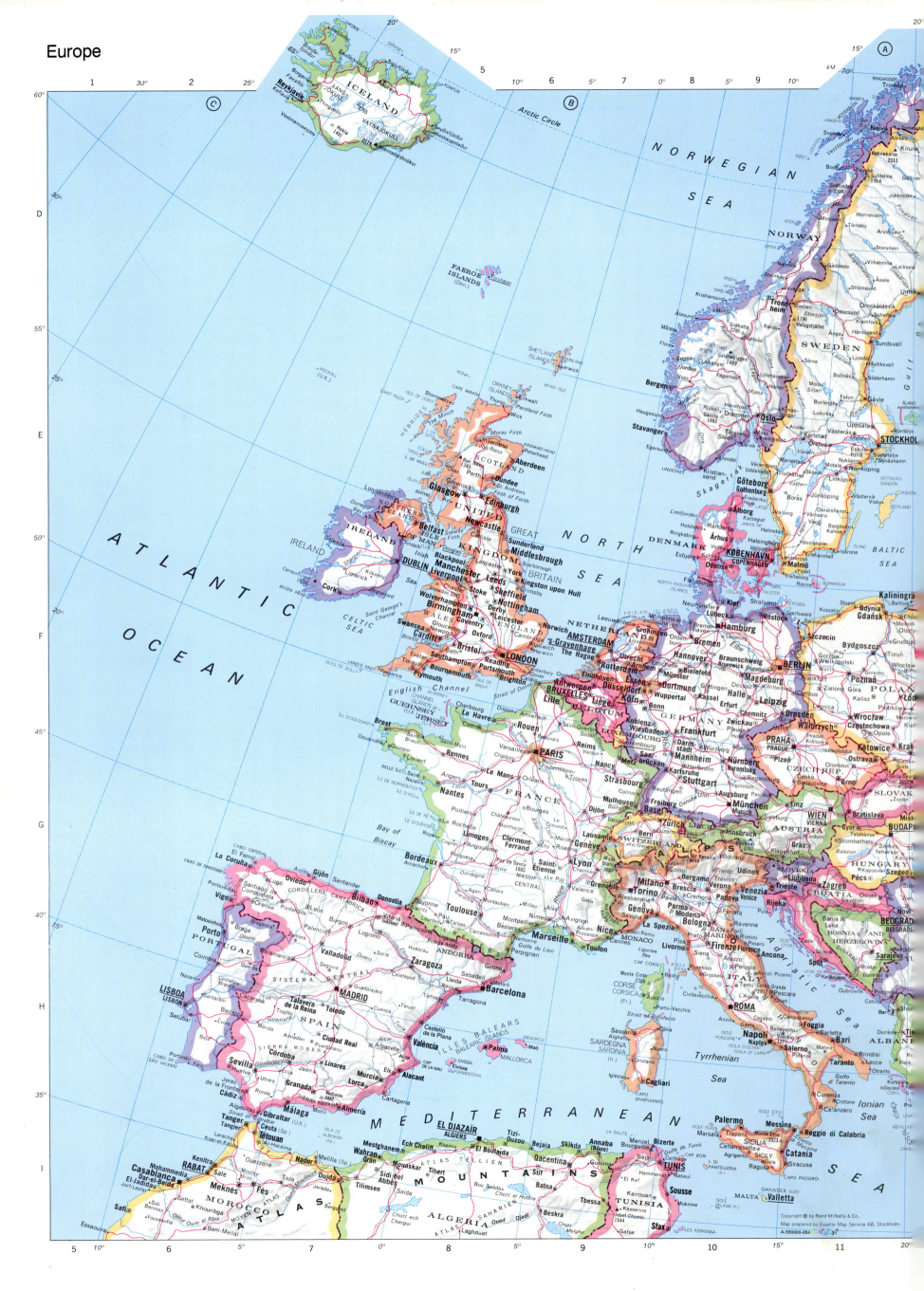

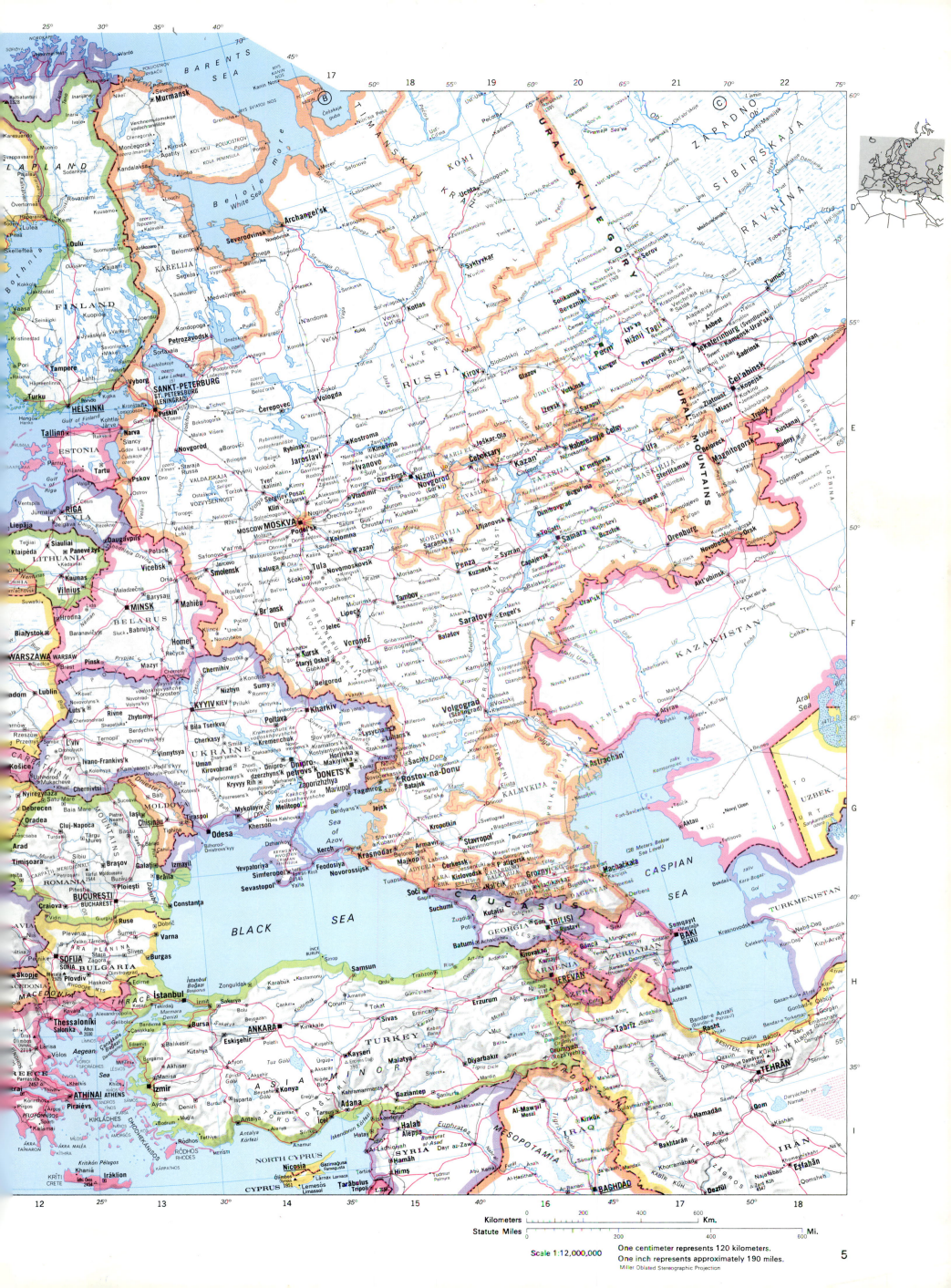

# British Isles

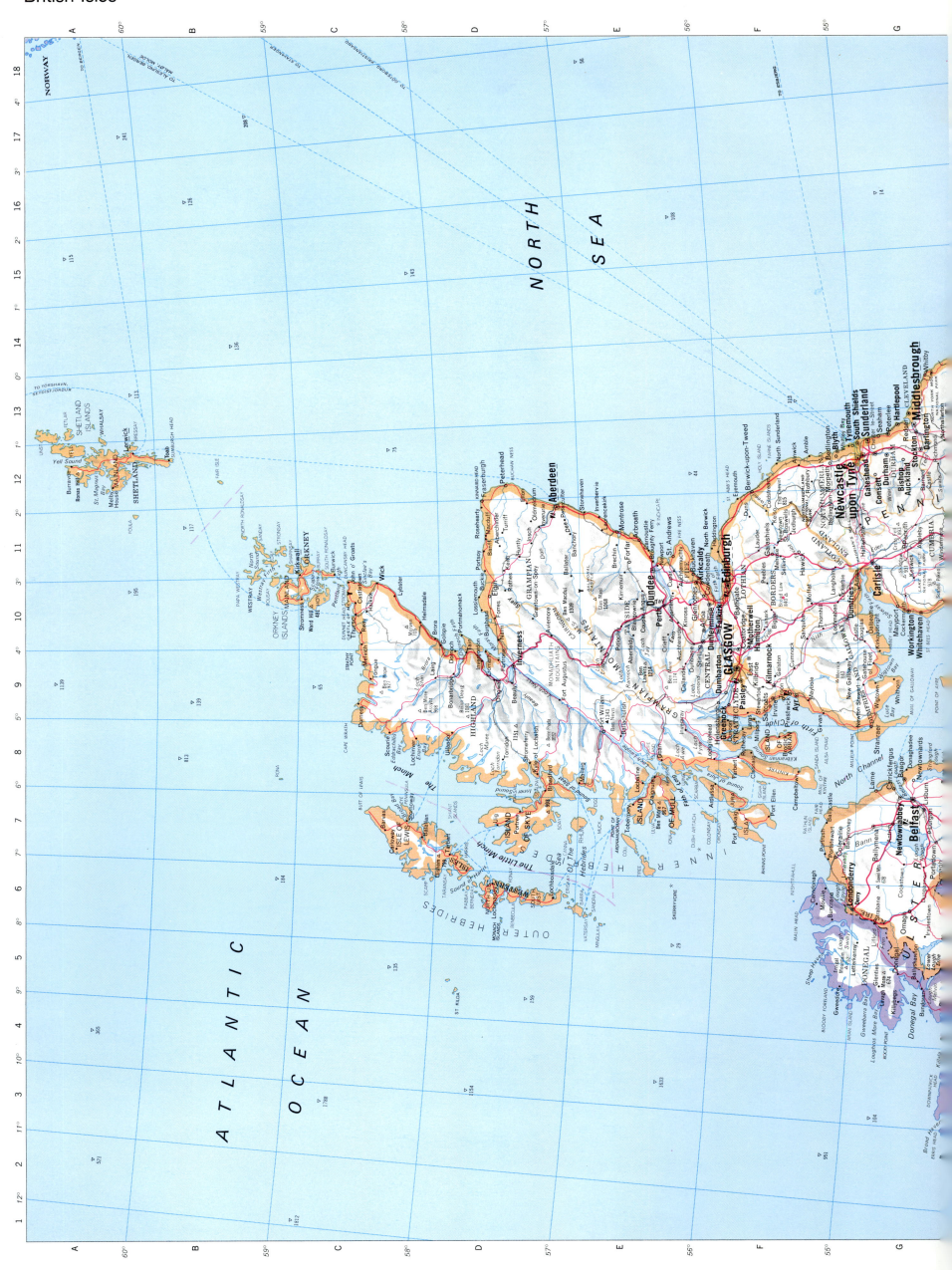

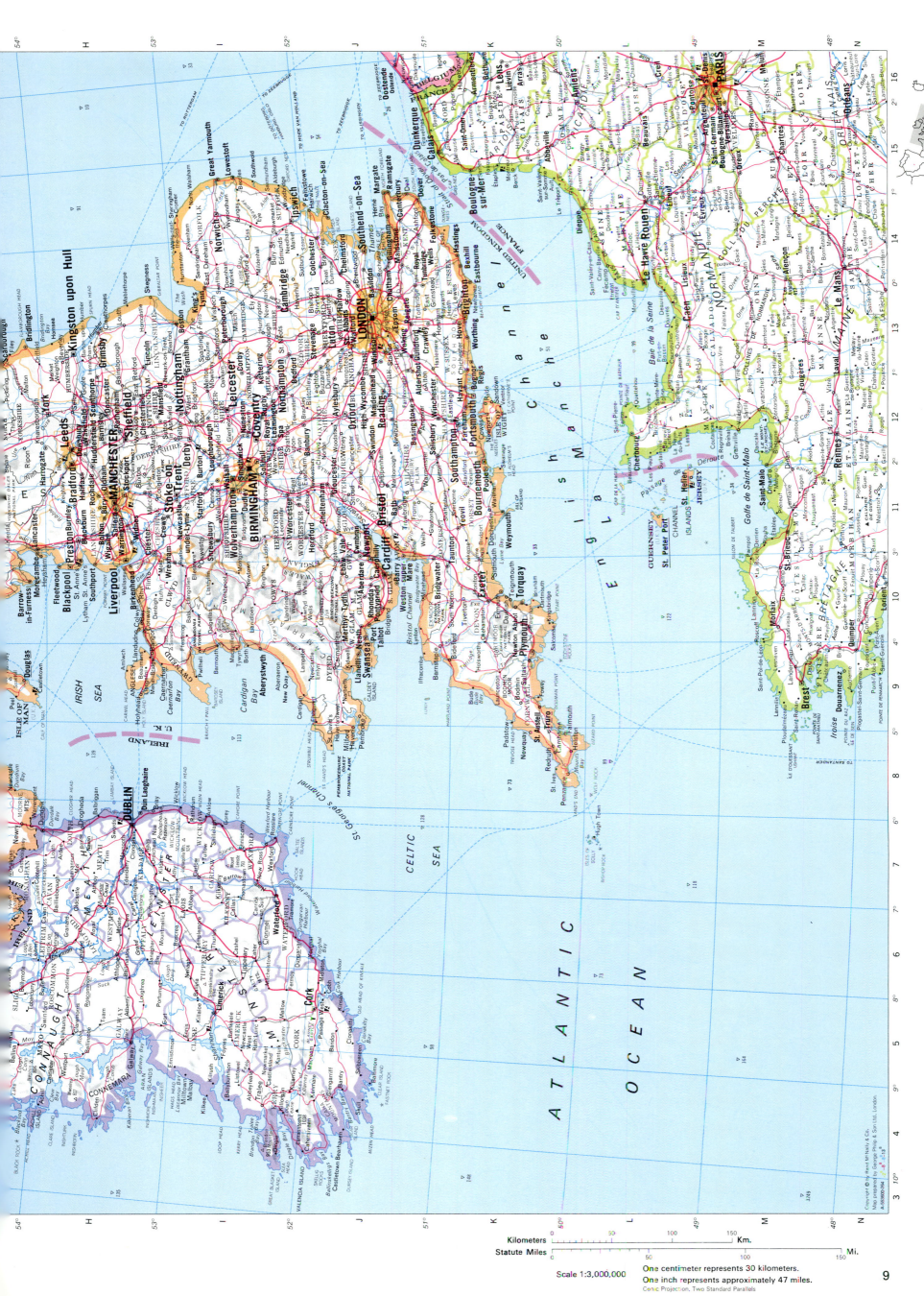

Kilometers
Statute Miles

One centimeter represents 30 kilometers.
One inch represents approximately 47 miles.
Scale 1:3,000,000
Conic Projection, Two Standard Parallels

Km.

Mi.

9

Kilometers
Statute Miles

Km.
Mi.

Scale 1:3,000,000

One centimeter represents 30 kilometers.
One inch represents approximately 47 miles.
Conic Projection, Two Standard Parallels.

# Belgium, Netherlands, and Luxembourg

NORTH SEA
NOORDZEE

Scale 1:1,500,000

One centimeter represents 15 kilometers.
One inch represents approximately 24 miles.
Lambert Conformal Conic Projection

Kilometers
Statute Miles

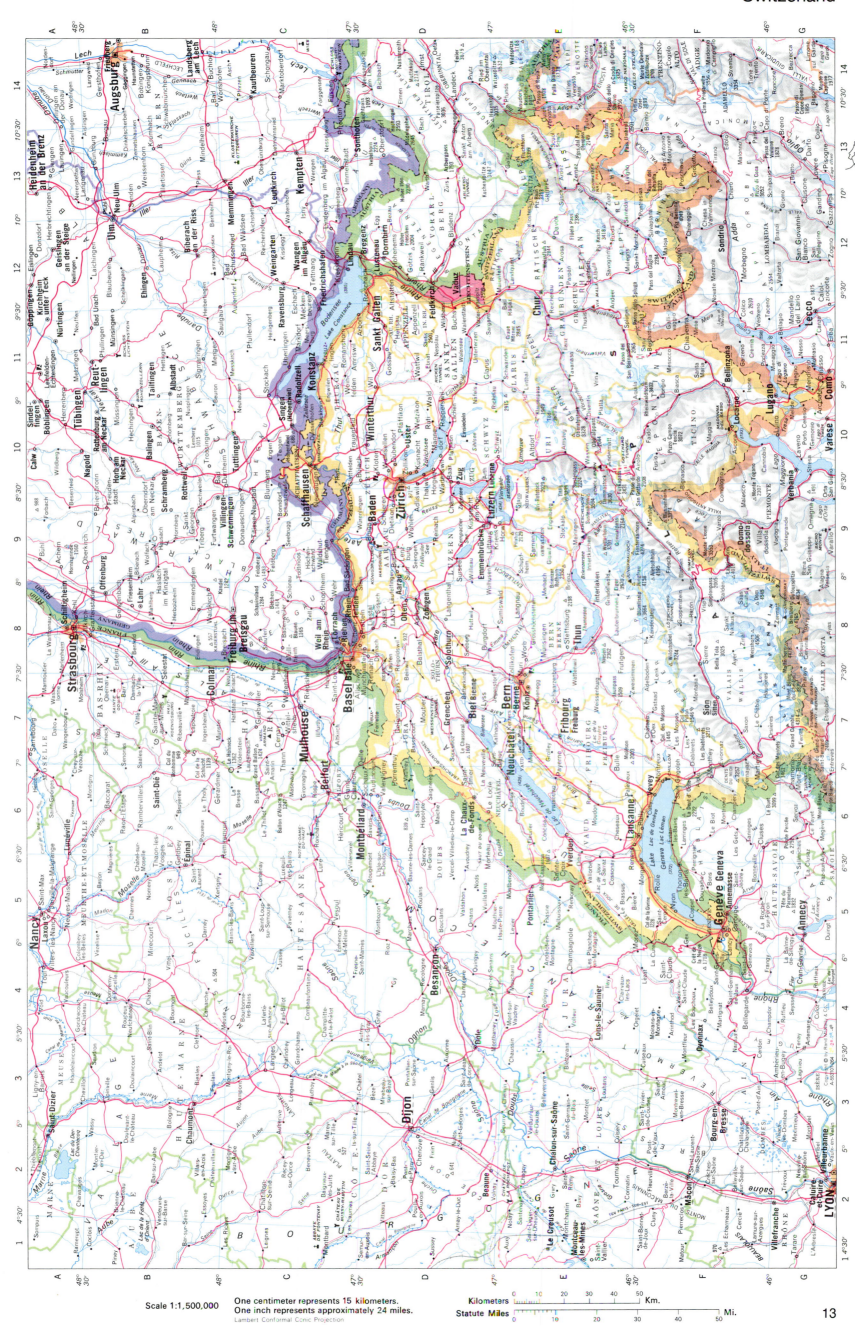

Scale 1:1,500,000

One centimeter represents 15 kilometers.
One inch represents approximately 24 miles.

Lambert Conformal Conic Projection

Kilometers

Statute Miles

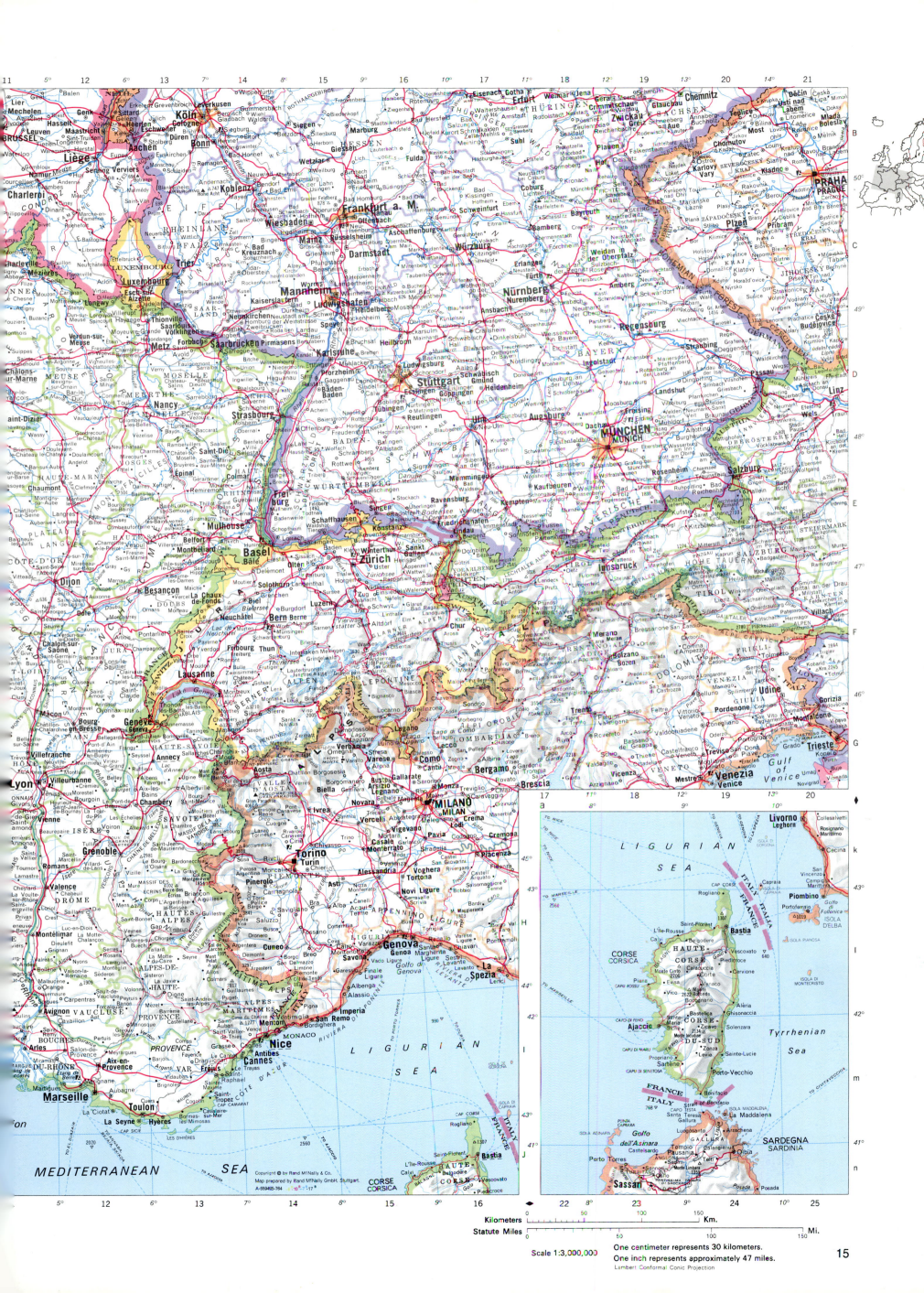

**MEDITERRANEAN SEA**

**LIGURIAN SEA**

*Tyrrhenian Sea*

**CORSE**
**CORSICA**

**SARDEGNA**
**SARDINIA**

Kilometers
Statute Miles

Scale 1:3,000,000
One centimeter represents 30 kilometers.
One inch represents approximately 47 miles.
Lambert Conformal Conic Projection

15

# Spain and Portugal

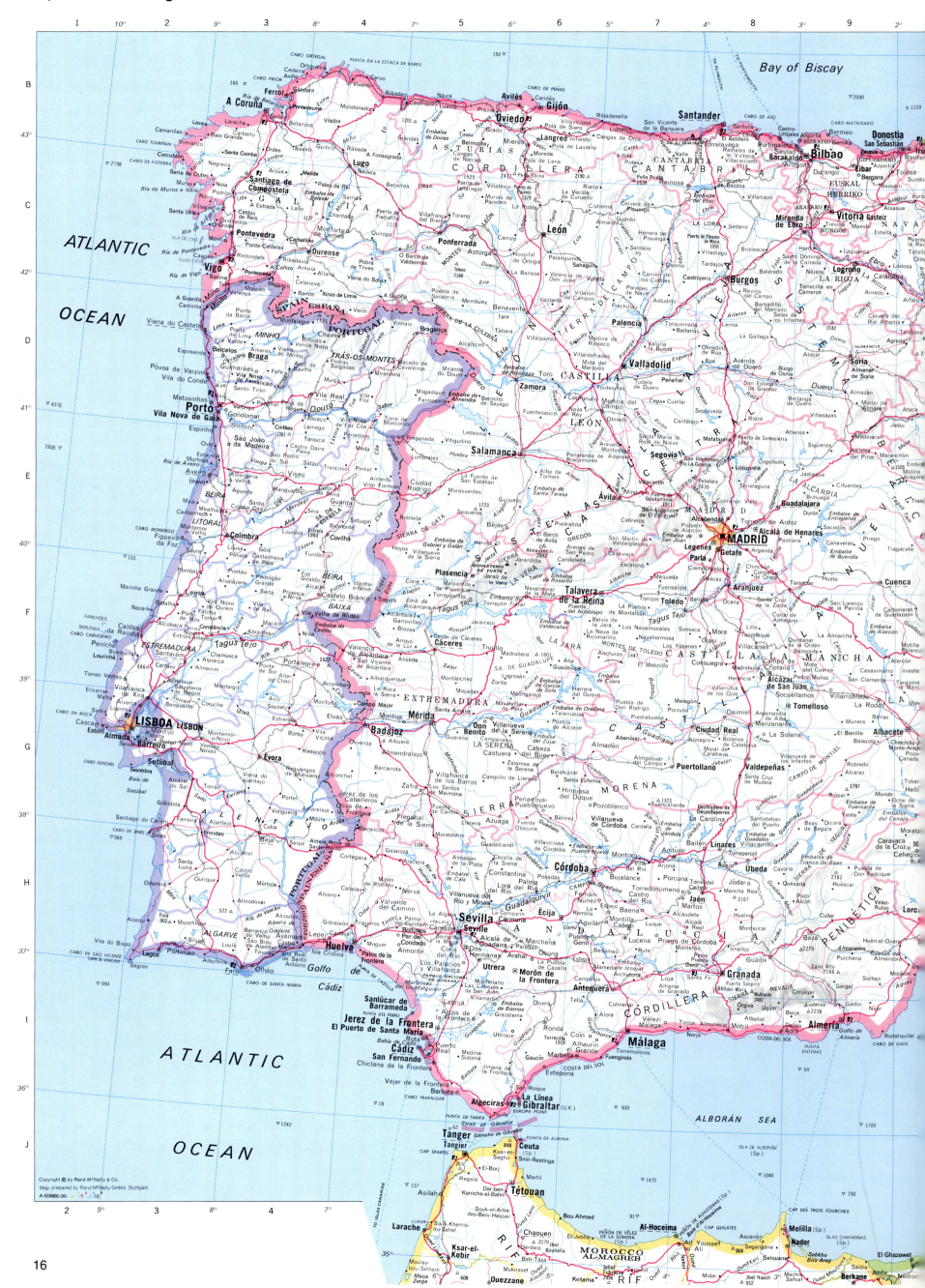

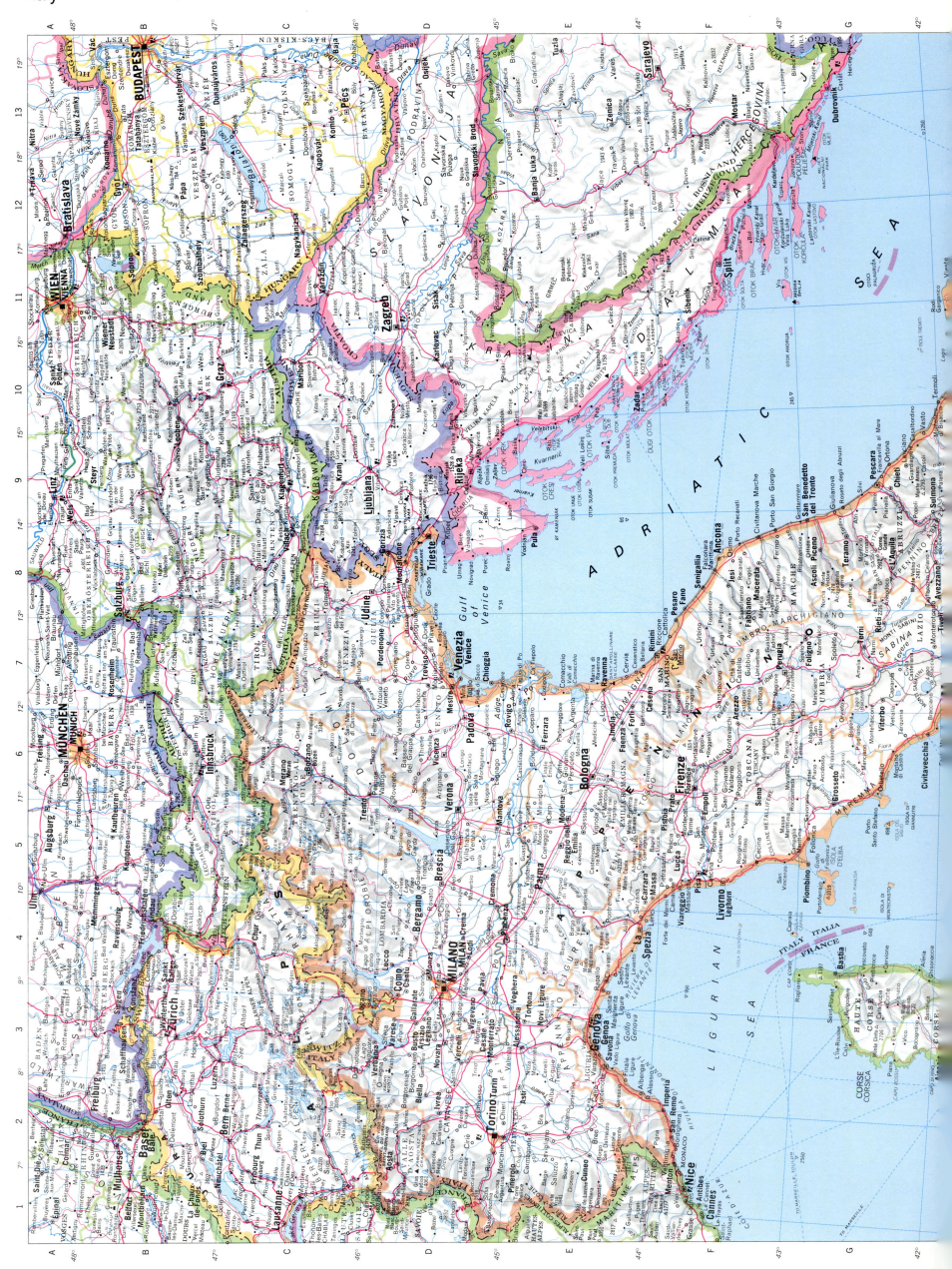

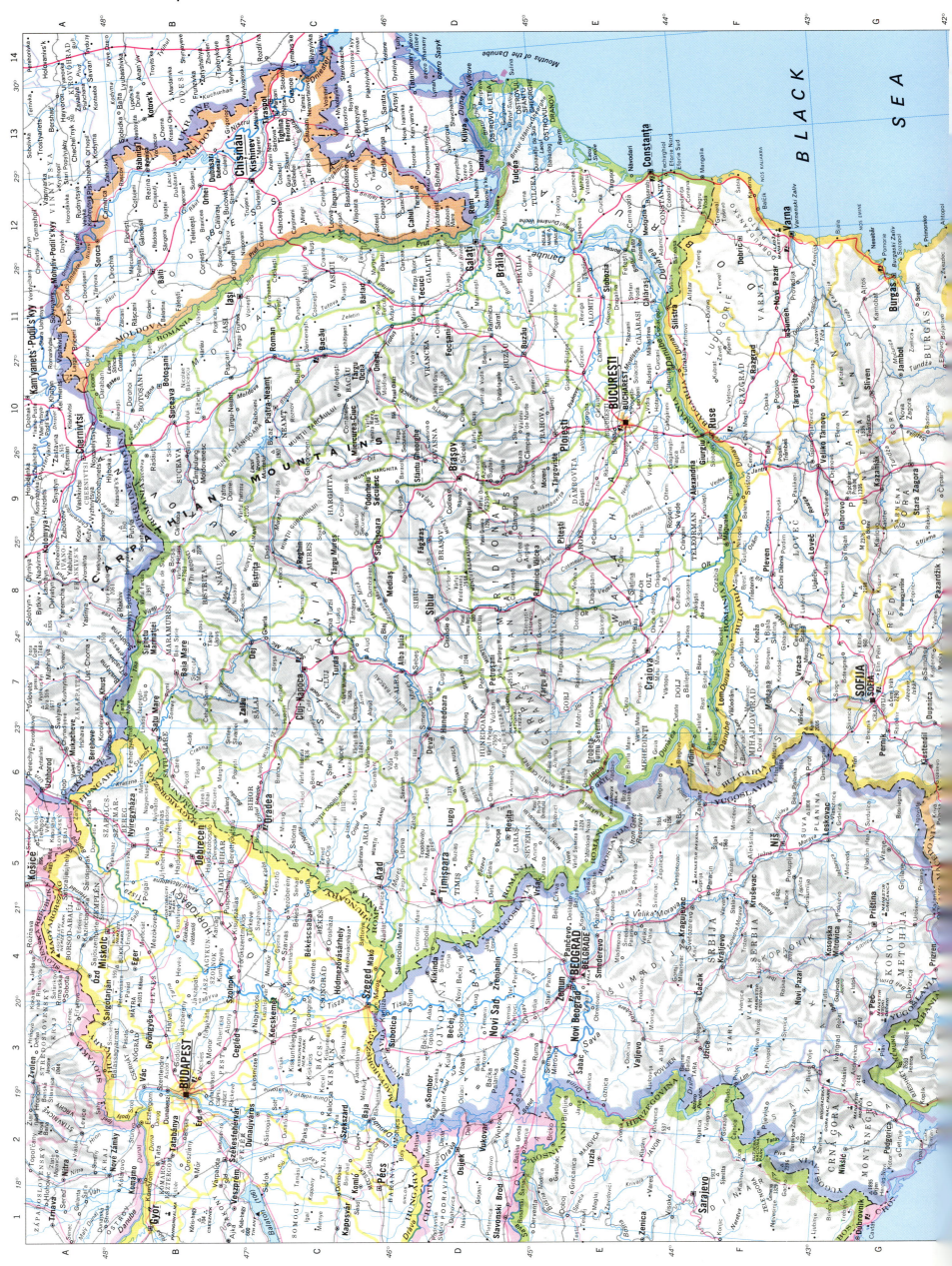

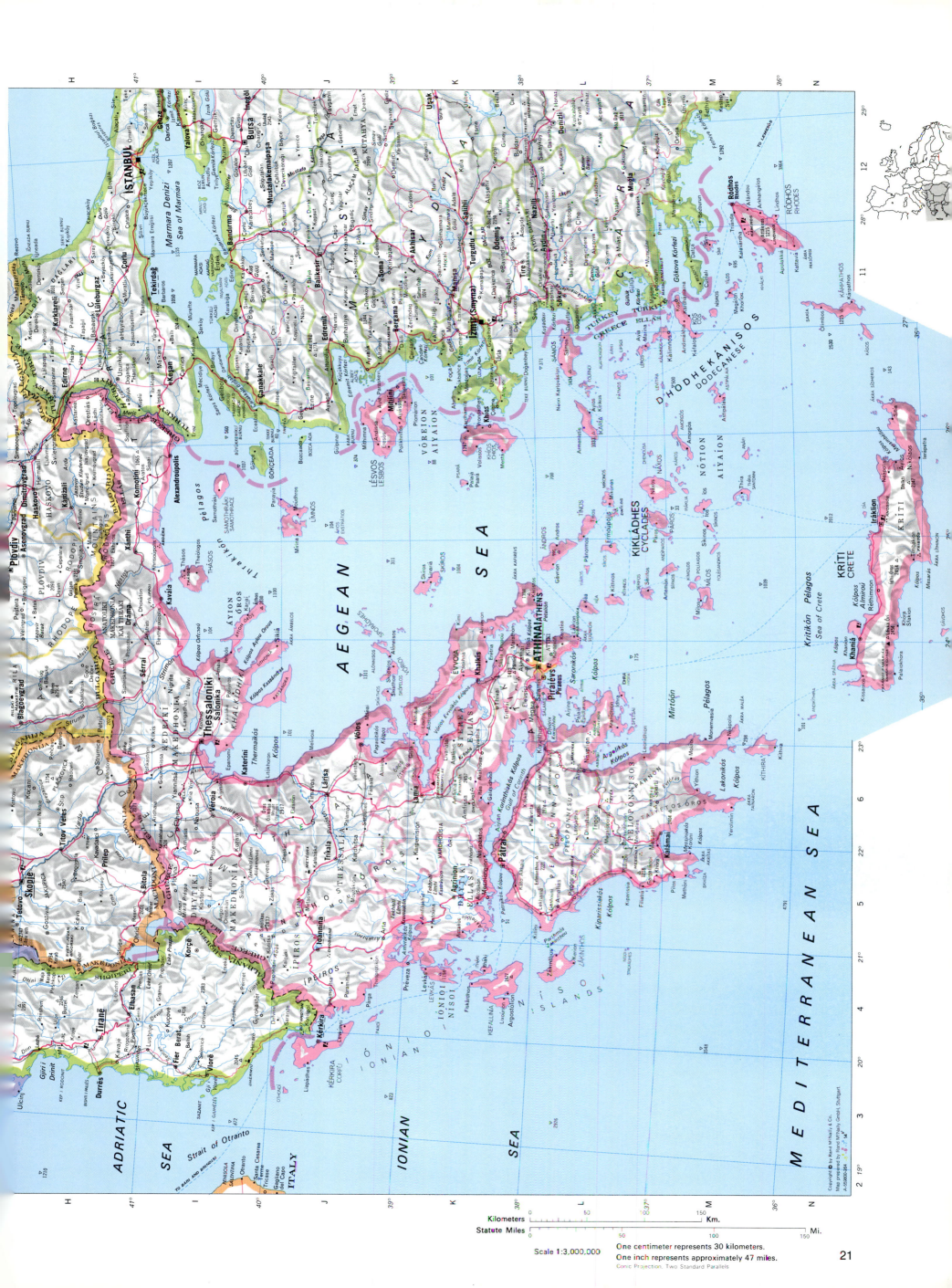

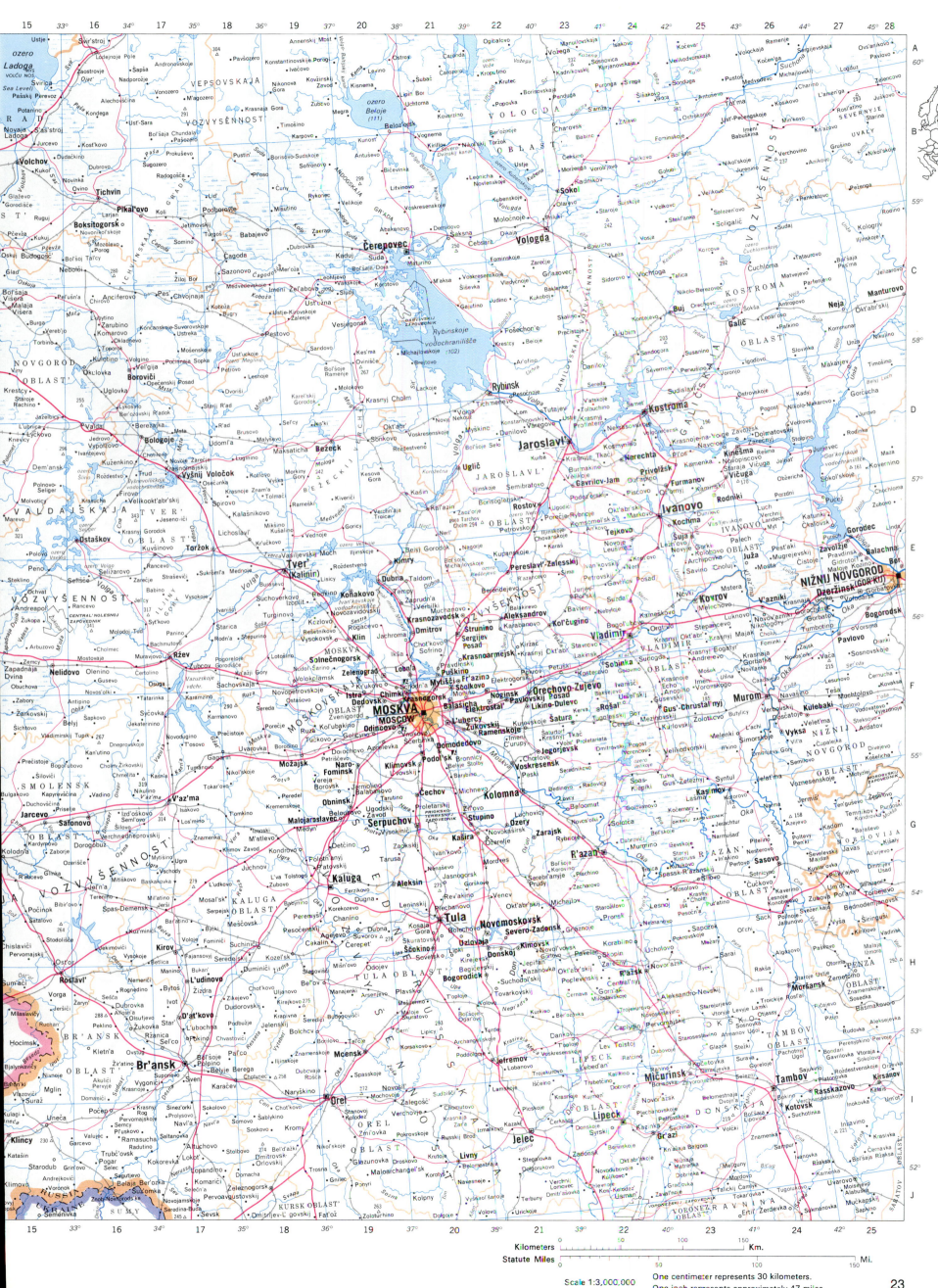

Scale 1:3,000,000

Kilometers
Statute Miles

One centimeter represents 30 kilometers.
One inch represents approximately 47 miles.
Lambert Conformal Conic Projection

23

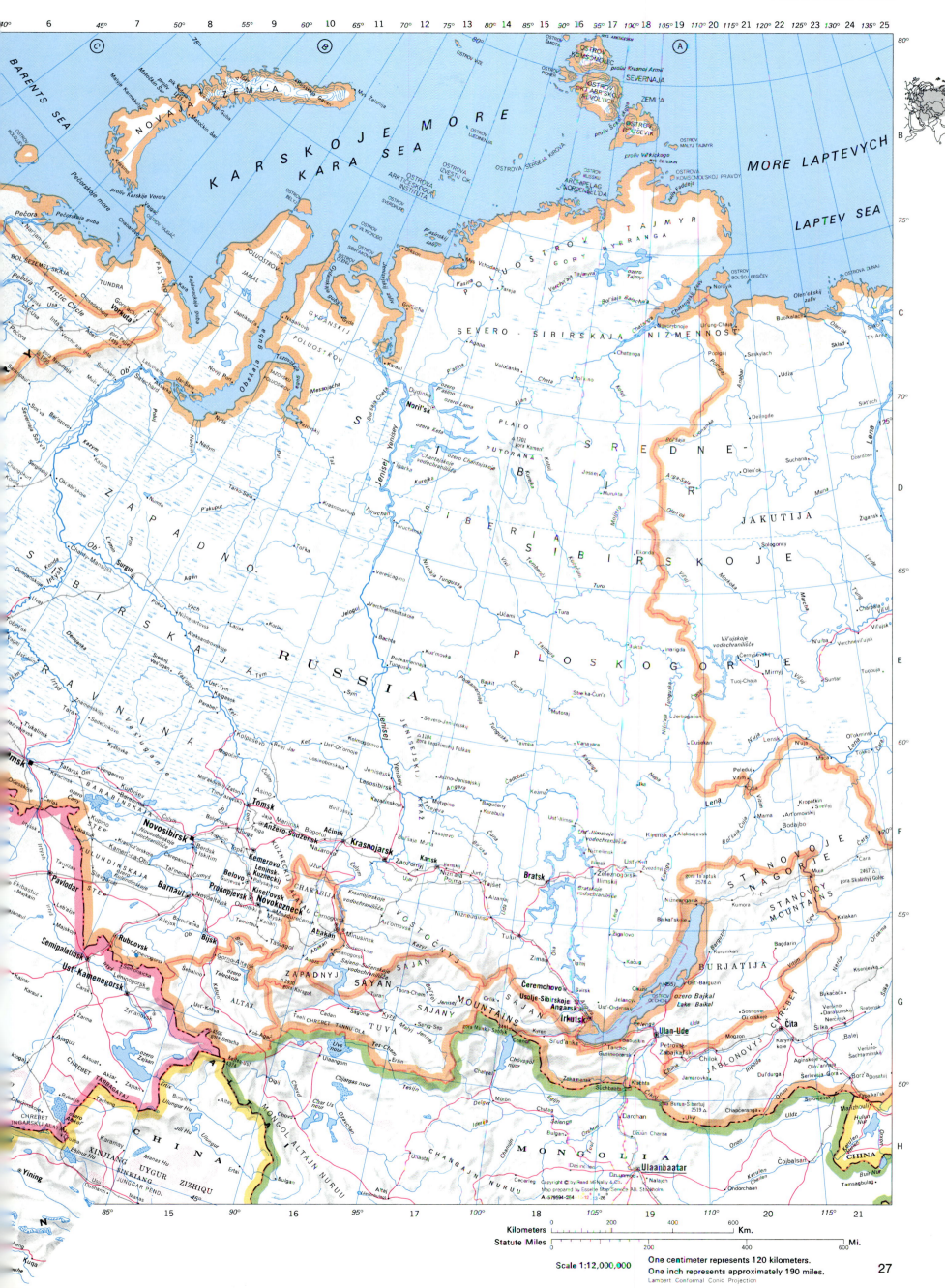

Scale 1:12,000,000

One centimeter represents 120 kilometers.
One inch represents approximately 190 miles.
Lambert Conformal Conic Projection

27

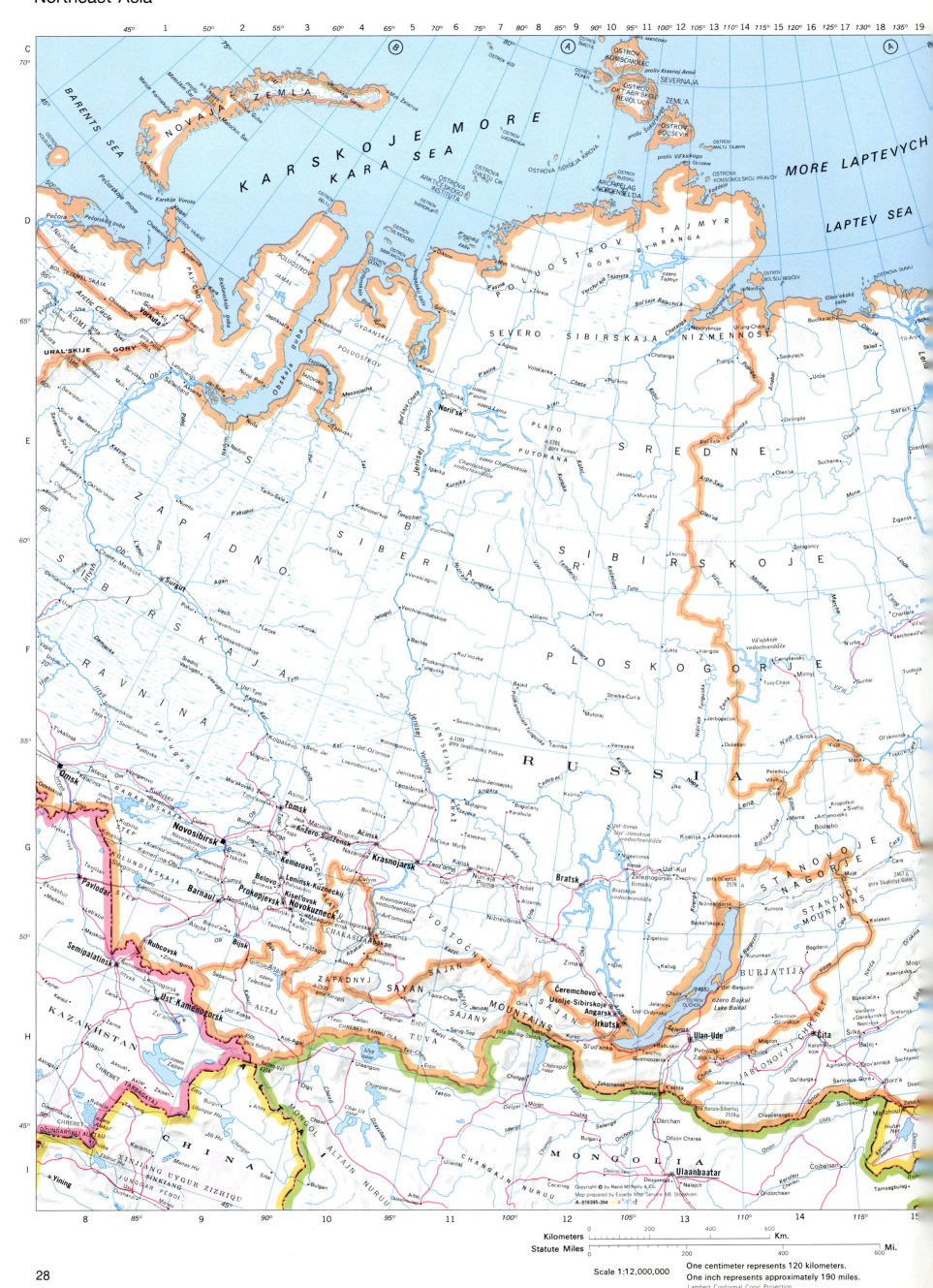

Kilometers
Statute Miles

Scale 1:12,000,000

One centimeter represents 120 kilometers.
One inch represents approximately 190 miles.
Lambert Conformal Conic Projection

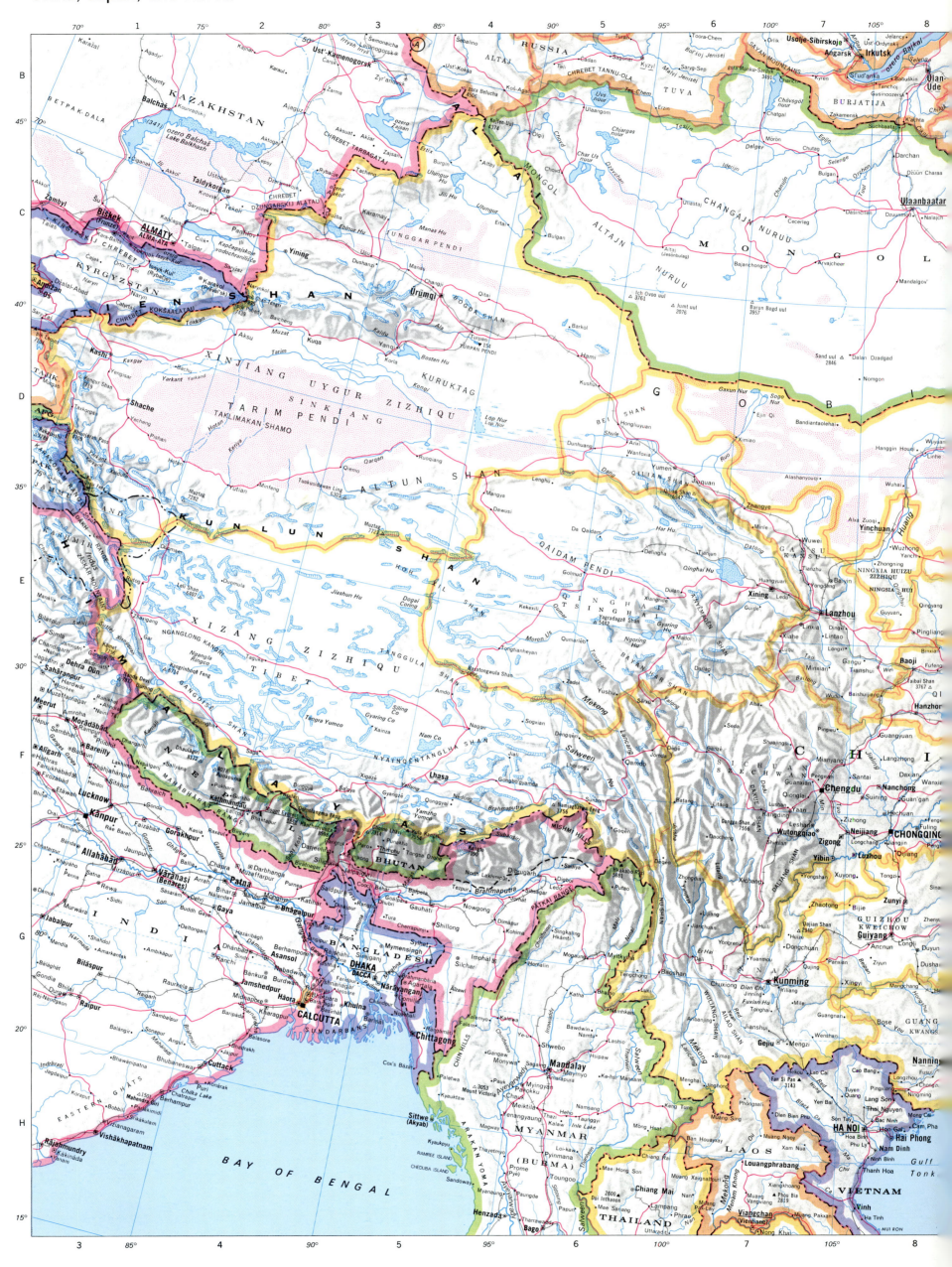

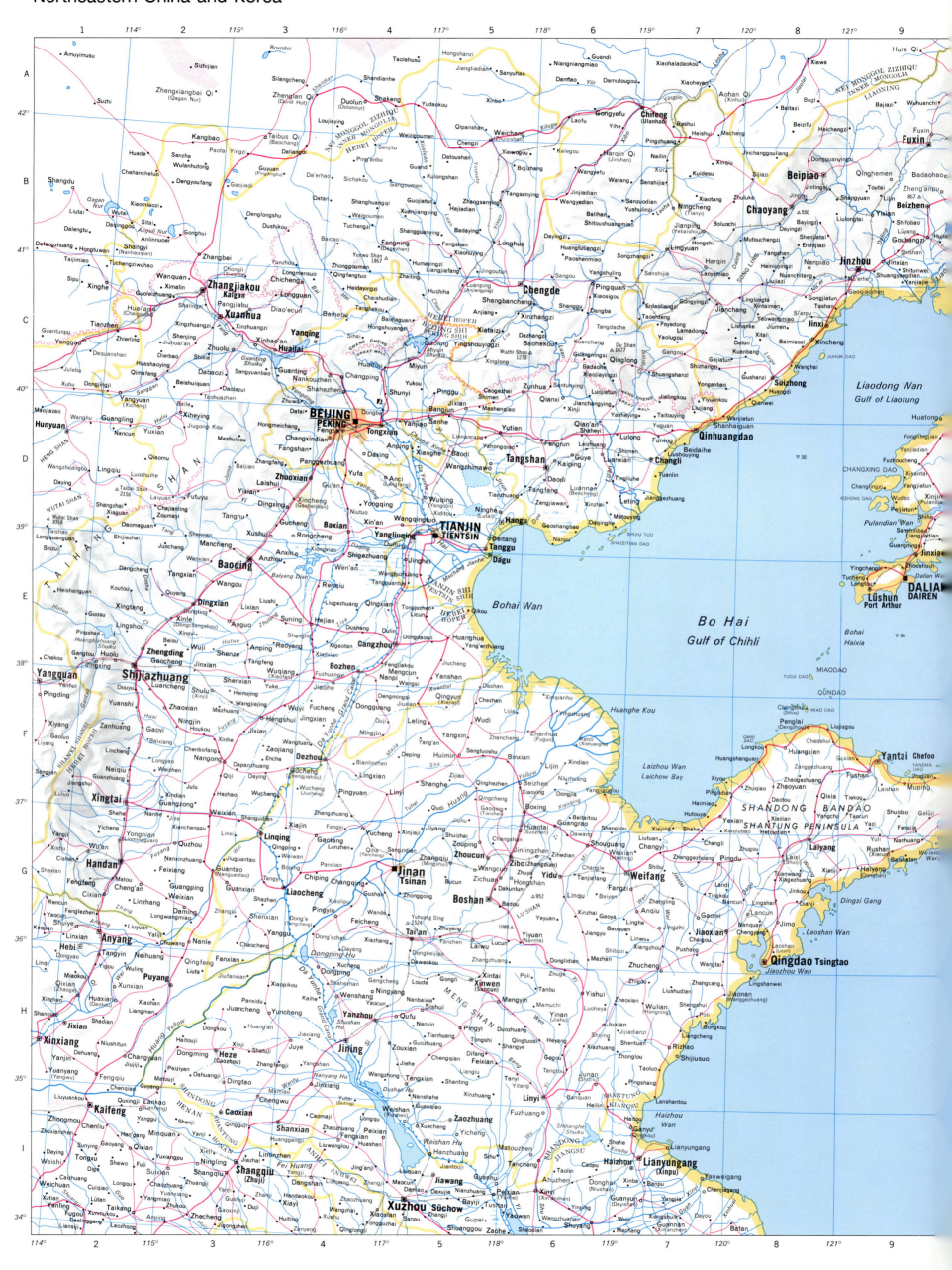

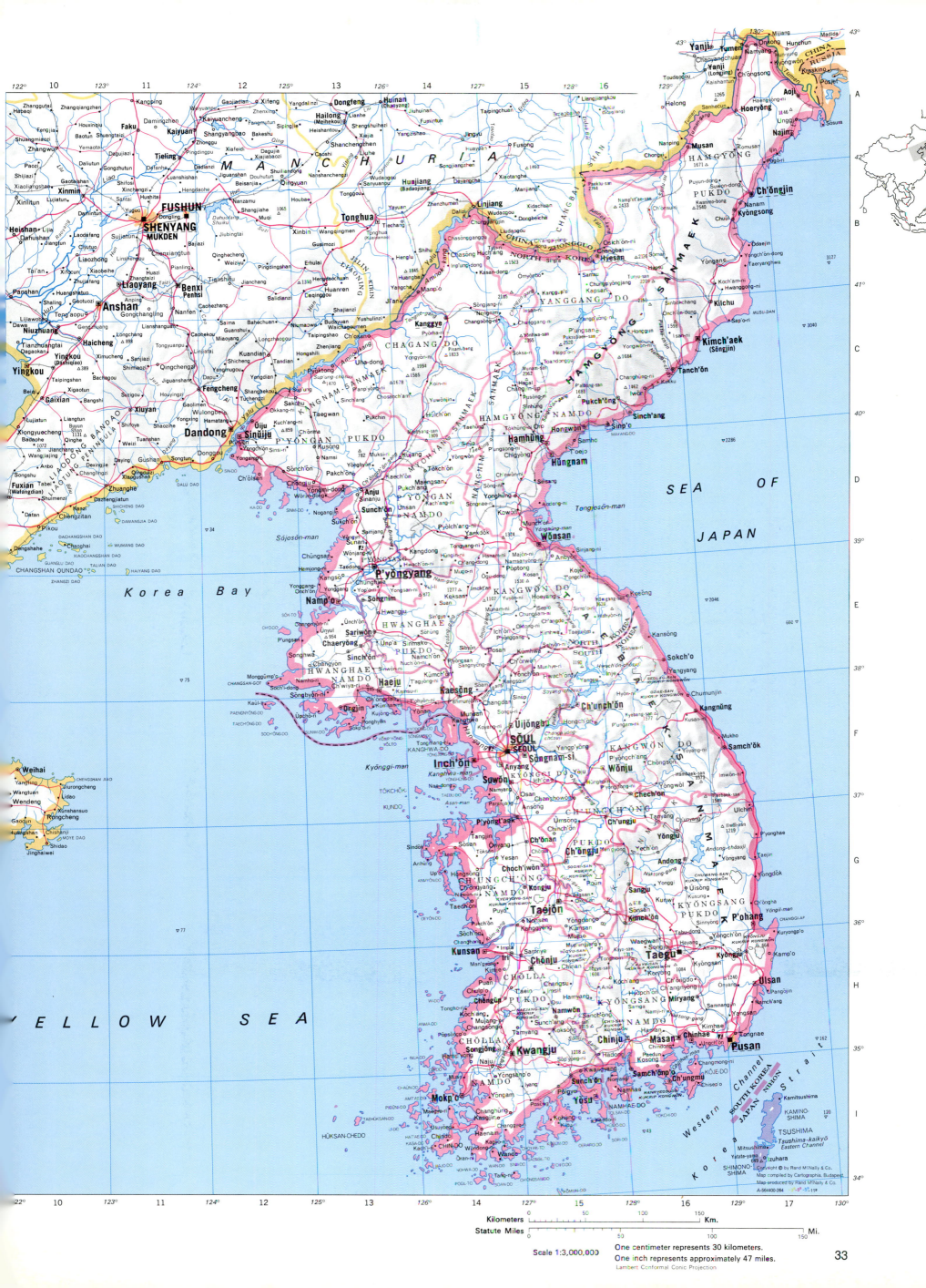

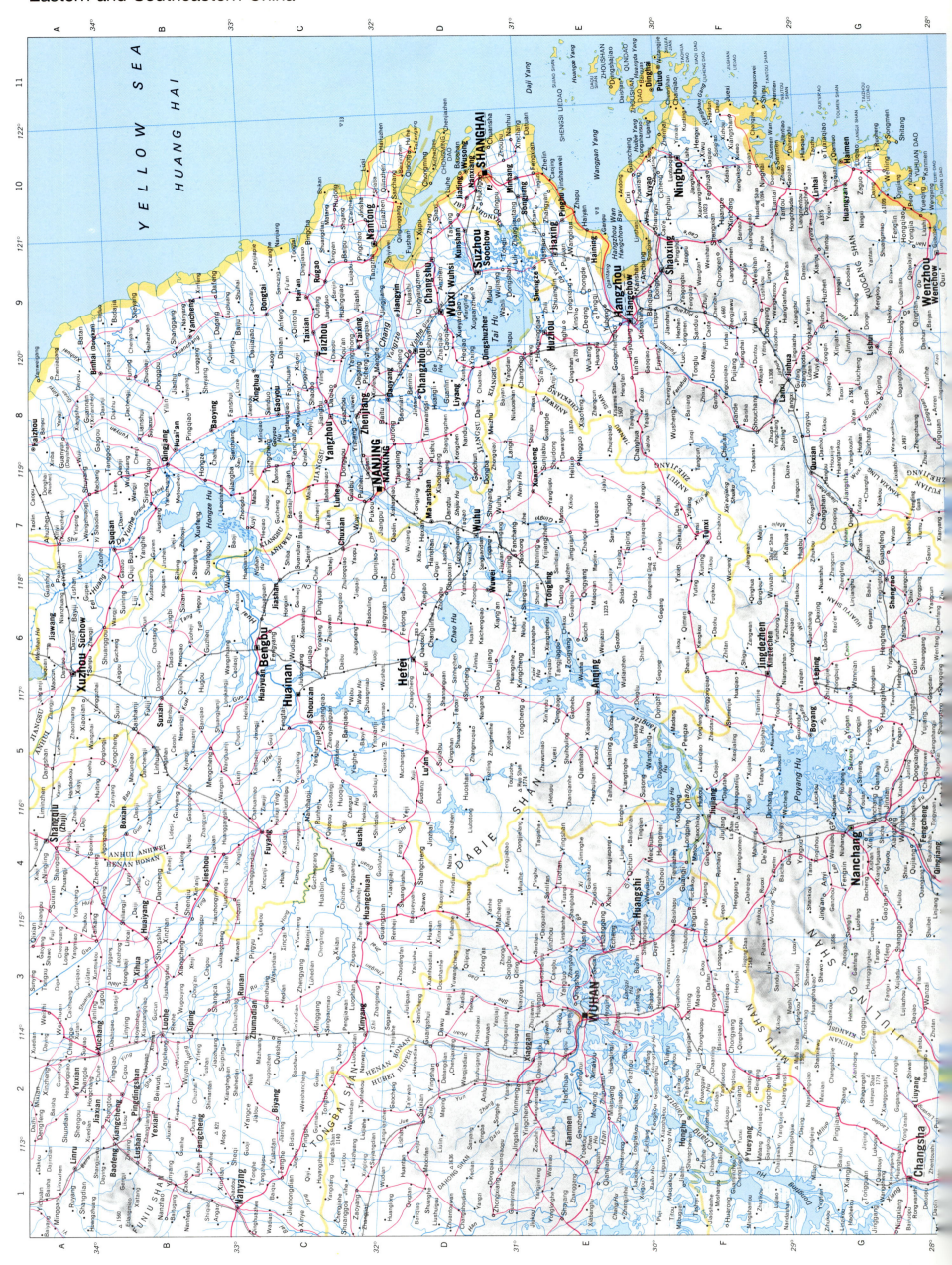

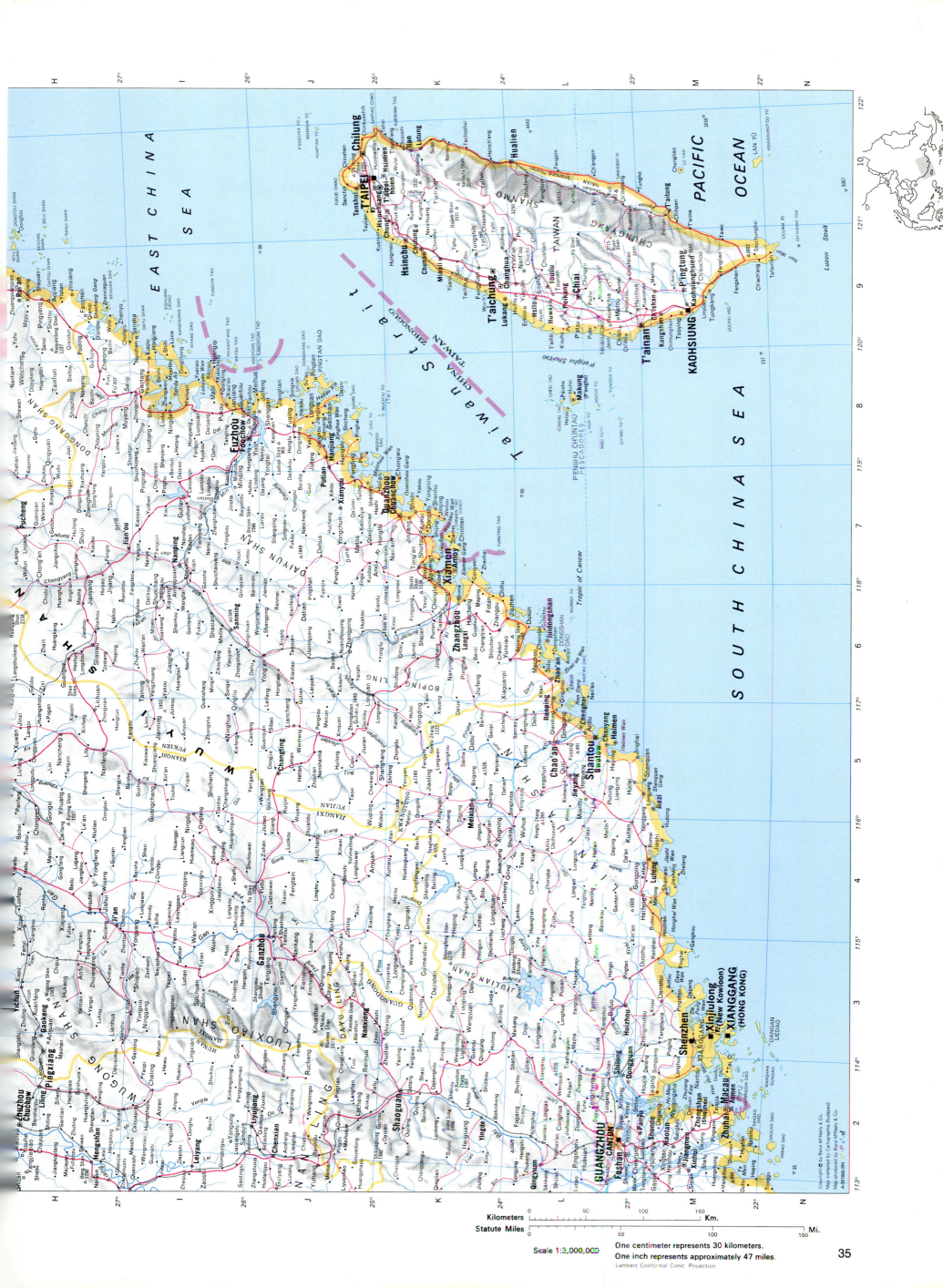

# Japan

PACIFIC OCEAN

SEA OF OKHOTSK

SEA OF JAPAN
NIHON-KAI

PACIFIC OCEAN

HOKKAIDŌ

HONSHŪ

**TŌKYŌ**

Sendai

**Sapporo**

Hakodate

Aomori

Akita

Morioka

Niigata

Nagano

Toyama

Kanazawa

Yokohama

Chiba

Asahikawa

Kushiro

Obihiro

Muroran

Tomakomai

Otaru

Ebetsu

Hachinohe

Hirosaki

Wakkanai

Nemuro

KURIL'SKIJE OSTROVA
KURIL'SKIE OSTROVA
CHISHIMA-RETTŌ
KURIL ISLANDS

OSTROV SACHALIN
SAKHALIN

RUSSIA
ROSSIJA

JAPAN
NIHON

La Pérouse Strait
Soyakaikyō

Tsugaru-kaikyō

KITAKAMI

KITAKAMI SANCHI

DEWA SANCHI

ECHIGO

ABUKUMA

KANTŌ

HIDA

HONSHŪ

TESHIO SANCHI

KITAMI SANCHI

ISHIKARI

HIDAKA-SAMMYAKU

HOKKAIDŌ

36

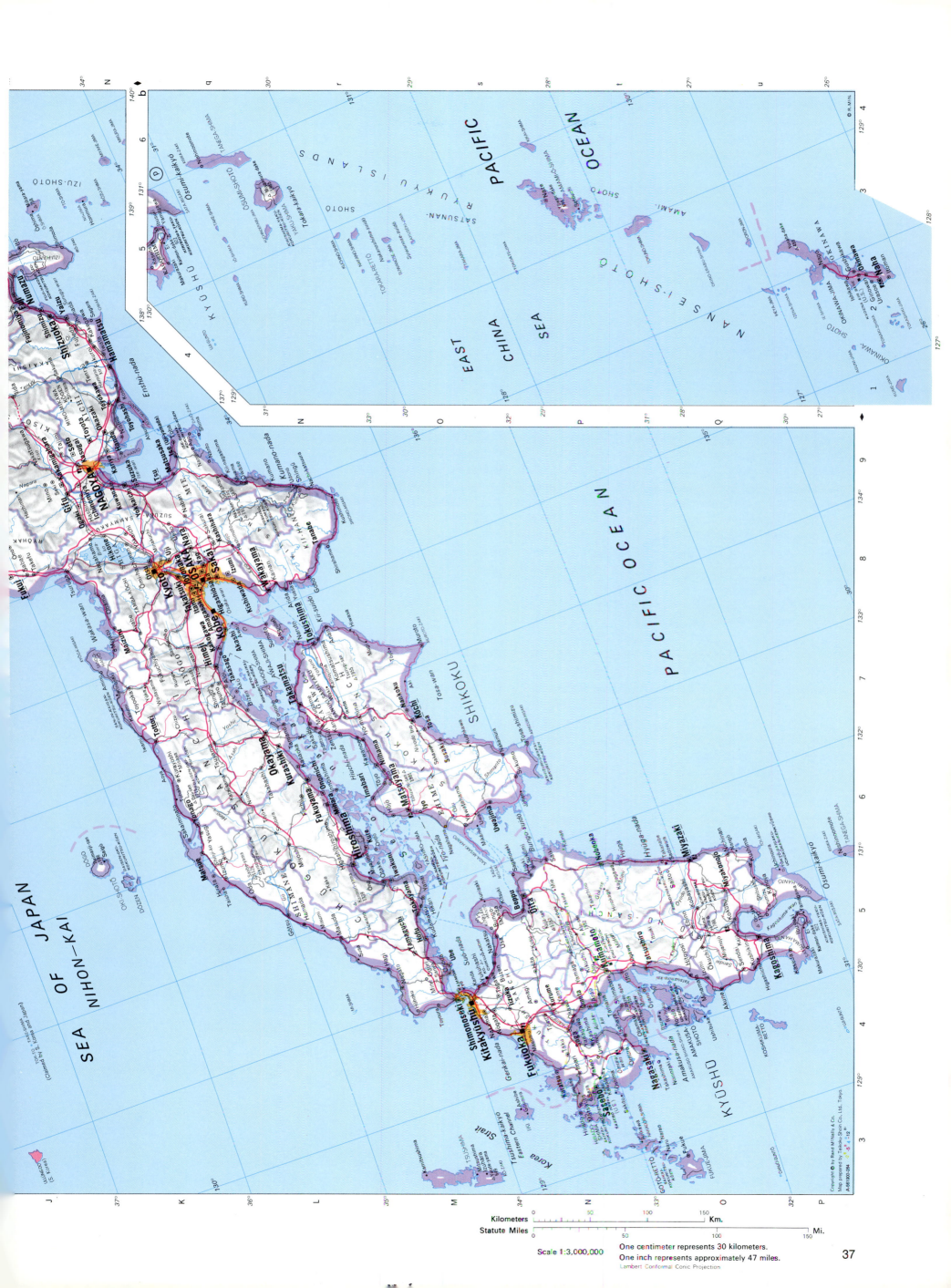

37

# Myanmar, Thailand, and Indochina

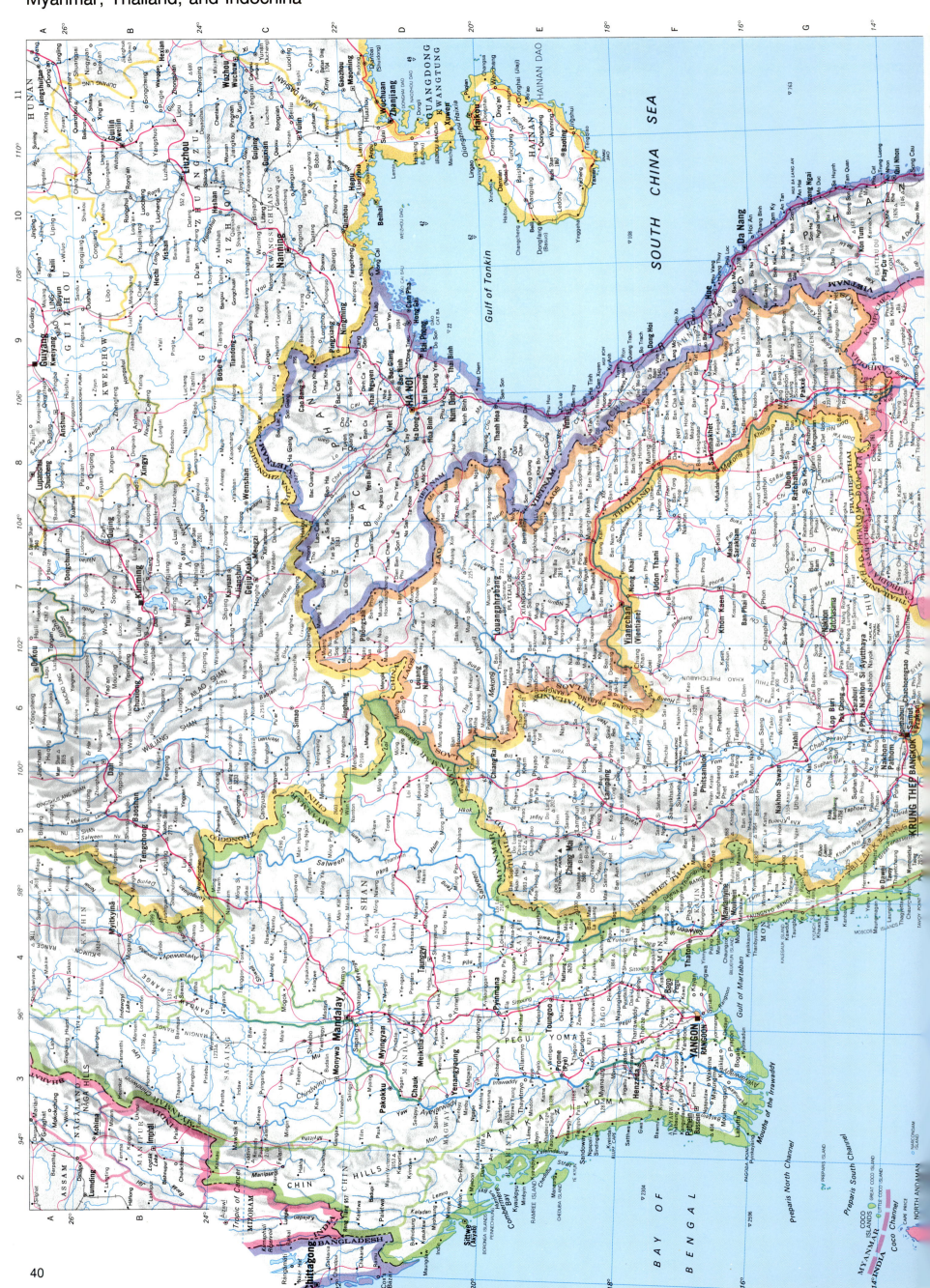

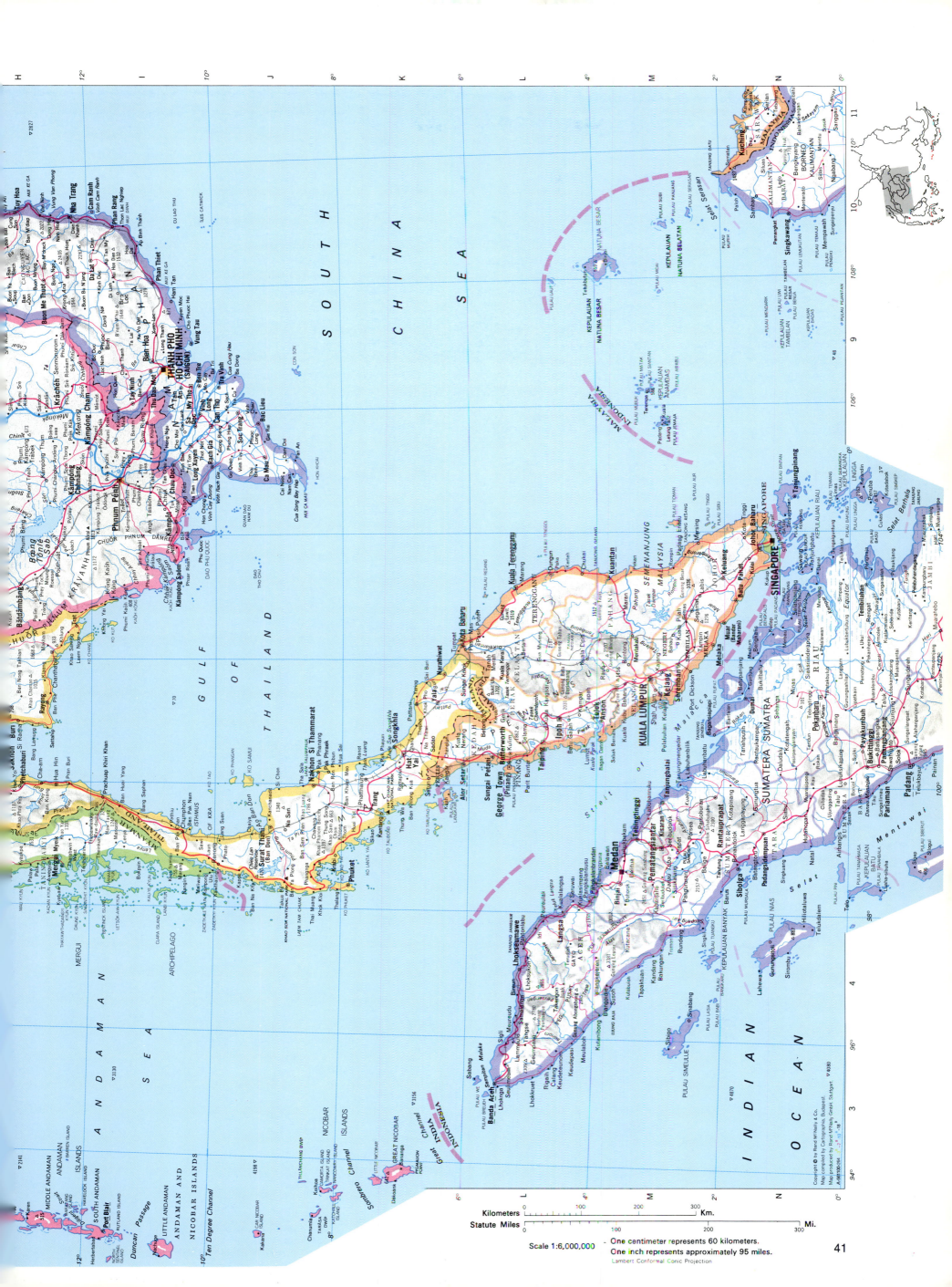

Kilometers
Statute Miles

Scale 1:12,000,000
One centimeter represents 120 kilometers.
One inch represents approximately 190 miles.
Lambert Conformal Conic Projection

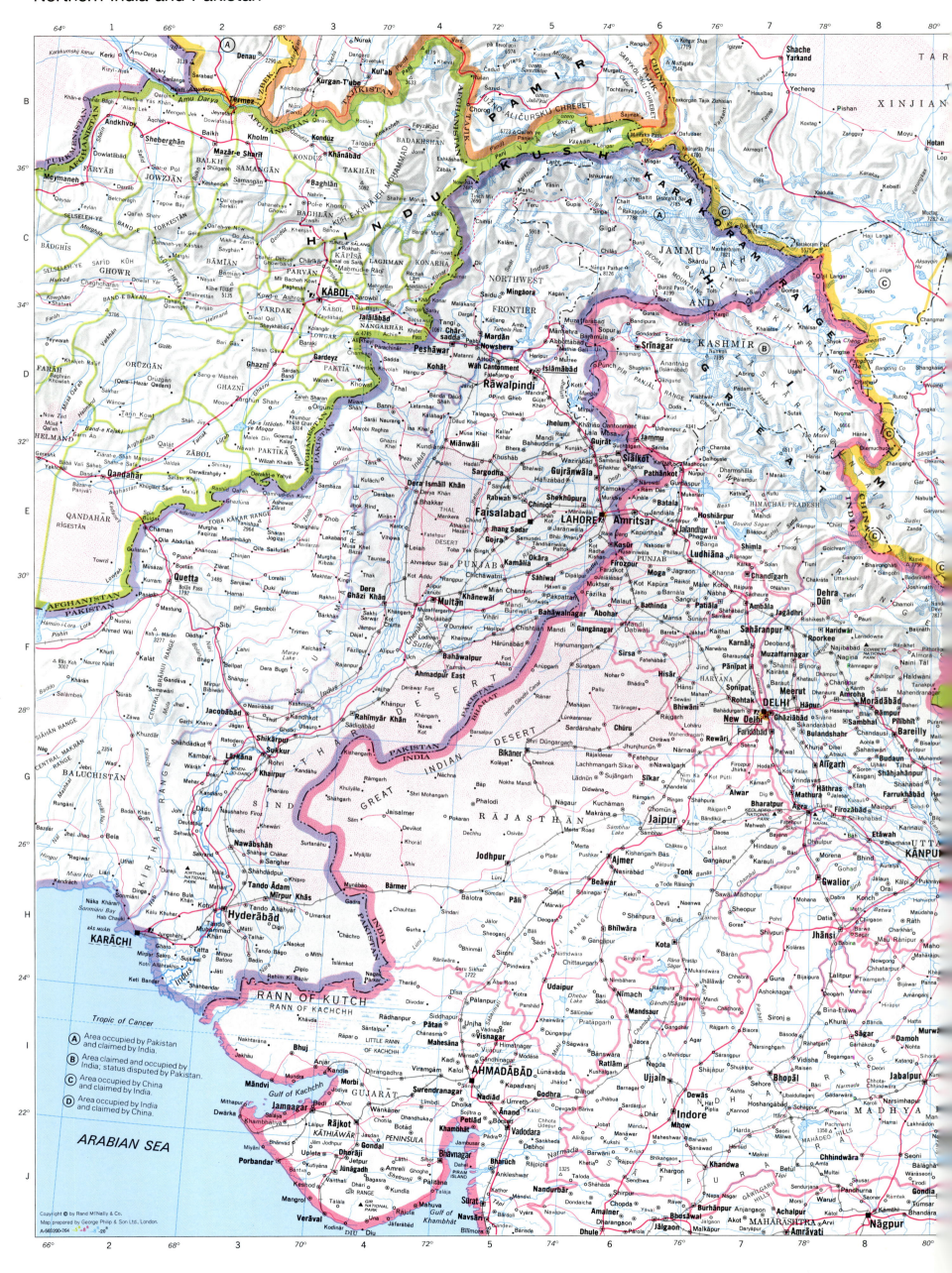

A Area occupied by Pakistan and claimed by India.
B Area claimed and occupied by India, status disputed by Pakistan.
C Area occupied by China and claimed by India.
D Area occupied by India and claimed by China.

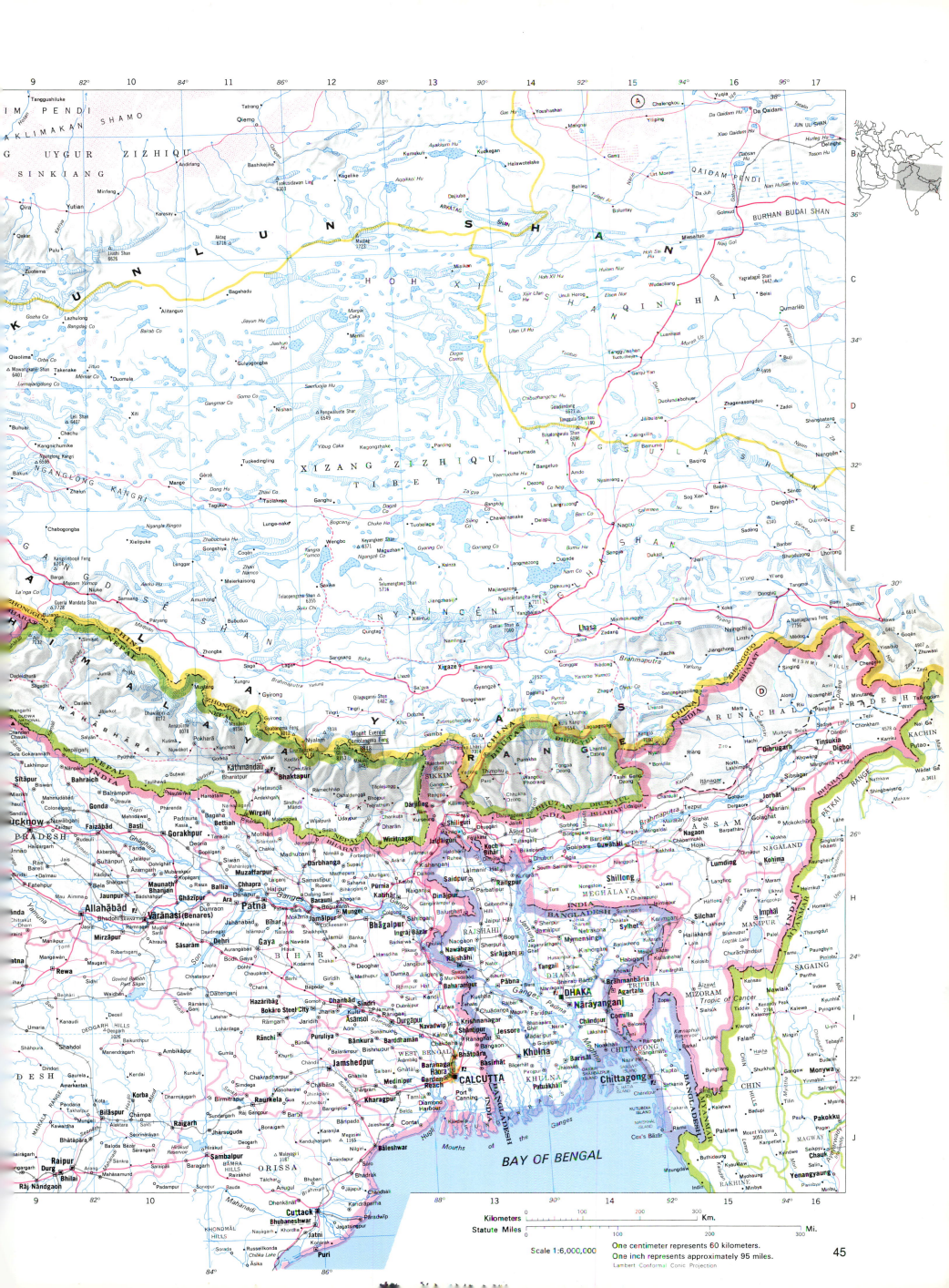

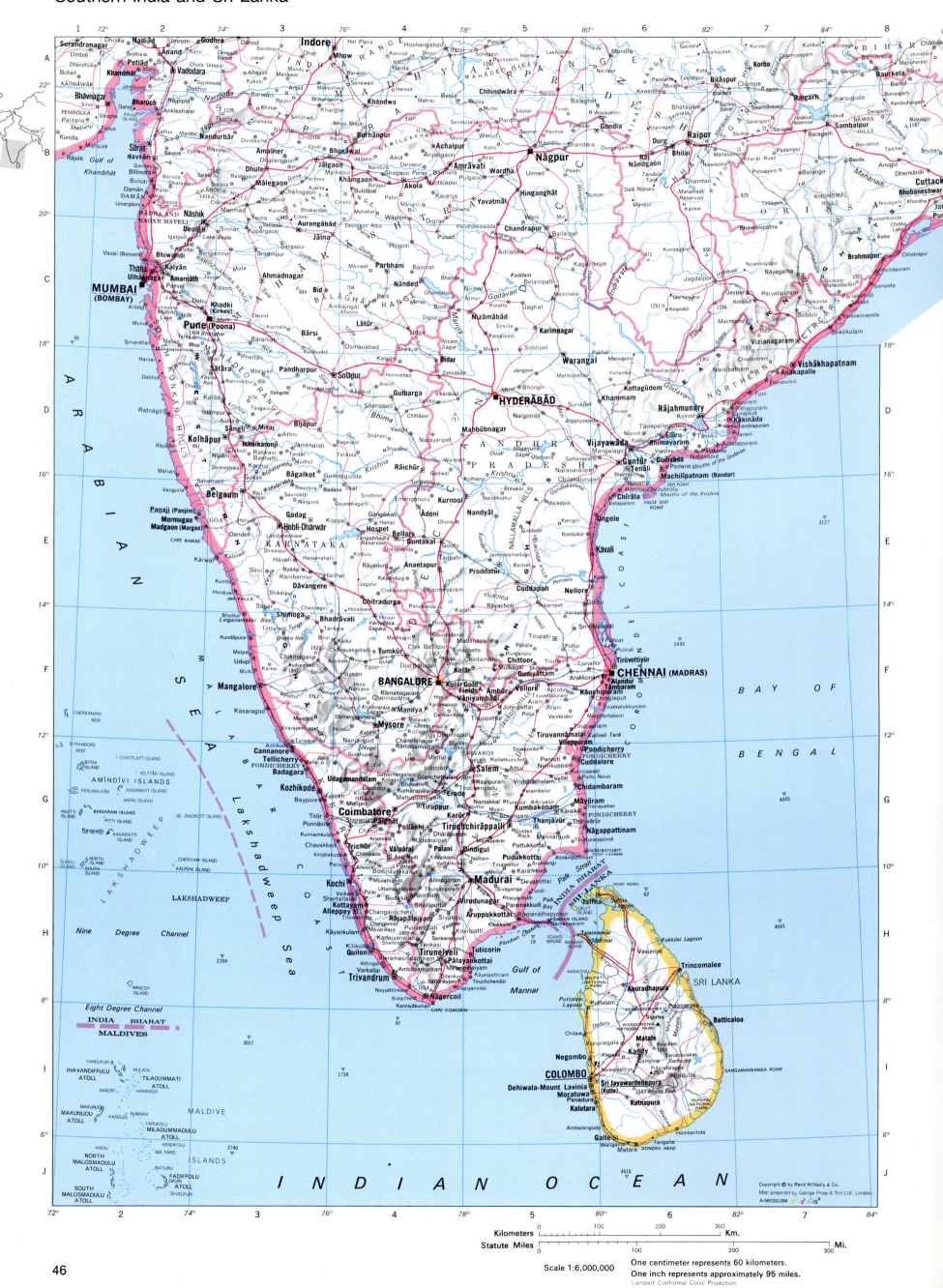

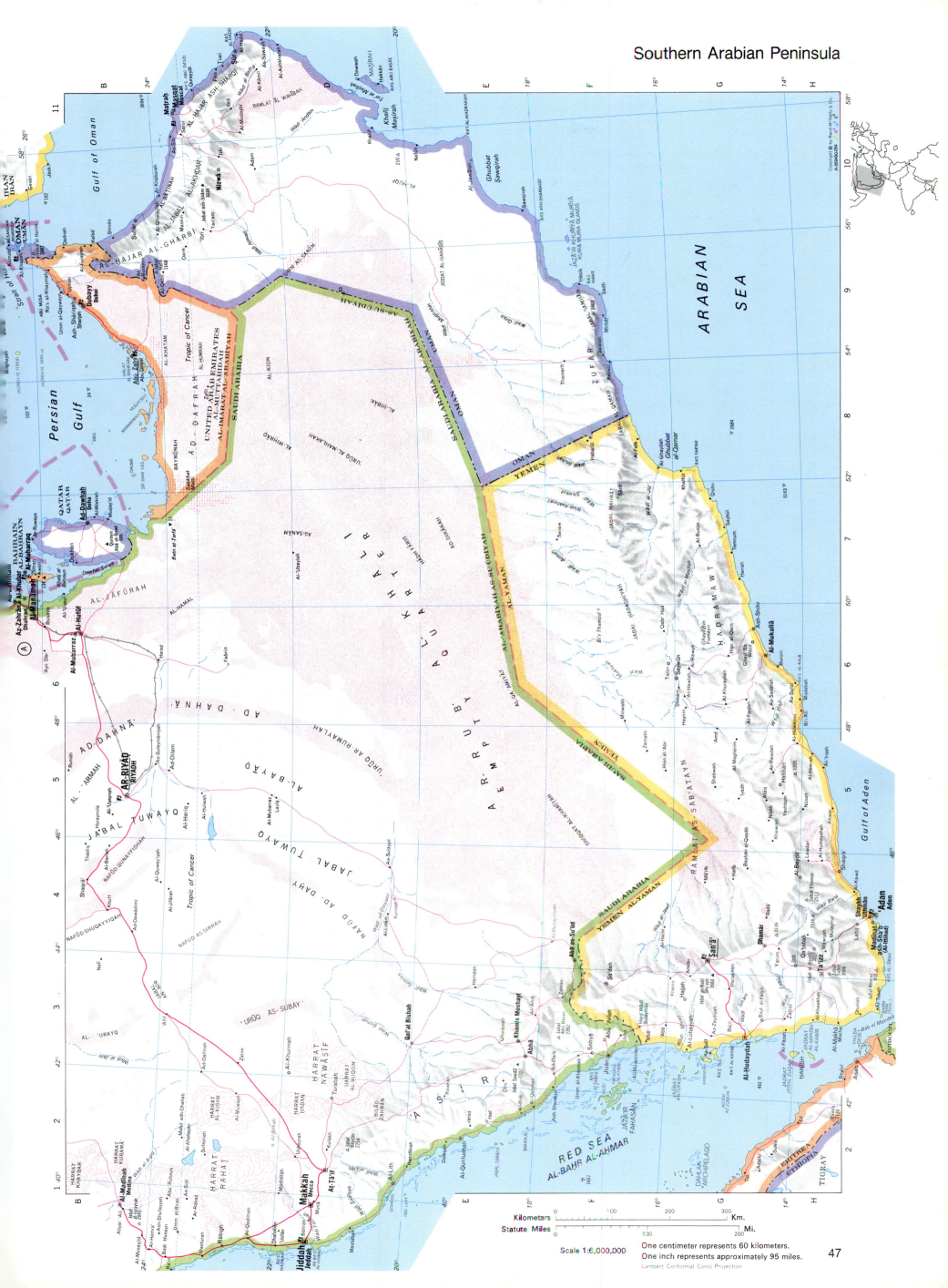

Southern Arabian Peninsula

# The Middle East

A Area occupied by United Nations
Disengagement Observer Force
since 1974.

B Golan Heights area. Occupied by Israel
since 1967. Unilaterally annexed by
Israel, 1981.

C West Bank area. Occupied by Israel
since 1967. Limited autonomy granted
to Jericho Area, 1994. A 1995 interim
agreement provides for the gradual
withdrawal of Israeli troops from
populated areas.

D East Jerusalem portion of West Bank.
Unilaterally annexed by Israel, 1980.

E Gaza Strip. Occupied by Israel in 1967.
Limited autonomy granted, 1994.
Permanent status to be determined.

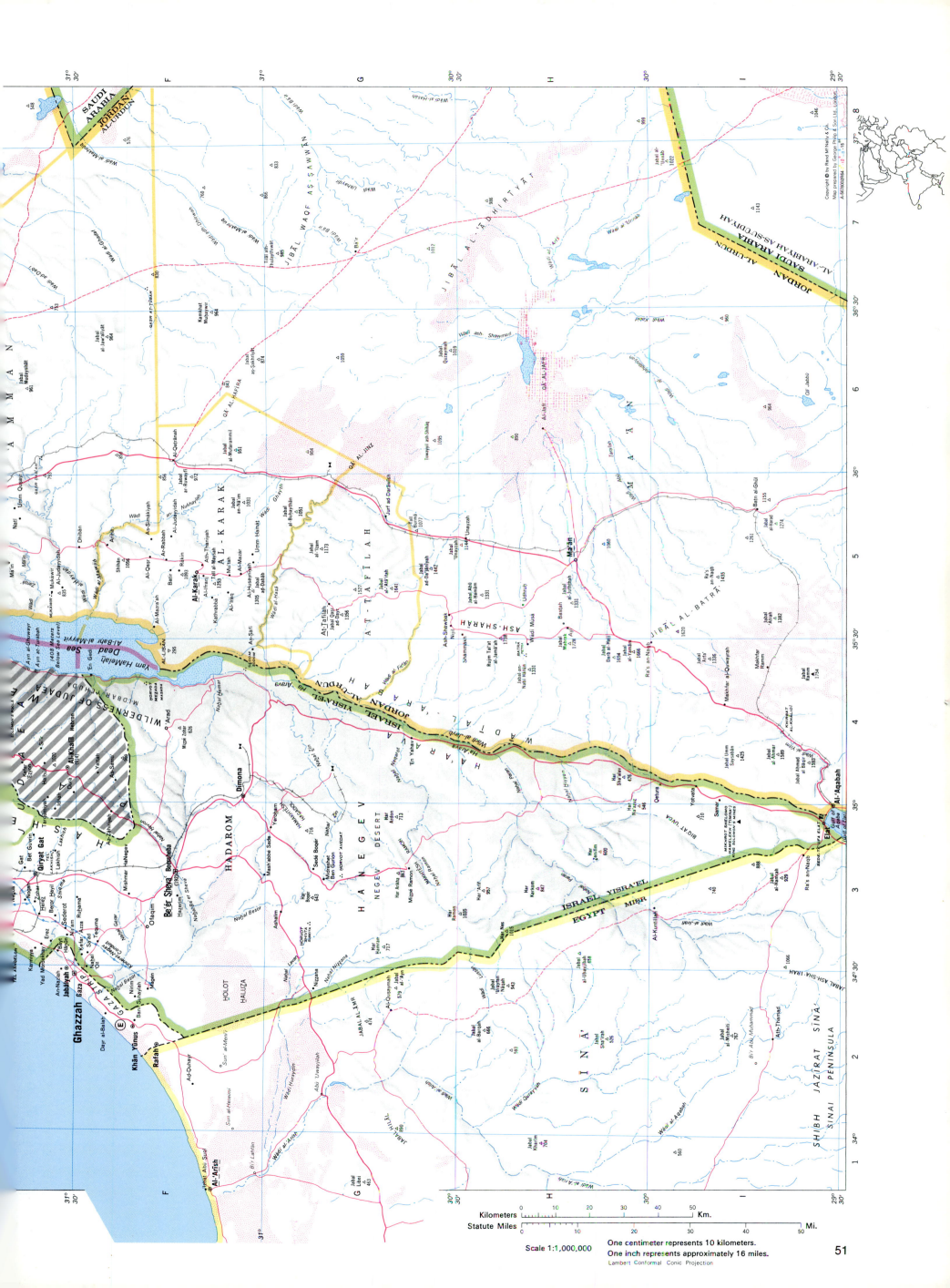

SAUDI ARABIA
AL-'ARABIYAH AS-SU'ŪDIYAH

JORDAN AL-URDUN

SAUDI ARABIA
JORDAN
AL-URDUN

A M M Ā N

M A 'Ā N

J I B Ā L   A L - A D H I R I Y Ā T

JIBĀL WAQF ASSAWWĀN

A L - K A R A K

A T - T A F Ī L A H

ASH-SHARĀH

JIBĀL AL-BATRĀ'

QĀ' AL-HAFĪRA

QĀ' AL-JINZ

QĀ' AL-JAFR

Al-Karak

At-Tafīlah

Ma'ān

Dead Sea
Al-Bahr al-Mayyit

Yam HaMelah

W E S T   B A N K

WILDERNESS OF JUDAEA
MIDBAR YEHUDA

Al-Khalīl

Be'ér Sheva'

Dimona

H A D A R O M

N E G E V   D E S E R T

HOLOT
HALUZA

HAR HANEGEV

Ghazzah

Gaza

Khān Yūnus

Rafah

Al-'Arīsh

S Ī N Ā'

S H I B H   J A Z Ī R A T   S Ī N Ā'
SINAI PENINSULA

JABAL ASH-SHA'ĪRAH

ISRAEL YISRA'EL
EGYPT MISR

ISRAEL YISRA'EL
JORDAN AL-URDUN

W Ā D Ī   A L - 'A R A B A H
HA 'Arava

Elat

Al-'Aqabah

Gulf of 'Aqaba

Kilometers 0 10 20 30 40 50 Km.
Statute Miles 0 10 20 30 40 50 Mi.

Scale 1:1,000,000
One centimeter represents 10 kilometers.
One inch represents approximately 16 miles.
Lambert Conformal Conic Projection

51

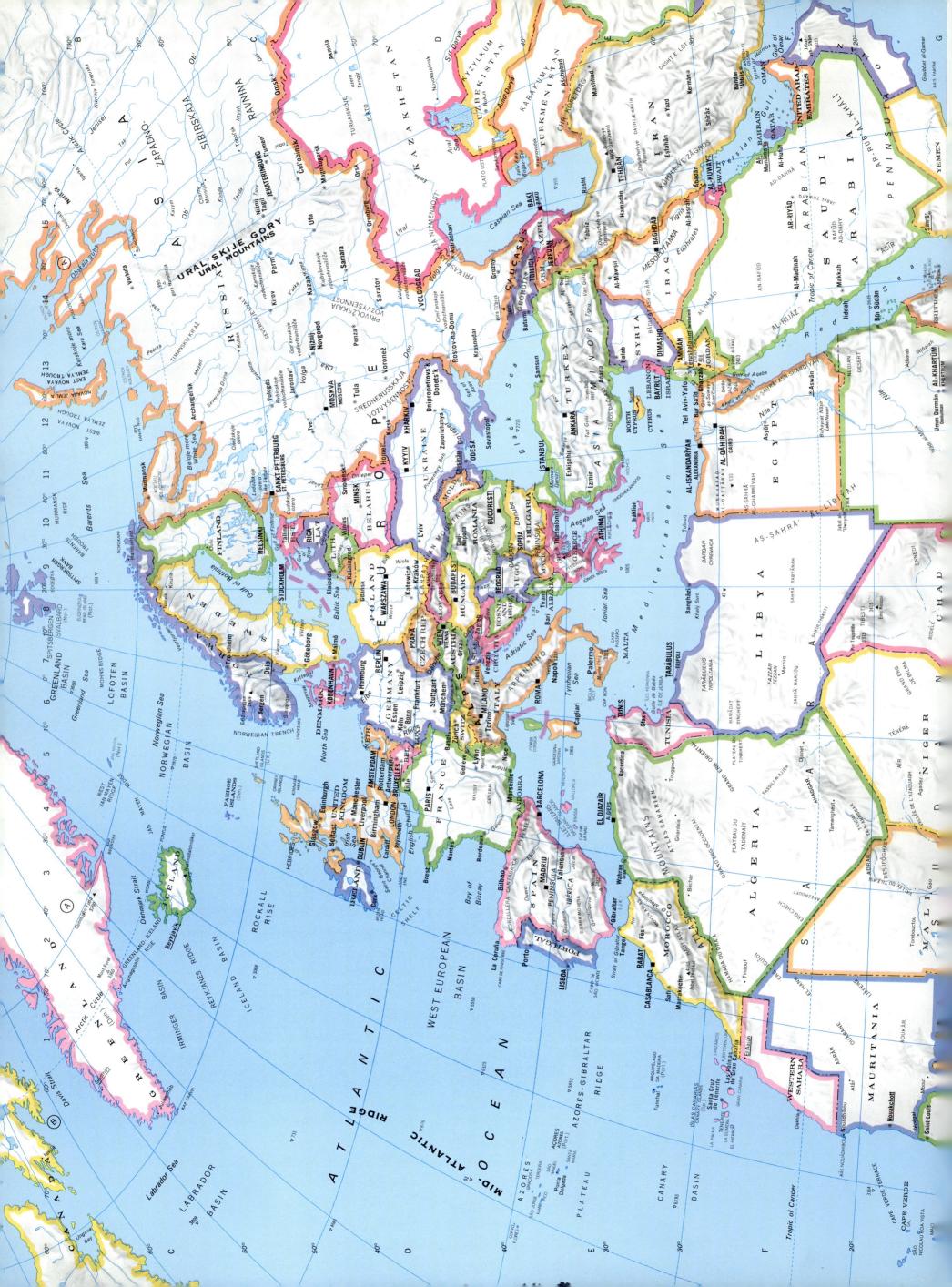

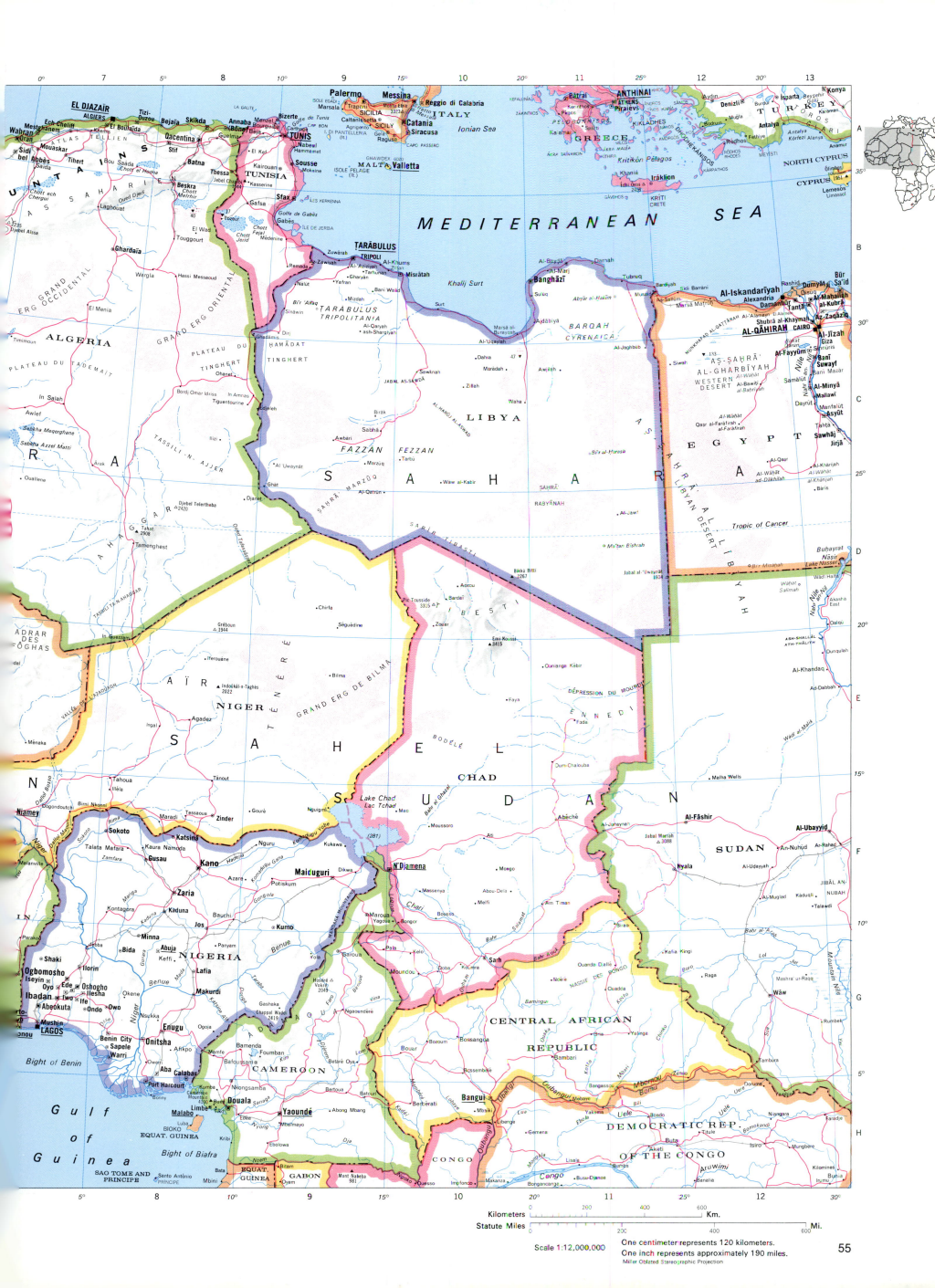

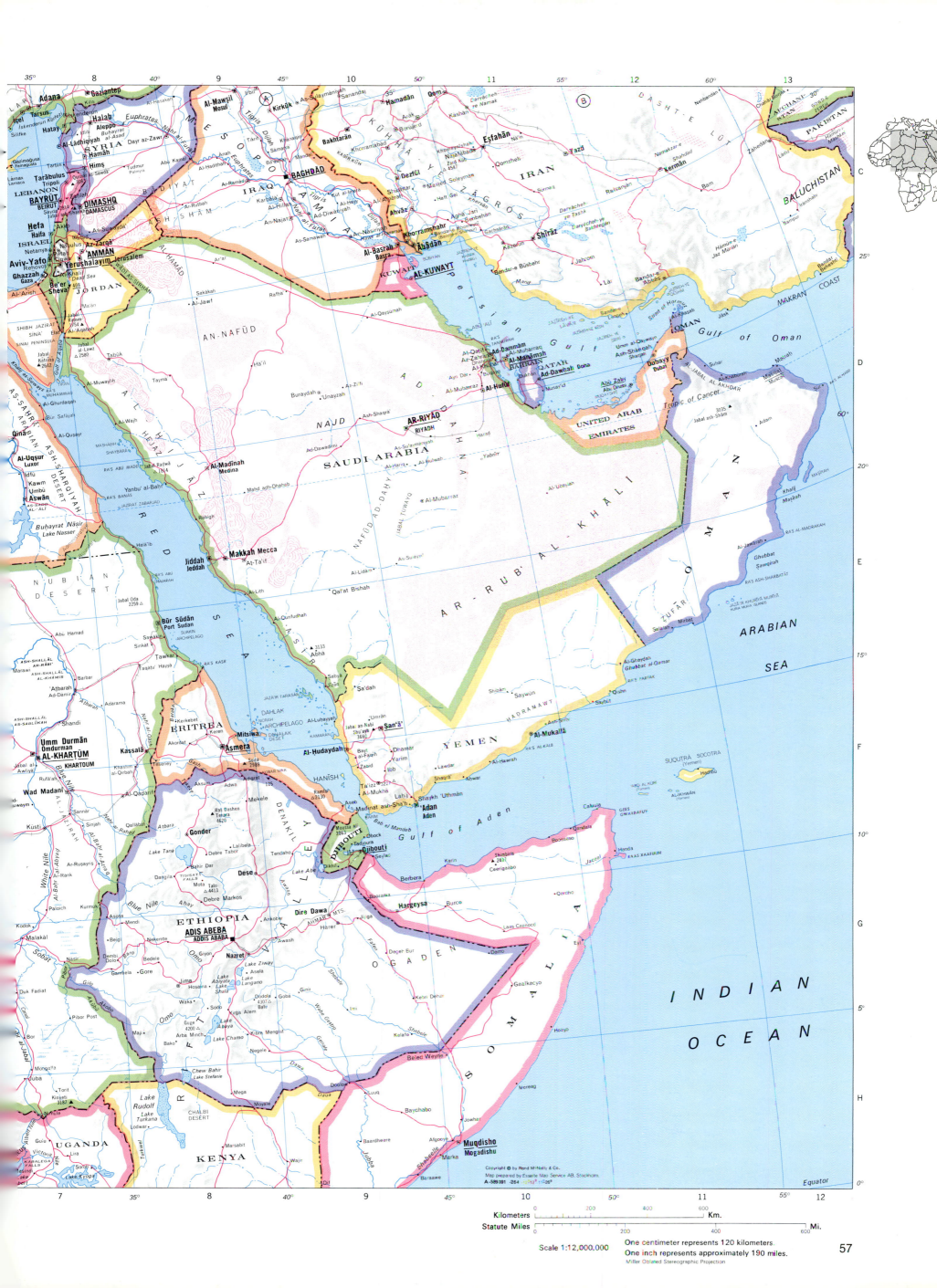

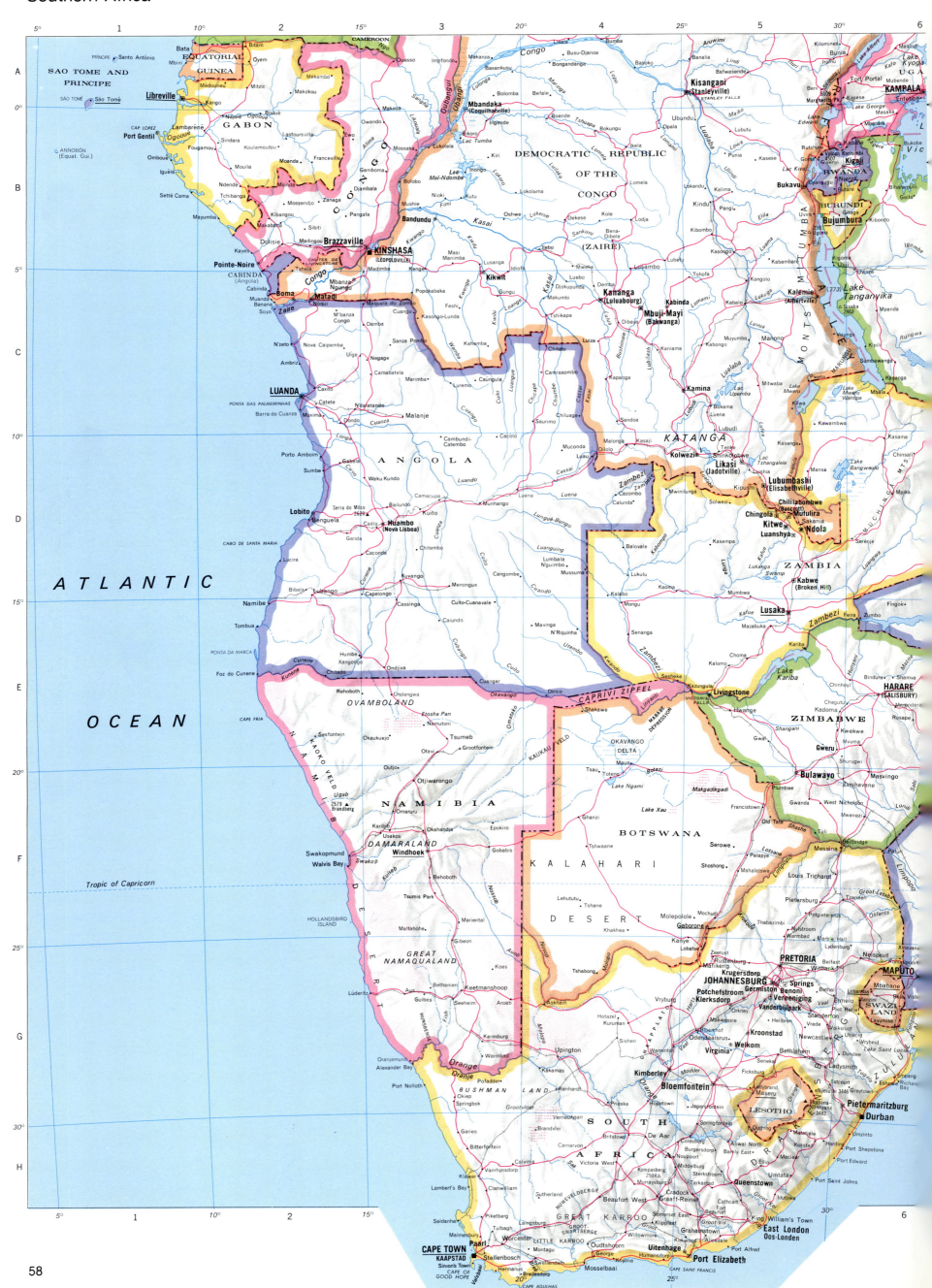

# Egypt and Sudan

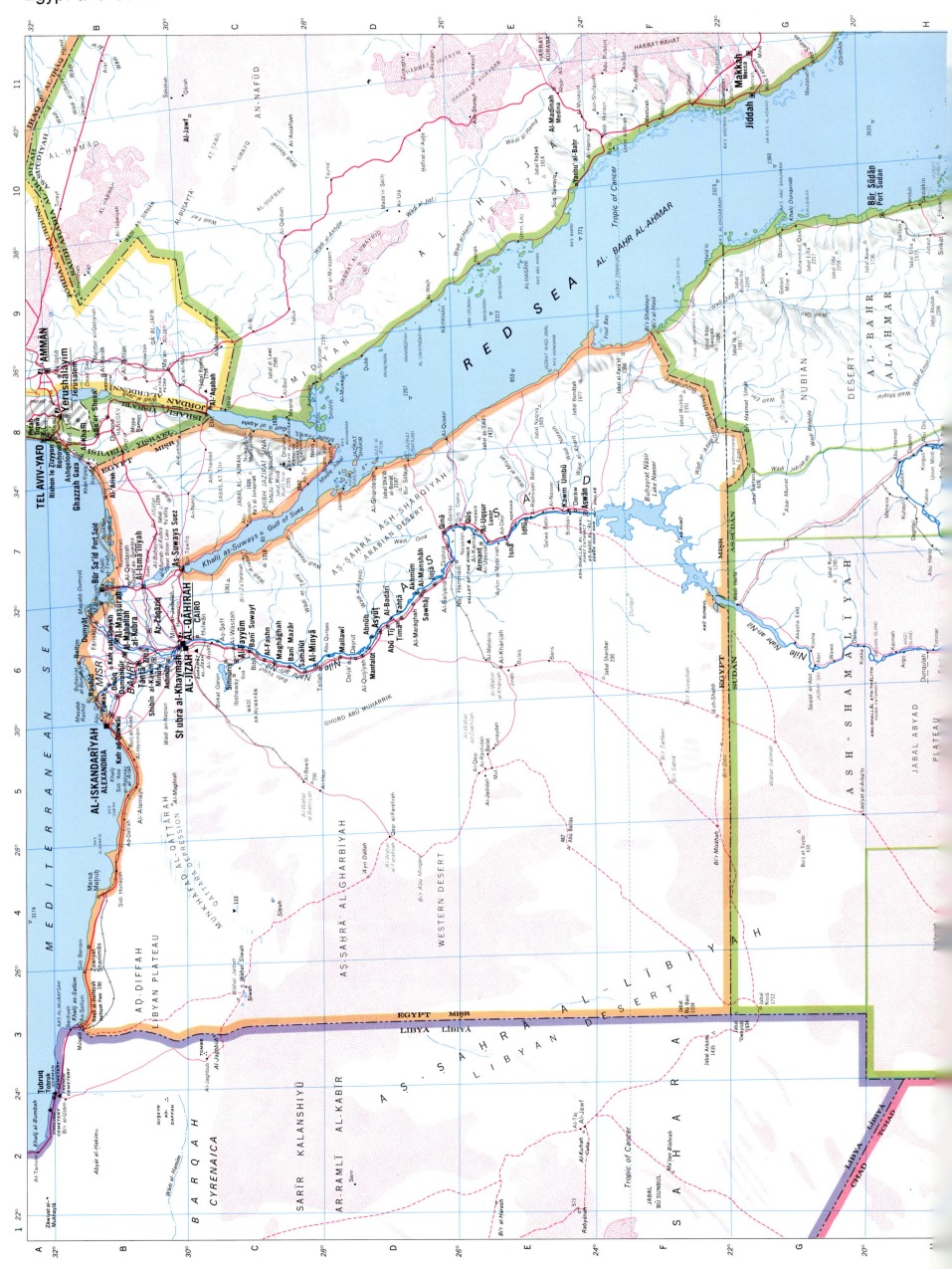

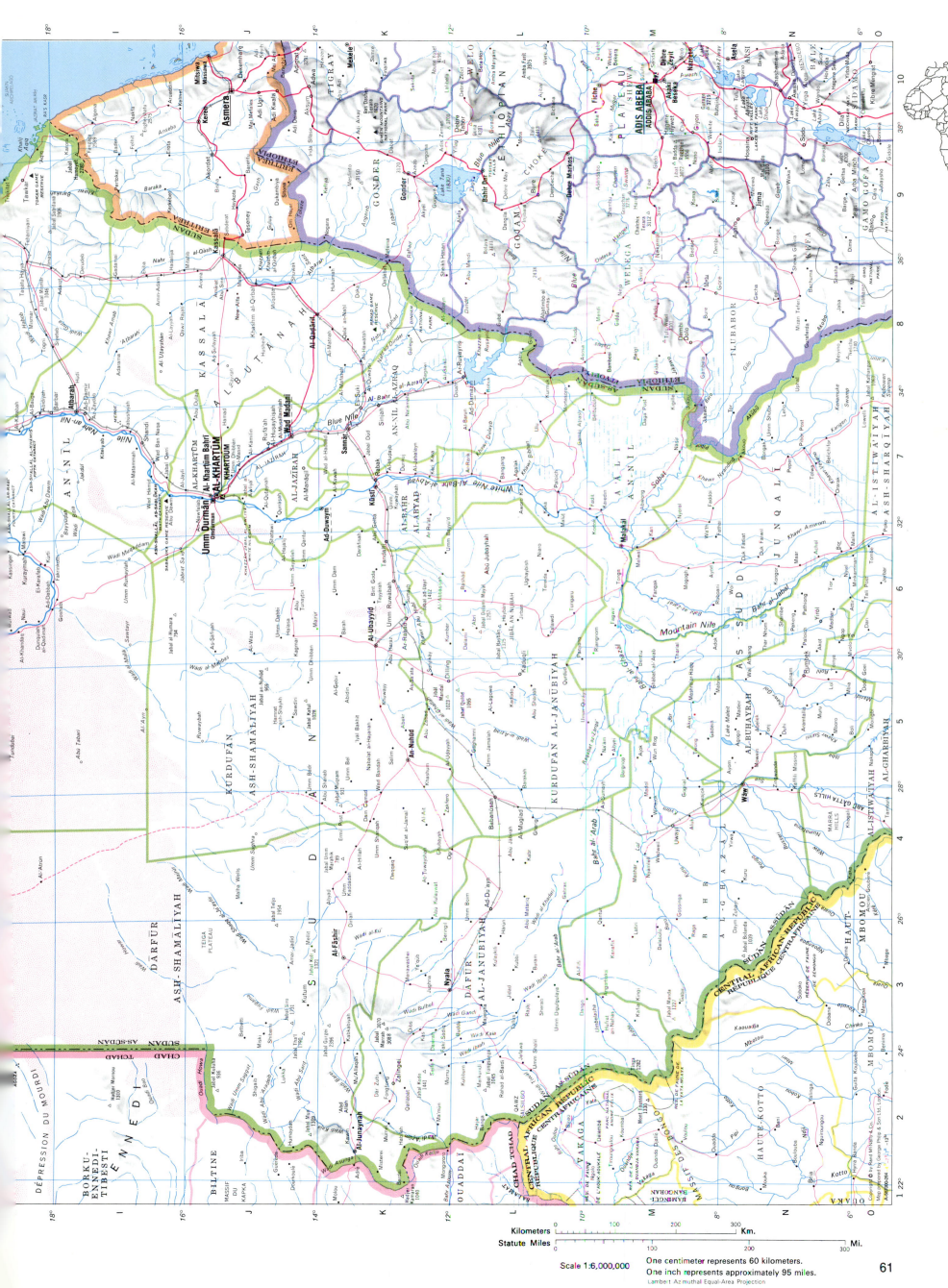

# Northwestern Africa

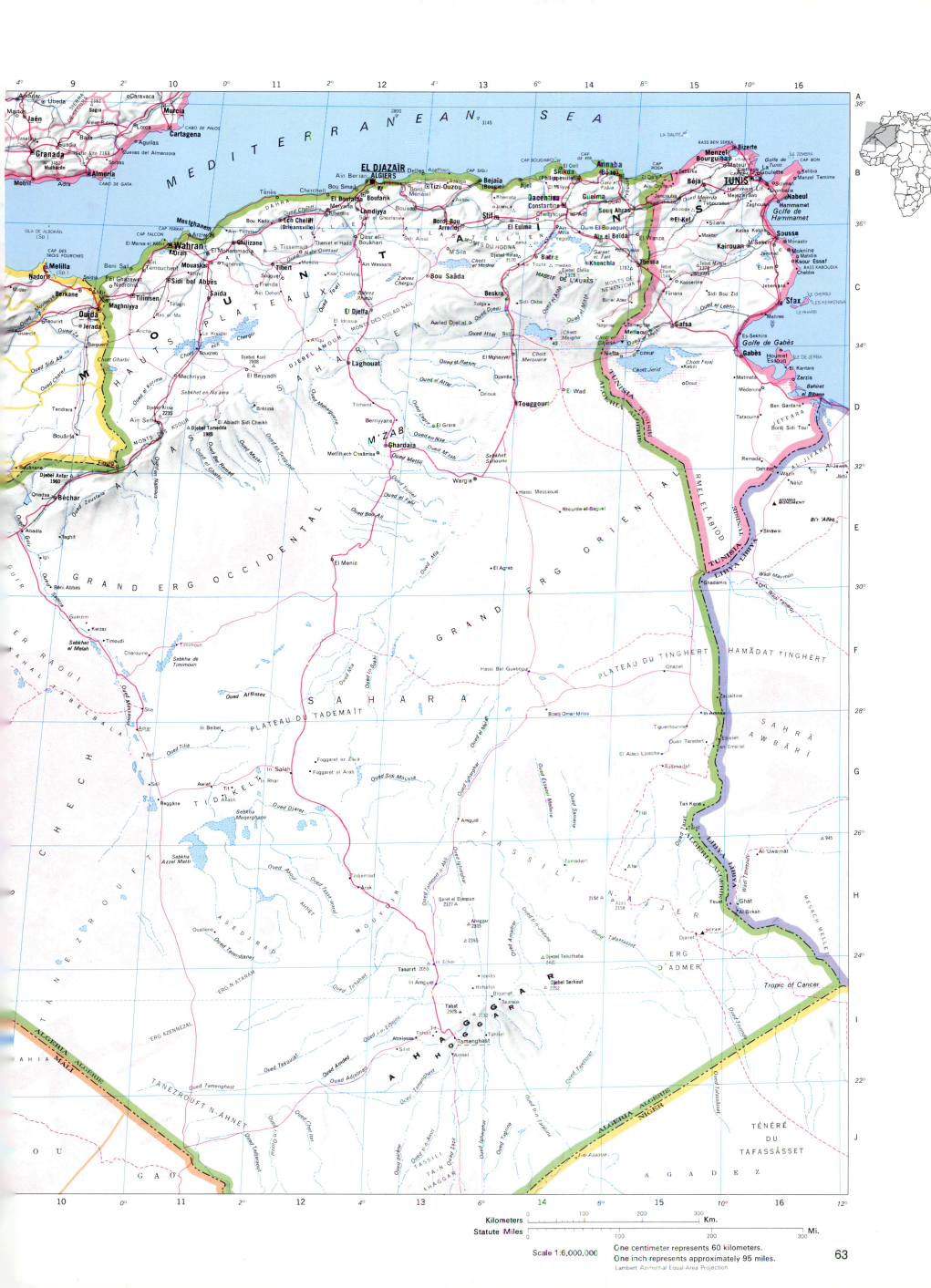

West Africa

64

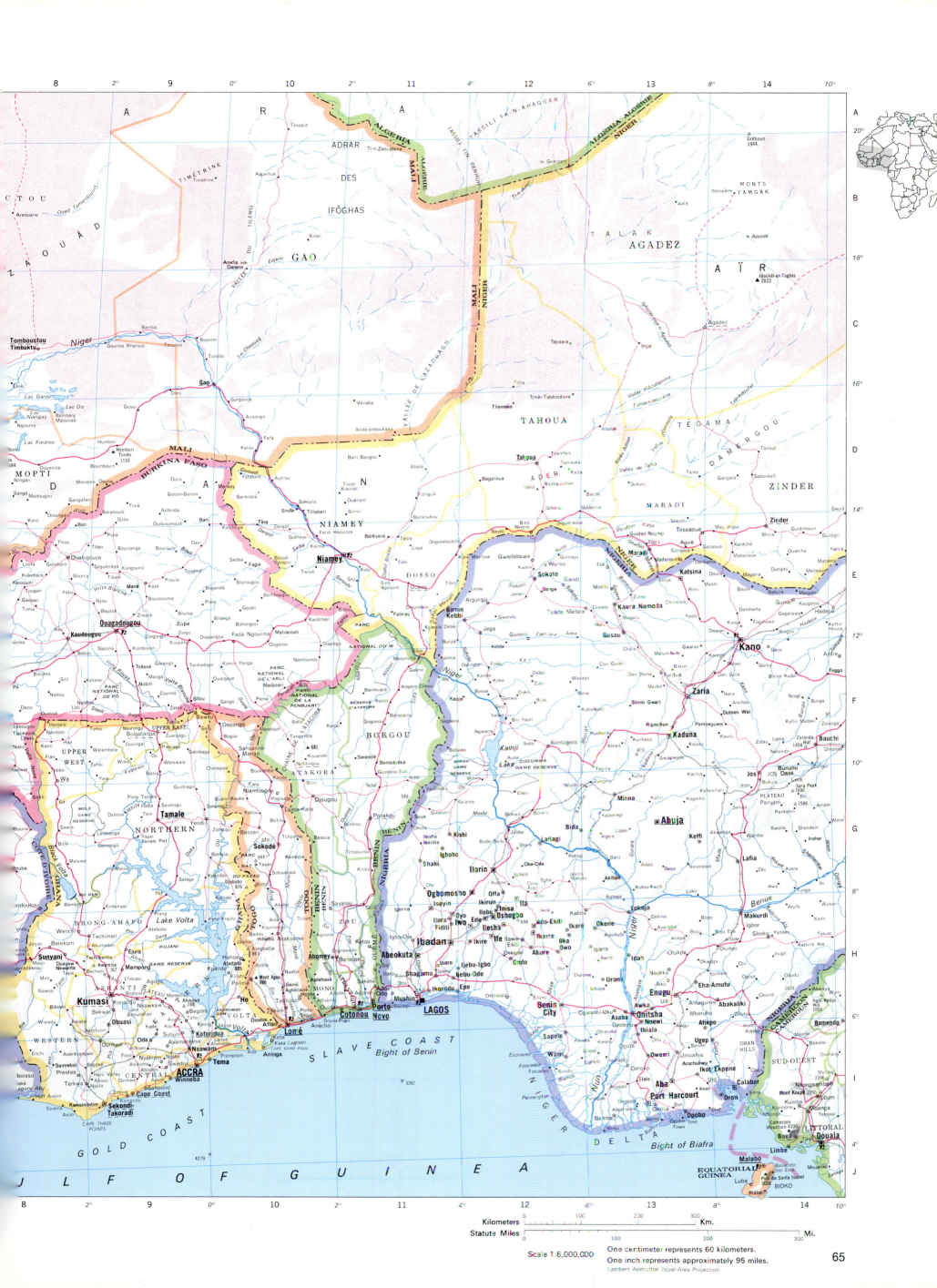

65

# Southern Africa and Madagascar

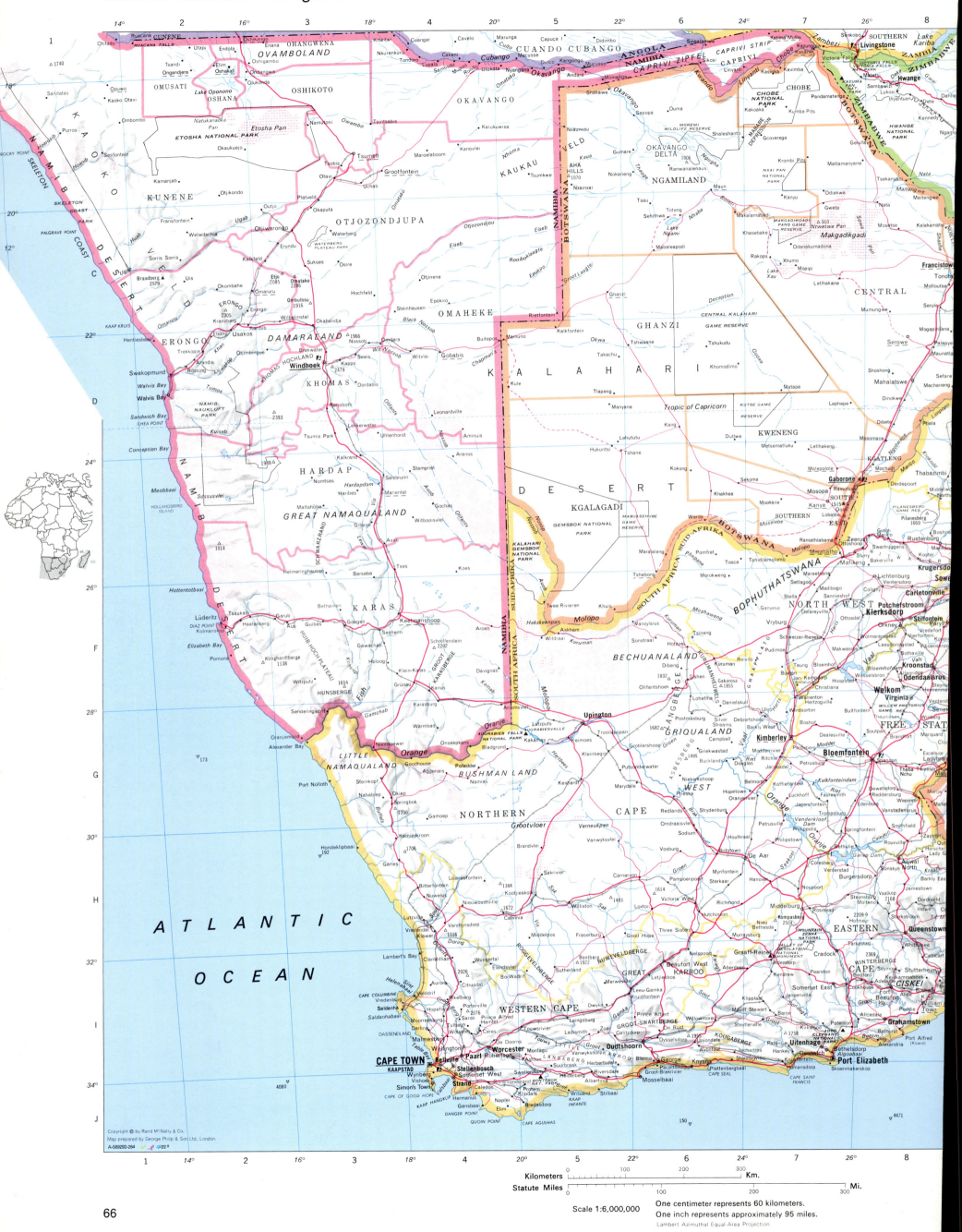

ATLANTIC

OCEAN

Kilometers

Statute Miles

Scale 1:6,000,000

One centimeter represents 60 kilometers.
One inch represents approximately 95 miles.

Lambert Azimuthal Equal-Area Projection

# Australia

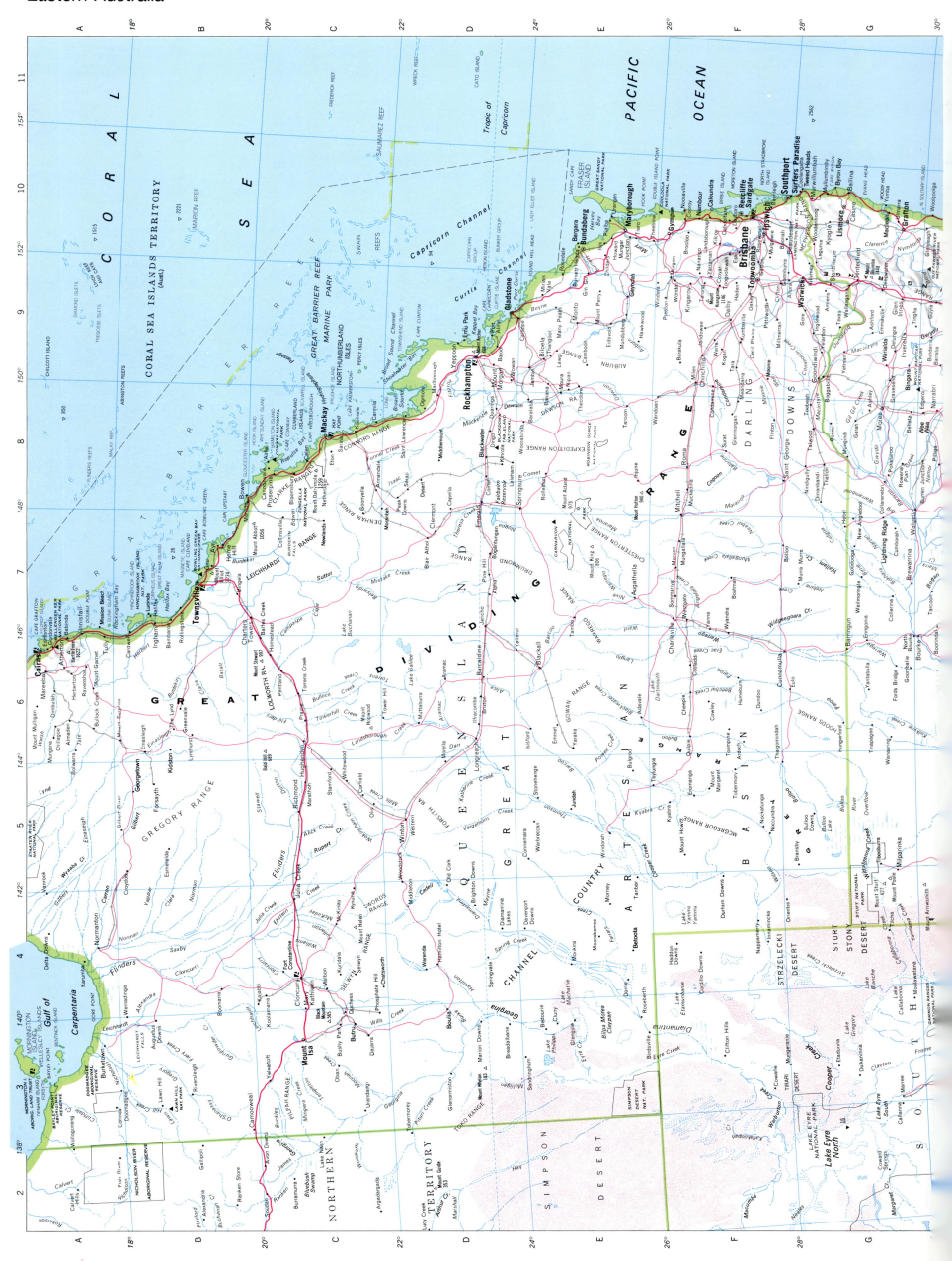

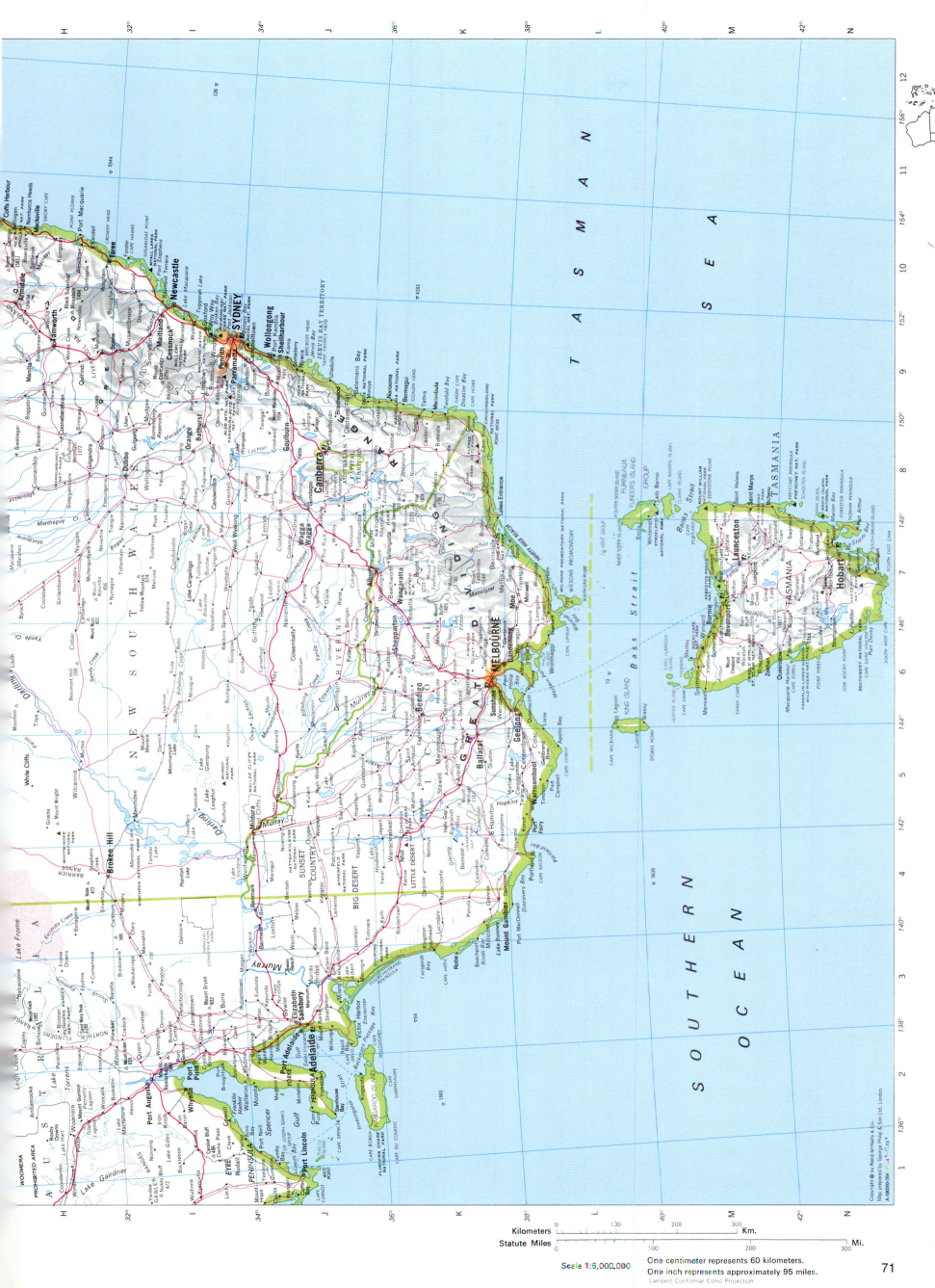

Kilometers
Statute Miles

Scale 1:6,000,000

One centimeter represents 60 kilometers.
One inch represents approximately 95 miles.
Lambert Conformal Conic Projection

71

# New Zealand

PACIFIC OCEAN

CAPE REINGA NORTH CAPE
Rangaunu Bay
Doubtless Bay
Ahipara Bay
TAUROA POINT CAPE BRETT
Okaihau
Opua
**Whangarei**
Dargaville Bream Bay
GREAT BARRIER ISLAND
Wellsford
Kaipara Harbour
Hauraki Gulf COROMANDEL PENINSULA
**Takapuna**
**Devonport**
**Auckland**
Manukau Harbour
Pukekohe Thames
Waiuku Waihi
Huntly Bay of Plenty CAPE RUNAWAY
Morrinsville **Tauranga** EAST CAPE
**Hamilton** Cambridge Whakatane
Te Awamutu **Rotorua** Opotiki
Kawhia Harbour Te Kuiti Murupara
Tokoroa
**NORTH** Taupo
**ISLAND** North Taranaki Bight Lake Taupo
Waitara Taumarunui **Gisborne**
**New Plymouth** Mt. Egmont 518 Tarawera Wairoa
Opunake Stratford Raetihi MAHIA PENINSULA
Hawera Ruapehu 2797 Hawke Bay
South Taranaki Bight Taihape **Napier** CAPE KIDNAPPERS
Patea **Hastings**
**Wanganui** Waipukurau
Dannevirke
**Palmerston North** Woodville
Levin Masterton
Otaki 1529 **Masterton**
**Lower Hutt**
**Wellington** Lake Wairarapa
CAPE PALLISER

**TASMAN SEA**

CAPE FAREWELL
Golden Bay D'URVILLE ISLAND
Takaka
Tasman Bay
Motueka Picton
CAPE CAMPBELL
Karamea Bight **Nelson**
Seddonville Richmond
1875 Mount Owen **Blenheim**
Westport CAPE FOULWIND Buller Cook Strait
Mt. Uriah 1501 Tapuaenuku 2885
Reefton 2337 Mount Travers 2610
**SOUTH** Mawheraiti
**Greymouth** Kaikoura
**ISLAND** Hokitika
Ross Waiau
Whataroa Mount Murchison 2400 Waipara
Oxford
Sheffield Pegasus Bay
**Christchurch**
Methven Little River
Mount Somers Southbridge BANKS PENINSULA
Fairlie
**Ashburton**
Mount Cook 3754
Lake Tekapo Canterbury Bight
Mount Aspiring 3035 Lake Wanaka
Mount Tutoko 2756 Lake Hawea Omarama **Timaru**
Mount Earnslaw 2819 Kurow Waimate
Doubtful Sound Queenstown Cromwell Ranfurly **Oamaru**
Te Anau Kingston Alexandra
RESOLUTION ISLAND Lake Wakatipu Roxburgh Palmerston
CAPE PROVIDENCE Mossburn Edievale Beaumont Port Chalmers
Nightcaps **Dunedin**
Otautau Winton Gore Milton
Riverton Kaitangata
**Invercargill** Tokanui Tahakopa
Te Waewae Bay Bluff
Foveaux Strait
Mt. Anglem 978
**STEWART ISLAND**

PACIFIC OCEAN

Copyright © by Rand McNally & Co.
A-591600-286

Scale 1:6,000,000
One centimeter represents 60 kilometers.
One inch represents approximately 95 miles.
Lambert Conformal Conic Projection

Kilometers
Statute Miles

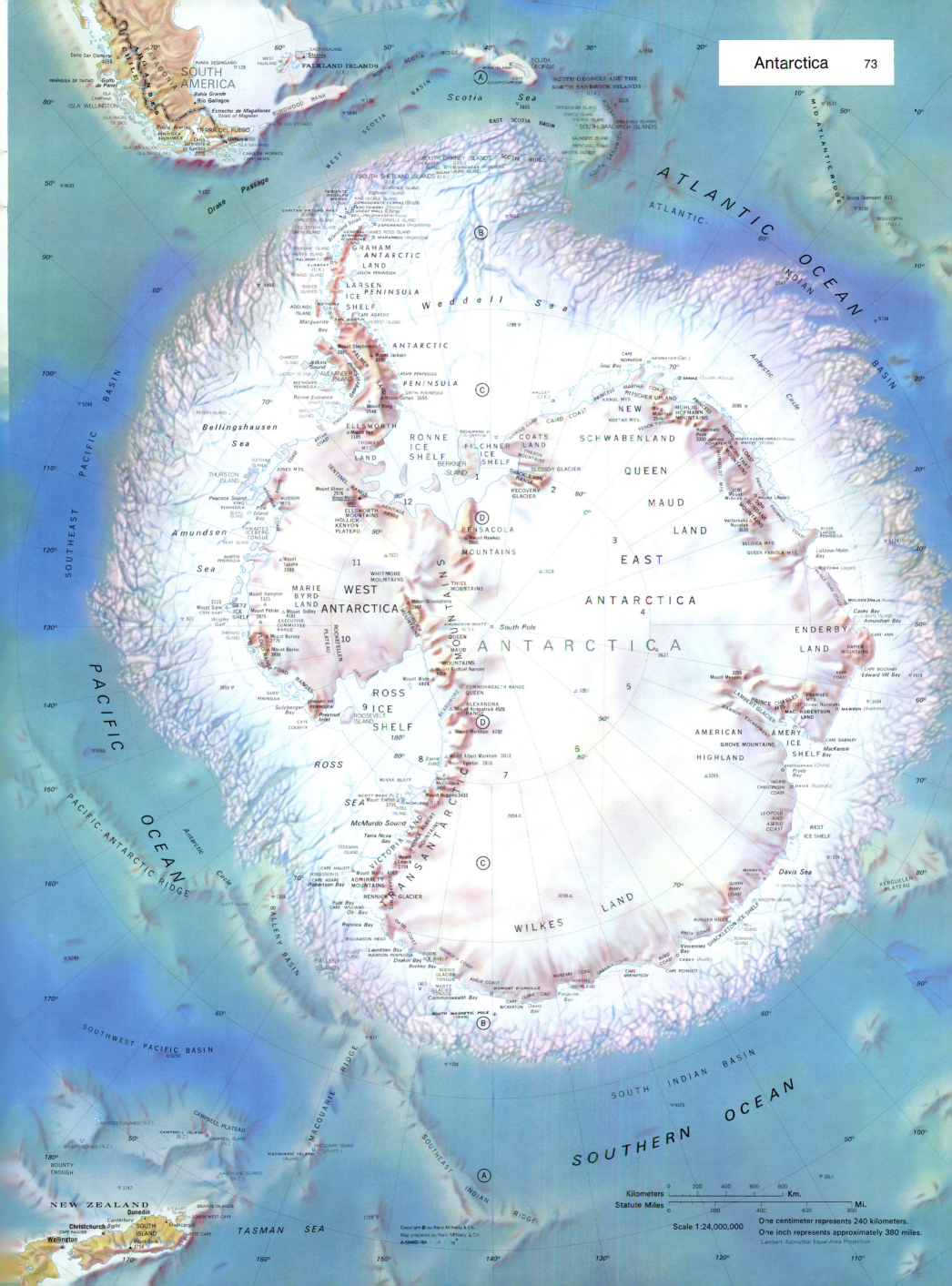

# Southern South America

Scale 1:12,000,000

Kilometers

Statute Miles

One centimeter represents 120 kilometers.
One inch represents approximately 190 miles.
Oblique Conic Conformal Projection

Copyright © by Rand McNally & Co.
Map prepared by Esselte Map Service AB, Stockholm.
A-549200-264

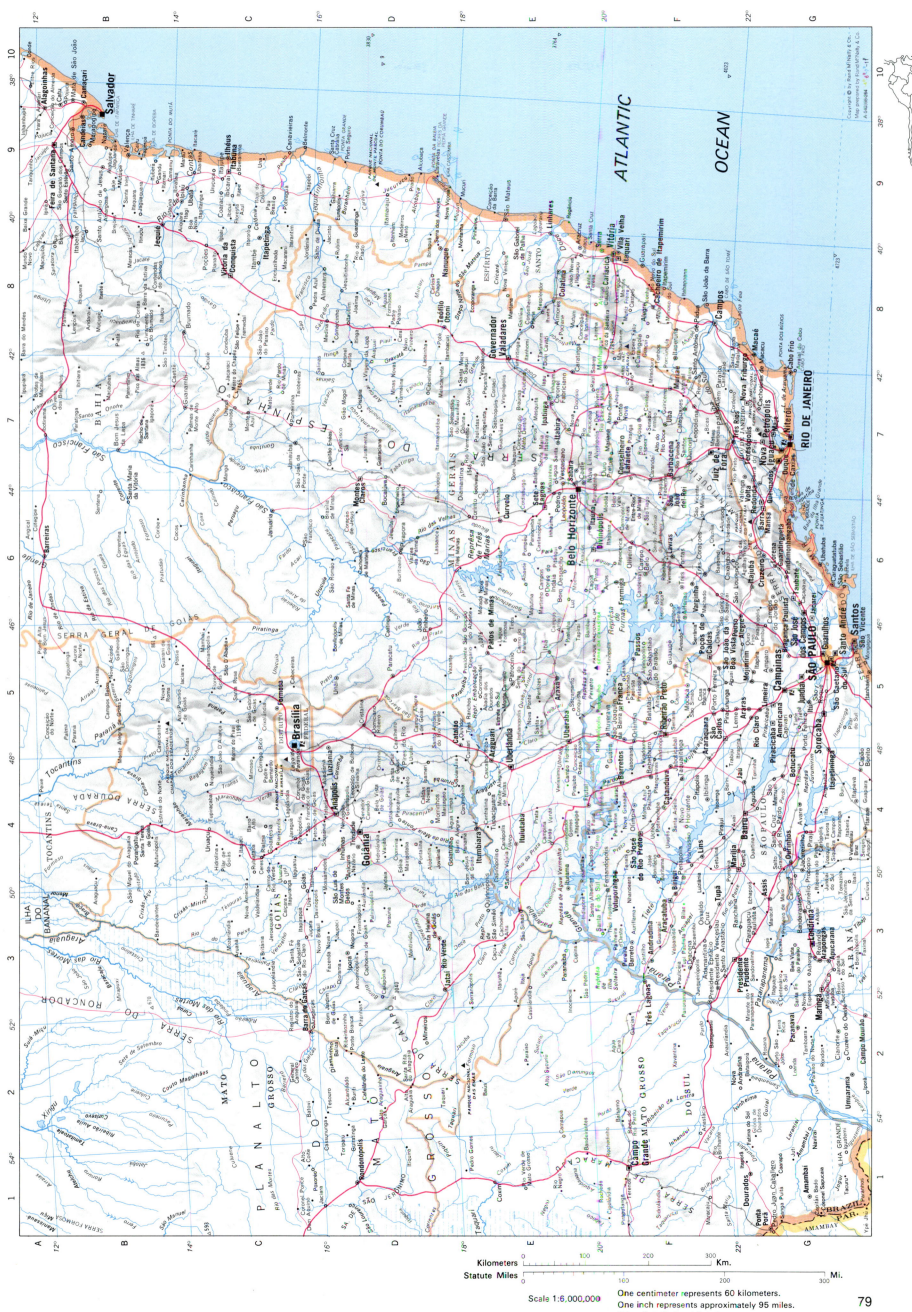

ATLANTIC OCEAN

Scale 1:6,000,000

One centimeter represents 60 kilometers.
One inch represents approximately 95 miles.

Oblique Conic Conformal Projection

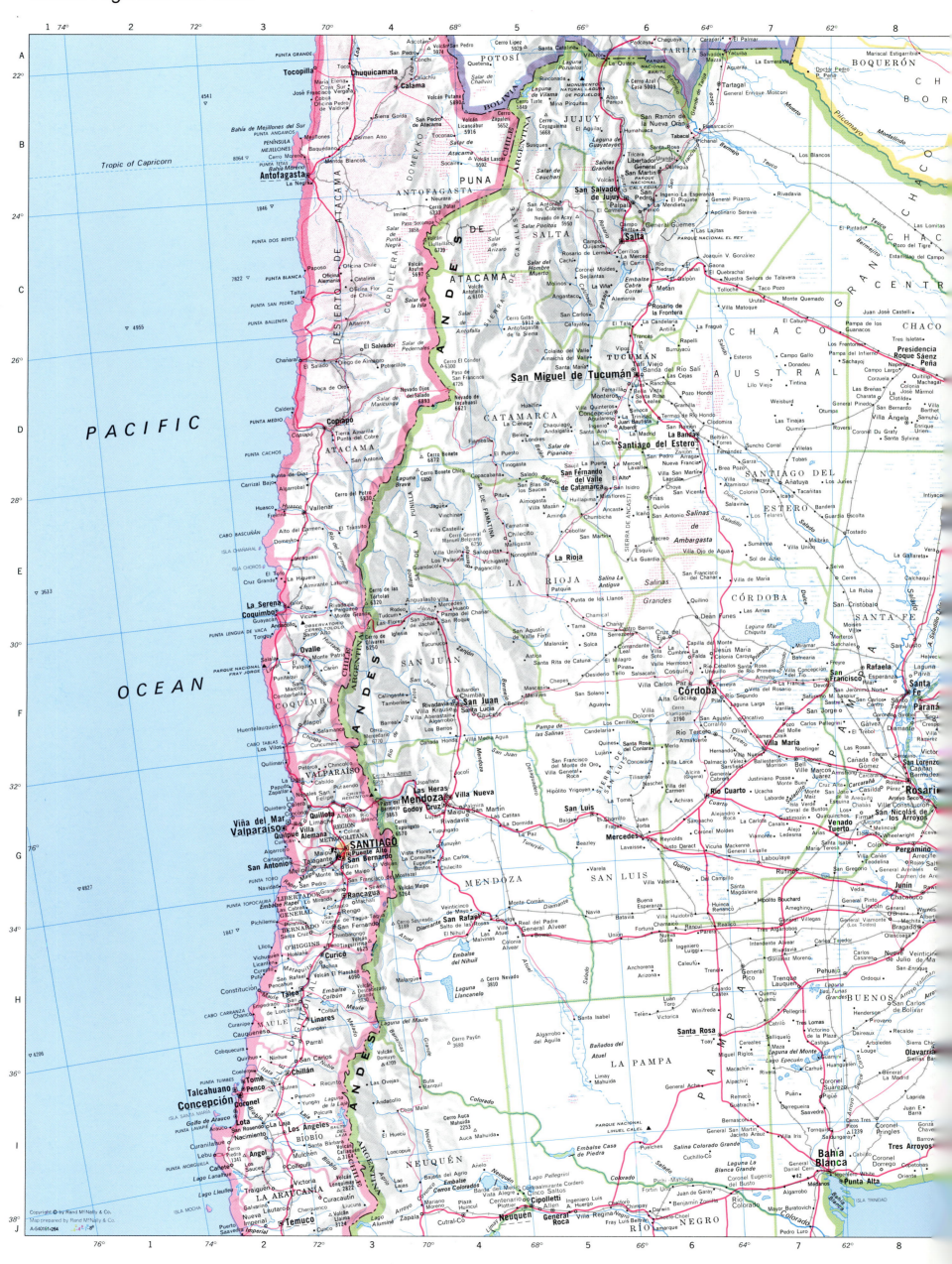

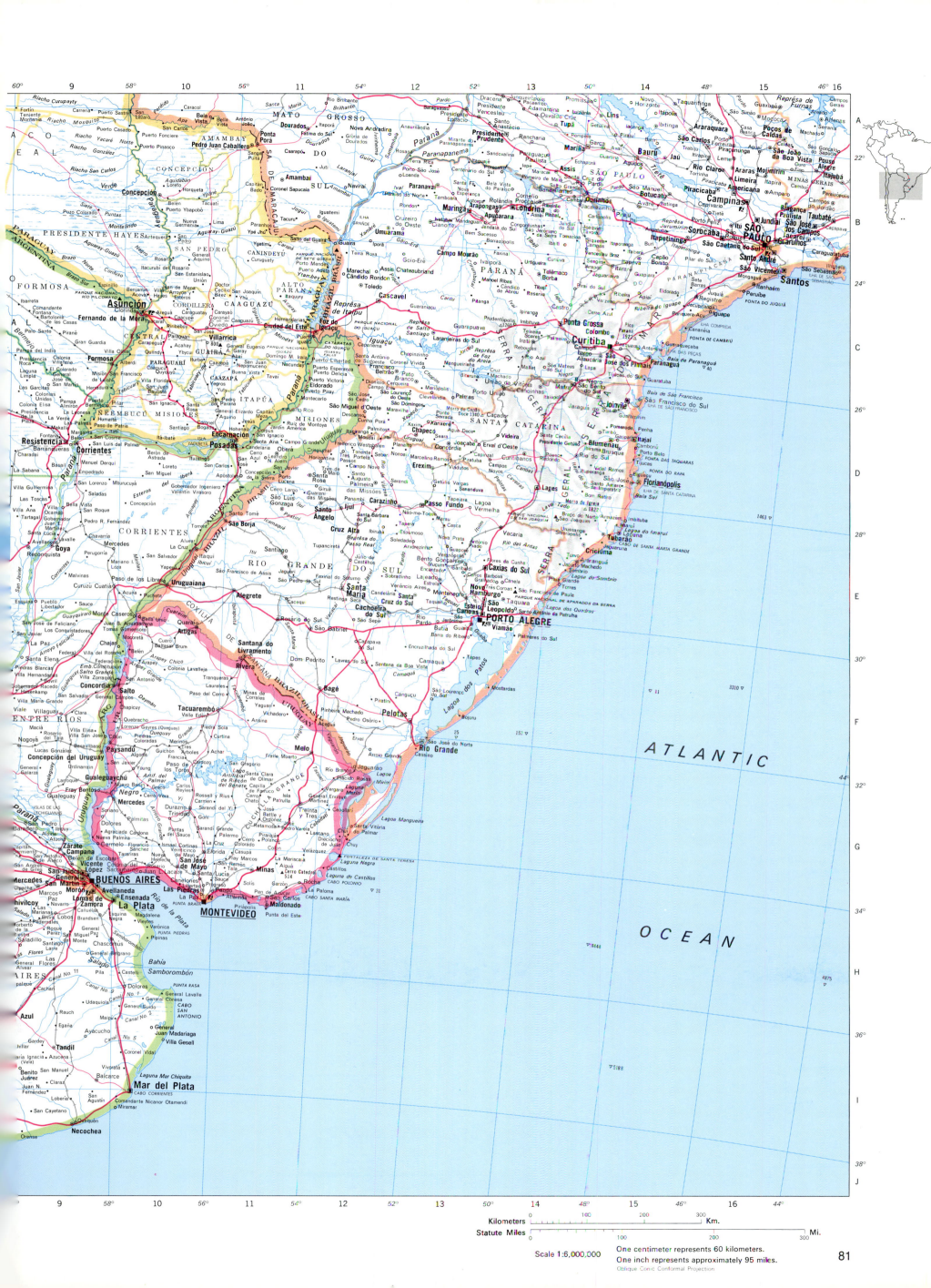

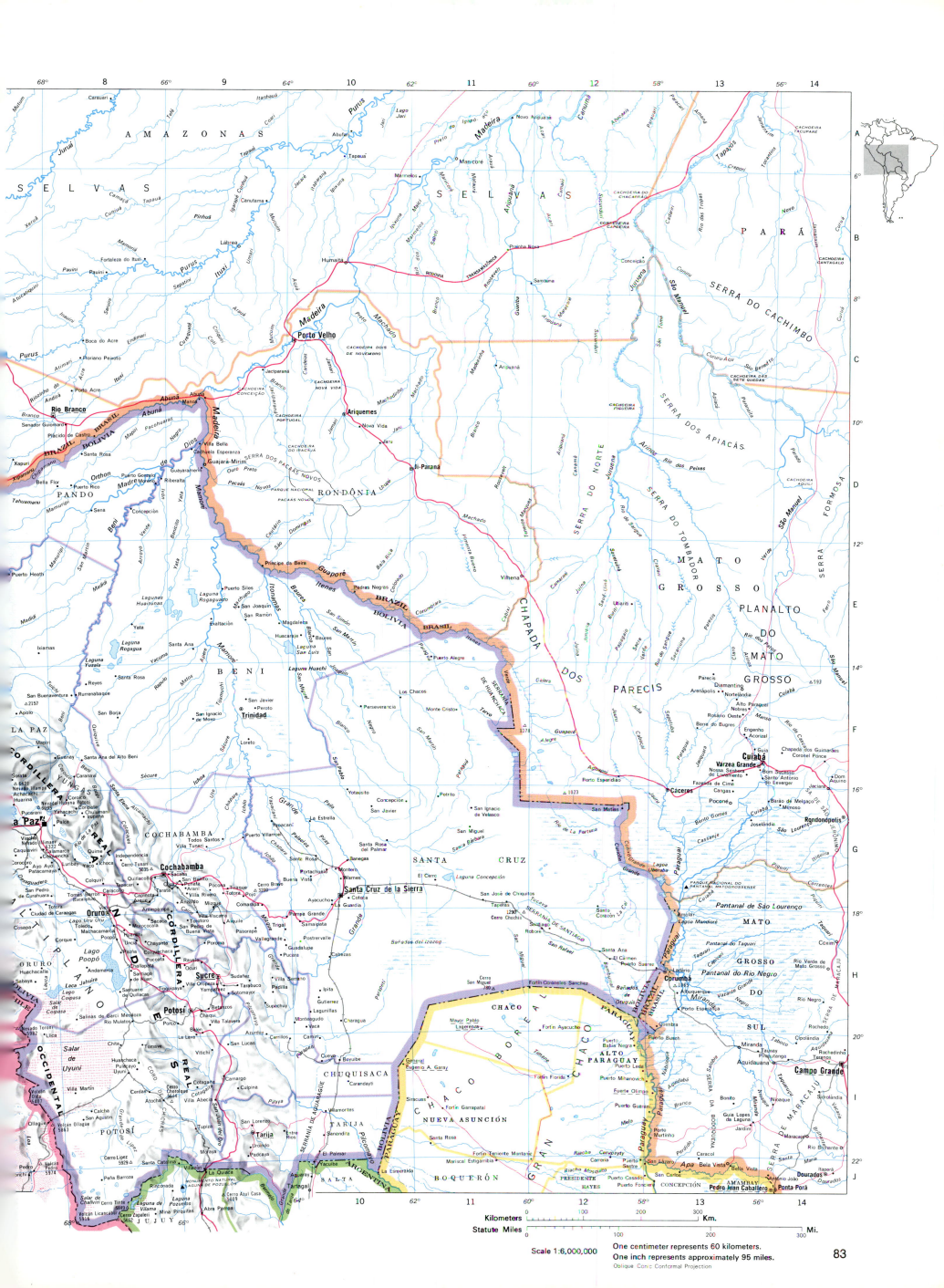

83

# Mexico

Kilometers

Statute Miles

Scale 1:6,000,000

One centimeter represents 60 kilometers.
One inch represents approximately 95 miles.
Lambert Conformal Conic Projection

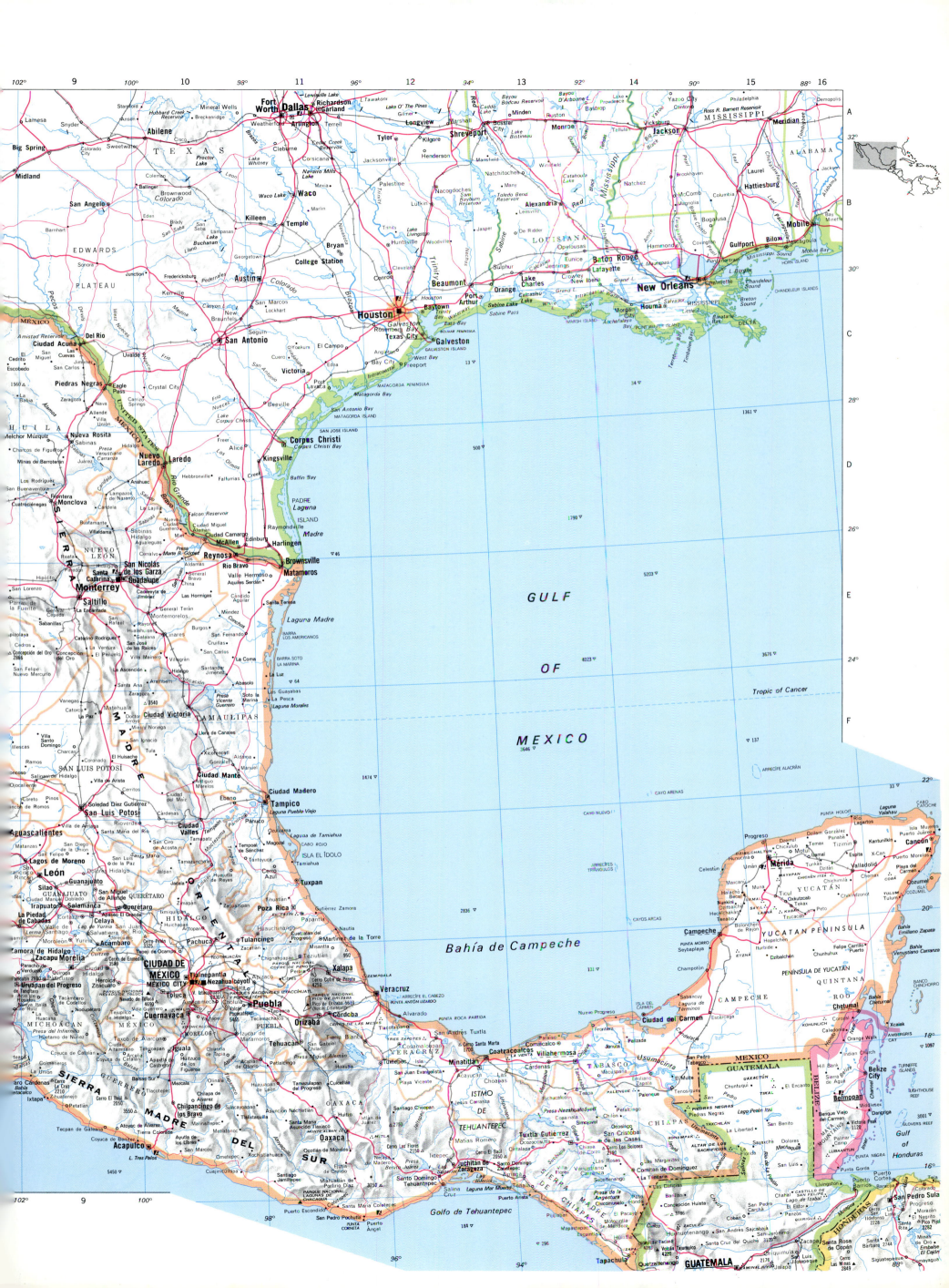

# Central America

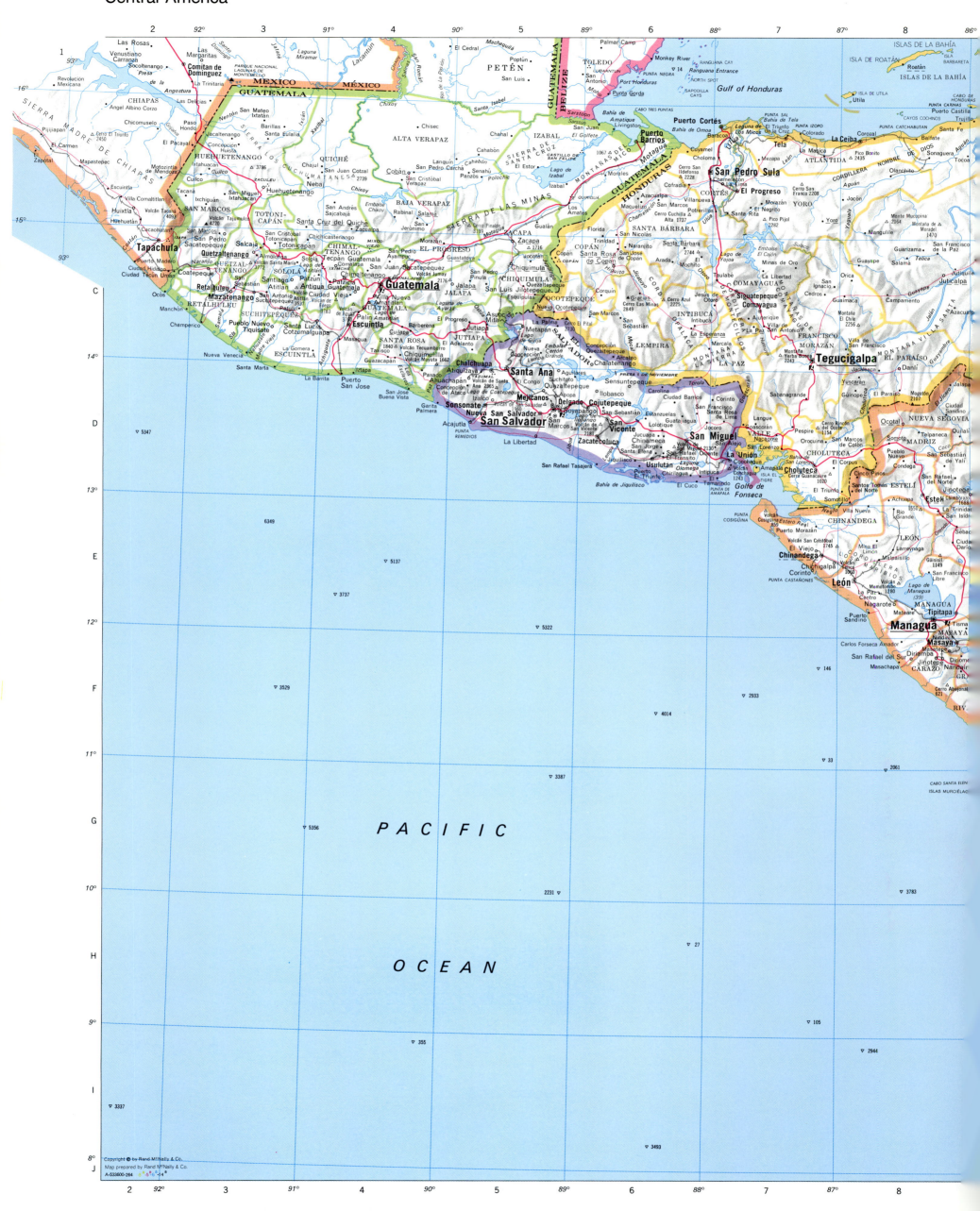

Caribbean Region

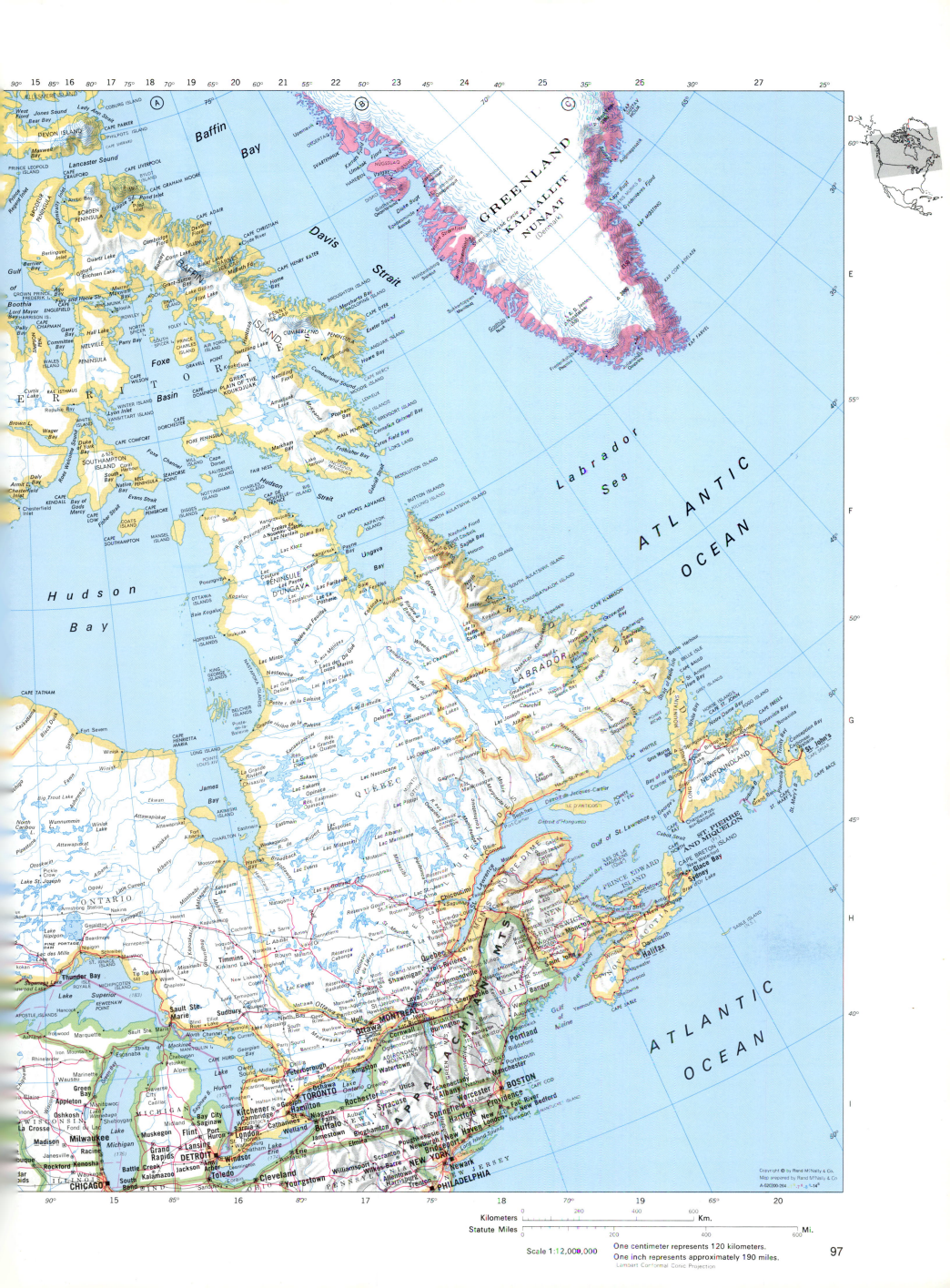

# United States of America

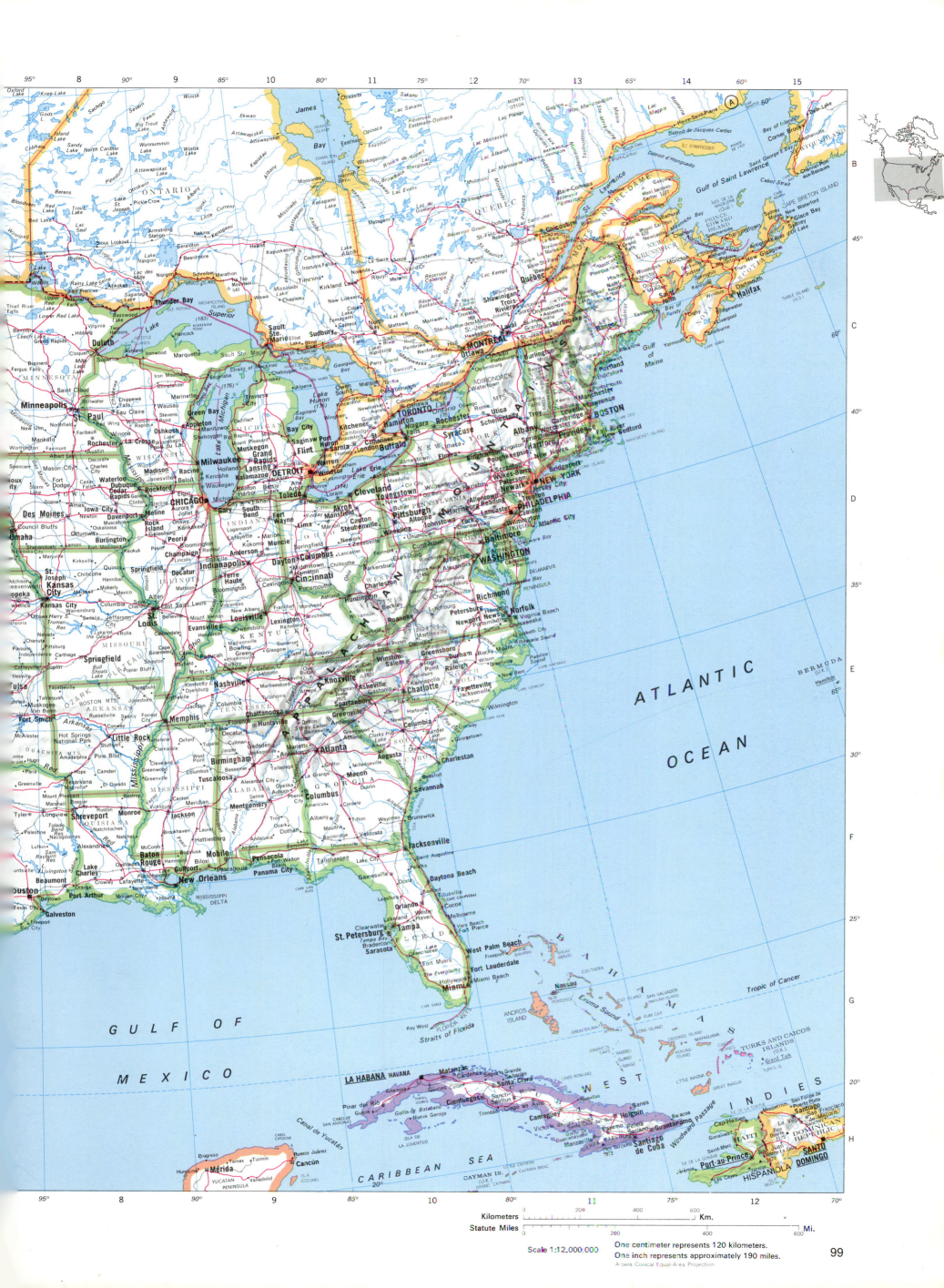

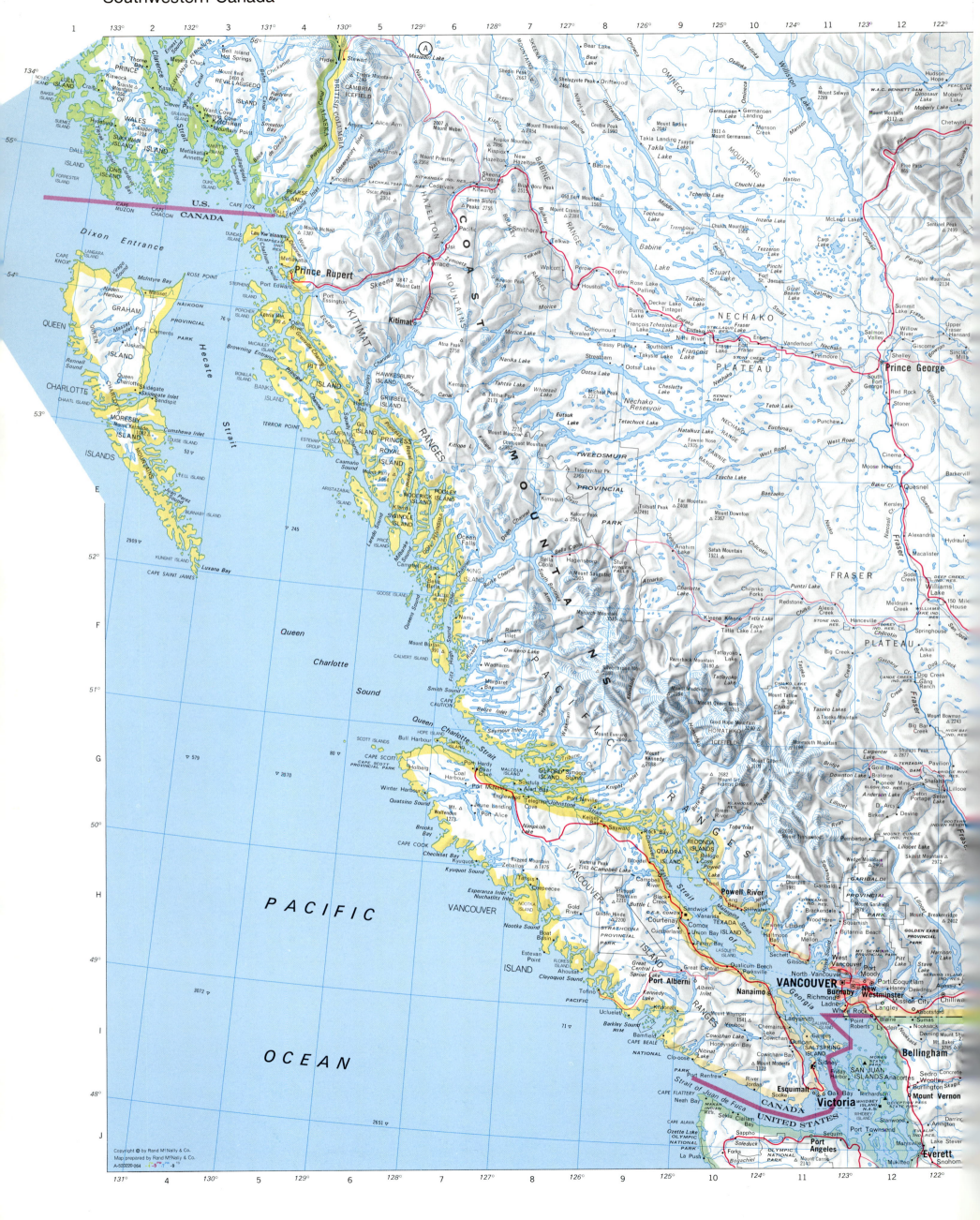

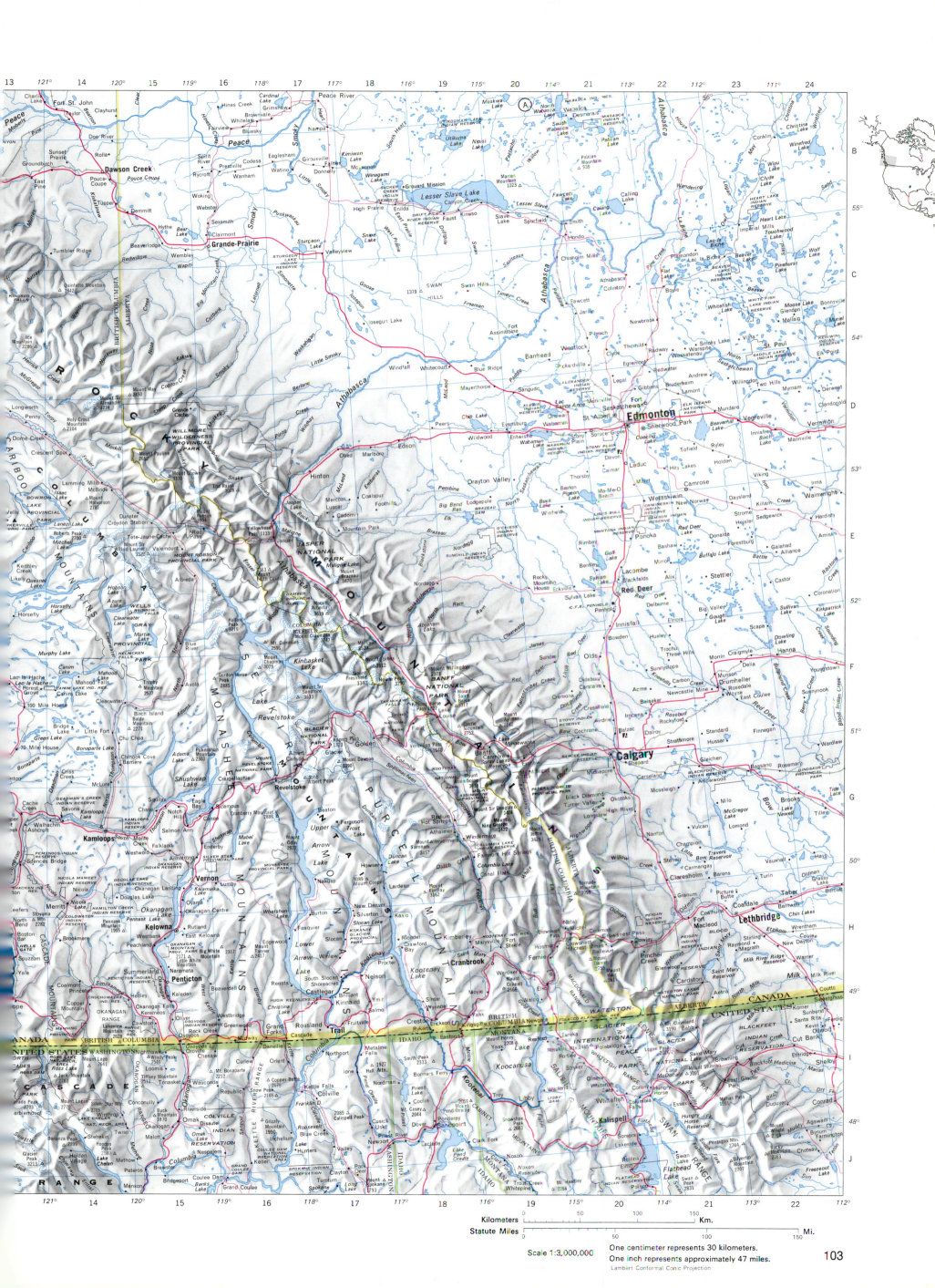

103

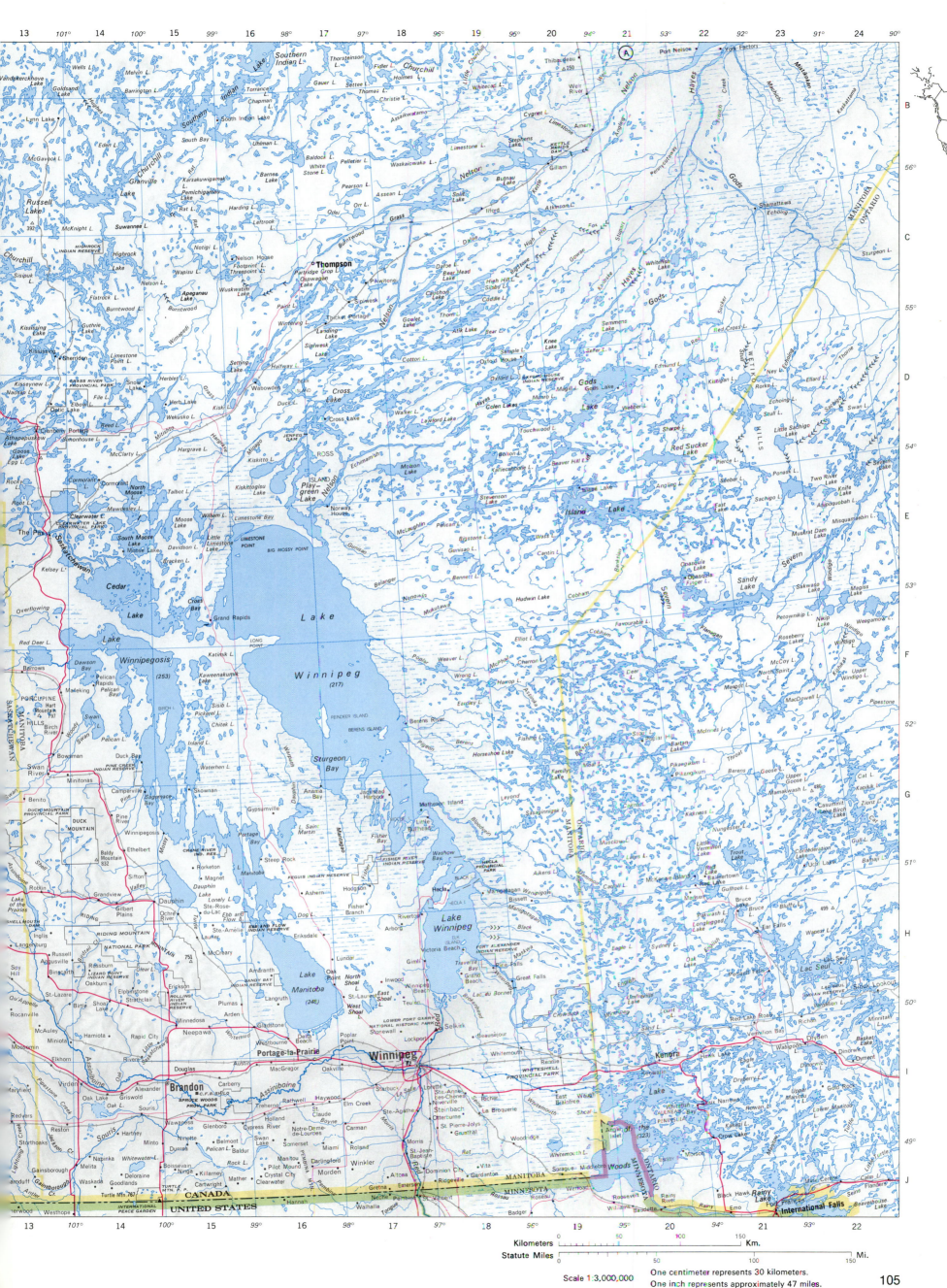

Kilometers                                    Km.
Statute Miles                                 Mi.
Scale 1:3,000,000
One centimeter represents 30 kilometers.
One inch represents approximately 47 miles.
Lambert Conformal Conic Projection

105

Copyright © by Rand McNally & Co.
Map prepared by Rand McNally
A-583596-264

One centimeter represents 30 kilometers.
One inch represents approximately 47 miles.
Scale 1:3,000,000
Albers Conical Equal-Area Projection

Kilometers
Statute Miles

109

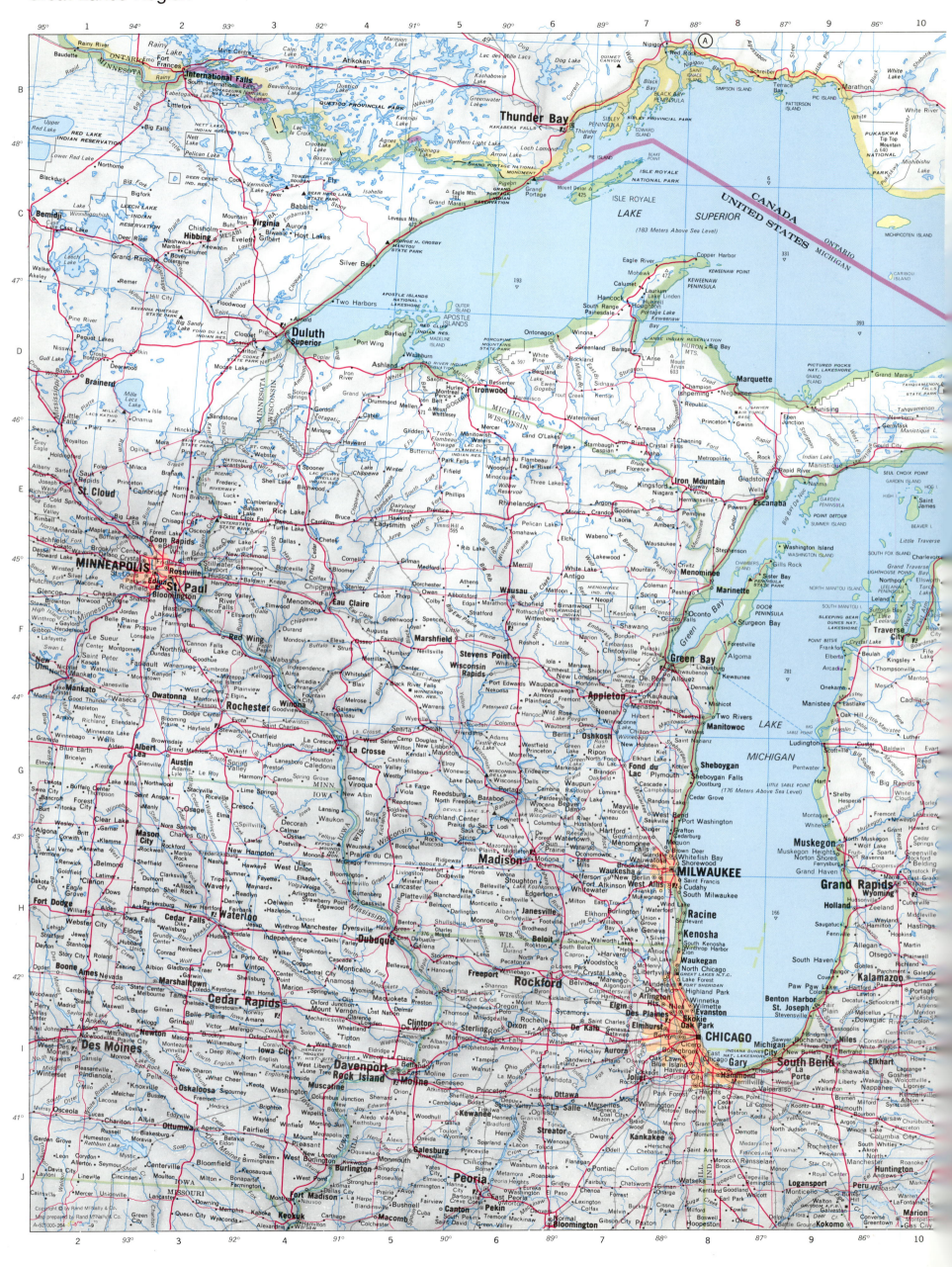

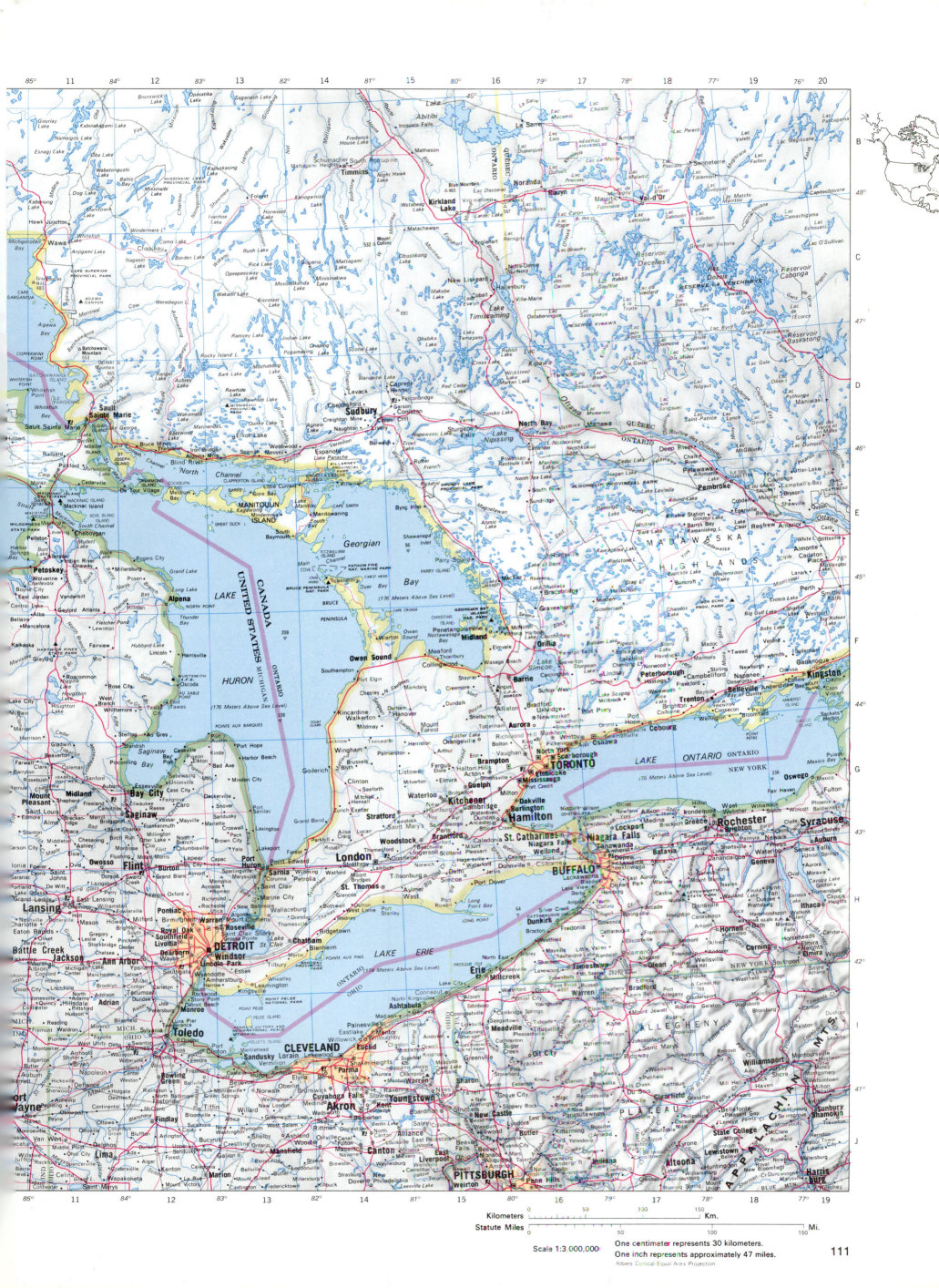

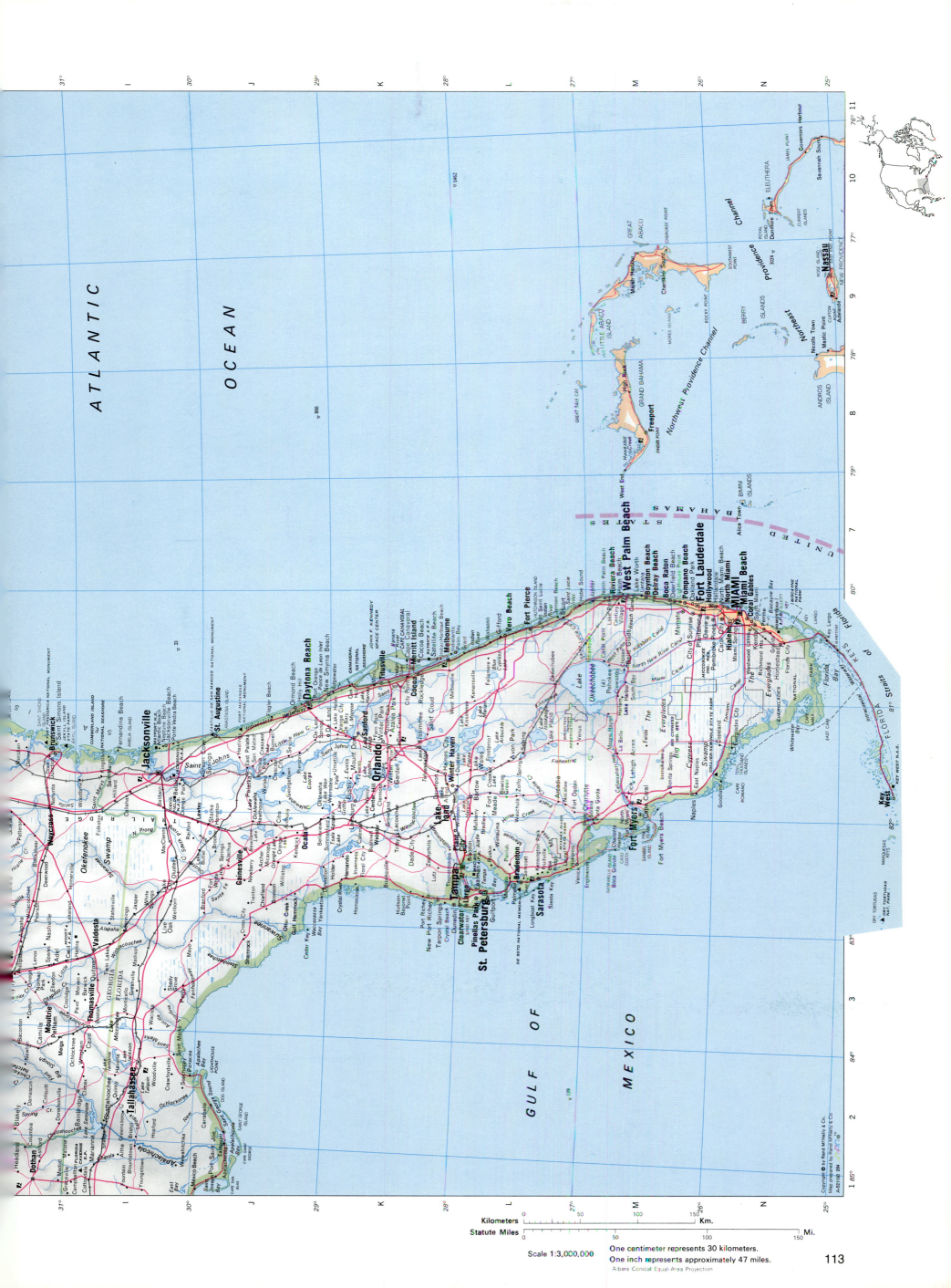

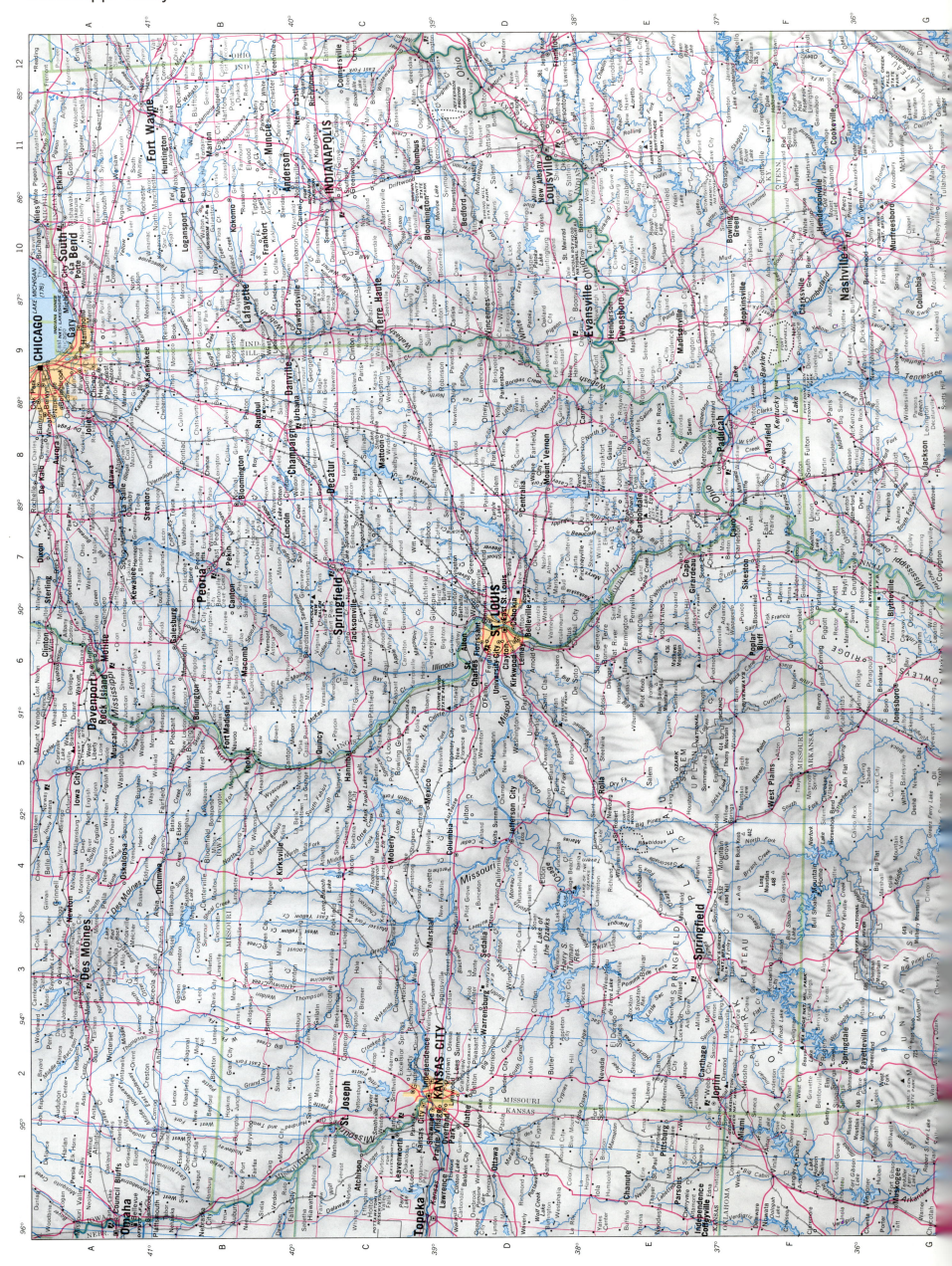

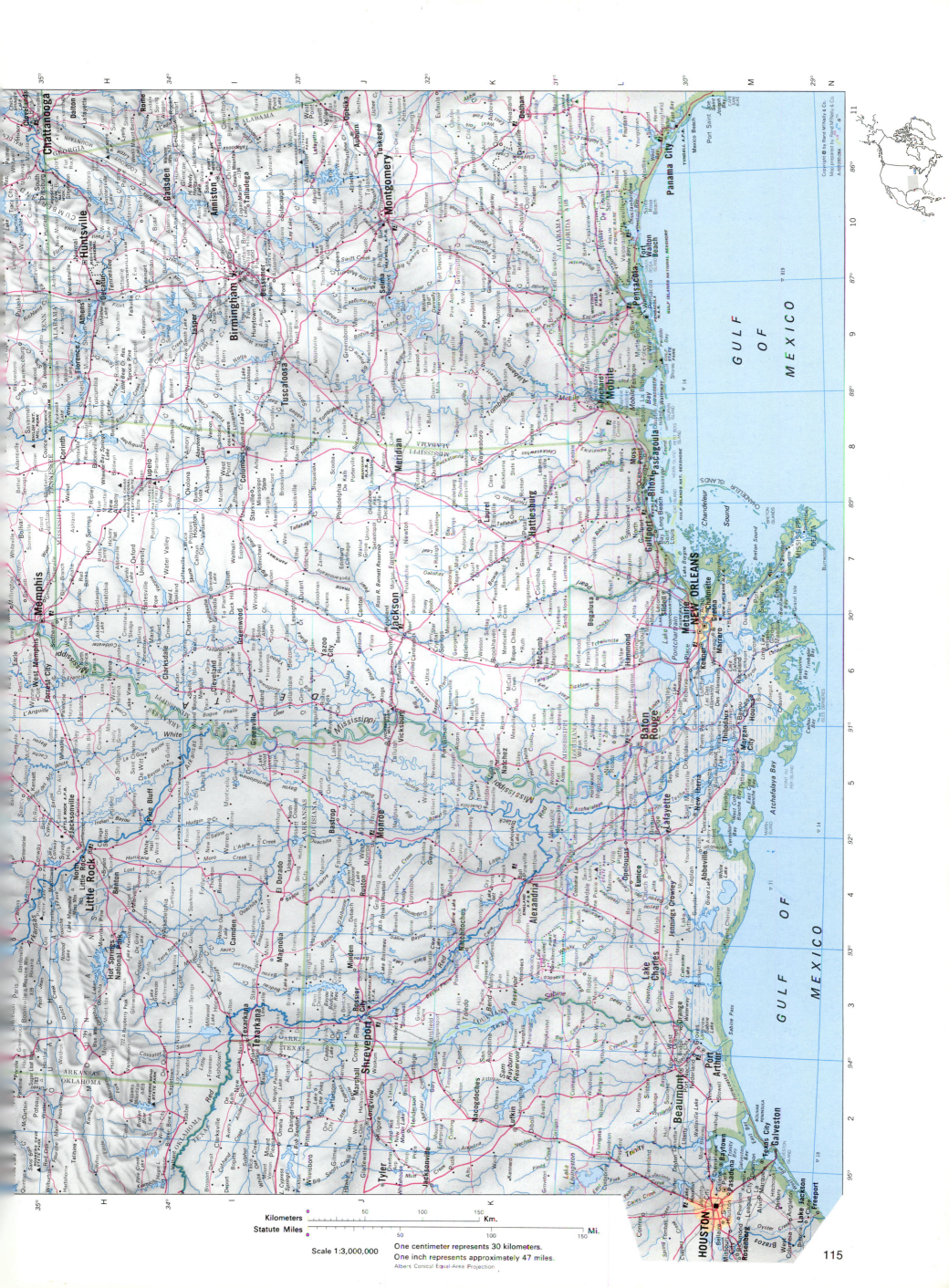

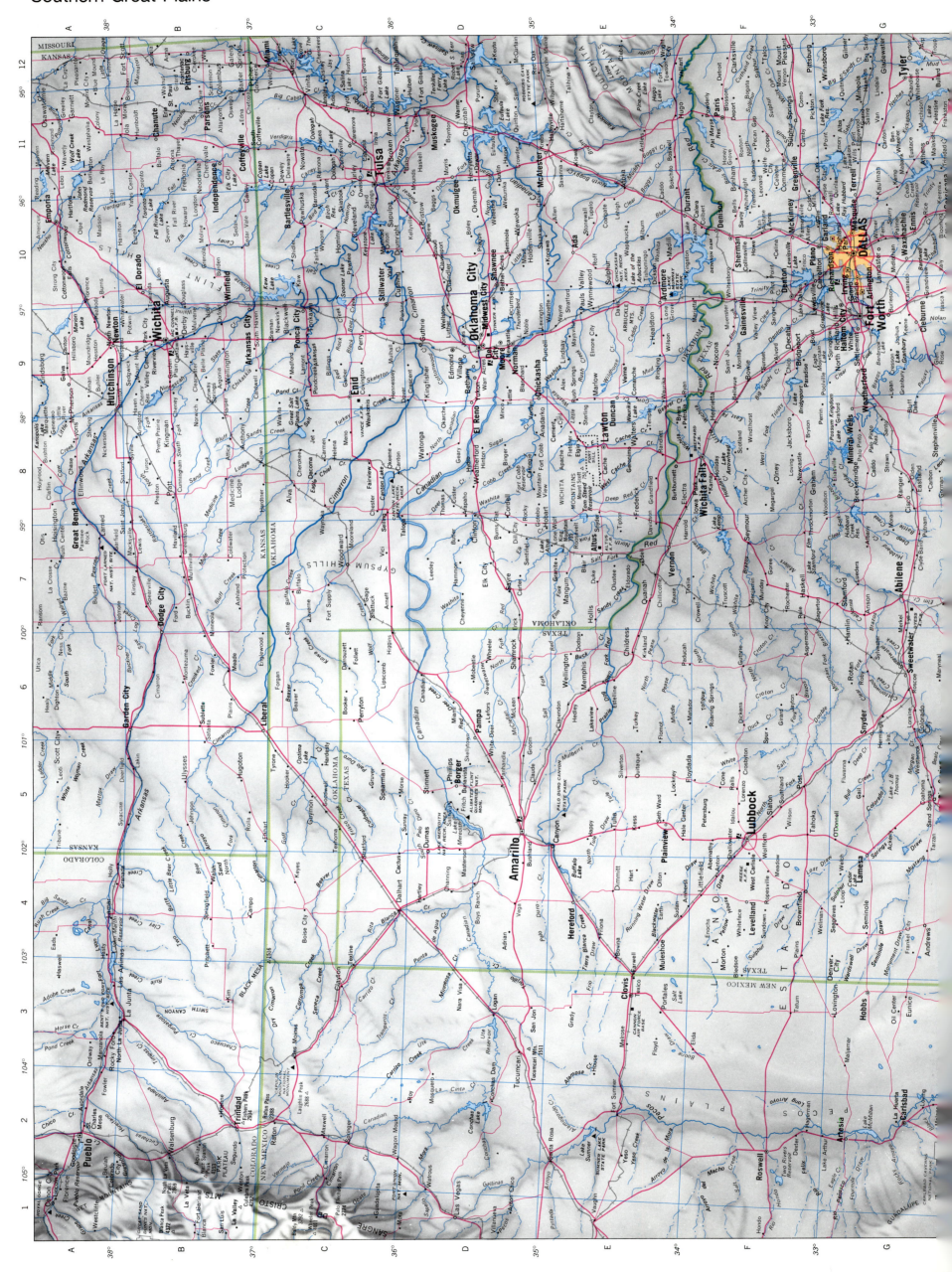

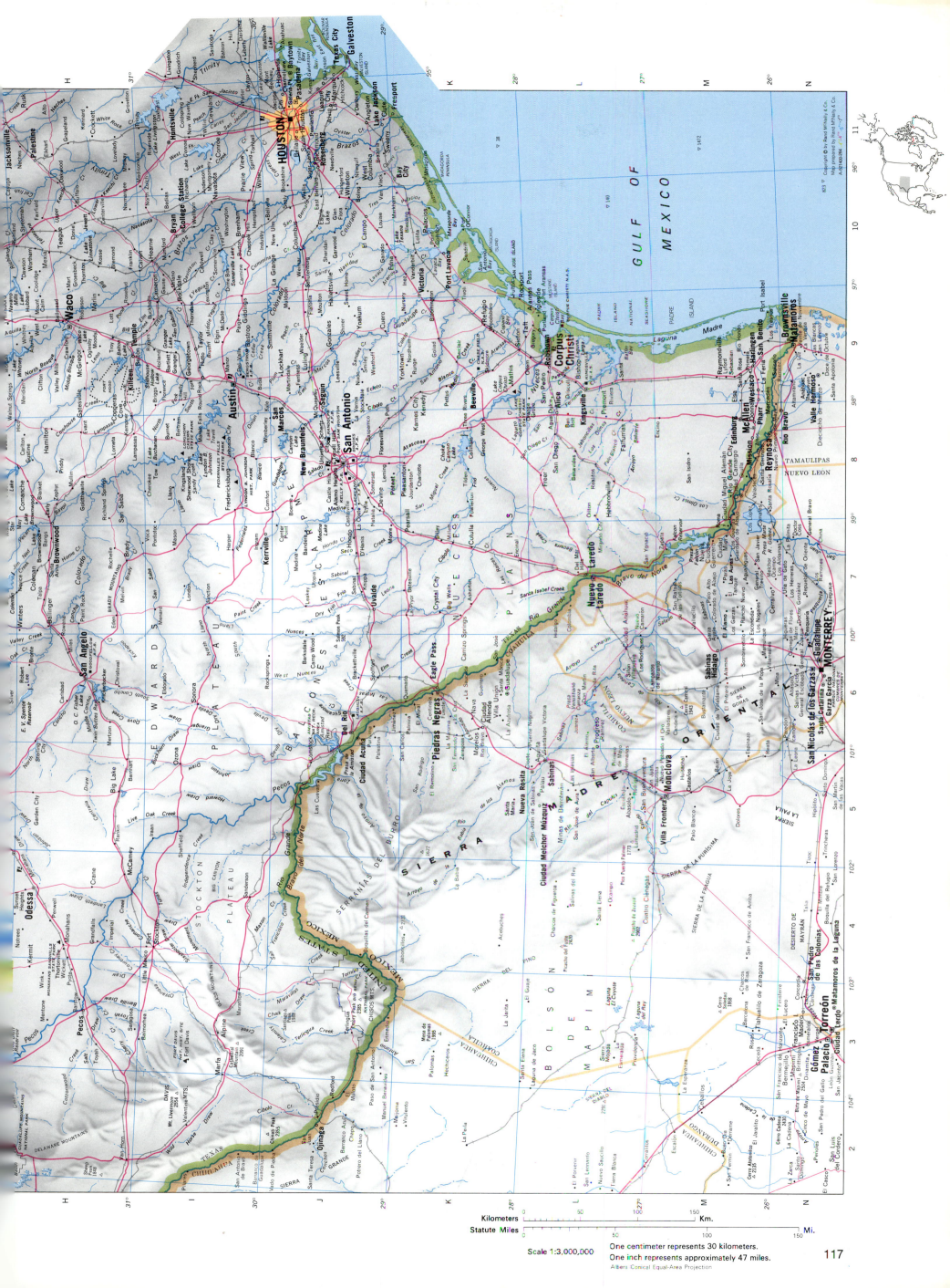

Scale 1:3,000,000
One centimeter represents 30 kilometers.
One inch represents approximately 47 miles.
Albers Conical Equal-Area Projection

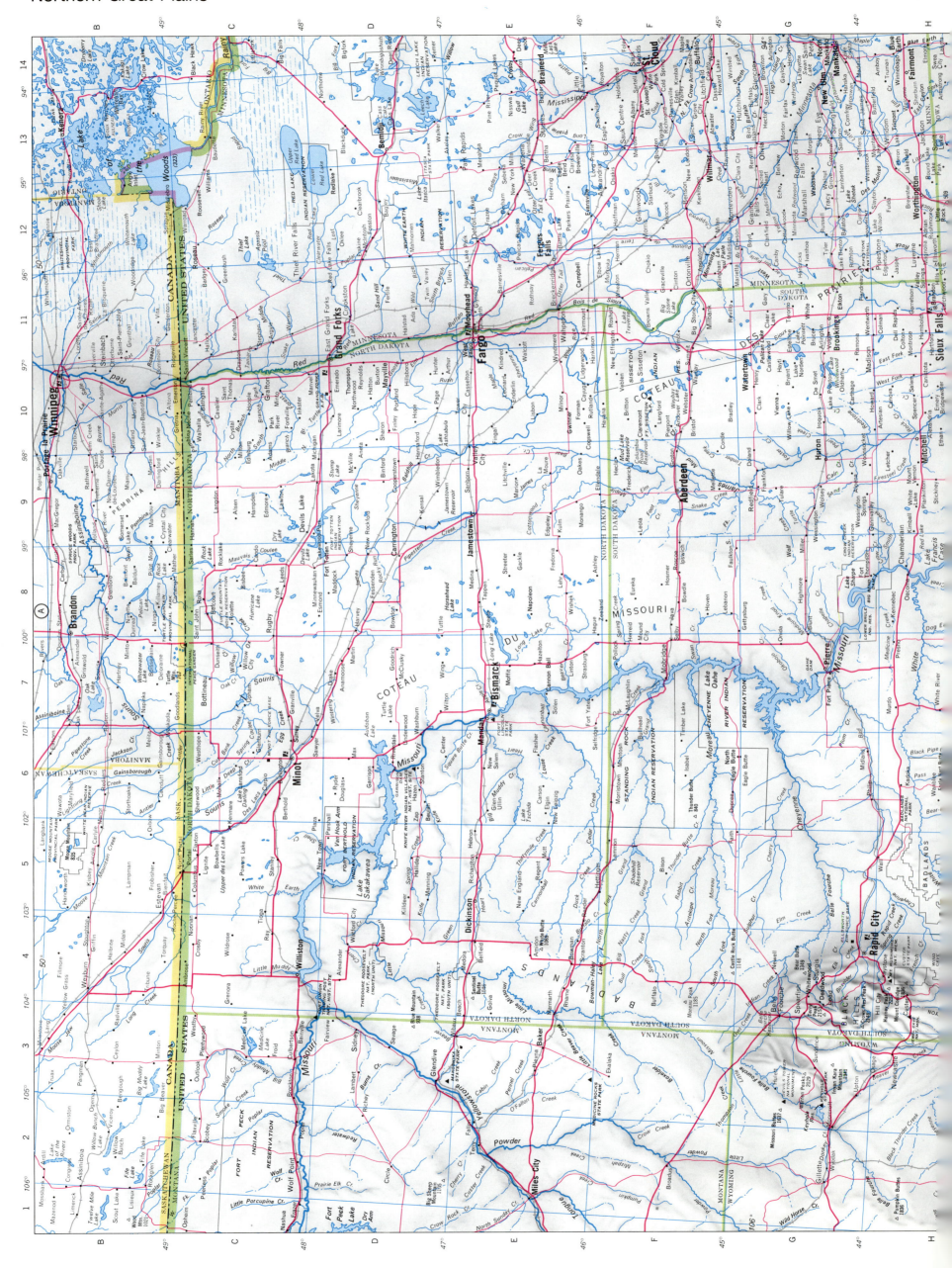

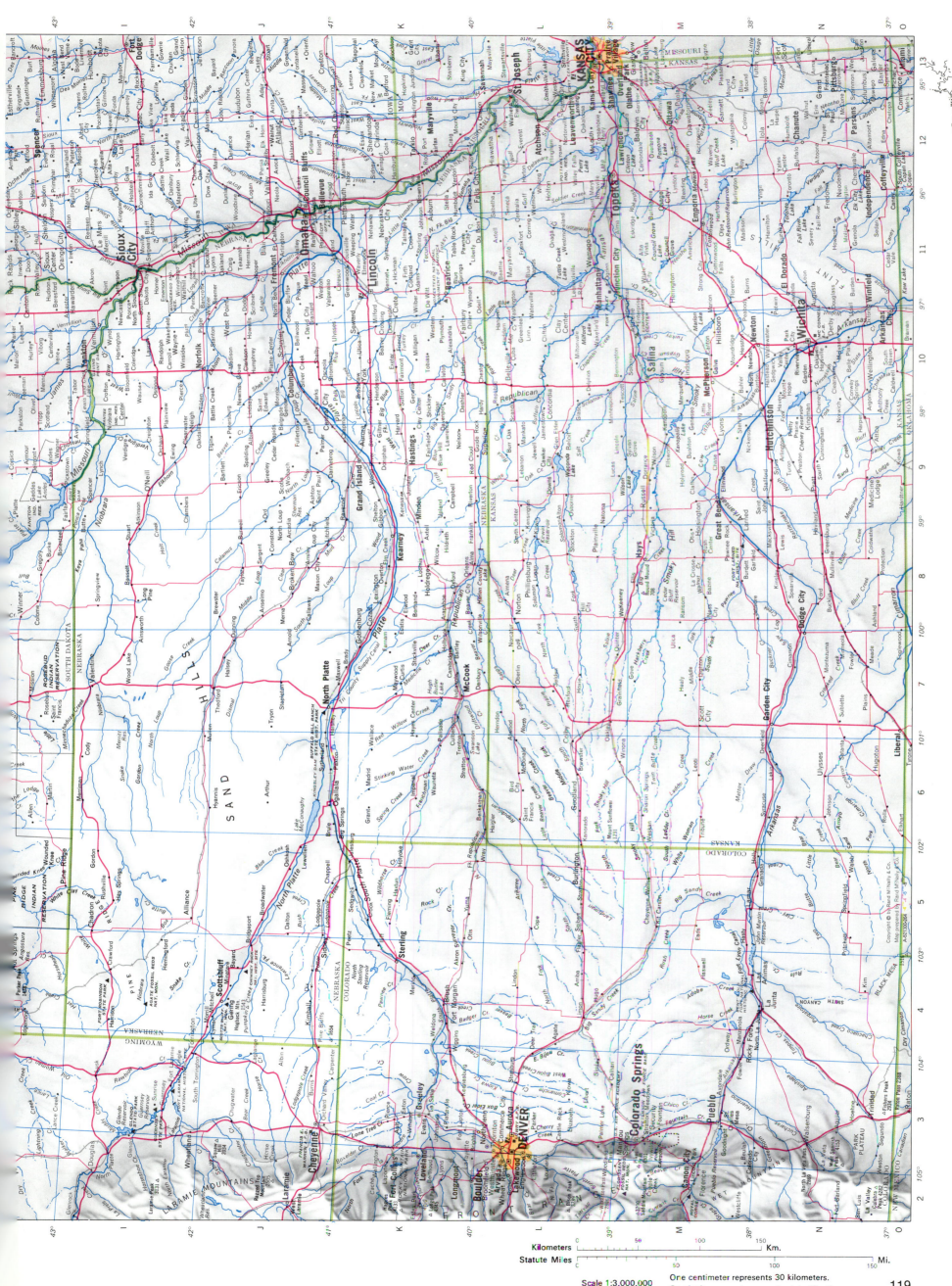

Kilometers

Statute Miles

Scale 1:3,000,000

One centimeter represents 30 kilometers.
One inch represents approximately 47 miles.
Albers Conical Equal-Area Projection

# Southern Rocky Mountains

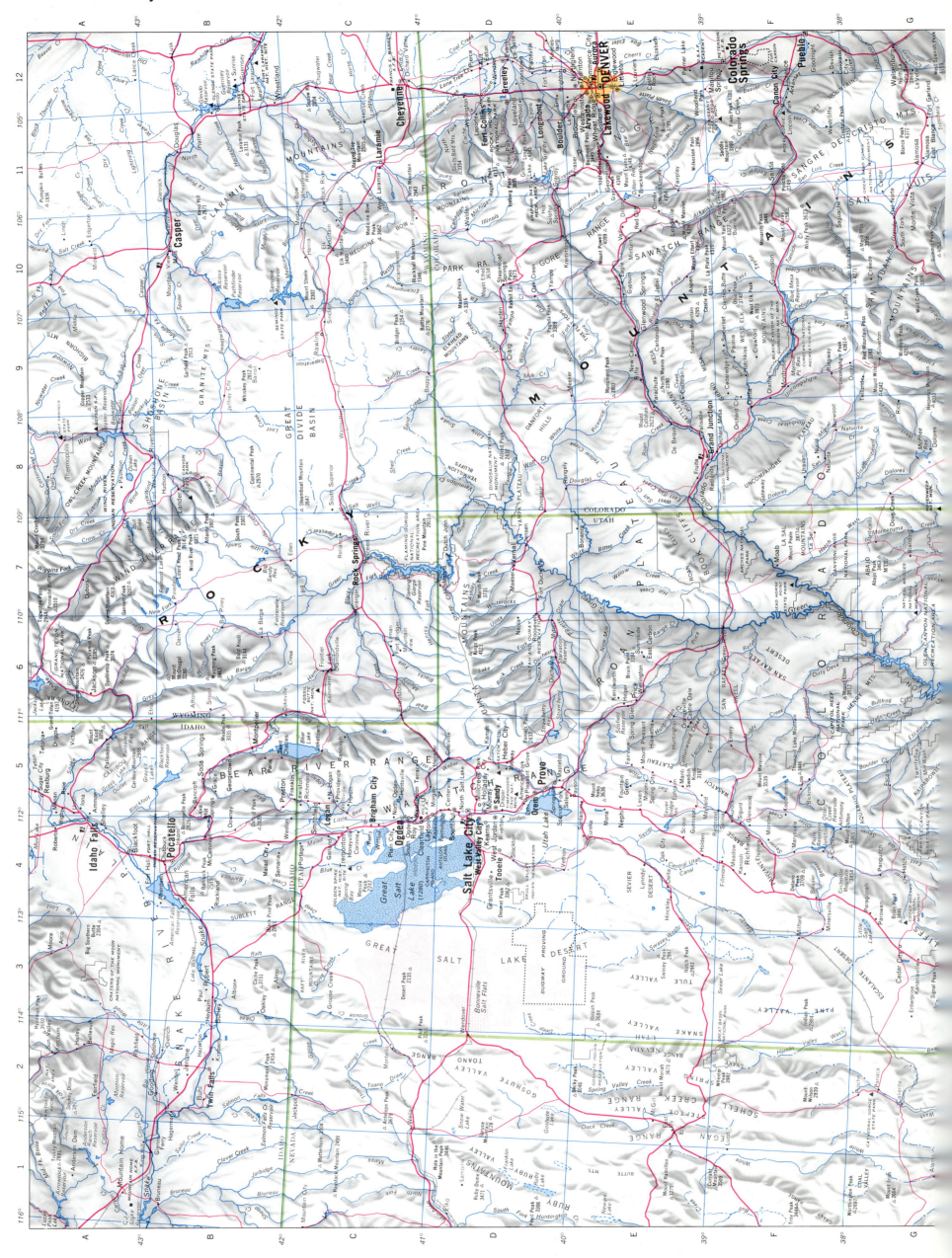

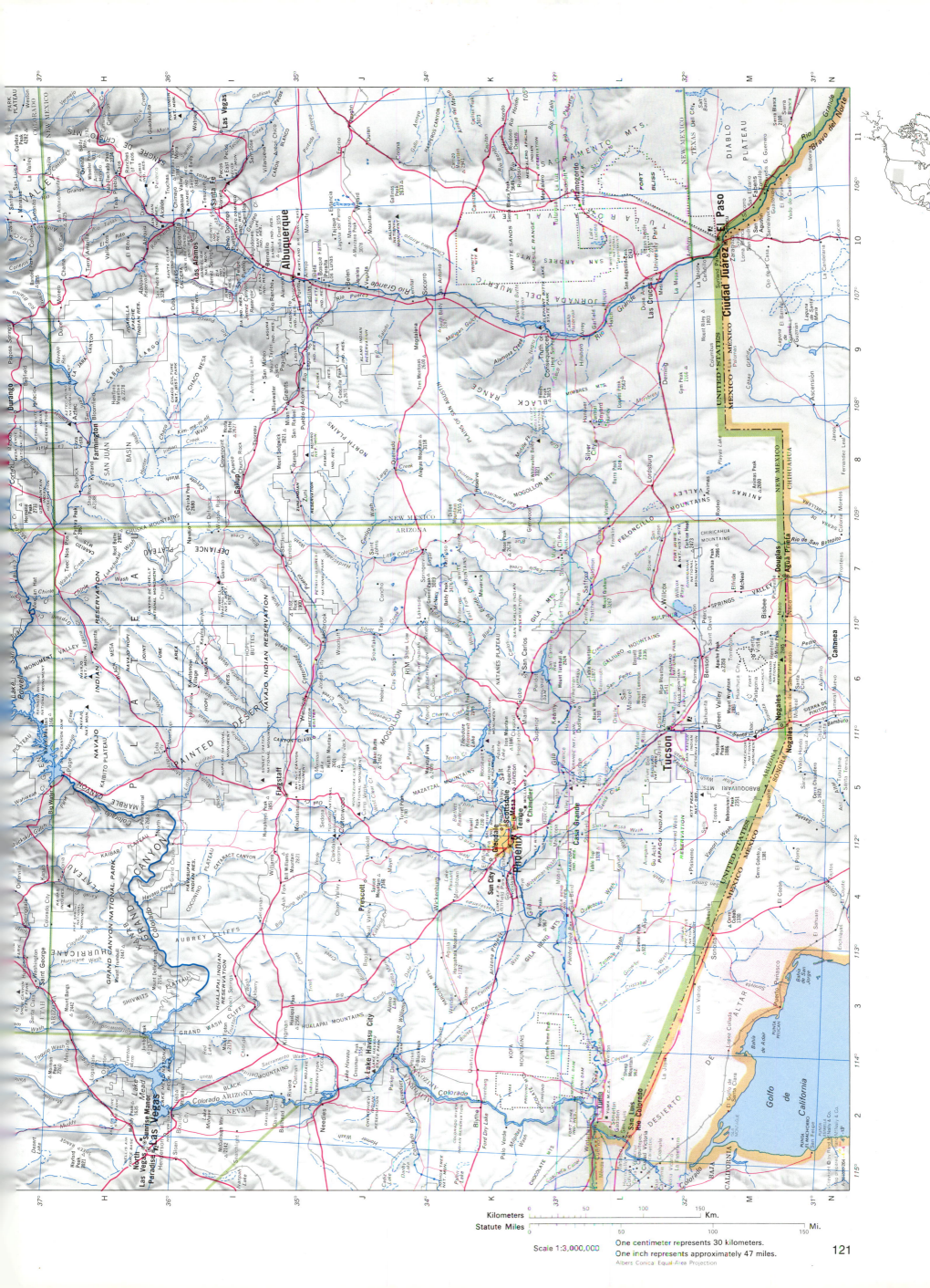

One centimeter represents 30 kilometers.
One inch represents approximately 47 miles.
Albers Conical Equal-Area Projection

Scale 1:3,000,000

Kilometers
Statute Miles
Km.
Mi.

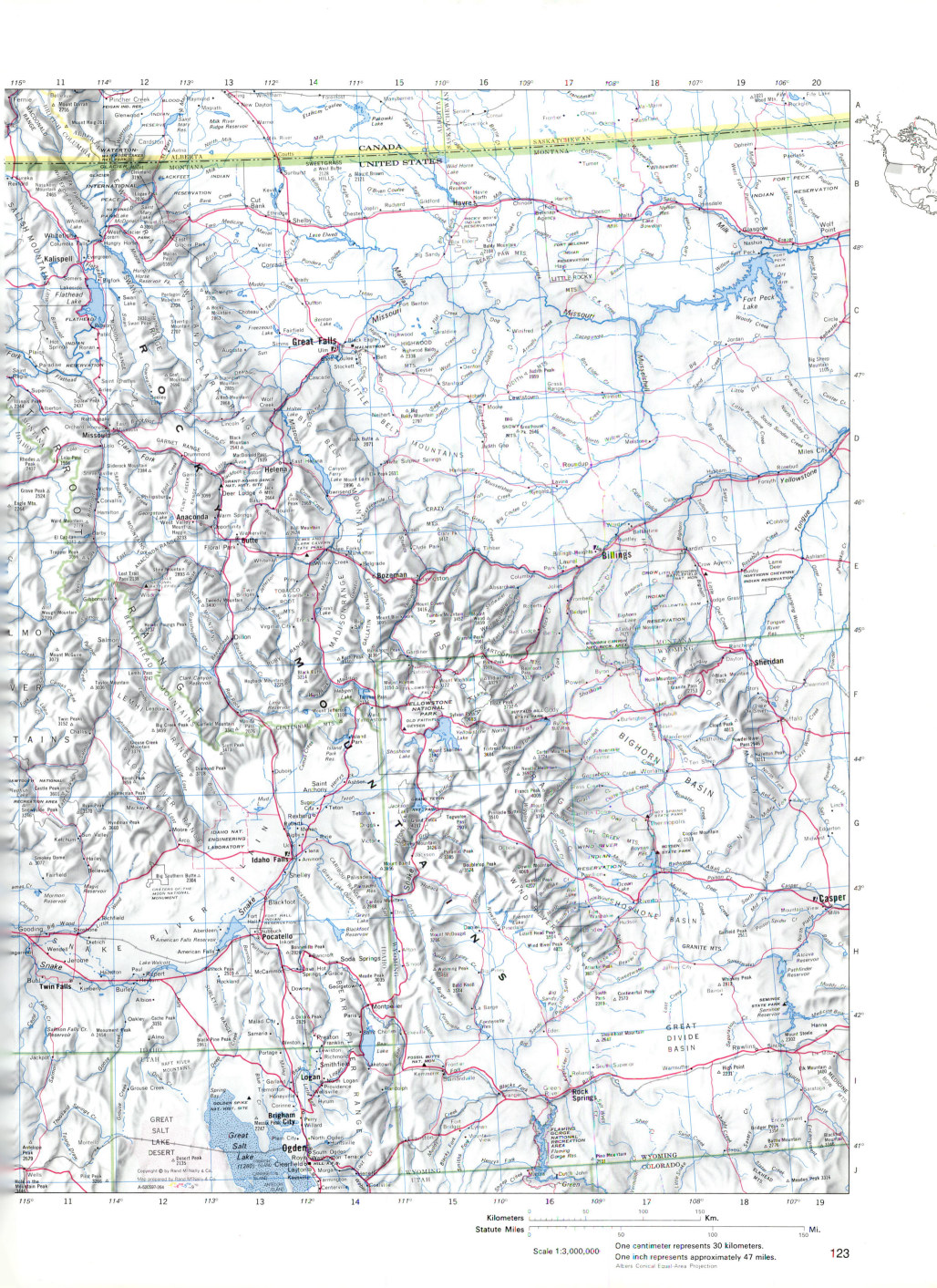

# Index to World Reference Maps

## Introduction to the Index

This universal index includes in a single alphabetical list over 52,000 names of features that appear on the reference maps. Each name is followed by the name of the country or continent in which it is located, a map-reference key and a page reference.

**Names** The names of cities appear in the index in regular type. The names of all other features appear in *italics*, followed by descriptive terms (hill, mtn., state) to indicate their nature.

Names that appear in shortened versions on the maps due to space limitations are spelled out in full in the index. The portions of these names omitted from the maps are enclosed in brackets — for example, Acapulco [de Juárez].

Abbreviations of names on the maps have been standardized as much as possible. Names that are abbreviated on the maps are generally spelled out in full in the index.

Country names and names of features that extend beyond the boundaries of one country are followed by the name of the continent in which each is located. Country designations follow the names of all other places in the index. The locations of places in the United States, Canada, and the United Kingdom are further defined by abbreviations that indicate the state, province, or political division in which each is located.

All abbreviations used in the index are defined in the List of Abbreviations below.

**Alphabetization** Names are alphabetized in the order of the letters of the English alphabet. Spanish *ll* and *ch*, for example, are not treated as distinct letters. Furthermore, diacritical marks are disregarded in alphabetization — German or Scandinavian *ä* or *ö* are treated as *a* or *o*.

The names of physical features may appear inverted, since they are always alphabetized under the proper, not the generic, part of the name, thus: 'Gibraltar, Strait of'. Otherwise every entry, whether consisting of one word or more, is alphabetized as a single continuous entity. 'Lakeland', for example, appears after 'La Crosse' and before 'La Salle'. Names beginning with articles (Le Havre, Den Helder, Al Manşūrah) are not inverted. Names beginning 'St.', 'Ste.' and 'Sainte' are alphabetized as though spelled 'Saint'.

In the case of identical names, towns are listed first, then political divisions, then physical features. Entries that are completely identical are listed alphabetically by country name.

**Map-Reference Keys and Page References** The map-reference keys and page references are found in the last two columns of each entry.

Each map-reference key consists of a letter and number. The letters appear along the sides of the maps. Lowercase letters indicate reference to inset maps. Numbers appear across the tops and bottoms of the maps.

Map reference keys for point features, such as cities and mountain peaks, indicate the locations of the symbols. For extensive areal features, such as countries or mountain ranges, locations are given for the approximate centers of the features. Those for linear features, such as canals and rivers, are given for the locations of the names.

The page number generally refers to the main map for the country in which the feature is located. Page references to two-page maps always refer to the left-hand page.

## List of Abbreviations

| | | | |
|---|---|---|---|
| Afg. | Afghanistan | Cyp. | Cyprus |
| Afr. | Africa | Czech. | Czech Republic |
| Ak., U.S. | Alaska, U.S. | D.C., U.S. | District of Columbia, U.S. |
| Al., U.S. | Alabama, U.S. | | |
| Alb. | Albania | De., U.S. | Delaware, U.S. |
| Alg. | Algeria | Den. | Denmark |
| Alta., Can. | Alberta, Can. | *dep.* | dependency, colony |
| Am. Sam. | American Samoa | *depr.* | depression |
| *anch.* | anchorage | *dept.* | department, district |
| And. | Andorra | *des.* | desert |
| Ang. | Angola | Dji. | Djibouti |
| Ant. | Antarctica | Dom. | Dominica |
| Antig. | Antigua and Barbuda | Dom. Rep. | Dominican Republic |
| | | D.R.C. | Democratic Republic of the Congo |
| Ar., U.S. | Arkansas, U.S. | | |
| Arg. | Argentina | Ec. | Ecuador |
| Arm. | Armenia | El Sal. | El Salvador |
| Aus. | Austria | Eng., U.K. | England, U.K. |
| Austl. | Australia | Eq. Gui. | Equatorial Guinea |
| Az., U.S. | Arizona, U.S. | Erit. | Eritrea |
| Azer. | Azerbaijan | *est.* | estuary |
| *b.* | bay, gulf, inlet, lagoon | Est. | Estonia |
| | | Eth. | Ethiopia |
| Bah. | Bahamas | Eur. | Europe |
| Bahr. | Bahrain | Faer. Is. | Faeroe Islands |
| Barb. | Barbados | Falk. Is. | Falkland Islands |
| B.C., Can. | British Columbia, Can. | Fin. | Finland |
| | | Fl., U.S. | Florida, U.S. |
| Bdi. | Burundi | *for.* | forest, moor |
| Bel. | Belgium | Fr. | France |
| Bela. | Belarus | Fr. Gu. | French Guiana |
| Ber. | Bermuda | Fr. Poly. | French Polynesia |
| Bhu. | Bhutan | Ga., U.S. | Georgia, U.S. |
| B.I.O.T. | British Indian Ocean Territory | Gam. | Gambia |
| | | Gaza | Gaza Strip and Jericho Area |
| Bngl. | Bangladesh | | |
| Bol. | Bolivia | Geor. | Georgia |
| Bos. | Bosnia and Herzegovina | Ger. | Germany |
| | | Gib. | Gibraltar |
| Bots. | Botswana | Golan | Golan Heights |
| Braz. | Brazil | Grc. | Greece |
| Bru. | Brunei | Gren. | Grenada |
| Br. Vir. Is. | British Virgin Islands | Grnld. | Greenland |
| Bul. | Bulgaria | Guad. | Guadeloupe |
| Burkina | Burkina Faso | Guat. | Guatemala |
| *c.* | cape, point | Gui. | Guinea |
| Ca., U.S. | California, U.S. | Gui.-B. | Guinea-Bissau |
| Cam. | Cameroon | Guy. | Guyana |
| Camb. | Cambodia | Hi., U.S. | Hawaii, U.S. |
| Can. | Canada | *hist.* | historic site, ruins |
| Cay. Is. | Cayman Islands | *hist. reg.* | historic region |
| Cen. Afr. Rep. | Central African Republic | Hond. | Honduras |
| | | Hung. | Hungary |
| Christ. I. | Christmas Island | *i.* | island |
| C. Iv. | Cote d'Ivoire | Ia., U.S. | Iowa, U.S. |
| *clf.* | cliff, escarpment | Ice. | Iceland |
| *co.* | county, parish | *ice* | ice feature, glacier |
| Co., U.S. | Colorado, U.S. | Id., U.S. | Idaho, U.S. |
| Col. | Colombia | Il., U.S. | Illinois, U.S. |
| Com. | Comoros | In., U.S. | Indiana, U.S. |
| *cont.* | continent | Indon. | Indonesia |
| C.R. | Costa Rica | I. of Man | Isle of Man |
| *crat.* | crater | Ire. | Ireland |
| Cro. | Croatia | *is.* | islands |
| Ct., U.S. | Connecticut, U.S. | Isr. | Israel |
| *ctry.* | country | Jam. | Jamaica |
| C.V. | Cape Verde | | |

| | | | |
|---|---|---|---|
| Jord. | Jordan | N. Ire., U.K. | Northern Ireland, U.K. |
| Kaz. | Kazakhstan | | |
| Kir. | Kiribati | N.J., U.S. | New Jersey, U.S. |
| Ks., U.S. | Kansas, U.S. | N. Kor. | North Korea |
| Kuw. | Kuwait | N.M., U.S. | New Mexico, U.S. |
| Ky., U.S. | Kentucky, U.S. | N. Mar. Is. | Northern Mariana Islands |
| Kyrg. | Kyrgyzstan | | |
| *l.* | lake, pond | Nmb. | Namibia |
| La., U.S. | Louisiana, U.S. | Nor. | Norway |
| Lat. | Latvia | Norf. I. | Norfolk Island |
| Leb. | Lebanon | N.S., Can. | Nova Scotia, Can. |
| Leso. | Lesotho | Nv., U.S. | Nevada, U.S. |
| Lib. | Liberia | N.W. Ter., Can. | Northwest Territories, Can. |
| Liech. | Liechtenstein | | |
| Lith. | Lithuania | N.Y., U.S. | New York, U.S. |
| Lux. | Luxembourg | N.Z. | New Zealand |
| Ma., U.S. | Massachusetts, U.S. | Oc. | Oceania |
| | | Oh., U.S. | Ohio, U.S. |
| Mac. | Macedonia | Ok., U.S. | Oklahoma, U.S. |
| Madag. | Madagascar | Ont., Can. | Ontario, Can. |
| Malay. | Malaysia | Or., U.S. | Oregon, U.S. |
| Mald. | Maldives | Pa., U.S. | Pennsylvania, U.S. |
| Man., Can. | Manitoba, Can. | Pak. | Pakistan |
| Marsh. Is. | Marshall Islands | Pan. | Panama |
| Mart. | Martinique | Pap. N. Gui. | Papua New Guinea |
| Maur. | Mauritania | Para. | Paraguay |
| May. | Mayotte | P.E.I., Can. | Prince Edward Island, Can. |
| Md., U.S. | Maryland, U.S. | | |
| Me., U.S. | Maine, U.S. | *pen.* | peninsula |
| Mex. | Mexico | Phil. | Philippines |
| Mi., U.S. | Michigan, U.S. | Pit. | Pitcairn |
| Micron. | Federated States of Micronesia | *pl.* | plain, flat |
| | | *plat.* | plateau, highland |
| Mid. Is. | Midway Islands | Pol. | Poland |
| *mil.* | military installation | Port. | Portugal |
| Mn., U.S. | Minnesota, U.S. | P.R. | Puerto Rico |
| Mo., U.S. | Missouri, U.S. | *prov.* | province, region |
| Mol. | Moldova | Que., Can. | Quebec, Can. |
| Mon. | Monaco | *reg.* | physical region |
| Mong. | Mongolia | *res.* | reservoir |
| Monts. | Montserrat | Reu. | Reunion |
| Mor. | Morocco | *rf.* | reef, shoal |
| Moz. | Mozambique | R.I., U.S. | Rhode Island, U.S. |
| Mrts. | Mauritius | Rom. | Romania |
| Ms., U.S. | Mississippi, U.S. | Rw. | Rwanda |
| Mt., U.S. | Montana, U.S. | S.A. | South America |
| *mth.* | river mouth or channel | S. Afr. | South Africa |
| | | Sask., Can. | Saskatchewan, Can. |
| *mtn.* | mountain | | |
| *mts.* | mountains | Sau. Ar. | Saudi Arabia |
| Mwi. | Malawi | S.C., U.S. | South Carolina, U.S. |
| Mya. | Myanmar | *sci.* | scientific station |
| N.A. | North America | Scot., U.K. | Scotland, U.K. |
| N.B., Can. | New Brunswick, Can. | S.D., U.S. | South Dakota, U.S. |
| | | Sen. | Senegal |
| N.C., U.S. | North Carolina, U.S. | Sey. | Seychelles |
| N. Cal. | New Caledonia | Sing. | Singapore |
| N. Cyp. | North Cyprus | S. Geor. | South Georgia |
| N.D., U.S. | North Dakota, U.S. | S. Kor. | South Korea |
| Ne., U.S. | Nebraska, U.S. | S.L. | Sierra Leone |
| Neth. | Netherlands | Slo. | Slovenia |
| Neth. Ant. | Netherlands Antilles | Slov. | Slovakia |
| Newf., Can. | Newfoundland, Can. | S. Mar. | San Marino |
| N.H., U.S. | New Hampshire, U.S. | Sol. Is. | Solomon Islands |
| | | Som. | Somalia |
| Nic. | Nicaragua | Sp. N. Afr. | Spanish North Africa |
| Nig. | Nigeria | | |

| | | |
|---|---|---|
| Sri L. | Sri Lanka | |
| *state* | state, republic, canton | |
| St. Hel. | St. Helena | |
| St. K./N | St. Kitts and Nevis | |
| St. Luc. | St. Lucia | |
| *stm.* | stream (river, creek) | |
| S. Tom./P. | Sao Tome and Principe | |
| St. P./M. | St. Pierre and Miquelon | |
| *strt.* | strait, channel, sound | |
| St. Vin. | St. Vincent and the Grenadines | |
| Sur. | Suriname | |
| *sw.* | swamp, marsh | |
| Swaz. | Swaziland | |
| Swe. | Sweden | |
| Switz. | Switzerland | |
| Tai. | Taiwan | |
| Taj. | Tajikistan | |
| Tan. | Tanzania | |
| T./C. Is. | Turks and Caicos Islands | |
| *ter.* | territory | |
| Thai. | Thailand | |
| Tn., U.S. | Tennessee, U.S. | |
| Tok. | Tokelau | |
| Trin. | Trinidad and Tobago | |
| Tun. | Tunisia | |
| Tur. | Turkey | |
| Turk. | Turkmenistan | |
| Tx., U.S. | Texas, U.S. | |
| U.A.E. | United Arab Emirates | |
| Ug. | Uganda | |
| U.K. | United Kingdom | |
| Ukr. | Ukraine | |
| Ur. | Uruguay | |
| U.S. | United States | |
| Ut., U.S. | Utah, U.S. | |
| Uzb. | Uzbekistan | |
| Va., U.S. | Virginia, U.S. | |
| *val.* | valley, watercourse | |
| Vat. | Vatican City | |
| Ven. | Venezuela | |
| Viet. | Vietnam | |
| V.I.U.S. | Virgin Islands (U.S.) | |
| *vol.* | volcano | |
| Vt., U.S. | Vermont, U.S. | |
| Wa., U.S. | Washington, U.S. | |
| Wal./F. | Wallis and Futuna | |
| W.B. | West Bank | |
| Wi., U.S. | Wisconsin, U.S. | |
| W. Sah. | Western Sahara | |
| W. Sam. | Western Samoa | |
| *wtfl.* | waterfall | |
| W.V., U.S. | West Virginia, U.S. | |
| Wy., U.S. | Wyoming, U.S. | |
| Yugo. | Yugoslavia | |
| Yukon, Can. | Yukon Territory, Can. | |
| Zam. | Zambia | |
| Zimb. | Zimbabwe | |

# Index

## A

| Name | Map Ref. | Page |
|---|---|---|

Aachen, Ger. — E6 10
Aalen, Ger. — G10 10
Aarau, Switz. — D9 13
Aarburg, Switz. — D8 13
Aare, stm., Switz. — C9 13
Aargau, state, Switz. — C9 13
Aarlen (Arlon), Bel. — I8 12
Aazanën, Mor. — J8 16
Aba, China — E7 30
Aba, Nig. — I13 64
Abā as-Su'ūd, Sau. Ar. — F4 47
Abacaxis, stm., Braz. — E7 76
Abaco, i., Bah. — A6 94
Abacou, Pointe, c., Haiti — E8 94
Ābādān, Iran — F10 48
Ābādeh, Iran — F12 48
Abadia dos Dourados, Braz. — E5 79
Abadiânia, Braz. — D4 79
Abadla, Alg. — E9 62
Abaeté, Braz. — E6 79
Abaeté, stm., Braz. — E6 79
Abaetetuba, Braz. — D9 76
Abagner Qi, China — C10 30
Abag Qi, China — C9 30
Abai, Para. — D11 80
Abaj, Kaz. — H12 26
Abaji, Nig. — G13 64
Abajo Peak, mtn., Ut., U.S. — G7 120
Abak, Nig. — I13 64
Abakaliki, Nig. — H14 64
Abakan, Russia — G10 28
Abakan, stm., Russia — G16 26
Abala, Niger — D11 64
Abalak, Niger — D13 64
Abalessa, Alg. — I13 62
Abancay, Peru — F4 82
Abā Kūh, Iran — F12 48
Abashiri, Japan — c19 36a
Abasolo, Mex. — E7 90
Abasolo, Mex. — E10 90
Abatimbo el Gumas, Eth. — L8 60
Abau, Pap. N. Gui. — B9 68
Abay see Blue Nile, stm., Afr. — K7 60
Abaya, Lake, l., Eth. — N9 60
Abaza, Russia — G16 26
Abbeville, Fr. — B8 14
Abbeville, Ga., U.S. — H3 112
Abbeville, La., U.S. — M4 114
Abbeville, S.C., U.S. — E4 112
Abbey, Sk., Can. — H6 104
Abbeyfeale, Ire. — I4 8
Abbiategrasso, Italy — D3 18
Abbot, Mount, mtn., Austl. — C7 70
Abbotsford, B.C., Can. — H12 102
Abbotsford, Wi., U.S. — F5 110
Abbottābād, Pak. — C5 44
'Abd al-Kūrī, i., Yemen — G5 42
'Abd Allāh, Sudan — K2 60
'Abd Allāh, Khawr, strt., Asia — G10 48
Abdulino, Russia — G8 26
Abe, Lake, l., Afr. — F9 56
Abéché, Chad — F5 56
Abéjar, Spain — D9 16
Abejorral, Col. — E5 84
Abejorral, Cerro, mtn., Nic. — F8 92
Abekr, Sudan — K5 60
Abelek, Sudan — N5 60
Abelti, Eth. — M9 60
Abengourou, C. Iv. — H8 64
Abenójar, Spain — G7 16
Abeokuta, Nig. — H11 64
Aberaeron see Port Talbot, Wales, U.K. — J10 8
Aberdeen, Id., U.S. — H13 122
Aberdeen, Md., U.S. — H10 108
Aberdeen, Ms., U.S. — I8 114
Aberdeen, N.C., U.S. — D7 112
Aberdeen, S. Afr. — I7 66
Aberdeen, Scot., U.K. — D11 8
Aberdeen, S.D., U.S. — F9 118
Aberdeen, Wa., U.S. — D2 122
Aberdeen Lake, l., N.T., Can. — D13 96
Abernathy, Tx., U.S. — F5 116
Abernethy, Sk., Can. — H11 104
Abetone, Italy — E5 18
Abez', Russia — D10 26
Abhā, Sau. Ar. — E3 47
Abhar, Iran — C10 48
Ābhē Bid Hāyk', l., Afr. — G3 42
'Abīdīyah, Sudan — H7 60
Abidjan, C. Iv. — I7 64
Abilene, Ks., U.S. — M10 118
Abilene, Tx., U.S. — G7 116
Abingdon, Il., U.S. — J5 110
Abingdon, Va., U.S. — C5 112
Abington Reefs, rf., Austl. — B8 70
Abiquiu, N.M., U.S. — H10 120
Abiseo, stm., Peru — B3 82
Abita Springs, La., U.S. — L6 114
Abitau, stm., Can. — D11 96
Abitibi, On., Can. — F16 96
Abitibi, Lake, l., Can. — G17 96
Abiy Adi, Eth. — K10 60
Abiyata, Lake, l., Eth. — N10 60
Abnūb, Egypt — D6 60
Abohar, India — E6 44
Abomey, Benin — H10 64
Abongabong, Gunung, mtn., Indon. — L4 40
Abong Mbang, Cam. — H9 54
Abonnema, Nig. — I13 64
Abony, Hung. — H20 10
Aborigen, pik, mtn., Russia — E21 28
Abou-Deïa, Chad — F4 56
Abraham Lake, res., Ab., Can. — E18 102
Abraka, Nig. — I13 64
Abrantes, Port. — F3 16
Abra Pampa, Arg. — B6 80
Abre-Campo, Braz. — F7 79
Ábrego, Col. — C6 84
Abreojos, Punta, c., Mex. — L6 60
'Abrī, Sudan — L6 60
Abruzzi, prov., Italy — G8 18
Abs, Yemen — G3 47
Absaroka Range, mts., U.S. — E16 122
Absarokee, Mt., U.S. — E16 122
Absecon, N.J., U.S. — H12 108
Abū 'Alī, i., Sau. Ar. — A11 48
Abū al-Khaṣīb, Iraq — F9 48
Abū 'Arīsh, Sau. Ar. — F3 47
Abū Dawm, Sudan — J6 60
Abu Dhabi see Abū Ẓaby, U.A.E. — B9 47
Abufari, Braz. — A10 82

Abū Gelba, Sudan — K6 60
Abū Hamad, Sudan — H7 60
Abuja, Nig. — G13 64
Abū Jubayhah, Sudan — L6 60
Abū Kamāl, Syria — D6 48
Abū Madd, Ra's, c., Sau. Ar. — I4 48
Abu Mendi, Eth. — L8 60
Abū Mūsá, i., Asia — H13 48
Abuna, Braz. — C9 82
Abunā (Abunã), stm., S.A. — C8 82
Abū Na'amah, Sudan — K8 60
Abū Qashsh, W.B. — E4 50
Abū Qurqāş, Egypt — D6 60
Abū Road, India — H5 44
Abū Rubayq, Sau. Ar. — C1 47
Abū Shajarah, Ra's, c., Sudan — G9 60
Abū Shanab, Sudan — K4 60
Abū Tīj, Egypt — D6 60
Abū Tunaytin, Sudan — J6 60
Abū Zabad, Sudan — K5 60
Abū Ẓaby, U.A.E. — B9 47
Abū Zanīmah, Egypt — C7 60
Abyad 'Alī, Sau. Ar. — B1 47
Acacias, Col. — F6 84
Acadia National Park, Me., U.S. — C18 108
Acadia Valley, Ab., Can. — G4 104
Acahay, Para. — C10 80
Acajutla, El Sal. — D5 92
Acámbaro, Mex. — G9 90
Acandí, Col. — C4 84
Acaponeta, Mex. — F7 90
Acaponeta, stm., Mex. — F7 90
Acapulco de Juárez, Mex. — I10 90
Acará, Lago, l., Braz. — I11 84
Acarai Mountains, mts., S.A. — G14 84
Acaraú, Braz. — D10 76
Acaray, stm., Para. — C11 80
Acarí, Peru — F4 82
Acarí, stm., Braz. — C6 79
Acari, stm., Braz. — A12 82
Acari, stm., Braz. — F4 82
Acarigua, Ven. — C8 84
Acatlán de Juárez, Mex. — G8 90
Acatlán de Osorio, Mex. — H10 90
Acay, Nevado de, mtn., Arg. — C5 80
Acayucan, Mex. — I12 90
Accomac, Va., U.S. — B11 112
Accoville, W.V., U.S. — B5 112
Accra, Ghana — I9 64
Acebuches, Mex. — C8 90
Aceguá, Braz. — F11 80
Acerra, Italy — I9 18
Acevedo, Arg. — G8 80
Achacachi, Bol. — G7 82
Achaguas, Ven. — D8 84
Achalpur, India — J7 44
Achar, Ur. — G10 80
Acheng, China — B12 30
Achern, Ger. — G8 10
Achí, Col. — C5 84
Achiguate, stm., Guat. — C4 92
Achill Island, i., Ire. — H3 8
Achiras, Arg. — G6 80
Achtuba, stm., Russia — H7 26
Achtubinsk, Russia — H7 26
Achuapa, Nic. — D8 92
Ačinsk, Russia — F10 28
Acipayam, Tur. — L13 20
Acireale, Italy — L10 18
Ačisaj, Kaz. — I11 26
Ackerly, Tx., U.S. — G5 116
Ackerman, Ms., U.S. — I7 114
Ackley, Ia., U.S. — H2 110
Acklins, i., Bah. — C9 94
Acklins, Bight of, Bah. — C7 94
Acme, Ab., Can. — F21 102
Acobamba, Peru — E4 82
Acolla, Peru — D4 82
Acomayo, Peru — E6 82
Acomayo, Peru — E3 82
Aconcagua, Cerro, mtn., Arg. — G3 80
Aconchi, Mex. — C4 90
Açores (Azores), is., Port. — k19 62a
Acoria, Peru — E4 82
Acorizal, Braz. — F13 82
Acornhoek, S. Afr. — E10 66
A Coruña, Spain — B3 16
Acoyapa, Nic. — F9 92
Acoyapa, stm., Nic. — F9 92
Acquapendente, Italy — G6 18
Acqui Terme, Italy — E3 18
Acre see 'Akko, Isr. — C4 50
Acre, stm., S.A. — C8 82
Acri, Italy — J11 18
Acrotambo, Cerro, mtn., Peru — C3 82
Acton, On., Can. — G15 110
Acton-Vale, P.Q., Can. — B14 108
Actopan, Mex. — G10 90
Açuã, stm., Braz. — B10 82
Açucena, Braz. — E7 79
Acuña, Arg. — E10 80
Acurauá, stm., Braz. — B6 82
Acworth, Ga., U.S. — E2 112
Ada, Mn., U.S. — D11 118
Ada, Oh., U.S. — G3 108
Ada, Ok., U.S. — E10 116
Ada, Yugo. — D4 20
Adaba, Eth. — N10 60
Adailo, Erit. — G2 47
Adair, Ok., U.S. — C11 116
Adair, Bahía, b., Mex. — B3 90
Adair, Cape, c., N.T., Can. — B18 96
Adairsville, Ga., U.S. — E2 112
Adairville, Ky., U.S. — F10 114
Adak, Ak., U.S. — K6 100
Adak Island, i., Ak., U.S. — K6 100
Adala, Tur. — K12 20
Ādam, Oman — C10 47
Adamantina, Braz. — F3 79
Adamaoua, mts., Afr. — G9 54
Adamclisi, Rom. — E11 20
Adamello, mtn., Italy — D5 18
Adami Tulu, Eth. — N10 60
Adamów, Pol. — D22 10
Adams, Mn., U.S. — G3 110
Adams, N.D., U.S. — C9 118
Adams, N.Y., U.S. — D10 108
Adams, Wi., U.S. — G6 110
Adams, Mount, mtn., Wa., U.S. — D4 122
Adams Bridge, rf., Asia — H5 46
Adams Lake, l., B.C., Can. — F15 102
Adams Peak, mtn., Sri L. — I6 46
Adamsville, Tn., U.S. — G8 114
'Adan (Aden), Yemen — H4 47
'Adan, Gulf of, b. — H4 47
Adarama, Sudan — J7 60
Adare, Cape, c., Ant. — C8 73
Adarot, Sudan — I9 60

Adavale, Austl. — E6 70
Adda, stm., Italy — D4 18
Ad-Dab'ah, Egypt — B5 60
Ad-Dabbah, Sudan — H6 60
Ad-Dafīnah, Sau. Ar. — C2 47
Ad-Dahnā', des., Sau. Ar. — C6 47
Ad-Damazin, Sudan — L8 60
Ad-Dammām, Sau. Ar. — A7 47
Ad-Dāmūr, Leb. — A4 50
Ad-Darb, Sau. Ar. — F3 47
Ad-Dawādimī, Sau. Ar. — B4 47
Ad-Dawhah (Doha), Qatar — I11 48
Ad-Dayr, Egypt — E7 60
Ad-Dilam, Sau. Ar. — C5 47
Addis, La., U.S. — L5 114
Addis Ababa see Adis Abeba, Eth. — G8 56
Addison, Mi., U.S. — I11 110
Ad-Dīwānīyah, Iraq — F8 48
Ad-Du'ayn, Sudan — L4 60
Ad-Duhayr, Egypt — F2 50
Ad-Duwayd, Sau. Ar. — F7 48
Ad-Duwaym, Sudan — J7 60
Adel, Ga., U.S. — H3 112
Adel, Ia., U.S. — I1 110
Adelaide, Austl. — J3 70
Adelaide, Bah. — B6 94
Adelaide, S. Afr. — I8 66
Adelaide Island, i., Ant. — B12 73
Adelaide Peninsula, pen., N.T., Can. — C13 96
Adélie Island, i., Ant. — C4 68
Adélie Coast, Ant. — B7 73
Adeta, Togo — H10 64
Ādhiriyāt, Jibāl al-, hills, Jord. — H7 50
Adi Arkay, Eth. — K9 60
Adi Dairo, Eth. — J10 60
Adieu, Cape, c., Austl. — F6 68
Adige, stm., Italy — D7 18
Adigrat, Eth. — J10 60
Adi Keyih, Erit. — J10 60
Adi Kwala, Erit. — J10 60
Adilābād, India — C5 46
Adin, Ca., U.S. — C5 124
Adirondack Mountains, mts., N.Y., U.S. — D12 108
Adis Abeba (Addis Ababa), Eth. — M10 60
Adis Zemen, Eth. — K9 60
Adi Ugri, Erit. — J10 60
Adiyaman, Tur. — C5 48
Adjohon, Benin — H11 64
Adjud, Rom. — C11 20
Adjuntas, Presa de las, res., Mex. — F10 90
Adliswil, Switz. — D10 13
Admer, Erg d', des., Alg. — H15 62
Admiral, Sk., Can. — I6 104
Admiralty Gulf, b., Austl. — B5 68
Admiralty Inlet, b., N.T., Can. — B15 96
Admiralty Island, i., Ak., U.S. — H27 100
Admiralty Island, i., N.T., Can. — C12 96
Admiralty Islands, is., Pap. N. Gui. — k16 68a
Admiralty Mountains, mts., Ant. — C8 73
Ado-Ekiti, Nig. — H12 64
Adok, Sudan — M6 60
Adolfo López Mateos, Mex. — C6 90
Adolfo López Mateos, Presa, res., Mex. — E6 90
Ādoni, India — D4 46
Ado-Odo, Nig. — H11 64
Adour, stm., Fr. — I5 14
Adra, Spain — I8 16
'Adrā, Syria — A7 50
Adrano, Italy — L9 18
Adrar, Alg. — G4 112
Adrar, reg., Maur. — J4 62
Adria, Italy — D7 18
Adrian, Mi., U.S. — I11 110
Adrian, Mn., U.S. — H12 118
Adrian, Mo., U.S. — D2 114
Adrian, Or., U.S. — G8 122
Adrian, Tx., U.S. — D4 116
Adrian, W.V., U.S. — I6 108
Adrianople see Edirne, Tur. — H10 20
Adriatic Sea, Eur. — G11 4
Advance, Mo., U.S. — E7 114
Advocate Harbour, N.S., Can. — G9 106
Adwa, Eth. — J10 60
Adycha, stm., Russia — D19 28
Adygea see Adygeja, state, Russia — I6 26
Adygeja, state, Russia — I6 26
Aegean Sea — J8 20
Aetna, Ab., Can. — G21 102
Afándou, Grc. — M12 20
Afar, reg., Afr. — H15 62
Afars and Issas see Djibouti, ctry., Afr. — F9 56
Affton, Mo., U.S. — D6 114
Afghanistan (Afghānestān), ctry., Asia — C8 42
Afikpo, Nig. — H13 64
Aflou, Alg. — C12 62
Afobaka, Sur. — B7 76
Afogados da Ingazeira, Braz. — E11 76
Afognak Island, i., Ak., U.S. — G18 100
Afonso Cláudio, Braz. — F8 79
Africa — G9 52
Afsluitdijk, Neth. — B7 12
Afton, Ia., U.S. — A2 114
Afton, N.Y., U.S. — E11 108
Afton, Ok., U.S. — C12 116
Afton, Wy., U.S. — H15 122
Afuá, Braz. — D8 76
Afula, Isr. — C4 50
Afyon, Tur. — H14 4
Agadez, Niger — F13 64
Agadir, Mor. — E6 62
Agadyr', Kaz. — H12 26
Agaie, Nig. — G13 64
Agalak, Sudan — L7 60
Agalega Islands, is., Mrts. — D11 58
Agano, stm., Japan — J11 36
Agapa, Russia — C10 28
Agaro, Eth. — N9 60
Agartala, India — H14 44
Agassiz, Cape, c., Ant. — B12 73
Agate, Co., U.S. — L4 118
Agate Beach, Or., U.S. — F1 122
Agawa Canyon, val., On., Can. — C11 110
Agboville, C. Iv. — I7 64
Agdam, Azer. — A9 48
Agde, Fr. — I10 14
Agen, Fr. — H7 14
Aghā Jārī, Iran — F10 48
Aginskoje, Russia — G14 28

Agogo, Sudan — N5 60
Agouna, Benin — H10 64
Āgra, India — G8 44
Agraciada, Ur. — G9 80
Agrado, Col. — F5 84
Agram see Zagreb, Cro. — D10 18
Agramunt, Spain — D12 16
Āgri Daği (Mount Ararat), mtn., Tur. — B8 48
Agrigento, Italy — L8 18
Agrinion, Grc. — K5 20
Agrio, stm., Arg. — J3 80
Agryz, Russia — F7 26
Agsu, Azer. — A10 48
Āīzawl, India — I15 44
Agua, Volcán de, vol., Guat. — C4 92
Agua Caliente, Mex. — F7 90
Agua Caliente, Mex. — C5 90
Agua Caliente Grande, Mex. — D5 90
Aguachica, Col. — C6 84
Aguada de Pasajeros, Cuba — C4 94
Aguadas, Col. — E5 84
Aguadilla, P.R. — E11 94
Água Doce, Braz. — D13 80
Aguadulce, Pan. — C2 84
Agua Dulce, Tx., U.S. — L9 116
Agua Fria, stm., Az., U.S. — K4 120
Aguaí, Braz. — G5 79
Agualeguas, Mex. — D10 90
Água Limpa, stm., Braz. — E4 79
Aguán, stm., Hond. — B8 92
Aguanaval, stm., Mex. — E8 90
Aguanish, P.Q., Can. — B11 106
Aguanus, stm., P.Q., Can. — B12 106
Aguapeí, stm., Braz. — F3 79
Aguapeí, stm., Braz. — F12 82
Aguapey, stm., Arg. — E10 80
Agua Preta, Igarapé, stm., Braz. — H10 84
Agua Prieta, Mex. — B5 90
Aguaray, Arg. — B7 80
Aguaray-Guazú, stm., Para. — B10 80
Aguaray-Guazú, stm., Para. — C9 80
A Guardia, Spain — D3 16
Aguarico, stm., S.A. — H4 84
Aguaruto, Mex. — E6 90
Aguas Formosas, Braz. — D8 79
Aguayo, Arg. — F6 80
Aguaytía, stm., Peru — C4 82
Agua Bay, b., N.T., Can. — B15 96
Agudos, Braz. — G4 79
Agueda, stm., Eur. — E5 16
Aguelhok, Mali — B10 64
Aguenar, Lac, l., P.Q., Can. — B5 106
Aguié, Niger — E13 64
Aguila, Az., U.S. — K3 120
Aguilar, Co., U.S. — N13 118
Aguilar, Spain — H7 16
Aguilares, Arg. — D6 80
Aguilares, El Sal. — D5 92
Aguilas, Arg. — H8 80
Aguilas, Spain — H10 16
Aguililla, mtn., Mex. — H8 90
Aguirre, stm., Ven. — C12 84
Aguja, Punta, c., Peru — A1 82
Agulhas, Cape, c., S. Afr. — J5 66
Agulhas Negras, Pico das, mtn., Braz. — G6 79
Agustín Codazzi, Col. — B6 84
Ahaggar (Hoggar), mts., Alg. — I13 62
Ahaggar, Tassili ta-n-, plat., Alg. — A12 64
Aha Hills, hills, Afr. — B5 66
Ahar, Iran — B9 48
Ahaus, Ger. — C7 10
Ahfir, Mor. — C9 62
Ahklun Mountains, mts., Ak., U.S. — G14 100
Ahlat, Tur. — B7 48
Ahlen, Ger. — D7 10
Ahmadābād, India — I5 44
Ahmadnagar, India — C3 46
Ahmadpur East, Pak. — F4 44
Ahmad Wāl, Pak. — F1 44
Ahmar Mountains, mts., Eth. — F9 56
Ahome, Mex. — E5 90
Ahoskie, N.C., U.S. — C10 112
Ahousat, B.C., Can. — H8 102
Ahuzhen, China — F10 32
Ahvāz, Iran — F10 48
Ahvenanmaa, prov., Fin. — K16 6
Ahwar, Yemen — H5 47
Aiapuá, Lago, l., Braz. — J11 84
Aigen im Mühlkreis, Aus. — F6 10
Aigle, Switz. — F6 13
Aigle, Lac à l', P.Q., Can. — A8 106
Aiguá, Ur. — H11 80
Aigueperse, Fr. — F10 14
Aiguillon, Fr. — H6 14
Aiguilles, Parc National d', Spain — C13 16
Aihui, China — A12 30
Aija, Peru — C2 82
Aiken, S.C., U.S. — F5 112
Ailao Shan, mts., China — B6 40
Ailsa Craig, On., Can. — G14 110
Aimogasta, Arg. — E5 80
Aimorés, Braz. — E8 79
Ain, stm., Fr. — F12 14
Ainaži, Lat. — D7 22
Aïn Beïda, Alg. — B14 62
Aïn Ben Tili, Maur. — J6 62
Aïn Berda, Alg. — C11 62
Aïn Deheb, Alg. — C11 62
Aïn Draham, Tun. — M3 18
Aïn el Beïda, Alg. — C14 62
Aïn Milia, Alg. — B14 62
Aïn Sefra, Alg. — D10 62
Ainslie Lake, l., N.S., Can. — F12 106
Aïn Tedelès, Alg. — B11 62
Aïn Témouchent, Alg. — C10 62
Aïn Touta, Alg. — C13 62
Aïn Wessara, Alg. — C12 62
Aiora, stm., Bol. — N9 60
Aipe, Col. — F5 84
Aiquara, Braz. — B9 79
Aiquile, Bol. — H9 82
Aïr, mts., Niger — C14 64
Airdrie, Ab., Can. — F20 102
Airdrie, Scot., U.K. — F10 8
Air Force Island, i., N.T., Can. — C18 96
Airvault, Fr. — E6 14
Aishihik Lake, l., Yk., Can. — F26 100
Aisne, dept., Fr. — C10 14

Aisne, stm., Fr. — C10 14
Aïssa, Djebel, mtn., Alg. — D10 62
Aitape, Pap. N. Gui. — F11 38
Aitkin, Mn., U.S. — D2 110
Aït-Melloul, Mor. — E6 62
Aït Youssef ou Ali, Mor. — C7 62
Aiud, Rom. — C7 20
Aiuruoca, Braz. — F6 79
Aix-en-Provence, Fr. — I12 14
Aix-la-Chapelle see Aachen, Ger. — E6 10
Aix-les-Bains, Fr. — G12 14
Aiyansh, B.C., Can. — B5 102
Aíyion, Grc. — K6 20
Aizkraukle, Lat. — E8 22
Aizpute, Lat. — E4 22
Aizu-wakamatsu, Japan — J14 36
Ajaccio, Fr. — m23 15a
Ajaguz, Kaz. — H8 28
Ajajú, stm., Col. — G6 84
Ajan, stm., Russia — C10 28
Ajanta, India — B3 46
Ajarani, stm., Braz. — F12 84
Ajax, On., Can. — G16 110
Ajdābiyā, Libya — B5 56
Ajibar, Eth. — L10 60
Ajka, Hung. — H17 10
'Ajlūn, Jord. — C5 50
Ajmer, India — G6 44
Ajo, Az., U.S. — L4 120
Ajok, Sudan — M5 60
Ajon, ostrov, i., Russia — D25 28
Ajoya, Mex. — E6 90
Ajtos, Bul. — G11 20
Ajuterique, Hond. — C7 92
Akabli, Alg. — G11 62
Akademii, zaliv, b., Russia — G19 28
Akaka Falls State Park, Hi., U.S. — r18 125a
Akaki Beseka, Eth. — M10 60
Akan, Japan — d19 36a
'Akasha East, Sudan — G6 60
Akashi, Japan — M9 36
Akbou, Alg. — B13 62
Akçadağ, Tur. — B4 48
Akçaova, Tur. — L12 20
Akcjaber'ski, Bela. — I11 22
Akdağmadeni, Tur. — B3 48
Akdhar, Al-Jabal al- mts., Oman — C10 47
Akhisar, Tur. — K11 20
Akhmīm, Egypt — D6 60
Akiachak, Ak., U.S. — F14 100
Akimiski Island, i., N.T., Can. — F16 96
Akita, Japan — H15 36
Akjoujt, Maur. — B2 64
Akkeshi, Japan — d19 36a
'Akko (Acre), Isr. — C4 50
Akkol', Kaz. — H12 26
Aklavik, N.T., Can. — B27 100
'Aklé 'Aouâna, reg., Afr. — B7 64
Akmeqit, China — B7 44
Akmola see Astana, Kaz. — G12 26
Aknīste, Lat. — E8 22
Aknoul, Mor. — C9 62
Akobo, Sudan — N7 60
Akobo (Akūbū), stm., Afr. — N8 60
Akola, India — B4 46
Akordat, Erit. — I8 56
Akot, India — B4 46
Akpatok Island, i., N.T., Can. — D19 96
Akranes, Ice. — B2 6a
Akrítas, Ákra, c., Grc. — M5 20
Akron, Co., U.S. — K4 118
Akron, In., U.S. — A10 114
Akron, N.Y., U.S. — D8 108
Akron, Oh., U.S. — F5 108
Akron, Pa., U.S. — G10 108
Aksaray, Tur. — B3 48
Aksarka, Russia — D5 28
Akşehir, Tur. — H14 4
Aksu, China — C3 30
Aksum, Eth. — J10 60
Aktau, Kaz. — I8 26
Aktogaj, Kaz. — H7 28
Aktubinsk, Kaz. — G9 26
Akt'ubinsk, Kaz. — G9 26
Akūbū (Akobo), stm., Afr. — G7 56
Akune, Japan — O5 36
Akwanga, Nig. — G14 64
Akwaya, Cam. — H14 64
Akyel, Eth. — K9 60
Akžar, Kaz. — H8 28
Al, China — C9 30
Alabama, state, U.S. — E9 98
Alabama, stm., Al., U.S. — K9 114
Alabaster, Al., U.S. — I10 114
Al-'Abbāsīyah, Sudan — L6 60
Āl-'Ābis, Sau. Ar. — E3 47
Alachua, Fl., U.S. — J4 112
Alacran, Arrecife, rf., Mex. — G15 90
Alacranes, Presa, res., Cuba — C4 94
Alagoa Grande, Braz. — E11 76
Alagoinhas, Braz. — B9 79
Alagón, Spain — D10 16
Alagón, stm., Spain — E5 16
Al-Ahmadī, Kuw. — G10 48
Alaior, Spain — F16 16
Al-Ait, Sudan — K4 60
Alajskij chrebet, mts., Asia — I12 26
Alajuela, C.R. — G10 92
Alajuela, prov., C.R. — G10 92
Alajuela, Lago, l., Pan. — H15 92
Alakamisy, Madag. — r22 67b
Alakol', ozero, l., Kaz. — H9 28
Al-'Alamayn, Egypt — B5 60
Al-'Amādīyah, Iraq — C7 48
Al-'Amārah, Iraq — F9 48
Alameda, Ca., U.S. — G3 124
Alameda, N.M., U.S. — I10 120
Alamein see Al-'Alamayn, Egypt — B5 60
Alamo, Nv., U.S. — G10 124
Alamo, stm., Ca., U.S. — K10 124
Alamogordo, N.M., U.S. — L11 120
Alamo Heights, Tx., U.S. — J8 116
Alamos, Mex. — D5 90
Alamos, stm., Mex. — G11 90
Alamosa, Co., U.S. — G11 120
Alamosa East, Co., U.S. — G11 120
Álamos de Márquez, Mex. — C8 90

Åland (Ahvenanmaa), is., Fin. — K16 6
Aland Islands see Åland, is., Fin. — K16 6
Alanje, Pan. — I12 92
Alanson, Mi., U.S. — E11 110
Alanya, Tur. — H14 4
Alaotra, Lac, l., Madag. — p23 67b
Alapaha, Ga., U.S. — H3 112
Alapaha, stm., U.S. — I3 112
Alapajevsk, Russia — F10 26
Alarcón, Embalse de, res., Spain — F9 16
Alarobia Vohiposa, Madag. — r22 67b
Alaşehir, Tur. — K12 20
Alashanyouqi, China — C7 30
Alaska, state, U.S. — D18 100
Alaska, Gulf of, b., Ak., U.S. — G22 100
Alaska Peninsula, pen., Ak., U.S. — H15 100
Alaska Range, mts., Ak., U.S. — E19 100
Alassio, Italy — E3 18
Älät, Azer. — B10 48
Alat, Uzb. — B17 48
Al-'Arīsh, Egypt — B7 60
Al-Atrūn, Sudan — G7 60
Alatyr', Russia — G7 26
Alausí, Ec. — I3 84
Alava, Cape, c., Wa., U.S. — B1 122
Alawa, Nig. — F13 64
Al-'Ayn, U.A.E. — I13 48
Al-'Ayyāṭ, Egypt — C6 60
Alazeja, stm., Russia — C22 28
Alba, Italy — E3 18
Alba, Tx., U.S. — F11 116
Alba Iulia, Rom. — C7 20
Al-Bādārī, Egypt — D6 60
Al-Badā'i', Sau. Ar. — D6 60
Al-Ballāṣ, Egypt — D7 60
Al-Balyanā, Egypt — D6 60
Albanel, Fr. — I9 14
Albanel, Lac, l., P.Q., Can. — F18 96
Albania (Shqipëri), ctry., Eur. — G12 4
Albano Laziale, Italy — H7 18
Albany, Austl. — G3 68
Albany, Ga., U.S. — H2 112
Albany, In., U.S. — B11 114
Albany, Ky., U.S. — F11 114
Albany, Mn., U.S. — E1 110
Albany, Mo., U.S. — B2 114
Albany, N.Y., U.S. — E13 108
Albany, Oh., U.S. — H4 108
Albany, Or., U.S. — F2 122
Albany, Tx., U.S. — G7 116
Albany, Wi., U.S. — H6 110
Albany, stm., On., Can. — F16 96
Albany, stm., On., Can. — D5 96
Albardão, Arg. — F4 80
Al-Barun, Sudan — L7 60
Al-Basrah (Basra), Iraq — F9 48
Al-Bāṭin, stm. — D3 48
Al-Bauga, Sudan — H7 60
Al-Bawītī, Egypt — C5 60
Albemarle, N.C., U.S. — D6 112
Albemarle Sound, strt., N.C., U.S. — C10 112
Albenga, Italy — E3 18
Alberdi, Para. — D9 80
Alberene, Va., U.S. — B8 112
Alberga Creek, stm., Austl. — E6 68
Alberni Inlet, b., B.C., Can. — H10 102
Albert, Fr. — B9 14
Albert, Lake, l., Afr. — A6 58
Alberta, prov., Can. — J9 114
Alberta, Mount, mtn., Ab., Can. — E17 102
Albert Canyon, B.C., Can. — F17 102
Albert City, Ia., U.S. — I13 118
Albert Edward Bay, b., N.T., Can. — C12 96
Alberti, Arg. — H8 80
Albertinia, S. Afr. — J5 66
Albertkanaal (Canal Albert), Bel. — G8 12
Albert Lea, Mn., U.S. — G2 110
Albert Markham, Mount, mtn., Ant. — D8 73
Albert Nile, stm., Ug. — H6 56
Alberton, Mt., U.S. — C11 122
Alberton, P.E., Can. — F9 106
Albert Peak, mtn., B.C., Can. — F17 102
Albertville, Al., U.S. — H10 114
Albertville, Fr. — G13 14
Albi, Fr. — I9 14
Albia, Ia., U.S. — I3 110
Albina, Sur. — B8 76
Albino, Italy — D4 18
Albion, Ca., U.S. — E2 124
Albion, Id., U.S. — H13 122
Albion, Il., U.S. — E8 114
Albion, In., U.S. — A11 114
Albion, Mi., U.S. — I11 110
Albion, Ne., U.S. — J9 118
Albion, N.Y., U.S. — D8 108
Albion, Pa., U.S. — E6 108
Al-Biqā' (Bekaa Valley), val., Leb. — A6 50
Alborán, Isla de, i., Spain — I8 16
Alborg, Den. — M11 6
Alborz, Reshteh-ye Kūhhā-ye (Elburz Mountains), mts., Iran — C12 48
Albreda, B.C., Can. — E15 102
Ālbū Gharz, Sabkhat, l., Asia — D6 48
Albufeira, Port. — H3 16
Albuñol, Spain — I8 16
Albuquerque, Braz. — H13 82
Albuquerque, N.M., U.S. — I10 120
Albuquerque, Cayos de, is., Col. — H4 94
Al-Buraymī, U.A.E. — B9 47
Albury, Austl. — K7 70
Al-Butaynah, Syria — C7 50
Alca, Peru — F5 82
Alcalá de Guadaira, Spain — H6 16
Alcalde, N.M., U.S. — H10 120
Alcamo, Italy — L7 18
Alcanar, Spain — E12 16
Alcañiz, Spain — D11 16
Alcañices, Spain — D5 16
Alcântara, Braz. — D10 76
Alcántara, Spain — F5 16

130

| Name | Map Ref. | Page |
|---|---|---|
| *Alcántara I, Embalse de, res., Spain* | F5 | 16 |
| Alcantarilla, Spain | H10 | 16 |
| Alcantilado, Braz. | D2 | 79 |
| Alcaudete, Spain | H7 | 16 |
| Alcázar de San Juan, Spain | F8 | 16 |
| Alcester, S.D., U.S. | H11 | 118 |
| Alcira (Gigena), Arg. | G6 | 80 |
| Alcoa, Tn., U.S. | D3 | 112 |
| Alcobaça, Braz. | D9 | 79 |
| Alcobaça, Port. | F3 | 16 |
| *Alcobaça, stm., Braz.* | D9 | 79 |
| Alcoi, Spain | G11 | 16 |
| Alcolu, S.C., U.S. | F6 | 112 |
| Alcorn, Ms., U.S. | K5 | 114 |
| Alcorta, Arg. | G8 | 80 |
| Alcoutim, Port. | H4 | 16 |
| *Alcovy, stm., Ga., U.S.* | F3 | 112 |
| *Aldabra Island, i., Sey.* | C9 | 58 |
| Aldama, Mex. | C7 | 90 |
| Aldama, Mex. | F10 | 90 |
| Aldan, Russia | F17 | 28 |
| *Aldan, stm., Russia* | F18 | 28 |
| *Aldanskoje nagorje, plat., Russia* | F17 | 28 |
| Aldeburgh, Eng., U.K. | I15 | 8 |
| Alden, Ia., U.S. | H2 | 110 |
| Alden, Mn., U.S. | G2 | 110 |
| *Alderney, i., Guernsey* | L11 | 8 |
| Aldershot, Eng., U.K. | J13 | 8 |
| Alderson, W.V., U.S. | B6 | 112 |
| Aledo, Il., U.S. | I5 | 110 |
| Alefa, Eth. | L9 | 60 |
| Aleg, Maur. | C3 | 64 |
| Alegre, Braz. | F8 | 79 |
| *Alegre, stm., Braz.* | F12 | 82 |
| *Alegres Mountain, mtn., N.M., U.S.* | J8 | 120 |
| Alegrete, Braz. | E11 | 80 |
| Alejandro Roca, Arg. | G7 | 80 |
| *Alejandro Selkirk, Isla, i., Chile* | H6 | 74 |
| Alejo Ledesma, Arg. | G7 | 80 |
| Alejsk, Russia | G8 | 28 |
| Aleknagik, Ak., U.S. | G15 | 100 |
| Aleksandro-Nevskij, Russia | H23 | 22 |
| Aleksandrov, Russia | E21 | 22 |
| Aleksandrov Gaj, Russia | G7 | 26 |
| Aleksandrovskoje, Russia | E13 | 26 |
| Aleksandrovsk-Sachalinskij, Russia | G20 | 28 |
| Aleksejevka, Kaz. | G12 | 26 |
| Aleksejevka, Russia | G5 | 26 |
| Aleksejevsk, Russia | F13 | 28 |
| Aleksin, Russia | G20 | 22 |
| Aleksinac, Yugo. | F5 | 20 |
| Alemania, Arg. | C6 | 80 |
| Além Paraíba, Braz. | F7 | 79 |
| Alençon, Fr. | D7 | 14 |
| Alenquer, Braz. | D8 | 76 |
| *Alentejo, hist. reg., Port.* | G3 | 16 |
| *Alenuihaha Channel, strt., Hi., U.S.* | q17 | 125a |
| Aleppo see Ḥalab, Syria | C4 | 48 |
| Aléria, Fr. | G4 | 18 |
| Alert, N.T., Can. | A13 | 86 |
| Alert Bay, B.C., Can. | G8 | 102 |
| Alès, Fr. | H11 | 14 |
| Alessandria, Italy | E3 | 18 |
| Ålesund, Nor. | J10 | 6 |
| *Aletschhorn, mtn., Switz.* | F9 | 13 |
| *Aleutian Islands, is., Ak., U.S.* | J6 | 100 |
| *Aleutian Range, mts., Ak., U.S.* | G17 | 100 |
| *Aleutian Trench* | D3 | 86 |
| *Alevina, mys, c., Russia* | F22 | 28 |
| Alex, Ok., U.S. | E9 | 116 |
| Alexander, Mb., Can. | I14 | 104 |
| Alexander, N.D., U.S. | D4 | 118 |
| *Alexander Archipelago, is., Ak., U.S.* | H27 | 100 |
| Alexander Bay, S. Afr. | G3 | 66 |
| Alexander City, Al., U.S. | J11 | 114 |
| *Alexander Indian Reserve, Ab., Can.* | D21 | 102 |
| *Alexander Island, i., Ant.* | C12 | 73 |
| Alexandra, N.Z. | F2 | 72 |
| *Alexandra, stm., Austl.* | B4 | 70 |
| *Alexandra Falls, wtfl, N.T., Can.* | D9 | 96 |
| Alexandretta see İskenderun, Tur. | C4 | 48 |
| *Alexandretta, Gulf of see İskenderun Körfezi, b., Tur.* | H15 | 4 |
| Alexandria, B.C., Can. | E12 | 102 |
| Alexandria see Al-Iskandarīyah, Egypt | B5 | 60 |
| Alexandria, In., U.S. | B11 | 114 |
| Alexandria, Ky., U.S. | I2 | 108 |
| Alexandria, La., U.S. | K4 | 114 |
| Alexandria, Mn., U.S. | F12 | 118 |
| Alexandria, Mo., U.S. | B5 | 114 |
| Alexandria, Ne., U.S. | K10 | 118 |
| Alexandria, On., Can. | B12 | 108 |
| Alexandria, Rom. | F9 | 20 |
| Alexandria, S.D., U.S. | H10 | 118 |
| Alexandria, Tn., U.S. | F10 | 114 |
| Alexandria, Va., U.S. | I9 | 108 |
| Alexandria Bay, N.Y., U.S. | C11 | 108 |
| *Alexandrina, Lake, l., Austl.* | J3 | 70 |
| Alexandroúpolis, Grc. | I9 | 20 |
| Alexis, Il., U.S. | I5 | 110 |
| Alexis Creek, B.C., Can. | E11 | 102 |
| *Alexis Indian Reserve, Ab., Can.* | D20 | 102 |
| Alfaro, Spain | C10 | 16 |
| Al-Fāshir, Sudan | K3 | 60 |
| Al-Fashn, Egypt | C6 | 60 |
| Al-Fāw, Iraq | G10 | 48 |
| Al-Fayyūm, Egypt | C6 | 60 |
| Alfeld, Ger. | D9 | 10 |
| Alfenas, Braz. | F6 | 79 |
| Al-Fifi, Sudan | L3 | 60 |
| *Alfiós, stm., Grc.* | L5 | 20 |
| *Alföld, pl., Hung.* | H20 | 10 |
| Alfred, Me., U.S. | D16 | 108 |
| Alfred, N.Y., U.S. | E9 | 108 |
| Alfred, On., Can. | B12 | 108 |
| Alga, Kaz. | H9 | 26 |
| Ålgård, Nor. | L9 | 6 |
| Al-Garef, Sudan | K8 | 60 |
| Algarrobal, Chile | E3 | 80 |
| Algarrobo, Arg. | J7 | 80 |
| Algarrobo, Arg. | F4 | 80 |
| Algarrobo, Chile | G3 | 80 |
| Algarrobo del Águila, Arg. | I5 | 80 |
| *Algarve, hist. reg., Port.* | H3 | 16 |
| Algasovo, Russia | H24 | 22 |
| Al-Gebir, Sudan | K5 | 60 |
| Algeciras, Col. | F5 | 84 |
| Algeciras, Spain | I6 | 16 |
| Algemesí, Spain | F11 | 16 |
| Algena, Erit. | I10 | 60 |
| Alger, Oh., U.S. | G3 | 108 |
| *Algeria (Algérie), ctry., Afr.* | C7 | 54 |
| Al-Ghāṭ, Sau. Ar. | H8 | 48 |
| *Al-Ghawr, val., Asia* | D5 | 50 |
| Al-Ghayḍah, Yemen | F8 | 47 |
| Al-Ghazālah, Sau. Ar. | H6 | 48 |
| Alghero, Italy | I3 | 18 |
| Al-Ghurayfah, Oman | B10 | 47 |
| Al-Ghurdaqah, Egypt | D7 | 60 |
| Algiers see El Djazaïr, Alg. | B12 | 62 |
| Alginet, Spain | F11 | 16 |
| *Algodón, stm., Peru* | I6 | 84 |
| Algodones, N.M., U.S. | I10 | 120 |
| Algoma, Wi., U.S. | F8 | 110 |
| Algoma Mills, On., Can. | D13 | 110 |
| Algona, Ia., U.S. | G1 | 110 |
| Algona, Wa., U.S. | C3 | 122 |
| Algonac, Mi., U.S. | H13 | 110 |
| Algonquin, Il., U.S. | H7 | 110 |
| Algood, Tn., U.S. | F11 | 114 |
| Algorta, Spain | B8 | 16 |
| Algorta, Ur. | G10 | 80 |
| Al-Ḥadīthah, Iraq | D7 | 48 |
| Al-Ḥadīthah, Sau. Ar. | E8 | 50 |
| *Al-Ḥajarah, reg., Asia* | F8 | 48 |
| Al Hajeb, Mor. | D8 | 62 |
| *Al-Ḥamād, pl., Sau. Ar.* | E5 | 48 |
| Alhama de Murcia, Spain | H10 | 16 |
| Al-Ḥammām, Egypt | B5 | 60 |
| Al-Ḥamrā', Sau. Ar. | C1 | 47 |
| Al-Ḥarīq, Sau. Ar. | C5 | 47 |
| *Al-Harūj al-Aswad, hills, Libya* | C4 | 56 |
| Al-Ḥasakah, Syria | C6 | 48 |
| Alhaurín el Grande, Spain | I7 | 16 |
| Al-Hawātah, Sudan | K8 | 60 |
| Al-Ḥawrah, Yemen | H5 | 47 |
| Al-Ḥawṭah, Yemen | G6 | 47 |
| Al-Ḥayy, Iraq | E9 | 48 |
| Al-Ḥayyānīyah, Sau. Ar. | G7 | 48 |
| Al-Ḥayz, Egypt | C5 | 60 |
| *Al-Ḥijāz, reg., Sau. Ar.* | I5 | 48 |
| Al-Ḥillah, Iraq | E8 | 48 |
| Al-Ḥillah, Sudan | K4 | 60 |
| Al-Hirmil, Leb. | D4 | 48 |
| Al-Ḥiṣn, Jord. | D5 | 50 |
| Al-Hoceïma, Mor. | A6 | 54 |
| *Al Hoceïma, Baie d', b., Afr.* | J8 | 16 |
| *Alhucemas, Peñón de, i., Sp. N. Afr.* | J8 | 16 |
| Al-Ḥudaydah, Yemen | G3 | 47 |
| Al-Hufūf, Sau. Ar. | B6 | 47 |
| Al-Ḥulwah, Sau. Ar. | J9 | 48 |
| Al-Humayshah, Yemen | H4 | 47 |
| Al-Ḥuṣayḥiṣah, Sudan | J7 | 60 |
| Al-Ḥuwaylizah, Golan | B5 | 50 |
| Al-Ḥuwayyiṭ, Sau. Ar. | I6 | 48 |
| 'Alīābād, Iran | C13 | 48 |
| Aliaga, Spain | E11 | 16 |
| *Aliákmon, stm., Grc.* | I6 | 20 |
| *Aliákmonos, Tekhnití Límni, res., Grc.* | I5 | 20 |
| 'Alī al-Gharbī, Iraq | E9 | 48 |
| Alībāg, India | C2 | 46 |
| Äli Bayramlı, Azer. | B10 | 48 |
| *Alibey, ozero, l., Ukr.* | D14 | 20 |
| Alibunar, Yugo. | D4 | 20 |
| Alice, S. Afr. | I8 | 66 |
| Alice, Tx., U.S. | L8 | 116 |
| Alice Arm, B.C., Can. | B5 | 102 |
| Alicedale, S. Afr. | I8 | 66 |
| Alice Springs, Austl. | D6 | 68 |
| Alice Town, Bah. | B5 | 94 |
| Aliceville, Al., U.S. | I8 | 114 |
| Alīgarh, India | G8 | 44 |
| Alīgūdarz, Iran | E10 | 48 |
| *Alijos, Islas, is., Mex.* | E2 | 90 |
| *Al-Ikhwān, is., Yemen* | G5 | 42 |
| Aliquippa, Pa., U.S. | G6 | 108 |
| Al-'Irāq, Jord. | F5 | 50 |
| Al-'Īsāwīyah, Sau. Ar. | F4 | 48 |
| Al-Iskandarīyah (Alexandria), Egypt | B5 | 60 |
| Al-Ismā'īlīyah, Egypt | B7 | 60 |
| Aliwal North, S. Afr. | H8 | 66 |
| Alix, Ab., Can. | E21 | 102 |
| Al-Jabalayn, Sudan | K7 | 60 |
| Al-Jadīdah, Egypt | E5 | 60 |
| Al-Jafr, Jord. | H6 | 50 |
| Al-Jaghbūb, Libya | C3 | 60 |
| Al-Jawf, Libya | E2 | 60 |
| Al-Jawf, Sau. Ar. | G5 | 48 |
| Al-Jaylī, Sudan | I7 | 60 |
| *Al-Jazīrah, reg., Sudan* | J7 | 60 |
| Aljezur, Port. | H3 | 16 |
| Al-Jifārah, Sau. Ar. | J8 | 48 |
| *Al-Jifārah (Jeffara), pl., Afr.* | D16 | 62 |
| Al-Jīzah, Egypt | B6 | 60 |
| Al-Jubayl, Sau. Ar. | H10 | 48 |
| Al-Jubayn, Sudan | K3 | 60 |
| Al-Judayyidah, Jord. | E5 | 50 |
| *Al-Julaydah, well, Asia* | G3 | 48 |
| Al-Junaynah, Sudan | K2 | 60 |
| Aljustrel, Port. | H3 | 16 |
| Al-Kafr, Syria | C7 | 50 |
| *Alkali Creek, stm., Ab., Can.* | G4 | 104 |
| Alkali Lake, B.C., Can. | F12 | 102 |
| Al-Kāmil, Oman | C11 | 47 |
| Al-Karabah, Sudan | H7 | 60 |
| Al-Karak, Jord. | F5 | 50 |
| Al-Karnak, Egypt | E7 | 60 |
| Al-Kawah, Sudan | K7 | 60 |
| Al-Khabrā', Sau. Ar. | H7 | 48 |
| Al-Khābūrah, Oman | C10 | 47 |
| Al-Khalīl (Hebrón), W.B. | E4 | 50 |
| Al-Khālis, Iraq | E8 | 48 |
| Al-Khandaq, Sudan | H6 | 60 |
| Al-Khārijah, Egypt | E6 | 60 |
| Al-Kharṭūm (Khartoum), Sudan | J7 | 60 |
| Al-Kharṭūm Baḥrī, Sudan | J7 | 60 |
| Al-Khaṣab, Oman | A10 | 47 |
| Al-Khubar, Sau. Ar. | A7 | 47 |
| Al-Khums, Libya | B3 | 56 |
| Al-Khuraybah, Jord. | C5 | 50 |
| Al-Khuraybah, Yemen | G6 | 47 |
| Al-Khurmah, Sau. Ar. | D3 | 47 |
| *Al-Kidn, reg., Asia* | C9 | 47 |
| Alkmaar, Neth. | C6 | 12 |
| Al-Kuntillah, Egypt | B8 | 60 |
| Al-Kūt, Iraq | E8 | 48 |
| Al-Kuwayt, Kuw. | G9 | 48 |
| Allada, Benin | H11 | 64 |
| Al-Lādhiqīyah (Latakia), Syria | D3 | 48 |
| Al-Lagowa, Sudan | L5 | 60 |
| Allahābād, India | H9 | 44 |
| Allan, Sk., Can. | G8 | 104 |
| Allanche, Fr. | G9 | 14 |
| Allanmyo, Myan. | E3 | 40 |
| *'Allāq, Bi'r, well, Libya* | E16 | 62 |
| *Allard, Lac, l., P.Q., Can.* | B10 | 106 |
| Allardt, Tn., U.S. | F12 | 114 |
| Al-Layyah, Sudan | I8 | 60 |
| Alldays, S. Afr. | D9 | 66 |
| Allegan, Mi., U.S. | H10 | 110 |
| Allegany, N.Y., U.S. | E8 | 108 |
| *Allegheny, stm., U.S.* | G7 | 108 |
| *Allegheny Mountains, mts., U.S.* | I6 | 108 |
| *Allegheny Plateau, plat., U.S.* | G8 | 108 |
| *Allegheny Reservoir, res., U.S.* | F8 | 108 |
| *Allemands, Lac Des, l., La., U.S.* | M6 | 114 |
| Allen, Arg. | J5 | 80 |
| Allen, Ne., U.S. | I11 | 118 |
| Allen, Ok., U.S. | E10 | 116 |
| Allen, S.D., U.S. | H6 | 118 |
| Allen, Tx., U.S. | F10 | 116 |
| *Allen, Mount, mtn., Ak., U.S.* | E23 | 100 |
| Allendale, Il., U.S. | D9 | 114 |
| Allendale, S.C., U.S. | F5 | 112 |
| Allende, Mex. | C9 | 90 |
| Allenstein see Olsztyn, Pol. | B20 | 10 |
| Allentown, Pa., U.S. | G11 | 108 |
| Allentsteig, Aus. | G15 | 10 |
| Alleppey, India | H4 | 46 |
| *Aller, stm., Ger.* | C9 | 10 |
| Allerton, Ia., U.S. | J2 | 110 |
| *Allgäu, reg., Ger.* | H10 | 10 |
| *Allgäuer Alpen, mts., Eur.* | E17 | 14 |
| Alliance, Ab., Can. | E23 | 102 |
| Alliance, Ne., U.S. | I5 | 118 |
| Alliance, Oh., U.S. | G5 | 108 |
| Al-Lidām, Sau. Ar. | D4 | 47 |
| *Allier, dept., Fr.* | F9 | 14 |
| *Allier, stm., Fr.* | F10 | 14 |
| *Alligator, stm., N.C., U.S.* | D10 | 112 |
| Allison, Ia., U.S. | H3 | 110 |
| Alliston, On., Can. | F16 | 110 |
| Al-Līth, Sau. Ar. | D2 | 47 |
| Alloa, Scot., U.K. | E10 | 8 |
| Allora, Austl. | G9 | 70 |
| Allouez, Wi., U.S. | F7 | 110 |
| Al-Luḥayyah, Yemen | G3 | 47 |
| Allyn, Wa., U.S. | C3 | 122 |
| Alma, Ar., U.S. | G2 | 114 |
| Alma, Ga., U.S. | H4 | 112 |
| Alma, Ks., U.S. | L11 | 118 |
| Alma, Mi., U.S. | G11 | 110 |
| Alma, N.B., Can. | G9 | 106 |
| Alma, Ne., U.S. | K8 | 118 |
| Alma, P.Q., Can. | D2 | 106 |
| Alma, Wi., U.S. | F4 | 110 |
| Alma-Ata see Alamty, Kaz. | I13 | 26 |
| Alma Center, Wi., U.S. | F5 | 110 |
| Almada, Port. | G2 | 16 |
| Almadén, Spain | G7 | 16 |
| Al-Madīnah (Medina), Sau. Ar. | B1 | 47 |
| Al-Mafāzah, Sudan | K8 | 60 |
| Al-Mafraq, Jord. | D6 | 50 |
| Almafuerte, Arg. | G6 | 80 |
| Almagro, Spain | G8 | 16 |
| Al-Maḥallah al-Kubrā, Egypt | B6 | 60 |
| Al-Maḥārīq, Egypt | E6 | 60 |
| Al Mahbas, W. Sah. | G6 | 62 |
| Al-Majma'ah, Sau. Ar. | I8 | 48 |
| Al-Makhā' (Mocha), Yemen | H3 | 47 |
| Almalyk, Uzb. | I11 | 26 |
| Al-Manāmah, Bahr. | H11 | 48 |
| Almansa, Spain | G10 | 16 |
| Al-Manshāh, Egypt | D6 | 60 |
| Al-Manṣūrah, Egypt | B6 | 60 |
| Al-Manzilah, Egypt | F1 | 48 |
| *Almanzor, mtn., Spain* | E6 | 16 |
| Al-Marāghah, Egypt | D6 | 60 |
| Al-Marj, Libya | B5 | 56 |
| *Almas, Pico das, mtn., Braz.* | B8 | 79 |
| Al-Masīd, Sudan | J7 | 60 |
| Almassora, Spain | F11 | 16 |
| Al-Matammah, Sudan | I7 | 60 |
| Al-Maṭarīyah, Egypt | B7 | 60 |
| Al-Matnah, Sudan | K8 | 60 |
| Almaty (Alma-Ata), Kaz. | I13 | 26 |
| Al-Mawṣil (Mosul), Iraq | C7 | 48 |
| Al-Mayādīn, Syria | D6 | 48 |
| Al-Mazār, Jord. | F5 | 50 |
| Al-Mazra'ah, Jord. | F5 | 50 |
| Almeida, Port. | E5 | 16 |
| Almeirim, Port. | F3 | 16 |
| Almelo, Neth. | D10 | 12 |
| Almena, Ks., U.S. | L8 | 118 |
| Almenara, Braz. | D8 | 79 |
| Almendralejo, Spain | G5 | 16 |
| Almería, Spain | I9 | 16 |
| *Almería, Golfo de, b., Spain* | I9 | 16 |
| Al'metjevsk, Russia | G8 | 26 |
| Al-Midhnab, Sau. Ar. | I8 | 48 |
| Al-Minyā, Egypt | C6 | 60 |
| Almira, Wa., U.S. | C7 | 122 |
| Almirante, Pan. | C1 | 84 |
| *Almirante, Bahía de, b., Pan.* | H12 | 92 |
| Almirante Latorre, Chile | E3 | 80 |
| Al-Mismīyah, Syria | B6 | 50 |
| Almo, Id., U.S. | H12 | 122 |
| Almodôvar, Port. | H3 | 16 |
| Almolonga, Guat. | C3 | 92 |
| Almond, Wi., U.S. | F6 | 110 |
| Almont, Mi., U.S. | H12 | 110 |
| Almonte, On., Can. | E19 | 110 |
| Almonte, Spain | H5 | 16 |
| Almora, India | F8 | 44 |
| Al-Mubarraz, Sau. Ar. | C5 | 47 |
| Al-Mubarraz, Sau. Ar. | B6 | 47 |
| Al-Mudawwarah, Jord. | G3 | 48 |
| Al-Muglad, Sudan | L4 | 60 |
| Al-Muḥarraq, Bahr. | H11 | 48 |
| Al-Mukallā, Yemen | G6 | 47 |
| Almuñécar, Spain | I8 | 16 |
| Al-Musallamīyah, Sudan | J7 | 60 |
| Al-Musayfirah, Syria | C6 | 50 |
| Al-Musayjid, Sau. Ar. | B1 | 47 |
| Al-Mutayn, Leb. | A5 | 50 |
| Al-Muwayh, Sau. Ar. | C2 | 47 |
| Al-Muwaylih, Sau. Ar. | H3 | 48 |
| Alnwick, Eng., U.K. | F12 | 8 |
| Aloândia, Braz. | D4 | 79 |
| Aloja, Lat. | D7 | 22 |
| *Alor, Pulau, i., Indon.* | G7 | 38 |
| Alor Setar, Malay. | K6 | 40 |
| Alosno, Spain | H4 | 16 |
| Alost (Aalst), Bel. | G5 | 12 |
| Alpachiri, Arg. | I7 | 80 |
| Alpaugh, Ca., U.S. | I6 | 124 |
| Alpena, Ar., U.S. | F3 | 114 |
| Alpena, Mi., U.S. | E12 | 110 |
| Alpena, S.D., U.S. | G9 | 118 |
| *Alpes-de-Haute-Provence, dept., Fr.* | H13 | 14 |
| *Alpes-Maritimes, dept., Fr.* | I14 | 14 |
| Alpha, Austl. | D7 | 70 |
| Alpha, Il., U.S. | I5 | 110 |
| Alpha, Mi., U.S. | D7 | 110 |
| Alpharetta, Ga., U.S. | E2 | 112 |
| Alpine, Az., U.S. | K7 | 120 |
| Alpine, Ca., U.S. | L9 | 124 |
| Alpine, Tx., U.S. | I3 | 116 |
| *Alpine National Park, Austl.* | K7 | 70 |
| Alpinópolis, Braz. | F5 | 79 |
| *Alps, mts., Eur.* | F10 | 4 |
| Al-Qābil, Oman | C9 | 47 |
| Al-Qaḍārif, Sudan | J8 | 60 |
| Al-Qadīmah, Sau. Ar. | C1 | 47 |
| Al-Qāhirah (Cairo), Egypt | B6 | 60 |
| Al-Qaḥmah, Sau. Ar. | E2 | 47 |
| Al-Qalībah, Sau. Ar. | G4 | 48 |
| Al-Qāmishlī, Syria | C6 | 48 |
| Al-Qanṭarah, Egypt | B7 | 60 |
| Al-Qaryah ash-Sharqīyah, Libya | B3 | 56 |
| Al-Qaṣr, Egypt | E5 | 60 |
| Al-Qaṣr, Jord. | F5 | 50 |
| Al-Qaṭīf, Sau. Ar. | A7 | 47 |
| Al-Qaṭrānah, Jord. | F6 | 50 |
| Al-Qaṭrūn, Libya | D3 | 56 |
| Al-Qayṣūmah, Sau. Ar. | G9 | 48 |
| Al-Qiṣfah, Jord. | C5 | 50 |
| Al-Quds see Yerushalayim, Isr. | E4 | 50 |
| Al-Qunayṭirah, Syria | B5 | 50 |
| Al-Qunfudhah, Sau. Ar. | E2 | 47 |
| Al-Qurnah, Iraq | F9 | 48 |
| Al-Quṣaymah, Egypt | G2 | 50 |
| Al-Quṣayr, Egypt | D8 | 60 |
| Al-Qūṣīyah, Egypt | D6 | 60 |
| Al-Quṭayfah, Syria | A7 | 50 |
| Al-Quṭaynah, Sudan | J7 | 60 |
| Al-Quway'īyah, Sau. Ar. | B4 | 47 |
| Al-Quwaysī, Sudan | K8 | 60 |
| *Alsace, hist. reg., Fr.* | D14 | 14 |
| Alsask, Sk., Can. | G5 | 104 |
| Alsea, Or., U.S. | F2 | 122 |
| *Alsea, stm., Or., U.S.* | F2 | 122 |
| *Alsek, stm., N.A.* | G25 | 100 |
| Alsen, N.D., U.S. | C9 | 118 |
| Alsfeld, Ger. | E9 | 10 |
| Alsina, Arg. | G9 | 80 |
| *Alstead, stm., Sk., Can.* | C7 | 104 |
| Alsunga, Lat. | E4 | 22 |
| Alta, Ia., U.S. | I12 | 118 |
| Alta Gracia, Arg. | F6 | 80 |
| Altagracia, Nic. | F9 | 92 |
| Altagracia, Ven. | B7 | 84 |
| Altagracia de Orituco, Ven. | C9 | 84 |
| *Altai, mts., Asia* | H16 | 26 |
| Altaj (Jesönbulag), Mong. | B6 | 30 |
| *Altaj, state, Russia* | G15 | 26 |
| *Altamaha, stm., Ga., U.S.* | H5 | 112 |
| Altamira, Braz. | D8 | 76 |
| Altamira, Chile | C4 | 80 |
| Altamira, C.R. | G10 | 92 |
| Altamont, Il., U.S. | C8 | 114 |
| Altamont, Ks., U.S. | N12 | 118 |
| Altamont, Or., U.S. | H4 | 122 |
| Altamont, Tn., U.S. | G11 | 114 |
| Altamura, Italy | I11 | 18 |
| *Altamura, Isla, i., Mex.* | E5 | 90 |
| Altar, Mex. | B4 | 90 |
| *Altar, stm., Mex.* | B4 | 90 |
| *Altar, Desierto de, des., Mex.* | B3 | 90 |
| *Altar de Los Sacrificios, hist., Guat.* | I14 | 90 |
| Altario, Ab., Can. | G4 | 104 |
| Altata, Mex. | E6 | 90 |
| *Alta Verapaz, dept., Guat.* | B4 | 92 |
| Alta Vista, Ks., U.S. | M11 | 118 |
| Altavista, Va., U.S. | B7 | 112 |
| Altay, China | B4 | 30 |
| *Altay see Altaj, state, Russia* | G15 | 26 |
| Altdorf, Switz. | E10 | 13 |
| Altenburg, Ger. | E12 | 10 |
| Altha, Fl., U.S. | I1 | 112 |
| Altheimer, Ar., U.S. | H5 | 114 |
| Althofen, Aus. | I14 | 10 |
| Altinópolis, Braz. | F5 | 79 |
| *Altiplano, plat., S.A.* | H7 | 82 |
| Altkirch, Fr. | E14 | 14 |
| *Altmark, reg., Ger.* | C11 | 10 |
| *Altmühl, stm., Ger.* | F10 | 10 |
| Alto, Tx., U.S. | H11 | 116 |
| Alto Araguaia, Braz. | D2 | 79 |
| Alto Cedro, Cuba | D7 | 94 |
| Alto Coité, Braz. | C1 | 79 |
| Alto del Carmen, Chile | E3 | 80 |
| Alto do Rio Doce, Braz. | F7 | 79 |
| Alto Garças, Braz. | D2 | 79 |
| Altomünster, Ger. | G11 | 10 |
| Alton, Ia., U.S. | I11 | 118 |
| Alton, Il., U.S. | D6 | 114 |
| Alton, Ks., U.S. | L9 | 118 |
| Alton, Mo., U.S. | F5 | 114 |
| Alton, N.H., U.S. | D15 | 108 |
| Altona, Mb., Can. | I17 | 104 |
| Altoona, Al., U.S. | H10 | 114 |
| Altoona, Ia., U.S. | I2 | 110 |
| Altoona, Ks., U.S. | N12 | 118 |
| Altoona, Pa., U.S. | G8 | 108 |
| Altoona, Wi., U.S. | F4 | 110 |
| Alto Paraguai, Braz. | F13 | 82 |
| *Alto Paraguay, dept., Para.* | I12 | 82 |
| Alto Paraíso de Goiás, Braz. | C5 | 79 |
| *Alto Paraná, dept., Para.* | C11 | 80 |
| Alto Parnaíba, Braz. | E9 | 76 |
| *Alto Purús, stm., Peru* | D6 | 82 |
| Alto Río Senguer, Arg. | F2 | 78 |
| Alto Sucuriú, Braz. | E2 | 79 |
| Altötting, Ger. | G12 | 10 |
| *Alto Yurua, stm., Peru* | C5 | 82 |
| Altstätten, Switz. | D12 | 13 |
| Altuchovo, Russia | I17 | 22 |
| Altunoluk, Tur. | J10 | 20 |
| *Altun Shan, mts., China* | D4 | 30 |
| Alturas, Ca., U.S. | C5 | 124 |
| Altus, Ar., U.S. | G3 | 114 |
| Altus, Ok., U.S. | E7 | 116 |
| Al-'Ubaylah, Sau. Ar. | D7 | 47 |
| Al-Ubayyiḍ, Sudan | K6 | 60 |
| Al-'Udaysāt, Egypt | E7 | 60 |
| Al-Uḍayyah, Sudan | K5 | 60 |
| Aluk, Sudan | M4 | 60 |
| Alūksne, Lat. | D10 | 22 |
| Al-'Ulā, Sau. Ar. | H4 | 48 |
| *Aluminé, Lago, l., Arg.* | J3 | 80 |
| Alum Rock, Ca., U.S. | G4 | 124 |
| Al-'Uqaylah, Libya | B4 | 56 |
| Al-'Uqayr, Sau. Ar. | B7 | 47 |
| Al-Uqṣur (Luxor), Egypt | E7 | 60 |
| Al-'Uwaynāt, Libya | C3 | 56 |
| Al-'Uyaynah, Sau. Ar. | B5 | 47 |
| Alva, Ok., U.S. | C8 | 116 |
| Alvarado, Mex. | H12 | 90 |
| Alvarado, Tx., U.S. | G9 | 116 |
| Alvarães, Braz. | I10 | 84 |
| *Álvaro Obregón, Presa, res., Mex.* | D5 | 90 |
| Alvdal, Nor. | J12 | 6 |
| Alvear, Arg. | E10 | 80 |
| *Alvernia, Mount, hill, Bah.* | B7 | 94 |
| Alvesta, Swe. | M14 | 6 |
| Alvin, Tx., U.S. | J11 | 116 |
| Alvinópolis, Braz. | F7 | 79 |
| Alvito, Port. | G4 | 16 |
| Älvkarleby, Swe. | K15 | 6 |
| Alvord, Tx., U.S. | F9 | 116 |
| Älvros, Swe. | J14 | 6 |
| *Älvsborgs Län, co., Swe.* | L13 | 6 |
| Al-Wajh, Sau. Ar. | H4 | 48 |
| Al-Wakrah, Qatar | I11 | 48 |
| Alwar, India | G7 | 44 |
| Al-Wāsiṭah, Egypt | C6 | 60 |
| Al-Wazz, Sudan | J6 | 60 |
| Alxa Zuoqi, China | D8 | 30 |
| Alytus, Lith. | G7 | 22 |
| Alzamaj, Russia | F11 | 28 |
| Alzira (Alcira), Spain | F11 | 16 |
| *Amacuro, stm., S.A.* | C12 | 84 |
| *Amadeus, Lake, l., Austl.* | D6 | 68 |
| *Amadjuak Lake, l., N.T., Can.* | C18 | 96 |
| Amagansett, N.Y., U.S. | G14 | 108 |
| Amagasaki, Japan | M10 | 36 |
| Amagi, Japan | N5 | 36 |
| Amagunze, Nig. | H13 | 64 |
| Amahai, Indon. | F8 | 38 |
| Amaichá del Valle, Arg. | D6 | 80 |
| *Amajac, stm., Mex.* | G10 | 90 |
| *Amaka, stm., Nic.* | C9 | 92 |
| *Amakusa-shotō, is., Japan* | O5 | 36 |
| *Amakuso-Shimo-shima, i., Japan* | O5 | 36 |
| Åmål, Swe. | L13 | 6 |
| Amalfi, Col. | D5 | 84 |
| Amalfi, Italy | I9 | 18 |
| Amaliás, Grc. | L5 | 20 |
| Amambaí, Braz. | G1 | 79 |
| *Amambaí, stm., Braz.* | G1 | 79 |
| *Amambay, dept., Para.* | B10 | 80 |
| *Amami-Ō-shima, i., Japan* | s4 | 37b |
| *Amami-shotō, is., Japan* | t3 | 37b |
| Amana, Ia., U.S. | I4 | 110 |
| *Amanã, stm., Braz.* | J14 | 84 |
| *Amana, stm., Ven.* | J13 | 94 |
| *Amanã, Lago, l., Braz.* | I10 | 84 |
| Amanda, Oh., U.S. | H4 | 108 |
| Amapá, Braz. | C8 | 76 |
| Amapala, Hond. | D7 | 92 |
| *Amapala, Punta de, c., El Sal.* | D7 | 92 |
| Amarante, Braz. | E10 | 76 |
| Amaranth, Mb., Can. | H16 | 104 |
| Amarapura, Myan. | D4 | 40 |
| 'Amārat Abū Sinn, Sudan | J8 | 60 |
| Amares, Port. | D3 | 16 |
| Amargosa, Braz. | B9 | 79 |
| *Amargosa, stm., U.S.* | H9 | 124 |
| *Amargosa Range, mts., Ca., U.S.* | H9 | 124 |
| Amarillo, Tx., U.S. | D5 | 116 |
| 'Amar Jadīd, Sudan | J3 | 60 |
| Amarkantak, India | G3 | 30 |
| Amarnāth, India | C2 | 46 |
| Amasa, Mi., U.S. | D7 | 110 |
| Amasya, Tur. | G15 | 4 |
| Amataurá, Braz. | I8 | 84 |
| Amatikulu, S. Afr. | G10 | 66 |
| *Amatique, Bahía de, b., N.A.* | B6 | 92 |
| Amatitlán, Guat. | C4 | 92 |
| *Amatitlán, Lago de, l., Guat.* | C4 | 92 |
| *Amazon (Solimões) (Amazonas), stm., S.A.* | D7 | 76 |
| *Amazonas, state, Braz.* | H10 | 84 |
| *Amazonas, dept., Col.* | H7 | 84 |
| *Amazonas, dept., Peru* | A2 | 82 |
| *Amazonas, ter., Ven.* | F9 | 84 |
| Ambakaka, Madag. | t22 | 67b |
| Ambāla, India | E7 | 44 |
| Ambalanjanakomby, Madag. | p22 | 67b |
| Ambalavao, Madag. | r22 | 67b |
| Amba Maryam, Eth. | L10 | 60 |
| Ambanja, Madag. | n23 | 67b |
| Ambar, Peru | D3 | 82 |
| Ambararata, Madag. | o23 | 67b |
| Ambarčik, Russia | D24 | 28 |
| *Ambargasta, Salinas de, pl., Arg.* | E6 | 80 |
| Ambarnyj, Russia | I23 | 6 |
| Ambato, Ec. | H3 | 84 |
| Ambatofinandrahana, Madag. | r22 | 67b |
| Ambatolampy, Madag. | q22 | 67b |
| Ambatondrazaka, Madag. | p23 | 67b |
| *Ámbelos, Ákra, c., Grc.* | J7 | 20 |
| Ambenja, Madag. | o22 | 67b |
| Amberg, Ger. | F11 | 10 |
| Amberg, Wi., U.S. | E8 | 110 |
| *Ambergris Cay, i., Belize* | H16 | 90 |
| Ambérieu-en-Bugey, Fr. | G12 | 14 |
| Ambert, Fr. | G10 | 14 |
| Ambevongo, Madag. | o22 | 67b |
| Ambikāpur, India | I10 | 44 |
| Ambilobe, Madag. | n23 | 67b |
| Ambinanindrano, Madag. | r23 | 67b |
| Ambivy, Madag. | r21 | 67b |
| Ambo, Peru | D3 | 82 |
| Amboahangy, Madag. | t22 | 67b |
| Ambodifototra, Madag. | p23 | 67b |
| Ambodiriana, Madag. | p23 | 67b |
| Ambohidray, Madag. | q23 | 67b |
| Ambohimahamasina, Madag. | r22 | 67b |
| Amboise, Fr. | E7 | 14 |
| Ambon, Indon. | F8 | 38 |
| Ambondro, Madag. | t21 | 67b |
| Ambositra, Madag. | r22 | 67b |
| Ambovombe, Madag. | t22 | 67b |
| Amboy, Il., U.S. | I6 | 110 |
| Amboy, Mn., U.S. | G1 | 110 |
| *Ambre, Cap d', c., Madag.* | m23 | 67b |
| Ambridge, Pa., U.S. | G6 | 108 |
| Ambrières, Fr. | D6 | 14 |
| Ambriz, Ang. | C2 | 58 |
| Ambrose, N.D., U.S. | C4 | 118 |
| Ambrosia Lake, N.M., U.S. | I9 | 120 |
| Ambunti, Pap. N. Gui. | F11 | 38 |
| *Amchitka Island, i., Ak., U.S.* | k4 | 101a |
| 'Amd, Yemen | G6 | 47 |
| Amderma, Russia | D10 | 26 |
| Amdo, China | E5 | 30 |
| Ameagle, W.V., U.S. | B5 | 112 |
| Ameca, Mex. | G7 | 90 |
| *Ameca, stm., Mex.* | G7 | 90 |
| Amecameca [de Juárez], Mex. | H10 | 90 |
| Ameghino, Arg. | H7 | 80 |
| *Ameland, i., Neth.* | B8 | 12 |
| Amelia, Italy | G7 | 18 |
| Amelia Court House, Va., U.S. | B9 | 112 |
| *Amelia Island, i., Fl., U.S.* | I5 | 112 |
| Āmer, India | G6 | 44 |
| Americana, Braz. | G5 | 79 |
| American Falls, Id., U.S. | H13 | 122 |
| *American Falls Reservoir, res., Id., U.S.* | H13 | 122 |
| American Fork, Ut., U.S. | D5 | 120 |
| *American Highland, plat., Ant.* | C5 | 73 |
| *American Samoa, dep., Oc.* | J22 | 126 |
| Americus, Ga., U.S. | G2 | 112 |
| Americus, Ks., U.S. | M11 | 118 |
| Amersfoort, Neth. | D7 | 12 |
| Amersfoort, S. Afr. | F9 | 66 |
| Amery, Mb., Can. | B20 | 104 |
| Amery, Wi., U.S. | E3 | 110 |
| *Amery Ice Shelf, Ant.* | B5 | 73 |
| Ames, Ia., U.S. | H2 | 110 |
| Amesbury, Ma., U.S. | E16 | 108 |
| *Amet Sound, strt., N.S., Can.* | G10 | 106 |
| Ámfissa, Grc. | K6 | 20 |
| Amga, Russia | E18 | 28 |
| *Amga, stm., Russia* | E18 | 28 |
| *Amguema, stm., Russia* | D27 | 28 |
| Amguid, Alg. | G13 | 62 |
| *Amgun', stm., Russia* | G19 | 28 |
| Amherst, Ma., U.S. | E14 | 108 |
| Amherst, N.S., Can. | G9 | 106 |
| Amherst, N.Y., U.S. | E8 | 108 |
| Amherst, Oh., U.S. | F4 | 108 |
| Amherst, Tx., U.S. | E4 | 116 |
| Amherst, Va., U.S. | B7 | 112 |
| Amherst, Wi., U.S. | F6 | 110 |
| Amherstburg, On., Can. | H12 | 110 |
| Amherstdale, W.V., U.S. | J5 | 108 |
| Amherstview, On., Can. | F19 | 110 |
| Amidon, N.D., U.S. | E4 | 118 |
| Amiens, Fr. | C9 | 14 |
| Amili, China | F16 | 44 |
| *Amīndīvi Islands, is., India* | G2 | 46 |
| Aminga, Arg. | E5 | 80 |
| Aminuis, Nmb. | D4 | 66 |
| *Amirante Islands, is., Sey.* | C10 | 58 |
| Amisk, Ab., Can. | E23 | 102 |
| *Amisk Lake, l., Sk., Can.* | D12 | 104 |
| *Amistad, Parque Internacional de la, C.R.* | H11 | 92 |
| *Amistad Reservoir (Presa de la Amistad), res., N.A.* | J5 | 116 |
| Amite, La., U.S. | L6 | 114 |
| *Amite, stm., La., U.S.* | L6 | 114 |
| Amity, Ar., U.S. | H3 | 114 |
| Amity, Or., U.S. | E2 | 122 |
| Amizmiz, Mor. | E6 | 62 |
| 'Amm-Adām, Sudan | I9 | 60 |
| 'Ammān, Jord. | E5 | 50 |
| Ammarnäs, Swe. | I15 | 6 |
| Ammon, Id., U.S. | G14 | 122 |
| *Ammonoosuc, stm., N.H., U.S.* | C15 | 108 |
| *Amne Machin Shan see A'nyêmaqên Shan, mts., China* | D6 | 30 |
| *Amnicon, stm., Wi., U.S.* | D4 | 110 |
| *Amnok-kang (Yalu), stm., Asia* | C13 | 32 |
| *Amo, stm., Asia* | G13 | 44 |
| Āmol, Iran | C12 | 48 |
| Amolar, Braz. | H13 | 82 |
| *Amorgós, i., Grc.* | M9 | 20 |
| Amorinópolis, Braz. | D3 | 79 |
| Amory, Ms., U.S. | I8 | 114 |
| Amoy see Xiamen, China | K7 | 34 |
| Ampanihy, Madag. | t21 | 67b |
| Amparihy, Madag. | s22 | 67b |
| Amparo, Braz. | G5 | 79 |
| *Ampato, Nevado, mtn., Peru* | F6 | 82 |
| Amper, Nig. | G14 | 64 |
| Ampombiantambo, Madag. | n23 | 67b |
| Amposta, Spain | E12 | 16 |
| Ampotaka, Madag. | t21 | 67b |
| Amqui, P.Q., Can. | D6 | 106 |
| 'Amrān, Yemen | G3 | 47 |
| Amrāvati, India | J7 | 44 |
| Amreli, India | J4 | 44 |
| Amritsar, India | E6 | 44 |
| Amroha, India | F8 | 44 |
| Amsel, Alg. | I13 | 62 |
| Åmsele, Swe. | I16 | 6 |
| Amsteg, Switz. | E10 | 13 |
| Amsterdam, Neth. | D6 | 12 |
| Amsterdam, N.Y., U.S. | E12 | 108 |
| Amsterdam, S. Afr. | F10 | 66 |
| *Amsterdam, Île, i., Afr.* | L11 | 126 |
| *Amsterdam-Rijnkanaal, Neth.* | E7 | 12 |
| Amstetten, Aus. | G14 | 10 |
| Am Timan, Chad | F5 | 56 |
| Amubri, C.R. | H12 | 92 |
| Amu-Darja, Turk. | C18 | 48 |
| *Amu Darya (Amudarja), stm., Asia* | B2 | 44 |
| *Amundsen Gulf, b., N.T., Can.* | B8 | 96 |
| *Amundsen-Scott, sci., Ant.* | D10 | 73 |
| *Amundsen Sea, Ant.* | C11 | 73 |
| Amuntai, Indon. | F6 | 38 |
| *Amur (Heilong), stm., Asia* | B14 | 30 |
| Amurrio, Spain | I3 | 14 |
| Amuzhong, China | E11 | 44 |
| *Amvrakikós Kólpos, b., Grc.* | K4 | 20 |
| *Anabar, stm., Russia* | C14 | 28 |
| Anaco, Ven. | C10 | 84 |
| Anacoco, La., U.S. | K3 | 114 |
| Anaconda, Mt., U.S. | D13 | 122 |
| Anacortes, Wa., U.S. | B3 | 122 |
| Anadarko, Ok., U.S. | D8 | 116 |
| Anadyr', Russia | E27 | 28 |
| *Anadyr', stm., Russia* | E26 | 28 |
| *Anadyrskij zaliv, b., Russia* | E28 | 28 |
| *Anadyrskoje ploskogorje, plat., Russia* | D26 | 28 |
| Anagni, Italy | H8 | 18 |
| 'Ānah, Iraq | D6 | 48 |
| Anaheim, Ca., U.S. | K8 | 124 |
| Anahim Lake, B.C., Can. | E9 | 102 |
| Anáhuac, Mex. | D9 | 90 |
| Anáhuac, Mex. | C6 | 90 |
| Anahuac, Tx., U.S. | J12 | 116 |
| *Ānai Mudi, mtn., India* | G4 | 46 |
| Analalava, Madag. | o22 | 67b |
| Analapatsy, Madag. | t22 | 67b |
| Anamã, Braz. | I12 | 84 |
| *Anamã, Lago, l., Braz.* | I12 | 84 |
| Anama Bay, Mb., Can. | G16 | 104 |
| *Ana María, Golfo de, b., Cuba* | D5 | 94 |
| *Anambas, Kepulauan, is., Indon.* | M9 | 40 |
| Anamoose, N.D., U.S. | D7 | 118 |
| Anamosa, Ia., U.S. | H4 | 110 |
| *Anamu, stm., Braz.* | G14 | 84 |
| Anamur, Tur. | C2 | 48 |
| Ānand, India | I5 | 44 |
| Ananea, Peru | F7 | 82 |
| Anantapur, India | E4 | 46 |
| Anantnāg (Islāmābād), India | D6 | 44 |
| Anan'yiv, Ukr. | B13 | 20 |
| Anápolis, Braz. | D4 | 79 |
| Anār, Iran | F13 | 48 |
| Anārak, Iran | E12 | 48 |
| Anār Darreh, Afg. | E16 | 48 |
| Anastácio, Braz. | F1 | 79 |
| *Anastasia Island, i., Fl., U.S.* | J5 | 112 |
| 'Anātā, W.B. | E4 | 50 |
| *Anatolikí Makedhonía kaí Thráki, prov., Grc.* | H9 | 20 |
| Añatuya, Arg. | E7 | 80 |
| *Anauá, stm., Braz.* | G12 | 84 |
| Anaurilândia, Braz. | G2 | 79 |
| *Anavilhanas, Arquipélago das, is., Braz.* | I12 | 84 |
| Anawalt, W.V., U.S. | B5 | 112 |
| Anbanjing, China | C6 | 40 |
| Anbu, China | L5 | 34 |
| Anbyŏn, N. Kor. | D15 | 32 |
| *Ancash, dept., Peru* | C3 | 82 |
| Ancaster, On., Can. | G15 | 110 |
| Ancasti, Arg. | E6 | 80 |
| *Ancasti, Sierra de, mts., Arg.* | E6 | 80 |
| Anchang, China | E9 | 34 |
| Anchorage, Ak., U.S. | F20 | 100 |
| Anchorena, Arg. | H6 | 80 |
| Anchor Point, Ak., U.S. | G19 | 100 |
| Anci (Langfang), China | D4 | 32 |
| Ancien Goubéré, C.A.R. | O4 | 60 |
| Anciferovo, Russia | C17 | 22 |
| Ancón, Peru | D3 | 82 |
| Ancona, Italy | F8 | 18 |
| *Ancón de Sardinas, Bahía de, b., S.A.* | G3 | 84 |
| Ancoraimes, Bol. | F7 | 82 |
| Ancud, Chile | E2 | 78 |
| *Ancud, Golfo de, b., Chile* | E2 | 78 |
| Anda, China | B12 | 30 |
| Andacollo, Arg. | I3 | 80 |
| Andacollo, Chile | F3 | 80 |
| Andahuaylas, Peru | E5 | 82 |
| Andalgalá, Arg. | D5 | 80 |
| Åndalsnes, Nor. | J10 | 6 |
| *Andalucía, state, Spain* | H7 | 16 |
| Andalusia, Al., U.S. | K10 | 114 |
| *Andaman Islands, is., India* | H2 | 40 |
| *Andaman Sea, Asia* | I3 | 40 |
| Andamarca, Bol. | H8 | 82 |

| Name | Map Ref. | Page |
|---|---|---|
| Andamarca, Peru | D4 | 82 |
| Andamooka, Austl. | H2 | 70 |
| Andapa, Madag. | o23 | 67b |
| Andaraí, Braz. | B8 | 79 |
| Andaray, Peru | F5 | 82 |
| Andeer, Switz. | E11 | 13 |
| Andelot, Fr. | D12 | 14 |
| Andenes, Nor. | G15 | 6 |
| Andéranboukane, Mali | D11 | 64 |
| Andermatt, Switz. | E10 | 13 |
| Andernach, Ger. | E7 | 10 |
| Anderson, Al., U.S. | H9 | 114 |
| Anderson, Ca., U.S. | D3 | 124 |
| Anderson, In., U.S. | B11 | 114 |
| Anderson, Mo., U.S. | F2 | 114 |
| Anderson, S.C., U.S. | E4 | 112 |
| Anderson, Tx., U.S. | I11 | 116 |
| Anderson, stm., N.T., Can. | B30 | 100 |
| Anderson Dam, Id., U.S. | G10 | 122 |
| Anderson Lake, l., B.C., Can. | G12 | 102 |
| Andes, Col. | E5 | 84 |
| Andes, mts., S.A. | G8 | 74 |
| Andevoranto, Madag. | q23 | 67b |
| Andhra Pradesh, state, India | D5 | 46 |
| Andikíthira, i., Grc. | N7 | 20 |
| Andimákhia, Grc. | M11 | 20 |
| Andīmeshk, Iran | E10 | 48 |
| Andirá, stm., Braz. | I14 | 84 |
| Andirá, Riozinho do, stm., Braz. | C8 | 82 |
| Andirlang, China | B10 | 44 |
| Ándissa, Grc. | J9 | 20 |
| Andižan, Uzb. | I12 | 26 |
| Andkhvoy, Afg. | B1 | 44 |
| Andoas, Peru | I4 | 84 |
| Andong, S. Kor. | G16 | 32 |
| Andorra, And. | C13 | 16 |
| Andorra, ctry., Eur. | G8 | 4 |
| Andover, Ma., U.S. | E15 | 108 |
| Andover, Me., U.S. | C16 | 108 |
| Andover, N.Y., U.S. | E9 | 108 |
| Andover, Oh., U.S. | F6 | 108 |
| Andover, S.D., U.S. | F10 | 118 |
| Andøya, i., Nor. | G14 | 6 |
| Andradina, Braz. | F3 | 79 |
| Andranopasy, Madag. | r20 | 67b |
| Andranovory, Madag. | s21 | 67b |
| Andreanof Islands, is., Ak., U.S. | J6 | 100 |
| Andreapol', Russia | E15 | 22 |
| Andrejevo, Russia | F24 | 22 |
| Andrew, Ab., Can. | D22 | 102 |
| Andrews, In., U.S. | B11 | 114 |
| Andrews, N.C., U.S. | D3 | 112 |
| Andrews, S.C., U.S. | F7 | 112 |
| Andrews, Tx., U.S. | G4 | 116 |
| Andria, Italy | H11 | 18 |
| Andriamena, Madag. | p22 | 67b |
| Andriandampy, Madag. | s21 | 67b |
| Andrijevica, Yugo. | G3 | 20 |
| Androka, Madag. | t21 | 67b |
| Ándros, Grc. | L8 | 20 |
| Andros, i., Bah. | B6 | 94 |
| Ándros, i., Grc. | L8 | 20 |
| Androscoggin, stm., Me., U.S. | C16 | 108 |
| Andros Town, Bah. | B6 | 94 |
| Āndrott Island, i., India | G2 | 46 |
| Andrychów, Pol. | F19 | 10 |
| Andújar, Spain | G7 | 16 |
| Anécho, Togo | H10 | 64 |
| Anegada, i., Br. Vir. Is. | E12 | 94 |
| Anegada Passage, strt., N.A. | E13 | 94 |
| Anegam, Az., U.S. | L4 | 120 |
| Añelo, Arg. | J4 | 80 |
| Aneroid, Sk., Can. | I7 | 104 |
| Aneta, N.D., U.S. | D10 | 118 |
| Aneto, Pico de, mtn., Spain | C12 | 16 |
| Anfeng, China | B9 | 34 |
| Anfeng, China | C9 | 34 |
| Anfengqiao, China | I7 | 34 |
| Anfu, China | H3 | 34 |
| Angamos, Punta, c., Chile | B3 | 80 |
| Ang'angxi, China | B11 | 30 |
| Angao, China | B1 | 34 |
| Angara, stm., Russia | F17 | 26 |
| Angara-Débou, Benin | F11 | 64 |
| Angarbaka, Sudan | M3 | 60 |
| Angarsk, Russia | G12 | 28 |
| Angastaco, Arg. | C5 | 80 |
| Angatuba, Braz. | G4 | 79 |
| Ángel, Salto (Angel Falls), wtfl, Ven. | E11 | 84 |
| Ángel de la Guarda, Isla, i., Mex. | C3 | 90 |
| Angeles, Phil. | n19 | 39b |
| Angel Falls see Ángel, Salto, wtfl, Ven. | E11 | 84 |
| Angelina, stm., Tx., U.S. | K2 | 114 |
| Angels Camp, Ca., U.S. | F5 | 124 |
| Angereb, stm., Afr. | K9 | 60 |
| Angermünde, Ger. | B14 | 10 |
| Angers, Fr. | E6 | 14 |
| Angerville, Fr. | D9 | 14 |
| Angical, Braz. | B6 | 79 |
| Angicos, Braz. | E11 | 76 |
| Angier, N.C., U.S. | D8 | 112 |
| Angijak Island, i., N.T., Can. | C20 | 96 |
| Angikuni Lake, l., N.T., Can. | D13 | 96 |
| Angkor Wat, hist., Camb. | H7 | 40 |
| Ângk Tasaôm, Camb. | I8 | 40 |
| Anglais, Baie des, b., P.Q., Can. | C5 | 106 |
| Angle Inlet, Mn., U.S. | B12 | 118 |
| Anglesey, i., Wales, U.K. | H9 | 8 |
| Angleton, Tx., U.S. | J11 | 116 |
| Angling, stm., Mb., Can. | B21 | 104 |
| Angling Lake, l., Mb., Can. | E21 | 104 |
| Angmagssalik, Grnld. | C16 | 86 |
| Angoche, Moz. | E7 | 58 |
| Angoche, Ilha, i., Moz. | E7 | 58 |
| Angol, Chile | I2 | 80 |
| Angola, In., U.S. | A12 | 114 |
| Angola, N.Y., U.S. | E7 | 108 |
| Angola, ctry., Afr. | D3 | 58 |
| Angoon, Ak., U.S. | H27 | 100 |
| Angora see Ankara, Tur. | B2 | 48 |
| Angoram, Pap. N. Gui. | F11 | 38 |
| Angostura, Mex. | E5 | 90 |
| Angostura, Presa de la, res., Mex. | I13 | 90 |
| Angoulême, Fr. | G7 | 14 |
| Angoumois, hist. reg., Fr. | G6 | 14 |
| Angra dos Reis, Braz. | G6 | 79 |
| Angren, Uzb. | I12 | 26 |
| Angualasto, Arg. | F4 | 80 |
| Anguciana, Cerro, mtn., C.R. | I11 | 92 |
| Anguilla, Ms., U.S. | J6 | 114 |
| Anguilla, dep., N.A. | E13 | 94 |
| Anguilla Cays, is., Bah. | C5 | 94 |
| Anguille, Cape, c., Nf., Can. | E14 | 106 |
| Anguo, China | E3 | 32 |
| Angus, On., Can. | F16 | 110 |
| Angusville, Mb., Can. | H13 | 104 |
| Angwin, Ca., U.S. | F3 | 124 |
| Anhai, China | K7 | 34 |
| Anhui (Anhwei), prov., China | E10 | 30 |
| Aniak, Ak., U.S. | F15 | 100 |
| Aniche, Fr. | H3 | 12 |
| Anicuns, Braz. | D4 | 79 |
| Anié, Togo | H10 | 64 |
| Animas, N.M., U.S. | M8 | 120 |
| Animas, stm., U.S. | H9 | 120 |
| Animas Peak, mtn., N.M., U.S. | M8 | 120 |
| Anina, Rom. | D5 | 20 |
| Anita, Ia., U.S. | J13 | 118 |
| Aniva, zaliv, b., Russia | H20 | 28 |
| Anivorano, Madag. | q23 | 67b |
| Anjangaon, India | B4 | 46 |
| Anjār, India | I4 | 44 |
| 'Anjar, Leb. | A5 | 50 |
| Anji, China | E8 | 34 |
| Anjiabe, Madag. | n23 | 67b |
| Anjiang, China | C5 | 32 |
| Anjou, hist. reg., Fr. | E6 | 14 |
| Anju, N. Kor. | D13 | 32 |
| Ankang, China | E8 | 30 |
| Ankara, Tur. | B2 | 48 |
| Ankaratra, mts., Madag. | q22 | 67b |
| Ankarimbelo, Madag. | s22 | 67b |
| Ankasakasa, Madag. | p21 | 67b |
| Ankavandra, Madag. | q21 | 67b |
| Ankazoabo, Madag. | s21 | 67b |
| Ankazobe, Madag. | q22 | 67b |
| Ankazomiriotra, Madag. | q22 | 67b |
| Ankeny, Ia., U.S. | I2 | 110 |
| Ankilimalinika, Madag. | s20 | 67b |
| Ankisabe, Madag. | q22 | 67b |
| Ankleshwar, India | B2 | 46 |
| Ankober, Eth. | G8 | 56 |
| Ankou, China | J2 | 34 |
| An'kovo, Russia | E22 | 22 |
| Ankpa, Nig. | H13 | 64 |
| Anliu, China | L4 | 34 |
| Anlu, China | D2 | 34 |
| Ann, Cape, c., Ant. | B4 | 73 |
| Anna, Il., U.S. | E7 | 114 |
| Anna, Tx., U.S. | F10 | 116 |
| Anna, Lake, res., Va., U.S. | A9 | 112 |
| Annaba (Bône), Alg. | B14 | 62 |
| Annaberg-Buchholz, Ger. | E13 | 10 |
| An-Nabk, Syria | D4 | 48 |
| An-Nafī, Sau. Ar. | B3 | 47 |
| An-Nafūd, des., Sau. Ar. | G6 | 48 |
| An-Najaf, Iraq | F8 | 48 |
| An-Nakhl, Egypt | C7 | 60 |
| Annamitique, Chaîne, mts., Asia | F9 | 40 |
| Annandale, Austl. | C8 | 70 |
| Annandale, Mn., U.S. | E1 | 110 |
| Annapolis, Md., U.S. | I10 | 108 |
| Annapolis Basin, b., N.S., Can. | H8 | 106 |
| Annapolis Royal, N.S., Can. | H8 | 106 |
| Annapūrṇa, mtn., Nepal | F10 | 44 |
| Ann Arbor, Mi., U.S. | H12 | 110 |
| Anna Regina, Guy. | D13 | 84 |
| An-Nāṣirīyah, Iraq | F9 | 48 |
| An-Nāṣirīyah, Syria | A7 | 50 |
| An-Nawfalāb, Sudan | J7 | 60 |
| Annecy, Fr. | G13 | 14 |
| Annemasse, Fr. | F13 | 14 |
| Annenskij Most, Russia | A20 | 22 |
| Annette, Ak., U.S. | I29 | 100 |
| An Nhon, Viet. | H10 | 40 |
| Anniston, Al., U.S. | I11 | 114 |
| Annobón, i., Eq. Gui. | B1 | 58 |
| Annonay, Fr. | G11 | 14 |
| An-Nuhūd, Sudan | K5 | 60 |
| An-Nu'mānīyah, Iraq | E8 | 48 |
| Annville, Ky., U.S. | B3 | 112 |
| Annville, Pa., U.S. | G10 | 108 |
| Anoka, Mn., U.S. | E2 | 110 |
| Anopino, Russia | F23 | 22 |
| Anori, Braz. | I12 | 84 |
| Anorí, Col. | D5 | 84 |
| Anping, China | D4 | 32 |
| Anpu, China | D11 | 40 |
| Anqing, China | E6 | 34 |
| Anqiu, China | G7 | 32 |
| Ansbach, Ger. | F10 | 10 |
| Anse-d'Hainault, Haiti | E7 | 94 |
| Anselmo, Ne., U.S. | J8 | 118 |
| Anserma, Col. | E5 | 84 |
| Anshan, China | B10 | 32 |
| Anshun, China | A8 | 40 |
| Ansina, Ur. | F11 | 80 |
| Ansley, Ne., U.S. | J8 | 118 |
| Anson, Tx., U.S. | G7 | 116 |
| Ansŏng, S. Kor. | F15 | 32 |
| Ansongo, Mali | D10 | 64 |
| Ansonville, N.C., U.S. | D6 | 112 |
| Ansted, W.V., U.S. | I5 | 108 |
| Anta, Peru | E5 | 82 |
| Antabamba, Peru | F5 | 82 |
| Antalaha, Madag. | o24 | 67b |
| Antalivtsi, Ukr. | G22 | 10 |
| Antalya, Tur. | H14 | 4 |
| Antalya Körfezi, b., Tur. | H14 | 4 |
| Antambohobe, Madag. | s22 | 67b |
| Antanambao Manampotsy, Madag. | q23 | 67b |
| Antananarivo, Madag. | q22 | 67b |
| Antanetibe, Madag. | q22 | 67b |
| Antanifotsy, Madag. | q22 | 67b |
| Antarctica | D5 | 73 |
| Antarctic Peninsula, pen., Ant. | B12 | 73 |
| Antas, Rio das, stm., Braz. | E13 | 80 |
| Antelope Island, i., Ut., U.S. | D4 | 120 |
| Antelope Mine, Zimb. | C9 | 66 |
| Antelope Peak, mtn., Nv., U.S. | C11 | 124 |
| Antequera, Para. | C10 | 80 |
| Antequera, Spain | H7 | 16 |
| Antevamena, Madag. | r21 | 67b |
| Anthon, Ia., U.S. | I12 | 118 |
| Anthony, Fl., U.S. | J4 | 112 |
| Anthony, Ks., U.S. | N9 | 118 |
| Anthony, N.M., U.S. | L10 | 120 |
| Anthony, Tx., U.S. | M10 | 120 |
| Anti-Atlas, mts., Mor. | E6 | 62 |
| Antibes, Fr. | I14 | 14 |
| Anticosti, Île d', i., P.Q., Can. | C10 | 106 |
| Antigo, Wi., U.S. | E6 | 110 |
| Antigonish, N.S., Can. | G12 | 106 |
| Antigua, i., Antig. | F14 | 94 |
| Antigua and Barbuda, ctry., N.A. | F14 | 94 |
| Antigua Guatemala, Guat. | C4 | 92 |
| Antiguo Morelos, Mex. | F10 | 90 |
| Anti-Lebanon see Sharqī, Al-Jabal ash-, mts., Asia | A6 | 50 |
| Antilla, Arg. | D6 | 80 |
| Antilla, Cuba | D7 | 94 |
| Antimony, Ut., U.S. | F5 | 120 |
| Antioch, Il., U.S. | H7 | 110 |
| Antioch see Hatay, Tur. | C4 | 48 |
| Antioquia, Col. | D5 | 84 |
| Antioquia, dept., Col. | D5 | 84 |
| Antipodes Islands, is., N.Z. | M21 | 126 |
| Antizana, vol., Ec. | H3 | 84 |
| Antler, stm., N.A. | I13 | 104 |
| Antlers, Ok., U.S. | E11 | 116 |
| Antofagasta, Chile | B3 | 80 |
| Antofagasta, prov., Chile | B4 | 80 |
| Antofagasta de la Sierra, Arg. | D5 | 80 |
| Antofalla, Salar de, pl., Arg. | C5 | 80 |
| Antofalla, Volcán, vol., Arg. | C5 | 80 |
| Antón, Pan. | C2 | 84 |
| Anton, Tx., U.S. | F4 | 116 |
| Anton Chico, N.M., U.S. | I11 | 120 |
| Antongila, Helodrano, b., Madag. | o23 | 67b |
| Antonina, Braz. | C14 | 80 |
| Antonio Amaro, Mex. | E7 | 90 |
| Antônio Prado, Braz. | E13 | 80 |
| Antonito, Co., U.S. | G10 | 120 |
| Antón Lizardo, Punta, c., Mex. | H12 | 90 |
| Antopal', Bela. | I7 | 22 |
| Antou, China | I7 | 34 |
| Antrain, Fr. | D5 | 14 |
| Antrim, N. Ire., U.K. | G7 | 8 |
| Antrodoco, Italy | G8 | 18 |
| Antropovo, Russia | C26 | 22 |
| Antsalova, Madag. | q21 | 67b |
| Antsenavolo, Madag. | r23 | 67b |
| Antsiafabositra, Madag. | p22 | 67b |
| Antsirabe, Madag. | o23 | 67b |
| Antsirabe, Madag. | q22 | 67b |
| Antsiranana, Madag. | n23 | 67b |
| Antsla, Est. | D9 | 22 |
| Antsohihy, Madag. | o22 | 67b |
| Antuševo, Russia | B20 | 22 |
| Antwerp see Antwerpen, Bel. | F5 | 12 |
| Antwerp, Oh., U.S. | F2 | 108 |
| Antwerpen (Anvers), Bel. | F5 | 12 |
| Antwerpen, prov., Bel. | F6 | 12 |
| Anugul, India | B8 | 46 |
| Anuradhapura, Sri L. | H6 | 46 |
| Anvers (Antwerpen), Bel. | F5 | 12 |
| Anvers Island, i., Ant. | B12 | 73 |
| Anvik, Ak., U.S. | E14 | 100 |
| Anvil Range, mts., Yk., Can. | E28 | 100 |
| Anxi, China | C6 | 30 |
| Anxi, China | J7 | 34 |
| Anxin, China | E3 | 32 |
| Anyama, C. Iv. | I7 | 64 |
| Anyang, China | G2 | 32 |
| A'nyêmaqên Shan, mts., China | D6 | 30 |
| Anyi, China | G4 | 34 |
| Anykščiai, Lith. | F8 | 22 |
| Anyox, B.C., Can. | B5 | 102 |
| Anyuan, China | H2 | 34 |
| Anzac, Ab., Can. | B3 | 104 |
| Anzaldo, Bol. | G9 | 82 |
| Anžero-Sudžensk, Russia | F15 | 26 |
| Anzhen, China | D9 | 34 |
| Anzhou, China | E3 | 32 |
| Anzin, Fr. | B10 | 14 |
| Anzio, Italy | H7 | 18 |
| Anzoátegui, state, Ven. | C10 | 84 |
| Anžu, ostrova, is., Russia | B20 | 28 |
| Aoga-shima, i., Japan | E14 | 30 |
| Aohan Qi (Xinhui), China | A7 | 32 |
| Aoji, N. Kor. | A18 | 32 |
| Aojiang, China | H9 | 34 |
| Aojiao, China | L6 | 34 |
| Aomori, Japan | G15 | 36 |
| Aóös (Vijosë), stm., Eur. | J4 | 20 |
| Aôral, Phnum, mtn., Camb. | H8 | 40 |
| Aosta, Italy | D2 | 18 |
| Aotou, China | M3 | 34 |
| Aouderas, Niger | C14 | 64 |
| Aouk, Bahr, stm., Afr. | G5 | 56 |
| Aoukâr, reg., Maur. | B5 | 64 |
| Aourou, Mali | D4 | 64 |
| Aozou, Chad | D4 | 56 |
| Apa, stm., S.A. | B10 | 80 |
| Apache, Ok., U.S. | E8 | 116 |
| Apache Junction, Az., U.S. | K5 | 120 |
| Apache Peak, mtn., Az., U.S. | M6 | 120 |
| Apalachicola, Fl., U.S. | J2 | 112 |
| Apalachicola, stm., Fl., U.S. | I1 | 112 |
| Apalachicola Bay, b., Fl., U.S. | J1 | 112 |
| Apanas, Laguna de, res., Nic. | D9 | 92 |
| Apaporis, stm., S.A. | H7 | 84 |
| Aparados da Serra, Parque Nacional de, Braz. | E13 | 80 |
| Aparri, Phil. | I19 | 39b |
| Apaseo El Grande, Mex. | G9 | 90 |
| Apatin, Yugo. | D2 | 20 |
| Apatity, Russia | D4 | 26 |
| Apatzingán de la Constitución, Mex. | H8 | 90 |
| Apaxtla de Castrejón, Mex. | H10 | 90 |
| Apayacu, stm., Peru | I6 | 84 |
| Ape, Lat. | D9 | 22 |
| Apeganau Lake, l., Mb., Can. | C15 | 104 |
| Apeldoorn, Neth. | D8 | 12 |
| Apennines see Appennino, mts., Italy | F7 | 18 |
| Apex, N.C., U.S. | D8 | 112 |
| Apex Mountain, mtn., Yk., Can. | E25 | 100 |
| Api, mtn., Nepal | F9 | 44 |
| Apía, Col. | E5 | 84 |
| Apia, W. Sam. | G1 | 2 |
| Apiacá, stm., Braz. | C13 | 82 |
| Apiacás, Serra dos, plat., Braz. | D13 | 82 |
| Apiaí, Braz. | C14 | 80 |
| Apiaú, stm., Braz. | F12 | 84 |
| Apizaco, Mex. | H10 | 90 |
| Apizolaya, Mex. | E8 | 90 |
| Aplahoué, Benin | H10 | 64 |
| Aplao, Peru | G5 | 82 |
| Apo, Mount, mtn., Phil. | D8 | 38 |
| Apolakkiá, Grc. | M11 | 20 |
| Apolda, Ger. | D11 | 10 |
| Apolinario Saravia, Arg. | C6 | 80 |
| Apollo, Pa., U.S. | G7 | 108 |
| Apolo, Bol. | F7 | 82 |
| Apón, stm., Ven. | B6 | 84 |
| Aponguao, stm., Ven. | E12 | 84 |
| Apopa, El Sal. | D5 | 92 |
| Aporé, Braz. | E2 | 79 |
| Aporé, stm., Braz. | E3 | 79 |
| Apostle Islands, is., Wi., U.S. | D5 | 110 |
| Apóstoles, Arg. | D11 | 80 |
| Apostolove, Ukr. | H4 | 26 |
| Appalachia, Va., U.S. | C4 | 112 |
| Appalachian Mountains, mts., N.A. | C11 | 98 |
| Appennino (Apennines), mts., Italy | F7 | 18 |
| Appenzell, Switz. | D11 | 13 |
| Appenzell-Ausserrhoden, state, Switz. | D11 | 13 |
| Apple, stm., U.S. | H5 | 110 |
| Apple, stm., Wi., U.S. | E3 | 110 |
| Applegate, stm., Or., U.S. | B2 | 124 |
| Appleton, Mn., U.S. | F11 | 118 |
| Appleton, Wi., U.S. | F7 | 110 |
| Appleton City, Mo., U.S. | D2 | 114 |
| Apple Valley, Ca., U.S. | J8 | 124 |
| Appling, Ga., U.S. | F4 | 112 |
| Appomattox, Va., U.S. | B8 | 112 |
| Appomattox, stm., Va., U.S. | B8 | 112 |
| Aprelevka, Russia | F20 | 22 |
| Apt, Fr. | I12 | 14 |
| Apuaú, stm., Braz. | I12 | 84 |
| Apucarana, Braz. | G3 | 79 |
| Apure, state, Ven. | D8 | 84 |
| Apure, stm., Ven. | D9 | 84 |
| Apurímac, dept., Peru | E5 | 82 |
| Apurímac, stm., Peru | E5 | 82 |
| Apurito, Ven. | D8 | 84 |
| Aqaba, Gulf of, b. | C8 | 60 |
| 'Aqīq, Sudan | H10 | 60 |
| Aquidabã, stm., Braz. | I13 | 82 |
| Aquidabán, stm., Para. | B10 | 80 |
| Aquidauana, Braz. | I14 | 82 |
| Aquidauana, stm., Braz. | I14 | 82 |
| Aquila, Mex. | H8 | 90 |
| Aquila, Switz. | E10 | 13 |
| Aquiles Serdán, Mex. | C7 | 90 |
| Aquiles Serdán, Mex. | E11 | 90 |
| Aquilla, Tx., U.S. | H9 | 116 |
| Aquin, Haiti | E8 | 94 |
| Aquio, stm., Col. | F9 | 84 |
| Ara, India | H11 | 44 |
| Arab, Al., U.S. | H10 | 114 |
| 'Arab, Baḥr al-, stm., Sudan | M4 | 60 |
| Arab, Shatt al-, stm., Asia | G10 | 48 |
| 'Arab, Wādī al-, val., Jord. | C5 | 50 |
| 'Arabah, Wādī al- (Ha'Arava), val., Asia | G4 | 50 |
| Arabako, prov., Spain | C9 | 16 |
| Arabelo, Ven. | E10 | 84 |
| Arabi, La., U.S. | M6 | 114 |
| Arabian Desert see Sharqīyah, Aṣ-Ṣaḥrā' ash-, des., Egypt | D7 | 60 |
| Arabian Gulf see Persian Gulf, b., Asia | H11 | 48 |
| Arabian Peninsula, pen., Asia | G5 | 24 |
| Arabian Sea | H7 | 24 |
| Araçá, stm., Braz. | G11 | 84 |
| Aracaju, Braz. | F11 | 76 |
| Aracataca, Col. | B5 | 84 |
| Aracati, Braz. | D11 | 76 |
| Araçatuba, Braz. | F3 | 79 |
| Aracena, Spain | H5 | 16 |
| Aracruz, Braz. | E8 | 79 |
| Araçuaí, Braz. | D7 | 79 |
| Araçuaí, stm., Braz. | D7 | 79 |
| Arad, Rom. | C5 | 20 |
| Arad, co., Rom. | C5 | 20 |
| Arada, Hond. | C6 | 92 |
| Arafura Sea | I17 | 126 |
| Aragarças, Braz. | C2 | 79 |
| Aragon, Ga., U.S. | E1 | 112 |
| Aragón, state, Spain | D10 | 16 |
| Aragón, stm., Spain | C10 | 16 |
| Aragua, state, Ven. | B9 | 84 |
| Araguacema, Braz. | E9 | 76 |
| Araguaçu, Braz. | B4 | 79 |
| Aragua de Barcelona, Ven. | C10 | 84 |
| Aragua de Maturín, Ven. | C11 | 84 |
| Araguaia, stm., Braz. | E9 | 76 |
| Araguaia, Braço Menor, stm., Braz. | B3 | 79 |
| Araguainha, Braz. | D2 | 79 |
| Araguao, Caño, mth., Ven. | C12 | 84 |
| Araguari, Braz. | E4 | 79 |
| Araguari, stm., Braz. | C8 | 76 |
| Araguari, stm., Braz. | E4 | 79 |
| Araguatins, Braz. | E9 | 76 |
| Arahal, Spain | H6 | 16 |
| Ârak, Alg. | H12 | 62 |
| Arāk, Iran | D10 | 48 |
| Arakan Yoma, mts., Myan. | E3 | 40 |
| Árakhthos, stm., Grc. | J4 | 20 |
| Aral Sea, Asia | H10 | 26 |
| Aral'sk, Kaz. | H10 | 26 |
| Aramac, Austl. | D6 | 70 |
| Aramac, stm., Austl. | D6 | 70 |
| Aramari, Braz. | B9 | 79 |
| Aramberri, Mex. | E10 | 90 |
| Arampampa, Bol. | G8 | 82 |
| Aramtalla, Sudan | N5 | 60 |
| Ārān, Iran | D11 | 48 |
| Aranda de Duero, Spain | D8 | 16 |
| Arandas, Mex. | G8 | 90 |
| Aranđelovac, Yugo. | E4 | 20 |
| Arandis, Nmb. | D2 | 66 |
| Arani, Bol. | G9 | 82 |
| Aran Islands, is., Ire. | H4 | 8 |
| Aranjuez, Spain | E8 | 16 |
| Aransas, stm., Tx., U.S. | K9 | 116 |
| Aransas Pass, Tx., U.S. | L9 | 116 |
| Aranyaprathet, Thai. | H7 | 40 |
| Arao, Japan | O5 | 36 |
| Araouane, Mali | E6 | 54 |
| Arapa, Laguna, l., Peru | F6 | 82 |
| Arapaho, Ok., U.S. | D8 | 116 |
| Arapahoe, Ne., U.S. | K8 | 118 |
| Arapey, Ur. | F10 | 80 |
| Arapey Chico, stm., Ur. | F10 | 80 |
| Arapey Grande, stm., Ur. | F10 | 80 |
| Arapiraca, Braz. | E11 | 76 |
| Arapkir, Tur. | B5 | 48 |
| Arapongas, Braz. | G3 | 79 |
| Arapoti, Braz. | H4 | 79 |
| 'Ar'ar, Sau. Ar. | F6 | 48 |
| 'Ar'ar, Wādī, val., Asia | B11 | 60 |
| Araranguá, Braz. | E14 | 80 |
| Araraquara, Braz. | F4 | 79 |
| Araras, Braz. | G5 | 79 |
| Ararat, Arm. | B8 | 48 |
| Ararat, Austl. | K5 | 70 |
| Ararat, Mount see Ağrı Dağı, mtn., Tur. | B8 | 48 |
| Ararirá, stm., Braz. | H10 | 84 |
| Araruama, Lagoa de, b., Braz. | G7 | 79 |
| Aras (Araz), stm., Asia | B10 | 48 |
| Áratos, Grc. | H9 | 20 |
| Aratuípe, Braz. | B9 | 79 |
| Arauã, stm., Braz. | C9 | 82 |
| Arauá, stm., Braz. | A11 | 82 |
| Arauá, stm., Braz. | J10 | 84 |
| Arauca, Col. | D7 | 84 |
| Arauca, dept., Col. | D7 | 84 |
| Arauca, stm., S.A. | D9 | 84 |
| Araucária, Braz. | C14 | 80 |
| Arauco, Chile | I2 | 80 |
| Arauco, Golfo de, b., Chile | I2 | 80 |
| Araújos, Braz. | E6 | 79 |
| Arauquita, Col. | D7 | 84 |
| Araure, Ven. | C8 | 84 |
| Arāvalli Range, mts., India | H5 | 44 |
| Araxá, Braz. | E5 | 79 |
| Araya, Ven. | B10 | 84 |
| Araya, Punta de, c., Ven. | B10 | 84 |
| Araz (Aras), stm., Asia | B10 | 48 |
| Arba Minch, Eth. | N9 | 60 |
| Arboga, Swe. | L14 | 6 |
| Arbois, Fr. | F12 | 14 |
| Arboledas, Arg. | I8 | 80 |
| Arboletes, Col. | C4 | 84 |
| Arbon, Switz. | C11 | 13 |
| Arborfield, Sk., Can. | E11 | 104 |
| Arborg, Mb., Can. | H17 | 104 |
| Arbroath, Scot., U.K. | E11 | 8 |
| Arbuckle, Ca., U.S. | E3 | 124 |
| Arc, Bayou des, stm., Ar., U.S. | G5 | 114 |
| Arcachon, Fr. | H5 | 14 |
| Arcade, Ca., U.S. | J7 | 124 |
| Arcade, N.Y., U.S. | E8 | 108 |
| Arcadia, Ca., U.S. | J7 | 124 |
| Arcadia, Fl., U.S. | L5 | 112 |
| Arcadia, Ia., U.S. | I12 | 118 |
| Arcadia, In., U.S. | B10 | 114 |
| Arcadia, Ks., U.S. | N13 | 118 |
| Arcadia, La., U.S. | J4 | 114 |
| Arcadia, Mi., U.S. | F9 | 110 |
| Arcadia, Mo., U.S. | E6 | 114 |
| Arcadia, Ne., U.S. | J8 | 118 |
| Arcadia, Pa., U.S. | G8 | 108 |
| Arcadia, S.C., U.S. | E5 | 112 |
| Arcadia, Wi., U.S. | F4 | 110 |
| Arcanum, Oh., U.S. | H2 | 108 |
| Arcas, Cayos, is., Mex. | G14 | 90 |
| Arcata, Ca., U.S. | D1 | 124 |
| Arcatao, El Sal. | C6 | 92 |
| Arc Dome, mtn., Nv., U.S. | F8 | 124 |
| Arcelia, Mex. | H9 | 90 |
| Archangel'sk, Russia | E6 | 26 |
| Archbold, Oh., U.S. | F2 | 108 |
| Archdale, N.C., U.S. | D7 | 112 |
| Archer, Fl., U.S. | J4 | 112 |
| Archer City, Tx., U.S. | F8 | 116 |
| Archidona, Spain | H7 | 16 |
| Archipovka, Russia | E24 | 22 |
| Arco, Id., U.S. | G12 | 122 |
| Arcola, Il., U.S. | C8 | 114 |
| Arcola, Ms., U.S. | I6 | 114 |
| Arcola, Sk., Can. | I12 | 104 |
| Arcos, Braz. | F6 | 79 |
| Arcos de la Frontera, Spain | I6 | 16 |
| Arcot, India | F5 | 46 |
| Arcoverde, Braz. | E11 | 76 |
| Arctic Bay, N.T., Can. | B15 | 96 |
| Arctic Ocean | A1 | 86 |
| Arctic Red, stm., N.T., Can. | C28 | 100 |
| Arctic Red River, N.T., Can. | C28 | 100 |
| Arctic Village, Ak., U.S. | B22 | 100 |
| Arctowski, sci., Ant. | B1 | 73 |
| Arcturus, Zimb. | A10 | 66 |
| Arda, stm., Eur. | H9 | 20 |
| Ardabīl, Iran | B10 | 48 |
| Ardahan, Tur. | G16 | 4 |
| Ardakān, Iran | F12 | 48 |
| Ardakān, Iran | E12 | 48 |
| Årdalstangen, Nor. | K10 | 6 |
| Ardatov, Russia | F26 | 22 |
| Ardèche, dept., Fr. | H11 | 14 |
| Arden, Ca., U.S. | F4 | 124 |
| Arden, Mb., Can. | H15 | 104 |
| Arden, Mount, mtn., Austl. | I2 | 70 |
| Ardennes, dept., Fr. | C11 | 14 |
| Ardennes, reg., Eur. | E5 | 10 |
| Ardestān, Iran | E12 | 48 |
| Ardila, stm., Eur. | G4 | 16 |
| Ardill, Sk., Can. | I9 | 104 |
| Ardino, Bul. | H9 | 20 |
| Ardlethan, Austl. | J7 | 70 |
| Ardmore, Al., U.S. | H10 | 114 |
| Ardmore, Ok., U.S. | E9 | 116 |
| Ardmore, Pa., U.S. | G11 | 108 |
| Ardoch, Austl. | F6 | 70 |
| Åre, Swe. | J13 | 6 |
| Areado, Braz. | F5 | 79 |
| Arecibo, P.R. | E11 | 94 |
| Areguá, Para. | C10 | 80 |
| Arèḫausk, Bela. | G13 | 22 |
| Areia, Ribeirão da, stm., Braz. | C6 | 79 |
| Areia Branca, Braz. | D11 | 76 |
| Arena, Punta, c., Mex. | F5 | 90 |
| Arena de la Ventana, Punta, c., Mex. | E5 | 90 |
| Arenal, C.R. | G10 | 92 |
| Arenal, Laguna de, l., C.R. | G10 | 92 |
| Arenal, Volcán, vol., C.R. | G10 | 92 |
| Arenápolis, Braz. | F13 | 82 |
| Arenas, Cayo, i., Mex. | F14 | 90 |
| Arendal, Nor. | L11 | 6 |
| Arenillas, Ec. | I2 | 84 |
| Arenys de Mar, Spain | D14 | 16 |
| Arequipa, Peru | G6 | 82 |
| Arequipa, dept., Peru | F5 | 82 |
| Arequito, Arg. | G8 | 80 |
| Arès, Fr. | H5 | 14 |
| Arezzo, Italy | F6 | 18 |
| Argadargada, Austl. | C2 | 70 |
| Arganda, Spain | E8 | 16 |
| Arga-Sala, stm., Russia | D13 | 28 |
| Argelès-Gazost, Fr. | I7 | 14 |
| Argelès-sur-Mer, Fr. | J10 | 14 |
| Argenta, Il., U.S. | C8 | 114 |
| Argenta, Italy | E6 | 18 |
| Argentan, Fr. | D6 | 14 |
| Argentat, Fr. | G8 | 14 |
| Argentera, mtn., Italy | E2 | 18 |
| Argentia, Nf., Can. | E20 | 106 |
| Argentina, ctry., S.A. | C4 | 78 |
| Argentino, Lago, l., Arg. | G2 | 78 |
| Argenton-Château, Fr. | F6 | 14 |
| Argenton-sur-Creuse, Fr. | F8 | 14 |
| Argeș, co., Rom. | E8 | 20 |
| Argeș, stm., Rom. | E9 | 20 |
| Arghandāb, stm., Afg. | D2 | 44 |
| Argo, Sudan | H6 | 60 |
| Argolikós Kólpos, b., Grc. | L6 | 20 |
| Argonia, Ks., U.S. | N10 | 118 |
| Argonne, Wi., U.S. | E7 | 110 |
| Argonne, reg., Fr. | C12 | 14 |
| Árgos, Grc. | L6 | 20 |
| Argos, In., U.S. | A10 | 114 |
| Argostólion, Grc. | K4 | 20 |
| Argun' (Ergun), stm., Asia | G16 | 28 |
| Argyle, Mn., U.S. | C11 | 118 |
| Argyle, Lake, res., Austl. | C5 | 68 |
| Århus, Den. | M12 | 6 |
| Ariana, Tun. | M5 | 18 |
| Ariano Irpino, Italy | H10 | 18 |
| Ariari, stm., Col. | F6 | 84 |
| Arias, Arg. | G7 | 80 |
| Ariaú, Braz. | I14 | 84 |
| Aribinda, Burkina | D9 | 64 |
| Arica, Chile | H6 | 82 |
| Arica, Col. | I7 | 84 |
| Arichat, N.S., Can. | G12 | 106 |
| Arichuna, Ven. | D9 | 84 |
| Arid, Cape, c., Austl. | F4 | 68 |
| Ariège, dept., Fr. | J8 | 14 |
| Ariguaní, stm., Col. | C6 | 84 |
| Arīḥā (Jericho), Gaza | E4 | 50 |
| Arīḥā, Jord. | F5 | 50 |
| Arikaree, stm., U.S. | L5 | 118 |
| Arima, Trin. | I14 | 94 |
| Arinos, stm., Braz. | D12 | 82 |
| Ario de Rosales, Mex. | H9 | 90 |
| Ariogala, Lith. | F6 | 22 |
| Ariporo, stm., Col. | D7 | 84 |
| Aripuanã, Braz. | C11 | 82 |
| Aripuanã, stm., Braz. | B11 | 82 |
| Ariquemes, Braz. | C10 | 82 |
| Arisa, stm., Ven. | D10 | 84 |
| 'Arīsh, Wādī al-, val., Egypt | B7 | 60 |
| Arismendi, Ven. | C8 | 84 |
| Aristazabal Island, i., B.C., Can. | E5 | 102 |
| Ariton, Al., U.S. | K11 | 114 |
| Arivonimamo, Madag. | q22 | 67b |
| Arizaro, Salar de, pl., Arg. | C5 | 80 |
| Arizgoiti, Spain | B9 | 16 |
| Arizona, Arg. | H6 | 80 |
| Arizona, state, U.S. | E4 | 98 |
| Arizpe, Mex. | B4 | 90 |
| Arjay, Ky., U.S. | C3 | 112 |
| Arjeplog, Swe. | H15 | 6 |
| Arjona, Col. | B5 | 84 |
| Arkadelphia, Ar., U.S. | H3 | 114 |
| Arkalyk, Kaz. | G11 | 26 |
| Arkansas, state, U.S. | D8 | 98 |
| Arkansas, stm., U.S. | D8 | 98 |
| Arkansas City, Ar., U.S. | I5 | 114 |
| Arkansas City, Ks., U.S. | N10 | 118 |
| Arkhangelsk see Archangel'sk, Russia | E6 | 26 |
| Arklow, Ire. | I7 | 8 |
| Arkoma, Ok., U.S. | G2 | 114 |
| Arkona, Kap, c., Ger. | A13 | 10 |
| Arkport, N.Y., U.S. | E9 | 108 |
| Arktičeskij, mys, c., Russia | A11 | 28 |
| Arktičeskogo Instituta, ostrova, is., Russia | B14 | 26 |
| Arlbergpass, Aus. | D13 | 13 |
| Arlberg-Tunnel, Aus. | D13 | 13 |
| Arlee, Mt., U.S. | C11 | 122 |
| Arles, Fr. | I11 | 14 |
| Arli, Burkina | F10 | 64 |
| Arlington, Ga., U.S. | H2 | 112 |
| Arlington, Ia., U.S. | H4 | 110 |
| Arlington, Ks., U.S. | N9 | 118 |
| Arlington, Ky., U.S. | F7 | 114 |
| Arlington, Mn., U.S. | F1 | 110 |
| Arlington, Ne., U.S. | J11 | 118 |
| Arlington, Oh., U.S. | G3 | 108 |
| Arlington, Or., U.S. | E5 | 122 |
| Arlington, S.D., U.S. | G10 | 118 |
| Arlington, Tn., U.S. | G7 | 114 |
| Arlington, Tx., U.S. | G9 | 116 |
| Arlington, Va., U.S. | I9 | 108 |
| Arlington, Vt., U.S. | D13 | 108 |
| Arlington, Wa., U.S. | B3 | 122 |
| Arlington Heights, Il., U.S. | H8 | 110 |
| Arlit, Niger | B13 | 64 |
| Arm, stm., Sk., Can. | H9 | 104 |
| Arma, Ks., U.S. | N13 | 118 |
| Armada, Mi., U.S. | H13 | 110 |
| Armageddon see Tel Megiddo, hist., Isr. | C4 | 50 |
| Armagh, N. Ire., U.K. | G7 | 8 |
| Armagnac, hist. reg., Fr. | I7 | 14 |
| Armant, Egypt | E7 | 60 |
| Armavir, Russia | H6 | 26 |
| Armazém, Braz. | E14 | 80 |
| Armenia, Col. | E5 | 84 |
| Armenia, ctry., Asia | I6 | 26 |
| Armentières, Fr. | B9 | 14 |
| Armería, Mex. | H8 | 90 |
| Armero, Col. | E5 | 84 |
| Armidale, Austl. | H9 | 70 |
| Armijo, N.M., U.S. | I10 | 120 |
| Armit Lake, l., N.T., Can. | D14 | 96 |
| Armona, Ca., U.S. | H6 | 124 |
| Armour, S.D., U.S. | H9 | 118 |
| Armstrong, Arg. | G8 | 80 |
| Armstrong, B.C., Can. | G15 | 102 |
| Armstrong, Ia., U.S. | H13 | 118 |
| Armstrong, Mo., U.S. | C4 | 114 |
| Armstrong, Mount, mtn., Yk., Can. | E28 | 100 |
| Armstrong Station, On., Can. | F15 | 96 |
| Arnaud, stm., P.Q., Can. | E18 | 96 |
| Arnaudville, La., U.S. | L5 | 114 |
| Arnay-le-Duc, Fr. | E11 | 14 |
| Arnedo, Spain | C9 | 16 |
| Årnes, Nor. | K12 | 6 |
| Arnett, Ok., U.S. | C7 | 116 |
| Arnhem, Neth. | E8 | 12 |
| Arnhem, Cape, c., Austl. | B7 | 68 |
| Arnhem Land, reg., Austl. | B6 | 68 |
| Árnissa, Grc. | I5 | 20 |
| Arno, stm., Italy | F5 | 18 |
| Arno Bay, Austl. | I2 | 70 |
| Arnold, Ca., U.S. | F5 | 124 |
| Arnold, Mn., U.S. | D3 | 110 |
| Arnold, Mo., U.S. | D6 | 114 |
| Arnold, Ne., U.S. | J7 | 118 |
| Arnolds Park, Ia., U.S. | H12 | 118 |
| Arnprior, On., Can. | E19 | 110 |
| Arnsberg, Ger. | D8 | 10 |
| Arnstadt, Ger. | E10 | 10 |
| Aro, stm., Ven. | D10 | 84 |
| Aroa, Ven. | B8 | 84 |
| Aroa, stm., Ven. | B8 | 84 |
| Aroab, Nmb. | F4 | 66 |
| Aroma, Sudan | J9 | 60 |
| Arona, Italy | D3 | 18 |
| Aroostook, stm., N.A. | F5 | 106 |
| Aros, stm., Mex. | C5 | 90 |
| Arosa, Switz. | E12 | 13 |
| Arp, Tx., U.S. | G11 | 116 |
| Arque, Bol. | G8 | 82 |
| Ar-Rabad, Sau. Ar. | K8 | 47 |
| Ar-Radīsīyah Baḥrī, Egypt | E7 | 60 |
| Arraga, Arg. | E6 | 80 |
| Ar-Rahad, Sudan | K6 | 60 |
| Arraial do Cabo, Braz. | G7 | 79 |
| Arraias, Braz. | B5 | 79 |
| Arraias, stm., Braz. | A1 | 79 |
| Arraias, stm., Braz. | B5 | 79 |
| Ar-Ramādī, Iraq | E7 | 48 |
| Ar-Ramthā, Jord. | C6 | 50 |
| Arran, Island of, i., Scot., U.K. | F8 | 8 |
| Ar-Rank, Sudan | L7 | 60 |
| Ar-Raqqah, Syria | D5 | 48 |
| Arras, Fr. | B9 | 14 |
| Ar-Rāshidah, Egypt | E5 | 60 |
| Ar-Rass, Sau. Ar. | I7 | 48 |
| Ar-Rawḍah, Sau. Ar. | H6 | 48 |
| Ar-Rāwuk, Yemen | G6 | 47 |
| Ar-Rayyān, Qatar | I11 | 48 |
| Arrecife, Spain | o27 | 17b |
| Arrecifes, Arg. | H8 | 80 |
| Arrey, N.M., U.S. | L9 | 120 |
| Arriaga, Mex. | I13 | 90 |
| Arriba, Co., U.S. | L4 | 118 |
| Ar-Rimāh, Sau. Ar. | B5 | 47 |
| Ar-Riyāḍ (Riyadh), Sau. Ar. | B5 | 47 |
| Arroio Grande, Braz. | G12 | 80 |
| Arrojado, stm., Braz. | B6 | 79 |
| Arronches, Port. | F4 | 16 |
| Arrowrock Reservoir, res., Id., U.S. | G10 | 122 |
| Arrowsmith, Mount, mtn., Austl. | H4 | 70 |
| Arrowwood, Ab., Can. | G21 | 102 |
| Arroyito, Arg. | F7 | 80 |
| Arroyo de la Luz, Spain | F5 | 16 |
| Arroyo Grande, Ca., U.S. | I5 | 124 |
| Arroyo Hondo, N.M., U.S. | H11 | 120 |
| Arroyo Seco, Arg. | G8 | 80 |
| Arroyos y Esteros, Para. | C10 | 80 |
| Ar-Ru'at, Sudan | K7 | 60 |
| Ar-Rub' al-Khālī (Empty Quarter), des., Asia | D7 | 47 |
| Ar-Rukhaymīyah, well, Asia | G8 | 48 |
| Ar-Rumaythah, Iraq | F8 | 48 |
| Ar-Rummān, Jord. | D5 | 50 |
| Ar-Ruṣayfah, Jord. | D6 | 50 |
| Ar-Ruṣayriṣ, Sudan | L8 | 60 |
| Ar-Ruṭbah, Iraq | E6 | 48 |
| Ar-Ruways, Qatar | H11 | 48 |
| Arsenault Lake, l., Sk., Can. | C6 | 104 |
| Arsenjev, Russia | I18 | 28 |
| Arsenjevo, Russia | H19 | 22 |
| Árta, Grc. | J4 | 20 |
| Artašat, Arm. | B8 | 48 |
| Arteaga, Mex. | H8 | 90 |
| Artemisa, Cuba | C3 | 94 |
| Artémou, Maur. | D3 | 64 |
| Artenay, Fr. | D8 | 14 |
| Artesia, Ms., U.S. | I8 | 114 |
| Artesia, N.M., U.S. | G2 | 116 |
| Artesian, S.D., U.S. | G10 | 118 |
| Arth, Switz. | D10 | 13 |
| Arthabaska, P.Q., Can. | A15 | 108 |

| Name | Map Ref. | Page |
|---|---|---|
| Arthur, Il., U.S. | C8 | 114 |
| Arthur, N.D., U.S. | D10 | 118 |
| Arthur, Ne., U.S. | J6 | 118 |
| Arthur, On., Can. | G15 | 110 |
| Arthur, Tn., U.S. | C3 | 112 |
| Arthur's Town, Bah. | B7 | 94 |
| Artibonite, stm., Haiti | E8 | 94 |
| Artigas, Ur. | F10 | 80 |
| Artik, Arm. | A7 | 48 |
| Artillery Lake, l., N.T., Can. | D11 | 96 |
| Artois, hist. reg., Fr. | B9 | 14 |
| Art'om, Russia | D8 | 122 |
| Art'omovsk, Russia | G10 | 28 |
| Art'omovskij, Russia | F10 | 26 |
| Artsyz, Ukr. | C13 | 20 |
| Artvin, Tur. | G16 | 4 |
| Artyk, Russia | E21 | 28 |
| Artyom, Azer. | A11 | 48 |
| Aru, Kepulauan, is., Indon. | G9 | 38 |
| Aruaḍdin, Erit. | I10 | 60 |
| Aruanã, Braz. | C3 | 79 |
| Aruba, dep., N.A. | H9 | 94 |
| Arunāchal Pradesh, state, India | F16 | 44 |
| Aruppukkottai, India | H5 | 46 |
| Arusha, Tan. | B7 | 58 |
| Aruwimi, stm., D.R.C. | H6 | 56 |
| Arvada, Co., U.S. | E11 | 120 |
| Arvajcheer, Mong. | B7 | 30 |
| Arvi, India | B5 | 46 |
| Arvida, P.Q., Can. | D2 | 106 |
| Arvidsjaur, Swe. | I16 | 6 |
| Arvika, Swe. | L13 | 6 |
| Arvin, Ca., U.S. | I7 | 124 |
| Arvon, Mount, mtn., Mi., U.S. | D7 | 110 |
| Arvonia, Va., U.S. | B8 | 112 |
| Arvorezinha, Braz. | E12 | 80 |
| Arxan, China | H15 | 28 |
| Arys', Kaz. | I11 | 26 |
| Arzachena, Italy | H4 | 18 |
| Arzamas, Russia | F26 | 8 |
| Arziw, Alg. | C10 | 62 |
| Aš, Czech Rep. | E12 | 10 |
| Aša, Russia | F26 | 8 |
| Asa, stm., Ven. | D11 | 84 |
| Asab, Nmb. | E3 | 66 |
| Asad, Buḩayrat al-, res., Syria | C5 | 48 |
| Asahikawa, Japan | d17 | 36a |
| Asamankese, Ghana | I9 | 64 |
| Asansol, India | I12 | 44 |
| Asbest, Russia | F10 | 26 |
| Asbestos, P.Q., Can. | B15 | 108 |
| Asbury Park, N.J., U.S. | G12 | 108 |
| Ascension, Mex. | B6 | 90 |
| Ascension, i., St. Hel. | I5 | 52 |
| Aščhabad (Ashgabat), Turk. | J9 | 26 |
| Aschach an der Donau, Aus. | A9 | 18 |
| Aschaffenburg, Ger. | F9 | 10 |
| Aschersleben, Ger. | D11 | 10 |
| Ascoli Piceno, Italy | G8 | 18 |
| Ascona, Switz. | F10 | 13 |
| Ascope, Peru | B2 | 82 |
| Ascotán, Chile | A4 | 80 |
| Aseb, Erit. | H3 | 47 |
| Aseda, Swe. | M14 | 6 |
| Asela, Eth. | N10 | 60 |
| Asele, Swe. | I15 | 6 |
| Asendabo, Eth. | M9 | 60 |
| Asenovgrad, Bul. | G8 | 20 |
| Asfūn al-Maṭā'inah, Egypt | E7 | 60 |
| Ashburn, Ga., U.S. | H3 | 112 |
| Ashburn, N.Z. | E3 | 72 |
| Ashburton, stm., Austl. | D3 | 68 |
| Ashcroft, B.C., Can. | G13 | 102 |
| Ashdod, Isr. | E3 | 50 |
| Ashdot Ya'aqov, Isr. | C3 | 73 |
| Ashdown, Ar., U.S. | I2 | 114 |
| Asheboro, N.C., U.S. | D7 | 112 |
| Ashern, Mb., Can. | G16 | 104 |
| Asherton, Tx., U.S. | K7 | 116 |
| Asheville, N.C., U.S. | D4 | 112 |
| Asheweig, stm., On., Can. | F15 | 96 |
| Ashford, Al., U.S. | K11 | 114 |
| Ashford, Austl. | G9 | 70 |
| Ash Fork, Az., U.S. | I4 | 120 |
| Ash Grove, Mo., U.S. | E3 | 114 |
| Ashibetsu, Japan | d17 | 36a |
| Ashikaga, Japan | K14 | 36 |
| Ashkhabad see Aščhabad, Turk. | J9 | 26 |
| Ashland, Al., U.S. | I11 | 114 |
| Ashland, Il., U.S. | D7 | 114 |
| Ashland, Ks., U.S. | N8 | 118 |
| Ashland, Ky., U.S. | I4 | 108 |
| Ashland, Mo., U.S. | H7 | 114 |
| Ashland, Ms., U.S. | E19 | 122 |
| Ashland, Ne., U.S. | J11 | 118 |
| Ashland, N.H., U.S. | D15 | 108 |
| Ashland, Oh., U.S. | G4 | 108 |
| Ashland, Or., U.S. | H3 | 122 |
| Ashland, Pa., U.S. | G10 | 108 |
| Ashland, Va., U.S. | B9 | 112 |
| Ashland, Wi., U.S. | D5 | 110 |
| Ashland, Mount, mtn., Or., U.S. | H3 | 122 |
| Ashland City, Tn., U.S. | I8 | 114 |
| Ashley, Il., U.S. | D7 | 114 |
| Ashley, Mi., U.S. | G11 | 110 |
| Ashley, N.D., U.S. | E8 | 118 |
| Ashley, Oh., U.S. | G4 | 108 |
| Ashmore, Il., U.S. | C8 | 114 |
| Ashmore Islands, is., Austl. | B4 | 68 |
| Ashmün, Egypt | B6 | 60 |
| Ashqelon, Isr. | E3 | 50 |
| Ash-Shajarah, Jord. | C5 | 50 |
| Ash-Shaqrā', Sau. Ar. | D3 | 47 |
| Ash-Shāriqah (Sharjah), U.A.E. | B9 | 47 |
| Ash-Sharmah, Sau. Ar. | G3 | 47 |
| Ash-Shaṭrah, Iraq | F9 | 48 |
| Ash-Shawbak, Jord. | G5 | 50 |
| Ash-Shawmarah, Leb. | B4 | 50 |
| Ash-Shiḩr, Yemen | G5 | 47 |
| Ash-Shufayyah, Sau. Ar. | C1 | 47 |
| Ash-Shumlul, Sau. Ar. | H9 | 48 |
| Ash-Shuqayq, Sau. Ar. | F3 | 47 |
| Ash-Shurayf, Sudan | H7 | 60 |
| Ashtabula, Oh., U.S. | S | |
| Ashtabula, Lake, l., N.D., U.S. | D10 | 118 |
| Ashton, Ia., U.S. | H12 | 118 |
| Ashton, Id., U.S. | F14 | 122 |
| Ashton, Il., U.S. | I6 | 110 |
| Ashton, Ne., U.S. | J9 | 118 |
| Ashton, S. Afr. | J4 | 66 |
| Ashuanipi Lake, l., Nf., Can. | F19 | 96 |
| Ashuelot, stm., N.H., U.S. | E14 | 108 |
| Ashville, Al., U.S. | I10 | 114 |
| Ashville, Oh., U.S. | H4 | 108 |
| Ashwaubenon, Wi., U.S. | F7 | 110 |
| Asi (Nahr al-'Āṣī), stm., Asia | D11 | 24 |
| Asia | | |
| Asia, Kepulauan, is., Indon. | F9 | 38 |
| Asia Minor, hist. reg., Tur. | H14 | 4 |
| Asilah, Mor. | C7 | 62 |
| Asino, Russia | F9 | 28 |
| Asipoquobah Lake, l., On., Can. | E23 | 104 |

| Name | Map Ref. | Page |
|---|---|---|
| Asipovičy, Bela. | H11 | 22 |
| 'Asīr, reg., Sau. Ar. | E2 | 47 |
| Aşkale, Tur. | B6 | 48 |
| Askham, S. Afr. | F5 | 66 |
| Asmār, Afg. | C4 | 44 |
| Asmara see Asmera, Erit. | E8 | 56 |
| Asmera, Erit. | E8 | 56 |
| Asmjany, Bela. | G8 | 22 |
| Asola, Italy | D5 | 18 |
| Asosa, Eth. | F7 | 56 |
| Asotin, Wa., U.S. | D8 | 122 |
| Asp, Spain | G11 | 16 |
| Aspang Markt, Aus. | H16 | 10 |
| Aspen, Co., U.S. | E10 | 120 |
| Aspen Butte, mtn., Or., U.S. | H3 | 122 |
| Aspermont, Tx., U.S. | F6 | 116 |
| Aspres-sur-Buëch, Fr. | H12 | 14 |
| Aspy Bay, b., N.S., Can. | F13 | 106 |
| Asquith, Sk., Can. | F7 | 104 |
| As-Sa'ata, Sudan | K5 | 60 |
| Aş-Şaff, Egypt | C6 | 60 |
| Aş-Şaffānīyah, Sau. Ar. | H10 | 43 |
| As-Şāfī, Jord. | F4 | 50 |
| Aş-Şāfīyah, Sudan | J6 | 60 |
| Assai, Braz. | G3 | 79 |
| Assaikwatamo, stm., Mb., Can. | B18 | 104 |
| 'Assāl al-Ward, Syria | A6 | 50 |
| As-Sallūm, Egypt | B3 | 60 |
| As-Salt, Jord. | D5 | 50 |
| Assam, state, India | G15 | 44 |
| As-Samāwah, Iraq | F8 | 48 |
| As-Sarīḩ, Jord. | C5 | 50 |
| Assateague Island, i., U.S. | I11 | 108 |
| Assean Lake, l., Mb., Can. | B18 | 104 |
| Assekaifaf, Alg. | G15 | 62 |
| Asseneede, Bel. | F4 | 12 |
| As-Sidr, Sau. Ar. | C1 | 47 |
| Assiniboia, Sk., Can. | I9 | 104 |
| Assiniboine, stm., Can. | I16 | 104 |
| Assiniboine, Mount, mtn., Can. | G19 | 102 |
| Assiniboine Indian Reserve, Sk., Can. | H11 | 104 |
| Assinika, stm., Mb., Can. | F19 | 104 |
| Assis, Braz. | G3 | 79 |
| Assisi, Italy | F7 | 18 |
| Assomada, C.V. | m17 | 64a |
| As-Sudd, reg., Sudan | N6 | 60 |
| Aş-Şufayyah, Sudan | J8 | 60 |
| As-Sulaymānīyah, Iraq | D8 | 48 |
| As-Sulaymānīyah, Sau. Ar. | B5 | 47 |
| As-Sulaymī, Sau. Ar. | H6 | 48 |
| As-Sulayyil, Sau. Ar. | D4 | 47 |
| As-Sumayh, Sudan | M4 | 60 |
| Assumption, Il., U.S. | C7 | 114 |
| Assumption Island, i., Sey. | C9 | 58 |
| As-Suwaydā', Syria | C7 | 50 |
| As-Suways (Suez), Egypt | C7 | 60 |
| Astaffort, Fr. | H7 | 14 |
| Āstāneh, Iran | C10 | 48 |
| Āstāneh, Iran | E10 | 48 |
| Astara, Azer. | J7 | 26 |
| Āstārā, Iran | B10 | 48 |
| Asti, Italy | E3 | 18 |
| Astica, Arg. | F5 | 80 |
| Astipálaia, Grc. | M10 | 20 |
| Astipálaia, i., Grc. | M10 | 20 |
| Astorga, Braz. | G3 | 79 |
| Astorga, Spain | C5 | 16 |
| Astoria, Il., U.S. | B6 | 114 |
| Astoria, Or., U.S. | D2 | 122 |
| Astrachan', Russia | H7 | 26 |
| Astraščyki Haradok, Bela. | G10 | 22 |
| Astroņa, Bela. | F12 | 22 |
| Asuka, sci., Ant. | C3 | 73 |
| Asunción, Para. | C10 | 80 |
| Asunción, Bahía, b., Mex. | D2 | 90 |
| Asunción Mita, Guat. | C5 | 92 |
| Asunción Nochixtlán, Mex. | I11 | 90 |
| Asunga, Wādī, val., Afr. | K2 | 60 |
| Asveja, Bela. | E11 | 22 |
| Aswān, Egypt | E7 | 60 |
| Aswān High Dam see 'Ālī, As-Sadd al-, Egypt | D7 | 60 |
| Asyūṭ, Egypt | D6 | 60 |
| Aszód, Hung. | H19 | 10 |
| Atabapo, stm., S.A. | F9 | 84 |
| Atacama, prov., Chile | D3 | 80 |
| Atacama, Desierto de (Atacama Desert), des., Chile | A3 | 78 |
| Atacama, Puna de, plat., S.A. | C5 | 80 |
| Atacama, Salar de, pl., Chile | B4 | 80 |
| Ataco, Col. | F5 | 84 |
| Atacuari, stm., Peru | I7 | 84 |
| Atakakup Indian Reserve, Sk., Can. | E8 | 104 |
| Atakpamé, Togo | H10 | 64 |
| Atalándi, Grc. | K7 | 20 |
| Atalaya, Pan. | I14 | 92 |
| Atalaya, Peru | D5 | 82 |
| Atalaya, Cerro, mtn., Peru | E6 | 82 |
| Atami, Japan | L14 | 36 |
| Atār, Maur. | A3 | 64 |
| Atascadero, Ca., U.S. | I5 | 124 |
| Atascosa, stm., Tx., U.S. | K8 | 116 |
| Atasu, Kaz. | H12 | 26 |
| Atauro, Pulau, i., Indon. | G8 | 38 |
| Atbara ('Atbarah), stm., Afr. | I8 | 60 |
| 'Atbarah, Sudan | I8 | 60 |
| 'Atbarah (Atbara), stm., Afr. | E7 | 56 |
| Atbasar, Kaz. | G11 | 26 |
| Atchafalaya, stm., La., U.S. | L5 | 114 |
| Atchafalaya Bay, b., La., U.S. | M5 | 114 |
| Atchison, Ks., U.S. | L12 | 118 |
| Ateca, Spain | D10 | 16 |
| Atebubu, Ghana | H9 | 64 |
| Atelchu, stm., Braz. | B1 | 79 |
| Atenguillo, Mex. | G7 | 90 |
| Ath (Aat), Bel. | G4 | 12 |
| Athabasca, Ab., Can. | C21 | 102 |
| Athabasca, stm., Ab., Can. | E10 | 96 |
| Athabasca, Lake, l., Can. | E10 | 96 |
| Athalmer, B.C., Can. | G18 | 102 |
| Athapapuskow Lake, l., Mb., Can. | D13 | 104 |
| Athārān Hazārī, Pak. | E5 | 44 |
| Athena, Or., U.S. | E7 | 122 |
| Athens, Al., U.S. | H10 | 114 |
| Athens see Athínai, Grc. | L7 | 20 |
| Athens, Ga., U.S. | F3 | 112 |
| Athens, Il., U.S. | C7 | 114 |
| Athens, La., U.S. | J3 | 114 |
| Athens, Mi., U.S. | H10 | 110 |
| Athens, N.Y., U.S. | E13 | 108 |
| Athens, Oh., U.S. | H4 | 108 |
| Athens, On., Can. | C11 | 108 |
| Athens, Pa., U.S. | F10 | 108 |
| Athens, Tn., U.S. | D2 | 112 |
| Athens, Tx., U.S. | G11 | 116 |
| Athens, Wi., U.S. | E5 | 110 |
| Athens, W.V., U.S. | B5 | 112 |
| Atherton, Austl. | A6 | 70 |
| Athiémé, Benin | H10 | 64 |
| Athínai (Athens), Grc. | L7 | 20 |
| Athlone, Ire. | H6 | 8 |
| Athok, Myan. | F3 | 40 |
| Athol, Ma., U.S. | E14 | 108 |

| Name | Map Ref. | Page |
|---|---|---|
| Áthos, mtn., Grc. | I8 | 20 |
| Ath-Thamad, Egypt | C8 | 60 |
| Ati, Chad | F4 | 56 |
| Atico, Peru | G5 | 82 |
| Aticonipi, Lac, l., P.Q., Can. | A14 | 106 |
| Atigun Pass, Ak., U.S. | B20 | 100 |
| Atik Lake, l., Mb., Can. | C18 | 104 |
| Atikokan, On., Can. | B4 | 110 |
| Atikonak Lake, l., Nf., Can. | F20 | 96 |
| Atimari, stm., Braz. | C8 | 82 |
| Atiparaná, stm., Braz. | I9 | 84 |
| Atiquizaya, El Sal. | D5 | 92 |
| Atitlán, Lago de, l., Guat. | C3 | 92 |
| Atitlán, Volcán, vol., Guat. | C3 | 92 |
| Atka, Ak., U.S. | J7 | 100 |
| Atka, Russia | E22 | 28 |
| Atkarsk, Russia | G7 | 26 |
| Atkins, Ar., U.S. | G4 | 114 |
| Atkinson, Il., U.S. | I5 | 110 |
| Atkinson, N.C., U.S. | E8 | 112 |
| Atkinson, Ne., U.S. | I9 | 118 |
| Atkinson Lake, l., Mb., Can. | C20 | 104 |
| Atlanta, Ga., U.S. | F2 | 112 |
| Atlanta, Il., U.S. | B7 | 114 |
| Atlanta, Mi., U.S. | E11 | 110 |
| Atlanta, Ne., U.S. | C4 | 114 |
| Atlanta, Tx., U.S. | I2 | 114 |
| Atlantic, Ia., U.S. | J12 | 118 |
| Atlantic, N.C., U.S. | E10 | 112 |
| Atlantic Beach, Fl., U.S. | I5 | 112 |
| Atlantic City, N.J., U.S. | H12 | 108 |
| Atlantic-Indian Ridge | N5 | 126 |
| Atlántico, dept., Col. | B5 | 84 |
| Atlantic Ocean | I11 | 128 |
| Atlantic Peak, mtn., Wy., U.S. | H16 | 122 |
| Atlántida, Ur. | H11 | 80 |
| Atlántida, dept., Hond. | B7 | 92 |
| Atlas Mountains, mts., Afr. | D11 | 62 |
| Atlas Saharien, mts., Alg. | C11 | 62 |
| Atlas Tellien, mts., Alg. | B12 | 62 |
| Atlin, B.C., Can. | G28 | 100 |
| Atlin Lake, l., Can. | G28 | 100 |
| 'Atlit, Isr. | C3 | 50 |
| Atmore, Al., U.S. | K9 | 114 |
| Atna Peak, mtn., B.C., Can. | D6 | 102 |
| Atnarko, stm., B.C., Can. | E6 | 102 |
| Atocha, Bol. | I8 | 82 |
| Atoka, Ok., U.S. | E10 | 116 |
| Atotonilco, Mex. | E8 | 90 |
| Atoui, Khatt (Khaṭṭ Atoui), val., Afr. | J3 | 62 |
| Atoyac, stm., Mex. | H10 | 90 |
| Atoyac de Álvarez, Mex. | I9 | 90 |
| Atoyaquillo, stm., Mex. | I11 | 90 |
| Atrak (Atrek), l., Asia | C12 | 48 |
| Atrato, stm., Col. | D4 | 84 |
| Atrek (Atrak), stm., Asia | C12 | 48 |
| Atsutoko, Japan | G8 | 18 |
| At-Ta'if, Sau. Ar. | D2 | 47 |
| At-Tāj, Libya | E2 | 60 |
| At-Tall, Syria | A6 | 50 |
| Attalla, Al., U.S. | H10 | 114 |
| Attapu, Laos | G9 | 40 |
| Attawapiskat, On., Can. | F16 | 96 |
| Attawapiskat, stm., On., Can. | F16 | 96 |
| Attawapiskat Lake, l., On., Can. | F15 | 96 |
| Attica, In., U.S. | B9 | 114 |
| Attica, Ks., U.S. | N9 | 118 |
| Attica, N.Y., U.S. | E8 | 108 |
| Attica, Oh., U.S. | F4 | 108 |
| Attigny, Fr. | C11 | 14 |
| Attikí, prov., Grc. | K7 | 20 |
| Attikí, hist. reg., Grc. | K7 | 20 |
| Attir, Sudan | N6 | 60 |
| Attleboro, Ma., U.S. | F15 | 108 |
| Attock, Pak. | D5 | 44 |
| Attoyac, stm., Tx., U.S. | K2 | 114 |
| Attu Island, i., Ak., U.S. | j1 | 101a |
| At-Tunayb, Jord. | E5 | 50 |
| At-Ţūr, Egypt | C7 | 60 |
| Attūr, India | G5 | 46 |
| At-Tuwayshah, Sudan | K4 | 60 |
| At-Tuwayyah, Sau. Ar. | H6 | 48 |
| Atucatiquini, stm., Braz. | B7 | 82 |
| Atucha, Arg. | G9 | 80 |
| Atuel, stm., Arg. | G5 | 80 |
| Atuel, Bañados del, sw., Arg. | I5 | 80 |
| Atuntaqui, Ec. | G3 | 84 |
| Atwater, Ca., U.S. | G5 | 124 |
| Atwater, Mn., U.S. | F13 | 118 |
| Atwater, Sk., Can. | H12 | 104 |
| Atwood, Il., U.S. | C8 | 114 |
| Atwood, Ks., U.S. | L6 | 118 |
| Atwood, On., Can. | G8 | 114 |
| Atyrau, Kaz. | H8 | 26 |
| Auari, stm., Braz. | F11 | 84 |
| Aubagne, Fr. | I12 | 14 |
| Aube, dept., Fr. | D11 | 14 |
| Aube, stm., Fr. | D11 | 14 |
| Aubenas, Fr. | H11 | 14 |
| Aubigny-sur-Nère, Fr. | E9 | 14 |
| Aubin, Fr. | H9 | 14 |
| Aubrey Cliffs, clf, Az., U.S. | I3 | 120 |
| Aubry Lake, l., N.T., Can. | C31 | 100 |
| Auburn, Al., U.S. | J11 | 114 |
| Auburn, Ca., U.S. | F4 | 124 |
| Auburn, Il., U.S. | C7 | 114 |
| Auburn, In., U.S. | A11 | 114 |
| Auburn, Ky., U.S. | E10 | 114 |
| Auburn, Me., U.S. | E15 | 108 |
| Auburn, Mi., U.S. | C16 | 108 |
| Auburn, Ne., U.S. | K12 | 118 |
| Auburn, N.Y., U.S. | E10 | 108 |
| Auburn, Wa., U.S. | C3 | 122 |
| Auburn, stm., Austl. | H9 | 104 |
| Auburn Range, mts., Austl. | E9 | 70 |
| Aubusson, Fr. | G9 | 14 |
| Auca Mahuida, Arg. | I4 | 80 |
| Auca Mahuida, Cerro, mtn., Arg. | I4 | 80 |
| Aucará, Peru | F4 | 82 |
| Auce, Lat. | E5 | 22 |
| Auch, Fr. | I7 | 14 |
| Aucilla, stm., U.S. | I3 | 112 |
| Auckland, N.Z. | B5 | 72 |
| Auckland Islands, is., N.Z. | N20 | 126 |
| Aude, dept., Fr. | I9 | 14 |
| Aude, stm., Fr. | I10 | 14 |
| Audierne, Fr. | D2 | 14 |
| Audincourt, Fr. | E13 | 14 |
| Audubon, Ia., U.S. | J13 | 118 |
| Aue, Ger. | E12 | 10 |
| Augathella, Austl. | E7 | 70 |
| Auglaize, stm., Oh., U.S. | F2 | 108 |
| Au Gres, Mi., U.S. | F12 | 110 |
| Au Gres, stm., Mi., U.S. | F12 | 110 |
| Augsburg, Ger. | G10 | 10 |
| Augstgrafne, Lat. | D8 | 22 |
| Augusta, Ar., U.S. | G5 | 114 |
| Augusta, Austl. | F3 | 68 |
| Augusta, Ga., U.S. | F4 | 112 |
| Augusta, Il., U.S. | B6 | 114 |
| Augusta, Italy | L10 | 18 |
| Augusta, Ks., U.S. | N10 | 118 |
| Augusta, Ky., U.S. | I3 | 108 |
| Augusta, Me., U.S. | C17 | 108 |
| Augusta, Mt., U.S. | C13 | 122 |
| Augusta, Wi., U.S. | F4 | 110 |

| Name | Map Ref. | Page |
|---|---|---|
| Augustów, Pol. | B22 | 10 |
| Auilla, Ribeirão, stm., Braz. | B2 | 79 |
| Aulander, N.C., U.S. | C9 | 112 |
| Aulnay, Fr. | F6 | 14 |
| Aulneau Peninsula, pen., On., Can. | I20 | 104 |
| Ault, Co., U.S. | D12 | 120 |
| Ault, Fr. | B8 | 14 |
| Aumale, Fr. | C8 | 14 |
| Auna, Nig. | F12 | 64 |
| Auneau, Fr. | D8 | 14 |
| Auob, stm., Afr. | F5 | 66 |
| Aurangābād, India | C3 | 46 |
| Auray, Fr. | E4 | 14 |
| Aurelia, Ia., U.S. | I12 | 118 |
| Aurès, Massif de l', mts., Alg. | C14 | 62 |
| Aurich, Ger. | B7 | 10 |
| Auriflama, Braz. | F3 | 79 |
| Aurilândia, Braz. | D3 | 79 |
| Aurillac, Fr. | H9 | 14 |
| Aurora, Co., U.S. | E12 | 120 |
| Aurora, Il., U.S. | I7 | 110 |
| Aurora, In., U.S. | C12 | 114 |
| Aurora, Mn., U.S. | C3 | 110 |
| Aurora, Mo., U.S. | F3 | 114 |
| Aurora, N.C., U.S. | D10 | 112 |
| Aurora, Ne., U.S. | K9 | 118 |
| Aurora, N.Y., U.S. | E10 | 108 |
| Aurora, Oh., U.S. | F5 | 108 |
| Aurora, On., Can. | F16 | 110 |
| Aurora, Ut., U.S. | F5 | 120 |
| Aurora do Norte, Braz. | B5 | 79 |
| Aurukun, Austl. | B8 | 68 |
| Aus, Nmb. | F3 | 66 |
| Au Sable, stm., Mi., U.S. | F12 | 110 |
| Au Sable Forks, N.Y., U.S. | C13 | 108 |
| Auschwitz see Oświęcim, Pol. | E19 | 10 |
| Aust-Agder, co., Nor. | L10 | 6 |
| Austin, In., U.S. | D11 | 114 |
| Austin, Mn., U.S. | I16 | 104 |
| Austin, Mn., U.S. | G3 | 110 |
| Austin, Nv., U.S. | E8 | 124 |
| Austin, Pa., U.S. | F8 | 108 |
| Austin, Tx., U.S. | I9 | 116 |
| Austin Channel, strt., N.T., Can. | A12 | 96 |
| Austinville, Va., U.S. | C6 | 112 |
| Australes, Îles, is., Fr. Poly. | K24 | 126 |
| Australia, ctry., Oc. | D7 | 68 |
| Australia Mountain, mtn., Yk., Can. | E25 | 100 |
| Australian Capital Territory, ter., Austl. | G9 | 68 |
| Austria (Österreich), ctry., Eur. | F10 | 4 |
| Autazes, Braz. | I13 | 84 |
| Autlán de Navarro, Mex. | H7 | 90 |
| Autun, Fr. | F11 | 14 |
| Auvergne, hist. reg., Fr. | G9 | 14 |
| Auxerre, Fr. | E10 | 14 |
| Auxier, Ky., U.S. | B4 | 112 |
| Auxi-le-Château, Fr. | B9 | 14 |
| Auxonne, Fr. | E12 | 14 |
| Auxvasse, Mo., U.S. | C5 | 114 |
| Auyán Tepuy, mtn., Ven. | E11 | 84 |
| Auzances, Fr. | F9 | 14 |
| Auzangate, Nevado, mtn., Peru | E6 | 82 |
| Ava, Il., U.S. | E7 | 114 |
| Ava, Mo., U.S. | F4 | 114 |
| Avaí, Braz. | G4 | 79 |
| Avallon, Fr. | E10 | 14 |
| Avalon, Ca., U.S. | K7 | 124 |
| Avalon Peninsula, pen., Nf., Can. | E20 | 106 |
| Ávalos, Braz. | C6 | 90 |
| Avanos, Tur. | B3 | 48 |
| Avant, Ok., U.S. | C10 | 116 |
| Avaré, Braz. | G4 | 79 |
| Avegbadje, mth., Afr. | H10 | 64 |
| Aveiro, Braz. | E3 | 84 |
| Aveiro, Port. | E3 | 16 |
| Avelgem, Bel. | G3 | 12 |
| Avellaneda, Arg. | H9 | 80 |
| Avellaneda, Arg. | E8 | 80 |
| Avellino, Italy | I9 | 18 |
| Avenal, Ca., U.S. | H5 | 124 |
| Aversa, Italy | I9 | 18 |
| Avery, Id., U.S. | C10 | 122 |
| Avery, Tx., U.S. | I2 | 114 |
| Avery Island, i., La., U.S. | M5 | 114 |
| Aveyron, dept., Fr. | H9 | 14 |
| Avezzano, Italy | G8 | 18 |
| Aviemore, Scot., U.K. | D10 | 8 |
| Avigliano, Italy | I10 | 18 |
| Avignon, Fr. | I11 | 14 |
| Ávila, Spain | E7 | 16 |
| Ávila, prov., Spain | E6 | 16 |
| Avilés, Spain | B6 | 16 |
| Avis, Pa., U.S. | F9 | 108 |
| Avispa, Cerro, mtn., Ven. | G10 | 84 |
| Aviz, Port. | F4 | 16 |
| Avoca, Ia., U.S. | J12 | 118 |
| Avoca, N.Y., U.S. | E9 | 108 |
| Avola, B.C., Can. | F15 | 102 |
| Avola, Italy | M10 | 18 |
| Avon, Il., U.S. | J5 | 110 |
| Avon, Mn., U.S. | F14 | 118 |
| Avon, N.C., U.S. | D11 | 112 |
| Avon, N.Y., U.S. | E9 | 108 |
| Avon, S.D., U.S. | H9 | 118 |
| Avon, co., Eng., U.K. | J11 | 8 |
| Avon, stm., Eng., U.K. | I12 | 8 |
| Avon, stm., N.S., Can. | H9 | 106 |
| Avondale, Az., U.S. | K4 | 120 |
| Avondale, Co., U.S. | M3 | 118 |
| Avon Downs, Austl. | C2 | 70 |
| Avonlea, Sk., Can. | H9 | 104 |
| Avon Park, Fl., U.S. | L5 | 112 |
| Avonmore, Pa., U.S. | G7 | 108 |
| Avontuur, S. Afr. | I6 | 66 |
| Avranches, Fr. | D5 | 14 |
| A'waj, Nahr al-, stm., Syria | B6 | 50 |
| Awali, Bahr. | H11 | 48 |
| Awash, stm., Eth. | N10 | 60 |
| Awash, Eth. | G9 | 56 |
| Awaso, Ghana | H8 | 64 |
| Awbārī, Libya | C3 | 56 |
| Awe, Nig. | G14 | 64 |
| Awegyun, Myan. | H5 | 40 |
| Awjilah, Libya | C4 | 56 |
| Awled Djellal, Alg. | C13 | 62 |
| Awlef, Alg. | G11 | 62 |
| Aworo Kit, Sudan | L7 | 60 |

| Name | Map Ref. | Page |
|---|---|---|
| Ayamonte, Spain | H4 | 16 |
| Ayangba, Nig. | H13 | 64 |
| Ayapel, Col. | C5 | 84 |
| Ayarza, Laguna de, l., Guat. | C4 | 92 |
| Ayaviri, Braz. | F6 | 82 |
| Ayaviri, stm., Peru | F6 | 82 |
| Ayden, N.C., U.S. | D9 | 112 |
| Aydın, Tur. | L11 | 20 |
| Ayer, Ma., U.S. | E15 | 108 |
| Ayers Rock (Uluru), mtn., Austl. | E6 | 68 |
| Ayeyarwady (Irrawaddy), stm., Myan. | F3 | 40 |
| Ayía Paraskeví, Grc. | J10 | 20 |
| Ayion Óros, pen., Grc. | I8 | 20 |
| Ayios Kírikos, Grc. | L10 | 20 |
| Ayios Nikólaos, Grc. | N9 | 20 |
| Ayiou Órous, Kólpos, b., Grc. | I8 | 20 |
| Ayl, Jord. | H5 | 50 |
| Aylmer, P.Q., Can. | B11 | 108 |
| Aylmer, Mount, mtn., Ab., Can. | F19 | 102 |
| Aylmer Lake, l., N.T., Can. | D11 | 96 |
| Aylmer West, On., Can. | H15 | 110 |
| Ayisham, Sk., Can. | E11 | 104 |
| 'Ayn Dār, Sau. Ar. | B6 | 47 |
| Aynor, S.C., U.S. | F7 | 112 |
| 'Aynūnah, Sau. Ar. | G3 | 48 |
| Ayo, Peru | F5 | 82 |
| Ayo Ayo, Bol. | G7 | 82 |
| Ayod, Sudan | M6 | 60 |
| Ayon, Sudan | N5 | 60 |
| Aurukun, Nmb. | F3 | 66 |
| 'Ayoûn el 'Atroûs, Maur. | C5 | 64 |
| Ayr, Austl. | B8 | 68 |
| Ayr, On., Can. | G15 | 110 |
| Ayr, Scot., U.K. | F9 | 8 |
| 'Aytā al-Fakhkhār, Leb. | A5 | 50 |
| Ayu, Kepulauan, is., Indon. | F9 | 38 |
| Ayutla, Mex. | G7 | 90 |
| Ayutla de los Libres, Mex. | I10 | 90 |
| Ayvacık, Tur. | J10 | 20 |
| Ayvalık, Tur. | J10 | 20 |
| Azacualpa, Hond. | C8 | 92 |
| Azacualpa, Hond. | B6 | 92 |
| Azalea Park, Fl., U.S. | K5 | 112 |
| Azambuja, Port. | F3 | 16 |
| Āzamgarh, India | G10 | 44 |
| Azángaro, Peru | F6 | 82 |
| Azángaro, stm., Peru | E6 | 82 |
| Azaouagh, Vallée de l', val., Afr. | D11 | 64 |
| Azapa, Quebrada de, stm., Chile | H6 | 82 |
| Azar, val., Afr. | C12 | 64 |
| Azare, Nig. | F15 | 64 |
| Āžar Shahr, Iran | B9 | 48 |
| Azaranj, Bela. | I12 | 22 |
| Azazga, Alg. | B13 | 62 |
| Azeffāl, dunes, Afr. | J4 | 62 |
| Azeffoun, Alg. | B13 | 62 |
| Azemmour, Mor. | D6 | 62 |
| Azerbaijan (Azārbaycan), ctry., Asia | I7 | 26 |
| Azerbaijan see Azerbaijan, ctry., Asia | I7 | 26 |
| Azēry, Bela. | H7 | 22 |
| Azezo, Eth. | K9 | 60 |
| Azogues, Ec. | I3 | 84 |
| Azores see Açores, is., Port. | k19 | 62a |
| Azoum, Bahr (Wādī 'Azūm), val., Afr. | K2 | 60 |
| Azov, Russia | H5 | 26 |
| Azov, Sea of, Eur. | H5 | 26 |
| Azpeitia, Spain | B9 | 16 |
| Azraq, Al-Baḩr al- see Blue Nile, stm., Afr. | K8 | 60 |
| Azrou, Mor. | D8 | 62 |
| Aztec, N.M., U.S. | H9 | 120 |
| Aztec Peak, mtn., Az., U.S. | K6 | 120 |
| Azua, Dom. Rep. | E9 | 94 |
| Azuaga, Spain | G6 | 16 |
| Azuay, prov., Ec. | I3 | 80 |
| Azucena, Arg. | I9 | 80 |
| Azuero, Peninsula de, pen., Pan. | D2 | 84 |
| Azul, Arg. | H9 | 80 |
| Azul, Cerro, mtn., C.R. | H9 | 92 |
| Azul, Cerro, mtn., Hond. | C6 | 92 |
| Azur, Côte d', Fr. | I14 | 14 |
| Azurduy, Bol. | H9 | 82 |
| Azure Lake, l., B.C., Can. | E14 | 102 |
| Az-Zabadānī, Syria | A6 | 50 |
| Az-Zahrān (Dhahran), Sau. Ar. | A7 | 47 |
| Az-Zaqāzīq, Egypt | B6 | 60 |
| Az-Zarqā', Jord. | D6 | 50 |
| Az-Zāwiyah, Libya | B3 | 56 |
| Az-Zaydīyah, Yemen | G3 | 47 |
| Azzel Matti, Sebkha, pl., Alg. | H11 | 62 |
| Az-Zilfī, Sau. Ar. | H8 | 48 |
| Az-Zubayr, Iraq | F9 | 48 |

**B**

| Name | Map Ref. | Page |
|---|---|---|
| Ba, stm., Viet. | H10 | 40 |
| Baar, Switz. | D10 | 13 |
| Baarderveen, som. | H9 | 56 |
| Baarle-Hertog (Baerle-Duc), Bel. | F6 | 12 |
| Baarle-Nassau, Bel. | F6 | 12 |
| Baba, Ec. | H3 | 84 |
| Babadağ, Tur. | L12 | 20 |
| Babahoyo, Ec. | H3 | 84 |
| Babailiqiao, China | C7 | 34 |
| Babajevo, Russia | B18 | 22 |
| Babana, Nig. | F11 | 64 |
| Babanango, S. Afr. | G10 | 66 |
| Babanūsah, Sudan | L4 | 60 |
| Babar, Kepulauan, is., Indon. | G8 | 38 |
| Babar, Pulau, i., Indon. | G8 | 38 |
| Babati, Tan. | B7 | 58 |
| Babbitt, Mn., U.S. | C4 | 110 |
| Babbitt, Nv., U.S. | F7 | 124 |
| Babel, stm., Russia | A5 | 106 |
| Bab el Mandeb see Mandeb, Bab el, strt. | H3 | 47 |
| Babimost, Pol. | C15 | 10 |
| Babina Greda, Cro. | A6 | 70 |
| Babine, B.C., Can. | B8 | 102 |
| Babine, stm., B.C., Can. | B8 | 102 |
| Babine Lake, l., B.C., Can. | C9 | 102 |
| Babine Range, mts., B.C., Can. | B7 | 102 |
| Babino, Russia | B14 | 22 |
| Babino, Russia | B23 | 22 |
| Babo, Indon. | F9 | 38 |
| Bābol, Iran | C12 | 48 |
| Bābol Sar, Iran | C12 | 48 |
| Baboquivari Peak, mtn., Az., U.S. | M5 | 120 |
| Babrujsk, Bela. | H12 | 22 |
| Babušnica, Russia | G13 | 28 |
| Babuyan Islands, is., Phil. | B7 | 38 |
| Babynino, Russia | G18 | 22 |
| Bacabal, Braz. | D10 | 76 |
| Bacadéhuachi, Mex. | C5 | 90 |
| Bacan, Pulau, i., Indon. | F8 | 38 |

| Name | Map Ref. | Page |
|---|---|---|
| Bacău, Rom. | C10 | 20 |
| Bacău, co., Rom. | C10 | 20 |
| Baccalieu Island, i., Nf., Can. | D21 | 106 |
| Bac Can, Viet. | C8 | 40 |
| Baccarat, Fr. | D13 | 14 |
| Bacerac, Mex. | B5 | 90 |
| Bac Giang, Viet. | D9 | 40 |
| Bachaquero, Ven. | C7 | 84 |
| Bacharden, Turk. | J9 | 26 |
| Bachi, China | K4 | 34 |
| Bachiniva, Mex. | C6 | 90 |
| Bachmutovo, Russia | E17 | 22 |
| Bachu, China | D2 | 30 |
| Back, stm., N.T., Can. | N8 | 60 |
| Backbone Ranges, mts., N.T., Can. | C13 | 96 |
| Bačka Palanka, Yugo. | D3 | 20 |
| Bačka Topola, Yugo. | D3 | 20 |
| Backbone Ranges, mts., N.T., Can. | E30 | 100 |
| Backnang, Ger. | G9 | 10 |
| Backstairs Passage, strt., Austl. | J2 | 70 |
| Bac Lieu, Viet. | J8 | 40 |
| Bac Ninh, Viet. | D9 | 40 |
| Bacoachi, Mex. | B5 | 90 |
| Bacolod, Phil. | C7 | 38 |
| Baconton, Ga., U.S. | H2 | 112 |
| Bacoor, Phil. | n19 | 39b |
| Bács-Kiskun, co., Hung. | I19 | 10 |
| Bácum, Mex. | D4 | 90 |
| Bad, stm., Mi., U.S. | G11 | 110 |
| Bad, stm., S.D., U.S. | G6 | 118 |
| Bad, stm., Wi., U.S. | D5 | 110 |
| Badagara, India | G3 | 46 |
| Badajia, China | B9 | 34 |
| Badajós, stm., Braz. | I11 | 84 |
| Badajós, Lago, l., Braz. | I11 | 84 |
| Badajoz, Spain | G5 | 16 |
| Badalona, Spain | D14 | 16 |
| Bādāmi, India | D3 | 46 |
| Badanah, Sau. Ar. | F8 | 48 |
| Badeohao, China | B9 | 32 |
| Badeohe, China | C10 | 32 |
| Bad Aussee, Aus. | H13 | 10 |
| Bad Axe, Mi., U.S. | G12 | 110 |
| Bad Bevensen, Ger. | B10 | 10 |
| Baddeck, N.S., Can. | F13 | 106 |
| Bad Doberan, Ger. | A11 | 10 |
| Bad Dürkheim, Ger. | F8 | 10 |
| Bad Dürrenberg, Ger. | D12 | 10 |
| Bad Ems, Ger. | E7 | 10 |
| Baden, Erit. | I9 | 60 |
| Baden, Switz. | D9 | 13 |
| Baden, Aus. | G8 | 10 |
| Baden-Baden, Ger. | G8 | 10 |
| Badenweiler, Ger. | H7 | 10 |
| Baden-Württemberg, state, Ger. | G8 | 10 |
| Badgastein, Aus. | H13 | 10 |
| Badger, Mn., U.S. | C11 | 118 |
| Badger, Nf., Can. | D17 | 106 |
| Bad Hall, Aus. | G14 | 10 |
| Bad Harzburg, Ger. | D10 | 10 |
| Bad Hersfeld, Ger. | E9 | 10 |
| Bad Homburg [vor der Höhe], Ger. | E8 | 10 |
| Baciraguato, Mex. | E6 | 90 |
| Bad Kissingen, Ger. | E10 | 10 |
| Bad Kreuznach, Ger. | F7 | 10 |
| Badlands, hills, S.D., U.S. | H5 | 118 |
| Badlands, hills, N.D., U.S. | E4 | 118 |
| Badlands National Park, S.D., U.S. | H5 | 118 |
| Bad Langensalza, Ger. | D10 | 10 |
| Bad Lauterberg, Ger. | D10 | 10 |
| Bad Leonfelden, Aus. | F9 | 10 |
| Bad Mergentheim, Ger. | F9 | 10 |
| Bad Muskau, Ger. | D14 | 10 |
| Bad Nauheim, Ger. | E8 | 10 |
| Bad Neustadt an der Saale, Ger. | E10 | 10 |
| Bad Oeynhausen, Ger. | C8 | 10 |
| Bad Oldesloe, Ger. | B10 | 10 |
| Badou, China | G5 | 32 |
| Badou, Togo | H10 | 64 |
| Badoumbé, Mali | E4 | 64 |
| Bad Pyrmont, Ger. | D9 | 10 |
| Bad Ragaz, Switz. | D12 | 13 |
| Bad Reichenhall, Ger. | H12 | 10 |
| Bad Hunayn, Sau. Ar. | C1 | 47 |
| Bad Salzuflen, Ger. | C8 | 10 |
| Bad Salzungen, Ger. | E10 | 10 |
| Bad Sankt Leonhard im Lavanttal, Aus. | I14 | 10 |
| Bad Schwalbach, Ger. | E8 | 10 |
| Bad Schwartau, Ger. | B10 | 10 |
| Bad Segeberg, Ger. | B10 | 10 |
| Bad Tölz, Ger. | H11 | 10 |
| Badu, China | I8 | 34 |
| Badulla, Sri L. | I6 | 46 |
| Badupi, Myan. | D2 | 40 |
| Bad Völslau, Aus. | H16 | 10 |
| Bad Waldsee, Ger. | H9 | 10 |
| Bad Wildungen, Ger. | D9 | 10 |
| Baediem, Maur. | D4 | 64 |
| Baena, Spain | H7 | 16 |
| Baependi, Braz. | F6 | 79 |
| Baeza, Ec. | H4 | 84 |
| Baezaeko, stm., B.C., Can. | E10 | 102 |
| Bafatá, Gui.-B. | E2 | 64 |
| Baffin Bay, b., N.A. | B13 | 86 |
| Baffin Bay, b., Tx., U.S. | L9 | 116 |
| Baffin Island, i., N.T., Can. | C18 | 96 |
| Bafing, stm., Afr. | F4 | 54 |
| Bafoulabé, Mali | E4 | 64 |
| Bafoussam, Cam. | G9 | 54 |
| Bāfq, Iran | F13 | 48 |
| Bafra, Tur. | G14 | 4 |
| Bafwasende, D.R.C. | A5 | 58 |
| Bagaces, C.R. | G9 | 92 |
| Bagagem, stm., Braz. | C4 | 79 |
| Bāgalkot, India | D3 | 46 |
| Baganliapiapi, Indon. | M6 | 40 |
| Baganuur, Tur. | L11 | 20 |
| Bagawi, Sudan | K8 | 60 |
| Bagdad, Az., U.S. | I3 | 120 |
| Bagdad, Fl., U.S. | L9 | 114 |
| Bagdarin, Russia | G14 | 28 |
| Bagé, Braz. | F11 | 80 |
| Baggs, Wy., U.S. | I18 | 122 |
| Baghdād, Iraq | E8 | 48 |
| Bagheria, Italy | K8 | 18 |
| Baghlān, Afg. | B9 | 44 |
| Bagley, Mn., U.S. | D12 | 118 |
| Bagnères-de-Bigorre, Fr. | I7 | 14 |
| Bagnères-de-Luchon, Fr. | J7 | 14 |
| Bagnols-sur-Cèze, Fr. | H11 | 14 |
| Bago (Pegu), Myan. | F4 | 40 |
| Bagotville, Base des Forces canadiennes, mil., P.Q., Can. | D3 | 106 |
| Bagrationovsk, Russia | G3 | 22 |
| Baguio, Phil. | m19 | 39b |
| Bahamas, ctry., N.A. | D9 | 88 |
| Bahār, Iran | D10 | 48 |
| Baharampur, India | H13 | 44 |
| Bahāwalnagar, Pak. | F5 | 44 |
| Bahāwalpur, Pak. | F5 | 44 |

| Name | Ref. | Page |
|---|---|---|
| Bahechuan, China | C12 | 32 |
| Bahia, state, Braz. | B7 | 79 |
| Bahía, Islas de la, is., Hond. | A8 | 92 |
| Bahía Azul, Pan. | H13 | 92 |
| Bahía Blanca, Arg. | J7 | 80 |
| Bahía Kino, Mex. | C4 | 90 |
| Bahir Dar, Eth. | L9 | 60 |
| Bahrah, Sau. Ar. | D1 | 47 |
| Bahraich, India | G9 | 44 |
| Bahrain (Al-Bahrayn), ctry., Asia | D5 | 42 |
| Bahrayn, Khalīj al-, b., Asia | B7 | 47 |
| Bāhū Kalāt, Iran | I16 | 48 |
| Bahuśbela, Bela. | G13 | 22 |
| Baï, Mali | E8 | 64 |
| Baia Mare, Rom. | B7 | 20 |
| Baía Rica, stm., Braz. | E10 | 82 |
| Baia Sprie, Rom. | B7 | 20 |
| Baicao, China | B4 | 32 |
| Baicheng, China | B11 | 30 |
| Baicheng, China | C3 | 30 |
| Baie-Comeau, P.Q., Can. | C5 | 106 |
| Baie-Comeau-Hauterive, Réserve, P.Q., Can. | B5 | 106 |
| Baie-des-Ha] Ha], P.Q., Can. | B15 | 106 |
| Baie-des-Moutons, P.Q., Can. | B14 | 106 |
| Baie-du-Renard, P.Q., Can. | C12 | 106 |
| Baie-Johan-Beetz, P.Q., Can. | B11 | 106 |
| Baie-Sainte-Claire, P.Q., Can. | C9 | 106 |
| Baie-Saint-Paul, P.Q., Can. | E3 | 106 |
| Baie-Trinité, P.Q., Can. | C6 | 106 |
| Baie Verte, Nf., Can. | C17 | 106 |
| Baigong, China | K5 | 34 |
| Baihebu, China | C4 | 32 |
| Baijian, China | D3 | 32 |
| Baiju, China | B9 | 34 |
| Baikal, Lake see Bajkal, ozero, l., Russia | G13 | 28 |
| Bailadores, Ven. | C7 | 84 |
| Baile, China | D2 | 32 |
| Baile Átha Cliath see Dublin, Ire. | H7 | 8 |
| Bǎile Govora, Rom. | D8 | 20 |
| Bailén, Spain | G8 | 16 |
| Bǎileşti, Rom. | E7 | 20 |
| Bailey, N.C., U.S. | D8 | 112 |
| Bailin, China | H9 | 34 |
| Bailique, Ilha, i., Braz. | C9 | 76 |
| Baillie, stm., N.T., Can. | D11 | 96 |
| Baile Islands, is., N.T., Can. | B7 | 96 |
| Bailong, stm., China | E7 | 30 |
| Bailundo, Ang. | D3 | 58 |
| Baimaguan, China | C4 | 32 |
| Baimashi, China | F7 | 34 |
| Baimiaozi, China | C8 | 32 |
| Bainbridge, Ga., U.S. | I2 | 112 |
| Bainbridge, N.Y., U.S. | E11 | 108 |
| Bainbridge, Oh., U.S. | H3 | 108 |
| Bain-de-Bretagne, Fr. | E5 | 14 |
| Bainiqiao, China | F3 | 34 |
| Bains-les-Bains, Fr. | D13 | 14 |
| Bainville, Mt., U.S. | C3 | 118 |
| Baipu, China | C9 | 34 |
| Baiquan, China | E11 | 34 |
| Baird, Tx., U.S. | G7 | 116 |
| Baird, Mount, mtn., Id., U.S. | G14 | 122 |
| Bairin Zuoqi, China | C10 | 30 |
| Bairnsdale, Austl. | K7 | 70 |
| Bairoil, Wy., U.S. | B9 | 120 |
| Bairuopu, China | G1 | 34 |
| Baisha, China | E10 | 40 |
| Baishanji, China | B5 | 34 |
| Baishatan, China | G9 | 32 |
| Baishuifan, China | E4 | 34 |
| Baishuijing, China | E8 | 30 |
| Baisogala, Lith. | F6 | 22 |
| Baitazi, China | A8 | 32 |
| Baitu, China | D8 | 34 |
| Baixa Grande, Braz. | A8 | 79 |
| Baixiang, China | F2 | 32 |
| Baiyin, China | D7 | 30 |
| Baizhongqu, China | B3 | 34 |
| Baja, Hung. | I18 | 10 |
| Baja, Punta c., Mex. | C2 | 90 |
| Baja California, state, Mex. | C2 | 90 |
| Baja California, pen., Mex. | C3 | 90 |
| Baja California Sur, state, Mex. | E4 | 90 |
| Bajada del Agrio, Arg. | J3 | 80 |
| Bajanaul, Kaz. | G13 | 26 |
| Bajanchongor, Mong. | B7 | 30 |
| Bajánsenye, Hung. | I16 | 10 |
| Baja Verapaz, dept., Guat. | B4 | 92 |
| Bajdarackaja guba, b., Russia | D11 | 26 |
| Bajestān, Iran | D15 | 48 |
| Bajíazi, China | B11 | 32 |
| Bajimba, Mount, mtn., Austl. | G10 | 70 |
| Bajkal, ozero (Lake Baikal), l., Russia | G13 | 28 |
| Bajkal'skoje, Russia | F13 | 28 |
| Bajmak, Russia | G9 | 26 |
| Bajo Baudó, Col. | E4 | 84 |
| Bajo Boquete, Pan. | C1 | 84 |
| Bajos de Haina, Dom. Rep. | E9 | 94 |
| Bajram-Ali, Turk. | J10 | 26 |
| Bakebe, Cam. | I14 | 64 |
| Bakel, Sen. | D3 | 64 |
| Baker, Ca., U.S. | I9 | 124 |
| Baker, La., U.S. | L10 | 114 |
| Baker, La., U.S. | L5 | 114 |
| Baker, Mt., U.S. | E3 | 118 |
| Baker, Or., U.S. | F8 | 122 |
| Baker, Mount, mtn., Wa., U.S. | B4 | 122 |
| Baker Butte, mtn., Az., U.S. | J5 | 120 |
| Baker Creek, stm., B.C., Can. | E12 | 102 |
| Baker Island, i., Oc. | H22 | 126 |
| Baker Lake, N.T., Can. | D13 | 96 |
| Baker Lake, l., N.T., Can. | D13 | 96 |
| Bakersfield, Ca., U.S. | I6 | 124 |
| Bakersville, N.C., U.S. | C4 | 112 |
| Bākhtarān (Kermānshāh), Iran | D9 | 48 |
| Bakhtegān, Daryācheh-ye, l., Iran | G13 | 48 |
| Bakı (Baku), Azer. | I7 | 26 |
| Bakkagerdi, Ice. | B7 | 6a |
| Baklanka, Russia | C23 | 22 |
| Bako, Eth. | M9 | 60 |
| Bakony, mts., Hung. | H17 | 10 |
| Baku see Bakı, Azer. | I7 | 26 |
| Bakun, China | D9 | 44 |
| Bala, Sen. | D3 | 64 |
| Balā, Tur. | B2 | 48 |
| Balabac Strait, strt., Asia | D6 | 38 |
| Ba'labakk, Leb. | D4 | 48 |
| Balabanovo, Russia | F19 | 22 |
| Balachna, Russia | E26 | 22 |
| Baladī, Iraq | B8 | 48 |
| Balaghāt, India | J9 | 44 |
| Balaguer, Spain | D12 | 16 |
| Balakirevo, Russia | E21 | 22 |
| Balaklava, Austl. | J3 | 70 |
| Balakovo, Russia | G7 | 26 |
| Balallan, Scot., U.K. | C7 | 8 |
| Bālā Morghāb, Afg. | D17 | 48 |
| Balāngīr, India | B7 | 46 |
| Balašicha, Russia | F20 | 22 |
| Balašov, Russia | G6 | 26 |
| Balassagyarmat, Hung. | G19 | 10 |
| Balāt, Egypt | E5 | 60 |
| Balatina, Mol. | B11 | 20 |
| Balaton, Mn., U.S. | G12 | 118 |
| Balaton, l., Hung. | I17 | 10 |
| Balayan, Phil. | o19 | 39b |
| Balbieriškis, Lith. | G6 | 22 |
| Balbirini, Austl. | C7 | 68 |
| Balboa, Pan. | I15 | 92 |
| Balbriggan, Ire. | H7 | 8 |
| Balcanoona, Austl. | H3 | 70 |
| Balcarce, Arg. | I9 | 80 |
| Balcarres, Sk., Can. | H11 | 104 |
| Balchaš, Kaz. | H12 | 26 |
| Balchaš, ozero (Lake Balkhash) l., Kaz. | H12 | 26 |
| Balcones Escarpment, clf, Tx., U.S. | J6 | 116 |
| Balde, Arg. | G5 | 80 |
| Baldim, Braz. | E7 | 79 |
| Bald Knob, Ar., U.S. | G5 | 114 |
| Baldone, Lat. | E7 | 22 |
| Baldur, Mb., Can. | I15 | 104 |
| Baldwin, Fl., U.S. | I5 | 112 |
| Baldwin, La., U.S. | M5 | 114 |
| Baldwin, Mi., U.S. | G10 | 110 |
| Baldwin, Wi., U.S. | F3 | 110 |
| Baldwin City, Ks., U.S. | M12 | 118 |
| Baldwin Peninsula, pen., Ak., U.S. | C13 | 100 |
| Baldwinsville, N.Y., U.S. | D10 | 108 |
| Baldwinville, Ma., U.S. | E14 | 108 |
| Baldwyn, Ms., U.S. | H8 | 114 |
| Baldy Mountain, mtn., B.C., Can. | F14 | 102 |
| Baldy Mountain, mtn., Mb., Can. | G14 | 104 |
| Baldy Mountain, mtn., Mt., U.S. | B16 | 122 |
| Baldy Mountain, mtn., N.M., U.S. | H11 | 120 |
| Baldy Peak, mtn., Az., U.S. | K7 | 120 |
| Balearic Islands see Balears, Illes, is., Spain | F15 | 16 |
| Balears, state, Spain | F15 | 16 |
| Balears, Illes (Balearic Islands), is., Spain | F15 | 16 |
| Baleia, Ponta da, c., Braz. | D9 | 79 |
| Baleine, Grande rivière de la, stm., P.Q., Can. | F18 | 96 |
| Baleine, Petite rivière de la, stm., P.Q., Can. | E18 | 96 |
| Baleine, Rivière à la, stm., P.Q., Can. | E19 | 96 |
| Balej, Russia | G15 | 28 |
| Baler, Phil. | n19 | 39b |
| Baleshwar, India | J12 | 44 |
| Baléyara, Niger | E11 | 64 |
| Balfate, Mol. | B8 | 92 |
| Balfes Creek, Austl. | C6 | 70 |
| Balfour, N.C., U.S. | D4 | 112 |
| Balhan, China | B6 | 32 |
| Bali, Laut (Bali Sea), Indon. | G6 | 38 |
| Bali, Selat, strt., Indon. | G5 | 38 |
| Balıkesir, Tur. | J11 | 20 |
| Balıkpapan, Indon. | F6 | 38 |
| Balimo, Pap. N. Gui. | G11 | 38 |
| Balingen, Ger. | G8 | 10 |
| Balintang Channel, strt., Phil. | B7 | 38 |
| Baliza, Braz. | D2 | 79 |
| Balkan Mountains see Stara Planina, mts., Eur. | G8 | 20 |
| Balkan Peninsula, pen., Eur. | D9 | 52 |
| Balkbrug, Neth. | C9 | 12 |
| Balkh, Afg. | B2 | 44 |
| Balkhash, Lake see Balchaš, ozero, l., Kaz. | H12 | 26 |
| Ball, La., U.S. | K4 | 114 |
| Ballachulish, Scot., U.K. | E8 | 8 |
| Ballangen, Nor. | G15 | 6 |
| Ballantine, Mt., U.S. | E17 | 122 |
| Ballarat, Austl. | K5 | 70 |
| Ballé, Mali | D5 | 64 |
| Ballenas, Bahía de, b., Mex. | D3 | 90 |
| Balleny Islands, is., Ant. | B8 | 73 |
| Balleroy, Fr. | C6 | 14 |
| Ballesteros, Arg. | G7 | 80 |
| Balleza, Mex. | D6 | 90 |
| Balleza, stm., Mex. | D6 | 90 |
| Ball Ground, Ga., U.S. | E2 | 112 |
| Ballia, India | H11 | 44 |
| Ballina, Austl. | G10 | 70 |
| Ballina, Ire. | G4 | 8 |
| Ballinasloe, Ire. | H5 | 8 |
| Ballinger, Tx., U.S. | H7 | 116 |
| Ballon, Fr. | M14 | 8 |
| Balls Pyramid, i., Austl. | F11 | 68 |
| Ballston Spa, N.Y., U.S. | D13 | 108 |
| Ballville, Oh., U.S. | F3 | 108 |
| Balmaceda, Chile | E4 | 84 |
| Balmertown, On., Can. | G21 | 104 |
| Balmorhea, Tx., U.S. | I3 | 116 |
| Balnearia, Arg. | F7 | 80 |
| Balonne, stm., Austl. | F8 | 70 |
| Bālotra, India | H5 | 44 |
| Balovale, Zam. | D4 | 58 |
| Baložži, Lat. | E7 | 22 |
| Balrāmpur, India | G10 | 44 |
| Balranald, Austl. | J5 | 70 |
| Balsam Lake, Wi., U.S. | E3 | 110 |
| Bálsamo, Braz. | F2 | 79 |
| Balsas, Braz. | E9 | 76 |
| Balsas, stm., Mex. | H8 | 90 |
| Balsas, stm., Mex. | I10 | 90 |
| Balsas, Rio das, stm., Braz. | E9 | 76 |
| Balsas Sur, Mex. | I10 | 90 |
| Bal'šavik, Bela. | I13 | 22 |
| Bålsta, Swe. | D8 | 13 |
| Balta, Ukr. | H3 | 26 |
| Baltasar Brum, Ur. | F10 | 80 |
| Bălţi, Mol. | B11 | 20 |
| Baltic Sea, Eur. | M16 | 6 |
| Baltijsk, Russia | G2 | 22 |
| Baltijskaja kosa, spit, Eur. | A19 | 10 |
| Baltīm, Egypt | B6 | 60 |
| Baltimore, Ire. | J4 | 8 |
| Baltimore, Md., U.S. | H10 | 108 |
| Baltimore, Oh., U.S. | H4 | 108 |
| Baltimore, S. Afr. | D9 | 66 |
| Baluarte, stm., Mex. | E6 | 90 |
| Balvi, Lat. | D10 | 22 |
| Balya, Tur. | J11 | 20 |
| Balykši, Kaz. | H8 | 26 |
| Bamberg, Ger. | F10 | 10 |
| Bamberg, S.C., U.S. | F5 | 112 |
| Bambesi, Eth. | M8 | 60 |
| Bamberzi, Zimb. | H6 | 66 |
| Bambuí, Braz. | F6 | 79 |
| Bamenda, Cam. | I14 | 64 |
| Bamfield, B.C., Can. | I9 | 102 |
| Bami, Turk. | B14 | 48 |
| Bamingui, stm., C.A.R. | G4 | 56 |
| Bampūr, Iran | H16 | 48 |
| Bamumo, China | D15 | 44 |
| Ba Na, Viet. | G9 | 40 |
| Banaba, i., Kir. | I20 | 126 |
| Banalia, D.R.C. | A5 | 58 |
| Banana, D.R.C. | C2 | 58 |
| Baode, China | D3 | 32 |
| Banana River, b., Fl., U.S. | K6 | 112 |
| Banarli, Tur. | H11 | 20 |
| Bands, Ra's c., Egypt | F8 | 60 |
| Banat, hist. reg., Eur. | D4 | 20 |
| Banbuji, China | B5 | 34 |
| Banco, Punta c., C.R. | I11 | 92 |
| Bancroft, Id., U.S. | H14 | 122 |
| Bancroft, Ne., U.S. | I11 | 118 |
| Bancroft, On., Can. | E18 | 110 |
| Banda, India | H9 | 44 |
| Banda, Kepulauan, is., Indon. | F8 | 38 |
| Banda, Laut (Banda Sea), Indon. | G8 | 38 |
| Banda Aceh, Indon. | L3 | 40 |
| Bānda Dāūd Shāh, Pak. | D4 | 44 |
| Banda del Río Salí, Arg. | D6 | 80 |
| Bandama, stm., C. Iv. | H7 | 64 |
| Bandama Blanc, stm., C. Iv. | G7 | 64 |
| Bandama Rouge, stm., C. Iv. | G6 | 64 |
| Bandar see Machilipatnam, India | D6 | 46 |
| Bandar Beheshtī, Iran | I16 | 48 |
| Bandar-e 'Abbās, Iran | H14 | 48 |
| Bandar-e Anzalī (Bandar-e Pahlavī), Iran | C10 | 48 |
| Bandar-e Būshehr, Iran | G11 | 48 |
| Bandar-e Deylam, Iran | F11 | 48 |
| Bandar-e Khomeynī (Bandar-e Shāhpūr), Iran | F10 | 48 |
| Bandar-e Māh Shahr, Iran | F10 | 48 |
| Bandar-e Rīg, Iran | G11 | 48 |
| Bandar-e Torkeman, Iran | C13 | 48 |
| Banded Peak, mtn., Co., U.S. | G10 | 120 |
| Bandeira, Pico da, mtn., Braz. | F8 | 79 |
| Bandeirantes, Braz. | B3 | 79 |
| Bandeirantes, Braz. | E1 | 79 |
| Bandera, Arg. | E7 | 80 |
| Bandera, Tx., U.S. | J7 | 116 |
| Bandera, Alto, mtn., Dom. Rep. | E9 | 94 |
| Banderas, Bahía de, b., Mex. | G7 | 90 |
| Bandiagara, Mali | D8 | 64 |
| Bandiantaolehai, China | C7 | 30 |
| Bandırma, Tur. | I11 | 20 |
| Bandon, Ire. | J5 | 8 |
| Bandon, Or., U.S. | G1 | 122 |
| Ban Don, Ao, b., Thai. | J5 | 40 |
| Bandula, Moz. | B11 | 66 |
| Bandundu, D.R.C. | B3 | 58 |
| Bandung, Indon. | j13 | 39a |
| Băneh, Iran | D8 | 48 |
| Banes, Cuba | D7 | 94 |
| Banff, Ab., Can. | F19 | 102 |
| Banff, Scot., U.K. | D11 | 8 |
| Banff National Park, Ab., Can. | F18 | 102 |
| Banfora, Burkina | F7 | 64 |
| Banga, D.R.C. | C4 | 58 |
| Bangaon, India | I13 | 44 |
| Banggai, Indon. | F7 | 38 |
| Banggai, Kepulauan, is., Indon. | F7 | 38 |
| Banghāzī, Libya | B5 | 56 |
| Bangil, Indon. | j16 | 39a |
| Bangjang, Sudan | L7 | 60 |
| Bangjun, China | D5 | 32 |
| Bangka, Pulau, i., Indon. | F4 | 38 |
| Bangkalan, Indon. | j16 | 39a |
| Bangkok see Krung Thep, Thai. | H6 | 40 |
| Bangladesh, ctry., Asia | E13 | 42 |
| Bang Mun Nak, Thai. | H6 | 40 |
| Bangolo, C. Iv. | H6 | 64 |
| Bangor, Me., U.S. | C18 | 108 |
| Bangor, Mi., U.S. | H9 | 110 |
| Bangor, N. Ire., U.K. | G8 | 8 |
| Bangor, Pa., U.S. | G11 | 108 |
| Bangor, Wales, U.K. | H9 | 8 |
| Bang Saphan, Thai. | I5 | 40 |
| Bangshi, China | C10 | 32 |
| Bangued, Phil. | m19 | 39b |
| Bangui, C.A.R. | H4 | 56 |
| Ban Hin Heup, Laos | E7 | 40 |
| Bangweulu, Lake, l., Zam. | D5 | 58 |
| Ban Houayxay, Laos | D6 | 40 |
| Bani, Burkina | E8 | 64 |
| Bani, Dom. Rep. | E9 | 94 |
| Bani, stm., Mali | D7 | 64 |
| Baniachang, Bngl. | H14 | 44 |
| Banikoara, Benin | F11 | 64 |
| Banī Mazār, Egypt | C6 | 60 |
| Banī Suwayf, Egypt | C6 | 60 |
| Banī Walīd, Libya | B4 | 56 |
| Bāniyās, Golan | B5 | 50 |
| Banja Luka, Bos. | E12 | 18 |
| Banjar, Indon. | j13 | 39a |
| Banjarmasin, Indon. | F5 | 38 |
| Banjul (Bathurst), Gam. | E1 | 64 |
| Bankas, Mali | D8 | 64 |
| Bankilaré, Niger | D8 | 64 |
| Banks, Al., U.S. | K11 | 114 |
| Banks Island, i., B.C., Can. | D4 | 102 |
| Banks Island, i., N.T., Can. | B8 | 96 |
| Banks Lake, res., Wa., U.S. | C6 | 122 |
| Banks Peninsula, pen., N.Z. | K4 | 72 |
| Banks Strait, strt., Austl. | M8 | 70 |
| Bankston, S. Afr. | D9 | 66 |
| Ban Mit, Laos | E6 | 40 |
| Bann, stm., N. Ire., U.K. | G7 | 8 |
| Ban Nahin, Laos | E8 | 40 |
| Ban Namnga, Laos | D7 | 40 |
| Ban Ngam, Laos | A5 | 40 |
| Banning, Ca., U.S. | K9 | 124 |
| Bannock Peak, mtn., Id., U.S. | H13 | 122 |
| Bannu, Pak. | D4 | 44 |
| Banon, Fr. | H12 | 14 |
| Baños, Ec. | H3 | 84 |
| Baños, Peru | B2 | 82 |
| Baños de Cerrato, Spain | D7 | 16 |
| Banpo, China | H4 | 32 |
| Banpu, China | E9 | 34 |
| Banqiao, China | E9 | 34 |
| Banqiaoji, China | C5 | 34 |
| Banquan, China | H6 | 32 |
| Banshi, China | C8 | 40 |
| Ban Songkhon, Laos | F8 | 40 |
| Bānswāra, India | I6 | 44 |
| Ban Thanoun, Laos | E6 | 40 |
| Bantry, Ire. | J4 | 8 |
| Ban Xènkhalôk, Laos | E6 | 40 |
| Banyak, Kepulauan, is., Indon. | M4 | 40 |
| Banyoles, Spain | C14 | 16 |
| Banzare Coast, Ant. | B7 | 73 |
| Banzi, China | K6 | 34 |
| Baode, China | D3 | 32 |
| Baoding, China | E3 | 32 |
| Baofeng, China | B2 | 34 |
| Bao Ha, Viet. | C8 | 40 |
| Baohekou, China | C6 | 32 |
| Baoji, China | E8 | 30 |
| Bao Lac, Viet. | I9 | 40 |
| Baonian, China | D8 | 34 |
| Baoqing, China | G7 | 32 |
| Baoshan, China | D10 | 34 |
| Baoshan, China | B5 | 40 |
| Baoting, China | H8 | 30 |
| Baowei, China | C9 | 40 |
| Baoxinji, China | C4 | 34 |
| Baoying, China | B8 | 34 |
| Bāpatla, India | E6 | 46 |
| Bapaume, Fr. | B9 | 14 |
| Bapchule, Az., U.S. | K5 | 120 |
| Bāqa el Gharbīya, Isr. | D4 | 50 |
| Baqên, China | E16 | 44 |
| B'aqlīn, Leb. | A5 | 50 |
| Ba'qūbah, Iraq | E8 | 48 |
| Baquedano, Chile | B4 | 80 |
| Bar, Yugo. | G3 | 20 |
| Baraawe, Som. | H9 | 56 |
| Barabinsk, Russia | F14 | 28 |
| Barabinskaja step', pl., Russia | F7 | 28 |
| Baraboo, Wi., U.S. | G6 | 110 |
| Baraboo, stm., Wi., U.S. | G6 | 110 |
| Baraboulé, Burkina | D9 | 64 |
| Baracaju, stm., Braz. | B3 | 79 |
| Barachit, Erit. | J10 | 60 |
| Barachois Pond Provincial Park, Nf., Can. | D15 | 106 |
| Baracoa, Cuba | D7 | 94 |
| Baradero, Arg. | G9 | 80 |
| Baradine, Austl. | H8 | 70 |
| Baragarh, India | B7 | 46 |
| Barahona, Dom. Rep. | E9 | 94 |
| Barak, Tur. | C4 | 48 |
| Baraka, val., Afr. | E8 | 56 |
| Barakaldo, Spain | B9 | 16 |
| Baralaba, Austl. | D9 | 70 |
| Baram, stm., Malay. | E5 | 38 |
| Barama, stm., Guy. | D13 | 84 |
| Baran', Bela. | G13 | 22 |
| Baranagar, India | I13 | 44 |
| Baranaviči, Bela. | H9 | 22 |
| Baranoa, Col. | B5 | 84 |
| Baranof Island, i., Ak., U.S. | H27 | 100 |
| Baranya, co., Hung. | J18 | 10 |
| Barão de Melgaço, Braz. | G14 | 82 |
| Baratang Island, i., India | H2 | 40 |
| Barataria, La., U.S. | M6 | 114 |
| Barataria Bay, b., La., U.S. | M7 | 114 |
| Barat Daya, Kepulauan, is., Indon. | G8 | 38 |
| Bar'atino, Russia | G17 | 22 |
| Barauana, stm., Braz. | G12 | 84 |
| Barauni, India | H11 | 44 |
| Baraut, India | F7 | 44 |
| Baravuha, Bela. | F11 | 22 |
| Barbacena, Braz. | F7 | 79 |
| Barbacoas, Col. | G3 | 84 |
| Barbados, ctry., N.A. | H15 | 94 |
| Barbar, Sudan | H7 | 60 |
| Barbarena, Isla, i., Hond. | A8 | 92 |
| Barbas, Cap, c., W. Sah. | I2 | 62 |
| Barbastro, Spain | C12 | 16 |
| Barbate, Spain | I6 | 16 |
| Barbeau, Peak, mtn., N.T., Can. | A12 | 86 |
| Barberena, Guat. | C4 | 92 |
| Barberton, Oh., U.S. | F5 | 108 |
| Barberton, S. Afr. | E10 | 66 |
| Barbezieux, Fr. | G6 | 14 |
| Barbil, India | I11 | 44 |
| Barbosa, Col. | D5 | 84 |
| Barbosa, Col. | E6 | 84 |
| Barbourville, W.V., U.S. | I4 | 108 |
| Barbourville, Ky., U.S. | C3 | 112 |
| Barby, Ger. | D11 | 10 |
| Barcaldine, Austl. | D6 | 70 |
| Barcău (Berettyó), stm., Eur. | B6 | 20 |
| Barce see Al-Marj, Libya | B5 | 56 |
| Barcelona, Mex. | D8 | 90 |
| Barcelona, Spain | D14 | 16 |
| Barcelona, Ven. | B10 | 84 |
| Barcelos, Braz. | H11 | 84 |
| Barcin, Pol. | C17 | 10 |
| Barcoo, stm., Austl. | E5 | 70 |
| Barcs, Hung. | J17 | 10 |
| Barczewo, Pol. | B20 | 10 |
| Bārda, Azer. | A9 | 48 |
| Barda del Medio, Arg. | J4 | 80 |
| Bardaī, Chad | D4 | 56 |
| Bardai, Sudan | K1 | 60 |
| Barddhamān, India | I12 | 44 |
| Bardejov, Slvk. | F21 | 10 |
| Bardi, Italy | E4 | 18 |
| Bardīyah, Libya | B5 | 56 |
| Bardo, Tun. | M5 | 18 |
| Bardonecchia, Italy | D1 | 18 |
| Bardstown, Ky., U.S. | E11 | 114 |
| Bardu, Nor. | G16 | 6 |
| Bardufoss, Nor. | G16 | 6 |
| Bardwell, Ky., U.S. | F7 | 114 |
| Barentin, Fr. | C7 | 14 |
| Barents Sea, Eur. | B4 | 24 |
| Barentu, Erit. | J9 | 60 |
| Barga, Eth. | N9 | 60 |
| Bargnop, Sudan | M5 | 60 |
| Barguzin, stm., Russia | G14 | 28 |
| Barguzin, Russia | G14 | 28 |
| Bar Harbor, Me., U.S. | C18 | 108 |
| Bari, Italy | H11 | 18 |
| Baria, Ven. | G9 | 84 |
| Barichara, Col. | D6 | 84 |
| Barika, Alg. | B13 | 62 |
| Barim (Perim), i., Yemen | H3 | 47 |
| Barinas, Ven. | C7 | 84 |
| Barinas, state, Ven. | C7 | 84 |
| Baring, Cape, c., N.T., Can. | B9 | 96 |
| Barinitas, Ven. | C7 | 84 |
| Bāripada, India | J12 | 44 |
| Bariri, Braz. | G4 | 79 |
| Bârîs, Egypt | E6 | 60 |
| Barisāl, Bngl. | I14 | 44 |
| Barisan, Pegunungan, mts., Indon. | F3 | 38 |
| Barito, stm., Indon. | F5 | 38 |
| Barjols, Fr. | I13 | 14 |
| Bark, stm., Wi., U.S. | H7 | 110 |
| Barkal, Bngl. | I15 | 44 |
| Barker, N.Y., U.S. | D8 | 108 |
| Barkerville Historic Park, B.C., Can. | D13 | 102 |
| Barkley, Lake, res., U.S. | F9 | 114 |
| Barkley Sound, strt., B.C., Can. | I9 | 102 |
| Barkly East, S. Afr. | H6 | 66 |
| Barkly Tableland, plat., Austl. | C7 | 68 |
| Barkly West, S. Afr. | G7 | 66 |
| Barkol, China | C5 | 30 |
| Bârlad, Rom. | C11 | 20 |
| Bar-le-Duc, Fr. | D12 | 14 |
| Barlee, Lake, l., Austl. | E3 | 68 |
| Barletta, Italy | H11 | 18 |
| Barling, Ar., U.S. | G2 | 114 |
| Barlow, Ky., U.S. | E7 | 114 |
| Bärmer, India | H4 | 44 |
| Barnard Castle, Eng., U.K. | G15 | 8 |
| Barnaul, Russia | G14 | 26 |
| Barnegat, N.J., U.S. | H12 | 108 |
| Barnegat Bay, b., N.J., U.S. | H12 | 108 |
| Barnes Ice Cap, N.T., Can. | B18 | 96 |
| Barnes Lake, l., Mb., Can. | B16 | 104 |
| Barnesville, Ga., U.S. | F2 | 112 |
| Barnesville, Mn., U.S. | E11 | 118 |
| Barnesville, Oh., U.S. | H5 | 108 |
| Barnsdall, Ok., U.S. | C10 | 116 |
| Barnstable, Ma., U.S. | F16 | 108 |
| Barnstaple, Eng., U.K. | J9 | 8 |
| Barnwell, Ab., Can. | H22 | 102 |
| Barnwell, S.C., U.S. | F5 | 112 |
| Baro, stm., Afr. | G8 | 56 |
| Barons, Ab., Can. | G21 | 102 |
| Barpeta, India | G14 | 44 |
| Barque, Canada Reef, rf., Asia | D5 | 38 |
| Barques, Pointe aux, c., Mi., U.S. | F13 | 110 |
| Barqah (Cyrenaica), hist. reg., Libya | C6 | 56 |
| Barquisimeto, Ven. | B8 | 84 |
| Barra, Braz. | F10 | 76 |
| Barra, Ponta da, c., Moz. | D12 | 66 |
| Barra, i., Scot., U.K. | D6 | 8 |
| Barra, stm., Braz. | B3 | 79 |
| Barraba, Austl. | H9 | 70 |
| Barrackville, W.V., U.S. | H6 | 108 |
| Barra da Estiva, Braz. | B8 | 79 |
| Barra do Bugres, Braz. | F13 | 82 |
| Barra do Corda, Braz. | E9 | 76 |
| Barra do Cuanza, Ang. | C2 | 58 |
| Barra do Garças, Braz. | D2 | 79 |
| Barra do Piraí, Braz. | G7 | 79 |
| Barra do Ribeiro, Braz. | F13 | 80 |
| Barra Falsa, Ponta da, c., Moz. | D12 | 66 |
| Barrafranca, Italy | L9 | 18 |
| Barra Mansa, Braz. | G6 | 79 |
| Barrancabermeja, Col. | D6 | 84 |
| Barranca, Peru | D3 | 82 |
| Barranca, Peru | A3 | 82 |
| Barrancas, Col. | B5 | 84 |
| Barrancas, Ven. | C7 | 84 |
| Barrancas, Ven. | C11 | 84 |
| Barrancas, stm., Arg. | I3 | 80 |
| Barranqueras, Arg. | D9 | 80 |
| Barranquilla, Col. | B5 | 84 |
| Barreal, Arg. | F4 | 80 |
| Barreiras, Braz. | B6 | 79 |
| Barreirinha, Braz. | I14 | 84 |
| Barreiro, Port. | G2 | 16 |
| Barreiro, stm., Braz. | C2 | 79 |
| Barren, stm., Ky., U.S. | E10 | 114 |
| Barren, Nosy, is., Madag. | q20 | 67b |
| Barren Islands, is., Ak., U.S. | G19 | 100 |
| Barren River Lake, res., Ky., U.S. | F10 | 114 |
| Barretos, Braz. | F4 | 79 |
| Barrhead, Ab., Can. | C20 | 102 |
| Barrhead, On., Can. | F16 | 110 |
| Barrie, On., Can. | F16 | 110 |
| Barrier Range, mts., Austl. | H4 | 70 |
| Barrington, N.S., Can. | I9 | 106 |
| Barrington Lake, l., Mb., Can. | B14 | 104 |
| Barrita Vieja, Guat. | C4 | 92 |
| Barro Alto, Braz. | C4 | 79 |
| Barron, Wi., U.S. | E4 | 110 |
| Barrow, Arg. | J8 | 80 |
| Barrow, Point, c., Ak., U.S. | A16 | 100 |
| Barrow, stm., Ire. | I6 | 8 |
| Barrow Creek, Austl. | D6 | 68 |
| Barrow-in-Furness, Eng., U.K. | G10 | 8 |
| Barrow Island, i., Austl. | D3 | 68 |
| Barrows, Mb., Can. | F13 | 104 |
| Barrow Strait, strt., N.T., Can. | B13 | 96 |
| Barry, Il., U.S. | C5 | 114 |
| Barrys Bay, On., Can. | E18 | 110 |
| Barryton, Mi., U.S. | G10 | 110 |
| Bārsi, India | C3 | 46 |
| Barsinghausen, Ger. | C9 | 10 |
| Barstow, Ca., U.S. | J8 | 124 |
| Barstow, Tx., U.S. | I3 | 116 |
| Bar-sur-Aube, Fr. | D11 | 14 |
| Bar-sur-Seine, Fr. | D11 | 14 |
| Bartang, stm., Taj. | A5 | 44 |
| Barthélemy, Col de, Viet. | E8 | 40 |
| Bartholomew, Bayou, stm., U.S. | J5 | 114 |
| Bartica, Guy. | D13 | 84 |
| Bartin, Tur. | G14 | 4 |
| Bartle Frere, mtn., Austl. | A5 | 70 |
| Bartlesville, Ok., U.S. | C11 | 116 |
| Bartlett, Ne., U.S. | J9 | 118 |
| Bartlett, N.H., U.S. | C15 | 108 |
| Bartlett, Tx., U.S. | H9 | 116 |
| Bartlett, Tn., U.S. | H4 | 114 |
| Bartletts Harbour, Nf., Can. | B16 | 106 |
| Barton Lake, l., On., Can. | F20 | 104 |
| Barton-upon-Humber, Eng., U.K. | H13 | 8 |
| Bartow, Fl., U.S. | L5 | 112 |
| Bartoszyce, Pol. | A20 | 10 |
| Bartow, Fl., U.S. | L5 | 112 |
| Barú, Volcán, vol., Pan. | I12 | 92 |
| Baruun-Urt, Mong. | B9 | 30 |
| Barview, Or., U.S. | G1 | 122 |
| Barwāni, India | I6 | 44 |
| Barwick, Ga., U.S. | I3 | 112 |
| Barwon, stm., Austl. | G8 | 70 |
| Barybino, Russia | F20 | 22 |
| Baryš, Russia | G7 | 26 |
| Barysau, Bela. | G11 | 22 |
| Basail, Arg. | D9 | 80 |
| Basankusu, D.R.C. | A3 | 58 |
| Basarabeasca, Mol. | C12 | 20 |
| Basarabi, Rom. | E12 | 20 |
| Basatongwula Shan, mtn., China | D14 | 44 |
| Basavilbaso, Arg. | G9 | 80 |
| Basco, Phil. | A7 | 38 |
| Bascuñán, Cabo, c., Chile | E3 | 80 |
| Basel (Bâle), Switz. | C8 | 13 |
| Basey, Phil. | C8 | 38 |
| Bashaw, Ab., Can. | E22 | 102 |
| Bashi Channel, strt., Asia | G11 | 30 |
| Bashkortostan see Baškirija, state, Russia | G9 | 26 |
| Basile, La., U.S. | L4 | 114 |
| Basilicata, prov., Italy | I11 | 18 |
| Basin, Mt., U.S. | D13 | 122 |
| Basin, Wy., U.S. | F17 | 122 |
| Basin Lake, l., Sk., Can. | F9 | 104 |
| Basin Lake, i., On., Can. | I22 | 104 |
| Baškirija, state, Russia | G9 | 26 |
| Baškmakovo, Russia | H26 | 22 |
| Basoko, D.R.C. | A4 | 58 |
| Basque Lands see Euskal Herriko, state, Spain | B9 | 16 |
| Basra see Al-Baṣrah, Iraq | F9 | 48 |
| Bas-Rhin, dept., Fr. | D14 | 14 |
| Bassano, Ab., Can. | G22 | 102 |
| Bassano del Grappa, Italy | D6 | 18 |
| Bassari, Togo | G10 | 64 |
| Bassas da India, rf., Afr. | E7 | 58 |
| Bassecourt, Switz. | D7 | 13 |
| Bassein see Pathein, Myan. | F3 | 40 |
| Bassein, mth., Myan. | F3 | 40 |
| Bassein, India | C2 | 46 |
| Basse-Terre, Guad. | F14 | 94 |
| Basseterre, St. K./N. | F13 | 94 |
| Basse-Terre, i., Guad. | F14 | 94 |
| Bassett, Va., U.S. | C7 | 112 |
| Bassett, Ne., U.S. | I8 | 118 |
| Bassett Peak, mtn., Az., U.S. | L6 | 120 |
| Bass Harbor, Me., U.S. | C18 | 108 |
| Bassikounou, Maur. | D7 | 64 |
| Bassila, Benin | G10 | 64 |
| Bass River, N.S., Can. | G10 | 106 |
| Bass Strait, strt., Austl. | L6 | 70 |
| Bastah, Jord. | H5 | 50 |
| Bastak, Iran | H13 | 48 |
| Bastelica, Fr. | I24 | 15a |
| Basti, India | G9 | 44 |
| Bastia, Fr. | I16 | 14 |
| Bastian, Va., U.S. | B5 | 112 |
| Bastimentos, Pan. | H12 | 92 |
| Bastimentos, Isla, i., Pan. | H12 | 92 |
| Bastogne (Bastenaken), Bel. | H8 | 12 |
| Bastrop, La., U.S. | J5 | 114 |
| Bastrop, Tx., U.S. | I9 | 116 |
| Bastuträsk, Swe. | I17 | 6 |
| Basutoland see Lesotho, ctry., Afr. | G5 | 58 |
| Bata, Eq. Gui. | A1 | 58 |
| Bataan Peninsula, pen., Phil. | n19 | 39b |
| Batabanó, Golfo de, b., Cuba | C3 | 94 |
| Bataguassu, Braz. | F2 | 79 |
| Bataiporã, Braz. | G2 | 79 |
| Batajsk, Russia | H5 | 26 |
| Batala, India | E6 | 44 |
| Batan, China | A9 | 34 |
| Batang, China | E6 | 30 |
| Batangas, Phil. | o19 | 39b |
| Batan Islands, is., Phil. | A7 | 38 |
| Bátaszék, Hung. | I18 | 10 |
| Batatais, Braz. | F5 | 79 |
| Batavia, Arg. | H6 | 80 |
| Batavia, Ia., U.S. | J3 | 110 |
| Batavia, Il., U.S. | I7 | 110 |
| Batavia, N.Y., U.S. | E8 | 108 |
| Batdâmbâng, Camb. | H7 | 40 |
| Batecikij, Russia | C13 | 22 |
| Batemans Bay, Austl. | J9 | 70 |
| Batesburg, S.C., U.S. | F5 | 112 |
| Batesville, In., U.S. | C11 | 114 |
| Batesville, Ms., U.S. | H7 | 114 |
| Batesville, Tx., U.S. | K7 | 116 |
| Bath, Eng., U.K. | J11 | 8 |
| Bath, N.B., Can. | F7 | 106 |
| Bath, N.Y., U.S. | E9 | 108 |
| Bathgate, N.D., U.S. | C10 | 118 |
| Bathinda, India | E6 | 44 |
| Bathsheba, Barb. | H15 | 94 |
| Bathurst, Austl. | I8 | 70 |
| Bathurst see Banjul, Gam. | E1 | 64 |
| Bathurst, S. Afr. | I8 | 66 |
| Bathurst, Cape, c., N.T., Can. | B7 | 96 |
| Bathurst Inlet, N.T., Can. | C11 | 96 |
| Bathurst Inlet, b., N.T., Can. | C11 | 96 |
| Bathurst Island, i., Austl. | B6 | 68 |
| Bathurst Island, i., N.T., Can. | A12 | 96 |
| Batia, Benin | F10 | 64 |
| Batié, Burkina | G8 | 64 |
| Bātin, Wādī al-, val., Asia | G9 | 48 |
| Batkanu, S.L. | G3 | 64 |
| Batlow, Austl. | J8 | 70 |
| Batman, Tur. | B6 | 48 |
| Batn al-Ghūl, Jord. | I5 | 50 |
| Batoche Rectory National Historic Site, hist., Sk., Can. | F8 | 104 |
| Baton Rouge, La., U.S. | L5 | 114 |
| Batouri, Cam. | H9 | 54 |
| Batovi, Braz. | C7 | 79 |
| Batrā (Petra), hist., Jord. | H4 | 50 |
| Batson, Tx., U.S. | I12 | 116 |
| Batticaloa, Sri L. | I6 | 46 |
| Battipaglia, Italy | I9 | 18 |
| Battle, stm., Can. | D13 | 104 |
| Battle Creek, Mi., U.S. | H10 | 110 |
| Battle Creek, stm., Can. | I11 | 104 |
| Battle Ground, In., U.S. | B10 | 114 |
| Battle Harbour, Nf., Can. | F21 | 96 |
| Battle Lake, Mn., U.S. | E12 | 118 |
| Battlement Mesa, mtn., Co., U.S. | E8 | 120 |
| Battle Mountain, Nv., U.S. | D9 | 124 |
| Battonya, Hung. | I21 | 10 |
| Batu, mtn., Eth. | N9 | 60 |
| Batu, Kepulauan, is., Indon. | O5 | 40 |
| Batumi, Geor. | I6 | 26 |
| Batu Pahat, Malay. | N7 | 40 |
| Baturité, Braz. | D11 | 76 |
| Bat Yam, Isr. | D3 | 50 |

| Name | Map Ref. | Page |
|---|---|---|
| Baubau, Indon. | G7 | 38 |
| Baud, Fr. | E3 | 14 |
| Baudette, Mn., U.S. | B1 | 110 |
| *Baudó, stm., Col.* | E4 | 84 |
| *Bauld, Cape, c., Nf., Can.* | A18 | 106 |
| Baume-les-Dames, Fr. | E13 | 14 |
| Baures, Bol. | E10 | 82 |
| *Baures, stm., Bol.* | E10 | 82 |
| Bauru, Braz. | G4 | 79 |
| Baús, Braz. | E2 | 79 |
| Bauska, Lat. | E7 | 22 |
| Bautzen, Ger. | D14 | 10 |
| Bauxite, Ar., U.S. | H4 | 114 |
| *Bavaria see Bayern, state, Ger.* | F11 | 10 |
| Bavispe, Mex. | B5 | 90 |
| *Bavispe, stm., Mex.* | C5 | 90 |
| Bavleny, Russia | E22 | 22 |
| Bawdwin, Myan. | C4 | 40 |
| Bawku, Ghana | F9 | 64 |
| Baxian, China | D4 | 32 |
| Baxley, Ga., U.S. | H4 | 112 |
| Baxter, Ia., U.S. | I2 | 110 |
| Baxter, Mn., U.S. | D1 | 110 |
| Baxter, Tn., U.S. | F11 | 114 |
| Baxter Springs, Ks., U.S. | N13 | 118 |
| Baxterville, Ms., U.S. | K7 | 114 |
| Bay, Ar., U.S. | G6 | 114 |
| Bayamo, Cuba | D6 | 94 |
| Bayamón, P.R. | E11 | 94 |
| *Bayan Har Shan, mts., China* | E6 | 30 |
| *Bayano, Lago, res., Pan.* | C3 | 84 |
| Bayan Obo, China | C9 | 30 |
| Bayard, Ia., U.S. | J13 | 118 |
| Bayard, Ne., U.S. | J4 | 118 |
| Bayard, N.M., U.S. | L8 | 120 |
| Bayard, W.V., U.S. | H7 | 108 |
| Bayboro, N.C., U.S. | D10 | 112 |
| Bay Bulls, Nf., Can. | E21 | 106 |
| Bayburt, Tur. | A6 | 48 |
| Bay City, Mi., U.S. | G12 | 110 |
| Bay City, Or., U.S. | E2 | 122 |
| Bay City, Tx., U.S. | K11 | 116 |
| Bay de Verde, Nf., Can. | D21 | 106 |
| Baydhabo, Som. | H9 | 56 |
| *Bay du Nord, stm., Nf., Can.* | E18 | 106 |
| *Bayerische Alpen, mts., Eur.* | H11 | 10 |
| *Bayern, state, Ger.* | F11 | 10 |
| Bayeux, Fr. | C6 | 14 |
| Bayfield, Co., U.S. | G9 | 120 |
| Bayfield, Wi., U.S. | D5 | 110 |
| *Bayfield, Île, i., P.Q., Can.* | A15 | 106 |
| Bayiji, China | A6 | 34 |
| Bayingzi, China | B8 | 32 |
| Bay L'Argent, Nf., Can. | E19 | 106 |
| Bay Minette, Al., U.S. | L9 | 114 |
| Bayombong, Phil. | m19 | 39b |
| Bayon, Fr. | D13 | 14 |
| Bayonne, Fr. | I5 | 14 |
| *Bayou Bodcau Reservoir, res., La., U.S.* | J3 | 114 |
| Bayou Cane, La., U.S. | M6 | 114 |
| *Bayou D'Arbonne Lake, res., La., U.S.* | J4 | 114 |
| Bayou La Batre, Al., U.S. | L8 | 114 |
| Bayovar, Peru | A1 | 82 |
| Bay Port, Mi., U.S. | G12 | 110 |
| Bayport, Mn., U.S. | E3 | 110 |
| Bayreuth, Ger. | F11 | 10 |
| Bayrischzell, Ger. | H12 | 10 |
| Bay Roberts, Nf., Can. | E20 | 106 |
| Bayrūt (Beirut), Leb. | A5 | 50 |
| Bay Saint Louis, Ms., U.S. | L7 | 114 |
| Bay Shore, N.Y., U.S. | G13 | 108 |
| Bayside, On., Can. | F18 | 110 |
| Bay Springs, Ms., U.S. | K7 | 114 |
| Bayt al-Faqīh, Yemen | G3 | 47 |
| Bayt Jinn, Syria | B5 | 50 |
| Bayt Laḥm (Bethlehem), W.B. | E4 | 50 |
| Bayt Mirī, Leb. | A5 | 50 |
| Baytown, Tx., U.S. | J12 | 116 |
| Bayzo, Niger | E12 | 64 |
| Baza, Spain | H9 | 16 |
| *Bazaruto, Ilha do, i., Moz.* | C12 | 66 |
| Bazas, Fr. | H6 | 14 |
| Bazdār, Pak. | G1 | 44 |
| Bazi, China | K2 | 34 |
| Bazine, Ks., U.S. | M8 | 118 |
| *Be, Nosy, i., Madag.* | n23 | 67b |
| Beach, N.D., U.S. | E3 | 118 |
| Beach Haven, N.J., U.S. | H12 | 108 |
| Beachville, On., Can. | G15 | 110 |
| Beacon, N.Y., U.S. | F13 | 108 |
| Beacon Hill, Wa., U.S. | D3 | 122 |
| Beaconsfield, Austl. | M7 | 70 |
| *Beagle Gulf, b., Austl.* | B6 | 68 |
| *Beagle Reef, rf., Austl.* | C4 | 68 |
| Bealanana, Madag. | o23 | 67b |
| *Beale, Cape, c., B.C., Can.* | I9 | 102 |
| *Bear, stm., Ca., U.S.* | E4 | 124 |
| *Bear, stm., Sk., Can.* | D10 | 104 |
| *Bear, stm., U.S.* | B5 | 120 |
| *Bear Bay, b., N.T., Can.* | A15 | 96 |
| Bear Cove, B.C., Can. | G7 | 102 |
| Bearden, Ar., U.S. | I4 | 114 |
| Beardmore, On., Can. | G15 | 96 |
| Beardstown, Il., U.S. | B6 | 114 |
| *Beardy and Okemasis Indian Reserves, Sk., Can.* | F8 | 104 |
| *Bear Head Lake, l., Mb., Can.* | C18 | 104 |
| *Bear Island, i., Ant.* | C11 | 73 |
| *Bear Island, i., Mb., Can.* | D16 | 104 |
| *Bear Island see Bjørnøya, i., Nor.* | B2 | 24 |
| Bear Lake, B.C., Can. | A8 | 102 |
| *Bear Lake, l., Ab., Can.* | B15 | 102 |
| *Bear Lake, l., B.C., Can.* | A8 | 102 |
| *Bear Lake, l., Mb., Can.* | C18 | 104 |
| *Bear Lake, l., U.S.* | C5 | 120 |
| *Bear Mountain, mtn., Or., U.S.* | G3 | 122 |
| *Béarn, hist. reg., Fr.* | I6 | 14 |
| Bear River, N.S., Can. | H8 | 106 |
| *Bear River Range, mts., U.S.* | C5 | 120 |
| *Beartooth Pass, Wy., U.S.* | F16 | 122 |
| Bear Town, Ms., U.S. | K6 | 114 |
| Beasain, Spain | B9 | 16 |
| Beas de Segura, Spain | G9 | 16 |
| *Beata, Cabo, c., Dom. Rep.* | F9 | 94 |
| *Beata, Isla, i., Dom. Rep.* | F9 | 94 |
| Beaton, B.C., Can. | G17 | 102 |
| Beatrice, Al., U.S. | K9 | 114 |
| Beatrice, Ne., U.S. | K11 | 118 |
| Beatrice, Zimb. | B10 | 66 |
| Beattie, Ks., U.S. | L11 | 118 |
| *Beatton, stm., B.C., Can.* | E8 | 96 |
| Beatty, Nv., U.S. | H9 | 124 |
| Beattyville, Ky., U.S. | B3 | 112 |
| Beaucaire, Fr. | I11 | 14 |
| *Beauce, reg., Fr.* | D8 | 14 |
| Beauceville, P.Q., Can. | A16 | 108 |
| Beaudesert, Austl. | F10 | 70 |
| Beaufort, N.C., U.S. | E10 | 112 |
| Beaufort, S.C., U.S. | G6 | 112 |
| *Beaufort Sea, N.A.* | B5 | 86 |
| Beaufort West, S. Afr. | I6 | 66 |
| Beaugency, Fr. | E8 | 14 |
| Beauharnois, P.Q., Can. | B13 | 108 |
| Beaumont, Ca., U.S. | K9 | 124 |
| Beaumont, Fr. | C5 | 14 |
| Beaumont, Ms., U.S. | K8 | 114 |
| Beaumont, Nf., Can. | C18 | 106 |
| Beaumont, Tx., U.S. | L2 | 114 |
| Beaumont-sur-Sarthe, Fr. | D7 | 14 |
| Beaune, Fr. | E11 | 14 |
| Beauport, P.Q., Can. | F2 | 106 |
| Beaupré, P.Q., Can. | E3 | 106 |
| Beaupréau, Fr. | E5 | 14 |
| *Beaupré Lake, l., Sk., Can.* | D7 | 104 |
| Beaurepaire, Fr. | G12 | 14 |
| Beauséjour, Mb., Can. | H18 | 104 |
| Beauvais, Fr. | C9 | 14 |
| Beauval, Sk., Can. | C7 | 104 |
| Beauvoir-sur-Mer, Fr. | F4 | 14 |
| Beaver, Ak., U.S. | C21 | 100 |
| Beaver, Ok., U.S. | C6 | 116 |
| Beaver, Pa., U.S. | G6 | 108 |
| Beaver, Ut., U.S. | F4 | 120 |
| Beaver, W.V., U.S. | B5 | 112 |
| *Beaver, stm., Can.* | D7 | 96 |
| *Beaver, stm., Can.* | D7 | 104 |
| *Beaver, stm., N.Y., U.S.* | D11 | 108 |
| *Beaver, stm., Pa., U.S.* | G6 | 108 |
| *Beaver, stm., Ut., U.S.* | F4 | 120 |
| Beaver City, Ne., U.S. | K8 | 118 |
| Beaver Creek, Yk., Can. | E24 | 100 |
| Beaver Crossing, Ne., U.S. | K10 | 118 |
| Beaver Dam, Ky., U.S. | E10 | 114 |
| Beaver Dam, Wi., U.S. | G7 | 110 |
| Beaverdell, B.C., Can. | H15 | 102 |
| Beaver Falls, Pa., U.S. | G6 | 108 |
| *Beaverhead, stm., Mt., U.S.* | E13 | 122 |
| *Beaverhead Mountains, mts., U.S.* | E12 | 122 |
| *Beaverhill Lake, l., Ab., Can.* | D22 | 102 |
| *Beaver Hill Lake, l., Mb., Can.* | D20 | 104 |
| *Beaver Island, i., Mi., U.S.* | E10 | 110 |
| *Beaver Lake, l., Ab., Can.* | C23 | 102 |
| *Beaver Lake, res., Ar., U.S.* | F3 | 114 |
| *Beaver Lake Indian Reserve, Ab., Can.* | C23 | 102 |
| Beaverlodge, Ab., Can. | B15 | 102 |
| *Beaver Mountains, mts., Ak., U.S.* | E16 | 100 |
| Beaverton, Mi., U.S. | G11 | 110 |
| Beaverton, On., Can. | F16 | 110 |
| Beaverton, Or., U.S. | E3 | 122 |
| Beāwar, India | G6 | 44 |
| Beazley, Arg. | G5 | 80 |
| Bebedouro, Braz. | F4 | 79 |
| Bebeji, Nig. | F14 | 64 |
| Becal, Mex. | G14 | 90 |
| *Bécancour, stm., P.Q., Can.* | A15 | 108 |
| Bečej, Yugo. | D4 | 20 |
| Beceni, Rom. | D10 | 20 |
| *Becerro, Cayos, is., Hond.* | B11 | 92 |
| Béchar, Alg. | E9 | 62 |
| Bechater, Tun. | L4 | 18 |
| Bechyně, Czech Rep. | F14 | 10 |
| Beckley, W.V., U.S. | J5 | 108 |
| Beckum, Ger. | D8 | 10 |
| Beckville, Tx., U.S. | J2 | 114 |
| *Becky Peak, mtn., Nv., U.S.* | E11 | 124 |
| Bédarieux, Fr. | I10 | 14 |
| Bedele, Eth. | M9 | 60 |
| *Bedeque Bay, b., P.E., Can.* | F10 | 106 |
| Bedford, Ia., U.S. | K13 | 118 |
| Bedford, In., U.S. | D10 | 114 |
| Bedford, Ky., U.S. | D11 | 114 |
| Bedford, Pa., U.S. | G8 | 108 |
| Bedford, P.Q., Can. | B14 | 108 |
| Bedford, Va., U.S. | B7 | 112 |
| *Bedfordshire, co., Eng., U.K.* | I13 | 8 |
| Bedias, Tx., U.S. | I11 | 116 |
| Bednodemjanovsk, Russia | H26 | 22 |
| Beebe, Ar., U.S. | G5 | 114 |
| *Beech, stm., Tn., U.S.* | G8 | 114 |
| Beech Creek, Ky., U.S. | E9 | 114 |
| Beecher, Il., U.S. | I8 | 110 |
| *Beech Fork, stm., Ky., U.S.* | E11 | 114 |
| Beech Grove, In., U.S. | C10 | 114 |
| Beechworth, Austl. | K7 | 70 |
| Beechy, Sk., Can. | H7 | 104 |
| *Beecroft Head, c., Austl.* | J9 | 70 |
| Beemer, Ne., U.S. | J11 | 118 |
| Beenleigh, Austl. | F10 | 70 |
| Bee Ridge, Fl., U.S. | L4 | 112 |
| Beersheba see Be'ér Sheva', Isr. | F3 | 50 |
| Beersheba Springs, Tn., U.S. | G11 | 114 |
| Be'ér Sheva' (Beersheba), Isr. | F3 | 50 |
| Beestekraal, S. Afr. | E8 | 66 |
| *Beethoven Peninsula, pen., Ant.* | C12 | 73 |
| *Beetz, Lac, l., P.Q., Can.* | B11 | 106 |
| Beeville, Tx., U.S. | K9 | 116 |
| Befale, D.R.C. | A4 | 58 |
| Befandriana, Madag. | o23 | 67b |
| Befasy, Madag. | r21 | 67b |
| Befotaka, Madag. | s22 | 67b |
| Bega, Austl. | K8 | 70 |
| *Bega (Begej), stm., Eur.* | D5 | 20 |
| *Begej (Bega), stm., Eur.* | D4 | 20 |
| Beggs, Ok., U.S. | D10 | 116 |
| Begičevskij, Russia | H21 | 22 |
| Begoro, Ghana | H9 | 64 |
| Begunicy, Russia | B12 | 22 |
| Begusarai, India | H12 | 44 |
| Behbahān, Iran | F11 | 48 |
| Behshahr, Iran | C12 | 48 |
| *Bei, stm., China* | K2 | 34 |
| Bei'an, China | B12 | 30 |
| Beida see Al-Bayḍā', Libya | E5 | 56 |
| Beidaihe, China | D7 | 32 |
| Beidun, China | I7 | 34 |
| Beigi, Eth. | M8 | 60 |
| Beihai, China | D10 | 40 |
| Beijing (Peking), China | D4 | 32 |
| *Beijing Shi (Peking Shih), China* | C10 | 30 |
| Beikan, China | C10 | 34 |
| Beiling, China | K4 | 34 |
| Beinwil, Switz. | D8 | 13 |
| *Beipan, stm., China* | F8 | 30 |
| Beipiao, China | B8 | 32 |
| Beiqi, China | C10 | 32 |
| Beira, Moz. | B12 | 66 |
| *Beira Baixa, hist. reg., Port.* | F4 | 16 |
| *Beira Litoral, hist. reg., Port.* | E3 | 16 |
| Beirut see Bayrūt, Leb. | A5 | 50 |
| Beiseker, Ab., Can. | F21 | 102 |
| Beishan, China | B10 | 40 |
| *Bei Shan, mts., China* | C6 | 30 |
| Beisu, China | E2 | 32 |
| Beitang, China | D5 | 32 |
| Beitbridge, Zimb. | D10 | 66 |
| Beixinzhen, China | D10 | 34 |
| Beizhen, China | B9 | 32 |
| Beja, Port. | G4 | 16 |
| Béja, Tun. | M4 | 18 |
| Bejaïa (Bougie), Alg. | B13 | 62 |
| Béjar, Spain | E6 | 16 |
| Bejuco, Pan. | C3 | 84 |
| Bejuma, Ven. | B8 | 84 |
| Bekabad, Uzb. | I11 | 26 |
| Bekdaš, Turk. | I8 | 26 |
| Békés, Hung. | I21 | 10 |
| *Békés, co., Hung.* | I20 | 10 |
| Békéscsaba, Hung. | I21 | 10 |
| Bekilli, Tur. | K13 | 20 |
| Bekily, Madag. | t21 | 67b |
| Bekitro, Madag. | t21 | 67b |
| Bekkaria, Alg. | N3 | 18 |
| Bekkevoort, Bel. | G6 | 12 |
| Bekodoka, Madag. | p21 | 67b |
| Bekoji, Eth. | N10 | 60 |
| Bela, India | H9 | 44 |
| Bela, Pak. | G2 | 44 |
| Belaazèrsk, Bela. | I8 | 22 |
| Belabolo, Sudan | M3 | 60 |
| Bela Crkva, Yugo. | E5 | 20 |
| Bel Air, Md., U.S. | H10 | 108 |
| *Belaja, stm., Russia* | G9 | 26 |
| Belaja Ber'ozka, Russia | I16 | 22 |
| *Bélanger, stm., Mb., Can.* | E17 | 104 |
| Bela Palanka, Yugo. | F6 | 20 |
| *Belarus, ctry., Eur.* | E13 | 4 |
| *Belau see Palau, ctry., Oc.* | E9 | 38 |
| Belavenona, Madag. | t22 | 67b |
| Bela Vista, Braz. | B10 | 80 |
| Bela Vista, Moz. | F11 | 66 |
| Bela Vista de Goiás, Braz. | D4 | 79 |
| Bela Vista do Paraíso, Braz. | G3 | 79 |
| Belawan, Indon. | M5 | 40 |
| Belbubulo, Sudan | M8 | 60 |
| Bełchatów, Pol. | D19 | 10 |
| Belcher, La., U.S. | J3 | 114 |
| Belcherāgh, Afg. | C1 | 44 |
| *Belcher Islands, is., N.T., Can.* | E17 | 96 |
| Belcourt, N.D., U.S. | C8 | 118 |
| Belding, Mi., U.S. | G10 | 110 |
| Beled Weyne, Som. | H10 | 56 |
| Belém, Braz. | D9 | 76 |
| Belén, Arg. | D5 | 80 |
| Belén, Chile | H7 | 82 |
| Belén, Col. | D6 | 84 |
| Belén, Nic. | F9 | 92 |
| Belen, N.M., U.S. | J10 | 120 |
| Belén, Para. | B10 | 80 |
| Belén, Ur. | F10 | 80 |
| *Belén, stm., Arg.* | D5 | 80 |
| Belén de Escobar, Arg. | H9 | 80 |
| Belfast, Me., U.S. | C17 | 108 |
| Belfast, N. Ire., U.K. | G8 | 8 |
| Belfast, S. Afr. | E10 | 66 |
| Belfield, N.D., U.S. | E4 | 118 |
| Belfort, Fr. | E13 | 14 |
| Belfry, Ky., U.S. | B4 | 112 |
| Belfry, Mt., U.S. | E16 | 122 |
| Belgaum, India | E3 | 46 |
| *Belgium, ctry., Eur.* | E8 | 4 |
| Belgorod, Russia | G5 | 26 |
| Belgrade, Mn., U.S. | F12 | 118 |
| Belgrade, Mt., U.S. | E14 | 122 |
| Belgrade, Ne., U.S. | J9 | 118 |
| Belgrade see Beograd, Yugo. | E4 | 20 |
| Belhaven, N.C., U.S. | D10 | 112 |
| *Beli Drim, stm., Eur.* | G4 | 20 |
| Beli Manastir, Cro. | D2 | 20 |
| Belington, W.V., U.S. | H7 | 108 |
| *Belitung, i., Indon.* | F4 | 38 |
| *Belize, ctry., N.A.* | I15 | 90 |
| *Belize, stm., Belize* | I15 | 90 |
| Belize City, Belize | I15 | 90 |
| *Belize Inlet, b., B.C., Can.* | F7 | 102 |
| *Belknap Crater, crat., Or., U.S.* | F4 | 122 |
| Belkofski, Ak., U.S. | I13 | 100 |
| *Bell, stm., P.Q., Can.* | G17 | 96 |
| *Bell, stm., Yk., Can.* | C26 | 100 |
| Bella Bella, B.C., Can. | E6 | 102 |
| Bellac, Fr. | F8 | 14 |
| Bella Coola, B.C., Can. | E8 | 102 |
| *Bella Coola, stm., B.C., Can.* | E8 | 102 |
| Bella Flor, Bol. | D8 | 82 |
| Bellair, Fl., U.S. | I5 | 112 |
| Bellaire, Mi., U.S. | F10 | 110 |
| Bellaire, Oh., U.S. | G6 | 108 |
| Bellaire, Tx., U.S. | J11 | 116 |
| Bellamy, Al., U.S. | J8 | 114 |
| Bellary, India | E4 | 46 |
| Bella Unión, Ur. | F10 | 80 |
| Bella Vista, Arg. | E9 | 80 |
| Bella Vista, Arg. | D6 | 80 |
| Bella Vista, Para. | B10 | 80 |
| Bellavista, Peru | A1 | 82 |
| Bellavista, Peru | B3 | 82 |
| Belle, Mo., U.S. | D5 | 114 |
| Bellé, Sen. | D3 | 64 |
| Belle, W.V., U.S. | I5 | 108 |
| *Belle, stm., Mi., U.S.* | H13 | 110 |
| *Belle Bay, b., Nf., Can.* | E18 | 106 |
| Bellefontaine, Oh., U.S. | G3 | 108 |
| Bellefonte, Pa., U.S. | G9 | 108 |
| Belle Fourche, S.D., U.S. | G4 | 118 |
| *Belle Fourche, stm., U.S.* | G5 | 118 |
| Bellegarde, Fr. | F12 | 14 |
| Belle Glade, Fl., U.S. | M6 | 112 |
| *Belle-Île, i., Fr.* | E3 | 14 |
| *Belle Isle, i., Nf., Can.* | F21 | 96 |
| *Belle Isle, Strait of, strt., Nf., Can.* | A17 | 106 |
| Bellême, Fr. | D7 | 14 |
| Belleoram, Nf., Can. | E18 | 106 |
| Belle Plaine, Ia., U.S. | I3 | 110 |
| Belle Plaine, Ks., U.S. | N10 | 118 |
| Belle Plaine, Mn., U.S. | F2 | 110 |
| Belle-Plaine, Sk., Can. | H9 | 104 |
| Belleview, Fl., U.S. | J4 | 112 |
| Belleville, Il., U.S. | D7 | 114 |
| Belleville, Ks., U.S. | L10 | 118 |
| Belleville, On., Can. | C9 | 108 |
| Belleville, Pa., U.S. | G9 | 108 |
| Belleville, Wi., U.S. | H6 | 110 |
| Belleville-sur-Saône, Fr. | F11 | 14 |
| Bellevue, Ab., Can. | H20 | 102 |
| Bellevue, Ia., U.S. | H5 | 110 |
| Bellevue, Id., U.S. | G11 | 122 |
| Bellevue, Mi., U.S. | H10 | 110 |
| Bellevue, Ne., U.S. | J12 | 118 |
| Bellevue, Oh., U.S. | F4 | 108 |
| Bellevue, Tx., U.S. | F8 | 116 |
| Bellevue, Wa., U.S. | C3 | 122 |
| Belley, Fr. | G12 | 14 |
| Bellingen, Austl. | H10 | 70 |
| Bellingham, Eng., U.K. | F11 | 8 |
| Bellingham, Mn., U.S. | F11 | 118 |
| Bellingham, Wa., U.S. | B3 | 122 |
| *Bellingshausen, sci., Ant.* | B1 | 73 |
| *Bellingshausen Sea, Ant.* | C11 | 73 |
| Bellinzona, Switz. | F11 | 13 |
| *Bell Island, i., Nf., Can.* | E21 | 106 |
| *Bell Island, i., Nf., Can.* | B18 | 106 |
| Bell Island Hot Springs, Ak., U.S. | B3 | 102 |
| Bellmead, Tx., U.S. | H9 | 116 |
| Bello, Col. | D5 | 84 |
| *Bellot Strait, strt., N.T., Can.* | B14 | 96 |
| Bellows Falls, Vt., U.S. | D14 | 108 |
| *Bell Peninsula, pen., N.T., Can.* | D16 | 96 |
| Bells, Tn., U.S. | G7 | 114 |
| Bells, Tx., U.S. | F10 | 116 |
| Bells Corners, On., Can. | B11 | 108 |
| Belluno, Italy | C7 | 18 |
| Bell Ville, Arg. | G7 | 80 |
| Bellville, Oh., U.S. | G4 | 108 |
| Bellville, Tx., U.S. | J10 | 116 |
| Bellwood, Ne., U.S. | J10 | 118 |
| Bellwood, Pa., U.S. | G8 | 108 |
| *Belly, stm., N.A.* | H21 | 102 |
| Belmond, Ia., U.S. | H2 | 110 |
| Belmont, Mb., Can. | I15 | 104 |
| Belmont, Ms., U.S. | H8 | 114 |
| Belmont, N.H., U.S. | D15 | 108 |
| Belmont, N.S., Can. | G10 | 106 |
| Belmont, N.Y., U.S. | E8 | 108 |
| Belmont, S. Afr. | G7 | 66 |
| Belmont, S.C., U.S. | E5 | 112 |
| Belmont, Wi., U.S. | H5 | 110 |
| Belmonte, Braz. | C9 | 79 |
| Belmonte, Port. | E4 | 16 |
| Belmopan, Belize | I15 | 90 |
| Belmullet, Ire. | G3 | 8 |
| Belo, Madag. | q21 | 67b |
| Belogorsk, Russia | G17 | 28 |
| Belo Horizonte, Braz. | E7 | 79 |
| Beloit, Ks., U.S. | L9 | 118 |
| Beloit, Wi., U.S. | H6 | 110 |
| *Beloje, ozero, l., Russia* | A20 | 22 |
| *Beloje more (White Sea), Russia* | D5 | 26 |
| Belomorsk, Russia | E4 | 26 |
| *Belomorsko-Baltijskij kanal, Russia* | I24 | 6 |
| Beloomut, Russia | G22 | 22 |
| Belorečensk, Russia | I5 | 26 |
| Beloreck, Russia | G9 | 26 |
| *Belorussia see Belarus, ctry., Eur.* | E13 | 4 |
| *Belot, Lac, l., N.T., Can.* | C31 | 100 |
| Belousovo, Russia | F19 | 22 |
| Bel'ov, Russia | H19 | 22 |
| Belo Vale, Braz. | F6 | 79 |
| Belovo, Russia | G9 | 28 |
| Beloz'orsk, Russia | A20 | 22 |
| Belpre, Oh., U.S. | H5 | 108 |
| Belspring, Va., U.S. | B6 | 112 |
| Belt, Mt., U.S. | C15 | 122 |
| Belton, Mo., U.S. | D2 | 114 |
| Belton, S.C., U.S. | E4 | 112 |
| Belton, Tx., U.S. | H9 | 116 |
| Beltrán, Arg. | D6 | 80 |
| *Belucha, gora, mtn., Asia* | H15 | 26 |
| Belūr, India | G10 | 42 |
| Belvès, Fr. | H8 | 14 |
| Belvidere, Il., U.S. | H7 | 110 |
| Belvidere, N.J., U.S. | G11 | 108 |
| Belview, Mn., U.S. | G12 | 118 |
| Belvís de la Jara, Spain | F7 | 16 |
| *Belyando, stm., Austl.* | C7 | 70 |
| Belyj, Russia | F15 | 22 |
| *Belyj, ostrov, i., Russia* | C12 | 26 |
| Belyje Berega, Russia | H17 | 22 |
| Belyje Stolby, Russia | F20 | 22 |
| Belyj Gorodok, Russia | E20 | 22 |
| *Belyj Luch, stm., Russia* | D27 | 22 |
| Belzoni, Ms., U.S. | I6 | 114 |
| Bemarivo, Madag. | r21 | 67b |
| Bemavo, Madag. | r21 | 67b |
| Bembéréké, Benin | F11 | 64 |
| Bement, Il., U.S. | C8 | 114 |
| Bemidji, Mn., U.S. | C1 | 110 |
| Bemis, Tn., U.S. | G8 | 114 |
| Benāb, Iran | C9 | 48 |
| Bena-Dibele, D.R.C. | B4 | 58 |
| Benagerie, Austl. | H4 | 70 |
| Benahmed, Mor. | D7 | 62 |
| Benalla, Austl. | K6 | 70 |
| Benares see Vārānasi, India | H10 | 44 |
| Ben Arous, Tun. | B16 | 62 |
| Benavente, Spain | C6 | 16 |
| Benavides, Tx., U.S. | L8 | 116 |
| Ben Badis, Alg. | K11 | 16 |
| Ben Bolt, Tx., U.S. | L8 | 116 |
| Bencubbin, Austl. | F3 | 68 |
| Bend, Or., U.S. | F4 | 122 |
| Bendaja, Lib. | H4 | 64 |
| Bende, Nig. | I13 | 64 |
| Bendemeer, Austl. | H9 | 70 |
| Bendigo, Austl. | K6 | 70 |
| Bendugu, S.L. | G4 | 64 |
| Bēne, Lat. | E6 | 22 |
| Bene Beraq, Isr. | D3 | 50 |
| Benedito Leite, Braz. | E10 | 76 |
| Benenitra, Madag. | s21 | 67b |
| Benešov, Czech Rep. | F14 | 10 |
| Benevento, Italy | H9 | 18 |
| Benfeld, Fr. | D14 | 14 |
| *Bengal, Bay of, b., Asia* | J14 | 44 |
| Ben Gardane, Tun. | D16 | 62 |
| Bengbu, China | C6 | 34 |
| Benghazi see Banghāzī, Libya | B5 | 56 |
| Ben Giang, Viet. | G9 | 40 |
| Bengkalis, Indon. | N7 | 40 |
| Bengkulu, Indon. | F3 | 38 |
| Bengough, Sk., Can. | I9 | 104 |
| Benguela, Ang. | D2 | 58 |
| Benguerir, Mor. | D7 | 62 |
| Benham, Ky., U.S. | C4 | 112 |
| Beni, D.R.C. | A5 | 58 |
| *Beni, dept., Bol.* | E9 | 82 |
| *Beni, stm., Bol.* | D9 | 82 |
| Béni Abbas, Alg. | E9 | 62 |
| Benicarló, Spain | E12 | 16 |
| *Benicito, stm., Bol.* | D9 | 82 |
| Benima, C.A.R. | O2 | 60 |
| Beni-Mellal, Mor. | D7 | 62 |
| *Benin (Bénin), ctry., Afr.* | G7 | 54 |
| *Benin, Bight of, Afr.* | G7 | 54 |
| Benin City, Nig. | H12 | 64 |
| Beni Saf, Alg. | J10 | 16 |
| Benissa, Spain | G12 | 16 |
| Benito, Mb., Can. | G13 | 104 |
| Benito Juárez, Arg. | I9 | 80 |
| *Benito Juárez, Presa, res., Mex.* | I12 | 90 |
| Benjakoni, Bela. | G8 | 22 |
| Benjamin, Tx., U.S. | F7 | 116 |
| Benjamín Aceval, Para. | C10 | 80 |
| Benjamin Constant, Braz. | J7 | 84 |
| Benjamín Hill, Mex. | B4 | 90 |
| Benjamín Zorrilla, Arg. | J6 | 80 |
| Benkelman, Ne., U.S. | K6 | 118 |
| Benld, Il., U.S. | C7 | 114 |
| Ben Lomond, Ca., U.S. | G3 | 124 |
| Ben Mehidi, Alg. | M2 | 18 |
| Benndale, Ms., U.S. | L8 | 114 |
| Bennet, Ne., U.S. | K11 | 118 |
| *Bennetta, ostrov, i., Russia* | B21 | 28 |
| *Bennett Lake, l., Can.* | F27 | 100 |
| *Bennett Lake, l., Mb., Can.* | E18 | 104 |
| Bennettsville, S.C., U.S. | E7 | 112 |
| Bennington, Ks., U.S. | L10 | 118 |
| Bennington, Vt., U.S. | E13 | 108 |
| Benniu, China | D8 | 34 |
| Benoit, Ms., U.S. | I5 | 114 |
| Benoni, S. Afr. | F9 | 66 |
| *Bénoué (Benue), stm., Afr.* | G9 | 54 |
| Benque Viejo del Carmen, Belize | I15 | 90 |
| Bensheim, Ger. | F8 | 10 |
| Ben-Slimane, Mor. | D7 | 62 |
| Ben Smih, Alg. | M2 | 18 |
| Benson, Az., U.S. | M6 | 120 |
| Benson, Mn., U.S. | F12 | 118 |
| Benson, N.C., U.S. | D8 | 112 |
| *Bentinck Island, i., Austl.* | C7 | 68 |
| Bentiu, Sudan | M5 | 60 |
| Bentley, Ab., Can. | E20 | 102 |
| *Bento Gomes, stm., Braz.* | G13 | 82 |
| Bento Gonçalves, Braz. | E13 | 80 |
| Benton, Ar., U.S. | H4 | 114 |
| Benton, Il., U.S. | E8 | 114 |
| Benton, Ky., U.S. | F8 | 114 |
| Benton, La., U.S. | J3 | 114 |
| Benton, Mo., U.S. | E7 | 114 |
| Benton, Ms., U.S. | J6 | 114 |
| Benton, Pa., U.S. | F10 | 108 |
| Benton, Tn., U.S. | D2 | 112 |
| Benton, Wi., U.S. | H5 | 110 |
| Benton City, Wa., U.S. | D6 | 122 |
| Bentong, Malay. | M6 | 40 |
| Benton Harbor, Mi., U.S. | H9 | 110 |
| Bentonia, Ms., U.S. | J6 | 114 |
| Bentonville, Ar., U.S. | F2 | 114 |
| Ben Tre, Viet. | I9 | 40 |
| *Benue (Bénoué), stm., Afr.* | G8 | 54 |
| Ben Wheeler, Tx., U.S. | G11 | 116 |
| Benxi (Penhsi), China | B11 | 32 |
| Beograd (Belgrade), Yugo. | E4 | 20 |
| Beowawe, Nv., U.S. | D9 | 124 |
| Beppu, Japan | N6 | 36 |
| *Bequia, i., St. Vin.* | H14 | 94 |
| Beramanja, Madag. | n23 | 67b |
| Berat, Alb. | I3 | 20 |
| *Berau, Teluk, b., Indon.* | F9 | 38 |
| Beravina, Madag. | q21 | 67b |
| Berazino, Bela. | H11 | 22 |
| Berazino, Bela. | G11 | 22 |
| Berbera, Som. | F10 | 56 |
| Berbérati, C.A.R. | H4 | 56 |
| *Berbice, stm., Guy.* | D14 | 84 |
| Berchtesgaden, Ger. | H13 | 10 |
| Berclair, Tx., U.S. | K9 | 116 |
| Berdigest'ach, Russia | E17 | 28 |
| Berdsk, Russia | G8 | 28 |
| Berdyans'k, Ukr. | H5 | 26 |
| Berdychiv, Ukr. | H3 | 26 |
| Berea, Ky., U.S. | B2 | 112 |
| Berea, Oh., U.S. | F5 | 108 |
| Berea, S.C., U.S. | E4 | 112 |
| Berehomet, Ukr. | A9 | 20 |
| Berehove, Ukr. | G22 | 10 |
| Berekua, Dom. | G14 | 94 |
| Berendejevo, Russia | E22 | 22 |
| *Berens, stm., Can.* | F18 | 104 |
| *Berens Island, i., Mb., Can.* | F17 | 104 |
| Berens River, Mb., Can. | F17 | 104 |
| Beresford, N.B., Can. | E8 | 106 |
| Beresford, S.D., U.S. | H11 | 118 |
| *Berettyó (Barcău), stm., Eur.* | B5 | 20 |
| Berevo, Madag. | q21 | 67b |
| Berezajka, Russia | D16 | 22 |
| Berezniki, Russia | F9 | 26 |
| Berezyne, Ukr. | C13 | 20 |
| Berg, Nor. | G15 | 6 |
| Berga, Spain | C13 | 16 |
| Bergama, Tur. | J11 | 20 |
| Bergamo, Italy | D4 | 18 |
| Bergantín, Ven. | B10 | 84 |
| Bergara, Spain | B9 | 16 |
| Bergby, Swe. | K15 | 6 |
| Bergen (Mons), Bel. | H4 | 12 |
| Bergen, Neth. | C6 | 12 |
| Bergen, Nor. | K9 | 6 |
| Bergen, N.Y., U.S. | D9 | 108 |
| Bergen aan Zee, Neth. | C6 | 12 |
| Bergen [auf Rügen], Ger. | A13 | 10 |
| Bergen op Zoom, Neth. | E5 | 12 |
| Bergerac, Fr. | H7 | 14 |
| Bergisch Gladbach, Ger. | E7 | 10 |
| Bergland, Mi., U.S. | D6 | 110 |
| Bergoo, W.V., U.S. | I6 | 108 |
| *Bergsche Maas, stm., Neth.* | E6 | 12 |
| Bergsjö, Swe. | K15 | 6 |
| Berguent, Mor. | C9 | 62 |
| Bergues, Fr. | B9 | 14 |
| *Berhala, Selat, strt., Indon.* | O8 | 40 |
| *Beringa, ostrov, i., Russia* | F25 | 28 |
| *Bering Glacier, Ak., U.S.* | F23 | 100 |
| *Bering Sea* | C2 | 86 |
| *Bering Strait, strt.* | D10 | 100 |
| Berja, Spain | I9 | 16 |
| Berkane, Mor. | C9 | 62 |
| Berkeley, Ca., U.S. | G3 | 124 |
| Berkeley Springs, W.V., U.S. | H8 | 108 |
| *Berkner Island, i., Ant.* | C1 | 73 |
| *Berkshire, co., Eng., U.K.* | J12 | 8 |
| *Berkshire Hills, hills, Ma., U.S.* | E13 | 108 |
| Berlaimont, Fr. | B10 | 14 |
| *Berland, stm., Ab., Can.* | C17 | 102 |
| Berlin, Ger. | C13 | 10 |
| Berlin, Md., U.S. | I11 | 108 |
| Berlin, N.H., U.S. | C15 | 108 |
| Berlin, N.J., U.S. | H12 | 108 |
| Berlin, Pa., U.S. | H8 | 108 |
| Berlin, S. Afr. | I8 | 66 |
| Berlin, Wi., U.S. | G7 | 110 |
| *Berlin, Mount, mtn., Ant.* | C10 | 73 |
| *Berlinguet Inlet, b., N.T., Can.* | B15 | 96 |
| *Berlin Lake, res., Oh., U.S.* | F5 | 108 |
| Bermejillo, Mex. | E8 | 90 |
| Bermejo, Arg. | F5 | 80 |
| *Bermejo, stm., Arg.* | F5 | 80 |
| *Bermejo, stm., S.A.* | C9 | 80 |
| *Bermejo, Paso del, S.A.* | G3 | 80 |
| *Bermen, Lac, l., P.Q., Can.* | F19 | 96 |
| Bermeo, Spain | B9 | 16 |
| *Bermuda, dep., N.A.* | B12 | 88 |
| Bern (Berne), Switz. | E7 | 13 |
| *Bern (Berne), state, Switz.* | E8 | 13 |
| Bernalda, Italy | I11 | 18 |
| Bernalillo, N.M., U.S. | I10 | 120 |
| Bernasconi, Arg. | I7 | 80 |
| Bernau bei Berlin, Ger. | C13 | 10 |
| Bernay, Fr. | C7 | 14 |
| Bernburg, Ger. | D11 | 10 |
| Berne, In., U.S. | B12 | 114 |
| *Berner Alpen, mts., Switz.* | F7 | 13 |
| Bernice, La., U.S. | J4 | 114 |
| Bernie, Mo., U.S. | F7 | 114 |
| *Bernier Bay, b., N.T., Can.* | B15 | 96 |
| *Bernina, mts., Eur.* | F12 | 13 |
| *Bernina, Passo del, Switz.* | F13 | 13 |
| *Bernina, Piz, mtn., Eur.* | F16 | 14 |
| Beromünster, Switz. | H8 | 10 |
| Berón de Astrada, Arg. | D10 | 80 |
| Beroroha, Madag. | r21 | 67b |
| Beroun, Czech Rep. | F14 | 10 |
| *Berounka, stm., Czech Rep.* | F13 | 10 |
| Berovo, Mac. | H6 | 20 |
| Ber'ozovo, Russia | E11 | 26 |
| Berrechid, Mor. | D7 | 62 |
| Berri, Austl. | J4 | 70 |
| Berrigan, Austl. | J6 | 70 |
| Berriyyane, Alg. | D12 | 62 |
| Berry, Al., U.S. | I9 | 114 |
| *Berry, hist. reg., Fr.* | E9 | 14 |
| *Berry Creek, stm., Ab., Can.* | F23 | 102 |
| *Berryessa, Lake, res., Ca., U.S.* | F3 | 124 |
| *Berry Islands, is., Bah.* | B6 | 94 |
| Berryville, Ar., U.S. | F3 | 114 |
| Berseba, Nmb. | F3 | 66 |
| Bersenbrück, Ger. | C7 | 10 |
| Bershad', Ukr. | A13 | 20 |
| *Berté, Lac, l., P.Q., Can.* | B5 | 106 |
| Bertha, Mn., U.S. | E12 | 118 |
| Berthold, N.D., U.S. | C6 | 118 |
| Berthoud, Co., U.S. | D11 | 120 |
| *Berthoud Pass, Co., U.S.* | E11 | 120 |
| Bertoua, Cam. | H9 | 54 |
| Bertram, Tx., U.S. | I8 | 116 |
| Bertrand, Mi., U.S. | A10 | 114 |
| Bertrand, Ne., U.S. | K8 | 118 |
| Beruri, Braz. | I12 | 84 |
| Berwick, La., U.S. | M5 | 114 |
| Berwick, Me., U.S. | D16 | 108 |
| Berwick, N.S., Can. | G9 | 106 |
| Berwick, Pa., U.S. | F10 | 108 |
| Berwick-upon-Tweed, Eng., U.K. | F11 | 8 |
| Berwyn, Il., U.S. | I8 | 110 |
| Besalampy, Madag. | p21 | 67b |
| Besançon, Fr. | E13 | 14 |
| Bešankovičy, Bela. | F12 | 22 |
| Besbes, Alg. | M2 | 18 |
| *Beskid Mountains, mts., Eur.* | F20 | 10 |
| Beskra, Alg. | C13 | 62 |
| *Besnard Lake, l., Sk., Can.* | C8 | 104 |
| Besni, Tur. | C4 | 48 |
| *Besor, Naḥal, val., Asia* | F2 | 50 |
| *Bessarabia, hist. reg., Mol.* | C12 | 20 |
| Besse, Nig. | F12 | 64 |
| Bessemer, Al., U.S. | I10 | 114 |
| Bessemer, Mi., U.S. | D5 | 110 |
| Bessemer, Pa., U.S. | G6 | 108 |
| Bessemer City, N.C., U.S. | D5 | 112 |
| Best'ach, Russia | E17 | 28 |
| Bestobe, Kaz. | G12 | 26 |
| Betafo, Madag. | q22 | 67b |
| Betanzos, Bol. | H9 | 82 |
| Betanzos, Spain | B3 | 16 |
| Betaré Oya, Cam. | G9 | 54 |
| Betbetti, Sudan | J3 | 60 |
| Bete Hor, Eth. | L10 | 60 |
| Bétera, Spain | F11 | 16 |
| Bétérou, Benin | G11 | 64 |
| Bet Guvrin, Isr. | E3 | 50 |
| Bet Ha'arava, W.B. | E5 | 50 |
| Bethal, S. Afr. | F9 | 66 |
| Bethalto, Il., U.S. | D6 | 114 |
| Bethanien, Nmb. | F3 | 66 |
| Bethany, Il., U.S. | C8 | 114 |
| Bethany, Mo., U.S. | B2 | 114 |
| Bethany, Ok., U.S. | D9 | 116 |
| Bethel, Ak., U.S. | F14 | 100 |
| Bethel, Ct., U.S. | F13 | 108 |
| Bethel, Me., U.S. | C16 | 108 |
| Bethel, N.C., U.S. | D9 | 112 |
| Bethel, Oh., U.S. | I2 | 108 |
| Bethel Acres, Ok., U.S. | D9 | 116 |
| Bethel Springs, Tn., U.S. | G8 | 114 |
| Bethesda, Oh., U.S. | G5 | 108 |
| Bethlehem, Pa., U.S. | G11 | 108 |
| Bethlehem, S. Afr. | G9 | 66 |
| Bethlehem see Bayt Laḥm, W.B. | E4 | 50 |
| Bethlehem, W.V., U.S. | G6 | 108 |
| Béthune, Fr. | B9 | 14 |
| Bethune, S.C., U.S. | E6 | 112 |
| Bethune, Sk., Can. | H9 | 104 |
| Betijoque, Ven. | C7 | 84 |
| Betioky, Madag. | s21 | 67b |
| Betlica, Russia | G16 | 22 |
| Betong, Thai. | L6 | 40 |
| Betoota, Austl. | E4 | 70 |
| *Betpak-Dala, des., Kaz.* | H12 | 26 |
| Betroka, Madag. | s22 | 67b |
| Bet Sh'ean, Isr. | C5 | 50 |
| Bet Shemesh, Isr. | E4 | 50 |
| Betsiamites, P.Q., Can. | D5 | 106 |
| *Betsiamites, stm., P.Q., Can.* | C4 | 106 |
| *Betsiamites, Barrage, P.Q., Can.* | C4 | 106 |
| *Betsiamites, Pointe de, c., P.Q., Can.* | D5 | 106 |
| *Betsiamites, Réserve indienne de, P.Q., Can.* | C5 | 106 |
| *Betsiboka, stm., Madag.* | p22 | 67b |
| Betsioky, Madag. | r21 | 67b |
| Betsy Layne, Ky., U.S. | B4 | 112 |
| Bettendorf, Ia., U.S. | I5 | 110 |
| Bettles Field, Ak., U.S. | C19 | 100 |
| Betūl, India | J7 | 44 |
| Betzdorf, Ger. | E7 | 10 |
| Beulah, Co., U.S. | F12 | 120 |
| Beulah, Mi., U.S. | F9 | 110 |
| Beulah, Ms., U.S. | I6 | 114 |
| Beulah, N.D., U.S. | D6 | 118 |
| Beulaville, N.C., U.S. | E9 | 112 |
| *B. Everett Jordan Lake, res., N.C., U.S.* | D7 | 112 |
| Beverley, Austl. | F3 | 68 |
| Beverley, Eng., U.K. | H13 | 8 |
| Beverly, Ma., U.S. | E16 | 108 |
| Beverly Hills, Ca., U.S. | J7 | 124 |
| *Beverly Lake, l., N.T., Can.* | D12 | 96 |
| Beverwijk, Neth. | D6 | 12 |
| Bevier, Mo., U.S. | C4 | 114 |
| Bexley, Oh., U.S. | H4 | 108 |
| Beyçayırı, Tur. | I10 | 20 |
| Beylul, Erit. | H3 | 47 |
| Beypazarı, Tur. | G14 | 4 |
| *Beyşehir Gölü, l., Tur.* | H14 | 4 |
| Bezaha, Madag. | s21 | 67b |
| Bežanicy, Russia | E12 | 22 |
| Bezau, Aus. | H9 | 10 |
| Bežeck, Russia | D19 | 22 |
| *Bezerra, stm., Braz.* | B5 | 79 |
| Béziers, Fr. | I10 | 14 |
| Bezmein, Turk. | B15 | 48 |
| Bhadrak, India | J12 | 44 |
| Bhadrāvati, India | F3 | 46 |
| Bhāg, Pak. | F2 | 44 |
| Bhāgalpur, India | H12 | 44 |
| Bhakkar, Pak. | E4 | 44 |
| Bhaktapur, Nepal | G11 | 44 |
| Bhamo, Myan. | B4 | 40 |
| Bhandāra, India | J8 | 44 |
| Bharatpur, India | G7 | 44 |
| Bharatpur, Nepal | G11 | 44 |
| Bharūch, India | J5 | 44 |
| Bhātāpāra, India | B6 | 46 |
| Bhātpāra, India | I13 | 44 |
| Bhāvnagar, India | J5 | 44 |
| Bhawānipatna, India | C7 | 46 |
| Bhera, Pak. | D5 | 44 |
| Bhilai, India | J9 | 44 |
| Bhīlwāra, India | H6 | 44 |
| Bhind, India | G8 | 44 |
| Bhiwandi, India | C2 | 46 |
| Bhiwāni, India | F7 | 44 |
| Bhongīr, India | D5 | 46 |
| Bhopāl, India | I7 | 44 |
| Bhubaneshwar, India | J11 | 44 |
| Bhuj, India | I3 | 44 |
| Bhusāwal, India | J6 | 44 |
| *Bhutan (Druk-Yul), ctry., Asia* | D13 | 42 |
| *Bia, stm., Afr.* | H8 | 64 |
| *Biá, stm., Braz.* | I9 | 84 |
| *Bia, Phou, mtn., Laos* | E7 | 40 |
| *Biabo, stm., Peru* | B3 | 82 |
| *Biafra, Bight of, Afr.* | H8 | 54 |

| Name | Map Ref. | Page |
|---|---|---|

Biak, i., Indon. — F10 38
Biała, Pol. — E17 10
Biała Podlaska, Pol. — C23 10
Biała Rawska, Pol. — D20 10
Białogard, Pol. — A16 10
Białystok, Pol. — B23 10
Bianco, Monte (Mont Blanc), mtn., Eur. — G13 14
Biarritz, Fr. — I5 14
Biasca, Switz. — F10 13
Bibā, Egypt — C6 60
Bibai, Japan — d16 36a
Bibala, Ang. — D2 58
Bibb City, Ga., U.S. — G2 112
Biberach an der Riss, Ger. — G9 10
Bibiani, Ghana — H8 64
Biblián, Ec. — I3 84
Bic, P.Q., Can. — D5 106
Bicas, Braz. — F7 79
Bicaz, Rom. — C10 20
Bičevinka, Russia — B20 22
Biche, Lac la, l., Ab., Can. — C22 102
Bichena, Eth. — L10 60
Bicknell, In., U.S. — D9 114
Bicknell, Ut., U.S. — F5 120
Bicol Peninsula, pen., Phil. — C7 38
Bicske, Hung. — H18 10
Bicudo, stm., Braz. — E6 79
Bīd, India — C3 46
Bida, Nig. — G13 64
Bīdar, India — D4 46
Biddeford, Me., U.S. — D16 108
Bidian, China — C2 34
Bidwell, Oh., U.S. — I4 108
Bieber, Ca., U.S. — C4 124
Biecz, Pol. — F21 10
Biedenkopf, Ger. — E8 10
Biel (Bienne), Switz. — D7 13
Bielawa, Pol. — E16 10
Bielefeld, Ger. — C8 10
Bieler Lake, l., N.T., Can. — B18 96
Bielersee, l., Switz. — D7 13
Biella, Italy — D3 18
Bielsko-Biała, Pol. — F19 10
Bielsk Podlaski, Pol. — C23 10
Bienfait, Sk., Can. — I12 104
Bien Hoa, Viet. — I9 40
Bienville, La., U.S. — J4 114
Bienville, Lac, l., P.Q., Can. — E18 96
Big, stm., Mo., U.S. — D6 114
Big, stm., N.T., Can. — B8 96
Big, stm., Sk., Can. — E7 104
Biga, Tur. — I11 20
Big Bald Mountain, mtn., N.B., Can. — E7 106
Big Bar Creek, B.C., Can. — F12 102
Big Bay, Mi., U.S. — D8 110
Big Bay De Noc, b., Mi., U.S. — E9 110
Big Bear Lake, Ca., U.S. — J9 124
Big Bear Lake, l., Ca., U.S. — J9 124
Big Beaver, Sk., Can. — I9 104
Big Belt Mountains, mts., Mt., U.S. — D14 122
Big Bend, Swaz. — F10 66
Big Bend National Park, Tx., U.S. — J3 116
Big Bend Reservoir, res., Ab., Can. — E19 102
Big Black, stm., Ms., U.S. — J6 114
Big Blue, stm., U.S. — L11 118
Big Canyon, val., Tx., U.S. — I4 116
Big Clifty, Ky., U.S. — E10 114
Big Creek, B.C., Can. — F11 102
Big Creek, Ca., U.S. — G6 124
Big Creek, stm., B.C., Can. — F11 102
Big Creek Peak, mtn., Id., U.S. — F12 122
Big Cypress Swamp, sw., Fl., U.S. — M5 112
Big Delta, Ak., U.S. — D22 100
Big Desert, des., Austl. — J4 70
Big Eau Pleine, stm., Wi., U.S. — F5 110
Bigelow Bight, Fl., U.S. — D16 108
Big Falls, Mn., U.S. — B2 110
Big Flat, Ar., U.S. — F4 114
Bigfork, Mn., U.S. — C2 110
Bigfork, Mt., U.S. — B11 122
Big Fork, stm., Mn., U.S. — B2 110
Big Frog Mountain, mtn., Tn., U.S. — D2 112
Biggar, Scot., U.K. — F9 8
Biggar, Sk., Can. — F6 104
Biggers, Ar., U.S. — F6 114
Biggs, Ca., U.S. — E4 124
Big Gully Creek, stm., Sk., Can. — E5 104
Big Hole, stm., Mt., U.S. — E12 122
Bighorn Basin, U.S. — F17 122
Bighorn Lake, res., U.S. — E17 122
Bighorn Mountains, mts., U.S. — F18 122
Big Island, i., N.T., Can. — D18 96
Big Island, i., On., Can. — I20 104
Big Lake, Mn., U.S. — E2 110
Big Lake, Tx., U.S. — H5 116
Big Lookout Mountain, mtn., Or., U.S. — F8 122
Big Lost, stm., Id., U.S. — G12 122
Big Mossy Point, c., Mb., Can. — E17 104
Big Mountain, mtn., B.C., Can. — H29 100
Big Mountain, mtn., Nv., U.S. — C6 124
Big Mountain Creek, stm., Ab., Can. — C16 102
Big Muddy Lake, l., Sk., Can. — I10 104
Bignasco, Switz. — F10 13
Bignona, Sen. — E1 64
Big Otter, stm., Va., U.S. — B7 112
Big Pine Mountain, mtn., Ca., U.S. — J6 124
Big Piney, Wy., U.S. — H15 122
Big Piney, stm., Mo., U.S. — E5 114
Bigpoint, Ms., U.S. — L8 114
Big Quill Lake, l., Sk., Can. — G10 104
Big Rapids, Mi., U.S. — G10 110
Big Rib, stm., Wi., U.S. — E6 110
Big River, Sk., Can. — E7 104
Big River Indian Reserve, Sk., Can. — E7 104
Big Sable, stm., Mi., U.S. — F9 110
Big Sable Point, c., Mi., U.S. — F9 110
Big Salmon, stm., Yk., Can. — F28 100
Big Salmon Range, mts., Can. — F28 100
Big Sand Lake, l., Mb., Can. — E13 96
Big Sandy, Tn., U.S. — F8 114
Big Sandy, Tx., U.S. — G11 116
Big Sandy, stm., Az., U.S. — J3 120
Big Sandy, stm., Tn., U.S. — F8 114
Big Sandy, stm., U.S. — I4 108
Big Sandy, stm., Wy., U.S. — I16 122

Big Sandy Lake, l., Sk., Can. — D10 104
Bigsby Island, i., On., Can. — I20 104
Big Sioux, stm., U.S. — I11 118
Big Sky, Mt., U.S. — E14 122
Big Smoky Valley, val., Nv., U.S. — F8 124
Big Spring, Tx., U.S. — G5 116
Big Springs, Ne., U.S. — J5 118
Big Spruce Knob, mtn., W.V., U.S. — I6 108
Bigstone, stm., Mb., Can. — C19 104
Big Stone City, S.D., U.S. — F11 118
Big Stone Gap, Va., U.S. — C4 112
Big Stone Lake, l., U.S. — F11 118
Big Sunflower, stm., Ms., U.S. — I6 114
Big Sur, reg., Ca., U.S. — I4 124
Big Thompson, stm., Co., U.S. — D11 120
Big Timber, Mt., U.S. — E16 122
Big Trout Lake, l., On., Can. — F14 96
Biguaçu, Braz. — D14 80
Big Valley, Ab., Can. — E22 102
Big Warrambool, stm., Austl. — G8 70
Big Water, Ut., U.S. — G5 120
Big Wells, Tx., U.S. — K7 116
Big White Mountain, mtn., B.C., Can. — H16 102
Big Wood, stm., Id., U.S. — G11 122
Bihać, Bos. — E10 18
Bihār, India — H11 44
Bihār, state, India — H11 44
Bihor, co., Rom. — B6 20
Bija, stm., Russia — G15 26
Bijagós, Arquipélago dos, is., Gui.-B. — F1 64
Bijār, Iran — D9 48
Bijeljina, Bos. — E3 20
Bijelo Polje, Yugo. — F3 20
Bijie, China — A9 40
Bijsk, Russia — G9 28
Bikāner, India — F5 44
Bikeqi, China — C9 30
Bikin, Russia — H18 28
Bikin, stm., Russia — H19 28
Bikini, atoll, Marsh. Is. — G20 126
Bīkkū Bīttī, mtn., Libya — D4 56
Bikoro, D.R.C. — B3 58
Bilac, Braz. — F3 79
Bilāspur, India — I10 44
Bila Tserkva, Ukr. — H4 26
Bilauktaung Range, mts., Asia — H5 40
Bilbao, Spain — B9 16
Bilhorod-Dnistrovs'kyy, Ukr. — H4 26
Bilian, China — G9 34
Bilimora, India — B2 46
Bilin, Myan. — F4 40
Bilina, Czech Rep. — E13 10
Billabong Creek, stm., Austl. — J6 70
Billings, Mo., U.S. — E4 114
Billings, Mt., U.S. — E17 122
Billings, Ok., U.S. — C9 116
Billings Heights, Mt., U.S. — E17 122
Billom, Fr. — G10 14
Bill Williams, stm., Az., U.S. — I3 120
Bill Williams Mountain, mtn., Az., U.S. — I4 120
Billy Chinook, Lake, res., Or., U.S. — F4 122
Bilma, Niger — E9 54
Biloela, Austl. — E9 70
Biloxi, Mn., U.S. — C3 110
Biloxi, Ms., U.S. — L8 114
Biloxi, stm., Ms., U.S. — L7 114
Biltmore Forest, N.C., U.S. — D4 112
Bilugyun Island, i., Myan. — F4 40
Bilwaskarma, Nic. — C11 92
Bilyayivka, Ukr. — C14 20
Bimbān, Egypt — E7 60
Bimini Islands, is., Bah. — B5 94
Binche, Bel. — H5 12
Bindloss, Ab., Can. — E6 58
Bindura, Zimb. — B10 66
Binéfar, Spain — D12 16
Binford, N.D., U.S. — D9 118
Binga, Monte, mtn., Afr. — B11 66
Bingara, Austl. — G9 70
Bingen, Ger. — F7 10
Binger, Ok., U.S. — D8 116
Bingham, Me., U.S. — B17 108
Binghamton, N.Y., U.S. — E11 108
Bingöl, Tur. — B6 48
Binhai (Dongkan), China — B8 34
Binjai, Indon. — M5 40
Binscarth, Mb., Can. — H13 104
Bintan, Pulau, i., Indon. — N8 40
Bintang, Gam. — E1 64
Bintimani, mtn., S.L. — G4 64
Bintulu, Malay. — E5 38
Binxian, China — D8 30
Binyamina, Isr. — C3 50
Binyang, China — C10 40
Bin Yauri, Nig. — F12 64
Biobío, prov., Chile — I3 80
Biobío, stm., Chile — I3 80
Bioko, i., Eq. Gui. — J14 64
Birao, C.A.R. — L2 60
Birāk, Libya — C3 56
Bi'r al-Uzam, Libya — B2 60
Biratnagar, Nepal — F4 30
Birch, stm., Ab., Can. — F9 104
Birch, stm., W.V., U.S. — I6 108
Birch Hills, Sk., Can. — F9 104
Birchford, Id., U.S. — G13 102
Birch Island, B.C., Can. — F15 102
Birch Island, i., Mb., Can. — F15 104
Birch Lake, l., Ab., Can. — D23 102
Birch Lake, l., On., Can. — G22 104
Birch Lake, l., Sk., Can. — C9 104
Birch Mountains, hills, Ab., Can. — E10 96
Birch River, Mb., Can. — F13 104
Birch Run, Mi., U.S. — G12 110
Birch Tree, Mo., U.S. — F5 114
Birchwood, Wi., U.S. — E6 110
Birchy Bay, Nf., Can. — C19 106
Bird City, Ks., U.S. — L6 118
Bird Island, Mn., U.S. — G13 118
Bird Island, sci., S. Geor. — A1 73
Bird Islet, i., Austl. — D11 68
Birds, Il., U.S. — D9 114
Birdsville, Austl. — E3 70
Birdtail Creek, stm., Mb., Can. — H14 104
Birdum, Austl. — C6 68
Birecik, Tur. — C4 48
Bir el Ater, Alg. — C15 62
Bir Enzaran, W. Sah. — I3 62
Birigui, Braz. — F3 79
Birilʹussy, Russia — F16 26
Birjand, Iran — E15 48
Birken, B.C., Can. — G12 102
Birkenhead, Eng., U.K. — H10 8
Birkfeld, Aus. — H15 10
Birmingham, Al., U.S. — I10 114
Birmingham, Eng., U.K. — I11 8
Birmingham, Ia., U.S. — J4 110
Birmingham, Mi., U.S. — H12 110

Birmitrapur, India — I11 44
Bīr Mogreïn (Fort-Trinquet), Maur. — H5 62
Birnamwood, Wi., U.S. — F6 110
Birni, Benin — F10 64
Birni Ngaouré, Niger — E11 64
Birnin Gwari, Nig. — F13 64
Birni Nkonni, Nig. — E12 64
Birnin Kudu, Nig. — F14 64
Birobidžan, Russia — H18 28
Birrie, stm., Austl. — G7 70
Birsk, Russia — F9 26
Birtle, Mb., Can. — H13 104
Bir'usa, stm., Russia — F17 26
Biržai, Lith. — E7 22
Bîrzava, stm., Eur. — D5 20
Bisbee, Az., U.S. — M7 120
Bisbee, N.D., U.S. — C8 118
Biscarrosse, Fr. — H5 14
Biscay, Bay of, b., Eur. — H3 14
Biscayne Bay, b., Fl., U.S. — N6 112
Bisceglie, Italy — H11 18
Bischofswerda, Ger. — D14 10
Biscoe, Ar., U.S. — H5 114
Biscoe, N.C., U.S. — D7 112
Biscoe Islands, is., Ant. — B12 73
Biscucuy, Ven. — C8 84
Bisha, Erit. — J9 60
Bishkek see Biškek, Kyrg. — I12 26
Bisho, S. Afr. — I8 66
Bishop, Ca., U.S. — G7 124
Bishop, Tx., U.S. — L9 116
Bishop Auckland, Eng., U.K. — G12 8
Bishop's Falls, Nf., Can. — C18 106
Bishopville, S.C., U.S. — E6 112
Bishrah, Ma'tan, well, Libya — F2 60
Biškek (Frunze), Kyrg. — I12 26
Bislig, Phil. — D8 38
Bismarck, Mo., U.S. — E6 114
Bismarck, N.D., U.S. — E7 118
Bismarck Archipelago, is., Pap. N. Gui. — k16 68a
Bismarck Range, mts., Pap. N. Gui. — m15 68a
Bismuna, Laguna, b., Nic. — C11 92
Bison, S.D., U.S. — F5 118
Bison Peak, mtn., Co., U.S. — E11 120
Bissau, Gui.-B. — F3 54
Bissett, Mb., Can. — G19 104
Bissikrima, Gui. — F4 64
Bissorã, Gui.-B. — E2 64
Bistcho Lake, l., Ab., Can. — E9 96
Bistineau, Lake, res., La., U.S. — J3 114
Bistrița, Rom. — B8 20
Bistrița, stm., Rom. — C10 20
Bistrița-Năsăud, co., Rom. — B8 20
Bisztynek, Pol. — A20 10
Bitam, Gabon — A2 58
Bitburg, Ger. — F6 10
Bitche, Fr. — C14 14
Bitlis, Tur. — B7 48
Bitola, Mac. — H5 20
Bitonto, Italy — H11 18
Bitterfeld, Ger. — D12 10
Bitter Lake, l., Sk., Can. — H5 104
Bittern Lake, l., Sk., Can. — E9 104
Bitterroot, stm., U.S. — D12 122
Bitterroot Range, mts., U.S. — D11 122
Bitti, Italy — I4 18
Bitung, Indon. — E8 38
Bituruna, Braz. — D13 80
Bivins, Tx., U.S. — I2 114
Biwabik, Mn., U.S. — C3 110
Biwa-ko, l., Japan — L11 36
Bixby, Ok., U.S. — D11 116
Biyang, China — C2 34
Bizana, S. Afr. — H9 66
Bizerte, Tun. — L4 18
Bizkaiko, prov., Spain — B9 16
Bjahomlʹ, Bela. — G11 22
Bjala Slatina, Bul. — H12 22
Bjalyničy, Bela. — H15 22
Bjalynkavičy, Bela. — I7 22
Bjaroza, Bela. — I5 22
Bjelovar, Cro. — D11 18
Björna, Swe. — J16 6
Bjørnøya (Bear Island), i., Nor. — B2 24
Bla, Mali — E7 64
Black, stm., Ak., U.S. — C23 100
Black (Lixian) (Da), stm., Asia — D8 40
Black, stm., Az., U.S. — K6 120
Black, stm., La., U.S. — K5 114
Black, stm., Mi., U.S. — H19 104
Black, stm., Mi., U.S. — G13 110
Black, stm., N.M., U.S. — G2 116
Black, stm., N.Y., U.S. — C11 108
Black, stm., S.C., U.S. — F7 112
Black, stm., U.S. — G5 114
Black, stm., Vt., U.S. — D14 108
Black, stm., Wi., U.S. — F5 110
Blackall, Austl. — E6 70
Black Bear Island Lake, l., Sk., Can. — C9 104
Black Birch Lake, l., Sk., Can. — B7 104
Black Butte, mtn., Mt., U.S. — F14 122
Black Diamond, Ab., Can. — G20 102
Black Diamond, Wa., U.S. — C3 122
Blackduck, Mn., U.S. — C1 110
Black Duck, stm., Can. — E15 96
Black Eagle, Mt., U.S. — C14 122
Blackfalds, Ab., Can. — E21 102
Blackfoot, Id., U.S. — G13 122
Blackfoot, stm., Mt., U.S. — D12 122
Blackfoot Indian Reserve, Ab., Can. — G21 102
Blackfoot Reservoir, res., Id., U.S. — H14 122
Black Forest see Schwarzwald, mts., Ger. — G8 10
Black Hawk, On., Can. — J21 104
Black Hawk Creek, stm., Ia., U.S. — H3 110
Blackhead Bay, b., Nf., Can. — D20 106
Black Hills, mts., U.S. — G4 118
Black Island, i., Mb., Can. — G18 104
Black Lake, l., N.Y., U.S. — C11 108
Black Lake, l., Sk., Can. — E11 96
Black Lake Bayou, stm., La., U.S. — J3 114
Black Mesa, mtn., Az., U.S. — H6 120
Blackmore, Mount, mtn., Mt., U.S. — E14 122
Black Mountain, mtn., Id., U.S. — D4 112
Black Mountain, mtn., U.S. — C4 112
Black Mountain, mtn., Wy., U.S. — F18 122
Black Mountains, mts., Az., U.S. — I2 120
Blackpool, Eng., U.K. — H10 8

Black Range, mts., N.M., U.S. — K9 120
Black River, N.Y., U.S. — C11 108
Black River Falls, Wi., U.S. — F5 110
Black Rock, Ar., U.S. — F5 114
Black Rock, rock, S. Geor. — G8 78
Black Rock Desert, des., Nv., U.S. — C7 124
Blacksburg, S.C., U.S. — D5 112
Blacksburg, Va., U.S. — B6 112
Black Sea — G15 4
Blacks Fork, stm., U.S. — C7 120
Blacks Harbour, N.B., Can. — G7 106
Blackshear, Ga., U.S. — H4 112
Blackstone, Va., U.S. — B9 112
Blackstone, stm., Yk., Can. — D26 100
Blackville, S.C., U.S. — F5 112
Black Volta (Volta Noire), stm., Afr. — G6 54
Black Warrior, stm., Al., U.S. — I9 114
Blackwater, stm., Mo., U.S. — D3 114
Blackwater Lake, l., N.T., Can. — D33 100
Blackwell, Ok., U.S. — C9 116
Blackwell, Tx., U.S. — G6 116
Bladel, Neth. — F7 12
Bladenboro, N.C., U.S. — E8 112
Bladgrond, S. Afr. — G4 66
Bladworth, Sk., Can. — G8 104
Blagodarnyj, Russia — H6 26
Blagoevgrad, Bul. — G7 20
Blagoveščensk, Russia — G17 28
Blain, Fr. — E5 14
Blaine, Mn., U.S. — E2 110
Blaine, Wa., U.S. — B3 122
Blaine Lake, Sk., Can. — F8 104
Blair, Ne., U.S. — J11 118
Blair, Ok., U.S. — E7 116
Blair, Wi., U.S. — F4 110
Blair Athol, Austl. — D7 70
Blairstown, Ia., U.S. — I3 110
Blairsville, Ga., U.S. — E3 112
Blairsville, Pa., U.S. — G7 108
Blakely, Ga., U.S. — H2 112
Blakesburg, Ia., U.S. — J3 110
Blanc, Mont (Monte Bianco), mtn., Eur. — G13 14
Blanc, Mont, mtn., P.Q., Can. — D7 106
Blanca, Bahía, b., Arg. — J7 80
Blanca, Isla, i., Peru — C2 82
Blanca, Punta, c., Chile — C3 80
Blanca Peak, mtn., Co., U.S. — G11 120
Blancas, Peñas, mtn., Nic. — D9 92
Blanchard, Ok., U.S. — D9 116
Blanchard, stm., Oh., U.S. — G3 108
Blanchardville, Wi., U.S. — H6 110
Blanche, Lake, l., Austl. — G3 70
Blanchester, Oh., U.S. — H3 108
Blanco, Tx., U.S. — I8 116
Blanco, stm., Bol. — E10 82
Blanco, stm., Ec. — G3 84
Blanco, stm., Tx., U.S. — I8 116
Blanco, Cabo, c., C.R. — H9 92
Blanco, Cañon, val., N.M., U.S. — I11 120
Blanco, Cape, c., Or., U.S. — H2 122
Blanco, Río, stm., Co., U.S. — G10 120
Blanc-Sablon, P.Q., Can. — A16 106
Bland, Mo., U.S. — D5 114
Bland, Va., U.S. — B5 112
Blanding, Ut., U.S. — G7 120
Blandinsville, Il., U.S. — J5 110
Blanes, Spain — D14 16
Blangy-sur-Bresle, Fr. — C8 14
Blankenberge, Bel. — F3 12
Blankenburg, Ger. — D10 10
Blanquilla, Isla, i., Ven. — B10 84
Blantyre, Mwi. — E7 58
Blarney Castle, hist., Ire. — J5 8
Blasdell, N.Y., U.S. — E8 108
Blatná, Czech Rep. — F13 10
Blaye-et-Sainte-Luce, Fr. — G6 14
Blayney, Austl. — I8 70
Bledsoe, Tx., U.S. — F3 116
Bleiburg, Aus. — I14 10
Blekinge Län, co., Swe. — M14 6
Blenheim, N.Z. — D4 72
Blenheim, On., Can. — H13 110
Blessing, Tx., U.S. — K10 116
Bletterans, Fr. — F12 14
Blind River, On., Can. — D13 110
Blissfield, Mi., U.S. — I12 110
Blitar, Indon. — k16 39a
Block Island, R.I., U.S. — F15 108
Block Island, i., R.I., U.S. — F15 108
Blockton, Ia., U.S. — K13 118
Bloedel, B.C., Can. — G9 102
Bloemfontein, S. Afr. — G8 66
Bloemhof, S. Afr. — F7 66
Blois, Fr. — E8 14
Blönduós, Ice. — B3 6a
Blood Indian Creek, stm., Ab., Can. — G3 104
Bloodvein, stm., Can. — E18 104
Bloomer, Wi., U.S. — E4 110
Bloomfield, Ia., U.S. — J3 110
Bloomfield, Ky., U.S. — E11 114
Bloomfield, Mo., U.S. — E7 114
Bloomfield, Ne., U.S. — I10 118
Bloomfield, N.M., U.S. — H9 120
Bloomfield, On., Can. — G18 110
Blooming Grove, Tx., U.S. — G10 116
Blooming Prairie, Mn., U.S. — G2 110
Bloomington, Il., U.S. — J7 110
Bloomington, In., U.S. — C10 114
Bloomington, Tx., U.S. — K10 116
Bloomsburg, Pa., U.S. — F10 108
Bloomville, Oh., U.S. — F3 108
Blora, Indon. — j15 39a
Blossburg, Pa., U.S. — F9 108
Blossom, Tx., U.S. — F11 116
Bloumet, Alg. — I14 62
Blountstown, Fl., U.S. — I1 112
Blountsville, Al., U.S. — H10 114
Blovice, Czech Rep. — F13 10
Blowering Reservoir, res., Austl. — J8 70
Blowing Rock, N.C., U.S. — C5 112
Bludenz, Aus. — H9 10
Blue, stm., Az., U.S. — K7 120
Blue, stm., In., U.S. — D10 114
Blue, stm., Ok., U.S. — E10 116
Blue Creek, Wa., U.S. — B8 122
Blue Earth, Mn., U.S. — G1 110
Blue Earth, stm., Mn., U.S. — G1 110
Bluefield, Va., U.S. — B5 112
Bluefield, W.V., U.S. — B5 112
Bluefields, Nic. — E11 92

Bluefields, Bahía de b., Nic. — F11 92
Blue Hill, Me., U.S. — C18 108
Blue Hill, Ne., U.S. — K9 118
Blue Hill Bay, b., Me., U.S. — C18 108
Blue Hills of Couteau, hills, Nf., Can. — E16 106
Blue Island, Il., U.S. — I8 110
Blue Mound, Ks., U.S. — M12 118
Blue Mountain, mtn., N.B., Can. — H7 106
Blue Mountain, mtn., Nf., Can. — B16 106
Blue Mountain, mtn., Pa., U.S. — G9 108
Blue Mountain Peak, mtn., Jam. — E6 94
Blue Mountains, mts., U.S. — F7 122
Blue Nile (Al-Baḥr al-Azraq) (Abay), stm., Afr. — F7 56
Bluenose Lake, l., N.T., Can. — B35 100
Blue Rapids, Ks., U.S. — L11 118
Blue Ridge, Ab., Can. — C19 102
Blue Ridge, Ga., U.S. — E2 112
Blue Ridge, mts., U.S. — D10 98
Blue River, B.C., Can. — E15 102
Bluesky, Ab., Can. — A16 102
Blue Springs, Ne., U.S. — K11 118
Bluestone, stm., U.S. — B5 112
Bluestone Lake, res., U.S. — B6 112
Bluewater, N.M., U.S. — I9 120
Bluff, N.Z. — G2 72
Bluff, Ut., U.S. — G7 120
Bluff City, Tn., U.S. — C4 112
Bluff Dale, Tx., U.S. — G8 116
Bluff Park, Al., U.S. — I10 114
Bluffs, Il., U.S. — C6 114
Bluffton, In., U.S. — B11 114
Bluffton, Oh., U.S. — G3 108
Bluffton, S.C., U.S. — G6 112
Bluffy Lake, l., On., Can. — H22 104
Blumberg, Ger. — H8 10
Blumenau, Braz. — D14 80
Blumenhof, Sk., Can. — H7 104
Blunt, S.D., U.S. — G8 118
Bly, Or., U.S. — H4 122
Blyth, On., Can. — G14 110
Blythe, Ca., U.S. — K11 124
Blytheville, Ar., U.S. — G7 114
Bø, Nor. — G14 6
Bo, S.L. — H4 64
Boaco, Nic. — E9 92
Boaco, dept., Nic. — E9 92
Boa Esperança, Braz. — F6 79
Board Camp, Ar., U.S. — H2 114
Boardman, Oh., U.S. — F6 108
Boardman, stm., Mi., U.S. — F10 110
Boat Basin, B.C., Can. — H8 102
Boatman, Austl. — F7 70
Boa Vista, Braz. — F12 84
Boa Vista, i., C.V. — m17 64a
Boavita, Col. — D6 84
Boaz, Al., U.S. — H10 114
Bobai, China — C10 40
Bobbili, India — C7 46
Bobcaygeon, On., Can. — F17 110
Böblingen, Ger. — G9 10
Bobo Dioulasso, Burkina — F7 64
Bobolice, Pol. — B16 10
Bobonaza, stm., Ec. — I4 84
Bobonong, Bots. — C9 66
Bobr, Bela. — G12 22
Bobtown, Pa., U.S. — H7 108
Bobures, Ven. — C7 84
Boby, Pic, mtn., Madag. — s22 67b
Boca Brava, Isla, i., Pan. — I12 92
Boca del Monte, Pan. — I12 92
Boca de Pozo, Ven. — B10 84
Boca de Quadra, strt., Ak., U.S. — B4 102
Boca do Acre, Braz. — C8 82
Boca Grande, Fl., U.S. — M4 112
Bocaiúva, Braz. — D7 79
Bocanda, C.Iv. — H7 64
Boca Raton, Fl., U.S. — M6 112
Bocas del Toro, Pan. — C1 84
Bocas del Toro, prov., Pan. — I12 92
Bocas del Toro, Archipiélago de, is., Pan. — H12 92
Bocay, Nic. — C9 92
Bocay, stm., Nic. — C9 92
Bochnia, Pol. — F20 10
Bocholt, Ger. — D6 10
Bochum, Ger. — D7 10
Bochum, S. Afr. — D9 66
Bocón, Carlo, stm., Col. — F8 84
Boconó, Ven. — C7 84
Bocşa, Rom. — D5 20
Bodajbo, Russia — F14 28
Bode, Ia., U.S. — H13 118
Bodegraven, Neth. — D6 12
Bodélé, reg., Chad — E4 56
Boden, Swe. — I17 6
Bodensee (Lake Constance), l., Eur. — E16 14
Bodh Gaya, India — H11 44
Bodināyakkanūr, India — G4 46
Bodine, Mount, mtn., Ab., Can. — B9 102
Bodmin, Eng., U.K. — K9 8
Bodø, Nor. — H14 6
Bodoquena, Serra da, plat., Braz. — I13 82
Bodrog, stm., Eur. — A5 20
Bodrum, Tur. — L11 20
Boende, D.R.C. — B4 58
Boerne, Tx., U.S. — J8 116
Bogale, Myan. — F3 40
Bogalusa, La., U.S. — L7 114
Bogan, stm., Austl. — H7 70
Bogandé, Burkina — E9 64
Bogart, Mount, mtn., Ab., Can. — G19 102
Bogata, Tx., U.S. — F11 116
Boğazlıyan, Tur. — B3 48
Bogda Shan, mts., China — C4 30
Boger City, N.C., U.S. — D5 112
Bogğabri, Austl. — H9 70
Boggy, stm., Ok., U.S. — E11 116
Bognor Regis, Eng., U.K. — K12 8
Bogo, Phil. — C7 38
Bogol'ubovo, Russia — E22 28
Bogong, Mount, mtn., Austl. — K7 70
Bogor, Indon. — j13 39a
Bogorodick, Russia — H21 22
Bogorodsk, Russia — E26 22
Bogotá see Santa Fe de Bogotá, Col. — C5 84
Bogotol, Russia — F9 28
Bogou, Togo — E9 64
Bogra, Bngl. — H13 44
Bogué, Maur. — H2 64
Bogue Chitto, Ms., U.S. — K6 114
Bogue Chitto, stm., U.S. — K6 114
Bogue Phalia, stm., Ms., U.S. — I6 114
Bo Hai (Gulf of Chihli), b., China — E8 32
Bohai Haixia, strt., China — E9 32
Bohain-en-Vermandois, Fr. — C10 14
Bohan, Bel. — I6 12

Bohemia see Čechy, hist. reg., Czech Rep. — F14 10
Bohemian Forest, mts., Eur. — F12 10
Bohicon, Benin — H11 64
Bohol, i., Phil. — D7 38
Bohol Sea, Phil. — D7 38
Boiaçu, Braz. — H12 84
Boiestown, N.B., Can. — F7 106
Boigu Island, i., Austl. — A8 68
Boiling Springs, N.C., U.S. — D5 112
Boipeba, Ilha de, i., Braz. — B9 79
Bois, Lac des, l., N.T., Can. — C32 100
Bois, Rio dos, stm., Braz. — E3 79
Bois Blanc Island, i., Mi., U.S. — E11 110
Bois de Sioux, stm., U.S. — E11 118
Boise, Id., U.S. — G9 122
Boise, stm., Id., U.S. — G9 122
Boise City, Ok., U.S. — C6 116
Boissevain, Mb., Can. — I14 104
Bojayá, stm., Col. — D4 84
Bojeador, Cape, c., Phil. — I19 39b
Bojnūrd, Iran — C14 48
Bojonegoro, Indon. — j15 39a
Boju, Nig. — H13 64
Bojuru, Braz. — F13 80
Bokani, Nig. — G12 64
Bokchito, Ok., U.S. — E10 116
Boké, Gui. — F2 64
Bokhara, stm., Austl. — G7 70
Bokino, Russia — I24 22
Bokkolako, Sen. — E3 64
Boksitogorsk, Russia — B16 22
Bokungu, D.R.C. — B4 58
Bol, Cro. — F11 18
Bolama, Gui.-B. — F2 64
Bolaños, stm., Mex. — F8 90
Bolaños de Calatrava, Spain — G8 16
Bolbec, Fr. — C7 14
Bolchov, Russia — H19 22
Boles, Ar., U.S. — H2 114
Bolesławiec, Pol. — D15 10
Boleszkowice, Pol. — C14 10
Boley, Ok., U.S. — D10 116
Bolgatanga, Ghana — F9 64
Bolhrad, Ukr. — D12 20
Boli, China — B13 30
Boli, Sudan — N5 60
Boligee, Al., U.S. — J8 114
Boling, Tx., U.S. — J11 116
Bolívar, Col. — E4 84
Bolívar, Mo., U.S. — E3 114
Bolívar, Tn., U.S. — G8 114
Bolívar, state, Ven. — D11 84
Bolívar, prov., Ec. — H3 84
Bolívar, dept., Col. — C5 84
Bolívar, Cerro, mtn., Ven. — D11 84
Bolívar, Pico, mtn., Ven. — C7 84
Bolívar Peninsula, pen., Tx., U.S. — J12 116
Bolivia, ctry., S.A. — G5 76
Bollène, Fr. — H11 14
Bollnäs, Swe. — K15 6
Bollon, Austl. — G7 70
Bollullos par del Condado, Spain — H5 16
Bolobo, D.R.C. — B3 58
Bolochovo, Russia — G20 22
Bologna, Italy — E6 18
Bolognesi, Peru — B5 82
Bologoje, Russia — D17 22
Bolomba, D.R.C. — A3 58
Bolonchén de Rejón, Mex. — G15 90
Bolotnoje, Russia — F14 26
Bolsena, Italy — G6 18
Bolsena, Lago di, l., Italy — G6 18
Bol'šereck, Russia — G23 28
Bol'ševik, ostrov, i., Russia — B12 28
Bol'ševik, Russia — E21 28
Bol'šezemel'skaja Tundra, reg., Russia — D9 26
Bol'šoj An'uj, stm., Russia — D24 28
Bol'šoj Begičev, ostrov, i., Russia — C14 28
Bol'šaja Balachn'a, stm., Russia — C12 28
Bol'šaja Četa, stm., Russia — D14 28
Bol'šaja Cuja, stm., Russia — F14 28
Bol'šaja Ižora, Russia — B12 22
Bol'šaja Kuonamka, stm., Russia — D13 28
Bol'šaja Lipovica, Russia — I24 22
Bol'šaja Murta, Russia — F16 26
Bol'šaja Višera, Russia — C15 22
Bol'šakovo, Russia — G4 22
Bol'šoje Michajlovskoje, Russia — E21 22
Bol'šoj Polpino, Russia — H17 22
Bol'šoj Jenisej, stm., Russia — G11 28
Bol'šoj L'achovskij, ostrov, i., Russia — C20 28
Bol'šoj Tal'cy, Russia — B16 22
Bol'šoj Tuters, ostrov, i., Russia — B10 22
Bol'šoj Uzen', stm., Eur. — H7 26
Bolton, Ms., U.S. — J6 114
Bolton, N.C., U.S. — E8 112
Bolton, On., Can. — G16 110
Bolton Lake, l., Mb., Can. — D19 104
Bolu, Tur. — G14 4
Boluntay, China — B7 34
Boluochi, China — B7 30
Bóly, Hung. — I18 10
Bolzano (Bozen), Italy — C6 18
Boma, D.R.C. — A2 58
Bomaderry, Austl. — J9 70
Bombala, Austl. — K8 70
Bombarral, Port. — F2 16
Bombay, India — C2 46
Bomberai, Semenanjung, pen., Indon. — F9 38
Bom Despacho, Braz. — E6 79
Bomei, China — M4 34
Bom Jardim de Goiás, Braz. — D2 79
Bom Jesus, Braz. — E10 76
Bom Jesus da Lapa, Braz. — B6 79
Bom Jesus de Goiás, Braz. — D14 80
Bom Retiro, Braz. — D14 80
Bom Sucesso, Braz. — F6 79
Bom Sucesso, Braz. — G3 79
Bomu (Mbomou), stm., Afr. — H5 56
Bon Air, Va., U.S. — B9 112
Bonaire, i., Neth. Ant. — H10 94
Bonampak, hist., Mex. — I14 90
Bonanza, Nic. — C10 92
Bonanza, Ut., U.S. — D7 120
Bonao, Dom. Rep. — E9 94
Bonaparte, Ia., U.S. — J4 110
Bonaparte, stm., B.C., Can. — F13 102
Bonaparte Archipelago, is., Austl. — B5 68
Bonaparte Lake, l., B.C., — F5 102
Bonarbridge, Scot., U.K. — D9 8
Bonárcado, Italy — I3 18

| Name | Map Ref. | Page |
|---|---|---|
| Bonaventure, P.Q., Can. | D8 | 106 |
| Bonaventure, stm., P.Q., Can. | D8 | 106 |
| Bonaventure, Île, i, P.Q., Can. | D9 | 106 |
| Bonavista, Nf., Can. | D20 | 106 |
| Bonavista, Cape, c., Nf., Can. | D20 | 106 |
| Bonavista Bay, b., Nf., Can. | D20 | 106 |
| Bond, Ms., U.S. | L7 | 114 |
| Bondeno, Italy | E6 | 18 |
| Bondo, D.R.C. | H5 | 56 |
| Bonduel, Wi., U.S. | F7 | 110 |
| Bondoukou, C. Iv. | G8 | 64 |
| Bone, Teluk, b., Indon. | F7 | 38 |
| Bonesteel, S.D., U.S. | H9 | 118 |
| Bonete, Cerro, mtn., Arg. | D4 | 80 |
| Bonete Chico, Cerro, mtn., Arg. | E4 | 80 |
| Bonga, Eth. | N9 | 60 |
| Bongak, Sudan | N7 | 60 |
| Bongandanga, D.R.C. | A4 | 58 |
| Bongo, Massif des, mts., C.A.R. | M2 | 60 |
| Bongor, Chad | F4 | 56 |
| Bongouanou, C. Iv. | H7 | 64 |
| Bonham, Tx., U.S. | F10 | 116 |
| Bonhomme, Morne, mtn., Haiti | E8 | 94 |
| Bonifacio, Fr. | m24 | 15a |
| Bonifacio, Strait of, strt., Eur. | H4 | 18 |
| Bonifay, Fl., U.S. | L11 | 114 |
| Bonilla Island, i., B.C., Can. | D4 | 102 |
| Bonita, La., U.S. | J5 | 114 |
| Bonita Springs, Fl., U.S. | M5 | 112 |
| Bonito, Braz. | I13 | 82 |
| Bonito, stm., Braz. | D3 | 79 |
| Bonito, Pico, mtn., Hond. | B8 | 92 |
| Bonito, Rio, stm., N.M., U.S. | K11 | 120 |
| Bonkoukou, Niger | D11 | 64 |
| Bonn, Ger. | E7 | 10 |
| Bonne Bay (Woody Point), Nf., Can. | C16 | 106 |
| Bonne Bay, b., Nf., Can. | C16 | 106 |
| Bonneia, Eth. | O9 | 60 |
| Bonner, Mt., U.S. | D12 | 122 |
| Bonners Ferry, Id., U.S. | B9 | 122 |
| Bonnet, Lac du, l., Mb., Can. | H19 | 104 |
| Bonnétable, Fr. | D7 | 14 |
| Bonne Terre, Mo., U.S. | E6 | 114 |
| Bonnet Plume, stm., Yk., Can. | D27 | 100 |
| Bonneval, Fr. | D8 | 14 |
| Bonneville, Fr. | F13 | 14 |
| Bonneville Peak, mtn., Id., U.S. | H13 | 122 |
| Bonneville Salt Flats, pl., Ut., U.S. | D3 | 120 |
| Bonnie Doone, N.C., U.S. | D8 | 112 |
| Bonnie Rock, Austl. | F3 | 68 |
| Bonny, Nig. | I13 | 64 |
| Bonnyville, Ab., Can. | C24 | 102 |
| Bonorva, Italy | I3 | 18 |
| Bono, Ar., U.S. | G6 | 114 |
| Bon Secour, Al., U.S. | L9 | 114 |
| Bonshaw, P.E., Can. | F10 | 106 |
| Bonthe, S.L. | H3 | 64 |
| Bontoc, Phil. | m19 | 39b |
| Bon Wier, Tx., U.S. | L3 | 114 |
| Bonyhád, Hung. | I18 | 10 |
| Bookaloo, Austl. | H2 | 70 |
| Book Cliffs, clf., U.S. | E7 | 120 |
| Booker, Tx., U.S. | C6 | 116 |
| Boola, Gui. | G5 | 64 |
| Boom, Bel. | F5 | 12 |
| Boomarra, Austl. | B4 | 70 |
| Boomer, W.V., U.S. | I5 | 108 |
| Boonah, Austl. | G10 | 70 |
| Boone, Ia., U.S. | H2 | 110 |
| Boone, N.C., U.S. | C5 | 112 |
| Boone, stm., Ia., U.S. | H2 | 110 |
| Boones Mill, Va., U.S. | B7 | 112 |
| Booneville, Ar., U.S. | G3 | 114 |
| Booneville, Ky., U.S. | B3 | 112 |
| Booneville, Ms., U.S. | H4 | 114 |
| Boonsboro, Md., U.S. | H9 | 108 |
| Boonville, Ca., U.S. | E2 | 124 |
| Boonville, In., U.S. | D9 | 114 |
| Boonville, Mo., U.S. | D4 | 114 |
| Boonville, N.Y., U.S. | D11 | 108 |
| Boopi, stm., Bol. | G8 | 82 |
| Boorama, Som. | G9 | 56 |
| Boorindal, Austl. | H7 | 70 |
| Boorowa, Austl. | J8 | 70 |
| Boosaaso, Som. | F10 | 56 |
| Bootahnie Indian Reserve, B.C., Can. | G13 | 102 |
| Booth, Al., U.S. | J10 | 114 |
| Boothbay Harbor, Me., U.S. | D17 | 108 |
| Boothia, Gulf of, b., N.T., Can. | B14 | 96 |
| Boothia Peninsula, pen., N.T., Can. | B14 | 96 |
| Boothville, La., U.S. | M7 | 114 |
| Booué, Gabon | B2 | 58 |
| Bophuthatswana, hist. reg., S. Afr. | F7 | 66 |
| Bopo, Nig. | H13 | 64 |
| Boquerón, Pan. | I12 | 92 |
| Boquerón, dept., Para. | B8 | 80 |
| Boquilla, Presa de la, res., Mex. | D7 | 90 |
| Boquillas del Carmen, Mex. | C8 | 90 |
| Bor, Czech Rep. | F12 | 10 |
| Bor, Russia | E27 | 22 |
| Bor, Sudan | N6 | 60 |
| Bor, Tur. | C3 | 48 |
| Bor, Yugo. | E6 | 20 |
| Boraha, Nosy, i., Madag. | p23 | 67b |
| Borah Peak, mtn., Id., U.S. | F12 | 122 |
| Borås, Swe. | M13 | 6 |
| Borāzjān, Iran | G11 | 48 |
| Borba, Braz. | J13 | 84 |
| Borba, Port. | G4 | 16 |
| Borda, Cape, c., Austl. | J2 | 70 |
| Bordeaux, Fr. | H6 | 14 |
| Borden, Sk., Can. | F7 | 104 |
| Borden Peninsula, pen., N.T., Can. | B16 | 96 |
| Borders, prov., Scot., U.K. | F10 | 8 |
| Bordertown, Austl. | K4 | 70 |
| Bordeyri, Ice. | B3 | 6a |
| Bordighera, Italy | F2 | 18 |
| Bordj Bou Arreridj, Alg. | B13 | 62 |
| Bordj Menaïel, Alg. | B12 | 62 |
| Bordj Omar Idriss, Alg. | F14 | 62 |
| Bordj Sidi Toui, Tun. | D16 | 62 |
| Boreda, Eth. | N9 | 60 |
| Borgå (Porvoo), Fin. | K19 | 6 |
| Borger, Tx., U.S. | D5 | 116 |
| Borgholm, Swe. | M15 | 6 |
| Borgne, Lake, b., U.S. | L7 | 114 |
| Borgosesia, Italy | D3 | 18 |
| Borimskoje, Russia | I22 | 22 |
| Borisoglebsk, Russia | G6 | 26 |
| Borisoglebskij, Russia | D22 | 22 |
| Borja, Peru | J4 | 84 |
| Borkavičy, Bela. | F11 | 22 |
| Borken, Ger. | D6 | 10 |
| Borkum, i., Ger. | B6 | 10 |
| Borlänge, Swe. | K14 | 6 |
| Bormes-les-Mimosas, Fr. | I13 | 14 |
| Bormio, Italy | C5 | 18 |
| Borna, Ger. | D13 | 10 |
| Borneo (Kalimantan), i., Asia | N11 | 40 |
| Bornholm, i., Den. | N14 | 6 |
| Boro, stm., Sudan | M3 | 60 |
| Borodarou, Benin | F11 | 64 |
| Borodino, Russia | F18 | 22 |
| Borodino, Ukr. | C13 | 20 |
| Borogoncy, Russia | E18 | 29 |
| Boromo, Burkina | F8 | 64 |
| Boron, Ca., U.S. | J8 | 124 |
| Borovichi, Russia | C16 | 22 |
| Borovsk, Russia | F19 | 22 |
| Borrachudo, stm., Braz. | E6 | 79 |
| Borriana, Spain | F11 | 16 |
| Borroloola, Austl. | C7 | 68 |
| Borş, Rom. | B5 | 20 |
| Borşa, Rom. | B8 | 20 |
| Borsad, India | I5 | 44 |
| Borsod-Abaúj-Zemplén, co., Hung. | G21 | 10 |
| Borth, Wales, U.K. | I9 | 8 |
| Bort-les-Orgues, Fr. | G9 | 14 |
| Boruca, C.R. | H11 | 92 |
| Borūjen, Iran | F11 | 43 |
| Borūjerd, Iran | E10 | 43 |
| Borz'a, Russia | G15 | 29 |
| Bosa, Italy | I3 | 18 |
| Bosanska Dubica, Bos. | D11 | 18 |
| Bosanska Gradiška, Bos. | D12 | 18 |
| Bosanski Novi, Bos. | D11 | 18 |
| Bosanski Šamac, Bos. | D2 | 20 |
| Bosavi, Mount, mtn., Pap. N. Gui. | G11 | 38 |
| Boscobel, Wi., U.S. | G5 | 110 |
| Bose, China | C9 | 40 |
| Boshan, China | G5 | 32 |
| Boshoek, S. Afr. | E8 | 66 |
| Boshrūyeh, Iran | E14 | 48 |
| Bosna, stm., Bos. | E13 | 18 |
| Bosna and Herzegovina, ctry., Eur. | G11 | 4 |
| Bosporus see İstanbul Boğazı, strt., Tur. | H13 | 20 |
| Bosque Farms, N.M., U.S. | J10 | 120 |
| Bossangoa, C.A.R. | G4 | 56 |
| Bossé Bangou, Niger | E10 | 64 |
| Bossembélé, C.A.R. | G4 | 56 |
| Bossier City, La., U.S. | J3 | 114 |
| Bosso, Dalal, val., Niger | E11 | 54 |
| Bosten Hu, l., China | C4 | 30 |
| Boston, Eng., U.K. | I13 | 8 |
| Boston, Ga., U.S. | I3 | 112 |
| Boston, Ma., U.S. | E15 | 108 |
| Boston Bar, B.C., Can. | H13 | 102 |
| Boston Mountains, mts., Ar., U.S. | G3 | 114 |
| Boswell, In., U.S. | B9 | 114 |
| Boswell, Ok., U.S. | E11 | 116 |
| Boswell, Pa., U.S. | G7 | 108 |
| Bosworth, Mo., U.S. | C3 | 114 |
| Botād, India | I4 | 44 |
| Botany Bay, b., Austl. | I9 | 70 |
| Boteti, stm., Bots. | C6 | 66 |
| Botha's Hill, S. Afr. | G10 | 66 |
| Bothaville, S. Afr. | F8 | 66 |
| Bothnia, Gulf of, b., Eur. | J17 | 6 |
| Bothwell, Austl. | m19 | 39b |
| Botija, Ilha da, i., Braz. | J11 | 84 |
| Botkins, Oh., U.S. | G2 | 108 |
| Botoşani, Rom. | B10 | 20 |
| Botoşani, co., Rom. | B10 | 20 |
| Botrange, mtn., Bel. | H9 | 12 |
| Botro, C. Iv. | H7 | 64 |
| Botswana, ctry., Afr. | F4 | 58 |
| Bottenhavet (Selkämeri), b., Eur. | K16 | 6 |
| Bottenviken (Perämeri), b., Eur. | I18 | 6 |
| Bottineau, N.D., U.S. | C7 | 118 |
| Botucatu, Braz. | G4 | 79 |
| Botwood, Nf., Can. | C18 | 106 |
| Bouaflé, C. Iv. | H7 | 64 |
| Bou Ahmed, Mor. | J6 | 16 |
| Bouaké, C. Iv. | H7 | 64 |
| Bouandougou, C. Iv. | G7 | 64 |
| Bouar, C.A.R. | G4 | 56 |
| Bou Arada, Tun. | M4 | 18 |
| Bouârfa, Mor. | D10 | 62 |
| Bouaye, Fr. | E5 | 14 |
| Bou Bernous, Alg. | G9 | 62 |
| Bouchegouf, Alg. | M2 | 18 |
| Boucher, stm., P.Q., Can. | C4 | 106 |
| Boucher, Lac, l., P.Q., Can. | A14 | 106 |
| Bouches-du-Rhône, dept., Fr. | I12 | 14 |
| Boudry, Switz. | E6 | 13 |
| Boufarik, Alg. | B12 | 62 |
| Bou Ficha, Tun. | M5 | 18 |
| Bougainville, i., Pap. N. Gui. | I19 | 126 |
| Bougouni, Mali | F6 | 64 |
| Bou Hadjar, Alg. | M3 | 18 |
| Bou Hajar, Alg. | N5 | 18 |
| Bouïra, Alg. | B12 | 62 |
| Boujad, Mor. | D7 | 62 |
| Boujdour, Cap, c., W. Sah. | G3 | 62 |
| Bou Kadir, Alg. | B11 | 62 |
| Bou Khadra, Alg. | N3 | 18 |
| Boukombé, Benin | F10 | 64 |
| Boularderie Island, i., N.S., Can. | F13 | 106 |
| Boulder, Co., U.S. | D11 | 120 |
| Boulder, Mt., U.S. | D13 | 122 |
| Boulder, stm., Mt., U.S. | D13 | 122 |
| Boulder City, Nv., U.S. | H11 | 124 |
| Bouli, stm., Burkina | E9 | 64 |
| Boulia, Austl. | D3 | 70 |
| Boulogne-Billancourt, Fr. | I7 | 14 |
| Boulogne-sur-Gesse, Fr. | I7 | 14 |
| Boulogne-sur-Mer, Fr. | B8 | 14 |
| Boulouba, C.A.R. | N2 | 60 |
| Boulouli, Mali | D5 | 64 |
| Boulsa, Burkina | E9 | 64 |
| Bouly, Maur. | D4 | 64 |
| Boumalne, Mor. | E8 | 62 |
| Boûmdeïd, Maur. | C5 | 64 |
| Bouna, C. Iv. | G8 | 64 |
| Boundary, Ak., U.S. | D24 | 100 |
| Boundary Peak, mtn., Nv., U.S. | G7 | 124 |
| Boundary Ranges, mts., N.A. | G27 | 100 |
| Bountiful, Ut., U.S. | D5 | 120 |
| Bounty Islands, is., N.Z. | M21 | 126 |
| Bouqteb, Alg. | C11 | 62 |
| Boura, Mali | E7 | 64 |
| Bourbeuse, stm., Mo., U.S. | D5 | 114 |
| Bourbon, In., U.S. | A10 | 114 |
| Bourbon, Mo., U.S. | D5 | 114 |
| Bourbon-Lancy, Fr. | F10 | 14 |
| Bourbonnais, hist. reg., Fr. | F9 | 14 |
| Bourbonne-les-Bains, Fr. | E12 | 14 |
| Bourem, Mali | D8 | 64 |
| Bourg, La., U.S. | M6 | 114 |
| Bourganeuf, Fr. | G8 | 14 |
| Bourg-en-Bresse, Fr. | F12 | 14 |
| Bourges, Fr. | E9 | 14 |
| Bourget, On., Can. | B11 | 108 |
| Bourgogne (Burgundy), hist. reg., Fr. | E11 | 14 |
| Bourgogne, Canal de, Fr. | E11 | 14 |
| Bourgoin, Fr. | G12 | 14 |
| Bourg-Saint-Andéol, Fr. | H11 | 14 |
| Bourg-Saint-Maurice, Fr. | G13 | 14 |
| Bourke, Austl. | H6 | 70 |
| Bourne, Eng., U.K. | I13 | 8 |
| Bournemouth, Eng., U.K. | K12 | 8 |
| Bourzanga, Burkina | E9 | 64 |
| Bou Saâda, Alg. | C13 | 62 |
| Bou Salem, Tun. | M3 | 18 |
| Bouse, Az., U.S. | K2 | 120 |
| Boussac, Fr. | F9 | 14 |
| Bousso, Chad | F4 | 56 |
| Boussouma, Burkina | E9 | 64 |
| Bouteldja, Alg. | M3 | 18 |
| Boutilimit, Maur. | C2 | 64 |
| Bouvetøya, i., Ant. | A3 | 73 |
| Bouza, Niger | D13 | 64 |
| Bou Zadjar, Alg. | J10 | 16 |
| Bovalino, Italy | K11 | 18 |
| Bovill, Id., U.S. | D9 | 122 |
| Bovina, Tx., U.S. | D4 | 116 |
| Bovril, Arg. | F9 | 80 |
| Bowang, China | D7 | 34 |
| Bowbells, N.D., U.S. | C5 | 118 |
| Bowden, Ab., U.S. | F20 | 102 |
| Bowdle, S.D., U.S. | F8 | 118 |
| Bowdon, Ga., U.S. | F1 | 112 |
| Bowdon, N.D., U.S. | D8 | 118 |
| Bowen, Arg. | H5 | 80 |
| Bowen, Austl. | C8 | 70 |
| Bowen, Il., U.S. | B5 | 114 |
| Bowie, Az., U.S. | L7 | 120 |
| Bowie, Md., U.S. | H10 | 108 |
| Bowie, Tx., U.S. | F9 | 116 |
| Bow Island, Ab., Can. | I3 | 104 |
| Bowling Green, Fl., U.S. | L5 | 112 |
| Bowling Green, Ky., U.S. | F10 | 114 |
| Bowling Green, Mo., U.S. | C5 | 114 |
| Bowling Green, Oh., U.S. | F3 | 108 |
| Bowling Green, Va., U.S. | A9 | 112 |
| Bowling Green, Cape, c., Austl. | B7 | 70 |
| Bowman, Ga., U.S. | E3 | 112 |
| Bowman, N.D., U.S. | E4 | 118 |
| Bowman, S.C., U.S. | F6 | 112 |
| Bowman, Mount, mtn., B.C., Can. | F10 | 102 |
| Bowmanville, On., Can. | G17 | 110 |
| Bowral, Austl. | J9 | 70 |
| Bowron, stm., B.C., Can. | D12 | 102 |
| Bowron Lake Provincial Park, B.C., Can. | D13 | 102 |
| Boxelder, Mt., U.S. | B15 | 122 |
| Boxey, Nf., Can. | E18 | 106 |
| Boxey Point, c., Nf., Can. | E18 | 106 |
| Boxian, China | B4 | 34 |
| Boxmeer, Neth. | E8 | 12 |
| Boxodoi, China | A3 | 32 |
| Boxtel, Neth. | E7 | 12 |
| Boyacá, dept., Col. | E6 | 84 |
| Boyalık, Tur. | H12 | 20 |
| Boyang, China | G5 | 34 |
| Boyce, La., U.S. | K4 | 114 |
| Boyceville, Wi., U.S. | E3 | 110 |
| Boyd, Mn., U.S. | G12 | 118 |
| Boyd, Tx., U.S. | F9 | 116 |
| Boyd's Cove, Nf., Can. | C19 | 106 |
| Boydton, Va., U.S. | C8 | 112 |
| Boyer, stm., Ia., U.S. | J12 | 118 |
| Boyertown, Pa., U.S. | G11 | 108 |
| Boykins, Va., U.S. | C9 | 112 |
| Boyle, Ab., Can. | C22 | 102 |
| Boyle, Ire. | H5 | 8 |
| Boyle, Ms., U.S. | I6 | 114 |
| Boylston, Al., U.S. | J10 | 114 |
| Boyne, stm., Austl. | E9 | 70 |
| Boyne, stm., Ire. | H7 | 8 |
| Boyne, stm., Mb., Can. | I16 | 104 |
| Boyne City, Mi., U.S. | E10 | 110 |
| Boynton, Ok., U.S. | D11 | 116 |
| Boynton Beach, Fl., U.S. | M6 | 112 |
| Boysen Reservoir, res., Wy., U.S. | G17 | 122 |
| Boys Ranch, Tx., U.S. | D4 | 116 |
| Boyuibe, Bol. | I10 | 82 |
| Bozel, Fr. | G13 | 14 |
| Bozeman, Mt., U.S. | E14 | 122 |
| Bozen see Bolzano, Italy | C6 | 18 |
| Bozhen, China | E4 | 32 |
| Bozoum, C.A.R. | G4 | 56 |
| Bozovici, Rom. | E5 | 20 |
| Bra, Italy | E2 | 18 |
| Brabant, prov., Bel. | G6 | 12 |
| Brabant Island, i., Ant. | B12 | 73 |
| Brabant Lake, l., Sk., Can. | B11 | 104 |
| Bracciano, Italy | G7 | 18 |
| Bracciano, Lago di, l., Italy | G7 | 18 |
| Bracebridge, On., Can. | E16 | 110 |
| Brackendale, B.C., Can. | H11 | 102 |
| Bracken Lake, l., Mb., Can. | E15 | 104 |
| Brackettville, Tx., U.S. | J6 | 116 |
| Braço do Norte, Braz. | E14 | 80 |
| Brad, Rom. | C6 | 20 |
| Bradenton, Fl., U.S. | L4 | 112 |
| Bradford, Ar., U.S. | G5 | 114 |
| Bradford, Il., U.S. | I6 | 110 |
| Bradford, Oh., U.S. | G2 | 108 |
| Bradford, On., Can. | F16 | 110 |
| Bradford, Pa., U.S. | F8 | 108 |
| Bradford, Tn., U.S. | H3 | 114 |
| Bradford, Vt., U.S. | D14 | 108 |
| Bradley, Ar., U.S. | I3 | 114 |
| Bradley, Fl., U.S. | L5 | 112 |
| Bradley, Il., U.S. | I8 | 110 |
| Bradley, S.D., U.S. | F10 | 118 |
| Bracore-Bay, P.Q., Can. | A16 | 106 |
| Bracshaw, Ne., U.S. | K10 | 118 |
| Bracshaw, W.V., U.S. | B5 | 112 |
| Brady, Mt., U.S. | B14 | 122 |
| Brady, Ne., U.S. | J7 | 118 |
| Brady, Tx., U.S. | H7 | 116 |
| Braga, Port. | D3 | 16 |
| Bragado, Arg. | H8 | 80 |
| Bragança, Braz. | D9 | 76 |
| Bragança, Port. | D5 | 16 |
| Bragança Paulista, Braz. | G5 | 79 |
| Braham, Mn., U.S. | E2 | 110 |
| Brahmanbaria, Bngl. | I14 | 44 |
| Brahmani, stm., India | J11 | 44 |
| Brahmapur, India | C8 | 46 |
| Brahmaputra (Yarlung), stm., Asia | G15 | 44 |
| Braich y Pwll, c., Wales, U.K. | I9 | 8 |
| Braidwood, Austl. | J8 | 70 |
| Braidwood, Il., U.S. | I7 | 110 |
| Brälla, Rom. | D11 | 20 |
| Brälla, co., Rom. | D11 | 20 |
| Brainerd, Mn., U.S. | E1 | 110 |
| Braine-l'Alleud (Eigenbrakel), Bel. | G5 | 12 |
| Braine-le-Comte ('s-Gravenbrakel), Bel. | G5 | 12 |
| Brainerd, Mn., U.S. | D1 | 110 |
| Brake, Ger. | B8 | 10 |
| Brakwater, Nmb. | D3 | 66 |
| Bralorne, B.C., Can. | G12 | 102 |
| Braman, Ok., U.S. | C9 | 116 |
| Brampton, On., Can. | G16 | 110 |
| Bramsche, Ger. | C7 | 10 |
| Branch, Nf., Can. | F20 | 106 |
| Branchville, S.C., U.S. | F6 | 112 |
| Branco, stm., Braz. | I13 | 82 |
| Branco, stm., Braz. | C7 | 82 |
| Branco, stm., Braz. | C11 | 82 |
| Branco, stm., Braz. | C9 | 82 |
| Branco, stm., Braz. | C11 | 82 |
| Branco, stm., Braz. | H12 | 84 |
| Brandberg, mtn., Nmb. | C2 | 66 |
| Brandbu, Nor. | K12 | 6 |
| Brandenburg, Ger. | C12 | 10 |
| Brandenburg, Ky., U.S. | D10 | 114 |
| Brandenburg, state, Ger. | C13 | 10 |
| Brand-Erbisdorf, Ger. | E13 | 10 |
| Brandon, Fl., U.S. | L4 | 112 |
| Brandon, Mb., Can. | I15 | 104 |
| Brandon, Ms., U.S. | J7 | 114 |
| Brandon, S.D., U.S. | H11 | 118 |
| Brandon, Vt., U.S. | D13 | 108 |
| Brandon, Wi., U.S. | G7 | 110 |
| Brandsen, Arg. | H9 | 80 |
| Brandvlei, S. Afr. | H5 | 66 |
| Brandýs nad Labem, Czech Rep. | E14 | 10 |
| Branford, Fl., U.S. | J4 | 112 |
| Braniewo, Pol. | A19 | 10 |
| Branquinho, stm., Braz. | A6 | 82 |
| Bransby, Austl. | G5 | 70 |
| Bransfield Strait, strt., Ant. | B12 | 73 |
| Branson, Mo., U.S. | F3 | 114 |
| Brantford, On., Can. | G15 | 110 |
| Brant Lake, N.Y., U.S. | D13 | 108 |
| Brantley, Al., U.S. | K10 | 114 |
| Brantville, N.B., Can. | E9 | 106 |
| Branxholme, Austl. | K4 | 70 |
| Bras d'Or Lake, l., N.S., Can. | G13 | 106 |
| Brasiléia, Braz. | D7 | 82 |
| Brasília, Braz. | C5 | 79 |
| Brasília, Parque Nacional de, Braz. | C4 | 79 |
| Brasília de Minas, Braz. | D6 | 79 |
| Braşov, Rom. | D9 | 20 |
| Braşov, co., Rom. | D8 | 20 |
| Brasstown Bald, mtn., Ga., U.S. | E3 | 112 |
| Bratca, Rom. | C6 | 20 |
| Bratislava, Slvk. | G17 | 10 |
| Bratsk, Russia | F12 | 29 |
| Bratskoje vodochranilišče, res., Russia | F13 | 29 |
| Brattleboro, Vt., U.S. | E14 | 108 |
| Braulio Carrillo, Parque Nacional, C.R. | G10 | 92 |
| Braúnas, Braz. | E7 | 79 |
| Braunau [am Inn], Aus. | G13 | 10 |
| Braunschweig (Brunswick), Ger. | C10 | 10 |
| Brava, i., C.V. | m16 | 64a |
| Brava, Costa, Spain | D15 | 16 |
| Brava, Laguna, l., Arg. | E4 | 80 |
| Brava, Punta, c., Ur. | H10 | 80 |
| Bravicea, Mol. | B12 | 20 |
| Bravo, Cerro, mtn., Bol. | G9 | 82 |
| Bravo, Cerro, mtn., Peru | A2 | 82 |
| Bravo del Norte (Rio Grande), stm., N.A. | F6 | 98 |
| Brawley, Ca., U.S. | L10 | 124 |
| Brawley Peaks, mts., Nv., U.S. | F7 | 124 |
| Bray, Ire. | H7 | 8 |
| Bray Island, i., N.T., Can. | C17 | 96 |
| Braymer, Mo., U.S. | C3 | 114 |
| Brazeau, stm., Ab., Can. | E18 | 102 |
| Brazeau, Mount, mtn., Ab., Can. | E17 | 102 |
| Brazeau Dam, Ab., Can. | E19 | 102 |
| Brazil, ctry., S.A. | F9 | 74 |
| Brazil, In., U.S. | C9 | 114 |
| Brazoria, Tx., U.S. | J11 | 116 |
| Brazos, stm., Tx., U.S. | J11 | 116 |
| Brazzaville, Congo | B3 | 58 |
| Brčko, Bos. | E2 | 20 |
| Brea, Ca., U.S. | K8 | 124 |
| Breadalbane, Austl. | D3 | 70 |
| Breakenridge, Mount, mtn., B.C., Can. | H13 | 102 |
| Breaux Bridge, La., U.S. | L5 | 114 |
| Breaza, Rom. | D9 | 20 |
| Brécey, Fr. | D5 | 14 |
| Brechin, Scot., U.K. | E11 | 8 |
| Breckenridge, Co., U.S. | E10 | 120 |
| Breckenridge, Mi., U.S. | G11 | 110 |
| Breckenridge, Mn., U.S. | E11 | 118 |
| Breckenridge, Tx., U.S. | G8 | 116 |
| Breclav, Czech Rep. | G16 | 10 |
| Brecon, Wales, U.K. | J10 | 8 |
| Breda, Neth. | E6 | 12 |
| Breda, Ia., U.S. | I13 | 118 |
| Bredasdorp, S. Afr. | J5 | 66 |
| Bredenbury, Sk., Can. | H12 | 104 |
| Breese, Il., U.S. | D7 | 114 |
| Breezand, Neth. | C6 | 12 |
| Bregenz, Aus. | H9 | 10 |
| Bréhal, Fr. | D5 | 14 |
| Breidafjördur, b., Ice. | B2 | 6a |
| Brejo, Braz. | D10 | 76 |
| Brejões, Braz. | B9 | 79 |
| Brekken, Nor. | J12 | 6 |
| Brekstad, Nor. | J11 | 6 |
| Bremen, Ger. | B8 | 10 |
| Bremen, Ga., U.S. | F1 | 112 |
| Bremen, In., U.S. | A10 | 114 |
| Bremen, state, Ger. | B8 | 10 |
| Bremerhaven, Ger. | B8 | 10 |
| Bremerton, Wa., U.S. | C3 | 122 |
| Bremervörde, Ger. | B9 | 10 |
| Bremond, Tx., U.S. | H10 | 116 |
| Brenham, Tx., U.S. | I10 | 116 |
| Brenner Pass, Eur. | H11 | 10 |
| Brent, Fl., U.S. | L9 | 114 |
| Brentford, Eng., U.K. | J13 | 8 |
| Brentwood, Tn., U.S. | H10 | 114 |
| Brescia, Italy | D5 | 18 |
| Breslau see Wrocław, Pol. | D17 | 10 |
| Bresse, reg., Fr. | F12 | 14 |
| Bressuire, Fr. | F6 | 14 |
| Brest, Bela. | C23 | 17 |
| Brest, Fr. | D2 | 14 |
| Breteuil, Fr. | C9 | 14 |
| Breteuil, Fr. | D7 | 14 |
| Breteuil-sur-Iton, Fr. | D7 | 14 |
| Breton, Ab., Can. | D20 | 102 |
| Breton islands, is., La., U.S. | M7 | 114 |
| Breton Sound, strt., La., U.S. | M7 | 114 |
| Brett, Cape, c., N.Z. | A5 | 72 |
| Bretten, Ger. | F8 | 10 |
| Breu, stm., Braz. | I9 | 84 |
| Breu, Rio do, stm., Braz. | I9 | 84 |
| Brevard, N.C., U.S. | D4 | 112 |
| Breves, Braz. | D8 | 76 |
| Brevoort Island, i., N.T., Can. | D20 | 96 |
| Brewarrina, Austl. | G7 | 70 |
| Brewer, Me., U.S. | C18 | 108 |
| Brewster, Ne., U.S. | J8 | 118 |
| Brewster, Oh., U.S. | G5 | 108 |
| Brewster, Wa., U.S. | B6 | 122 |
| Brewster, Kap, c., Grnld. | B17 | 86 |
| Brewster, Lake, l., Austl. | H7 | 70 |
| Brewton, Al., U.S. | K9 | 114 |
| Brežice, Slvn. | D10 | 18 |
| Breznik, Bul. | G6 | 20 |
| Bria, C.A.R. | N1 | 60 |
| Brian Boru Peak, mtn., Can. | H18 | 104 |
| Briançon, Fr. | H13 | 14 |
| Brian Head, mtn., Ut., U.S. | F4 | 120 |
| Briare, Fr. | E9 | 14 |
| Bricelyn, Mn., U.S. | G2 | 110 |
| Briceni, Mol. | A11 | 20 |
| Briceville, Tn., U.S. | C12 | 112 |
| Briçonnet, Lac, l., P.Q., Can. | A13 | 106 |
| Bricquebec, Fr. | C5 | 14 |
| Bridge, stm., B.C., Can. | G11 | 102 |
| Bridge City, Tx., U.S. | L3 | 114 |
| Bridge Lake, B.C., Can. | F14 | 102 |
| Bridgeport, Al., U.S. | H11 | 114 |
| Bridgeport, Ca., U.S. | F6 | 124 |
| Bridgeport, Ct., U.S. | F13 | 108 |
| Bridgeport, Il., U.S. | D9 | 114 |
| Bridgeport, Mi., U.S. | G12 | 110 |
| Bridgeport, Ne., U.S. | J4 | 118 |
| Bridgeport, On., Can. | G15 | 110 |
| Bridgeport, Tx., U.S. | F9 | 116 |
| Bridgeport, Wa., U.S. | B6 | 122 |
| Bridgeport, W.V., U.S. | H6 | 108 |
| Bridgeport, Lake, res., Tx., U.S. | F9 | 116 |
| Bridgeton, Mt., U.S. | E17 | 122 |
| Bridgetown, Austl. | F3 | 68 |
| Bridgetown, Barb. | H15 | 94 |
| Bridgetown, N.S., Can. | H8 | 106 |
| Bridgetown, De., U.S. | I11 | 108 |
| Bridgewater, Austl. | N7 | 70 |
| Bridgewater, Ma., U.S. | F15 | 108 |
| Bridgewater, N.S., Can. | H9 | 106 |
| Bridgewater, S.D., U.S. | H10 | 118 |
| Bridgewater, Va., U.S. | I8 | 108 |
| Bridgman, Mi., U.S. | I9 | 110 |
| Bridgton, Me., U.S. | C16 | 108 |
| Bridgwater, Eng., U.K. | J10 | 8 |
| Brie, reg., Fr. | D10 | 14 |
| Briec, Fr. | D2 | 14 |
| Brienne-le-Château, Fr. | D11 | 14 |
| Brienz, Switz. | E9 | 13 |
| Brienzersee, l., Switz. | E9 | 13 |
| Brier Island, i., N.S., Can. | H7 | 106 |
| Briey, Fr. | C12 | 14 |
| Brig, Switz. | F9 | 13 |
| Brigg, Eng., U.K. | H13 | 8 |
| Briggs, Tx., U.S. | I9 | 116 |
| Brigham City, Ut., U.S. | C4 | 120 |
| Bright, Austl. | K7 | 70 |
| Brighton, Eng., U.K. | K13 | 8 |
| Brighton, Ia., U.S. | I4 | 110 |
| Brighton, Il., U.S. | C6 | 114 |
| Brighton, Mi., U.S. | H12 | 110 |
| Brighton, N.Y., U.S. | D9 | 108 |
| Brighton Downs, Austl. | D4 | 70 |
| Brightsand Lake, l., Sk., Can. | E6 | 104 |
| Brignoles, Fr. | I13 | 14 |
| Brigus, Nf., Can. | E20 | 106 |
| Brikama, Gam. | E1 | 64 |
| Brilhante, stm., Braz. | F1 | 79 |
| Brilliant, Al., U.S. | H9 | 114 |
| Brilliant, B.C., Can. | H17 | 102 |
| Brillion, Wi., U.S. | F7 | 110 |
| Brilon, Ger. | D8 | 10 |
| Brindisi, Italy | I12 | 18 |
| Brinje, Cro. | D10 | 18 |
| Brinkley, Ar., U.S. | H5 | 114 |
| Brion, Île, i., P.Q., Can. | E12 | 106 |
| Brioude, Fr. | G10 | 14 |
| Briouze, Fr. | D6 | 14 |
| Brisbane, Austl. | F10 | 70 |
| Bristol, Eng., U.K. | J11 | 8 |
| Bristol, Fl., U.S. | I2 | 112 |
| Bristol, N.H., U.S. | D15 | 108 |
| Bristol, Pa., U.S. | G12 | 108 |
| Bristol, R.I., U.S. | F15 | 108 |
| Bristol, S.D., U.S. | F10 | 118 |
| Bristol, Tn., U.S. | C4 | 112 |
| Bristol, Vt., U.S. | C13 | 108 |
| Bristol Bay, b., Ak., U.S. | G15 | 100 |
| Bristol Lake, l., Ca., U.S. | I10 | 124 |
| Bristow, Ok., U.S. | D10 | 116 |
| Britânia, Braz. | C3 | 79 |
| Britannia Beach, B.C., Can. | H11 | 102 |
| British Columbia, prov., Can. | F7 | 96 |
| British Honduras see Belize, ctry., N.A. | I15 | 90 |
| British Indian Ocean Territory, dep., Afr. | J8 | 24 |
| British Mountains, mts., N.A. | B24 | 100 |
| British Virgin Islands, dep., N.A. | E12 | 94 |
| Brits, S. Afr. | E8 | 66 |
| Britstown, S. Afr. | H6 | 66 |
| Britt, Ia., U.S. | G2 | 110 |
| Brittany see Bretagne, hist. reg., Fr. | D3 | 14 |
| Britton, S.D., U.S. | F10 | 118 |
| Brive-la-Gaillarde, Fr. | G8 | 14 |
| Brixton, Austl. | D6 | 70 |
| Brno, Czech Rep. | F16 | 10 |
| Broa, Ensenada de la, b., Cuba | C3 | 94 |
| Broad, stm., U.S. | E5 | 112 |
| Broadback, stm., P.Q., Can. | F17 | 96 |
| Broadford, Scot., U.K. | D8 | 8 |
| Broad Sound, strt., Austl. | D9 | 70 |
| Broad Sound Channel, strt., Austl. | D9 | 70 |
| Broadus, Mt., U.S. | E4 | 122 |
| Broadview, Sk., Can. | H12 | 104 |
| Broadwater, Ne., U.S. | J5 | 118 |
| Broadway, Va., U.S. | I8 | 108 |
| Brochet, Mb., Can. | E12 | 96 |
| Brochet, Lac au, l., P.Q., Can. | C4 | 106 |
| Brochet, Lac, l., Mb., Can. | D12 | 96 |
| Brock, Sk., Can. | G6 | 104 |
| Brockport, N.Y., U.S. | D9 | 108 |
| Brockton, Ma., U.S. | E15 | 108 |
| Brockville, On., Can. | C11 | 108 |
| Brockway, Pa., U.S. | F8 | 108 |
| Brocton, N.Y., U.S. | E7 | 108 |
| Brodeur Peninsula, pen., N.T., Can. | B15 | 96 |
| Brodhead, Ky., U.S. | B2 | 112 |
| Brodhead, Wi., U.S. | H6 | 110 |
| Brodnax, Va., U.S. | C8 | 112 |
| Brodnica, Pol. | B19 | 10 |
| Brogan, Or., U.S. | F8 | 122 |
| Broken Arrow, Ok., U.S. | C11 | 116 |
| Broken Bay, b., Austl. | I9 | 70 |
| Broken Bow, Ne., U.S. | J8 | 118 |
| Broken Bow, Ok., U.S. | H2 | 114 |
| Broken Bow Lake, res., Ok., U.S. | H2 | 114 |
| Brokenhead, stm., Mb., Can. | H18 | 104 |
| Broken Hill, Austl. | H4 | 70 |
| Brokopondo, Sur. | B8 | 76 |
| Brokopondo Stuwmeer, res., Sur. | C7 | 76 |
| Bromptonville, P.Q., Can. | B15 | 108 |
| Brønlund Peak, mtn., B.C., Can. | E7 | 96 |
| Bronnae, Bela. | I13 | 22 |
| Bronnicy, Russia | F21 | 22 |
| Bronson, Fl., U.S. | J4 | 112 |
| Bronson, Ks., U.S. | N12 | 118 |
| Bronson, Mi., U.S. | I10 | 110 |
| Bronson, Tx., U.S. | K2 | 114 |
| Bronson Lake, l., Sk., Can. | E5 | 104 |
| Brontë, Italy | L9 | 18 |
| Brontë, Tx., U.S. | H6 | 116 |
| Bronwood, Ga., U.S. | H2 | 112 |
| Brooch, Lac, l., P.Q., Can. | B6 | 106 |
| Brook, In., U.S. | B9 | 114 |
| Brookeland, Tx., U.S. | K2 | 114 |
| Brooker, Fl., U.S. | J4 | 112 |
| Brookfield, Mo., U.S. | C3 | 114 |
| Brookfield, N.S., Can. | G10 | 106 |
| Brookfield, Wi., U.S. | G7 | 110 |
| Brookford, N.C., U.S. | D5 | 112 |
| Brookhaven, Ms., U.S. | K6 | 114 |
| Brookings, Or., U.S. | H1 | 122 |
| Brookings, S.D., U.S. | G11 | 118 |
| Brookland, Ar., U.S. | G5 | 114 |
| Brooklet, Ga., U.S. | G5 | 112 |
| Brooklyn, Ia., U.S. | I3 | 110 |
| Brooklyn, Mi., U.S. | H11 | 110 |
| Brooklyn, Ms., U.S. | K7 | 114 |
| Brooklyn, N.S., Can. | H9 | 106 |
| Brooklyn Center, Mn., U.S. | E2 | 110 |
| Brookmere, B.C., Can. | H14 | 102 |
| Brookneal, Va., U.S. | B8 | 112 |
| Brookport, Il., U.S. | E8 | 114 |
| Brooks, Ab., Can. | G23 | 102 |
| Brooks, Me., U.S. | C17 | 108 |
| Brooks, Mount, mtn., Ak., U.S. | E19 | 100 |
| Brooks Bay, b., B.C., Can. | G7 | 102 |
| Brookshire, Tx., U.S. | J11 | 116 |
| Brooks Range, mts., Ak., U.S. | C16 | 100 |
| Brooksville, Fl., U.S. | K4 | 112 |
| Brooksville, Ky., U.S. | I2 | 110 |
| Brooksville, Ms., U.S. | I8 | 114 |
| Brookton, Austl. | F3 | 68 |
| Brookville, In., U.S. | C11 | 114 |
| Brookville, Pa., U.S. | F7 | 108 |
| Brookville Lake, res., in., U.S. | C11 | 114 |
| Broome, Austl. | C4 | 68 |
| Broomfield, Co., U.S. | E11 | 120 |
| Broons, Fr. | D4 | 14 |
| Brora, Scot., U.K. | C10 | 8 |
| Brotas de Macaúbas, Braz. | B7 | 79 |
| Brou, Fr. | D8 | 14 |
| Broughton Island, i., N.T., Can. | C20 | 96 |
| Broughty Ferry, Scot., U.K. | E11 | 8 |
| Brouwersdam, Neth. | E4 | 12 |
| Brouwershaven, Neth. | E4 | 12 |
| Browerville, Mn., U.S. | E1 | 110 |
| Brown City, Mi., U.S. | G13 | 110 |
| Brown Deer, Wi., U.S. | G8 | 110 |
| Browne Bay, b., N.T., Can. | B13 | 96 |
| Brownfield, Tx., U.S. | F4 | 116 |
| Browning, Mo., U.S. | B3 | 114 |
| Browning Entrance, b., B.C., Can. | D4 | 102 |
| Brown Lake, l., N.T., Can. | C14 | 96 |
| Brownlee Reservoir, res., U.S. | F8 | 122 |
| Brownsburg, In., U.S. | C10 | 114 |
| Brownsburg, P.Q., Can. | B12 | 108 |
| Brownsdale, Mn., U.S. | G3 | 110 |
| Brownstown, Il., U.S. | D8 | 114 |
| Brownstown, In., U.S. | D10 | 114 |
| Browns Valley, Mn., U.S. | F11 | 118 |
| Brownsville, Ky., U.S. | E10 | 114 |
| Brownsville, La., U.S. | J4 | 114 |
| Brownsville, Or., U.S. | F3 | 122 |
| Brownsville, Pa., U.S. | G7 | 108 |
| Brownsville, Tn., U.S. | G7 | 114 |
| Brownsville, Tx., U.S. | N9 | 116 |
| Brownton, Mn., U.S. | F1 | 110 |
| Brownvale, Ab., Can. | A17 | 102 |
| Brownville, Me., U.S. | B17 | 108 |
| Brownville Junction, Me., U.S. | B17 | 108 |
| Brownwood, Tx., U.S. | H8 | 116 |
| Browse Island, i., Austl. | B4 | 68 |
| Broxton, Ga., U.S. | H4 | 112 |
| Broža, Bela. | I12 | 22 |
| Bruay-en-Artois, Fr. | B9 | 14 |
| Bruce, S.D., U.S. | G11 | 118 |
| Bruce, Wi., U.S. | E4 | 110 |
| Bruce, Mount, mtn., Austl. | D3 | 68 |
| Bruce Lake, On., Can. | H21 | 104 |
| Bruce Mines, On., Can. | D12 | 110 |
| Bruce Peninsula, pen., On., Can. | E14 | 110 |
| Bruce Peninsula National Park, On., Can. | E14 | 110 |
| Bruchsal, Ger. | F8 | 10 |
| Bruck an der Mur, Aus. | H15 | 10 |
| Bruderheim, Ab., Can. | D22 | 102 |
| Bruges (Brugge), Bel. | F3 | 12 |
| Brugg, Switz. | D9 | 13 |
| Brugge (Bruges), Bel. | F3 | 12 |
| Brühl, Ger. | E6 | 10 |
| Bruinisse, Neth. | E5 | 12 |
| Bruin Point, mtn., Ut., U.S. | E5 | 120 |
| Bruja, Cerro, mtn., Pan. | H15 | 92 |
| Brule, stm., U.S. | E7 | 110 |
| Brumadinho, Braz. | F6 | 79 |
| Brumado, Braz. | C8 | 79 |
| Brumath, Fr. | D14 | 14 |
| Brundidge, Al., U.S. | K11 | 114 |
| Bruneau, Id., U.S. | H10 | 122 |
| Bruneau, stm., U.S. | H10 | 122 |
| Brunei, ctry., Asia | E6 | 36 |
| Brunette Island, i., Nf., Can. | E18 | 106 |
| Bruni, Tx., U.S. | M8 | 116 |
| Brunico, Italy | C6 | 18 |
| Bruno, Sk., Can. | F9 | 104 |
| Bruno, S.C., U.S. | F9 | 112 |
| Brunswick see Braunschweig, Ger. | C10 | 10 |
| Brunswick, Ga., U.S. | H5 | 112 |

Brunswick, Md., U.S. — H9 108
Brunswick, Oh., U.S. — D17 108
Brunswick, Mo., U.S. — C3 114
Brunswick, Oh., U.S. — F5 108
Brunswick, Peninsula, pen., Chile — G2 78
Bruntál, Czech Rep. — F17 10
Brus, Laguna de, b., Hond. — B10 92
Brush, Co., U.S. — K4 118
Brus Laguna, Hond. — B10 92
Brusovo, Russia — D18 22
Brusque, Braz. — D14 80
Brussels see Bruxelles, Bel. — G5 12
Brussels, On., Can. — G14 110
Brusy, Pol. — B17 10
Bruthen, Austl. — K7 70
Bruxelles (Brussel) (Brussels), Bel. — G5 12
Bruyères, Fr. — D13 14
Brucual, Ven. — C8 84
Bryan, Tx., U.S. — F2 108
Bryan, Tx., U.S. — I10 116
Bryansk see Br'ansk, Russia — H17 22
Bryant, Ar., U.S. — H4 114
Bryant, S.D., U.S. — G10 118
Bryce Canyon National Park, U.S. — G4 120
Bryson, P.Q., Can. — B10 108
Bryson, Tx., U.S. — F8 116
Bryson City, N.C., U.S. — D3 112
Brzeg, Pol. — E17 10
Brzesko, Pol. — F20 10
Brzeziny, Pol. — D19 10
Bsharrī, Leb. — A6 48
Bua Yai, Thai. — G7 40
Buba, Gui.-B. — F2 64
Bū Bārīl, Jabal, mtn., Afr. — F3 60
Bubaque, Gui.-B. — F2 64
Būbiyān, I., Kuw. — G10 48
Bucaramanga, Col. — D6 84
Buccaneer Archipelago, is., Austl. — C4 68
Buccino, Italy — I10 18
Buchanan, Ga., U.S. — F1 112
Buchanan, Lib. — I4 64
Buchanan, Mi., U.S. — I3 110
Buchanan, Sk., Can. — G12 104
Buchanan, Va., U.S. — B7 112
Buchanan, Lake, I., Austl. — C6 70
Buchanan, Lake, res., Tx., U.S. — I8 116
Buchans, Nf., Can. — D17 106
Buchara, Uzb. — J10 26
Bucharest see București, Rom. — E10 20
Buchholz, Ger. — B9 10
Buchloe, Ger. — G10 10
Buchs, Switz. — D11 13
Buchy, Fr. — C8 14
Buckatunna, Ms., U.S. — K8 114
Bückeburg, Ger. — C9 10
Buckeye, Az., U.S. — K4 120
Buckeye Lake, Oh., U.S. — H4 108
Buckhannon, W.V., U.S. — I6 108
Buckhaven, Scot., U.K. — E10 8
Buckholts, Tx., U.S. — I9 116
Buckie, Scot., U.K. — D11 8
Buckingham, P.Q., Can. — B11 108
Buckingham, Va., U.S. — B8 112
Buckingham Bay, b., Austl. — B7 68
Buckinghamshire, co., Eng., U.K. — J13 8
Buck Lake, I., Ab., Can. — D20 102
Buckland, Ak., U.S. — D14 100
Bucklands, S. Afr. — G6 66
Buckley, Il., U.S. — J7 110
Buckley, Wa., U.S. — C3 122
Buckley, stm., Austl. — C3 70
Bucklin, Ks., U.S. — N8 118
Bucklin, Mo., U.S. — C5 114
Buckow, Ger. — C14 10
Bucksport, Me., U.S. — C18 108
Bucovăţ, Mol. — B12 20
Bucun, China — G5 32
București (Bucharest), Rom. — E10 20
Bucyrus, Oh., U.S. — G4 108
Buda, Il., U.S. — I6 110
Buda, Tx., U.S. — I9 116
Budalin, Myan. — C3 40
Budapest, Hung. — H19 10
Búðardalur, Ice. — B3 6a
Budaun, India — F8 44
Buddu, Sudan — L3 60
Bude, Ms., U.S. — K6 114
Büdingen, Ger. — E9 10
Búðir, Ice. — B7 6a
Budogošč', Russia — B15 22
Bud'onnovsk, Russia — I6 26
Budweis see České Budějovice, Czech Rep. — G14 10
Buea, Cam. — I14 64
Buena Esperanza, Arg. — H6 80
Buenaventura, Col. — F4 84
Buenaventura, Mex. — C6 90
Buena Vista, Bol. — G10 82
Buena Vista, Co., U.S. — F10 120
Buena Vista, Ga., U.S. — G2 112
Buena Vista, Ms., U.S. — I8 114
Buena Vista, Para. — D10 80
Buena Vista, Va., U.S. — B7 112
Buendia, Embalse de, res., Spain — E9 16
Buenópolis, Braz. — D6 79
Buenos Aires, Arg. — H9 80
Buenos Aires, Col. — F4 84
Buenos Aires, C.R. — H11 92
Buenos Aires, prov., Arg. — I8 80
Buenos Aires (Lago General Carrera), I., S.A. — F2 78
Buerarema, Braz. — C9 79
Buesaco, Col. — G4 84
Buffalo, Ks., U.S. — N12 118
Buffalo, Mn., U.S. — E2 110
Buffalo, Mo., U.S. — E3 114
Buffalo, N.Y., U.S. — E8 108
Buffalo, Oh., U.S. — H5 108
Buffalo, Ok., U.S. — C7 116
Buffalo, S.C., U.S. — E5 112
Buffalo, S.D., U.S. — F4 118
Buffalo, Wy., U.S. — F19 122
Buffalo, stm., Ar., U.S. — F4 114
Buffalo, stm., Can. — E10 96
Buffalo, stm., Mn., U.S. — D1 118
Buffalo, stm., Ms., U.S. — K5 114
Buffalo, stm., Tn., U.S. — G10 114
Buffalo, stm., Wi., U.S. — F4 110
Buffalo Center, Ia., U.S. — G2 110
Buffalo Lake, Il., U.S. — G13 118
Buffalo Lake, I., Ab., Can. — E22 102
Buffalo Lake, I., Sk., Can. — D9 96
Buffalo Narrows, Sk., Can. — C6 104
Buffalo Pound Lake, I., Sk., Can. — H9 104
Buffalo Pound Provincial Park, Sk., Can. — H9 104
Buford, Ga., U.S. — E2 112
Bug, stm., Eur. — E18 4
Buga, Col. — F4 84
Buga, Nig. — G13 64
Bugalagrande, Col. — E4 84

Bugeat, Fr. — G8 14
Bugojno, Bos. — E12 18
Bugry, Russia — C18 22
Bugt, China — B11 30
Bugt, China — A8 32
Buguruslan, Russia — G8 26
Buhera, Zimb. — B10 66
Buhl, Id., U.S. — H12 122
Buhl, Mn., U.S. — C3 110
Buhuşi, Rom. — C10 20
Builth Wells, Wales, U.K. — I10 8
Buin, Chile — G3 80
Buin, Piz, mtn., Eur. — E13 13
Buir Nuur, I., Asia — B10 30
Buj, Russia — C24 22
Bujalance, Spain — H7 16
Buji, China — D16 44
Bujnaksk, Russia — I7 26
Bujumbura, Bdi. — B5 58
Bukačača, Russia — G15 28
Bukama, D.R.C. — C5 58
Būkān, Iran — O6 40
Bukavu, D.R.C. — B5 58
Bukittinggi, Indon. — O6 40
Bukovina, hist. reg., Eur. — B9 20
Bülach, Switz. — C10 13
Bukmarino, Russia — D23 22
Bulan, Phil. — o20 39b
Bulandshahr, India — F7 44
Bûlâq, Egypt — E6 60
Bulawayo, Zimb. — C9 66
Buldibuyo, Peru — C3 82
Bulgan, Mong. — B5 30
Bulgan, Mong. — B7 30
Bulgaria (Bâlgarija), ctry., Eur. — G13 4
Bûlki, Russia — N9 60
Bulkley, stm., B.C., Can. — C7 102
Bulkley Ranges, mts., B.C., Can. — C7 102
Bull, stm., B.C., Can. — H19 102
Bullard, Tx., U.S. — G11 116
Bullas, Spain — G10 16
Buller, Mount, mtn., Austl. — K7 70
Bullfinch, Austl. — F3 68
Bull Harbour, B.C., Can. — G7 102
Bullhead, S.D., U.S. — F6 118
Bullhead City, Az., U.S. — I2 120
Bull Mountain, mtn., Mt., U.S. — D13 122
Bullock, N.C., U.S. — C8 112
Bullock Creek, Austl. — A6 70
Bulloo, stm., Austl. — G5 70
Bullpound Creek, stm., Ab., Can. — F23 102
Bulls Gap, Tn., U.S. — C3 112
Bull Shoals, Ar., U.S. — F4 114
Bull Shoals Lake, res., U.S. — F4 114
Bulnes, Chile — I2 80
Bultfontein, S. Afr. — G8 66
Bulukumba, Indon. — G7 38
Bumba, D.R.C. — A4 58
Bumbuna, S.L. — G4 64
Bumpus, Mount, hill, N.T., Can. — C10 96
Buna, Tx., U.S. — L3 114
Bunavista, Tx., U.S. — D5 116
Bunbury, Austl. — F3 68
Bunceton, Mo., U.S. — D4 114
Bundaberg, Austl. — E10 70
Bünde, Ger. — C8 10
Bundi, India — H6 44
Bungo-suidō, strt., Japan — N7 36
Bunia, D.R.C. — A6 58
Bunker Group, is., Austl. — D10 70
Bunker Hill, Il., U.S. — C7 114
Bunker Hill, In., U.S. — B10 114
Bunker Hill, Or., U.S. — G8 122
Bunker Hill, mtn., Nv., U.S. — E8 124
Bunkie, La., U.S. — L4 114
Bunnell, Fl., U.S. — J5 112
Buntok, Indon. — F5 38
Bünyan, Tur. — B3 48
Bunyola, Spain — F11 16
Bunza, Nig. — E11 64
Buon Me Thuot, Viet. — H10 40
Buor-Chaja, guba, b., Russia — C18 28
Buor-Chaja, mys, c., Russia — C18 28
Buqayq, Sau. Ar. — B6 47
Bura, Kenya — B7 58
Buram, Sudan — L3 60
Burang, China — E9 30
Buranhém, stm., Braz. — D9 79
Buras, La., U.S. — M7 114
Buraydah, Sau. Ar. — H7 48
Burbank, Ca., U.S. — J7 124
Burbank, Wa., U.S. — D6 122
Burco, Som. — G10 56
Burdekin, stm., Austl. — B7 70
Burden, Ks., U.S. — N11 118
Burdett, Ab., Can. — H23 102
Burdett, Ks., U.S. — M8 118
Burdur, Tur. — H14 4
Bure, Eth. — L9 60
Bure, Eth. — M8 60
Bureinskij chrebet, mts., Russia — G18 28
Bureja, stm., Russia — G18 28
Büren, Ger. — D8 10
Burford, On., Can. — G15 110
Bür Fu'ād, Egypt — F2 48
Burg [auf Fehmarn], Ger. — A11 10
Burgas, Bul. — G11 20
Burgaw, N.C., U.S. — E9 112
Burg [bei Magdeburg], Ger. — C11 10
Burgdorf, Switz. — D8 13
Burgenland, state, Aus. — H13 10
Burgeo, Nf., Can. — E16 106
Burgersdorp, S. Afr. — H8 66
Burgess, Va., U.S. — B10 112
Burgettstown, Pa., U.S. — G6 108
Burgin, China — B4 30
Burgin, Ky., U.S. — E12 114
Burglengenfeld, Ger. — F12 10
Burgos, Mex. — E10 90
Burgos, Spain — C8 16
Burgos, prov., Spain — C8 16
Burgstädt, Ger. — E12 10
Burgundy see Bourgogne, hist. reg., Fr. — E11 14
Burhaniye, Tur. — J10 20
Burhänpur, India — J7 44
Buri, Braz. — G4 79
Burjassot, Spain — F11 16
Burica, Punta, c., N.A. — C3 92
Buri Ram, Thai. — G7 40
Buritama, Braz. — F3 79
Buriti, Braz. — E12 82
Buriti Alegre, Braz. — E4 79
Buritirama, Braz. — D6 79
Buritizeiro, Braz. — D6 79
Burjatija, state, Russia — G20 28

Burke, S.D., U.S. — H8 118
Burke, stm., Austl. — D3 70
Burke Channel, strt., B.C., Can. — E7 102
Burkesville, Ky., U.S. — F11 114
Burketown, Austl. — B2 70
Burkina Faso, ctry., Afr. — F6 54
Burleson, Tx., U.S. — G9 116
Burley, Id., U.S. — H12 122
Burlingame, Ca., U.S. — G3 124
Burlington, Co., U.S. — L5 118
Burlington, Ia., U.S. — J4 110
Burlington, Ks., U.S. — M12 118
Burlington, N.C., U.S. — C7 112
Burlington, N.D., U.S. — C6 118
Burlington, Nf., Can. — C17 106
Burlington, N.J., U.S. — G12 108
Burlington, On., Can. — G16 110
Burlington, Vt., U.S. — C13 108
Burlington, Wa., U.S. — B3 122
Burlington, Wi., U.S. — H7 110
Burlington, Wy., U.S. — F17 122
Burlington Junction, Mo., U.S. — B1 114
Burma see Myanmar, ctry., Asia — A2 38
Burmā, Tall, mtn., Jord. — G5 50
Burmakino, Russia — D23 22
Burnaby, B.C., Can. — H12 102
Burnaby Island, i., B.C., Can. — E3 102
Burnet, Tx., U.S. — I8 116
Burnett, stm., Austl. — E10 70
Burnett Bay, b., N.T., Can. — D4 124
Burney, Ca., U.S. — D4 124
Burnham, Pa., U.S. — G9 108
Burnie, Austl. — M6 70
Burnley, Eng., U.K. — H11 8
Burns, Ks., U.S. — M11 118
Burns, Or., U.S. — G6 122
Burns, Tn., U.S. — F9 114
Burns, Wy., U.S. — J3 118
Burns Flat, Ok., U.S. — D7 116
Burnside, stm., N.T., Can. — C11 96
Burns Lake, B.C., Can. — C9 102
Burnsville, Ms., U.S. — J10 114
Burnsville, Ms., U.S. — H8 114
Burnsville, N.C., U.S. — D4 112
Burnt, stm., Or., U.S. — F8 122
Burnt Island, Nf., Can. — E15 106
Burnt Pond, I., Nf., Can. — D16 106
Burntwood, stm., Mb., Can. — C17 104
Burntwood Lake, I., Mb., Can. — C14 104
Burra, Austl. — I3 70
Burragorang, Lake, res., Austl. — I9 70
Burramurra, Austl. — C2 70
Burrendong Reservoir, res., Austl. — I8 70
Burriñuck Reservoir, res., Austl. — J7 70
Burr Oak, Ks., U.S. — L9 118
Burro Burro, stm., Guy. — E13 84
Burro Peak, mtn., N.M., U.S. — L8 120
Burton, Ks., U.S. — M10 118
Burton, Mi., U.S. — G12 110
Burton, Tx., U.S. — I10 116
Burton, B.C., Can. — G12 110
Burt Lake, I., Mi., U.S. — E11 110
Burträsk, Swe. — I14 6
Burundi, ctry., Afr. — B6 58
Burūm, Yemen — G6 47
Burwash, On., Can. — D15 110
Burwash Landing, Yk., Can. — F25 100
Burwell, Ne., U.S. — J8 118
Bury Saint Edmunds, Eng., U.K. — I14 8
Busby, Mt., U.S. — E19 122
Busca, Italy — E2 18
Bush, stm., S.C., U.S. — E5 112
Bushland, Tx., U.S. — D4 116
Bush Lot, Guy. — D14 84
Bushnell, Fl., U.S. — K4 112
Bushnell, Il., U.S. — J5 110
Bushton, Ks., U.S. — M9 118
Bushtyna, Ukr. — A7 20
Buskerud, co., Nor. — K11 6
Busko Zdrój, Pol. — E20 10
Buşra al-Harīrī (Bosor), Syria — C6 50
Buşrá ash-Shām, Syria — C6 50
Busselton, Austl. — F3 68
Bussum, Neth. — D7 12
Bustamante, Mex. — D9 90
Busto Arsizio, Italy — D3 18
Busu-Djanoa, D.R.C. — A4 58
Bušuicha, Russia — B23 22
Buta, D.R.C. — H5 56
Butajira, Eth. — M10 60
Buta Ranquil, Arg. — I4 80
Butare, Rw. — B5 58
Bute Inlet, b., B.C., Can. — G10 102
Butera, Italy — L9 18
Butere, Kenya — A6 58
Butha Qi, China — B11 30
Butiá, Braz. — F13 80
Butler, Al., U.S. — J8 114
Butler, Ga., U.S. — G2 112
Butler, In., U.S. — A12 114
Butler, Mo., U.S. — D2 114
Butler, Pa., U.S. — G7 108
Butnau Lake, I., Mb., Can. — B19 104
Butner, N.C., U.S. — C8 112
Butru, Pulau, i., Indon. — F8 38
Butte, Mt., U.S. — D13 122
Butte, Ne., U.S. — I8 118
Butte Creek, stm., Ca., U.S. — E4 124
Butte du Lion, hist., Bel. — F2 64
Butte Falls, Or., U.S. — H3 122
Butterfield, Mn., U.S. — H13 118
Butternut, Wi., U.S. — D5 110
Butterworth, S. Afr. — H8 66
Buttle Lake, I., B.C., Can. — H9 102
Button Islands, is., N.T., Can. — D20 96
Buttonwillow, Ca., U.S. — I6 124
Butuan, Phil. — D8 38

Butylicy, Russia — F24 22
Butzbach, Ger. — E8 10
Bützow, Ger. — B11 10
Buurgplaatz, mtn., Lux. — H9 12
Buxtehude, Ger. — B9 10
Buxton, Guy. — D13 84
Buxton, N.C., U.S. — D11 112
Buxton, N.D., U.S. — D10 118
Buxton, S. Afr. — F7 66
Buxton, Mount, mtn., B.C., Can. — F7 102
Buxy, Fr. — F11 14
Buyo, C.I. — H6 64
Buzançais, Fr. — F8 14
Buzău, Rom. — D10 20
Buzău, co., Rom. — D10 20
Buzău, stm., Rom. — D11 20
Buzen, Japan — N6 36
Búzios, Ponta dos, c., Braz. — G8 79
Buzuluk, Russia — G8 26
Byam Channel, strt., N.T., Can. — A11 96
Byam Martin Channel, strt., N.T., Can. — A12 96
Byam Martin Island, i., N.T., Can. — A12 96
Bydgoszcz, Pol. — B18 10
Byelorussia see Belarus, ctry., Eur. — E13 4
Byers, Tx., U.S. — E8 116
Byesville, Oh., U.S. — H5 108
Bygdin, Nor. — K11 6
Byhalia, Ms., U.S. — H7 114
Byhau, Bela. — H13 22
Bykle, Nor. — L10 6
Bylas, Az., U.S. — K6 120
Bylot Island, i., N.T., Can. — B17 96
Byng Inlet, On., Can. — E15 110
Bynum, N.C., U.S. — D7 112
Byrdstown, Tn., U.S. — F11 114
Byron, Ga., U.S. — G3 112
Byron, Il., U.S. — H6 110
Byron, Wy., U.S. — F17 122
Byron, Cape, c., Austl. — G10 70
Byron Bay, Austl. — G10 70
Byrranga, gory, mts., Russia — B12 28
Bystřice, Czech Rep. — F14 10
Bystrzyca Kłodzka, Pol. — E16 10
Bytantaj, stm., Russia — D18 28
Bytkiv, Ukr. — A8 20
Bytom (Beuthen), Pol. — E18 10
Bytoš', Russia — H17 22
Bytów, Pol. — A17 10

## C

Ca, stm., Asia — E8 40
Caacupé, Para. — C10 80
Caaguazú, Para. — C10 80
Caaguazú, dept., Para. — C11 80
Caála, Ang. — D3 58
Caamaño Sound, strt., B.C., Can. — E5 102
Caapiranga, Braz. — I12 84
Caapucú, Para. — D10 80
Caarapó, Braz. — G1 79
Caazapá, Para. — D10 80
Caazapá, dept., Para. — D10 80
Cabaçal, stm., Braz. — F12 82
Cabaiguán, Cuba — C5 94
Cabanaconde, Peru — F6 82
Cabanatuan, Phil. — n19 39b
Cabano, P.Q., Can. — E5 106
Cabeceiras, Braz. — C5 79
Cabedelo, Braz. — E12 76
Cabeza del Buey, Spain — G6 16
Cabezas, Bol. — H10 82
Cabildo, Arg. — J8 80
Cabildo, Chile — G3 80
Cabimas, Ven. — B6 84
Cabinda, Ang. — C2 58
Cabinda, dept., Ang. — C2 58
Cabixi, stm., Braz. — E11 82
Cable, Wi., U.S. — D4 110
Cabo, Braz. — E11 76
Cabo Frio, Braz. — G7 79
Cabo Gracias a Dios, Nic. — C11 92
Cabool, Mo., U.S. — E4 114
Caboolture, Austl. — F10 70
Cabora Bassa Dam, Moz. — E6 58
Caborca, Mex. — B3 90
Cabot, Ar., U.S. — H4 114
Cabot Strait, strt., Can. — E14 106
Cabra, Spain — H7 16
Cabrera, stm., Col. — F5 84
Cabrera, Illa de, i., Spain — F14 16
Cabruta, Ven. — D9 84
Cabure, Ven. — B8 84
Cabuya, C.R. — H9 92
Cabuyaro, Col. — E6 84
Caçador, Braz. — D13 80
Čačak, Yugo. — F4 20
Cacahoatán, Mex. — J13 90
Cacaoui, Lac, l., P.Q., Can. — G7 106
Caçapava, Braz. — G6 79
Caçapava do Sul, Braz. — F12 80
Cacapon, stm., W.V., U.S. — H8 108
Caccamo, Italy — L8 18
Cáceres, Braz. — G13 82
Cáceres, Col. — D5 84
Cáceres, Spain — F5 16
Cáceres, prov., Spain — F6 16
Cačersk, Bela. — H13 22
Čačevičy, Bela. — H12 22
Cacharí, Arg. — I9 80
Cache, stm., Il., U.S. — E7 114
Cache Creek, B.C., Can. — G13 102
Cache Peak, mtn., Id., U.S. — H12 122
Cacheu, Gui.-B. — E1 64
Cachi, Arg. — C5 80
Cachimbo, Serra do, mts., Braz. — C13 82
Cachoeira, Braz. — B9 79
Cachoeira Alta, Braz. — E3 79
Cachoeira de Goiás, Braz. — D3 79
Cachoeira do Sul, Braz. — F12 80
Cachoeiras de Macacu, Braz. — G7 79
Cachoeiro de Itapemirim, Braz. — F8 79
Cachuela Esperanza, Bol. — D9 82
Cacine, Gui.-B. — F2 64
Cacólo, Ang. — D3 58
Caconda, Ang. — D3 58
Cacra, Peru — E4 82
Cactus, Tx., U.S. — C4 116
Cactus Peak, mtn., Nv., U.S. — G9 124
Caçu, Braz. — E3 79
Caculé, Braz. — C7 79
Çadan, Russia — G16 26
Cadereyta de Jiménez, Mex. — E9 90
Cadillac, Mi., U.S. — F10 110
Cadillac, Sk., Can. — I7 104
Cadiz, Ky., U.S. — F9 114
Cádiz, Spain — I5 16
Cádiz, Golfo de, b., Eur. — I4 16
Cadiz Lake, res., Ca., U.S. — J11 124
Cadomin, Ab., Can. — D17 102
Cadott, Wi., U.S. — F4 110
Cadwell, Ga., U.S. — G3 112
Caen, Fr. — C6 14
Caernarvon, Wales, U.K. — H9 8
Caesarea see Qesari, Horbat, hist., Isr. — C3 50
Caetaninópolis, Braz. — E6 79
Caeté, Braz. — E7 79
Caeté, stm., Braz. — C7 82
Caetité, Braz. — C7 79
Cafayate, Arg. — D6 80
Cafelândia do Leste, Braz. — G14 82
Cafuini, stm., Braz. — H13 84
Cagayan de Oro, Phil. — D7 38
Cagayan, stm., Phil. — n19 39b
Çağış, Tur. — J12 20
Cagli, Italy — F7 18
Cagliari, Italy — J4 18
Cagliari, Golfo di, b., Italy — J4 18
Cagnes, Fr. — I14 14
Čagoda, Russia — B18 22
Caguán, stm., Col. — G5 84
Caguas, P.R. — E11 94
Cahaba, stm., Al., U.S. — J9 114
Cahabón, Guat. — B5 92
Cahabón, stm., Guat. — B5 92
Cahokia, Il., U.S. — D6 114
Cahors, Fr. — H8 14
Cahuinari, stm., Col. — H7 84
Cahuita, Punta, c., C.R. — H12 92
Cahul, Mol. — F13 4
Cai, stm., Braz. — E13 80
Caia, stm., Eur. — F4 16
Caiabis, Serra dos, mts., Braz. — D2 79
Caiapó, stm., Braz. — D3 79
Caiapó, Serra do, mts., Braz. — D2 79
Caiaponia, Braz. — D3 79
Caibarién, Cuba — C5 94
Cai Bau, Dao, i., Viet. — D9 40
Caiçara, Braz. — C3 79
Caicara, Caño, stm., Ven. — D6 84
Caicara de Maturín, Ven. — C11 84
Caicara de Orinoco, Ven. — D9 84
Caicedonia, Col. — E5 84
Caicó, Braz. — E11 76
Caicos Islands, is., T./C. Is. — D9 94
Caicos Passage, strt., N.A. — B3 34
Caimanera, Cuba — E7 94
Caine, stm., Bol. — G9 82
Cains, stm., N.B., Can. — F7 106
Caird Coast, Ant. — C2 73
Cairns, Austl. — A5 70
Cairns Lake, I., On., Can. — G20 104
Cairo see Al-Qāhirah, Egypt — B6 60
Cairo, Ga., U.S. — I2 112
Cairo, Il., U.S. — E7 114
Cairo, Ne., U.S. — J9 118
Cairo, W.V., U.S. — H5 108
Cairu, Braz. — B9 79
Caiundo, Ang. — E3 58
Cajabamba, Peru — B2 82
Cajamarca, Peru — B2 82
Cajamarca, dept., Peru — B2 82
Cajacay, Peru — D3 82
Cajazeiras, Braz. — E11 76
Çajek, Kyrg. — I12 26
Cajkovskij, Russia — F8 26
Cajones, Cayos, rf., Hond. — A11 92
Cajon Summit, Ca., U.S. — J8 124
Cajuru, Braz. — F5 79
Čakeni, Russia — A4 66
Čakovec, Cro. — C11 18
Cala, S. Afr. — H8 66
Calabar, Nig. — I14 64
Calabozo, Ven. — C9 84
Calabria, prov., Italy — J11 18
Calafat, Rom. — F6 20
Calahorra, Spain — C10 16
Calais, Fr. — B8 14
Calais, Me., U.S. — B19 108
Calais, Pas de (Strait of Dover), strt., Eur. — J15 8
Calalaste, Sierra de, mts., Arg. — C5 80
Calama, Chile — B4 80
Calamar, Col. — B5 84
Calamar, Col. — G6 84
Calamian Group, is., Phil. — C6 38
Calamocha, Spain — D10 16
Calan, Rom. — D6 20
Calang, Indon. — M3 40
Calapan, Phil. — n19 39b
Călăraşi, Rom. — E11 20
Calatafimi, Italy — L7 18
Calatayud, Spain — D10 16
Calau, Ger. — D13 10
Calavon, stm., Fr. — I12 14
Calbayog, Phil. — C8 38
Calçoene, Braz. — C8 76
Calceta, Ec. — H2 84
Calchaquí, Arg. — E8 80
Calcutta, India — I13 44
Caldas, Col. — E4 84
Caldas, dept., Col. — E5 84
Caldas da Rainha, Port. — F2 16
Caldas Novas, Braz. — D4 79
Caldera, Chile — D3 80
Caldwell, Id., U.S. — G9 122
Caldwell, Ks., U.S. — N10 118
Caldwell, Oh., U.S. — H5 108
Caldwell, Tx., U.S. — I10 116
Caledon, stm., Afr. — H8 66
Caledonia, Belize — B15 90
Caledonia, Mn., U.S. — G4 110
Caledonia, Ms., U.S. — I8 114
Caledonia, N.S., Can. — H8 106
Caledonia, N.Y., U.S. — E8 108
Caledonia, On., Can. — G16 110
Calella, Spain — D14 16
Calera, Al., U.S. — I10 114
Calera, Ok., U.S. — E10 116
Caleta del Sebo, Spain — o23 17b
Caleufú, Arg. — H6 80
Calexico, Ca., U.S. — L10 124

Calfkiller, stm., Tn., U.S. — F11 114
Calfpasture, stm., Va., U.S. — I7 108
Calgary, Ab., Can. — F20 102
Calhan, Co., U.S. — L3 118
Calhoun, Al., U.S. — J10 114
Calhoun, Ga., U.S. — E2 112
Calhoun, Ky., U.S. — E9 114
Calhoun, Mo., U.S. — D3 114
Calhoun, Tn., U.S. — D2 112
Calhoun City, Ms., U.S. — I7 114
Calhoun Falls, S.C., U.S. — E4 112
Cali, Col. — F4 84
Calico Rock, Ar., U.S. — F4 114
Calicut see Kozhikode, India — G3 46
Caliente, Nv., U.S. — G11 124
California, Mo., U.S. — D4 114
California, Pa., U.S. — G7 108
California, state, U.S. — D2 98
California, Golfo de, b., Mex. — D4 90
California Aqueduct, Ca., U.S. — H5 124
Calimere, Point, c., India — G5 46
Calingasta, Arg. — F4 80
Calion, Ar., U.S. — I4 114
Calipatria, Ca., U.S. — K10 124
Calispell Peak, mtn., Wa., U.S. — B8 122
Calistoga, Ca., U.S. — F3 124
Calitri, Italy — I10 18
Callabonna, Lake, I., Austl. — G4 70
Callac, Fr. — D3 14
Callaghan, Mount, mtn., Nv., U.S. — E9 124
Callahan, Fl., U.S. — I5 112
Callander, On., Can. — D16 110
Callanmarca, Peru — E4 82
Callanna, Austl. — G2 70
Callao, Peru — E3 82
Callaway, Ne., U.S. — J8 118
Calling Lake, Ab., Can. — B21 102
Calling Lake, I., Ab., Can. — B21 102
Callosa d'En Sarrià, Spain — G11 16
Callosa de Segura, Spain — G11 16
Calmar, Ab., Can. — D21 102
Calmar, Ia., U.S. — G4 110
Calobre, Pan. — I14 92
Caloosahatchee, stm., Fl., U.S. — M5 112
Caloundra, Austl. — F10 70
Calp, Spain — G12 16
Caltanissetta, Italy — L9 18
Calumet, Mi., U.S. — C7 110
Calumet, Mn., U.S. — C2 110
Calumet City, Il., U.S. — I8 110
Calunda, Ang. — D4 58
Caluula, Som. — F11 56
Calvados, dept., Fr. — C6 14
Calvert, Tx., U.S. — I10 116
Calvert Island, i., B.C., Can. — F6 102
Calvi, Fr. — I23 15a
Calvia, Spain — F14 16
Calvillo, Mex. — G8 90
Calvin, Ok., U.S. — E10 116
Calvinia, S. Afr. — H4 66
Calw, Ger. — G8 10
Calypso, N.C., U.S. — D8 112
Calzada, Peru — B2 82
Camabatela, Ang. — C3 58
Camaçã, Braz. — B8 79
Camaçari, Braz. — B9 79
Camacupa, Ang. — D3 58
Camaguán, Ven. — C9 84
Camagüey, Cuba — D6 94
Camaiore, Italy — F5 18
Camajuaní, Cuba — C5 94
Camamu, Braz. — B9 79
Camaná, Peru — G5 82
Camaná, stm., Peru — G5 82
Camanaú, stm., Braz. — H12 84
Camanche, Ia., U.S. — I5 110
Camaquã, Braz. — F13 80
Camaquã, stm., Braz. — F12 80
Camará, Braz. — I11 84
Camararé, stm., Braz. — E12 82
Camarès, Fr. — I9 14
Camargo, Mex. — E9 90
Camargue, reg., Fr. — I11 14
Camarillo, Ca., U.S. — J7 124
Camarón, Cabo, c., Hond. — A9 92
Camarones, Arg. — E3 78
Camas, Spain — H5 16
Ca Mau, Viet. — J8 40
Ca Mau, Mui, c., Viet. — J8 40
Cambará, Braz. — G3 79
Cambodia (Kâmpŭchéa), ctry., Asia — C4 38
Camboon, Austl. — E9 70
Camboriú, Braz. — D14 80
Cambrai, Fr. — B10 14
Cambria, Ca., U.S. — I5 124
Cambria, Wi., U.S. — G6 110
Cambria Ice Field, B.C., Can. — B5 102
Cambrian Mountains, mts., Wales, U.K. — I10 8
Cambridge, Eng., U.K. — I14 8
Cambridge, Ia., U.S. — I2 110
Cambridge, Id., U.S. — F9 122
Cambridge, Il., U.S. — I6 110
Cambridge, Ma., U.S. — E15 108
Cambridge, Md., U.S. — I10 108
Cambridge, Mn., U.S. — E2 110
Cambridge, N.Y., U.S. — D13 108
Cambridge, N.Z. — B5 72
Cambridge, Oh., U.S. — H5 108
Cambridge, On., Can. — G15 110
Cambridge City, In., U.S. — C11 114
Cambridge Fiord, N.T., Can. — B18 96
Cambridgeshire, co., Eng., U.K. — I13 8
Cambridge Springs, Pa., U.S. — F6 108
Cambuí, Ponta de, c., Braz. — C15 80
Cambundi-Catembo, Ang. — D3 58
Camden, Al., U.S. — K9 114
Camden, Austl. — I9 70
Camden, Ar., U.S. — I4 114
Camden, Me., U.S. — C17 108
Camden, N.J., U.S. — H11 108
Camden, N.Y., U.S. — D11 108
Camden, N.C., U.S. — C10 112
Camden, Oh., U.S. — H2 108
Camden, S.C., U.S. — E6 112
Camden, Tn., U.S. — F8 114
Camden, Mo., U.S. — A12 114
Camenca, Mol. — A12 20

| Name | Map Ref. | Page |
|---|---|---|
| Cameron, La., U.S. | M3 | 114 |
| Cameron, Mo., U.S. | C2 | 114 |
| Cameron, S.C., U.S. | F6 | 112 |
| Cameron, Tx., U.S. | I10 | 116 |
| Cameron, Wi., U.S. | E4 | 110 |
| Cameron, W.V., U.S. | H6 | 108 |
| Cameron Hills, hills, Can. | E9 | 96 |
| Cameroon (Cameroun), ctry., Afr. | G9 | 54 |
| Cameroon Mountain, Cam. | I14 | 64 |
| Cametá, Braz. | D9 | 76 |
| Camiling, Phil. | n19 | 39b |
| Camilla, Ga., U.S. | H2 | 112 |
| Camiña, Chile | H7 | 82 |
| Camino, Ca., U.S. | F5 | 124 |
| Camiranga, Braz. | D9 | 76 |
| Camiri, Bol. | I10 | 82 |
| Camisea, stm., Peru | D5 | 82 |
| Camissombo, Ang. | C4 | 58 |
| Camoapa, Nic. | E9 | 92 |
| Camocim, Braz. | D10 | 76 |
| Camooweal, Austl. | B3 | 70 |
| Camorta Island, i., India | J2 | 40 |
| Campaign, Tn., U.S. | G11 | 114 |
| Campamento, Hond. | C8 | 92 |
| Campana, Arg. | H9 | 80 |
| Campana, Isla, i., Chile | E1 | 78 |
| Campana, Spain | G6 | 16 |
| Campanario, Cerro de, mtn., Peru | A3 | 82 |
| Campanero, Cerro, mtn., Ven. | E10 | 84 |
| Campania, prov., Italy | I9 | 18 |
| Campania Island, i., B.C., Can. | D5 | 102 |
| Campbell, Ca., U.S. | G4 | 124 |
| Campbell, Mn., U.S. | E11 | 118 |
| Campbell, Mo., U.S. | F6 | 114 |
| Campbell, Ne., U.S. | K9 | 118 |
| Campbell, Cape, c., N.Z. | D5 | 72 |
| Campbellford, Pa., U.S. | F18 | 110 |
| Campbell Hill, hill, Oh., U.S. | G3 | 108 |
| Campbell Island, B.C., Can. | E6 | 102 |
| Campbell Island, i., N.Z. | N20 | 126 |
| Campbell Range, mts., Yk., Can. | F30 | 100 |
| Campbell River, B.C., Can. | G9 | 102 |
| Campbell's-Bay, P.Q., Can. | B10 | 108 |
| Campbellsport, Wi., U.S. | G7 | 110 |
| Campbellsville, Ky., U.S. | E11 | 114 |
| Campbellton, Fl., U.S. | I1 | 112 |
| Campbellton, N.B., Can. | D7 | 106 |
| Campbellton, Nf., Can. | C19 | 106 |
| Campbellton, P.E., Can. | F9 | 106 |
| Campbelltown, Austl. | J9 | 70 |
| Campbell Town, Austl. | M7 | 70 |
| Camp Douglas, Wi., U.S. | G5 | 110 |
| Campeche, Mex. | H14 | 90 |
| Campeche, Bahía de, b., Mex. | H12 | 90 |
| Campechuela, Cuba | D6 | 94 |
| Camperdown, Austl. | L5 | 70 |
| Camperville, Mb., Can. | G14 | 104 |
| Cam Pha, Viet. | D9 | 40 |
| Camp Hill, Al., U.S. | J11 | 114 |
| Camp Hill, Pa., U.S. | G10 | 108 |
| Campillos, Spain | H7 | 16 |
| Câmpina, Rom. | D9 | 20 |
| Campina Grande, Braz. | E11 | 76 |
| Campinas, Braz. | G5 | 79 |
| Campina Verde, Braz. | E4 | 79 |
| Campo, Co., U.S. | N5 | 118 |
| Campo Alegre de Goiás, Braz. | D5 | 79 |
| Campobasso, Italy | H9 | 18 |
| Campo Belo, Braz. | F6 | 79 |
| Campo de Criptana, Spain | F8 | 16 |
| Campo de la Cruz, Col. | B5 | 84 |
| Campo Erê, Braz. | D12 | 80 |
| Campo Florido, Braz. | E4 | 79 |
| Campo Gallo, Arg. | D7 | 80 |
| Campo Grande, Arg. | D11 | 80 |
| Campo Grande, Braz. | F1 | 79 |
| Campo Largo, Arg. | D8 | 80 |
| Campo Largo, Braz. | C14 | 80 |
| Campo Maior, Braz. | D10 | 76 |
| Campo Mourão, Braz. | H2 | 79 |
| Campo Novo, Braz. | D12 | 80 |
| Campo Quijano, Arg. | C6 | 80 |
| Camporredondo, Peru | B2 | 82 |
| Campos, Braz. | F8 | 79 |
| Campos Altos, Braz. | E5 | 79 |
| Campos Santo, Arg. | C6 | 80 |
| Campos Belos, Braz. | G6 | 79 |
| Campos do Jordão, Braz. | G6 | 79 |
| Campos Gerais, Braz. | F6 | 79 |
| Campos Novos, Braz. | D13 | 80 |
| Campo Point, Il., U.S. | B5 | 114 |
| Campti, La., U.S. | K3 | 114 |
| Campton, Ky., U.S. | B3 | 112 |
| Câmpulung, Rom. | D9 | 20 |
| Câmpulung Moldovenesc, Rom. | B9 | 20 |
| Campuya, stm., Peru | H5 | 84 |
| Camp Verde, Az., U.S. | J5 | 120 |
| Camp Wood, Tx., U.S. | J6 | 116 |
| Cam Ranh, Viet. | I10 | 40 |
| Cam Ranh, Vinh, b., Viet. | I10 | 40 |
| Camrose, Ab., Can. | D22 | 102 |
| Camsell, stm., N.T., Can. | C9 | 96 |
| Can, Tur. | I10 | 20 |
| Canaan, Ct., U.S. | E13 | 108 |
| Canaan, Vt., U.S. | C15 | 108 |
| Canaan, stm., N.B., Can. | F8 | 106 |
| Cana-brava, Braz. | B4 | 79 |
| Cana-brava, stm., Braz. | B4 | 79 |
| Canaçarí, Lago, l., Braz. | I13 | 84 |
| Canada, ctry., N.A. | D13 | 96 |
| Cañada de Gómez, Arg. | G8 | 80 |
| Cañada Honda, Arg. | F4 | 80 |
| Canadian, Tx., U.S. | D6 | 116 |
| Canadian, stm., U.S. | D10 | 120 |
| Canadian, stm., U.S. | D10 | 116 |
| Canaguá, stm., Ven. | C7 | 84 |
| Canaima, Ven. | D11 | 84 |
| Canaima, Parque Nacional, Ven. | E11 | 84 |
| Canajoharie, N.Y., U.S. | E12 | 108 |
| Çanakkale, Tur. | I10 | 20 |
| Çanakkale Boğazı (Dardanelles), strt., Tur. | I10 | 20 |
| Canal Flats, B.C., Can. | G19 | 102 |
| Canal Fulton, Oh., U.S. | G5 | 108 |
| Canal Point, Fl., U.S. | M6 | 112 |
| Canals, Arg. | G7 | 80 |
| Canal Winchester, Oh., U.S. | H4 | 108 |
| Canandaigua, N.Y., U.S. | E9 | 108 |
| Cananea, Mex. | B4 | 90 |
| Cananéia, Braz. | C15 | 80 |
| Canápolis, Braz. | E4 | 79 |
| Cañar, Ec. | I3 | 84 |
| Cañar, prov., Ec. | I3 | 84 |
| Canarias, Islas (Canary Islands), is., Spain | o25 | 17b |
| Canarreos, Archipiélago de los, is., Cuba | D4 | 94 |
| Canary Islands see Canarias, Islas, is., Spain | C3 | 54 |
| Cañas, C.R. | G9 | 92 |
| Cañasgordas, Col. | D4 | 84 |
| Canaseraga, N.Y., U.S. | E9 | 108 |
| Canastota, N.Y., U.S. | D11 | 108 |
| Canatlán, Mex. | E7 | 90 |
| Canaveral, Cape, c., Fl., U.S. | K6 | 112 |
| Canavieiras, Braz. | C9 | 79 |
| Cañazas, Pan. | C2 | 84 |
| Canberra, Austl. | J8 | 70 |
| Canby, Ca., U.S. | C5 | 124 |
| Canby, Mn., U.S. | G11 | 118 |
| Canby, Or., U.S. | E3 | 122 |
| Cancale, Fr. | D5 | 14 |
| Canchaque, Peru | A2 | 82 |
| Cancún, Mex. | G16 | 90 |
| Cancún, Punta, c., Mex. | D1 | 94 |
| Candarave, Peru | G6 | 82 |
| Candás, Spain | B6 | 16 |
| Candé, Fr. | E5 | 14 |
| Candeias, Braz. | B9 | 79 |
| Candeias, Braz. | F6 | 79 |
| Candeias, stm., Braz. | C10 | 82 |
| Candela, Mex. | D9 | 90 |
| Candela, stm., Mex. | D9 | 90 |
| Candelaria, Arg. | D11 | 80 |
| Candelaria, Arg. | G6 | 80 |
| Candelária, Braz. | E12 | 80 |
| Candelaria, Col. | F2 | 84 |
| Candelaria, Cuba | C3 | 94 |
| Candelaria, stm., Mex. | H14 | 90 |
| Candeleda, Spain | E6 | 16 |
| Cándido Aguilar, Mex. | E10 | 90 |
| Cándido de Abreu, Braz. | C13 | 80 |
| Candle, Ak., U.S. | D14 | 100 |
| Candle Lake, l., Sk., Can. | E9 | 104 |
| Candlemas Islands, is., S. Geor. | J12 | 74 |
| Candlestick, Ms., U.S. | J6 | 114 |
| Candlewood, Lake, l., Ct., U.S. | F13 | 108 |
| Cando, Sk., Can. | C8 | 104 |
| Cando, N.D., U.S. | D7 | 118 |
| Candor, N.C., U.S. | D7 | 112 |
| Candor, N.Y., U.S. | E10 | 108 |
| Cane, stm., La., U.S. | K4 | 114 |
| Canea see Khaniá, Grc. | N8 | 20 |
| Canela, Braz. | E13 | 80 |
| Canelas, Mex. | E6 | 90 |
| Canelones, Ur. | H10 | 80 |
| Canelli, Italy | E3 | 18 |
| Cañete, Chile | I2 | 80 |
| Cañete, Spain | E10 | 16 |
| Caney, Ks., U.S. | N12 | 118 |
| Caney, stm., U.S. | C11 | 116 |
| Cangallo, Peru | E4 | 82 |
| Cangas, Braz. | G13 | 82 |
| Cangamba, Ang. | D3 | 58 |
| Cangombe, Ang. | D3 | 58 |
| Canguçu, Braz. | F12 | 80 |
| Cangzhou, China | E4 | 32 |
| Caniapiscau, stm., P.Q., Can. | E19 | 96 |
| Caniapiscau, Lac, l., P.Q., Can. | F19 | 96 |
| Canicattì, Italy | L8 | 18 |
| Canim Lake, B.C., Can. | F14 | 102 |
| Canim Lake Indian Reserve, B.C., Can. | F14 | 102 |
| Canindeyú, dept., Para. | C11 | 80 |
| Canisteo, N.Y., U.S. | E9 | 108 |
| Canisteo, stm., N.Y., U.S. | E9 | 108 |
| Cañitas de Felipe Pescador, Mex. | F8 | 90 |
| Canmore, Ab., Can. | F19 | 102 |
| Cannanore, India | G3 | 46 |
| Cannel City, Ky., U.S. | B3 | 112 |
| Cannelton, In., U.S. | E10 | 114 |
| Cannes, Fr. | I14 | 14 |
| Canning, N.S., Can. | E9 | 106 |
| Cannington, On., Can. | F16 | 110 |
| Cannon, stm., Mn., U.S. | F3 | 110 |
| Cannon Ball, N.D., U.S. | E7 | 118 |
| Cannonball, stm., N.D., U.S. | E7 | 118 |
| Cannon Beach, Or., U.S. | E2 | 122 |
| Cannon Falls, Mn., U.S. | F3 | 110 |
| Cann River, Austl. | K8 | 70 |
| Caño, Isla del, i., C.R. | I11 | 92 |
| Canoas, Braz. | E13 | 80 |
| Canoas, stm., Braz. | D13 | 80 |
| Canoe, stm., B.C., Can. | G15 | 102 |
| Canoe, stm., B.C., Can. | E16 | 102 |
| Canoe Creek Indian Reserve, B.C., Can. | F12 | 102 |
| Canoe Lake, l., Sk., Can. | C6 | 104 |
| Canoe Lake Indian Reserve, Sk., Can. | C6 | 104 |
| Canoinhas, Braz. | D13 | 80 |
| Canol, N.T., Can. | D31 | 100 |
| Canon, Ga., U.S. | E3 | 112 |
| Canon City, Co., U.S. | F11 | 120 |
| Caño Negro, C.R. | G10 | 92 |
| Canonsburg, Pa., U.S. | G6 | 108 |
| Canoochee, stm., Ga., U.S. | G5 | 112 |
| Canora, Sk., Can. | G12 | 104 |
| Canosa [di Puglia], Italy | H11 | 18 |
| Canossa, hist., Italy | E5 | 18 |
| Canouan, i., St. Vin. | H14 | 94 |
| Canova, S.D., U.S. | H10 | 118 |
| Canova Beach, Fl., U.S. | K6 | 112 |
| Canowindra, Austl. | I8 | 70 |
| Cansado, Maur. | J2 | 62 |
| Canso, N.S., Can. | G12 | 106 |
| Canso, Strait of, strt., N.S., Can. | G12 | 106 |
| Canta, Peru | D3 | 82 |
| Cantabria, state, Spain | B7 | 16 |
| Cantábrica, Cordillera, Spain | B6 | 16 |
| Cantagalo, Braz. | F7 | 79 |
| Cantal, dept., Fr. | G9 | 14 |
| Cantanhede, Port. | E3 | 16 |
| Cantaura, Ven. | C10 | 84 |
| Canterbury, Eng., U.K. | J15 | 8 |
| Canterbury, N.B., Can. | G6 | 106 |
| Canterbury Bight, N.Z. | F4 | 72 |
| Can Tho, Viet. | I8 | 40 |
| Canton see Guangzhou, China | L2 | 34 |
| Canton, Ga., U.S. | E2 | 112 |
| Canton, Il., U.S. | J5 | 110 |
| Canton, Ks., U.S. | M10 | 118 |
| Canton, Mn., U.S. | G4 | 110 |
| Canton, Mo., U.S. | B5 | 114 |
| Canton, Ms., U.S. | J7 | 114 |
| Canton, N.C., U.S. | D3 | 112 |
| Canton, N.Y., U.S. | C11 | 108 |
| Canton, Oh., U.S. | G5 | 108 |
| Canton, Ok., U.S. | C8 | 116 |
| Canton, S.D., U.S. | H11 | 118 |
| Canton, Tx., U.S. | G11 | 116 |
| Canton Lake, res., Ok., U.S. | C8 | 116 |
| Cantonment, Fl., U.S. | L9 | 114 |
| Cantù, Italy | D4 | 18 |
| Cantu, stm., Braz. | C12 | 80 |
| Cantwell, Ak., U.S. | E20 | 100 |
| Cañuelas, Arg. | H9 | 80 |
| Canumã, Braz. | J13 | 84 |
| Canumã, stm., Braz. | J13 | 84 |
| Canutama, Braz. | B9 | 82 |
| Canutillo, Tx., U.S. | M10 | 120 |
| Çany, ozero, l., Russia | G13 | 26 |
| Cany-Barville, Fr. | C7 | 14 |
| Canyon, Tx., U.S. | E5 | 116 |
| Canyon, Yk., Can. | F26 | 100 |
| Canyon City, Or., U.S. | F7 | 122 |
| Canyon Creek, Ab., Can. | B19 | 102 |
| Canyon Ferry Lake, res., Mt., U.S. | D14 | 122 |
| Canyonlands National Park, Ut., U.S. | F7 | 120 |
| Canyonville, Or., U.S. | H2 | 122 |
| Cao Bang, Viet. | C9 | 40 |
| Caojun, China | F5 | 34 |
| Caomji, China | I4 | 32 |
| Caoping, China | G7 | 34 |
| Caoqiao, China | Q8 | 34 |
| Caota, China | F9 | 34 |
| Caoxian, China | I3 | 32 |
| Caoyangxi, China | I7 | 34 |
| Cap, Pointe du, c., St. Luc. | D5 | — |
| Capac, Mi., U.S. | G13 | 110 |
| Capão Bonito, Braz. | G4 | 79 |
| Capão Doce, Morro do, mtn., Braz. | D13 | 80 |
| Capaotigamau, Lac, l., P.Q. | B5 | 106 |
| Caparaó, Parque Nacional do, Braz. | F8 | 79 |
| Caparo Viejo, stm., Ven. | D7 | 84 |
| Capatárida, Ven. | B7 | 84 |
| Cap-aux-Meules (Grindstone Island), P.Q. | E12 | 106 |
| Cap aux Meules, Île du, i., P.Q., Can. | E12 | 106 |
| Cap-Chat, P.Q., Can. | C7 | 106 |
| Cape, stm., Austl. | C7 | 70 |
| Cape Arid National Park, Austl. | F4 | 68 |
| Cape Barren Island, i., Austl. | M8 | 70 |
| Cape Breton Highlands National Park, N.S., Can. | F13 | 106 |
| Cape Breton Island, i., N.S., Can. | F13 | 106 |
| Cape Broyle, Nf., Can. | E21 | 106 |
| Cape Canaveral, Fl., U.S. | K6 | 112 |
| Cape Charles, Va., U.S. | B10 | 112 |
| Cape Coast, Ghana | I9 | 64 |
| Cape Cod Bay, b., Ma., U.S. | F16 | 108 |
| Cape Dorset, N.T., Can. | D17 | 96 |
| Cape Elizabeth, Me., U.S. | D16 | 108 |
| Cape Fear, stm., N.C., U.S. | E8 | 112 |
| Cape Girardeau, Mo., U.S. | E7 | 114 |
| Cape LaHave Island, i., N.S., Can. | H9 | 106 |
| Cape la Hune, Nf., Can. | E17 | 106 |
| Capelinha, Braz. | J13 | 20 |
| Cape Lisburne, Ak., U.S. | B11 | 100 |
| Capel'ka, Russia | C11 | 22 |
| Capelle [aan den IJssel], Neth. | E6 | 12 |
| Capelongo, Ang. | D3 | 58 |
| Cape May, N.J., U.S. | I12 | 108 |
| Cape May Court House, N.J., U.S. | H12 | 108 |
| Cape Pole, Ak., U.S. | I28 | 100 |
| Cape Porpoise, Me., U.S. | D16 | 108 |
| Capernaum see Kefar Naḥum, hist., Isr. | C4 | 50 |
| Cape Romanzof, Ak., U.S. | F12 | 100 |
| Cape Sable island, i., N.S., Can. | I8 | 106 |
| Cape Scott Provincial Park, Can. | G6 | 102 |
| Cape Tormentine, N.B., Can. | F10 | 106 |
| Cape Town (Kaapstad), S. Afr. | I4 | 66 |
| Cape Verde (Cabo Verde), ctry., Afr. | E2 | 54 |
| Cape Vincent, N.Y., U.S. | C10 | 108 |
| Cape Yakataga, Ak., U.S. | F23 | 100 |
| Cape York Peninsula, pen., Austl. | B8 | 68 |
| Cap-Haïtien, Haiti | E8 | 94 |
| Capilla de Farruco, Ur. | G11 | 80 |
| Capilla del Monte, Arg. | F5 | 80 |
| Capim, stm., Braz. | D9 | 76 |
| Capinópolis, Braz. | E4 | 79 |
| Capinota, Bol. | G8 | 82 |
| Capira, Pan. | C3 | 84 |
| Capitan, N.M., U.S. | K11 | 120 |
| Capitán Arturo Prat, sci., Ant. | B1 | 73 |
| Capitán Bado, Para. | C10 | 80 |
| Capitán Bermúdez, Arg. | G8 | 80 |
| Capitán Meza, Para. | C11 | 80 |
| Capitán Peak, mtn., N.M., U.S. | K11 | 120 |
| Capitán Sarmiento, Arg. | H9 | 80 |
| Capitola, Ca., U.S. | H4 | 124 |
| Capitol Peak, mtn., Nv., U.S. | C8 | 124 |
| Capitol Reef National Park, Ut., U.S. | F5 | 120 |
| Capivara, Braz. | B8 | 79 |
| Capivari, Braz. | H13 | 82 |
| Capivari, stm., Braz. | C7 | 79 |
| Caplan, P.Q., Can. | D8 | 106 |
| Caplina, stm., Peru | H22 | 82 |
| Čaplygin, Russia | H22 | 26 |
| Carabobo, state, Ven. | B7 | 84 |
| Caracal, Rom. | E8 | 20 |
| Caracaraí, Braz. | G12 | 84 |
| Caracas, Ven. | B9 | 84 |
| Carache, Ven. | C7 | 84 |
| Caracol, Braz. | B10 | 80 |
| Caracollo, Bol. | G8 | 82 |
| Caraga, Phil. | D8 | 38 |
| Caraguatatuba, Braz. | G6 | 79 |
| Caraguatay, Para. | C10 | 80 |
| Caraí, Braz. | D8 | 79 |
| Caraíbamba, Peru | E5 | 82 |
| Caraigres, Cerro, mtn., C.R. | H10 | 92 |
| Carajás, Serra dos, mts., Braz. | E8 | 76 |
| Caranavi, Bol. | F8 | 82 |
| Carandaí, Braz. | F7 | 79 |
| Carangola, Braz. | F7 | 79 |
| Caransebeş, Rom. | D6 | 20 |
| Carapá, stm., Para. | C11 | 80 |
| Cara-Paraná, stm., Col. | H6 | 84 |
| Carapeguá, Para. | C10 | 80 |
| Carapó, stm., Ven. | D11 | 84 |
| Caraquet, N.B., Can. | E9 | 106 |
| Caráquez, Ec. | H2 | 84 |
| Carare, stm., Col. | D5 | 84 |
| Carari, Col. | D5 | 20 |
| Caratasca, Laguna de, l., Hond. | B11 | 92 |
| Caratinga, Braz. | E7 | 79 |
| Carauari, Braz. | J9 | 84 |
| Caravaca de la Cruz, Spain | G10 | 16 |
| Caravaggio, Italy | D4 | 18 |
| Caraveli, Peru | F5 | 82 |
| Caraway, Ar., U.S. | B5 | 114 |
| Carballido, Spain | C10 | 80 |
| Carbó, Mex. | C4 | 90 |
| Carbon, Tx., U.S. | G8 | 116 |
| Carbondale, Co., U.S. | E9 | 120 |
| Carbondale, Il., U.S. | E7 | 114 |
| Carbondale, Ks., U.S. | M12 | 118 |
| Carbondale, Pa., U.S. | F11 | 108 |
| Carbonear, Nf., Can. | E20 | 106 |
| Carbonia, Italy | J3 | 18 |
| Carcaixent, Spain | F11 | 16 |
| Carcajou, Ab., Can. | D90 | 100 |
| Carcarañá, Arg. | G8 | 80 |
| Carcarañá, stm., Arg. | G8 | 80 |
| Carcassonne, Fr. | I9 | 14 |
| Carchi, prov., Ec. | G3 | 84 |
| Carcross, Yk., Can. | F27 | 100 |
| Čardarinskoje vodochranilišče, res., Asia | I11 | 26 |
| Cárdenas, Cuba | C4 | 94 |
| Cárdenas, Mex. | F10 | 90 |
| Cárdenas, Mex. | H13 | 90 |
| Cárdenas, Nic. | F9 | 92 |
| Cárdenas, Bahía de, b., Cuba | C4 | 94 |
| Cardi, Tur. | J13 | 20 |
| Cardiel, Lago, l., Arg. | F2 | 78 |
| Cardiff, Wales, U.K. | J10 | 8 |
| Cardigan, P.E., Can. | F11 | 106 |
| Cardigan Bay, b., Can. | F11 | 106 |
| Cardigan Bay, b., Wales, U.K. | I9 | 8 |
| Cardinal, On., Can. | C11 | 108 |
| Cardinal Lake, l., Ab., Can. | A17 | 102 |
| Cardington, Oh., U.S. | G4 | 108 |
| Cardona, Ur. | G10 | 80 |
| Cardona, Spain | D13 | 16 |
| Cardoso, Braz. | F4 | 79 |
| Cardoso, Ilha do, i., Braz. | C14 | 80 |
| Cardston, Ab., Can. | H21 | 102 |
| Cardwell, Austl. | B7 | 70 |
| Cardwell, Mo., U.S. | F6 | 114 |
| Careen Lake, l., Sk., Can. | A6 | 104 |
| Carei, Rom. | B6 | 20 |
| Careiro, Braz. | I13 | 84 |
| Careiro, Ilha do, i., Braz. | I13 | 84 |
| Carén, Chile | D2 | 80 |
| Carencro, La., U.S. | L4 | 114 |
| Carentan, Fr. | C5 | 14 |
| Carey, stm., Spain | B7 | 16 |
| Caretta, W.V., U.S. | B5 | 112 |
| Carey, Lake, l., Austl. | E4 | 68 |
| Careysburg, Lib. | H4 | 64 |
| Carhaix-Plouguer, Fr. | D3 | 14 |
| Carhué, Arg. | I7 | 80 |
| Caria, hist. reg., Tur. | L11 | 20 |
| Cariacica, Braz. | F8 | 79 |
| Cariamanga, Ec. | J3 | 84 |
| Cariban, Punta, c., Col. | B4 | 84 |
| Caribbean Sea | G8 | 94 |
| Caribou, stm., B.C., Can. | E13 | 102 |
| Caribou, Me., U.S. | B5 | 106 |
| Caribou Mountains, mts., B.C., Can. | D13 | 102 |
| Caribou, N.S., Can. | G11 | 106 |
| Caribou Lake, l., On., Can. | A11 | 108 |
| Caribou Mountain, mtn., Id., U.S. | G15 | 122 |
| Caribou Mountains, mts., Ab., Can. | A9 | 96 |
| Carichic, Mex. | D6 | 90 |
| Carignan, Fr. | C12 | 14 |
| Carinhanha, Braz. | C7 | 79 |
| Carinhanha, stm., Braz. | C5 | 79 |
| Carini, Italy | K8 | 18 |
| Caripe, Ven. | B11 | 84 |
| Caripito, Ven. | B11 | 84 |
| Carleton, Mi., U.S. | H12 | 110 |
| Carleton, Ne., U.S. | K10 | 118 |
| Carleton, Mount, mtn., N.B., Can. | E7 | 106 |
| Carleton Place, On., Can. | E19 | 124 |
| Carlin, Nv., U.S. | D9 | 124 |
| Carlinville, Il., U.S. | C7 | 114 |
| Carlisle, Ar., U.S. | H5 | 114 |
| Carlisle, Eng., U.K. | G11 | 8 |
| Carlisle, In., U.S. | D9 | 114 |
| Carlisle, Ky., U.S. | I2 | 108 |
| Carlisle, Pa., U.S. | G9 | 108 |
| Carlisle, S.C., U.S. | E5 | 112 |
| Carl Junction, Mo., U.S. | E2 | 114 |
| Carlópolis, Braz. | G4 | 79 |
| Carlos Barbosa, Braz. | E13 | 80 |
| Carlos Casares, Arg. | H8 | 80 |
| Carlos Chagas, Braz. | D8 | 79 |
| Carlos Forseca Amador, Nic. | F8 | 92 |
| Carlos Pellegrini, Arg. | G8 | 80 |
| Carlos Reyles, Ur. | G10 | 80 |
| Carlos Tejedor, Arg. | H7 | 80 |
| Carlow, Ire. | I6 | 8 |
| Carlow, co., Ire. | I6 | 8 |
| Carlsbad, Ca., U.S. | K8 | 124 |
| Carlsbad see Karlovy Vary, Czech Rep. | E12 | 10 |
| Carlsbad, N.M., U.S. | G2 | 116 |
| Carlsbad, Tx., U.S. | H6 | 116 |
| Carlsbad Caverns National Park, N.M., U.S. | G2 | 116 |
| Carlton, Mn., U.S. | D3 | 110 |
| Carlton, Or., U.S. | E2 | 122 |
| Carlton, Tx., U.S. | H8 | 116 |
| Carlyle, Il., U.S. | D7 | 114 |
| Carlyle, Sk., Can. | I12 | 104 |
| Carlyle Lake, res., Il., U.S. | D7 | 114 |
| Carmacks, Yk., Can. | E26 | 100 |
| Carmagnola, Italy | E2 | 18 |
| Carman, Mb., Can. | I16 | 104 |
| Carmangay, Ab., Can. | G21 | 102 |
| Carmanville, Nf., Can. | C19 | 106 |
| Carmaux, Fr. | H9 | 14 |
| Carmel, Ca., U.S. | H4 | 124 |
| Carmel, In., U.S. | C10 | 114 |
| Carmel, N.Y., U.S. | F13 | 108 |
| Carmel, Mount see Karmel, Har, Isr. | C4 | 50 |
| Carmelo, Ur. | H9 | 80 |
| Carmel Valley, Ca., U.S. | H4 | 124 |
| Carmel Woods, Ca., U.S. | H4 | 124 |
| Carmen, Ok., U.S. | C8 | 116 |
| Carmen, stm., Mex. | G10 | 90 |
| Carmen, Isla, i., Mex. | E4 | 90 |
| Carmen, Isla del, i., Mex. | H14 | 90 |
| Carmen Alto, Chile | B4 | 80 |
| Carmen de Apicalá, Col. | E5 | 84 |
| Carmen de Areco, Arg. | H9 | 80 |
| Carmen de Patagones, Arg. | E4 | 78 |
| Carmi, Il., U.S. | D8 | 114 |
| Carmichael, Ca., U.S. | F4 | 124 |
| Carmine, Tx., U.S. | H10 | 116 |
| Carmo de Paranaíba, Braz. | E6 | 79 |
| Carmo do Rio Verde, Braz. | C4 | 79 |
| Carmona, Spain | H6 | 16 |
| Carmópolis de Minas, Braz. | F6 | 79 |
| Carnarvon, Austl. | D2 | 68 |
| Carnarvon, S. Afr. | H6 | 66 |
| Carnatic, hist. reg., India | G10 | 42 |
| Carnduff, Sk., Can. | I13 | 104 |
| Carnegie, Ok., U.S. | D8 | 116 |
| Carnegie, Lake, l., Austl. | E4 | 68 |
| Carnic Alpi, mts., Eur. | C8 | 18 |
| Car Nicobar Island, i., India | J2 | 40 |
| Carnot, Cen. Afr. Rep. | H4 | 54 |
| Carnoustie, Scot., U.K. | E11 | 8 |
| Carnsore Point, c., Ire. | I7 | 8 |
| Carnwath, stm., N.T., Can. | C30 | 100 |
| Carol City, Fl., U.S. | N6 | 112 |
| Carolbeen, N.C., U.S. | C5 | 112 |
| Carolina, Braz. | E9 | 76 |
| Carolina, Col. | D5 | 84 |
| Carolina, El Sal. | D6 | 92 |
| Carolina, P.R. | E15 | 94 |
| Carolina Beach, N.C., U.S. | E9 | 112 |
| Caroline Islands, is., Oc. | H18 | 126 |
| Caron, Sk., Can. | H6 | 104 |
| Carora, Ven. | B7 | 84 |
| Carouge, Switz. | F5 | 13 |
| Carp, On., Can. | E19 | 110 |
| Carp, stm., Mi., U.S. | D11 | 110 |
| Carpathian Mountains, mts., Eur. | F12 | 4 |
| Carpați Meridionali, mts., Rom. | D8 | 20 |
| Carpentaria, Gulf of, b., Austl. | B7 | 68 |
| Carpenter, Wy., U.S. | J3 | 118 |
| Carpenter Lake, l., B.C., Can. | G12 | 102 |
| Carpentersville, Il., U.S. | H7 | 110 |
| Carpentras, Fr. | H12 | 14 |
| Carpi, Italy | E5 | 18 |
| Cărpineni, Mol. | C12 | 20 |
| Carpinteria, Ca., U.S. | J6 | 124 |
| Carpio, Mo., U.S. | C6 | 118 |
| Carp Lake, l., B.C., Can. | C11 | 102 |
| Carpolac, Austl. | K4 | 70 |
| Carrabelle, Fl., U.S. | J2 | 112 |
| Carranza, Cabo, c., Chile | H2 | 80 |
| Carrao, stm., Ven. | D11 | 84 |
| Čardžou, Turk. | J10 | 26 |
| Carrara, Italy | E5 | 18 |
| Carrboro, N.C., U.S. | D7 | 112 |
| Carraria, Para. | A9 | 80 |
| Carreta, Punta, c., Peru | F3 | 82 |
| Carriacou, i., Gren. | H14 | 94 |
| Carrick on Shannon, Ire. | H5 | 8 |
| Carrick on Suir, Ire. | I6 | 8 |
| Carrières-sur-Seine, Fr. | L7 | 14 |
| Carriers Mills, Il., U.S. | E8 | 114 |
| Carrillo, C.R. | H9 | 92 |
| Carrillo, Mex. | D7 | 90 |
| Carrión de los Condes, Spain | C7 | 16 |
| Carrizal Bajo, Chile | E3 | 80 |
| Carrizo Mountain, mtn., N.M., U.S. | K11 | 120 |
| Carrizo Springs, Tx., U.S. | K7 | 116 |
| Carrizozo, N.M., U.S. | K11 | 120 |
| Carroll, Ia., U.S. | I13 | 118 |
| Carroll Lake, l., On., Can. | G19 | 104 |
| Carrollton, Al., U.S. | I8 | 114 |
| Carrollton, Ga., U.S. | F1 | 112 |
| Carrollton, Il., U.S. | C6 | 114 |
| Carrollton, Ky., U.S. | D11 | 114 |
| Carrollton, Mi., U.S. | G12 | 110 |
| Carrollton, Mo., U.S. | C3 | 114 |
| Carrollton, Oh., U.S. | G5 | 108 |
| Carrollton, Tx., U.S. | G10 | 116 |
| Carrolltown, Pa., U.S. | G8 | 108 |
| Carrot, stm., Ab., U.S. | E12 | 104 |
| Carrot River, Sk., Can. | E11 | 104 |
| Carruthers, Ab., Can. | D11 | — |
| Çarşamba, Tur. | A8 | 44 |
| Carseland, Ab., Can. | G21 | 102 |
| Čarsk, Russia | H14 | 26 |
| Carson, N.D., U.S. | E6 | 118 |
| Carson, Wa., U.S. | E4 | 122 |
| Carson, stm., Nv., U.S. | E6 | 124 |
| Carson City, Mi., U.S. | G11 | 110 |
| Carson City, Nv., U.S. | E6 | 124 |
| Carson Range, mts., Nv., U.S. | E6 | 124 |
| Carson Sink, l., Nv., U.S. | E7 | 124 |
| Carstairs, Ab., Can. | F20 | 102 |
| Cartagena, Chile | G3 | 80 |
| Cartagena, Col. | B4 | 84 |
| Cartagena, Spain | H11 | 16 |
| Cartago, Col. | E5 | 84 |
| Cartago, prov., C.R. | H11 | 92 |
| Cartaxo, Port. | F3 | 16 |
| Cartaya, Spain | H4 | 16 |
| Carter, co., Mo. | E6 | 114 |
| Carter Lake, Ia., U.S. | J12 | 118 |
| Carteret, N.J., U.S. | F16 | 122 |
| Cartersville, Ga., U.S. | E1 | 112 |
| Carthage, Ar., U.S. | H4 | 114 |
| Carthage, Il., U.S. | B5 | 114 |
| Carthage, In., U.S. | C11 | 114 |
| Carthage, Mo., U.S. | E2 | 114 |
| Carthage, N.C., U.S. | D7 | 112 |
| Carthage, N.Y., U.S. | D11 | 108 |
| Carthage, S.D., U.S. | G10 | 118 |
| Carthage, Tn., U.S. | F11 | 114 |
| Carthage, Tx., U.S. | J2 | 114 |
| Carthage, Tun. | M5 | 18 |
| Carthage, hist., Tun. | M5 | 18 |
| Carter Islands, is., Austl. | A6 | 68 |
| Cartier, Mb., Can. | I16 | 104 |
| Cartwright, Mb., Can. | F21 | 96 |
| Caruaru, Braz. | E11 | 76 |
| Carumas, Peru | G6 | 82 |
| Carúpano, Ven. | B11 | 84 |
| Carutapera, Braz. | D9 | 76 |
| Caruthersville, Mo., U.S. | F6 | 114 |
| Carutu, stm., Ven. | E11 | 84 |
| Carvin, Fr. | B9 | 14 |
| Carvoeiro, Braz. | H12 | 84 |
| Cary, Ms., U.S. | J6 | 114 |
| Cary, N.C., U.S. | C7 | 112 |
| Caryville, Fl., U.S. | L11 | 114 |
| Caryville, Tn., U.S. | C2 | 112 |
| Casablanca (Dar-el-Beida), Mor. | D7 | 62 |
| Casa Branca, Braz. | F5 | 79 |
| Casa Grande, Az., U.S. | L5 | 120 |
| Casale Monferrato, Italy | D3 | 18 |
| Casanare, state, Col. | D6 | 84 |
| Casanare, stm., Col. | D7 | 84 |
| Casanay, Ven. | B11 | 84 |
| Casas Adobes, Az., U.S. | L6 | 120 |
| Casas Grandes, stm., Mex. | B6 | 90 |
| Casas-Ibáñez, Spain | F10 | 16 |
| Casasimarro, Spain | F9 | 16 |
| Casavieja, Spain | E7 | 16 |
| Casbas, Arg. | I7 | 80 |
| Casca, Braz. | E13 | 80 |
| Casca, Rio da, stm., Braz. | F14 | 82 |
| Cascade, B.C., Can. | H16 | 102 |
| Cascade, Ia., U.S. | H4 | 110 |
| Cascade, Id., U.S. | F9 | 122 |
| Cascade, Mt., U.S. | C14 | 122 |
| Cascade, Wi., U.S. | G7 | 110 |
| Cascade Locks, Or., U.S. | E4 | 122 |
| Cascade Range, mts., N.A. | C2 | 98 |
| Cascade Reservoir, res., Id., U.S. | F9 | 122 |
| Cascais, Port. | G2 | 16 |
| Cascalho Rico, Braz. | E5 | 79 |
| Cascapédia, stm., P.Q., Can. | D7 | 106 |
| Cascavel, Braz. | C12 | 80 |
| Cascina, Italy | F5 | 18 |
| Casco Bay, b., Me., U.S. | D16 | 108 |
| Cascumpeque Bay, b., P.E., Can. | — | — |
| Caserta, Italy | H9 | 18 |
| Caseville, Mi., U.S. | G12 | 110 |
| Casey, Ia., U.S. | J13 | 118 |
| Casey, Il., U.S. | C9 | 114 |
| Cashel, Ire. | I6 | 8 |
| Cashiers, N.C., U.S. | D3 | 112 |
| Cashmere, Wa., U.S. | C5 | 122 |
| Cashton, Wi., U.S. | G5 | 110 |
| Casigua, Ven. | C6 | 84 |
| Casilda, Arg. | G8 | 80 |
| Casillas del Angel, Spain | o27 | 17b |
| Casino, Austl. | G10 | 70 |
| Casiquiare, stm., Ven. | F9 | 84 |
| Čáslav, Czech Rep. | F15 | 10 |
| Casma, Peru | C2 | 82 |
| Čašniki, Bela. | G12 | 22 |
| Casnovia, Mi., U.S. | G10 | 110 |
| Casoli, Italy | G9 | 18 |
| Caspe, Spain | D11 | 16 |
| Casper, Wy., U.S. | B10 | 120 |
| Caspian, Mi., U.S. | D7 | 110 |
| Caspian Sea | E5 | 26 |
| Cass, stm., Mi., U.S. | G12 | 110 |
| Cassai (Kasai), stm., Afr. | C4 | 58 |
| Cassange, stm., Braz. | G13 | 82 |
| Cass City, Mi., U.S. | G12 | 110 |
| Casselman, On., Can. | B11 | 108 |
| Casselton, N.D., U.S. | E10 | 118 |
| Cássia, Braz. | F5 | 79 |
| Cassiar, B.C., Can. | E30 | 100 |
| Cassiar Mountains, mts., Can. | E7 | 96 |
| Cassilândia, Braz. | E3 | 79 |
| Cassinga, Ang. | E3 | 58 |
| Cassino, Braz. | F12 | 80 |
| Cassino, Italy | H8 | 18 |
| Cass Lake, Mn., U.S. | C11 | 110 |
| Cassopolis, Mi., U.S. | I9 | 110 |
| Cassummba, Ilha, i., Braz. | D7 | 79 |
| Cassununga, Braz. | D2 | 79 |
| Cassville, Mo., U.S. | F3 | 114 |
| Cassville, Wi., U.S. | H5 | 110 |
| Castalia, Ia., U.S. | F4 | 108 |
| Castanheira de Pêra, Port. | E3 | 16 |
| Castaños, Punta, c., Nic. | E7 | 92 |
| Castelfiorentino, Italy | F5 | 18 |
| Castelfranco Veneto, Italy | C6 | 18 |
| Castellammare del Golfo, Italy | K7 | 18 |
| Castellammare [di Stabia], Italy | I9 | 18 |
| Castellaneta, Italy | I11 | 18 |
| Castelli, Arg. | I10 | 80 |
| Castelló, prov., Spain | E11 | 16 |
| Castellón de la Plana, Spain | F11 | 16 |
| Castelmassa, Italy | D6 | 18 |
| Castelnaudary, Fr. | I8 | 14 |
| Castelo, Braz. | F8 | 79 |
| Castelo Branco, Port. | F4 | 16 |
| Castelsarrasin, Fr. | H8 | 14 |
| Castets, Fr. | I5 | 14 |
| Castile, N.Y., U.S. | E8 | 108 |
| Castilho, Braz. | F3 | 79 |
| Castilla, Peru | A1 | 82 |
| Castilla-La Mancha, state, Spain | F8 | 16 |
| Castilla la Nueva, hist. reg., Spain | F8 | 16 |
| Castilla la Vieja, hist. reg., Spain | D6 | 16 |
| Castilla-León, state, Spain | D6 | 16 |
| Castillo del Romeral, Spain | p25 | 17b |
| Castillo Incaico de Ingapirca, hist., Ec. | I3 | 84 |
| Castillos, Ur. | H12 | 80 |
| Castine, Me., U.S. | D18 | 108 |
| Castle Dale, Ut., U.S. | E6 | 120 |
| Castleberry, Al., U.S. | K9 | 114 |
| Castle Douglas, Scot., U.K. | G10 | 8 |
| Castlegar, B.C., Can. | H17 | 102 |
| Castle Hills, Austl. | K6 | 70 |
| Castlemaine, Austl. | L6 | 70 |
| Castle Mountain, mtn., Yk., Can. | D27 | 100 |
| Castle Peak, mtn., Co., U.S. | E10 | 120 |
| Castlereagh, Ire. | H5 | 8 |
| Castlereagh, stm., Austl. | H7 | 70 |
| Castle Rock, Co., U.S. | E12 | 120 |

| Name | Map Ref. | Page |
|---|---|---|
| Castle Rock, Wa., U.S. | D3 | 122 |
| Castle Rock, mtn., Or., U.S. | F7 | 122 |
| Castle Rock Lake, res., Wi., U.S. | G6 | 110 |
| Castleton, Vt., U.S. | D13 | 108 |
| Castletown, Scot., U.K. | C10 | 8 |
| Castlewood, S.D., U.S. | G10 | 118 |
| Castlewood, Va., U.S. | C4 | 112 |
| Castor, Ab., Can. | E23 | 102 |
| Castor, stm., Mo., U.S. | E6 | 114 |
| Castres, Fr. | I9 | 14 |
| Castricum, Neth. | C6 | 12 |
| Castries, St. Luc. | G14 | 94 |
| Castro, Braz. | C13 | 80 |
| Castro, Chile | E2 | 78 |
| Castro Barros, Arg. | F6 | 80 |
| Castro del Río, Spain | H7 | 16 |
| Castro-Urdiales, Spain | B8 | 16 |
| Castro Verde, Port. | H3 | 16 |
| Castroville, Ca., U.S. | H4 | 124 |
| Castroville, Tx., U.S. | J8 | 116 |
| Castuera, Spain | G6 | 16 |
| Casummit Lake, On., Can. | G22 | 104 |
| Casupá, Ur. | H11 | 80 |
| Cat, stm., On., Can. | G23 | 104 |
| Catacamas, Hond. | C9 | 92 |
| Catacaos, Peru | A1 | 82 |
| Catacocha, Ec. | J3 | 84 |
| Cataguases, Braz. | F7 | 79 |
| Catahoula Lake, l., La., U.S. | K4 | 114 |
| Catalão, Braz. | E5 | 79 |
| Çatalca, Tur. | H12 | 20 |
| Catalina, Chile | C4 | 80 |
| Catalina, Nf., Can. | D20 | 106 |
| Catalonia see Catalunya, prov., Spain | D13 | 16 |
| Catalunya, state, Spain | D13 | 16 |
| Catamarca, prov., Arg. | D5 | 80 |
| Catamayo, Ec. | J3 | 84 |
| Catamayo, stm., Ec. | J3 | 84 |
| Catanduva, Braz. | F4 | 79 |
| Catania, Italy | L10 | 18 |
| Catania, Golfo di, b., Italy | L10 | 18 |
| Catanzaro, Italy | K11 | 18 |
| Catarama, Ec. | H3 | 84 |
| Cataraman, Phil. | C7 | 38 |
| Catarroja, Spain | F11 | 16 |
| Catatumbo, stm., Ven. | C7 | 84 |
| Catawba, stm., U.S. | E6 | 112 |
| Catawissa, Pa., U.S. | G10 | 108 |
| Cat Ba, Dao, i., Viet. | D9 | 40 |
| Catbalogan, Phil. | C7 | 38 |
| Catchabutan, Punta, c., Hond. | B8 | 92 |
| Caterino Rodríguez, Mex. | E9 | 90 |
| Catete, Ang. | C2 | 58 |
| Cathcart, S. Afr. | I8 | 66 |
| Cathedral City, Ca., U.S. | K9 | 124 |
| Cathlamet, Wa., U.S. | D2 | 122 |
| Ca' Tiepolo, Italy | E7 | 18 |
| Cat Island, i., Bah. | B7 | 94 |
| Cat Island, i., Ms., U.S. | L7 | 114 |
| Cat Lake, l., On., Can. | G23 | 104 |
| Catlettsburg, Ky., U.S. | I4 | 108 |
| Catlin, Il., U.S. | B9 | 114 |
| Catnip Mountain, mtn., Nv., U.S. | C6 | 124 |
| Catoche, Cabo, c., Mex. | G16 | 90 |
| Cato Island, i., Austl. | D11 | 70 |
| Catonsville, Md., U.S. | H10 | 108 |
| Catoosa, Ok., U.S. | C11 | 116 |
| Catorce, Mex. | F9 | 90 |
| Catriló, Arg. | I7 | 80 |
| Catrimani, stm., Braz. | G11 | 84 |
| Catskill, N.Y., U.S. | E13 | 108 |
| Catskill Mountains, mts., N.Y., U.S. | E12 | 108 |
| Catt, Mount, mtn., B.C., Can. | C6 | 102 |
| Cattaraugus, N.Y., U.S. | E8 | 108 |
| Cattolica, Italy | F7 | 18 |
| Catu, Braz. | B9 | 79 |
| Catwick, Iles, is., Viet. | I10 | 40 |
| Cauaburi, stm., Braz. | G9 | 84 |
| Caubvick, Mount (Mont d'Iberville), mtn., Can. | E20 | 96 |
| Cauca, dept., Col. | F4 | 84 |
| Cauca, stm., Col. | D5 | 84 |
| Caucasia, Col. | C5 | 84 |
| Caucasus, mts. | I6 | 26 |
| Caucete, Arg. | F4 | 80 |
| Cauchari, Salar de, pl., Arg. | B5 | 80 |
| Cauchon Lake, l., Mb., Can. | C18 | 104 |
| Caudry, Fr. | B10 | 14 |
| Caulonia, Italy | K11 | 18 |
| Çaúngula, Ang. | C3 | 58 |
| Čaúnskaja guba, b., Russia | D25 | 28 |
| Cauquenes, Chile | H2 | 80 |
| Caura, stm., Ven. | D10 | 84 |
| Caurés, stm., Braz. | H11 | 84 |
| Causapscal, P.Q., Can. | D6 | 106 |
| Caussade, Fr. | H8 | 14 |
| Cautário, stm., Braz. | D9 | 82 |
| Caution, Cape, c., B.C., Can. | F7 | 102 |
| Cauto, stm., Cuba | D6 | 94 |
| Caux, Pays de, reg., Fr. | C7 | 14 |
| Cavaillon, Fr. | I12 | 14 |
| Cavalaire-sur-Mer, Fr. | I13 | 14 |
| Cavalcante, Braz. | B5 | 79 |
| Cavalheiro, Braz. | D4 | 79 |
| Cavalier, N.D., U.S. | C10 | 118 |
| Cavalla (Cavally), stm., Afr. | G5 | 54 |
| Cavan, Ire. | G6 | 8 |
| Cavan, co., Ire. | H6 | 8 |
| Cavarzere, Italy | D7 | 18 |
| Cave City, Ar., U.S. | G5 | 114 |
| Cave City, Ky., U.S. | E11 | 114 |
| Cave in Rock, Il., U.S. | E8 | 114 |
| Caveiras, stm., Braz. | D13 | 80 |
| Cavelo, Ang. | A4 | 66 |
| Cavendish, Vt., U.S. | K5 | 70 |
| Cave Run Lake, res., Ky., U.S. | I3 | 108 |
| Cave Spring, Ga., U.S. | E1 | 112 |
| Caviana de Fora, Ilha, i., Braz. | C8 | 76 |
| Çavite, Phil. | n19 | 39b |
| Čavusy, Bela. | H13 | 22 |
| Cawker City, Ks., U.S. | L9 | 118 |
| Cawood, Ky., U.S. | C3 | 112 |
| Cawston, B.C., Can. | H15 | 102 |
| Caxambu, Braz. | F6 | 79 |
| Caxias, Braz. | D10 | 76 |
| Caxias do Sul, Braz. | E13 | 80 |
| Caxinas, Punta, c., Hond. | A8 | 92 |
| Caxito, Ang. | C2 | 58 |
| Cayambe, Ec. | G3 | 84 |
| Cayambe, vol., Ec. | G3 | 84 |
| Cayce, S.C., U.S. | F5 | 112 |
| Cayenne, Fr. Gu. | C8 | 76 |
| Cayey, P.R. | E11 | 94 |
| Cayman Brac, i., Cay. Is. | E5 | 94 |
| Cayman Islands, dep., N.A. | E4 | 94 |
| Cayman Trench | H11 | 86 |
| Cayna, Peru | D3 | 82 |
| Cayo Agua, Isla, i., Pan. | H12 | 92 |
| Cayucos, Ca., U.S. | I5 | 124 |
| Cayuga, In., U.S. | C9 | 114 |
| Cayuga, N.D., U.S. | E10 | 118 |
| Cayuga, On., Can. | H16 | 110 |
| Cayuga, Tx., U.S. | H11 | 116 |
| Cayuga Heights, N.Y., U.S. | E10 | 108 |
| Cayuga Lake, l., N.Y., U.S. | E10 | 108 |
| Cazaclia, Mol. | C12 | 20 |
| Cazenovia, N.Y., U.S. | E11 | 108 |
| Cazères, Fr. | I8 | 14 |
| Cazin, Bos. | E10 | 18 |
| Cazombo, Ang. | D4 | 58 |
| Cazorla, Spain | H8 | 16 |
| Cazorla, Ven. | C9 | 84 |
| Ccapi, Peru | E5 | 82 |
| Ceanannus Mór, Ire. | H7 | 8 |
| Ceará-Mirim, Braz. | E11 | 76 |
| Cebaco, Isla De, i., Pan. | D2 | 84 |
| Ceballos, Mex. | D7 | 90 |
| Cebollar, Arg. | E5 | 80 |
| Cebollas, Mex. | F7 | 90 |
| Cebollati, Ur. | G12 | 80 |
| Cebollatí, stm., Ur. | G11 | 80 |
| Cebu, Phil. | C7 | 38 |
| Cebu, i., Phil. | C7 | 38 |
| Ceccano, Italy | H8 | 18 |
| Cecerleg, Mong. | B7 | 30 |
| Cechovo, Russia | F20 | 22 |
| Čechtice, Czech Rep. | F15 | 10 |
| Čechy, hist. reg., Czech Rep. | F14 | 10 |
| Cecil, Ga., U.S. | H3 | 112 |
| Cecilia, Ky., U.S. | E11 | 114 |
| Cecina, Italy | F5 | 18 |
| Čečňa-Inguśetija, state, Russia | I7 | 26 |
| Cedar, stm., Mi., U.S. | F11 | 110 |
| Cedar, stm., Ne., U.S. | J9 | 118 |
| Cedar, stm., N.Y., U.S. | D12 | 108 |
| Cedar Bluff Reservoir, res., Ks., U.S. | M8 | 118 |
| Cedar Bluffs, Ne., U.S. | J11 | 118 |
| Cedar City, Mo., U.S. | D4 | 114 |
| Cedar City, Ut., U.S. | G3 | 120 |
| Cedar Creek Reservoir, res., Tx., U.S. | G10 | 116 |
| Cedaredge, Co., U.S. | F9 | 120 |
| Cedar Falls, Ia., U.S. | H3 | 110 |
| Cedar Grove, Wi., U.S. | G8 | 110 |
| Cedar Grove, W.V., U.S. | I5 | 108 |
| Cedar Hill, Tn., U.S. | F10 | 114 |
| Cedar Key, Fl., U.S. | J3 | 112 |
| Cedar Lake, l., In., U.S. | A9 | 114 |
| Cedar Lake, res., Mb., Can. | E14 | 104 |
| Cedar Mountain, mtn., Ca., U.S. | C5 | 124 |
| Cedar Rapids, Ia., U.S. | I4 | 110 |
| Cedar Rapids, Ne., U.S. | J9 | 118 |
| Cedar Springs, Mi., U.S. | G10 | 110 |
| Cedartown, Ga., U.S. | E1 | 112 |
| Cedarvale, B.C., Can. | B6 | 102 |
| Cedar Vale, Ks., U.S. | N11 | 118 |
| Cedarville, Ca., U.S. | C5 | 124 |
| Cedarville, Mi., U.S. | D11 | 110 |
| Cedarville, N.J., U.S. | H11 | 108 |
| Cedillo, Embalse de, res., Eur. | F4 | 16 |
| Cedros, Hond. | C7 | 92 |
| Cedros, Mex. | E5 | 90 |
| Cedros, Isla, i., Mex. | C2 | 90 |
| Ceduna, Austl. | F6 | 68 |
| Ceepeecee, B.C., Can. | H8 | 102 |
| Ceerigaabo, Som. | F10 | 56 |
| Cefalù, Italy | K9 | 18 |
| Cegdomyn, Russia | G18 | 28 |
| Cegléd, Hung. | H19 | 10 |
| Cehegín, Spain | G10 | 16 |
| Cehu Silvaniei, Rom. | B7 | 20 |
| Cekalin, Russia | G19 | 22 |
| Cekunda, Russia | J26 | 6 |
| Cel'abinsk, Russia | F10 | 26 |
| Celano, Italy | G8 | 18 |
| Celaya, Mex. | G9 | 90 |
| Celebes see Sulawesi, i., Indon. | F7 | 38 |
| Celebes Sea, Asia | E7 | 38 |
| Çeleken, Turk. | J8 | 26 |
| Celendín, Peru | B2 | 82 |
| Celeste, Tx., U.S. | F10 | 116 |
| Celestún, Mex. | G14 | 90 |
| Celica, Ec. | J3 | 84 |
| Celina, Oh., U.S. | G2 | 108 |
| Celina, Tn., U.S. | F11 | 114 |
| Celina, Tx., U.S. | F10 | 116 |
| Celjahany, Bela. | I8 | 22 |
| Celje, Sln. | C10 | 18 |
| Celkar, Kaz. | H9 | 26 |
| Celle, Ger. | C10 | 10 |
| Celtic Sea, Eur. | J7 | 8 |
| Cel'uskin, mys, c., Russia | B18 | 26 |
| Cement, Ok., U.S. | E8 | 116 |
| Cenderawasih, Teluk, b., Indon. | F10 | 38 |
| Cenepa, stm., Peru | J3 | 84 |
| Centenario, Arg. | J4 | 80 |
| Centenario do Sul, Braz. | G3 | 79 |
| Centennial Mountains, mts., U.S. | E12 | 122 |
| Center, Co., U.S. | G10 | 120 |
| Center, Mo., U.S. | C5 | 114 |
| Center, N.D., U.S. | D6 | 118 |
| Center, Ne., U.S. | I10 | 118 |
| Center, Tx., U.S. | K2 | 114 |
| Centerburg, Oh., U.S. | G4 | 108 |
| Center Hill, Fl., U.S. | K5 | 112 |
| Center Hill Lake, res., Tn., U.S. | F11 | 114 |
| Center Moriches, N.Y., U.S. | G14 | 108 |
| Center Mountain, mtn., Id., U.S. | E10 | 122 |
| Center Point, Al., U.S. | I10 | 114 |
| Center Point, Ia., U.S. | H4 | 110 |
| Center Point, Tx., U.S. | J7 | 116 |
| Centerville, Ia., U.S. | I3 | 110 |
| Centerville, In., U.S. | C12 | 114 |
| Centerville, Mo., U.S. | E6 | 114 |
| Centerville, Pa., U.S. | G8 | 108 |
| Centerville, S.D., U.S. | H11 | 118 |
| Centerville, Tn., U.S. | G9 | 114 |
| Centerville, Tx., U.S. | H11 | 116 |
| Centerville, Ut., U.S. | C5 | 120 |
| Cento, Italy | E6 | 18 |
| Central, Az., U.S. | L7 | 120 |
| Central, N.M., U.S. | L7 | 120 |
| Central, dept., Para. | C10 | 80 |
| Central, prov., Kenya | B7 | 58 |
| Central, prov., Zam. | D5 | 58 |
| Central, dept., Bots. | C8 | 66 |
| Central, prov., Scot., U.K. | E8 | 8 |
| Central, Cordillera, mts., Col. | E5 | 84 |
| Central, Cordillera, mts., C.R. | G10 | 92 |
| Central, Cordillera, mts., Pan. | I13 | 92 |
| Central, Cordillera, mts., Peru | B3 | 82 |
| Central, Cordillera, mts., P.R. | E11 | 94 |
| Central Central, reg., Arg. | C8 | 80 |
| Central, Massif, mts., Fr. | G10 | 14 |
| Central, Planalto, plat., Braz. | G9 | 76 |
| Central, Sistema, mts., Spain | E6 | 16 |
| Central African Republic, ctry., Afr. | G5 | 56 |
| Central Brāhui Range, mts., Pak. | F2 | 44 |
| Central Butte, Sk., Can. | H8 | 104 |
| Central City, Ia., U.S. | H4 | 110 |
| Central City, Il., U.S. | D7 | 114 |
| Central City, Ky., U.S. | E9 | 114 |
| Central City, Ne., U.S. | J9 | 118 |
| Central City, Pa., U.S. | G8 | 108 |
| Central Heights, Az., U.S. | K6 | 120 |
| Centralia, Il., U.S. | D7 | 114 |
| Centralia, Ks., U.S. | L11 | 118 |
| Centralia, Mo., U.S. | C4 | 114 |
| Centralia, Wa., U.S. | D3 | 122 |
| Centralina, Braz. | E4 | 79 |
| Central Kalahari Game Reserve, Bots. | D6 | 66 |
| Central Lake, Mi., U.S. | E10 | 110 |
| Central Makrān Range, mts., Pak. | G1 | 44 |
| Central'nyj, Russia | H22 | 22 |
| Central Point, Or., U.S. | H3 | 122 |
| Central Range, mts., Leso. | G9 | 66 |
| Central Square, N.Y., U.S. | D10 | 108 |
| Central Valley, Ca., U.S. | D3 | 124 |
| Centre, Al., U.S. | H11 | 114 |
| Centre, Canal du, Fr. | F11 | 14 |
| Centre Peak, mtn., B.C., Can. | B8 | 102 |
| Centreville, Al., U.S. | J9 | 114 |
| Centreville, Md., U.S. | H10 | 108 |
| Centreville, Mi., U.S. | I10 | 110 |
| Centreville, Ms., U.S. | K5 | 114 |
| Century, Fl., U.S. | L9 | 114 |
| Century, W.V., U.S. | H6 | 108 |
| Century Village, Fl., U.S. | M6 | 112 |
| Cenxi, China | B6 | 34 |
| Cepu, Indon. | j15 | 39a |
| Cerahoŋka, Bela. | I14 | 22 |
| Ceram see Seram, i., Indon. | F8 | 38 |
| Ceram Sea see Seram, Laut, Indon. | F8 | 38 |
| Čerčany, Czech Rep. | F14 | 10 |
| Cerdas, Bol. | I8 | 82 |
| Cère, stm., Fr. | H9 | 14 |
| Cereal, Ab., Can. | I7 | 80 |
| Cereales, Arg. | I8 | 80 |
| Čeremchovo, Russia | G18 | 28 |
| Čeremšanka, Russia | G14 | 26 |
| Cerepet', Russia | F20 | 22 |
| Čerepovec, Russia | B20 | 22 |
| Ceres, Arg. | E8 | 80 |
| Ceres, Braz. | C4 | 79 |
| Ceres, S. Afr. | I4 | 66 |
| Ceresco, Ne., U.S. | J11 | 118 |
| Ceresole Reale, Italy | D2 | 18 |
| Cereté, Col. | C5 | 84 |
| Cerignola, Italy | H10 | 18 |
| Čerkassy, Russia | I6 | 26 |
| Čerkessk, Russia | I6 | 26 |
| Čerknica, Slvn. | D9 | 18 |
| Čerlak, Russia | G12 | 26 |
| Čern', Russia | H19 | 22 |
| Cermei, Rom. | C5 | 20 |
| Čern'achovsk (Insterburg), Russia | G4 | 22 |
| Čern'aŭcycy, Bela. | I6 | 22 |
| Černavodă, Rom. | E12 | 20 |
| Cernay, Fr. | E14 | 14 |
| Černogorsk, Russia | G10 | 28 |
| Čern'ovo, Russia | C11 | 22 |
| Černyševskij, Russia | E14 | 28 |
| Cerralvo, Mex. | D10 | 90 |
| Cerralvo, Isla, i., Mex. | E5 | 90 |
| Cerrillos, Arg. | C6 | 80 |
| Cerrillos, N.M., U.S. | I10 | 120 |
| Cerritos, Mex. | F9 | 90 |
| Cerro Azul, Arg. | D11 | 80 |
| Cerro Azul, Braz. | C14 | 80 |
| Cerro Azul, Peru | E3 | 82 |
| Cerro Azul, Ur. | G11 | 80 |
| Cerro Chato, Ur. | G11 | 80 |
| Cerro Colorado, Ur. | G11 | 80 |
| Cerro de las Mesas, hist., Mex. | H11 | 90 |
| Cerro de Pasco, Peru | D3 | 82 |
| Cerro Gordo, Il., U.S. | C8 | 114 |
| Cerro Largo, Braz. | E11 | 80 |
| Cerro Moreno, Chile | B3 | 80 |
| Cerrón, Cerro, mtn., Ven. | B7 | 84 |
| Cerrón Grande, Embalse, res., El Sal. | C5 | 92 |
| Cerros Colorados, Embalse, res., Arg. | J4 | 80 |
| Cerro Vera, Ur. | G10 | 80 |
| Čerskogo, chrebet, mts., Russia | E21 | 28 |
| Čerusti, Russia | F23 | 22 |
| Červen', Bela. | H11 | 22 |
| Cervera Briag, Bul. | F8 | 20 |
| Cervera, Spain | D13 | 16 |
| Cervia, Italy | E7 | 18 |
| Cervione, Fr. | I24 | 15a |
| Čeŕykau, Bela. | H14 | 22 |
| Cesar, dept., Col. | C6 | 84 |
| Cesar, stm., Col. | B6 | 84 |
| Cesena, Italy | E7 | 18 |
| Cesenatico, Italy | E7 | 18 |
| Cēsis, Lat. | D8 | 22 |
| Česká Lípa, Czech Rep. | E14 | 10 |
| České Budějovice, Czech Rep. | G14 | 10 |
| Českomoravská vrchovina, plat., Czech Rep. | F15 | 10 |
| Český Brod, Czech Rep. | E14 | 10 |
| Český Krumlov, Czech Rep. | G14 | 10 |
| Češskaja guba, b., Russia | D7 | 26 |
| Cessnock, Austl. | I9 | 70 |
| Cestos, stm., Lib. | I5 | 64 |
| Cesvaine, Lat. | E9 | 22 |
| Cetinje, Yugo. | G2 | 20 |
| Ceuta, Sp. N. Afr. | C8 | 62 |
| Cévennes, mts., Fr. | H10 | 14 |
| Ceylon, Mn., U.S. | H13 | 118 |
| Ceylon, Sk., Can. | I10 | 104 |
| Chaanling, China | F2 | 34 |
| Chaatl Island, i., B.C., Can. | D2 | 102 |
| Chabanais, Fr. | G7 | 14 |
| Chabarovsk, Russia | H19 | 28 |
| Chablais, reg., Fr. | F13 | 14 |
| Chablis, Fr. | E10 | 14 |
| Chacabuco, Arg. | H8 | 80 |
| Chacayán, Peru | D3 | 82 |
| Chachani, Nevado, mtn., Peru | G6 | 82 |
| Chachas, Peru | F5 | 82 |
| Chachoengsao, Thai. | H6 | 40 |
| Chachu, China | D9 | 44 |
| Chaco, prov., Arg. | D8 | 80 |
| Chaco, dept., Para. | H12 | 82 |
| Chaco, stm., N.M., U.S. | H8 | 120 |
| Chaco Austral, reg., Arg. | D7 | 80 |
| Chaco Boreal, reg., Para. | B8 | 80 |
| Chaco Central, reg., Arg. | C8 | 80 |
| Chacon, Cape, c., Ak., U.S. | C2 | 102 |
| Chad (Tchad), ctry., Afr. | E4 | 56 |
| Chad, Lake (Lac Tchad), l., Afr. | F3 | 56 |
| Chadbourn, N.C., U.S. | E8 | 112 |
| Chadron, Ne., U.S. | I4 | 118 |
| Chadwick, Il., U.S. | H6 | 110 |
| Chaeryŏng, N. Kor. | E13 | 32 |
| Chafe, Nig. | F13 | 64 |
| Chaffee, Mo., U.S. | E7 | 114 |
| Chāgai Hills, hills, Asia | G18 | 48 |
| 'Chaghcharān, Afg. | C1 | 44 |
| Chagny, Fr. | F11 | 14 |
| Chagoda, Russia | B21 | 22 |
| Chagos Archipelago, is., B.I.O.T. | J8 | 24 |
| Chaguaramas, Ven. | C9 | 84 |
| Chagrin Falls, Oh., U.S. | F5 | 108 |
| Chāh Bahār, India | I11 | 44 |
| Chai Nat, Thai. | G6 | 40 |
| Chaiqiao, China | F10 | 34 |
| Chaiyaphum, Thai. | G7 | 40 |
| Chajari, Arg. | F10 | 80 |
| Chajian, China | C7 | 34 |
| Chajiaqiao, China | A3 | 34 |
| Chajul, Guat. | B3 | 92 |
| Chakasija, state, Russia | G15 | 26 |
| Chakdaha, India | I13 | 44 |
| Chakradharpur, India | I11 | 44 |
| Chakwāl, Pak. | C5 | 44 |
| Chala, Peru | F4 | 82 |
| Chalatenango, El Sal. | C6 | 92 |
| Chalchuapa, El Sal. | D5 | 92 |
| Chalcis see Khalkís, Grc. | K7 | 20 |
| Chalengkou, China | B15 | 44 |
| Chaleur Bay, b., Can. | E8 | 106 |
| Chalhuanca, Peru | F5 | 82 |
| Chaling, China | H2 | 34 |
| Chālisgaon, India | B3 | 46 |
| Chalk River, On., Can. | D18 | 110 |
| Chalkyitsik, Ak., U.S. | C23 | 100 |
| Challapata, Bol. | H8 | 82 |
| Challenger Deep | G18 | 126 |
| Challis, Id., U.S. | F11 | 122 |
| Challviri, Salar de, pl., Bol. | J8 | 82 |
| Chalmette, La., U.S. | M7 | 114 |
| Châlons-sur-Marne, Fr. | D11 | 14 |
| Chalon-sur-Saône, Fr. | F11 | 14 |
| Chalosse, reg., Fr. | I6 | 14 |
| Chaltel, Cerro (Monte Fitzroy), mtn., S.A. | F2 | 78 |
| Cham, Ger. | F12 | 10 |
| Chama, N.M., U.S. | H10 | 120 |
| Chama, Rio, stm., U.S. | H10 | 120 |
| Chama, stm., Ven. | C7 | 84 |
| Chamaicó, Arg. | H6 | 80 |
| Chaman, Pak. | E2 | 44 |
| Chamaya, stm., Peru | A2 | 82 |
| Chambal, stm., India | G7 | 44 |
| Chamberlain, S.D., U.S. | H8 | 118 |
| Chamberlain, Sk., Can. | H9 | 104 |
| Chambers, Az., U.S. | I7 | 120 |
| Chambers, Ne., U.S. | I9 | 118 |
| Chambersburg, Pa., U.S. | H9 | 108 |
| Chambéry, Fr. | G12 | 14 |
| Chambi, Jebel, mtn., Tun. | C15 | 62 |
| Chambira, stm., Peru | I5 | 84 |
| Chambira, stm., Peru | I5 | 84 |
| Chamblee, Ga., U.S. | F2 | 112 |
| Chame, Pan. | I15 | 92 |
| Chame, Punta, c., Pan. | I15 | 92 |
| Chamelecón, Hond. | B6 | 92 |
| Chamelecón, stm., Hond. | B6 | 92 |
| Chamical, Arg. | F5 | 80 |
| Chamo, Lake, l., Eth. | O9 | 60 |
| Chamois, Mo., U.S. | D5 | 114 |
| Chamonix-Mont-Blanc, Fr. | G13 | 14 |
| Chāmpa, India | I10 | 44 |
| Champagne, Yk., Can. | F26 | 100 |
| Champagne, hist. reg., Fr. | D11 | 14 |
| Champagne Castle, mtn., S. Afr. | G9 | 66 |
| Champagnole, Fr. | F12 | 14 |
| Champaign, Il., U.S. | B8 | 114 |
| Champaqui, Cerro, mtn., Arg. | F6 | 80 |
| Champasak, Laos | G8 | 40 |
| Champdoré, Lac, l., P.Q., Can. | E19 | 96 |
| Champeix, Fr. | G10 | 14 |
| Champerico, Guat. | C3 | 92 |
| Champéry, Switz. | F13 | 13 |
| Champion, Ab., Can. | G21 | 102 |
| Champion, Mi., U.S. | D8 | 110 |
| Champion, Oh., U.S. | F5 | 108 |
| Champlain, N.Y., U.S. | C13 | 108 |
| Champlain, Lake, l., N.A. | C13 | 108 |
| Champlitte-et-le-Prélot, Fr. | E12 | 14 |
| Champotón, Mex. | H14 | 90 |
| Chamusca, Port. | F3 | 16 |
| Chañar, Arg. | F6 | 80 |
| Chañaral, Chile | D3 | 80 |
| Chañaral, Isla, i., Chile | D3 | 80 |
| Chancay, Peru | D3 | 82 |
| Chancay, stm., Peru | D3 | 82 |
| Chanch, Mong. | A7 | 30 |
| Chanco, Chile | H2 | 80 |
| Chandalar, stm., Ak., U.S. | C21 | 100 |
| Chandausi, India | F8 | 44 |
| Chandeleur Islands, is., La., U.S. | M8 | 114 |
| Chandeleur Sound, strt., La., U.S. | M7 | 114 |
| Chandigarh, India | E7 | 44 |
| Chandler, Az., U.S. | K5 | 120 |
| Chandler, In., U.S. | D9 | 114 |
| Chandler, Ok., U.S. | D10 | 116 |
| Chandler, P.Q., Can. | D9 | 106 |
| Chandler, Tx., U.S. | G11 | 116 |
| Chandler Lake, l., Ak., U.S. | B18 | 100 |
| Chandlerville, Il., U.S. | B6 | 114 |
| Chandless, stm., S.A. | C6 | 82 |
| Chāndpur, India | F8 | 44 |
| Chandrapur, India | B5 | 46 |
| Chandyga, Russia | E19 | 28 |
| Changane, stm., Moz. | D11 | 66 |
| Changbai Shan, mts., Asia | B15 | 32 |
| Chang Cheng (Great Wall), hist., China | C4 | 32 |
| Chang Chenmo, stm., Asia | C8 | 44 |
| Changchou see Zhangzhou, China | K6 | 34 |
| Changchun, China | C12 | 30 |
| Changde (Sihou), China | F8 | 32 |
| Change Islands, Nf., Can. | C19 | 106 |
| Changguandian, China | A7 | 34 |
| Changhua, Tai. | L9 | 34 |
| Changhūng, S. Kor. | I14 | 32 |
| Changji, China | C3 | 30 |
| Changjiang, China | J2 | 34 |
| Changli, China | D7 | 32 |
| Changlingzi, China | D10 | 32 |
| Ch'angnyŏng, S. Kor. | H16 | 32 |
| Changsha, China | G2 | 34 |
| Changshan, China | G7 | 34 |
| Changshoujie, China | G2 | 34 |
| Changshu, China | D9 | 34 |
| Changsŏng, S. Kor. | H14 | 32 |
| Changsu, S. Kor. | H15 | 32 |
| Changting, China | J5 | 34 |
| Changuinola, Pan. | H12 | 92 |
| Changxing, China | D8 | 34 |
| Changyŏn, N. Kor. | E13 | 32 |
| Changzhi, China | D9 | 30 |
| Changzhou (Changchow), China | D8 | 34 |
| Chanino, Russia | G19 | 22 |
| Channel Country, reg., Austl. | E4 | 70 |
| Channel Islands, is., Ca., U.S. | K6 | 124 |
| Channel Islands, is., Eur. | L11 | 8 |
| Channel-Port-aux-Basques, Nf., Can. | E14 | 106 |
| Channelview, Tx., U.S. | J11 | 116 |
| Channing, Mi., U.S. | D7 | 110 |
| Channing, Tx., U.S. | D4 | 116 |
| Chantada, Spain | C3 | 16 |
| Chantajskoje, ozero, l., Russia | D10 | 28 |
| Chantajskoje vodochranilišče, res., Russia | D15 | 26 |
| Chantang, China | B6 | 34 |
| Chanthaburi, Thai. | H7 | 40 |
| Chantilly, Fr. | C9 | 14 |
| Chantrey Inlet, b., N.T., Can. | C13 | 96 |
| Chanute, Ks., U.S. | N12 | 118 |
| Chao, Isla, i., Peru | C2 | 82 |
| Chao'an, China | L5 | 34 |
| Chao Hu, l., China | E10 | 30 |
| Chao Phraya, stm., Thai. | G6 | 40 |
| Chaoshui, China | F8 | 32 |
| Chaouen, Mor. | C8 | 62 |
| Chaoyang, China | L5 | 34 |
| Chaoyang, China | A17 | 32 |
| Chapada dos Guimarães, Braz. | F14 | 82 |
| Chapala, Mex. | G8 | 90 |
| Chapala, Laguna de, l., Mex. | G8 | 90 |
| Chapare, stm., Bol. | G9 | 82 |
| Chaparral, Col. | F5 | 84 |
| Chapčeranga, Russia | H14 | 28 |
| Chapecó, Braz. | D12 | 80 |
| Chapel Hill, N.C., U.S. | D7 | 112 |
| Chapel Hill, Tn., U.S. | G10 | 114 |
| Chapicuy, Ur. | F10 | 80 |
| Chapimarca, Peru | E5 | 82 |
| Chapin, Il., U.S. | C6 | 114 |
| Chapleau, On., Can. | C12 | 110 |
| Chaplin, Sk., Can. | H8 | 104 |
| Chaplin, Ky., U.S. | E11 | 114 |
| Chaplin Lake, l., Sk., Can. | H8 | 104 |
| Chaplygin, Russia | I23 | 22 |
| Chapman, Ks., U.S. | M10 | 118 |
| Chapman, Cape, c., N.T., Can. | C15 | 96 |
| Chapman, Mount, mtn., B.C., Can. | F16 | 102 |
| Chapman Lake, l., Mb., Can. | B16 | 104 |
| Chapman's (Okwa), stm., Afr. | D4 | 66 |
| Chapmanville, W.V., U.S. | J4 | 108 |
| Chappell, Ne., U.S. | J5 | 118 |
| Chappell Hill, Tx., U.S. | I10 | 116 |
| Chaqui, Bol. | H9 | 82 |
| Chaquiago, Arg. | D5 | 80 |
| Charadai, Arg. | D9 | 80 |
| Charagua, Bol. | H10 | 82 |
| Charalá, Col. | D6 | 84 |
| Charaña, Bol. | G7 | 82 |
| Charata, Arg. | D8 | 80 |
| Charcana, Peru | F5 | 82 |
| Charcas, Mex. | F9 | 90 |
| Charco Azul, Bahía de, b., Pan. | I12 | 92 |
| Charcos de Figueroa, Mex. | D8 | 90 |
| Chardon, Oh., U.S. | F5 | 108 |
| Charente, dept., Fr. | G7 | 14 |
| Charente, stm., Fr. | G6 | 14 |
| Charente-Maritime, dept., Fr. | G6 | 14 |
| Chari, stm., Afr. | F4 | 56 |
| Chārīkār, Afg. | C3 | 44 |
| Chariton, Ia., U.S. | I2 | 110 |
| Chariton, stm., U.S. | C4 | 114 |
| Charity, Guy. | D13 | 84 |
| Charleroi, Bel. | H5 | 12 |
| Charleroi, Pa., U.S. | G7 | 108 |
| Charles, Cape, c., Va., U.S. | B11 | 112 |
| Charles City, Ia., U.S. | G3 | 110 |
| Charles City, Va., U.S. | B9 | 112 |
| Charles Island, i., N.T., Can. | D18 | 96 |
| Charles Mound, hill, Il., U.S. | H5 | 110 |
| Charleston, Ar., U.S. | G2 | 114 |
| Charleston, Il., U.S. | C8 | 114 |
| Charleston, Ms., U.S. | H6 | 114 |
| Charleston, Mo., U.S. | E7 | 114 |
| Charleston, S.C., U.S. | F7 | 112 |
| Charleston, W.V., U.S. | I5 | 108 |
| Charleston Peak, mtn., Nv., U.S. | H10 | 124 |
| Charlestown, N.H., U.S. | D14 | 108 |
| Charlestown, S. Afr. | F9 | 66 |
| Charlestown, St. K./N. | F13 | 94 |
| Charleville, Austl. | F7 | 70 |
| Charleville-Mézières, Fr. | C11 | 14 |
| Charlevoix, Mi., U.S. | E10 | 110 |
| Charlevoix, Lake, l., Mi. | E10 | 110 |
| Charlotte, Mi., U.S. | H11 | 110 |
| Charlotte, N.C., U.S. | D5 | 112 |
| Charlotte, Tn., U.S. | F9 | 114 |
| Charlotte, Tx., U.S. | K8 | 116 |
| Charlotte Amalie, V.I.U.S. | E12 | 94 |
| Charlotte Court House, Va., U.S. | B8 | 112 |
| Charlotte Harbor, b., Fl. | M4 | 112 |
| Charlottesville, Va., U.S. | A8 | 112 |
| Charlottetown, P.E.I., Can. | F10 | 106 |
| Charlton Island, i., N.T., Can. | E16 | 96 |
| Charlu, Russia | K22 | 6 |
| Charlue, China | F10 | 34 |
| Charouine, Alg. | E10 | 62 |
| Charron Lake, l., Mb., Can. | F19 | 104 |
| Charsadda, Pak. | C4 | 44 |
| Charter Oak, Ia., U.S. | I12 | 118 |
| Charters Towers, Austl. | C7 | 70 |
| Chartres, Fr. | D8 | 14 |
| Chasav'urt, Russia | I7 | 26 |
| Chascomús, Arg. | H9 | 80 |
| Chase, Ks., U.S. | M9 | 118 |
| Chase, B.C., Can. | G15 | 102 |
| Chase, Mn., U.S. | F2 | 110 |
| Chase City, Va., U.S. | C8 | 112 |
| Chaska, Mn., U.S. | F2 | 110 |
| Chasŏng, N. Kor. | B14 | 32 |
| Chasuta, Peru | B3 | 82 |
| Chatanbulag, Mong. | C7 | 30 |
| Chatanga, stm., Russia | C12 | 28 |
| Chatangskij zaliv, b., Russia | C13 | 28 |
| Chatanika, stm., Ak., U.S. | D20 | 100 |
| Château-Chinon, Fr. | E5 | 14 |
| Château-d'Oex, Switz. | F7 | 13 |
| Château-du-Loir, Fr. | E7 | 14 |
| Châteaudun, Fr. | D8 | 14 |
| Chateauguay, stm., N.A. | B12 | 108 |
| Châteaulin, Fr. | D2 | 14 |
| Châteauneuf-sur-Charente, Fr. | G6 | 14 |
| Château-Renault, Fr. | E7 | 14 |
| Château-Richer, P.Q., Can. | F2 | 106 |
| Chateauroux, Fr. | F8 | 14 |
| Château-Salins, Fr. | D13 | 14 |
| Château-Thierry, Fr. | C10 | 14 |
| Châtellerault, Fr. | F7 | 14 |
| Châtel-sur-Moselle, Fr. | D13 | 14 |
| Chatfield, Mn., U.S. | G3 | 110 |
| Chatgal, Mong. | A7 | 30 |
| Chatham, Il., U.S. | C7 | 114 |
| Chatham, La., U.S. | J4 | 114 |
| Chatham, Ma., U.S. | F17 | 108 |
| Chatham, N.B., Can. | E8 | 106 |
| Chatham, N.Y., U.S. | E13 | 108 |
| Chatham, On., Can. | H14 | 110 |
| Chatham, Va., U.S. | C7 | 112 |
| Chatham Head, N.B., Can. | E8 | 106 |
| Chatham Islands, is., N.Z. | M22 | 126 |
| Chatham Sound, strt., B.C., Can. | C4 | 102 |
| Chatham Strait, strt., Ak., U.S. | H27 | 100 |
| Châtillon, Italy | D2 | 18 |
| Châtillon-sur-Chalaronne, Fr. | F11 | 14 |
| Châtillon-sur-Indre, Fr. | F8 | 14 |
| Châtillon-sur-Seine, Fr. | E11 | 14 |
| Chatom, Al., U.S. | K8 | 114 |
| Chatsquot Mountain, mtn., B.C., Can. | D7 | 102 |
| Chatsworth, Ga., U.S. | E2 | 112 |
| Chatsworth, Il., U.S. | J7 | 110 |
| Chatsworth, Zimb. | B10 | 66 |
| Chattahoochee, Fl., U.S. | I2 | 112 |
| Chattahoochee, stm., U.S. | G11 | 112 |
| Chattanooga, Tn., U.S. | G11 | 114 |
| Chattaroy, W.V., U.S. | B4 | 112 |
| Chaudière, stm., P.Q., Can. | F2 | 106 |
| Chauk, Mya. | D3 | 40 |
| Chaukan Pass, Asia | E5 | 82 |
| Chaumont, Fr. | D12 | 14 |
| Chaumont-en-Vexin, Fr. | C8 | 14 |
| Chauncey, Oh., U.S. | H4 | 108 |
| Chaungwabyin, Myan. | H5 | 40 |
| Chauny, Fr. | C10 | 14 |
| Chaussin, Fr. | F12 | 14 |
| Chautauqua Lake, l., N.Y., U.S. | E7 | 108 |
| Chauvin, Ab., Can. | F4 | 104 |
| Chauvin, La., U.S. | M6 | 114 |
| Chavakkad, India | G4 | 46 |
| Chavantes, Braz. | G3 | 79 |
| Chavarría, Arg. | E9 | 80 |
| Chaviña, Peru | F5 | 82 |
| Cháviva, Col. | E6 | 84 |
| Chayanta, Bol. | H8 | 82 |
| Chazy, N.Y., U.S. | C13 | 108 |
| Cheaha Mountain, mtn., Al., U.S. | I11 | 114 |
| Cheakamus Indian Reserve, B.C., Can. | H11 | 102 |
| Cheat, stm., U.S. | H7 | 108 |
| Cheat, Shavers Fork, stm., W.V., U.S. | I7 | 108 |
| Cheb, Czech Rep. | E12 | 10 |
| Chebanse, Il., U.S. | I8 | 110 |
| Chebba, Tun. | C16 | 62 |
| Chebogue Point, c., N.S., Can. | I7 | 106 |
| Cheboygan, Mi., U.S. | E11 | 110 |
| Chech, Erg, des., Afr. | D6 | 54 |
| Chechnya see Čečnja-Inguśetija, state, Russia | I7 | 26 |
| Chech'on, S. Kor. | F16 | 32 |
| Chęciny, Pol. | E20 | 10 |
| Checleset Bay, b., B.C., Can. | G7 | 102 |
| Checotah, Ok., U.S. | D11 | 116 |
| Chedabucto Bay, b., N.S. | G12 | 106 |
| Cheduba Island, i., Myan. | E2 | 40 |
| Checktowaga, N.Y., U.S. | E8 | 108 |
| Chefornak, Ak., U.S. | F12 | 100 |
| Chehalis, Wa., U.S. | D2 | 122 |
| Chehalis, stm., Wa., U.S. | D2 | 122 |
| Chehe, China | B9 | 40 |
| Cheju, S. Kor. | E12 | 30 |
| Chekiang see Zhejiang, prov., China | F11 | 30 |
| Chelan, Wa., U.S. | C5 | 122 |
| Chelan, Lake, l., Wa., U.S. | C5 | 122 |
| Chelektu, S. Kor. | N10 | 60 |
| Chelforó, Arg. | J5 | 80 |
| Chelghoum el Aïd, Alg. | B14 | 62 |
| Chéliff, Oued, stm., Alg. | B11 | 62 |
| Chełm, Pol. | D23 | 10 |
| Chełmno, Pol. | B18 | 10 |
| Chelmsford, On., Can. | D14 | 110 |
| Chełmza, Pol. | B18 | 10 |
| Chelsea, Ia., U.S. | I3 | 110 |
| Chelsea, Mi., U.S. | H11 | 110 |
| Chelsea, Ok., U.S. | C11 | 116 |
| Chelsea, Vt., U.S. | D13 | 108 |
| Chelyabinsk see Čel'abinsk, Russia | F10 | 26 |
| Chemainus, B.C., Can. | I11 | 102 |
| Chemax, Mex. | G16 | 90 |
| Chemnitz, Ger. | E12 | 10 |
| Chemult, Or., U.S. | G4 | 122 |
| Chemung, stm., U.S. | E9 | 108 |
| Chenab, stm., Asia | E5 | 44 |
| Chenachane, Alg. | D7 | 62 |
| Chenango, stm., N.Y., U.S. | E11 | 108 |
| Chenango Bridge, N.Y., U.S. | E11 | 108 |
| Chenārān, Iran | C15 | 48 |
| Cheney, Ks., U.S. | N10 | 118 |
| Cheney, Wa., U.S. | C8 | 122 |
| Cheney Reservoir, res., Ks., U.S. | N10 | 118 |
| Chengde, China | C5 | 32 |
| Chengdu, China | E7 | 30 |
| Chenghai, China | L5 | 34 |
| Chengjiang, China | B7 | 40 |

| Name | Map Ref. | Page |
|---|---|---|
| Chengshan Jiao, c., China | F10 | 32 |
| Chengtu see Chengdu, China | E7 | 30 |
| Chengzitan, China | D10 | 32 |
| Chenil, Lac, l., P.Q., Can. | A14 | 106 |
| Chennai (Madras), India | F6 | 46 |
| Chenoa, Il., U.S. | J7 | 110 |
| Chenxian, China | J1 | 34 |
| Cheo Reo, Viet. | H10 | 40 |
| Chepén, Peru | B2 | 82 |
| Chepes, Arg. | F5 | 80 |
| Chepo, Pan. | C3 | 84 |
| Cher, dept., Fr. | E9 | 14 |
| Cher, stm., Fr. | E8 | 14 |
| Cheraw, S.C., U.S. | E7 | 112 |
| Cherbourg, Fr. | C5 | 14 |
| Cherchell, Alg. | B12 | 62 |
| Chergui, Chott ech, l., Alg. | C11 | 62 |
| Cheriton, Va., U.S. | B11 | 112 |
| Cherkasy, Ukr. | H4 | 26 |
| Chernihiv, Ukr. | G4 | 26 |
| Chernivtsi, Ukr. | A9 | 20 |
| Chernobyl see Chornobyl', Ukr. | G4 | 26 |
| Cherokee, Al., U.S. | H9 | 114 |
| Cherokee, Ia., U.S. | I12 | 118 |
| Cherokee, Ks., U.S. | N13 | 118 |
| Cherokee, Ok., U.S. | C8 | 116 |
| Cherokee, Tx., U.S. | I8 | 116 |
| Cherokee Lake, res., Tn., U.S. | C3 | 112 |
| Cherokees, Lake O' The, res., Ok., U.S. | C12 | 116 |
| Cherokee Village, Ar., U.S. | F5 | 114 |
| Cherquenco, Chile | J2 | 80 |
| Cherrapunji, India | H14 | 44 |
| Cherry Hill, N.J., U.S. | H11 | 108 |
| Cherryvale, Ks., U.S. | N12 | 118 |
| Cherry Valley, Ar., U.S. | G6 | 114 |
| Cherryville, N.C., U.S. | D5 | 112 |
| Chervonoarmiys'ke, Ukr. | D12 | 20 |
| Chervonohrad, Ukr. | G2 | 26 |
| Chesaning, Mi., U.S. | G11 | 110 |
| Chesapeake, Va., U.S. | C10 | 112 |
| Chesapeake Bay, b., U.S. | D11 | 98 |
| Chesapeake Beach, Md., U.S. | I10 | 108 |
| Chesapeake City, Md., U.S. | H11 | 108 |
| Cheseaux, Switz. | E6 | 13 |
| Cheshire, Ma., U.S. | E13 | 108 |
| Cheshire, co., Eng., U.K. | H11 | 8 |
| Cheslatta Lake, l., B.C., Can. | D9 | 102 |
| Chesley, On., Can. | F14 | 110 |
| Chesnee, S.C., U.S. | D5 | 112 |
| Chester, Ca., U.S. | D4 | 124 |
| Chester, Eng., U.K. | H11 | 8 |
| Chester, Il., U.S. | E7 | 114 |
| Chester, Mt., U.S. | B15 | 122 |
| Chester, Ne., U.S. | K10 | 118 |
| Chester, Ok., U.S. | C8 | 116 |
| Chester, Pa., U.S. | H11 | 108 |
| Chester, S.C., U.S. | E5 | 112 |
| Chester, Va., U.S. | B9 | 112 |
| Chester, Vt., U.S. | D14 | 108 |
| Chester Basin, N.S., Can. | H9 | 106 |
| Chesterfield, S.C., U.S. | E6 | 112 |
| Chesterfield, Va., U.S. | B9 | 112 |
| Chesterfield, Îles, is., N. Cal. | C11 | 68 |
| Chesterfield, Nosy, i., Madag. | E8 | 58 |
| Chesterfield Inlet, N.T., Can. | D14 | 96 |
| Chesterfield Inlet, b., N.T., Can. | D14 | 96 |
| Chesterhill, Oh., U.S. | H5 | 108 |
| Chester-le-Street, Eng., U.K. | G12 | 8 |
| Chesterton, In., U.S. | A9 | 114 |
| Chesterton Range, mts., Austl. | E7 | 70 |
| Chestertown, Md., U.S. | H10 | 108 |
| Chesterville, On., Can. | B11 | 108 |
| Chesuncook Lake, l., Me., U.S. | A17 | 108 |
| Cheta, stm., Russia | C11 | 28 |
| Chetaibi, Alg. | L2 | 18 |
| Chetco, stm., Or., U.S. | B1 | 124 |
| Chetek, Wi., U.S. | E4 | 110 |
| Chéticamp, N.S., Can. | F12 | 106 |
| Chetopa, Ks., U.S. | N12 | 118 |
| Chetumal, Mex. | H15 | 90 |
| Chetumal, Bahía, b., N.A. | H15 | 90 |
| Chetwynd, B.C., Can. | B13 | 102 |
| Chevak, Ak., U.S. | F12 | 100 |
| Cheviot, Oh., U.S. | H2 | 108 |
| Chewaucan, stm., Or., U.S. | H5 | 122 |
| Chew Bahir (Lake Stefanie), l., Afr. | H8 | 56 |
| Chewelah, Wa., U.S. | B8 | 122 |
| Cheyenne, Ok., U.S. | D7 | 116 |
| Cheyenne, Wy., U.S. | C12 | 120 |
| Cheyenne, stm., U.S. | G6 | 118 |
| Cheyenne Wells, Co., U.S. | M5 | 118 |
| Chezhen, China | F5 | 32 |
| Chhapra, India | H11 | 44 |
| Chhatak, Bngl. | H14 | 44 |
| Chhatarpur, India | H8 | 44 |
| Chhatrapur, India | C8 | 46 |
| Chhèb Kândal, Camb. | H8 | 40 |
| Chhindwāra, India | I8 | 44 |
| Chhukha Dzong, Bhu. | G13 | 44 |
| Chi, stm., Thai. | G8 | 40 |
| Chía, Col. | E5 | 84 |
| Chiai, Tai. | L9 | 34 |
| Chiali, Tai. | L9 | 34 |
| Chiang Kham, Thai. | E6 | 40 |
| Chiang Khan, Thai. | F6 | 40 |
| Chiang Mai, Thai. | E5 | 40 |
| Chiang Rai, Thai. | E5 | 40 |
| Chiapa, India | H7 | 82 |
| Chiapa de Corzo, Mex. | I13 | 90 |
| Chiapas, state, Mex. | I14 | 90 |
| Chiari, Italy | D4 | 18 |
| Chiasso, Switz. | G11 | 13 |
| Chiautla de Tapia, Mex. | H10 | 90 |
| Chiavari, Italy | E4 | 18 |
| Chiavenna, Italy | C4 | 18 |
| Chiba, Japan | L15 | 36 |
| Chibougamau, P.Q., Can. | G18 | 96 |
| Chibuto, Moz. | E11 | 66 |
| Chicago, Il., U.S. | I8 | 110 |
| Chicago Heights, Il., U.S. | I8 | 110 |
| Chicama, Peru | B2 | 82 |
| Chicapa, stm., Afr. | C4 | 58 |
| Chic-Chocs, Monts, mts., P.Q., Can. | D8 | 106 |
| Chichagof Island, i., Ak., U.S. | H27 | 100 |
| Chichas, Cordillera de, mts., Bol. | I8 | 82 |
| Chicheng, China | C3 | 32 |
| Chichén Itzá, hist., Mex. | G15 | 90 |
| Chichester, Eng., U.K. | K13 | 8 |
| Chichi, Tai. | L9 | 34 |
| Chichibu, Japan | L14 | 36 |
| Chichica, Pan. | I13 | 92 |
| Chichicastenango, Guat. | C3 | 92 |
| Chichigalpa, Nic. | E7 | 92 |
| Chichihualco, Mex. | I9 | 90 |
| Chichimilá, Mex. | G15 | 90 |
| Chichiriviche, Ven. | B8 | 84 |
| Chickahominy, stm., Va., U.S. | B9 | 112 |
| Chickaloon, Ak., U.S. | F20 | 100 |
| Chickamauga, Ga., U.S. | E1 | 112 |
| Chickamauga Lake, res., Tn., U.S. | D1 | 112 |
| Chickasaw, Al., U.S. | L8 | 114 |
| Chickasaw Bogue, stm., Al., U.S. | J9 | 114 |
| Chickasawhay, stm., Ms., U.S. | K8 | 114 |
| Chickasha, Ok., U.S. | D9 | 116 |
| Chiclana de la Frontera, Spain | I5 | 16 |
| Chiclayo, Peru | B2 | 82 |
| Chico, Ca., U.S. | E4 | 124 |
| Chico, Tx., U.S. | F9 | 116 |
| Chico, stm., Arg. | F3 | 78 |
| Chico, stm., Arg. | E3 | 78 |
| Chico, stm., Pan. | I14 | 92 |
| Chicomo, Moz. | E12 | 66 |
| Chicomuselo, Mex. | J13 | 90 |
| Chicopee, Ga., U.S. | E3 | 112 |
| Chicopee, Ma., U.S. | E14 | 108 |
| Chicoutimi, P.Q., Can. | D2 | 106 |
| Chicoutimi, stm., P.Q., Can. | D2 | 106 |
| Chicoutimi, Réserve, P.Q., Can. | D3 | 106 |
| Chicú, Cerro, mtn., Pan. | C15 | 92 |
| Chicxulub, Mex. | G15 | 90 |
| Chidambaram, India | G5 | 46 |
| Chiefland, Fl., U.S. | J4 | 112 |
| Chiemsee, l., Ger. | H12 | 10 |
| Chieri, Italy | D2 | 18 |
| Chiers, stm., Eur. | I7 | 12 |
| Chifeng (Ulanhad), China | A7 | 32 |
| Chigasaki, Japan | L14 | 36 |
| Chignahuapan, Mex. | H10 | 90 |
| Chignecto, Cape, c., N.S., Can. | G9 | 106 |
| Chignecto Bay, b., Can. | G9 | 106 |
| Chignik, Ak., U.S. | H15 | 100 |
| Chignik Lake, Ak., U.S. | H15 | 100 |
| Chigorodó, Col. | D4 | 84 |
| Chigyong, N. Kor. | D15 | 32 |
| Chihli, Gulf of see Bo Hai, b., China | E8 | 32 |
| Chihsi see Jixi, China | B13 | 30 |
| Chihuahua, Mex. | C6 | 90 |
| Chihuahua, state, Mex. | C6 | 90 |
| Chihuahuan Desert, des., N.A. | F9 | 86 |
| Chikaskia, stm., U.S. | B9 | 116 |
| Chik Ballāpur, India | F4 | 46 |
| Chikindzonot, Mex. | G15 | 90 |
| Chikmagalūr, India | F3 | 46 |
| Chikou, China | E6 | 34 |
| Chilakalūrupet, India | D6 | 46 |
| Chilako, stm., B.C., Can. | D11 | 102 |
| Chilanko Forks, B.C., Can. | E10 | 102 |
| Chilapa de Álvarez, Mex. | I10 | 90 |
| Chilas, Pak. | C6 | 44 |
| Chilca, Peru | E3 | 82 |
| Chilca, Peru | E4 | 82 |
| Chilca, Punta, c., Peru | E3 | 82 |
| Chilcotin, stm., B.C., Can. | F12 | 102 |
| Chilcott Island, i., Austl. | A8 | 70 |
| Childers, Austl. | E10 | 70 |
| Childersburg, Al., U.S. | I10 | 114 |
| Childress, Tx., U.S. | E6 | 116 |
| Chile, ctry., S.A. | C2 | 78 |
| Chile Chico, Chile | F2 | 78 |
| Chilecito, Arg. | E5 | 80 |
| Chilecito, Arg. | G4 | 80 |
| Chilete, Peru | B2 | 82 |
| Chilhowie, Va., U.S. | C5 | 112 |
| Chili, stm., Peru | G6 | 82 |
| Chilika Lake, l., India | C3 | 46 |
| Chilko, stm., B.C., Can. | E11 | 102 |
| Chilko Lake, l., B.C., Can. | F10 | 102 |
| Chilko Lake Indian Reserve, B.C., Can. | F10 | 102 |
| Chillagoe, Austl. | A6 | 70 |
| Chillán, Chile | I2 | 80 |
| Chillar, Arg. | I9 | 80 |
| Chillicothe, Il., U.S. | J6 | 110 |
| Chillicothe, Mo., U.S. | C3 | 114 |
| Chillicothe, Oh., U.S. | H4 | 108 |
| Chillicothe, Tx., U.S. | E7 | 116 |
| Chilliwack, B.C., Can. | H13 | 102 |
| Chillón, stm., Peru | D3 | 82 |
| Chillón, hist., Switz. | F6 | 13 |
| Chiloé, Isla Grande de, i., Chile | E2 | 78 |
| Chilok, Russia | G14 | 28 |
| Chilok, stm., Russia | G13 | 28 |
| Chilón, Mex. | I13 | 90 |
| Chiloquin, Or., U.S. | H4 | 122 |
| Chilpancingo de los Bravo, Mex. | I10 | 90 |
| Chilton, Wi., U.S. | F7 | 110 |
| Chiluage, Ang. | C4 | 58 |
| Chilung, Tai. | J10 | 34 |
| Chilwa, Lake, l., Afr. | E7 | 58 |
| Chimaltenango, Guat. | C4 | 92 |
| Chimaltenango, dept., Guat. | C4 | 92 |
| Chimán, Pan. | C3 | 84 |
| Chimayo, N.M., U.S. | H11 | 120 |
| Chimbarongo, Chile | H3 | 80 |
| Chimbas, Arg. | F4 | 80 |
| Chimbay, Uzb. | I8 | 44 |
| Chimborazo, prov., Ec. | H3 | 84 |
| Chimborazo, mtn., Ec. | D9 | 92 |
| Chimborazo, vol., Ec. | H3 | 84 |
| Chimbote, Peru | C2 | 82 |
| Chimichagua, Col. | C6 | 84 |
| Chimkent see Symkent, Kaz. | I11 | 26 |
| Chimki, Russia | F20 | 22 |
| Chimoio, Moz. | B11 | 66 |
| Chimpay, Arg. | J5 | 80 |
| China, Mex. | E10 | 90 |
| China (Zhongguo), ctry., Asia | D8 | 30 |
| Chinácota, Col. | D6 | 84 |
| Chinandega, Nic. | E7 | 92 |
| Chinandega, dept., Nic. | E8 | 92 |
| Chinati Peak, mtn., Tx., U.S. | J2 | 116 |
| Chincha Alta, Peru | E3 | 82 |
| Chinchaga, stm., Can. | E9 | 96 |
| Chincheros, Peru | E5 | 82 |
| Chinchilla, Austl. | F9 | 70 |
| Chinchiná, Col. | E5 | 84 |
| Chinch'ŏn, S. Kor. | G15 | 32 |
| Chinchón, Spain | E8 | 16 |
| Chinchorro, Banco, Mex. | G3 | 80 |
| Chincolco, Chile | G3 | 80 |
| Chincoteague, Va., U.S. | B11 | 112 |
| Chinde, Moz. | B13 | 66 |
| Chindo, S. Kor. | I14 | 32 |
| Chindwinn, stm., Myan. | C3 | 40 |
| Chingola, Zam. | D5 | 58 |
| Chinguetti, Maur. | A3 | 64 |
| Chinhae, S. Kor. | H16 | 32 |
| Chinhae-man, b., S. Kor. | H16 | 32 |
| Chin Hills, Myan. | C2 | 40 |
| Chinhoyi, Zimb. | E6 | 58 |
| Chiniot, Pak. | E5 | 44 |
| Chinju, S. Kor. | H16 | 32 |
| Chinkiang see Zhenjiang, China | E10 | 30 |
| Chinko, stm., C.A.R. | G5 | 56 |
| Chin Lakes, l., Ab., Can. | H22 | 102 |
| Chinle, Az., U.S. | H7 | 120 |
| Chon Buri, Thai. | H6 | 40 |
| Chinmen, China | K7 | 34 |
| Chinmen Tao, i., Tai. | K7 | 34 |
| Chino, Ca., U.S. | J8 | 124 |
| Chinook, Ab., Can. | G4 | 104 |
| Chinook, Mt., U.S. | B17 | 122 |
| Chinook Cove, B.C., Can. | F14 | 102 |
| Chino Valley, Az., U.S. | J4 | 120 |
| Chinquapin, N.C., U.S. | E9 | 112 |
| Chinsali, Zam. | D6 | 58 |
| Chintāmani, India | F5 | 46 |
| Chinú, Col. | C5 | 84 |
| Chiny, Bel. | I7 | 12 |
| Chioggia, Italy | D7 | 18 |
| Chios see Khíos, Grc. | K10 | 20 |
| Chipao, Peru | F5 | 82 |
| Chipata, Zam. | D6 | 58 |
| Chiperceni, Mol. | B12 | 20 |
| Chipinge, Zimb. | C11 | 66 |
| Chip Lake, l., Ab., Can. | D19 | 102 |
| Chipley, Fl., U.S. | L11 | 114 |
| Chipman, N.B., Can. | F8 | 106 |
| Chippewa, stm., Mi., U.S. | G11 | 110 |
| Chippewa, stm., Mn., U.S. | F12 | 118 |
| Chippewa, stm., Wi., U.S. | F4 | 110 |
| Chippewa, Lake, l., Wi., U.S. | E4 | 110 |
| Chippewa Falls, Wi., U.S. | F4 | 110 |
| Chiquián, Peru | D3 | 82 |
| Chiquimula, Guat. | C5 | 92 |
| Chiquimula, dept., Guat. | C5 | 92 |
| Chiquimulilla, Guat. | C4 | 92 |
| Chiquinquirá, Col. | E6 | 84 |
| Chiquintirca, Peru | E5 | 82 |
| Chiquito, stm., Mex. | H9 | 90 |
| Chira, stm., S.A. | J2 | 84 |
| Chira, Isla, i., C.R. | G9 | 92 |
| Chireno, Tx., U.S. | K2 | 114 |
| Chirfa, Niger | D9 | 54 |
| Chiriaco, stm., Peru | A2 | 82 |
| Chiricahua Mountains, mts., Az., U.S. | M7 | 120 |
| Chiricahua Peak, mtn., Az., U.S. | M7 | 120 |
| Chiriguaná, Col. | C6 | 84 |
| Chirikof Island, i., Ak., U.S. | I17 | 100 |
| Chirilagua, El Sal. | D6 | 92 |
| Chirinos, Peru | A2 | 82 |
| Chiriquí, Pan. | I12 | 92 |
| Chiriquí, prov., Pan. | I12 | 92 |
| Chiriquí, Golfo de, b., Pan. | I12 | 92 |
| Chiriquí, Laguna de, b., Pan. | H12 | 92 |
| Chiriquí Grande, Pan. | C1 | 84 |
| Chiriquí Viejo, stm., Pan. | I11 | 92 |
| Chiromo, Mwi. | E7 | 58 |
| Chirripó, stm., C.R. | G11 | 92 |
| Chirripó, stm., C.R. | H11 | 92 |
| Chirripó, Parque Nacional, C.R. | H11 | 92 |
| Chisago City, Mn., U.S. | E3 | 110 |
| Chisasibi, P.Q., Can. | F17 | 96 |
| Chiscas, Col. | D6 | 84 |
| Chisec, Guat. | B4 | 92 |
| Chi'shan, Tai. | M9 | 34 |
| Chisholm, Al., U.S. | J10 | 114 |
| Chisholm, Me., U.S. | C16 | 108 |
| Chisholm, Mn., U.S. | C5 | 110 |
| Chisholm Mills, Ab., Can. | C20 | 102 |
| Chishtiān Mandi, Pak. | F5 | 44 |
| Chişinău (Kishinev), Mol. | B12 | 20 |
| Chislaviči, Russia | G15 | 22 |
| Chisos Mountains, mts., Tx., U.S. | J3 | 116 |
| Chistochina, Ak., U.S. | E22 | 100 |
| Chita, Russia | G14 | 28 |
| Chitado, Ang. | A1 | 66 |
| Chitagá, Col. | D6 | 84 |
| Chitato, Ang. | C4 | 58 |
| Chitcani, Mol. | C13 | 20 |
| Chitek, stm., Sk., Can. | D7 | 104 |
| Chitek Lake, l., Mb., Can. | F15 | 104 |
| Chitek Lake, l., Sk., Can. | E7 | 104 |
| Chitembo, Ang. | D3 | 58 |
| Chitina, Ak., U.S. | F22 | 100 |
| Chitina, stm., Ak., U.S. | F23 | 100 |
| Chitipa, Mwi. | C6 | 58 |
| Chitradurga, India | F4 | 46 |
| Chitrāl, Pak. | B4 | 44 |
| Chittagong, Bngl. | I14 | 44 |
| Chittaurgarh, India | H6 | 44 |
| Chittoor, India | F5 | 46 |
| Chittūr, India | G4 | 46 |
| Chitu, Eth. | M9 | 60 |
| Chiuchiu, Chile | B4 | 80 |
| Chiume, stm., Afr. | C4 | 58 |
| Chiúta, Lake, l., Afr. | E7 | 58 |
| Chiva, Uzb. | I10 | 26 |
| Chivacoa, Ven. | B8 | 84 |
| Chivasso, Italy | D2 | 18 |
| Chivato, Punta, c., Mex. | D4 | 90 |
| Chivay, Peru | F6 | 82 |
| Chivhu, Zimb. | B10 | 66 |
| Chivilcoy, Arg. | H8 | 80 |
| Chiwata, Tan. | D7 | 58 |
| Chixoy (Salinas), stm., N.A. | J14 | 90 |
| Chixoy, Embalse, res., Guat. | B4 | 92 |
| Chlevnoje, Russia | I22 | 22 |
| Chloride, Az., U.S. | I2 | 120 |
| Chôâm Khsant, Camb. | G8 | 40 |
| Chobe, dept., Bots. | B7 | 66 |
| Chobe, stm., Afr. | A7 | 66 |
| Chobe National Park, Bots. | B7 | 66 |
| Chochis, Cerro, mtn., Bol. | H11 | 82 |
| Choch'iwŏn, S. Kor. | G15 | 32 |
| Chocó, dept., Col. | D4 | 84 |
| Chocolate Mountains, mts., U.S. | K10 | 124 |
| Chocontá, Col. | E6 | 84 |
| Chocope, Peru | C2 | 82 |
| Choco Grove, N.C., U.S. | D6 | 112 |
| Choctawhatchee, stm., Al., U.S. | D6 | 112 |
| Choctawhatchee Bay, b., Fl., U.S. | L10 | 114 |
| Chodecz, Pol. | C19 | 10 |
| Chodźakala, Turk. | B14 | 48 |
| Chodzież, Pol. | C16 | 10 |
| Choele-Choel, Arg. | J6 | 80 |
| Choiceland, Sk., Can. | E10 | 104 |
| Choiseul, i., Sol. Is. | I19 | 126 |
| Choix, Mex. | D5 | 90 |
| Chojnice, Pol. | B17 | 10 |
| Chojnów, Pol. | D15 | 10 |
| Chokio, Mn., U.S. | F11 | 118 |
| Cholet, Fr. | E6 | 14 |
| Cholm, Russia | E16 | 22 |
| Cholmec, Russia | E16 | 22 |
| Cholmsk, Russia | H20 | 28 |
| Choloma, Hond. | B7 | 92 |
| Ch'ŏlsan, N. Kor. | D12 | 32 |
| Choluj, Russia | E24 | 22 |
| Cholula (de Rivadabia), Mex. | H10 | 90 |
| Choluteca, Hond. | D7 | 92 |
| Choluteca, dept., Hond. | D7 | 92 |
| Choluteca, stm., Hond. | D8 | 92 |
| Choma, Zam. | E5 | 58 |
| Chomo Lhari, mtn., Asia | G13 | 44 |
| Chomŭm, India | G6 | 44 |
| Chomutov, Czech Rep. | E13 | 10 |
| Chomutovo, Russia | I20 | 22 |
| Ch'ŏnan, S. Kor. | G15 | 32 |
| Chone, Ec. | H2 | 84 |
| Chŏngdan, N. Kor. | F13 | 32 |
| Chŏngjin, N. Kor. | B17 | 32 |
| Chŏngju, N. Kor. | D13 | 32 |
| Chongoyape, Peru | B2 | 82 |
| Chongqing, China | F8 | 30 |
| Chongqing, China | H9 | 34 |
| Chongos Bajo, Peru | E4 | 82 |
| Ch'ŏngsong, N. Kor. | B17 | 32 |
| Chongzuo, China | G8 | 30 |
| Chŏnju, S. Kor. | H15 | 32 |
| Chonos, Archipiélago de los, is., Chile | F2 | 78 |
| Chontaleña, Cordillera, mts., Nic. | F10 | 92 |
| Chontales, dept., Nic. | E9 | 92 |
| Chop, Ukr. | A6 | 20 |
| Chopda, India | B3 | 46 |
| Chopim, stm., Braz. | D12 | 80 |
| Chopinzinho, Braz. | C12 | 80 |
| Chop'or, stm., Russia | G6 | 26 |
| Chopu, mtn., Asia | F12 | 44 |
| Chor, stm., Russia | H19 | 28 |
| Chorlovo, Russia | F21 | 22 |
| Chorna, Ukr. | B13 | 20 |
| Chornobyl' (Chernobyl), Ukr. | G4 | 26 |
| Chorog, Taj. | J12 | 26 |
| Chorolque, Cerro, mtn., Bol. | I8 | 82 |
| Choros, Isla, i., Chile | E3 | 80 |
| Chorreras, Mex. | C7 | 90 |
| Ch'ŏrwŏn, S. Kor. | E15 | 32 |
| Chorzele, Pol. | H3 | 22 |
| Chorzów, Pol. | E18 | 10 |
| Chos, mtn., N. Kor. | C13 | 32 |
| Chosen, Fl., U.S. | M6 | 112 |
| Chōshi, Japan | L15 | 36 |
| Choshui, stm., Tai. | L9 | 34 |
| Chosica, Peru | D3 | 82 |
| Chos Malal, Arg. | I3 | 80 |
| Choszczno, Pol. | B15 | 10 |
| Chota, Peru | B2 | 82 |
| Choteau, Mt., U.S. | C13 | 122 |
| Chotěboř, Czech Rep. | F15 | 10 |
| Chotynec, Russia | H18 | 22 |
| Choûm, Maur. | J4 | 62 |
| Chouteau, Ok., U.S. | C11 | 116 |
| Chovd, Mong. | B5 | 30 |
| Chövsgöl Nuur, l., Mong. | A7 | 30 |
| Chowan, stm., N.C., U.S. | C10 | 112 |
| Chowchilla, Ca., U.S. | G5 | 124 |
| Chown, Mount, mtn., Ab., Can. | B15 | 102 |
| Choya, Arg. | E6 | 80 |
| Chrisman, Il., U.S. | C9 | 114 |
| Christchurch, N.Z. | E4 | 72 |
| Christian, Cape, c., N.T., Can. | B19 | 96 |
| Christiana, S. Afr. | F7 | 66 |
| Christiansburg, Va., U.S. | B6 | 112 |
| Christiansted, V.I.U.S. | F12 | 94 |
| Christie, Mount, mtn., Yk., Can. | E30 | 100 |
| Christie Bay, b., N.T., Can. | D10 | 96 |
| Christie Lake, l., Mb., Can. | B18 | 104 |
| Christina, stm., Ab., U.S. | B3 | 104 |
| Christina Lake, l., Ab., Can. | B24 | 102 |
| Christina Lake, l., B.C., Can. | H16 | 102 |
| Christmas Island, dep., Oc. | E7 | 114 |
| Christopher, Il., U.S. | E7 | 114 |
| Christoval, Tx., U.S. | H6 | 116 |
| Chromtau, Kaz. | G9 | 26 |
| Chrudim, Czech Rep. | F15 | 10 |
| Chrzanów, Pol. | E19 | 10 |
| Chu (Xam), stm., Asia | E8 | 40 |
| Chuanliao, China | B9 | 34 |
| Chubbuck, Id., U.S. | H13 | 122 |
| Chubut, stm., Arg. | E3 | 78 |
| Chuchi Lake, l., B.C., Can. | B10 | 102 |
| Chu Chua, B.C., Can. | F14 | 102 |
| Chuchuwayha Indian Reserve, B.C., Can. | H14 | 102 |
| Chucuito, Peru | F7 | 82 |
| Chucunaque, stm., Pan. | C3 | 84 |
| Chudžand (Leninabad), Taj. | I11 | 26 |
| Chugach Islands, is., Ak., U.S. | G19 | 100 |
| Chugach Mountains, mts., Ak., U.S. | F21 | 100 |
| Chugwater, Wy., U.S. | C12 | 120 |
| Chugwater Creek, stm., Wy., U.S. | C11 | 120 |
| Chuhuichupa, Mex. | C5 | 90 |
| Chui, Braz. | G12 | 80 |
| Chuius Mountain, mtn., B.C., Can. | C10 | 102 |
| Chukai, Malay. | L7 | 40 |
| Chukchi Sea | C2 | 86 |
| Chula Vista, Ca., U.S. | L8 | 124 |
| Chulucanas, Peru | A1 | 82 |
| Chulumani, Bol. | G8 | 82 |
| Chuma, Bol. | F7 | 82 |
| Chumbicha, Arg. | E6 | 80 |
| Chumphon, Thai. | I5 | 40 |
| Chumpi, Peru | F5 | 82 |
| Chum Saeng, Thai. | G6 | 40 |
| Churan, Tai. | K9 | 34 |
| Chunchi, Ec. | I3 | 84 |
| Ch'unch'ŏn, S. Kor. | F15 | 32 |
| Chunchula, Al., U.S. | L8 | 114 |
| Chunghwa, N. Kor. | E13 | 32 |
| Ch'ungju, S. Kor. | G15 | 32 |
| Chungking see Chongqing, China | F8 | 30 |
| Chungli, Tai. | K10 | 34 |
| Chŭngsan, N. Kor. | D13 | 32 |
| Chungyang Shanmo, mts., Tai. | L10 | 34 |
| Chunhuhux, Mex. | H15 | 90 |
| Chunhugui, Guat. | I14 | 90 |
| Chuôr Phnum Krâvanh, mts., Asia | H7 | 40 |
| Chupaca, Peru | E4 | 82 |
| Chuquibamba, Peru | F5 | 82 |
| Chuquibambilla, Peru | F5 | 82 |
| Chuquicamata, Chile | B4 | 80 |
| Chuquisaca, dept., Bol. | H9 | 82 |
| Chur, Switz. | E4 | 82 |
| Churcampa, Peru | E4 | 82 |
| Churchill, Mb., Can. | E14 | 96 |
| Churchill, stm., Nf., Can. | F20 | 96 |
| Churchill, stm., Can. | E14 | 96 |
| Churchill, Cape, c., Mb., Can. | E14 | 96 |
| Churchill, Mount, mtn., B.C., Can. | H11 | 102 |
| Churchill Falls, wtfl, Nf., Can. | F20 | 96 |
| Churchill Lake, l., Sk., Can. | C6 | 104 |
| Church Point, La., U.S. | L4 | 114 |
| Church Point, N.S., Can. | H8 | 106 |
| Church Rock, N.M., U.S. | I8 | 120 |
| Churdan, Ia., U.S. | I13 | 118 |
| Churn Creek, stm., B.C., Can. | F12 | 102 |
| Chūru, India | F6 | 44 |
| Churubusco, In., U.S. | A11 | 114 |
| Churuguara, Ven. | B8 | 84 |
| Chushan, Tai. | L9 | 34 |
| Chuska Peak, mtn., N.M., U.S. | I8 | 120 |
| Chutag, Mong. | B7 | 30 |
| Chutung, Tai. | K10 | 34 |
| Chuuk, is., Micron. | H19 | 126 |
| Chuvashia see Čuvašija, state, Russia | F7 | 26 |
| Chuwang, China | G2 | 32 |
| Chuxiong, China | B6 | 40 |
| Chuy, Ur. | G12 | 80 |
| Chvalynsk, Russia | G7 | 26 |
| Chvojnaja, Russia | C17 | 22 |
| Ch'wiya-ri, N. Kor. | E13 | 32 |
| Chynadyjeve, Ukr. | A6 | 20 |
| Ciadâr Lunga, Mol. | C12 | 20 |
| Cianjur, Indon. | j13 | 39a |
| Cianorte, Braz. | G22 | 79 |
| Cibecue, Az., U.S. | J6 | 120 |
| Cicero, In., U.S. | B10 | 114 |
| Cicero, Il., U.S. | I8 | 110 |
| Ciechanów, Pol. | C20 | 10 |
| Ciechocinek, Pol. | C18 | 10 |
| Ciego de Ávila, Cuba | D5 | 94 |
| Ciempozuelos, Spain | E8 | 16 |
| Ciénaga, Col. | B5 | 84 |
| Ciénaga de Oro, Col. | C5 | 84 |
| Cienfuegos, Cuba | C4 | 94 |
| Cierna [nad Tisou], Slvk. | G22 | 10 |
| Cieszyn, Pol. | F18 | 10 |
| Cieza, Spain | G10 | 16 |
| Çiganak, Kaz. | H12 | 26 |
| Cigüela, stm., Spain | F8 | 16 |
| Cihanbeyli, Tur. | B2 | 48 |
| Çili, Kaz. | I11 | 26 |
| Čikoj, stm., Asia | G19 | 28 |
| Cikou, China | F3 | 34 |
| Cilacap, Indon. | j14 | 39a |
| Cilik, Kaz. | I13 | 26 |
| Çilov ada, i., Azer. | A11 | 48 |
| Cimarron, Ks., U.S. | N7 | 118 |
| Cimarron, N.M., U.S. | H12 | 120 |
| Cimarron, stm., N.M., U.S. | H11 | 120 |
| Cimarron, stm., U.S. | D9 | 116 |
| Cîmbaj, Uzb. | I9 | 26 |
| Cimişlia, Mol. | C12 | 20 |
| Ciml'anskoje vodochranilišče, res., Russia | H6 | 26 |
| Cincinnati, Ia., U.S. | J3 | 110 |
| Cincinnati, Oh., U.S. | H2 | 108 |
| Cinco, Canal Numero, Arg. | I10 | 80 |
| Cinco Saltos, Arg. | J4 | 80 |
| Cinco Pinos, Nic. | D8 | 92 |
| Cinema, B.C., Can. | D12 | 102 |
| Cine, Tur. | L12 | 20 |
| Cingoli, Italy | F8 | 18 |
| Cinto, Monte, mtn., Fr. | m23 | 15a |
| Cipa, stm., Russia | F15 | 28 |
| Cipó, stm., Braz. | E6 | 79 |
| Cipolândia, Braz. | F1 | 79 |
| Cipolletti, Arg. | J5 | 80 |
| Circle, Ak., U.S. | D22 | 100 |
| Circle, Mt., U.S. | C20 | 122 |
| Circleville, Oh., U.S. | H4 | 108 |
| Circleville, Ut., U.S. | F4 | 120 |
| Circleville Mountain, mtn., Ut., U.S. | F4 | 120 |
| Cirebon, Indon. | j14 | 39a |
| Ciremay, Gunung, mtn., Indon. | j14 | 39a |
| Cirey-sur-Vezouze, Fr. | D13 | 14 |
| Ciriè, It. | D2 | 18 |
| Ciriquiri, stm., Braz. | C9 | 82 |
| Cirpan, Bul. | G9 | 20 |
| Cisco, Tx., U.S. | G8 | 116 |
| Ciskei, hist. reg., S. Afr. | I8 | 66 |
| Cisne, Il., U.S. | D8 | 114 |
| Cisneros, Col. | D5 | 84 |
| Cissna Park, Il., U.S. | J8 | 110 |
| Cistern Point, c., Bah. | C6 | 94 |
| Čistoje, Russia | E28 | 22 |
| Citac, Nevado, mtn., Peru | E4 | 82 |
| Citra, Fl., U.S. | J4 | 112 |
| Citronelle, Al., U.S. | K8 | 114 |
| Citrus Heights, Ca., U.S. | F4 | 124 |
| Cittadella, Italy | D6 | 18 |
| Città di Castello, Italy | F7 | 18 |
| Cittanova, Italy | K11 | 18 |
| City of Refuge see Pu'uhonua o Honaunau National Historical Park, hist., Hi., U.S. | r18 | 125a |
| City Point, Fl., U.S. | K6 | 112 |
| Ciudad Acuña, Mex. | C9 | 90 |
| Ciudad Altamirano, Mex. | H9 | 90 |
| Ciudad Barrios, El Sal. | D6 | 92 |
| Ciudad Bolívar, Ven. | C11 | 84 |
| Ciudad Bolivia, Ven. | C7 | 84 |
| Ciudad Camargo, Mex. | D10 | 90 |
| Ciudad Constitución, Mex. | E4 | 90 |
| Ciudad Cortés, C.R. | I11 | 92 |
| Ciudad Darío, Nic. | E8 | 92 |
| Ciudad del Carmen, Mex. | H14 | 90 |
| Ciudad del Este, Para. | C11 | 80 |
| Ciudad del Maíz, Mex. | F10 | 90 |
| Ciudad de México (Mexico City), Mex. | H10 | 90 |
| Ciudad de Nutrias, Ven. | C8 | 84 |
| Ciudad Guayana, Ven. | C11 | 84 |
| Ciudad Guzmán, Mex. | H8 | 90 |
| Ciudad Hidalgo, Mex. | H9 | 90 |
| Ciudad Juárez, Mex. | B6 | 90 |
| Ciudad Lerdo, Mex. | E8 | 90 |
| Ciudad Madero, Mex. | F11 | 90 |
| Ciudad Manuel Doblado, Mex. | G9 | 90 |
| Ciudad Miguel Alemán, Mex. | D10 | 90 |
| Ciudad Moreios, Mex. | A2 | 90 |
| Ciudad Obregón, Mex. | D5 | 90 |
| Ciudad Ojeda (Lagunillas), Ven. | B7 | 84 |
| Ciudad Piar, Ven. | D11 | 84 |
| Ciudad Real, Spain | G8 | 16 |
| Ciudad Rodrigo, Spain | E5 | 16 |
| Ciudad Sandino, Nic. | D8 | 92 |
| Ciudad Trujillo see Santo Domingo, Dom. Rep. | E10 | 94 |
| Ciudad Valles, Mex. | G10 | 90 |
| Ciudad Victoria, Mex. | F10 | 90 |
| Ciudad Vieja, Guat. | C4 | 92 |
| Civitanova Marche, Italy | F8 | 18 |
| Civitavecchia, Italy | F7 | 18 |
| Civray, Fr. | F7 | 14 |
| Cizre, Tur. | C7 | 48 |
| Čkalovsk, Russia | E26 | 22 |
| Clackamas, stm., Or., U.S. | E3 | 122 |
| Clacton-on-Sea, Eng., U.K. | J14 | 8 |
| Claflin, Ks., U.S. | M9 | 118 |
| Claiborne, Al., U.S. | K9 | 114 |
| Claire, Lake, l., Ab., Can. | E10 | 96 |
| Clair Engle Lake, res., Ca., U.S. | D3 | 124 |
| Clairmont, Ab., Can. | B16 | 102 |
| Clairton, Pa., U.S. | G7 | 108 |
| Clairvaux-les-Lacs, Fr. | F12 | 14 |
| Clam, stm., Mi., U.S. | F10 | 110 |
| Clam Lake, l., Sk., Can. | C9 | 104 |
| Clandonald, Ab., Can. | D24 | 102 |
| Clanton, Al., U.S. | J10 | 114 |
| Clanwilliam, S. Afr. | I4 | 66 |
| Clara, Arg. | F9 | 80 |
| Clara City, Mn., U.S. | G12 | 118 |
| Claraz, Arg. | I9 | 80 |
| Clare, Austl. | I3 | 70 |
| Clare, Mi., U.S. | G11 | 110 |
| Clare, co., Ire. | I4 | 8 |
| Claremont, Ca., U.S. | J8 | 124 |
| Claremont, N.H., U.S. | D14 | 108 |
| Claremont, S.D., U.S. | F9 | 118 |
| Claremont, mtn., U.S. | E5 | 124 |
| Claremore, Ok., U.S. | C11 | 116 |
| Clarence, Ia., U.S. | I4 | 110 |
| Clarence, Mo., U.S. | C4 | 114 |
| Clarence, stm., Austl. | G10 | 70 |
| Clarence, i., Chile | B1 | 73 |
| Clarence Strait, strt., Austl. | B6 | 68 |
| Clarence Town, Bah. | C7 | 94 |
| Clarendon, Ar., U.S. | H5 | 114 |
| Clarendon, Pa., U.S. | F7 | 108 |
| Clarendon, Tx., U.S. | E6 | 116 |
| Claresholm, Ab., Can. | G21 | 102 |
| Clarie Coast, Ant. | B7 | 73 |
| Clarinda, Ia., U.S. | K12 | 118 |
| Clarines, Ven. | C10 | 84 |
| Clarion, Ia., U.S. | H2 | 110 |
| Clarion, Pa., U.S. | F7 | 108 |
| Clarión, Isla, i., Mex. | H2 | 90 |
| Clarissa, Mn., U.S. | E1 | 118 |
| Clark, S.D., U.S. | G10 | 118 |
| Clark, Lake, l., Ak., U.S. | F17 | 100 |
| Clark, Mount, mtn., N.T., Can. | D32 | 100 |
| Clarkdale, Az., U.S. | J4 | 120 |
| Clarke City, P.Q., Can. | B7 | 106 |
| Clarke Island, i., Austl. | M8 | 70 |
| Clarke Lake, l., Sk., Can. | D8 | 104 |
| Clarke Range, mts., Austl. | C8 | 70 |
| Clarkesville, Ga., U.S. | E3 | 112 |
| Clark Fork, Id., U.S. | B9 | 122 |
| Clark Fork, stm., U.S. | C10 | 122 |
| Clarks, La., U.S. | J4 | 114 |
| Clarks, Ne., U.S. | J10 | 118 |
| Clarks, stm., Ky., U.S. | F8 | 114 |
| Clarksburg, W.V., U.S. | H6 | 108 |
| Clarksdale, Ms., U.S. | H6 | 114 |
| Clark's Harbour, N.S., Can. | I8 | 106 |
| Clarks Hill Lake, res., U.S. | E4 | 112 |
| Clarkson, Ky., U.S. | E10 | 114 |
| Clarks Point, Ak., U.S. | G15 | 100 |
| Clarks Summit, Pa., U.S. | F11 | 108 |
| Clarksville, Ar., U.S. | G3 | 114 |
| Clarksville, Ia., U.S. | H3 | 110 |
| Clarksville, Tn., U.S. | D11 | 114 |
| Clarksville, Tx., U.S. | F11 | 116 |
| Clarkton, Mo., U.S. | C7 | 114 |
| Clarkton, N.C., U.S. | E8 | 112 |
| Claro, stm., Braz. | C3 | 79 |
| Claro, stm., Braz. | E5 | 79 |
| Claro, stm., Braz. | B9 | 82 |
| Clatskanie, Or., U.S. | D2 | 122 |
| Claude, Tx., U.S. | E5 | 116 |
| Clavet, Sk., Can. | F8 | 104 |
| Claxton, Ga., U.S. | E5 | 112 |
| Clay, Ky., U.S. | E9 | 114 |
| Clay, Tx., U.S. | I10 | 116 |
| Clay, W.V., U.S. | I5 | 108 |
| Clay Center, Ks., U.S. | L10 | 118 |
| Clay Center, Ne., U.S. | K9 | 118 |
| Clay City, Il., U.S. | D9 | 114 |
| Clay City, In., U.S. | C9 | 114 |
| Clay City, Ky., U.S. | B3 | 112 |
| Clayhurst, B.C., Can. | A14 | 102 |
| Claymont, De., U.S. | H11 | 108 |
| Claypool, Az., U.S. | K6 | 120 |
| Clay Springs, Az., U.S. | J6 | 120 |
| Clayton, Al., U.S. | K11 | 114 |
| Clayton, De., U.S. | H11 | 108 |
| Clayton, Ga., U.S. | E3 | 112 |
| Clayton, La., U.S. | K5 | 114 |
| Clayton, N.C., U.S. | D8 | 112 |
| Clayton, N.J., U.S. | H11 | 108 |
| Clayton, N.Y., U.S. | C10 | 108 |
| Clayton, Ok., U.S. | E11 | 116 |
| Clayton, stm., Ab., Can. | A15 | 102 |
| Clearbrook, Mn., U.S. | D12 | 118 |
| Clearfield, Pa., U.S. | F8 | 108 |
| Clearfield, Ut., U.S. | C4 | 120 |
| Clearlake, Ca., U.S. | F3 | 124 |
| Clear Lake Reservoir, res., Ca., U.S. | C4 | 124 |
| Clearmont, Mo., U.S. | F12 | 122 |
| Clearmont, Wy., U.S. | F19 | 122 |
| Clearwater, Fl., U.S. | L4 | 112 |
| Clearwater, Ks., U.S. | N10 | 118 |
| Clearwater, stm., Ab., Can. | I15 | 104 |
| Clearwater, stm., B.C., Can. | E14 | 102 |
| Clearwater, stm., Mn., U.S. | B4 | 118 |
| Clearwater, stm., U.S. | C12 | 122 |
| Clearwater Lake, l., B.C., Can. | E14 | 102 |
| Clearwater Lake, l., Mb., Can. | D13 | 104 |
| Clearwater Lake Provincial Park, Mb., Can. | D13 | 104 |
| Clearwater Mountains, mts., Id., U.S. | D10 | 122 |
| Cle Elum, Wa., U.S. | C4 | 122 |
| Cle Elum, stm., Wa., U.S. | C4 | 122 |
| Clefmont, Fr. | D12 | 14 |
| Clementsport, N.S., Can. | H8 | 106 |
| Clemson, S.C., U.S. | E4 | 112 |
| Clendenin, W.V., U.S. | I5 | 108 |
| Clermont, Austl. | D7 | 70 |

| Name | Map Ref. | Page |
|---|---|---|
| Clermont, Fl., U.S. | K5 | 112 |
| Clermont, Fr. | C9 | 14 |
| Clermont, P.Q., Can. | E3 | 106 |
| Clermont-en-Argonne, Fr. | C12 | 14 |
| Clermont-Ferrand, Fr. | G10 | 14 |
| Cles, Italy | C6 | 18 |
| Cleveland, Al., U.S. | I10 | 114 |
| Cleveland, Ga., U.S. | E3 | 112 |
| Cleveland, Ms., U.S. | I6 | 114 |
| Cleveland, N.C., U.S. | D6 | 112 |
| Cleveland, Oh., U.S. | F5 | 108 |
| Cleveland, Tn., U.S. | C10 | 116 |
| Cleveland, Tn., U.S. | I11 | 116 |
| Cleveland, Tx., U.S. | I11 | 116 |
| Cleveland, Va., U.S. | G17 | 110 |
| Cleveland, Cape, c., Austl. | B7 | 70 |
| Cleveland, Mount, mtn., Mt., U.S. | B12 | 122 |
| Cleveländia, Braz. | D12 | 80 |
| Clew Bay, b., Ire. | H4 | 8 |
| Clewiston, Fl., U.S. | M6 | 112 |
| Clifton, Az., U.S. | K7 | 120 |
| Clifton, Il., U.S. | J8 | 110 |
| Clifton, Ks., U.S. | L10 | 118 |
| Clifton, Tn., U.S. | G9 | 114 |
| Clifton, Tx., U.S. | H9 | 116 |
| Clifton Forge, Va., U.S. | B7 | 112 |
| Climax, Co., U.S. | E10 | 120 |
| Climax, Ga., U.S. | I2 | 112 |
| Climax, Mn., U.S. | H10 | 110 |
| Climax, Sk., Can. | I6 | 104 |
| Clinch, stm., U.S. | C3 | 112 |
| Clinchco, Va., U.S. | B4 | 112 |
| Clingmans Dome, mtn., U.S. | D3 | 112 |
| Clinton, Al., U.S. | J8 | 114 |
| Clinton, Ar., U.S. | G4 | 114 |
| Clinton, B.C., Can. | F13 | 102 |
| Clinton, Ct., U.S. | F14 | 108 |
| Clinton, Ia., U.S. | I5 | 110 |
| Clinton, Il., U.S. | B8 | 114 |
| Clinton, In., U.S. | C9 | 114 |
| Clinton, Ky., U.S. | F9 | 114 |
| Clinton, La., U.S. | L5 | 114 |
| Clinton, Ma., U.S. | E15 | 108 |
| Clinton, Me., U.S. | C17 | 108 |
| Clinton, Mi., U.S. | H12 | 110 |
| Clinton, Mn., U.S. | F11 | 118 |
| Clinton, Mo., U.S. | D3 | 114 |
| Clinton, Ms., U.S. | J6 | 114 |
| Clinton, N.C., U.S. | E8 | 112 |
| Clinton, Ok., U.S. | D8 | 116 |
| Clinton, On., Can. | G14 | 110 |
| Clinton, S.C., U.S. | E5 | 112 |
| Clinton, Tn., U.S. | C2 | 112 |
| Clinton, Wi., U.S. | H7 | 110 |
| Clinton, Cape, c., Austl. | D9 | 70 |
| Clinton-Colden Lake, l., N.T., Can. | D11 | 96 |
| Clinton Lake, res., Ks., U.S. | M12 | 118 |
| Clintonville, Wi., U.S. | F7 | 110 |
| Clintwood, Va., U.S. | B4 | 112 |
| Clio, Al., U.S. | K11 | 114 |
| Clio, Mi., U.S. | G12 | 110 |
| Clio, S.C., U.S. | E7 | 112 |
| Clipperton, Île, atoll, Oc. | E5 | 14 |
| Clisson, Fr. | E5 | 14 |
| Clodomira, Arg. | D6 | 80 |
| Cloncurry, Austl. | B4 | 70 |
| Cloncurry, stm., Austl. | B4 | 70 |
| Clonmel, Ire. | I6 | 8 |
| Cloppenburg, Ger. | C8 | 10 |
| Cloquet, Mn., U.S. | C3 | 110 |
| Cloquet, stm., Mn., U.S. | C3 | 110 |
| Clorinda, Arg. | C10 | 80 |
| Cloudcroft, N.M., U.S. | L11 | 120 |
| Cloud Peak, mtn., Wy., U.S. | F18 | 122 |
| Clover, S.C., U.S. | D5 | 112 |
| Cloverdale, Al., U.S. | H9 | 114 |
| Cloverdale, Ca., U.S. | F2 | 124 |
| Cloverdale, In., U.S. | C10 | 114 |
| Clover Pass, Ak., U.S. | I29 | 100 |
| Cloverport, Ky., U.S. | E10 | 114 |
| Clovis, Ca., U.S. | H6 | 124 |
| Clovis, N.M., U.S. | E3 | 116 |
| Cluj, co., Rom. | C7 | 20 |
| Cluj-Napoca, Rom. | C7 | 20 |
| Clunes, Austl. | K5 | 70 |
| Cluny, Fr. | F11 | 14 |
| Cluses, Fr. | F13 | 14 |
| Clusone, Italy | D4 | 18 |
| Clute, Tx., U.S. | J11 | 116 |
| Clwyd, co., Wales, U.K. | H10 | 8 |
| Clyde, Ab., Can. | C21 | 102 |
| Clyde, Ks., U.S. | L10 | 118 |
| Clyde, N.C., U.S. | D4 | 112 |
| Clyde, N.Y., U.S. | D10 | 108 |
| Clyde, Oh., U.S. | F4 | 108 |
| Clyde, Tx., U.S. | G7 | 116 |
| Clyde, stm., N.S., Can. | H4 | 110 |
| Clyde, stm., Scot., U.K. | F10 | 8 |
| Clyde, Vt., U.S. | C14 | 108 |
| Clyde, Firth of, est., Scot., U.K. | F8 | 8 |
| Clyde Lake, l., Ab., Can. | B23 | 102 |
| Clyde Park, Mt., U.S. | E15 | 122 |
| Clyde River, N.T., Can. | B19 | 96 |
| Clymer, Pa., U.S. | G7 | 108 |
| Cna, stm., Russia | G25 | 22 |
| Coachella, Ca., U.S. | K9 | 124 |
| Coacoyole, Mex. | E6 | 90 |
| Coahoma, Tx., U.S. | G5 | 116 |
| Coahuila, state, Mex. | C8 | 90 |
| Coal, stm., Can. | F31 | 100 |
| Coal City, Il., U.S. | I7 | 110 |
| Coalcomán de Matamoros, Mex. | H8 | 90 |
| Coaldale, Ab., Can. | H22 | 102 |
| Coal Fork, W.V., U.S. | I5 | 108 |
| Coalgate, Ok., U.S. | E10 | 116 |
| Coal Grove, Oh., U.S. | I4 | 108 |
| Coal Harbour, B.C., Can. | G7 | 102 |
| Coal Hill, Ar., U.S. | G4 | 114 |
| Coalhurst, Ab., Can. | H22 | 102 |
| Coalinga, Ca., U.S. | H5 | 124 |
| Coalmont, B.C., Can. | H14 | 102 |
| Coalport, Pa., U.S. | G8 | 108 |
| Coal River, B.C., Can. | G31 | 100 |
| Coalspur, Ab., Can. | D17 | 102 |
| Coalville, Ut., U.S. | D5 | 120 |
| Coamo, P.R. | E11 | 94 |
| Coaraci, Braz. | C9 | 79 |
| Coari, Braz. | J11 | 84 |
| Coari, stm., Braz. | J11 | 84 |
| Coari, Lago de, l., Braz. | J11 | 84 |
| Coast Mountains, mts., N.A. | E6 | 96 |
| Coast Ranges, mts., U.S. | C2 | 98 |
| Coatbridge, Scot., U.K. | F9 | 8 |
| Coatepeque, Guat. | C3 | 92 |
| Coatepeque, Lago de, l., El Sal. | D5 | 92 |
| Coatesville, Pa., U.S. | H11 | 108 |
| Coaticook, P.Q., Can. | B15 | 108 |
| Coats Island, i., N.T., Can. | D16 | 96 |
| Coats Land, reg., Ant. | C2 | 73 |
| Coatzacoalcos, Mex. | H12 | 90 |
| Coayllo, Peru | E3 | 82 |
| Cobá, hist., Mex. | G16 | 90 |
| Cobadin, Rom. | E12 | 20 |
| Coballo Cocha, Peru | I7 | 84 |
| Cobalt, On., Can. | C16 | 110 |
| Cobán, Guat. | B4 | 92 |
| Cobar, Austl. | H6 | 70 |
| Cobberas, Mount, mtn., Austl. | K8 | 70 |
| Cobden, Il., U.S. | E7 | 114 |
| Cobden, On., Can. | E19 | 110 |
| Cobh, Ire. | J5 | 8 |
| Cobham, stm., Can. | E20 | 104 |
| Cobija, Bol. | D7 | 82 |
| Cobija, Chile | B3 | 80 |
| Cobleskill, N.Y., U.S. | E12 | 108 |
| Cobourg, On., Can. | G17 | 110 |
| Cobourg Peninsula, pen., Austl. | B6 | 68 |
| Cobquecura, Chile | I2 | 80 |
| Cobram, Austl. | J6 | 70 |
| Cobre, stm., Pan. | I13 | 92 |
| Cobre, Barranca del, val., Mex. | D6 | 90 |
| Cobué, Moz. | D6 | 58 |
| Coburg, Ger. | E10 | 10 |
| Coburg Island, i., N.T., Can. | A17 | 96 |
| Coca, stm., Ec. | H4 | 84 |
| Cocachacra, Peru | G6 | 82 |
| Cocentaina, Spain | G11 | 16 |
| Cochabamba, Bol. | G8 | 82 |
| Cochabamba, dept., Bol. | G9 | 82 |
| Coche, Isla, i., Ven. | B11 | 84 |
| Cochin see Kochi, India | H4 | 46 |
| Cochinos, Cayos, is., Hond. | B8 | 92 |
| Cochise Head, mtn., Az., U.S. | L7 | 120 |
| Cochran, Ga., U.S. | G3 | 112 |
| Cochrane, Ab., Can. | F20 | 102 |
| Cochrane, On., Can. | G16 | 96 |
| Cochrane, Wi., U.S. | F4 | 110 |
| Cochrane, stm., Can. | E12 | 96 |
| Cochrane, Lago (Lago Pueyrredón), l., S.A. | F2 | 78 |
| Cochranton, Pa., U.S. | F6 | 108 |
| Cockburn Island, i., On., Can. | E12 | 110 |
| Coclé, prov., Pan. | I14 | 92 |
| Coclé del Norte, stm., Pan. | I14 | 92 |
| Coco, stm., N.A. | G3 | 94 |
| Coco, Cayo, i., Cuba | C5 | 94 |
| Coco, Isla del, i., C.R. | J12 | 92 |
| Cocoa, Fl., U.S. | K6 | 112 |
| Cocoa Beach, Fl., U.S. | K6 | 112 |
| Coco Channel, strt., Asia | C1 | 38 |
| Coco Islands, is., Myan. | G2 | 40 |
| Coconino Plateau, plat., Az., U.S. | I4 | 120 |
| Cocorocuma, Cayos, rf., Hond. | B11 | 92 |
| Cocos, Braz. | C6 | 79 |
| Cocos (Keeling) Islands, dep., Oc. | K10 | 24 |
| Cocuiza, stm., Ven. | B7 | 84 |
| Cocula, Mex. | G8 | 90 |
| Cod, Cape, pen., Ma., U.S. | F16 | 108 |
| Codăeşti, Rom. | C11 | 20 |
| Codajás, Braz. | I11 | 84 |
| Coderre, Sk., Can. | H8 | 104 |
| Codó, Braz. | D10 | 76 |
| Codogno, Italy | D4 | 18 |
| Codpa, Chile | H7 | 82 |
| Codroy, Nf., Can. | E14 | 106 |
| Codroy Pond, Nf., Can. | D15 | 106 |
| Cody, Ne., U.S. | I6 | 118 |
| Cody, Wy., U.S. | F16 | 122 |
| Coeburn, Va., U.S. | C4 | 112 |
| Coelemu, Chile | I2 | 80 |
| Coen, Austl. | B8 | 68 |
| Coén, stm., C.R. | H11 | 92 |
| Coeroeni (Corentyne), stm., S.A. | F14 | 84 |
| Coetivy Island, i., Sey. | C11 | 58 |
| Coeur d'Alene, Id., U.S. | C9 | 122 |
| Coeur d'Alene, stm., Id., U.S. | C9 | 122 |
| Coeur d'Alene Lake, l., Id., U.S. | C9 | 122 |
| Coevorden, Neth. | C10 | 12 |
| Coffeen, Il., U.S. | C7 | 114 |
| Coffeeville, Ms., U.S. | I7 | 114 |
| Coffeyville, Ks., U.S. | N12 | 118 |
| Coffs Harbour, Austl. | H10 | 70 |
| Cofradía, Hond. | B6 | 92 |
| Cofre de Perote, Cerro, mtn., Mex. | H11 | 90 |
| Cofre de Perote, Parque Nacional, Mex. | H11 | 90 |
| Coggon, Ia., U.S. | H4 | 110 |
| Cognac, Fr. | G6 | 14 |
| Cogolin, Fr. | I13 | 14 |
| Cogoon, stm., Austl. | F8 | 70 |
| Cohengua, stm., Peru | D5 | 82 |
| Cohocton, stm., N.Y., U.S. | E9 | 108 |
| Cohoes, N.Y., U.S. | E13 | 108 |
| Cohuna, Austl. | J6 | 70 |
| Coiba, Isla de, i., Pan. | J12 | 92 |
| Coig, stm., Arg. | G2 | 78 |
| Coihaique, Chile | F2 | 78 |
| Coimbatore, India | G4 | 46 |
| Coimbra, Braz. | F7 | 79 |
| Coimbra, Port. | E3 | 16 |
| Coin, Ia., U.S. | K12 | 118 |
| Coín, Spain | I7 | 16 |
| Coipasa, Lago, l., Bol. | H7 | 82 |
| Coipasa, Salar de, pl., S.A. | H7 | 82 |
| Cojbalsan, Mong. | B9 | 30 |
| Cojedes, Ven. | C8 | 84 |
| Cojedes, state, Ven. | C8 | 84 |
| Cojutepeque, El Sal. | D6 | 92 |
| Cokato, Mn., U.S. | E1 | 110 |
| Cokeville, Wy., U.S. | H15 | 122 |
| Colac, Austl. | L5 | 70 |
| Colatina, Braz. | E8 | 79 |
| Colbeck, Cape, c., Ant. | C9 | 73 |
| Colbert, Ok., U.S. | F10 | 116 |
| Colborne, On., Can. | F18 | 110 |
| Colbún, Chile | H3 | 80 |
| Colby, Ks., U.S. | L6 | 118 |
| Colby, Wi., U.S. | F5 | 110 |
| Colca, stm., Peru | F4 | 82 |
| Colchester, Ct., U.S. | F14 | 108 |
| Colchester, Eng., U.K. | J14 | 8 |
| Colchester, Il., U.S. | J5 | 110 |
| Cold Bay, Ak., U.S. | H13 | 100 |
| Cold Lake, Ab., Can. | D4 | 104 |
| Cold Lake, Canadian Forces Base, mil., Ab., Can. | D4 | 104 |
| Cold Lake Indian Reserve, Ab., Can. | D4 | 104 |
| Cold Spring, Mn., U.S. | E1 | 110 |
| Coldspring, Tx., U.S. | I11 | 116 |
| Coldstream, Scot., U.K. | F11 | 8 |
| Coldwater, Ks., U.S. | N8 | 118 |
| Coldwater, Mi., U.S. | I10 | 110 |
| Coldwater, Ms., U.S. | H7 | 114 |
| Coldwater, Oh., U.S. | G2 | 108 |
| Coldwater, stm., Ms., U.S. | H6 | 114 |
| Coldwater Indian Reserve, B.C., Can. | G14 | 102 |
| Colebrook, N.H., U.S. | C15 | 108 |
| Cole Camp, Mo., U.S. | D3 | 114 |
| Coleman, Ab., Can. | H20 | 102 |
| Coleman, Fl., U.S. | K4 | 112 |
| Coleman, Mi., U.S. | G11 | 110 |
| Coleman, Tx., U.S. | H7 | 116 |
| Coleman, Wi., U.S. | E7 | 110 |
| Coleman, stm., Austl. | B8 | 68 |
| Coleman, Lake, res., Tx., U.S. | G7 | 116 |
| Colen Lakes, l., Mb., Can. | D19 | 104 |
| Coleraine, Austl. | K4 | 70 |
| Coleraine, Mn., U.S. | C3 | 110 |
| Coleridge, Ne., U.S. | I10 | 118 |
| Coles, Ms., U.S. | K5 | 114 |
| Coles, Punta, c., Peru | G6 | 82 |
| Colesberg, S. Afr. | H7 | 66 |
| Coleville, Sk., Can. | G5 | 104 |
| Colfax, Ca., U.S. | F4 | 124 |
| Colfax, Ia., U.S. | I2 | 110 |
| Colfax, Il., U.S. | J7 | 110 |
| Colfax, In., U.S. | B10 | 114 |
| Colfax, La., U.S. | K4 | 114 |
| Colfax, Wa., U.S. | D8 | 122 |
| Colfax, Wi., U.S. | F4 | 110 |
| Colhué Huapí, Lago, l., Arg. | F3 | 78 |
| Colico, Italy | C4 | 18 |
| Colima, Mex. | H8 | 90 |
| Colima, state, Mex. | H8 | 90 |
| Colima, Nevado de, mtn., Mex. | H8 | 90 |
| Colimes, stm., Ec. | H2 | 84 |
| Colina, Chile | G3 | 80 |
| Colinas, Braz. | E10 | 76 |
| Colinas, Braz. | C4 | 79 |
| Colinet, Nf., Can. | E20 | 106 |
| Colinton, Ab., Can. | C21 | 102 |
| Collarenebri, Austl. | G8 | 70 |
| Collbran, Co., U.S. | E9 | 120 |
| College, Ak., U.S. | D21 | 100 |
| Collegedale, Tn., U.S. | G11 | 114 |
| College Park, Md., U.S. | F2 | 112 |
| College Place, Wa., U.S. | D7 | 122 |
| College Station, Ar., U.S. | G4 | 114 |
| College Station, Tx., U.S. | I10 | 116 |
| Collegeville, In., U.S. | B9 | 114 |
| Collerina, Austl. | G7 | 70 |
| Colleymount, B.C., Can. | C8 | 102 |
| Colleyville, Tx., U.S. | G9 | 116 |
| Collie, Austl. | F3 | 68 |
| Collier Bay, b., Austl. | C4 | 68 |
| Collier Range National Park, Austl. | D3 | 68 |
| Collierville, Tn., U.S. | G7 | 114 |
| Collingwood, On., Can. | F15 | 110 |
| Collins, Ga., U.S. | G4 | 112 |
| Collins, Ia., U.S. | I2 | 110 |
| Collins, Ms., U.S. | K7 | 114 |
| Collins, stm., U.S. | G11 | 114 |
| Collins Bay, On., Can. | F19 | 110 |
| Collinston, La., U.S. | J5 | 114 |
| Collinsville, Al., U.S. | H11 | 114 |
| Collinsville, Austl. | C7 | 70 |
| Collinsville, Ms., U.S. | J8 | 114 |
| Collinsville, Ok., U.S. | C11 | 116 |
| Collinsville, Tx., U.S. | F10 | 116 |
| Collinwood, Tn., U.S. | G9 | 114 |
| Collipulli, Chile | I2 | 80 |
| Collister, Id., U.S. | G12 | 122 |
| Colman, S.D., U.S. | H11 | 118 |
| Colmar, Fr. | E14 | 14 |
| Colmenar de Oreja, Spain | E8 | 16 |
| Colmenar Viejo, Spain | E8 | 16 |
| Colmeneros, Mex. | H9 | 90 |
| Colmesneil, Tx., U.S. | L2 | 114 |
| Colo, Ia., U.S. | H2 | 110 |
| Cologne see Köln, Ger. | E6 | 10 |
| Cologne, Mn., U.S. | F2 | 110 |
| Coloio, Nevado, mtn., Bol. | F7 | 82 |
| Coloma, Mi., U.S. | H9 | 110 |
| Coloma, Wi., U.S. | F6 | 110 |
| Colombey-les-Belles, Fr. | D12 | 14 |
| Colômbia, Braz. | F4 | 79 |
| Colombia, Col. | F5 | 84 |
| Colombia, ctry., S.A. | C4 | 76 |
| Colombo, Braz. | C7 | 79 |
| Colombo, Sri L. | I5 | 46 |
| Colome, S.D., U.S. | H8 | 118 |
| Colón, Arg. | G8 | 80 |
| Colón, Cuba | C4 | 94 |
| Colón, Mi., U.S. | I10 | 110 |
| Colón, Pan. | C3 | 84 |
| Colón, dept., Hond. | C10 | 92 |
| Colón, Archipiélago de (Galapagos Islands), is., Ec. | j13 | 84a |
| Colón, Isla, i., Pan. | H12 | 92 |
| Colón, Montañas de, mts., Hond. | C10 | 92 |
| Colona, Austl. | F5 | 68 |
| Colonia Alvear, Arg. | H5 | 80 |
| Colonia del Sacramento, Ur. | H10 | 80 |
| Colonia Dora, Arg. | E7 | 80 |
| Colonia Elisa, Arg. | D8 | 80 |
| Colonia José Mármol, Arg. | D8 | 80 |
| Colonia Lavalleja, Ur. | G9 | 80 |
| Colonial Heights, Va., U.S. | B9 | 112 |
| Colonia Vicente Guerrero, Mex. | D9 | 90 |
| Colonia Villafañe, Arg. | C8 | 80 |
| Colonsay, Sk., Can. | G9 | 104 |
| Colony, Ks., U.S. | M12 | 118 |
| Colorada Grande, Salina, pl., Arg. | J7 | 80 |
| Colorado, C.R. | H11 | 92 |
| Colorado, Hond. | B7 | 92 |
| Colorado, state, U.S. | D5 | 98 |
| Colorado, stm., Arg. | J7 | 80 |
| Colorado, stm., Braz. | E10 | 82 |
| Colorado, stm., N.A. | M1 | 120 |
| Colorado, stm., Tx., U.S. | J10 | 116 |
| Colorado City, Az., U.S. | H4 | 120 |
| Colorado City, Co., U.S. | G12 | 120 |
| Colorado City, Tx., U.S. | G6 | 116 |
| Colorado River Aqueduct, Ca., U.S. | K10 | 124 |
| Colorado Springs, Co., U.S. | F12 | 120 |
| Colotepec, stm., Mex. | J11 | 90 |
| Colotlán, Mex. | F8 | 90 |
| Colquechaca, Bol. | H8 | 82 |
| Colquiri, Bol. | G7 | 82 |
| Colquitt, Ga., U.S. | H2 | 112 |
| Colt, Ar., U.S. | G6 | 114 |
| Colta, Peru | F5 | 82 |
| Coltauco, Chile | G3 | 80 |
| Colton, Ca., U.S. | J8 | 124 |
| Colton, S.D., U.S. | H11 | 118 |
| Columbia, Al., U.S. | I1 | 112 |
| Columbia, Ca., U.S. | F5 | 124 |
| Columbia, Il., U.S. | D6 | 114 |
| Columbia, Ky., U.S. | E11 | 114 |
| Columbia, La., U.S. | J4 | 114 |
| Columbia, Md., U.S. | H10 | 108 |
| Columbia, Mo., U.S. | D4 | 114 |
| Columbia, Ms., U.S. | K7 | 114 |
| Columbia, N.C., U.S. | D10 | 112 |
| Columbia, Pa., U.S. | G10 | 108 |
| Columbia, S.C., U.S. | E5 | 112 |
| Columbia, Tn., U.S. | G9 | 114 |
| Columbia, stm., N.A. | G8 | 96 |
| Columbia, Cape, c., N.T., Can. | A12 | 86 |
| Columbia, Mount, mtn., Can. | E17 | 102 |
| Columbia City, In., U.S. | A11 | 114 |
| Columbia Falls, Me., U.S. | C19 | 108 |
| Columbia Falls, Mt., U.S. | B11 | 122 |
| Columbia Icefield, Can. | E17 | 102 |
| Columbia Lake, l., B.C., Can. | G19 | 102 |
| Columbia Mountains, mts., N.A. | D14 | 102 |
| Columbiana, Oh., U.S. | G6 | 108 |
| Columbiaville, Mi., U.S. | G12 | 110 |
| Columbus, Ga., U.S. | G2 | 112 |
| Columbus, In., U.S. | C11 | 114 |
| Columbus, Ks., U.S. | N13 | 118 |
| Columbus, Ms., U.S. | I8 | 114 |
| Columbus, Mt., U.S. | E16 | 122 |
| Columbus, N.C., U.S. | D4 | 112 |
| Columbus, N.D., U.S. | C5 | 118 |
| Columbus, Ne., U.S. | J10 | 118 |
| Columbus, Oh., U.S. | H4 | 108 |
| Columbus, Tx., U.S. | J10 | 116 |
| Columbus, Wi., U.S. | G6 | 110 |
| Columbus Grove, Oh., U.S. | G2 | 108 |
| Columbus Junction, Ia., U.S. | I4 | 110 |
| Columbus Point, c., Bah. | B7 | 94 |
| Coluna, Braz. | E7 | 79 |
| Colusa, Ca., U.S. | E3 | 124 |
| Colville, Wa., U.S. | B8 | 122 |
| Colville, stm., Ak., U.S. | B19 | 100 |
| Colville Lake, l., N.T., Can. | C31 | 100 |
| Comacchio, Italy | E7 | 18 |
| Comala, Mex. | H8 | 90 |
| Comalapa, Nic. | E9 | 92 |
| Comalcalco, Mex. | H13 | 90 |
| Coman, Mount, mtn., Ant. | C12 | 73 |
| Comanche, Ok., U.S. | E9 | 116 |
| Comanche, Tx., U.S. | H8 | 116 |
| Comandante Ferraz, sci., Ant. | B1 | 73 |
| Comandante Fontana, Arg. | C9 | 80 |
| Comandante Leal, Arg. | F6 | 80 |
| Comandante Nicanor Otamendi, Arg. | J10 | 80 |
| Comarapa, Bol. | G9 | 82 |
| Comas, Peru | D4 | 82 |
| Comayagua, Hond. | C7 | 92 |
| Comayagua, dept., Hond. | C7 | 92 |
| Comayagua, Montañas de, mts., Hond. | C7 | 92 |
| Combahee, stm., S.C., U.S. | G6 | 112 |
| Combarbalá, Chile | F3 | 80 |
| Combeaufontaine, Fr. | E12 | 14 |
| Combourg, Fr. | D5 | 14 |
| Comboyne, Austl. | H10 | 70 |
| Combronde, Fr. | G10 | 14 |
| Come by Chance, Nf., Can. | E20 | 106 |
| Comendador, Dom. Rep. | E9 | 94 |
| Comendador Gomes, Braz. | E4 | 79 |
| Comer, Ga., U.S. | E3 | 112 |
| Comercinho, Braz. | D8 | 79 |
| Comfort, N.C., U.S. | D9 | 112 |
| Comfort, Tx., U.S. | J8 | 116 |
| Comfort, Cape, c., N.T., Can. | C16 | 96 |
| Comfrey, Mn., U.S. | G13 | 118 |
| Comilla, Bngl. | I14 | 44 |
| Comino, Italy | M9 | 18 |
| Comiso, Italy | M9 | 18 |
| Comitán de Dominguez, Mex. | I13 | 90 |
| Commentry, Fr. | F9 | 14 |
| Commerce, Ga., U.S. | E3 | 112 |
| Commerce, Ok., U.S. | C12 | 116 |
| Commerce, Tx., U.S. | F11 | 116 |
| Commerce City, Co., U.S. | E12 | 120 |
| Commercy, Fr. | D12 | 14 |
| Comminges, reg., Fr. | I7 | 14 |
| Committee Bay, b., N.T., Can. | C15 | 96 |
| Como, Italy | D4 | 18 |
| Como, Ms., U.S. | H7 | 114 |
| Como, Tx., U.S. | F11 | 116 |
| Como, Lago di, l., Italy | C4 | 18 |
| Comodoro Rivadavia, Arg. | F3 | 78 |
| Comores, Archipel des, is., Afr. | D8 | 58 |
| Comorin, Cape, c., India | H4 | 46 |
| Comoros (Comores), ctry., Afr. | D8 | 58 |
| Comox, B.C., Can. | H10 | 102 |
| Comox, Canadian Forces Base, mil., B.C., Can. | H10 | 102 |
| Compiègne, Fr. | C9 | 14 |
| Compostela, Mex. | G7 | 90 |
| Comprida, Ilha, i., Braz. | C15 | 80 |
| Compton, Ca., U.S. | K7 | 124 |
| Comrat, Mol. | C12 | 20 |
| Comstock, Ne., U.S. | J8 | 118 |
| Comstock, Tx., U.S. | J5 | 116 |
| Comstock Park, Mi., U.S. | G10 | 110 |
| Čona, stm., Russia | E13 | 28 |
| Conakry, Gui. | G3 | 64 |
| Conambo, stm., Ec. | H4 | 84 |
| Concarán, Arg. | G6 | 80 |
| Concarneau, Fr. | E3 | 14 |
| Conceição, Braz. | E9 | 76 |
| Conceição da Barra, Braz. | E9 | 79 |
| Conceição das Alagoas, Braz. | E4 | 79 |
| Conceição de Ipanema, Braz. | E8 | 79 |
| Conceição do Almeida, Braz. | B9 | 79 |
| Conceição do Araguaia, Braz. | E9 | 76 |
| Conceição do Maú, Braz. | F13 | 84 |
| Conceição do Norte, Braz. | B5 | 79 |
| Concepción, Arg. | E10 | 80 |
| Concepción, Bol. | F10 | 82 |
| Concepción, Bol. | G10 | 82 |
| Concepción, Chile | I2 | 80 |
| Concepción, Col. | D6 | 84 |
| Concepción, Pan. | I11 | 92 |
| Concepción, Para. | B10 | 80 |
| Concepción, Peru | D4 | 82 |
| Concepción, Bahía, b., Mex. | D4 | 90 |
| Concepción, Laguna, l., Bol. | G11 | 82 |
| Concepción, Volcán, vol., Nic. | F9 | 92 |
| Concepción de Ataco, El Sal. | D5 | 92 |
| Concepción de la Sierra, Arg. | D11 | 80 |
| Concepción del Oro, Mex. | E9 | 90 |
| Concepción del Uruguay, Arg. | G9 | 80 |
| Concepción Huista, Guat. | B3 | 92 |
| Concepción Quezaltepeque, El Sal. | C6 | 92 |
| Conception Bay, b., Nf., Can. | E20 | 106 |
| Conception Bay, b., Nmb. | D2 | 66 |
| Conception Island, i., Bah. | C7 | 94 |
| Conchagua, Volcán, vol., El Sal. | D7 | 92 |
| Conchas, stm., N.M., U.S. | D2 | 116 |
| Conchas Dam, N.M., U.S. | D2 | 116 |
| Conche, Nf., Can. | B18 | 106 |
| Conches-en-Ouche, Fr. | D7 | 14 |
| Conchi, Chile | B4 | 80 |
| Concho, Az., U.S. | J7 | 120 |
| Concho, stm., Tx., U.S. | H7 | 116 |
| Conchos, stm., Mex. | C7 | 90 |
| Conchos, stm., Mex. | E10 | 90 |
| Concise, Switz. | E6 | 13 |
| Concón, Chile | G3 | 124 |
| Concord, Ca., U.S. | F12 | 124 |
| Concord, Ga., U.S. | F2 | 112 |
| Concord, Mi., U.S. | H11 | 110 |
| Concord, N.C., U.S. | D6 | 112 |
| Concord, N.H., U.S. | D15 | 108 |
| Concórdia, Arg. | F9 | 80 |
| Concórdia, Braz. | D12 | 80 |
| Concordia, Ks., U.S. | L10 | 118 |
| Concórdia, Mo., U.S. | D3 | 114 |
| Concórdia, Peru | J5 | 84 |
| Concrete, Wa., U.S. | B4 | 122 |
| Conde, Braz. | A10 | 79 |
| Condé, Fr. | D6 | 14 |
| Conde, S.D., U.S. | F9 | 118 |
| Condega, Nic. | D8 | 92 |
| Condeúba, Braz. | C8 | 79 |
| Condobolin, Austl. | I7 | 70 |
| Condom, Fr. | I7 | 14 |
| Condon, Or., U.S. | E5 | 122 |
| Condoto, Col. | E4 | 84 |
| Cone, Tx., U.S. | F5 | 116 |
| Conecuh, stm., U.S. | K10 | 114 |
| Conegliano, Italy | D7 | 18 |
| Conejos, stm., Co., U.S. | G10 | 120 |
| Confederation Lake, l., On., Can. | G22 | 104 |
| Confluence, Pa., U.S. | H7 | 108 |
| Confolens, Fr. | F7 | 14 |
| Confusion Bay, b., Nf., Can. | C18 | 106 |
| Confuso, stm., Para. | C9 | 80 |
| Congaz, Mol. | C12 | 20 |
| Congaree, stm., S.C., U.S. | F6 | 112 |
| Congo, ctry., Afr. | B3 | 58 |
| Congo (Zaire) (Zaïre), stm., Afr. | C2 | 58 |
| Congo, Democratic Republic of (Zaire), ctry., Afr. | B4 | 58 |
| Congo Basin, Afr. | H9 | 52 |
| Congress, Ks., U.S. | I8 | 104 |
| Conitaca, Mex. | E6 | 90 |
| Conjeeveram see Kānchipuram, India | F5 | 46 |
| Conklin, Ab., Can. | B23 | 102 |
| Connaught, hist. reg., Ire. | H4 | 8 |
| Conneaut, Oh., U.S. | F6 | 108 |
| Conneautville, Pa., U.S. | F6 | 108 |
| Connecticut, state, U.S. | C12 | 98 |
| Connecticut, stm., U.S. | F14 | 108 |
| Connell, Wa., U.S. | D7 | 122 |
| Connellsville, Pa., U.S. | H7 | 108 |
| Connemara, reg., Ire. | H4 | 8 |
| Connersville, In., U.S. | C11 | 114 |
| Connors Range, mts., Austl. | C8 | 70 |
| Cononaco, stm., Ec. | H4 | 84 |
| Conover, N.C., U.S. | D5 | 112 |
| Conquest, Sk., Can. | G7 | 104 |
| Conquista, Braz. | E5 | 79 |
| Conrad, Ia., U.S. | H3 | 110 |
| Conrad, Mt., U.S. | B14 | 122 |
| Conroe, Tx., U.S. | I11 | 116 |
| Conroe, Lake, res., Tx., U.S. | I11 | 116 |
| Consecon, On., Can. | F18 | 110 |
| Conselheiro Lafaiete, Braz. | F7 | 79 |
| Conselheiro Pena, Braz. | E8 | 79 |
| Consolación del Sur, Cuba | C3 | 94 |
| Con Son, i., Viet. | J9 | 40 |
| Constance, Lake see Bodensee, l., Eur. | E16 | 14 |
| Constância, co., Rom. | E12 | 20 |
| Constanța, Rom. | E12 | 20 |
| Constantina, Spain | H6 | 16 |
| Constantine, Mi., U.S. | I10 | 110 |
| Constantinople see İstanbul, Tur. | H12 | 20 |
| Constitución, Chile | H2 | 80 |
| Constitución, Ur. | F8 | 80 |
| Consul, Sk., Can. | I5 | 104 |
| Contamana, Peru | B4 | 82 |
| Contas, stm., Braz. | C9 | 79 |
| Contendas do Sincorá, Braz. | B8 | 79 |
| Continental, Oh., U.S. | F2 | 108 |
| Contralmirante Cordero, Arg. | J4 | 80 |
| Contratación, Col. | D6 | 84 |
| Contumazá, Peru | B2 | 82 |
| Contwoyto Lake, l., N.T., Can. | C10 | 96 |
| Conty, Fr. | C9 | 14 |
| Convención, Col. | C6 | 84 |
| Convento, C.R. | H11 | 92 |
| Conversano, Italy | I11 | 18 |
| Conway, Ar., U.S. | G4 | 114 |
| Conway, N.C., U.S. | C9 | 112 |
| Conway, N.H., U.S. | D15 | 108 |
| Conway, P.E., Can. | F10 | 106 |
| Conway, S.C., U.S. | F7 | 112 |
| Conway Springs, Ks., U.S. | N10 | 118 |
| Conyers, Ga., U.S. | F2 | 112 |
| Cook, Ne., U.S. | K11 | 118 |
| Cook, Cape, c., B.C., Can. | G6 | 102 |
| Cookes Peak, mtn., N.M., U.S. | L9 | 120 |
| Cookeville, Tn., U.S. | F11 | 114 |
| Cookhouse, S. Afr. | I7 | 66 |
| Cooking Lake, l., Ab., Can. | D21 | 102 |
| Cook Inlet, b., Ak., U.S. | F18 | 100 |
| Cook Islands, dep., Oc. | J23 | 126 |
| Cook's Harbour, Nf., Can. | A18 | 106 |
| Cook Strait, strt., N.Z. | D5 | 72 |
| Cooktown, Austl. | C9 | 68 |
| Coolah, Austl. | H8 | 70 |
| Coolamon, Austl. | J7 | 70 |
| Coolangatta, Austl. | G10 | 70 |
| Cooleemee, N.C., U.S. | D6 | 112 |
| Coolgardie, Austl. | F4 | 68 |
| Coolidge, Az., U.S. | L5 | 120 |
| Coolidge, Ga., U.S. | H3 | 112 |
| Coolidge, Tx., U.S. | H10 | 116 |
| Coolin, Id., U.S. | B9 | 122 |
| Cooma, Austl. | K8 | 70 |
| Coonabarabran, Austl. | H8 | 70 |
| Coonamble, Austl. | H8 | 70 |
| Coonoor, India | G4 | 46 |
| Coon Rapids, Ia., U.S. | J13 | 118 |
| Coon Rapids, Mn., U.S. | E2 | 110 |
| Coon Valley, Wi., U.S. | G4 | 110 |
| Cooper, Tx., U.S. | F11 | 116 |
| Cooper, Mount, mtn., B.C., Can. | G17 | 102 |
| Cooper Creek, stm., Austl. | G3 | 70 |
| Cooper Landing, Ak., U.S. | F20 | 100 |
| Cooper Mountain, mtn., B.C., Can. | F20 | 100 |
| Coopers, Al., U.S. | J10 | 114 |
| Cooperstown, N.D., U.S. | C9 | 118 |
| Cooperstown, N.Y., U.S. | E12 | 108 |
| Coopersville, Mi., U.S. | G10 | 110 |
| Cooroy, Austl. | F10 | 70 |
| Coosa, stm., U.S. | J10 | 114 |
| Coosawhatchie, stm., S.C., U.S. | G5 | 112 |
| Coos Bay, Or., U.S. | G1 | 122 |
| Coos Bay, b., Or., U.S. | G1 | 122 |
| Cootamundra, Austl. | J8 | 70 |
| Copacabana, Arg. | E5 | 80 |
| Copacabana, Bol. | G7 | 82 |
| Copainalá, Mex. | I13 | 90 |
| Copán, Hond. | C5 | 92 |
| Copan, Ok., U.S. | C11 | 116 |
| Copán, hist., Hond. | C6 | 92 |
| Copán, dept., Hond. | C5 | 92 |
| Cope, Co., U.S. | L5 | 118 |
| Copeá, Paraná, mth., Braz. | I11 | 84 |
| Copeau, stm., Sk., Can. | F11 | 104 |
| Copeland, Fl., U.S. | N5 | 112 |
| Copenhagen see København, Den. | N13 | 6 |
| Copenhagen, N.Y., U.S. | D11 | 108 |
| Copertino, Italy | I13 | 18 |
| Copiapó, Chile | D3 | 80 |
| Copiapó, stm., Chile | D3 | 80 |
| Copley, Austl. | H3 | 70 |
| Copparo, Italy | E6 | 18 |
| Copper, stm., Ak., U.S. | F22 | 100 |
| Copper Butte, mtn., Wa., U.S. | B7 | 122 |
| Copper Canyon see Cobre, Barranca del, val., Mex. | D6 | 90 |
| Copper Cliff, On., Can. | D14 | 110 |
| Copper Harbor, Mi., U.S. | C8 | 110 |
| Coppermine, N.T., Can. | C9 | 96 |
| Coppermine, stm., N.T., Can. | C10 | 96 |
| Copper Mountain, B.C., Can. | H14 | 102 |
| Coppet, Switz. | F5 | 13 |
| Copton Creek, stm., Ab., Can. | C15 | 102 |
| Coquille, Or., U.S. | G1 | 122 |
| Coquille, stm., Or., U.S. | G1 | 122 |
| Coquimbo, Chile | E3 | 80 |
| Coquimbo, prov., Chile | F3 | 80 |
| Coração de Jesus, Braz. | D6 | 79 |
| Coração de Maria, Braz. | B9 | 79 |
| Coracora, Peru | F4 | 82 |
| Coral Gables, Fl., U.S. | N6 | 112 |
| Coral Harbour, N.T., Can. | D16 | 96 |
| Coral Lake, l., N.T., Can. | B18 | 96 |
| Coralaque, stm., Peru | G6 | 82 |
| Coral Sea, Oc. | J19 | 126 |
| Coral Sea Islands Territory, ter., Austl. | B9 | 70 |
| Coralville, Ia., U.S. | I4 | 110 |
| Coralville Lake, res., Ia., U.S. | I4 | 110 |
| Coram, Mt., U.S. | B11 | 122 |
| Corangamite, Lake, l., Austl. | L5 | 70 |
| Corbeil-Essonnes, Fr. | D9 | 14 |
| Corbin, Ky., U.S. | C2 | 112 |
| Corcoran, Ca., U.S. | H6 | 124 |
| Corcovado, Golfo, b., Chile | E2 | 78 |
| Corcovado, Parque Nacional, C.R. | I11 | 92 |
| Cordeiro, Braz. | F7 | 79 |
| Cordele, Ga., U.S. | H3 | 112 |
| Cordell, Ok., U.S. | D8 | 116 |
| Cordell Hull Reservoir, res., Tn., U.S. | F11 | 114 |
| Corder, Mo., U.S. | C3 | 114 |
| Cordillera, dept., Para. | C10 | 80 |
| Cordillo Downs, Austl. | F4 | 70 |
| Cordisburgo, Braz. | E6 | 79 |
| Córdoba, Arg. | F6 | 80 |
| Córdoba, Mex. | H11 | 90 |
| Córdoba, Spain | H7 | 16 |
| Córdoba, prov., Arg. | F7 | 80 |
| Córdoba, dept., Col. | C5 | 84 |
| Cordova, Al., U.S. | I9 | 114 |
| Córdoba, Peru | F4 | 82 |
| Corentyne (Corantijn), stm., S.A. | E14 | 84 |
| Corerepe, Mex. | E5 | 90 |
| Corfu see Kérkira, Grc. | J3 | 20 |
| Corfu see Kérkira, i., Grc. | J3 | 20 |
| Coria, Spain | F5 | 16 |
| Coria del Río, Spain | H5 | 16 |
| Coribe, Braz. | C8 | 79 |
| Corigliano Calabro, Italy | J11 | 18 |
| Corinda, Austl. | A3 | 70 |
| Corinne, W.V., U.S. | B5 | 112 |
| Corinne, Ut., U.S. | C4 | 120 |
| Corinth, Ms., U.S. | H8 | 114 |
| Corinth, N.Y., U.S. | D13 | 108 |
| Corinth, Gulf of see Korinthiakós Kólpos, b., Grc. | K6 | 20 |
| Corinto, Braz. | E6 | 79 |
| Corinto, El Sal. | D7 | 92 |
| Corinto, Nic. | E7 | 92 |
| Coripata, Bol. | G7 | 82 |
| Corire, Peru | G5 | 82 |
| Coris, Peru | J5 | 84 |
| Cork, Ire. | J5 | 8 |
| Cork, co., Ire. | I5 | 8 |

| Name | Map Ref. | Page |
|---|---|---|

Corlay, Fr. — D3 14
Corleone, Italy — L8 18
Çorlu, Tur. — H11 20
Cormeilles, Fr. — C7 14
Cormorant, Mb., Can. — D14 104
Cormorant Lake, l., Mb., Can. — D14 104
Cornelia, Ga., U.S. — E3 112
Cornélio Procópio, Braz. — G3 79
Cornelius, N.C., U.S. — D6 112
Cornelius Grinnell Bay, b., N.T., Can. — D20 96
Cornell, Wi., U.S. — E4 110
Corner Brook, Nf., Can. — D16 106
Connersville, U.S. — G10 114
Corneşti, Mol. — B11 20
Corneta, Punta, c., Mex. — J11 90
Corning, Ar., U.S. — F6 114
Corning, Ca., U.S. — E3 124
Corning, Ia., U.S. — K13 118
Corning, Ks., U.S. — L11 118
Corning, N.Y., U.S. — E9 108
Corning, Oh., U.S. — H4 108
Cornish, Me., U.S. — D16 108
Corno Grande, mtn., Italy — G8 18
Cornwall, On., Can. — B12 108
Cornwall, co., Eng., U.K. — K9 8
Cornwallis Island, i., N.T., Can. — A14 96
Coro, Ven. — A7 84
Coro, Golfete de b., Ven. — I10 94
Coroaci, Braz. — E7 79
Corocoro, Bol. — G7 82
Corocoro Island, i., S.A. — C12 84
Coroico, Bol. — G8 82
Coroico, stm., Bol. — F8 82
Coromandel, Braz. — E5 79
Coromandel Coast, India — F6 46
Coromandel Peninsula, pen., N.Z. — B5 72
Corona, Ca., U.S. — K8 124
Corona, N.M., U.S. — J11 120
Coronado, Ca., U.S. — L8 124
Coronado, Mex. — F9 90
Coronado, Bahía de b., C.R. — H11 92
Coronation, Ab., Can. — E23 102
Coronation Gulf, b., N.T., Can. — C10 96
Coronation Island, i., Ant. — B1 73
Coronda, Arg. — F8 80
Coronel, Chile — I2 80
Coronel Bogado, Para. — D10 80
Coronel Dorrego, Arg. — I6 80
Coronel Du Graty, Arg. — D8 80
Coronel Eugenio del Busto, Arg. — J6 80
Coronel Fabriciano, Braz. — E7 79
Coronel Moldes, Arg. — C6 80
Coronel Moldes, Arg. — G6 80
Coronel Murta, Braz. — D7 79
Coronel Oviedo, Para. — C10 80
Coronel Ponce, Braz. — C1 79
Coronel Pringles, Arg. — I6 80
Coronel Sapucaia, Braz. — G1 79
Coronel Suárez, Arg. — I8 80
Coronel Vidal, Arg. — I10 80
Coronel Vivida, Braz. — C12 80
Corongo, Peru — C3 82
Coronie, dept., Sur. — E14 84
Coropuna, Nevado, vol., Peru — F5 82
Corowa, Austl. — K7 70
Corozal, Belize — H15 90
Corozal, Col. — C5 84
Corozal, Hond. — B8 92
Corps, Fr. — H12 14
Corpus, Arg. — D11 80
Corpus Christi, Tx., U.S. — L9 116
Corpus Christi, Lake, res., Tx., U.S. — K9 116
Corpus Christi Bay, b., Tx., U.S. — L9 116
Corque, Bol. — H8 82
Corqüín, Hond. — D6 92
Corral, Chile — D2 78
Corral de Almaguer, Spain — E8 16
Corral de Bustos, Arg. — G7 80
Corralejo, Braz. — o27 17b
Correctionville, Ia., U.S. — I12 118
Correggio, Italy — E5 18
Córrego Rico, Braz. — C5 79
Corrente, stm., Braz. — E3 79
Corrente, stm., Braz. — B6 79
Corrente, stm., Braz. — B7 79
Correntina, Braz. — B6 79
Corrib, Lough, l., Ire. — H4 8
Corrientes, Arg. — E10 80
Corrientes, prov., Arg. — B2 80
Corrientes, stm., Arg. — E10 80
Corrientes, stm., S.A. — I5 84
Corrientes, Bahía de b., Cuba — D2 94
Corrientes, Cabo, c., Arg. — J10 80
Corrientes, Cabo, c., Col. — E4 84
Corrientes, Cabo, c., Cuba — D2 94
Corrientes, Cabo, c., Mex. — G6 90
Corrigan, Tx., U.S. — L2 114
Corriverton, Guy. — E14 84
Corry, Pa., U.S. — F7 108
Corse (Corsica), i., Fr. — I24 15a
Corse, Cap, c., Fr. — m24 15a
Corse-du-Sud, dept., Fr. — m24 15a
Corsica, S.D., U.S. — H9 118
Corsica see Corse, i., Fr. — I24 15a
Corsicana, Tx., U.S. — G10 116
Cortazar, Mex. — G9 90
Corte, Fr. — I24 15a
Cortegana, Spain — H5 16
Cortés, dept., Hond. — D6 92
Cortez, Co., U.S. — G8 120
Cortez, Sea of see California, Golfo de b., Mex. — D4 90
Cortina d'Ampezzo, Italy — C7 18
Cortland, Ne., U.S. — K11 118
Cortland, N.Y., U.S. — E10 108
Cortland, Oh., U.S. — F5 108
Cortona, Italy — F6 18
Corubal (Koliba), stm., Afr. — F2 64
Çoruh, stm., Asia — A6 48
Çorum, Tur. — J12 20
Corumbá, Braz. — H13 82
Corumbá, stm., Braz. — C4 79
Corumbá de Goiás, Braz. — C4 79
Corumbaíba, Braz. — E4 79
Corumbataí, stm., Braz. — C13 80
Corumbaú, Ponta do, c., Braz. — D9 79
Corumbiara, stm., Braz. — E11 82
Coruña, stm., Ven. — D12 84
Coruña, Mi., U.S. — H11 110
Coruripe, Braz. — F11 76
Corvallis, Mt., U.S. — D11 122
Corvallis, Or., U.S. — F2 122
Corwith, Ia., U.S. — H2 110
Corydon, In., U.S. — D10 114
Corydon, Ia., U.S. — J3 118
Corydon, Ky., U.S. — E9 114
Corzuela, Arg. — D8 80
Cosamaloapan [de Carpio], Mex. — H12 90

Cosapa, Bol. — H7 82
Cosenza, Italy — J11 18
Coshocton, Oh., U.S. — G5 108
Cosigüina, Punta, c., Nic. — E7 92
Cosigüina, Volcán, vol., Nic. — C9 53
Cosmeledo Island, i., Sey. — C9 58
Cosmos, Mn., U.S. — G13 118
Cosne-Cours-sur-Loire, Fr. — E9 14
Cospán, Peru — B2 82
Cosquín, Arg. — F6 80
Cossatot, stm., Ar., U.S. — H2 114
Cossonay, Switz. — E6 13
Costa Mesa, Ca., U.S. — K8 124
Costa Rica, ctry., N.A. — G10 92
Costa Rica, Mex. — E6 90
Costeşti, Mol. — C12 20
Costigan Lake, l., Sk., Can. — B9 104
Costilla, N.M., U.S. — H11 120
Cosumnes, stm., Ca., U.S. — F4 124
Coswig, Ger. — D12 10
Cotabambas, Peru — E5 82
Cotabato, Phil. — D7 38
Cotacajes, stm., Bol. — G8 82
Cotagaita, Bol. — I9 82
Cotagaita, Bol. — I9 82
Cotahuasi, Peru — F5 82
Cotati, Ca., U.S. — F3 124
Coteaux, Haiti — E7 54
Cote d'Ivoire (Ivory Coast), ctry., Afr. — G5 54
Côte-d'Or, dept., Fr. — E11 14
Cotegipe, Braz. — B6 79
Cote Indian Reserve, Sk., Can. — G13 104
Cotentin, pen., Fr. — C5 14
Côtes-d'Armor, dept., Fr. — C4 14
Coti, stm., Braz. — C9 82
Cotija de la Paz, Mex. — H8 90
Cotingo, stm., Braz. — E12 84
Cotiujeni, Mol. — B12 20
Cotoca, Bol. — G10 82
Cotonou, Benin — H11 64
Cotopaxi, prov., Ec. — H3 84
Cotopaxi, vol., Ec. — H3 84
Cotswold Hills, hills, Eng., U.K. — J11 8
Cottage Grove, Or., U.S. — G2 122
Cottageville, S.C., U.S. — G6 112
Cottbus, Ger. — D14 10
Cottel Island, i., Nf., Can. — D20 106
Cotter, Ar., U.S. — F4 114
Cottian Alps (Alpi Cozie), mts., Eur. — E1 18
Cottondale, Al., U.S. — I10 114
Cottondale, Fl., U.S. — I1 112
Cotton Lake, l., Mb., Can. — C18 104
Cotton Plant, Ar., U.S. — G5 114
Cotton Valley, La., U.S. — J3 114
Cottonwood, Az., U.S. — J4 120
Cottonwood, Ca., U.S. — D3 124
Cottonwood, Id., U.S. — D9 122
Cottonwood, Mn., U.S. — G12 118
Cottonwood, stm., Ks., U.S. — M11 118
Cottonwood, stm., Mn., U.S. — G12 118
Cottonwood Falls, Ks., U.S. — M11 118
Cotuhé, stm., Col. — I7 84
Cotui, Dom. Rep. — E9 94
Cotulla, Tx., U.S. — K7 116
Coudekerque, Fr. — B8 14
Coudres, Île aux, i., P.Q., Can. — E3 106
Couhé, Fr. — F7 14
Coulee City, Wa., U.S. — C6 122
Coulee Dam, Wa., U.S. — C7 122
Coulommiers, Fr. — D10 14
Coulterville, Ca., U.S. — G5 124
Coulterville, Il., U.S. — D7 114
Counce, Tn., U.S. — G8 114
Council, Id., U.S. — F9 122
Council Bluffs, Ia., U.S. — J12 118
Council Grove, Ks., U.S. — M11 118
Country Homes, Wa., U.S. — B8 122
Coupeville, Wa., U.S. — B3 122
Courcelles, Bel. — H5 12
Couronnement, Île du see Coronation Island, i., Ant. — B1 73
Courtalain, Fr. — D8 14
Courtenay, B.C., Can. — H9 102
Courtland, Al., U.S. — H9 114
Courtland, Va., U.S. — C9 112
Courtrai (Kortrijk), Bel. — G3 12
Coushatta, La., U.S. — J3 114
Coutances, Fr. — C5 14
Couto Magalhães, stm., Braz. — B2 79
Coutts, Ab., Can. — H23 102
Couture, Lac, l., P.Q., Can. — D17 96
Couvin, Bel. — H5 12
Covasna, co., Rom. — D9 20
Cove, Or., U.S. — E8 122
Covelo, Ca., U.S. — E2 124
Coventry, Eng., U.K. — I12 8
Covered Wells, Az., U.S. — M5 120
Covert, Mi., U.S. — H9 110
Covilhã, Port. — E4 16
Covington, Ga., U.S. — F3 112
Covington, In., U.S. — B9 114
Covington, Ky., U.S. — H2 108
Covington, La., U.S. — L6 114
Covington, Oh., U.S. — G2 108
Covington, Tn., U.S. — G7 114
Covington, Va., U.S. — B7 112
Covunco, Arroyo, stm., Arg. — J4 80
Cowal, Lake l., Austl. — I7 70
Cowan, Tn., U.S. — G10 114
Cowan Lake, l., Austl. — F4 68
Cowan Lake, l., Sk., Can. — D22 104
Cowansville, P.Q., Can. — B14 108
Coward, S.C., U.S. — F6 112
Coward Springs, Austl. — G2 70
Cowden, Il., U.S. — C8 114
Cowdenbeath, Scot., U.K. — E10 8
Cowell, Austl. — I2 70
Cowen, W.V., U.S. — I6 108
Cowen, Mount, mtn., Mt., U.S. — E15 122
Cowes, Eng., U.K. — K11 8
Coweta, Ok., U.S. — D11 116
Cowgill, Mo., U.S. — C3 114
Cowichan Lake, l., B.C., Can. — H11 102
Cowlitz, stm., Wa., U.S. — D3 122
Cowpasture, stm., Va., U.S. — I7 108
Cowpens, S.C., U.S. — D5 112
Cowra, Austl. — I8 70
Coxá, stm., Braz. — C6 79
Coxim, Braz. — E1 79
Coxim, stm., Braz. — E1 79
Coxsackie, N.Y., U.S. — E13 108
Cox's Cove, Nf., Can. — C15 106
Coyaguaima, Cerro, mtn., Arg. — B5 80
Coyame, Mex. — C7 90
Coya Sur, Chile — B4 80

Coyuca de Benítez, Mex. — I9 90
Coyuca de Catalán, Mex. — I8 90
Cozad, Ne., U.S. — K8 118
Cozie, Alpi (Alpes Cottiennes), mts., Eur. — E2 18
Cozumel, Mex. — G16 90
Cozumel, Isla, i., Mex. — G16 90
Crab Orchard, Ky., U.S. — B2 112
Crab Orchard, Tn., U.S. — D2 112
Cradock, S. Afr. — I7 66
Craig, Ak., U.S. — B1 102
Craig, Co., U.S. — D9 120
Craig, Ne., U.S. — J11 118
Craigellachie, Scot., U.K. — D10 8
Craigmont, Id., U.S. — D9 122
Craigmyle, Ab., Can. — F22 102
Craignure, Scot., U.K. — E8 8
Craigsville, Va., U.S. — I7 108
Craik, Sk., Can. — G9 104
Crailsheim, Ger. — F10 10
Craiova, Rom. — E7 20
Cranberry Mountain, mtn., B.C., Can. — G16 102
Cranberry Portage, Mb., Can. — D13 104
Cranbrook, B.C., Can. — H19 102
Crandon, Wi., U.S. — E7 110
Crane, Az., U.S. — L2 120
Crane, In., U.S. — D10 114
Crane, Mo., U.S. — E3 114
Crane, Tx., U.S. — H4 116
Crane Lake, l., Sk., Can. — H5 104
Crane Mountain, mtn., Or., U.S. — H5 122
Crane River Indian Reserve, Mb., Can. — G15 104
Crângeni, Rom. — E8 20
Cranston, R.I., U.S. — F15 108
Craon, Fr. — E6 14
Craonne, Fr. — C10 14
Craponne, Fr. — G10 14
Crasna, Rom. — C11 20
Crasna (Kraszna), stm., Eur. — B6 20
Crasnoe, Mol. — C13 20
Crater Lake, l., Or., U.S. — H3 122
Crater Lake National Park, Or., U.S. — H3 122
Crateús, Braz. — E10 76
Cravari, stm., Braz. — E13 82
Craven, Sk., Can. — H10 104
Cravinhos, Braz. — F5 79
Cravo Norte, Col. — D7 84
Cravo Norte, stm., Col. — D7 84
Cravo Sur, stm., Col. — E7 84
Crawford, Co., U.S. — F9 120
Crawford, Ms., U.S. — I8 114
Crawford, Ne., U.S. — I4 118
Crawford, Tx., U.S. — H9 116
Crawford Bay, B.C., Can. — H18 102
Crawfordsville, Ar., U.S. — G6 114
Crawfordsville, In., U.S. — B10 114
Crawfordville, Fl., U.S. — I2 112
Crawfordville, Ga., U.S. — F4 112
Crazy Woman Creek, stm., Wy., U.S. — F19 122
Creal Springs, Il., U.S. — E8 114
Crean Lake, l., Sk., Can. — E8 104
Creede, Co., U.S. — G10 120
Creedmoor, N.C., U.S. — C8 112
Creel, Mex. — D6 90
Creemore, On., Can. — F15 110
Creighton, Ne., U.S. — I10 118
Creighton Mine, On., Can. — D14 110
Creil, Fr. — C9 14
Crema, Italy — E4 18
Cremona, Ab., Can. — F20 102
Cremona, Italy — E4 18
Crenshaw, Ms., U.S. — H6 114
Crepori, stm., Braz. — A13 82
Cres, Otok, i., Cro. — E9 18
Cresaptown, Md., U.S. — H8 108
Crescent, Ok., U.S. — D9 116
Crescent, Or., U.S. — G4 122
Crescent City, Ca., U.S. — C1 124
Crescent City, Fl., U.S. — J5 112
Crescent Spur, B.C., Can. — D14 102
Cresco, Ia., U.S. — G3 110
Crespo, Arg. — F8 80
Cresson, Pa., U.S. — G8 108
Cresson, Tx., U.S. — G9 116
Crested Butte, Co., U.S. — F10 120
Crestline, Ca., U.S. — J8 124
Crestline, Oh., U.S. — G4 108
Creston, B.C., Can. — H18 102
Creston, Ia., U.S. — J13 118
Creston, Ne., U.S. — J10 118
Crestone Peak, mtn., Co., U.S. — G11 120
Crestview, Fl., U.S. — L10 114
Crestwood Hills, Tn., U.S. — D2 112
Creswell, Or., U.S. — G3 122
Creswell Bay, b., N.T., Can. — B14 96
Creswick, Austl. — K5 70
Crete, Il., U.S. — B8 114
Crete, Ne., U.S. — K11 118
Crete see Kríti, i., Grc. — N8 20
Crêteville, Tun. — M5 18
Creus, Cap de c., Spain — C15 16
Creuse, dept., Fr. — F9 14
Creve Coeur, Il., U.S. — J7 110
Crevillent, Spain — G11 16
Crewe, Eng., U.K. — H11 8
Crewe, Va., U.S. — B8 112
Crewkerne, Eng., U.K. — K11 8
Cricamola, stm., Pan. — H13 92
Cricaré, stm., Braz. — E8 79
Criciúma, Braz. — E14 80
Cricket, N.C., U.S. — C5 112
Cridersville, Oh., U.S. — G2 108
Crieff, Scot., U.K. — E10 8
Crikvenica, Cro. — D9 18
Crimean Peninsula see Kryms'kyy pivostriv, pen., Ukr. — H4 26
Crimmitschau, Ger. — E12 10
Cripple Creek, Co., U.S. — F11 120
Crisfield, Md., U.S. — J11 108
Criss Creek, B.C., Can. — F14 102
Cristalândia, Braz. — F9 76
Cristália, Braz. — D7 79
Cristalina, Braz. — C5 79
Cristalino, stm., Braz. — B3 79
Cristianópolis, Braz. — C4 79
Cristóbal, Pan. — C3 84
Cristóbal Colón, Pico, mtn., Col. — B6 84
Crişul Alb, stm., Eur. — C5 20
Crişul Negru, stm., Eur. — C5 20
Crişul Repede (Sebeş Körös), stm., Eur. — C5 20
Crivitz, Wi., U.S. — E7 110
Crixás, Braz. — C4 79
Crixás-Açu, stm., Braz. — B4 79
Crixás-Mirim, stm., Braz. — C3 79
Crna Gora, state, Yugo. — G3 20
Črnomelj, Slvn. — D10 18
Croatia (Hrvatska), ctry., Eur. — D10 18

Crocker, Mo., U.S. — E4 114
Crockett, Tx., U.S. — H11 116
Crofton, Ky., U.S. — E9 114
Crofton, Ne., U.S. — I10 118
Croghan, N.Y., U.S. — D11 108
Croix, Lac à la, l., P.Q., Can. — A3 106
Croker, Tx., U.S. — J9 116
Croker, Cape, c., Austl. — B6 68
Croker Island, i., Austl. — B6 68
Cromarty, Scot., U.K. — D9 8
Cromínia, Braz. — D4 79
Cromwell, Al., U.S. — J8 114
Cromwell, N.Z. — F2 72
Cronin, Mount, mtn., B.C., Can. — C8 102
Crook, Co., U.S. — K5 118
Crooked, stm., B.C., Can. — C12 102
Crooked, stm., Mo., U.S. — C2 114
Crooked Creek, Ak., U.S. — F15 100
Crooked Island, i., Bah. — C7 94
Crooked Island Passage, strt., Bah. — C7 94
Crooked Lake, l., On., Can. — D17 106
Crooked Lake, l., Sk., Can. — H12 104
Crooked River, Sk., Can. — F11 104
Crookston, Mn., U.S. — D11 118
Crooksville, Oh., U.S. — H4 108
Crookwell, Austl. — J8 70
Crosby, Mn., U.S. — D2 110
Crosby, Ms., U.S. — K5 114
Crosby, N.D., U.S. — C4 118
Crosby, Mount, mtn., Wy., U.S. — G16 122
Crosbyton, Tx., U.S. — F5 116
Cross, stm., Afr. — I14 64
Cross Bay, b., Mb., Can. — E15 104
Cross City, Fl., U.S. — J3 112
Crossett, Ar., U.S. — I5 114
Crossfield, Ab., Can. — F20 102
Cross Lake, l., Mb., Can. — D17 104
Cross Lake, l., Mb., Can. — D17 104
Cross Plains, Tn., U.S. — G7 116
Cross Plains, Wi., U.S. — G6 110
Cross Sound, strt., Ak., U.S. — G26 100
Crossville, Il., U.S. — D8 114
Crossville, Tn., U.S. — D11 114
Croswell, Mi., U.S. — G13 110
Crothersville, In., U.S. — D11 114
Crotone, Italy — J12 18
Crow, stm., Mn., U.S. — E2 110
Crow Agency, Mt., U.S. — E18 122
Crowder, Ms., U.S. — H6 114
Crowder, Ok., U.S. — D11 116
Crowduck Lake, l., Mb., Can. — H19 104
Crowell, Tx., U.S. — F7 116
Crowley, La., U.S. — L4 114
Crow Lake, l., On., Can. — I21 104
Crowley, Lake, res., Ca., U.S. — G6 124
Crowleys Ridge, mtn., U.S. — G6 114
Crown Point, In., U.S. — A9 114
Crown Point, N.M., U.S. — I8 120
Crown Point, N.Y., U.S. — D13 108
Crown Prince Frederik Island, i., N.T., Can. — B15 96
Crowsnest, stm., Ab., Can. — H20 102
Crowsnest Pass, Ab., Can. — H20 102
Crowsnest Pass, Can. — H20 102
Crow Wing, stm., Mn., U.S. — E13 118
Croydon, Austl. — B5 70
Croydon Station, B.C., Can. — D15 102
Crozet, Va., U.S. — I8 108
Crozet, Archipel, is., Afr. — M9 126
Crucero, Peru — F6 82
Cruces, Cuba — C6 94
Cruger, Ms., U.S. — I6 114
Cruillas, Mex. — E10 90
Cruz, Cabo, c., Cuba — E6 94
Cruz Alta, Arg. — G8 80
Cruz Alta, Braz. — E12 80
Cruz del Eje, Arg. — F6 80
Cruzeiro, Braz. — G6 79
Cruzeiro do Oeste, Braz. — G2 79
Cruzeiro do Sul, Braz. — B5 82
Cruz Grande, Chile — E3 80
Cruzília, Braz. — F6 79
Cruz Machado, Braz. — D13 80
Crysler, On., Can. — B11 108
Crystal, Mn., U.S. — m12 110
Crystal, N.D., U.S. — C10 118
Crystal Beach, Fl., U.S. — K4 112
Crystal City, Mb., Can. — I16 104
Crystal City, Mo., U.S. — D6 114
Crystal City, Tx., U.S. — K7 116
Crystal Falls, Mi., U.S. — D7 110
Crystal Lake, l., Ia., U.S. — H7 110
Crystal River, Fl., U.S. — K4 112
Crystal Springs, Ms., U.S. — K5 114
Csongrád, Hung. — I20 10
Csongrád, co., Hung. — I20 10
Csurgó, Hung. — I17 10
Cu, stm., Asia — I12 26
Cúa, Ven. — B9 84
Cuajinicuilapa, Mex. — I10 90
Cuajone, Peru — G6 82
Cuamba, Moz. — D7 58
Cuando (Kwando), stm., Afr. — D4 58
Cuangar, Ang. — A4 66
Cuango, Ang. — C3 58
Cuango (Kwango), stm., Afr. — C3 58
Cuanza, stm., Ang. — C3 58
Cuao, stm., Ven. — E9 84
Cuareim (Quaraí), stm., S.A. — F10 80
Cuaró, Ur. — F10 80
Cuatrociénegas, Mex. — D8 90
Cuauhtémoc, Mex. — C6 90
Cuautitlán [de Romero Rubio], Mex. — H10 90
Cuba, Al., U.S. — J8 114
Cuba, Il., U.S. — J5 110
Cuba, Mo., U.S. — D5 114
Cuba, N.M., U.S. — H10 120
Cuba, N.Y., U.S. — E8 108
Cuba, Port. — G4 16
Cuba, ctry., N.A. — C5 94
Cubagua, Isla, i., Ven. — B10 84
Cubango (Okavango), stm., Afr. — D3 58
Cub Hills, hills, Sk., Can. — D10 104
Cuchilla Alta, Cerro, mtn., Hond. — B6 92
Cuchillo-Có, Arg. — J6 80
Cuchumatanes, Sierra los, mts., Guat. — B3 92
Čučkovo, Russia — E25 22
Cucúi, Braz. — G9 84
Cúcuta, Col. — D6 84
Cudahy, Wi., U.S. — H8 110
Cuddalore, India — F5 46
Cuddapah, India — E5 46
Čudovo, Russia — C15 22
Čudskoje ozero (Peipsi järv), l., Eur. — C10 22
Cudworth, Sk., Can. — F9 104

Cue, Austl. — E3 68
Cuéllar, Spain — D7 16
Cuenca, Ec. — I3 84
Cuenca, Spain — E9 16
Cuencamé [de Ceniceros], Mex. — E8 90
Cuernavaca, Mex. — H10 90
Cuero, Tx., U.S. — J9 116
Cuers, Fr. — I13 14
Cuesta Pass, Ca., U.S. — I5 124
Cueto, Cuba — D7 94
Cuetzalan del Progreso, Mex. — G11 90
Cuevo, Bol. — I10 82
Cugir, Rom. — D7 20
Cuiabá, Braz. — F13 82
Cuiabá, stm., Braz. — G13 82
Cuiari, Braz. — G8 84
Cuicatlán, Mex. — I11 90
Cuieiras, stm., Braz. — I12 84
Cuijk, Neth. — E8 12
Cuilapa, Guat. — C4 92
Cuilco, Guat. — B3 92
Cuilco (Grijalva), stm., N.A. — B3 92
Cuilo (Kwilu), stm., Afr. — C3 58
Cuiseaux, Fr. — F12 14
Cuito-Cuanavale, Ang. — E3 58
Cuiuni, stm., Braz. — H11 84
Čukotskij, mys, c., Russia — E29 28
Čukotskij poluostrov, pen., Russia — D28 28
Čukurca, Tur. — C7 48
Culbertson, Mt., U.S. — C3 118
Culbertson, Ne., U.S. — K7 118
Culiacán, Mex. — E6 90
Culiacancito, Mex. — E6 90
Culión, Nevado, mtn., Peru — F7 82
Cullen, La., U.S. — J3 114
Cullera, Spain — F11 16
Culleoka, Tn., U.S. — G10 114
Cullman, Al., U.S. — H10 114
Cullowhee, N.C., U.S. — D3 112
Culman, Russia — F17 28
Culpeper, Va., U.S. — I9 108
Culuene, stm., Braz. — A2 79
Culver, In., U.S. — A10 114
Culverden, N.Z. — E4 72
Cully, Switz. — F6 13
Čulym, Russia — F14 26
Čulym, stm., Russia — F9 28
Čulym, stm., Russia — F9 28
Culzeo, Laguna de, l., Mex. — H9 90
Cumaná, Ven. — B10 84
Cumanacoa, Ven. — B11 84
Cumare, Cerro, hill, Col. — G6 84
Cumari, Braz. — E4 79
Cumberland, B.C., Can. — H9 102
Cumberland, Ia., U.S. — J13 118
Cumberland, Ky., U.S. — C4 112
Cumberland, Md., U.S. — H8 108
Cumberland, Wi., U.S. — E3 110
Cumberland, stm., U.S. — D9 98
Cumberland, Lake, res., Ky., U.S. — F12 114
Cumberland City, Tn., U.S. — F9 114
Cumberland Gap, U.S. — C3 112
Cumberland House, Sk., Can. — E12 104
Cumberland Indian Reserve, Sk., Can. — E10 104
Cumberland Islands, is., Austl. — C8 70
Cumberland Lake, l., Sk., Can. — D12 104
Cumberland Peninsula, pen., N.T., Can. — C19 96
Cumberland Sound, strt., N.T., Can. — C19 96
Cumbria, state, Eng., U.K. — G11 8
Cumby, Tx., U.S. — F11 116
Cumming, Ga., U.S. — E2 112
Cummins, Austl. — J1 70
Cummins, Mount, mtn., B.C., Can. — E16 102
Cumpas, Mex. — B5 90
Cumuripa, Mex. — C5 90
Čumyš, stm., Russia — G15 28
Cunani, Braz. — C8 76
Cunani, stm., Braz. — H1 84
Cunaviche, Ven. — D9 84
Cunco, Chile — J2 80
Cuncumén, Chile — F2 80
Cundinamarca, dept., Col. — E5 84
Cunene (Kunene), stm., Afr. — E2 58
Cuneo, Italy — E2 18
Cunha Porã, Braz. — D12 80
Cunhinga, Igarapé, stm., Braz. — B9 82
Cunnamulla, Austl. — G8 70
Cunucunuma, stm., Ven. — F10 84
Cupar, Sk., Can. — H10 104
Cupica, Golfo de b., Col. — D4 84
Cupins, Braz. — E3 79
Ćuprija, Yugo. — F5 20
Cúpula, Pico, mtn., Mex. — E4 90
Curaçá, Braz. — E11 76
Curaçao, i., Neth. Ant. — H10 94
Curacautín, Chile — I2 80
Curaçavi, Chile — G3 80
Curanilahue, Chile — I2 80
Curanipe, Chile — H2 80
Curapça, Russia — E18 28
Curaray, stm., S.A. — H5 84
Curepto, Chile — H2 80
Curequeté, stm., Braz. — B9 82
Curiapo, Ven. — C12 84
Curicó, Chile — H3 80
Curicuriari, stm., Braz. — H9 84
Curicurú, stm., Braz. — B9 82
Curiseví, stm., Braz. — A2 79
Curitiba, Braz. — C14 80
Curitibanos, Braz. — D13 80
Curiuaú, stm., Braz. — H12 84
Curlewis, Austl. — H8 70
Currais Novos, Braz. — E11 76
Currant Mountain, mtn., Nv., U.S. — F10 124
Current, stm., U.S. — E5 98
Currie, Austl. — L5 70
Currie, Mn., U.S. — G12 118

Currituck, N.C., U.S. — C10 112
Currituck Sound, strt., N.C., U.S. — C11 112
Curtea de Argeş, Rom. — D8 20
Curtina, Ur. — G10 80
Curtis, Ne., U.S. — K7 118
Curtis, Port, Austl. — D9 70
Curtis Channel, strt., Austl. — D9 70
Curtis Island, i., Austl. — D9 70
Curtis Lake, l., N.T., Can. — C15 96
Curuá, stm., Braz. — D8 76
Curuá, stm., Braz. — C3 79
Curuá, stm., Braz. — B14 82
Curuá, Ilha do, i., Braz. — C8 76
Curuaés, stm., Braz. — B2 79
Curuçá, stm., Braz. — J7 84
Čurug, Yugo. — D4 20
Curuguaty, Para. — C11 80
Curupayty, Riacho, stm., Para. — I12 82
Cururu, Canal, Braz. — B13 82
Curuzú Cuatiá, Arg. — E9 80
Curvelo, Braz. — E6 79
Curwensville, Pa., U.S. — G8 108
Cusco, Peru — F5 82
Cusco, dept., Peru — E5 82
Cushabatay, stm., Peru — B4 82
Cushing, Ok., U.S. — D10 116
Cushing, Tx., U.S. — K2 114
Cushman, Ar., U.S. — F5 114
Cusiana, stm., Col. — E6 84
Cusihuiriáchic, Mex. — C6 90
Cusovoj, Russia — F9 26
Cusseta, Ga., U.S. — G2 112
Custer, Mi., U.S. — G9 110
Custer, Mt., U.S. — D18 122
Custer, Ok., U.S. — D8 116
Custer, S.D., U.S. — H4 118
Cut Bank, Mt., U.S. — B13 122
Cutbank, stm., Ab., Can. — C16 102
Cut Beaver Lake, l., Sk., Can. — E12 104
Cuthbert, Ga., U.S. — H2 112
Cut Knife, Sk., Can. — F5 104
Cutler, Ca., U.S. — H6 124
Cutlerville, Mi., U.S. — H10 110
Cutral-Có, Arg. — J4 80
Cutro, Italy — J11 18
Cuttack, India — J11 44
Cutzamala, stm., Mex. — H9 90
Cuvašija, state, Russia — F7 26
Cuxhaven, Ger. — B8 10
Cuyahoga Falls, Oh., U.S. — F5 108
Cuyamel, Hond. — B6 92
Cuyubini, stm., Ven. — C12 84
Cuyuni, stm., S.A. — D13 84
Cuyuni-Mazaruni, prov., Guy. — D12 84
Cyangugu, Rw. — B5 58
Cyclades see Kikládhes, is., Grc. — L9 20
Cygnet Lake, l., Mb., Can. — B20 104
Cynthiana, Ky., U.S. — I2 108
Cypress, La., U.S. — K3 114
Cypress Hills Provincial Park, Ab., Can. — I4 104
Cypress Hills Provincial Park, Sk., Can. — I5 104
Cypress Lake, l., Sk., Can. — I5 104
Cypress River, Mb., Can. — I15 104
Cyprus, ctry., Asia — H14 4
Cyprus, North (Kuzey Kıbrıs), ctry., Asia — H14 4
Cyril, On., Can. — E8 116
Cyrus Field Bay, b., N.T., Can. — D20 96
Czarna Woda, Pol. — B18 10
Czech Republic (Česká Republika), ctry., Eur. — F11 4
Częstochowa, Pol. — E19 10
Człuchów, Pol. — B17 10

**D**

Dabajuro, Ven. — B7 84
Dabat, Eth. — K9 60
Dabeiba, Col. — D4 84
Daberas, Nmb. — E4 66
Dabhoi, India — I5 44
Dabie Shan, mts., China — D4 34
Dabnou, Niger — D12 64
Dabola, Gui. — F4 64
Daboya, Gui. — G4 64
Dąbrowa Tarnowska, Pol. — E21 10
Dacca see Dhaka, Bngl. — I14 44
Dachau, Ger. — G11 10
Dac Lac, Cao Nguyen, plat., Viet. — H10 40
Dacoma, Ok., U.S. — C8 116
Dadanawa, Guy. — F13 84
Dade City, Fl., U.S. — K4 112
Daceville, Fl., U.S. — J11 114
Dādra and Nagar Haveli, i., China — B11 30
Dādra and Nagar Haveli, ter., India — B2 46
Dadu, Pak. — G2 44
Dadu, stm., China — F7 30
Daet, Phil. — n20 39b
Dafoe, Sk., Can. — G10 104
Dafoe Lake, l., Mb., Can. — C18 104
Dagana, Sen. — C2 64
Dagang, China — M2 34
Daga Post, Sudan — M7 60
Dagash, Sudan — H7 60
Dagda, Lat. — E10 22
Dagestan, state, Russia — I7 26
Daghfall, Sudan — H7 60
Dagu, China — E5 32
Dagua, Pap. N. Gui. — F11 38
Daguan, China — F8 30
Dagupan, Phil. — m19 39b
Dahana Dao (Lantau Island), i., China — M2 34
Da Hinggan Ling, mts., China — B11 30
Dahlak Archipelago, is., Erit. — G3 47
Dahlgren, Il., U.S. — D8 114
Dahlonega, Ga., U.S. — E3 112
Dāhod, India — I6 44
Dahomey see Benin, ctry., Afr. — G7 54
Dahra, Libya — C4 56
Dahūk, Iraq — D4 47
Dahy, Nafūd ad-, des., Sau. Ar. — D4 47
Dailekh, Nepal — F8 16
Daimiel, Spain — F8 16
Daingerfield, Tx., U.S. — I2 114
Daireaux, Arg. — I7 80
Daisetta, Tx., U.S. — I12 116
Dajabón, Dom. Rep. — E8 94
Dajarra, Austl. — C3 70
Dak, stm., China — F9 30
Dakar, Sen. — D1 64
Dakeng, China — I4 34

| Name | Map Ref. | Page |
|---|---|---|
| Dak Gle, Viet. | G9 | 40 |
| Dakhla, W. Sah. | I3 | 62 |
| Dakingari, Nig. | F12 | 64 |
| Dakoro, Niger | D13 | 64 |
| Dakota City, Ia., U.S. | I13 | 118 |
| Dakota City, Ne., U.S. | I11 | 118 |
| Dakovica, Yugo. | G4 | 20 |
| Dalaba, Gui. | F3 | 64 |
| Dalan Dzadgad, Mong. | C7 | 30 |
| Dalao, Gui. | F3 | 64 |
| Da Lat, Viet. | I10 | 40 |
| Dālbandin, Pak. | G18 | 48 |
| Dalby, Austl. | F9 | 70 |
| Dale, In., U.S. | D10 | 114 |
| Dale, Nor. | K9 | 6 |
| Dale, Nor. | K9 | 6 |
| *Dale Hollow Lake, res., U.S.* | C1 | 112 |
| Dalen, Nor. | L11 | 6 |
| Dalet, Myan. | E2 | 40 |
| Daleville, Al., U.S. | K11 | 114 |
| Daleville, In., U.S. | B11 | 114 |
| Dalhart, Tx., U.S. | C4 | 116 |
| Dalhousie, N.B., Can. | D7 | 106 |
| *Dalhousie, Cape, c., N.T., Can.* | A30 | 100 |
| Dali, China | B6 | 40 |
| Dalian (Dairen), China | E9 | 32 |
| *Daliang Shan, mts., China* | F7 | 30 |
| Daliuzhuang, China | B3 | 34 |
| Daliyat et Karmil, Isr. | C4 | 50 |
| Dalj, Cro. | D2 | 20 |
| Daljā', Egypt | D6 | 60 |
| Dallas, Al., U.S. | I10 | 114 |
| Dallas, Ga., U.S. | F2 | 112 |
| Dallas, N.C., U.S. | D5 | 112 |
| Dallas, Or., U.S. | F2 | 122 |
| Dallas, Pa., U.S. | F11 | 108 |
| Dallas, Tx., U.S. | G10 | 116 |
| Dallas, Wi., U.S. | E4 | 110 |
| Dallas Center, Ia., U.S. | I2 | 110 |
| Dallas City, Il., U.S. | J4 | 110 |
| *Dall Island, i., Ak., U.S.* | C2 | 102 |
| *Dalmacija, hist. reg., Eur.* | F11 | 18 |
| Dalmacio Vélez Sarsfield, Arg. | G7 | 80 |
| *Dalmatia see Dalmacija, hist. reg., Eur.* | F11 | 18 |
| Dalmeny, Sk., Can. | F8 | 104 |
| Dal'negorsk, Russia | I19 | 28 |
| Dal'nerečensk, Russia | H18 | 28 |
| Daloa, C. Iv. | H6 | 64 |
| Dalqū, Sudan | G6 | 60 |
| Dalroy, Ab., Can. | F21 | 102 |
| *Dalrymple, Mount, mtn., Austl.* | C8 | 70 |
| Dāltenganj, India | H11 | 44 |
| Dalton, Ga., U.S. | E2 | 112 |
| Dalton, Ma., U.S. | E13 | 108 |
| Dalton, Ne., U.S. | J5 | 118 |
| Dalton, Pa., U.S. | F11 | 108 |
| Dalton Gardens, Id., U.S. | C9 | 122 |
| Dalvík, Ice. | B4 | 6a |
| Dalwallinu, Austl. | F3 | 68 |
| *Daly, stm., Austl.* | B6 | 68 |
| *Daly Bay, b., N.T., Can.* | D15 | 96 |
| Daly City, Ca., U.S. | G3 | 124 |
| *Daly Lake, l., Sk., Can.* | B9 | 104 |
| Daly Waters, Austl. | C6 | 68 |
| Dāmā, Syria | C6 | 50 |
| Damān, India | B2 | 46 |
| *Damān, ter., India* | B2 | 46 |
| Damanhūr, Egypt | B6 | 60 |
| *Damar, Pulau, i., Indon.* | G8 | 38 |
| *Damaraland, hist. reg., Nmb.* | D3 | 66 |
| Damascus, Ar., U.S. | G4 | 114 |
| Damascus, Ga., U.S. | E2 | 112 |
| Damascus, Md., U.S. | H9 | 108 |
| Damascus see Dimashq, Syria | A6 | 50 |
| Damascus, Va., U.S. | C5 | 112 |
| *Damāvand, Qolleh-ye, mtn., Iran* | D12 | 48 |
| Damba, Ang. | C3 | 58 |
| *Dâmboviţa, co., Rom.* | E9 | 20 |
| *Dâmboviţa, stm., Rom.* | E9 | 20 |
| Dam Gamad, Sudan | K4 | 60 |
| Dāmghān, Iran | C13 | 48 |
| Damianópolis, Braz. | C5 | 79 |
| Damietta see Dumyāţ, Egypt | B6 | 60 |
| Dammartin-en-Goële, Fr. | C9 | 14 |
| Damoh, India | I8 | 44 |
| Damongo, Ghana | G9 | 64 |
| Dampier, Austl. | D3 | 68 |
| *Dampier, Selat, strt., Indon.* | F9 | 38 |
| *Dampier Archipelago, is., Austl.* | D3 | 68 |
| *Dan, stm., U.S.* | C7 | 112 |
| Dana, In., U.S. | C9 | 114 |
| Da Nang, Viet. | F10 | 40 |
| Danbury, Ct., U.S. | F13 | 108 |
| Danbury, Ia., U.S. | I12 | 118 |
| Danbury, N.C., U.S. | C6 | 112 |
| Danbury, Ne., U.S. | K7 | 118 |
| Danbury, Tx., U.S. | J11 | 116 |
| *Danby Lake, l., Ca., U.S.* | J10 | 124 |
| Dandenong, Austl. | K6 | 70 |
| Dandong, China | C12 | 32 |
| Dandridge, Tn., U.S. | C3 | 112 |
| Dan Dume, Nig. | F13 | 64 |
| Danforth, Me., U.S. | B19 | 108 |
| *Danforth Hills, mts., Co., U.S.* | D8 | 120 |
| *Dang, stm., China* | D6 | 30 |
| Dangba, China | C6 | 32 |
| *Danggali Conservation Park, Austl.* | I4 | 70 |
| Dangila, Eth. | L9 | 60 |
| Dango, Sudan | L3 | 60 |
| Dangriga, Belize | I15 | 90 |
| Dangtu, China | D7 | 34 |
| Dan Gulbi, Nig. | F13 | 64 |
| Daniel, Wy., U.S. | B6 | 120 |
| *Daniel-Johnson, Barrage, P.Q., Can.* | B5 | 106 |
| Daniel's Harbour, Nf., Can. | B16 | 106 |
| Danielson, Ct., U.S. | F15 | 108 |
| *Daniels Pass, Ut., U.S.* | D5 | 120 |
| Danielsville, Ga., U.S. | E3 | 112 |
| Danilov, Russia | C23 | 22 |
| Dänizkänarı, Azer. | A10 | 48 |
| Dank, Oman | C10 | 47 |
| Dankov, Russia | H22 | 22 |
| Danlí, Hond. | C8 | 92 |
| Dannebrog, Ne., U.S. | J9 | 118 |
| Dannemora, N.Y., U.S. | C13 | 108 |
| Dannenberg, Ger. | B11 | 10 |
| Dannevirke, N.Z. | D6 | 72 |
| Dannhauser, S. Afr. | G10 | 66 |
| Dansville, N.Y., U.S. | E9 | 108 |
| Dante, Va., U.S. | C4 | 112 |
| *Danube, stm., Eur.* | G13 | 4 |
| *Danube, Mouths of the, mth., Eur.* | D13 | 20 |
| Danubyu, Myan. | F3 | 40 |
| Danvers, Il., U.S. | J6 | 110 |
| Danville, Ar., U.S. | G3 | 114 |
| Danville, Ga., U.S. | G3 | 112 |
| Danville, Il., U.S. | B9 | 114 |
| Danville, In., U.S. | C10 | 114 |
| Danville, Ky., U.S. | E12 | 114 |
| Danville, Pa., U.S. | G10 | 108 |
| Danville, P.Q., Can. | B14 | 108 |
| Danville, Va., U.S. | C7 | 112 |
| Danville, Vt., U.S. | C14 | 108 |
| Danyang, China | C8 | 34 |
| Danzig see Gdańsk, Pol. | A18 | 10 |
| Daocheng, China | F7 | 30 |
| Daolin, China | H1 | 34 |
| Daoukro, C. Iv. | H8 | 64 |
| Daoulas, Fr. | D2 | 14 |
| *Daoura, Oued, val., Alg.* | F9 | 62 |
| Dapango, Togo | F10 | 64 |
| Daphne, Al., U.S. | L9 | 114 |
| Da Qaidam, China | B16 | 44 |
| Daqing, China | D6 | 32 |
| Daqqāq, Sudan | K4 | 60 |
| Dara, Sen. | D2 | 64 |
| Dar'ā, Syria | C6 | 50 |
| Dārāb, Iran | G13 | 48 |
| Darabani, Rom. | A10 | 20 |
| Daraina, Madag. | n23 | 67b |
| Darāw, Egypt | E7 | 60 |
| Dārayyā, Syria | B6 | 50 |
| Darbhanga, India | G11 | 44 |
| Darby, Mt., U.S. | D11 | 122 |
| Darchan, Mong. | B8 | 30 |
| D'Arcy, B.C., Can. | G12 | 102 |
| Dardanelle, Ar., U.S. | G3 | 114 |
| Dardanelle, Ca., U.S. | F6 | 124 |
| *Dardanelle Lake, res., Ar., U.S.* | G3 | 114 |
| *Dardanelles see Çanakkale Boğazı, strt., Tur.* | I10 | 20 |
| Dardara, Mor. | J6 | 16 |
| Dar-el-Beida see Casablanca, Mor. | D7 | 62 |
| Darende, Tur. | B4 | 48 |
| Dar es Salaam, Tan. | C7 | 58 |
| Dargai, Pak. | C4 | 44 |
| Dargan-Ata, Turk. | I10 | 26 |
| Dargaville, N.Z. | A4 | 72 |
| Dargol, Niger | E10 | 64 |
| Darién, Col. | F4 | 84 |
| Darien, Ga., U.S. | H5 | 112 |
| *Darién, Serranía del, mts.* | C4 | 84 |
| *Dariense, Cordillera, mts., Nic.* | E9 | 92 |
| Dariganga, Mong. | B9 | 30 |
| Dārjiling, India | G13 | 44 |
| Darlag, China | E6 | 30 |
| Darling, Ms., U.S. | H6 | 114 |
| Darling, S. Afr. | I4 | 66 |
| *Darling, stm., Austl.* | I5 | 70 |
| *Darling Downs, reg., Austl.* | F9 | 70 |
| Darlingford, Mb., Can. | I16 | 104 |
| *Darling Range, mts., Austl.* | F3 | 68 |
| Darlington, S.C., U.S. | E7 | 112 |
| Darlington, Wi., U.S. | H5 | 110 |
| Darłowo, Pol. | A16 | 10 |
| Darmstadt, Ger. | F8 | 10 |
| Darnah, Libya | B5 | 56 |
| Darnétal, Fr. | C8 | 14 |
| Darney, Fr. | D13 | 14 |
| *Darnley, Cape, c., Ant.* | B5 | 73 |
| *Darnley Bay, b., N.T., Can.* | C8 | 96 |
| Daroca, Spain | D10 | 16 |
| Dar-Ould-Zidouh, Mor. | D7 | 62 |
| Darou Mousti, Sen. | D1 | 64 |
| *Darrah, Mount, mtn., Can.* | H20 | 102 |
| Darregueira, Arg. | I7 | 80 |
| Darreh Gaz, Iran | C15 | 48 |
| Darrington, Wa., U.S. | B4 | 122 |
| Darrouzett, Tx., U.S. | C6 | 116 |
| *Dart, Cape, c., Ant.* | C10 | 73 |
| *Dartmoor, for., Eng., U.K.* | K9 | 8 |
| Dartmouth, Eng., U.K. | K10 | 8 |
| Dartmouth, N.S., Can. | H10 | 106 |
| *Dartmouth, stm., P.Q., Can.* | C9 | 106 |
| *Dartmouth, Lake, l., Austl.* | F6 | 70 |
| Daru, Pap. N. Gui. | A8 | 68 |
| Daru, S.L. | H4 | 64 |
| Daruvar, Cro. | D12 | 18 |
| Darwin, Arg. | J6 | 80 |
| Darwin, Austl. | B6 | 68 |
| *Dās, i., U.A.E.* | B8 | 47 |
| Dashaping, China | F2 | 34 |
| *Dasht, stm., Pak.* | I16 | 48 |
| Dasiji, China | B4 | 34 |
| Dašinčilen, Mong. | B7 | 30 |
| Daškauka, Bela. | H13 | 22 |
| Dassel, Mn., U.S. | E1 | 110 |
| Date, Japan | e15 | 36a |
| Datia, India | H8 | 44 |
| Datian, China | K5 | 34 |
| D'at'kovo, Russia | H17 | 22 |
| Datong, China | C9 | 30 |
| *Datong, stm., China* | D7 | 30 |
| Datoushan, China | B5 | 32 |
| *Datu, Tanjung, c., Asia* | M10 | 40 |
| *Daua (Dawa), stm., Afr.* | H9 | 56 |
| Daugai, Lith. | G7 | 22 |
| *Daugava (Zahodnjaja Dzvina), stm., Eur.* | E7 | 22 |
| Daugavpils, Lat. | F9 | 22 |
| Daule, Ec. | G2 | 84 |
| Daule, Ec. | H3 | 84 |
| *Daule, stm., Ec.* | H2 | 84 |
| Daun, Ger. | E6 | 10 |
| Dauphin, Mb., Can. | G14 | 104 |
| *Dauphin, stm., Mb., Can.* | G16 | 104 |
| *Dauphiné, hist. reg., Fr.* | H12 | 14 |
| Dauphin Island, Al., U.S. | L8 | 114 |
| *Dauphin Island, i., Al., U.S.* | L8 | 114 |
| *Dauphin Lake, l., Mb., Can.* | G15 | 104 |
| Daura, Nig. | E14 | 64 |
| *D'Auteuil, Lac, l., P.Q., Can.* | B12 | 106 |
| Dāvangere, India | E3 | 46 |
| Davant, La., U.S. | M7 | 114 |
| Davao, Phil. | D8 | 38 |
| *Davao Gulf, b., Phil.* | D8 | 38 |
| Dāvar Panāh, Iran | H17 | 48 |
| Davel, S. Afr. | F9 | 66 |
| Davenport, Fl., U.S. | K5 | 112 |
| Davenport, Ia., U.S. | I5 | 110 |
| Davenport, Ne., U.S. | K10 | 118 |
| Davenport, Ok., U.S. | D10 | 116 |
| Davenport, Wa., U.S. | C7 | 122 |
| *Davey, Port, b., Austl.* | N6 | 70 |
| David, Pan. | C1 | 84 |
| David City, Ne., U.S. | J10 | 118 |
| Davidson, N.C., U.S. | D6 | 112 |
| Davidson, Ok., U.S. | E7 | 116 |
| Davidson, Sk., Can. | G9 | 104 |
| *Davidson Lake, l., Mb., Can.* | E15 | 104 |
| Davie, Fl., U.S. | M6 | 112 |
| *Davin Lake, l., Sk., Can.* | B11 | 104 |
| Davinópolis, Braz. | C3 | 79 |
| Davis, Ca., U.S. | F4 | 124 |
| Davis, N.C., U.S. | E10 | 112 |
| Davis, Ok., U.S. | E9 | 116 |
| Davis, W.V., U.S. | H7 | 108 |
| *Davis, Mount, mtn., Pa., U.S.* | H7 | 108 |
| Davisboro, Ga., U.S. | G4 | 112 |
| Davis City, Ia., U.S. | J2 | 110 |
| Davis Cove, Nf., Can. | E19 | 106 |
| Davis Dam, Az., U.S. | I2 | 120 |
| *Davis Strait, strt., N.A.* | C21 | 96 |
| Davlekanovo, Russia | G9 | 26 |
| Davos, Switz. | E12 | 13 |
| Davutlar, Tur. | L11 | 20 |
| Davy, W.V., U.S. | B5 | 112 |
| *Dawa (Daua), stm., Afr.* | H9 | 56 |
| *Dawāsir, Wādī ad-, val., Sau. Ar.* | D4 | 47 |
| Dawei (Tavoy), Myan. | G5 | 40 |
| *Dawna Range, mts., Myan.* | F5 | 40 |
| Dawqah, Sau. Ar. | E2 | 47 |
| Dawrah, Sudan | K3 | 60 |
| Dawson, Ga., U.S. | H2 | 112 |
| Dawson, Mn., U.S. | G11 | 118 |
| Dawson, Ne., U.S. | K12 | 118 |
| Dawson, Tx., U.S. | H10 | 116 |
| Dawson, Yk., Can. | D25 | 100 |
| *Dawson, stm., Austl.* | E8 | 70 |
| *Dawson, Isla, i., Chile* | G2 | 78 |
| *Dawson, Mount, mtn., B.C., Can.* | F17 | 102 |
| *Dawson Bay, b., Mb., Can.* | F14 | 104 |
| Dawson Creek, B.C., Can. | B14 | 102 |
| *Dawson Inlet, b., N.T., Can.* | D14 | 96 |
| *Dawson Range, mts., Austl.* | E8 | 70 |
| *Dawson Range, mts., Yk., Can.* | E25 | 100 |
| Dawson Springs, Ky., U.S. | E9 | 114 |
| Dawsonville, Ga., U.S. | E2 | 112 |
| Dawusi, China | D5 | 30 |
| Dax, Fr. | I5 | 14 |
| Daxian, China | E8 | 30 |
| Daxing, China | D4 | 32 |
| *Daxue Shan, mts., China* | E7 | 30 |
| Daye, China | E3 | 34 |
| Daying, China | D1 | 32 |
| *Daying (Taping), stm., Asia* | B5 | 40 |
| Daylesford, Austl. | K6 | 70 |
| *Daymán, stm., Ur.* | F10 | 80 |
| Daym Zubayr, Sudan | N4 | 60 |
| Dayr Abū Sa'īd, Jord. | C5 | 50 |
| Dayr 'Alī, Syria | B6 | 50 |
| Dayr az-Zawr, Syria | D6 | 48 |
| Dayr Qānūn, Syria | A6 | 50 |
| Dayrūţ, Egypt | D6 | 60 |
| Daysland, Ab., Can. | E22 | 102 |
| *Day Star Indian Reserve, Sk., Can.* | G10 | 104 |
| Dayton, Ia., U.S. | H1 | 110 |
| Dayton, Oh., U.S. | H2 | 108 |
| Dayton, Or., U.S. | E2 | 122 |
| Dayton, Pa., U.S. | G7 | 108 |
| Dayton, Tn., U.S. | G11 | 114 |
| Dayton, Tx., U.S. | I12 | 116 |
| Dayton, Va., U.S. | I8 | 108 |
| Dayton, Wa., U.S. | D8 | 122 |
| Dayton, Wy., U.S. | F18 | 122 |
| Daytona Beach, Fl., U.S. | J5 | 112 |
| Dayu, China | J3 | 34 |
| *Dayu Ling, mts., China* | J3 | 34 |
| *Da Yunhe (Grand Canal), China* | E10 | 30 |
| Dayville, Or., U.S. | F6 | 122 |
| Dazui, China | E3 | 34 |
| Dcheïra, Mor. | E6 | 62 |
| De Aar, S. Afr. | H7 | 66 |
| *Dead, stm., Mi., U.S.* | D8 | 110 |
| *Deadman, stm., B.C., Can.* | F14 | 102 |
| Deadman's Cay, Bah. | C7 | 94 |
| *Deadman's Creek Indian Reserve, B.C., Can.* | G14 | 102 |
| *Dead Sea (Al-Baḥr al-Mayyit) (Yam HaMelaḥ), l., Asia* | F4 | 50 |
| Deadwood, S.D., U.S. | G4 | 118 |
| *Deadwood, stm., Id., U.S.* | F10 | 122 |
| Deakin, Austl. | F5 | 68 |
| Deal, Eng., U.K. | J15 | 8 |
| Deale, Md., U.S. | I10 | 108 |
| Deal Island, Md., U.S. | I11 | 108 |
| *Dean, stm., B.C., Can.* | E8 | 102 |
| *Dean Channel, strt., B.C., Can.* | E7 | 102 |
| Deán Funes, Arg. | F6 | 80 |
| *Deans Dundas Bay, b., N.T., Can.* | B9 | 96 |
| Dearborn, Mi., U.S. | H12 | 110 |
| *Dearborn, stm., Mt., U.S.* | C13 | 122 |
| *Dease, stm., B.C., Can.* | G30 | 100 |
| *Dease Arm, b., N.T., Can.* | C34 | 100 |
| *Dease Lake, l., B.C., Can.* | G29 | 100 |
| *Dease Strait, strt., N.T., Can.* | C11 | 96 |
| Death Valley, Ca., U.S. | H9 | 124 |
| *Death Valley, val., Ca., U.S.* | H9 | 124 |
| Deatsville, Al., U.S. | J10 | 114 |
| Deauville, Fr. | C7 | 14 |
| Debar, Mac. | H4 | 20 |
| De Bary, Fl., U.S. | K5 | 112 |
| De Beque, Co., U.S. | E8 | 120 |
| De Berry, Tx., U.S. | J2 | 114 |
| Dębica, Pol. | E21 | 10 |
| Dęblin, Pol. | D21 | 10 |
| Debrecen, Hung. | H21 | 10 |
| Debre Markos, Eth. | L9 | 60 |
| Debre May, Eth. | L9 | 60 |
| Debre Tabor, Eth. | L10 | 60 |
| Debre Zebit, Eth. | L10 | 60 |
| Debre Zeyit, Eth. | M10 | 60 |
| Debrzno, Pol. | B17 | 10 |
| Decatur, Al., U.S. | H10 | 114 |
| Decatur, Ga., U.S. | F2 | 112 |
| Decatur, Il., U.S. | C8 | 114 |
| Decatur, In., U.S. | B12 | 114 |
| Decatur, Mi., U.S. | H10 | 110 |
| Decatur, Ms., U.S. | J7 | 114 |
| Decatur, Ne., U.S. | I11 | 118 |
| Decatur, Tn., U.S. | D2 | 112 |
| Decatur, Tx., U.S. | F9 | 116 |
| Decaturville, Tn., U.S. | G8 | 114 |
| Decazeville, Fr. | H9 | 14 |
| *Deccan, plat., India* | D5 | 46 |
| *Deception, stm., Bots.* | C6 | 66 |
| *Deception Island, i., Ant.* | B12 | 73 |
| *Deception Lake, l., Sk., Can.* | B10 | 104 |
| *Dechêne, Lac, l., P.Q., Can.* | A6 | 106 |
| Decherd, Tn., U.S. | G10 | 114 |
| Děčín, Czech Rep. | E14 | 10 |
| Decize, Fr. | F10 | 14 |
| Decker Lake, B.C., Can. | C9 | 102 |
| Deckerville, Mi., U.S. | G13 | 110 |
| De Cocksdorp, Neth. | B6 | 12 |
| Decorah, Ia., U.S. | G4 | 110 |
| Decs, Hung. | I18 | 10 |
| Deda, Rom. | C8 | 20 |
| De Doorns, S. Afr. | I4 | 66 |
| Dédougou, Burkina | E8 | 64 |
| Dedovsk, Russia | F20 | 22 |
| *Dee, stm., Scot., U.K.* | D11 | 8 |
| *Dee, stm., U.K.* | H10 | 8 |
| Deenwood, Ga., U.S. | H4 | 112 |
| *Deep Bay, b., Sk., Can.* | B11 | 104 |
| *Deep Creek Indian Reserve, B.C., Can.* | E12 | 102 |
| Deep River, Ct., U.S. | F14 | 108 |
| Deep River, Ia., U.S. | I3 | 110 |
| Deep River, On., Can. | D18 | 110 |
| Deepwater, Mo., U.S. | D3 | 114 |
| Deer Creek, Mn., U.S. | E12 | 118 |
| Deerfield, Il., U.S. | H8 | 110 |
| Deerfield, Ks., U.S. | N6 | 118 |
| Deerfield Beach, Fl., U.S. | M6 | 112 |
| *Deer Island, i., N.B., Can.* | H7 | 106 |
| Deer Isle, Me., U.S. | C18 | 108 |
| Deer Lake, Nf., Can. | C16 | 106 |
| *Deer Lake, l., Nf., Can.* | C16 | 106 |
| *Deer Lake, l., On., Can.* | F20 | 104 |
| Deer Lodge, Mt., U.S. | D13 | 122 |
| Deer Park, Al., U.S. | K8 | 114 |
| Deer Park, Wa., U.S. | C8 | 122 |
| *Deerpass Bay, b., N.T., Can.* | D33 | 100 |
| *Deer Pond, l., Nf., Can.* | D19 | 106 |
| Deer River, Mn., U.S. | C2 | 110 |
| Deer Trail, Co., U.S. | L3 | 118 |
| Deerwood, Mn., U.S. | D2 | 110 |
| Defiance, Ia., U.S. | J12 | 118 |
| Defiance, Oh., U.S. | F2 | 108 |
| De Forest, Wi., U.S. | G6 | 110 |
| De Funiak Springs, Fl., U.S. | L10 | 114 |
| Dêgê, China | E6 | 30 |
| Degeh Bur, Eth. | G9 | 56 |
| Dégelis (Sainte-Rose-du-Dégelis), P.Q., Can. | E5 | 106 |
| Degerfors, Swe. | L14 | 6 |
| Deggendorf, Ger. | G12 | 10 |
| *Degh, stm., Asia* | D6 | 44 |
| Degoma, Eth. | K9 | 60 |
| De Graff, Oh., U.S. | G3 | 108 |
| *De Gray Lake, res., Ar., U.S.* | H3 | 114 |
| *De Grey, stm., Austl.* | D4 | 68 |
| *Dehalak Deset, i., Erit.* | E9 | 56 |
| Deh Bīd, Iran | F12 | 48 |
| Dehibat, Tun. | D16 | 62 |
| Dehiwala-Mount Lavinia, Sri L. | I5 | 46 |
| Deh Kord, Iran | E10 | 48 |
| Dehlorān, Iran | E9 | 48 |
| Dehra Dūn, India | E8 | 44 |
| Dehri, India | H11 | 44 |
| Dehua, China | J7 | 34 |
| Dehui, China | C12 | 30 |
| Dej, Rom. | B7 | 20 |
| Dejnau, Turk. | J10 | 26 |
| De Kalb, Il., U.S. | I7 | 110 |
| De Kalb, Ms., U.S. | J8 | 114 |
| De Kalb, Tx., U.S. | I2 | 114 |
| Dekemhare, Erit. | J10 | 60 |
| Dekese, D.R.C. | B4 | 58 |
| Dekina, Nig. | H13 | 64 |
| *De La Blanche, Lac, l., P.Q., Can.* | B4 | 106 |
| De Land, Fl., U.S. | J5 | 112 |
| Delano, Ca., U.S. | I6 | 124 |
| Delano, Mn., U.S. | E2 | 110 |
| *Delano Peak, mtn., Ut., U.S.* | F4 | 120 |
| Delārām, Afg. | E17 | 48 |
| Delareyville, S. Afr. | F7 | 66 |
| *Delaronde Lake, l., Sk., Can.* | D7 | 104 |
| Delavan, Il., U.S. | B7 | 114 |
| Delaware, Oh., U.S. | G3 | 108 |
| Delaware, Ok., U.S. | C11 | 116 |
| *Delaware, state, U.S.* | D11 | 98 |
| *Delaware, stm., Ks., U.S.* | L12 | 118 |
| *Delaware, stm., U.S.* | F12 | 108 |
| *Delaware Bay, b., U.S.* | H11 | 108 |
| Delaware City, De., U.S. | H11 | 108 |
| Delburne, Ab., Can. | E21 | 102 |
| Delcambre, La., U.S. | M5 | 114 |
| Del Campillo, Arg. | H6 | 80 |
| Del City, Ok., U.S. | D9 | 116 |
| Delegate, Austl. | K8 | 70 |
| Délembé, C.A.R. | M2 | 60 |
| Delémont, Switz. | D7 | 13 |
| De Leon, Tx., U.S. | G8 | 116 |
| De Leon Springs, Fl., U.S. | J5 | 112 |
| Delfinópolis, Braz. | F5 | 79 |
| Delft, Neth. | D5 | 12 |
| Delfzijl, Neth. | B10 | 12 |
| Delgado, El Sal. | D5 | 92 |
| *Delgado, Cabo, c., Moz.* | D8 | 58 |
| Delhi, Ia., U.S. | H4 | 110 |
| Delhi, India | F7 | 44 |
| Delhi, La., U.S. | J5 | 114 |
| Delhi, N.Y., U.S. | E12 | 108 |
| Delhi, On., Can. | H15 | 110 |
| *Delhi, ter., India* | F7 | 44 |
| Delia, Ab., Can. | F22 | 102 |
| Delicias, Mex. | C7 | 90 |
| Delight, Ar., U.S. | H3 | 114 |
| Delingde, Russia | C14 | 28 |
| Delingha, China | D6 | 30 |
| Delisle, Sk., Can. | G7 | 104 |
| Delitzsch, Ger. | D12 | 10 |
| Dell City, Tx., U.S. | M11 | 120 |
| Delle, Fr. | E14 | 14 |
| Delles, Alg. | B12 | 62 |
| Dell Rapids, S.D., U.S. | H11 | 118 |
| Del Mar, Ca., U.S. | L8 | 124 |
| Delmar, De., U.S. | I11 | 108 |
| Delmar, Ia., U.S. | H5 | 110 |
| Delmar, Md., U.S. | I11 | 108 |
| Del Mar Hills, Tx., U.S. | L7 | 116 |
| *Delmarva Peninsula, pen., U.S.* | I11 | 108 |
| Delmas, Sk., Can. | F6 | 104 |
| Delmenhorst, Ger. | B8 | 10 |
| Delmont, S.D., U.S. | H9 | 118 |
| Del Norte, Co., U.S. | G10 | 120 |
| *De-Longa, ostrova, is., Russia* | B22 | 28 |
| Deloraine, Austl. | M7 | 70 |
| Deloraine, Mb., Can. | I14 | 104 |
| *Delorme, Lac, l., P.Q., Can.* | F19 | 96 |
| Delphi, In., U.S. | J9 | 110 |
| *Delphi see Dhelfoí, hist., Grc.* | K6 | 20 |
| Delphos, Ks., U.S. | L10 | 118 |
| Delphos, Oh., U.S. | G2 | 108 |
| Delray Beach, Fl., U.S. | M6 | 112 |
| Del Rio, Tx., U.S. | J6 | 116 |
| Delta, Co., U.S. | F8 | 120 |
| Delta, Mo., U.S. | E7 | 114 |
| Delta, Oh., U.S. | F2 | 108 |
| Delta, Ut., U.S. | E4 | 120 |
| *Delta Amacuro, ter., Ven.* | C12 | 84 |
| Delta Beach, Mb., Can. | H16 | 104 |
| Delta City, Ms., U.S. | I6 | 114 |
| Delta Downs, Austl. | A4 | 70 |
| Delta Junction, Ak., U.S. | D22 | 100 |
| *Delta Peak, mtn., B.C., Can.* | H30 | 100 |
| Del Valle, Tx., U.S. | I9 | 116 |
| Delyatyn, Ukr. | A8 | 20 |
| Dem'ansk, Russia | D15 | 22 |
| *Demarcation Point, c., Ak., U.S.* | B24 | 100 |
| Demba, D.R.C. | C4 | 58 |
| Dembecha, Eth. | L9 | 60 |
| Dembéni, Com. | k15 | 67a |
| Dembi, Eth. | M9 | 60 |
| Dembi Dolo, Eth. | M8 | 60 |
| *Demerara, stm., Guy.* | D13 | 84 |
| Demidov, Russia | F14 | 22 |
| Deming, N.M., U.S. | L9 | 120 |
| *Demini, stm., Braz.* | H11 | 84 |
| Demirci, Tur. | J12 | 20 |
| Demirtaş, Tur. | I13 | 20 |
| *Demjanka, stm., Russia* | F6 | 28 |
| Demjanskoje, Russia | F11 | 26 |
| Demmin, Ger. | B13 | 10 |
| Demmitt, Ab., Can. | B15 | 102 |
| Demnate, Mor. | E7 | 62 |
| Demopolis, Al., U.S. | J9 | 114 |
| Demorest, Ga., U.S. | E3 | 112 |
| Demotte, In., U.S. | A9 | 114 |
| Denain, Fr. | B10 | 14 |
| *Denakil, reg., Afr.* | F9 | 56 |
| Denali National Park, Ak., U.S. | E20 | 100 |
| *Denali National Park, Ak., U.S.* | E19 | 100 |
| Denare Beach, Sk., Can. | D12 | 104 |
| Denau, Uzb. | J11 | 26 |
| Denbigh, Wales, U.K. | H10 | 8 |
| *Dender (Dendre), stm., Bel.* | G4 | 12 |
| Dendermonde (Termonde), Bel. | F5 | 12 |
| Dendron, S. Afr. | D9 | 66 |
| Deneba, Eth. | M10 | 60 |
| Dengcheng, China | B3 | 34 |
| Dêngqên, China | E6 | 30 |
| Dengshahe, China | D10 | 32 |
| Denham, Austl. | E2 | 68 |
| *Denham, Mount, mtn., Jam.* | E6 | 94 |
| *Denham Island, i., Austl.* | A3 | 70 |
| *Denham Range, mts., Austl.* | C7 | 70 |
| Denham Springs, La., U.S. | L6 | 114 |
| Den Helder, Neth. | C6 | 12 |
| Dénia, Spain | G12 | 16 |
| Dénié, Mali | F6 | 64 |
| Deniliquin, Austl. | J6 | 70 |
| Denison, Ia., U.S. | I12 | 118 |
| Denison, Tx., U.S. | F10 | 116 |
| Denizli, Tur. | L13 | 20 |
| Denmark, Austl. | F3 | 68 |
| Denmark, S.C., U.S. | F5 | 112 |
| Denmark, Wi., U.S. | F8 | 110 |
| *Denmark (Danmark), ctry., Eur.* | D10 | 4 |
| *Denmark Bay, b., N.T., Can.* | B12 | 96 |
| *Denmark Strait, strt.* | C17 | 86 |
| Dennison, Oh., U.S. | G5 | 108 |
| Dennis Port, Ma., U.S. | F16 | 108 |
| Denpasar, Indon. | G6 | 38 |
| Denton, Md., U.S. | I11 | 108 |
| Denton, Mt., U.S. | C16 | 122 |
| Denton, N.C., U.S. | D6 | 112 |
| Denton, Tx., U.S. | F9 | 116 |
| *D'Entrecasteaux, Point, c., Austl.* | F3 | 68 |
| *D'Entrecasteaux Islands, is., Pap. N. Gui.* | A10 | 68 |
| Denver, Co., U.S. | E12 | 120 |
| Denver, Ia., U.S. | H3 | 110 |
| Denver, Pa., U.S. | G10 | 108 |
| Denver City, Tx., U.S. | G4 | 116 |
| Deoghar, India | H12 | 44 |
| Deolāli, India | C2 | 46 |
| Deoria, India | G10 | 44 |
| De Pere, Wi., U.S. | F7 | 110 |
| Depew, N.Y., U.S. | E8 | 108 |
| Depew, Ok., U.S. | D10 | 116 |
| Depoe Bay, Or., U.S. | F1 | 122 |
| Depok, Indon. | j13 | 39a |
| Deport, Tx., U.S. | F11 | 116 |
| Deposit, N.Y., U.S. | E11 | 108 |
| Depue, Il., U.S. | I6 | 110 |
| Dêqên, China | F6 | 30 |
| De Queen, Ar., U.S. | H2 | 114 |
| De Quincy, La., U.S. | L3 | 114 |
| *Dera, Lach, val., Afr.* | A8 | 58 |
| Dera Ghāzi Khān, Pak. | E4 | 44 |
| Dera Ismāīl Khān, Pak. | E4 | 44 |
| Derbent, Russia | I7 | 26 |
| Derby, Austl. | M7 | 70 |
| Derby, Eng., U.K. | I12 | 8 |
| Derby, Ks., U.S. | N10 | 118 |
| Derby, Me., U.S. | B18 | 108 |
| Derby, N.Y., U.S. | E8 | 108 |
| Derby Line, Vt., U.S. | B14 | 108 |
| *Derbyshire, co., Eng., U.K.* | H12 | 8 |
| Derdepoort, S. Afr. | E8 | 66 |
| Derecske, Hung. | H21 | 10 |
| Derev'anka, Russia | K24 | 6 |
| De Ridder, La., U.S. | L3 | 114 |
| Derik, Tur. | C6 | 48 |
| Dermott, Ar., U.S. | I5 | 114 |
| *Dernieres, Isles, is., La., U.S.* | M6 | 114 |
| *Déroute, Passage de la, strt., Eur.* | L11 | 8 |
| Derry, N.H., U.S. | E15 | 108 |
| Derry see Londonderry, N. Ire., U.K. | F6 | 8 |
| Derudeb, Sudan | I9 | 60 |
| De Rust, S. Afr. | I6 | 66 |
| Derval, Fr. | E5 | 14 |
| Derventa, Bos. | E1 | 20 |
| Derwent, Ab., Can. | D24 | 102 |
| *Derwent, stm., Austl.* | N7 | 70 |
| Deržavinsk, Kaz. | G11 | 26 |
| *Desaguadero, stm., Arg.* | G5 | 80 |
| *Desaguadero, stm., Bol.* | G7 | 82 |
| Des Allemands, La., U.S. | M6 | 114 |
| Des Arc, Ar., U.S. | H5 | 114 |
| *Descabezado Grande, Volcán, vol., Chile* | H3 | 80 |
| Descanso, Braz. | D12 | 80 |
| Descanso, Ca., U.S. | L9 | 124 |
| Descartes, Fr. | F7 | 14 |
| Deschambault Lake, Sk., Can. | D11 | 104 |
| *Deschambault Lake, l., Sk., Can.* | D11 | 104 |
| *Descharme Lake, l., Sk., Can.* | A5 | 104 |
| *Deschutes, stm., Or., U.S.* | E5 | 122 |
| *Deschutes, stm., Wa., U.S.* | D3 | 122 |
| Desdunes, Haiti | E8 | 94 |
| Dese, Eth. | F8 | 56 |
| *Deseado, stm., Arg.* | F3 | 78 |
| *Desengaño, Punta, c., Arg.* | F3 | 78 |
| Desenzano del Garda, Italy | D5 | 18 |
| *Deseret Peak, mtn., Ut., U.S.* | D4 | 120 |
| Deseronto, On., Can. | F18 | 110 |
| *Desertas, Ilhas, is., Port.* | m21 | 17a |
| Desert Hot Springs, Ca., U.S. | K9 | 124 |
| *Desert Peak, mtn., Ut., U.S.* | C3 | 120 |
| Desha, Ar., U.S. | G5 | 114 |
| Desheng, China | B10 | 40 |
| Deshler, Ne., U.S. | K10 | 118 |
| Deshler, Oh., U.S. | F3 | 108 |
| Desiderio Tello, Arg. | F5 | 80 |
| Desloge, Mo., U.S. | E6 | 114 |
| Desmarais, Ab., Can. | B21 | 102 |
| De Smet, S.D., U.S. | G10 | 118 |
| Des Moines, Ia., U.S. | I2 | 110 |
| Des Moines, N.M., U.S. | C3 | 116 |
| *Des Moines, stm., U.S.* | J3 | 110 |
| *Desna, stm., Eur.* | G4 | 26 |
| *Desolación, Isla, i., Chile* | G2 | 78 |
| De Soto, Il., U.S. | E7 | 114 |
| De Soto, Mo., U.S. | D6 | 114 |
| Des Plaines, Il., U.S. | H8 | 110 |
| *Desroches, Île, i., Sey.* | C10 | 58 |
| Dessau, Ger. | D12 | 10 |
| Destin, Fl., U.S. | L10 | 114 |
| Destruction Bay, Yk., Can. | F25 | 100 |
| Desvres, Fr. | B8 | 14 |
| Deta, Rom. | D5 | 20 |
| Detčino, Russia | G19 | 22 |
| Dete, Zimb. | B8 | 66 |
| Detmold, Ger. | D8 | 10 |
| *Detour, Point, c., Mi., U.S.* | E9 | 110 |
| De Tour Village, Mi., U.S. | D12 | 110 |
| Detroit, Mi., U.S. | H12 | 110 |
| Detroit, Or., U.S. | F3 | 122 |
| Detroit, Tx., U.S. | I1 | 114 |
| Detroit Beach, Mi., U.S. | I12 | 110 |
| Detroit Lakes, Mn., U.S. | E12 | 118 |
| Deurne, Bel. | F5 | 12 |
| Deurne, Neth. | F8 | 12 |
| *Deutsche Bucht, b., Ger.* | A7 | 10 |
| *Deux-Sèvres, dept., Fr.* | F6 | 14 |
| Deva, Rom. | D6 | 20 |
| Devakottai, India | H5 | 46 |
| De Valls Bluff, Ar., U.S. | H5 | 114 |
| Dev'atiny, Russia | K25 | 6 |
| Dévaványa, Hung. | H20 | 10 |
| Devecser, Hung. | H17 | 10 |
| Deventer, Neth. | D9 | 12 |
| *De View, Bayou, stm., Ar., U.S.* | G5 | 114 |
| *Devils, stm., Tx., U.S.* | J5 | 116 |
| *Devils Island see Diable, Île du, i., Fr. Gu.* | B8 | 76 |
| Devils Lake, N.D., U.S. | C9 | 118 |
| *Devils Lake, l., N.D., U.S.* | C8 | 118 |
| *Devils Paw, mtn., N.A.* | G28 | 100 |
| *Devils Tower, mtn., Wy., U.S.* | G3 | 118 |
| Devine, B.C., Can. | G12 | 102 |
| Devine, Tx., U.S. | J8 | 116 |
| Devon, Ab., Can. | D21 | 102 |
| *Devon, co., Eng., U.K.* | K10 | 8 |
| *Devon Island, i., N.T., Can.* | B11 | 86 |
| Devonport, Austl. | M7 | 70 |
| Devonport, N.Z. | B5 | 72 |
| Devoto, Arg. | F7 | 80 |
| Dewar, Ok., U.S. | D11 | 116 |
| Dewās, India | I7 | 44 |
| Dewetsdorp, S. Afr. | G8 | 66 |
| Dewey, Ok., U.S. | C11 | 116 |
| Deweyville, Tx., U.S. | L3 | 114 |
| De Witt, Ar., U.S. | H5 | 114 |
| De Witt, Ia., U.S. | I5 | 110 |
| De Witt, Mi., U.S. | H11 | 110 |
| De Witt, Ne., U.S. | K11 | 118 |
| De Witt, N.Y., U.S. | D10 | 108 |
| Dexter, Me., U.S. | B17 | 108 |
| Dexter, Mi., U.S. | E3 | 108 |
| Dexter, Mo., U.S. | F7 | 114 |
| Dexter, N.M., U.S. | F2 | 116 |
| Dexter, N.Y., U.S. | C10 | 108 |
| *Dexterity Fiord, N.T., Can.* | B18 | 96 |
| Deyhūk, Iran | E14 | 48 |
| Deyyer, Iran | H11 | 48 |
| Dezfūl, Iran | E10 | 48 |
| Dezhou, China | F4 | 32 |
| *Dežneva, mys, c., Russia* | D30 | 28 |
| Dháfni, Grc. | L6 | 20 |
| Dhahab, Egypt | C8 | 60 |
| Dhahabān, Sau. Ar. | D1 | 47 |
| Dhahran see Aẓ-Ẓahrān, Sau. Ar. | A7 | 47 |
| Dhaka, Bngl. | I14 | 44 |
| Dhamār, Yemen | G4 | 47 |
| Dhamtari, India | B6 | 46 |
| Dhanbād, India | I12 | 44 |
| Dhangaḍhī, Nepal | F9 | 44 |
| D'Hanis, Tx., U.S. | J7 | 116 |
| Dhār, India | I6 | 44 |
| Dharangaon, India | B3 | 46 |
| Dhārāpuram, India | G4 | 46 |
| Dharmavaram, India | E4 | 46 |
| Dharmshāla, India | D7 | 44 |
| Dhaulpur, India | G7 | 44 |
| *Dhawlāgiri, mtn., Nepal* | F10 | 44 |
| *Dhelfoí, hist., Grc.* | K6 | 20 |
| Dhībān, Jord. | E5 | 50 |
| *Dhodhekánisos (Dodecanese), is., Grc.* | M10 | 20 |
| Dholka, India | I5 | 44 |
| Dhorāji, India | J4 | 44 |
| Dhuburi, India | G13 | 44 |
| Dhule, India | J6 | 44 |
| *Dhytikí Ellás, prov., Grc.* | K5 | 20 |
| *Dhytikí Makedhonía, prov., Grc.* | I5 | 20 |
| *Diable, Île du, i., Fr. Gu.* | B8 | 76 |
| *Diablo, Pico del, mtn., Mex.* | B2 | 90 |
| *Diablo Range, mts., Ca., U.S.* | G4 | 124 |
| *Diablotins, Morne, mtn., Dom.* | G14 | 94 |
| Diagonal, Ia., U.S. | K13 | 118 |
| *Diaka, mth., Mali* | D7 | 64 |
| Dialakoto, Sen. | E3 | 64 |
| Diamante, Arg. | G8 | 80 |
| *Diamante, stm., Arg.* | H5 | 80 |
| Diamantina, Braz. | E7 | 79 |
| *Diamantina, stm., Austl.* | F3 | 70 |
| Diamantino, Braz. | F13 | 82 |
| *Diamantino, stm., Braz.* | D2 | 79 |
| Diamond, Mo., U.S. | E2 | 114 |
| Diamond Harbour, India | I13 | 44 |
| *Diamond Islets, is., Austl.* | A9 | 70 |
| *Diamond Peak, mtn., Id., U.S.* | F12 | 122 |
| *Diamond Peak, mtn., Or., U.S.* | G3 | 122 |
| Diamondville, Wy., U.S. | C6 | 120 |
| *Diana Bay, b., Can.* | D19 | 96 |
| *Dian Chi, l., China* | B7 | 40 |
| Diangounté Kamara, Mali | D5 | 64 |
| Dianhu, China | B8 | 34 |
| Dianópolis, Braz. | F9 | 76 |
| Diapaga, Burkina | E10 | 64 |
| Diaz, Ar., U.S. | G5 | 114 |
| Dibaya, D.R.C. | C4 | 58 |
| Dibeng, S. Afr. | F6 | 66 |
| D'Iberville, Ms., U.S. | L8 | 114 |
| Dibete, Bots. | D8 | 66 |
| Diboll, Tx., U.S. | K2 | 114 |
| Dibrugarh, India | G16 | 44 |
| Dickens, Tx., U.S. | F6 | 116 |
| Dickinson, N.D., U.S. | E5 | 118 |
| Dickinson, Tx., U.S. | J11 | 116 |
| Dickson, Ok., U.S. | E10 | 116 |
| Dickson, Tn., U.S. | F9 | 114 |
| Didimbo, Ang. | A5 | 66 |
| Didsbury, Ab., Can. | F20 | 102 |
| Die, Fr. | H12 | 14 |
| Diébougou, Burkina | F8 | 64 |
| Dieciocho de Julio, Ur. | G12 | 80 |
| *Diefenbaker, Lake, res., Sk., Can.* | G8 | 104 |
| Diego de Almagro, Chile | D3 | 80 |
| *Diego de Ocampo, Pico, mtn., Dom. Rep.* | E9 | 94 |
| *Diego Garcia, i., B.I.O.T.* | J8 | 24 |
| *Diego Ramírez, Islas, is., Chile* | H3 | 78 |
| Diembéring, Sen. | E1 | 64 |
| Dien Bien Phu, Viet. | D7 | 40 |
| Dieppe, Fr. | L15 | 8 |
| Dieppe, N.B., Can. | F9 | 106 |
| Dieren, Neth. | D9 | 12 |
| Dierks, Ar., U.S. | H2 | 114 |
| Diessenhofen, Switz. | C10 | 13 |
| Dietikon, Switz. | D9 | 13 |
| Dietrich, Id., U.S. | H11 | 122 |
| Dieulefit, Fr. | H12 | 14 |
| Dieuze, Fr. | D13 | 14 |
| Diez de Octubre, Mex. | E7 | 90 |
| Dif, Kenya | A8 | 58 |
| Difang, China | H5 | 32 |
| Differdange, Lux. | I8 | 12 |
| Digboi, India | G16 | 44 |
| Digby, N.S., Can. | H8 | 106 |
| *Digby Neck, pen., N.S., Can.* | H7 | 106 |
| *Digges Islands, is., N.T., Can.* | D17 | 96 |

| Name | Map Ref. | Page |
|---|---|---|
| Dighton, Ks., U.S. | M7 | 118 |
| Digne, Fr. | H13 | 14 |
| Digoin, Fr. | F10 | 14 |
| Digras, India | B4 | 46 |
| Digri, Pak. | H3 | 44 |
| *Digul, stm., Indon.* | G11 | 38 |
| Dijon, Fr. | E12 | 14 |
| Dikaja, Russia | B22 | 22 |
| Dike, Ia., U.S. | H3 | 110 |
| Dikhil, Dji. | F9 | 56 |
| Dikili, Tur. | J10 | 20 |
| Dikodougou, C. Iv. | G7 | 64 |
| Diksmuide (Dixmude), Bel. | F2 | 12 |
| Dikson, Russia | C8 | 28 |
| Dikwa, Nig. | F9 | 54 |
| Dila, Eth. | N10 | 60 |
| Dili, Indon. | G8 | 38 |
| Dill City, Ok., U.S. | D7 | 116 |
| Diller, Ne., U.S. | K11 | 118 |
| Dilley, Tx., U.S. | K7 | 116 |
| Dilling, Sudan | K5 | 60 |
| Dillingen [an der Donau], Ger. | G10 | 10 |
| Dillingham, Ak., U.S. | G15 | 100 |
| Dillon, Co., U.S. | E10 | 120 |
| Dillon, Mt., U.S. | E13 | 122 |
| Dillon, S.C., U.S. | E7 | 112 |
| *Dillon, stm., Can.* | C5 | 104 |
| *Dillon Lake, l., Sk., Can.* | C5 | 104 |
| *Dillon Lake, res., Oh., U.S.* | G4 | 108 |
| *Dillon Mountain, mtn., N.M., U.S.* | K8 | 120 |
| Dillwyn, Va., U.S. | B8 | 112 |
| Dilly, Mali | D6 | 64 |
| Dilolo, D.R.C. | D4 | 58 |
| Dilworth, Mn., U.S. | E11 | 118 |
| Dimāpur, India | H15 | 44 |
| Dimashq (Damascus), Syria | A6 | 50 |
| Dimboola, Austl. | K5 | 70 |
| Dime, Eth. | N9 | 60 |
| Dime Box, Tx., U.S. | I10 | 116 |
| Dimitrovgrad, Bul. | G9 | 20 |
| Dimitrovgrad, Russia | G7 | 26 |
| Dimmitt, Tx., U.S. | E4 | 116 |
| Dimona, Isr. | F4 | 50 |
| Dinājpur, Bngl. | H13 | 44 |
| Dinan, Fr. | D4 | 14 |
| Dinant, Bel. | H6 | 12 |
| *Dinara (Dinaric Alps), mts., Eur.* | F11 | 18 |
| Dinard, Fr. | D4 | 14 |
| *Dinaric Alps see Dinara, mts., Eur.* | F11 | 18 |
| *Dindar, Nahr ad- (Dinder), stm., Afr.* | K8 | 60 |
| Dindigul, India | G4 | 46 |
| Dindima, Nig. | F15 | 64 |
| *Dingalan Bay, b., Phil.* | n19 | 39b |
| Dinggyê, China | F4 | 30 |
| Dinghai, China | E11 | 34 |
| *Dingle Bay, b., Ire.* | I3 | 8 |
| Dingnan, China | K3 | 34 |
| Dingolfing, Ger. | G12 | 10 |
| Dingshuzhen, China | D8 | 34 |
| Dinguiraye, Gui. | F4 | 64 |
| Dingwall, N.S., Can. | F13 | 106 |
| Dingxi, China | D7 | 30 |
| Dingxian, China | E2 | 32 |
| Dingyuan, China | C6 | 34 |
| Dinh Lap, Viet. | D9 | 40 |
| Dinkelsbühl, Ger. | F10 | 10 |
| Dinokwe, Bots. | D8 | 66 |
| Dinorwic, On., Can. | I22 | 104 |
| *Dinorwic Lake, l., On., Can.* | I22 | 104 |
| Dinosaur, Co., U.S. | D7 | 120 |
| *Dinosaur Lake, res., B.C., Can.* | B12 | 102 |
| *Dinosaur Provincial Park, Ab., Can.* | G23 | 102 |
| Dinsmore, Sk., Can. | G7 | 104 |
| Dinuba, Ca., U.S. | H6 | 124 |
| Dinwiddie, Va., U.S. | B9 | 112 |
| Dioïla, Mali | E6 | 64 |
| Diomede, Ak., U.S. | D10 | 100 |
| Dionísio, Braz. | E7 | 79 |
| Dionísio Cerqueira, Braz. | D12 | 80 |
| *Dionne, Lac, l., P.Q., Can.* | C6 | 106 |
| Diorama, Braz. | D3 | 79 |
| Diouloulou, Sen. | E1 | 64 |
| Dioundiou, Niger | E11 | 64 |
| Dioura, Mali | D7 | 64 |
| Diourbel, Sen. | D1 | 64 |
| Dipkarpaz, N. Cyp. | D3 | 48 |
| Dipolog, Phil. | D7 | 38 |
| Dippoldiswalde, Ger. | E13 | 10 |
| Dīr, Pak. | C4 | 44 |
| Dire Dawa, Eth. | G9 | 56 |
| Diriamba, Nic. | F8 | 92 |
| Dirico, Ang. | A5 | 66 |
| Diriomo, Nic. | F8 | 92 |
| Dirj, Libya | E16 | 62 |
| *Dirk Hartog Island, i., Austl.* | E2 | 68 |
| Dirrah, Sudan | K4 | 60 |
| Dirranbandi, Austl. | G8 | 70 |
| Dirs, Sau. Ar. | E3 | 47 |
| *Dirty Devil, stm., Ut., U.S.* | F6 | 120 |
| *Disappointment, Cape, c., S. Geor.* | J11 | 74 |
| *Disappointment, Cape, c., Wa., U.S.* | D1 | 122 |
| *Disappointment, Lake, l., Austl.* | D4 | 68 |
| *Disaster Bay, b., Austl.* | K9 | 70 |
| *Discovery Bay, b., Austl.* | L4 | 70 |
| *Discovery Passage, strt., B.C., Can.* | G9 | 102 |
| Disentis, Switz. | E10 | 13 |
| Dishman, Wa., U.S. | C8 | 122 |
| Dishnā, Egypt | D7 | 60 |
| *Disko, i., Grnld.* | C22 | 96 |
| *Dismal, stm., Ne., U.S.* | J7 | 118 |
| *Dismal Lakes, l., N.T., Can.* | C9 | 96 |
| Disney, Ok., U.S. | C11 | 116 |
| Disraeli, P.Q., Can. | B15 | 108 |
| *Dissimieux, Lac, l., P.Q., Can.* | C4 | 106 |
| *Distrito Federal, dept., Braz.* | C5 | 79 |
| *Distrito Federal, dept., Ven.* | B9 | 84 |
| Disūq, Egypt | B6 | 60 |
| Diu, India | J4 | 44 |
| Divalá, Pan. | I12 | 92 |
| Divenskaja, Russia | B13 | 22 |
| Divernon, Il., U.S. | C7 | 114 |
| Divinhe, Moz. | C12 | 66 |
| Divino, Braz. | F7 | 79 |
| Divinópolis, Braz. | F6 | 79 |
| *Divisor, Serra do (Cordillera Ultraoriental), plat., S.A.* | C5 | 82 |
| Divnoje, Russia | H6 | 26 |
| Divriği, Tur. | B5 | 48 |
| Dix, Ne., U.S. | J4 | 118 |
| *Dix, stm., Ky., U.S.* | B2 | 112 |
| Dixfield, Me., U.S. | C16 | 108 |
| *Dixie Valley, val., Nv., U.S.* | D7 | 124 |
| Dixmude (Diksmuide), Bel. | F2 | 12 |
| Dixon, Ca., U.S. | F4 | 124 |
| Dixon, Il., U.S. | I6 | 110 |
| Dixon, Ky., U.S. | E9 | 114 |
| Dixon, Mo., U.S. | E4 | 114 |
| Dixon, N.M., U.S. | H11 | 120 |
| *Dixon Entrance, strt., N.A.* | C2 | 102 |
| Dixons Mills, Al., U.S. | J9 | 114 |
| *Diyālā (Sīrvān), stm., Asia* | E8 | 48 |
| Diyarbakır, Tur. | C6 | 48 |
| Dizhou, China | C9 | 40 |
| *Dja, stm., Afr.* | H9 | 54 |
| Djakarta see Jakarta, Indon. | j13 | 39a |
| Djamâa, Alg. | D13 | 62 |
| Djambala, Congo | B2 | 58 |
| Djanet, Alg. | H15 | 62 |
| *Djedi, Oued, val., Alg.* | C13 | 62 |
| Djema, C.A.R. | N3 | 60 |
| *Djemila, hist., Alg.* | B13 | 62 |
| Djénné, Mali | E7 | 64 |
| *Djérem, stm., Cam.* | G9 | 54 |
| Djibo, Burkina | D9 | 64 |
| Djibouti, Dji. | F9 | 56 |
| *Djibouti, ctry., Afr.* | F9 | 56 |
| Djokupunda, D.R.C. | C4 | 58 |
| Djougou, Benin | G10 | 64 |
| Djúpivogur, Ice. | B6 | 6a |
| Djurås, Swe. | K14 | 6 |
| *Dmitrija Lapteva, proliv, strt., Russia* | C20 | 28 |
| Dmitrijevka, Russia | I23 | 22 |
| Dmitrijev-L'govskij, Russia | I18 | 22 |
| Dmitrov, Russia | E20 | 22 |
| Dmitrovskij Pogost, Russia | F22 | 22 |
| Dmitrovsk-Orlovskij, Russia | I18 | 22 |
| Dnepropetrovsk see Dnipropetrovs'k, Ukr. | H4 | 26 |
| *Dnieper, stm., Eur.* | H4 | 26 |
| Dniprodzerzhyns'k, Ukr. | H4 | 26 |
| Dnipropetrovs'k, Ukr. | H4 | 26 |
| *Dnister, stm., Eur.* | F13 | 4 |
| *Dnistrovs'kyy lyman, l., Ukr.* | C14 | 20 |
| *Dnjaprouska Buhski, kanal, Bela.* | I7 | 22 |
| Dno, Russia | D12 | 22 |
| Doaktown, N.B., Can. | F7 | 106 |
| Doany, Madag. | o23 | 67b |
| Doba, Chad | E4 | 56 |
| Dobane, C.A.R. | N3 | 60 |
| Dobbiaco, Italy | C7 | 18 |
| Dobczyce, Pol. | F20 | 10 |
| Dobele, Lat. | E6 | 22 |
| Döbeln, Ger. | D13 | 10 |
| *Doberai, Jazirah, pen., Indon.* | F9 | 38 |
| Doboj, Bos. | E2 | 20 |
| Dobr'anka, Russia | F9 | 26 |
| Dobrič, Bul. | F11 | 20 |
| Dobrinka, Russia | I23 | 22 |
| Dobříš, Czech Rep. | F14 | 10 |
| Dobromyl', Ukr. | F22 | 10 |
| *Dobrudžansko plato, plat., Bul.* | F11 | 20 |
| *Dobruja, hist. reg., Eur.* | E12 | 20 |
| Dobruš, Bela. | I14 | 22 |
| Dobson, N.C., U.S. | C6 | 112 |
| *Doce, stm., Braz.* | E8 | 79 |
| *Doce, stm., Braz.* | E3 | 79 |
| Dock Junction, Ga., U.S. | H5 | 112 |
| Doctor Arroyo, Mex. | F9 | 90 |
| Doctor Cecilio Báez, Para. | C10 | 80 |
| Doctor Pedro P. Peña, Para. | B7 | 80 |
| Dod Ballāpur, India | F4 | 46 |
| Doddridge, Ar., U.S. | I3 | 114 |
| Doddsville, Ms., U.S. | I6 | 114 |
| *Dodecanese see Dhodhekánisos, is., Grc.* | M10 | 20 |
| Dodge, Ne., U.S. | J11 | 118 |
| Dodge Center, Mn., U.S. | F3 | 110 |
| Dodge City, Ks., U.S. | N7 | 118 |
| Dodgeville, Wi., U.S. | H5 | 110 |
| Dodola, Eth. | N10 | 60 |
| Dodoma, Tan. | C7 | 58 |
| Dodsland, Sk., Can. | G6 | 104 |
| Dodson, La., U.S. | J4 | 114 |
| Dodson, Mt., U.S. | B17 | 122 |
| Dodson, Tx., U.S. | E6 | 116 |
| Doe River, B.C., Can. | A14 | 102 |
| Doerun, Ga., U.S. | H3 | 112 |
| Doetinchem, Neth. | E9 | 12 |
| *Dogai Coring, l., China* | C13 | 44 |
| Dog Creek, B.C., Can. | F12 | 102 |
| *Dog Creek, stm., B.C., Can.* | F12 | 102 |
| *Dog Island, i., Anguilla* | E13 | 94 |
| *Dog Lake, l., Mb., Can.* | G16 | 104 |
| *Dōgo, i., Japan* | K8 | 36 |
| Do Gonbadān, Iran | F11 | 48 |
| Dogondoutchi, Niger | E12 | 64 |
| *Dogpound Creek, stm., Ab., Can.* | F20 | 102 |
| Doğubayazıt, Tur. | B8 | 48 |
| Doha see Ad-Dawḥah, Qatar | B7 | 47 |
| *Doiran, Lake, l., Eur.* | H6 | 20 |
| *Dois de Novembro, Cachoeira, wtfl, Braz.* | C10 | 82 |
| Dokka, Nor. | K12 | 6 |
| Doksy, Czech Rep. | E14 | 10 |
| Dokšycy, Bela. | G10 | 22 |
| Doland, S.D., U.S. | G9 | 118 |
| Dolbeau, P.Q., Can. | G18 | 96 |
| Dol-de-Bretagne, Fr. | D5 | 14 |
| Dole, Fr. | E12 | 14 |
| Dolega, Pan. | C1 | 84 |
| Dolgeville, N.Y., U.S. | D12 | 108 |
| Dolgoje, Russia | I20 | 22 |
| Dolgorukovo, Russia | I21 | 22 |
| Dolinsk, Russia | H20 | 28 |
| Dolisie, Congo | B2 | 58 |
| *Dolj, co., Rom.* | E7 | 20 |
| *Dollard, b., Eur.* | B11 | 12 |
| Dolmatovskij, Russia | D25 | 22 |
| *Dolomites see Dolomiti, mts., Italy* | C6 | 18 |
| *Dolomiti, mts., Italy* | C6 | 18 |
| Dolores, Arg. | I10 | 80 |
| Dolores, Co., U.S. | G8 | 120 |
| Dolores, Col. | F5 | 84 |
| Dolores, Guat. | I15 | 90 |
| Dolores, Ur. | G9 | 80 |
| Dolores, Ven. | C8 | 84 |
| *Dolores, stm., U.S.* | F8 | 120 |
| Dolores Hidalgo, Mex. | G9 | 90 |
| *Dolphin and Union Strait, strt., N.T., Can.* | C9 | 96 |
| Dolzhak, Ukr. | A10 | 20 |
| Dom Aquino, Braz. | C1 | 79 |
| Domažlice, Czech Rep. | F12 | 10 |
| Dombarovskij, Russia | G9 | 26 |
| Dombås, Nor. | J11 | 6 |
| Dombrád, Hung. | G21 | 10 |
| Dom Cavati, Braz. | E7 | 79 |
| Dome Creek, B.C., Can. | D13 | 102 |
| Domeyko, Chile | E3 | 80 |
| *Domeyko, Cordillera, mts., Chile* | B4 | 80 |
| Domfront, Fr. | D6 | 14 |
| Domiciano Ribeiro, Braz. | D5 | 79 |
| Domíngo M. Irala, Para. | C11 | 80 |
| Domingos Martins, Braz. | F8 | 79 |
| *Dominica, ctry., N.A.* | G14 | 94 |
| Dominical, C.R. | H11 | 92 |
| *Dominican Republic (República Dominicana), ctry., N.A.* | E9 | 94 |
| *Dominica Passage, strt., N.A.* | G14 | 94 |
| Dominion, N.S., Can. | F13 | 106 |
| *Dominion, Cape, c., N.T., Can.* | C18 | 96 |
| Dominion City, Mb., Can. | I17 | 104 |
| Dom Joaquim, Braz. | E7 | 79 |
| Domo, Eth. | G10 | 56 |
| Domodedovo, Russia | F20 | 22 |
| Domodossola, Italy | C3 | 18 |
| Domoni, Com. | I16 | 67a |
| Dom Pedrito, Braz. | F11 | 80 |
| Domremy, Sk., Can. | F9 | 104 |
| Dom Silvério, Braz. | F7 | 79 |
| *Domuyo, Volcán, vol., Arg.* | I3 | 80 |
| *Don, stm., Russia* | H6 | 26 |
| *Don, stm., Scot., U.K.* | D11 | 8 |
| Dona Ana, N.M., U.S. | L10 | 120 |
| Donadeu, Arg. | D7 | 80 |
| Donald, Austl. | K5 | 70 |
| Donalda, Ab., Can. | E22 | 102 |
| Donaldson, Ar., U.S. | H4 | 114 |
| Donaldsonville, La., U.S. | L6 | 114 |
| Donalsonville, Ga., U.S. | H2 | 112 |
| *Doñana, Parque Nacional de, Spain* | H5 | 16 |
| Donaueschingen, Ger. | H8 | 10 |
| Donauwörth, Ger. | G10 | 10 |
| Don Benito, Spain | G6 | 16 |
| Doncaster, Eng., U.K. | H12 | 8 |
| Dondo, Ang. | C2 | 58 |
| Dondo, Moz. | B12 | 66 |
| *Dondra Head, c., Sri L.* | J6 | 46 |
| Dondușeni, Mol. | A11 | 20 |
| Donegal, Ire. | G5 | 8 |
| *Donegal, co., Ire.* | G5 | 8 |
| *Donegal Bay, b., Ire.* | G5 | 8 |
| Doneraile, S.C., U.S. | E7 | 112 |
| Donets'k, Ukr. | H5 | 26 |
| *Dong, stm., China* | L6 | 34 |
| *Donga, stm., Nig.* | G15 | 64 |
| Dong'an, China | B3 | 34 |
| Dongara, Austl. | E2 | 68 |
| Dongba, China | D8 | 34 |
| Dongchuan, China | A7 | 40 |
| Dongdaoan, China | E5 | 32 |
| Dong'ezhen, China | G4 | 32 |
| Dongfang (Basuo), China | E10 | 40 |
| Dongfeng, China | A13 | 32 |
| Donggu, China | I4 | 34 |
| Dongguan, China | L2 | 34 |
| Dongguanyingzi, China | B8 | 32 |
| *Donghai Dao, i., China* | D11 | 40 |
| Dong Hoi, Viet. | F9 | 40 |
| Dongmen, China | G3 | 34 |
| *Dong Nai, stm., Viet.* | I9 | 40 |
| Dongshi, China | K7 | 34 |
| Dongtai, China | C9 | 34 |
| *Dongting Hu, l., China* | G1 | 34 |
| Dongyang, China | F9 | 34 |
| Dongzhi, China | E5 | 34 |
| Donie, Tx., U.S. | H10 | 116 |
| Doniphan, Mo., U.S. | F6 | 114 |
| Doniphan, Ne., U.S. | K9 | 118 |
| *Donjek, stm., Yk., Can.* | F25 | 100 |
| Donji Vakuf, Bos. | E12 | 18 |
| Don Matías, Col. | D5 | 84 |
| Donna, Tx., U.S. | M8 | 116 |
| Donnelly, Ab., Can. | B17 | 102 |
| Donnelly, Id., U.S. | F9 | 122 |
| Donner, La., U.S. | M6 | 114 |
| *Donner Pass, Ca., U.S.* | E5 | 124 |
| *Donner und Blitzen, stm., Or., U.S.* | G7 | 122 |
| Donora, Pa., U.S. | G7 | 108 |
| Donostia (San Sebastián), Spain | B10 | 16 |
| *Don Peninsula, pen., B.C., Can.* | E6 | 102 |
| Donskoj, Russia | H21 | 22 |
| Donskoje, Russia | I22 | 22 |
| Doolow, Som. | H9 | 56 |
| Doomadgee, Austl. | A3 | 70 |
| Doon, Ia., U.S. | H11 | 118 |
| Doornik (Tournai), Bel. | G3 | 12 |
| *Door Peninsula, pen., Wi., U.S.* | F8 | 110 |
| Dora, Al., U.S. | I9 | 114 |
| Doraville, Ga., U.S. | F2 | 112 |
| *Dorcheat, Bayou, stm., U.S.* | I3 | 114 |
| Dorchester, Eng., U.K. | K11 | 8 |
| Dorchester, N.B., Can. | G9 | 106 |
| Dorchester, Ne., U.S. | K10 | 118 |
| Dorchester, On., Can. | H14 | 110 |
| Dorchester, Wi., U.S. | E5 | 110 |
| *Dorchester, Cape, c., N.T., Can.* | C17 | 96 |
| Dorchester Crossing, N.B., Can. | F9 | 106 |
| *Dordogne, dept., Fr.* | G7 | 14 |
| *Dordogne, stm., Fr.* | H8 | 14 |
| Dordrecht, Neth. | E6 | 12 |
| Dordrecht, S. Afr. | H8 | 66 |
| *Doré, stm., Sk., Can.* | D7 | 104 |
| Doré Lake, Sk., Can. | D7 | 104 |
| *Doré Lake, l., Sk., Can.* | D7 | 104 |
| Dorena, Or., U.S. | G3 | 122 |
| Dores do Indaiá, Braz. | E6 | 79 |
| Dornach, Switz. | D8 | 13 |
| Dornbirn, Aus. | H9 | 10 |
| Doro, Mali | C9 | 64 |
| Dorochovo, Russia | F19 | 22 |
| Dorog, Hung. | H18 | 10 |
| Dorogobuž, Russia | G16 | 22 |
| Dorohoi, Rom. | B10 | 20 |
| Dorrance, Ks., U.S. | M9 | 118 |
| *Dorre Island, i., Austl.* | E2 | 68 |
| Dorrigo, Austl. | H10 | 70 |
| Dorris, Ca., U.S. | C4 | 124 |
| *Dorset, co., Eng., U.K.* | K11 | 8 |
| Dortmund, Ger. | D7 | 10 |
| Dorton, Ky., U.S. | B4 | 112 |
| Dörtyol, Tur. | C4 | 48 |
| Do Rūd, Iran | E10 | 48 |
| Doruma, D.R.C. | H6 | 56 |
| *Dos, Canal Numero, Arg.* | I10 | 80 |
| Dosatuj, Russia | G15 | 28 |
| *Dos Bahías, Cabo, c., Arg.* | E3 | 78 |
| Doščatoje, Russia | F25 | 22 |
| Dos Hermanas, Spain | H6 | 16 |
| Dos Palos, Ca., U.S. | H5 | 124 |
| Dos Quebradas, Col. | E5 | 84 |
| Dossor, Kaz. | H8 | 26 |
| Dothan, Al., U.S. | K11 | 114 |
| Doting Cove, Nf., Can. | C20 | 106 |
| Dotnuva, Lith. | F6 | 22 |
| Douai, Fr. | B10 | 14 |
| Douala, Cam. | I14 | 64 |
| Douarnenez, Fr. | D2 | 14 |
| *Double, Lac, l., P.Q., Can.* | B3 | 106 |
| *Double Island Point, c., Austl.* | E10 | 70 |
| *Double Point, c., Austl.* | A7 | 70 |
| Double Springs, Al., U.S. | H9 | 114 |
| *Doubletop Peak, mtn., Wy., U.S.* | G15 | 122 |
| *Doubs, dept., Fr.* | E13 | 14 |
| *Doubs, stm., Eur.* | E12 | 14 |
| *Doubs, Saut de, wtfl, Eur.* | D6 | 13 |
| Doudeville, Fr. | C7 | 14 |
| Douentza, Mali | D8 | 64 |
| Douglas, Ak., U.S. | G27 | 100 |
| Douglas, Az., U.S. | M7 | 120 |
| Douglas, Ga., U.S. | H4 | 112 |
| Douglas, I. of Man | G9 | 8 |
| Douglas, Mb., Can. | I15 | 104 |
| Douglas, N.D., U.S. | D6 | 118 |
| Douglas, Wy., U.S. | B11 | 120 |
| *Douglas, Cape, c., Ak., U.S.* | G18 | 100 |
| *Douglas, Mount, mtn., Ak., U.S.* | G18 | 100 |
| *Douglas Channel, strt., B.C., Can.* | D5 | 102 |
| Douglas Lake, B.C., Can. | G14 | 102 |
| *Douglas Lake, res., Tn., U.S.* | C3 | 112 |
| *Douglas Lake Indian Reserve, B.C., Can.* | G14 | 102 |
| Douglass, Ks., U.S. | N10 | 118 |
| Douglasville, Ga., U.S. | F2 | 112 |
| Doulaincourt, Fr. | D12 | 14 |
| Doulevant-le-Château, Fr. | D11 | 14 |
| Doullens, Fr. | B9 | 14 |
| Doumanaba, Mali | F7 | 64 |
| Doura, Mali | E7 | 64 |
| *Dourada, Serra, plat., Braz.* | B4 | 79 |
| Dourados, Braz. | G1 | 79 |
| *Dourados, stm., Braz.* | G1 | 79 |
| Dourdan, Fr. | D9 | 14 |
| Dourkoulé, Chad | J2 | 60 |
| *Douro (Duero), stm., Eur.* | D4 | 16 |
| Doushanhe, China | D3 | 34 |
| Douz, Tun. | D15 | 62 |
| Dove Creek, Co., U.S. | G8 | 120 |
| Dover, Ar., U.S. | G3 | 114 |
| Dover, Austl. | N7 | 70 |
| Dover, De., U.S. | H11 | 108 |
| Dover, Eng., U.K. | J15 | 8 |
| Dover, Id., U.S. | B9 | 122 |
| Dover, N.C., U.S. | D9 | 112 |
| Dover, N.H., U.S. | D16 | 108 |
| Dover, N.J., U.S. | G12 | 108 |
| Dover, Oh., U.S. | G5 | 108 |
| Dover, Ok., U.S. | D9 | 116 |
| Dover, Tn., U.S. | F9 | 114 |
| *Dover, Strait of (Pas de Calais), strt., Eur.* | J15 | 8 |
| Dover-Foxcroft, Me., U.S. | B17 | 108 |
| Dovre, Nor. | K11 | 6 |
| Dovsk, Bela. | H13 | 22 |
| Dowagiac, Mi., U.S. | I9 | 110 |
| *Dowagiac, stm., Mi., U.S.* | H9 | 110 |
| Dow City, Ia., U.S. | J12 | 118 |
| Dowlatābād, Afg. | B2 | 44 |
| Dowlatābād, Afg. | B1 | 44 |
| Dowlat Yār, Afg. | C1 | 44 |
| *Dowling Lake, l., Ab., Can.* | F22 | 102 |
| Downey, Id., U.S. | H13 | 122 |
| Downieville, Ca., U.S. | E5 | 124 |
| Downing, Mo., U.S. | B4 | 114 |
| Downingtown, Pa., U.S. | G11 | 108 |
| Downs, Ks., U.S. | L9 | 118 |
| *Downs Mountain, mtn., Wy., U.S.* | G16 | 122 |
| Downsville, N.Y., U.S. | E12 | 108 |
| *Downton, Mount, mtn., B.C., Can.* | E10 | 102 |
| *Downton Lake, l., B.C., Can.* | G11 | 102 |
| Dows, Ia., U.S. | H2 | 110 |
| Dowshī, Afg. | C3 | 44 |
| Doyle, Ca., U.S. | D5 | 124 |
| Doyles, Nf., Can. | E14 | 106 |
| Doylestown, Oh., U.S. | G5 | 108 |
| Doylestown, Pa., U.S. | G11 | 108 |
| Doyline, La., U.S. | J3 | 114 |
| *Dōzen, is., Japan* | K8 | 36 |
| Dozier, Al., U.S. | K10 | 114 |
| *Dra'a, Hamada du, des., Alg.* | F7 | 62 |
| *Drâa, Oued, val., Afr.* | F5 | 62 |
| Dracena, Braz. | F3 | 79 |
| Dracut, Ma., U.S. | E15 | 108 |
| Drăgășani, Rom. | E8 | 20 |
| *Dragons Mouths, strt.* | B12 | 84 |
| Dragoon, Az., U.S. | L6 | 120 |
| Draguignan, Fr. | I13 | 14 |
| Drahičyn, Bela. | I8 | 22 |
| Drain, Or., U.S. | G2 | 122 |
| Drake, N.D., U.S. | D7 | 118 |
| *Drakensberg, mts., Afr.* | F9 | 66 |
| *Drake Passage, strt.* | J8 | 74 |
| *Drake Peak, mtn., Or., U.S.* | H5 | 122 |
| Drakesboro, Ky., U.S. | E9 | 114 |
| Drakes Branch, Va., U.S. | C8 | 112 |
| Dráma, Grc. | H8 | 20 |
| Drammen, Nor. | L12 | 6 |
| *Drang, stm., Asia* | H9 | 40 |
| Draper, N.C., U.S. | C7 | 112 |
| Draper, Ut., U.S. | D5 | 120 |
| *Drau (Drava) (Dráva), stm., Eur.* | C8 | 18 |
| *Drava (Drau) (Dráva), stm., Eur.* | D13 | 18 |
| Drawno, Pol. | B15 | 10 |
| Drayton, N.D., U.S. | C10 | 118 |
| Drayton, S.C., U.S. | E5 | 112 |
| Drayton Valley, Ab., Can. | D20 | 102 |
| Drean, Alg. | M2 | 18 |
| *Drenthe, prov., Neth.* | C10 | 12 |
| Dresden, Ger. | D13 | 10 |
| Dresden, Oh., U.S. | G4 | 108 |
| Dresden, On., Can. | H13 | 110 |
| Dresden, Tn., U.S. | F8 | 114 |
| Drètun', Bela. | F12 | 22 |
| Dreux, Fr. | D8 | 14 |
| Drew, Ms., U.S. | I6 | 114 |
| *Driftpile, stm., Ab., Can.* | B19 | 102 |
| *Drift Pile River Indian Reserve, Ab., Can.* | B19 | 102 |
| Driftwood, B.C., Can. | B8 | 102 |
| *Driftwood, stm., B.C., Can.* | B8 | 102 |
| *Driftwood, stm., In., U.S.* | C10 | 114 |
| Driggs, Id., U.S. | G14 | 122 |
| *Drin, stm., Alb.* | H3 | 20 |
| *Drina, stm., Eur.* | E3 | 20 |
| *Drini i Zi, stm., Eur.* | H4 | 20 |
| *Drinit, Gjiri i, b., Alb.* | H3 | 20 |
| Driscoll, Tx., U.S. | L9 | 116 |
| *Driskill Mountain, hill, La., U.S.* | J4 | 114 |
| Drobeta-Turnu Severin, Rom. | E6 | 20 |
| Drochia, Mol. | A11 | 20 |
| Drogheda, Ire. | H7 | 8 |
| Drohiczyn, Pol. | C22 | 10 |
| Drohobych, Ukr. | H2 | 26 |
| *Drôme, dept., Fr.* | H12 | 14 |
| Droskovo, Russia | I20 | 22 |
| Druja, Bela. | F10 | 22 |
| Drumheller, Ab., Can. | F22 | 102 |
| Drummond, Mt., U.S. | D12 | 122 |
| Drummond, Wi., U.S. | D4 | 110 |
| *Drummond Island, i., Mi., U.S.* | D12 | 110 |
| *Drummond Range, mts., Austl.* | E7 | 70 |
| Drummondville, P.Q., Can. | B14 | 108 |
| Drumright, Ok., U.S. | D10 | 116 |
| Druskininkai, Lith. | G6 | 22 |
| Družba, Kaz. | H14 | 26 |
| Drvar, Bos. | E11 | 18 |
| *Dry Bay, b., Ak., U.S.* | G25 | 100 |
| *Dryberry Lake, l., On., Can.* | I21 | 104 |
| *Dry Cimarron, stm., U.S.* | C3 | 116 |
| *Dry Creek Mountain, mtn., Nv., U.S.* | C9 | 124 |
| Dryden, On., Can. | I22 | 104 |
| *Dry Devils, stm., Tx., U.S.* | J6 | 116 |
| *Dry Fork, stm., Mo., U.S.* | E5 | 114 |
| Dry Prong, La., U.S. | K4 | 114 |
| Dry Ridge, Ky., U.S. | I2 | 108 |
| *Drysdale, stm., Austl.* | C5 | 68 |
| *Drysdale River National Park, Austl.* | B5 | 68 |
| *Dry Tortugas, is., Fl., U.S.* | O4 | 112 |
| Dschang, Cam. | I15 | 64 |
| Du, Ghana | F9 | 64 |
| *Duarte, Pico, mtn., Dom. Rep.* | E9 | 94 |
| Duartina, Braz. | G4 | 79 |
| Dubā, Sau. Ar. | H3 | 48 |
| Dubach, La., U.S. | J4 | 114 |
| Dubai see Dubayy, U.A.E. | B9 | 47 |
| Dubăsari (Dubesar'), Mol. | B13 | 20 |
| *Dubăsari, Lacul, res., Mol.* | B13 | 20 |
| *Dubawnt, stm., N.T., Can.* | D12 | 96 |
| *Dubawnt Lake, l., N.T., Can.* | D12 | 96 |
| Dubayy (Dubai), U.A.E. | B9 | 47 |
| Dubbo, Austl. | I8 | 70 |
| Dübendorf, Switz. | D10 | 13 |
| Dublin, Ga., U.S. | G4 | 112 |
| Dublin (Baile Átha Cliath), Ire. | H7 | 8 |
| Dublin, Tx., U.S. | G8 | 116 |
| Dublin, Va., U.S. | B6 | 112 |
| *Dublin, co., Ire.* | H7 | 8 |
| Dubna, Russia | E20 | 22 |
| Dubois, Id., U.S. | F13 | 122 |
| Dubois, In., U.S. | D10 | 114 |
| Du Bois, Ne., U.S. | K11 | 118 |
| Du Bois, Pa., U.S. | F8 | 108 |
| Dubois, Wy., U.S. | A7 | 120 |
| Dubovka, Russia | H6 | 26 |
| Dubréka, Gui. | G3 | 64 |
| Dubrouna, Bela. | G13 | 22 |
| Dubrovka, Russia | H16 | 22 |
| Dubrovka, Russia | B13 | 22 |
| Dubrovnik, Cro. | G2 | 20 |
| Dubuque, Ia., U.S. | H5 | 110 |
| Duchcov, Czech Rep. | E13 | 10 |
| Duchesne, Ut., U.S. | D6 | 120 |
| *Duchesne, stm., Ut., U.S.* | D6 | 120 |
| Duchess, Austl. | C3 | 70 |
| Duchovščina, Russia | F15 | 22 |
| *Duck, stm., Tn., U.S.* | G9 | 114 |
| Duck Bay, Mb., Can. | F14 | 104 |
| Duck Hill, Ms., U.S. | I7 | 114 |
| Duck Lake, Sk., Can. | F8 | 104 |
| *Duck Lake, l., Mb., Can.* | D16 | 104 |
| *Duck Mountain, mtn., Mb., Can.* | G13 | 104 |
| *Duck Mountain Provincial Park, Mb., Can.* | G14 | 104 |
| *Duck Mountain Provincial Park, Sk., Can.* | G13 | 104 |
| *Du Couedic, Cape, c., Austl.* | K2 | 70 |
| *Duda, stm., Col.* | F5 | 84 |
| Dudelange, Lux. | J9 | 12 |
| Duderstadt, Ger. | D10 | 10 |
| Dudinka, Russia | D9 | 28 |
| Dudleyville, Az., U.S. | L6 | 120 |
| Dudorovskij, Russia | H18 | 22 |
| Duékoué, C. Iv. | H6 | 64 |
| *Duerna, stm., Spain* | C5 | 16 |
| *Duero (Douro), stm., Eur.* | D5 | 16 |
| Due West, S.C., U.S. | E4 | 112 |
| *Duffer Peak, mtn., Nv., U.S.* | C7 | 124 |
| *Dufourspitze, mtn., Eur.* | G14 | 14 |
| Dufur, Or., U.S. | E4 | 122 |
| *Duga-Zapadnaja, mys, c., Russia* | F21 | 28 |
| *Dugdemona, stm., La., U.S.* | J4 | 114 |
| Dugger, In., U.S. | C9 | 114 |
| *Dugi Otok, i., Cro.* | E10 | 18 |
| *Du Gué, stm., P.Q., Can.* | E18 | 96 |
| Duhi, Sudan | N5 | 60 |
| *Duida, Cerro, mtn., Ven.* | F10 | 84 |
| Duisburg, Ger. | D6 | 10 |
| Duitama, Col. | E6 | 84 |
| Duiwelskloof, S. Afr. | D10 | 66 |
| Dukambiya, Erit. | J9 | 60 |
| Duke, Ok., U.S. | E7 | 116 |
| *Duke of York Bay, b., N.T., Can.* | C16 | 96 |
| Duk Fadiat, Sudan | N6 | 60 |
| Duk Faiwil, Sudan | N6 | 60 |
| Dukhān, Qatar | B7 | 47 |
| Duki, Pak. | E3 | 44 |
| *Dukla Pass, Eur.* | F21 | 10 |
| Dūkštas, Lith. | F9 | 22 |
| Duku, Nig. | F12 | 64 |
| Dulan, China | D6 | 30 |
| Dul'apino, Russia | D23 | 22 |
| Dulce, N.M., U.S. | H10 | 120 |
| *Dulce, stm., Arg.* | F7 | 80 |
| *Dulce, Golfo, b., C.R.* | I11 | 92 |
| Dulce Nombre de Culmí, Hond. | B9 | 92 |
| Dul'durga, Russia | G14 | 28 |
| Dulkaninna, Austl. | G3 | 70 |
| Dulovka, Russia | D11 | 22 |
| Dulovo, Bul. | F11 | 20 |
| Duluth, Ga., U.S. | E2 | 112 |
| Duluth, Mn., U.S. | D3 | 110 |
| Duma, Bots. | B6 | 66 |
| Dūmā, Syria | A6 | 50 |
| Dumaguete, Phil. | D7 | 38 |
| *Dumaresq, stm., Austl.* | G9 | 70 |
| Dumaring, Indon. | E6 | 38 |
| Dumas, Ar., U.S. | I5 | 114 |
| Dumas, Tx., U.S. | D5 | 116 |
| Ḍumayr, Syria | A7 | 50 |
| Dumbarton, Scot., U.K. | F9 | 8 |
| Dumei, China | K6 | 34 |
| Dumfries, Scot., U.K. | F10 | 8 |
| *Dumfries and Galloway, prov., Scot., U.K.* | F9 | 8 |
| Duminiči, Russia | H18 | 22 |
| Dumka, India | H12 | 44 |
| Dumont, Ia., U.S. | H3 | 110 |
| Dumraon, India | H11 | 44 |
| Dumyāṭ, Egypt | B6 | 60 |
| *Dumyāṭ, Maṣabb, mth., Egypt* | F1 | 48 |
| Dunaföldvár, Hung. | I18 | 10 |
| Dunaharaszti, Hung. | H19 | 10 |
| *Dunajec, stm., Eur.* | E20 | 10 |
| Dunakeszi, Hung. | H19 | 10 |
| Dunaújváros, Hung. | I18 | 10 |
| Dunbar, W.V., U.S. | I5 | 108 |
| Dunblane, Sk., Can. | G8 | 104 |
| Duncan, Az., U.S. | L7 | 120 |
| Duncan, B.C., Can. | I11 | 102 |
| Duncan, Ms., U.S. | H6 | 114 |
| Duncan, Ok., U.S. | E9 | 116 |
| *Duncan, stm., B.C., Can.* | G17 | 102 |
| *Duncan Lake, res., B.C., Can.* | G18 | 102 |
| Duncannon, Pa., U.S. | G9 | 108 |
| *Duncan Passage, strt., India* | I2 | 40 |
| *Duncansby Head, c., Scot., U.K.* | C10 | 8 |
| Dundaga, Lat. | D5 | 22 |
| Dundalk, Ire. | G7 | 8 |
| Dundalk, Md., U.S. | H10 | 108 |
| Dundalk, On., Can. | F15 | 110 |
| Dundas, Mn., U.S. | F2 | 110 |
| Dundas, On., Can. | G16 | 110 |
| *Dundas Island, i., B.C., Can.* | C4 | 102 |
| *Dundas Peninsula, pen., N.T., Can.* | B10 | 96 |
| Dundee, Fl., U.S. | K5 | 112 |
| Dundee, Mi., U.S. | I12 | 110 |
| Dundee, Ms., U.S. | H6 | 114 |
| Dundee, N.Y., U.S. | E10 | 108 |
| Dundee, S. Afr. | G10 | 66 |
| Dundee, Scot., U.K. | E11 | 8 |
| Dundurn, Sk., Can. | G8 | 104 |
| Dunedin, Fl., U.S. | K4 | 112 |
| Dunedin, N.Z. | F3 | 72 |
| Dunedoo, Austl. | I8 | 70 |
| Dunfermline, Scot., U.K. | E10 | 8 |
| Dungannon, Va., U.S. | C4 | 112 |
| Dungas, Niger | E14 | 64 |
| Dungog, Austl. | I9 | 70 |
| Dungun, Malay. | L7 | 40 |
| Dunhua, China | C12 | 30 |
| Dunhuang, China | C5 | 30 |
| Dunilovo, Russia | D21 | 22 |
| Dunkerque, Fr. | A9 | 14 |
| Dunkirk see Dunkerque, Fr. | A9 | 14 |
| Dunkirk, In., U.S. | B11 | 114 |
| Dunkirk, N.Y., U.S. | E7 | 108 |
| Dunkirk, Oh., U.S. | G3 | 108 |
| Dunkuj, Sudan | K7 | 60 |
| Dunkwa, Ghana | I9 | 64 |
| Dún Laoghaire, Ire. | H7 | 8 |
| Dunlap, Ia., U.S. | J12 | 118 |
| Dunlap, Tn., U.S. | G11 | 114 |
| Dunleary see Dún Laoghaire, Ire. | H7 | 8 |
| Dunmore, Pa., U.S. | F11 | 108 |
| Dunmore Town, Bah. | B6 | 94 |
| Dunn, N.C., U.S. | D8 | 112 |
| Dunnellon, Fl., U.S. | J4 | 112 |
| Dunning, Ne., U.S. | J7 | 118 |
| Dunnville, On., Can. | H16 | 110 |
| Dunqulah, Sudan | H6 | 60 |
| Dunqulah al-Qadīmah, Sudan | H6 | 60 |
| Dunqunāb, Sudan | G9 | 60 |
| Dunrea, Mb., Can. | I15 | 104 |
| Duns, Scot., U.K. | F11 | 8 |
| Dunseith, N.D., U.S. | C7 | 118 |
| Dunsmuir, Ca., U.S. | C3 | 124 |
| Dunster, B.C., Can. | D15 | 102 |
| Dun-sur-Auron, Fr. | F9 | 14 |
| Dun-sur-Meuse, Fr. | C12 | 14 |
| Dunville, Nf., Can. | E20 | 106 |
| Duolun (Dolonnur), China | A4 | 32 |
| Duolundabohuer, China | D15 | 44 |
| Duomaer, China | E2 | 30 |
| Duomula, China | E3 | 30 |
| Duozhu, China | M3 | 34 |
| *Du Page, stm., Il., U.S.* | I7 | 110 |
| Dupnica, Bul. | G7 | 20 |
| Dupree, S.D., U.S. | F6 | 118 |
| Duque de Caxias, Braz. | G7 | 79 |
| DuQuoin, Il., U.S. | E7 | 114 |
| *Durack Ranges, mts., Austl.* | C5 | 68 |
| Duran, N.M., U.S. | J11 | 120 |
| *Durance, stm., Fr.* | I12 | 14 |
| Durand, Il., U.S. | H6 | 110 |
| Durand, Mi., U.S. | H12 | 110 |
| Durand, Wi., U.S. | F4 | 110 |
| Durango, Co., U.S. | G9 | 120 |
| Durango, Mex. | E7 | 90 |
| Durango, Spain | B9 | 16 |
| *Durango, state, Mex.* | E7 | 90 |
| Durant, Ia., U.S. | I5 | 110 |
| Durant, Ms., U.S. | I7 | 114 |
| Durant, Ok., U.S. | F10 | 116 |
| Durazno, Ur. | G10 | 80 |
| Durban, S. Afr. | G10 | 66 |
| Durbe, Lat. | E4 | 22 |
| Durbin, W.V., U.S. | I7 | 108 |
| Đurđevac, Cro. | C12 | 18 |
| Düren, Ger. | E6 | 10 |
| Durg, India | J9 | 44 |
| Durgāpur, India | I12 | 44 |
| Durham, Ca., U.S. | E4 | 124 |
| Durham, N.C., U.S. | D8 | 112 |
| Durham, N.H., U.S. | D16 | 108 |
| Durham, On., Can. | F15 | 110 |
| *Durham, co., Eng., U.K.* | G12 | 8 |
| *Durham Heights, mtn., N.T., Can.* | B8 | 96 |
| Durlești, Mol. | B12 | 20 |
| *Durmitor, mtn., Yugo.* | F3 | 20 |
| Durness, Scot., U.K. | C9 | 8 |
| Dürnkrut, Aus. | G16 | 10 |
| Durrell, Nf., Can. | C19 | 106 |
| Durrës, Alb. | H3 | 20 |
| Dursunbey, Tur. | J12 | 20 |
| *D'Urville, Tanjung, c., Indon.* | F10 | 38 |
| *D'Urville Island, i., N.Z.* | D4 | 72 |
| Dušak, Turk. | C16 | 48 |
| Dušanbe, Taj. | J11 | 26 |
| Dusetos, Lith. | F8 | 22 |
| Dushan, China | B9 | 40 |
| Dushanbe see Dušanbe, Taj. | J11 | 26 |
| Dushanzi, China | C3 | 30 |
| Dusheng, China | E4 | 32 |
| Dushore, Pa., U.S. | F10 | 108 |
| Duson, La., U.S. | L4 | 114 |
| Düsseldorf, Ger. | D6 | 10 |
| Dustin, Ok., U.S. | D10 | 116 |
| *Dutch Creek, stm., B.C., Can.* | G18 | 102 |
| Dutch Harbor, Ak., U.S. | J11 | 100 |
| Dutch John, Ut., U.S. | D7 | 120 |
| Dutlwe, Bots. | D6 | 66 |
| Dutou, China | M4 | 34 |
| Dutton, Mt., U.S. | C14 | 122 |
| Dutton, On., Can. | H14 | 110 |
| *Dutton, stm., Austl.* | C5 | 70 |
| *Dutton, Mount, mtn., Ut., U.S.* | F4 | 120 |
| Duyun, China | A9 | 40 |
| Duze, China | F7 | 34 |
| *Dvinskaja guba, b., Russia* | I26 | 6 |
| *Dvuch Cirkov, gora, mtn., Russia* | D25 | 28 |
| Dvůr Králové [nad Labem], Czech Rep. | E15 | 10 |
| Dwārka, India | I3 | 44 |
| Dwight, Il., U.S. | I7 | 110 |
| *Dworshak Reservoir, res., Id., U.S.* | D10 | 122 |
| Dyer, Tn., U.S. | F8 | 114 |
| *Dyer, Cape, c., N.T., Can.* | C20 | 96 |
| Dyersburg, Tn., U.S. | F7 | 114 |
| Dyersville, Ia., U.S. | H4 | 110 |
| *Dyfed, co., Wales, U.K.* | J9 | 8 |
| *Dyje (Thaya), stm., Eur.* | G16 | 10 |
| Dyment, On., Can. | I22 | 104 |
| Dynów, Pol. | F22 | 10 |
| Dysart, Ia., U.S. | H3 | 110 |
| Dysart, Sk., Can. | H10 | 104 |
| Dyviziya, Ukr. | D13 | 20 |
| Džalal-Abad, Kyrg. | I12 | 26 |
| Džalinda, Russia | G16 | 28 |
| Džambejty, Kaz. | G8 | 26 |
| Džanga, Turk. | A12 | 48 |
| Džanybek, Kaz. | H7 | 26 |
| Dzaoudzi, May. | I16 | 67a |
| *Dzavchan, stm., Mong.* | B5 | 30 |
| Džebel, Turk. | B13 | 48 |
| Dzemul, Mex. | G15 | 90 |
| Dzeržinsk, Russia | E26 | 22 |
| Dzeržinskoje, Kaz. | H14 | 26 |
| Džetygara, Kaz. | G10 | 26 |
| Dzhankoy, Ukr. | H4 | 26 |
| Dzhuryn, Ukr. | A12 | 20 |
| Dzibalchén, Mex. | H15 | 90 |
| *Dzibilchaltun, hist., Mex.* | G15 | 90 |
| Dzierżoniów (Reichenbach), Pol. | E16 | 10 |

Name — Map Ref. — Page


Dzilam González, Mex. G15 90
Dzioua, Alg. D13 62
Dzisna, Bela. F11 22
Dzitás, Mex. G15 90
Dzitbalché, Mex. G14 90
Dzivin, Bela. J7 22
Džizak, Uzb. I11 26
Dzjaržynsk, Bela. H10 22
Dzjatlava, Bela. H8 22
Džugdžur, chrebet, mts., Russia F19 28
Dzungarian Basin see Junggar Pendi, China B4 30
Džungarskij Alatau, chrebet, mts., Asia H8 28
Džusaly, Kaz. H10 26
Džüün Charaa, Mong. B8 30
Dzuunmod, Mong. B8 30
Dzyhivka, Ukr. A12 20


## E


Eads, Co., U.S. M5 118
Eagar, Az., U.S. J7 120
Eagle, Ak., U.S. D24 100
Eagle, Co., U.S. E10 120
Eagle, stm., Co., U.S. E10 120
Eagle, stm., Nf., Can. F21 96
Eagle, stm., Yk., Can. C26 100
Eagle Bay, B.C., Can. G15 102
Eagle Bend, Mn., U.S. E12 118
Eagle Butte, S.D., U.S. F6 118
Eagle Creek, stm., Sk., Can. G7 104
Eagle Grove, Ia., U.S. H2 110
Eaglehawk, Austl. K6 70
Eagle Lake, Tx., U.S. J10 116
Eagle Lake, l., B.C., Can. F10 102
Eagle Lake, l., Ca., U.S. D5 124
Eagle Lake, l., On., Can. H20 104
Eagle Lake, l., On., Can. I21 104
Eagle Mountain, Ca., U.S. K10 124
Eagle Mountain, mtn., Id., U.S. D10 122
Eagle Mountain, hill, Mn., U.S. C5 110
Eagle Pass, Tx., U.S. K6 116
Eagle Peak, mtn., Ca., U.S. C5 124
Eagle River, Mi., U.S. C7 110
Eagle River, Wi., U.S. E6 110
Eagle Rock, Va., U.S. B7 112
Eaglesham, Ab., Can. B17 102
Eagleton Village, Tn., U.S. D3 112
Eagletown, Ok., U.S. H2 114
Eagle Village, Ak., U.S. D24 100
Eardley Lake, l., Mb., Can. F18 104
Ear Falls, On., Can. H21 104
Earle, Ar., U.S. G6 114
Earl Grey, Sk., Can. H10 104
Earlham, Ia., U.S. A2 114
Earlimart, Ca., U.S. I6 124
Earlington, Ky., U.S. E9 114
Earl Park, In., U.S. B9 114
Earlville, Il., U.S. I7 110
Earlville, N.Y., U.S. E11 108
Early, Ia., U.S. I12 118
Early, Tx., U.S. H8 116
Earth, Tx., U.S. E4 116
Easley, S.C., U.S. E4 112
East Alton, Il., U.S. D6 114
East-Angus, P.Q., Can. B15 108
East Aurora, N.Y., U.S. E8 108
East Bay, b., Tx., U.S. J12 116
East Bend, N.C., U.S. C6 112
East Berbice-Corentyne, prov., Guy. E13 84
East Berlin, Pa., U.S. H10 108
East Bernard, Tx., U.S. J10 116
East Bernstadt, Ky., U.S. B2 112
East Brady, Pa., U.S. G7 108
East Braintree, Mb., Can. I19 104
East Brewton, Al., U.S. K9 114
East Caicos, i., T./C. Is. D9 94
East Cape, c., N.Z. B7 72
East Carbon, Ut., U.S. E6 120
East Channel, mth., N.T., Can. B28 100
East Chicago, In., U.S. A9 114
East China Sea, Asia r3 37b
East Coulee, Ab., Can. F22 102
East Dublin, Ga., U.S. G4 112
East Dubuque, Il., U.S. H5 110
East Ely, Nv., U.S. E11 124
Eastend, Sk., Can. I6 104
Easter Island see Pascua, Isla de, i., Chile G4 74
Eastern Cape, prov., S. Afr. I8 66
Eastern Ghāts, mts., India F5 46
East Falkland, i., Falk. Is. G5 78
East Fayetteville, N.C., U.S. D8 112
East Flat Rock, N.C., U.S. D4 112
East Frisian Islands see Ostfriesische Inseln, is., Ger. B7 10
East Gaffney, S.C., U.S. D5 112
East Gallatin, stm., Mt., U.S. E14 122
East Glacier Park, Mt., U.S. B12 122
East Grand Forks, Mn., U.S. D10 118
East Grand Rapids, Mi., U.S. H10 110
East Greenwich, R.I., U.S. F15 108
Easthampton, Ma., U.S. E14 108
East Helena, Mt., U.S. D14 122
East Jordan, Mi., U.S. E10 110
East Kelowna, B.C., Can. H15 102
East Kilbride, Scot., U.K. F9 8
Eastlake, Mi., U.S. F9 110
Eastlake, Oh., U.S. F5 108
East Lake, l., On., Can. E21 104
Eastland, Tx., U.S. G8 116
East Lansing, Mi., U.S. H11 110
East Laurinburg, N.C., U.S. E7 112
East Liverpool, Oh., U.S. G6 108
East London (Oos-Londen), S. Afr. I8 66
East Lynn Lake, res., W.V., U.S. I4 108
Eastmain, P.Q., Can. F17 96
Eastmain, stm., P.Q., Can. F17 96
Eastmain-Opinaca, Réservoir, res., P.Q., Can. F17 96
Eastman, Ga., U.S. G3 112
East Millinocket, Me., U.S. B18 108
East Missoula, Mt., U.S. D12 122
East Moline, Il., U.S. I5 110
East Naples, Fl., U.S. M5 112
East Nishnabotna, stm., Ia., U.S. K12 118
East Olympia, Wa., U.S. D3 122
Easton, Md., U.S. I10 108
Easton, Pa., U.S. G11 108
Eastover, S.C., U.S. F6 112
East Palatka, Fl., U.S. J5 112
East Palestine, Oh., U.S. G6 108
East Pecos, N.M., U.S. I11 120
East Peoria, Il., U.S. J6 110
East Pine, B.C., Can. B13 102
Eastpoint, Fl., U.S. J2 112
East Point, Ga., U.S. F2 112
East Point, c., P.E., Can. F12 106
Eastport, Id., U.S. A9 122
Eastport, Me., U.S. C20 108
Eastport, Nf., Can. D20 106
East Porterville, Ca., U.S. H7 124
East Prairie, Mo., U.S. F7 114
East Prairie, stm., Ab., Can. B18 102
East Rockingham, N.C., U.S. E7 112
East Saint Louis, Il., U.S. D6 114
East Shoal Lake, l., Mb., Can. H17 104
East Siberian Sea see Vostočno-Sibirskoje more, Russia C23 28
East Spencer, N.C., U.S. D6 112
East Stroudsburg, Pa., U.S. G11 108
East Tawas, Mi., U.S. F12 110
East Troy, Wi., U.S. H7 110
Eastville, Va., U.S. B11 112
East Wenatchee, Wa., U.S. C5 122
East Wilmington, N.C., U.S. E9 112
Eaton, Co., U.S. D12 120
Eaton, In., U.S. B11 114
Eaton, Oh., U.S. H2 108
Eatonia, Sk., Can. G5 104
Eaton Rapids, Mi., U.S. H11 110
Eatonton, Ga., U.S. F3 112
Eatonville, Wa., U.S. D3 122
Eau Claire, Wi., U.S. F4 110
Eau Claire, stm., Wi., U.S. F4 110
Eau Claire, Lac à l', l., P.Q., Can. E18 96
Eau Galle, stm., Wi., U.S. F3 110
Eauze, Fr. I7 14
Eban, Nig. G12 64
Ebano, Mex. F10 90
Ebb and Flow Indian Reserve, Mb., Can. G15 104
Ebb and Flow Lake, l., Mb., Can. G16 104
Ebbw Vale, Wales, U.K. J10 8
Eben Junction, Mi., U.S. D9 110
Ebensburg, Pa., U.S. G8 108
Ebensee, Aus. H13 10
Eberbach, Ger. F8 10
Ebermannstadt, Ger. F11 10
Eberndorf, Aus. I14 10
Ebersbach, Ger. D14 10
Ebersberg, Ger. G11 10
Eberstein, Aus. I14 10
Eberswalde-Finow, Ger. C13 10
Ebetsu, Japan d16 36a
Ebinur Hu, l., China C3 30
Ebnat, Switz. D11 13
Eboli, Italy I10 18
Ebolowa, Cam. H9 54
Ebony, Nmb. D2 66
Ebro (Ebre), stm., Spain E12 16
Ebro, Embalse del, res., Spain B8 16
Eccles, W.V., U.S. B5 112
Echaporã, Braz. G3 79
Ech Cheliff (Orléansville), Alg. B11 62
Echimamish, stm., Mb., Can. D17 104
Echo, Mn., U.S. G12 118
Echo Bay, N.T., Can. C9 96
Echoing, stm., Can. C23 104
Echoing Lake, l., On., Can. D22 104
Echt, Neth. F8 12
Echuca, Austl. K6 70
Écija, Spain H6 16
Eckernförde, Ger. A9 10
Eckville, Ab., Can. E20 102
Eclectic, Al., U.S. J10 114
Eclipse Sound, strt., N.T., Can. B17 96
Ečmiadzin, Arm. I6 26
Écrins, Barre des, mtn., Fr. H13 14
Ecru, Ms., U.S. H7 114
Ecstall, stm., B.C., Can. D5 102
Ecuador, ctry., S.A. D3 76
Ecum Secum, N.S., Can. H11 106
Ed, Erit. H2 47
Edam, Neth. C7 12
Edam, Sk., Can. E6 104
Eddystone Point, c., Austl. M8 70
Eddyville, Ia., U.S. I3 110
Eddyville, Ky., U.S. E8 114
Ede, Nig. H12 64
Edéa, Cam. H9 54
Edehon Lake, l., N.T., Can. D13 96
Edéia, Braz. D4 79
Edelény, Hung. G20 10
Eden, Austl. K8 70
Eden, Ms., U.S. J6 114
Eden, Tx., U.S. H7 116
Eden, Wy., U.S. B7 120
Edenburg, S. Afr. G7 66
Eden Lake, l., Mb., Can. B14 104
Edenton, N.C., U.S. C10 112
Eden Valley, Mn., U.S. E1 110
Edenville, S. Afr. F8 66
Edeowie, Austl. H3 70
Eder, stm., Ger. D8 10
Edfu see Idfū, Egypt E7 60
Edgar, Ne., U.S. K10 118
Edgar, Wi., U.S. F6 110
Edgard, La., U.S. L6 114
Edgartown, Ma., U.S. F16 108
Edgefield, S.C., U.S. F5 112
Edgeley, N.D., U.S. E9 118
Edgemont, S.D., U.S. H4 118
Edgeøya, i., Nor. B3 24
Edgerton, Ab., Can. F4 104
Edgerton, Mn., U.S. H11 118
Edgerton, Oh., U.S. F2 108
Edgerton, Wi., U.S. H6 110
Edgerton, Wy., U.S. A10 120
Edgewater, Al., U.S. I10 114
Edgewater, Fl., U.S. K6 112
Edgewood, B.C., Can. H16 102
Edgewood, Ia., U.S. H4 110
Edgewood, Il., U.S. D8 114
Edgewood, Md., U.S. H10 108
Edgewood, Tx., U.S. G11 116
Édhessa, Grc. I6 20
Edina, Mn., U.S. F2 110
Edina, Mo., U.S. B4 114
Edinboro, Pa., U.S. F6 108
Edinburg, Il., U.S. C7 114
Edinburg, In., U.S. C11 114
Edinburg, Ms., U.S. J7 114
Edinburg, N.D., U.S. C10 118
Edinburg, Tx., U.S. M8 116
Edinburg, Va., U.S. I8 108
Edinburgh, Scot., U.K. F10 8
Edinburgh, Arrecife, rf., Nic. C12 92
Edinburgh Channel, strt., Nic. C12 92
Edincik, Tur. I11 20
Edirne, Tur. H10 20
Edison, Ga., U.S. H2 112
Edisto, stm., S.C., U.S. G6 112
Edisto Island, i., S.C., U.S. G6 112
Edith Cavell, Mount, mtn., Ab., Can. E16 102
Edjeleh, Alg. G15 62
Edmond, Ok., U.S. D9 116
Edmonds, Wa., U.S. C3 122
Edmonton, Ab., Can. D21 102
Edmonton, Austl. A6 70
Edmonton, Ky., U.S. F11 114
Edmore, Mi., U.S. G10 110
Edmore, N.D., U.S. C9 118
Edmund Lake, l., Mb., Can. D21 104
Edmundston, N.B., Can. E5 106
Edna, Ks., U.S. N12 118
Edna, Tx., U.S. K10 116
Edna Bay, Ak., U.S. I28 100
Edolo, Italy C5 18
Edremit, Tur. J11 20
Edsbro, Swe. L16 6
Edsbyn, Swe. K14 6
Edson, Ab., Can. D18 102
Eduardo Castex, Arg. H6 80
Eduni, Mount, mtn., N.T., Can. D30 100
Edward, Lake, l., Afr. B5 58
Edwards, Ms., U.S. J6 114
Edwards, N.Y., U.S. C11 108
Edwards, stm., Il., U.S. I5 110
Edwards Plateau, plat., Tx., U.S. I6 116
Edwardsville, Il., U.S. D7 114
Edward VII Peninsula, pen., Ant. C9 73
Edziza, Mount, mtn., B.C., Can. H29 100
Eek, Ak., U.S. F13 100
Eeklo, Bel. F4 12
Eel, stm., Ca., U.S. D1 124
Eel, stm., In., U.S. B10 114
Eel, stm., In., U.S. C9 114
Effingham, Il., U.S. C8 114
Effingham, Ks., U.S. L12 118
Ega, stm., Spain C9 16
Egadi, Isole, is., Italy L7 18
Egaña, Arg. I9 80
Egan Range, mts., Nv., U.S. E11 124
Eganville, On., Can. E18 110
Egegik, Ak., U.S. G16 100
Eger see Cheb, Czech Rep. E12 10
Eger, Hung. H20 10
Egeria Mountain, mtn., B.C., Can. D4 102
Egersund, Nor. L10 6
Eggenburg, Aus. G15 10
Egg Harbor City, N.J., U.S. H12 108
Egg Lake, l., Mb., Can. D13 104
Egg Lake, l., Sk., Can. C9 104
Egilsstaðir, Ice. B6 6a
Egmont, Mount, mtn., N.Z. C4 72
Egmont Bay, b., P.E., Can. F9 106
Egremont, Ab., Can. C21 102
Éguas, Rio das, stm., Braz. B6 79
Egypt (Mişr), ctry., Afr. C7 56
Ehrenberg, Az., U.S. K2 120
Ehrhardt, S.C., U.S. F5 112
Eibar, Spain B9 16
Eichstätt, Ger. G11 10
Eidsvåg, Nor. J11 6
Eidsvold, Austl. E9 70
Eifel, mts., Ger. E6 10
Eiger, mtn., Switz. E9 13
Eight Degree Channel, strt., Asia I2 46
Eights Coast, Ant. C11 73
Eighty Mile Beach, Austl. C4 68
Eildon, Austl. K6 70
Eildon, Lake, res., Austl. K6 70
Eilenburg, Ger. D12 10
Einasleigh, Austl. B6 70
Einasleigh, stm., Austl. A5 70
Einbeck, Ger. D9 10
Eindhoven, Neth. F7 12
Einsiedeln, Switz. D10 13
Eiru, stm., Braz. B6 82
Eirunepé, Braz. B7 82
Eisden, Bel. G8 12
Eisenach, Ger. E10 10
Eisenberg, Ger. E11 10
Eisenerz, Aus. H14 10
Eisenhüttenstadt, Ger. C14 10
Eisenkappel, Aus. I14 10
Eisenstadt, Aus. H16 10
Eišiškės, Lith. G8 22
Eitorf, Ger. E7 10
Eivissa, Spain G13 16
Eivissa (Ibiza), i., Spain G13 16
Ejea de los Caballeros, Spain C10 16
Ejeda, Madag. t21 67b
Ejido, Ven. C7 84
Ejido Jaboncillos, Mex. C8 90
Ejin Qi, China C7 30
Ejutla de Crespo, Mex. I11 90
Ekalaka, Mt., U.S. F3 118
Eket, Nig. I13 64
Ekibastuz, Kaz. G7 28
Ekpoma, Nig. H13 64
Eksjö, Swe. M14 6
Ekwan, stm., On., Can. F16 96
Ekwok, Ak., U.S. G16 100
Ela, Myan. E4 40
El Aaiún (La'youn), W. Sah. G4 62
El Abiadh Sidi Cheikh, Alg. D11 62
El Adeb Larache, Alg. G15 62
El Adelanto, Guat. C5 92
El Agreb, Alg. E13 62
El Aguilar, Arg. B6 80
Elaine, Ar., U.S. H6 114
El Alamein see Al-'Alamayn, Egypt B5 60
El Alia, Tun. L5 18
El Alto, Arg. E6 80
El Alto, Peru J2 84
El Amparo de Apure, Ven. D7 84
Elandsvlei, S. Afr. I4 66
El Angel, Ec. G4 84
El Aouinet, Alg. N2 18
El Arco, Mex. C3 90
El Aricha, Alg. C10 62
El Aroussa, Tun. M4 18
El Astillero, Spain B8 16
Elat, Isr. I3 50
El Ávila, Parque Nacional, Ven. B9 84
Elazığ, Tur. B5 48
Elba, Al., U.S. K10 114
Elba, Isola d', i., Italy G5 18
El Banco, Col. C6 84
Elbasan, Alb. H4 20
El Baúl, Ven. C8 84
El Baúl, Cerro, mtn., Mex. I9 90
El Baúl, Cerro, mtn., Mex. I12 90
Elbe (Labe), stm., Eur. B9 10
Elbert, Co., U.S. L3 118
Elbert, Mount, mtn., Co., U.S. E10 120
Elberta, Mi., U.S. F9 110
Elberton, Ga., U.S. E4 112
Elbeuf, Fr. C8 14
El Beyyadh, Alg. D11 62
Elbistan, Tur. B4 48
Elbląg (Elbing), Pol. A19 10
El Bluff, Nic. F11 92
El-Borouj, Mor. D7 62
El Boulaïda, Alg. B12 62
Elbow, Sk., Can. G8 104
Elbow, stm., Ab., Can. G20 102
Elbow Cay, i., Bah. C4 94
Elbow Lake, Mn., U.S. F12 118
Elbow Lake, l., Mb., Can. D14 104
El'brus, gora, mtn., Russia I6 26
Elbrus, Mount see El'brus, gora, mtn., Russia I6 26
El Cabezo, Arrecife, rf., Mex. H12 90
El Caburé, Arg. D7 80
El Caimanero, Laguna, b., Mex. F6 90
El Cajon, Ca., U.S. L9 124
El Cajón, Embalse, res., Hond. B7 92
El Calafate, Arg. G2 78
El Callao, Ven. D12 84
El Calvario, Col. E6 84
El Calvario, Ven. C9 84
El Campo, Tx., U.S. J10 116
El Capitan, mtn., Mt., U.S. D11 122
El Carmen, Arg. C6 80
El Cármen, Bol. H12 82
El Carmen, Col. C6 84
El Carmen, Peru E3 82
El Carmen, stm., Mex. B6 90
El Carmen de Bolívar, Col. C5 84
El Carricito, Mex. C8 90
El Carril, Arg. C6 80
El Castillo de La Concepción, Nic. F10 92
El Cedral, Guat. A4 92
El Cedrito, Mex. C9 90
El Centro, Ca., U.S. L10 124
El Cerrito, Col. F4 84
El Cerro, Bol. G11 82
El Chile, Montaña, mtn., Hond. C8 92
Elcho, Wi., U.S. E6 110
El Chorrillo, Arg. G5 80
El Cocuy, Col. D6 84
El Colorado, Arg. D9 80
El Cóndor, Cerro, mtn., Arg. D4 80
El Congo, El Sal. D5 92
El Corazón, Ec. H3 84
El Corpus, Hond. D7 92
El Coyote, stm., Mex. B3 90
El Cozón, Mex. B3 90
El Cuco, El Sal. D6 92
El Cuervo, Laguna, l., Mex. C7 90
Elda, Spain G11 16
El Dátil, Mex. B3 90
El Desemboque, Mex. C3 90
El Desemboque, Mex. B3 90
El'dikan, Russia E19 28
El Diviso, Col. G3 84
El Djazaïr (Algiers), Alg. B12 62
El Djelfa, Alg. C12 62
Eldon, Ia., U.S. J3 110
Eldon, Mo., U.S. D4 114
Eldora, Ia., U.S. H2 110
El Dorado, Ar., U.S. I4 114
Eldorado, Arg. D11 80
Eldorado, Braz. C14 80
Eldorado, Il., U.S. E8 114
El Dorado, Ks., U.S. N11 118
El Dorado, Mex. E6 90
Eldorado, Ok., U.S. E7 116
Eldorado, Tx., U.S. I6 116
El Dorado, Ven. D12 84
El Dorado Springs, Mo., U.S. E2 114
Eldoret, Kenya A7 58
Eldred, Pa., U.S. F8 108
Eldridge, Ia., U.S. I5 110
Eleanor, W.V., U.S. I5 108
Electra, Tx., U.S. E8 116
Electric City, Wa., U.S. C6 122
Elefante, Isla del see Elephant Island, i., Ant. B1 73
Elefantes, Rio dos (Olifants), stm., Afr. E11 66
Elei, Wādī, val., Sudan G8 60
Eleja, Lat. E6 22
Elektrogorsk, Russia F21 22
Elektrostal', Russia F21 22
El Encanto, Col. H6 84
El Encanto, Guat. I15 90
Elephant Butte Reservoir, res., N.M., U.S. K9 120
Elephant Island, i., Ant. K9 74
El Estor, Guat. B5 92
El Eulma, Alg. B13 62
Eleuthera, i., Bah. B6 94
Eleuthera Point, c., Bah. B6 94
Eleva, Wi., U.S. F4 110
Eleven Point, stm., U.S. F5 114
Elevsís, Grc. K7 20
El Fahs, Tun. M4 18
Elfrida, Az., U.S. M7 120
Elfros, Sk., Can. G11 104
El Fuerte, Mex. D5 90
El Galpón, Arg. C6 80
El Ghazawet, Alg. C10 62
Elgin, Ia., U.S. H4 110
Elgin, Il., U.S. H7 110
Elgin, Mn., U.S. F3 110
Elgin, N.D., U.S. E6 118
Elgin, Ne., U.S. J9 118
Elgin, Ok., U.S. E8 116
Elgin, Or., U.S. E8 122
Elgin, Scot., U.K. D10 8
Elgin, Tx., U.S. I9 116
El Golfete, l., Guat. B6 92
Elgon, Mount, mtn., Afr. A6 58
El Grara, Alg. D13 62
El Guaje, Mex. D8 90
El Guaje, Laguna, l., Mex. C8 90
El Guamo, Col. B5 84
El Guapo, Ven. B10 84
El Guayabo de Abajo, Mex. D6 90
El Hadjar, Alg. M2 18
El Hank, clf, Afr. D5 54
El Haouaria, Tun. L6 18
El Hierro, i., Spain p22 17b
Elhovo, Bul. G10 20
El Huecú, Arg. I3 80
El Huisache, Mex. F9 90
Eliasville, Tx., U.S. G8 116
Elida, N.M., U.S. F3 116
El Ídolo, Isla, i., Mex. G11 90
El Idrissia, Alg. C12 62
Elim, Ak., U.S. D13 100
El Infiernillo, Canal, strt., Mex. C3 90
Eliot, Me., U.S. D16 108
Élisabethville see Lubumbashi, D.R.C. D5 58
Elisenvaara, Russia K21 6
Elista, Russia H6 26
Elizabeth, Austl. J3 70
Elizabeth, Co., U.S. E12 120
Elizabeth, Il., U.S. H5 110
Elizabeth, La., U.S. L4 114
Elizabeth, N.J., U.S. G12 108
Elizabeth, W.V., U.S. H5 108
Elizabeth City, N.C., U.S. C10 112
Elizabethton, Tn., U.S. C4 112
Elizabethtown, Il., U.S. E8 114
Elizabethtown, Ky., U.S. E11 114
Elizabethtown, N.C., U.S. E8 112
Elizabethtown, N.Y., U.S. C13 108
Elizabethtown, Pa., U.S. G10 108
El-Jadida (Mazagan), Mor. D6 62
El Jaralito, Mex. D7 90
El Jebel, Co., U.S. E9 120
El-Jebha, Mor. J7 16
El Jem, Tun. N5 18
El Jícaro, stm., Nic. D8 92
Ełk, Pol. B22 10
Elk, stm., Ab., Can. E19 102
Elk, stm., B.C., Can. H19 102
Elk, stm., Co., U.S. D10 120
Elk, stm., Ks., U.S. N11 118
Elk, stm., Mn., U.S. E2 110
Elk, stm., Mo., U.S. F2 114
Elk, stm., U.S. G10 114
Elk, stm., Wi., U.S. E5 110
Elk, stm., W.V., U.S. I5 108
Elkader, Ia., U.S. H4 110
El Kantara, Tun. D16 62
El-Karafab, Sudan H6 60
Elk City, Ok., U.S. D7 116
Elk Creek, Ca., U.S. E3 124
El Kef, Tun. M3 18
El-Kelâa-des-Srarhna, Mor. D7 62
El Kerma, Alg. J11 16
Elk Grove, Ca., U.S. F4 124
Elkhart, In., U.S. A11 114
Elkhart, Ks., U.S. N6 118
Elkhart, Tx., U.S. H11 116
Elkhart Lake, Wi., U.S. G7 110
Elkhead Mountains, mts., Co., U.S. D9 120
Elk Horn, Ia., U.S. J12 118
Elkhorn, Mb., Can. I13 104
Elkhorn, Wi., U.S. H7 110
Elkhorn, stm., Ne., U.S. J10 118
Elkhorn City, Ky., U.S. B4 112
Elkhorn Mountain, mtn., B.C., Can. H9 102
Elkin, N.C., U.S. C6 112
Elkins, W.V., U.S. I7 108
Elk Island, i., Mb., Can. H18 104
Elk Island National Park, Ab., Can. D22 102
Elkland, Pa., U.S. F9 108
Elk Mountain, Wy., U.S. C10 120
Elk Mountain, mtn., Wy., U.S. C10 120
Elko, B.C., Can. H19 102
Elko, Nv., U.S. D10 124
El Kouif, Alg. N3 18
Elk Point, Ab., Can. D24 102
Elk Point, S.D., U.S. I11 118
Elk Rapids, Mi., U.S. F10 110
El Krib, Tun. M4 18
Elk River, Id., U.S. D9 122
Elk River, Mn., U.S. E2 110
Elkton, Ky., U.S. F9 114
Elkton, Md., U.S. H11 108
Elkton, Mi., U.S. G12 110
Elkton, S.D., U.S. G11 118
Elkton, Va., U.S. I8 108
Elkville, Il., U.S. E7 114
Ellard Lake, l., On., Can. D23 104
Ellaville, Ga., U.S. G2 112
Ellef Ringnes Island, i., N.T., Can. B9 86
Ellen, Mount, mtn., Ut., U.S. F6 120
Ellendale, Mn., U.S. G2 110
Ellendale, N.D., U.S. E9 118
Ellensburg, Wa., U.S. D5 122
Ellenton, Ga., U.S. H3 112
Ellenville, N.Y., U.S. F12 108
Ellerbe, N.C., U.S. D7 112
Ellès, Tun. N4 18
Ellesmere Island, i., N.T., Can. A11 86
Ellettsville, In., U.S. C10 114
Ellice, stm., N.T., Can. C12 96
Ellice Islands see Tuvalu, ctry., Oc. I21 126
Ellichpur see Achalpur, India J7 44
Ellicott City, Md., U.S. H10 108
Ellicottville, N.Y., U.S. E8 108
Ellijay, Ga., U.S. E2 112
El Limón de Teachi, Mex. E6 90
Ellington, Mo., U.S. E6 114
Ellinwood, Ks., U.S. M9 118
Elliot, S. Afr. H8 66
Elliotdale, S. Afr. H9 66
Elliot Lake, On., Can. D13 110
Elliot Lake, l., Mb., Can. F19 104
Elliott, Ia., U.S. J12 118
Elliott, Ms., U.S. I7 114
Elliott Key, i., Fl., U.S. N6 112
Ellis, Ks., U.S. M8 118
Ellisras, S. Afr. D8 66
Elliston, Mt., U.S. D13 122
Elliston, Nf., Can. D20 106
Ellisville, Ms., U.S. K7 114
Ellore see Elūru, India D6 46
Elloree, S.C., U.S. F6 112
Ellsworth, Ks., U.S. M9 118
Ellsworth, Me., U.S. C18 108
Ellsworth, Mi., U.S. E10 110
Ellsworth, Mn., U.S. H11 118
Ellsworth, Wi., U.S. F3 110
Ellsworth Land, reg., Ant. C12 73
Ellsworth Mountains, mts., Ant. C12 73
Ellwangen, Ger. G10 10
Ellwood City, Pa., U.S. G6 108
Elm, Switz. E11 13
Elm, stm., N.D., U.S. D10 118
Elm, stm., U.S. F9 118
Elma, Ia., U.S. G3 110
Elma, Wa., U.S. C2 122
El Mahdia, Tun. C16 62
El Malah, Alg. J10 16
El Maneadero, Mex. B1 90
El Manteco, Ven. D11 84
El Marsa el Kebir, Alg. C10 62
Elm City, N.C., U.S. D9 112
Elm Creek, Mb., Can. I16 104
Elm Creek, Ne., U.S. K8 118
El Médano, Mex. E4 90
El Menia, Alg. E12 62
Elmer, N.J., U.S. H11 108
El Mghayyar, Alg. D13 62
Elmhurst, Il., U.S. I8 110
El Milagro, Arg. F6 80
El Miliyya, Alg. B14 62
Elmina, Ghana I9 64
Elmira, N.Y., U.S. E10 108
Elmira, On., Can. G15 110
Elmira, P.E., Can. F11 106
El Mirage, Az., U.S. K4 120
Elmira Heights, N.Y., U.S. E10 108
El Mochito, Hond. C6 92
El Mohammadia, Alg. C11 62
El Molinillo, Spain F7 16
El Monte, Chile G3 80
Elmore, Austl. K6 70
Elmore, Mn., U.S. G1 110
Elmore, Oh., U.S. F3 108
Elmore City, Ok., U.S. E9 116
Elmsdale, N.S., Can. H10 106
Elmshorn, Ger. B9 10
Elm Springs, Ar., U.S. F2 114
El Multe, Mex. I14 90
Elmvale, On., Can. F16 110
Elmwood, Il., U.S. J6 110
Elmwood, Ne., U.S. K11 118
Elmwood, Wi., U.S. F3 110
Elne, Fr. J9 14
El Negrito, Hond. B7 92
El Nihuil, Arg. H4 80
El Nopal, Cerro, mtn., Mex. C6 90
Elnora, Ab., Can. F21 102
Elnora, In., U.S. D9 114
El Ocote, Cerro, mtn., Mex. E6 90
Eloise, Fl., U.S. L5 112
Elora, On., Can. G15 110
Elora, Tn., U.S. G10 114
El Oro, prov., Ec. I3 84
Elortondo, Arg. G8 80
Elorza, Ven. D8 84
Eloy, Az., U.S. L5 120
Eloy Alfaro, Ec. I3 84
El Pacayal, Mex. J13 90
El Palmar, Bol. I10 82
El Palmar, Ven. D12 84
El Palqui, Chile F3 80
El Pao, Ven. C11 84
El Pao, Ven. C8 84
El Paraíso, Hond. D8 92
El Paraíso, dept., Hond. C8 92
El Paso, Il., U.S. J6 110
El Paso, Spain o23 17b
El Paso, Tx., U.S. M10 120
El Peñuelo, Mex. E9 90
El Perú, Ven. D12 84
Elphinstone, Mb., Can. H14 104
El Pilar, Ven. B11 84
El Piñón, Col. B5 84
El Pintado, Arg. C8 80
El Piquete, Arg. C6 80
El Pital, Cerro, mtn., N.A. C5 92
El Portal, Ca., U.S. G6 124
El Prat de Llobregat, Spain D14 16
El Progreso, Guat. C5 92
El Progreso, Hond. B7 92
El Progreso, dept., Guat. C4 92
El Puerto de Santa María, Spain I5 16
El Puesto, Arg. D5 80
El Qala, Alg. B15 62
El Qoll, Alg. B14 62
El Quebrachal, Arg. C6 80
El Quelite, Mex. F6 90
Elqui, stm., Chile E3 80
El Rastro, Ven. C9 84
El Real de Santa María, Pan. C4 84
El Reno, Ok., U.S. D9 116
El Rey, Parque Nacional, Arg. C6 80
El Rio, Ca., U.S. J6 124
El Rito, N.M., U.S. H10 120
El Rito, stm., N.M., U.S. H10 120
El Roble, Mesa, mtn., Mex. B2 90
El Rom, Golan B5 50
El Rosarito, Mex. C2 90
Elrose, Sk., Can. G6 104
Elroy, Wi., U.S. G5 110
Elsa, Tx., U.S. M9 116
Elsa, Yk., Can. E27 100
El Salado, Chile D3 80
El Salitre, Ec. H3 84
El Salto, Mex. F7 90
El Salvador, ctry., N.A. D6 92
El Samán de Apure, Ven. D8 84
El Sauz, Mex. C6 90
El Sauzal, Mex. B1 90
Elsberry, Mo., U.S. C6 114
El Seibo, Dom. Rep. E10 94
Elsie, Mi., U.S. G11 110
Elsinore, Ut., U.S. F4 120
Elsmere, De., U.S. H11 108
El Socorro, Ven. C10 84
El Sombrero, Ven. C9 84
Elst, Neth. E8 12
Elsterwerda, Ger. D13 10
El Sueco, Mex. C6 90
El Tagarete, Cerro, mtn., Mex. D7 90
El Tajín, hist., Mex. G11 90
El Tala, Arg. D6 80
El Tamarindo, El Sal. D7 92
El Tambo, Col. G4 84
El Tarf, Alg. M3 18
El Tecuán, Mex. E6 90
El Tigre, Ven. C10 84
El Tigre, Isla, i., Hond. D7 92
Eltmann, Ger. F10 10
El Tocuyo, Ven. C8 84
El Tofo, Chile E3 80
Elton, La., U.S. L4 114
El Tránsito, Chile E3 80
El Tránsito, El Sal. D6 92
El Trébol, Arg. G8 80
El Triunfo, Hond. D7 92
El Triunfo, Mex. F4 90
El Triunfo, Cerro, mtn., Mex. B2 92
El Triunfo de la Cruz, Hond. B7 92
El Tunal, Arg. C6 80
El Turbio, Arg. G2 78
Elūru, India D6 46
Elva, Est. C9 22
El Valle, Pan. C2 84
Elvas, Port. G4 16
El Vendrell, Spain D13 16
El Viejo, Nic. E7 92
El Vigía, Ven. C7 84
El Vigía, Cerro, mtn., Mex. G7 90
Elvins, Mo., U.S. E6 114
Elvira, Arg. H9 80
El Volcán, Chile G3 80
El Wad, Alg. D14 62
El Wanza, Alg. C15 62
Elwell, Lake, res., Mt., U.S. B14 122
Elwood, In., U.S. B11 114
Elwood, Ks., U.S. L13 118
Elwood, Ne., U.S. K8 118
Elx, Spain G11 16
Ely, Mn., U.S. C4 110
Ely, Nv., U.S. E11 124
El Yagual, Ven. D8 84
Elyria, Oh., U.S. F4 108
Emāmshahr (Shāhrūd), Iran C13 48
Emas, Parque Nacional das, Braz. E2 79
Emba, Kaz. H9 26
Emba, stm., Kaz. H9 26
Embarcación, Arg. B6 80
Embarras, stm., Ab., Can. D18 102
Embarras, stm., Il., U.S. D9 114
Embarrass, Wi., U.S. F7 110
Embarrass, stm., Mn., U.S. C3 110
Embarrass, stm., Wi., U.S. F7 110
Embreeville, Tn., U.S. C4 112
Embrun, Fr. H13 14
Embrun, On., Can. B11 108
Emden, Ger. B7 10
Emden, Il., U.S. B7 114
Emelle, Al., U.S. J8 114
Emerado, N.D., U.S. D10 118
Emerald, Austl. D8 70
Emerson, Ar., U.S. I3 114
Emerson, Ga., U.S. E2 112
Emerson, Ia., U.S. J12 118
Emerson, Mb., Can. I17 104
Emerson, Ne., U.S. I11 118
Emery, S.D., U.S. H10 118
Emery, Ut., U.S. F5 120
Emet, Tur. J13 20
Emiliano Zapata, Mex. I14 90
Emiliano Zapata, Bahía, b., Mex. H16 90
Emilia-Romagna, prov., Italy E6 18
Emine, nos, c., Bul. G11 20
Eminence, Ky., U.S. D11 114
Eminence, Mo., U.S. E5 114
Emlembe, mtn., Afr. E10 66

| Name | Map Ref. | Page |
|---|---|---|
| Emlenton, Pa., U.S. | F7 | 108 |
| Emmaus, Pa., U.S. | G11 | 108 |
| Emmaville, Austl. | G9 | 70 |
| Emmeline Lake, l., Sk., Can. | C8 | 104 |
| Emmeloord, Neth. | C8 | 12 |
| Emmen, Neth. | C10 | 12 |
| Emmenbrücke, Switz. | D9 | 13 |
| Emmendingen, Ger. | G7 | 10 |
| Emmer-Compascuum, Neth. | C11 | 12 |
| Emmerich, Ger. | D6 | 10 |
| Emmet, Ar., U.S. | I3 | 114 |
| Emmetsburg, Ia., U.S. | H13 | 118 |
| Emmett, Id., U.S. | G9 | 122 |
| Emmiganūru, India | E4 | 46 |
| Emmitsburg, Md., U.S. | H9 | 108 |
| Emmonak, Ak., U.S. | E12 | 100 |
| Emo, On., Can. | J21 | 104 |
| Emory, Tx., U.S. | G11 | 116 |
| Emory, stm., Tn., U.S. | C2 | 112 |
| Emory Peak, mtn., Tx., U.S. | J16 | 116 |
| Empalme, Mex. | D4 | 90 |
| Empangeni, S. Afr. | G10 | 66 |
| Empedrado, Arg. | D9 | 80 |
| Empedrado, Chile | H2 | 114 |
| Empire, La., U.S. | M7 | 114 |
| Empire, Nv., U.S. | D6 | 124 |
| Empoli, Italy | F5 | 18 |
| Emporia, Ks., U.S. | M11 | 118 |
| Emporia, Va., U.S. | C9 | 112 |
| Emporium, Pa., U.S. | F8 | 108 |
| Empress, Ab., Can. | H4 | 104 |
| Empty Quarter see Ar-Rub' al-Khālī, des., Asia | D7 | 47 |
| Ems, stm., Eur. | C7 | 10 |
| Emsdetten, Ger. | C7 | 10 |
| Emure-Ekiti, Nig. | H12 | 64 |
| En (Inn), stm., Eur. | F17 | 14 |
| Encampment, Wy., U.S. | C10 | 120 |
| Encampment, stm., U.S. | C10 | 120 |
| Encarnación, Para. | E13 | 80 |
| Encinal, Tx., U.S. | D11 | 80 |
| Encinal, Tx., U.S. | K7 | 116 |
| Encinitas, Ca., U.S. | K8 | 124 |
| Encino, N.M., U.S. | J11 | 120 |
| Encino, Tx., U.S. | M8 | 116 |
| Encontrados, Ven. | C6 | 84 |
| Encounter Bay, b., Austl. | J3 | 70 |
| Encruzilhada, Braz. | C8 | 79 |
| Encruzilhada do Sul, Braz. | F12 | 80 |
| Encs, Hung. | G21 | 10 |
| Endako, B.C., Can. | C9 | 102 |
| Endako, stm., B.C., Can. | C9 | 102 |
| Ende, Indon. | G7 | 38 |
| Endeavor, Wi., U.S. | G6 | 110 |
| Endeavour, Sk., Can. | F12 | 104 |
| Endeavour Strait, strt., Austl. | B8 | 68 |
| Enderby, B.C., Can. | G15 | 102 |
| Enderby Land, reg., Ant. | B4 | 73 |
| Enderlin, N.D., U.S. | E10 | 118 |
| Endicott, N.Y., U.S. | E10 | 108 |
| Endicott, Wa., U.S. | D8 | 122 |
| Endimari, stm., Braz. | B7 | 82 |
| Endola, Nmb. | A2 | 66 |
| Ene, stm., Peru | D4 | 82 |
| Enewetak, atoll, Marsh. Is. | G20 | 126 |
| Enez, Tur. | I10 | 20 |
| Enfida, Tun. | M5 | 18 |
| Enfield, N.C., U.S. | C9 | 112 |
| Enfield, N.H., U.S. | D14 | 108 |
| Engaño, Cabo, c., Dom. Rep. | E10 | 94 |
| Engcobo, S. Afr. | H9 | 66 |
| Engelberg, Switz. | E9 | 13 |
| Engelhard, N.C., U.S. | D11 | 112 |
| Engel's, Russia | G7 | 26 |
| Engen, B.C., Can. | C10 | 102 |
| Engenho, Braz. | F13 | 82 |
| 'En Gedi, Isr. | F4 | 50 |
| 'En Gev, Isr. | C5 | 50 |
| Enggano, Pulau, i., Indon. | H5 | 114 |
| England, ctry., U.K. | I12 | 8 |
| England, Nf., Can. | B17 | 106 |
| Englefield, Cape, c., N.T., Can. | C15 | 92 |
| Englehart, On., Can. | C16 | 110 |
| Englewood, B.C., Can. | G8 | 102 |
| Englewood, Co., U.S. | E12 | 120 |
| Englewood, Fl., U.S. | M4 | 112 |
| Englewood, Ks., U.S. | N8 | 118 |
| Englewood, Tn., U.S. | D2 | 112 |
| English, In., U.S. | D10 | 114 |
| English, stm., In., U.S. | I4 | 110 |
| English, stm., On., Can. | G14 | 96 |
| English Bay, Ak., U.S. | G19 | 100 |
| English Channel (La Manche), strt., Eur. | K12 | 8 |
| English Coast, Ant. | C12 | 73 |
| English Harbour West, Nf., Can. | E18 | 106 |
| Enguera, Spain | G11 | 16 |
| Engure, Lat. | D6 | 22 |
| Engwilen, Switz. | C11 | 13 |
| 'En Harod, Isr. | C4 | 50 |
| Enid, Ok., U.S. | C9 | 116 |
| Enilda, Ab., Can. | B18 | 102 |
| Enka, N.C., U.S. | D4 | 112 |
| eNjesuthi, mtn., Afr. | G9 | 66 |
| Enkhuizen, Neth. | C7 | 12 |
| Enmedio, Cerro de, mtn., Mex. | H9 | 90 |
| Enna, Italy | L9 | 18 |
| Ennadai Lake, l., N.T., Can. | D12 | 96 |
| Ennedi, plat., Chad | E5 | 56 |
| Ennis, Mt., U.S. | E14 | 122 |
| Ennis, Tx., U.S. | G10 | 116 |
| Enniskillen, N. Ire., U.K. | G6 | 8 |
| Enns, Aus. | G14 | 10 |
| Enns, stm., Aus. | F14 | 10 |
| Enochs, Tx., U.S. | F4 | 116 |
| Enon, Oh., U.S. | H3 | 108 |
| Enosburg Falls, Vt., U.S. | C14 | 108 |
| Enrique Urien, Arg. | D8 | 80 |
| Enriquillo, Dom. Rep. | F9 | 94 |
| Enriquillo, Lago, l., Dom. Rep. | E9 | 94 |
| Enschede, Neth. | D10 | 12 |
| Ensenada, Arg. | H10 | 80 |
| Ensenada, Mex. | B1 | 90 |
| Enshi, China | E8 | 30 |
| Entebbe, Ug. | A6 | 58 |
| Enterprise, Al., U.S. | K11 | 114 |
| Enterprise, Ca., U.S. | E4 | 124 |
| Enterprise, Guy. | D13 | 84 |
| Enterprise, Ms., U.S. | M10 | 118 |
| Enterprise, Ms., U.S. | J8 | 114 |
| Enterprise, Or., U.S. | E8 | 122 |
| Enterprise, Ut., U.S. | G3 | 120 |
| Entiat, stm., Wa., U.S. | C5 | 122 |
| Entrée, Île d' l', i., P.Q., Can. | E12 | 106 |
| Entre Rios, Bol. | I9 | 82 |
| Entre Rios, Braz. | A9 | 79 |
| Entre Rios, prov., Arg. | F9 | 80 |
| Entre-Rios, Cordillera, mts., Hond. | C9 | 92 |
| Entre-Rios de Minas, Braz. | F6 | 79 |
| Entroncamento, Port. | F3 | 16 |
| Entwistle, Ab., Can. | D19 | 102 |
| Enugu, Nig. | H13 | 64 |
| Enumclaw, Wa., U.S. | C4 | 122 |
| Envalira, Port d', Eur. | C13 | 16 |
| Envermeu, Fr. | C8 | 14 |
| Envigado, Col. | D5 | 84 |
| Envira, Braz. | B6 | 82 |
| Envira, stm., Braz. | B6 | 82 |
| Eo, stm., Spain | B4 | 16 |
| Eolia, Mo., U.S. | C5 | 114 |
| Eolie, Isole, is., Italy | K9 | 18 |
| Epe, Nig. | H11 | 64 |
| Epecuén, Lago, l., Arg. | I7 | 80 |
| Épehy, Fr. | H3 | 12 |
| Épernay, Fr. | C10 | 14 |
| Ephesus, hist., Tur. | L11 | 20 |
| Ephraim, Ut., U.S. | E5 | 120 |
| Ephrata, Pa., U.S. | G10 | 108 |
| Ephrata, Wa., U.S. | C6 | 122 |
| Épinal, Fr. | D13 | 14 |
| Epirus see Ípeiros, hist. reg., Grc. | J4 | 20 |
| Epokiro, Nmb. | C4 | 66 |
| Epping, Eng., U.K. | J14 | 8 |
| Epping, N.H., U.S. | D15 | 108 |
| Epsom, Eng., U.K. | J13 | 8 |
| Epukiro, stm., Afr. | C5 | 66 |
| Eqlīd, Iran | F12 | 48 |
| Equality, Il., U.S. | E8 | 114 |
| Equatorial Guinea, ctry., Afr. | H8 | 54 |
| Erath, La., U.S. | M4 | 114 |
| Erciş, Tur. | B7 | 48 |
| Erciyes Dağı, mtn., Tur. | B3 | 48 |
| Érd, Hung. | H18 | 10 |
| Erdaoliangzi, China | C7 | 32 |
| Erdene, Mong. | C9 | 30 |
| Erebato, stm., Ven. | E10 | 84 |
| Erebus, Mount, mtn., Ant. | C8 | 73 |
| Ereğli, Tur. | C3 | 48 |
| Ereğli, Tur. | C9 | 30 |
| Erenhot, China | C9 | 30 |
| Erepecuru, Lago do, l., Braz. | H14 | 84 |
| Eressós, Grc. | J9 | 20 |
| Erexim, Braz. | K7 | 20 |
| Erexim, Braz. | D12 | 80 |
| Erfoud, Mor. | E8 | 62 |
| Erft, stm., Ger. | F5 | 10 |
| Erfurt, Ger. | E11 | 10 |
| Erges (Erjas), stm., Eur. | F5 | 16 |
| Ergun (Argun'), stm., Asia | A11 | 30 |
| Er Hai, l., China | B6 | 40 |
| Erhlin, Tai. | L9 | 34 |
| Eriba, Sudan | I9 | 60 |
| Erice, Italy | K7 | 18 |
| Erichsen Lake, l., N.T., Can. | B16 | 96 |
| Erick, Ok., U.S. | D7 | 116 |
| Erickson, B.C., Can. | H18 | 102 |
| Erickson, Mb., Can. | H15 | 104 |
| Ericson, Ne., U.S. | J9 | 118 |
| Erie, Co., U.S. | D11 | 120 |
| Erie, Il., U.S. | I5 | 110 |
| Erie, Pa., U.S. | E6 | 108 |
| Erie, Lake, l., N.A. | H15 | 110 |
| Erie Canal see New York State Barge Canal, N.Y., U.S. | D8 | 108 |
| Eriksdale, Mb., Can. | H16 | 104 |
| Erimo-misaki, c., Japan | f18 | 36a |
| Erin, On., Can. | G15 | 110 |
| Erin, Tn., U.S. | F9 | 114 |
| Eritrea, ctry., Afr. | E8 | 56 |
| Erjas (Erges), stm., Eur. | F5 | 16 |
| Erjiazhen, China | C10 | 34 |
| Erkelenz, Ger. | D6 | 10 |
| Erkowit, Sudan | H9 | 60 |
| Erlangen, Ger. | F11 | 10 |
| Ermelo, Neth. | D8 | 12 |
| Ermelo, S. Afr. | F9 | 66 |
| Ermenek, Tur. | C2 | 48 |
| Ermineskin Indian Reserve, Ab., Can. | E21 | 102 |
| Ermoúpolis, Grc. | L8 | 20 |
| Ernée, Fr. | D6 | 14 |
| Erode, India | G4 | 46 |
| Eromanga, Austl. | F5 | 70 |
| Erongo, Nmb. | C2 | 66 |
| Erota, Erit. | I9 | 60 |
| Er-Rachidia, Mor. | E8 | 62 |
| Errol Heights, Or., U.S. | E3 | 122 |
| Erskine, Mn., U.S. | D11 | 118 |
| Erskine Inlet, b., N.T., Can. | A12 | 96 |
| Erstein, Fr. | D14 | 14 |
| Ertai, China | B5 | 30 |
| Ertil', Russia | J23 | 22 |
| Ertix (Irtyš), stm., Asia | H9 | 28 |
| Ertuğrul, Tur. | J11 | 20 |
| Erudina, Austl. | H3 | 70 |
| Eruwa, Nig. | H11 | 64 |
| Erval, Braz. | G12 | 80 |
| Erval d'Oeste, Braz. | D13 | 80 |
| Erwin, N.C., U.S. | D8 | 112 |
| Erwin, Tn., U.S. | C4 | 112 |
| Erwood, Sk., Can. | F12 | 104 |
| Eryuan, China | A5 | 40 |
| Erzgebirge (Krušné hory), mts., Eur. | E13 | 10 |
| Erzin, Russia | G17 | 26 |
| Erzincan, Tur. | B5 | 48 |
| Erzurum, Tur. | B6 | 48 |
| Esa'ala, Pap. N. Gui. | A10 | 68 |
| Esashi, Japan | F15 | 36 |
| Esashi, Japan | H16 | 36 |
| Esbjerg, Den. | N11 | 6 |
| Esca, stm., Spain | J5 | 14 |
| Escalante, Ut., U.S. | G5 | 120 |
| Escalante, stm., Ut., U.S. | G5 | 120 |
| Escalante Desert, des., Ut., U.S. | G3 | 120 |
| Escalon, Ca., U.S. | G4 | 124 |
| Escalón, Mex. | D7 | 90 |
| Escanaba, Mi., U.S. | D8 | 110 |
| Escanaba, stm., Mi., U.S. | C7 | 110 |
| Escárcega, Mex. | H14 | 90 |
| Escarpada Point, c., Phil. | I20 | 39b |
| Escatawpa, stm., U.S. | L8 | 114 |
| Escaut (Schelde), stm., Eur. | B8 | 14 |
| Esch-sur-Alzette, Lux. | I8 | 12 |
| Eschwege, Ger. | D10 | 10 |
| Eschweiler, Ger. | E6 | 10 |
| Escobal, Pan. | H15 | 92 |
| Escobedo, Mex. | C8 | 90 |
| Escocesa, Bahía, b., Dom. Rep. | E10 | 94 |
| Escondida, Ca., U.S. | K8 | 124 |
| Escondido, stm., Nic. | E11 | 92 |
| Escondido, Río de Veraguas, Isla, i., Pan. | H13 | 92 |
| Escuinapa de Hidalgo, Mex. | F7 | 90 |
| Escuintla, Guat. | C4 | 92 |
| Escuintla, Mex. | J13 | 90 |
| Escuintla, dept., Guat. | C3 | 92 |
| Escuminac, Point, c., N.B., Can. | E9 | 106 |
| Ese-Suki, Sudan | K7 | 60 |
| Eşfahān (Isfahan), Iran | E11 | 48 |
| Esfarāyen, Iran | C14 | 48 |
| Eshkāshem, Afg. | B4 | 44 |
| Eshowe, S. Afr. | G10 | 66 |
| Esigodini, Zimb. | C9 | 66 |
| Esk, Austl. | F10 | 70 |
| Eskdale, W.V., U.S. | I5 | 108 |
| Eskifjörður, Ice. | B7 | 6a |
| Eskilstuna, Swe. | L15 | 6 |
| Eskimo Lakes, l., N.T., Can. | B28 | 100 |
| Eskimo Point, N.T., Can. | D14 | 96 |
| Eskişehir, Tur. | H14 | 4 |
| Eskridge, Ks., U.S. | M11 | 118 |
| Esla, stm., Spain | C6 | 16 |
| Eslāmābād, Iran | D9 | 48 |
| Eslāmshahr, Iran | D11 | 48 |
| Esmeralda, Austl. | B5 | 70 |
| Esmeralda, Cuba | D5 | 94 |
| Esmeraldas, Ec. | G3 | 84 |
| Esmeraldas, prov., Ec. | G3 | 84 |
| Esmeraldas, stm., Ec. | G3 | 84 |
| Esmond, N.D., U.S. | C8 | 118 |
| Esneux, Bel. | H8 | 12 |
| Espada, Punta, c., Col. | A7 | 84 |
| Espalion, Fr. | H9 | 14 |
| Espanola, N.M., U.S. | I10 | 120 |
| Espanola, On., Can. | D14 | 110 |
| Esparza, C.R. | H10 | 92 |
| Espejo, Spain | H7 | 16 |
| Espera Feliz, Braz. | F8 | 79 |
| Esperança, Braz. | J8 | 84 |
| Esperance, Austl. | F4 | 68 |
| Esperance Bay, b., Austl. | F4 | 68 |
| Esperanza, Arg. | F8 | 80 |
| Esperanza, Mex. | D5 | 90 |
| Esperanza Inlet, b., B.C., Can. | H8 | 102 |
| Espinal, Col. | E5 | 84 |
| Espinhaço, Serra do, mts., Braz. | C7 | 79 |
| Espinho, Port. | D3 | 16 |
| Espinillo, Braz. | C9 | 80 |
| Espino, Ven. | C9 | 84 |
| Espinosa, Braz. | C7 | 79 |
| Espírito Santo, state, Braz. | F8 | 79 |
| Espíritu Santo, Isla, i., Mex. | E4 | 90 |
| Espita, Mex. | G15 | 90 |
| Espoir, Bay d', b., Nf., Can. | E18 | 106 |
| Espoo (Esbo), Fin. | K19 | 6 |
| El Port de Pollença, Spain | F15 | 16 |
| Espumoso, Braz. | E12 | 80 |
| Espungabera, Moz. | B11 | 66 |
| Esquel, Arg. | E2 | 78 |
| Esquimalt, B.C., Can. | I11 | 102 |
| Esquina, Arg. | F9 | 80 |
| Esquina Negra, Arg. | H9 | 80 |
| Esquipulas, Guat. | C5 | 92 |
| Esquipulas, Nic. | E9 | 92 |
| Esquiú, Arg. | E6 | 80 |
| Essaouira (Mogador), Mor. | E6 | 62 |
| Es-Sekhira, Tun. | C16 | 62 |
| Essen, Bel. | F5 | 12 |
| Essen, Ger. | D7 | 10 |
| Essequibo, stm., Guy. | E13 | 84 |
| Essequibo Islands-West Demerara, prov., Guy. | D13 | 84 |
| Es Sers, Tun. | M4 | 18 |
| Essex, Ia., U.S. | K12 | 118 |
| Essex, Md., U.S. | H10 | 108 |
| Essex, Mt., U.S. | B12 | 122 |
| Essex, On., Can. | H13 | 110 |
| Essex, co., Eng., U.K. | J14 | 8 |
| Essex Junction, Vt., U.S. | C13 | 108 |
| Essexville, Mi., U.S. | G12 | 110 |
| Esslingen, Ger. | G9 | 10 |
| Es Smala es Souassi, Tun. | N5 | 18 |
| Essonne, dept., Fr. | D9 | 14 |
| Essoyes, Fr. | D11 | 14 |
| Est, Île de l', i., P.Q., Can. | E12 | 106 |
| Est, Pointe de l', c., P.Q., Can. | C12 | 106 |
| Estacada, Or., U.S. | E4 | 122 |
| Estacado, Llano, pl., U.S. | F4 | 116 |
| Estados, Isla de los, i., Arg. | G4 | 78 |
| Eṣṭahbān, Iran | G13 | 48 |
| Estância, Braz. | F11 | 76 |
| Estancia, N.M., U.S. | J10 | 120 |
| Estanislao del Campo, Arg. | C8 | 80 |
| Estanzuelas, El Sal. | D6 | 92 |
| Estats, Pique d', mtn., Eur. | C13 | 16 |
| Estcourt, S. Afr. | G9 | 66 |
| Este, Italy | D6 | 18 |
| Esteio, Braz. | E13 | 80 |
| Esteli, Nic. | D8 | 92 |
| Esteli, dept., Nic. | D8 | 92 |
| Estella, Spain | C9 | 16 |
| Estelline, S.D., U.S. | G11 | 118 |
| Estelline, Tx., U.S. | E6 | 116 |
| Estepa, Spain | H7 | 16 |
| Estepona, Spain | I6 | 16 |
| Esteros, Arg. | D7 | 80 |
| Estes Park, Co., U.S. | D11 | 120 |
| Estevan, Sk., Can. | I12 | 104 |
| Estevan Group, is., B.C., Can. | D5 | 102 |
| Estevan Point, B.C., Can. | H8 | 102 |
| Estherville, Ia., U.S. | H13 | 118 |
| Estill, S.C., U.S. | G5 | 112 |
| Estiva, Rio da, stm., Braz. | B6 | 79 |
| Eston, Sk., Can. | G6 | 104 |
| Estonia (Eesti), ctry., Eur. | G17 | 26 |
| Estrela, Braz. | E13 | 80 |
| Estrela, Port. | E4 | 16 |
| Estrela do Norte, Braz. | B4 | 79 |
| Estrela do Sul, Braz. | E5 | 79 |
| Estremadura, hist. reg., Port. | F2 | 16 |
| Estremoz, Port. | G4 | 16 |
| Estuary, Sk., Can. | H5 | 104 |
| Esztergom, Hung. | H18 | 10 |
| Étables, Fr. | D4 | 14 |
| Etadunna, Austl. | G3 | 70 |
| Etah, Grnld. | B12 | 86 |
| Etah, India | G8 | 44 |
| Étain, Fr. | C12 | 14 |
| Étamaniou, stm., P.Q., Can. | B13 | 106 |
| Étampes, Fr. | D9 | 14 |
| Étaples, Fr. | B8 | 14 |
| Etāwah, India | G8 | 44 |
| Etchemin, stm., P.Q., Can. | F3 | 106 |
| Etchojoa, Mex. | D5 | 90 |
| Ethan, S.D., U.S. | H10 | 118 |
| Ethel, Ms., U.S. | I7 | 114 |
| Ethelbert, Mb., Can. | G14 | 104 |
| Ethel Lake, l., Yk., Can. | E26 | 100 |
| Ethiopia (Ityopiya), ctry., Afr. | G8 | 56 |
| Ethridge, Tn., U.S. | G9 | 114 |
| Etna, Ca., U.S. | C3 | 124 |
| Etna, Wy., U.S. | A5 | 120 |
| Etna, Monte, vol., Italy | L10 | 18 |
| Etobicoke, On., Can. | G16 | 110 |
| Etomami, stm., Sk., Can. | F12 | 104 |
| Etosha Pan, pl., Nmb. | A2 | 66 |
| Etowah, Tn., U.S. | D2 | 112 |
| Etowah, stm., Ga., U.S. | E1 | 112 |
| Étretat, Fr. | C7 | 14 |
| Ettelbruck, Lux. | I9 | 12 |
| Et Tidra, i., Maur. | B1 | 64 |
| Ettlingen, Ger. | G8 | 10 |
| Ettrick, Va., U.S. | B9 | 112 |
| Etzatlán, Mex. | G7 | 90 |
| Etzikom Coulee, stm., Ab., Can. | I3 | 104 |
| Etzná, hist., Mex. | H14 | 90 |
| Eu, Fr. | B8 | 14 |
| Euchiniko, stm., B.C., Can. | D10 | 102 |
| Eucla, Austl. | F5 | 68 |
| Euclid, Oh., U.S. | F5 | 108 |
| Eucumbene, Lake, res., Austl. | K8 | 70 |
| Eudora, Ar., U.S. | I5 | 114 |
| Eudora, Ks., U.S. | M12 | 118 |
| Eudunda, Austl. | J3 | 70 |
| Eufaula, Al., U.S. | K11 | 114 |
| Eufaula, Ok., U.S. | D11 | 116 |
| Eufaula Lake, res., Ok., U.S. | D11 | 116 |
| Eugene, Or., U.S. | F2 | 122 |
| Eugenia, Punta, c., Mex. | D2 | 90 |
| Eugenio Bustos, Arg. | G4 | 80 |
| Eugowra, Austl. | I8 | 70 |
| Eumungerie, Austl. | H8 | 70 |
| Eunice, La., U.S. | L4 | 114 |
| Eunice, N.M., U.S. | G3 | 116 |
| Eupen, Bel. | G9 | 12 |
| Euphrates (Firat) (Nahr al-Furāt), stm., Asia | F9 | 48 |
| Eupora, Ms., U.S. | I7 | 114 |
| Eure, dept., Fr. | C7 | 14 |
| Eure, stm., Fr. | D8 | 14 |
| Eure-et-Loir, dept., Fr. | D8 | 14 |
| Eureka, Ca., U.S. | D1 | 124 |
| Eureka, Il., U.S. | J6 | 110 |
| Eureka, Ks., U.S. | N11 | 118 |
| Eureka, Mt., U.S. | B10 | 122 |
| Eureka, Nv., U.S. | E10 | 124 |
| Eureka, S.C., U.S. | F5 | 112 |
| Eureka, S.D., U.S. | F8 | 118 |
| Eureka, Ut., U.S. | E4 | 120 |
| Eureka Springs, Ar., U.S. | F3 | 114 |
| Euroa, Austl. | K6 | 70 |
| Europa, Île, i., Afr. | F8 | 58 |
| Europa Point, c., Gib. | I6 | 16 |
| Europe | C9 | 52 |
| Europoort, Neth. | E5 | 12 |
| Euskal Herriko, state, Spain | B9 | 16 |
| Euskirchen, Ger. | E6 | 10 |
| Eustace, Tx., U.S. | G10 | 116 |
| Eustis, Fl., U.S. | K5 | 112 |
| Eustis, Ne., U.S. | K7 | 118 |
| Eutaw, Al., U.S. | J9 | 114 |
| Eutsuk Lake, l., B.C., Can. | D8 | 102 |
| Eva, Al., U.S. | H10 | 114 |
| Evadale, Tx., U.S. | L2 | 114 |
| Evans, Co., U.S. | D12 | 120 |
| Evans, Lac, l., P.Q., Can. | F17 | 96 |
| Evans, Mount, mtn., Co., U.S. | E11 | 120 |
| Evansburg, Ab., Can. | D19 | 102 |
| Evans City, Pa., U.S. | G6 | 108 |
| Evansdale, Ia., U.S. | H3 | 110 |
| Evans Head, c., Austl. | G10 | 70 |
| Evans Strait, strt., N.T., Can. | D16 | 96 |
| Evanston, Il., U.S. | H8 | 110 |
| Evanston, Wy., U.S. | C6 | 120 |
| Evansville, Il., U.S. | D7 | 114 |
| Evansville, In., U.S. | E9 | 114 |
| Evansville, Mn., U.S. | E12 | 118 |
| Evansville, Wi., U.S. | H6 | 110 |
| Evansville, Wy., U.S. | B10 | 120 |
| Evant, Tx., U.S. | H8 | 116 |
| Evart, Mi., U.S. | G10 | 110 |
| Evarts, Ky., U.S. | C3 | 112 |
| Eveleth, Mn., U.S. | C3 | 118 |
| Evening Shade, Ar., U.S. | F5 | 114 |
| Everard, Lake, l., Austl. | F7 | 68 |
| Everard, Mount, mtn., B.C., Can. | F9 | 102 |
| Everest, Ks., U.S. | L12 | 118 |
| Everest, Mount (Qomolangma Feng), mtn., Asia | G12 | 44 |
| Everett, Pa., U.S. | G8 | 108 |
| Everett, Wa., U.S. | C3 | 122 |
| Everglades, The, sw., Fl., U.S. | M6 | 112 |
| Everglades City, Fl., U.S. | N5 | 112 |
| Everglades National Park, Fl., U.S. | N6 | 112 |
| Evergreen, Al., U.S. | K10 | 114 |
| Evergreen, Ca., U.S. | I5 | 124 |
| Evergreen, Mt., U.S. | B11 | 122 |
| Everly, Ia., U.S. | H12 | 118 |
| Everman, vol., Mex. | H4 | 90 |
| Evesham, Sk., Can. | F5 | 104 |
| Évian-les-Bains, Fr. | F13 | 14 |
| Evionnaz, Switz. | F7 | 13 |
| Evisa, Fr. | G3 | 18 |
| Évora, Port. | G4 | 16 |
| Évreux, Fr. | C8 | 14 |
| Évros (Marica) (Meriç), stm., Eur. | H10 | 20 |
| Évry, Fr. | D9 | 14 |
| Évvoia, i., Grc. | K7 | 20 |
| Ewa, Hi., U.S. | p15 | 125a |
| Ewen, Mi., U.S. | D6 | 110 |
| Ewing, Ne., U.S. | I9 | 118 |
| Ewing, Va., U.S. | C3 | 112 |
| Ewo, Congo | B2 | 58 |
| Exaltación, Bol. | E9 | 82 |
| Excelsior Mountain, mtn., Ca., U.S. | F6 | 124 |
| Excelsior Springs, Mo., U.S. | H6 | 124 |
| Exeter, Ca., U.S. | H6 | 124 |
| Exeter, Eng., U.K. | K10 | 8 |
| Exeter, Ne., U.S. | K10 | 118 |
| Exeter, N.H., U.S. | E16 | 108 |
| Exeter, On., Can. | G14 | 110 |
| Exeter Sound, strt., N.T., Can. | C20 | 96 |
| Exira, Ia., U.S. | J13 | 118 |
| Exmore, Va., U.S. | B11 | 112 |
| Exmouth, Austl. | D2 | 68 |
| Exmouth, Eng., U.K. | K10 | 8 |
| Exmouth Gulf, b., Austl. | D2 | 68 |
| Expedition Range, mts., Austl. | E8 | 70 |
| Experiment, Ga., U.S. | F2 | 112 |
| Exploits, stm., Nf., Can. | D17 | 106 |
| Exploits, Bay of, b., Nf., Can. | C18 | 106 |
| Exploits Dam, Nf., Can. | D17 | 106 |
| Exshaw, Ab., Can. | F19 | 102 |
| Extremadura, state, Spain | F5 | 16 |
| Exuma Cays, is., Bah. | B6 | 94 |
| Exuma Sound, strt., Bah. | B6 | 94 |
| Eyebrow, Sk., Can. | H8 | 104 |
| Eyehill Creek, stm., Can. | F4 | 104 |
| Eyl, Som. | G10 | 56 |
| Eymoutiers, Fr. | G8 | 14 |
| Eyota, Mn., U.S. | G16 | 110 |
| Eyrarbakki, Ice. | C3 | 6a |
| Eyre, Austl. | F5 | 68 |
| Eyre North, Lake, l., Austl. | G2 | 70 |
| Eyre Peninsula, pen., Austl. | I1 | 70 |
| Eyre South, Lake, l., Austl. | G2 | 70 |
| Eysturoy, i., Faer. Is. | D8 | 6b |
| Ezine, Tur. | J10 | 20 |
| Ezjaryšča, Bela. | F12 | 22 |

**F**

| Fabens, Tx., U.S. | M10 | 120 |
|---|---|---|
| Faber Lake, l., N.T., Can. | D9 | 96 |
| Fábrega, Cerro, mtn., Pan. | H12 | 92 |
| Fabriano, Italy | F7 | 18 |
| Facatativá, Col. | E5 | 84 |
| Factoryville, Pa., U.S. | F11 | 108 |
| Fada, Chad | E5 | 56 |
| Fada Ngourma, Burkina | E10 | 64 |
| Fadd, Hung. | I18 | 10 |
| Faddeja, zaliv, b., Russia | B13 | 28 |
| Fadit, Sudan | M7 | 60 |
| Faenza, Italy | E6 | 18 |
| Faeroe Islands (Føroyar), dep., Eur. | D8 | 6b |
| Fafa, Mali | D10 | 64 |
| Fafakourou, Sen. | E2 | 64 |
| Fafen, stm., Eth. | G9 | 56 |
| Faga, stm., Burkina | E10 | 64 |
| Fagaras, Rom. | D8 | 20 |
| Fagernes, Nor. | K11 | 6 |
| Faget, Rom. | D6 | 20 |
| Fagulbine, Lac, l., Mali | C8 | 64 |
| Fagurhólsmýri, Ice. | C5 | 6a |
| Faido, Switz. | F10 | 13 |
| Fairbairn Reservoir, res., Austl. | D8 | 70 |
| Fairbank, Az., U.S. | M6 | 120 |
| Fairbanks, Ak., U.S. | D21 | 100 |
| Fairbanks, La., U.S. | J4 | 114 |
| Fair Bluff, N.C., U.S. | E7 | 112 |
| Fairborn, Oh., U.S. | H2 | 108 |
| Fairburn, Ga., U.S. | F2 | 112 |
| Fairbury, Il., U.S. | J7 | 110 |
| Fairbury, Ne., U.S. | K10 | 118 |
| Fairchance, Pa., U.S. | H7 | 108 |
| Fairchild, Wi., U.S. | F5 | 110 |
| Fairfax, Al., U.S. | J11 | 114 |
| Fairfax, Mn., U.S. | G13 | 118 |
| Fairfax, Mo., U.S. | B1 | 114 |
| Fairfax, Ok., U.S. | C10 | 116 |
| Fairfax, S.C., U.S. | G5 | 112 |
| Fairfax, S.D., U.S. | H9 | 118 |
| Fairfax, Va., U.S. | I9 | 108 |
| Fairfax, Vt., U.S. | C13 | 108 |
| Fairfield, Al., U.S. | I10 | 114 |
| Fairfield, Ca., U.S. | F3 | 124 |
| Fairfield, Ia., U.S. | I4 | 110 |
| Fairfield, Id., U.S. | G11 | 122 |
| Fairfield, Il., U.S. | D8 | 114 |
| Fairfield, Me., U.S. | C17 | 108 |
| Fairfield, Mt., U.S. | C14 | 122 |
| Fairfield, Ne., U.S. | K9 | 118 |
| Fairfield, Oh., U.S. | H2 | 108 |
| Fairfield, Tx., U.S. | H10 | 116 |
| Fairgrove, Mi., U.S. | G12 | 110 |
| Fairhaven, Ma., U.S. | F16 | 108 |
| Fair Haven, N.Y., U.S. | D10 | 108 |
| Fairhope, Al., U.S. | L9 | 114 |
| Fairland, In., U.S. | C11 | 114 |
| Fairland, Ok., U.S. | C12 | 116 |
| Fairlie, N.Z. | F3 | 72 |
| Fairmont, Mn., U.S. | H13 | 118 |
| Fairmont, Ne., U.S. | K10 | 118 |
| Fairmont, W.V., U.S. | H6 | 108 |
| Fairmont Hot Springs, B.C., Can. | G19 | 102 |
| Fairmount, Ga., U.S. | E1 | 112 |
| Fairmount, Il., U.S. | B9 | 114 |
| Fairmount, In., U.S. | B11 | 114 |
| Fairmount, N.D., U.S. | E11 | 118 |
| Fair Ness, c., N.T., Can. | D18 | 96 |
| Fair Oaks, Ca., U.S. | F4 | 124 |
| Fair Plain, Mi., U.S. | H9 | 110 |
| Fairplains, N.C., U.S. | C5 | 112 |
| Fairplay, Co., U.S. | E10 | 120 |
| Fairview, Ab., Can. | A16 | 102 |
| Fairview, Ga., U.S. | E1 | 112 |
| Fairview, Il., U.S. | J5 | 110 |
| Fairview, Ks., U.S. | L12 | 118 |
| Fairview, Mi., U.S. | F11 | 110 |
| Fairview, Mt., U.S. | D3 | 118 |
| Fairview, Ok., U.S. | C8 | 116 |
| Fairview, Tn., U.S. | G9 | 114 |
| Fairview, Ut., U.S. | E5 | 120 |
| Fairview Park, In., U.S. | C9 | 114 |
| Fairview Peak, mtn., Nv., U.S. | E7 | 124 |
| Fairweather Mountain, mtn., N.A. | G26 | 100 |
| Faisalabad, Pak. | E5 | 44 |
| Faison, N.C., U.S. | D8 | 112 |
| Faith, S.D., U.S. | F5 | 118 |
| Faiyum see Al-Fayyūm, Egypt | C6 | 60 |
| Faizābād, India | G10 | 44 |
| Fajardo, P.R. | E12 | 94 |
| Fakfak, Indon. | F9 | 38 |
| Faku, China | A11 | 32 |
| Falam, Myan. | C2 | 40 |
| Falcon, state, Ven. | B8 | 84 |
| Falconara Marittima, Italy | F8 | 18 |
| Falconbridge, On., Can. | D15 | 110 |
| Falcon Heights, Or., U.S. | H4 | 122 |
| Falcon Reservoir (Presa Falcón), res., N.A. | M7 | 116 |
| Falémé, stm., Afr. | F4 | 54 |
| Faleşti, Mol. | B11 | 20 |
| Falfurrias, Tx., U.S. | L8 | 116 |
| Falher, Ab., Can. | B17 | 102 |
| Falkensee, Ger. | C13 | 10 |
| Falkenstein, Ger. | E12 | 10 |
| Falkirk, Scot., U.K. | E10 | 8 |
| Falkland, B.C., Can. | G15 | 102 |
| Falkland Islands, dep., S.A. | G5 | 78 |
| Falkland Sound, strt., Falk. Is. | G5 | 78 |
| Falkville, Al., U.S. | H10 | 114 |
| Fall, stm., Ks., U.S. | N12 | 118 |
| Fallais, Bel. | G7 | 12 |
| Fallbrook, Ca., U.S. | K8 | 124 |
| Fall Creek, Wi., U.S. | F4 | 110 |
| Fallentimber Creek, stm., Ab., Can. | F19 | 102 |
| Fallon, Mt., U.S. | E2 | 118 |
| Fallon, Nv., U.S. | E7 | 124 |
| Fall River, Ks., U.S. | N11 | 118 |
| Fall River, Wi., U.S. | G6 | 110 |
| Fall River Mills, Ca., U.S. | C4 | 124 |
| Falls City, Ne., U.S. | K12 | 118 |
| Falls Creek, Pa., U.S. | F8 | 108 |
| Falmouth, Eng., U.K. | K8 | 8 |
| Falmouth, Jam. | E6 | 94 |
| Falmouth, Ky., U.S. | I2 | 108 |
| Falmouth, Me., U.S. | D16 | 108 |
| Falmouth, Va., U.S. | I9 | 108 |
| False Divi Point, c., India | E6 | 46 |
| Falso, Cabo, c., Dom. Rep. | E8 | 94 |
| Falso, Cabo, c., Hond. | B11 | 92 |
| Falster, i., Den. | N12 | 6 |
| Fălticeni, Rom. | B10 | 20 |
| Falun, Swe. | K14 | 6 |
| Famaillá, Arg. | D6 | 80 |
| Famatina, Arg. | E5 | 80 |
| Famatina, Sierra de, mts., Arg. | E5 | 80 |
| Family Lake, l., Mb., Can. | G19 | 104 |
| Fana, Mali | E6 | 64 |
| Fanado, stm., Braz. | D7 | 79 |
| Fanambana, Madag. | n24 | 67b |
| Fanchon, Pointe, c., Haiti | E7 | 94 |
| Fanchuan, China | C8 | 34 |
| Fandriana, Madag. | r22 | 67b |
| Fang, Thai. | E5 | 40 |
| Fangak, Sudan | M6 | 60 |
| Fangcheng, China | H7 | 34 |
| Fangdao, China | G3 | 34 |
| Fanipol', Bela. | H10 | 22 |
| Fanny, Mount, mtn., Or., U.S. | E8 | 122 |
| Fanny Bay, B.C., Can. | H10 | 102 |
| Fano, Italy | F8 | 18 |
| Fan Si Pan, mtn., Viet. | C7 | 40 |
| Fanxian, China | H3 | 32 |
| Faraday, sci., Ant. | B12 | 73 |
| Faradje, D.R.C. | H6 | 56 |
| Faradofay, Madag. | t22 | 67b |
| Farafangana, Madag. | s22 | 67b |
| Farāh, Afg. | E17 | 48 |
| Farahalana, Madag. | o24 | 67b |
| Farā'id, Jabal al-, mtn., Egypt | J3 | 48 |
| Farallon Islands, is., Ca., U.S. | G2 | 124 |
| Faramana, Burkina | E7 | 64 |
| Faranah, Gui. | F4 | 64 |
| Farasān, Jazā'ir, is., Sau. Ar. | F2 | 47 |
| Faratsiho, Madag. | q22 | 67b |
| Farewell, Cape, c., N.Z. | D4 | 72 |
| Fargo, N.D., U.S. | E11 | 118 |
| Faribault, Mn., U.S. | F2 | 110 |
| Faribault, Lac, l., P.Q., Can. | E18 | 96 |
| Farīdkot, India | E6 | 44 |
| Farīdpur, Bngl. | I13 | 44 |
| Farīdpur, India | D15 | 48 |
| Farīmān, Iran | D15 | 48 |
| Farina, Il., U.S. | D8 | 114 |
| Fāriskūr, Egypt | B6 | 60 |
| Farley, Ia., U.S. | H4 | 110 |
| Farmer City, Il., U.S. | B8 | 114 |
| Farmersburg, In., U.S. | C9 | 114 |
| Farmersville, Il., U.S. | C7 | 114 |
| Farmersville, Tx., U.S. | F10 | 116 |
| Farmerville, La., U.S. | J4 | 114 |
| Farmington, Ia., U.S. | J4 | 110 |
| Farmington, Il., U.S. | J5 | 110 |
| Farmington, Me., U.S. | C16 | 108 |
| Farmington, Mo., U.S. | E6 | 114 |
| Farmington, N.H., U.S. | D15 | 108 |
| Farmington, N.M., U.S. | H8 | 120 |
| Farmington, Ut., U.S. | D5 | 120 |
| Far Mountain, mtn., B.C., Can. | E9 | 102 |
| Farmville, N.C., U.S. | D9 | 112 |
| Farmville, Va., U.S. | B8 | 112 |
| Farnam, Ne., U.S. | K7 | 118 |
| Farnham, P.Q., Can. | B14 | 108 |
| Farnham, Mount, mtn., B.C., Can. | G18 | 102 |
| Farnhamville, Ia., U.S. | I13 | 118 |
| Faro, Braz. | I14 | 84 |
| Faro, Port. | H4 | 16 |
| Faro, stm., Afr. | G9 | 54 |
| Farquhar Group, is., Sey. | D10 | 58 |
| Farragut, Ia., U.S. | K12 | 118 |
| Farrāshband, Iran | G12 | 48 |
| Farrell, Pa., U.S. | F6 | 108 |
| Farrukhābād, India | G8 | 44 |
| Fārsī, Afg. | E17 | 48 |
| Farsund, Nor. | L10 | 6 |
| Fartak, Ra's, c., Yemen | G8 | 47 |
| Farvel, Kap, c., Grnld. | E24 | 96 |
| Farwell, Mi., U.S. | G11 | 110 |
| Farwell, Tx., U.S. | I3 | 116 |
| Fasā, Iran | G12 | 48 |
| Fasano, Italy | I12 | 18 |
| Fatehpur, India | G6 | 44 |
| Fathai, Sudan | M6 | 60 |
| Fathom Five National Marine Park, On., Can. | E14 | 110 |
| Fatick, Sen. | D1 | 64 |
| Fátima, Port. | F3 | 16 |
| Fatoto, Gam. | E3 | 64 |
| Fatʹož, Russia | I18 | 22 |
| Faulkton, S.D., U.S. | F8 | 118 |
| Faulquemont, Fr. | C13 | 14 |
| Fauquier, B.C., Can. | H16 | 102 |
| Fauske, Nor. | H14 | 6 |
| Faust, Ab., Can. | B19 | 102 |
| Fauvillers, Bel. | I8 | 12 |
| Faux-Cap, Madag. | t21 | 67b |
| Favara, Italy | L8 | 18 |
| Faverges, Fr. | G13 | 14 |
| Favourable Lake, l., On., Can. | F21 | 104 |
| Fawcett, Ab., Can. | C20 | 102 |
| Fawcett Lake, l., Ab., Can. | B21 | 102 |
| Fawn, stm., On., Can. | F15 | 96 |
| Fawnie Nose, mtn., B.C., Can. | D9 | 102 |
| Fawnie Range, mts., B.C., Can. | D10 | 102 |
| Faxaflói, b., Ice. | B2 | 6a |
| Faxinal, Braz. | G3 | 79 |
| Faxinal do Soturno, Braz. | E12 | 80 |
| Faya, Chad | E4 | 56 |
| Fayd, Sau. Ar. | H7 | 48 |
| Fayette, Al., U.S. | I9 | 114 |
| Fayette, Ia., U.S. | H4 | 110 |
| Fayette, Mo., U.S. | C4 | 114 |
| Fayette, Ms., U.S. | K5 | 114 |
| Fayette, Oh., U.S. | F2 | 108 |
| Fayetteville, Ar., U.S. | F2 | 114 |
| Fayetteville, Ga., U.S. | F2 | 112 |
| Fayetteville, N.C., U.S. | D8 | 112 |
| Fayetteville, Tn., U.S. | G10 | 114 |
| Fayetteville, W.V., U.S. | I5 | 108 |
| Fayl-Billot, Fr. | E12 | 14 |
| Fazenda de Cima, Braz. | F13 | 82 |
| Fazenda Nova, Braz. | D3 | 79 |
| Fǎzilka, India | E6 | 44 |
| Fǎzilpur, Pak. | F4 | 44 |
| Fazzān (Fezzan), hist. reg., Libya | C3 | 56 |
| Fdérik, Maur. | I4 | 62 |
| Fear, Cape, c., N.C., U.S. | F9 | 112 |
| Feather, stm., Ca., U.S. | E4 | 124 |
| Feathertop, Mount, mtn., Austl. | K7 | 70 |
| Fécamp, Fr. | C7 | 14 |
| Federación, Arg. | F10 | 80 |
| Federal, Arg. | F9 | 80 |
| Federalsburg, Md., U.S. | I11 | 108 |
| Fehérgyarmat, Hung. | H22 | 10 |
| Fehmarn, i., Ger. | A11 | 10 |
| Fehmarnbelt, strt., Eur. | A11 | 10 |
| Feia, Lagoa, b., Braz. | G8 | 79 |
| Feijó, Braz. | C6 | 82 |
| Feira, Zam. | E6 | 58 |
| Feira de Santana, Braz. | B9 | 79 |
| Feixiang, China | G2 | 32 |
| Fejér, co., Hung. | H18 | 10 |
| Felanitx, Spain | F15 | 16 |
| Felda, Fl., U.S. | M5 | 112 |
| Feldbach, Aus. | I15 | 10 |

| Name | Map Ref. | Page |
|---|---|---|
| Feldkirch, Aus. | H9 | 10 |
| Felhit, Erit. | I10 | 60 |
| Feliciano, Arroyo, stm., Arg. | F9 | 80 |
| Felix, Cape, c., N.T., Can. | C13 | 96 |
| Felix, Rio, stm., N.M., U.S. | K11 | 120 |
| Feliklândia, Braz. | E6 | 79 |
| Felixstowe, Eng., U.K. | J15 | 8 |
| Felixton, S. Afr. | G10 | 66 |
| Félix U. Gómez, Mex. | C4 | 90 |
| Fellbach, Ger. | G9 | 10 |
| Fellsmere, Fl., U.S. | L6 | 112 |
| Feltre, Italy | C6 | 18 |
| Femund, l., Nor. | J12 | 6 |
| Femundsenden, Nor. | K12 | 6 |
| Fen, stm., China | D9 | 30 |
| Fenelon Falls, On., Can. | F17 | 110 |
| Fengcheng, China | C12 | 32 |
| Fengcheng, China | G4 | 34 |
| Fengdu, China | F8 | 30 |
| Fengfeng, China | G2 | 32 |
| Fenghuanjing, China | D6 | 34 |
| Fengjiazhen, China | F9 | 32 |
| Fenglin, Tai. | L10 | 34 |
| Fengxin, China | G4 | 34 |
| Fengyang, China | E10 | 30 |
| Fengyüan, Tai. | K9 | 34 |
| Fengzhen, China | C9 | 30 |
| Feni, Bngl. | I14 | 44 |
| Fennimore, Wi., U.S. | H5 | 110 |
| Fennville, Mi., U.S. | H9 | 110 |
| Fenoarivo Atsinanana, Madag. | p23 | 67b |
| Fenshui'ao, China | J3 | 34 |
| Fenton, Mi., U.S. | H12 | 110 |
| Fentress, Tx., U.S. | J9 | 116 |
| Fenwick, W.V., U.S. | I6 | 108 |
| Fenyang, China | D9 | 30 |
| Feodosiya, Ukr. | H5 | 26 |
| Ferdinand, In., U.S. | D10 | 114 |
| Ferdows, Iran | D15 | 48 |
| Fergana, Uzb. | I12 | 26 |
| Fergus, On., Can. | G15 | 110 |
| Fergus Falls, Mn., U.S. | E11 | 118 |
| Ferguson, B.C., Can. | G17 | 102 |
| Ferguson, Ky., U.S. | B2 | 112 |
| Ferguson, Mo., U.S. | D6 | 114 |
| Fériana, Tun. | C15 | 62 |
| Ferkéssédougou, C. Iv. | G7 | 64 |
| Ferlo, Vallée du, val., Sen. | D2 | 64 |
| Fermo, Italy | F8 | 18 |
| Fermont, P.Q., Can. | F19 | 96 |
| Fernández, Arg. | D7 | 80 |
| Fernandina, Isla, i., Ec. | j13 | 84a |
| Fernandina Beach, Fl., U.S. | I5 | 112 |
| Fernando de Mora, Arg. | C10 | 80 |
| Fernando de Noronha, Ilha, i., Braz. | D12 | 76 |
| Fernandópolis, Braz. | F3 | 79 |
| Fernando Póo see Bioko, i., Eq. Gui. | J14 | 64 |
| Fernán-Núñez, Spain | H7 | 16 |
| Ferndale, Ca., U.S. | D1 | 124 |
| Ferndale, Wa., U.S. | B3 | 122 |
| Fernie, B.C., Can. | H19 | 102 |
| Fernley, Nv., U.S. | E6 | 124 |
| Fern Park, Fl., U.S. | K5 | 112 |
| Fernwood, Id., U.S. | C9 | 122 |
| Ferolle Point, c., Nf., Can. | A16 | 106 |
| Ferrara, Italy | E6 | 18 |
| Ferreñafe, Peru | B2 | 82 |
| Ferreyra, Arg. | F6 | 80 |
| Ferriday, La., U.S. | K5 | 114 |
| Ferrières, Fr. | D9 | 14 |
| Ferris, Tx., U.S. | G10 | 116 |
| Ferrol, Spain | B3 | 16 |
| Ferrol, Península de, pen., Peru | C2 | 82 |
| Ferron, Ut., U.S. | E5 | 120 |
| Ferros, Braz. | E7 | 79 |
| Ferryland, Nf., Can. | E21 | 106 |
| Ferrysburg, Mi., U.S. | G9 | 110 |
| Fertile, Mn., U.S. | D11 | 118 |
| Fès, Mor. | C8 | 62 |
| Feshi, D.R.C. | C3 | 58 |
| Fessenden, N.D., U.S. | D8 | 118 |
| Festus, Mo., U.S. | D6 | 114 |
| Fété Bowé, Sen. | D3 | 64 |
| Feteşti, Rom. | E11 | 20 |
| Fethiye, Tur. | M13 | 20 |
| Feuchtwangen, Ger. | F10 | 10 |
| Feuet, Libya | H16 | 62 |
| Feuilles, Baie aux, b., P.Q., Can. | E19 | 96 |
| Feuilles, Rivière aux, stm., P.Q., Can. | E18 | 96 |
| Feyzābād, Afg. | B4 | 44 |
| Fez see Fès, Mor. | C8 | 62 |
| Fiambalá, Arg. | D5 | 80 |
| Fianarantsoa, Madag. | r22 | 67b |
| Fiantsonana, Madag. | q22 | 67b |
| Fiche, Eth. | M10 | 60 |
| Fichtelberg, mtn., Ger. | E12 | 10 |
| Fichtelgebirge, mts., Eur. | E11 | 10 |
| Ficksburg, S. Afr. | G8 | 66 |
| Fidenza, Italy | E5 | 18 |
| Fidler Lake, l., Mb., Can. | A18 | 104 |
| Field, B.C., Can. | F18 | 102 |
| Fieldale, Va., U.S. | C7 | 112 |
| Fier, Alb. | I3 | 20 |
| Fiesch, Switz. | F9 | 13 |
| Fife, prov., Scot., U.K. | E10 | 8 |
| Fife Lake, Mi., U.S. | F10 | 110 |
| Fife Lake, Sk., Can. | I9 | 104 |
| Fife Lake, l., Sk., Can. | I9 | 104 |
| Fifield, Wi., U.S. | E5 | 110 |
| Figeac, Fr. | H9 | 14 |
| Figueira da Foz, Port. | E3 | 16 |
| Figueres, Spain | C14 | 16 |
| Figuig, Mor. | D10 | 62 |
| Fiji, ctry., Oc. | J21 | 126 |
| Filabusi, Zimb. | C9 | 66 |
| Filadelfia, C.R. | G9 | 92 |
| Filchner Ice Shelf, Ant. | C1 | 73 |
| File Lake, l., Mb., Can. | D14 | 104 |
| Filingué, Niger | D11 | 64 |
| Fillmore, Ca., U.S. | J7 | 124 |
| Fillmore, Sk., Can. | I11 | 104 |
| Fillmore, Ut., U.S. | F4 | 120 |
| Finale Ligure, Italy | E3 | 18 |
| Finarwa, Eth. | K10 | 60 |
| Fincastle, Va., U.S. | B7 | 112 |
| Findlay, Il., U.S. | C8 | 114 |
| Findlay, Oh., U.S. | F3 | 108 |
| Findlay, Mount, mtn., B.C., Can. | G18 | 102 |
| Fingal, N.D., U.S. | E10 | 118 |
| Finger Lake, l., On., Can. | E21 | 104 |
| Fingoè, Moz. | E6 | 58 |
| Finike, Tur. | M13 | 20 |
| Finistère, dept., Fr. | D2 | 14 |
| Finke, Austl. | E6 | 68 |
| Finke, stm., Austl. | E7 | 68 |
| Finland (Suomi), ctry., Eur. | C13 | 4 |
| Finland, Gulf of, b., Eur. | L20 | 6 |
| Finlay, stm., B.C., Can. | J6 | 70 |
| Finley, Austl. | J6 | 70 |
| Finley, N.D., U.S. | D10 | 118 |
| Finmoore, B.C., Can. | D11 | 102 |
| Finn, stm., Eur. | G6 | 8 |
| Finnegan, Ab., Can. | F22 | 102 |
| Finnmark, co., Nor. | F19 | 6 |
| Fins, Oman | C11 | 47 |
| Finsteraarhorn, mtn., Switz. | F9 | 13 |
| Finsterwalde, Ger. | D13 | 10 |
| Fiora, stm., Italy | G6 | 18 |
| Fiq, Golan | C5 | 50 |
| Firavitoba, Col. | E6 | 84 |
| Firebaugh, Ca., U.S. | H5 | 124 |
| Firenze (Florence), Italy | F6 | 18 |
| Firminópolis, Braz. | D3 | 79 |
| Firminy, Fr. | G11 | 14 |
| Firovo, Russia | D16 | 22 |
| Firozābād, India | G8 | 44 |
| Firozpur, India | E6 | 44 |
| Firth, Ne., U.S. | K11 | 118 |
| Firth, stm., N.A. | B24 | 100 |
| Firūzābād, Iran | G12 | 48 |
| Firūz Kūh, Iran | D12 | 48 |
| Fish, stm., Ak., U.S. | L9 | 114 |
| Fish (Vis), stm., Nmb. | F3 | 66 |
| Fisher, Ar., U.S. | H5 | 114 |
| Fisher, Il., U.S. | B8 | 114 |
| Fisher, La., U.S. | K3 | 114 |
| Fisher, stm., Mb., Can. | G17 | 104 |
| Fisher, stm., Mb., Can. | B10 | 122 |
| Fisher Bay, b., Mb., Can. | G17 | 104 |
| Fisher Branch, Mb., Can. | G17 | 104 |
| Fisher Channel, strt., B.C., Can. | E7 | 102 |
| Fisher River Indian Reserve, Mb., Can. | G17 | 104 |
| Fishers Island, i., N.Y., U.S. | F15 | 108 |
| Fisher Strait, strt., N.T., Can. | D16 | 96 |
| Fishing Creek, Md., U.S. | I10 | 108 |
| Fishing Lake, l., Mb., Can. | F19 | 104 |
| Fishing Lake, l., Sk., Can. | G11 | 104 |
| Fisk, Mo., U.S. | F6 | 114 |
| Fismes, Fr. | C10 | 14 |
| Fisterra, Cabo de, c., Spain | C2 | 16 |
| Fitchburg, Ma., U.S. | E15 | 108 |
| Fitzgerald, Ga., U.S. | H3 | 112 |
| Fitzgerald River National Park, Austl. | F3 | 68 |
| Fitz Hugh Sound, strt., B.C., Can. | F7 | 102 |
| Fitzroy, stm., Austl. | C4 | 68 |
| Fitzroy, stm., Austl. | D9 | 70 |
| Fitzroy, Monte (Cerro Chaltel), mtn., S.A. | F2 | 78 |
| Fitzroy Crossing, Austl. | C5 | 68 |
| Fiume see Rijeka, Cro. | D9 | 18 |
| Fiumicino, Italy | H7 | 18 |
| Five Islands, N.S., Can. | G9 | 106 |
| Five Points, N.M., U.S. | I10 | 120 |
| Fizi, D.R.C. | B5 | 58 |
| Fkih-Ben-Salah, Mor. | D7 | 62 |
| Flagler, Co., U.S. | L4 | 118 |
| Flagler Beach, Fl., U.S. | J5 | 112 |
| Flagstaff, Az., U.S. | I5 | 120 |
| Flagstaff Lake, res., Me., U.S. | B16 | 108 |
| Flambeau, stm., Wi., U.S. | E4 | 110 |
| Flaming Gorge Reservoir, res., U.S. | C7 | 120 |
| Flanagan, Il., U.S. | J7 | 110 |
| Flanagan, stm., On., Can. | F21 | 104 |
| Flanders, On., Can. | B3 | 110 |
| Flanders (Flandre), hist. reg., Eur. | G2 | 12 |
| Flandes, Col. | E5 | 84 |
| Flandreau, S.D., U.S. | G11 | 118 |
| Flasher, N.D., U.S. | E6 | 118 |
| Flat, Tx., U.S. | H9 | 116 |
| Flat, stm., Mi., U.S. | G10 | 110 |
| Flat, stm., N.T., Can. | F31 | 100 |
| Flat Bay, Nf., Can. | D15 | 106 |
| Flatey, Ice. | B2 | 6a |
| Flateyri, Ice. | B2 | 6a |
| Flathead, Mt., U.S. | I20 | 102 |
| Flathead Lake, res., Mt., U.S. | C11 | 122 |
| Flat Lake, l., Ab., Can. | C22 | 102 |
| Flat Lick, Ky., U.S. | C3 | 112 |
| Flat River, Mo., U.S. | E6 | 114 |
| Flat River, P.E., Can. | F11 | 106 |
| Flat Rock, Al., U.S. | H11 | 114 |
| Flat Rock, Il., U.S. | D9 | 114 |
| Flatrock Lake, l., Mb., Can. | C14 | 104 |
| Flattery, Cape, c., Wa., U.S. | B1 | 122 |
| Flatwood, Al., U.S. | J10 | 114 |
| Flatwoods, Ky., U.S. | I4 | 108 |
| Flaxcombe, Sk., Can. | G5 | 104 |
| Flaxton, N.D., U.S. | C5 | 118 |
| Flaxville, Mt., U.S. | C11 | 122 |
| Fleetwood, Eng., U.K. | G10 | 8 |
| Fleetwood, Pa., U.S. | G11 | 108 |
| Fleming, Co., U.S. | K5 | 118 |
| Fleming-Neon, Ky., U.S. | B4 | 112 |
| Flemingsburg, Ky., U.S. | I3 | 108 |
| Flensburg, Ger. | A9 | 10 |
| Fletcher, N.C., U.S. | D4 | 112 |
| Fletcher Pond, res., Mi., U.S. | F12 | 110 |
| Fleurance, Fr. | I7 | 14 |
| Fleur-de-Lys, Nf., Can. | B17 | 106 |
| Fleurier, Switz. | E6 | 13 |
| Flevoland, prov., Neth. | D7 | 12 |
| Flin Flon, Mb., Can. | D13 | 104 |
| Flinders, stm., Austl. | A4 | 70 |
| Flinders Island, i., Austl. | M8 | 70 |
| Flinders Reefs, rf., Austl. | A8 | 70 |
| Flint, Mi., U.S. | G12 | 110 |
| Flint, stm., Ga., U.S. | I2 | 112 |
| Flint, stm., Mi., U.S. | G12 | 110 |
| Flint, stm., Wi., U.S. | H10 | 114 |
| Flint, stm., N.T., Can. | C18 | 96 |
| Flintville, Tn., U.S. | G10 | 114 |
| Flippin, Ar., U.S. | F4 | 114 |
| Flisa, Nor. | K13 | 6 |
| Flize, Fr. | C11 | 14 |
| Flomaton, Al., U.S. | K9 | 114 |
| Flomot, Tx., U.S. | E6 | 116 |
| Floodwood, Mn., U.S. | D11 | 118 |
| Flora, Il., U.S. | B10 | 114 |
| Flora, In., U.S. | B10 | 114 |
| Flora, Ms., U.S. | J6 | 114 |
| Florac, Fr. | H10 | 14 |
| Florala, Al., U.S. | K10 | 114 |
| Floral City, Fl., U.S. | K4 | 112 |
| Floral Park, Mt., U.S. | E13 | 122 |
| Flora Vista, N.M., U.S. | H8 | 120 |
| Florence see Firenze, Italy | F6 | 18 |
| Florence, Al., U.S. | H9 | 114 |
| Florence, Co., U.S. | F11 | 120 |
| Florence, Ks., U.S. | M11 | 118 |
| Florence, Or., U.S. | G1 | 122 |
| Florence, S.C., U.S. | E7 | 112 |
| Florence, Tx., U.S. | I9 | 116 |
| Florence, Wi., U.S. | E7 | 110 |
| Florencia, Col. | G5 | 84 |
| Florencio Sánchez, Ur. | G11 | 80 |
| Flores, Braz. | E11 | 76 |
| Flores, i., Indon. | G7 | 38 |
| Flores, i., Port. | k18 | 62a |
| Flores, Laut (Flores Sea), Indon. | G7 | 38 |
| Flores de Goiás, Braz. | C5 | 79 |
| Flores de Cunha, Braz. | E13 | 80 |
| Flores Island, i., B.C., Can. | H8 | 102 |
| Floresta Azul, Braz. | C9 | 79 |
| Foreşti, Mol. | B12 | 20 |
| Floresville, Tx., U.S. | J8 | 116 |
| Floriano, Braz. | E10 | 76 |
| Floriano Peixoto, Braz. | C8 | 82 |
| Florianópolis, Braz. | D14 | 80 |
| Florida, Col. | F4 | 84 |
| Florida, Cuba | D5 | 94 |
| Florida, Hond. | B6 | 92 |
| Florida, Peru | A3 | 82 |
| Florida, state, U.S. | F10 | 98 |
| Florida, stm., Co., U.S. | G9 | 120 |
| Florida, Straits of, strt., N.A. | B4 | 94 |
| Florida Bay, b., Fl., U.S. | N6 | 112 |
| Floridablanca, Col. | D6 | 84 |
| Florida City, Fl., U.S. | N6 | 112 |
| Florida Keys, is., Fl., U.S. | O5 | 112 |
| Floridia, Italy | L10 | 18 |
| Florido, stm., Mex. | D7 | 90 |
| Florin, La., U.S. | K3 | 114 |
| Flórina, Grc. | I5 | 20 |
| Florissant, Mo., U.S. | D6 | 114 |
| Florø, Nor. | K9 | 6 |
| Flotten Lake, l., Sk., Can. | C15 | 122 |
| Flower's Cove, Nf., Can. | A17 | 106 |
| Flowery Branch, Ga., U.S. | E3 | 112 |
| Floyd, N.M., U.S. | E3 | 116 |
| Floyd, Va., U.S. | C6 | 112 |
| Floyd, stm., Ia., U.S. | I11 | 118 |
| Floydada, Tx., U.S. | F5 | 116 |
| Floyds Fork, stm., Ky., U.S. | D11 | 114 |
| Fluchthorn, mtn., Eur. | E13 | 13 |
| Flushing, Mi., U.S. | G12 | 110 |
| Fluvanna, Tx., U.S. | G5 | 116 |
| Fly, stm. | m15 | 68a |
| Foam Lake, Sk., Can. | G11 | 104 |
| Foča, Bos. | F2 | 20 |
| Focşani, Rom. | D11 | 20 |
| Fodé, C.A.R. | O2 | 60 |
| Fodécontea, Gui. | F2 | 64 |
| Foggaret el Arab, Alg. | G12 | 62 |
| Foggaret ez Zoua, Alg. | G12 | 62 |
| Foggia, Italy | H10 | 18 |
| Fogo, Nf., Can. | C19 | 106 |
| Fogo, Cape, c., Nf., Can. | C19 | 106 |
| Fogo, I., C.V. | m16 | 64a |
| Fogo Island, i., Nf., Can. | C19 | 106 |
| Fogolawa, Nig. | E14 | 64 |
| Fohnsdorf, Aus. | H14 | 10 |
| Foix, Fr. | J8 | 14 |
| Foix, hist. reg., Fr. | J8 | 14 |
| Fokino, Russia | H17 | 22 |
| Folakara, Madag. | q21 | 67b |
| Foley, Al., U.S. | L9 | 114 |
| Foley, Mn., U.S. | E2 | 110 |
| Foleyet, On., Can. | B13 | 110 |
| Foley Island, i., N.T., Can. | C17 | 96 |
| Folkestone, Eng., U.K. | J15 | 8 |
| Folkston, Ga., U.S. | I4 | 112 |
| Follett, Tx., U.S. | C6 | 116 |
| Follonica, Italy | G5 | 18 |
| Follonica, Golfo di, b., Italy | G5 | 18 |
| Folsom, Ca., U.S. | F4 | 124 |
| Folsom Lake, res., Ca., U.S. | F4 | 124 |
| Fomboni, Com. | I15 | 67a |
| Fonda, Ia., U.S. | I13 | 118 |
| Fonda, N.Y., U.S. | E12 | 108 |
| Fond du Lac, Sk., Can. | E11 | 96 |
| Fond du Lac, stm., Sk., Can. | E11 | 96 |
| Fondi, Italy | H8 | 18 |
| Fondouk el Aouareb, Tun. | N4 | 18 |
| Fonni, Italy | I4 | 18 |
| Fonseca, Col. | B6 | 84 |
| Fonseca, Golfo de, b., N.A. | D7 | 92 |
| Fontainebleau, Fr. | D9 | 14 |
| Fontana, Arg. | D9 | 80 |
| Fontana Lake, res., N.C., U.S. | D3 | 112 |
| Fontanelle, Ia., U.S. | J13 | 118 |
| Fontarabie, Lac, l., P.Q., Can. | A7 | 106 |
| Fontas, stm., Can. | E8 | 96 |
| Fonte Boa, Braz. | I9 | 84 |
| Fontenelle, P.Q., Can. | A9 | 106 |
| Fontenelle Lac, l., P.Q., Can. | A12 | 106 |
| Fontur, c., Ice. | A6 | 6a |
| Fonyód, Hung. | I17 | 10 |
| Foochow see Fuzhou, China | I8 | 34 |
| Foothills, Ab., Can. | D18 | 102 |
| Footprint Lake, l., Mb., Can. | C14 | 104 |
| Footville, Wi., U.S. | H6 | 110 |
| Foraker, Mount, mtn., Ak., U.S. | E19 | 100 |
| Forbach, Fr. | C13 | 14 |
| Forbes, Austl. | I8 | 70 |
| Forbes, Mount, mtn., Ab., Can. | F18 | 102 |
| Forchheim, Ger. | F11 | 10 |
| Ford, Ks., U.S. | N8 | 118 |
| Ford, stm., Mi., U.S. | E2 | 110 |
| Ford City, Ca., U.S. | I6 | 124 |
| Ford City, Pa., U.S. | G7 | 108 |
| Ford Ranges, mts., Ant. | C10 | 73 |
| Fordsville, Ky., U.S. | E10 | 114 |
| Fordville, N.D., U.S. | C10 | 118 |
| Fordyce, Ar., U.S. | I4 | 114 |
| Forel, Mont, mtn., Grnld. | C16 | 86 |
| Foreman, Ar., U.S. | I2 | 114 |
| Foremost, Ab., Can. | H22 | 102 |
| Forest, Ms., U.S. | J7 | 114 |
| Forest, On., Can. | G13 | 110 |
| Forest Acres, S.C., U.S. | E6 | 112 |
| Forest City, Ia., U.S. | G2 | 110 |
| Forest City, N.C., U.S. | D5 | 112 |
| Forest City, Pa., U.S. | F11 | 108 |
| Forest Grove, B.C., Can. | E13 | 102 |
| Foresthill, Ca., U.S. | E5 | 124 |
| Forest Home, Al., U.S. | K10 | 114 |
| Forest Lake, Mn., U.S. | E3 | 110 |
| Forest Park, Ga., U.S. | I2 | 112 |
| Forestville, P.Q., Can. | D4 | 106 |
| Forestville, Wi., U.S. | F8 | 110 |
| Forfar, Scot., U.K. | E11 | 8 |
| Forgan, Ok., U.S. | C6 | 116 |
| Forillon, Parc National de, P.Q., Can. | D9 | 106 |
| Forked Deer, stm., Tn. | G7 | 114 |
| Forks, Wa., U.S. | C1 | 122 |
| Forlì, Italy | E7 | 18 |
| Forman, N.D., U.S. | E10 | 118 |
| Formentera, i., Spain | G13 | 16 |
| Formia, Italy | H8 | 18 |
| Formiga, Braz. | F6 | 79 |
| Formosa, Arg. | D5 | 79 |
| Formosa, Braz. | C5 | 79 |
| Formosa, prov., Arg. | C9 | 80 |
| Formosa see Taiwan, ctry., Asia | I8 | 34 |
| Formosa, Serra, plat., Braz. | F13 | 76 |
| Formoso, stm., Braz. | E18 | 80 |
| Formoso, stm., Braz. | E2 | 79 |
| Fornosovo, Russia | B13 | 22 |
| Forney, Arg. | D7 | 80 |
| Forrest, Austl. | F5 | 68 |
| Forrest, stm., Austl. | D7 | 68 |
| Forrest City, Ar., U.S. | G6 | 114 |
| Forreston, Il., U.S. | H6 | 110 |
| Forsan, Tx., U.S. | G5 | 116 |
| Forsayth, Austl. | B5 | 70 |
| Forst, Ger. | D14 | 10 |
| Forster, Austl. | I10 | 70 |
| Forsyth, Ga., U.S. | F3 | 112 |
| Forsyth, Mo., U.S. | F3 | 114 |
| Forsyth, Mt., U.S. | D19 | 122 |
| Forsyth Range, mts., Austl. | D5 | 70 |
| Fort Adams, Ms., U.S. | K5 | 114 |
| Fort Albany, On., Can. | F16 | 96 |
| Fort Alexander Indian Reserve, Mb., Can. | H18 | 104 |
| Fort Amherst National Historic Park, P.E., Can. | F10 | 106 |
| Fort Anne National Historic Park, N.S., Can. | H8 | 106 |
| Fort Assiniboine, Ab., Can. | C20 | 102 |
| Fort Atkinson, Wi., U.S. | H7 | 110 |
| Fort Battleford National Historic Park, Sk., Can. | F6 | 104 |
| Fort Beaufort, S. Afr. | I8 | 66 |
| Fort Beauséjour National Historic Park, N.B., Can. | G9 | 106 |
| Fort Benton, Mt., U.S. | C15 | 122 |
| Fort Bidwell, Ca., U.S. | E2 | 124 |
| Fort Bragg, Ca., U.S. | D1 | 124 |
| Fort Branch, In., U.S. | D9 | 114 |
| Fort Bridger, Wy., U.S. | C6 | 120 |
| Fort Calhoun, Ne., U.S. | J11 | 118 |
| Fort-Carnot, Madag. | r22 | 67b |
| Fort Chipewyan, Ab., Can. | E10 | 96 |
| Fort Cobb, Ok., U.S. | D8 | 116 |
| Fort Collins, Co., U.S. | D11 | 120 |
| Fort-Coulonge, P.Q., Can. | B10 | 108 |
| Fort Covington, N.Y., U.S. | C12 | 108 |
| Fort Davis, Al., U.S. | J11 | 114 |
| Fort Davis, Tx., U.S. | I3 | 116 |
| Fort Defiance, Az., U.S. | I7 | 120 |
| Fort Deposit, Al., U.S. | K10 | 114 |
| Fort Dodge, Ia., U.S. | H1 | 110 |
| Fort Duchesne, Ut., U.S. | D7 | 120 |
| Forteau, Nf., Can. | A17 | 106 |
| Fort Edward, N.Y., U.S. | D13 | 108 |
| Fort Erie, On., Can. | H17 | 110 |
| Fortescue, stm., Austl. | D3 | 68 |
| Fortezza, Italy | C6 | 18 |
| Fort Fitzgerald, Ab., Can. | E10 | 96 |
| Fort Frances, On., Can. | B2 | 110 |
| Fort Franklin, N.T., Can. | D33 | 100 |
| Fort Fraser, B.C., Can. | C10 | 102 |
| Fort Gaines, Ga., U.S. | H1 | 112 |
| Fort Garland, Co., U.S. | G11 | 120 |
| Fort Gay, W.V., U.S. | I4 | 108 |
| Fort Gibson, Ok., U.S. | D11 | 116 |
| Fort Gibson Lake, res., Ok., U.S. | C11 | 116 |
| Fort Good Hope, N.T., Can. | C30 | 100 |
| Fort Hall, Id., U.S. | G13 | 122 |
| Fortín, Lac, l., P.Q., Can. | B6 | 106 |
| Fortín Ayacucho, Para. | H12 | 82 |
| Fortín Coroneles Sanchez, Para. | H12 | 82 |
| Fortín Garrapatal, Para. | I11 | 82 |
| Fortín Teniente Montania, Para. | B9 | 80 |
| Fortín Uno, Arg. | J6 | 80 |
| Fort Jones, Ca., U.S. | C3 | 124 |
| Fort Klamath, Or., U.S. | H4 | 122 |
| Fort-Lamy see N'Djamena, Chad | F4 | 56 |
| Fort Laramie, Wy., U.S. | B12 | 120 |
| Fort Lauderdale, Fl., U.S. | M6 | 112 |
| Fort-Liberté, Haiti | E9 | 94 |
| Fort Loramie, Oh., U.S. | G2 | 108 |
| Fort Loudoun Lake, res., Tn., U.S. | D2 | 112 |
| Fort Lupton, Co., U.S. | D12 | 120 |
| Fort Macleod, Ab., Can. | H21 | 102 |
| Fort Madison, Ia., U.S. | J4 | 110 |
| Fort McMurray, Ab., Can. | B3 | 104 |
| Fort McPherson, N.T., Can. | C27 | 100 |
| Fort Meade, Fl., U.S. | L5 | 112 |
| Fort Mill, S.C., U.S. | D6 | 112 |
| Fort Mitchell, Al., U.S. | G1 | 112 |
| Fort Morgan, Co., U.S. | K4 | 118 |
| Fort Myers, Fl., U.S. | M5 | 112 |
| Fort Myers Beach, Fl., U.S. | M5 | 112 |
| Fort Nelson, B.C., Can. | E8 | 96 |
| Fort Nelson, stm., B.C., Can. | E8 | 96 |
| Fort Norman, N.T., Can. | D32 | 100 |
| Fort Ogden, Fl., U.S. | L5 | 112 |
| Fort Payne, Al., U.S. | H11 | 114 |
| Fort Peck, Mt., U.S. | B19 | 122 |
| Fort Peck Lake, res., Mt., U.S. | C19 | 122 |
| Fort Pierce, Fl., U.S. | L6 | 112 |
| Fort Pierre, S.D., U.S. | G7 | 118 |
| Fort Plain, N.Y., U.S. | E12 | 108 |
| Fort Portal, Ug. | A6 | 58 |
| Fort Providence, N.T., Can. | D9 | 96 |
| Fort Qu'Appelle, Sk., Can. | H11 | 104 |
| Fort Recovery, Oh., U.S. | G2 | 108 |
| Fort Resolution, N.T., Can. | D10 | 96 |
| Fortress Mountain, mtn., Wy., U.S. | F16 | 122 |
| Fortress of Louisbourg National Historic Park, N.S., Can. | G14 | 106 |
| Fort Saint James, B.C., Can. | C10 | 102 |
| Fort Saskatchewan, Ab., Can. | D21 | 102 |
| Fort Scott, Ks., U.S. | N13 | 118 |
| Fort-Ševčenko, Kaz. | I8 | 26 |
| Fort Severn, On., Can. | E15 | 96 |
| Fort Simpson, N.T., Can. | D8 | 96 |
| Fort Smith, Ar., U.S. | G2 | 114 |
| Fort Smith, N.T., Can. | D10 | 96 |
| Fort Steele, B.C., Can. | H19 | 102 |
| Fort Stockton, Tx., U.S. | I4 | 116 |
| Fort Sumner, N.M., U.S. | E2 | 116 |
| Fort Supply, Ok., U.S. | C7 | 116 |
| Fort Thomas, Az., U.S. | K7 | 120 |
| Fort Thompson, S.D., U.S. | G8 | 118 |
| Fort Totten, N.D., U.S. | D9 | 118 |
| Fort Towson, Ok., U.S. | E11 | 116 |
| Fortuna, Arg. | H6 | 80 |
| Fortuna, Ca., U.S. | D1 | 124 |
| Fortuna, prov., Arg. | C9 | 80 |
| Fortuna, Río de la, stm., Bol. | G12 | 82 |
| Fortune, Nf., Can. | E18 | 106 |
| Fortune Bay, b., Nf., Can. | E18 | 106 |
| Fortune Harbour, Nf., Can. | C18 | 106 |
| Fort Valley, Ga., U.S. | G3 | 112 |
| Fort Vermilion, Ab., Can. | E9 | 96 |
| Fort Walton Beach, Fl., U.S. | A11 | 114 |
| Fort Washakie, Wy., U.S. | H2 | 108 |
| Fort Wayne, In., U.S. | A11 | 114 |
| Fort Wellington, Guy. | D14 | 84 |
| Fort White, Fl., U.S. | J4 | 112 |
| Fort William see Thunder Bay, On., Can. | B6 | 110 |
| Fort William, Scot., U.K. | E8 | 8 |
| Fort Worth, Tx., U.S. | G9 | 116 |
| Fort Yates, N.D., U.S. | E7 | 118 |
| Fortymile, N.T., Can. | D24 | 100 |
| Fort Yukon, Ak., U.S. | C22 | 100 |
| Foshan, China | L2 | 34 |
| Fossano, Italy | E2 | 18 |
| Fossil, Or., U.S. | F5 | 122 |
| Fosston, Mn., U.S. | D12 | 118 |
| Foster, Austl. | L7 | 70 |
| Foster, stm., Sk., Can. | C9 | 104 |
| Foster, Mount, mtn., N.A. | G27 | 100 |
| Fosters, Al., U.S. | I9 | 114 |
| Fostoria, Oh., U.S. | F3 | 108 |
| Fouesnant, Fr. | E2 | 14 |
| Fougamou, Gabon | B2 | 58 |
| Fougères, Fr. | D5 | 14 |
| Fouke, Ar., U.S. | I3 | 114 |
| Foul Bay, b., Egypt | J3 | 48 |
| Foulpointe, Madag. | p23 | 67b |
| Foulwind, Cape, c., N.Z. | D3 | 72 |
| Foumban, Cam. | G9 | 54 |
| Foumbouni, Com. | k15 | 67a |
| Foum-el-Hisn, Mor. | F6 | 62 |
| Foum-Zguid, Mor. | E7 | 62 |
| Foundiougne, Sen. | D1 | 64 |
| Fountain, Co., U.S. | M3 | 118 |
| Fountain, Fl., U.S. | I11 | 114 |
| Fountain City, Wi., U.S. | F4 | 110 |
| Fountain Green, Ut., U.S. | E5 | 120 |
| Fountain Inn, S.C., U.S. | E4 | 112 |
| Fountain Peak, mtn., Ca., U.S. | J10 | 124 |
| Fountain Place, La., U.S. | L5 | 114 |
| Fourche LaFave, stm., Ar., U.S. | H4 | 114 |
| Fourche Maline, stm., Ok., U.S. | E12 | 116 |
| Fourchu, N.S., Can. | G13 | 106 |
| Four Corners, Wy., U.S. | F23 | 122 |
| Fourmies, Fr. | B11 | 14 |
| Four Mountains, Islands of, is., Ak., U.S. | J9 | 100 |
| Fournier, Lac, l., P.Q., Can. | A8 | 106 |
| Four Oaks, N.C., U.S. | D8 | 112 |
| Fouta Djalon, reg., Gui. | F3 | 64 |
| Foux, Cap à, c., Haiti | E8 | 94 |
| Foveaux Strait, strt., N.Z. | G1 | 72 |
| Fowler, Ca., U.S. | H6 | 124 |
| Fowler, Co., U.S. | M3 | 118 |
| Fowler, In., U.S. | B9 | 114 |
| Fowler, Ks., U.S. | N7 | 118 |
| Fowler, Mi., U.S. | G11 | 110 |
| Fowlerton, Tx., U.S. | K8 | 116 |
| Fowlerville, Mi., U.S. | H11 | 110 |
| Fowman, Iran | C10 | 48 |
| Fox, stm., Il., U.S. | D8 | 114 |
| Fox, stm., Mb., Can. | C20 | 104 |
| Fox, stm., Wi., U.S. | B5 | 114 |
| Fox, stm., Wi., U.S. | F7 | 110 |
| Fox Harbour, Nf., Can. | E20 | 106 |
| Fox Islands, is., Ak., U.S. | J10 | 100 |
| Fox Lake, Il., U.S. | H7 | 110 |
| Fox Lake, Wi., U.S. | G7 | 110 |
| Fox Mountain, mtn., Yk., Can. | F28 | 100 |
| Fox Valley, Sk., Can. | H5 | 104 |
| Foxpark, Wy., U.S. | C10 | 120 |
| Foxworth, Ms., U.S. | K7 | 114 |
| Foyle, Lough, b., Eur. | F6 | 8 |
| Foyil, Ok., U.S. | C11 | 116 |
| Foz do Cunene, Ang. | E2 | 58 |
| Foz do Iguaçu, Braz. | C11 | 80 |
| Foz do Jordão, Braz. | C6 | 82 |
| Foz Giraldo, Port. | E4 | 16 |
| Foziling, China | D5 | 34 |
| Fraga, Arg. | G6 | 80 |
| Fraile Muerto, Ur. | G11 | 80 |
| Framingham, Ma., U.S. | E15 | 108 |
| Frampol, Pol. | E22 | 10 |
| Franca, Braz. | F5 | 79 |
| Franca-Iosifa, Zeml'a (Franz Josef Land), is., Russia | A6 | 24 |
| Francavilla Fontana, Italy | I12 | 18 |
| France, ctry., Eur. | F8 | 4 |
| Frances, stm., Yk., Can. | F30 | 100 |
| Frances Lake, l., Yk., Can. | F30 | 100 |
| Francés Viejo, Cabo, c., Dom. Rep. | E10 | 94 |
| Francesville, In., U.S. | B9 | 114 |
| Franceville, Gabon | B2 | 58 |
| Franche-Comté, hist. reg., Fr. | F12 | 14 |
| Francia, Sk., Can. | H11 | 104 |
| Francis Case, Lake, res., S.D., U.S. | H8 | 118 |
| Francisco Beltrão, Braz. | D12 | 80 |
| Francisco I. Madero, Mex. | E8 | 90 |
| Francisco I. Madero, Mex. | E7 | 90 |
| Francisco Morazán, dept., Hond. | C7 | 92 |
| Francisco Murguía, Mex. | E8 | 90 |
| Francisco Sá, Braz. | D7 | 79 |
| Francistown, Bots. | C8 | 66 |
| Francofonte, Italy | L9 | 18 |
| François, Nf., Can. | E17 | 106 |
| François, Lacs à, l., P.Q., Can. | A8 | 106 |
| François Lake, B.C., Can. | C9 | 102 |
| François Lake, l., B.C., Can. | C9 | 102 |
| Francs Peak, mtn., Wy., U.S. | G16 | 122 |
| Frangy, Fr. | F12 | 14 |
| Frankel City, Tx., U.S. | G4 | 116 |
| Frankenmuth, Mi., U.S. | G12 | 110 |
| Frankford, Mo., U.S. | C5 | 114 |
| Frankford, On., Can. | F18 | 110 |
| Frankfort, In., U.S. | B10 | 114 |
| Frankfort, Ks., U.S. | L11 | 118 |
| Frankfort, Ky., U.S. | D12 | 114 |
| Frankfort, Mi., U.S. | F9 | 110 |
| Frankfort, N.Y., U.S. | D11 | 108 |
| Frankfort, S. Afr. | F9 | 66 |
| Frankfort, S.D., U.S. | G9 | 118 |
| Frankfurt, Ger. | C14 | 10 |
| Frankfurt am Main, Ger. | E8 | 10 |
| Franklin, Ga., U.S. | F1 | 112 |
| Franklin, Id., U.S. | H14 | 122 |
| Franklin, In., U.S. | C10 | 114 |
| Franklin, Ky., U.S. | F10 | 114 |
| Franklin, La., U.S. | M5 | 114 |
| Franklin, Ma., U.S. | E15 | 108 |
| Franklin, N.C., U.S. | D3 | 112 |
| Franklin, Ne., U.S. | K9 | 118 |
| Franklin, N.H., U.S. | D15 | 108 |
| Franklin, N.J., U.S. | F12 | 108 |
| Franklin, Oh., U.S. | H2 | 108 |
| Franklin, Pa., U.S. | F7 | 108 |
| Franklin, Tn., U.S. | G10 | 114 |
| Franklin, Tx., U.S. | H10 | 116 |
| Franklin, Va., U.S. | C10 | 112 |
| Franklin, Wi., U.S. | H7 | 110 |
| Franklin, W.V., U.S. | I7 | 108 |
| Franklin Bay, b., N.T., Can. | C7 | 96 |
| Franklin D. Roosevelt Lake, res., Wa., U.S. | B7 | 122 |
| Franklin Grove, Il., U.S. | I6 | 110 |
| Franklin Harbor, b., Austl. | I2 | 70 |
| Franklin Lake, l., N.T., Can. | C13 | 96 |
| Franklin Mountains, mts., N.T., Can. | D31 | 100 |
| Franklin Strait, strt., N.T., Can. | B13 | 96 |
| Franklinton, La., U.S. | L6 | 114 |
| Franklinton, N.C., U.S. | C8 | 112 |
| Franklinville, N.Y., U.S. | E8 | 108 |
| Frankston, In., U.S. | B11 | 114 |
| Frankville, Al., U.S. | K8 | 114 |
| Franz Josef Land see Franca Iosifa, Zeml'a, is., Russia | A6 | 24 |
| Frascati, Italy | H7 | 18 |
| Fraser, Co., U.S. | E11 | 120 |
| Fraser, stm., B.C., Can. | G13 | 102 |
| Fraser, stm., B.C., Can. | D11 | 102 |
| Fraser, stm., Nf., Can. | E20 | 96 |
| Fraserburg, S. Afr. | H5 | 66 |
| Fraser Island, i., Austl. | E10 | 70 |
| Fraser Lake, l., B.C., Can. | C10 | 102 |
| Fraser Plateau, plat., B.C., Can. | E11 | 102 |
| Frauenfeld, Switz. | C10 | 13 |
| Fray Bentos, Ur. | G9 | 80 |
| Fray Luis Beltrán, Arg. | J6 | 80 |
| Fray Marcos, Ur. | H11 | 80 |
| Frazee, Mn., U.S. | E12 | 118 |
| Frazer, Mt., U.S. | B19 | 122 |
| Fr'azino, Russia | F21 | 22 |
| Frederic, Wi., U.S. | E3 | 110 |
| Frederica, De., U.S. | H11 | 108 |
| Fredericia, Den. | N11 | 6 |
| Frederick, Md., U.S. | H9 | 108 |
| Frederick, Ok., U.S. | E7 | 116 |
| Frederick Reef, rf., Austl. | C11 | 70 |
| Fredericksburg, Tx., U.S. | I8 | 116 |
| Fredericksburg, Va., U.S. | I9 | 108 |
| Fredericktown, Mo., U.S. | E6 | 114 |
| Frederico Westphalen, Braz. | D12 | 80 |
| Fredericton Junction, N.B., Can. | G7 | 106 |
| Fredericton, N.B., Can. | G7 | 106 |
| Frederikshavn, Den. | M12 | 6 |
| Frederiksted, V.I.U.S. | F12 | 94 |
| Frederik Willem IV Vallen, wtfl, Sur. | F14 | 84 |
| Fredonia, Az., U.S. | H4 | 120 |
| Fredonia, Col. | E5 | 84 |
| Fredonia, Ks., U.S. | N12 | 118 |
| Fredonia, N.D., U.S. | E8 | 118 |
| Fredonia, N.Y., U.S. | E8 | 108 |
| Fredrikstad, Nor. | L12 | 6 |
| Freeburg, Il., U.S. | D7 | 114 |
| Freeburg, Mo., U.S. | D5 | 114 |
| Freehold, N.J., U.S. | G12 | 108 |
| Freeland, Mi., U.S. | G12 | 110 |
| Freeland, Pa., U.S. | F11 | 108 |
| Freels, Cape, c., Nf., Can. | C20 | 106 |
| Freels, Cape, c., Nf., Can. | F20 | 106 |
| Freeman, S.D., U.S. | H10 | 118 |
| Freeman, stm., Ab., Can. | C19 | 102 |
| Freeport, Bah. | A5 | 94 |
| Freeport, Il., U.S. | H6 | 110 |
| Freeport, Me., U.S. | D16 | 108 |
| Freeport, N.S., Can. | H7 | 106 |
| Freeport, N.Y., U.S. | G13 | 108 |
| Freeport, Pa., U.S. | G7 | 108 |
| Freeport, Tx., U.S. | K11 | 116 |
| Freer, Tx., U.S. | L8 | 116 |
| Free State, prov., S. Afr. | G8 | 66 |
| Freetown, S.L. | G3 | 64 |
| Fregenal de la Sierra, Spain | G5 | 16 |
| Freiberg, Ger. | E13 | 10 |
| Freiberg [im Breisgau], Ger. | H7 | 10 |
| Freiburg (Freiburg), Switz. | F7 | 13 |
| Freire, Chile | D2 | 78 |
| Freising, Ger. | G11 | 10 |
| Freistadt, Aus. | G14 | 10 |
| Freital, Ger. | D13 | 10 |
| Fréjus, Fr. | I13 | 14 |
| Fremantle, Austl. | F3 | 68 |
| Fremont, Ca., U.S. | G4 | 124 |
| Fremont, In., U.S. | A12 | 114 |
| Fremont, Mi., U.S. | G10 | 110 |
| Fremont, N.C., U.S. | D9 | 112 |
| Fremont, Ne., U.S. | J11 | 118 |
| Fremont, Oh., U.S. | F3 | 108 |
| Fremont, Wi., U.S. | F7 | 110 |
| Fremont, stm., Ut., U.S. | F6 | 120 |
| Fremont Lake, l., Wy., U.S. | B16 | 122 |
| French Broad, stm., U.S. | D4 | 112 |
| Frenchburg, Ky., U.S. | B3 | 112 |
| French Creek, stm., Mb., Can. | B22 | 104 |
| French Guiana (Guyane français), dep., S.A. | C8 | 76 |
| French Island, i., Austl. | L6 | 70 |
| French Lick, In., U.S. | D10 | 114 |
| Frenchman Bay, b., Me., U.S. | C18 | 108 |
| Frenchman Butte, Sk., Can. | E5 | 104 |
| Frenchmans Cap, mtn., Austl. | N6 | 70 |
| French Polynesia, dep., Oc. | J25 | 126 |
| Frenda, Alg. | C11 | 62 |
| Fresco, stm., Braz. | E8 | 76 |
| Freshfield, Mount, mtn., Can. | F18 | 102 |
| Fresnes-Saint-Mamès, Fr. | E12 | 14 |
| Fresnes-en-Woëvre, Fr. | C12 | 14 |
| Fresnillo, Mex. | F8 | 90 |
| Fresno, Ca., U.S. | H6 | 124 |
| Fresno, Col. | E5 | 84 |
| Fresno Reservoir, res., Mt., U.S. | B16 | 122 |
| Frewsburg, N.Y., U.S. | E7 | 108 |
| Freycinet Peninsula, pen., Austl. | N8 | 70 |
| Freyre, Arg. | F7 | 80 |
| Fria, Cape, c., Nmb. | E2 | 58 |
| Fria, Gui. | F2 | 64 |
| Friant, Ca., U.S. | H6 | 124 |
| Friars Point, Ms., U.S. | H6 | 114 |
| Frías, Arg. | D6 | 80 |
| Frías, Peru | A2 | 82 |
| Fribourg (Freiburg), Switz. | F7 | 13 |
| Fribourg, state, Switz. | F7 | 13 |
| Friday Harbor, Wa., U.S. | B2 | 122 |
| Fridley, Mn., U.S. | E2 | 110 |
| Fridtjof Nansen, Mount, mtn., Ant. | D9 | 73 |
| Friedberg, Aus. | H16 | 10 |
| Friedberg, Ger. | G10 | 10 |
| Friedland, Ger. | B13 | 10 |
| Friedrichshafen, Ger. | H9 | 10 |

| Name | Map Ref. | Page |
|---|---|---|
| *Friedrichsort, Ger.* | A10 | 10 |
| Friedrichstadt, Ger. | A9 | 10 |
| Friend, Ne., U.S. | K10 | 118 |
| Friendship, N.Y., U.S. | E8 | 108 |
| Friendship, Tn., U.S. | G7 | 114 |
| Friendship, Wi., U.S. | G6 | 110 |
| Fries, Va., U.S. | C6 | 112 |
| Friesach, Aus. | I14 | 10 |
| *Friesland, prov., Neth.* | B8 | 12 |
| Friguia, Gui. | E4 | 64 |
| *Frio, stm., N.A.* | G10 | 92 |
| *Frio, stm., Tx., U.S.* | K8 | 116 |
| *Frio, Cabo, c., Braz.* | G7 | 79 |
| Friona, Tx., U.S. | E4 | 116 |
| Frisco, Tx., U.S. | F10 | 116 |
| Frisco City, Al., U.S. | K9 | 114 |
| *Frisian Islands, is., Eur.* | E9 | 4 |
| Fritch, Tx., U.S. | D5 | 116 |
| *Friuli-Venezia-Giulia, prov., Italy* | C7 | 18 |
| *Friza, proliv, strt., Russia* | H21 | 28 |
| Frobisher, Sk., Can. | I12 | 104 |
| *Frobisher Bay, b., N.T., Can.* | D19 | 96 |
| *Frobisher Lake, l., Sk., Can.* | B6 | 104 |
| *Frog Lake, l., Ab., Can.* | E4 | 104 |
| Frohnleiten, Aus. | H15 | 10 |
| Froid, Mt., U.S. | C3 | 118 |
| Frolovo, Russia | H6 | 26 |
| Fromberg, Mt., U.S. | E17 | 122 |
| Frombork, Pol. | A19 | 10 |
| *Frome, stm., Austl.* | G3 | 70 |
| *Frome, Lake, l., Austl.* | H3 | 70 |
| Frontenac, Ks., U.S. | N13 | 118 |
| Frontera, Mex. | D9 | 90 |
| Frontera, Mex. | H13 | 90 |
| Frontier, Sk., Can. | I6 | 104 |
| Frontier, Wy., U.S. | C6 | 120 |
| Frontino, Col. | D4 | 84 |
| *Frontino, Páramo, mtn., Col.* | D4 | 84 |
| *Front Range, mts., Co., U.S.* | D11 | 120 |
| Front Royal, Va., U.S. | I8 | 108 |
| Frosinone, Italy | H8 | 18 |
| Frost, Tx., U.S. | G10 | 116 |
| Frostburg, Md., U.S. | H8 | 108 |
| Frostproof, Fl., U.S. | L5 | 112 |
| *Frøya, i., Nor.* | J11 | 6 |
| Fruges, Fr. | B9 | 14 |
| Fruita, Co., U.S. | E8 | 120 |
| Fruitdale, Al., U.S. | K8 | 114 |
| Fruitdale, Or., U.S. | H2 | 122 |
| Fruithurst, Al., U.S. | I11 | 114 |
| Fruitland, Id., U.S. | F9 | 122 |
| Fruitland, Md., U.S. | I11 | 108 |
| Fruitport, Mi., U.S. | G9 | 110 |
| Fruitvale, B.C., Can. | H17 | 102 |
| Fruitvale, Wa., U.S. | D5 | 122 |
| Fruitville, Fl., U.S. | L4 | 112 |
| Frunze see Bišhek, Kyrg. | I12 | 26 |
| Frunzivka, Ukr. | B13 | 20 |
| Frutal, Braz. | F4 | 79 |
| Frutigen, Switz. | E8 | 13 |
| Frýdek-Místek, Czech Rep. | F18 | 10 |
| Fryeburg, Me., U.S. | C16 | 108 |
| *Fryingpan, stm., Co., U.S.* | E10 | 120 |
| Fuchang, China | E2 | 34 |
| Fuchū, Japan | M8 | 36 |
| *Fuchun, stm., China* | F8 | 34 |
| Fuding, China | H9 | 34 |
| *Fuego, Volcán de, vol., Guat.* | C4 | 92 |
| Fuencaliente de la Palma, Spain | o23 | 17b |
| Fuensalida, Spain | E7 | 16 |
| Fuente de Cantos, Spain | G5 | 16 |
| Fuente de Oro, Col. | F6 | 84 |
| Fuentesaúco, Spain | D6 | 16 |
| *Fuerte, stm., Mex.* | D5 | 90 |
| Fuerte Olimpo, Para. | I13 | 82 |
| *Fuerteventura, i., Spain* | o26 | 17b |
| Fufeng, China | E8 | 30 |
| Fuhe, China | L2 | 34 |
| Fuhu, China | F7 | 34 |
| Fuji, Japan | L13 | 36 |
| *Fujian (Fukien), prov., China* | F10 | 30 |
| Fujieda, Japan | M13 | 36 |
| Fujin, China | B13 | 30 |
| Fujinomiya, Japan | L13 | 36 |
| *Fuji-san (Fujiyama), vol., Japan* | L13 | 36 |
| Fujisawa, Japan | L14 | 36 |
| *Fujiyama see Fuji-san, vol., Japan* | L13 | 36 |
| Fuji-yoshida, Japan | L13 | 36 |
| Fukagawa, Japan | d17 | 36a |
| Fukou, China | I6 | 34 |
| Fukuchiyama, Japan | L10 | 36 |
| *Fukue-jima, i., Japan* | O3 | 36 |
| Fukui, Japan | K11 | 36 |
| Fukuoka, Japan | N5 | 36 |
| Fukushima, Japan | J15 | 36 |
| Fukuyama, Japan | M8 | 36 |
| Fulacunda, Gui.-B. | F2 | 64 |
| *Fūlādī, Kūh-e, mtn., Afg.* | C2 | 44 |
| Fulda, Ger. | E9 | 10 |
| Fulda, Mn., U.S. | H12 | 118 |
| *Fulda, stm., Ger.* | D9 | 10 |
| Fulechang, China | B8 | 40 |
| Fuling, China | F8 | 30 |
| Fullerton, Ca., U.S. | K8 | 124 |
| Fullerton, Ne., U.S. | J10 | 118 |
| Fulpmes, Aus. | H11 | 10 |
| Fulton, Al., U.S. | K9 | 114 |
| Fulton, Ar., U.S. | I3 | 114 |
| Fulton, Il., U.S. | I5 | 110 |
| Fulton, Ks., U.S. | M13 | 118 |
| Fulton, Ky., U.S. | F8 | 114 |
| Fulton, Mo., U.S. | D5 | 114 |
| Fulton, Ms., U.S. | H8 | 114 |
| Fulton, N.Y., U.S. | D10 | 108 |
| Fulton, Tx., U.S. | K9 | 116 |
| *Fulton, stm., B.C., Can.* | C8 | 102 |
| Fultondale, Al., U.S. | I10 | 114 |
| Fumay, Fr. | C11 | 14 |
| Fumel, Fr. | H7 | 14 |
| Fumintun, China | A14 | 32 |
| Funabashi, Japan | L14 | 36 |
| Funchal, Port. | m21 | 17a |
| Fundación, Col. | B5 | 84 |
| *Fundy, Bay of, b., Can.* | H8 | 106 |
| *Fundy National Park, N.B., Can.* | G8 | 106 |
| Funhalouro, Moz. | D12 | 66 |
| Funing, China | B8 | 34 |
| *Funk Island, i., Nf., Can.* | C20 | 106 |
| Funtua, Nig. | F13 | 64 |
| Funza, Col. | E5 | 84 |
| Fuqikou, China | F6 | 34 |
| Fuquay-Varina, N.C., U.S. | D8 | 112 |
| Furano, Japan | d17 | 36a |
| Fürg, Iran | G13 | 48 |
| Furmanov, Russia | D24 | 22 |
| *Furnas, Represa de, res., Braz.* | F5 | 79 |
| *Furneaux Group, is., Austl.* | L8 | 70 |
| Furnes (Veurne), Bel. | F2 | 12 |
| Furqlus, Syria | D4 | 48 |
| Fürstenfeldbruck, Ger. | G11 | 10 |
| Fürstenwalde, Ger. | C14 | 10 |
| Fürth, Ger. | F10 | 10 |
| Furth im Wald, Ger. | F12 | 10 |
| Furudal, Swe. | K14 | 6 |
| Furukawa, Japan | I15 | 36 |
| Furukawa, Japan | K12 | 36 |
| *Fury and Hecla Strait, strt., N.T., Can.* | C15 | 96 |
| Fusagasugá, Col. | E5 | 84 |
| Fushan, China | D9 | 34 |
| Fushuigang, China | D2 | 34 |
| Fushun, China | B11 | 32 |
| Fusilier, Sk., Can. | G5 | 104 |
| Fusui, China | G8 | 30 |
| Futianpu, China | H1 | 34 |
| Futuyu, China | D2 | 32 |
| Fuwah, Egypt | B6 | 60 |
| Fuxi, China | J2 | 34 |
| Fuxian, China | D8 | 30 |
| Fuxian (Wafangdian), China | D10 | 32 |
| *Fuxian Hu, l., China* | B7 | 40 |
| Fuxin, China | A9 | 32 |
| Fuyang, China | C4 | 34 |
| Fuyu, China | B11 | 30 |
| Fuzhai, China | F9 | 34 |
| Fuzhou, China | G5 | 34 |
| Fuzhou (Foochow), China | I8 | 34 |
| Fuzhuang, China | I6 | 32 |
| Füzuli, Azer. | B9 | 48 |
| *Fyn, i., Den.* | N12 | 6 |

## G

| Name | Map Ref. | Page |
|---|---|---|
| Gaalkacyo, Som. | G10 | 56 |
| Gabarus, N.S., Can. | G13 | 106 |
| *Gabarus Bay, b., N.S., Can.* | G13 | 106 |
| *Gabas, stm., Fr.* | I6 | 14 |
| Gabbs, Nv., U.S. | F8 | 124 |
| Gabela, Ang. | D2 | 58 |
| Gabès, Tun. | D16 | 62 |
| *Gabès, Golfe de, b., Tun.* | C16 | 62 |
| Gabiarra, Braz. | D9 | 79 |
| Gabir, Sudan | M3 | 60 |
| *Gable Mountain, mtn., B.C., Can.* | C13 | 102 |
| *Gabon, ctry., Afr.* | B2 | 58 |
| Gaborone, Bots. | E7 | 66 |
| *Gabriel Strait, strt., N.T., Can.* | D19 | 96 |
| Gabrovo, Bul. | G9 | 20 |
| Gacé, Fr. | D7 | 14 |
| Gachetá, Col. | E6 | 84 |
| Gachsārān, Iran | F11 | 48 |
| Gackle, N.D., U.S. | E8 | 118 |
| Gadag, India | E3 | 46 |
| Gadamai, Sudan | I9 | 60 |
| Gäddede, Swe. | I14 | 6 |
| Gadsden, Al., U.S. | H10 | 114 |
| Gadsden, Az., U.S. | L2 | 120 |
| Gaeta, Italy | H8 | 18 |
| *Gaeta, Golfo di, b., Italy* | H8 | 18 |
| Gaffney, S.C., U.S. | D5 | 112 |
| Gafour, Tun. | M4 | 18 |
| Gafsa, Tun. | C15 | 62 |
| Gagarin, Russia | F18 | 22 |
| Gage, Ok., U.S. | C7 | 116 |
| Gagetown, N.B., Can. | G7 | 106 |
| *Gagetown, Canadian Forces Base, mil., N.B., Can.* | G7 | 106 |
| Gaggenau, Ger. | G8 | 10 |
| Gaghamni, Sudan | L5 | 60 |
| *Gagnoa, C. Iv.* | H7 | 64 |
| Gagnon, P.Q., Can. | F19 | 96 |
| Gagra, Geor. | I6 | 26 |
| Gaibandha, Bngl. | H13 | 44 |
| Gail, Tx., U.S. | G5 | 116 |
| Gaillac, Fr. | I8 | 14 |
| *Gaillard, Lac, l., P.Q., Can.* | B5 | 106 |
| Gaillon, Fr. | C8 | 14 |
| Gainesboro, Tn., U.S. | F11 | 114 |
| Gainesville, Fl., U.S. | J4 | 112 |
| Gainesville, Ga., U.S. | E3 | 112 |
| Gainesville, Mo., U.S. | F4 | 114 |
| Gainesville, Tx., U.S. | F9 | 116 |
| Gainsborough, Sk., Can. | I13 | 104 |
| *Gainsborough Creek, stm., Can.* | I13 | 104 |
| *Gairdner, Lake, l., Austl.* | F7 | 68 |
| *Gaital, Cerro, mtn., Pan.* | I14 | 92 |
| Gaithersburg, Md., U.S. | H9 | 108 |
| Gaixian, China | C10 | 32 |
| Gajny, Russia | E8 | 26 |
| Gajutino, Russia | C21 | 22 |
| Galaassija, Uzb. | B18 | 48 |
| Galahad, Ab., Can. | E23 | 102 |
| *Galán, Cerro, mtn., Arg.* | C5 | 80 |
| *Galapagos Islands see Colón, Archipiélago de, is., Ec.* | j13 | 84a |
| Galashiels, Scot., U.K. | F11 | 8 |
| Galați, Rom. | D12 | 20 |
| *Galați, co., Rom.* | D11 | 20 |
| Galatia, Il., U.S. | E8 | 114 |
| Galatina, Italy | I13 | 18 |
| Galax, Va., U.S. | C6 | 112 |
| Gáldar, Spain | o25 | 17b |
| *Galdhøpiggen, mtn., Nor.* | K11 | 6 |
| Galeana, Mex. | B6 | 90 |
| Galeana, Mex. | E9 | 90 |
| Galela, Indon. | E8 | 38 |
| Galena, Ak., U.S. | D16 | 100 |
| Galena, Il., U.S. | H5 | 110 |
| Galena, Ks., U.S. | N13 | 118 |
| Galena, Mo., U.S. | F3 | 114 |
| Galena Park, Tx., U.S. | J11 | 116 |
| *Galeota Point, c., Trin.* | I14 | 94 |
| *Galera, stm., Braz.* | F12 | 82 |
| *Galera, Punta, c., Ec.* | G2 | 84 |
| *Galera Point, c., Trin.* | I14 | 94 |
| Galesburg, Il., U.S. | J5 | 110 |
| Galesburg, Mi., U.S. | H10 | 110 |
| Galesville, Wi., U.S. | F4 | 110 |
| Galeton, Pa., U.S. | F9 | 108 |
| Galheiros, Braz. | B5 | 79 |
| Gali, Geor. | C25 | 22 |
| *Galicia, state, Spain* | C3 | 16 |
| *Galicia, hist. reg., Eur.* | F12 | 4 |
| *Galilee, Lake, l., Austl.* | D6 | 70 |
| *Galilee, Sea of see Kinneret, Yam, l., Isr.* | C5 | 50 |
| Galiléia, Braz. | E8 | 79 |
| Galion, Oh., U.S. | G4 | 108 |
| *Galiuro Mountains, mts., Az., U.S.* | L6 | 120 |
| Gallarate, Italy | D3 | 18 |
| Gallatin, Mo., U.S. | C3 | 114 |
| Gallatin, Tn., U.S. | F10 | 114 |
| *Gallatin, stm., U.S.* | E14 | 122 |
| Galle, Sri L. | I6 | 46 |
| Galliano, La., U.S. | M6 | 114 |
| Galliate, Italy | D3 | 18 |
| *Gallinas, stm., N.M., U.S.* | D2 | 116 |
| *Gallinas, Punta, c., Col.* | A7 | 84 |
| *Gallinas Peak, mtn., N.M., U.S.* | J11 | 120 |
| Gallipoli, Austl. | B2 | 70 |
| Gallipoli, Italy | I12 | 18 |
| Gallipoli see Gelibolu, Tur. | I10 | 20 |
| *Gallipoli Peninsula see Gelibolu Yarımadası, pen., Tur.* | I10 | 20 |
| Gallipolis, Oh., U.S. | I4 | 108 |
| Gällivare, Swe. | H17 | 6 |
| *Galloway, Mull of, c., Scot., U.K.* | G9 | 8 |
| Gallup, N.M., U.S. | I8 | 120 |
| Galougo, Mali | E4 | 64 |
| Galt, Ca., U.S. | F4 | 124 |
| Galtat Zemmour, W. Sah. | H4 | 62 |
| *Galty Mountains, mts., Ire.* | I5 | 8 |
| Galva, Ia., U.S. | I12 | 118 |
| Galva, Il., U.S. | I5 | 110 |
| Galva, Ks., U.S. | M10 | 118 |
| Galvarino, Chile | J2 | 80 |
| Galveston, In., U.S. | B10 | 114 |
| Galveston, Tx., U.S. | J12 | 116 |
| *Galveston Bay, b., Tx., U.S.* | J12 | 116 |
| *Galveston Island, i., Tx., U.S.* | J12 | 116 |
| Gálvez, Arg. | G8 | 80 |
| Galway, Ire. | H4 | 8 |
| *Galway, co., Ire.* | H5 | 8 |
| *Galway Bay, b., Ire.* | H4 | 8 |
| Gamagōri, Japan | M12 | 36 |
| Gamaliel, Ky., U.S. | F11 | 114 |
| Gamarra, Col. | C6 | 84 |
| Gambaga, Ghana | F9 | 64 |
| Gambela, Eth. | M8 | 60 |
| Gambell, Ak., U.S. | E9 | 100 |
| *Gambia, ctry., Afr.* | F3 | 54 |
| *Gambia (Gambie), stm., Afr.* | F3 | 54 |
| Gambī Atrash, Sudan | L7 | 60 |
| Gambier, Oh., U.S. | G4 | 108 |
| *Gambier, Îles, is., Fr. Poly.* | K26 | 126 |
| Gambo, Nf., Can. | D19 | 106 |
| Gamboa, Pan. | C3 | 84 |
| Gamboma, Congo | B3 | 58 |
| *Gammon, stm., Can.* | G19 | 104 |
| Gamoep, S. Afr. | G4 | 66 |
| Gamon, Sen. | E3 | 64 |
| *Gan, stm., China* | A11 | 30 |
| *Gan, stm., China* | G4 | 34 |
| Ganado, Az., U.S. | I7 | 120 |
| Ganado, Tx., U.S. | J10 | 116 |
| Gananoque, On., Can. | F19 | 110 |
| Ganāveh, Iran | G11 | 48 |
| Gäncä, Azer. | I7 | 26 |
| Gand (Gent), Bel. | F4 | 12 |
| Ganda, Ang. | D2 | 58 |
| *Gandak (Nārāyani), stm., Asia* | G11 | 44 |
| Gander, Nf., Can. | D19 | 106 |
| *Gander, stm., Nf., Can.* | D19 | 106 |
| Gander Bay, Nf., Can. | C19 | 106 |
| *Gander Bay, b., Nf., Can.* | C19 | 106 |
| Ganderkesee, Ger. | B8 | 10 |
| *Gander Lake, l., Nf., Can.* | D19 | 106 |
| *Gāndhi Sāgar, res., India* | H6 | 44 |
| Ganda, Nig. | E12 | 64 |
| Gandia, Spain | G11 | 16 |
| Gandu, Braz. | B9 | 79 |
| Ganfang, China | G3 | 34 |
| Gangānagar, India | F5 | 44 |
| Gangāpur, India | G7 | 44 |
| Gangaw, Myan. | C3 | 40 |
| *Gangdisê Shan, mts., China* | E9 | 44 |
| Ganges, B.C., Can. | I11 | 102 |
| Ganges, Fr. | I10 | 14 |
| *Ganges (Ganga) (Padma), stm., Asia* | I13 | 44 |
| Ganghu, China | D12 | 44 |
| Gangi, Italy | L9 | 18 |
| Gangkou, China | F4 | 34 |
| Gangotri, India | E8 | 44 |
| Gangotri, India | E8 | 44 |
| Gangou, China | C7 | 32 |
| Gangoumen, China | B4 | 32 |
| Gang Ranch, B.C., Can. | F12 | 102 |
| Gangtok, India | G13 | 44 |
| Gangu, China | E8 | 30 |
| *Gannett Peak, mtn., Wy., U.S.* | G16 | 122 |
| Gannvalley, S.D., U.S. | G9 | 118 |
| Ganq, China | B15 | 44 |
| *Gansu (Kansu), prov., China* | D7 | 30 |
| Gantt, Al., U.S. | K10 | 114 |
| Ganxi, China | G7 | 34 |
| Ganzê, China | E7 | 30 |
| Ganzhou, China | J3 | 34 |
| Ganzo Azul, Peru | C4 | 82 |
| Gao, Mali | C9 | 64 |
| Gaobu, China | H6 | 34 |
| Gaocun, China | F10 | 32 |
| Gaohe, China | M1 | 34 |
| Gaokeng, China | H2 | 34 |
| Gaoling, China | C5 | 32 |
| Gaona, Arg. | C6 | 80 |
| Gaoqiaozhen, China | C9 | 32 |
| Gaoshan, China | J8 | 34 |
| Gaotan, China | E6 | 34 |
| Gaotingsi, China | I1 | 34 |
| Gaoua, Burkina | F8 | 64 |
| Gaoxinji, China | A4 | 34 |
| Gaoya, China | G6 | 32 |
| Gaoyou, China | C8 | 34 |
| *Gaoyou Hu, l., China* | C8 | 34 |
| Gap, Fr. | H13 | 14 |
| Gar, China | E3 | 30 |
| Garachiné, Pan. | C3 | 84 |
| Garagoa, Col. | E6 | 84 |
| Garanhuns, Braz. | E11 | 76 |
| Garara, Pap. N. Gui. | A9 | 68 |
| Garber, Ok., U.S. | C9 | 116 |
| Garberville, Ca., U.S. | D2 | 124 |
| Gârbovu, Rom. | E7 | 20 |
| Garça, Braz. | G4 | 79 |
| *Garças, Rio das, stm., Braz.* | C2 | 79 |
| García, Mex. | C5 | 90 |
| *García de Sola, Embalse de, res., Spain* | F6 | 16 |
| Garcias, Braz. | F2 | 79 |
| *Gard, dept., Fr.* | I11 | 14 |
| Garda, Italy | D5 | 18 |
| *Garda, Lago di, l., Italy* | D5 | 18 |
| Gardelegen, Ger. | C11 | 10 |
| Garden City, Ga., U.S. | G5 | 112 |
| Garden City, Ks., U.S. | N7 | 118 |
| Garden City, Mo., U.S. | D2 | 114 |
| Garden City, Tx., U.S. | H5 | 116 |
| Gardendale, Al., U.S. | I10 | 114 |
| Garden Grove, Ca., U.S. | K8 | 124 |
| Garden Grove, Ia., U.S. | J2 | 110 |
| *Garden Lakes, Ga., U.S.* | E1 | 112 |
| *Garden Peninsula, pen., Mi., U.S.* | E9 | 110 |
| Garden Plain, Ks., U.S. | N10 | 118 |
| Garden Reach, India | I13 | 44 |
| Gardenton, Mb., Can. | I18 | 104 |
| Gardey, Arg. | I9 | 80 |
| Gardeyz, Afg. | D3 | 44 |
| Gardiner, Me., U.S. | C17 | 108 |
| Gardiner, Mt., U.S. | E15 | 122 |
| Gardiner, Or., U.S. | G1 | 122 |
| *Gardiner Dam, Sk., Can.* | G8 | 104 |
| *Gardiners Bay, b., N.Y., U.S.* | F14 | 108 |
| Gardner, Ks., U.S. | M13 | 118 |
| Gardner, Ma., U.S. | E15 | 108 |
| *Gardner Canal, b., B.C., Can.* | D6 | 102 |
| Gardnerville, Nv., U.S. | F6 | 124 |
| Gardone Val Trompia, Italy | D5 | 18 |
| Garešnica, Cro. | D11 | 18 |
| Garfield, Ks., U.S. | M8 | 118 |
| Garfield, N.M., U.S. | L9 | 120 |
| Garfield, Wa., U.S. | C8 | 122 |
| *Garfield Mountain, mtn., Mt., U.S.* | F13 | 122 |
| Gargouna, Mali | D10 | 64 |
| Gargždai, Lith. | F4 | 22 |
| Garibaldi, B.C., Can. | H11 | 102 |
| Garibaldi, Braz. | E13 | 80 |
| Garibaldi, Or., U.S. | E2 | 122 |
| *Garibaldi, Mount, mtn., B.C., Can.* | H11 | 102 |
| *Garibaldi Provincial Park, B.C., Can.* | G12 | 102 |
| Garies, S. Afr. | H4 | 66 |
| Garissa, Kenya | B7 | 58 |
| Garita Palmera, El Sal. | D4 | 92 |
| Garko, Nig. | F14 | 64 |
| Garland, Al., U.S. | K10 | 114 |
| Garland, Tx., U.S. | G10 | 116 |
| Garland, Ut., U.S. | C4 | 120 |
| Garlasco, Italy | D3 | 18 |
| Garliava, Lith. | G6 | 22 |
| Garlin, Fr. | I6 | 14 |
| Garm, Taj. | J12 | 26 |
| Garmisch-Partenkirchen, Ger. | H11 | 10 |
| Garnavillo, Ia., U.S. | H4 | 110 |
| Garner, Ia., U.S. | G2 | 110 |
| Garner, N.C., U.S. | D8 | 112 |
| Garnett, Ks., U.S. | M12 | 118 |
| Garnish, Nf., Can. | E18 | 106 |
| *Garonne, stm., Eur.* | H6 | 14 |
| Garoua, Cam. | G9 | 54 |
| Garretson, S.D., U.S. | H11 | 118 |
| Garrett, In., U.S. | A11 | 114 |
| Garrett, Ky., U.S. | B4 | 112 |
| Garrison, Mt., U.S. | D13 | 122 |
| Garrison, N.D., U.S. | D6 | 118 |
| Garrison, Tx., U.S. | K2 | 114 |
| Garrovillas, Spain | F5 | 16 |
| *Garry Bay, b., N.T., Can.* | C15 | 96 |
| *Garry Lake, l., N.T., Can.* | C12 | 96 |
| Garson, On., Can. | D15 | 110 |
| *Garson Lake, l., Can.* | B4 | 104 |
| Garub, Nmb. | F3 | 66 |
| Garut, Indon. | j13 | 39a |
| Garwin, Ia., U.S. | H3 | 110 |
| Garwolin, Pol. | D21 | 10 |
| Garwood, Tx., U.S. | J10 | 116 |
| Gary, In., U.S. | A9 | 114 |
| Gary, S.D., U.S. | G11 | 118 |
| Gary, Tx., U.S. | J2 | 114 |
| Gary, W.V., U.S. | B5 | 112 |
| Garyarsa, China | E9 | 44 |
| Garza, Arg. | E7 | 80 |
| Garzón, Col. | F5 | 84 |
| Garzón, Ur. | H11 | 80 |
| Gas City, In., U.S. | B11 | 114 |
| *Gascogne, hist. reg., Fr.* | H6 | 14 |
| *Gasconade, stm., Mo., U.S.* | D5 | 114 |
| *Gascoyne, stm., Austl.* | E2 | 68 |
| *Gash (Nahr al-Qāsh), stm., Afr.* | F8 | 56 |
| Gashaka, Nig. | G9 | 54 |
| Gaspar, Braz. | D14 | 80 |
| *Gaspard Creek, stm., B.C., Can.* | F12 | 102 |
| Gaspé, P.Q., Can. | D9 | 106 |
| *Gaspé, Baie de, b., P.Q., Can.* | D9 | 106 |
| *Gaspé, Cap, c., P.Q., Can.* | D9 | 106 |
| *Gaspé Peninsula see Gaspésie, Péninsule de la, pen., P.Q., Can.* | D8 | 106 |
| Gaspereau Lake, l., N.S., Can. | H9 | 106 |
| *Gaspésie, Parc Provincial de la, P.Q., Can.* | D8 | 106 |
| *Gaspésie, Péninsule de la, pen., P.Q., Can.* | D8 | 106 |
| Gassaway, W.V., U.S. | I6 | 108 |
| Gaston, N.C., U.S. | C9 | 112 |
| *Gaston, Lake, res., U.S.* | C8 | 112 |
| Gastonia, N.C., U.S. | D5 | 112 |
| Gastre, Arg. | E3 | 78 |
| *Gata, Cabo de, c., Spain* | I9 | 16 |
| *Gátas, Akrotírion, c., Cyp.* | D2 | 48 |
| Gatčina, Russia | B13 | 22 |
| Gate, Ok., U.S. | C6 | 116 |
| Gate City, Va., U.S. | C4 | 112 |
| Gateshead, Eng., U.K. | G12 | 8 |
| *Gateshead Island, i., N.T., Can.* | B12 | 96 |
| Gatesville, N.C., U.S. | C10 | 112 |
| Gatesville, Tx., U.S. | H9 | 116 |
| Gateway, Co., U.S. | F8 | 120 |
| Gatineau, P.Q., Can. | B11 | 108 |
| *Gatineau, stm., P.Q., Can.* | G17 | 96 |
| *Gatineau, Parc de la, P.Q., Can.* | B10 | 108 |
| Gatlinburg, Tn., U.S. | D3 | 112 |
| Gattinara, Italy | D3 | 18 |
| Gatton, Austl. | F10 | 70 |
| *Gatún, Esclusas de, Pan.* | H15 | 92 |
| *Gatún, Lago, res., Pan.* | H15 | 92 |
| *Gauer Lake, l., Mb., Can.* | A17 | 104 |
| *Gauley, stm., W.V., U.S.* | I5 | 108 |
| Gauley Bridge, W.V., U.S. | I5 | 108 |
| Gaultois, Nf., Can. | E18 | 106 |
| *Gaurīśaṅkar, mtn., Asia* | G12 | 44 |
| Gause, Tx., U.S. | I10 | 116 |
| *Gauteng, prov., S. Afr.* | F9 | 66 |
| Gauting, Ger. | G11 | 10 |
| Gavà, Spain | D14 | 16 |
| *Gávdhos, i., Grc.* | O8 | 20 |
| *Gavião, stm., Braz.* | C8 | 79 |
| Gävle, Swe. | K15 | 6 |
| *Gävleborgs Län, co., Swe.* | K15 | 6 |
| Gavrilov-Jam, Russia | D22 | 22 |
| Gavrilov Posad, Russia | E23 | 22 |
| Gawler, Austl. | J3 | 70 |
| *Gawler Ranges, mts., Austl.* | F7 | 68 |
| *Gaxun Nur, l., China* | C7 | 30 |
| Gaya, India | H11 | 44 |
| Gaylord, Mi., U.S. | E11 | 110 |
| Gaylord, Mn., U.S. | F1 | 110 |
| Gayndah, Austl. | E9 | 70 |
| Gays Mills, Wi., U.S. | G5 | 110 |
| Gaza see Ghazzah, Gaza | F3 | 48 |
| *Gaza Strip, hist. reg., Gaza* | F2 | 50 |
| Gaziantep, Tur. | C4 | 48 |
| Gazimağusa (Famagusta), N. Cyp. | D2 | 48 |
| Gbangbatok, S.L. | H3 | 64 |
| *Gbanhala, stm., Afr.* | G5 | 64 |
| Gbarnga, Lib. | H5 | 64 |
| Gbongan, Nig. | H12 | 64 |
| Gcoverega, Bots. | B7 | 66 |
| Gdańsk (Danzig), Pol. | A18 | 10 |
| *Gdańsk, Gulf of, b., Eur.* | A19 | 10 |
| Gdov, Russia | C10 | 22 |
| Gdyel, Alg. | J11 | 16 |
| Gdynia, Pol. | A18 | 10 |
| *Gearhart Mountain, mtn., Or., U.S.* | H5 | 122 |
| Geary, N.B., Can. | G7 | 106 |
| Geary, Ok., U.S. | D8 | 116 |
| *Geba, stm., Afr.* | F4 | 54 |
| Gebeit Mine, Sudan | G9 | 60 |
| Gebze, Tur. | I13 | 20 |
| Gecha, Eth. | N8 | 60 |
| Geddes, S.D., U.S. | H9 | 118 |
| Gedera, Isr. | E3 | 50 |
| Gediz, Tur. | J13 | 20 |
| Gedo, Eth. | M9 | 60 |
| Gedun, China | H7 | 34 |
| Geel, Bel. | F7 | 12 |
| Geelong, Austl. | L6 | 70 |
| Geesthacht, Ger. | B10 | 10 |
| Geeveston, Austl. | N7 | 70 |
| Gegong, China | E6 | 34 |
| Geiger, Al., U.S. | J8 | 114 |
| *Geikie, stm., Sk., Can.* | E12 | 96 |
| Geilo, Nor. | K11 | 6 |
| Geiranger, Nor. | J10 | 6 |
| Geislingen, Ger. | G9 | 10 |
| Geistown, Pa., U.S. | G8 | 108 |
| Gejiu (Kokiu), China | C7 | 40 |
| Gejiatun, China | C7 | 32 |
| Gela, Italy | L9 | 18 |
| *Gelderland, prov., Neth.* | D8 | 12 |
| Geldermalsen, Neth. | E7 | 12 |
| Geldrop, Neth. | F8 | 12 |
| Gelenbe, Tur. | J11 | 20 |
| Gelgaudiškis, Lith. | F6 | 22 |
| Gelibolu, Tur. | I10 | 20 |
| *Gelibolu Yarımadası (Gallipoli Peninsula), pen., Tur.* | I10 | 20 |
| Gelsenkirchen, Ger. | D7 | 10 |
| Geltsa, Eth. | N9 | 60 |
| Gemena, D.R.C. | H4 | 56 |
| Gemlik, Tur. | I13 | 20 |
| *Gemsbok National Park, Bots.* | E5 | 66 |
| Gemünden, Ger. | E9 | 10 |
| *Gen, stm., China* | A11 | 30 |
| *Genale (Jubba), stm., Afr.* | G9 | 56 |
| Gençay, Fr. | F7 | 14 |
| *General, stm., C.R.* | H11 | 92 |
| General Acha, Arg. | I6 | 80 |
| General Alvear, Arg. | I8 | 80 |
| General Alvear, Arg. | H5 | 80 |
| General Aquino, Para. | C10 | 80 |
| General Arenales, Arg. | H8 | 80 |
| General Belgrano, Arg. | H9 | 80 |
| General Bravo, Mex. | E10 | 90 |
| General Cabrera, Arg. | G7 | 80 |
| General Campos, Arg. | F9 | 80 |
| General Carneiro, Braz. | C2 | 79 |
| *General Carrera, Lago (Lago Buenos Aires), l., S.A.* | F2 | 78 |
| General Cepeda, Mex. | E9 | 90 |
| General Conesa, Arg. | I10 | 80 |
| General Daniel Cerri, Arg. | J7 | 80 |
| General Elizardo Aquino, Para. | D10 | 80 |
| General Enrique Martínez, Ur. | G12 | 80 |
| General Enrique Mosconi, Arg. | B7 | 80 |
| General Escobedo, Mex. | E7 | 90 |
| General Eugenio A. Garay, Para. | C10 | 80 |
| General Eugenio A. Garay, Para. | I10 | 82 |
| General Galarza, Arg. | G9 | 80 |
| General Güemes, Arg. | C6 | 80 |
| General Guido, Arg. | I10 | 80 |
| General José de San Martín, Arg. | D9 | 80 |
| General Juan José Ríos, Mex. | E5 | 90 |
| General Juan Madariaga, Arg. | I10 | 80 |
| General La Madrid, Arg. | I8 | 80 |
| General Lavalle, Arg. | I10 | 80 |
| General Leonidas Plaza Gutiérrez, Ec. | I3 | 84 |
| General Levalle, Arg. | H7 | 80 |
| *General Manuel Belgrano, Cerro, mtn., Arg.* | E5 | 80 |
| General O'Brien, Arg. | H8 | 80 |
| General Paz, Arg. | H9 | 80 |
| General Pico, Arg. | H7 | 80 |
| General Pinedo, Arg. | D8 | 80 |
| General Pinto, Arg. | H8 | 80 |
| General Pizarro, Arg. | C6 | 80 |
| General Roca, Arg. | J5 | 80 |
| General San Martín, Arg. | H9 | 80 |
| General San Martín, Arg. | I7 | 80 |
| General Santos, Phil. | D8 | 38 |
| General Terán, Mex. | E10 | 90 |
| General Viamonte (Los Toldos), Arg. | H8 | 80 |
| General Villegas, Arg. | H7 | 80 |
| Genesee, Id., U.S. | D9 | 122 |
| *Genesee, stm., U.S.* | H18 | 110 |
| Geneseo, Il., U.S. | I5 | 110 |
| Geneseo, Ks., U.S. | M9 | 118 |
| Geneseo, N.Y., U.S. | E9 | 108 |
| Geneva, Al., U.S. | K11 | 114 |
| Geneva, Il., U.S. | I7 | 110 |
| Geneva, In., U.S. | B12 | 114 |
| Geneva, Ne., U.S. | K10 | 118 |
| Geneva, N.Y., U.S. | E9 | 108 |
| Geneva, Oh., U.S. | F6 | 108 |
| Geneva see Genève, Switz. | F13 | 14 |
| *Geneva, Lake, l., Eur.* | F13 | 14 |
| Genève (Geneva), Switz. | F5 | 13 |
| *Genève, state, Switz.* | F5 | 13 |
| *Genévriers, Île des, i., P.Q., Can.* | A15 | 106 |
| Gengma, China | C5 | 40 |
| Genk, Bel. | G8 | 12 |
| Genlis, Fr. | E12 | 14 |
| *Genoa, Il., U.S.* | H7 | 110 |
| Genoa see Genova, Italy | E3 | 18 |
| Genoa, Ne., U.S. | J10 | 118 |
| Genoa, Oh., U.S. | F3 | 108 |
| Genoa, Wi., U.S. | G4 | 110 |
| Genova (Genoa), Italy | E3 | 18 |
| *Genova, Golfo di, b., Italy* | F3 | 18 |
| *Genrietty, ostrov, i., Russia* | B23 | 28 |
| Gent (Gand), Bel. | F4 | 12 |
| Genthin, Ger. | C12 | 10 |
| Gentry, Ar., U.S. | F2 | 114 |
| *Geographe Bay, b., Austl.* | F3 | 68 |
| *Geographe Channel, strt., Austl.* | D2 | 68 |
| Geok-Tepe, Turk. | B14 | 48 |
| George, Ia., U.S. | H11 | 118 |
| George, S. Afr. | I6 | 66 |
| *George, stm., P.Q., Can.* | E19 | 96 |
| *George, Cape, c., N.S., Can.* | G12 | 106 |
| *George, Lake, l., Austl.* | J8 | 70 |
| *George, Lake, l., Fl., U.S.* | J5 | 112 |
| *George, Lake, l., N.Y., U.S.* | D13 | 108 |
| *George, Lake, l., Ug.* | B6 | 58 |
| *Georges Bank* | E13 | 86 |
| George Town, Austl. | M7 | 70 |
| George Town, Cay. Is. | E4 | 94 |
| Georgetown, Co., U.S. | E11 | 120 |
| Georgetown, De., U.S. | I11 | 108 |
| Georgetown, Ga., U.S. | H1 | 112 |
| Georgetown, Gam. | E2 | 64 |
| Georgetown, Guy. | D13 | 84 |
| Georgetown, Id., U.S. | H14 | 122 |
| Georgetown, Il., U.S. | C9 | 114 |
| Georgetown, Ky., U.S. | I2 | 108 |
| George Town (Pinang), Malay. | L6 | 40 |
| Georgetown, Ms., U.S. | K6 | 114 |
| Georgetown, Oh., U.S. | I3 | 108 |
| Georgetown, P.E., Can. | F11 | 106 |
| Georgetown, S.C., U.S. | F7 | 112 |
| Georgetown, St. Vin. | H14 | 94 |
| Georgetown, Tx., U.S. | I9 | 116 |
| *George V Coast, Ant.* | B7 | 73 |
| *George VI Sound, strt., Ant.* | C12 | 73 |
| George West, Tx., U.S. | K8 | 116 |
| *Georgia, ctry., Asia* | I6 | 26 |
| *Georgia, state, U.S.* | E10 | 98 |
| *Georgia, Strait of, strt., N.A.* | H11 | 102 |
| Georgiana, Al., U.S. | K10 | 114 |
| *Georgian Bay, b., On., Can.* | E14 | 110 |
| *Georgian Bay Islands National Park, On., Can.* | F16 | 110 |
| Georgijevsk, Russia | I6 | 26 |
| *Georgina, stm., Austl.* | D3 | 70 |
| Gera, Ger. | E12 | 10 |
| *Geral, Serra, clf, Braz.* | D14 | 80 |
| Gerald, Mo., U.S. | D5 | 114 |
| *Geral de Goiás, Serra, clf, Braz.* | B5 | 79 |
| Geraldine, Mt., U.S. | C15 | 122 |
| Geraldton, Austl. | E2 | 68 |
| Geraldton, On., Can. | G15 | 96 |
| Gérardmer, Fr. | D13 | 14 |
| Gerber, Ca., U.S. | D3 | 124 |
| *Gerdine, Mount, mtn., Ak., U.S.* | F18 | 100 |
| Gereshk, Afg. | E1 | 44 |
| Gering, Ne., U.S. | J4 | 118 |
| *Gerlachovský štít, mtn., Slvk.* | F20 | 10 |
| *Germain, Grand lac, l., P.Q., Can.* | A7 | 106 |
| *Germansen, Mount, mtn., B.C., Can.* | B10 | 102 |
| *Germansen Lake, l., B.C., Can.* | B10 | 102 |
| Germansen Landing, B.C., Can. | B10 | 102 |
| Germantown, Il., U.S. | D7 | 114 |
| Germantown, Tn., U.S. | G7 | 114 |
| Germantown, Wi., U.S. | G7 | 110 |
| *Germany (Deutschland), ctry., Eur.* | E9 | 4 |
| Germfask, Mi., U.S. | D10 | 110 |
| Germiston, S. Afr. | F9 | 66 |
| Gernikao (Guernica), Spain | B9 | 16 |
| Geronimo, Ok., U.S. | E8 | 116 |
| *Gers, dept., Fr.* | I7 | 14 |
| Gerufa, Bots. | B8 | 66 |
| Gêrzê, China | D11 | 44 |
| Gesher HaZiw, Isr. | B4 | 50 |
| Getafe, Spain | E8 | 16 |
| Gettysburg, Pa., U.S. | H9 | 108 |
| Gettysburg, S.D., U.S. | F8 | 118 |
| Getulina, Braz. | F4 | 79 |
| Getúlio Vargas, Braz. | D12 | 80 |
| Gevgelija, Mac. | H6 | 20 |
| *Gévora, stm., Eur.* | F4 | 16 |
| Gex, Fr. | F13 | 14 |
| Geyikli, Tur. | J10 | 20 |
| Geyser, Mt., U.S. | C15 | 122 |
| Geyserville, Ca., U.S. | F3 | 124 |
| *Ghaapplato, plat., S. Afr.* | F7 | 66 |
| Ghadāmis, Libya | E15 | 62 |
| *Ghāghara, stm., Asia* | G10 | 44 |
| *Ghana, ctry., Afr.* | G6 | 54 |
| Ghanzi, Bots. | C5 | 66 |
| *Ghanzi, dept., Bots.* | D6 | 66 |
| *Gharbi, Oued el, val., Alg.* | D11 | 62 |
| *Gharbīyah, Aṣ-Ṣaḥrā' al- (Western Desert), des., Egypt* | D4 | 60 |
| Ghardaïa, Alg. | D12 | 62 |
| Ghardimaou, Tun. | M3 | 18 |
| Gharig, Sudan | L4 | 60 |
| Gharyān, Libya | B3 | 56 |
| Ghasm, Syria | C6 | 50 |
| Ghāt, Libya | H16 | 62 |
| Ghātāl, India | I12 | 44 |
| *Għawdex (Gozo), i., Malta* | M9 | 18 |
| *Ghawr ash-Sharqīyah, Qanāt al- (East Ghor Canal), Jord.* | D5 | 50 |
| *Ghayth, Wādī, val., Jord.* | G5 | 50 |
| *Ghazāl, Bahr al-, stm., Sudan* | M5 | 60 |
| *Ghazal, Bahr el, val., Chad* | F4 | 56 |
| Ghāziābād, India | F7 | 44 |
| Ghāzīpur, India | H10 | 44 |
| Ghazlūna, Pak. | E2 | 44 |
| Ghaznī, Afg. | D3 | 44 |
| Ghazzah (Gaza), Gaza | F3 | 48 |
| Ghedi, Italy | D5 | 18 |
| Ghent see Gent, Bel. | F4 | 12 |
| Gheorgheni, Rom. | C9 | 20 |
| Gherla, Rom. | B7 | 20 |
| Ghilizane, Alg. | C11 | 62 |
| Ghisonaccia, Fr. | I24 | 15a |
| *Ghudāf, Wādī al-, val., Iraq* | E7 | 48 |
| Ghūrīān, Afg. | D16 | 48 |
| *Giant's Castle, mtn., Afr.* | G9 | 66 |
| Giarre, Italy | L10 | 18 |
| Gibara, Cuba | D6 | 94 |
| Gibbon, Mn., U.S. | F1 | 110 |
| Gibbon, Ne., U.S. | K9 | 118 |
| Gibbons, Ab., Can. | D21 | 102 |
| Gibbonsville, Id., U.S. | E12 | 122 |
| Gibeon, Nmb. | E3 | 66 |
| Gibraleón, Spain | H5 | 16 |
| Gibraltar, Gib. | I6 | 16 |
| *Gibraltar, dep., Eur.* | H6 | 4 |
| *Gibraltar, Strait of (Estrecho de Gibraltar), strt.* | J6 | 16 |
| Gibsland, La., U.S. | J3 | 114 |
| Gibson, Ga., U.S. | F4 | 112 |
| Gibson City, Il., U.S. | J7 | 110 |
| *Gibson Desert, des., Austl.* | D5 | 68 |
| Gibsons, B.C., Can. | H11 | 102 |
| Gidami, Eth. | M8 | 60 |
| Gidda, Eth. | M8 | 60 |
| Giddings, Tx., U.S. | I10 | 116 |
| Gideon, Mo., U.S. | F7 | 114 |
| Gidole, Eth. | O9 | 60 |
| Gidrotorf, Russia | E26 | 22 |
| Gien, Fr. | E9 | 14 |
| Giessen, Ger. | E8 | 10 |
| Gifford, Fl., U.S. | L6 | 112 |
| *Gifford, stm., N.T., Can.* | B16 | 96 |
| Gifhorn, Ger. | C10 | 10 |
| Gifu, Japan | L11 | 36 |
| *Giganta, Sierra de la, mts., Mex.* | E4 | 90 |
| Gigante, Col. | F5 | 84 |
| Gijón, Spain | B6 | 16 |
| *Gila, stm., U.S.* | L2 | 120 |
| Gila Bend, Az., U.S. | L4 | 120 |
| *Gila Bend Mountains, mts., Az., U.S.* | K3 | 120 |
| *Gila Mountains, mts., Az., U.S.* | K7 | 120 |
| Gilbert, La., U.S. | J5 | 114 |
| Gilbert, Mn., U.S. | C3 | 110 |
| *Gilbert, stm., Austl.* | A4 | 70 |
| *Gilbert, Mount, mtn., B.C., Can.* | G10 | 102 |
| Gilbertown, Al., U.S. | K8 | 114 |
| Gilbert Plains, Mb., Can. | G14 | 104 |
| *Gilboa', Haré, hills, Asia* | D4 | 50 |
| Gilbués, Braz. | E9 | 76 |
| Gildford, Mt., U.S. | B15 | 122 |
| *Gilford Island, i., B.C., Can.* | G8 | 102 |
| Gilgandra, Austl. | H8 | 70 |
| Gilgit, Pak. | C6 | 44 |
| *Gilgit, stm., Pak.* | B5 | 44 |
| *Gil Island, i., B.C., Can.* | D5 | 102 |
| Gillam, Mb., Can. | B20 | 104 |
| *Gilles, Lake, l., Austl.* | I2 | 70 |
| Gillespie, Il., U.S. | C7 | 114 |
| Gillett, Ar., U.S. | H5 | 114 |

| Name | Map Ref. | Page |
|---|---|---|
| Gillett, Wi., U.S. | F7 | 110 |
| Gillette, Wy., U.S. | G2 | 118 |
| Gillian, Lake, l., N.T., Can. | C17 | 96 |
| Gills Rock, Wi., U.S. | E8 | 110 |
| Gilman, Ia., U.S. | I3 | 110 |
| Gilman, Il., U.S. | J8 | 110 |
| Gilman, Wi., U.S. | E5 | 110 |
| Gilmer, Tx., U.S. | G12 | 116 |
| Gilmore City, Ia., U.S. | I13 | 118 |
| Gilroy, Ca., U.S. | G4 | 124 |
| Giltner, Ne., U.S. | K9 | 118 |
| Giluwe, Mount, mtn., Pap. N. Gui. | m15 | 68a |
| Gimbi, Eth. | M8 | 60 |
| Gimie, Mount, mtn., St. Luc. | H14 | 94 |
| Gimli, Mb., Can. | H18 | 104 |
| Gimoly, Russia | J23 | 6 |
| Gimont, Fr. | I7 | 14 |
| Gin Gin, Austl. | E9 | 70 |
| Ginir, Eth. | G9 | 56 |
| Ginosa, Italy | I11 | 18 |
| Gioia del Colle, Italy | I11 | 18 |
| Gioia Tauro, Italy | K10 | 18 |
| Gipuzkoako, prov., Spain | B9 | 16 |
| Girard, Il., U.S. | C7 | 114 |
| Girard, Ks., U.S. | N13 | 118 |
| Girard, Oh., U.S. | F6 | 108 |
| Girard, Pa., U.S. | E6 | 108 |
| Girard, Tx., U.S. | F6 | 116 |
| Girardot, Col. | E5 | 84 |
| Girgarre, Austl. | K6 | 70 |
| Giridih, India | H12 | 44 |
| Girne, N. Cyp. | D2 | 48 |
| Giromagny, Fr. | E13 | 14 |
| Girón, Ec. | I3 | 84 |
| Girona, Spain | D14 | 16 |
| Gironde, dept., Fr. | G6 | 14 |
| Gironde, stm., Fr. | G6 | 14 |
| Girouxville, Ab., Can. | B17 | 102 |
| Giru, Austl. | B7 | 70 |
| Giruá, Braz. | E11 | 80 |
| Girvas, Russia | J23 | 6 |
| Gisborne, N.Z. | C7 | 72 |
| Gisborne Lake, l., Nf., Can. | E19 | 106 |
| Giscome, B.C., Can. | C12 | 102 |
| Gisenyi, Rw. | B5 | 58 |
| Gisors, Fr. | C8 | 14 |
| Giswil, Switz. | E9 | 13 |
| Gitega, Bur. | B5 | 58 |
| Giugliano [in Campania], Italy | I9 | 18 |
| Giulianova, Italy | G8 | 18 |
| Giurgiu, Rom. | F9 | 20 |
| Giurgiu, co., Rom. | E10 | 20 |
| Giv'atayim, Isr. | D3 | 50 |
| Givet, Fr. | B11 | 14 |
| Givors, Fr. | G11 | 14 |
| Givry, Fr. | F11 | 14 |
| Giyon, Eth. | M9 | 60 |
| Giza see Al-Jīzah, Egypt | B6 | 60 |
| Gizáb, Afg. | D2 | 44 |
| Gižduvan, Uzb. | I10 | 26 |
| Gizen, Sudan | L8 | 60 |
| Gižiginskaja guba, b., Russia | E23 | 28 |
| Gizycko, Pol. | A21 | 10 |
| Gjirokastër, Alb. | I4 | 20 |
| Gjoa Haven, N.T., Can. | C13 | 96 |
| Gjøvik, Nor. | K12 | 6 |
| Gjuhëzës, Kepi i, c., Alb. | I3 | 20 |
| Glace Bay, N.S., Can. | F14 | 106 |
| Glacier, B.C., Can. | F17 | 102 |
| Glacier Bay, b., Ak., U.S. | G26 | 100 |
| Glacier National Park, B.C., Can. | F17 | 102 |
| Glacier National Park, Mt., U.S. | B12 | 122 |
| Glacier Peak, mtn., Wa., U.S. | B4 | 122 |
| Gladbach see Mönchengladbach, Ger. | D6 | 10 |
| Gladbrook, Ia., U.S. | H3 | 110 |
| Glade Spring, Va., U.S. | C5 | 112 |
| Gladewater, Tx., U.S. | G12 | 116 |
| Gladstone, Austl. | D9 | 70 |
| Gladstone, Austl. | I3 | 70 |
| Gladstone, Mb., Can. | H16 | 104 |
| Gladstone, Mi., U.S. | E8 | 110 |
| Gladstone, Mo., U.S. | C2 | 114 |
| Gladwin, Mi., U.S. | G11 | 110 |
| Gladys Lake, l., B.C., Can. | G28 | 100 |
| Glåma, stm., Nor. | K12 | 6 |
| Glarner Alpen, mts., Switz. | E10 | 13 |
| Glarus, Switz. | D11 | 13 |
| Glarus, state, Switz. | E11 | 13 |
| Glasco, Ks., U.S. | L10 | 118 |
| Glasgow, Ky., U.S. | F11 | 114 |
| Glasgow, Mo., U.S. | C4 | 114 |
| Glasgow, Mt., U.S. | B19 | 122 |
| Glasgow, Scot., U.K. | F9 | 8 |
| Glaslyn, Sk., Can. | B7 | 112 |
| Glassboro, N.J., U.S. | E6 | 104 |
| Glassboro, N.J., U.S. | H11 | 108 |
| Glattfelden, Switz. | C10 | 13 |
| Glauchau, Ger. | E12 | 10 |
| Glažević, Bos. | B15 | 22 |
| Glazov, Russia | F8 | 26 |
| Glazunovka, Russia | I19 | 22 |
| Gleason, Tn., U.S. | F8 | 114 |
| Gleichen, Ab., Can. | G21 | 102 |
| Gleisdorf, Aus. | H15 | 10 |
| Glen Alpine, N.C., U.S. | D5 | 112 |
| Glenavon, Sk., Can. | H11 | 104 |
| Glenboro, Mb., Can. | I15 | 104 |
| Glenburn, N.D., U.S. | C6 | 118 |
| Glen Burnie, Md., U.S. | H10 | 108 |
| Glen Canyon, val., U.S. | G5 | 120 |
| Glencoe, Al., U.S. | I11 | 114 |
| Glencoe, Austl. | K4 | 70 |
| Glencoe, Mn., U.S. | F1 | 110 |
| Glencoe, On., Can. | H14 | 110 |
| Glen Cove, N.Y., U.S. | G13 | 108 |
| Glendale, Az., U.S. | K4 | 120 |
| Glendale, Ca., U.S. | J7 | 124 |
| Glendale, Ms., U.S. | K7 | 114 |
| Glendale, Or., U.S. | H2 | 122 |
| Glendale, Ut., U.S. | G4 | 120 |
| Glendale, Wi., U.S. | G8 | 110 |
| Glendive, Mt., U.S. | D3 | 118 |
| Glendo, Wy., U.S. | B11 | 120 |
| Gleneden Beach, Or., U.S. | C23 | 102 |
| | F1 | 122 |
| Glen Elder, Ks., U.S. | L9 | 118 |
| Glen Flora, Tx., U.S. | J10 | 116 |
| Glen Innes, Austl. | G9 | 70 |
| Glen Lyon, Pa., U.S. | F10 | 108 |
| Glenmora, La., U.S. | L4 | 114 |
| Glenmorgan, Austl. | F8 | 70 |
| Glennallen, Ak., U.S. | E22 | 100 |
| Glenns Ferry, Id., U.S. | H10 | 122 |
| Glennville, Ga., U.S. | H5 | 112 |
| Glenoma, Wa., U.S. | D3 | 122 |
| Glenormiston, Austl. | D3 | 70 |
| Glenreagh, Austl. | H10 | 70 |
| Glen Robertson, On., Can. | B12 | 108 |
| Glen Rock, Pa., U.S. | H10 | 108 |
| Glen Rose, Tx., U.S. | G9 | 116 |
| Glens Falls, N.Y., U.S. | D13 | 108 |
| Glenties, Ire. | G5 | 8 |
| Glen Ullin, N.D., U.S. | E6 | 118 |
| Glenville, W.V., U.S. | I6 | 108 |
| Glen White, W.V., U.S. | B5 | 112 |

| Name | Map Ref. | Page |
|---|---|---|
| Glenwood, Ab., Can. | H21 | 102 |
| Glenwood, Al., U.S. | K10 | 114 |
| Glenwood, Ar., U.S. | H3 | 114 |
| Glenwood, Ga., U.S. | G4 | 112 |
| Glenwood, Ia., U.S. | J12 | 118 |
| Glenwood, Mn., U.S. | F12 | 118 |
| Glenwood, Nf., Can. | D19 | 106 |
| Glenwood, N.M., U.S. | K8 | 120 |
| Glenwood, Ut., U.S. | F5 | 120 |
| Glenwood, Va., U.S. | C7 | 112 |
| Glenwood City, Wi., U.S. | E3 | 110 |
| Glenwood Springs, Co., U.S. | E9 | 120 |
| Glidden, Ia., U.S. | I13 | 118 |
| Glidden, Wi., U.S. | D5 | 110 |
| Glide, Or., U.S. | G2 | 122 |
| Glinka, Russia | G15 | 22 |
| Gliwice (Gleiwitz), Pol. | E18 | 10 |
| Globe, Az., U.S. | K5 | 120 |
| Gloggnitz, Aus. | H15 | 10 |
| Gloria, Pol. | D16 | 10 |
| Glória de Dourados, Braz. | G1 | 79 |
| Glorieta, N.M., U.S. | I11 | 120 |
| Glorieuses, Îles, is., Afr. | D9 | 58 |
| Gloster, Ms., U.S. | K5 | 114 |
| Gloucester, Austl. | H9 | 70 |
| Gloucester, Eng., U.K. | J11 | 8 |
| Gloucester, Ma., U.S. | E16 | 108 |
| Gloucester, Va., U.S. | B10 | 112 |
| Gloucester Island, i., Austl. | C8 | 70 |
| Gloucestershire, co., Eng., U.K. | J11 | 8 |
| Glouster, Oh., U.S. | H4 | 108 |
| Glover, Ok., U.S. | E12 | 116 |
| Glover Island, i., Nf., Can. | D16 | 106 |
| Glovers Reef, rf., Belize | I16 | 90 |
| Gloversville, N.Y., U.S. | D12 | 108 |
| Glovertown, Nf., Can. | D19 | 106 |
| Głowno, Pol. | D19 | 10 |
| Głubczyce, Pol. | E17 | 10 |
| Głuchołazy, Pol. | E17 | 10 |
| Glückstadt, Ger. | B9 | 10 |
| Glyndon, Mn., U.S. | E11 | 118 |
| Gmünd, Aus. | G14 | 10 |
| Gmunden, Aus. | H13 | 10 |
| Gnalta, Austl. | H5 | 70 |
| Gnezdovo, Russia | G14 | 22 |
| Gniew, Pol. | B18 | 10 |
| Gniewkowo, Pol. | C18 | 10 |
| Gniezno, Pol. | C17 | 10 |
| Gnjilane, Yugo. | G5 | 20 |
| Gnowangerup, Austl. | F3 | 68 |
| Goa, state, India | E2 | 46 |
| Goalen Head, c., Austl. | K9 | 70 |
| Goālpāra, India | G14 | 44 |
| Goan, Mali | E7 | 64 |
| Goascorán, Hond. | D7 | 92 |
| Goascorán, stm., N.A. | D7 | 92 |
| Goat Mountain, mtn., Mt., U.S. | C12 | 122 |
| Goba, Eth. | G9 | 56 |
| Gobabis, Nmb. | D4 | 66 |
| Gobernador Gregores, Arg. | F2 | 78 |
| Gobernador Ingeniero Valentín Virasoro, Arg. | E10 | 80 |
| Gobernador Juan E. Martínez, Arg. | E9 | 80 |
| Gobernador Racedo, Arg. | F8 | 80 |
| Gobi, des., Asia | C7 | 30 |
| Gobles, In., U.S. | H10 | 110 |
| Gobō, Japan | N10 | 36 |
| Goce Delčev, Bul. | H7 | 20 |
| Gochas, Nmb. | E4 | 66 |
| Goch, Ger. | D6 | 10 |
| Godāvari, stm., India | D6 | 46 |
| Godbout, P.Q., Can. | C6 | 106 |
| Godbout, stm., P.Q., Can. | C6 | 106 |
| Goderich, On., Can. | G14 | 110 |
| Goderville, Fr. | C7 | 14 |
| Godfrey, Il., U.S. | D6 | 114 |
| Godhavn (Qeqertarsuaq), Grnld. | C22 | 96 |
| Godhra, India | I5 | 44 |
| Godiane, Bel. | H6 | 12 |
| Godoy Cruz, Arg. | G4 | 80 |
| Gods, stm., Mb., Can. | B22 | 104 |
| Gods Lake, Mb., Can. | D20 | 104 |
| Gods Lake, l., Mb., Can. | D20 | 104 |
| Gods Mercy, Bay of, b., N.T., Can. | D15 | 96 |
| Godthåb (Nuuk), Grnld. | D22 | 96 |
| Godwin Austen see K2, mtn., Asia | C7 | 44 |
| Goéland, Lac au, l., P.Q., Can. | G17 | 96 |
| Goélands, Lac aux, l., P.Q., Can. | E20 | 96 |
| Goes, Neth. | E4 | 12 |
| Goff, Ks., U.S. | L12 | 118 |
| Goffstown, N.H., U.S. | E4 | 46 |
| Gogebic, Lake, l., Mi., U.S. | D6 | 110 |
| Gogland, ostrov, i., Russia | A10 | 22 |
| Gogonou, Benin | F11 | 64 |
| Gohad, India | G8 | 44 |
| Gohtafla, C. Iv. | H7 | 64 |
| Goiana, Braz. | E12 | 76 |
| Goianápolis, Braz. | D4 | 79 |
| Goiandira, Braz. | E4 | 79 |
| Goianésia, Braz. | C4 | 79 |
| Goiânia, Braz. | D4 | 79 |
| Goiás, Braz. | C3 | 79 |
| Goiás, state, Braz. | B4 | 79 |
| Goiatuba, Braz. | E4 | 79 |
| Goio-Erê, Braz. | C12 | 80 |
| Gôio-Erê, stm., Braz. | B12 | 80 |
| Goito, Italy | D5 | 18 |
| Gojō, Japan | M10 | 36 |
| Gokāk, India | D3 | 46 |
| Gol, Nor. | K11 | 6 |
| Gol, Russia | A22 | 10 |
| Goläghāt, India | G15 | 44 |
| Golan Heights, clf, Golan | G5 | 50 |
| Golbāf, Iran | G14 | 48 |
| Golconda, Il., U.S. | E8 | 114 |
| Golconda, Nv., U.S. | D8 | 124 |
| Gölcük, Tur. | J11 | 20 |
| Gołdap, Pol. | A22 | 10 |
| Gold Beach, Or., U.S. | H1 | 122 |
| Goldboro, N.S., Can. | G12 | 106 |
| Gold Bridge, B.C., Can. | G12 | 102 |
| Gold Coast, Ghana | I9 | 64 |
| Gold Creek, stm., B.C., Can. | H19 | 102 |
| Golden, B.C., Can. | F18 | 102 |
| Golden, Co., U.S. | E11 | 120 |
| Golden, Il., U.S. | B5 | 114 |
| Golden City, Mo., U.S. | E2 | 114 |
| Goldendale, Wa., U.S. | E5 | 122 |
| Golden Ears Provincial Park, B.C., Can. | H12 | 102 |
| Golden Hinde, mtn., B.C., Can. | H9 | 102 |
| Goldfield, Ia., U.S. | H2 | 110 |
| Goldfield, Nv., U.S. | G8 | 124 |
| Goldonna, La., U.S. | J4 | 114 |
| Gold River, B.C., Can. | H8 | 102 |
| Gold Rock, On., Can. | I22 | 104 |
| Goldsand Lake, l., Mb., Can. | A13 | 104 |
| Goldsboro, N.C., U.S. | D9 | 112 |
| Goldsmith, Tx., U.S. | H4 | 116 |
| Goldston, N.C., U.S. | D7 | 112 |

| Name | Map Ref. | Page |
|---|---|---|
| Goldsworthy, Austl. | D3 | 68 |
| Goldthwaite, Tx., U.S. | H8 | 116 |
| Golela, S. Afr. | F10 | 66 |
| Goleniów, Pol. | B14 | 10 |
| Goleta, Ca., U.S. | J6 | 124 |
| Golfito, C.R. | I11 | 92 |
| Golfo de Santa Clara, Mex. | B2 | 90 |
| Goliad, Tx., U.S. | K9 | 116 |
| Golicyno, Russia | F19 | 22 |
| Golmud, China | D5 | 30 |
| Golo, stm., Fr. | J16 | 14 |
| Golovin, Ak., U.S. | D13 | 100 |
| Golpāyegān, Iran | E11 | 48 |
| Golva, N.D., U.S. | E4 | 118 |
| Golynki, Russia | G14 | 22 |
| Golyšmanovo, Russia | F11 | 26 |
| Goma, D.R.C. | B5 | 58 |
| Gómez Farías, Mex. | C6 | 90 |
| Gómez Palacio, Mex. | E8 | 90 |
| Gómez Plata, Col. | D5 | 84 |
| Gonābād, Iran | D15 | 48 |
| Gonaïves, Haiti | E8 | 94 |
| Gonâve, Golfe de la, b., Haiti | E8 | 94 |
| Gonâve, Île de la, i., Haiti | E8 | 94 |
| Gonbad-e Qābūs, Iran | C13 | 48 |
| Gonda, India | G9 | 44 |
| Gondal, India | J4 | 44 |
| Gondarbal, India | C6 | 44 |
| Gonder, Eth. | K9 | 60 |
| Gondia, India | J9 | 44 |
| Gondrecourt-le-Château, Fr. | D12 | 14 |
| Gönen, Tur. | I11 | 20 |
| Gongbo'gyamda, China | F5 | 30 |
| Gongchenqiao, China | E9 | 34 |
| Gongchuan, China | I6 | 34 |
| Gongdian, China | G5 | 34 |
| Gongga Shan, mtn., China | F7 | 30 |
| Gongko, China | H7 | 32 |
| Gongola, stm., Nig. | F9 | 54 |
| Gongpingxu, China | I1 | 34 |
| Gongxian, China | E9 | 30 |
| Gongyingzi, China | C7 | 32 |
| Goñi, Ur. | G10 | 80 |
| Goniądz, Pol. | B22 | 10 |
| Gonzales, Ca., U.S. | H4 | 124 |
| Gonzales, La., U.S. | L6 | 114 |
| Gonzales, Tx., U.S. | J9 | 116 |
| González, Mex. | F10 | 90 |
| González, Riacho, stm., Para. | B9 | 80 |
| González Chaves, Arg. | J8 | 80 |
| González Moreno, Arg. | H7 | 80 |
| Gonzanamá, Ec. | J3 | 84 |
| Goochland, Va., U.S. | B9 | 112 |
| Goodenough, Mount, mtn., N.T., Can. | C27 | 100 |
| Gooderham, On., Can. | F17 | 110 |
| Goodeve, Sk., Can. | G11 | 104 |
| Good Hope, S. Afr. | H5 | 66 |
| Good Hope, Cape of, c., S. Afr. | J4 | 66 |
| Good Hope Mountain, mtn., B.C., Can. | F10 | 102 |
| Goodhue, Mn., U.S. | F3 | 110 |
| Gooding, Id., U.S. | H11 | 122 |
| Goodland, In., U.S. | N5 | 112 |
| Goodland, Ks., U.S. | B9 | 114 |
| Goodlands, Mb., Can. | I14 | 104 |
| Goodman, Ms., U.S. | J7 | 114 |
| Goodman, Wi., U.S. | E7 | 110 |
| Goodnews Bay, Ak., U.S. | G14 | 100 |
| Goodnight, Co., U.S. | F12 | 120 |
| Goodrich, N.D., U.S. | D7 | 118 |
| Goodrich, Tx., U.S. | I12 | 116 |
| Good Spirit Lake, l., Sk., Can. | G12 | 104 |
| Good Spirit Lake Provincial Park, Sk., Can. | G12 | 104 |
| Good Thunder, Mn., U.S. | F1 | 110 |
| Goodview, Mn., U.S. | F4 | 110 |
| Goodwell, Ok., U.S. | C10 | 116 |
| Goodyear, Az., U.S. | K4 | 120 |
| Googong, Austl. | I6 | 70 |
| Googowi, Austl. | I6 | 70 |
| Goombalie, Austl. | G6 | 70 |
| Goomeri, Austl. | C2 | 114 |
| Goondiwindi, Austl. | G9 | 70 |
| Goose, stm., Ab., Can. | C18 | 102 |
| Goose, stm., N.D., U.S. | D10 | 118 |
| Goose Bay see Happy Valley-Goose Bay, Nf., Can. | F20 | 96 |
| Goose Creek, S.C., U.S. | G6 | 112 |
| Goose Island, i., B.C., Can. | F6 | 102 |
| Goose Lake, l., Mb., Can. | D13 | 104 |
| Goose Lake, l., On., Can. | G21 | 104 |
| Goose Lake, l., Sk., Can. | G7 | 104 |
| Goose Lake, l., U.S. | B8 | 124 |
| Gooty, India | E4 | 46 |
| Gopālpur, India | C20 | 104 |
| Gopālpur, India | E4 | 46 |
| Gopālpur, India | E4 | 46 |
| Gopālpettipālayam, India | G4 | 46 |
| Goppenstein, Switz. | F8 | 13 |
| Göppingen, Ger. | G9 | 10 |
| Goqên, China | F6 | 30 |
| Góra, Pol. | D16 | 10 |
| Goradit, Eth. | L10 | 60 |
| Gorakhpur, India | G10 | 44 |
| Goražde, Bos. | F2 | 20 |
| Gorbatov, Russia | E26 | 22 |
| Gorbatovka, Russia | E26 | 22 |
| Gorčucha, Russia | D26 | 22 |
| Gorda, Punta, c., Chile | H6 | 82 |
| Gorda, Punta, c., Cuba | C3 | 94 |
| Gorda, Punta, c., Nic. | F11 | 92 |
| Gorda, Punta, c., Nic. | C11 | 92 |
| Gordo, Al., U.S. | I9 | 114 |
| Gordon, Ga., U.S. | G3 | 112 |
| Gordon, Ne., U.S. | I5 | 118 |
| Gordon, Wi., U.S. | D4 | 110 |
| Gordon, Lake, res., Austl. | N7 | 70 |
| Gordon Horne Peak, mtn., B.C., Can. | F16 | 102 |
| Gordon Indian Reserve, Sk., Can. | G10 | 104 |
| Gordonvale, Austl. | A6 | 70 |
| Gore, Eth. | M8 | 60 |
| Gore, N.S., Can. | G10 | 106 |
| Gore, N.Z. | G2 | 72 |
| Gore Bay, On., Can. | E13 | 110 |
| Goree, Tx., U.S. | F7 | 116 |
| Gore Point, c., Austl. | A3 | 70 |
| Goreville, Il., U.S. | E8 | 114 |
| Gorgān, Iran | C13 | 48 |
| Gorgona, Isla i., Col. | F3 | 84 |
| Gorgor, Peru | D3 | 82 |
| Gorham, Ks., U.S. | K9 | 60 |
| Gorham, Me., U.S. | D16 | 108 |
| Gorham, N.H., U.S. | C15 | 108 |
| Gori, Geor. | I6 | 26 |
| Goricy, Russia | D19 | 22 |
| Gorinchem, Neth. | E7 | 12 |
| Goris, Arm. | B9 | 48 |
| Gorizia, Italy | D8 | 18 |
| Gorj, co., Rom. | E7 | 20 |
| Gor'kovskoje vodochranilišče, res., Russia | D26 | 22 |
| Gorky see Nižnij Novgorod, Russia | E27 | 22 |
| Gorlice, Pol. | F21 | 10 |

| Name | Map Ref. | Page |
|---|---|---|
| Görlitz, Ger. | D14 | 10 |
| Gorlovka see Horlivka, Ukr. | H5 | 26 |
| Gorlovo, Russia | H22 | 22 |
| Gorman, Tx., U.S. | G8 | 116 |
| Gorn'ackij, Russia | D10 | 26 |
| Gorn'ak, Russia | H22 | 22 |
| Gornji Milanovac, Yugo. | E4 | 20 |
| Gorno-Altajsk, Russia | G9 | 28 |
| Gornozavodsk, Russia | H20 | 28 |
| Gorochovec, Russia | E25 | 22 |
| Gorodec, Russia | E26 | 22 |
| Gorodec, Russia | C12 | 22 |
| Goroka, Pap. N. Gui. | G12 | 38 |
| Gorontalo, Indon. | E7 | 38 |
| Gorouol, stm., Afr. | D10 | 64 |
| Gorutuba, stm., Braz. | C7 | 79 |
| Górzow Wielkopolski (Landsberg an der Warthe), Pol. | C15 | 10 |
| Gosford, Austl. | I9 | 70 |
| Goshabi, Sudan | I6 | 60 |
| Goshen, Ca., U.S. | H6 | 124 |
| Goshen, In., U.S. | A11 | 114 |
| Goshen, N.S., Can. | G12 | 106 |
| Goshen, N.Y., U.S. | F12 | 108 |
| Goslar, Ger. | D10 | 10 |
| Gosport, In., U.S. | C10 | 114 |
| Gossas, Sen. | D1 | 64 |
| Gossi, Mali | D9 | 64 |
| Gostivar, Mac. | H4 | 20 |
| Gostyń, Pol. | D17 | 10 |
| Gostynin, Pol. | C19 | 10 |
| Göta älv, stm., Swe. | M13 | 6 |
| Gotebo, Ok., U.S. | D8 | 116 |
| Göteborg (Gothenburg), Swe. | M12 | 6 |
| Göteborgs och Bohus län, co., Swe. | L12 | 6 |
| Gotemba, Japan | L13 | 36 |
| Goteshti, Mol. | C12 | 20 |
| Gotha, Ger. | E10 | 10 |
| Gothenburg, Ne., U.S. | K7 | 118 |
| Gothenburg see Göteborg, Swe. | M12 | 6 |
| Gotland, i., Swe. | M16 | 6 |
| Gotlands Län, co., Swe. | M16 | 6 |
| Gotō-rettō, is., Japan | O3 | 36 |
| Gotō-rettō, i., Japan | O3 | 36 |
| Göttingen, Ger. | D9 | 10 |
| Gouarec, Fr. | D3 | 14 |
| Gouda, Neth. | D6 | 12 |
| Goudge, Arg. | H4 | 80 |
| Goudiry, Arg. | D3 | 64 |
| Gough Island, i., St. Hel. | M6 | 52 |
| Gough Lake, l., Ab., Can. | E22 | 102 |
| Goulburn, Austl. | J8 | 70 |
| Goulburn Islands, is., Austl. | B6 | 68 |
| Gould, Ar., U.S. | I5 | 114 |
| Gould City, Mi., U.S. | D10 | 110 |
| Goulds, Fl., U.S. | N6 | 112 |
| Goulet Lake, l., Mb., Can. | C18 | 104 |
| Goulimime, Mor. | F5 | 62 |
| Goundam, Mali | D8 | 64 |
| Gourdon, Fr. | H8 | 14 |
| Gouré, Niger | E15 | 64 |
| Gourma Rharous, Mali | C9 | 64 |
| Gournay-en-Bray, Fr. | C8 | 14 |
| Gouveia, Braz. | E7 | 79 |
| Gouverneur, N.Y., U.S. | C11 | 108 |
| Govan, Sk., Can. | G9 | 104 |
| Govena, mys, c., Russia | F25 | 28 |
| Govenlock, Sk., Can. | I5 | 104 |
| Governador Valadares, Braz. | E8 | 79 |
| Governor's Harbour, Bah. | B6 | 94 |
| Govind Ballabh Pant Sāgar, res., India | H10 | 44 |
| Govind Sāgar, res., India | C20 | 104 |
| Gowanda, N.Y., U.S. | E8 | 108 |
| Gowan Range, mts., Austl. | E6 | 70 |
| Gower, Mo., U.S. | C2 | 114 |
| Gowmal (Gumal), stm., Asia | D3 | 44 |
| Gowrie, Ia., U.S. | I13 | 118 |
| Goya, Arg. | E9 | 80 |
| Göyçay, Azer. | I7 | 26 |
| Goyelle, Lac, l., P.Q., Can. | B13 | 106 |
| Göytäpä, Azer. | B10 | 48 |
| Gozo see Għawdex, i., Malta | M9 | 19 |
| Graaff-Reinet, S. Afr. | I7 | 66 |
| Grabo, C. Iv. | I6 | 64 |
| Grabowiec, Pol. | E23 | 10 |
| Grace, Id., U.S. | H14 | 122 |
| Gračanica, Bos. | E2 | 20 |
| Gracefield, P.Q., Can. | A10 | 108 |
| Graceville, Fl., U.S. | I11 | 114 |
| Graceville, Mn., U.S. | F11 | 118 |
| Gracias, Hond. | D6 | 92 |
| Gracias a Dios, dept., Hond. | B10 | 92 |
| Gracias a Dios, Cabo, c., N.A. | B11 | 92 |
| Gradačac, Bos. | E2 | 20 |
| Gradaús, Braz. | E6 | 76 |
| Grado, Italy | D8 | 18 |
| Grady, Ar., U.S. | H5 | 114 |
| Grady, N.M., U.S. | I9 | 114 |
| Graettinger, Ia., U.S. | H13 | 118 |
| Grafenau, Ger. | G13 | 10 |
| Gräfenhainichen, Ger. | C11 | 10 |
| Grafing bei München, Ger. | G11 | 10 |
| Graford, Tx., U.S. | G8 | 116 |
| Grafton, Austl. | G10 | 70 |
| Grafton, N.D., U.S. | C10 | 118 |
| Grafton, Wi., U.S. | H6 | 108 |
| Grafton, W.V., U.S. | H6 | 108 |
| Grafton, Cape, c., Austl. | A6 | 70 |
| Graham, N.C., U.S. | C7 | 112 |
| Graham, Tx., U.S. | F8 | 116 |
| Graham, Mount, mtn., Az., U.S. | L7 | 120 |
| Graham Island, i., B.C., Can. | D2 | 102 |
| Graham Land, reg., Ant. | B12 | 73 |
| Graham Moore, Cape, c., N.T., Can. | B17 | 96 |
| Graham Moore Bay, b., N.T., Can. | A12 | 96 |
| Grahamstown, S. Afr. | I8 | 66 |
| Grain Coast, hist. reg., Afr. | I5 | 64 |
| Grainfield, Ks., U.S. | L7 | 118 |
| Grajagan, stm., Braz. | D9 | 76 |
| Grajaú, stm., Braz. | D9 | 76 |
| Grajewo, Pol. | B22 | 10 |
| Gramada, Bul. | F6 | 20 |
| Gramado, Braz. | E13 | 80 |
| Gramalote, Col. | D6 | 84 |
| Grambling, La., U.S. | J4 | 114 |
| Gramilla, Arg. | D6 | 80 |
| Grammichele, Italy | L9 | 18 |
| Grampian, prov., Scot., U.K. | D11 | 8 |
| Grampian Mountains, mts., Scot., U.K. | E9 | 8 |
| Grampians National Park, Austl. | K5 | 70 |
| Granada, Co., U.S. | M5 | 118 |
| Granada, Col. | F6 | 84 |

| Name | Map Ref. | Page |
|---|---|---|
| Granada, Nic. | F9 | 92 |
| Granada, Spain | H8 | 16 |
| Granada, dept., Nic. | F8 | 92 |
| Granadilla de Abona, Spain | o24 | 17b |
| Granby, Co., U.S. | D11 | 120 |
| Granby, Mo., U.S. | F2 | 114 |
| Granby, P.Q., Can. | B14 | 108 |
| Granby, stm., B.C., Can. | H16 | 102 |
| Granby, Lake, res., Co., U.S. | D11 | 120 |
| Gran Canaria, i., Spain | o25 | 17b |
| Gran Chaco, reg., S.A. | C8 | 80 |
| Grand, stm., Oh., U.S. | F5 | 108 |
| Grand, stm., S.D., U.S. | C3 | 114 |
| Grand, stm., Wi., U.S. | G7 | 110 |
| Grand Bahama, i., Bah. | A5 | 94 |
| Grand Bank, Nf., Can. | E18 | 106 |
| Grand Banks of Newfoundland | E14 | 86 |
| Grand-Bassam, C. Iv. | I8 | 64 |
| Grand Bay, Al., U.S. | L8 | 114 |
| Grand Bay, N.B., Can. | G7 | 106 |
| Grand Beach, Mb., Can. | H18 | 104 |
| Grand Bend, On., Can. | G14 | 110 |
| Grand Blanc, Mi., U.S. | H12 | 110 |
| Grand Bruit, Nf., Can. | E15 | 106 |
| Grand Canal see Da Yunhe, China | E10 | 30 |
| Grand Canal, Ire. | H6 | 8 |
| Grand Cane, La., U.S. | J3 | 114 |
| Grand Canyon, Az., U.S. | H4 | 120 |
| Grand Canyon, val., Az., U.S. | H4 | 120 |
| Grand Canyon National Park, Az., U.S. | H4 | 120 |
| Grand Cayman, i., Cay. Is. | E4 | 94 |
| Grand Cess, Lib. | I5 | 64 |
| Grand Chenier, La., U.S. | M4 | 114 |
| Grand Combin, mtn., Switz. | G7 | 13 |
| Grand Coulee, Wa., U.S. | C6 | 122 |
| Grand Coulee, val., Wa., U.S. | | |
| Grand Coulee Dam, Wa., U.S. | C6 | 122 |
| Grand-Couronne, Fr. | C8 | 14 |
| Grande, stm., Arg. | I4 | 80 |
| Grande, stm., Arg. | C6 | 80 |
| Grande, stm., Bol. | G9 | 82 |
| Grande, stm., Braz. | F10 | 76 |
| Grande, stm., Braz. | E8 | 79 |
| Grande, stm., Chile | F3 | 80 |
| Grande, stm., Nic. | E8 | 92 |
| Grande, stm., Pan. | I14 | 92 |
| Grande, stm., Peru | F4 | 82 |
| Grande, Arroyo, stm., Ur. | G10 | 80 |
| Grande, Bahía, b., Arg. | G3 | 78 |
| Grande, Boca, mth., Ven. | C12 | 84 |
| Grande, Cerro, mtn., Mex. | E8 | 90 |
| Grande, Cerro, mtn., Mex. | G8 | 90 |
| Grande, Corixa, stm., S.A. | G8 | 82 |
| Grande, Corixa (Curiche Grande), stm., S.A. | G12 | 82 |
| Grande, Cuchilla, mts., Ur. | G11 | 80 |
| Grande, Ilha, i., Braz. | G6 | 79 |
| Grande, Ponta, c., Braz. | D9 | 79 |
| Grande, Punta, c., Chile | A3 | 80 |
| Grande, Rio (Bravo del Norte), stm., N.A. | F7 | 98 |
| Grande-Anse, N.B., Can. | E8 | 106 |
| Grande Cache, Ab., Can. | D15 | 102 |
| Grande Cayemite, i., Haiti | E8 | 94 |
| Grande de Lipez, stm., Bol. | G8 | 82 |
| Grande de Manacapuru, Lago, l., Braz. | I12 | 84 |
| Grande de Matagalpa, stm., Nic. | D11 | 92 |
| Grande de Santiago, stm., Mex. | G7 | 90 |
| Grande de Tarija, stm., S.A. | J9 | 82 |
| Grande de Térraba, stm., C.R. | I11 | 92 |
| Grande do Gurupá, Ilha, i., Braz. | D8 | 76 |
| Grand-Entrée, P.Q., Can. | E12 | 106 |
| Grand-Prairie, Ab., Can. | B16 | 102 |
| Grand Erg de Bilma, des., Niger | E9 | 54 |
| Grand Erg Occidental, des., Alg. | E11 | 62 |
| Grand Erg Oriental, des., Alg. | E14 | 62 |
| Grande-Rivière, P.Q., Can. | D9 | 106 |
| Grande-Rivière, La, stm., P.Q., Can. | F17 | 96 |
| Grande Ronde, stm., U.S. | F8 | 122 |
| Grandes, Salinas, pl., Arg. | F6 | 80 |
| Grandes, Salinas, pl., Arg. | B6 | 80 |
| Grand-Étang, N.S., Can. | F12 | 106 |
| Grande-Terre, i., Guad. | F14 | 94 |
| Grand Falls, N.B., Can. | E6 | 106 |
| Grand Falls, Nf., Can. | D18 | 106 |
| Grandfalls, Tx., U.S. | H4 | 116 |
| Grandfield, Ok., U.S. | C19 | 116 |
| Grand Forks, B.C., Can. | H16 | 102 |
| Grand Forks, N.D., U.S. | D10 | 118 |
| Grand Haven, Mi., U.S. | H9 | 110 |
| Grand Hers, stm., Fr. | I7 | 14 |
| Grandin, Lac, l., N.T., Can. | D9 | 96 |
| Grand Island, Ne., U.S. | K9 | 118 |
| Grand Island, i., Mi., U.S. | D9 | 110 |
| Grand Isle, La., U.S. | M7 | 114 |
| Grand Junction, Co., U.S. | E8 | 120 |
| Grand Junction, Ia., U.S. | I13 | 118 |
| Grand Junction, Tn., U.S. | G7 | 114 |
| Grand-Lahou, C. Iv. | I7 | 64 |
| Grand Lake, Co., U.S. | D11 | 120 |
| Grand Lake, l., La., U.S. | M5 | 114 |
| Grand Lake, l., La., U.S. | L4 | 114 |
| Grand Lake, l., N.B., Can. | G6 | 106 |
| Grand Lake, l., Nf., Can. | D16 | 106 |
| Grand Lake, l., Oh., U.S. | G2 | 108 |
| Grand Lake, l., U.S. | H11 | 110 |
| Grand Manan Channel, strt., N.A. | H7 | 106 |
| Grand Manan Island, i., N.B., Can. | H7 | 106 |
| Grand Marais, Mi., U.S. | D10 | 110 |
| Grand Marais, Mn., U.S. | C5 | 110 |
| Grand Meadow, Mn., U.S. | G3 | 110 |
| Grand-Mère, P.Q., Can. | G18 | 96 |
| Grand Mesa, mtn., Co., U.S. | E9 | 120 |
| Grandmesnil, Lac, l., P.Q., Can. | A6 | 106 |
| Grand Pabos, Rivière de, stm., P.Q., Can. | D9 | 106 |
| Grand Portage, Mn., U.S. | C6 | 110 |
| Grand Pré National Historic Park, N.S., Can. | G9 | 106 |
| Grand Rapids, Mb., Can. | E15 | 104 |
| Grand Rapids, Mi., U.S. | H10 | 110 |
| Grand Rapids, Mn., U.S. | C2 | 110 |
| Grandrieu, Bel. | H5 | 12 |
| Grand-Saint-Bernard, Col du, Eur. | G7 | 13 |

| Name | Map Ref. | Page |
|---|---|---|
| Grand-Saint-Bernard, Tunnel du, Eur. | G14 | 14 |
| Grand Strand, Tx., U.S. | G11 | 116 |
| Grand Teton, mtn., Wy., U.S. | A6 | 120 |
| Grand Teton National Park, Wy., U.S. | G15 | 122 |
| Grand Tower, Il., U.S. | E7 | 114 |
| Grand Traverse Bay, b., Mi., U.S. | E10 | 110 |
| Grand Turk, T./C. Is. | D9 | 94 |
| Grandview, Mb., Can. | G4 | 104 |
| Grandview, Mo., U.S. | D2 | 114 |
| Grandview, Wa., U.S. | D6 | 122 |
| Grand View, Wi., U.S. | D4 | 110 |
| Graneros, Chile | H3 | 80 |
| Granger, Tx., U.S. | I9 | 116 |
| Granger, Wa., U.S. | D5 | 122 |
| Grangeville, Id., U.S. | E9 | 122 |
| Gran Guardia, Arg. | C9 | 80 |
| Granite, Ok., U.S. | E7 | 116 |
| Granite City, Il., U.S. | D6 | 114 |
| Granite Falls, Mn., U.S. | G12 | 118 |
| Granite Falls, N.C., U.S. | D5 | 112 |
| Granite Falls, Wa., U.S. | B4 | 122 |
| Granite Lake, res., Nf., Can. | D16 | 106 |
| Granite Peak, mtn., Mt., U.S. | E16 | 122 |
| Graniteville, S.C., U.S. | F5 | 112 |
| Graniteville, Vt., U.S. | C14 | 108 |
| Granollers, Spain | D14 | 16 |
| Gran Pajonal, reg., Peru | D4 | 82 |
| Gran Paradiso, mtn., Italy | D2 | 18 |
| Gran Sasso d'Italia, mts., Italy | G8 | 18 |
| Grant, Fl., U.S. | L6 | 112 |
| Grant, Mi., U.S. | G10 | 110 |
| Grant, Ne., U.S. | K6 | 118 |
| Grant, stm., Wi., U.S. | H5 | 110 |
| Grant, Mount, mtn., Nv., U.S. | F7 | 124 |
| Gran Tarajal, Spain | o26 | 17b |
| Grant City, Mo., U.S. | B2 | 114 |
| Grant Park, Il., U.S. | I8 | 110 |
| Grant, point, c., N.T., Can. | C13 | 96 |
| Grants, N.M., U.S. | I9 | 120 |
| Grantsburg, Wi., U.S. | E3 | 110 |
| Grants Pass, Or., U.S. | H2 | 122 |
| Grant-Suttie Bay, b., N.T., Can. | C17 | 96 |
| Grantsville, W.V., U.S. | I5 | 108 |
| Grantville, Ga., U.S. | F2 | 112 |
| Granum, Ab., Can. | H21 | 102 |
| Granville, Fr. | D5 | 14 |
| Granville, Il., U.S. | I6 | 110 |
| Granville, N.D., U.S. | C7 | 118 |
| Granville, N.Y., U.S. | D13 | 108 |
| Granville, Oh., U.S. | G4 | 108 |
| Granville, W.V., U.S. | H7 | 108 |
| Granville Lake, l., Mb., Can. | A13 | 104 |
| Granvin, Nor. | K10 | 6 |
| Grão Mogol, Braz. | D7 | 79 |
| Grapeland, Tx., U.S. | H11 | 116 |
| Grapevine Lake, res., Tx., U.S. | | |
| Gras, Lac de l., N.T., Can. | D10 | 96 |
| Grasmere, B.C., Can. | F8 | 66 |
| Grasonville, Md., U.S. | I10 | 108 |
| Grass, stm., Mb., Can. | B18 | 104 |
| Grass, stm., N.Y., U.S. | C11 | 108 |
| Grass Creek, Wy., U.S. | G17 | 122 |
| Grasse, Fr. | I13 | 14 |
| Grassflat, Pa., U.S. | F8 | 108 |
| Grass Lake, Mi., U.S. | H11 | 110 |
| Grass Range, Mt., U.S. | C17 | 122 |
| Grass River Provincial Park, Mb., Can. | D14 | 104 |
| Grass Valley, Ca., U.S. | E4 | 124 |
| Grassy, Austl. | M6 | 70 |
| Grassy Island Lake, l., Ab., Can. | G4 | 104 |
| Grassy Lake, Ab., Can. | H23 | 102 |
| Grassy Plains, B.C., Can. | D9 | 102 |
| Grates Point, c., Nf., Can. | D21 | 106 |
| Graubünden (Grischun), state, Switz. | E11 | 13 |
| Gravatá, Braz. | E11 | 76 |
| Gravatá, stm., Braz. | D7 | 79 |
| Gravatal, Braz. | D9 | 79 |
| Gravelbourg, Sk., Can. | I8 | 104 |
| Gravelines, Fr. | B9 | 14 |
| Gravel Point, l., N.T., Can. | C17 | 96 |
| Gravenhurst, On., Can. | F16 | 110 |
| Grave Peak, mtn., Id., U.S. | D11 | 122 |
| Gravette, Ar., U.S. | F2 | 114 |
| Gravina in Puglia, Italy | I11 | 18 |
| Gray, Fr. | E12 | 14 |
| Gray, Ga., U.S. | F3 | 112 |
| Gray, Ky., U.S. | C2 | 112 |
| Grayback Mountain, mtn., Or., U.S. | H2 | 122 |
| Grayling, Ak., U.S. | E14 | 100 |
| Grayling, Mi., U.S. | F11 | 110 |
| Grays Harbor, b., Wa., U.S. | D1 | 122 |
| Grayson, Ky., U.S. | I4 | 108 |
| Grayson, La., U.S. | J4 | 114 |
| Grayson, Sk., Can. | H12 | 104 |
| Grays Peak, mtn., Co., U.S. | E11 | 120 |
| Graysville, Tn., U.S. | G11 | 114 |
| Grayville, Il., U.S. | E8 | 114 |
| Graz, Aus. | H15 | 10 |
| Grazalema, Spain | I6 | 16 |
| Gr'aznoje, Russia | I22 | 22 |
| Gr'azovec, Russia | C23 | 22 |
| Great Artesian Basin, Austl. | E5 | 70 |
| Great Australian Bight, Austl. | F5 | 68 |
| Great Barrier Island, i., N.Z. | B5 | 72 |
| Great Barrier Reef, rf., Austl. | C9 | 68 |
| Great Barrier Reef Marine Park, Austl. | C9 | 68 |
| Great Barrington, Ma., U.S. | E13 | 108 |
| Great Basin, reg., U.S. | C3 | 98 |
| Great Bear, stm., N.T., Can. | D32 | 100 |
| Great Bear Lake, l., N.T., Can. | | |
| Great Beaver Lake, l., B.C., Can. | C11 | 102 |
| Great Bend, Ks., U.S. | M9 | 118 |
| Great Britain, i., U.K. | E7 | 4 |
| Great Burnt Lake, l., Nf., Can. | D17 | 106 |
| Great Central, B.C., Can. | H10 | 102 |
| Great Central Lake, l., B.C., Can. | H9 | 102 |
| Great Channel, strt., Asia | K3 | 40 |
| Great Dismal Swamp, sw., U.S. | C10 | 112 |
| Great Divide Basin, Wy., U.S. | H17 | 122 |
| Great Dividing Range, mts., Austl. | E9 | 68 |
| Greater Antilles, is., N.A. | D7 | 94 |
| Greater Khingan Range see Da Hinggan Ling, mts., China | B11 | 30 |
| Greater Sunda Islands, is., Asia | F5 | 38 |
| Great Exuma, i., Bah. | C7 | 94 |

| Name | Map Ref. | Page |
|---|---|---|

Great Falls, Mb., Can. . . . . H18 104
Great Falls, Mt., U.S. . . . . C14 122
Great Falls, S.C., U.S. . . . E6 112
Great Guana Cay, i., Bah. . B6 94
Great Inagua, i., Bah. . . . . D8 94
Great Indian Desert (Thar Desert), des., Asia . . . . G4 44
Great Karroo, plat., S. Afr. . I6 66
Great Lake, l., Austl. . . . . M7 70
Great Miami, stm., U.S. . . . H2 108
Great Namaqualand, hist. reg., Nmb. . . . . . . . . E3 66
Great Nicobar, i., India . . . K2 40
Great Palm Island, i., Austl. B7 70
Great Pee Dee, stm., S.C., U.S. . . . . . . . . . . . F7 112
Great Plain of the Koukdjuak, pl., N.T., Can. C18 96
Great Plains, l., N.A. . . . . E9 86
Great Pubnico Lake, l., N.S., Can. . . . . . . . . . I8 106
Great Ruaha, stm., Tan. . . C7 58
Great Sacandaga Lake, l., N.Y., U.S. . . . . . . . . D12 108
Great Saint Bernard Pass see Grand-Saint-Bernard, Col du, Eur. . . . . . . . . G7 13
Great Salt Lake, l., Ut., U.S. C4 120
Great Salt Lake Desert, des., U.S. . . . . . . . . D3 120
Great Sand Hills, hills, Sk., Can. . . . . . . . . . . . H5 104
Great Sandy Desert, des., Austl. . . . . . . . . . . D4 68
Great Scarcies (Kolenté), stm., Afr. . . . . . . . . G3 64
Great Slave Lake, l., N.T., Can. . . . . . . . . . . . D10 96
Great Smoky Mountains, mts., U.S. . . . . . . . . D3 112
Great Smoky Mountains National Park, U.S. . . . D3 112
Great Victoria Desert, des., Austl. . . . . . . . . . . E5 68
Great Wall, sci., Ant. . . . . B1 73
Great Wall see Chang Cheng, hist., China . . . . C4 32
Great Yarmouth, Eng., U.K. I15 8
Great Zab (Büyükzap) (Az-Zāb al-Kabīr), stm., Asia C7 48
Gréboun, mtn., Niger . . . . A14 64
Grecia, C.R. . . . . . . . . . G10 92
Greco, It. . . . . . . . . . . . I9 18
Greece, N.Y., U.S. . . . . . D9 108
Greece (Ellás), ctry., Eur. . H12 4
Greeley, Co., U.S. . . . . . D12 120
Greeley, Ne., U.S. . . . . . J9 118
Greeleyville, S.C., U.S. . . . E7 112
Green, stm., Il., U.S. . . . . I6 110
Green, stm., Ky., U.S. . . . E10 114
Green, stm., N.B., Can. . . . E5 106
Green, stm., N.D., U.S. . . . E5 118
Green, stm., Ut., U.S. . . . . F7 120
Green, stm., Wa., U.S. . . . C3 122
Greenacres, Wa., U.S. . . . C8 122
Green Bay, b., Nf., Can. . . F7 110
Green Bay, b., U.S. . . . . . C18 106
Greenbrier, Ar., U.S. . . . . G4 114
Green Brier, Tn., U.S. . . . . F10 114
Greenbrier, stm., W.V., U.S. J6 108
Greenburg, La., U.S. . . . . L6 114
Greenbush, Mn., U.S. . . . . C11 118
Greencastle, In., U.S. . . . . C10 114
Greencastle, Pa., U.S. . . . H9 108
Green City, Mo., U.S. . . . . B4 114
Green Cove Springs, Fl., U.S. . . . . . . . . . . . J5 112
Greendale, In., U.S. . . . . C12 114
Greene, Ia., U.S. . . . . . . H3 110
Greene, N.Y., U.S. . . . . . E11 108
Greeneville, Tn., U.S. . . . . C4 112
Greenfield, Ca., U.S. . . . . H4 124
Greenfield, Ia., U.S. . . . . J13 118
Greenfield, Il., U.S. . . . . . C6 114
Greenfield, Ma., U.S. . . . . E14 108
Greenfield, Mo., U.S. . . . . E3 114
Greenfield, Oh., U.S. . . . . H3 108
Greenfield, Tn., U.S. . . . . F8 114
Green Forest, Ar., U.S. . . . F3 114
Green Head, c., Austl. . . . F2 68
Green Lake, Sk., Can. . . . D7 104
Green Lake, Wi., U.S. . . . . G7 110
Green Lake, l., B.C., Can. . F13 102
Green Lake, l., Sk., Can. . . D7 104
Greenland, Ar., U.S. . . . . G2 114
Greenland, Mi., U.S. . . . . D6 110
Greenland (Kalaallit Nunaat), dep., N.A. . . . . . . . B15 86
Greenland Sea . . . . . . . B20 86
Greenleaf, Ks., U.S. . . . . L11 118
Green Mountains, mts., N.A. . . . . . . . . . . . D14 108
Green Peter Lake, res., Or., U.S. . . . . . . . . . . . F3 122
Green Pond, Al., U.S. . . . . I9 114
Greenport, N.Y., U.S. . . . F14 108
Green River, Ut., U.S. . . . F6 120
Green River, Wy., U.S. . . . C7 120
Green River Lake, res., Ky., U.S. . . . . . . . . . . . E11 114
Greensboro, Al., U.S. . . . . J9 114
Greensboro, Ga., U.S. . . . I2 112
Greensboro, Ga., U.S. . . . F3 112
Greensboro, Md., U.S. . . . I11 108
Greensboro, N.C., U.S. . . . C11 114
Greensburg, In., U.S. . . . . C12 114
Greensburg, Ks., U.S. . . . N8 118
Greensburg, Ky., U.S. . . . E11 114
Greensburg, Pa., U.S. . . . G7 108
Greens Peak, mtn., Az., U.S. . . . . . . . . . . . J7 120
Greenspond, Nf., Can. . . . C20 106
Green Springs, Fl., U.S. . . F3 108
Green Swamp, sw., N.C., U.S. . . . . . . . . . . . E8 112
Greentown, In., U.S. . . . . B11 114
Greenup, Il., U.S. . . . . . . D9 114
Greenup, Ky., U.S. . . . . . I4 108
Greenvale, Austl. . . . . . . B5 70
Green Valley, Az., U.S. . . . M6 120
Green Valley, Il., U.S. . . . . J6 110
Greenview, Il., U.S. . . . . . B7 114
Greenville, Al., U.S. . . . . . K10 114
Greenville, Ca., U.S. . . . . D5 124
Greenville, Fl., U.S. . . . . . I3 112
Greenville, Ga., U.S. . . . . F2 112
Greenville, Il., U.S. . . . . . E9 114
Greenville, Lib., U.S. . . . . I5 64
Greenville, Me., U.S. . . . . B17 108
Greenville, Mi., U.S. . . . . G10 110
Greenville, Mo., U.S. . . . . E7 114
Greenville, Ms., U.S. . . . . I5 114
Greenville, N.C., U.S. . . . . D9 112
Greenville, N.H., U.S. . . . . E15 108
Greenville, Oh., U.S. . . . . G2 108
Greenville, Pa., U.S. . . . . F6 108
Greenville, S.C., U.S. . . . . E4 112
Greenville, Tx., U.S. . . . . . F10 116
Greenwater Lake Provincial Park, Sk., Can. . . . . F11 104
Greenwich, Ct., U.S. . . . . F13 108

Greenwich, N.Y., U.S. . . . . D13 108
Greenwich, Oh., U.S. . . . . F4 108
Greenwood, Ar., U.S. . . . . G2 114
Greenwood, B.C., Can. . . . H16 102
Greenwood, In., U.S. . . . . C10 114
Greenwood, Ms., U.S. . . . I6 114
Greenwood, Ne., U.S. . . . . K11 118
Greenwood, S.C., U.S. . . . E4 112
Greenwood, Wi., U.S. . . . F5 110
Greenwood, Lake, res., S.C., U.S. . . . . . . . . E4 112
Greer, S.C., U.S. . . . . . . E4 112
Greers Ferry Lake, res., Ar., U.S. . . . . . . . . . . . G4 114
Gregoire Lake Indian Reserve, Ab., Can. . . . B3 104
Gregório, stm., Braz. . . . . B6 82
Gregory, Mi., U.S. . . . . . . H11 110
Gregory, S.D., U.S. . . . . . H8 118
Gregory, Tx., U.S. . . . . . . L9 116
Gregory, stm., Austl. . . . . B7 70
Gregory, Lake, l., Austl. . . G3 70
Gregory Range, mts., Austl. A13 70
Greifswald, Ger. . . . . . . . E12 10
Greiz, Ger. . . . . . . . . . . E12 10
Gruziya see Georgia, ctry., Asia . . . . . . . . . . . . I6 26
Grem'ačinsk, Russia . . . . . F9 26
Grenada, ctry., N.A. . . . . I7 114
Grenada, i., U.S. . . . . . . H14 94
Grenadines, is., N.A. . . . . H14 94
Grenchen, Switz. . . . . . . D7 13
Grenfell, Austl. . . . . . . . . I8 70
Grenfell, Sk., Can. . . . . . H12 104
Grenoble, Fr. . . . . . . . . . G12 14
Grenola, Ks., U.S. . . . . . . N11 118
Grenora, N.D., U.S. . . . . . C4 118
Grenville, Cape, c., Austl. . B8 68
Grenville Channel, strt., B.C., Can. . . . . . . . . D5 102
Gréoux-les-Bains, Fr. . . . . I12 14
Gresham, Or., U.S. . . . . . E3 122
Gresham Park, Ga., U.S. . . F2 112
Gresik, Indon. . . . . . . . . j16 39a
Gresten, Aus. . . . . . . . . G15 10
Gretna, La., U.S. . . . . . . M6 114
Gretna, Mb., Can. . . . . . . I17 104
Gretna, Va., U.S. . . . . . . C7 112
Greven, Ger. . . . . . . . . . C7 10
Grevená, Ger. . . . . . . . . I5 20
Grevenbroich, Ger. . . . . . D6 10
Greville Bay, b., N.S., Can. E17 106
Grey, stm., Nf., Can. . . . . E17 106
Greybull, Wy., U.S. . . . . . F17 122
Greybull, stm., Wy., U.S. . . F17 122
Grey Eagle, Mn., U.S. . . . F1 110
Grey Islands, is., Nf., Can. . B18 106
Greylock, Mount, mtn., Ma., U.S. . . . . . . . . . . . D13 108
Greymouth, N.Z. . . . . . . . E3 72
Grey Range, mts., Austl. . . G5 70
Grey River, Nf., Can. . . . . E16 106
Greys, stm., Wy., U.S. . . . G15 122
Greytown, S. Afr. . . . . . . G10 66
Gribanovskij, Russia . . . . I7 26
Gribbel Island, i., B.C., Can. D5 102
Gridley, Ca., U.S. . . . . . . E4 124
Gridley, Il., U.S. . . . . . . . J7 110
Griesbach, Ger. . . . . . . . G13 10
Griesheim, Ger. . . . . . . . F8 10
Griffin, Ga., U.S. . . . . . . F2 112
Griffin, Sk., Can. . . . . . . I11 104
Griffith, Austl. . . . . . . . . J7 70
Griffith Island, i., N.T., Can. B13 96
Grifton, N.C., U.S. . . . . . . D9 112
Griggsville, Il., U.S. . . . . . C6 114
Grignan, Fr. . . . . . . . . . H11 14
Grigoriopol, Mol. . . . . . . B13 20
Grijalva, stm., Mex. . . . . . I13 90
Grijalva (Cuilco), stm., N.A. H14 90
Grijpskerk, Neth. . . . . . . B9 12
Grim, Cape, c., Austl. . . . M6 70
Grimsby, Eng., U.K. . . . . . H13 8
Grimsby, On., Can. . . . . . G16 110
Grimselpass, Switz. . . . . . E9 13
Grimshaw, Ab., Can. . . . . A17 102
Grímsstaðir, Ice. . . . . . . . B5 6a
Grimstad, Nor. . . . . . . . . L11 6
Grímsvötn, mtn., Ice. . . . . B5 6a
Grindelwald, Switz. . . . . . E9 13
Grindstone Island see Cap-aux-Meules, P.Q., Can. . E12 106
Grinnell, Ia., U.S. . . . . . . I3 110
Grinnell Peninsula, pen., N.T., Can. . . . . . . . . A13 96
Gris-Nez, Cap, c., Fr. . . . . B8 14
Griswold, Ia., U.S. . . . . . J12 118
Griswold, Mb., Can. . . . . I14 104
Grizzly Bear Mountain, mtn., N.T., Can. . . . . . C8 96
Grizzly Bear's Head and Lead Man Indian Reserve, Sk., Can. . . . . F6 104
Groais Island, i., Nf., Can. . B18 106
Grobina, Lat. . . . . . . . . . E4 22
Groblersdal, S. Afr. . . . . . E9 66
Groblershoop, S. Afr. . . . . G5 66
Grodków, Pol. . . . . . . . . E17 10
Grodzisk Mazowiecki, Pol. . C20 10
Groede, Neth. . . . . . . . . F4 12
Groenlo, Neth. . . . . . . . . D10 12
Groesbeck, Tx., U.S. . . . . H10 116
Groesbeek, Neth. . . . . . . E8 12
Gróiec, Pol. . . . . . . . . . E4 12
Grombalia, Tun. . . . . . . . M5 18
Gronau, Ger. . . . . . . . . . C7 10
Groningen, Neth. . . . . . . B10 12
Groningen, prov., Neth. . . . B10 12
Gronlid, Sk., Can. . . . . . . E10 104
Groom, Tx., U.S. . . . . . . . D5 116
Groot-Brakrivier, S. Afr. . . . J5 66
Groote Eylandt, i., Austl. . . B7 68
Grootfontein, Nmb. . . . . . B4 66
Groot Karasberge, mts., Nmb. . . . . . . . . . . . F4 66
Groot-Kei, stm., S. Afr. . . . I9 66
Groot Laagte, stm., Afr. . . C5 66
Groot-Marico, S. Afr. . . . . E8 66
Groot-Vis, stm., S. Afr. . . . I8 66
Gros Mécatina, Cap de l', P.Q., Can. . . . . . . . B14 106
Gros Morne, mtn., Nf., Can. B16 106
Gros Morne National Park, Nf., Can. . . . . . . . . C16 106
Grosse Île, i., P.Q., Can. . . E12 106
Grosse Pointe, Mi., U.S. . . H13 110
Großer Bärensee, l., N.T., Can. . . . . . . . . . . . C8 96
Grosseto, Italy . . . . . . . . G6 18
Gross-Gerau, Ger. . . . . . . F8 10
Grossglockner, mtn., Aus. . H12 10
Grosshöchstetten, Switz. . . D8 13
Großräschen, Ger. . . . . . . D14 10
Gros Ventre, stm., Wy., U.S. . . . . . . . . . . . G15 122
Groswater Bay, b., Nf., Can. . . . . . . . . . . . F21 96
Groton, Ct., U.S. . . . . . . . F14 108
Groton, N.Y., U.S. . . . . . . E10 108
Groton, S.D., U.S. . . . . . . F9 118
Grottaglie, Italy . . . . . . . I12 18
Grottoes, Va., U.S. . . . . . I8 108
Grouard Mission, Ab., Can. B18 102

Groundbirch, B.C., Can. . . B14 102
Groundhog, stm., On., Can. G16 96
Grove, Ok., U.S. . . . . . . . C12 116
Grove City, Mn., U.S. . . . . F13 118
Grove City, Oh., U.S. . . . . H3 108
Grove City, Pa., U.S. . . . . F6 108
Grove Hill, Al., U.S. . . . . . K9 114
Grover City, Ca., U.S. . . . . I5 124
Groveland, Fl., U.S. . . . . . K5 112
Grover, Co., U.S. . . . . . . J3 120
Groves, Tx., U.S. . . . . . . M3 114
Groveton, N.H., U.S. . . . . C15 108
Groveton, Tx., U.S. . . . . . H11 116
Grovetown, Ga., U.S. . . . . F4 112
Groznyj, Russia . . . . . . . I7 26
Grudziądz, Pol. . . . . . . . B18 10
Gruetli-Laager, Tn., U.S. . . G11 114
Gruitrode, Bel. . . . . . . . . F8 12
Grulla, Tx., U.S. . . . . . . . M8 116
Grünau, Nmb. . . . . . . . . F4 66
Grünau [im Almtal], Aus. . H13 10
Grundy, Va., U.S. . . . . . . B4 112
Grundy Center, Ia., U.S. . . H3 110
Grunthal, Mb., Can. . . . . . I18 104
Gruver, Tx., U.S. . . . . . . . C5 116
Gruziya see Georgia, ctry., Asia . . . . . . . . . . . . I6 26
Grybów, Pol. . . . . . . . . . F20 10
Gryfice, Pol. . . . . . . . . . B15 10
Gstaad, Switz. . . . . . . . . F7 13
Guabito, Pan. . . . . . . . . H12 92
Guacanayabo, Golfo de, b., Cuba . . . . . . . . . . . D6 94
Guacara, Ven. . . . . . . . . B9 84
Guacarí, Col. . . . . . . . . . F4 84
Gu Achi, Az., U.S. . . . . . . L4 120
Guachiría, stm., Col. . . . . E7 84
Guachochi, Mex. . . . . . . . D6 90
Guaçuí, Braz. . . . . . . . . F8 79
Guadalajara, Mex. . . . . . . G8 90
Guadalajara, Spain . . . . . E8 16
Guadalcanal, i., Sol. Is. . . . I20 126
Guadalén, stm., Spain . . . G8 16
Guadalén, Embalse de, res., Spain . . . . . . . . . . . G8 16
Guadalmena, stm., Spain . G9 16
Guadalquivir, stm., Spain . . H6 16
Guadalupe, Bol. . . . . . . . H9 82
Guadalupe, Ca., U.S. . . . . I5 124
Guadalupe, Col. . . . . . . . F5 84
Guadalupe, C.R. . . . . . . . H10 92
Guadalupe, Mex. . . . . . . E9 90
Guadalupe, Peru . . . . . . . B2 82
Guadalupe [Bravos], Mex. . B6 90
Guadalupe Mountains National Park, Tx., U.S. . H2 116
Guadalupe Peak, mtn., Tx., U.S. . . . . . . . . . . . H2 116
Guadalupe Victoria, Mex. . E7 90
Guadalupe, N.M., U.S. . . . H11 120
Guadarrama, Sierra de, mts., Spain . . . . . . . E7 16
Guadiana, stm., Eur. . . . . H4 16
Guacix, Spain . . . . . . . . H8 16
Guaíba, Braz. . . . . . . . . F13 80
Guaíba, est., Braz. . . . . . F13 80
Guaihe, China . . . . . . . . B1 34
Guaimaca, Hond. . . . . . . C8 92
Guaimoreto, Laguna de, b., Hond. . . . . . . . . . . . B9 92
Guainía, dept., Col. . . . . . F8 84
Guainía, stm., S.A. . . . . . . F9 84
Guakuinima, Cerro, mtn., Ven. . . . . . . . . . . . . E11 84
Guaíra, Braz. . . . . . . . . . F4 79
Guaíra, Braz. . . . . . . . . . C11 80
Guaíra, dept., Para. . . . . . C10 80
Guáitara, stm., Col. . . . . . G4 84
Guajaba, Cayo i., Cuba . . . D6 94
Guajará-Mirim, Braz. . . . . D1 82
Guaca, Pan. . . . . . . . . . C1 84
Guacao, Ec. . . . . . . . . . I3 84
Guaiala, Ca., U.S. . . . . . . F2 124
Gualán, Guat. . . . . . . . . C4 92
Gualaquiza, Ec. . . . . . . . I3 84
Gualdo Tadino, Italy . . . . F7 18
Gualeguay, Arg. . . . . . . . G8 80
Gualeguay, stm., Arg. . . . . G8 80
Gualeguaychú, Arg. . . . . . G8 80
Guelicho, Salina del, pl., Arg. . . . . . . . . . . . . E3 78
Guam, dep., Oc. . . . . . . . G18 126
Guamal, Col. . . . . . . . . . F6 84
Guamal, Col. . . . . . . . . . E5 84
Guamini, Arg. . . . . . . . . I7 80
Guamo, Col. . . . . . . . . . E5 84
Guamote, Ec. . . . . . . . . H3 84
Guamúchil, Mex. . . . . . . . E5 90
Guamués, stm., Col. . . . . . G4 84
Guanacaste, Cordillera de, mts., C.R. . . . . . . . . G9 92
Guanacaste, Parque Nacional, C.R. . . . . . . G9 92
Guanacaure, Cerro, mtn., Hond. . . . . . . . . . . . D7 92
Guanacevi, Mex. . . . . . . . E7 90
Guanache, stm., Peru . . . . B4 82
Guanahacabibes, Golfo de, b., Cuba . . . . . . . . . C2 94
Guanaja, Hond. . . . . . . . A9 92
Guanaja, Isla de, i., Hond. . A9 92
Guanajay, Cuba . . . . . . . C3 94
Guanajuato, Mex. . . . . . . G9 90
Guanajuato, state, Mex. . . G9 90
Guanambi, Braz. . . . . . . . C7 79
Guanaparo, Caño, stm., Ven. . . . . . . . . . . . . C8 84
Guañape, Islas, is., Peru . . C2 82
Guanare, Ven. . . . . . . . . C8 84
Guanarito, Ven. . . . . . . . C8 82
Guanay, Bol. . . . . . . . . . G8 82
Guanay, Cerro, mtn., Ven. . E9 84
Guanbuqiao, China . . . . . B9 34
Guandacol, Arg. . . . . . . . E4 80
Guandanghu, China . . . . . E2 34
Guandian, China . . . . . . . C7 34
Guane, Cuba . . . . . . . . . C2 94
Guangde, China . . . . . . . E8 34
Guangdong (Kwangtung), prov., China . . . . . . . G9 30
Guanghua, China . . . . . . E8 34
Guangnan, China . . . . . . B8 30
Guangrao, China . . . . . . . F5 32
Guangxi Zhuangzu Zizhiqu (Kwangsi Chuang), prov., China . . . . . . . . . . . G8 30
Guangyuan, China . . . . . . E8 32
Guangzhou (Canton), China L2 34
Guanhães, Braz. . . . . . . . E7 79
Guanipa, stm., Ven. . . . . . C11 84
Guano, Ec. . . . . . . . . . . H3 84
Guanqian, China . . . . . . . E8 34
Guanqiaocu, China . . . . . B10 34
Guanta, Ven. . . . . . . . . . B10 84
Guantánamo, Cuba . . . . . D7 94

Guantao (Nanguantao) China . . . . . . . . . . . G3 32
Guantou, China . . . . . . . G9 34
Guanxian, China . . . . . . . E7 30
Guanyintang, China . . . . . D1 34
Guanzhuang, China . . . . . F2 32
Guanzhuang, China . . . . . C3 34
Guapi, Col. . . . . . . . . . . F4 84
Guapiara, Braz. . . . . . . . H4 79
Guápiles, C.R. . . . . . . . . G11 92
Guaporé, Braz. . . . . . . . . F3 79
Guaporé (Itenes), stm., S.A. E10 82
Guaqui, Bol. . . . . . . . . . G7 82
Guará, stm., Braz. . . . . . . B6 79
Guarabira, Braz. . . . . . . . E11 75
Guaraçaí, Braz. . . . . . . . F3 79
Guaraci, Braz. . . . . . . . . F4 79
Guaraciama, Braz. . . . . . . D7 79
Guaramirim, Braz. . . . . . . D14 80
Guaranda, Ec. . . . . . . . . H3 84
Guaraniaçu, Braz. . . . . . . C12 80
Guarani das Missões, Braz. E11 80
Guarani de Goiás, Braz. . . B5 79
Guarapari, Braz. . . . . . . . C13 80
Guarapuava, Braz. . . . . . . C13 80
Guararapes, Braz. . . . . . . F3 79
Guararé, Pan. . . . . . . . . D2 84
Guaratinguetá, Braz. . . . . G6 79
Guaratuba, Braz. . . . . . . C14 80
Guarda, Port. . . . . . . . . . E4 16
Guardaful, Cape see Gwardafuy, Gees, c., Som. . . . . . . . . . . . F11 56
Guardavalle, Italy . . . . . . . K11 18
Guardia Escolta, Arg. . . . . E7 80
Guardiagrele, Italy . . . . . . G9 18
Guardo, Spain . . . . . . . . C7 16
Guareña, Spain . . . . . . . . G5 16
Guarenas, Ven. . . . . . . . B9 84
Guariba, stm., Braz. . . . . . C11 82
Guarico, Ven. . . . . . . . . . C8 84
Guárico, state, Ven. . . . . . C9 84
Guárico, stm., Ven. . . . . . C9 84
Guárico, Embalse del, res., Ven. . . . . . . . . . . . . C9 84
Guariquito, stm., Ven. . . . . D9 84
Guarulhos, Braz. . . . . . . . G5 79
Guasave, Mex. . . . . . . . . E5 90
Guasdualito, Ven. . . . . . . D7 84
Guasipati, Ven. . . . . . . . . D12 84
Guastalla, Italy . . . . . . . . E5 18
Guastatoya, Guat. . . . . . . C4 92
Guatajiagua, El Sal. . . . . . D6 92
Guatemala, Guat. . . . . . . C4 92
Guatemala, dept., Guat. . . C4 92
Guatemala, ctry., N.A. . . . . E6 88
Guateque, Col. . . . . . . . . E6 84
Guatimozin, Arg. . . . . . . . G7 80
Guatopo, Parque Nacional, Ven. . . . . . . . . . . . . C9 84
Guatraché, Arg. . . . . . . . I7 80
Guaviare, ter., Col. . . . . . F6 84
Guaviare, stm., Col. . . . . . F8 84
Guaxupé, Braz. . . . . . . . . F5 79
Guayabal, Col. . . . . . . . . D6 94
Guayabal, Ven. . . . . . . . . C9 84
Guayabero, stm., Col. . . . . F6 84
Guayacán, Chile . . . . . . . E3 80
Guayama, P.R. . . . . . . . . F11 94
Guayambre, stm., Hond. . . C8 92
Guayape, Hond. . . . . . . . C8 92
Guayape, stm., Hond. . . . . C9 92
Guayapo, stm., Ven. . . . . . E9 84
Guayaquil, Ec. . . . . . . . . D3 76
Guayaquil, Golfo de, b., S.A. . . . . . . . . . . . . I2 84
Guayaramerín, Bol. . . . . . D9 82
Guayas, prov., Ec. . . . . . . H2 84
Guayas, stm., Col. . . . . . . G5 84
Guayas, stm., Ec. . . . . . . I3 84
Guayatayacu, Laguna de, l., Arg. . . . . . . . . . . . . B6 80
Guaycora, Mex. . . . . . . . C5 90
Guaymas, Mex. . . . . . . . . D4 90
Guaymi, stm., Col. . . . . . . F8 84
Guayquiraró, stm., Arg. . . . F9 80
Guayuriba, stm., Col. . . . . F6 84
Guazacapán, Guat. . . . . . C4 92
Guazapares, Mex. . . . . . . D5 90
Guazárachi, Mex. . . . . . . D6 90
Guba, Eth. . . . . . . . . . . L8 60
Gubacha, Russia . . . . . . . F9 26
Gubbio, Italy . . . . . . . . . F7 18
Guben, Ger. . . . . . . . . . . D14 10
Gubin, Pol. . . . . . . . . . . D14 10
Gubkin, Russia . . . . . . . . G5 26
Gucheng, China . . . . . . . E4 34
Güdalür, India . . . . . . . . H4 46
Gudenå, stm., Den. . . . . . I3 6
Gudermes, Russia . . . . . . I7 26
Gudianzi, China . . . . . . . D5 34
Gudiyāttam, India . . . . . . F5 46
Güdür, India . . . . . . . . . E5 46
Guebwiller, Fr. . . . . . . . . E14 14
Gŭeltat-Zemmour, W. Sah. . E4 62
Guelma, Alg. . . . . . . . . . B14 62
Guelph, On., Can. . . . . . . G15 110
Guémené-sur-Scorff, Fr. . . E4 14
Guémé, Benin . . . . . . . . F11 64
Guénange, Fr. . . . . . . . . . C13 14
Guercif, Mor. . . . . . . . . . C9 62
Guéréda, Chad . . . . . . . . F4 60
Guéret, Fr. . . . . . . . . . . . F8 14
Guerneville, Ca., U.S. . . . . F2 124
Guernsey, Wy., U.S. . . . . . B12 120
Guernsey, dep., Eur. . . . . C5 14
Guerrero, Mex. . . . . . . . . C6 90
Guerrero, state, Mex. . . . . I9 90
Guerzim, Alg. . . . . . . . . . F10 62
Guessou-Sud, Benin . . . . . F11 64
Gueydan, La., U.S. . . . . . L4 114
Gugang, China . . . . . . . . B9 34
Guge, mtn., Eth. . . . . . . . N9 60
Guía, Braz. . . . . . . . . . . F13 82
Guía de Isora, Spain . . . . o24 17b
Guía Lopes da Laguna, Braz. . . . . . . . . . . . I13 82
Guibes, Nmb. . . . . . . . . . F3 66
Güicán, Col. . . . . . . . . . D6 84
Guichen, Fr. . . . . . . . . . . E5 14
Guichón, Ur. . . . . . . . . . G10 80
Guidan Roumji, Niger . . . . E13 64
Guide, China . . . . . . . . . D7 30
Guide Rock, Ne., U.S. . . . . K9 118
Guider, Cam. . . . . . . . . . G9 64
Guiding, China . . . . . . . . A9 34
Guidimouni, Niger . . . . . . E14 64
Guifujie, China . . . . . . . . H9 34
Guiglo, C. Iv. . . . . . . . . . H6 64
Güija, Lago de, l., N.A. . . . C5 92
Guildford, Eng., U.K. . . . . J13 8
Guildhall, Vt., U.S. . . . . . . C15 108
Guilford, Me., U.S. . . . . . . B17 108
Guilin (Kweilin), China . . . B11 30
Guillaume-Delisle, Lac, l., P.Q., Can. . . . . . . . . E17 96
Guimarães, Braz. . . . . . . . D10 75
Guimarães, Port. . . . . . . . D3 16
Guin, Al., U.S. . . . . . . . . I9 114
Guinea (Guinée), ctry., Afr. . F3 54
Guinea, Gulf of, b., Afr. . . . H7 52

Guinea-Bissau (Guiné-Bissau), ctry., Afr. . . . . F3 54
Guinecourt, Lac, l., P.Q., Can. . . . . . . . . . . . B4 106
Güines, Cuba . . . . . . . . . C3 94
Güines, Fr. . . . . . . . . . . B8 14
Guingamp, Fr. . . . . . . . . D3 14
Güinope, Hond. . . . . . . . D8 92
Guines, Punta, c., C.R. . . . H9 92
Guiping, China . . . . . . . . C11 40
Guir, Hammada du, des., Afr. . . . . . . . . . . . . E9 62
Guir, Oued, val., Afr. . . . . . E9 62
Güira de Melena, Cuba . . . C3 94
Guirai, stm., Braz. . . . . . . G2 79
Guiratinga, Braz. . . . . . . . D2 79
Güiria, Ven. . . . . . . . . . . B11 84
Guiricema, Braz. . . . . . . . F7 79
Güisisil, mtn., Nic. . . . . . . E8 92
Guita Koulouba, C.A.R. . . . O2 60
Guitou, China . . . . . . . . . K2 34
Güitres, Fr. . . . . . . . . . . C8 14
Guixian, Phil. . . . . . . . . . C11 40
Guixi, China . . . . . . . . . . G6 34
Guixian, China . . . . . . . . C10 40
Guiyang (Kweiyang) China . A9 40
Güiza, stm., Col. . . . . . . . G3 84
Guizhou (Kweichow), prov., China . . . . . . . . . . . F8 30
Gujarāt, state, India . . . . . I4 44
Gujrānwāla, Pak. . . . . . . . D6 44
Gujrāt, Pak. . . . . . . . . . . D6 44
Gulbarga, India . . . . . . . . D4 46
Gulbene, Lat. . . . . . . . . . D9 22
Guledagudda, India . . . . . D3 46
Guleitou, China . . . . . . . . L6 34
Gulf Hammock, Fl., U.S. . . J4 112
Gulfport, Fl., U.S. . . . . . . L4 112
Gulfport, Ms., U.S. . . . . . L7 114
Gulf Shores, Al., U.S. . . . . L9 114
Guigong, Austl. . . . . . . . . I8 70
Gulistan, Pak. . . . . . . . . E2 44
Gulistan, Uzb. . . . . . . . . I11 26
Gull Lake, Sk., Can. . . . . . H6 104
Gull Lake, l., Ab., Can. . . . E21 102
Gull Lake, l., On., Can. . . . G23 104
Gullrock Lake, l., On., Can. . H21 104
Güllük, Tur. . . . . . . . . . . L11 20
Gülpinar, Tur. . . . . . . . . . J10 20
Guluy, Erit. . . . . . . . . . . J9 60
Gumal (Gowmal), stm., Asia D12 84
Gumare, Bots. . . . . . . . . B6 66
Gumiao, China . . . . . . . . C2 34
Gummersbach, Ger. . . . . . D7 10
Gummi, Nig. . . . . . . . . . E12 64
Gümüshane, Tur. . . . . . . . A5 48
Guna, India . . . . . . . . . . H7 44
Gundagai, Austl. . . . . . . . J8 70
Gundelsheim, Ger. . . . . . . F9 10
Gungu, D.R.C. . . . . . . . . C3 58
Gunisao, stm., Mb., Can. . . C18 104
Gunisao Lake, l., Mb., Can. E18 104
Gunnar, Sk., Can. . . . . . . E7 104
Gunnbjørn Fjeld, mtn., Grnld. . . . . . . . . . . . C17 86
Gunnedah, Austl. . . . . . . H9 70
Gunnison, Co., U.S. . . . . . F10 120
Gunnison, Ut., U.S. . . . . . E5 120
Gunnison, Co., U.S. . . . . . F10 120
Guntakal, India . . . . . . . . E4 46
Guntersville, Al., U.S. . . . . I10 114
Guntersville Lake, res., Al., U.S. . . . . . . . . . . . H10 114
Guntūr, India . . . . . . . . . D6 46
Gunungsitoli, Indon. . . . . N4 40
Gunzenhausen, Ger. . . . . . F10 10
Guolutan, China . . . . . . . C4 34
Guozhuang, China . . . . . . H5 32
Gupei, China . . . . . . . . . I5 32
Guraferda, Eth. . . . . . . . . N8 60
Gura Galbehei, Mol. . . . . . C12 20
Gurara, stm., Nig. . . . . . . F12 64
Gurdāspur, India . . . . . . . D6 44
Gurdon, Ar., U.S. . . . . . . I3 114
Güre, Tur. . . . . . . . . . . . K13 20
Gurgueia, stm., Braz. . . . . D4 90
Guri, Embalse de, res., Ven. D11 84
Gurjevsk, Russia . . . . . . . G3 22
Gurjevsk, Russia . . . . . . . G15 26
Gurupá, Braz. . . . . . . . . . D8 76
Gurupi, stm., Braz. . . . . . . D9 76
Gurupi, Braz. . . . . . . . . . E13 64
Gusau, Nig. . . . . . . . . . . E12 64
Gus'-Chrustal'nyj, Russia . . F23 22
Gusev, Russia . . . . . . . . G5 22
Gusevskij, Russia . . . . . . F23 22
Gushanzi, China . . . . . . . C4 34
Gushi, China . . . . . . . . . C4 34
Gushikawa, Japan . . . . . . u2 37b
Gusino, Russia . . . . . . . . G14 22
Gusinoozersk, Russia . . . . G13 26
Guspini, Italy . . . . . . . . . J3 18
Güstine, Ca., U.S. . . . . . . G4 124
Gustavus, Ak., U.S. . . . . . G27 100
Güstrow, Ger. . . . . . . . . B12 10
Gus'-Železnyj, Russia . . . . F24 22
Gütersloh, Ger. . . . . . . . . D8 10
Guthrie, Ky., U.S. . . . . . . F9 114
Guthrie, Ok., U.S. . . . . . . D9 116
Guthrie, Tx., U.S. . . . . . . E6 116
Guthrie Center, Ia., U.S. . . J13 118
Guthrie Lake, l., Mb., Can. . C14 104
Gutian, China . . . . . . . . . I7 34
Gutierrez, Bol. . . . . . . . . H10 82
Gutiérrez Zamora, Mex. . . F12 124
Guttenberg, Ia., U.S. . . . . H4 110
Gutu, Zimb. . . . . . . . . . B10 66
Guwāhāti, India . . . . . . . . G14 44
Guxian, China . . . . . . . . F9 32
Guxian, China . . . . . . . . C5 34
Guyana, ctry., S.A. . . . . . . C13 76
Guyandotte, stm., W.V., U.S. . . . . . . . . . . . . I4 108
Guyi, China . . . . . . . . . . J7 34
Guymon, Ok., U.S. . . . . . . C5 116
Guyot, Mount, mtn., U.S. . . D3 112
Guysborough, N.S., Can. . . G5 112
Guyton, Ga., U.S. . . . . . . G4 112
Guyuan, China . . . . . . . . J11 26
Guzar, Uzb. . . . . . . . . . . J11 26
Guzhu, China . . . . . . . . . I7 34
Guzmán, Mex. . . . . . . . . B6 90
Guzmán, Laguna, l., Mex. . . C6 90
Gvardejsk, Russia . . . . . . G4 22
Gwa, Myan. . . . . . . . . . . F3 40
Gwadabawa, Nig. . . . . . . E12 64
Gwādar, Pak. . . . . . . . . . B8 66
Gwai, Zimb. . . . . . . . . . B8 66
Gwâl Haidarzai, Pak. . . . . E3 44
Gwalior, India . . . . . . . . . G8 44
Gwanda, Zimb. . . . . . . . . C9 66
Gwandu, Nig. . . . . . . . . . E12 64
Gwardafuy, Gees, c., Asia . . F11 56
Gwātar Bay, b., Asia . . . . . J11 48
Gwent, co., Wales, U.K. . . . J11 8
Gweru, Zimb. . . . . . . . . . B9 66
Gweta, Bots. . . . . . . . . . C7 66
Gwinner, N.D., U.S. . . . . . E10 118
Gwynedd, co., Wales, U.K. . H9 8
Gy, Fr. . . . . . . . . . . . . . E12 14
Gyangzê, China . . . . . . . . F4 30

Gyaring Co, l., China . . . . E13 44
Gyaring Hu, l., China . . . . E6 30
Gydanskaja guba, b., Russia . . . . . . . . . . . C13 26
Gydanskij poluostrov, pen., Russia . . . . . . . . . . . C13 26
Gyirong, China . . . . . . . . F11 44
Gym Peak, mtn., N.M., U.S. L9 120
Gympie, Austl. . . . . . . . . F10 70
Gyobingauk, Myan. . . . . . E3 40
Gyoma, Hung. . . . . . . . . I20 10
Gyöngyös, Hung. . . . . . . . H19 10
Győr, Hung. . . . . . . . . . . H17 10
Győr-Moson-Sopron, co., Hung. . . . . . . . . . . . H17 10
Gypsum, Co., U.S. . . . . . . E10 120
Gypsum, Ks., U.S. . . . . . . M10 118
Gypsum Point, c., N.T., Can. . . . . . . . . . . . . D10 96
Gypsumville, Mb., Can. . . . G16 104
Gyula, Hung. . . . . . . . . . I21 10

**H**

Haag in Oberbayern, Ger. . G12 10
Haalenberg, Nmb. . . . . . . F2 66
Haaltert, Bel. . . . . . . . . . G5 12
Haapajärvi, Fin. . . . . . . . J19 6
Haapamäki, Fin. . . . . . . . J19 6
Haapsalu, Est. . . . . . . . . C6 22
Ha'Arava (Wādī al-Jayb), val., Asia . . . . . . . . . H4 50
Ha'Arava (Wādī al-'Arabah), val., Asia . . . . . . . . . G4 50
Haarlem, Neth. . . . . . . . . D6 12
Habarūt, Yemen . . . . . . . F8 47
Habban, Yemen . . . . . . . G5 47
Habbūsh, Leb. . . . . . . . . B4 50
Habermehl Peak, mtn., Ant. C3 73
Habiganj, Bngl. . . . . . . . . H14 44
Habomai-shotō see Malaja Kuril'skaja Gr'ada, is., Russia . . . . . . . . . . . d21 36a
Hache, Lac La, l., B.C., Can. F13 102
Hachijō-jima, i., Japan . . . . E14 36
Hachinohe, Japan . . . . . . G16 36
Hachiōji, Japan . . . . . . . . L14 36
Hacienda Miravalles, C.R. . G9 92
Hacienda Murciélago, C.R. . G9 92
Hackberry, Az., U.S. . . . . . I3 120
Hackberry, La., U.S. . . . . . M3 114
Hackensack, N.J., U.S. . . . G12 108
Hackett, Ar., U.S. . . . . . . G2 114
Hackettstown, N.J., U.S. . . G12 108
Hackleburg, Al., U.S. . . . . H9 114
Hadaliya, Sudan . . . . . . . I9 60
Hadd, Ra's al-, c., Oman . . C11 47
Haddam, Ks., U.S. . . . . . . L10 118
Haddington, Scot., U.K. . . . F11 8
Haddock, Ga., U.S. . . . . . F3 112
Hadejia, Nig. . . . . . . . . . E14 64
Hadejia, stm., Nig. . . . . . . E14 64
Hadera, Isr. . . . . . . . . . . D3 50
Hadera, stm., Asia . . . . . . D3 50
Hadley Bay, b., N.T., Can. . B11 96
Hadlock, Wa., U.S. . . . . . B3 122
Ha Dong, Viet. . . . . . . . . D8 40
Hedramawt, reg., Yemen . . G6 47
Hedzilavičy, Bela. . . . . . . H13 22
Heeju, N. Kor. . . . . . . . . E13 32
Haenam, S. Kor. . . . . . . . H14 32
Hafford, Sk., Can. . . . . . . F7 104
Haffouz, Tun. . . . . . . . . . N4 18
Hafīrat al-'Ayda, Sau. Ar. . . H5 48
Hafnarfjörður, Ice. . . . . . . B3 6a
Haft Gel, Iran . . . . . . . . . F10 48
Hagen, Ger. . . . . . . . . . . D7 10
Hagensborg, B.C., Can. . . . E9 102
Hagere Hiywet, Eth. . . . . . M9 60
Hagere Selam, Eth. . . . . . N10 60
Hagerman, Id., U.S. . . . . . H11 122
Hagerman, N.M., U.S. . . . . F2 116
Hagerstown, In., U.S. . . . . C11 114
Hagerstown, Md., U.S. . . . H9 108
Hagersville, On., Can. . . . . H15 110
Hagetmau, Fr. . . . . . . . . I6 14
Haggin, Mount, mtn., Mt., U.S. . . . . . . . . . . . . D12 122
Ha Giang, Viet. . . . . . . . . C8 40
Hagondange, Fr. . . . . . . . C13 14
Hague, N.D., U.S. . . . . . . E8 118
Hague, Sk., Can. . . . . . . . F8 104
Hague, Cap de la, c., Fr. . . C5 14
Haguenau, Fr. . . . . . . . . D14 14
Hagues Peak, mtn., Co., U.S. . . . . . . . . . . . . D11 120
Hahaïa, Com. . . . . . . . . . k15 67a
Hahira, Ga., U.S. . . . . . . . I3 112
Haian Shanmo, mts., Tai. . L10 34
Haicheng, China . . . . . . . C10 32
Haidra, Tun. . . . . . . . . . N3 18
Haifa see Hefa, Isr. . . . . . C4 50
Haifeng, China . . . . . . . . M4 34
Haig, Austl. . . . . . . . . . . F5 68
Haig, Mount, mtn., Can. . . H20 102
Haigler, Ne., U.S. . . . . . . K6 118
Haikang (Leizhou), China . . D11 40
Haikou, China . . . . . . . . . D11 40
Hā'il, Sau. Ar. . . . . . . . . . H6 48
Hailākāndi, India . . . . . . . H15 44
Hailar, China . . . . . . . . . B10 30
Hailar, stm., China . . . . . . B11 30
Hailey, Id., U.S. . . . . . . . . G12 122
Haileybury, On., Can. . . . . C16 110
Haileyville, Ok., U.S. . . . . E11 116
Hailong (Meihekou), China . A13 32
Hailun, China . . . . . . . . . B12 30
Haimen, China . . . . . . . . G10 34
Haimen, China . . . . . . . . E8 34
Hainan, prov., China . . . . . H8 30
Hainan Dao, i., China . . . . E10 40
Hainaut, prov., Bel. . . . . . G4 12
Hainaut, hist. reg., Eur. . . . H4 12
Haines, Or., U.S. . . . . . . . F8 122
Haines, Ak., U.S. . . . . . . . G27 100
Haines City, Fl., U.S. . . . . K5 112
Hainfeld, Aus. . . . . . . . . G15 10
Hai Phong, Viet. . . . . . . . D9 40
Haiti (Haïti), ctry., N.A. . . . E9 94
Haitou, China . . . . . . . . . I7 32
Haiyaopu, China . . . . . . . A6 40
Haizhou, China . . . . . . . . A8 34
Hajdú-Bihar, co., Hung. . . . H21 10
Hajdúböszörmény, Hung. . . H21 10
Hajdúnánás, Hung. . . . . . H21 10
Hajeb el Ayoun, Tun. . . . . N4 18
Haji Langar, China . . . . . . C8 44
Hājīpur, India . . . . . . . . . H11 44
Hajjah, Yemen . . . . . . . . G3 47
Hajnówka, Pol. . . . . . . . . C23 10
Hakim, Abyār al-, well, Libya . . . . . . . . . . . . B2 60
Hakkâri, Tur. . . . . . . . . . C6 48
Hakodate, Japan . . . . . . . f15 36a
Hakui, Japan . . . . . . . . . K11 36
Halab (Aleppo), Syria . . . . C4 48
Halabjah, Iraq . . . . . . . . . D8 48
Halachó, Mex. . . . . . . . . G15 90
Halā'ib, Egypt . . . . . . . . . F9 60
Halaula, Hi., U.S. . . . . . . . q18 125a

| Name | Map Ref. | Page |
|---|---|---|
| *Halawa, Cape, c., Hi., U.S.* | p17 | 125a |
| Halawotelake, China | B14 | 44 |
| Halberstadt, Ger. | D11 | 10 |
| Halbrite, Sk., Can. | I11 | 104 |
| Haldwāni, India | F8 | 44 |
| Hale, Mo., U.S. | C3 | 114 |
| *Haleakala Crater, crat., Hi., U.S.* | q17 | 125a |
| *Haleakala National Park, Hi., U.S.* | q17 | 125a |
| Hale Center, Tx., U.S. | E5 | 116 |
| Haleyville, Al., U.S. | H9 | 114 |
| Halfmoon Bay, B.C., Can. | H11 | 102 |
| Halfway, Md., U.S. | H9 | 108 |
| Halfway, Or., U.S. | F8 | 122 |
| *Halfway, stm., B.C., Can.* | E8 | 96 |
| *Halfway Lake, l., Mb., Can.* | C16 | 104 |
| Haliburton, On., Can. | E17 | 110 |
| Halifax, Austl. | B7 | 70 |
| Halifax, N.C., U.S. | C9 | 112 |
| Halifax, N.S., Can. | H10 | 106 |
| Halifax, Va., U.S. | C8 | 112 |
| *Halifax, Canadian Forces Base, mil., N.S., Can.* | H10 | 106 |
| *Halifax Bay, b., Austl.* | B7 | 70 |
| *Halifax Citadel National Historic Park, N.S., Can.* | H10 | 106 |
| *Halifax Harbour, b., N.S., Can.* | H10 | 106 |
| *Hallam Peak, mtn., B.C., Can.* | E16 | 102 |
| Hallandale, Fl., U.S. | N6 | 112 |
| *Hallands Län, co., Swe.* | M13 | 6 |
| *Halla-san, mtn., S. Kor.* | E12 | 30 |
| Halle (Hal), Bel. | G5 | 12 |
| Halle, Ger. | D11 | 10 |
| Hallein, Aus. | H13 | 10 |
| Hallettsville, Tx., U.S. | J10 | 116 |
| Halliday, N.D., U.S. | D5 | 118 |
| Hall in Tirol, Aus. | H11 | 10 |
| *Hall Lake, l., N.T., Can.* | C16 | 96 |
| Hällnäs, Swe. | I16 | 6 |
| Hallock, Mn., U.S. | C11 | 118 |
| Hallowell, Me., U.S. | C17 | 108 |
| *Hall Peninsula, pen., N.T., Can.* | D19 | 96 |
| Halls, Tn., U.S. | G7 | 114 |
| Hallsberg, Swe. | L14 | 6 |
| Halls Creek, Austl. | C5 | 68 |
| Hallstavik, Swe. | K16 | 6 |
| Hallstead, Pa., U.S. | F11 | 108 |
| Hallsville, Mo., U.S. | C4 | 114 |
| Hallsville, Tx., U.S. | J2 | 114 |
| Halma, Bel. | H7 | 12 |
| *Halmahera, i., Indon.* | E8 | 38 |
| *Halmahera, Laut (Halmahera Sea), Indon.* | F8 | 38 |
| Halmstad, Swe. | M13 | 6 |
| Halsey, Ne., U.S. | J7 | 118 |
| Halsey, Or., U.S. | F2 | 122 |
| Hälsingborg see Helsingborg, Swe. | M13 | 6 |
| Halstad, Mn., U.S. | D11 | 118 |
| Halstead, Ks., U.S. | M10 | 118 |
| Haltern, Ger. | D7 | 10 |
| *Haltiatunturi, mtn., Eur.* | G17 | 6 |
| Haltom City, Tx., U.S. | G9 | 116 |
| Halton Hills, On., Can. | G16 | 110 |
| *Halvorson, Mount, mtn., B.C., Can.* | D14 | 102 |
| Hamad, Sudan | J7 | 60 |
| Hamada, Japan | M7 | 36 |
| Hamadān, Iran | D10 | 48 |
| Ḥamāh, Syria | D4 | 48 |
| Hamale, Ghana | F8 | 64 |
| Hamamatsu, Japan | M12 | 36 |
| Hamar, Nor. | K12 | 6 |
| *Hamāṭah, Jabal, mtn., Egypt* | I3 | 48 |
| *Hamber Provincial Park, B.C., Can.* | E17 | 102 |
| Hamburg, Ar., U.S. | I5 | 114 |
| Hamburg, Ger. | B9 | 10 |
| Hamburg, Ia., U.S. | K12 | 118 |
| Hamburg, N.J., U.S. | F12 | 108 |
| Hamburg, N.Y., U.S. | E8 | 108 |
| Hamburg, Pa., U.S. | G11 | 108 |
| Hamdānah, Sau. Ar. | E2 | 47 |
| Hamden, Ct., U.S. | F14 | 108 |
| Hamden, Oh., U.S. | H4 | 108 |
| *Hämeen lääni, prov., Fin.* | K19 | 6 |
| Hämeenlinna, Fin. | K19 | 6 |
| Hameln, Ger. | C9 | 10 |
| *Hamersley Range, mts., Austl.* | D3 | 68 |
| *Hamersley Range National Park, Austl.* | D3 | 68 |
| Hamhŭng, N. Kor. | D15 | 32 |
| Hami, China | C5 | 30 |
| Hamilton, Al., U.S. | H9 | 114 |
| Hamilton, Austl. | K5 | 70 |
| Hamilton, Ber. | B12 | 88 |
| Hamilton, Ga., U.S. | G2 | 112 |
| Hamilton, Il., U.S. | J4 | 110 |
| Hamilton, Ks., U.S. | N11 | 118 |
| Hamilton, Mi., U.S. | H9 | 110 |
| Hamilton, Mo., U.S. | C3 | 114 |
| Hamilton, Mt., U.S. | D11 | 122 |
| Hamilton, N.C., U.S. | D9 | 112 |
| Hamilton, N.Y., U.S. | E11 | 108 |
| Hamilton, N.Z. | B5 | 72 |
| Hamilton, Oh., U.S. | H2 | 108 |
| Hamilton, On., Can. | G16 | 110 |
| Hamilton, Scot., U.K. | F9 | 8 |
| Hamilton, Tx., U.S. | H8 | 116 |
| *Hamilton, stm., Austl.* | D4 | 70 |
| *Hamilton, Mount, mtn., Nv., U.S.* | E10 | 124 |
| Hamilton City, Ca., U.S. | E3 | 124 |
| *Hamilton Creek Indian Reserve, B.C., Can.* | G14 | 102 |
| Hamilton Dome, Wy., U.S. | A8 | 120 |
| Hamilton Hotel, Austl. | D4 | 70 |
| *Hamilton Inlet, b., Nf., Can.* | F21 | 96 |
| *Hamilton Sound, strt., Nf., Can.* | C19 | 106 |
| Hamina, Fin. | K20 | 6 |
| Hamiota, Mb., Can. | H14 | 104 |
| *Hamīr, Wādī, val., Asia* | F7 | 48 |
| Hamīrpur, India | H9 | 44 |
| Hamlet, N.C., U.S. | E7 | 112 |
| Hamlin, Tx., U.S. | G6 | 116 |
| Hamlin, W.V., U.S. | I4 | 108 |
| Hamm, Ger. | D7 | 10 |
| Hammamet, Alg. | N2 | 18 |
| Hammamet, Tun. | M5 | 18 |
| *Hammamet, Golfe de, b., Tun.* | M5 | 18 |
| Hammam Lif, Tun. | M5 | 18 |
| *Hammār, Hawr al-, l., Iraq* | F9 | 48 |
| Hamme, Bel. | F5 | 12 |
| Hammerdal, Swe. | J14 | 6 |
| Hammerfest, Nor. | F18 | 6 |
| Hammon, Ok., U.S. | D7 | 116 |
| Hammond, In., U.S. | A9 | 114 |
| Hammond, La., U.S. | L6 | 114 |
| Hammond, Wi., U.S. | F3 | 110 |
| Hammondsport, N.Y., U.S. | E9 | 108 |
| Hammonton, N.J., U.S. | H12 | 108 |
| *Hamoyet, Jabal, mtn., Afr.* | I10 | 60 |
| Hampden, Me., U.S. | C18 | 108 |
| Hampden, N.D., U.S. | C9 | 118 |
| Hampden, Nf., Can. | C17 | 106 |
| Hampden Sydney, Va., U.S. | B8 | 112 |
| Hampshire, Il., U.S. | H7 | 110 |
| *Hampshire, co., Eng., U.K.* | J12 | 8 |
| Hampstead, N.C., U.S. | E9 | 112 |
| Hampton, Ar., U.S. | I4 | 114 |
| Hampton, Fl., U.S. | J4 | 112 |
| Hampton, Ga., U.S. | F2 | 112 |
| Hampton, Ia., U.S. | H2 | 110 |
| Hampton, N.B., Can. | G8 | 106 |
| Hampton, Ne., U.S. | K10 | 118 |
| Hampton, N.H., U.S. | E16 | 108 |
| Hampton, N.J., U.S. | G12 | 108 |
| Hampton, S.C., U.S. | G5 | 112 |
| Hampton, Tn., U.S. | C4 | 112 |
| Hampton, Va., U.S. | B10 | 112 |
| Hampton Bays, N.Y., U.S. | G14 | 108 |
| *Hampton Butte, mtn., Or., U.S.* | G5 | 122 |
| *Hamra, As Saquia al, val., W. Sah.* | G4 | 62 |
| *Hams Fork, stm., Wy., U.S.* | C6 | 120 |
| Hamyang, S. Kor. | H15 | 32 |
| *Han, stm., China* | E9 | 30 |
| Hana, Hi., U.S. | q18 | 125a |
| Hanahan, S.C., U.S. | G6 | 112 |
| Hanamaki, Japan | H16 | 36 |
| Hanapepe, Hi., U.S. | p14 | 125a |
| Hanau, Ger. | E8 | 10 |
| *Hanbury, stm., N.T., Can.* | D11 | 96 |
| Hancavičy, Bela. | I9 | 22 |
| Hâncești, Mol. | C12 | 20 |
| Hanceville, Al., U.S. | H10 | 114 |
| Hanceville, B.C., Can. | F11 | 102 |
| Hancheng, China | D9 | 30 |
| Hancock, Md., U.S. | H8 | 108 |
| Hancock, Mi., U.S. | C7 | 110 |
| Hancock, Mn., U.S. | F12 | 118 |
| Hancock, N.Y., U.S. | F11 | 108 |
| Hancock, Wi., U.S. | F6 | 110 |
| Handa, Japan | M11 | 36 |
| Handa, Som. | F11 | 56 |
| Handan, China | G2 | 32 |
| Handsworth, Sk., Can. | I11 | 104 |
| Handub, Sudan | H9 | 60 |
| *HaNegev (Negev Desert), reg., Isr.* | G3 | 50 |
| Haney, B.C., Can. | H12 | 102 |
| Hanford, Ca., U.S. | H6 | 124 |
| Han'gang, China | I2 | 32 |
| *Han-gang, stm., Asia* | F14 | 32 |
| Hangchow see Hangzhou, China | E9 | 34 |
| Hanggin Houqi, China | C8 | 30 |
| Hanggin Qi, China | D8 | 30 |
| Hangö (Hanko), Fin. | L18 | 6 |
| Hangu, China | D5 | 32 |
| Hangu, Pak. | D4 | 44 |
| Hangzhou (Hangchow), China | E9 | 34 |
| *Hangzhou Wan (Hangchow Bay), b., China* | E10 | 34 |
| Hani, Tur. | B6 | 48 |
| *Ḥanīsh, is., Yemen* | H3 | 47 |
| Ḥanita, Isr. | B4 | 50 |
| Hanjiang, China | J8 | 34 |
| Hankey, S. Afr. | I7 | 66 |
| Hankinson, N.D., U.S. | E11 | 118 |
| Hanko see Hangö, Fin. | D12 | 4 |
| Hankow see Wuhan, China | E3 | 34 |
| Hanley, Sk., Can. | G8 | 104 |
| Hanmer, On., Can. | D15 | 110 |
| Hanna, Ab., Can. | F23 | 102 |
| Hanna, Ok., U.S. | D11 | 116 |
| Hanna, Wy., U.S. | C10 | 120 |
| Hanna City, Il., U.S. | J6 | 110 |
| Hannaford, N.D., U.S. | D9 | 118 |
| Hannah, N.D., U.S. | C9 | 118 |
| *Hannah Bay, b., On., Can.* | F17 | 96 |
| Hannibal, Mo., U.S. | C5 | 114 |
| Hannover, Ger. | C9 | 10 |
| Ha Noi, Viet. | D8 | 40 |
| Hanover see Hannover, Ger. | C9 | 10 |
| Hanover, Il., U.S. | H5 | 110 |
| Hanover, In., U.S. | D11 | 114 |
| Hanover, Ks., U.S. | L11 | 118 |
| Hanover, N.H., U.S. | D14 | 108 |
| Hanover, N.M., U.S. | L8 | 120 |
| Hanover, On., Can. | F14 | 110 |
| Hanover, Pa., U.S. | H10 | 108 |
| Hanover, Va., U.S. | B9 | 112 |
| Hansard, B.C., Can. | C13 | 102 |
| Hānsi, India | F6 | 44 |
| Hanska, Mn., U.S. | G13 | 118 |
| *Hanson Lake, l., Sk., Can.* | D12 | 104 |
| Hant's Harbour, Nf., Can. | D20 | 106 |
| Hantsport, N.S., Can. | G9 | 106 |
| *Hantzsch, stm., N.T., Can.* | C18 | 96 |
| Hanumangarh, India | F6 | 44 |
| Hanušovice, Czech Rep. | E16 | 10 |
| Hanwood, Austl. | J7 | 70 |
| Hanzhong, China | E8 | 30 |
| Hanzhuang, China | I5 | 32 |
| Haohekou, China | G1 | 34 |
| Hāora, India | I13 | 44 |
| Hapeville, Ga., U.S. | F2 | 112 |
| Happy, Tx., U.S. | E5 | 116 |
| Happy Camp, Ca., U.S. | C2 | 124 |
| Happy Jack, Az., U.S. | J5 | 120 |
| Happy Valley-Goose Bay, Nf., Can. | F20 | 96 |
| Hāpur, India | F7 | 44 |
| Haquira, Peru | F5 | 82 |
| Haraḍ, Sau. Ar. | B6 | 47 |
| *Ḥaraḍ, Jabal al-, mtn., Jord.* | I5 | 50 |
| Haradok, Bela. | F12 | 22 |
| Haradzeja, Bela. | H9 | 22 |
| Haradzišča, Bela. | H9 | 22 |
| Harany, Bela. | F12 | 22 |
| Harare (Salisbury), Zimb. | A10 | 66 |
| *Ḥarash, Bi'r al-, well, Libya* | E2 | 60 |
| Harbavičy, Bela. | H13 | 22 |
| Harbin, China | B12 | 30 |
| Harbor, Or., U.S. | H1 | 122 |
| Harbor Beach, Mi., U.S. | G13 | 110 |
| Harbor Springs, Mi., U.S. | E11 | 110 |
| Harbour Breton, Nf., Can. | E18 | 106 |
| Harbour Buffett, Nf., Can. | E19 | 106 |
| Harbour Deep, Nf., Can. | B17 | 106 |
| Harbour Grace, Nf., Can. | E20 | 106 |
| Harbourville, N.S., Can. | G9 | 106 |
| *Harcuvar Mountains, mts., Az., U.S.* | K3 | 120 |
| Harda, India | I7 | 44 |
| *Hardangerfjorden, Nor.* | K10 | 6 |
| Hardeeville, S.C., U.S. | G5 | 112 |
| Harderwijk, Neth. | D8 | 12 |
| Hardesty, Ok., U.S. | C5 | 116 |
| Hardin, Il., U.S. | C6 | 114 |
| Hardin, Mt., U.S. | E18 | 122 |
| Harding, S. Afr. | H9 | 66 |
| *Harding Lake, l., Mb., Can.* | B16 | 104 |
| Hardinsburg, Ky., U.S. | E10 | 114 |
| Hardisty, Ab., Can. | E23 | 102 |
| *Hardisty Lake, l., N.T., Can.* | D9 | 96 |
| Hardoi, India | G9 | 44 |
| Hardtner, Ks., U.S. | N9 | 118 |
| Hardwick, Ga., U.S. | F3 | 112 |
| Hardwick, Vt., U.S. | C14 | 108 |
| Hardwood, La., U.S. | L5 | 114 |
| Hardy, Ar., U.S. | F5 | 114 |
| Hardy, Ne., U.S. | K10 | 118 |
| *Hardy Bay, b., N.T., Can.* | A9 | 96 |
| *Hare, Mount, mtn., Yk., Can.* | C26 | 100 |
| Hare Bay, Nf., Can. | D19 | 106 |
| *Hare Bay, b., Nf., Can.* | A18 | 106 |
| *Hare Indian, stm., N.T., Can.* | C31 | 100 |
| Harer, Eth. | G9 | 56 |
| Hareto, Eth. | M9 | 60 |
| Hargeysa, Som. | G9 | 56 |
| *Harghita, co., Rom.* | C9 | 20 |
| *Hargrave, stm., Mb., Can.* | D15 | 104 |
| *Hargrave Lake, l., Mb., Can.* | D15 | 104 |
| *Har Hu, l., China* | D6 | 30 |
| *Hari, stm., Indon.* | F3 | 38 |
| Haría, Spain | n27 | 17b |
| Haridwār, India | F8 | 44 |
| Harihar, India | E3 | 46 |
| *Haringvliet, strt., Neth.* | E5 | 12 |
| *Harīrūd (Tedžen), stm., Asia* | C16 | 48 |
| Harkers Island, N.C., U.S. | E10 | 112 |
| Harlan, Ia., U.S. | J12 | 118 |
| Harlan, Ky., U.S. | C3 | 112 |
| *Harlan County Lake, res., Ne., U.S.* | K8 | 118 |
| Harlem, Fl., U.S. | M6 | 112 |
| Harlem, Ga., U.S. | F4 | 112 |
| Harlem, Mt., U.S. | B17 | 122 |
| Harlingen, Neth. | B7 | 12 |
| Harlingen, Tx., U.S. | M9 | 116 |
| Harlowton, Mt., U.S. | D16 | 122 |
| Harman, W.V., U.S. | I7 | 108 |
| Harmanli, Bul. | H9 | 20 |
| Harmony, In., U.S. | C9 | 114 |
| Harmony, Mn., U.S. | G3 | 110 |
| *Harney Peak, mtn., S.D., U.S.* | H4 | 118 |
| Härnösand, Swe. | J15 | 6 |
| Haro, Spain | C9 | 16 |
| *Haro, Cabo, c., Mex.* | D4 | 90 |
| Harper, Ks., U.S. | N9 | 118 |
| Harper, Lib. | I6 | 64 |
| Harper, Tx., U.S. | I7 | 116 |
| Harqin Qi (Jinshan), China | B6 | 32 |
| Ḥarrān al-'Awāmīd, Syria | B7 | 50 |
| Harrell, Ar., U.S. | I4 | 114 |
| *Harricana, stm., Can.* | F17 | 96 |
| Harriman, Tn., U.S. | D2 | 112 |
| Harrington, De., U.S. | I11 | 108 |
| Harrington, Me., U.S. | C19 | 108 |
| Harrington, Wa., U.S. | C7 | 122 |
| Harris, Mn., U.S. | E3 | 110 |
| Harris, Sk., Can. | G7 | 104 |
| Harrisburg, Ar., U.S. | G6 | 114 |
| Harrisburg, Il., U.S. | E8 | 114 |
| Harrisburg, Ne., U.S. | J4 | 118 |
| Harrisburg, Or., U.S. | F2 | 122 |
| Harrisburg, Pa., U.S. | G10 | 108 |
| Harrismith, S. Afr. | G9 | 66 |
| Harrison, Ar., U.S. | F3 | 114 |
| Harrison, Id., U.S. | C9 | 122 |
| Harrison, Mi., U.S. | F11 | 110 |
| Harrison, Ne., U.S. | I4 | 118 |
| *Harrison, Cape, c., Nf., Can.* | F21 | 96 |
| Harrisonburg, La., U.S. | K5 | 114 |
| Harrisonburg, Va., U.S. | I8 | 108 |
| *Harrison Islands, is., N.T., Can.* | C14 | 96 |
| *Harrison Lake, l., B.C., Can.* | H13 | 102 |
| Harrisonville, Mo., U.S. | D2 | 114 |
| Harriston, Ms., U.S. | K5 | 114 |
| Harriston, On., Can. | G15 | 110 |
| Harrisville, Mi., U.S. | F12 | 110 |
| Harrisville, N.Y., U.S. | C11 | 108 |
| Harrisville, W.V., U.S. | H5 | 108 |
| Harrodsburg, Ky., U.S. | E12 | 114 |
| Harrogate, Eng., U.K. | G12 | 8 |
| Harrold, Tx., U.S. | E7 | 116 |
| *Harrop Lake, l., Mb., Can.* | F19 | 104 |
| Harrow, On., Can. | H13 | 110 |
| Harrowsmith, On., Can. | F19 | 110 |
| *Harry S. Truman Reservoir, res., Mo., U.S.* | D3 | 114 |
| Harsīn, Iran | D9 | 48 |
| Hart, Mi., U.S. | G9 | 110 |
| Hart, Tx., U.S. | E4 | 116 |
| *Hart, stm., Yk., Can.* | D26 | 100 |
| *Hart, Lake, l., Austl.* | H2 | 70 |
| Hartberg, Aus. | H15 | 10 |
| Hartford, Al., U.S. | K11 | 114 |
| Hartford, Ar., U.S. | G2 | 114 |
| Hartford, Ct., U.S. | F14 | 108 |
| Hartford, Ks., U.S. | M12 | 118 |
| Hartford, Ky., U.S. | E10 | 114 |
| Hartford, Mi., U.S. | H9 | 110 |
| Hartford, S.D., U.S. | H11 | 118 |
| Hartford, Wi., U.S. | G7 | 110 |
| Hartford City, In., U.S. | B11 | 114 |
| Hartington, Ne., U.S. | I10 | 118 |
| Hartland, Me., U.S. | C17 | 108 |
| Hartland, N.B., Can. | F6 | 106 |
| Hartlepool, Eng., U.K. | G12 | 8 |
| Hartley, Ia., U.S. | H12 | 118 |
| Hartley, Tx., U.S. | D4 | 116 |
| Hartley Bay, B.C., Can. | D5 | 102 |
| *Hart Mountain, mtn., Mb., Can.* | F13 | 104 |
| Hartney, Mb., Can. | I14 | 104 |
| *Harts, stm., S. Afr.* | G7 | 66 |
| Hartselle, Al., U.S. | H10 | 114 |
| Hartshorne, Ok., U.S. | E11 | 116 |
| Hartsville, S.C., U.S. | E6 | 112 |
| Hartsville, Tn., U.S. | F10 | 114 |
| Hartville, Mo., U.S. | E4 | 114 |
| Hartwell, Ga., U.S. | E4 | 112 |
| *Hartwell Lake, res., U.S.* | E4 | 112 |
| Harvard, Il., U.S. | H7 | 110 |
| Harvard, Ne., U.S. | K9 | 118 |
| Harvey, Il., U.S. | I8 | 110 |
| Harvey, N.B., Can. | G9 | 106 |
| Harvey, N.D., U.S. | D8 | 118 |
| Harwich, Eng., U.K. | J15 | 8 |
| *Haryāna, state, India* | F7 | 44 |
| *Harz, mts., Eur.* | D10 | 10 |
| *Ḥaṣā, Bi'r al-, well, Sudan* | J3 | 48 |
| Hasan Kīādeh, Iran | C10 | 48 |
| *Ḥāṣbānī, Nahr al-, stm., Asia* | B5 | 50 |
| Hasenkamp, Arg. | F9 | 80 |
| *Ḥashā', Jabal al-, mtn., Yemen* | H4 | 47 |
| Hāsilpur, Pak. | F5 | 44 |
| Haskell, Ok., U.S. | D11 | 116 |
| Haskell, Tx., U.S. | F7 | 116 |
| Haskovo, Bul. | H9 | 20 |
| *Hasperos Canyon, val., N.M., U.S.* | K11 | 120 |
| Hassan, India | F4 | 46 |
| Hasselt, Bel. | G7 | 12 |
| Hassi Bel Guebbour, Alg. | F14 | 62 |
| Hassi el Ghella, Alg. | J10 | 16 |
| Hassi Messaoud, Alg. | E13 | 62 |
| Hassi Zehana, Alg. | J11 | 16 |
| Hässleholm, Swe. | M13 | 6 |
| Hastings, Eng., U.K. | K14 | 8 |
| Hastings, Fl., U.S. | J5 | 112 |
| Hastings, Mi., U.S. | H10 | 110 |
| Hastings, Mn., U.S. | F3 | 110 |
| Hastings, Ne., U.S. | K9 | 118 |
| Hastings, N.Z. | C6 | 72 |
| Hastings, On., Can. | F18 | 110 |
| Hasty, Co., U.S. | M5 | 118 |
| Haswell, Co., U.S. | M4 | 118 |
| Hatay, Tur. | C4 | 48 |
| Hatch, N.M., U.S. | L9 | 120 |
| Hatch, Ut., U.S. | G4 | 120 |
| Hatchet Lake, N.S., Can. | H10 | 106 |
| *Hatchie, stm., U.S.* | G7 | 114 |
| Hatfield, Ar., U.S. | H2 | 114 |
| Hatfield, Ma., U.S. | E14 | 108 |
| Hāthras, India | G8 | 44 |
| Ha Tien, Viet. | I8 | 40 |
| Ha Tinh, Viet. | E8 | 40 |
| Hato Mayor [del Rey], Dom. Rep. | E10 | 94 |
| Hatteras, N.C., U.S. | D11 | 112 |
| *Hatteras, Cape, c., N.C., U.S.* | D11 | 112 |
| *Hatteras Island, i., N.C., U.S.* | D11 | 112 |
| Hattiesburg, Ms., U.S. | K7 | 114 |
| Hatton, Al., U.S. | H9 | 114 |
| Hatton, N.D., U.S. | D10 | 118 |
| Hatvan, Hung. | H19 | 10 |
| Hat Yai, Thai. | K6 | 40 |
| Haubstadt, In., U.S. | D9 | 114 |
| Hauge, Nor. | L10 | 6 |
| Haugesund, Nor. | L9 | 6 |
| Haugsdorf, Aus. | G16 | 10 |
| *Haultain, stm., Sk., Can.* | B8 | 104 |
| *Hauraki Gulf, b., N.Z.* | B5 | 72 |
| *Haut Atlas, mts., Mor.* | E7 | 62 |
| *Haute-Corse, dept., Fr.* | I24 | 15a |
| *Haute-Garonne, dept., Fr.* | I8 | 14 |
| *Haute-Loire, dept., Fr.* | G10 | 14 |
| *Haute-Marne, dept., Fr.* | D12 | 14 |
| Hauterive, P.Q., Can. | C5 | 106 |
| *Hautes-Alpes, dept., Fr.* | H13 | 14 |
| *Haute-Saône, dept., Fr.* | E13 | 14 |
| *Haute-Savoie, dept., Fr.* | F13 | 14 |
| *Hautes Fagnes, mts., Eur.* | E6 | 10 |
| *Hautes-Pyrénées, dept., Fr.* | I7 | 14 |
| *Haute-Vienne, dept., Fr.* | G8 | 14 |
| *Haut-Folin, mtn., Fr.* | E11 | 14 |
| Hautmont, Fr. | B10 | 14 |
| *Haut-Rhin, dept., Fr.* | E14 | 14 |
| Hauula, Hi., U.S. | p16 | 125a |
| Havana, Ar., U.S. | G3 | 114 |
| Havana see La Habana, Cuba | C3 | 94 |
| Havana, Fl., U.S. | I2 | 112 |
| Havana, Il., U.S. | B6 | 114 |
| Havana, N.D., U.S. | F10 | 118 |
| *Havasu, Lake, res., U.S.* | J2 | 120 |
| Havelock, N.C., U.S. | E10 | 112 |
| Havelock, On., Can. | F18 | 110 |
| Haven, Ks., U.S. | N10 | 118 |
| Haverhill, Ma., U.S. | E15 | 108 |
| Hāveri, India | E3 | 46 |
| Haviland, Ks., U.S. | N8 | 118 |
| Havířov, Czech Rep. | F18 | 10 |
| Havlíčkův Brod, Czech Rep. | F15 | 10 |
| Havre, Mt., U.S. | B16 | 122 |
| Havre-Aubert, P.Q., Can. | E12 | 106 |
| *Havre Aubert, Île du, i., P.Q., Can.* | E12 | 106 |
| *Havre aux Maisons, Île du, i., P.Q., Can.* | E12 | 106 |
| Havre de Grace, Md., U.S. | H10 | 108 |
| Havre North, Mt., U.S. | B16 | 122 |
| Havre-Saint-Pierre, P.Q., Can. | B10 | 106 |
| Havsa, Tur. | H10 | 20 |
| *Haw, stm., N.C., U.S.* | D7 | 112 |
| *Hawaii, state, U.S.* | q16 | 125a |
| *Hawaii, i., Hi., U.S.* | r18 | 125a |
| *Hawaiian Islands, is., Hi., U.S.* | q16 | 125a |
| *Hawaiian Ridge* | F22 | 126 |
| *Hawaii Volcanoes National Park, Hi., U.S.* | r18 | 125a |
| Hawarden, Ia., U.S. | I11 | 118 |
| Hawarden, Sk., Can. | G8 | 104 |
| *Hawea, Lake, l., N.Z.* | F2 | 72 |
| Hawera, N.Z. | C5 | 72 |
| Hawesville, Ky., U.S. | E10 | 114 |
| Hawi, Hi., U.S. | q18 | 125a |
| Hawick, Scot., U.K. | F11 | 8 |
| *Hawke, Cape, c., Austl.* | I10 | 70 |
| *Hawke Bay, b., N.Z.* | C6 | 72 |
| Hawker, Austl. | H3 | 70 |
| *Hawkes, Mount, mtn., Ant.* | D1 | 73 |
| Hawkesbury, On., Can. | B12 | 108 |
| *Hawkesbury Island, i., B.C., Can.* | D5 | 102 |
| Hawkins, Tx., U.S. | G11 | 116 |
| Hawkins, Wi., U.S. | E5 | 110 |
| Hawkinsville, Ga., U.S. | G3 | 112 |
| Hawk Junction, On., Can. | B11 | 110 |
| Hawk Lake, On., Can. | I21 | 104 |
| *Hawksbill, mtn., Va., U.S.* | I8 | 108 |
| *Hawks Nest Point, c., Bah.* | B7 | 94 |
| Hawley, Mn., U.S. | E11 | 118 |
| Hawley, Pa., U.S. | F11 | 108 |
| Hawthorne, Fl., U.S. | J4 | 112 |
| Hawthorne, Nv., U.S. | F7 | 124 |
| Ḥawwārah, Jord. | C5 | 50 |
| Hawza, W. Sah. | G5 | 62 |
| Haxtun, Co., U.S. | K5 | 118 |
| Hay, Austl. | J6 | 70 |
| *Hay, stm., Austl.* | D2 | 70 |
| *Hay, stm., Can.* | E9 | 96 |
| *Hay, stm., Wi., U.S.* | E4 | 110 |
| *Hay, Cape, c., N.T., Can.* | B10 | 96 |
| *Hay, Mount, mtn., N.A.* | G26 | 100 |
| Hayange, Fr. | C13 | 14 |
| Haybān, Sudan | L6 | 60 |
| Hayden, Az., U.S. | K6 | 120 |
| Hayden, Co., U.S. | D9 | 120 |
| Haydenville, Oh., U.S. | H4 | 108 |
| Hayes, La., U.S. | L4 | 114 |
| *Hayes, stm., Mb., Can.* | B22 | 104 |
| *Hayes, stm., N.T., Can.* | C14 | 96 |
| *Hayes, Mount, mtn., Ak., U.S.* | E21 | 100 |
| Hayes Center, Ne., U.S. | K6 | 118 |
| Hayesville, N.C., U.S. | D3 | 112 |
| Hayesville, Or., U.S. | F3 | 122 |
| Hayfield, Mn., U.S. | G3 | 110 |
| Hayfork, Ca., U.S. | D2 | 124 |
| Haykota, Erit. | J9 | 60 |
| Hay Lakes, Ab., Can. | D21 | 102 |
| Haymana, Tur. | B2 | 48 |
| Haynes, Ar., U.S. | H6 | 114 |
| Haynesville, La., U.S. | J3 | 114 |
| Hayneville, Al., U.S. | J10 | 114 |
| Hay River, N.T., Can. | D9 | 96 |
| Hays, Ab., Can. | G23 | 102 |
| Hays, Ks., U.S. | M8 | 118 |
| Hays, Mt., U.S. | C17 | 122 |
| Hay Springs, Ne., U.S. | I5 | 118 |
| *Haystack Mountain, mtn., Nv., U.S.* | C10 | 124 |
| Haysville, Ks., U.S. | N10 | 118 |
| Hayti, Mo., U.S. | F7 | 114 |
| Hayti, S.D., U.S. | G10 | 118 |
| Hayvoron, Ukr. | A13 | 20 |
| Hayward, Ca., U.S. | G3 | 124 |
| Hayward, Wi., U.S. | D4 | 110 |
| Haywood, Mb., Can. | I16 | 104 |
| Hazard, Ky., U.S. | B3 | 112 |
| Hazārībāg, India | I11 | 44 |
| Hazebrouck, Fr. | B9 | 14 |
| *Hazel, stm., Va., U.S.* | I9 | 108 |
| Hazel Green, Wi., U.S. | H5 | 110 |
| Hazelton, B.C., Can. | B7 | 102 |
| Hazelton, Id., U.S. | H11 | 122 |
| Hazelton, N.D., U.S. | E7 | 118 |
| *Hazelton Mountains, mts., B.C., Can.* | C6 | 102 |
| Hazelwood, N.C., U.S. | D3 | 112 |
| Hazen, Ar., U.S. | H5 | 114 |
| Hazen, N.D., U.S. | D6 | 118 |
| Hazlehurst, Ga., U.S. | H4 | 112 |
| Hazlehurst, Ms., U.S. | K6 | 114 |
| Hazlet, Sk., Can. | H6 | 104 |
| Hazleton, Ia., U.S. | H4 | 110 |
| Hazleton, Pa., U.S. | G11 | 108 |
| Ḥazor HaGelilit, Isr. | C5 | 50 |
| Head Bay d'Espoir, Nf., Can. | E18 | 106 |
| Headland, Al., U.S. | K11 | 114 |
| *Headley, Mount, mtn., Mt., U.S.* | C10 | 122 |
| Healdsburg, Ca., U.S. | F3 | 124 |
| Healdton, Ok., U.S. | E9 | 116 |
| Healesville, Austl. | K6 | 70 |
| Healy, Ak., U.S. | E20 | 100 |
| Healy, Ks., U.S. | M7 | 118 |
| Heany Junction, Zimb. | C9 | 66 |
| *Heard Island, i., Austl.* | N11 | 126 |
| Hearne, Tx., U.S. | I10 | 116 |
| Hearst, On., Can. | G16 | 96 |
| *Hearst Island, i., Ant.* | B12 | 73 |
| *Heart, stm., Ab., Can.* | A17 | 102 |
| *Heart, stm., N.D., U.S.* | E6 | 118 |
| *Heart Lake, l., Ab., Can.* | B23 | 102 |
| *Heart Lake Indian Reserve, Ab., Can.* | B23 | 102 |
| Heart's Content, Nf., Can. | E20 | 106 |
| *Heath, stm., S.A.* | E7 | 82 |
| *Heath, Pointe, c., P.Q., Can.* | C12 | 106 |
| Heathcote, Austl. | K6 | 70 |
| Heath Springs, S.C., U.S. | E6 | 112 |
| Heathsville, Va., U.S. | B10 | 112 |
| Heavener, Ok., U.S. | H2 | 114 |
| Hebbronville, Tx., U.S. | L8 | 116 |
| *Hebei (Hopeh), prov., China* | D10 | 30 |
| Heber, Az., U.S. | J6 | 120 |
| Heber, Ca., U.S. | L10 | 124 |
| Heber City, Ut., U.S. | D5 | 120 |
| Heber Springs, Ar., U.S. | G4 | 114 |
| Hebi, China | H2 | 32 |
| *Hebrides, is., Scot., U.K.* | D6 | 4 |
| Hebron, Il., U.S. | H7 | 110 |
| Hebron, In., U.S. | A9 | 114 |
| Hebron, Md., U.S. | I11 | 108 |
| Hebron, N.D., U.S. | E5 | 118 |
| Hebron, Ne., U.S. | K10 | 118 |
| Hebron, Nf., Can. | E20 | 96 |
| Hebron see Al-Khalīl, W.B. | E4 | 50 |
| Hebu, China | H4 | 34 |
| *Hecate Strait, strt., B.C., Can.* | D3 | 102 |
| Hecelchakán, Mex. | G14 | 90 |
| Hechi, China | B10 | 40 |
| Hechingen, Ger. | G8 | 10 |
| Hechuan, China | E8 | 30 |
| Hecla, Mb., Can. | G18 | 104 |
| Hecla, S.D., U.S. | F9 | 118 |
| *Hecla Island, i., Mb., Can.* | G18 | 104 |
| *Hecla Provincial Park, Mb., Can.* | G18 | 104 |
| Hectanooga, N.S., Can. | H7 | 106 |
| Hector, Mn., U.S. | G13 | 118 |
| Hédé, Fr. | D5 | 14 |
| *He Devil, mtn., Id., U.S.* | E9 | 122 |
| Hedian, China | C3 | 34 |
| Hedley, B.C., Can. | H14 | 102 |
| Hedley, Tx., U.S. | E6 | 116 |
| *Hedmark, co., Nor.* | K12 | 6 |
| Hedrick, Ia., U.S. | I3 | 110 |
| Heerenveen, Neth. | C8 | 12 |
| Heerlen, Neth. | G8 | 12 |
| Ḥefa (Haifa), Isr. | C4 | 50 |
| Hefei, China | D6 | 34 |
| Heflin, Al., U.S. | I11 | 114 |
| Hegang, China | B13 | 30 |
| Heho, Myan. | D4 | 40 |
| Heichengzi, China | A9 | 32 |
| Heide, Ger. | A9 | 10 |
| Heidelberg, Ger. | F8 | 10 |
| Heidelberg, Ms., U.S. | K8 | 114 |
| Heidelberg, S. Afr. | I4 | 66 |
| Heidelberg, S. Afr. | F9 | 66 |
| Heidenheim, Ger. | F10 | 10 |
| Heidenreichstein, Aus. | G15 | 10 |
| Heilbad Heiligenstadt, Ger. | D10 | 10 |
| Heilbron, S. Afr. | F8 | 66 |
| Heilbronn, Ger. | F9 | 10 |
| Heilin, China | H6 | 32 |
| *Heilong (Amur), stm., Asia* | A12 | 30 |
| *Heilongjiang (Heilungkiang), prov., China* | B12 | 30 |
| *Heimaey, i., Ice.* | C3 | 6a |
| Heirnkut, Myan. | H16 | 44 |
| Heishan, China | B10 | 32 |
| Heishantou, China | A13 | 32 |
| Heisler, Ab., Can. | E22 | 102 |
| Hejian, China | E4 | 32 |
| *Hekla, vol., Ice.* | C4 | 6a |
| Hekou, China | C7 | 40 |
| Hel, Pol. | A18 | 10 |
| *Helen, Mount, mtn., Austl.* | C4 | 70 |
| Helena, Ar., U.S. | H6 | 114 |
| Helena, Mt., U.S. | D13 | 122 |
| Helena, Ok., U.S. | C8 | 116 |
| Helensburgh, Scot., U.K. | E9 | 8 |
| Helenwood, Tn., U.S. | C2 | 112 |
| *Helgoland, i., Ger.* | A7 | 10 |
| *Helgoländer Bucht, b., Ger.* | A8 | 10 |
| Heliuji, China | B5 | 34 |
| Hellertown, Pa., U.S. | G11 | 108 |
| Hellín, Spain | G10 | 16 |
| *Hell Point, c., N.S., Can.* | H9 | 106 |
| *Hells Canyon, val., U.S.* | E9 | 122 |
| *Hells Gate, val., B.C., Can.* | H13 | 102 |
| Hell-Ville, Madag. | n23 | 67b |
| *Helmand, stm., Asia* | D1 | 44 |
| *Helmcken Falls, wtfl, B.C., Can.* | F14 | 102 |
| Helmond, Neth. | F8 | 12 |
| Helmstedt, Ger. | C11 | 10 |
| Helper, Ut., U.S. | E6 | 120 |
| Helsingborg, Swe. | M13 | 6 |
| Helsingfors see Helsinki, Fin. | K19 | 6 |
| Helsingør (Elsinore), Den. | M13 | 6 |
| Helsinki (Helsingfors), Fin. | K19 | 6 |
| *Helska, Mierzeja, spit, Pol.* | A18 | 10 |
| Helvecia, Arg. | F8 | 80 |
| Hemau, Ger. | F11 | 10 |
| Hemel Hempstead, Eng., U.K. | J13 | 8 |
| Hemet, Ca., U.S. | K9 | 124 |
| Hemford, N.S., Can. | H9 | 106 |
| Hemingford, Ne., U.S. | I4 | 118 |
| Hemingway, S.C., U.S. | F7 | 112 |
| Hemphill, Tx., U.S. | K3 | 114 |
| Hempstead, Tx., U.S. | I10 | 116 |
| Hemujing, China | F3 | 32 |
| *Henan (Honan), prov., China* | E9 | 30 |
| Henderson, Arg. | I8 | 80 |
| Henderson, Ky., U.S. | E9 | 114 |
| Henderson, Mn., U.S. | F2 | 110 |
| Henderson, N.C., U.S. | C8 | 112 |
| Henderson, Ne., U.S. | K10 | 118 |
| Henderson, Nv., U.S. | H11 | 124 |
| Henderson, Tn., U.S. | G8 | 114 |
| Henderson, Tx., U.S. | J2 | 114 |
| *Henderson Island, i., Pit.* | K27 | 126 |
| Hendersonville, N.C., U.S. | D4 | 112 |
| Hendersonville, Tn., U.S. | F10 | 114 |
| Hendījān, Iran | F10 | 48 |
| Hendricks, Mn., U.S. | G11 | 118 |
| Hendricks, W.V., U.S. | H7 | 108 |
| Henefer, Ut., U.S. | C5 | 120 |
| Hengdaohe, China | A11 | 32 |
| Hengelo, Neth. | D10 | 12 |
| Henggang, China | F4 | 34 |
| Hengshan, China | D8 | 30 |
| Hengshan, China | H1 | 34 |
| Hengshui, China | F3 | 32 |
| Hengxian, China | C10 | 40 |
| Hengyang, China | F9 | 30 |
| *Henlopen, Cape, c., De., U.S.* | I11 | 108 |
| Hennaya, Alg. | K10 | 16 |
| Hennebont, Fr. | E3 | 14 |
| Hennef, Ger. | E7 | 10 |
| Hennenman, S. Afr. | F8 | 66 |
| Hennepin, Il., U.S. | I6 | 110 |
| Hennessey, Ok., U.S. | C9 | 116 |
| Henniker, N.H., U.S. | D15 | 108 |
| Henning, Mn., U.S. | E12 | 118 |
| Henning, Tn., U.S. | G7 | 114 |
| *Henri, Cap, c., P.Q., Can.* | C9 | 106 |
| Henri-Chapelle (Hendrik-Kapelle), Bel. | G8 | 12 |
| Henrietta, N.C., U.S. | D5 | 112 |
| Henrietta, N.Y., U.S. | D9 | 108 |
| Henrietta, Tx., U.S. | F8 | 116 |
| *Henrietta Maria, Cape, c., On., Can.* | E16 | 96 |
| *Henri Pittier, Parque Nacional, Ven.* | B9 | 84 |
| Henry, Il., U.S. | I6 | 110 |
| Henry, S.D., U.S. | G10 | 118 |
| *Henry, Cape, c., Va., U.S.* | C10 | 112 |
| *Henry, Mount, mtn., Mt., U.S.* | B10 | 122 |
| Henryetta, Ok., U.S. | D11 | 116 |
| *Henry Kater, Cape, c., N.T., Can.* | C19 | 96 |
| *Henrys Fork, stm., U.S.* | C6 | 120 |
| Hensall, On., Can. | G14 | 110 |
| Hensley, Ar., U.S. | H4 | 114 |
| Hentiesbaai, Nmb. | D2 | 66 |
| Henty, Austl. | J7 | 70 |
| Henzada, Myan. | F3 | 40 |
| Hepburn, Sk., Can. | F8 | 104 |
| Hephzibah, Ga., U.S. | F4 | 112 |
| Heping, China | K3 | 34 |
| Heppenheim, Ger. | F8 | 10 |
| Heppner, Or., U.S. | E6 | 122 |
| Hepu (Lianzhou), China | D10 | 40 |
| Heqiao, China | D8 | 34 |
| Herāt, Afg. | D17 | 48 |
| *Hérault, dept., Fr.* | I10 | 14 |
| Herbert, Sk., Can. | H7 | 104 |
| *Herbert, stm., Austl.* | B6 | 70 |
| Herberton, Austl. | A6 | 70 |
| Herbignac, Fr. | E4 | 14 |
| Herb Lake, Mb., Can. | D15 | 104 |
| *Herblet Lake, l., Mb., Can.* | D15 | 104 |
| Herceg-Novi, Yugo. | G2 | 20 |
| Herculaneum, Mo., U.S. | D6 | 114 |
| Hércules, Mex. | C8 | 90 |
| Heredia, C.R. | G10 | 92 |
| *Heredia, prov., C.R.* | G10 | 92 |
| Hereford, Az., U.S. | M6 | 120 |
| Hereford, Tx., U.S. | E4 | 116 |
| *Hereford and Worcester, co., Eng., U.K.* | I11 | 8 |
| Herencia, Spain | F8 | 16 |
| Herentals, Bel. | F6 | 12 |
| Herford, Ger. | C8 | 10 |
| Hergla, Tun. | M5 | 18 |
| Herington, Ks., U.S. | M11 | 118 |
| Herisau, Switz. | D11 | 13 |
| Herkimer, N.Y., U.S. | D12 | 108 |
| Herleshausen, Ger. | D10 | 10 |
| Herlong, Ca., U.S. | D5 | 124 |
| Herman, Mn., U.S. | F11 | 118 |
| Herman, Ne., U.S. | J11 | 118 |
| Hermann, Mo., U.S. | D5 | 114 |
| Hermansville, Mi., U.S. | E8 | 110 |
| Hermanus, S. Afr. | J4 | 66 |
| Hermanville, Ms., U.S. | K6 | 114 |
| Hermiston, Or., U.S. | E6 | 122 |
| Hermitage, Ar., U.S. | I4 | 114 |
| Hermitage, Mo., U.S. | E3 | 114 |
| Hermitage, Nf., Can. | E18 | 106 |
| *Hermitage Bay, b., Nf., Can.* | E17 | 106 |
| Hermleigh, Tx., U.S. | G6 | 116 |
| *Hermon, Mount see Shaykh, Jabal ash-, mtn., Asia* | B5 | 50 |
| Hermosillo, Mex. | C4 | 90 |
| *Hermoso, Cerro, mtn., Ec.* | H3 | 84 |
| *Hernád, stm., Eur.* | G21 | 10 |
| Hernandarias, Para. | C11 | 80 |
| Hernando, Arg. | G7 | 80 |
| Hernando, Fl., U.S. | K4 | 112 |
| Hernando, Ms., U.S. | H7 | 114 |
| Herndon, Ks., U.S. | L7 | 118 |
| Herndon, Pa., U.S. | G10 | 108 |
| Heroica Zitácuaro, Mex. | H9 | 90 |
| *Heron Island, i., Austl.* | D9 | 70 |
| Heron Lake, Mn., U.S. | H12 | 118 |
| Herradura, Arg. | D9 | 80 |
| Herreid, S.D., U.S. | F7 | 118 |
| Herrera, Arg. | E7 | 80 |
| *Herrera, prov., Pan.* | I14 | 92 |
| *Herrick Creek, stm., B.C., Can.* | C13 | 102 |
| Herrin, Il., U.S. | E7 | 114 |
| Herring Cove, Ak., U.S. | I29 | 100 |
| Herring Cove, N.S., Can. | H10 | 106 |
| Herschel, Sk., Can. | G6 | 104 |
| *Herschel Island, i., Yk., Can.* | B25 | 100 |
| Herscher, Il., U.S. | I7 | 110 |
| Hershey, Ne., U.S. | J6 | 118 |
| Hershey, Pa., U.S. | G10 | 108 |
| Herstal, Bel. | G8 | 12 |
| Hertford, N.C., U.S. | C10 | 112 |
| *Hertfordshire, co., Eng., U.K.* | J13 | 8 |
| *Hervey Bay, b., Austl.* | E10 | 70 |
| Herzberg, Ger. | D13 | 10 |
| Herzberg [am Harz], Ger. | D10 | 10 |
| Herzliyya, Isr. | D3 | 50 |
| Hesdin, Fr. | B9 | 14 |
| Heshangqiao, China | A2 | 34 |
| Heshi, China | J7 | 34 |
| Heshuijian, China | E5 | 34 |
| Hesperia, Mi., U.S. | G9 | 110 |
| *Hesperus Mountain, mtn., Co., U.S.* | G8 | 120 |
| *Hess, stm., Yk., Can.* | E28 | 100 |
| *Hessen, state, Ger.* | E9 | 10 |
| Hesston, Ks., U.S. | M10 | 118 |
| Hetang, China | I8 | 34 |
| *Hetch Hetchy Aqueduct, Ca., U.S.* | G4 | 124 |
| Hetou, China | K2 | 34 |
| Hettinger, N.D., U.S. | E5 | 118 |
| Hettstedt, Ger. | D11 | 10 |
| Hetupu, China | E5 | 34 |
| Heuvelton, N.Y., U.S. | C11 | 108 |
| Heves, Hung. | H20 | 10 |
| *Heves, co., Hung.* | H20 | 10 |
| *Ḥevron, Naḥal, val., Asia* | F3 | 50 |

| Name | Map Ref. | Page |
|---|---|---|
| Hexi, China | K6 | 34 |
| Hexian, China | G9 | 30 |
| Heyang, China | H6 | 32 |
| Heyburn, Id., U.S. | H12 | 122 |
| Heywood, Austl. | L4 | 70 |
| Heyworth, Il., U.S. | B8 | 114 |
| Heze (Caozhou), China | H3 | 32 |
| Hezhen, China | F9 | 34 |
| Hialeah, Fl., U.S. | N6 | 112 |
| Hiawassee, Ga., U.S. | E3 | 112 |
| Hiawatha, Ks., U.S. | L12 | 118 |
| Hiawatha, Ut., U.S. | E5 | 120 |
| Hibbing, Mn., U.S. | C3 | 110 |
| *Hibbs, Point, c., Austl.* | N6 | 70 |
| *Hibernia Reef, rf., Austl.* | B4 | 68 |
| Hickman, Ky., U.S. | F7 | 114 |
| Hickman, Ne., U.S. | K11 | 118 |
| Hickman's Harbour, Nf., Can. | D20 | 106 |
| Hickory, Ms., U.S. | J7 | 114 |
| Hickory, N.C., U.S. | D5 | 112 |
| Hickory Flat, Ms., U.S. | H7 | 114 |
| *Hicks, Point, c., Austl.* | K8 | 70 |
| *Hickson Lake, l., Sk., Can.* | B10 | 104 |
| Hicksville, Oh., U.S. | F2 | 108 |
| Hico, Tx., U.S. | H8 | 116 |
| Hidalgo, Mex. | D10 | 90 |
| Hidalgo, Mex. | E9 | 90 |
| Hidalgo, Mex. | E10 | 90 |
| Hidalgo, Mex. | F8 | 90 |
| *Hidalgo, state, Mex.* | G10 | 90 |
| Hidalgo del Parral, Mex. | D7 | 90 |
| *Hida-sammyaku, mts., Japan* | K12 | 36 |
| Hidrolândia, Braz. | D4 | 79 |
| Hidrolina, Braz. | C4 | 79 |
| Hieflau, Aus. | H14 | 10 |
| Higashine, Japan | I15 | 36 |
| Higashiōsaka, Japan | M10 | 36 |
| Higbee, Mo., U.S. | C4 | 114 |
| Higgins, Tx., U.S. | C6 | 116 |
| Higginsville, Mo., U.S. | C3 | 114 |
| *High Bar Indian Reserve, B.C., Can.* | F13 | 102 |
| *High Hill, stm., Can.* | B4 | 104 |
| *High Hill, stm., Mb., Can.* | C20 | 104 |
| *High Hill Lake, l., Mb., Can.* | C19 | 104 |
| Highland, Ca., U.S. | J8 | 124 |
| Highland, Il., U.S. | D7 | 114 |
| Highland, In., U.S. | A9 | 114 |
| Highland, Ks., U.S. | L12 | 118 |
| *Highland, prov., Scot., U.K.* | D8 | 8 |
| Highland Home, Al., U.S. | K10 | 114 |
| Highland Park, Il., U.S. | H8 | 110 |
| Highland Park, Tx., U.S. | G10 | 116 |
| Highlands, N.C., U.S. | D3 | 112 |
| Highlands, N.J., U.S. | G13 | 108 |
| Highlands, Tx., U.S. | J11 | 116 |
| Highland Springs, Va., U.S. | B9 | 112 |
| Highmore, S.D., U.S. | G8 | 118 |
| High Point, N.C., U.S. | D6 | 112 |
| *High Point, mtn., N.J., U.S.* | F12 | 108 |
| High Prairie, Ab., Can. | B18 | 102 |
| High River, Ab., Can. | G21 | 102 |
| *Highrock Indian Reserve, Mb., Can.* | C14 | 104 |
| *Highrock Lake, l., Mb., Can.* | C14 | 104 |
| *Highrock Lake, l., Sk., Can.* | A9 | 104 |
| *High Rock Lake, res., N.C., U.S.* | D6 | 112 |
| High Springs, Fl., U.S. | J4 | 112 |
| Hightstown, N.J., U.S. | G12 | 108 |
| Highwood, Mt., U.S. | C15 | 122 |
| *Highwood, stm., Ab., Can.* | G20 | 102 |
| High Wycombe, Eng., U.K. | J13 | 8 |
| Higuera de Abuya, Mex. | E6 | 90 |
| Higuera de Zaragoza, Mex. | E5 | 90 |
| *Higüero, Punta, c., P.R.* | E11 | 94 |
| Higüey, Dom. Rep. | E10 | 94 |
| *Higuito, stm., Hond.* | C6 | 92 |
| *Hiiumaa, i., Est.* | C5 | 22 |
| Hikone, Japan | L11 | 36 |
| Hilbert, Wi., U.S. | F7 | 110 |
| Hilda, Ab., Can. | H4 | 104 |
| Hildburghausen, Ger. | E10 | 10 |
| Hildesheim, Ger. | C9 | 10 |
| Hildreth, Ne., U.S. | K8 | 118 |
| *Hillaby, Mount, mtn., Barb.* | H15 | 94 |
| Hill Bank, Belize | I15 | 90 |
| Hill City, Ks., U.S. | L8 | 118 |
| Hill City, Mn., U.S. | D2 | 110 |
| Hill City, S.D., U.S. | H4 | 118 |
| Hillcrest Center, Ca., U.S. | I7 | 124 |
| Hillcrest Mines, Ab., Can. | H20 | 102 |
| Hilli, Bngl. | H13 | 44 |
| Hilliard, Fl., U.S. | I5 | 112 |
| *Hill Island Lake, l., N.T., Can.* | D11 | 96 |
| Hillister, Tx., U.S. | L2 | 114 |
| Hillman, Mi., U.S. | E12 | 110 |
| Hills, Mn., U.S. | H11 | 118 |
| Hillsboro, Il., U.S. | C7 | 114 |
| Hillsboro, Ks., U.S. | M10 | 118 |
| Hillsboro, Mo., U.S. | D6 | 114 |
| Hillsboro, N.D., U.S. | D10 | 118 |
| Hillsboro, N.H., U.S. | D15 | 108 |
| Hillsboro, N.M., U.S. | L9 | 120 |
| Hillsboro, Oh., U.S. | H3 | 108 |
| Hillsboro, Or., U.S. | E3 | 122 |
| Hillsboro, Tx., U.S. | G9 | 116 |
| Hillsboro, Wi., U.S. | G5 | 110 |
| *Hillsboro Canal, Fl., U.S.* | M6 | 112 |
| Hillsborough, N.B., Can. | G9 | 106 |
| Hillsborough, N.C., U.S. | C7 | 112 |
| *Hillsborough, stm., Fl., U.S.* | K4 | 112 |
| *Hillsborough, Cape, c., Austl.* | C8 | 70 |
| *Hillsborough Bay, b., P.E., Can.* | F10 | 106 |
| Hillsdale, Mi., U.S. | I11 | 110 |
| *Hillsdale Lake, res., Ks., U.S.* | M13 | 118 |
| Hillston, Austl. | I6 | 70 |
| Hillsville, Va., U.S. | C6 | 112 |
| Hilo, Hi., U.S. | r18 | 125a |
| *Hilo Bay, b., Hi., U.S.* | r18 | 125a |
| Hilton, N.Y., U.S. | D9 | 108 |
| *Hilton Head Island, i., S.C., U.S.* | G6 | 112 |
| Hilversum, Neth. | D7 | 12 |
| Hima, Ky., U.S. | B3 | 112 |
| *Himāchal Pradesh, state, India* | E7 | 44 |
| *Himalayas, mts., Asia* | F11 | 44 |
| Himeji, Japan | M9 | 36 |
| Himi, Japan | K11 | 36 |
| Ḥimṣ (Homs), Syria | D4 | 48 |
| Hinche, Haiti | E8 | 94 |
| *Hinchinbrook Entrance, strt., Ak., U.S.* | F21 | 100 |
| *Hinchinbrook Island, i., Ak., U.S.* | F21 | 100 |
| *Hinchinbrook Island, i., Austl.* | B7 | 70 |
| Hinckley, Il., U.S. | I7 | 110 |
| Hinckley, Mn., U.S. | D3 | 110 |
| Hinckley, Ut., U.S. | E4 | 120 |
| Hindaun, India | G7 | 44 |
| Hindman, Ky., U.S. | B4 | 112 |
| *Hindmarsh, Lake, l., Austl.* | K4 | 70 |
| *Hinds Lake, l., Nf., Can.* | D17 | 106 |
| *Hindu Kush, mts., Asia* | B4 | 44 |
| Hindupur, India | F4 | 46 |
| Hines, Or., U.S. | G6 | 122 |
| Hines Creek, Ab., Can. | A16 | 102 |
| *Hines Creek, stm., Ab., Can.* | A16 | 102 |
| Hinesville, Ga., U.S. | H5 | 112 |
| Hinganghāt, India | B5 | 46 |
| Hingham, Ma., U.S. | E16 | 108 |
| *Hingol, stm., Pak.* | H1 | 44 |
| Hingoli, India | C4 | 46 |
| Hınıs, Tur. | B6 | 48 |
| *Hinnøya, i., Nor.* | G14 | 6 |
| Hinojosa del Duque, Spain | G6 | 16 |
| Hinsdale, Mt., U.S. | B18 | 122 |
| Hinsdale, N.H., U.S. | E14 | 108 |
| *Hinterrhein, stm., Switz.* | E11 | 13 |
| Hinton, Ab., Can. | D17 | 102 |
| Hinton, Ok., U.S. | D8 | 116 |
| Hinton, W.V., U.S. | B6 | 112 |
| Hipólito, Mex. | E9 | 90 |
| Hipólito Yrigoyen, Arg. | G5 | 80 |
| Hirado, Japan | N4 | 36 |
| *Hīrākud Reservoir, res., India* | B7 | 46 |
| Hiram, Me., U.S. | D16 | 108 |
| Hirata, Japan | L7 | 36 |
| Hiratsuka, Japan | L14 | 36 |
| Hirhafok, Alg. | I13 | 62 |
| Ḥirjillah, Syria | B6 | 50 |
| Hirosaki, Japan | G15 | 36 |
| Hiroshima, Japan | M7 | 36 |
| Hirson, Fr. | C11 | 14 |
| Hisār, India | F6 | 44 |
| Ḥisbān, Jord. | E5 | 50 |
| Ḥiṣn al-Qarn, Yemen | G6 | 47 |
| *Hispaniola, i., N.A.* | E9 | 94 |
| Hita, Japan | N5 | 36 |
| Hitachi, Japan | K15 | 36 |
| Hitchcock, Tx., U.S. | J11 | 116 |
| Hitchins, Ky., U.S. | I4 | 108 |
| Hitoyoshi, Japan | O5 | 36 |
| *Hitra, i., Nor.* | J11 | 6 |
| *Hiva Oa, i., Fr. Poly.* | I26 | 126 |
| Hiwannee, Ms., U.S. | K8 | 114 |
| *Hiwassee, stm., U.S.* | D2 | 112 |
| Hixon, B.C., Can. | D12 | 102 |
| Hixson, Tn., U.S. | G11 | 114 |
| *Hkakabo Razi, mtn., Myan.* | F6 | 30 |
| *Hkok (Kok), stm., Asia* | D5 | 40 |
| Hlatikulu, Swaz. | F10 | 66 |
| Hlegu, Myan. | F4 | 40 |
| Hlinsko, Czech Rep. | F15 | 10 |
| Hlobane, S. Afr. | F10 | 66 |
| Hlohovec, Slvk. | G17 | 10 |
| Hluboká nad Vltavou, Czech Rep. | F14 | 10 |
| Hlučín, Czech Rep. | F18 | 10 |
| Hluša, Bela. | H11 | 22 |
| Hlusk, Bela. | I11 | 22 |
| Hlyboka, Ukr. | A9 | 20 |
| Hlybokae, Bela. | F10 | 22 |
| Hmawbi, Myan. | F4 | 40 |
| Ho, Ghana | H10 | 64 |
| Hoa Binh, Viet. | D8 | 40 |
| *Hoare Bay, b., N.T., Can.* | C20 | 96 |
| *Hoback, stm., Wy., U.S.* | G15 | 122 |
| Hobart, Austl. | N7 | 70 |
| Hobart, Ok., U.S. | D7 | 116 |
| Hobbs, N.M., U.S. | G3 | 116 |
| Hobe Sound, Fl., U.S. | L6 | 112 |
| Hobgood, N.C., U.S. | C9 | 112 |
| Hobo, Col. | F5 | 84 |
| Hoboken, Bel. | F5 | 12 |
| Hobson, Mt., U.S. | C16 | 122 |
| *Hobson Lake, l., B.C., Can.* | E14 | 102 |
| Hobyo, Som. | G10 | 56 |
| *Hochalmspitze, mtn., Aus.* | H13 | 10 |
| Ho Chi Minh City see Thanh Pho Ho Chi Minh, Viet. | I9 | 40 |
| *Hochkönig, mtn., Aus.* | H13 | 10 |
| Höchstadt an der Aisch, Ger. | F10 | 10 |
| Hocimsk, Bela. | H15 | 22 |
| Hockenheim, Ger. | F8 | 10 |
| *Hocking, stm., Oh., U.S.* | H5 | 108 |
| Hodeida see Al-Ḥudaydah, Yemen | G3 | 47 |
| Hodge, La., U.S. | J4 | 114 |
| Hodgenville, Ky., U.S. | E11 | 114 |
| *Hodges Hill, hill, Nf., Can.* | C18 | 106 |
| Hodgeville, Sk., Can. | H8 | 104 |
| Hodgson, Mb., Can. | G17 | 104 |
| Hódmezővásárhely, Hung. | I20 | 10 |
| *Hodna, Chott el, l., Alg.* | C13 | 62 |
| Hodonín, Czech Rep. | G17 | 10 |
| Hoehne, Co., U.S. | N3 | 118 |
| Hoek van Holland, Neth. | E5 | 12 |
| Hoeryŏng, N. Kor. | A17 | 32 |
| Hoeyang, N. Kor. | E15 | 32 |
| Hof, Ger. | E11 | 10 |
| Hof, Ice. | B6 | 6a |
| Hoffman, Mn., U.S. | F12 | 118 |
| Hofmeyr, S. Afr. | H7 | 66 |
| Höfn, Ice. | B6 | 6a |
| Hofors, Swe. | K15 | 6 |
| Hōfu, Japan | M6 | 36 |
| Hofuf see Al-Hufūf, Sau. Ar. | I10 | 48 |
| Hogansville, Ga., U.S. | F2 | 112 |
| *Hoggar see Ahaggar, mts., Alg.* | I13 | 62 |
| Högsby, Swe. | M15 | 6 |
| *Hoh, stm., Wa., U.S.* | C1 | 122 |
| Hohenau, Para. | D11 | 80 |
| Hohenau an der March, Aus. | G16 | 10 |
| Hohenthurn, Aus. | I13 | 10 |
| Hohenwald, Tn., U.S. | G9 | 114 |
| *Hoher Dachstein, mtn., Aus.* | H13 | 10 |
| *Hohe Tauern, mts., Aus.* | H12 | 10 |
| Hohhot, China | C9 | 30 |
| Hohoe, Ghana | H10 | 64 |
| *Hoh Xil Shan, mts., China* | C13 | 44 |
| Hoi An, Viet. | G10 | 40 |
| Hoisington, Ks., U.S. | M9 | 118 |
| Hojāi, India | G15 | 44 |
| Hokah, Mn., U.S. | G4 | 110 |
| Hokes Bluff, Al., U.S. | I11 | 114 |
| Hokitika, N.Z. | E3 | 72 |
| *Hokkaidō, i., Japan* | d17 | 36a |
| Holberg, B.C., Can. | G6 | 102 |
| Holbrook, Austl. | J7 | 70 |
| Holbrook, Az., U.S. | J6 | 120 |
| Holbrook, Ne., U.S. | K7 | 118 |
| Holden, Ab., Can. | D22 | 102 |
| Holden, Mo., U.S. | D3 | 114 |
| Holden, Ut., U.S. | E4 | 120 |
| Holden, W.V., U.S. | J4 | 108 |
| Holdenville, Ok., U.S. | D10 | 116 |
| Holder, Fl., U.S. | K4 | 112 |
| Holdfast, Sk., Can. | H9 | 104 |
| Holdingford, Mn., U.S. | E1 | 110 |
| Holdrege, Ne., U.S. | K8 | 118 |
| *Hole in the Mountain Peak, mtn., Nv., U.S.* | D10 | 124 |
| Holgate, Oh., U.S. | F2 | 108 |
| Holguín, Cuba | D6 | 94 |
| Holíč, Slvk. | G17 | 10 |
| Hollabrunn, Aus. | G16 | 10 |
| Holladay, Ut., U.S. | D5 | 120 |
| Holland, Mb., Can. | I16 | 104 |
| Holland, Mi., U.S. | H9 | 110 |
| Holland, Tx., U.S. | I9 | 116 |
| *Holland see Netherlands, ctry., Eur.* | E9 | 4 |
| Hollandale, Ms., U.S. | I6 | 114 |
| *Hollandsbird Island, i., Nmb.* | E2 | 66 |
| *Hollandsch Diep, strt., Neth.* | E5 | 12 |
| Holley, N.Y., U.S. | D8 | 108 |
| Holliday, Tx., U.S. | F8 | 116 |
| Hollidaysburg, Pa., U.S. | G8 | 108 |
| Hollins, Va., U.S. | B7 | 112 |
| Hollis, Ok., U.S. | E7 | 116 |
| Hollister, Ca., U.S. | H4 | 124 |
| Hollow Rock, Tn., U.S. | F8 | 114 |
| Holly, Co., U.S. | M5 | 118 |
| Holly Grove, Ar., U.S. | H5 | 114 |
| Holly Hill, Fl., U.S. | J5 | 112 |
| Holly Hill, S.C., U.S. | F6 | 112 |
| Holly Springs, Ms., U.S. | H7 | 114 |
| Hollywood, Fl., U.S. | M6 | 112 |
| Holman, N.T., Can. | B9 | 96 |
| Holmen, Wi., U.S. | G4 | 110 |
| *Holmes, Mount, mtn., Wy., U.S.* | F15 | 122 |
| *Holmes Lake, l., Mb., Can.* | A18 | 104 |
| Holmestrand, Nor. | L12 | 6 |
| Holmia, Guy. | E13 | 84 |
| Holod, Rom. | C6 | 20 |
| *Holoit, Punta, c., Mex.* | G15 | 90 |
| Ḥolon, Isr. | D3 | 50 |
| Holoog, Nmb. | F3 | 66 |
| Holovanivs'k, Ukr. | A14 | 20 |
| Holstebro, Den. | M11 | 6 |
| Holstein, Ia., U.S. | I12 | 118 |
| *Holston, stm., Tn., U.S.* | C3 | 112 |
| *Holston High Knob, mtn., Tn., U.S.* | C4 | 112 |
| Holt, Al., U.S. | I9 | 114 |
| Holt, Fl., U.S. | L10 | 114 |
| Holt, Mi., U.S. | H11 | 110 |
| Holton, Ks., U.S. | L12 | 118 |
| Holts Summit, Mo., U.S. | D4 | 114 |
| Holtville, Ca., U.S. | L10 | 124 |
| Holy Cross, Ak., U.S. | E15 | 100 |
| *Holy Cross Mountain, mtn., B.C., Can.* | D14 | 102 |
| Holyoke, Co., U.S. | K5 | 118 |
| Holyoke, Ma., U.S. | E14 | 108 |
| Holyrood, Ks., U.S. | M9 | 118 |
| Holzkirchen, Ger. | H11 | 10 |
| Holzminden, Ger. | D9 | 10 |
| Homalin, Myan. | B3 | 40 |
| *Homathko, stm., B.C., Can.* | F10 | 102 |
| *Homathko Icefield, B.C., Can.* | F10 | 102 |
| Homberg, Ger. | D9 | 10 |
| *Hombori Tondo, mtn., Mali* | D9 | 64 |
| *Hombre Muerto, Salar del, pl., Arg.* | C5 | 80 |
| Homburg see Bad Homburg vor der Höhe, Ger. | E8 | 10 |
| Homburg, Ger. | F7 | 10 |
| *Home Bay, b., N.T., Can.* | C19 | 96 |
| Homedale, Id., U.S. | G9 | 122 |
| Home Hill, Austl. | B7 | 70 |
| Homel', Bela. | I14 | 22 |
| Homeland Park, S.C., U.S. | E4 | 112 |
| Homer, Ak., U.S. | G19 | 100 |
| Homer, Ga., U.S. | E3 | 112 |
| Homer, La., U.S. | J3 | 114 |
| Homer, Mi., U.S. | H11 | 110 |
| Homer, Ne., U.S. | I11 | 118 |
| Homer, N.Y., U.S. | E10 | 108 |
| Homer City, Pa., U.S. | G7 | 108 |
| Homerville, Ga., U.S. | H4 | 112 |
| Homestead, Fl., U.S. | N6 | 112 |
| Homewood, Al., U.S. | I10 | 114 |
| Hominy, Ok., U.S. | C10 | 116 |
| *Homochitto, stm., Ms., U.S.* | K5 | 114 |
| Homosassa, Fl., U.S. | K4 | 112 |
| Homs see Al-Khums, Libya | B3 | 56 |
| Homs see Ḥimṣ, Syria | D4 | 48 |
| Honaker, Va., U.S. | B5 | 112 |
| *Honan see Henan, prov., China* | E9 | 30 |
| Honaz, Tur. | L13 | 20 |
| Honda, Col. | E5 | 84 |
| *Honda, Bahía, b., Col.* | A7 | 84 |
| Hondeklipbaai, S. Afr. | H3 | 66 |
| Hondo, Ab., Can. | B20 | 102 |
| Hondo, N.M., U.S. | K11 | 120 |
| Hondo, Tx., U.S. | J7 | 116 |
| *Hondo, stm., N.A.* | H15 | 90 |
| *Hondo, Rio, stm., N.M., U.S.* | F2 | 116 |
| *Hondsrug, hills, Neth.* | C10 | 12 |
| *Honduras, ctry., N.A.* | B8 | 92 |
| *Honduras, Cabo de, c., Hond.* | A8 | 92 |
| *Honduras, Gulf of, b., N.A.* | E7 | 88 |
| *Honduras, Port, b., Belize* | A6 | 92 |
| Honea Path, S.C., U.S. | E4 | 112 |
| Hønefoss, Nor. | K12 | 6 |
| Honesdale, Pa., U.S. | F11 | 108 |
| Honey Grove, Tx., U.S. | F11 | 116 |
| *Honey Lake, l., Ca., U.S.* | D5 | 124 |
| Honeyville, Ut., U.S. | C4 | 120 |
| Honfleur, Fr. | C7 | 14 |
| *Hong see Red, stm., Asia* | C8 | 40 |
| Hon Gai, Viet. | D9 | 40 |
| Hong'an, China | D3 | 34 |
| Hongch'ŏn, S. Kor. | F15 | 32 |
| Hongcun, China | H5 | 34 |
| Honghu, China | F2 | 34 |
| Hongjiang, China | F8 | 30 |
| Hong Kong see Xianggang | G9 | 30 |
| Honglai, China | J7 | 34 |
| Hongliuyuan, China | C6 | 30 |
| Honglu, China | J8 | 34 |
| Hongmendu, China | A7 | 40 |
| Hong Ngu, Viet. | I8 | 40 |
| Hongshi, China | B7 | 32 |
| *Hongshui, stm., China* | C10 | 40 |
| Hongshuyangzi, China | C4 | 32 |
| Hongsŏng, S. Kor. | G14 | 32 |
| Hongtong, China | D9 | 30 |
| *Honguedo, Détroit d', strt., P.Q., Can.* | C10 | 106 |
| Hongwŏn, N. Kor. | C15 | 32 |
| Hongxingqiao, China | E8 | 34 |
| Hongyang, China | L5 | 34 |
| *Hongze Hu, l., China* | B7 | 34 |
| Honiara, Sol. Is. | I19 | 126 |
| Honokaa, Hi., U.S. | q18 | 125a |
| Honolulu, Hi., U.S. | p16 | 125a |
| Honomu, Hi., U.S. | r18 | 125a |
| Hon Quan, Viet. | I9 | 40 |
| *Honshū, i., Japan* | K13 | 36 |
| *Hood, stm., N.T., Can.* | C10 | 96 |
| *Hood, Mount, mtn., Or., U.S.* | E4 | 122 |
| *Hood Canal, b., Wa., U.S.* | C2 | 122 |
| *Hoodoo Peak, mtn., Wa., U.S.* | B5 | 122 |
| *Hood Point, c., Austl.* | F3 | 68 |
| Hood River, Or., U.S. | E4 | 122 |
| Hoodsport, Wa., U.S. | C2 | 122 |
| *Hoods Range, mts., Austl.* | G6 | 70 |
| Hooker, Ok., U.S. | C5 | 116 |
| Hookina, Austl. | H3 | 70 |
| *Hook Island, i., Austl.* | C8 | 70 |
| Hooks, Tx., U.S. | I2 | 114 |
| Hoolehua, Hi., U.S. | p16 | 125a |
| Hoonah, Ak., U.S. | G27 | 100 |
| Hoopa, Ca., U.S. | C2 | 124 |
| Hooper, Ne., U.S. | J11 | 118 |
| Hooper Bay, Ak., U.S. | F11 | 100 |
| Hoopeston, Il., U.S. | J8 | 110 |
| Hooping Harbour, Nf., Can. | B17 | 106 |
| Hoople, N.D., U.S. | C10 | 118 |
| Hoosick Falls, N.Y., U.S. | E13 | 108 |
| *Hoover Dam, U.S.* | H2 | 120 |
| Hooversville, Pa., U.S. | G8 | 108 |
| Hopatcong, N.J., U.S. | G12 | 108 |
| Hope, Ar., U.S. | I3 | 114 |
| Hope, B.C., Can. | H13 | 102 |
| Hope, In., U.S. | C11 | 114 |
| Hope, N.D., U.S. | D10 | 118 |
| *Hope, Point, c., Ak., U.S.* | B11 | 100 |
| Hopedale, Il., U.S. | B7 | 114 |
| Hopedale, La., U.S. | M7 | 114 |
| Hopedale, Nf., Can. | E20 | 96 |
| Hopefield, S. Afr. | I4 | 66 |
| *Hope Island, i., B.C., Can.* | G7 | 102 |
| Hopelchén, Mex. | H15 | 90 |
| Hope Mills, N.C., U.S. | E8 | 112 |
| *Hopes Advance, Cap, c., P.Q., Can.* | D19 | 96 |
| Hopetoun, Austl. | F4 | 68 |
| Hopetoun, Austl. | J5 | 70 |
| Hopetown, S. Afr. | G7 | 66 |
| Hope Valley, R.I., U.S. | F15 | 108 |
| Hopewell, Va., U.S. | B9 | 112 |
| *Hopewell Islands, is., N.T., Can.* | E17 | 96 |
| Hopkins, Mi., U.S. | H10 | 110 |
| Hopkins, Mo., U.S. | B2 | 114 |
| Hopkinsville, Ky., U.S. | F9 | 114 |
| Hopkinton, Ia., U.S. | H4 | 110 |
| Hopland, Ca., U.S. | F2 | 124 |
| Hopólito Bouchard, Arg. | H7 | 80 |
| *Hopwood, Mount, mtn., Austl.* | C6 | 70 |
| Hoquiam, Wa., U.S. | D2 | 122 |
| Horancia, Eth. | N10 | 60 |
| Horatio, Ar., U.S. | I2 | 114 |
| Horconcitos, Pan. | I12 | 92 |
| *Hordaland, co., Nor.* | K10 | 6 |
| Horezu, Rom. | D7 | 20 |
| Horgen, Switz. | D10 | 13 |
| Horicon, Wi., U.S. | G7 | 110 |
| Horizontina, Braz. | D11 | 80 |
| Horki, Bela. | G13 | 22 |
| *Horlick Mountains, mts., Ant.* | D10 | 73 |
| Horlivka, Ukr. | H5 | 26 |
| *Hormuz, Strait of, strt., Asia* | H14 | 48 |
| Horn, Aus. | G15 | 10 |
| *Horn, c., Ice.* | A2 | 6a |
| *Horn, stm., N.T., Can.* | D9 | 96 |
| *Horn, Cape see Hornos, Cabo de, c., Chile* | H3 | 78 |
| *Hornaday, stm., N.T., Can.* | B33 | 100 |
| Hornbeak, Tn., U.S. | F7 | 114 |
| Hornbeck, La., U.S. | K3 | 114 |
| Hornbrook, Ca., U.S. | C3 | 124 |
| *Hornby Bay, b., N.T., Can.* | C9 | 96 |
| Hornell, N.Y., U.S. | E9 | 108 |
| Hornepayne, On., Can. | G16 | 96 |
| *Horn Island, i., Ms., U.S.* | L8 | 114 |
| *Hornito, Cerro, mtn., Pan.* | I12 | 92 |
| Horn Lake, Ms., U.S. | H6 | 114 |
| *Hornos, Cabo de (Cape Horn), c., Chile* | H3 | 78 |
| *Horn Plateau, plat., N.T., Can.* | D9 | 96 |
| Horodenka, Ukr. | A9 | 20 |
| Horodkivka, Ukr. | A12 | 20 |
| Horodne, Ukr. | D12 | 20 |
| Horqin Youyi Qianqi, China | B11 | 30 |
| Horqueta, Para. | B10 | 80 |
| *Horse, stm., Ab., Can.* | B3 | 104 |
| Horse Cave, Ky., U.S. | E11 | 114 |
| Horse Creek, Wy., U.S. | C11 | 120 |
| Horsefly, B.C., Can. | E13 | 102 |
| *Horsefly Lake, l., B.C., Can.* | E14 | 102 |
| Horseheads, N.Y., U.S. | E10 | 108 |
| *Horse Islands, is., Nf., Can.* | B18 | 106 |
| Horsens, Den. | N11 | 6 |
| Horseshoe Bend, Ar., U.S. | F5 | 114 |
| Horseshoe Bend, Id., U.S. | G9 | 122 |
| *Horseshoe Lake, l., Mb., Can.* | F19 | 104 |
| *Horse Shoe Reef, rf., Br. Vir. Is.* | E12 | 94 |
| Horsham, Austl. | K5 | 70 |
| Horsham, Eng., U.K. | J13 | 8 |
| Horst, Neth. | F9 | 12 |
| Horton, Ks., U.S. | L12 | 118 |
| *Horton, stm., N.T., Can.* | B31 | 100 |
| *Horton Lake, l., N.T., Can.* | C33 | 100 |
| Hortonville, Wi., U.S. | E7 | 110 |
| Hosaina, Eth. | N9 | 60 |
| *Hoséré Vokré, mtn., Cam.* | G9 | 54 |
| Hosford, Fl., U.S. | I2 | 112 |
| Hoshangābād, India | I7 | 44 |
| Hoshiārpur, India | E6 | 44 |
| Hosmer, B.C., Can. | H20 | 102 |
| Hosmer, S.D., U.S. | F8 | 118 |
| Hospers, Ia., U.S. | H12 | 118 |
| Hospet, India | E4 | 46 |
| Hossegor, Fr. | I5 | 14 |
| Hosston, La., U.S. | J3 | 114 |
| *Hosta Butte, mtn., N.M., U.S.* | I8 | 120 |
| *Hoste, Isla, i., Chile* | H3 | 78 |
| Hot, Thai. | E5 | 40 |
| Hotan, China | D2 | 30 |
| *Hotan, stm., China* | D3 | 30 |
| Hotazel, S. Afr. | F6 | 66 |
| Hotchkiss, Co., U.S. | F9 | 120 |
| Hotevilla, Az., U.S. | I6 | 120 |
| *Hotham Inlet, b., Ak., U.S.* | C14 | 100 |
| Hot Springs, Mt., U.S. | C11 | 122 |
| Hot Springs, N.C., U.S. | D4 | 112 |
| Hot Springs see Truth or Consequences, N.M., U.S. | K9 | 120 |
| Hot Springs, S.D., U.S. | H4 | 118 |
| Hot Springs, Va., U.S. | B7 | 112 |
| Hot Springs National Park, Ar., U.S. | H3 | 114 |
| Hot Sulphur Springs, Co., U.S. | D10 | 120 |
| *Hottah Lake, l., N.T., Can.* | C9 | 96 |
| *Hottentotbaai, b., Nmb.* | F2 | 66 |
| Houbao, China | B13 | 32 |
| Houdan, Fr. | D8 | 14 |
| Houghton, Mi., U.S. | C7 | 110 |
| Houghton, N.Y., U.S. | E8 | 108 |
| Houghton Lake, Mi., U.S. | F11 | 110 |
| *Houghton Lake, l., Mi., U.S.* | F11 | 110 |
| *Houghton Lake, l., Sk., Can.* | F9 | 104 |
| Houjie, China | M2 | 34 |
| Houlka, Ms., U.S. | H7 | 114 |
| Houlton, Me., U.S. | A19 | 108 |
| Houma, China | D9 | 30 |
| Houma, La., U.S. | M6 | 114 |
| Houndé, Burkina | F8 | 64 |
| Housatonic, Ma., U.S. | E13 | 108 |
| House, N.M., U.S. | E3 | 116 |
| *House, stm., Ab., Can.* | C2 | 104 |
| Houston, B.C., Can. | C8 | 102 |
| Houston, Mn., U.S. | G4 | 110 |
| Houston, Mo., U.S. | E5 | 114 |
| Houston, Ms., U.S. | I8 | 114 |
| Houston, Tx., U.S. | J11 | 116 |
| *Houston, stm., La., U.S.* | L3 | 114 |
| *Houston, Lake, res., Tx., U.S.* | J11 | 116 |
| *Houtman Abrolhos, is., Austl.* | E2 | 68 |
| Houtzdale, Pa., U.S. | G8 | 108 |
| Houxijie, China | G7 | 34 |
| Houxinqiu, China | A10 | 32 |
| Hoven, S.D., U.S. | F8 | 118 |
| *Howar, Wādī (Ouadi Howa), val., Afr.* | I3 | 60 |
| Howard, Austl. | E10 | 70 |
| Howard, Ks., U.S. | N11 | 118 |
| Howard, Pa., U.S. | F9 | 108 |
| Howard, S.D., U.S. | G10 | 118 |
| Howard, Wi., U.S. | F7 | 110 |
| Howard City, Mi., U.S. | G10 | 110 |
| Howard Lake, Mn., U.S. | E1 | 110 |
| Howe, In., U.S. | A11 | 114 |
| Howe, Tx., U.S. | F10 | 116 |
| *Howe, Cape, c., Austl.* | K8 | 70 |
| Howeke, Lib. | I6 | 64 |
| Howell, Mi., U.S. | H12 | 110 |
| Howells, Ne., U.S. | J10 | 118 |
| *Howe Sound, strt., B.C., Can.* | H11 | 102 |
| Howick, S. Afr. | G10 | 66 |
| *Howitt, Mount, mtn., Austl.* | K7 | 70 |
| Howland, Me., U.S. | B18 | 108 |
| *Howland Island, i., Oc.* | H22 | 126 |
| Howley, Nf., Can. | C16 | 106 |
| *Howley, Mount, mtn., Nf., Can.* | D15 | 106 |
| *Howse Peak, mtn., Can.* | F18 | 102 |
| Howser, B.C., Can. | G18 | 102 |
| *Howson Peak, mtn., B.C., Can.* | C7 | 102 |
| Hoxie, Ar., U.S. | F6 | 114 |
| Hoxie, Ks., U.S. | L7 | 118 |
| Höxter, Ger. | D9 | 10 |
| Høyanger, Nor. | K10 | 6 |
| Hoyerswerda, Ger. | D14 | 10 |
| Hoyleton, Il., U.S. | D7 | 114 |
| Hoyt Lakes, Mn., U.S. | C3 | 110 |
| Hradec Králové, Czech Rep. | E15 | 10 |
| Hrandzičy, Bela. | H6 | 22 |
| Hranice, Czech Rep. | F17 | 10 |
| Hrodna, Bela. | H6 | 22 |
| *Hron, stm., Slvk.* | G18 | 10 |
| Hronov, Czech Rep. | E16 | 10 |
| Hrubieszów, Pol. | E23 | 10 |
| Hrynyavka, Ukr. | B8 | 20 |
| Hsihu, Tai. | L9 | 34 |
| Hsilo, Tai. | L9 | 34 |
| Hsinchu, Tai. | K9 | 34 |
| Hsinchuang, Tai. | J10 | 34 |
| Hsinhua, Tai. | L9 | 34 |
| Hsintien, Tai. | K10 | 34 |
| Hsipaw, Myan. | C4 | 40 |
| Hsüehchia, Tai. | L9 | 34 |
| Hua'an, China | J6 | 34 |
| Huacaña, Peru | F4 | 82 |
| Huacaraje, Bol. | E10 | 82 |
| Huachacalla, Bol. | H7 | 82 |
| Huacheng, China | K4 | 34 |
| *Huachi, Laguna, l., Bol.* | F10 | 82 |
| Huacho, Peru | D3 | 82 |
| Huachón, Peru | D4 | 82 |
| Huachos, Peru | E4 | 82 |
| Huachuca City, Az., U.S. | M6 | 120 |
| Huaco, Arg. | F4 | 80 |
| Huacrachuco, Peru | C3 | 82 |
| Huadian, China | C12 | 30 |
| Hua Hin, Thai. | H5 | 40 |
| *Huai, stm., China* | C6 | 34 |
| Huai'an, China | B8 | 34 |
| Huaibin, China | C4 | 34 |
| Huaide, China | C11 | 30 |
| Huailai, China | C3 | 32 |
| Huaillati, Peru | F5 | 82 |
| Huainan, China | C6 | 34 |
| Huaining, China | E5 | 34 |
| *Huaitunas, Lagunas, l., Bol.* | E8 | 82 |
| Huaiyang, China | B3 | 34 |
| Huaiyuan, China | C6 | 34 |
| Huajuapan de León, Mex. | I11 | 90 |
| Huakou, China | J6 | 34 |
| Hualahuises, Mex. | E10 | 90 |
| *Hualalai, vol., Hi., U.S.* | r18 | 125a |
| Hualañé, Chile | H3 | 80 |
| *Hualapai Peak, mtn., Az., U.S.* | I3 | 120 |
| Hualfín, Arg. | D5 | 80 |
| Hualgayoc, Peru | B2 | 82 |
| Hualien, Tai. | L10 | 34 |
| *Huallaga, stm., Peru* | A4 | 82 |
| Huallanca, Peru | C3 | 82 |
| Huallanca, Peru | C3 | 82 |
| *Huallayabamba, stm., Peru* | B3 | 82 |
| Huamanquiquia, Peru | E4 | 82 |
| Huambo (Nova Lisboa), Ang. | D3 | 58 |
| Huambos, Peru | B2 | 82 |
| Huancabamba, Peru | D4 | 82 |
| Huancabamba, Peru | A2 | 82 |
| Huancané, Peru | F7 | 82 |
| Huancapi, Peru | E4 | 82 |
| Huancarama, Peru | E5 | 82 |
| Huancarqui, Peru | G5 | 82 |
| Huancavelica, Peru | E4 | 82 |
| *Huancavelica, dept., Peru* | E4 | 82 |
| Huancaybamba, Peru | C3 | 82 |
| Huancayo, Peru | E4 | 82 |
| Huanchaca, Bol. | I8 | 82 |
| *Huanchaca, Serranía de, mts., S.A.* | F11 | 82 |
| Huando, Peru | E4 | 82 |
| *Huang, stm., Asia* | F6 | 40 |
| *Huang (Yellow), stm., China* | D10 | 30 |
| Huang'an, China | H3 | 32 |
| Huangbai, China | B14 | 32 |
| Huangchuan, China | C4 | 34 |
| Huangdu, China | D10 | 34 |
| Huanggang, China | E3 | 34 |
| Huangguoshu, China | A8 | 40 |
| Huanghua, China | E5 | 32 |
| Huangkeng, China | H6 | 34 |
| Huangling, China | D8 | 30 |
| Huangmao, China | G3 | 34 |
| Huangnihe, China | D6 | 34 |
| Huangqi, China | I8 | 34 |
| Huangqiao, China | C9 | 34 |
| Huangshapu, China | J1 | 34 |
| Huangshatuo, China | B10 | 32 |
| Huangshi, China | E4 | 34 |
| Huangshiguan, China | I4 | 34 |
| Huangtankou, China | G7 | 34 |
| Huangtianfan, China | F9 | 34 |
| Huangtugang, China | D4 | 34 |
| Huanguelén, Arg. | I8 | 80 |
| Huangyan, China | G10 | 34 |
| Huangyuan, China | D7 | 30 |
| Huangzhuang, China | A1 | 34 |
| Huanjiang, China | B10 | 40 |
| Huanta, Peru | E4 | 82 |
| Huántar, Peru | C3 | 82 |
| Huánuco, Peru | C3 | 82 |
| *Huánuco, dept., Peru* | C4 | 82 |
| Huanuni, Bol. | H8 | 82 |
| Huanxi, China | I2 | 34 |
| *Huanzo, Cordillera de, mts., Peru* | F5 | 82 |
| *Huapí, Serranías, mts., Nic.* | E10 | 92 |
| Huara, Chile | H7 | 82 |
| Huaral, Peru | D3 | 82 |
| Huaráz, Peru | C3 | 82 |
| Huari, Peru | C3 | 82 |
| Huariaca, Peru | D3 | 82 |
| Huaribamba, Peru | E4 | 82 |
| Huarina, Bol. | G7 | 82 |
| Huarmey, Peru | D2 | 82 |
| Huarochirí, Peru | E3 | 82 |
| Huarocondo, Peru | E5 | 82 |
| *Huasaga, stm., S.A.* | I4 | 84 |
| *Huascarán, Nevado, mtn., Peru* | C3 | 82 |
| Huasco, Chile | E3 | 80 |
| *Huasco, stm., Chile* | E3 | 80 |
| Huashan, China | I4 | 32 |
| Huashi, China | D9 | 34 |
| Huatabampo, Mex. | D5 | 90 |
| Huatong, China | C9 | 32 |
| Huauchinango, Mex. | G10 | 90 |
| Huaura, Peru | D3 | 82 |
| *Huaura, stm., Peru* | D3 | 82 |
| Huautla, Mex. | H11 | 90 |
| Huaxian, China | L2 | 34 |
| Huayllay, Peru | D3 | 82 |
| *Huayna Potosí, Nevado, mtn., Bol.* | G7 | 82 |
| Huaytará, Peru | E4 | 82 |
| Huayuanzui, China | B7 | 34 |
| *Huayunca, Nevado, mtn., Peru* | F5 | 82 |
| *Huayuri, Pampa de, pl., Peru* | F4 | 82 |
| Huazhou, China | D11 | 40 |
| Hubbard, Ia., U.S. | H2 | 110 |
| Hubbard, Tx., U.S. | H10 | 116 |
| *Hubbard Creek Reservoir, res., Tx., U.S.* | G7 | 116 |
| *Hubbard Lake, l., Mi., U.S.* | F12 | 110 |
| Hubbards, N.S., Can. | H9 | 106 |
| Hubbell, Mi., U.S. | C7 | 110 |
| *Hubei (Hupeh), prov., China* | E9 | 30 |
| Huberdeau, P.Q., Can. | B12 | 108 |
| Hubli-Dhārwār, India | E3 | 46 |
| Huch'ang, N. Kor. | B15 | 32 |
| Huchi, China | D6 | 34 |
| Huddersfield, Eng., U.K. | H12 | 8 |
| Hūdī, Sudan | I8 | 60 |
| Hudiksvall, Swe. | K15 | 6 |
| Hudson, Ia., U.S. | H3 | 110 |
| Hudson, Ma., U.S. | E15 | 108 |
| Hudson, Mi., U.S. | I11 | 110 |
| Hudson, N.C., U.S. | D5 | 112 |
| Hudson, N.H., U.S. | E15 | 108 |
| Hudson, N.Y., U.S. | E13 | 108 |
| Hudson, Oh., U.S. | F5 | 108 |
| Hudson, S.D., U.S. | H11 | 118 |
| Hudson, Wi., U.S. | F3 | 110 |
| Hudson, Wy., U.S. | B8 | 120 |
| *Hudson, stm., U.S.* | F12 | 108 |
| *Hudson, Lake, res., Ok., U.S.* | C11 | 116 |
| Hudson Bay, Sk., Can. | F12 | 104 |
| *Hudson Bay, b., Can.* | D15 | 96 |
| Hudson-Bayonet Point, Fl., U.S. | K4 | 112 |
| Hudson Falls, N.Y., U.S. | D13 | 108 |
| Hudson Hope, B.C., Can. | A13 | 102 |
| *Hudson Strait, strt., Can.* | D18 | 96 |
| Hudsonville, Mi., U.S. | H10 | 110 |
| *Hudwin Lake, l., Mb., Can.* | E19 | 104 |
| Hue, Viet. | F9 | 40 |
| Huehuetán, Mex. | B2 | 92 |
| Huehuetenango, Guat. | B3 | 92 |
| *Huehuetenango, dept., Guat.* | B3 | 92 |
| Huejutla de Reyes, Mex. | G10 | 90 |
| Huelgoat, Fr. | D3 | 14 |
| Huelva, Spain | H5 | 16 |
| *Huenque, stm., Peru* | G7 | 82 |
| Huentelauquén, Chile | F3 | 80 |
| Huércal-Overa, Spain | H10 | 16 |
| *Huerfano, stm., Co., U.S.* | M3 | 118 |
| *Huerfano Mountain, mtn., N.M., U.S.* | H9 | 120 |
| *Huerva, stm., Spain* | D10 | 16 |
| Huesca, Spain | C11 | 16 |
| Huéscar, Spain | H9 | 16 |
| Huetamo de Núñez, Mex. | H9 | 90 |
| Hueytown, Al., U.S. | I10 | 114 |
| *Huggins, Mount, mtn., Ant.* | C8 | 73 |
| *Hugh Butler Lake, res., Ne., U.S.* | K7 | 118 |
| Hughenden, Austl. | C6 | 70 |
| Hughes, Ak., U.S. | C17 | 100 |
| Hughes, Ar., U.S. | H6 | 114 |
| *Hughes, stm., Mb., Can.* | B14 | 104 |
| Hughes Springs, Tx., U.S. | I2 | 114 |
| Hughesville, Pa., U.S. | F10 | 108 |
| *Hugh Keenleyside Dam, B.C., Can.* | H17 | 102 |
| Hughson, Ca., U.S. | G5 | 124 |
| Hugh Town, Eng., U.K. | L7 | 8 |
| *Hugli, stm., India* | J12 | 44 |
| Hugo, Co., U.S. | L4 | 118 |
| Hugo, Ok., U.S. | E11 | 116 |
| Hugoton, Ks., U.S. | N6 | 118 |
| Hugou, China | B6 | 34 |
| Huichang, China | J4 | 34 |
| Huichapan, Mex. | G10 | 90 |
| Hŭich'ŏn, N. Kor. | C14 | 32 |
| Huicungo, Peru | B3 | 82 |
| Huidong, China | A7 | 40 |
| *Huila, dept., Col.* | F5 | 84 |
| *Huila, Nevado del, mtn., Col.* | F4 | 84 |
| Huili, China | A7 | 40 |
| Huillapima, Arg. | E6 | 80 |
| Huilong, China | K2 | 34 |
| Huimin, China | F5 | 32 |
| Huinan (Chaoyang), China | A14 | 32 |
| *Huínaymarca, Lago, l., S.A.* | G7 | 82 |
| Huinca Renancó, Arg. | H6 | 80 |
| Huisduinen, Neth. | C6 | 12 |
| Huiting, China | I4 | 32 |
| Huitzo, Mex. | I11 | 90 |
| Huitzuco de los Figueroa, Mex. | H10 | 90 |
| Huixtla, Mex. | J13 | 90 |
| Huiyang, China | A5 | 38 |
| Huize, China | A7 | 40 |
| Huizen, Neth. | D7 | 12 |
| Huizhou, China | L3 | 34 |
| Hukeng, China | H3 | 34 |
| Ḥukūmah, Sudan | K9 | 60 |
| Hukuntsi, Bots. | E5 | 66 |
| Hulan, China | B12 | 30 |
| Hulan Ergi, China | B11 | 30 |
| Hulbert, Mi., U.S. | D10 | 110 |
| Hulbert, Ok., U.S. | G1 | 114 |
| Hulett, Wy., U.S. | G3 | 118 |
| Hulin, China | B13 | 30 |
| Hull see Kingston upon Hull, Eng., U.K. | H13 | 8 |
| Hull, Ia., U.S. | H11 | 118 |
| Hull, Il., U.S. | C5 | 114 |
| Hull, P.Q., Can. | B11 | 108 |
| Hull, Tx., U.S. | I12 | 116 |
| *Hulun Nur, l., China* | B10 | 30 |
| Ḥulwān, Egypt | C6 | 60 |
| Huma, China | A12 | 30 |
| *Huma, stm., China* | A11 | 30 |
| Humacao, P.R. | E12 | 94 |
| Humahuaca, Arg. | B6 | 80 |
| Humaitá, Braz. | B10 | 82 |
| Humaitá, Para. | D9 | 80 |
| *Humaitá, stm., Braz.* | C5 | 82 |
| Humansdorp, S. Afr. | J7 | 66 |
| Humansville, Mo., U.S. | E3 | 114 |
| Humayingzi, China | B4 | 32 |

| Name | Map Ref. | Page |
|---|---|---|
| Humbe, Ang. | E2 | 58 |
| Humber, stm., Eng., U.K. | H13 | 8 |
| Humberside, co., Eng., U.K. | H13 | 8 |
| Humbird, Wi., U.S. | F5 | 110 |
| Humboldt, Az., U.S. | J4 | 120 |
| Humboldt, Ia., U.S. | I13 | 118 |
| Humboldt, Ks., U.S. | C8 | 114 |
| Humboldt, Ne., U.S. | N12 | 118 |
| Humboldt, Ne., U.S. | K12 | 118 |
| Humboldt, S.D., U.S. | H10 | 118 |
| Humboldt, Sk., Can. | F9 | 104 |
| Humboldt, Tn., U.S. | G8 | 114 |
| Humboldt, stm., Nv., U.S. | D7 | 124 |
| Hume, Ca., U.S. | H7 | 124 |
| Hume, Lake, res., Austl. | K7 | 70 |
| Humenné, Slvk. | G21 | 10 |
| Humeston, Ia., U.S. | J2 | 110 |
| Humphrey, Ar., U.S. | H5 | 114 |
| Humphrey, Ne., U.S. | J10 | 118 |
| Humphreys, Mount, mtn., Ca., U.S. | G7 | 124 |
| Humphreys Peak, mtn., Az., U.S. | I5 | 120 |
| Humptulips, stm., Wa., U.S. | C2 | 122 |
| Humpty Doo, Austl. | B6 | 68 |
| Humuya, stm., Hond. | C7 | 92 |
| Húnaflói, b., Ice. | B3 | 6a |
| Hunan, prov., China | F9 | 30 |
| Hunchun, China | A18 | 32 |
| Hundred, W.V., U.S. | H6 | 108 |
| Hunedoara, Rom. | D6 | 20 |
| Hunedoara, co., Rom. | D6 | 20 |
| Hünfeld, Ger. | E9 | 10 |
| Hungary (Magyarország), ctry., Eur. | F12 | 4 |
| Hungerford, Tx., U.S. | J10 | 116 |
| Hüngnam, N. Kor. | D15 | 32 |
| Hungry Horse, Mt., U.S. | B11 | 122 |
| Hungry Horse Reservoir, res., Mt., U.S. | B12 | 122 |
| Hung Yen, Viet. | D9 | 40 |
| Huningue, Fr. | E14 | 14 |
| Hunjiang (Badaojiang), China | B14 | 32 |
| Hunkurâb, Ra's, c., Egypt | I3 | 48 |
| Hunlen Falls, wtfl, B.C., Can. | E9 | 102 |
| Hunsberge, mts., Nmb. | F3 | 66 |
| Hunsrück, mts., Ger. | F6 | 10 |
| Hunter, N.D., U.S. | D10 | 118 |
| Hunter, Mount, mtn., Ak., U.S. | E19 | 100 |
| Hunter Island, i., Austl. | M6 | 70 |
| Hunter Island, i., B.C., Can. | F6 | 102 |
| Hunter River, P.E., Can. | F10 | 106 |
| Hunters Road, Zimb. | B9 | 66 |
| Huntersville, N.C., U.S. | D6 | 112 |
| Huntingburg, In., U.S. | D10 | 114 |
| Huntingdon, Pa., U.S. | G8 | 108 |
| Huntingdon, P.Q., Can. | B12 | 108 |
| Huntingdon, Tn., U.S. | F8 | 114 |
| Huntington, In., U.S. | B11 | 114 |
| Huntington, N.Y., U.S. | G13 | 108 |
| Huntington, Or., U.S. | F9 | 122 |
| Huntington, Tx., U.S. | K2 | 114 |
| Huntington, Ut., U.S. | E6 | 120 |
| Huntington, W.V., U.S. | I4 | 108 |
| Huntington Beach, Ca., U.S. | K8 | 124 |
| Huntland, Tn., U.S. | G10 | 114 |
| Huntley, Mt., U.S. | E17 | 122 |
| Huntly, N.Z. | B5 | 72 |
| Hunt Mountain, mtn., Wy., U.S. | F18 | 122 |
| Huntsville, Al., U.S. | H10 | 114 |
| Huntsville, Ar., U.S. | F3 | 114 |
| Huntsville, Mo., U.S. | C4 | 114 |
| Huntsville, On., Can. | E16 | 110 |
| Huntsville, Tn., U.S. | C2 | 112 |
| Huntsville, Tx., U.S. | I11 | 116 |
| Huntsville, Ut., U.S. | C5 | 120 |
| Hunyani, stm., Afr. | E6 | 58 |
| Hunyuan, China | D1 | 32 |
| Huon Gulf, b., Pap. N. Gui. | m16 | 68a |
| Huonville, Austl. | N7 | 70 |
| Huoqiu, China | C5 | 34 |
| Huotong, China | I8 | 34 |
| Hupeh see Hubei, prov., China | E9 | 30 |
| Huraymilā, Sau. Ar. | B5 | 47 |
| Hurd, Cape, c., On., Can. | E14 | 110 |
| Hure Qi, China | A9 | 32 |
| Huriel, Fr. | F9 | 14 |
| Hurley, Ms., U.S. | L8 | 114 |
| Hurley, N.M., U.S. | L8 | 120 |
| Hurley, Wi., U.S. | D5 | 110 |
| Hurlock, Md., U.S. | I11 | 108 |
| Huron, Ca., U.S. | H5 | 124 |
| Huron, Oh., U.S. | F4 | 108 |
| Huron, S.D., U.S. | G9 | 118 |
| Huron, stm., Mi., U.S. | H12 | 110 |
| Huron, Lake, l., N.A. | F13 | 110 |
| Hurricane, Ut., U.S. | G3 | 120 |
| Hurricane, W.V., U.S. | I4 | 108 |
| Hurricane Cliffs, clf, U.S. | H3 | 120 |
| Hurstbridge, Austl. | K6 | 70 |
| Hurt, Va., U.S. | B7 | 112 |
| Hurtado, stm., Chile | F3 | 80 |
| Hurtsboro, Al., U.S. | J11 | 114 |
| Húsavík, Faer. Is. | E8 | 6b |
| Húsavík, Ice. | A5 | 6a |
| Husheib, Sudan | J6 | 60 |
| Hushina, China | C4 | 32 |
| Huşi, Rom. | C12 | 20 |
| Huslia, Ak., U.S. | D16 | 100 |
| Hussar, Ab., Can. | F22 | 102 |
| Hustisford, Wi., U.S. | G7 | 110 |
| Husum, Ger. | A9 | 10 |
| Husum, Swe. | J16 | 6 |
| Hutanopan, Indon. | N5 | 40 |
| Hutchinson, Ks., U.S. | M10 | 118 |
| Hutchinson, Mn., U.S. | F1 | 110 |
| Hutchinson, S. Afr. | H6 | 66 |
| Hutouya, China | F7 | 32 |
| Hutsonville, Il., U.S. | C9 | 114 |
| Hutte Sauvage, Lac de la, l., P.Q., Can. | E20 | 106 |
| Huttig, Ar., U.S. | I4 | 114 |
| Hutto, Tx., U.S. | D8 | 13 |
| Huttwil, Switz. | D8 | 13 |
| Huwei, Tai. | L9 | 34 |
| Huwwārah, W.B. | D4 | 50 |
| Huxford, Al., U.S. | K9 | 114 |
| Huxley, Ia., U.S. | I2 | 110 |
| Huxley, Mount, mtn., B.C. | F21 | 102 |
| Huyangzhen, China | C1 | 34 |
| Hüzgän, Iran | F10 | 48 |
| Huzhou, China | E9 | 34 |
| Hvannadalshnúkur, mtn., Ice. | B5 | 6a |
| Hvar, Cro. | F11 | 18 |
| Hvar, Otok, i., Cro. | F11 | 18 |
| Hveragerdi, Ice. | B3 | 6a |
| Hvizdets', Ukr. | A9 | 20 |
| Hvolsvöllur, Ice. | C3 | 6a |
| Hwang Ho see Huang, stm., China | D10 | 30 |
| Hwangju, N. Kor. | E13 | 32 |
| Hyannis, Ma., U.S. | E16 | 108 |
| Hyannis, Ne., U.S. | I6 | 118 |
| Hyattville, Wy., U.S. | F18 | 122 |
| Hyco, stm., U.S. | C8 | 112 |
| Hydaburg, Ak., U.S. | I28 | 100 |
| Hyden, Austl. | F3 | 68 |
| Hyden, Ky., U.S. | B3 | 112 |
| Hyde Park, Guy. | D13 | 84 |
| Hyde Park, N.Y., U.S. | F13 | 108 |
| Hyde Park, Vt., U.S. | C14 | 108 |
| Hyderābād, India | D5 | 46 |
| Hyderābād, Pak. | H3 | 44 |
| Hydra see Idhra, i., Grc. | L7 | 20 |
| Hydraulic, B.C., Can. | E13 | 102 |
| Hydro, Ok., U.S. | D8 | 116 |
| Hydrographers Passage, strt., Austl. | C8 | 70 |
| Hyères, Fr. | I13 | 14 |
| Hyères, Îles d', is., Fr. | B18 | 16 |
| Hyesan, N. Kor. | B16 | 32 |
| Hyland, stm., Can. | F30 | 100 |
| Hymaya, stm., Mex. | E6 | 90 |
| Hymera, In., U.S. | C9 | 114 |
| Hyndman, Pa., U.S. | H8 | 108 |
| Hyndman Peak, mtn., Id., U.S. | G11 | 122 |
| Hyŏpch'ŏn, S. Kor. | H16 | 32 |
| Hyrra Banda, C.A.R. | O2 | 60 |
| Hyrum, Ut., U.S. | C5 | 120 |
| Hysham, Mt., U.S. | D18 | 122 |
| Hythe, Ab., Can. | B15 | 102 |
| **I** | | |
| Iacanga, Braz. | F4 | 79 |
| Iaciara, Braz. | C5 | 79 |
| Iaco (Yaco), stm., S.A. | C7 | 82 |
| Iaçu, Braz. | B8 | 79 |
| Iaeger, W.V., U.S. | B5 | 112 |
| Ialomița, co., Rom. | E11 | 20 |
| Ialomița, stm., Rom. | E11 | 20 |
| Ianakafy, Madag. | s21 | 67b |
| Iapó, stm., Braz. | C13 | 80 |
| Iapu, Braz. | E7 | 79 |
| Iargara, Mol. | C12 | 20 |
| Iaşi, Rom. | B11 | 20 |
| Iaşi, co., Rom. | B11 | 20 |
| Iauaretê, Braz. | G8 | 84 |
| Ibadan, Nig. | H11 | 64 |
| Ibagué, Col. | E5 | 84 |
| Ibaiti, Braz. | G3 | 79 |
| Ibans, Laguna de, b., Hond. | B10 | 92 |
| Ibapah Peak, mtn., Ut., U.S. | E3 | 120 |
| Ibarra, Ec. | G3 | 84 |
| Ibb, Yemen | G4 | 47 |
| Ibbenbüren, Ger. | C7 | 10 |
| Iberia, Mo., U.S. | D4 | 114 |
| Ibérico, Sistema, mts., Spain | D9 | 16 |
| Iberville, Mont d' (Mount Caubvick), mtn., Can. | E20 | 96 |
| Ibeto, Nig. | F12 | 64 |
| Ibiá, Braz. | E5 | 79 |
| Ibicaraí, Braz. | C9 | 79 |
| Ibicuí, Braz. | E10 | 80 |
| Ibicuí, stm., Braz. | E10 | 80 |
| Ibicuy, Arg. | G9 | 80 |
| Ibiquera, Braz. | B8 | 79 |
| Ibiraci, Braz. | F5 | 79 |
| Ibiraçu, Braz. | E8 | 79 |
| Ibirama, Braz. | D14 | 80 |
| Ibirapuitã, stm., Braz. | F11 | 80 |
| Ibirataia, Braz. | C9 | 79 |
| Ibirubá, Braz. | E12 | 80 |
| Ibitiara, Braz. | B7 | 79 |
| Ibitinga, Braz. | F4 | 79 |
| Ibo, Moz. | D8 | 58 |
| Ibotirama, Braz. | B7 | 79 |
| 'Ibrī, Oman | C10 | 47 |
| Ibshaway, Egypt | C6 | 60 |
| Ibusuki, Japan | P5 | 36 |
| Ica, Peru | F4 | 82 |
| Ica, dept., Peru | F4 | 82 |
| Içá (Putumayo), stm., S.A. | I8 | 84 |
| Icabarú, stm., Ven. | E11 | 84 |
| Icamaquã, stm., Braz. | E11 | 80 |
| Içana, Braz. | G9 | 84 |
| Içana (Isana), stm., S.A. | G9 | 84 |
| Icaño, Arg. | E6 | 80 |
| Icaño, Arg. | E7 | 80 |
| Iceberg Pass, Co., U.S. | D11 | 120 |
| İçel, Tur. | C3 | 48 |
| Iceland (Island), ctry., Eur. | B4 | 4 |
| Icém, Braz. | F4 | 79 |
| Ice Mountain, mtn., B.C., Can. | C13 | 102 |
| Ichaikaranji, India | D3 | 46 |
| Ichikawa, Japan | L14 | 36 |
| Ichilo, stm., Bol. | G9 | 82 |
| Ichinomiya, Japan | L11 | 36 |
| Ichinoseki, Japan | I16 | 36 |
| Ichkeul, Lac, l., Tun. | L4 | 18 |
| Ichoa, stm., Bol. | F9 | 82 |
| Ichoca, Bol. | G8 | 82 |
| Ich'ŏn, N. Kor. | E14 | 32 |
| Ich'ŏn, S. Kor. | F15 | 32 |
| Ičinskaja Sopka, vulkan, vol., Russia | F23 | 28 |
| Icó, Braz. | E11 | 76 |
| Iconha, Braz. | F8 | 79 |
| Icy Bay, b., Ak., U.S. | F24 | 100 |
| Ida, Mn., U.S. | I12 | 110 |
| Idabel, Ok., U.S. | I12 | 114 |
| Ida Grove, Ia., U.S. | I12 | 118 |
| Idah, Nig. | H13 | 64 |
| Idaho, state, U.S. | C4 | 98 |
| Idaho City, Id., U.S. | G10 | 122 |
| Idaho Falls, Id., U.S. | G13 | 122 |
| Idaho Springs, Co., U.S. | E11 | 120 |
| Idalou, Tx., U.S. | F5 | 116 |
| Idanre, Nig. | H12 | 64 |
| Idappādi, India | G4 | 46 |
| Idar-Oberstein, Ger. | F7 | 10 |
| Idelès, Alg. | I13 | 62 |
| Idfū, Egypt | E7 | 60 |
| Ídhi Óros, mtn., Grc. | N8 | 20 |
| Idhra (Hydra), i., Grc. | L7 | 20 |
| Idi, Indon. | L4 | 40 |
| Idiofa, D.R.C. | C3 | 58 |
| Idlib, Syria | D4 | 48 |
| Idoûkâl-n-Taghès, mtn., Niger | C14 | 64 |
| Idre, Swe. | K13 | 6 |
| Idrica, Russia | E11 | 22 |
| Idrija, Slvn. | C9 | 18 |
| Idutywa, S. Afr. | I9 | 66 |
| Idyllwild, Ca., U.S. | K9 | 124 |
| Iecava, Lat. | E7 | 22 |
| Iepê, Braz. | G3 | 79 |
| Ieper (Ypres), Bel. | G2 | 12 |
| Ierisós, Grc. | I7 | 20 |
| Ife, Nig. | H12 | 64 |
| Iferouâne, Niger | B14 | 64 |
| Ifni, hist. reg., Mor. | F5 | 62 |
| Ifôghas, Adrar des, mts., Afr. | E7 | 54 |
| Ifon-Oshogbo, Nig. | H12 | 64 |
| Igal, Hung. | I17 | 10 |
| Iganga, Ug. | H11 | 64 |
| Igapora, Braz. | B7 | 79 |
| Igara Paraná, stm., Col. | H6 | 84 |
| Igarka, Russia | D9 | 28 |
| Igbosa-Odo, Nig. | H11 | 64 |
| İğdır, Tur. | B8 | 48 |
| Igharghar, Oued, val., Afr. | J14 | 62 |
| Igizyar, China | A7 | 44 |
| Iglesia, Arg. | F4 | 80 |
| Iglesias, Italy | J3 | 18 |
| Igli, Alg. | E9 | 62 |
| Igloolik, N.T., Can. | C16 | 96 |
| Ignacio, Co., U.S. | G9 | 120 |
| Ignacio Zaragoza, Mex. | C6 | 90 |
| Ignalina, Lith. | F9 | 22 |
| Ignaței, Mol. | B12 | 20 |
| Iğneada, Tur. | H11 | 20 |
| Iguaçu, Cataratas do (Iguassu Falls), wtfl, S.A. | C11 | 80 |
| Iguaí, Braz. | C8 | 79 |
| Igualada, Spain | D13 | 16 |
| Iguana, stm., Ven. | C10 | 84 |
| Iguape, Braz. | C15 | 80 |
| Iguassu Falls see Iguaçu, Cataratas do, wtfl, S.A. | C11 | 80 |
| Iguatemi, Braz. | G1 | 79 |
| Iguatemi, stm., Braz. | G1 | 79 |
| Iguatu, Braz. | E11 | 76 |
| Iguazú, Parque Nacional, S.A. | C11 | 80 |
| Iguéla, Gabon | B1 | 58 |
| Iguídi, 'Erg, dunes, Afr. | C5 | 54 |
| Igžei, Russia | G12 | 28 |
| Iheya-shima, i., Japan | t2 | 37b |
| Ihiala, Nig. | I13 | 64 |
| Ihosy, Madag. | s22 | 67b |
| Ihtiman, Bul. | G7 | 20 |
| Iida, Japan | L12 | 36 |
| Iisaku, Est. | B10 | 22 |
| Ii-shima, i., Japan | F12 | 30 |
| Iiyama, Japan | K13 | 36 |
| Iizuka, Japan | N5 | 36 |
| Ijâfene, des., Afr. | D5 | 54 |
| Ijaji, Eth. | M9 | 60 |
| Ijebu-Igbo, Nig. | H12 | 64 |
| IJmuiden, Neth. | D6 | 12 |
| IJssel, stm., Neth. | C8 | 12 |
| IJsselmeer (Zuiderzee), Neth. | C7 | 12 |
| IJsselstein, Neth. | D7 | 12 |
| Ijuí, Braz. | E12 | 80 |
| Ijuí, stm., Braz. | E11 | 80 |
| Ikalamavony, Madag. | r22 | 67b |
| Ikang, Nig. | I14 | 64 |
| Ikaría, i., Grc. | L10 | 20 |
| Ikeja, Nig. | H11 | 64 |
| Ikela, D.R.C. | B4 | 58 |
| Ikirun, Nig. | H12 | 64 |
| Ikot Ekpene, Nig. | I13 | 64 |
| Ikša, Russia | E20 | 22 |
| Ilabaya, Peru | G6 | 82 |
| Ilagan, Phil. | m19 | 39b |
| Ilaka, Madag. | q23 | 67b |
| Ilām, Iran | E9 | 48 |
| Ilām, Nepal | D11 | 44 |
| Ilan, Tai. | K10 | 34 |
| Ilanskij, Russia | F17 | 26 |
| Ilanz, Switz. | E11 | 13 |
| Ilaro, Nig. | H11 | 64 |
| Iława, Pol. | B19 | 10 |
| Ilbenge, Russia | E16 | 28 |
| Île-à-la-Crosse, Sk., Can. | C7 | 104 |
| Île-à-la-Crosse, Lac, l., Sk., Can. | C7 | 104 |
| Îlebo, D.R.C. | B4 | 58 |
| Île-de-France, hist. reg., Fr. | C9 | 14 |
| Ilek, stm., Asia | G8 | 26 |
| Îles, Lac des, l., Sk., Can. | D5 | 104 |
| Ilesha, Nig. | H12 | 64 |
| Ilesha Ibarada, Nig. | G11 | 64 |
| Ilford, Mb., Can. | B19 | 104 |
| Ilfracombe, Austl. | D6 | 70 |
| Ilhabela, Braz. | G6 | 79 |
| Ilha Grande, Baía da, b., Braz. | G6 | 79 |
| Ilhéus, Braz. | C9 | 79 |
| Ili, stm., Asia | H12 | 26 |
| Ilia, Rom. | D7 | 94 |
| Iliamna, Ak., U.S. | G17 | 100 |
| Iliamna Lake, l., Ak., U.S. | G17 | 100 |
| Ilicínia, Braz. | F6 | 79 |
| Iliff, Co., U.S. | K4 | 118 |
| Iligan, Phil. | D7 | 38 |
| Ilimsk, Russia | F12 | 28 |
| Ilinza, mtn., Ec. | H3 | 84 |
| Ilion, N.Y., U.S. | D11 | 108 |
| Ilizi, Alg. | G15 | 62 |
| Iljinskij, Russia | H20 | 28 |
| Iljinskoje, Russia | D21 | 22 |
| Iljinskoje, Russia | E20 | 22 |
| Iljinskoje-Chovanskoje, Russia | E22 | 22 |
| Ilkal, India | E4 | 46 |
| Il'kino, Russia | H11 | 22 |
| Illampu, Nevado, mtn., Bol. | F7 | 82 |
| Illapel, Chile | F3 | 80 |
| Ille-et-Vilaine, dept., Fr. | D5 | 14 |
| Illéla, Niger | D12 | 64 |
| Illescas, Mex. | F8 | 90 |
| Illescas, Spain | E8 | 16 |
| Illiers, Fr. | D8 | 14 |
| Illimani, Nevado, mtn., Bol. | G8 | 82 |
| Illimo, Peru | B2 | 82 |
| Illinois, state, U.S. | D9 | 98 |
| Illinois, stm., Or., U.S. | H2 | 122 |
| Illinois, stm., U.S. | C9 | 114 |
| Illinois Peak, mtn., U.S. | C10 | 122 |
| Illiopolis, Il., U.S. | C7 | 114 |
| Il'men', ozero, l., Russia | C14 | 22 |
| Ilo, Peru | G6 | 82 |
| Ilobasco, El Sal. | D6 | 92 |
| Iloilo, Phil. | C7 | 38 |
| Ilopango, Lago de, l., El Sal. | D6 | 92 |
| Ilora, Nig. | H11 | 64 |
| Ilorin, Nig. | G12 | 64 |
| Iłukste, Lat. | F9 | 22 |
| Ilwaki, Indon. | G8 | 38 |
| Ilych, stm., Russia | E7 | 26 |
| Imabari, Japan | M8 | 36 |
| Imandra, ozero, l., Russia | H23 | 6 |
| Imari, Japan | N4 | 36 |
| Imaruí, Braz. | E14 | 80 |
| Imaruí, Lagoa do, b., Braz. | E14 | 80 |
| Imatra, Fin. | K21 | 6 |
| Imbabura, prov., Ec. | G3 | 84 |
| Imbituba, Braz. | E14 | 80 |
| Imbituva, Braz. | C13 | 80 |
| Imboden, Ar., U.S. | F5 | 114 |
| Imeni Babuškina, Russia | B26 | 22 |
| Imeni C'urupy, Russia | E27 | 22 |
| Imeni Vorovskogo, Russia | F24 | 22 |
| Imeni Zel'androsa, Madag. | p23 | 67b |
| Imerimandroso, Madag. | p23 | 67b |
| Imi, Eth. | G9 | 56 |
| Imías, Cuba | D7 | 94 |
| Imilac, Chile | C4 | 80 |
| Imin-t'Anout, Mor. | E6 | 62 |
| Imişli, Azer. | B10 | 48 |
| Imlay, Nv., U.S. | C7 | 124 |
| Imlay City, Mi., U.S. | G12 | 110 |
| Immenstadt, Ger. | H10 | 10 |
| Immokalee, Fl., U.S. | M5 | 112 |
| Imola, Italy | E6 | 18 |
| Imotski, Cro. | F12 | 18 |
| Imperatriz, Braz. | E9 | 76 |
| Imperia, Italy | F3 | 18 |
| Imperial, Ca., U.S. | L10 | 124 |
| Imperial, Ne., U.S. | K6 | 118 |
| Imperial, Peru | E3 | 82 |
| Imperial, Sk., Can. | G9 | 104 |
| Imperial, Tx., U.S. | H4 | 116 |
| Imperial Beach, Ca., U.S. | L8 | 124 |
| Imperial Mills, Ab., Can. | B23 | 102 |
| Imperial Valley, val., Ca., U.S. | L10 | 124 |
| Impfondo, Congo | A3 | 58 |
| Imphal, India | H15 | 44 |
| Impilachti, Russia | K22 | 6 |
| Imst, Aus. | H11 | 10 |
| Imuris, Mex. | B4 | 90 |
| Ina, Japan | L12 | 36 |
| Ina, stm., Japan | L12 | 36 |
| Inambari, stm., Peru | E7 | 82 |
| In Amguel, Alg. | I13 | 62 |
| In Amnas, Alg. | D15 | 62 |
| Inari, Fin. | G20 | 6 |
| Inarijärvi, l., Fin. | G20 | 6 |
| Inauini, stm., Braz. | C8 | 82 |
| Inawashiro-ko, l., Japan | J15 | 36 |
| In Belbel, Alg. | G11 | 62 |
| Inca, Spain | F14 | 16 |
| Inca de Oro, Chile | D4 | 80 |
| Incaguasi, Chile | E3 | 80 |
| Incesu, Tur. | B3 | 48 |
| Inch'ŏn, S. Kor. | F14 | 32 |
| Incline Village, Nv., U.S. | E6 | 124 |
| Incomáti (Komati), stm., Afr. | E11 | 66 |
| Indaiá, stm., Braz. | E6 | 79 |
| Inda Silase, Eth. | J10 | 60 |
| Indaw, Myan. | C3 | 40 |
| Indé, Mex. | E7 | 90 |
| Independence, Ca., U.S. | H7 | 124 |
| Independence, Ia., U.S. | H4 | 110 |
| Independence, Ks., U.S. | N12 | 118 |
| Independence, Ky., U.S. | I2 | 108 |
| Independence, Mo., U.S. | C2 | 114 |
| Independence, Or., U.S. | F2 | 122 |
| Independence, Va., U.S. | C5 | 112 |
| Independence, Wi., U.S. | F4 | 110 |
| Independence, stm., N.Y., U.S. | D11 | 108 |
| Independence Mountains, mts., Nv., U.S. | C9 | 124 |
| Independencia, Bol. | G8 | 82 |
| Independencia, Isla, i., Peru | F3 | 82 |
| India (Bhārat), ctry., Asia | E10 | 42 |
| Indialantic, Fl., U.S. | K6 | 112 |
| Indian, stm., Mi., U.S. | D9 | 110 |
| Indiana, Pa., U.S. | G7 | 108 |
| Indiana, state, U.S. | C9 | 98 |
| Indiana Dunes National Lakeshore, In., U.S. | A9 | 114 |
| Indianapolis, In., U.S. | C10 | 114 |
| Indian Brook, N.S., Can. | F13 | 106 |
| Indian Church, Belize | I15 | 90 |
| Indian Head, Sk., Can. | H11 | 104 |
| Indian Lake, N.Y., U.S. | D12 | 108 |
| Indian Ocean | J11 | 126 |
| Indianola, Ia., U.S. | I2 | 110 |
| Indianola, Ms., U.S. | I6 | 114 |
| Indianola, Ne., U.S. | K7 | 118 |
| Indianópolis, Braz. | E5 | 79 |
| Indian Peak, mtn., Ut., U.S. | F3 | 120 |
| Indian Peak, mtn., Wy., U.S. | F16 | 122 |
| Indian River, Mi., U.S. | E11 | 110 |
| Indian River, b., Fl., U.S. | K6 | 112 |
| Indian Springs, Nv., U.S. | H10 | 124 |
| Indiantown, Fl., U.S. | L6 | 112 |
| Indiaporã, Braz. | E3 | 79 |
| Indibir, Eth. | M9 | 60 |
| Indigirka, stm., Russia | D21 | 28 |
| Indija, Serb. | D4 | 20 |
| Indio, Ca., U.S. | K9 | 124 |
| Indio, stm., Nic. | H12 | 92 |
| Indio, stm., Pan. | H14 | 92 |
| Indira Gandhi Canal, India | F5 | 44 |
| Indispensable Reefs, rf., Sol. Is. | B12 | 68 |
| Indochina, reg., Asia | B3 | 38 |
| Indonesia, ctry., Asia | G7 | 38 |
| Indore, India | I6 | 44 |
| Indragiri, stm., Indon. | O7 | 40 |
| Indramayu, Indon. | G5 | 38 |
| Indravati, stm., India | C6 | 46 |
| Indre, dept., Fr. | F8 | 14 |
| Indre-et-Loire, dept., Fr. | E7 | 14 |
| Indus, stm., Asia | H4 | 42 |
| Industry, Il., U.S. | B6 | 114 |
| Industry, Tx., U.S. | J10 | 116 |
| Indwe, S. Afr. | H8 | 66 |
| Inece, Tur. | H11 | 20 |
| In Ecker, Alg. | H13 | 62 |
| Inegöl, Tur. | I13 | 20 |
| Inez, Ky., U.S. | B4 | 112 |
| Inez, Tx., U.S. | K10 | 116 |
| Inferior, Laguna, b., Mex. | I12 | 90 |
| Infiernillo, Presa del, res., Mex. | H9 | 90 |
| Ingal, Niger | C13 | 64 |
| Ingelheim, Ger. | F8 | 10 |
| Ingelmunster, Bel. | G3 | 12 |
| Ingende, D.R.C. | B3 | 58 |
| Ingeniero Luiggi, Arg. | H6 | 80 |
| Ingeniero Luis A. Huergo, Arg. | J5 | 80 |
| Ingeniero White, Arg. | J7 | 80 |
| Ingenio La Esperanza, Arg. | C6 | 80 |
| Ingenio Santa Ana, Arg. | D6 | 80 |
| Ingersoll, On., Can. | G15 | 110 |
| Ingham, Austl. | B7 | 70 |
| Ingleside, Tx., U.S. | L9 | 116 |
| Inglewood, Austl. | G9 | 70 |
| Inglewood, Ca., U.S. | K7 | 124 |
| Inglis, Mb., Can. | H13 | 104 |
| Ingoda, stm., Russia | G14 | 28 |
| Ingolstadt, Ger. | G11 | 10 |
| Ingonish, N.S., Can. | F13 | 106 |
| Ingonachoix Bay, b., Nf., Can. | B16 | 106 |
| Ingraj Bāzār, India | H13 | 44 |
| Ingram, Tx., U.S. | I7 | 116 |
| In Guezzam, Alg. | B14 | 64 |
| Inhaca, Ilha da, i., Moz. | F11 | 66 |
| Inhafenga, Moz. | C11 | 66 |
| Inhambane, Moz. | D12 | 66 |
| Inhambane, prov., Moz. | C12 | 66 |
| Inhambupe, Braz. | B9 | 79 |
| Inhaminga, Moz. | B12 | 66 |
| Inhandui, stm., Braz. | F1 | 79 |
| Inhapim, Braz. | E7 | 79 |
| Inharrime, Moz. | D12 | 66 |
| Inhaúma, Braz. | E6 | 79 |
| Inhumas, Braz. | D4 | 79 |
| Inimutaba, Braz. | E6 | 79 |
| Inírida, Col. | F9 | 84 |
| Inírida, stm., Col. | F9 | 84 |
| Inisa, Nig. | H12 | 64 |
| Inishmore, i., Ire. | H4 | 8 |
| Injibara, Eth. | L9 | 60 |
| Injune, Austl. | E8 | 70 |
| Inkom, Id., U.S. | H13 | 122 |
| Inkster, Mi., U.S. | G12 | 110 |
| Inland Lake, l., Mb., Can. | F15 | 104 |
| Inland Sea see Seto-naikai, Japan | M7 | 36 |
| Inle Lake, l., Myan. | D4 | 40 |
| Inman, Ks., U.S. | M10 | 118 |
| Inman, S.C., U.S. | D4 | 112 |
| Inman Mills, S.C., U.S. | D4 | 112 |
| Inn (En), stm., Eur. | D20 | 14 |
| Innamincka, Austl. | F4 | 70 |
| Inner Channel, strt., Belize | I15 | 90 |
| Inner Hebrides, is., Scot., U.K. | E7 | 8 |
| Inner Mongolia see Nei Monggol Zizhiqu, prov., China | C10 | 30 |
| Innertkirchen, Switz. | E9 | 13 |
| Innisfail, Ab., Can. | E21 | 102 |
| Innisfail, Austl. | A7 | 70 |
| Innisfree, Ab., Can. | D23 | 102 |
| Innsbruck, Aus. | H11 | 10 |
| Inocência, Braz. | E3 | 79 |
| Inola, Ok., U.S. | C11 | 116 |
| Inongo, D.R.C. | B3 | 58 |
| Inowrocław, Pol. | C18 | 10 |
| In Rhar, Alg. | G11 | 62 |
| In Salah, Alg. | G12 | 62 |
| Inspiration, Az., U.S. | K6 | 120 |
| Instow, Sk., Can. | I6 | 104 |
| Inta, Russia | D10 | 26 |
| Intendente Alvear, Arg. | H7 | 80 |
| Intepe, Tur. | I10 | 20 |
| Interlaken, Switz. | E8 | 13 |
| Interlândia, Braz. | D4 | 79 |
| International Falls, Mn., U.S. | B2 | 110 |
| Inthanon, Doi, mtn., Thai. | E5 | 40 |
| Intibucá, Hond. | C6 | 92 |
| Intibucá, dept., Hond. | C6 | 92 |
| Intipucá, El Sal. | D6 | 92 |
| Intracoastal Waterway, U.S. | H5 | 112 |
| Intracoastal Waterway, U.S. | K10 | 116 |
| Intuto, Peru | I5 | 84 |
| Inukjuak, P.Q., Can. | B28 | 100 |
| Inuvik, N.T., Can. | C10 | 96 |
| Inuya, stm., Peru | D5 | 82 |
| Invercargill, N.Z. | G2 | 72 |
| Inverell, Austl. | G9 | 70 |
| Invergordon, Scot., U.K. | D9 | 8 |
| Invermay, Sk., Can. | G11 | 104 |
| Invermere, B.C., Can. | G18 | 102 |
| Inverness, Ca., U.S. | F3 | 124 |
| Inverness, Fl., U.S. | K4 | 112 |
| Inverness, Ms., U.S. | I6 | 114 |
| Inverness, N.S., Can. | F12 | 106 |
| Inverness, Scot., U.K. | D9 | 8 |
| Investigator Group, is., Austl. | F6 | 68 |
| Investigator Strait, strt., Austl. | J2 | 70 |
| Inwood, Ia., U.S. | H11 | 118 |
| Inwood, Mb., Can. | H17 | 104 |
| Inyangani, mtn., Zimb. | B11 | 66 |
| Inyantue, Zimb. | B8 | 66 |
| Inyati, Zimb. | B9 | 66 |
| Inyokern, Ca., U.S. | I8 | 124 |
| Inywa, Myan. | C4 | 40 |
| Inza, Russia | G7 | 26 |
| Inzana Lake, l., B.C., Can. | C10 | 102 |
| Inzhavino, Russia | I25 | 22 |
| Ioánnina, Grc. | J4 | 20 |
| Iō-jima (Iwo Jima), i., Japan | F18 | 126 |
| Iola, Ks., U.S. | N12 | 118 |
| Iola, Wi., U.S. | F6 | 110 |
| Iolotan', Turk. | J10 | 26 |
| Iona, N.S., Can. | F12 | 106 |
| Iona, stm., Ang. | G14 | 28 |
| Ione, Ca., U.S. | F5 | 124 |
| Ione, Or., U.S. | E6 | 122 |
| Ione, Wa., U.S. | B8 | 122 |
| Ionia, Mi., U.S. | H10 | 110 |
| Ionian Islands see Iónioi Nísoi, is., Grc. | K4 | 20 |
| Ionian Sea, Eur. | H11 | 4 |
| Iónioi Nísoi, prov., Grc. | K4 | 20 |
| Iónioi Nísoi, is., Grc. | K4 | 20 |
| Íos, i., Grc. | M9 | 20 |
| Iosegun, stm., Ab., Can. | C18 | 102 |
| Iosegun Lake, l., Ab., Can. | C18 | 102 |
| Iota, La., U.S. | L4 | 114 |
| Iowa, state, U.S. | C8 | 98 |
| Iowa, stm., Ia., U.S. | I4 | 110 |
| Iowa City, Ia., U.S. | I4 | 110 |
| Iowa Falls, Ia., U.S. | H2 | 110 |
| Iowa Park, Tx., U.S. | F8 | 116 |
| Ipameri, Braz. | D5 | 79 |
| Ipatinga, Braz. | E7 | 79 |
| Ipatovo, Russia | B6 | 48 |
| Ipauçu, Braz. | G4 | 79 |
| Ipel' (Ipoly), stm., Eur. | G19 | 10 |
| Ipiales, Col. | G4 | 84 |
| Ipiaú, Braz. | C9 | 79 |
| Ipirá, Braz. | B9 | 79 |
| Ipiranga, Braz. | C13 | 80 |
| Ipiros, hist. reg., Grc. | J4 | 20 |
| Ipita, Bol. | H10 | 82 |
| Ipixuna, Braz. | B5 | 82 |
| Ipixuna, stm., Braz. | B10 | 82 |
| Ipixuna, stm., Braz. | B10 | 82 |
| Ipoh, Malay. | L6 | 40 |
| Ipoly (Ipel'), stm., Eur. | G18 | 10 |
| Iporá, Braz. | D3 | 79 |
| Iporã, Braz. | G2 | 79 |
| Ipoti-Ekiti, Nig. | H12 | 64 |
| Ipswich, Austl. | F10 | 70 |
| Ipswich, Eng., U.K. | I14 | 8 |
| Ipswich, S.D., U.S. | F8 | 118 |
| Ipu, Braz. | D10 | 76 |
| Ipupiara, Braz. | A7 | 79 |
| Iqaluit, N.T., Can. | D19 | 96 |
| Iquique, Chile | I6 | 82 |
| Iquitos, Peru | I6 | 84 |
| Ira, Tx., U.S. | G5 | 116 |
| Iraan, Tx., U.S. | I5 | 116 |
| Iracajá, Cachoeira do, wtfl, Braz. | D9 | 82 |
| Iraí, Braz. | D12 | 80 |
| Iráklion, Grc. | N9 | 20 |
| Iran (Īrān), ctry., Asia | E8 | 42 |
| Iran, Pegunungan, mts., Indon. | E5 | 38 |
| Īrānshahr, Iran | H16 | 48 |
| Irapa, Ven. | B11 | 84 |
| Irapuato, Mex. | G9 | 90 |
| Iraq (Al-'Irāq), ctry., Asia | C3 | 42 |
| Irará, Braz. | B9 | 79 |
| Irati, Braz. | C13 | 80 |
| Irazú, Volcán, vol., C.R. | H11 | 92 |
| Irbeni väin (Irbes jūras šaurums), strt., Eur. | D5 | 22 |
| Irbes jūras šaurums (Irbeni väin), strt., Eur. | D5 | 22 |
| Irbid, Jord. | C5 | 50 |
| Irbil, Iraq | C8 | 48 |
| Irbit, Russia | F10 | 26 |
| Ireland (Éire), ctry., Eur. | E9 | 4 |
| Irene, S. Afr. | E9 | 66 |
| Irene, Tx., U.S. | H10 | 116 |
| Ireng (Maú), stm., S.A. | E13 | 84 |
| Ireton, Ia., U.S. | I11 | 118 |
| Irgiz, Kaz. | H10 | 26 |
| Iriba, Chad | J2 | 60 |
| Irîgui, reg., Afr. | C7 | 64 |
| Iringa, Tan. | C7 | 58 |
| Iriona, Hond. | B9 | 92 |
| Iriri, stm., Braz. | D8 | 76 |
| Irish, Mount, mtn., Nv., U.S. | G10 | 124 |
| Irish Sea, Eur. | H8 | 8 |
| Irkutsk, Russia | G12 | 28 |
| Irma, Ab., Can. | E23 | 102 |
| Irma, Wi., U.S. | D5 | 110 |
| Iron Belt, Wi., U.S. | D5 | 110 |
| Iron Bridge, On., Can. | D12 | 110 |
| Iron City, Tn., U.S. | G9 | 114 |
| Iron Creek, stm., Ab., Can. | D23 | 102 |
| Irondale, Al., U.S. | I10 | 114 |
| Irondale, Mo., U.S. | E6 | 114 |
| Irondequoit, N.Y., U.S. | D9 | 108 |
| Iron Gate, val., Eur. | E6 | 20 |
| Iron Gate Reservoir, res., Eur. | E6 | 20 |
| Iron Knob, Austl. | I2 | 70 |
| Iron Mountain, Mi., U.S. | E7 | 110 |
| Iron Mountain, mts., U.S. | C5 | 112 |
| Iron Mountains, mts., U.S. | C5 | 112 |
| Iron Range, Austl. | B8 | 68 |
| Iron River, Mi., U.S. | D7 | 110 |
| Iron River, Wi., U.S. | D4 | 110 |
| Ironton, Mo., U.S. | E6 | 114 |
| Ironton, Oh., U.S. | I4 | 108 |
| Ironwood, Mi., U.S. | D5 | 110 |
| Iroquois, On., Can. | C11 | 108 |
| Iroquois, S.D., U.S. | G10 | 118 |
| Iroquois, stm., U.S. | J8 | 110 |
| Iroquois Falls, On., Can. | B15 | 110 |
| Irrawaddy see Ayeyarwady, stm., Myan. | F3 | 40 |
| Irricana, Ab., Can. | F21 | 102 |
| Irrigon, Or., U.S. | E6 | 122 |
| Irshava, Ukr. | A7 | 20 |
| Irtysh (Irtyš) (Ertix), stm., Asia | E11 | 26 |
| Irtyšsk, Kaz. | G13 | 26 |
| Irumu, D.R.C. | A5 | 58 |
| Irún, Spain | B10 | 16 |
| Irupana, Bol. | G8 | 82 |
| Irurzun, Spain | C10 | 16 |
| Irvine, Ab., Can. | I4 | 104 |
| Irvine, Ky., U.S. | B3 | 112 |
| Irvine, Scot., U.K. | F9 | 8 |
| Irvines Landing, B.C., Can. | H10 | 102 |
| Irving, Il., U.S. | C7 | 114 |
| Irving, Tx., U.S. | G10 | 116 |
| Irvington, Ky., U.S. | E10 | 114 |
| Irwinton, Ga., U.S. | G3 | 112 |
| Isaac, stm., Austl. | D8 | 70 |
| Isaac Lake, l., B.C., Can. | D14 | 102 |
| Isabel, S.D., U.S. | F6 | 118 |
| Isabela, Phil. | D7 | 38 |
| Isabela, Cabo, c., Dom. Rep. | E9 | 94 |
| Isabela, Isla, i., Ec. | j13 | 84a |
| Isabela, Isla, i., Mex. | G7 | 90 |
| Isabela, Cordillera, mts., Nic. | D9 | 92 |
| Isabella, Mn., U.S. | C4 | 110 |
| Isaccea, Rom. | A2 | 6a |
| Ísafjördur, Ice. | A2 | 6a |
| Isahaya, Japan | O5 | 36 |
| Isa Khel, Pak. | D4 | 44 |
| Isalnița, Rom. | E7 | 20 |
| Iṣana (Içana), stm., S.A. | G8 | 84 |
| Isanti, Mn., U.S. | E2 | 110 |
| Isar, stm., Eur. | G11 | 10 |
| Isara, stm., Eur. | H11 | 64 |
| Ischia, Italy | I8 | 18 |
| Ischia, Isola d', i., Italy | I8 | 18 |
| Iscuandé, stm., Col. | F4 | 84 |
| Ise (Uji-yamada), Japan | M11 | 36 |
| Iseo, Lago d', l., Italy | D5 | 18 |
| Isère, dept., Fr. | G12 | 14 |
| Isère, stm., Fr. | G12 | 14 |
| Iserlohn, Ger. | D7 | 10 |
| Isernia, Italy | H9 | 18 |
| Iset', stm., Russia | F11 | 26 |
| Iseyin, Nig. | H11 | 64 |
| Isherton, Guy. | F13 | 84 |
| Ishinomaki, Japan | I16 | 36 |
| Ishioka, Japan | K15 | 36 |
| Ishpeming, Mi., U.S. | D8 | 110 |
| Isigny, Fr. | C5 | 14 |
| Isil'kul', Russia | G12 | 26 |
| Išim, Russia | F11 | 26 |
| Išim, stm., Asia | F12 | 26 |
| Išimbaj, Russia | G9 | 26 |
| Isiolo, Kenya | A7 | 58 |
| Isipingo, S. Afr. | H10 | 66 |
| Isiro, D.R.C. | H6 | 56 |
| Isisford, Austl. | E5 | 70 |
| Iskăr, stm., Bul. | F8 | 20 |
| Iskăr, Jazovir, res., Bul. | G7 | 20 |
| Iskele, N. Cyp. | D2 | 48 |
| Iskenderun, Tur. | C4 | 48 |
| İskenderun Körfezi, b., Tur. | H15 | 4 |
| İskitim, Russia | G8 | 28 |
| Iskut, stm., B.C., Can. | H29 | 100 |
| Isla, Mex. | I12 | 90 |
| Isla, Salar de la, pl., Chile | C4 | 80 |
| Isla Cristina, Spain | H4 | 16 |
| Isla de Maipo, Chile | G3 | 80 |
| Islāmābād, Pak. | D5 | 44 |
| Islāmkot, Pak. | H4 | 44 |
| Islāmpur, India | G12 | 44 |
| Isla Mujeres, Mex. | G16 | 90 |
| Island, Ky., U.S. | E10 | 114 |
| Island Falls, Me., U.S. | A18 | 108 |
| Island Falls, Sk., Can. | C12 | 104 |
| Island Lagoon, l., Austl. | H2 | 70 |
| Island Lake, Mb., Can. | E20 | 104 |
| Island Lake, l., Mb., Can. | E20 | 104 |
| Island Park, Id., U.S. | F14 | 122 |
| Island Park Reservoir, res., Id., U.S. | F14 | 122 |
| Island Pond, Vt., U.S. | C15 | 108 |
| Islands, Bay of, b., Nf., Can. | D17 | 106 |
| Isla Patrulla, Ur. | G11 | 80 |
| Islas de la Bahía, dept., Hond. | A8 | 92 |
| Isla Verde, Arg. | G7 | 80 |
| Isla Vista, Ca., U.S. | J6 | 124 |
| Islay, i., Scot., U.K. | F7 | 8 |
| Islay, Punta, c., Peru | G5 | 82 |
| Isle-aux-Morts, Nf., Can. | E15 | 106 |
| Isle of Hope, Ga., U.S. | H5 | 112 |
| Isle of Man, dep., Eur. | E7 | 4 |
| Isle of Palms, S.C., U.S. | G7 | 112 |
| Isle of Wight, co., Eng., U.K. | K12 | 8 |
| Isle Royale National Park, U.S. | B7 | 110 |
| Islesboro Island, i., Me., U.S. | C18 | 108 |
| Isleta, N.M., U.S. | J10 | 120 |
| Isleton, Ca., U.S. | F4 | 124 |
| Islets-Caribou, P.Q., Can. | C6 | 106 |
| Islón, Chile | E3 | 80 |
| Ismael Cortinas, Ur. | G10 | 80 |
| Ismailia see Al-Ismā'īlīya, Egypt | B7 | 60 |
| Ismā'īlīya, Egypt | E7 | 60 |
| Ismalı, Tur. | K11 | 20 |
| Isna, Egypt | E7 | 60 |
| Isojoki, Fin. | J17 | 6 |
| Isola, Ms., U.S. | I6 | 114 |
| Isone, Switz. | F10 | 13 |

| Name | Map Ref. | Page |
|---|---|---|
| Isparta, Tur. | H14 | 4 |
| İspir, Tur. | A6 | 48 |
| Israel (Yisra'el), ctry., Asia | C2 | 42 |
| Israel, stm., N.H., U.S. | C15 | 108 |
| Issano, Guy. | E13 | 84 |
| Issoire, Fr. | G10 | 14 |
| Issoudun, Fr. | F9 | 14 |
| Is-sur-Tille, Fr. | E12 | 14 |
| Issyk-Kul' (Rybačje), Kyrg. | I13 | 26 |
| Issyk-Kul', ozero, l., Kyrg. | I13 | 26 |
| İstanbul, Tur. | H12 | 20 |
| İstanbul Boğazı (Bosporus), strt., Tur. | H13 | 20 |
| Istmina, Col. | E4 | 84 |
| Isto, Mount, mtn., Ak., U.S. | B23 | 100 |
| Istokpoga, Lake, l., Fl., U.S. | I15 | 112 |
| Istra, Russia | F19 | 22 |
| Istra, pen., Eur. | D8 | 18 |
| Istria see Istra, pen., Eur. | D8 | 18 |
| Itá, Para. | C10 | 80 |
| Itabaiana, Braz. | E11 | 76 |
| Itabaiana, Braz. | F11 | 76 |
| Itabapoana, Braz. | F8 | 79 |
| Itaberá, Braz. | G4 | 79 |
| Itaberaba, Braz. | B8 | 79 |
| Itaberaí, Braz. | D4 | 79 |
| Itabira, Braz. | E7 | 79 |
| Itabuna, Braz. | C9 | 79 |
| Itacambiruçu, stm., Braz. | D7 | 79 |
| Itacaré, Braz. | C9 | 79 |
| Itacoatiara, Braz. | I13 | 84 |
| Itacurubí del Rosario, Para. | C10 | 80 |
| Itaeté, Braz. | B8 | 79 |
| Itagi, Braz. | C8 | 79 |
| Itaguaçu, Braz. | E8 | 79 |
| Itaguajé, Braz. | G3 | 79 |
| Itaguara, Braz. | F6 | 79 |
| Itaguari, stm., Braz. | C6 | 79 |
| Itaguaru, Braz. | C4 | 79 |
| Itagüí, Col. | D5 | 84 |
| Itaí, Braz. | G4 | 79 |
| Itá-Ibaté, Arg. | D10 | 80 |
| Itaiópolis, Braz. | D14 | 80 |
| Itaituba, Braz. | D7 | 76 |
| Itajá, Braz. | E3 | 79 |
| Itajaí, Braz. | D14 | 80 |
| Itajaí do Sul, stm., Braz. | D14 | 80 |
| Itajubá, Braz. | G6 | 79 |
| Itaju do Colônia, Braz. | C9 | 79 |
| Itaiuipe, Braz. | C9 | 79 |
| Italy, Tx., U.S. | G10 | 116 |
| Italy (Italia), ctry., Eur. | G10 | 4 |
| Itamaraju, Braz. | D9 | 79 |
| Itamarandiba, Braz. | D7 | 79 |
| Itamarandiba, stm., Braz. | D7 | 79 |
| Itamari, Braz. | B9 | 79 |
| Itambacuri, Braz. | E8 | 79 |
| Itambé, Braz. | C8 | 79 |
| Itami, Japan | M10 | 36 |
| Itanhaém, Braz. | H5 | 79 |
| Itanhauã, stm., Braz. | A9 | 82 |
| Itanhém, Braz. | D8 | 79 |
| Itanhomi, Braz. | E8 | 79 |
| Itaobim, Braz. | D8 | 79 |
| Itapaci, Braz. | C4 | 79 |
| Itapagipe, Braz. | E4 | 79 |
| Itaparana, stm., Braz. | B10 | 82 |
| Itaparica, Ilha de, i., Braz. | B9 | 79 |
| Itapaya, Bol. | G8 | 82 |
| Itapebi, Braz. | C9 | 79 |
| Itapemirim, Braz. | F8 | 79 |
| Itapecerica, Braz. | F6 | 79 |
| Itapecuru-Mirim, Braz. | D10 | 76 |
| Itapemirim, Braz. | F8 | 79 |
| Itaperuna, Braz. | F8 | 79 |
| Itapetinga, Braz. | G4 | 79 |
| Itapetininga, stm., Braz. | G5 | 79 |
| Itapeva, Braz. | G4 | 79 |
| Itapicuru, Braz. | D10 | 76 |
| Itapicuru, stm., Braz. | F11 | 76 |
| Itapira, Braz. | G5 | 79 |
| Itapiranga, Braz. | D12 | 80 |
| Itapiranga, Braz. | I13 | 84 |
| Itapitanga, Braz. | C3 | 79 |
| Itápolis, Braz. | F4 | 79 |
| Itaporã, Braz. | G1 | 79 |
| Itaporanga, Braz. | G4 | 79 |
| Itapúa, dept., Para. | D11 | 80 |
| Itapuranga, Braz. | C4 | 79 |
| Itaquaí, stm., Braz. | J7 | 84 |
| Itaquara, Braz. | B9 | 79 |
| Itaquari, Braz. | F8 | 79 |
| Itaqui, Braz. | E10 | 80 |
| Itaquyry, Para. | C11 | 80 |
| Itarantim, Braz. | C8 | 79 |
| Itararé, Braz. | H4 | 79 |
| Itärsi, India | I7 | 44 |
| Itarumã, Braz. | E3 | 79 |
| Itasca, Tx., U.S. | G9 | 116 |
| Itasca, Lake, l., Mn., U.S. | D12 | 118 |
| Itata, stm., Chile | I2 | 80 |
| Itatí, Arg. | D9 | 80 |
| Itatiaia, Parque Nacional do, Braz. | G6 | 79 |
| Itatinga, Braz. | G4 | 79 |
| Itaúna, Braz. | F6 | 79 |
| Itenes (Guaporé), stm., S.A. | E10 | 82 |
| Ithaca, Mi., U.S. | G11 | 110 |
| Ithaca, N.Y., U.S. | E10 | 108 |
| Itháki, Grc. | K4 | 20 |
| Itháki, i., Grc. | K4 | 20 |
| Itinga, Braz. | D1 | 79 |
| Itinga, stm., Braz. | D8 | 79 |
| Itiquira, Braz. | G5 | 79 |
| Itirapina, Braz. | G5 | 79 |
| Itiruçu, Braz. | B8 | 79 |
| Itō, Japan | M14 | 36 |
| Itoigawa, Japan | J12 | 36 |
| Itomamo, Lac, l., P.Q., Can. | C3 | 106 |
| Itonamas, stm., Bol. | E9 | 82 |
| Itororó, Braz. | C8 | 79 |
| Itsä, Egypt | C6 | 60 |
| Itta Bena, Ms., U.S. | I6 | 114 |
| Itú, Braz. | G5 | 79 |
| Ituaçu, Braz. | E11 | 80 |
| Ituango, Col. | D5 | 84 |
| Ituberá, Braz. | B9 | 79 |
| Itucumã, stm., Braz. | B7 | 82 |
| Itueta, Braz. | E8 | 79 |
| Itui, stm., Braz. | J7 | 84 |
| Ituiutaba, Braz. | E13 | 80 |
| Itumbiara, Braz. | E4 | 79 |
| Ituna, Sk., Can. | G11 | 104 |
| Ituni, Guy. | E13 | 84 |
| Ituporanga, Braz. | D14 | 80 |
| Iturama, Braz. | E3 | 79 |
| Iturbe, Para. | D10 | 80 |
| Iturbide, Mex. | H15 | 90 |
| Iturup, ostrov (Etorofu-tō), i., Russia | c22 | 36a |
| Ituverava, Braz. | F5 | 79 |
| Ituxi, stm., Braz. | B9 | 82 |
| Ituzaingó (Argbče), Arg. | D10 | 80 |
| Itzehoe, Ger. | B9 | 10 |
| Iye, Bela. | H8 | 114 |
| Iuka, Ms., U.S. | H11 | 110 |
| Iúna, Braz. | F8 | 79 |
| Iva, S.C., U.S. | E4 | 112 |
| Ivacevičy, Bela. | I8 | 22 |
| Ivahona, Madag. | s22 | 67b |
| Ivaí, stm., Braz. | G2 | 79 |
| Ivaiporã, Braz. | C13 | 80 |
| Ivanava, Bela. | I8 | 22 |
| Ivane-Puste, Ukr. | A10 | 20 |
| Ivangorod, Russia | B11 | 22 |
| Ivanhoe, Austl. | I6 | 70 |
| Ivanhoe, Ca., U.S. | H6 | 124 |
| Ivanhoe, Mn., U.S. | G11 | 118 |
| Ivanhoe, Va., U.S. | C6 | 112 |
| Ivan'kovo, Russia | G20 | 22 |
| Ivan'kovskij, Russia | E23 | 22 |
| Ivan'kovskoje vodochranilišče, res., Russia | E19 | 22 |
| Ivano-Frankivs'k, Ukr. | H2 | 26 |
| Ivanovo, Russia | D23 | 22 |
| Ivato, Madag. | r22 | 67b |
| Ivatuba, Braz. | G2 | 79 |
| Ivdel', Russia | E10 | 25 |
| Ivinheima, stm., Braz. | G2 | 79 |
| Ivjanec, Bela. | H9 | 22 |
| Ivón, stm., Bol. | D8 | 82 |
| Ivory Coast see Cote d'Ivoire, ctry., Afr. | G5 | 54 |
| Ivory Coast, C. Iv. | I7 | 64 |
| Ivrea, Italy | D2 | 18 |
| Ivrindi, Tur. | J11 | 20 |
| Ivujivik, P.Q., Can. | D17 | 96 |
| Iwaki (Taira), Japan | J15 | 36 |
| Iwakuni, Japan | M7 | 36 |
| Iwamizawa, Japan | d16 | 36a |
| Iwanai, Japan | e15 | 36a |
| Iwo, Nig. | H12 | 54 |
| Iwo Jima see Iō-jima, i., Japan | F18 | 126 |
| Iwŏn, N. Kor. | C16 | 32 |
| Ixcán, stm., N.A. | B3 | 92 |
| Ixchiguán, Guat. | B3 | 92 |
| Ixiamas, Bol. | E7 | 82 |
| Iximché, hist., Guat. | C4 | 92 |
| Iximiquilpan, Mex. | G10 | 90 |
| Ixopo, S. Afr. | H10 | 66 |
| Ixtahuacán, Guat. | B3 | 92 |
| Ixtapa, Mex. | I9 | 90 |
| Ixtepec, Mex. | I12 | 90 |
| Ixtlán de Juárez, Mex. | I11 | 90 |
| Ixtlán del Río, Mex. | G7 | 90 |
| 'Iyäl Bakhīt, Sudan | K5 | 60 |
| Iyo-mishima, Japan | N8 | 36 |
| Izabal, Guat. | B5 | 92 |
| Izabal, dept., Guat. | B5 | 92 |
| Izabal, Lago de, l., Guat. | B5 | 92 |
| 'Izäd Khvāst, Iran | F12 | 48 |
| Izalco, El Sal. | D5 | 92 |
| Izamal, Mex. | G15 | 90 |
| Izapa, hist., Mex. | J13 | 90 |
| Izberbaš, Russia | I7 | 26 |
| Izbica, Pol. | A17 | 10 |
| Izd'oškovo, Russia | F16 | 22 |
| Izegem, Bel. | G3 | 12 |
| Īžeh, Iran | F10 | 48 |
| Iževsk, Russia | F8 | 26 |
| Izkī, Oman | C10 | 47 |
| Ižma, stm., Russia | E8 | 26 |
| Izmalkovo, Russia | I20 | 22 |
| Izmayil, Ukr. | H3 | 26 |
| İzmir (Smyrna), Tur. | K11 | 20 |
| İzmit, Tur. | G13 | 4 |
| Iznajar, Embalse de, res., Spain | H7 | 16 |
| Izoplit, Russia | E19 | 22 |
| Izopo, Punta, c., Hond. | B7 | 92 |
| Izozog, Bañados del, sw., Bol. | H10 | 82 |
| Izra', Syria | C6 | 50 |
| Izsák, Hung. | I19 | 10 |
| Iztaccíhuatl, Volcán, vol., Mex. | H10 | 90 |
| Iztaccíhuatl y Popocatépti, Parques Nacionales, Mex. | H10 | 90 |
| Iztapa, Guat. | D4 | 92 |
| Izucar de Matamoros, Mex. | H10 | 90 |
| Izuhara, Japan | M4 | 36 |
| Izumi, Japan | C5 | 36 |
| Izumi, Japan | M10 | 36 |
| Izumi, Japan | I15 | 36 |
| Izumo, Japan | L7 | 36 |
| Izu-shotō, is., Japan | E15 | 36 |
| Izvestij CIK, ostrova, is., Russia | B14 | 26 |
| Izyum, Ukr. | H5 | 26 |

## J

| Jaba, Eth. | N8 | 60 |
| Jabal al-Awliyā', Sudan | J7 | 60 |
| Jabalpur, India | I8 | 44 |
| Jabālyah, Gaza | E2 | 50 |
| Jabiru, Austl. | B6 | 68 |
| Jabjabah, Wādī, val., Afr. | G7 | 60 |
| Jablah, Syria | D3 | 48 |
| Jablonec nad Nisou, Czech Rep. | E15 | 10 |
| Jabłonka, Pol. | E19 | 10 |
| Jablonovyj chrebet, mts., Russia | G14 | 28 |
| Jaboatão, Braz. | E11 | 76 |
| Jaborandi, Braz. | F4 | 79 |
| Jaboticabal, Braz. | F4 | 79 |
| Jabung, Tanjung, c., Indon. | O8 | 40 |
| Jaca, Spain | C11 | 16 |
| Jacala, Mex. | G10 | 90 |
| Jacaleapa, Hond. | C8 | 92 |
| Jacaltenango, Guat. | B3 | 92 |
| Jacaraci, Braz. | C7 | 79 |
| Jacaré, stm., Braz. | B8 | 79 |
| Jacaré, Braz. | B10 | 82 |
| Jacareí, Braz. | G6 | 79 |
| Jacarezinho, Braz. | G4 | 79 |
| Jaceel, val., Som. | F11 | 56 |
| Jáchal, stm., Arg. | F4 | 80 |
| Jachroma, Russia | E20 | 22 |
| Jaciara, Braz. | C1 | 79 |
| Jacinto, Braz. | D8 | 79 |
| Jacinto Aráuz, Arg. | J7 | 80 |
| Jacinto City, Tx., U.S. | J11 | 116 |
| Jacinto Machado, Braz. | E14 | 80 |
| Jaciparaná, Braz. | C9 | 82 |
| Jaciparaná, stm., Braz. | D9 | 82 |
| Jackfish Lake, l., Sk., Can. | E6 | 104 |
| Jackhead Harbour, Mb., Can. | G17 | 104 |
| Jackman, Me., U.S. | B16 | 108 |
| Jack Mountain, mtn., Wa., U.S. | B5 | 122 |
| Jackpot, Nv., U.S. | C11 | 124 |
| Jacksboro, Tn., U.S. | C2 | 112 |
| Jacksboro, Tx., U.S. | F8 | 116 |
| Jacks Fork, stm., Mo., U.S. | E5 | 114 |
| Jackson, Al., U.S. | K9 | 114 |
| Jackson, Ca., U.S. | F5 | 124 |
| Jackson, Ga., U.S. | E3 | 112 |
| Jackson, Ky., U.S. | B3 | 112 |
| Jackson, La., U.S. | L5 | 114 |
| Jackson, Mi., U.S. | H11 | 110 |
| Jackson, Mn., U.S. | H13 | 118 |
| Jackson, Mo., U.S. | E7 | 114 |
| Jackson, Ms., U.S. | J6 | 114 |
| Jackson, N.C., U.S. | C9 | 112 |
| Jackson, Oh., U.S. | H4 | 108 |
| Jackson, S.C., U.S. | F5 | 112 |
| Jackson, Tn., U.S. | G8 | 114 |
| Jackson, Wy., U.S. | A6 | 120 |
| Jackson, Mount, mtn., Ant. | C12 | 73 |
| Jackson Center, Oh., U.S. | G2 | 108 |
| Jackson Creek, stm., Can. | I13 | 104 |
| Jackson Lake, l., Wy., U.S. | G15 | 122 |
| Jackson's Arm, Nf., Can. | C17 | 106 |
| Jacksonville, Al., U.S. | I11 | 114 |
| Jacksonville, Ar., U.S. | H4 | 114 |
| Jacksonville, Fl., U.S. | I5 | 112 |
| Jacksonville, Il., U.S. | D7 | 114 |
| Jacksonville, N.C., U.S. | C9 | 112 |
| Jacksonville, Or., U.S. | H3 | 122 |
| Jacksonville, Tx., U.S. | H11 | 116 |
| Jacksonville Beach, Fl., U.S. | I5 | 112 |
| Jacmel, Haiti | E8 | 94 |
| Jaco, Mex. | D7 | 90 |
| Jacobābād, Pak. | F3 | 44 |
| Jacobina, Braz. | F10 | 76 |
| Jacobsdal, S. Afr. | G7 | 66 |
| Jacques, Lac à, l., N.T., Can. | C31 | 100 |
| Jacques-Cartier, Détroit de, strt., P.Q., Can. | C10 | 106 |
| Jacques-Cartier, Mont, mtn., P.Q., Can. | D8 | 106 |
| Jacquet River, N.B., Can. | E7 | 106 |
| Jacqueville, C. Iv. | I7 | 64 |
| Jacuba, stm., Braz. | E2 | 79 |
| Jacuí, stm., Braz. | F12 | 80 |
| Jacuípe, stm., Braz. | B9 | 79 |
| Jacumba, Ca., U.S. | L9 | 124 |
| Jacupiranga, Braz. | C14 | 80 |
| Jaén, Peru | A2 | 82 |
| Jaén, Spain | H8 | 16 |
| Jäfaräbäd, India | B1 | 46 |
| Jaffa, Cape, c., Austl. | K3 | 70 |
| Jaffa, Tel Aviv- see Tel Aviv-Yafo, Isr. | D3 | 50 |
| Jaffna, Sri L. | H6 | 46 |
| Jaffrey, N.H., U.S. | E14 | 108 |
| Jafr, Qā'ai-, depr., Jord. | H6 | 50 |
| Jagädhri, India | E7 | 44 |
| Jagdalpur, India | C7 | 46 |
| Jagersfontein, S. Afr. | G7 | 66 |
| Jagodnoje, Russia | E21 | 28 |
| Jagraon, India | E6 | 44 |
| Jagtiäl, India | C5 | 46 |
| Jaguaquara, Braz. | B9 | 79 |
| Jaguarão, Braz. | G12 | 80 |
| Jaguarão (Yaguarón), stm., S.A. | G12 | 80 |
| Jaguari, Braz. | E11 | 80 |
| Jaguariaíva, Braz. | C14 | 80 |
| Jaguaribe, stm., Braz. | E11 | 76 |
| Jaguaruna, Braz. | E14 | 80 |
| Jaglé, Arg. | E4 | 80 |
| Jagüey Grande, Cuba | C4 | 94 |
| Jahänäbäd, India | H11 | 44 |
| Jahrom, Iran | G12 | 48 |
| Jailolo, Indon. | E8 | 38 |
| Jaipur, India | G6 | 44 |
| Jaisalmer, India | G4 | 44 |
| Jaja, Russia | F15 | 26 |
| Jájapur, India | J12 | 44 |
| Jajce, Bos. | E12 | 18 |
| Jakarta, Indon. | j13 | 39a |
| Jake Creek Mountain, mtn., Nv., U.S. | C9 | 124 |
| Jakobstad (Pietarsaari), Fin. | J18 | 6 |
| Jakša, Russia | E9 | 26 |
| Jakutija, state, Russia | D18 | 28 |
| Jakutsk, Russia | E17 | 28 |
| Jal, N.M., U.S. | G3 | 116 |
| Jaläläbäd, Afg. | C4 | 44 |
| Jalälïd, Sau. Ar. | B10 | 60 |
| Jalán, stm., Hond. | C8 | 92 |
| Jalandhar, India | E6 | 44 |
| Jalapa, Guat. | C5 | 92 |
| Jalapa, Nic. | D8 | 92 |
| Jalapa, dept., Guat. | C5 | 92 |
| Jälçaon, India | J6 | 44 |
| Jalisco, state, Mex. | G7 | 90 |
| Jalizava, Bela. | H12 | 22 |
| Jälna, India | C3 | 46 |
| Jälor, India | H5 | 44 |
| Jalostotitlán, Mex. | G8 | 90 |
| Jalpa, Mex. | G8 | 90 |
| Jälpäigurí, India | G13 | 44 |
| Jalpan, Mex. | G10 | 90 |
| Jaltepec, stm., Mex. | I12 | 90 |
| Jalutorovsk, Russia | F11 | 26 |
| Jamaame, Som. | A8 | 58 |
| Jamaica, ctry., N.A. | E7 | 94 |
| Jamaica Channel, strt., N.A. | E7 | 94 |
| Jamal, poluostrov, pen., Russia | C12 | 26 |
| Jamälpur, Bngl. | H13 | 44 |
| Jamälpur, India | H12 | 44 |
| Jamantau, gora, mtn., Russia | G9 | 26 |
| Jamanxim, stm., Braz. | A13 | 82 |
| Jamari, stm., Braz. | C10 | 82 |
| Jamarovka, Russia | G14 | 28 |
| Jambeli, Canal de, strt., Ec. | I2 | 84 |
| Jambi, Indon. | F3 | 38 |
| Jambol, Bul. | G10 | 20 |
| James, Ab., Can. | F20 | 102 |
| James, stm., Mo., U.S. | E3 | 114 |
| James, stm., U.S. | H10 | 118 |
| James, stm., Va., U.S. | B9 | 112 |
| James Bay, b., Can. | F16 | 96 |
| James City, N.C., U.S. | D9 | 112 |
| James Craik, Arg. | G7 | 80 |
| James Island, S.C., U.S. | G7 | 112 |
| Jamestown, Mo., U.S. | C3 | 114 |
| James Ross, Cape, c., N.T., Can. | B10 | 96 |
| James Ross Strait, strt., N.T., Can. | C13 | 96 |
| James Smith Indian Reserve, Sk., Can. | E10 | 104 |
| Jamestown, Austl. | I3 | 70 |
| Jamestown, Ca., U.S. | G5 | 124 |
| Jamestown, Ks., U.S. | L10 | 118 |
| Jamestown, Ky., U.S. | F11 | 114 |
| Jamestown, N.Y., U.S. | D7 | 112 |
| Jamestown, N.D., U.S. | E9 | 118 |
| Jamestown, Oh., U.S. | H3 | 108 |
| Jamestown, S. Afr. | H8 | 66 |
| Jamestown, Tn., U.S. | F12 | 114 |
| Jamestown Reservoir, res., N.D., U.S. | D9 | 118 |
| Jaminauä, stm., Braz. | C8 | 82 |
| Jamkhandi, India | D3 | 46 |
| Jamm, Russia | C11 | 22 |
| Jammu, India | D6 | 44 |
| Jammu and Kashmir, dep., Asia | C10 | 42 |
| Jamnagar, India | I4 | 44 |
| Jamsah, Egypt | D7 | 60 |
| Jamshedpur, India | I12 | 44 |
| Jämtlands Län, co., Swe. | J13 | 6 |
| Jamūi, India | H12 | 44 |
| Jamuna, stm., Bngl. | H13 | 44 |
| Jamundí, Col. | F4 | 84 |
| Jana, stm., Russia | C19 | 28 |
| Janauacá, Lago, l., Braz. | I12 | 84 |
| Janaúba, Braz. | C7 | 79 |
| Janasucu, Ilha, i., Braz. | C8 | 76 |
| Janaviščy, Bela. | F13 | 22 |
| Jand, Pak. | D5 | 44 |
| Jandaia, Braz. | D3 | 79 |
| Jandaia do Sul, Braz. | G3 | 79 |
| Jandaq, Iran | D13 | 48 |
| Jandïäla, India | E6 | 44 |
| Jandïäla, India | E6 | 44 |
| Janeiro, Rio de, stm., Braz. | A6 | 79 |
| Janesville, Ca., U.S. | D5 | 124 |
| Janesville, Mn., U.S. | F2 | 110 |
| Janesville, Wi., U.S. | H6 | 110 |
| Jangipur, India | H13 | 44 |
| Janin, W.B. | D4 | 50 |
| Janjina, Madag. | r21 | 67b |
| Jan Kempdorp (Andalusia), S. Afr. | F7 | 66 |
| Jan Lake, l., Sk., Can. | D12 | 104 |
| Jan Mayen, i., Nor. | B19 | 86 |
| Janos, Mex. | B5 | 90 |
| Jánoshalma, Hung. | I19 | 10 |
| Jánosháza, Hung. | H17 | 10 |
| Jansen, Sk., Can. | G10 | 104 |
| Janskij zaliv, b., Russia | C19 | 28 |
| Jantarnyj, Russia | G2 | 22 |
| Januária, Braz. | C6 | 79 |
| Janzé, Fr. | E5 | 14 |
| Jaora, India | I6 | 44 |
| Japan (Nihon), ctry., Asia | D14 | 30 |
| Japan, Sea of (Nihon-kai), Asia | K7 | 36 |
| Japim, Braz. | B5 | 82 |
| Japurá (Caquetá), stm., S.A. | H8 | 84 |
| Jaqué, Pan. | D3 | 84 |
| Jaqui, Peru | F4 | 82 |
| Jarābulus, Syria | C5 | 48 |
| Jarad, Sau. Ar. | E2 | 47 |
| Jaraguá, Braz. | C4 | 79 |
| Jaraguá do Sul, Braz. | D14 | 80 |
| Jaraiz de la Vera, Spain | E6 | 16 |
| Jarales, N.M., U.S. | J10 | 120 |
| Jarama, stm., Spain | E8 | 16 |
| Jaramänah, Syria | B6 | 50 |
| Jaransk, Russia | F7 | 26 |
| Jarash, Jord. | D5 | 50 |
| Jarbidge, stm., U.S. | H10 | 122 |
| Jarcevo, Russia | F15 | 22 |
| Jardim, Braz. | I13 | 82 |
| Jardín América, Arg. | D11 | 80 |
| Jardine River National Park, Austl. | B8 | 68 |
| Jardines de la Reina, Archipiélago de los, is., Cuba | D5 | 94 |
| Jardinópolis, Braz. | F5 | 79 |
| Jaredi, Nig. | E12 | 64 |
| Jarensk, Russia | E7 | 26 |
| Jargeau, Fr. | E9 | 14 |
| Jari, stm., Braz. | A10 | 82 |
| Jari, stm., Braz. | J11 | 84 |
| Jaridih, India | I12 | 44 |
| Jarnac, Fr. | G6 | 14 |
| Jarocin, Pol. | D17 | 10 |
| Jaroměř, Czech Rep. | E15 | 10 |
| Jaroslavl', Russia | D22 | 22 |
| Jarosław, Pol. | F22 | 10 |
| Jarratt, Va., U.S. | B9 | 112 |
| Jarreau, La., U.S. | L5 | 114 |
| Jaru, Braz. | D10 | 82 |
| Jaru, stm., Braz. | D10 | 82 |
| Järva-Jaani, Est. | B8 | 22 |
| Järvenpää, Fin. | K19 | 6 |
| Jarvie, Ab., Can. | C21 | 102 |
| Jarvis, On., Can. | H15 | 110 |
| Jarvisburg, N.C., U.S. | C11 | 112 |
| Jarvis Island, i., Oc. | I23 | 126 |
| Jaša Tomić, Yugo. | D4 | 20 |
| Jasikan, Ghana | H10 | 64 |
| Jäsk, Iran | I14 | 48 |
| Jasło, Pol. | F21 | 10 |
| Jasnogorsk, Russia | G20 | 22 |
| Jason Islands, is., Falk. Is. | G4 | 78 |
| Jasonville, In., U.S. | C9 | 114 |
| Jasper, Ab., Can. | E16 | 102 |
| Jasper, Al., U.S. | I9 | 114 |
| Jasper, Ar., U.S. | F3 | 114 |
| Jasper, Fl., U.S. | I4 | 112 |
| Jasper, Ga., U.S. | E2 | 112 |
| Jasper, In., U.S. | D10 | 114 |
| Jasper, Mn., U.S. | H11 | 118 |
| Jasper, Mo., U.S. | E2 | 114 |
| Jasper, Tn., U.S. | G11 | 114 |
| Jasper, Tx., U.S. | L3 | 114 |
| Jasper National Park, Ab., Can. | E17 | 102 |
| Jászapáti, Hung. | H20 | 10 |
| Jászberény, Hung. | H19 | 10 |
| Jász-Nagykun-Szolnok, co., Hung. | H20 | 10 |
| Jataí, Braz. | D3 | 79 |
| Jatapu, stm., Braz. | H13 | 84 |
| Jataté, stm., Mex. | I14 | 90 |
| Jatni, India | J11 | 44 |
| Jatobá, stm., Braz. | B1 | 79 |
| Jaú, Braz. | G4 | 79 |
| Jauaperi, stm., Braz. | H12 | 84 |
| Jauja, Peru | D4 | 82 |
| Jaunelgava, Lat. | D7 | 22 |
| Jaungulbene, Lat. | D9 | 22 |
| Jaunjelgava, Lat. | E8 | 22 |
| Jaunpiebalga, Lat. | D9 | 22 |
| Jaunpur, India | H10 | 44 |
| Jaupaci, Braz. | D3 | 79 |
| Jauru, stm., Braz. | F13 | 82 |
| Jauru, stm., Braz. | G13 | 82 |
| Java, S.D., U.S. | F8 | 118 |
| Java see Jawa, i., Indon. | j15 | 39a |
| Javari (Yavari), stm., S.A. | D4 | 76 |
| Javas, Russia | G25 | 22 |
| Java Sea see Jawa, Laut, Indon. | G5 | 38 |
| Java Trench | J11 | 24 |
| Java (Jawa), i., Indon. | j15 | 39a |
| Jawa, Laut (Java Sea), Indon. | G5 | 38 |
| Jawbar, Syria | A6 | 50 |
| Jawor, Pol. | D16 | 10 |
| Jaworzno, Pol. | E19 | 10 |
| Jay, Fl., U.S. | L9 | 114 |
| Jay, Ok., U.S. | C12 | 116 |
| Jaya, Puncak, mtn., Indon. | F10 | 38 |
| Jayanca, Peru | B2 | 82 |
| Jayapura (Sukarnapura), Indon. | F11 | 38 |
| Jayb, Wādī al- (Ha'Arava), val., Asia | H4 | 50 |
| Jaynes, Az., U.S. | L5 | 120 |
| Jaypur, India | C7 | 46 |
| Jayton, Tx., U.S. | F6 | 116 |
| Jazïr-ye Kharg, Iran | D11 | 47 |
| Jaželbicy, Russia | C15 | 22 |
| Jeanerette, La., U.S. | M5 | 114 |
| Jeanne, Nig. | E12 | 64 |
| Jebenianä, Tun. | D16 | 62 |
| Jebercos, Peru | A3 | 82 |
| Jechegnadzor, Arm. | B8 | 48 |
| Jeddore Lake, res., Nf., Can. | D18 | 106 |
| Jette, Bel. | B5 | 12 |
| Jedrzejów, Pol. | E20 | 10 |
| Jefawa, Sudan | L2 | 60 |
| Jeffara (Al-Jifärah), pl., Afr. | D16 | 62 |
| Jeffers, Mn., U.S. | G12 | 118 |
| Jefferson, Ga., U.S. | E3 | 112 |
| Jefferson, Ia., U.S. | I13 | 118 |
| Jefferson, N.C., U.S. | C5 | 112 |
| Jefferson, Oh., U.S. | F6 | 108 |
| Jefferson, Or., U.S. | F2 | 122 |
| Jefferson, S.C., U.S. | E6 | 112 |
| Jefferson, S.D., U.S. | I11 | 118 |
| Jefferson, Tx., U.S. | J2 | 114 |
| Jefferson, Wi., U.S. | G7 | 110 |
| Jefferson, stm., Mt., U.S. | E13 | 122 |
| Jefferson, Mount, mtn., Nv., U.S. | F9 | 124 |
| Jefferson, Mount, mtn., Or., U.S. | F4 | 122 |
| Jefferson, Mount, mtn., U.S. | F14 | 122 |
| Jefferson City, Mo., U.S. | D4 | 114 |
| Jefferson City, Tn., U.S. | C3 | 112 |
| Jeffersonton, Va., U.S. | I9 | 108 |
| Jeffersontown, Ky., U.S. | D11 | 114 |
| Jeffersonville, Ga., U.S. | G3 | 112 |
| Jeffersonville, In., U.S. | D11 | 114 |
| Jeffersonville, Oh., U.S. | H3 | 108 |
| Jeffrey City, Wy., U.S. | B9 | 120 |
| Jefimovskij, Russia | L24 | 6 |
| Jefremov, Russia | G5 | 26 |
| Jega, Nig. | E12 | 54 |
| Jegenstorf, Switz. | D8 | 13 |
| Jegorjevsk, Russia | F22 | 22 |
| Jëkabpils, Lat. | E8 | 22 |
| Jekaterinburg, Russia | F10 | 26 |
| Jekateriny, proliv, strt., Russia | I21 | 28 |
| Jekimoviči, Russia | G16 | 22 |
| Jekyll Island, i., Ga., U.S. | H5 | 112 |
| Jelabuga, Russia | F8 | 26 |
| Jelancy, Russia | G13 | 28 |
| Jel'cy, Russia | E16 | 22 |
| Jelec, Russia | I21 | 22 |
| Jelenia Góra (Hirschberg), Pol. | E15 | 10 |
| Jelenskij, Russia | H18 | 22 |
| Jelgava, Lat. | E6 | 22 |
| Jelizarovo, Russia | C27 | 22 |
| Jel'niki, Russia | G20 | 28 |
| Jelizovo, mys, c., Russia | C2 | 112 |
| Jel'na, Russia | G16 | 22 |
| Jeinat', Russia | D25 | 22 |
| Jefoguj, stm., Russia | E15 | 28 |
| Ješava, Slvk. | G20 | 10 |
| Jemanželinsk, Russia | G10 | 26 |
| Jember, Indon. | G5 | 38 |
| Jemca, Russia | J27 | 6 |
| Jemez, stm., N.M., U.S. | I10 | 120 |
| Jemez Springs, N.M., U.S. | I10 | 120 |
| Jemmal, Tun. | N5 | 18 |
| Jena, Ger. | E11 | 10 |
| Jena, La., U.S. | K4 | 114 |
| Jenakijeve, Ukr. | H5 | 26 |
| Jenašimskij Poikan, gora, mtn., Russia | F16 | 26 |
| Jenbach, Aus. | H11 | 10 |
| Jandouba (Souk el Arba), Tun. | M3 | 18 |
| Jenisej (Yenisey), stm., Russia | D15 | 26 |
| Jenisejsk, Russia | F10 | 28 |
| Jenisejskij kr'ąž, mts., Russia | F16 | 26 |
| Jenisejskij zaliv, b., Russia | C8 | 28 |
| Jenkins, Ky., U.S. | B4 | 112 |
| Jenkinsville, S.C., U.S. | E5 | 112 |
| Jenkintown, Pa., U.S. | G11 | 108 |
| Jenks, Ok., U.S. | C11 | 116 |
| Jennersdorf, Aus. | I16 | 10 |
| Jennings, Fl., U.S. | I3 | 112 |
| Jennings, La., U.S. | L4 | 114 |
| Jensen, Ut., U.S. | D7 | 120 |
| Jensen Beach, Fl., U.S. | M6 | 112 |
| Jens Munk Island, i., N.T., Can. | C17 | 96 |
| Jepart, Austl. | K4 | 70 |
| Jepelacio, Peru | B3 | 82 |
| Jepifan', Russia | H21 | 22 |
| Jequié, Braz. | F7 | 79 |
| Jequetepeque, stm., Peru | B2 | 82 |
| Jequitaí, Braz. | B8 | 79 |
| Jequitinhonha, Braz. | D6 | 79 |
| Jequitinhonha, stm., Braz. | D9 | 79 |
| Jerada, Mor. | C9 | 62 |
| Jeradou, Tun. | M5 | 18 |
| Jerba, Île de, i., Tun. | D16 | 62 |
| Jerécuaro, Mex. | G9 | 90 |
| Jérémie, Haiti | E7 | 94 |
| Jeremoabo, Braz. | F11 | 76 |
| Jerevan, Arm. | I6 | 26 |
| Jerez de García Salinas, Mex. | F8 | 90 |
| Jerez de la Frontera, Spain | I5 | 16 |
| Jerez de los Caballeros, Spain | G5 | 16 |
| Jergeni, hills, Russia | H6 | 26 |
| Jericho see Arīhä, Gaza | E5 | 84 |
| Jeriänï (Tsinan), China | — | — |
| Jeric, Chott, sw., Tun. | D15 | 62 |
| Jerilderie, Austl. | J6 | 70 |
| Jerimoth Hill, hill, R.I., U.S. | F15 | 108 |
| Jermiš', Russia | G25 | 22 |
| Jermolajevo (Kumertau), Russia | G9 | 26 |
| Jermolino, Russia | F19 | 22 |
| Jeroaquara, Braz. | C3 | 79 |
| Jerofej Pavlovič, Russia | G16 | 28 |
| Jerome, Az., U.S. | J4 | 120 |
| Jerome, Id., U.S. | H11 | 122 |
| Jersey, state, Eur. | F7 | 4 |
| Jersey City, N.J., U.S. | G12 | 108 |
| Jersey Mountain, mtn., Id., U.S. | E10 | 122 |
| Jersey Shore, Pa., U.S. | F9 | 108 |
| Jerseyville, Il., U.S. | C6 | 114 |
| Jershov, Russia | G7 | 26 |
| Jerusalem see Yerushalayim, Isr. | E4 | 50 |
| Jervis, Cape, c., Austl. | J3 | 70 |
| Jervis Bay, b., Austl. | J9 | 70 |
| Jervis Inlet, b., B.C., Can. | H10 | 102 |
| Jesenice, Czech Rep. | E13 | 10 |
| Jesi, Italy | F8 | 18 |
| Jesil', Kaz. | G11 | 26 |
| Jessentuki, Russia | I6 | 26 |
| Jessore, Bngl. | I13 | 44 |
| Jessup, Ga., U.S. | H5 | 112 |
| Jessup, Md., U.S. | H11 | 108 |
| Jesup, Ga., U.S. | H5 | 112 |
| Jesús, Para. | D11 | 80 |
| Jesús Carranza, Mex. | I12 | 90 |
| Jesús de Otoro, Hond. | C7 | 92 |
| Jesús María, Arg. | F7 | 80 |
| Jesús María, Mex. | E6 | 90 |
| Jesús María, Mex. | F7 | 90 |
| Jesús Menéndez, Cuba | D6 | 94 |
| Jetpur, India | J4 | 44 |
| Jever, Ger. | B7 | 10 |
| Jewell, Ia., U.S. | H2 | 110 |
| Jewell, Ks., U.S. | L9 | 118 |
| Jewell Ridge, Va., U.S. | B5 | 112 |
| Jewett, Il., U.S. | C8 | 114 |
| Jewett, Tx., U.S. | H10 | 116 |
| Jewett City, Ct., U.S. | F15 | 108 |
| Jewett Lake, l., Sk., Can. | B10 | 104 |
| Jezerce, mtn., Alb. | G3 | 20 |
| Jeziorany, Pol. | B20 | 10 |
| Jhābua, India | I6 | 44 |
| Jhäläwär, India | H7 | 44 |
| Jhal Jhao, Pak. | E4 | 44 |
| Jhang Sadar, Pak. | E5 | 44 |
| Jhänsi, India | H8 | 44 |
| Jharia, India | I12 | 44 |
| Jhärsuguda, India | B8 | 46 |
| Jhelum, Pak. | D5 | 44 |
| Jhelum, stm., Asia | E5 | 44 |
| Jhok Rind, Pak. | E4 | 44 |
| Jhunjhunūn, India | F6 | 44 |
| Jiaban, China | B9 | 40 |
| Jiading, China | D10 | 34 |
| Jiägañj, India | H13 | 44 |
| Jiakou, China | E8 | 34 |
| Jiali, China | E5 | 30 |
| Jialing, stm., China | E8 | 30 |
| Jialu, China | D2 | 34 |
| Jiamusi, China | B13 | 30 |
| Ji'an, China | H3 | 34 |
| Jianchang, China | B12 | 32 |
| Jianchuan, China | A5 | 40 |
| Jiangbeixu, China | I4 | 40 |
| Jiangbianzhai, China | C6 | 40 |
| Jiangcun, China | G6 | 34 |
| Jiangdihe, China | B6 | 40 |
| Jiangduo, China | C9 | 34 |
| Jiangge, China | D7 | 32 |
| Jiangji, China | C4 | 34 |
| Jiangkou, China | F8 | 30 |
| Jiangkou, China | G9 | 30 |
| Jiangkou, China | H7 | 34 |
| Jiangkouji, China | C5 | 34 |
| Jiangliadian, China | D10 | 34 |
| Jiangmen, China | M2 | 34 |
| Jiangsu (Kiangsu), prov., China | E10 | 30 |
| Jiangtun, China | B10 | 32 |
| Jiangxi (Kiangsi), prov., China | F10 | 30 |
| Jiangxiang, China | C6 | 34 |
| Jiangyin, China | D9 | 34 |
| Jiangzhasiji, China | E13 | 44 |
| Jianli, China | F1 | 34 |
| Jianning, China | I5 | 34 |
| Jian'ou, China | H7 | 34 |
| Jianshan, China | F9 | 34 |
| Jianshui, China | C7 | 40 |
| Jiantouji, China | I5 | 32 |
| Jiaohe, China | C12 | 32 |
| Jiaomei, China | K6 | 34 |
| Jiaoshanhe, China | F1 | 34 |
| Jiaoxian, China | G7 | 32 |
| Jiaozuo, China | D9 | 30 |
| Jieshun Hu, l., China | C12 | 44 |
| Jiewang, China | A5 | 34 |
| Jiexian, China | B2 | 34 |
| Jiexiu, China | F3 | 34 |
| Jiazi, China | M5 | 34 |
| Jibiya, Nig. | E13 | 64 |
| Jiboa, stm., El Sal. | D5 | 92 |
| Jicarón, Isla, i., Pan. | D2 | 84 |
| Jicatuyo, stm., Hond. | C6 | 92 |
| Jiddah (Jeddah), Sau. Ar. | D1 | 47 |
| Jidingxilin, China | D15 | 44 |
| Jiedong, China | I2 | 34 |
| Jiehe, China | H5 | 32 |
| Jieji, China | B7 | 34 |
| Jiepai, China | E4 | 34 |
| Jiesheng, China | M4 | 34 |
| Jieshou, China | B4 | 34 |
| Jieyang, China | L5 | 34 |
| Jiezna, Lith. | G7 | 22 |
| Jigongzhen, China | A4 | 34 |
| Jiguaní, Cuba | D6 | 94 |
| Jiguanshan, China | A12 | 32 |
| Jigüey, Bahía de, b., Cuba | F15 | 90 |
| Jihlava, Czech Rep. | F15 | 10 |
| Jijel, Alg. | B13 | 62 |
| Jijiadianzi, China | H6 | 32 |
| Jikawo, Eth. | M7 | 60 |
| Jikawo, stm., Afr. | M8 | 60 |
| Jilib, Som. | A8 | 58 |
| Jili Hu, l., China | B4 | 30 |
| Jilin, China | C12 | 30 |
| Jilin (Kirin), prov., China | C12 | 30 |
| Jill, Kediet ej, mtn., Maur. | I4 | 62 |
| Jima, Eth. | N9 | 60 |
| Jimbolia, Rom. | D4 | 20 |
| Jiménez, Mex. | D7 | 90 |
| Jiménez, Mex. | F7 | 90 |
| Jiménez del Téul, Mex. | G8 | 32 |
| Jim Thorpe, Pa., U.S. | G11 | 108 |
| Jimo, China | G8 | 32 |
| Jin (Gam), stm., Asia | C8 | 40 |
| Jinäh, Egypt | E6 | 60 |
| Jinan (Tsinan), China | G7 | 32 |
| Jincheng, China | D9 | 30 |
| Jīnd, India | F7 | 44 |
| Jindřichův Hradec, Czech Rep. | F15 | 10 |
| Jingangtou, China | H2 | 34 |
| Jingcheng, China | K6 | 32 |
| Jingdezhen (Kingtechen), China | F6 | 34 |
| Jinggang, China | C3 | 34 |
| Jinggangshan (Ciping), China | I3 | 34 |
| Jinghai, China | E4 | 32 |
| Jinghaiwei, China | G10 | 32 |
| Jinghong, China | C6 | 40 |
| Jingjiang, China | B8 | 34 |
| Jingning, China | C9 | 40 |
| Jingxi, China | C9 | 40 |
| Jingxian, China | F4 | 32 |
| Jingyu, China | A14 | 32 |
| Jingzhi, China | G7 | 32 |
| Jinhua, China | C9 | 30 |
| Jining, China | F4 | 32 |
| Jinja, Ug. | A6 | 58 |
| Jinjiang, China | B6 | 34 |
| Jinkeng, China | G7 | 34 |
| Jinkou, China | G8 | 32 |
| Jinlingzhen, China | G6 | 32 |
| Jinmu Jiao, c., China | H8 | 30 |
| Jinning, China | B7 | 40 |
| Jinotega, Nic. | D8 | 92 |
| Jinotega, dept., Nic. | D8 | 92 |
| Jinotepe, Nic. | E8 | 92 |
| Jinping, China | A10 | 40 |
| Jinping, China | C8 | 40 |
| Jinsha, stm., China | E6 | 30 |
| Jinshan, China | C10 | 34 |
| Jinshi, China | F9 | 34 |
| Jintian, China | G6 | 34 |
| Jinxi, China | D9 | 34 |
| Jinxian, China | D9 | 34 |
| Jinyun, China | G9 | 34 |

**Name — Map Ref. — Page**

Jinzhaizhen, China — D4 34
Jinzhou (Chinchou), China — B9 32
Ji-Paraná, Braz. — D11 82
Jipijapa, Ec. — H2 84
Jiquilisco, El Sal. — D6 92
Jiquilisco, Bahía de b., El Sal. — D6 92
Jiquiriçá, stm., Braz. — B8 79
Jirāfī, Wādī al- (Naḥal Paran), val. — I3 50
Jirbān, Sudan — L6 60
Jirjā, Egypt — D6 60
Jirkov, Czech Rep. — E13 10
Jiroft, Iran — G14 48
Jisr ash-Shughūr, Syria — D6 48
Jitan, China — K4 34
Jitaúna, Braz. — C9 79
Jiu, stm., Rom. — F7 20
Jiubao, China — J4 34
Jiucheng, China — E5 32
Jiuguan, China — F9 32
Jiuhu, China — F5 32
Jiuhuaxian, China — L2 34
Jiujiang, China — F4 34
Jiukou, China — E1 34
Jiulian Shan, mts., China — K3 34
Jiuling Shan, mts., China — G3 34
Jiulong, China — K1 34
Jiumianyang, China — E2 34
Jiuningyang, China — J6 34
Jiuquan, China — D6 30
Jiushangshui, China — B3 34
Jiutai, China — C12 30
Jiuxian, China — B2 34
Jiuxiangcheng, China — B3 34
Jixi, China — B13 30
Jixian, China — H2 32
Jixian, China — C5 32
Jixingji, China — C5 34
Jiyang, China — G5 32
Jīzān, Sau. Ar. — F3 47
Joaçaba, Braz. — D13 80
Joaíma, Braz. — D8 79
Joanna, S.C., U.S. — E5 112
João Neiva, Braz. — E8 79
João Pessoa, Braz. — E12 76
João Pinheiro, Braz. — D5 79
Joaquim Távora, Braz. — G4 79
Joaquín, Tx., U.S. — K2 114
Joaquín V. González, Arg. — C6 80
Job Peak, mtn., Nv., U.S. — E7 124
Jocolí, Arg. — G4 80
Jocón, Hond. — B8 92
Jocoro, El Sal. — D6 92
Jocotán, Guat. — C5 92
Jódar, Spain — H8 16
Jodhpur, India — G5 44
Joe Batt's Arm, Nf., Can. — C19 106
Joensuu, Fin. — J21 6
Joetsu, Japan — J13 36
Joffre, Mount, mtn., Can. — G19 102
Jõgeva, Est. — C9 22
Jog Falls, wtfl, India — E3 46
Joggins, N.S., Can. — G9 106
Jogui, stm., Braz. — G1 79
Johannesburg, Ca., U.S. — I8 124
Johannesburg, S. Afr. — F9 66
John Day, Or., U.S. — F7 122
John Day, stm., Or., U.S. — E5 122
John H. Kerr Reservoir, res., U.S. — C8 112
John Martin Reservoir, res., Co., U.S. — M4 118
John o' Groats, Scot., U.K. — C10 8
John Redmond Reservoir, res., Ks., U.S. — M12 118
Johnson, Ar., U.S. — F2 114
Johnson, Ks., U.S. — N6 118
Johnson, Ne., U.S. — K12 118
Johnson, Vt., U.S. — C14 108
Johnsonburg, Pa., U.S. — F8 108
Johnson City, N.Y., U.S. — E11 108
Johnson City, Tn., U.S. — C4 112
Johnson City, Tx., U.S. — I8 116
Johnsondale, Ca., U.S. — I7 124
Johnsons Crossing, Yk., Can. — F28 100
Johnsonville, S.C., U.S. — F7 112
Johnston, Ia., U.S. — I2 110
Johnston, S.C., U.S. — F5 112
Johnston Atoll, atoll, Oc. — G23 126
Johnston City, Il., U.S. — E8 114
Johnstone Strait, strt., B.C., Can. — G8 102
Johnstown, Co., U.S. — D12 108
Johnstown, N.Y., U.S. — D12 108
Johnstown, Oh., U.S. — G4 108
Johnstown, Pa., U.S. — G8 108
Johor Baharu, Malay. — N7 40
Joigny, Fr. — E10 14
Joiner, Ar., U.S. — H6 114
Joinville, Braz. — D14 80
Joinville, Fr. — D12 14
Joinville Island, i., Ant. — B1 73
Jokkmokk, Swe. — H16 6
Jolärpettai, India — F5 46
Jolfā, Iran — B8 48
Joliet, Il., U.S. — I7 110
Joliet, Mt., U.S. — E17 122
Joliette, P.Q., Can. — A13 108
Jolo, Phil. — D7 38
Jomda, China — E6 30
Jonava, Lith. — F7 22
Jones, Ok., U.S. — D9 116
Jonesboro, Ar., U.S. — G6 114
Jonesboro, Ga., U.S. — F2 112
Jonesboro, Il., U.S. — E7 114
Jonesboro, In., U.S. — B11 114
Jonesboro, La., U.S. — J4 114
Jonesboro, Tn., U.S. — C4 112
Jonesburg, Mo., U.S. — D5 114
Jones Mill, Ar., U.S. — H4 114
Jonesport, Me., U.S. — C19 108
Jones Sound, strt., N.T., Can. — A15 96
Jonestown, Ms., U.S. — H6 114
Jonestown, Pa., U.S. — K5 114
Jonesville, La., U.S. — K5 114
Jonesville, Mi., U.S. — I11 110
Jonesville, N.C., U.S. — C6 112
Jonesville, S.C., U.S. — E5 112
Jonesville, Va., U.S. — C3 112
Joniškėlis, Lith. — E7 22
Joniškis, Lith. — E6 22
Jönköping, Swe. — M14 6
Jonquière, P.Q., Can. — D2 106
Jonuta, Mex. — H13 90
Joplin, Mo., U.S. — E2 114
Joplin, Mt., U.S. — B15 122
Joppa, Il., U.S. — E8 114
Jordan, Mn., U.S. — F2 110
Jordan, N.Y., U.S. — D10 108
Jordan (Al-Urdun), ctry., Asia — C2 42
Jordan (Nahr al-Urdun) (HaYarden), stm., Asia — E5 50
Jordan, stm., Ut., U.S. — D5 120
Jordânia, Braz. — C8 79
Jordanów, Pol. — F19 10
Jordan Valley, Or., U.S. — H8 122
Jordet, Nor. — K13 6
Jorhāt, India — G16 44

Jornado del Muerto, des., N.M., U.S. — K10 120
José Battle y Ordóñez, Ur. — G11 80
José Bonifácio, Braz. — F4 79
José Francisco Vergara, Chile — B4 80
Joselândia, Braz. — G13 82
José Pedro Varela, Ur. — G11 80
Joseph, Or., U.S. — E8 122
Joseph, Lac, l., Nf., Can. — F19 96
Joseph Bonaparte Gulf, b., Austl. — B5 68
Joseph City, Az., U.S. — J6 120
Joshua, Tx., U.S. — G9 116
Joshua Tree, Ca., U.S. — J9 124
Joškar-Ola, Russia — F7 26
Josselin, Fr. — E4 14
Joubertina, S. Afr. — I6 66
Jourdanton, Tx., U.S. — K8 116
Jovellanos, Cuba — C4 94
Joviânia, Braz. — D4 79
Jowhar, Som. — H10 56
Joy, Il., U.S. — I5 110
Joy, Mount, mtn., Yk., Can. — E28 100
Joyce, Ca., U.S. — K4 114
Józefów, Pol. — C21 10
J. Percy Priest Lake, res., Tn., U.S. — F10 114
Juami, stm., Braz. — H9 84
Juan Aldama, Mex. — E8 90
Juan B. Arruabarrena, Arg. — F9 80
Juan Bautista Alberdi, Arg. — D6 80
Juan de Fuca, Strait of, strt., N.A. — I10 102
Juan de Mena, Para. — C10 80
Juan de Nova, Île, i., Afr. — E8 58
Juan Eugenio, Mex. — E8 90
Juan Fernández, Archipiélago, is., Chile — C1 79
Juangriego, Ven. — B11 84
Juan Guerra, Peru — B3 82
Juan Jorba, Arg. — G6 80
Juan José Castelli, Arg. — C8 80
Juanjuí, Peru — B3 82
Juan L. Lacaze, Ur. — H10 80
Juan N. Fernández, Arg. — J9 80
Juan Pérez Sound, strt., Can. — E3 102
Juan Viñas, C.R. — H11 92
Juárez, Mex. — D9 90
Juárez, Mex. — B5 90
Juárez see Ciudad Juárez, Mex. — B6 90
Juárez, Sierra de, mts., Mex. — B2 90
Juatinga, Ponta de, c., Braz. — G6 79
Juàzeiro, Braz. — E10 76
Juazeiro do Norte, Braz. — E11 76
Jūbā, Sudan — H7 56
Juba, stm., Braz. — F12 82
Jūbāl, Sudan — D7 60
Jūbāl, Maḍīq, strt., Egypt — D7 60
Jubayb, Eth. — O9 60
Jubayt, Sudan — H9 60
Jubba (Genale), stm., Afr. — H9 56
Jubbah, Sau. Ar. — G6 48
Jubilee Lake, l., Nf., Can. — D18 106
Jubones, stm., Ec. — I3 84
Juby, Cap, c., Mor. — G4 62
Júcar (Xúquer), stm., Spain — F10 16
Jucás, Braz. — C3 79
Júcaro, Cuba — D5 94
Juchipila, Mex. — G8 90
Juchitán de Zaragoza, Mex. — I12 90
Jucurucu, stm., Braz. — D9 79
Jucuapa, El Sal. — D6 92
Judaea, hist. reg., Asia — E4 50
Judas, Punta, c., C.R. — H10 92
Jude Island, i., Nf., Can. — E19 106
Judenburg, Aus. — H14 10
Judique, N.S., Can. — G12 106
Judith, stm., Mt., U.S. — C16 122
Judith Gap, Mt., U.S. — D16 122
Judith Mountains, mts., Mt., U.S. — C16 122
Judson, S.C., U.S. — E4 112
Judsonia, Ar., U.S. — G5 114
Juexi, China — F10 34
Jufari, stm., Braz. — H11 84
Jugon, Fr. — D4 14
Juhā, Sau. Ar. — F3 47
Juhavič, Bela. — E11 22
Juidongshan, China — L6 34
Juigalpa, Nic. — E9 92
Juína, stm., Braz. — E12 82
Juiz de Fora, Braz. — F7 79
Jujuy, prov., Arg. — B5 80
Jukagirskoje ploskogorje, plat., Russia — D23 28
Julesburg, Co., U.S. — K5 118
Juli, Peru — G7 82
Juliaca, Peru — G6 82
Julia Creek, Austl. — C4 70
Julianakanaal, Neth. — F8 12
Julian Alps, mts., Eur. — C8 18
Julianehåb (Qaqortoq), Grnld. — D23 96
Jülich, Ger. — E6 12
Júlio de Castilhos, Braz. — E12 80
Julu, China — F3 32
Juma, Russia — I23 6
Jumay, Volcán, vol., Guat. — C5 92
Jumbilla, Peru — A3 82
Jumboo, Som. — B8 58
Jumentos Cays, is., Bah. — C7 94
Jumet, Bel. — H5 12
Jumilla, Spain — G10 16
Jump, stm., Wi., U.S. — E5 110
Junaynah, Ra's al-, mtn., Egypt — I4 48
Junction, Tx., U.S. — I7 116
Junction, Ut., U.S. — F4 120
Junction City, Ar., U.S. — I4 114
Junction City, Ks., U.S. — L11 118
Junction City, Ky., U.S. — E12 114
Junction City, Or., U.S. — F3 122
Juneau, Ak., U.S. — G27 100a
Juneau, Wi., U.S. — G7 110
June, Austl. — J7 70
June Lake, Ca., U.S. — G6 124
Jungfrau, mtn., Switz. — E8 13
Junggar Pendi, China — B4 30
Jungshāhi, Pak. — H2 44
Juniata, stm., Pa., U.S. — G9 108
Junín, Arg. — H2 84
Junín, Ec. — H2 84
Junín, Peru — D3 82
Junín, dépt., Peru — D3 82
Junín, lago de, l., Peru — D3 82
Juniper, Can. — F6 106

Juniville, Fr. — C11 14
Jos, Nig. — G14 64
Juntas, C.R. — G9 92
Junxian, China — E9 30
Juparanã, Lagoa l., Braz. — C5 92
Jupilingo, stm., Guat. — C5 92
Jupiter, Fl., U.S. — M6 112
Jupiter, stm., P.Q., Can. — C10 106
Juquiá, Braz. — C15 80
Juquiá, Ponta do, c., Braz. — C15 80
Juquiá, stm., Braz. — B12 80
Jura, state, Switz. — D7 13
Jura, dépt., Fr. — F12 14
Jura, mts., Eur. — F13 14
Jura, i., Scot., U.K. — E8 8
Juraciški, Bela. — G8 22
Jurbarkas, Lith. — F5 22
Jurf ad-Darāwīsh, Jord. — G5 50
Jurga, Russia — F8 28
Juruá, Braz. — I9 84
Juruá, stm., S.A. — D5 76
Juruena, stm., Braz. — B12 82
Jurupari, stm., Braz. — C7 82
Jur'uzan', Russia — G9 26
Juscelândia, Braz. — C3 79
Jusepín, Ven. — C11 84
Juskatla, B.C., Can. — D2 102
Jussey, Fr. — E12 14
Justiniano Posse, Arg. — G7 80
Justo Daract, Arg. — G6 80
Jutaí, Braz. — A7 82
Jutaí, stm., Braz. — D5 76
Jüterbog, Ger. — D13 10
Juti, Braz. — G1 79
Jutiapa, Guat. — C5 92
Jutiapa, dépt., Guat. — C5 92
Juticalpa, Hond. — C8 92
Jutiquile, Hond. — C8 92
Jutland see Jylland, pen., Den. — M11 6
Juva, Fin. — K20 6
Juventud, Isla de la (Isla de Pinos), i., Cuba — D3 94
Juxi, China — H8 34
Juža, Russia — E25 22
Južno-Sachalinsk, Russia — H20 28
Južno-Ural'sk, Russia — G10 26
Južnyj, mys, c., Russia — F23 28
Jwayyā, Leb. — B4 50
Jylland, reg., Den. — M11 6
Jyväskylä, Fin. — J19 6

**K**

K2 (Qogir Feng), mtn., Asia — C7 44
Kaachka, Turk. — C15 48
Kaala, mtn., Hi., U.S. — p15 125a
Kaapstad see Cape Town, S. Afr. — I4 66
Kabah, hist., Mex. — G15 90
Kabale, Ug. — B5 58
Kabalo, D.R.C. — C5 58
Kabambare, D.R.C. — B5 58
Kabangu, D.R.C. — C5 58
Kabetogama Lake, l., Mn., U.S. — B2 110
Kabinda, D.R.C. — C4 58
Kabkābīyah, Sudan — K3 60
Kabna, Sudan — H7 60
Kābol, Afg. — C3 44
Kābol, stm., Asia — C4 44
Kabompo, stm., Zam. — D4 58
Kabongo, D.R.C. — C5 58
Kabot, Gui. — F2 64
Kabou, Togo — G10 64
Kabr, Sudan — L4 60
Kābul see Kābol, Afg. — C3 44
Kaburuang, Pulau, i., Indon. — E8 38
Kabwe (Broken Hill), Zam. — D5 58
Kačanik, Yugo. — G5 20
Kačerginė, Lith. — G6 22
Kachchh, Gulf of, b., India — I3 44
Kachemak Bay, b., Ak., U.S. — G19 100
Kachisi, Eth. — M9 60
K'achta, Russia — G13 28
Kačug, Russia — G13 28
Kadaiyanallūr, India — H4 46
Kadanai (Kadaney), stm., Asia — E2 44
Kadaney (Kadanai), stm., Asia — E2 44
Kade, Ghana — H9 64
Kadi, India — I5 44
Kadiana, Mali — F6 64
Kadina, Austl. — I2 70
Kadirli, Tur. — C4 48
Kadja, Ouadi (Wādī Kaja), val., Afr. — L3 60
Kadnikov, Russia — B23 22
Kadnikovskij, Russia — A23 22
Kadodo, Sudan — L5 60
Kadoka, S.D., U.S. — H6 118
Kadoma, Zimb. — B9 66
Kaduj, Russia — B20 22
Kaduna, Nig. — F13 64
Kaduna, stm., Nig. — G12 64
Kādūqlī, Sudan — L5 60
Kadyčkan, Russia — E21 28
Kadžerom, Russia — H9 26
Kaech'on, N. Kor. — D13 32
Kaédi, Maur. — C3 64
Kaegudeck Lake, l., Nf., Can. — D18 106
Kaena Point, c., Hi., U.S. — p15 125a
Kaesŏng, N. Kor. — F14 32
Kāf, Sau. Ar. — F4 48
Kafan, Arm. — B9 48
Kafanchan, Nig. — G14 64
Kaffrine, Sen. — D2 64
Kafia Kingi, Sudan — M3 60
Kafin Madaki, Nig. — F14 64
Kafirévs, Ákra, c., Grc. — K8 20
Kafr ad-Dawwār, Egypt — B6 60
Kafr ash-Shaykh, Egypt — B6 60
Kafue, stm., Zam. — D5 58
Kafue, Zam. — E5 58
Kaga, Japan — K11 36
Kagan, Uzb. — J10 26
Kagaznagar, India — B5 46
Kagera, stm., Afr. — B6 58
Kağızman, Tur. — A7 48
Kagmar, Sudan — K6 60
Kagoshima, Japan — P5 36
Kagoshima-wan, b., Japan — P5 36
Kahama, Tan. — B6 58
Kahayan, stm., Indon. — F5 38
Kahemba, D.R.C. — C3 58
Kahnūj, Iran — H14 48
Kahoka, Mo., U.S. — B5 114

Kahoolawe, i., Hi., U.S. — q17 125a
Kahramanmaraş, Tur. — C4 48
Kahuku, Hi., U.S. — p16 125a
Kahuku Point, c., Hi., U.S. — p16 125a
Kahului Bay, b., Hi., U.S. — q17 125a
Kai, Kepulauan, is., Indon. — G9 38
Kaiama, Nig. — G11 64
Kaibab Plateau, plat., Az., U.S. — H4 120
Kaibito Plateau, plat., Az., U.S. — H5 120
Kaidu, stm., China — C4 30
Kaieteur Fall, wtfl, Guy. — E13 84
Kaifeng, China — E4 32
Kaikoura, S.L. — G4 64
Kaili, China — A9 40
Kailu, China — C11 30
Kailua, Hi., U.S. — p16 125a
Kailua Kona, Hi., U.S. — r18 125a
Kaimanawa Mountains, mts., N.Z. — C5 72
Kainan, Japan — M10 36
Kaipara Harbour, b., N.Z. — B5 72
Kaiping, China — G9 30
Kairāna, India — F7 44
Kairouan, Tun. — N5 18
Kaiserslautern, Ger. — F7 10
Kaishantun, China — A17 32
Kaišiadorys, Lith. — G7 22
Kaitangata, N.Z. — G2 72
Kaithal, India — F7 44
Kaituma, stm., Guy. — D13 84
Kaiwi Channel, strt., Hi., U.S. — p16 125a
Kaiyuan, China — A9 40
Kaja, Wādī (Ouadi Kadja), val., Afr. — L3 60
Kajaani, Fin. — I20 6
Kajang, Malay. — M6 40
Kajnar, Kaz. — H13 26
Kaka, C.A.R. — N4 60
Kākā, Sudan — L7 60
Kakadu National Park, Austl. — B6 68
Kakagi Lake, l., On., Can. — I21 104
Kakamas, S. Afr. — G5 66
Kake, Ak., U.S. — H28 100
Kakegawa, Japan — M13 36
Kakhovs'ke vodoskhovyshche, res., Ukr. — H4 26
Kākināda, India — D7 46
Kakisa Lake, l., N.T., Can. — D9 96
Kako, stm., Guy. — E12 84
Kakoaka, Bots. — B7 66
Kakogawa, Japan — M9 36
Kaktovik, Ak., U.S. — A23 100
Kakwa, stm., Ab., Can. — C15 102
Kalaa Kebira, Tun. — N5 18
Kalaallit Nunaat see Greenland, dep., N.A. — B15 86
Kalaa Sghira, Tun. — N5 18
Kālābāgh, Pak. — D4 44
Kalabo, Zam. — D4 58
Kalač, Russia — G6 26
Kalač-na-Donu, Russia — H6 26
Kaladan, stm., Asia — D2 40
Kalae, c., Hi., U.S. — s18 125a
Kalahari Desert, des., Afr. — C4 58
Kalai-Chumb, Taj. — A4 44
Kalai-Mor, Turk. — D17 48
Kalajoki, Fin. — I18 6
Kalakamate, Bots. — C8 66
Kalām, Pak. — C5 44
Kalama, Wa., U.S. — D3 122
Kalámai, Grc. — L6 20
Kalamalka Lake, l., B.C., Can. — G15 102
Kalamazoo, Mi., U.S. — H10 110
Kalamazoo, stm., Mi., U.S. — H9 110
Kalapana, Hi., U.S. — r19 125a
Kalár, stm., Russia — F17 28
Kalašnikovo, Russia — D18 22
Kalāt, Pak. — F2 44
Kalaw, Myan. — D4 40
Kal'azin, Russia — D20 22
Kalb, Ra's al-, c., Yemen — G6 47
Kalbarri, Austl. — E2 68
Kaleden, B.C., Can. — H15 102
Kalemie (Albertville), D.R.C. — C5 58
Kalemyo, Myan. — C2 40
Kaletwa, Myan. — D2 40
Kalewa, Myan. — C2 40
Kālfafell, Ice. — C5 6a
Kalgan see Zhangjiakou, China — C4 32
Kalgoorlie-Boulder, Austl. — F4 68
Kali, stm., India — E4 46
Kaliakra, nos, c., Bul. — F12 20
Kalibo, Phil. — C7 38
Kalima, D.R.C. — B5 58
Kalimantan see Borneo, i., Asia — E5 38
Kálimnos, Grc. — M10 20
Kālimpang, India — G13 44
Kalinin see Tver', Russia — E18 22
Kaliningrad (Königsberg), Russia — G3 22
Kalininkavičy, Bela. — I12 22
Kalinkavičy, Bela. — I12 22
Kalispell, Mt., U.S. — B11 122
Kalisz, Pol. — D18 10
Kalkaska, Mi., U.S. — F10 110
Kalkfontein, Bots. — D5 66
Kallaste, Est. — C10 22
Kallavesi, l., Fin. — J20 6
Kalliecahoolie Lake, l., Mb., Can. — D19 104
Kalmar, Swe. — M15 6
Kalmykia see Kalmykija, state, Russia — H7 26
Kalmykija, state, Russia — H7 26
Kālna, India — I13 44
Kālol, India — I5 44
Kalomo, Zam. — D5 58
Kalone Peak, mtn., B.C., Can. — I4 110
Kalpeni Island, i., India — g2 46a
Kalskag, Ak., U.S. — F14 100
Kaltag, Ak., U.S. — D15 100
Kaluga, Russia — G19 22
Kalundborg, Den. — N12 6
Kałuszyn, Pol. — C21 10
Kalutara, Sri L. — I5 46
Kalvarija, Lith. — G6 22
Kalyān, India — C2 46
Kama, stm., Russia — F8 26
Kamaishi, Japan — H16 36
Kamakou, mtn., Hi., U.S. — p17 125a
Kamanjab, Nmb. — B2 66

Kamarān, i., Yemen — G3 47
Kamarang, stm., S.A. — E12 84
Kamas, Ut., U.S. — D5 120
Kamatsi Lake, l., Sk., Can. — B12 104
Kamay, Tx., U.S. — F8 116
Kamba, Nig. — F11 64
Kambam, India — H4 46
Kambar, Pak. — G3 44
Kambarka, Russia — E4 72
Kambia, S.L. — G3 64
Kamčatka, poluostrov (Kamchatka), pen., Russia — F24 28
Kamčatskij zaliv, b., Russia — F25 28
Kamchatka see Kamčatka, poluostrov, pen., Russia — F24 28
Kamčija, stm., Bul. — I8 20
Kamen', gora, mtn., Russia — D16 26
Kamenka, Russia — G6 26
Kamen'-na-Obi, Russia — G8 28
Kamennogorsk, Russia — K21 6
Kamensk-Ural'skij, Russia — F10 26
Kameškovo, Russia — E24 22
Kamět, mtn., Asia — B5 44
Kamiah, Id., U.S. — D9 122
Kamienna Góra, Pol. — E16 10
Kamień, Pol. — D19 10
Kamilukuak Lake, l., N.T., Can. — D12 96
Kaminak Lake, l., N.T., Can. — D13 96
Kaminoyama, Japan — H15 36
Kaminskij, Russia — D24 22
Kaminuriak Lake, l., N.T., Can. — D13 96
Kamishak Bay, b., Ak., U.S. — G18 100
Kamisunagawa, Japan — d17 36a
Kamjanec, Bela. — I6 22
Kamloops, B.C., Can. — G14 102
Kamloops Indian Reserve, B.C., Can. — G14 102
Kamloops Lake, l., B.C., Can. — G14 102
Kamo, Arm. — A8 48
Kamoa Mountains, mts., Guy. — G13 84
Kampala, Ug. — A6 58
Kampar, Malay. — L6 40
Kampar, stm., Indon. — N7 40
Kamphaeng Phet, Thai. — F5 40
Kâmpông Cham, Camb. — H8 40
Kâmpông Chhnăng, Camb. — H8 40
Kâmpông Saôm, Camb. — I7 40
Kâmpông Saôm, Chhâk, b., Camb. — I7 40
Kâmpông Thum, Camb. — H8 40
Kâmpôt, Camb. — I8 40
Kâmpúchéa see Cambodia, ctry., Asia — C4 38
Kamsack, Sk., Can. — G13 104
Kamskoe vodohranilišče, res., Russia — F9 26
Kāmthi, India — B5 46
Kamuchawie Lake, l., Sk., Can. — B8 104
Kamuela (Waimea), Hi., U.S. — q18 125a
Kámuk, Cerro, mtn., C.R. — H11 92
Kam'yanets'-Podil's'kyy, Ukr. — H3 26
Kamyšin, Russia — G7 26
Kamyšlov, Russia — F10 26
Kanaaupscow, stm., P.Q., Can. — F17 96
Kanab, Ut., U.S. — G4 120
Kanab Plateau, plat., Az., U.S. — H4 120
Kanafis, Sudan — M3 60
Kanaga Volcano, vol., Ak., U.S. — K6 100
Kananga (Luluabourg), D.R.C. — C4 58
Kanarraville, Ut., U.S. — G3 120
Kanaš, Russia — F7 26
Kanawha, Ia., U.S. — H2 110
Kanawha, stm., W.V., U.S. — I4 108
Kanazawa, Japan — K11 36
Kanchanaburi, Thai. — G5 40
Kānchenjunga, mtn., Asia — G13 44
Kānchipuram, India — F5 46
Kandahār, Sk., Can. — G10 104
Kandalakša, Russia — D4 26
Kandalakšskaja guba, b., Russia — H23 6
Kandangan, Indon. — F6 38
Kandava, Lat. — D5 22
Kandersteg, Switz. — F8 13
Kandi, Benin — F11 64
Kandiāro, Pak. — G3 44
Kandik, stm., N.A. — D24 100
Kandla, India — I3 44
Kandos, Austl. — I8 70
Kandrāch, Pak. — H1 44
Kandy, Sri L. — I6 46
Kane, Pa., U.S. — F8 108
Kāne'ohe Bay, b., Hi., U.S. — p16 125a
Kang, Bots. — D6 66
Kangal, Tur. — B4 48
Kangar, Malay. — K6 40
Kangaroo Island, i., Austl. — J2 70
Kangding, China — E7 30
Kangdong, N. Kor. — D14 32
Kangean, Kepulauan, is., Indon. — G6 38
Kanggye, N. Kor. — C14 32
Kanghwa-man, b., S. Kor. — F14 32
Kangiqsualujjuaq, P.Q., Can. — E19 96
Kangirsuk, P.Q., Can. — D18 96
Kango, Gabon — A2 58
Kangsŏ, N. Kor. — E13 32
Kangto, mtn., Asia — F15 44
Kangyidaung, Myan. — F2 40
Kani, Myan. — C2 40
Kaniama, D.R.C. — C4 58
Kanin, poluostrov, pen., Russia — D7 26
Kanin Nos, mys, c., Russia — D6 26
Kaniva, Austl. — K4 70
Kanjiža, Yugo. — C4 20
Kankakee, Il., U.S. — I8 110
Kankakee, stm., U.S. — A8 114
Kankan, Gui. — F4 64
Kankossa, Maur. — D4 64
Kanmaw Kyun, i., Myan. — I5 40

Kannapolis, N.C., U.S. — D6 112
Kannauj, India — G8 44
Kano, Nig. — E14 64
Kanonji, Japan — M8 36
Kanopolis, Ks., U.S. — M9 118
Kanorado, Ks., U.S. — L5 118
Kanosh, Ut., U.S. — F4 120
Kanoya, Japan — P5 36
Kānpur, India — G9 44
Kansas, Il., U.S. — C9 114
Kansas, state, U.S. — D7 98
Kansas, stm., Ks., U.S. — L11 118
Kansas City, Ks., U.S. — L13 118
Kansas City, Mo., U.S. — C2 114
Kanshan, China — E9 34
Kansk, Russia — F12 28
Kansu see Gansu, prov., China — D7 30
Kant, Kyrg. — I12 26
Kantang, Thai. — K5 40
Kantchè, Niger — E14 64
Kantishna, stm., Ak., U.S. — D19 100
Kantō-sanchi, mts., Japan — K13 36
Kantunilkin, Mex. — G16 90
Kanuku Mountains, mts., Guy. — F13 84
Kanuma, Japan — K14 36
Kanus, Nmb. — F4 66
Kan'utino, Russia — F16 22
Kanye, Bots. — E7 66
Kanyu, D.R.C. — C7 66
Kaohsiung, Tai. — M9 34
Kaohsiunghsien, Tai. — M9 34
Kaoko Veld, plat., Nmb. — B1 66
Kaolack, Sen. — D1 64
Kaoma, Zam. — D4 58
Kaoshanpu, China — e3 34
Kapaa, Hi., U.S. — o14 125a
Kapadvanj, India — I5 44
Kapanga, D.R.C. — C4 58
Kapčagaj, Kaz. — I13 26
Kapčagajskoje vodochranilišče, res., Kaz. — I13 26
Kapcevičy, Bela. — H15 10
Kapfenberg, Aus. — H15 10
Kapikik Lake, l., On., Can. — G23 104
Kapiskau, stm., On., Can. — F16 96
Kaplan, La., U.S. — L4 114
Kapoe, Thai. — J5 40
Kaposvár, Hung. — I17 10
Kappeln, Ger. — A9 10
Kapps, Nmb. — D3 66
Kaprun, Aus. — H12 10
Kapsan, N. Kor. — B16 32
Kapuas, stm., Indon. — F4 38
Kapuas Hulu, Pegunungan, mts., Asia — E5 38
Kapunda, Austl. — J3 70
Kapūrthala, India — E6 44
Kapuskasing, On., Can. — G16 96
Kapuskasing, stm., On., Can. — G16 96
Kapuvár, Hung. — H17 10
Kapyl', Bela. — H10 22
Kara, stm., Afr. — G10 64
Kara-Balta, Kyrg. — I12 26
Karabanovo, Russia — E21 22
Karabekaul, Turk. — B18 48
Kara-Bogaz-Gol, zaliv, b., Turk. — I8 48
Karabük, Tur. — G14 4
Karacabey, Tur. — I12 20
Karačev, Russia — H18 22
Karāchi, Pak. — H2 44
Kārād, India — C2 46
Karaganda, Kaz. — H12 26
Karaginskij, ostrov, i., Russia — F24 28
Karaginskij zaliv, b., Russia — G19 102
Karagoš, gora, mtn., Russia — G15 26
Kārāikāl, India — G5 46
Kāraikkudi, India — G5 46
Karaj, Iran — D11 48
Karakax, stm., China — B8 44
Karakelong, Pulau, i., Indon. — E8 38
Karakol (Prževal'sk), Kyrg. — I13 26
Karakoram Pass, Asia — C7 44
Karakoram Range, mts., Asia — C7 44
Karakoro, stm., Afr. — D4 64
Karakumskij kanal, Turk. — C16 48
Karakumy, des., Turk. — J9 26
Karaman, Tur. — L13 20
Karamay, China — B3 30
Karamea Bight, N.Z. — D3 72
Karamürsel, Tur. — I13 20
Karamyševo, Russia — D11 22
Kāranja, India — B4 46
Karapınar, Tur. — L14 20
Karasburg, Nmb. — G4 66
Kara Sea see Karskoje more, Russia — C11 26
Karasjok, Nor. — G19 6
Karasu, stm., Tur. — B5 48
Karasuk, Russia — G7 28
Karaton, Kaz. — H8 26
Karauli, India — G7 44
Karawang, Tanjung, c., Indon. — j13 39a
Karawanken, mts., Eur. — C9 18
Karaya, Nig. — F14 64
Karazal, Kaz. — H12 26
Karbalā', Iraq — E8 48
Karcag, Hung. — H20 10
Kardhitsa, Grc. — J5 20
Kärdla, Est. — C5 22
Kardymovo, Russia — G15 22
Karelia see Karelija, state, Russia — E4 26
Karelia, hist. reg., Eur. — J22 6
Karelija, state, Russia — E4 26
Karesuando, Swe. — G18 6
Karia-ba-Mohammed, Mor. — C8 62
Kariba, Zimb. — A9 66
Kariba, Lake, res., Afr. — E5 58
Karibib, Nmb. — C2 66
Karigasniemi, Fin. — G19 6
Karimata, Kepulauan, is., Indon. — F4 38
Karimata, Selat (Karimata Strait), strt., Indon. — F4 38
Karimnagar, India — C5 46
Karimunjawa, Kepulauan, is., Indon. — G5 38
Karin, Som. — F10 56
Karis (Karjaa), Fin. — K18 6
Karisimbi, Volcan, vol., Afr. — B5 58
Kariya, Japan — M11 36
Kārīz, Iran — D16 48
Karkaralinsk, Kaz. — H13 26

Name — Map Ref. — Page

Karl-Marx-Stadt see Chemnitz, Ger. E12 10
*Karloske, stm., Mb., Can.* C20 104
Karlovac, Cro. D10 18
Karlovo, Bul. G8 20
Karlovy Vary, Czech Rep. E12 10
Karlsborg, Swe. I18 6
Karlskoga, Swe. L14 6
Karlskrona, Swe. M14 6
Karlsruhe, Ger. F8 10
Karlstad, Mn., U.S. C11 118
Karlstadt, Ger. F9 10
Karma, Niger E10 64
Karmah, Sudan H6 60
*Karmel, Har (Mount Carmel), mtn., Isr.* C4 50
Karmiyya, Isr. E3 50
Karnack, Tx., U.S. J2 114
Karnak see Al-Karnak, Egypt E7 60
Karnak, Il., U.S. E8 114
Karnāl, India F7 44
*Karṇāli, stm., Asia* F9 44
*Karnātaka, state, India* E3 46
Karnes City, Tx., U.S. K9 116
Karnobat, Bul. G10 20
*Kärnten, state, Aus.* I13 10
Karonga, Mwi. C6 58
Karora, Sudan I10 60
*Kárpathos, i., Grc.* N11 20
Karpenísion, Grc. K5 20
Karpinsk, Russia F10 26
Karpogory, Russia E6 26
Karratha, Austl. D3 68
Kars, Tur. A7 48
Karsakpaj, Kaz. H11 26
*Karsakuwigamak Lake, l., Mb., Can.* B15 104
Kärsämäki, Fin. J19 6
Kārsava, Lat. E10 22
Karši, Uzb. J11 26
Karsin, Pol. B17 10
*Karskije Vorota, proliv, strt., Russia* C9 26
*Karskoje more (Kara Sea), Russia* C11 26
Kartaly, Russia G10 26
Karthaus, Pa., U.S. F8 108
Kartuzy, Pol. A18 10
Karukuwisa, Nmb. B4 66
Karūr, India G5 46
Karviná, Czech Rep. F18 10
Kārwār, India E3 46
Karymskoje, Russia G14 28
Kas, Sudan K3 60
Kasaan, Ak., U.S. I28 100
*Kasai (Cassai), stm., Afr.* B3 58
Kasaji, D.R.C. D4 58
Kasama, Zam. D6 58
Kasan, Uzb. B18 48
Kasane, Bots. A7 66
Kasanga, Tan. C6 58
Kasaoka, Japan M8 36
Kāsaragod, India F3 46
*Kasba Lake, l., N.T., Can.* D12 96
Kasba-Tadla, Mor. D7 62
Kascjukoŭka, Bela. I13 22
Kascjukovičy, Bela. H15 22
Kaseda, Japan P5 36
Kasempa, Zam. D5 58
Kasenga, D.R.C. D5 58
Kasese, D.R.C. B5 58
Kāsganj, India G8 44
Kāshān, Iran K8 26
Kashgar see Kashi, China D2 30
Kashi, China D2 30
Kashihara, Japan M10 36
Kashima, Japan N5 36
Kāshīpur, India F8 44
Kashiwazaki, Japan J13 36
Kāshmar, Iran D15 48
*Kashmir see Jammu and Kashmīr, dep., Asia* C10 42
Kashmor, Pak. F3 44
*Kashunuk, stm., Ak., U.S.* F12 100
Kasigluk, Ak., U.S. F13 100
Kasimov, Russia G24 22
Kašin, Russia D20 22
Kasinka, Bots. B7 66
Kašira, Russia G21 22
*Kasiruta, Pulau, i., Indon.* F8 38
*Kaskaskia, stm., Il., U.S.* D7 114
*Kaskattama, stm., Mb., Can.* E14 96
Kaskö (Kaskinen), Fin. J17 6
Kasli, Russia F10 26
Kaslo, B.C., Can. H18 102
Kasn'a, Russia F17 22
Kasongo, D.R.C. B5 58
Kasongo-Lunda, D.R.C. C3 58
*Kásos, i., Grc.* N10 20
Kasota, Mn., U.S. F2 110
Kaspijsk, Russia I7 26
Kaspijskij, Russia H7 26
*Kasr, Ra's, c., Afr.* H10 60
Kassalā, Sudan J9 60
*Kassándra, pen., Grc.* I7 20
*Kassándras, Kólpos, b., Grc.* I7 20
Kassel, Ger. D9 10
Kasserine, Tun. C15 62
*Kassikaityu, stm., Guy.* G13 84
Kassinger, Sudan H6 60
Kasson, Mn., U.S. F3 110
Kastamonu, Tur. G14 4
Kastoriá, Grc. I5 20
*Kastrávion, Tekhnití Límni, res., Grc.* K5 20
Kasūr, Pak. E6 44
Kataeregi, Nig. G13 64
*Katahdin, Mount, mtn., Me., U.S.* B18 108
*Katanga, hist. reg., D.R.C.* D5 58
*Katanga, stm., Russia* F12 28
Katanning, Austl. F3 68
*Katchall Island, i., India* K2 40
Katélé, Mali F7 64
Katepwa Beach, Sk., Can. H11 104
Kateríni, Grc. I6 20
*Kates Needle, mtn., N.A.* H28 100
Katha, Myan. B4 40
Katherine, Austl. B6 68
*Kāthiāwār Peninsula, pen., India* I4 44
Kāṭhmāṇḍau, Nepal G11 44
Kathrabbā, Jord. F5 50
Katihār, India F4 30
*Katimik Lake, l., Mb., Can.* F15 104
Katiola, C. Iv. G7 64
Katmandu see Kāṭhmāṇḍau, Nepal G11 44
Katoomba, Austl. I9 70
Katoúna, Grc. K5 20
Katowice, Pol. E19 10
*Kātrīnā, Jabal, mtn., Egypt* C7 60
Katsepe, Madag. o22 67b
Katsina, Nig. E13 64
Katsina Ala, Nig. H14 64
*Katsina Ala, stm., Afr.* G8 54
Katsuta, Japan K15 36
Katsuura, Japan L15 36
Katsuyama, Japan K11 36
Kattakurgan, Uzb. J11 26
Kattaviá, Grc. N11 20
*Kattegat, strt., Eur.* M12 6
*Katun', stm., Russia* G9 28
Katunki, Russia E26 22
Kātwa, India I13 44
Katwijk aan Zee, Neth. D5 12
Katyn, Russia G14 22
*Kauai, i., Hi., U.S.* o14 125a
*Kauai Channel, strt., Hi., U.S.* p15 125a
*Kau Desert, des., Hi., U.S.* r18 125a
Kaufbeuren, Ger. H10 10
Kaufman, Tx., U.S. G10 116
Kaukauna, Wi., U.S. F7 110
*Kaukau Veld, plat., Afr.* B5 66
Kauliranta, Fin. H18 6
Kaumalapau, Hi., U.S. q17 125a
Kaunakakai, Hi., U.S. p16 125a
Kaunas, Lith. G6 22
Kaura Namoda, Nig. E13 64
Kauru, Nig. F14 64
Kaustinen, Fin. J18 6
Kautokeino, Nor. G18 6
Kavacık, Tur. J12 20
Kavajë, Alb. H3 20
Kavála, Grc. I8 20
Kavalerovo, Russia I19 28
Kāvali, India E5 46
*Kavaratti Island, i., India* G2 46
*Kāveri, stm., India* G5 46
*Kāveri Falls, wtfl, India* F4 46
Kaverino, Russia G24 22
Kavieng, Pap. N. Gui. k17 68a
Kavimba, Bots. B7 66
*Kavīr, Dasht-e, des., Iran* D13 48
Kaw, Ok., U.S. C10 116
Kawagoe, Japan L14 36
Kawaguchi, Japan L14 36
*Kawaihae Bay, b., Hi., U.S.* q18 125a
*Kawaikini, mtn., Hi., U.S.* o14 125a
Kawambwa, Zam. C5 58
Kawara Débé, Niger E11 64
Kawasaki, Japan L14 36
Kawdut, Myan. G4 40
*Kaweenakumik Lake, l., Mb., Can.* F15 104
*Kawich Peak, mtn., Nv., U.S.* G9 124
*Kaw Lake, res., Ok., U.S.* C10 116
Kawludo, Myan. E4 40
Kawm Umbū, Egypt E7 60
Kawthaung, Myan. J5 40
*Kaxgar, stm., China* D2 30
Kaya, Burkina E9 64
*Kayak Island, i., Ak., U.S.* G22 100
Kayan, Myan. F4 40
*Kayan, stm., Indon.* E6 38
Kāyankulam, India H4 46
Kaycee, Wy., U.S. A10 120
Kayenta, Az., U.S. H6 120
Kayes, Congo B2 58
Kayes, Mali D4 64
*Kay Point, c., Yk., Can.* B25 100
*Kayser Gebergte, mts., Sur.* F14 84
Kayseri, Tur. B3 48
Kaysville, Ut., U.S. C5 120
*Kazachskij melkosopočnik, hills, Kaz.* H12 26
Kazačinskoje, Russia F16 26
*Kazakhstan, ctry., Asia* H11 26
Kazaki, Russia I21 22
*Kazakstan see Kazakhstan, ctry., Asia* H11 26
Kazalinsk, Kaz. H10 26
Kazan', Russia F7 26
*Kazan, stm., N.T., Can.* D13 96
Kazandžik, Turk. J9 26
Kazanlăk, Bul. G9 20
*Kazan Lake, l., Sk., Can.* E6 104
Kazanovka, Russia H21 22
*Kazbek, gora, mtn.* I6 26
Kāzerūn, Iran G11 48
Kazimierza Wielka, Pol. E20 10
Kazincbarcika, Hung. G20 10
Kazinka, Russia I22 22
Kazloŭščyna, Bela. H8 22
Kazlų Rūda, Lith. G6 22
Kazungula, Zam. A7 66
*Kazym, stm., Russia* E5 28
*Kazyr, stm., Russia* G17 26
Kcynia, Pol. B17 10
Kdyně, Czech Rep. F13 10
*Kéa, i., Grc.* L8 20
Keaau, Hi., U.S. r18 125a
*Keahole Point, c., Hi., U.S.* r17 125a
*Kealakekua Bay, b., Hi., U.S.* r18 125a
Kearns Canyon, Az., U.S. I6 120
Kearney, Mo., U.S. C2 114
Kearney, Ne., U.S. K8 118
Kearns, Ut., U.S. D5 120
Kearny, Az., U.S. K6 120
Kebeiti, China B8 44
Kébémer, Sen. D1 64
Kebili, Tun. D15 62
*Kebnekaise, mtn., Swe.* H16 6
Kebri Dehar, Eth. G9 56
Kecel, Hung. I19 10
*Kech, stm., Pak.* H17 48
*Kechika, stm., B.C., Can.* E7 96
Kecskemét, Hung. I19 10
Kėdainiai, Lith. F7 22
Kedgwick, N.B., Can. E6 106
*Kedgwick, stm., Can.* E6 106
Kediri, Indon. j16 39a
Kédougou, Sen. E3 64
*Kedrikí Makedhonía, prov., Grc.* I7 20
Kędzierzyn Kozle, Pol. E18 10
Keefers, B.C., Can. G13 102
*Keele, stm., N.T., Can.* D31 100
*Keele Peak, mtn., Yk., Can.* E29 100
*Keeley Lake, l., Sk., Can.* D6 104
*Keeling Islands see Cocos Islands, dep., Oc.* K10 24
Keels, Nf., Can. D20 106
Keene, Ky., U.S. B2 112
Keene, N.H., U.S. E14 108
Keene, Tx., U.S. G9 116
Keenesburg, Co., U.S. D12 120
Keerbergen, Bel. F6 12
Keeseville, N.Y., U.S. C13 108
Keetmanshoop, Nmb. F4 66
Keewatin, Mn., U.S. C2 110
Keewatin, On., Can. I20 104
*Kefallinía, i., Grc.* K4 20
Kefar Blum, Isr. B5 50
Kefar 'Ezyon, W.B. E4 50
*Kefar Naḥum (Capernaum), hist., Isr.* C5 50
Kefar Sava, Isr. D3 50
Keffi, Nig. G13 64
Keffin Hausa, Nig. E14 64
Keflavík, Ice. B2 6a
Keftya, Eth. K9 60
*Ke Ga, Mui, c., Viet.* H10 40
Kégashka, P.Q., Can. B12 106
*Kégashka, Lac, l., P.Q., Can.* B12 106
Keg River, Ab., Can. E9 96
Kegums, Lat. E7 22
*Kehiwin Indian Reserve, Ab., Can.* C24 102
Kehra, Est. B8 22
Ke-hsi Mānsām, Myan. D4 40
Keila, Est. B7 22
Keimoes, S. Afr. G5 66
Keiser, Ar., U.S. G6 114
Keith, Scot., U.K. D11 8
*Keith Arm, b., N.T., Can.* C8 96
Keithley Creek, B.C., Can. E13 102
Keithsburg, Il., U.S. I5 110
Keizer, Or., U.S. F2 122
*Kejimkujik National Park, N.S., Can.* H8 106
Kekaha, Hi., U.S. p14 125a
*Kékes, mtn., Hung.* H20 10
Kekexili, China D5 30
Kelafo, Eth. G9 56
Kelang, Malay. M6 40
*Kelantan, stm., Malay.* L7 40
Kelegou, China B6 32
Kelibia, Tun. M6 18
Kellerberrin, Austl. F3 68
*Keller Lake, l., N.T., Can.* D8 96
*Keller Lake, l., Sk., Can.* B8 104
*Kellett, Cape, c., N.T., Can.* B7 96
*Kelleys Island, i., Oh., U.S.* F4 108
Kelliher, Sk., Can. G11 104
Kellogg, Ia., U.S. I3 110
Kellogg, Id., U.S. C9 122
Kellogg, Mn., U.S. F4 110
*Kelly Lake, l., N.T., Can.* D31 100
Kellyville, Ok., U.S. D10 116
Kelmė, Lith. F5 22
Kel'mentsi, Ukr. A10 20
Kelmet, Erit. I10 60
Kelo, Chad G4 56
Kelolokan, Indon. E6 38
Kelowna, B.C., Can. H15 102
Kelsey Bay, B.C., Can. G9 102
*Kelsey Lake, l., Mb., Can.* E13 104
Kelseyville, Ca., U.S. F3 124
Kelso, Wa., U.S. D3 122
Keluang, Malay. M7 40
Kelvington, Sk., Can. F11 104
Kem', Russia E4 26
Kemah, Tx., U.S. J11 116
Kemalpaşa, Tur. K11 20
Kemano, B.C., Can. D7 102
*Kemer Barajı, res., Tur.* L12 20
Kemerovo, Russia F9 28
Kemi, Fin. I19 6
Kemijärvi, Fin. H20 6
*Kemijoki, stm., Fin.* H19 6
Kemmerer, Wy., U.S. C6 120
Kemnath, Ger. F11 10
Kemp, Tx., U.S. G10 116
*Kemp, Lake, res., Tx., U.S.* F7 116
Kemparana, Mali E7 64
Kempele, Fin. I19 6
Kempner, Tx., U.S. H8 116
Kemps Bay, Bah. B6 94
Kempsey, Austl. H10 70
*Kempt, Lac, l., P.Q., Can.* G18 96
Kempten [Allgäu], Ger. H10 10
Kemptville, On., Can. B11 108
Kenai, Ak., U.S. F19 100
*Kenai Peninsula, pen., Ak., U.S.* G19 100
Kenansville, Fl., U.S. L6 112
Kenansville, N.C., U.S. E9 112
Kenaston, Sk., Can. G8 104
Kenbridge, Va., U.S. C8 112
Kendal, S. Afr. F9 66
Kendal, Sk., Can. H11 104
Kendall, Fl., U.S. N6 112
Kendall, Wi., U.S. G5 110
*Kendall, Cape, c., N.T., Can.* D15 96
Kendallville, In., U.S. A11 114
Kendari, Indon. F7 38
Kendrāpāra, India J12 44
Kendrick, Fl., U.S. J4 112
Kendrick, Id., U.S. D9 122
Kenedy, Tx., U.S. K9 116
Kenema, S.L. H4 64
Kenesaw, Ne., U.S. K9 118
Kenge, D.R.C. B3 58
Kengtian, China J8 34
Kēng Tung, Myan. D5 40
Kenhardt, S. Afr. G5 66
Kenilworth, Ut., U.S. E6 120
Kenitra, Mor. C7 62
Kenly, N.C., U.S. D8 112
Kenmare, N.D., U.S. C5 118
Kennard, Tx., U.S. H11 116
Kennebec, S.D., U.S. H8 118
*Kennebec, stm., Me., U.S.* C17 108
*Kennebecasis Bay, b., N.B., Can.* G8 106
Kennebunk, Me., U.S. D16 108
Kennedy, Al., U.S. I9 114
Kennedy, Zimb. B8 66
*Kennedy, Cape see Canaveral, Cape, c., Fl., U.S.* K6 112
*Kennedy, Mount, mtn., B.C., Can.* G9 102
*Kennedy, Mount, mtn., Yk., Can.* F25 100
*Kennedy Entrance, strt., Ak., U.S.* G18 100
*Kennedy Lake, l., B.C., Can.* H9 102
Kenner, La., U.S. M6 114
Kennetcook, N.S., Can. G10 106
Kennett, Mo., U.S. F6 114
Kennett Square, Pa., U.S. H11 108
Kennewick, Wa., U.S. D6 122
*Kenney Dam, B.C., Can.* D10 102
*Kenn Reef, rf., Austl.* D11 68
Kénogami, P.Q., Can. D2 106
*Kenogami, stm., On., Can.* G15 96
*Kénogami, Lac, l., P.Q., Can.* D2 106
Keno Hill, Yk., Can. E27 100
Kenora, On., Can. I20 104
Kenosha, Wi., U.S. H8 110
Kenova, W.V., U.S. I4 108
Kensal, N.D., U.S. D9 118
Kensett, Ar., U.S. G5 114
Kensington, Ks., U.S. L8 118
Kensington, P.E., Can. F10 106
Kensington Park, Fl., U.S. L4 112
Kent, Oh., U.S. F5 108
Kent, S.L. G3 64
Kent, Wa., U.S. C3 122
*Kent, co., Eng., U.K.* J14 8
Kentau, Kaz. I11 26
*Kent Group, is., Austl.* L7 70
Kentland, In., U.S. B9 114
Kenton, Mi., U.S. D7 110
Kenton, Oh., U.S. G3 108
Kenton, Tn., U.S. F7 114
*Kent Peninsula, pen., N.T., Can.* C11 96
*Kentucky, state, U.S.* D9 98
*Kentucky, stm., Ky., U.S.* D11 114
*Kentucky Lake, res., U.S.* F8 114
Kentville, N.S., Can. G9 106
Kentwood, La., U.S. L6 114
*Kenya, ctry., Afr.* B7 58
*Kenya, Mount see Kirinyaga, mtn., Kenya* E7 58
Kenyon, Mn., U.S. F3 110
Keokea, Hi., U.S. q17 125a
Keokuk, Ia., U.S. J4 110
*Keo Neua, Col de, Asia* E8 40
Keosauqua, Ia., U.S. J4 110
Keota, Ia., U.S. I4 110
Keota, Ok., U.S. D12 116
Kępice, Pol. A16 10
Kępno, Pol. D17 10
*Keppel Bay, b., Austl.* D9 70
Kequan, China G2 32
*Kerala, state, India* G4 46
Kerang, Austl. J5 70
Kerby, Or., U.S. H2 122
Kerch, Ukr. H5 26
Keremeos, B.C., Can. H15 102
Keren, Erit. J10 60
Kerend, Iran D9 48
Kerens, Tx., U.S. G10 116
*Keret', ozero, l., Russia* I23 6
Kerewan, Gam. E1 64
*Kerguélen, Îles, is., Afr.* M10 126
Kericho, Kenya B7 58
Keri Kera, Sudan K7 60
*Kerinci, Gunung, mtn., Indon.* F3 38
*Keriya, stm., China* B9 44
Kerkebet, Erit. I9 60
*Kerkenna, Îles, is., Tun.* C16 62
Kerkhoven, Mn., U.S. F12 118
Kerki, Turk. J11 26
Kérkira (Corfu), Grc. J3 20
*Kérkira (Corfu), i., Grc.* J3 20
Kerkrade, Neth. G9 12
*Kermadec Islands, is., N.Z.* K22 126
Kerman, Ca., U.S. H5 124
Kermān, Iran F14 48
Kermit, Tx., U.S. H3 116
*Kermode, Mount, mtn., B.C., Can.* E3 102
*Kern, stm., Ca., U.S.* I7 124
Kernersville, N.C., U.S. C6 112
Kernville, Ca., U.S. I7 124
Kérou, Benin F11 64
Kerrobert, Sk., Can. G5 104
Kerrville, Tx., U.S. I7 116
*Kerry, co., Ire.* I4 8
Kershaw, S.C., U.S. E6 112
Kersley, B.C., Can. E12 102
*Kerulen (Cherlen) (Herlen), stm., Asia* B10 30
Kerzaz, Alg. F10 62
Kerzers, Switz. E7 13
*Kesagami Lake, l., On., Can.* F16 96
Keşan, Tur. I10 20
Kesennuma, Japan I16 36
Keshena, Wi., U.S. F7 110
Keshendeh, Afg. B2 44
Keshod, India J4 44
Keskin, Tur. B2 48
*Keski-Suomen lääni, prov., Fin.* J19 6
Keskozero, Russia K23 6
Kes'ma, Russia C20 22
Kesova Gora, Russia D20 22
Kesra, Tun. N4 18
Kesten'ga, Russia I22 6
Keszthely, Hung. I17 10
*Ket', stm., Russia* F8 28
Keta, Ghana I10 64
*Keta, ozero, l., Russia* D10 28
Ketama, Mor. K7 16
Ketang, China M4 34
Ketchikan, Ak., U.S. I29 100
Ketchum, Id., U.S. G11 122
Kete Krachi, Ghana H9 64
Kétou, Benin H11 64
Kętrzyn (Rastenburg), Pol. A21 10
Kettering, Eng., U.K. I13 8
Kettering, Oh., U.S. H2 108
*Kettle, stm., Mb., Can.* B20 104
*Kettle, stm., Mn., U.S.* D3 110
*Kettle, stm., N.A.* H16 102
Kettle Falls, Wa., U.S. B7 122
*Kettle Rapids Dam, Mb., Can.* B20 104
*Keuka Lake, l., N.Y., U.S.* E9 108
Kevin, Mt., U.S. B14 122
Kew, T./C. Is. D8 94
Kewanee, Il., U.S. I6 110
Kewanna, In., U.S. A10 114
Kewaunee, Wi., U.S. F8 110
*Keweenaw Bay, b., Mi., U.S.* C7 110
*Keweenaw Peninsula, pen., Mi., U.S.* C7 110
*Keweenaw Point, c., Mi., U.S.* C8 110
*Keya Paha, stm., U.S.* I8 118
Keyes, Ok., U.S. C4 116
Key Largo, Fl., U.S. N6 112
*Key Largo, i., Fl., U.S.* N6 112
Keyser, W.V., U.S. H8 108
Keystone, Ia., U.S. I3 110
Keystone, S.D., U.S. H4 118
Keystone, W.V., U.S. B5 112
*Keystone Lake, res., Ok., U.S.* C10 116
Keysville, Va., U.S. B8 112
Keytesville, Mo., U.S. C4 114
Key West, Fl., U.S. O5 112
Kežmarok, Slvk. F20 10
*Kgalagadi, dept., Bots.* E5 66
*Kgatleng, dept., Bots.* E8 66
*Khābūr, Nahr al-, stm., Asia* D6 48
Khadki (Kirkee), India C2 46
Khairpur, Pak. G3 44
Khajrāho, India H8 44
*Khakassia see Chakasija, state, Russia* G15 26
Khakhea, Bots. E6 66
Khalkhalah, Syria B7 50
*Khalkidhikí, hist. reg., Grc.* I7 20
Khalkís, Grc. K7 20
Khalūf, Oman D11 47
Khambhāliya, India I3 44
Khambhāt, India I5 44
*Khambhāt, Gulf of, b., India* J5 44
Khāmgaon, India B4 46
Khamir, Yemen F3 47
Khamīs Mushayṭ, Sau. Ar. E3 47
Khamkeut, Laos E8 40
Khammam, India D6 46
Khānābād, Afg. B3 44
Khān al-Baghdādī, Iraq E7 48
Khānaqīn, Iraq D8 48
Khancoban, Austl. K8 70
Khandwa, India J7 44
Khānewāl, Pak. E4 44
Khāngarh, Pak. F4 44
Khaniá, Grc. N8 20
Khānpur, Pak. F4 44
Khān Yūnus, Gaza F2 50
Kharagpur, India I12 44
Kharānoq, Iran E13 48
*Kharg Island see Khārk, Jazīreh-ye, i., Iran* G11 48
Khargon, India J6 44
Khāriān Cantonment, Pak. D5 44
Khar'kiv (Kharkov), Ukr. G5 26
Kharkov see Khar'kiv, Ukr. G5 26
Khartoum see Al-Khartūm, Sudan J7 60
Khartoum North see Al-Kharṭūm Baḥrī, Sudan J7 60
Khartūm see Al-Kharṭūm, Sudan J7 60
Khasebake, Bots. C7 66
Khāsh, Afg. F17 48
Khāsh, Iran G16 48
Khashm al-Qirbah, Sudan J8 60
*Khatt, Oued al, val., W. Sah.* G4 62
Khawsa, Myan. G4 40
Khemis, Alg. B12 62
Khemmarat, Thai. F8 40
Khenchela, Alg. C14 62
Khenifra, Mor. D8 62
Kherrata, Alg. B13 62
Kherson, Ukr. H4 26
Khíos, Grc. K10 20
*Khíos (Chios), i., Grc.* K10 20
Khirbet 'Awwād, Syria D7 50
Khlong Thom, Thai. K5 40
Khmel'nyts'kyy, Ukr. H3 26
Kholm, Afg. B2 44
Khomeyn, Iran E11 48
Khomeynīshahr, Iran E11 48
Khomodimo, Bots. D6 66
Khon Kaen, Thai. F7 40
Khóra, Grc. L5 20
Khorramābād, Iran E10 48
Khorramshahr, Iran F10 48
Khossanto, Sen. E4 64
Khotyn, Ukr. A10 20
Khouribga, Mor. D7 62
Khowst, Afg. D3 44
Khuff, Sau. Ar. B4 47
Khugaung, Myan. A5 40
Khuis, Bots. F5 66
Khu Khan, Thai. G8 40
Khulna, Bngl. I13 44
*Khūnjerāb Pass, Asia* B6 44
Khurai, India H8 44
*Khurīyā Murīyā, Jazā'ir, is., Oman* F10 47
Khurja, India F7 44
Khust, Ukr. H2 26
Khuzdār, Pak. G2 44
Khvāf, Iran D16 48
Khvor, Iran E13 48
Khvormūj, Iran G11 48
Khvoy, Iran B8 48
*Khwae Noi, stm., Thai.* G5 40
*Khyber Pass, Asia* C4 44
Khyriv, Ukr. F22 10
Kiama, Austl. J9 70
*Kiamichi, stm., Ok., U.S.* E11 116
Kiana, Ak., U.S. C14 100
*Kiangarow, Mount, mtn., Austl.* F9 70
*Kiangsi see Jiangxi, prov., China* F10 30
*Kiangsu see Jiangsu, prov., China* E10 30
Kibangou, Congo B2 58
Kibombo, D.R.C. B5 58
Kibre Mengist, Eth. O10 60
Kičevo, Mac. H4 20
*Kickapoo, stm., Wi., U.S.* G5 110
*Kicking Horse Pass, Can.* F18 102
Kidal, Mali B10 64
Kidira, Sen. D3 64
Kiel, Ger. A10 10
Kiel, Wi., U.S. G7 110
*Kiel Canal see Nord-Ostsee-Kanal, Ger.* A9 10
Kielce, Pol. E20 10
*Kieler Bucht, b., Ger.* A10 10
Kiester, Mn., U.S. G2 110
Kiev see Kyyiv, Ukr. G4 26
Kiffa, Maur. C4 64
Kifisiá, Grc. K7 20
Kifrī, Iraq D8 48
Kigali, Rw. B6 58
Kigille, Sudan M8 60
Kigoma, Tan. B5 58
Kihei, Hi., U.S. q17 125a
Kihniö, Fin. J18 6
*Kihnu, i., Est.* C6 22
*Kii-suidō, strt., Japan* N9 36
Kikerino, Russia B12 22
*Kikerk Lake, l., N.T., Can.* C10 96
Kikinda, Yugo. D4 20
*Kikládhes (Cyclades), is., Grc.* L9 20
Kikori, Pap. N. Gui. G11 38
Kikwit, D.R.C. C3 58
*Kilambé, Cerro, mtn., Nic.* D9 92
Kilauea, Hi., U.S. o14 125a
*Kilauea Crater, crat., Hi., U.S.* r18 125a
Kilchu, N. Kor. C17 32
Kilcoy, Austl. F10 70
Kildare, Ire. H7 8
*Kildare, co., Ire.* H7 8
*Kildare, Cape, c., P.E., Can.* F10 106
*Kil'din, ostrov, i., Russia* G24 6
Kil'dinstroj, Russia G23 6
Kildonan, B.C., Can. H9 102
Kilgore, Tx., U.S. J2 114
*Kilian Island, i., N.T., Can.* B11 96
Kilibo, Benin G11 64
Kilikollūr, India H4 46
*Kilimanjaro, mtn., Tan.* B7 58
Kilimavony, Madag. s20 67b
Kilingi-Nõmme, Est. C7 22
Kilis, Tur. C4 48
Kiliya, Ukr. D13 20
Kilkenny, Ire. I6 8
*Kilkenny, co., Ire.* I6 8
Kilkís, Grc. H6 20
Killaloe, Ire. I5 8
Killaloe Station, On., Can. E18 110
Killam, Ab., Can. E23 102
Killarney, Ire. I4 8
Killarney, Mb., Can. I15 104
Killarney, On., Can. E14 110
Killbuck, Oh., U.S. G5 108
Killdeer, N.D., U.S. D5 118
Killeen, Tx., U.S. H9 116
Killen, Al., U.S. H9 114
*Killington Peak, mtn., Vt., U.S.* D14 108
*Killiniq Island, i., Can.* D20 96
Killinkoski, Fin. J18 6
Kilmarnock, Scot., U.K. F9 8
Kilmarnock, Va., U.S. B10 112
Kilmichael, Ms., U.S. I7 114
Kilomines, D.R.C. A6 58
Kilosa, Tan. C7 58
Kilpisjärvi, Fin. G17 6
Kilrush, Ire. I4 8
*Kilttān Island, i., India* G2 46
Kilwa, D.R.C. C5 58
Kim, Co., U.S. N4 118
*Kim, stm., Cam.* G9 54
Kimba, Austl. I2 70
Kimball, Mn., U.S. E1 110
Kimball, Ne., U.S. J4 118
Kimball, S.D., U.S. H9 118
Kimberley, B.C., Can. H19 102
Kimberley, S. Afr. G7 66
*Kimberley Plateau, plat., Austl.* C5 68
Kimberling City, Mo., U.S. F3 114
Kimberly, Id., U.S. H11 122
Kimberly, Wi., U.S. F7 110
Kimch'aek (Sŏngjin), N. Kor. C17 32
Kimch'ŏn, S. Kor. G16 32
Kimito (Kemiö), Fin. K18 6
*Kimiwan Lake, l., Ab., Can.* B18 102
Kimje, S. Kor. H14 32
Kimovsk, Russia H21 22
Kimry, Russia E20 22
Kimsquit, B.C., Can. E8 102
*Kinabalu, Gunong, mtn., Malay.* D6 38
*Kinbasket Lake, res., B.C., Can.* F17 102
Kincaid, Il., U.S. C7 114
Kincaid, Sk., Can. I7 104
Kincardine, On., Can. F14 110
Kincolith, B.C., Can. B5 102
Kindberg, Aus. H15 10
Kinde, Mi., U.S. G13 110
Kinder, La., U.S. L4 114
Kindersley, Sk., Can. G5 104
Kindia, Gui. F3 64
Kindred, N.D., U.S. E10 118
Kindu, D.R.C. B5 58
Kinel', Russia G8 26
Kinešma, Russia D25 22
King, N.C., U.S. C6 112
King and Queen Court House, Va., U.S. B10 112
Kingaroy, Austl. F9 70
King City, Ca., U.S. H4 124
King City, Mo., U.S. B2 114
King City, On., Can. G16 110
King Cove, Ak., U.S. I13 100
Kingfield, Me., U.S. C16 108
Kingfisher, Ok., U.S. D9 116
King George, Va., U.S. I9 108
*King George, Mount, mtn., B.C., Can.* G19 102
*King George Island, i., Ant.* B1 73
*King George Islands, is., N.T., Can.* E17 96
King Hill, Id., U.S. G10 122
Kingisepp, Russia B11 22
*King Island, i., Austl.* L6 70
*King Island, i., B.C., Can.* E7 102
*King Lear Peak, mtn., Nv., U.S.* C7 124
*King Leopold Ranges, mts., Austl.* C5 68
Kingman, Az., U.S. I2 120
Kingman, Ks., U.S. N9 118
*Kingman Reef, rf., Oc.* H23 126
*King Mountain, mtn., B.C., Can.* G30 100
*King Mountain, mtn., Or., U.S.* G7 122
Kings, Ms., U.S. J6 114
*Kings, stm., Ar., U.S.* F3 114
*Kings, stm., Ca., U.S.* H6 124
*Kings, stm., Nv., U.S.* C7 124
King Salmon, Ak., U.S. G16 100
Kings Beach, Ca., U.S. E5 124
Kingsburg, Ca., U.S. H6 124
*Kings Canyon National Park, Ca., U.S.* H7 124
Kingscote, Austl. J2 70
Kingsford, Mi., U.S. E7 110
Kingsgate, B.C., Can. H18 102
Kingsland, Ar., U.S. I4 114
Kingsland, Ga., U.S. I5 112
Kingsland, Tx., U.S. I8 116
Kingsley, Ia., U.S. I12 118
Kingsley, Mi., U.S. F10 110
King's Lynn, Eng., U.K. I14 8
*Kingsmere Lake, l., Sk., Can.* D8 104
Kings Mountain, N.C., U.S. D5 112
*King Solomon's Mines see Mikhrot Shelomo Hamelekh, hist., Isr.* I3 50
*King Sound, strt., Austl.* C4 68
*Kings Peak, mtn., Ut., U.S.* D6 120
King's Point, Nf., Can. C17 106
Kingsport, Tn., U.S. C4 112
Kingston, Ga., U.S. E2 112
Kingston, Jam. E6 94
Kingston, Ma., U.S. F16 108
Kingston, Mo., U.S. C2 114
Kingston, N.S., Can. H9 106
Kingston, N.Y., U.S. F13 108
Kingston, N.Z. F2 72
Kingston, Oh., U.S. H4 108
Kingston, Ok., U.S. F10 116
Kingston, On., Can. F19 110
Kingston, Pa., U.S. F11 108
Kingston, Tn., U.S. D2 112
Kingston Southeast, Austl. K3 70
Kingston upon Hull, Eng., U.K. H13 8
Kingstown, St. Vin. H14 94
Kingstree, S.C., U.S. F7 112
Kingsville, On., Can. H13 110
Kingsville, Tx., U.S. L9 116
King William, Va., U.S. B9 112
*King William Island, i., N.T., Can.* C13 96
King William's Town, S. Afr. I8 66
Kingwood, W.V., U.S. H7 108
Kinistino, Sk., Can. F9 104
*Kinkony, Lac, l., Madag.* p21 67b
Kinmundy, Il., U.S. D8 114
Kinnaird, B.C., Can. H17 102
*Kinnaird Head, c., Scot., U.K.* D11 8
*Kinneret, Yam (Sea of Galilee), l., Isr.* C5 50
*Kinsale, Old Head of, c., Ire.* J5 8
Kinshasa (Léopoldville), D.R.C. B3 58
Kinsley, Ks., U.S. N8 118
Kinsman, Oh., U.S. F6 108
Kinston, Al., U.S. K10 114
Kinston, N.C., U.S. D9 112
Kintampo, Ghana G9 64
*Kintyre, pen., Scot., U.K.* F8 8
*Kintyre, Mull of, c., Scot., U.K.* F8 8
*Kinuseo Falls, wtfl, B.C., Can.* C13 102
Kinuso, Ab., Can. B19 102
*Kinyeti, mtn., Sudan* H7 56
Kinzua, Or., U.S. F5 122
Kiowa, Co., U.S. L3 118
Kiowa, Ks., U.S. N9 118
Kiowa, Ok., U.S. E11 116
*Kipahigan Lake, l., Can.* C12 104
*Kipengere Range, mts., Tan.* C6 58
Kipling, Sk., Can. H12 104
Kipnuk, Ak., U.S. G12 100
Kipushi, D.R.C. D5 58
Kirane, Mali D4 64
Kiraŭsk, Bela. H12 22
Kirazlı, Tur. I10 20
Kirbyville, Tx., U.S. L3 114
Kirchberg, Ger. F9 10
Kirchheimbolanden, Ger. F8 10
Kirchmöser, Ger. C12 10
Kirchschlag in der Buckligen Welt, Aus. H16 10
Kirejevsk, Russia H20 22
*Kirenga, stm., Russia* F13 28
Kirensk, Russia F13 28
*Kirghizia see Kyrgyzstan, ctry., Asia* I13 26
*Kirgizskij chrebet, mts., Asia* I12 26

| Name | Map Ref. | Page |
|---|---|---|
| Kiri, D.R.C. | B3 | 58 |
| *Kiribati, ctry., Oc.* | I22 | 126 |
| Kırıkhan, Tur. | C4 | 48 |
| Kırıkkale, Tur. | B2 | 48 |
| Kirillov, Russia | B21 | 22 |
| Kirillovskoje, Russia | A12 | 22 |
| Kirin see Jilin, China | C12 | 30 |
| *Kirin see Jilin, prov., China* | C12 | 30 |
| *Kirinyaga, mtn., Kenya* | B7 | 58 |
| Kiriši, Russia | B15 | 22 |
| *Kiriwina Islands, is., Pap. N. Gui.* | A10 | 68 |
| Kırkağaç, Tur. | J11 | 20 |
| Kirkcaldy, Scot., U.K. | E10 | 8 |
| Kirkcudbright, Scot., U.K. | G9 | 8 |
| Kirkenes, Nor. | G22 | 6 |
| Kirkjubæjarklaustur, Ice. | C4 | 6a |
| Kirkland, Il., U.S. | H7 | 110 |
| Kirkland, Tx., U.S. | E6 | 116 |
| Kirkland, Wa., U.S. | C3 | 122 |
| Kirkland Lake, On., Can. | B15 | 110 |
| Kırklareli, Tur. | H11 | 20 |
| Kirklin, In., U.S. | B10 | 114 |
| *Kirkness Lake, l., On., Can.* | G21 | 104 |
| *Kirkpatrick, Mount, mtn., Ant.* | D8 | 73 |
| *Kirkpatrick Lake, l., Ab., Can.* | F23 | 102 |
| Kirksville, Mo., U.S. | B4 | 114 |
| Kirkūk, Iraq | D8 | 48 |
| Kirkwall, Scot., U.K. | C11 | 8 |
| Kirkwood, Il., U.S. | J5 | 110 |
| Kirkwood, Mo., U.S. | D6 | 114 |
| Kirkwood, S. Afr. | I7 | 66 |
| Kirov, Russia | G17 | 22 |
| Kirov, Russia | F7 | 26 |
| Kirovakan, Arm. | I6 | 26 |
| Kirovgrad, Russia | F10 | 26 |
| Kirovohrad, Ukr. | H4 | 26 |
| Kirovsk, Russia | B14 | 22 |
| Kirovsk, Russia | D4 | 26 |
| Kirovskij, Kaz. | I13 | 26 |
| Kirs, Russia | F8 | 26 |
| Kirsanov, Russia | I25 | 22 |
| Kırşehir, Tur. | B3 | 48 |
| *Kīrthar Range, mts., Pak.* | G2 | 44 |
| Kirtland, N.M., U.S. | H8 | 120 |
| Kiruna, Swe. | H17 | 6 |
| Kirwin, Ks., U.S. | L8 | 118 |
| Kiryū, Japan | K14 | 36 |
| Kiržač, Russia | E21 | 22 |
| Kisa, Swe. | M14 | 6 |
| Kisangani (Stanleyville), D.R.C. | A5 | 58 |
| Kisarazu, Japan | L14 | 36 |
| Kisbey, Sk., Can. | I12 | 104 |
| Kisel'ovsk, Russia | G9 | 28 |
| Kishanganj, India | G12 | 44 |
| Kishangarh Bās, India | G6 | 44 |
| Kishi, Nig. | G11 | 64 |
| *Kishikas, stm., On., Can.* | F23 | 104 |
| Kishinev see Chişinău, Mol. | B12 | 20 |
| Kishiwada, Japan | M10 | 36 |
| Kishorganj, Bngl. | H14 | 44 |
| Kisii, Kenya | B6 | 58 |
| *Kiska Island, i., Ak., U.S.* | j3 | 101a |
| *Kiskatinaw, stm., B.C., Can.* | B14 | 102 |
| *Kiski Lake, l., Mb., Can.* | D16 | 104 |
| *Kiskittogisu Lake, l., Mb., Can.* | D16 | 104 |
| *Kiskitto Lake, l., Mb., Can.* | D16 | 104 |
| Kiskunfélegyháza, Hung. | I19 | 10 |
| Kiskunhalas, Hung. | I19 | 10 |
| Kiskunmajsa, Hung. | I19 | 10 |
| Kislovodsk, Russia | I6 | 26 |
| Kismaayo, Som. | B8 | 58 |
| *Kiso-sammyaku, mts., Japan* | L12 | 36 |
| Kispiox, B.C., Can. | B7 | 102 |
| *Kispiox, stm., B.C., Can.* | B7 | 102 |
| *Kispiox Mountain, mtn., B.C., Can.* | B7 | 102 |
| *Kisseynew Lake, l., Can.* | D13 | 104 |
| Kissidougou, Gui. | G4 | 64 |
| Kissimmee, Fl., U.S. | K5 | 112 |
| *Kissimmee, stm., Fl., U.S.* | L6 | 112 |
| *Kissimmee, Lake, l., Fl., U.S.* | L5 | 112 |
| Kississing, Mb., Can. | C13 | 104 |
| *Kississing Lake, l., Mb., Can.* | C13 | 104 |
| *Kistigan Lake, l., Mb., Can.* | D22 | 104 |
| Kisújszállás, Hung. | H20 | 10 |
| Kisumu, Kenya | B6 | 58 |
| Kisvárda, Hung. | G22 | 10 |
| Kita, Mali | E5 | 64 |
| *Kita-Daitō-jima, i., Japan* | F13 | 30 |
| Kitaibaraki, Japan | K15 | 36 |
| Kitakata, Japan | J14 | 36 |
| Kitakyūshū, Japan | N5 | 36 |
| Kitale, Kenya | A7 | 58 |
| Kitami, Japan | d18 | 36a |
| *Kitami-sanchi, mts., Japan* | c17 | 36a |
| Kit Carson, Co., U.S. | M5 | 118 |
| Kitchener, On., Can. | G15 | 110 |
| Kiteiyab, Sudan | I7 | 60 |
| Kíthira, Grc. | M7 | 20 |
| *Kíthira, i., Grc.* | M6 | 20 |
| *Kíthnos, i., Grc.* | L8 | 20 |
| Kitimat, B.C., Can. | C6 | 102 |
| *Kitimat, stm., B.C., Can.* | C6 | 102 |
| *Kitimat Ranges, mts., B.C., Can.* | D5 | 102 |
| *Kitlope, stm., B.C., Can.* | D7 | 102 |
| *Kitlope Lake, l., B.C., Can.* | D7 | 102 |
| Kitscoty, Ab., Can. | E4 | 104 |
| Kitsman', Ukr. | A9 | 20 |
| Kittanning, Pa., U.S. | G7 | 108 |
| Kittery, Me., U.S. | D16 | 108 |
| Kittilä, Fin. | H19 | 6 |
| Kittitas, Wa., U.S. | D5 | 122 |
| Kitui, Kenya | B7 | 58 |
| Kitwanga, B.C., Can. | B6 | 102 |
| *Kitwangar Indian Reserve, B.C., Can.* | B6 | 102 |
| Kitwe, Zam. | D5 | 58 |
| Kitwitwi, Nmb. | A4 | 66 |
| Kitzbühel, Aus. | H12 | 10 |
| Kitzingen, Ger. | F10 | 10 |
| Kiukiang see Jiujiang, China | F4 | 34 |
| Kiviõli, Est. | B9 | 22 |
| *Kivu, Lac, l., Afr.* | B5 | 58 |
| Kıyıköy, Tur. | H12 | 20 |
| *Kiyiu Lake, l., Sk., Can.* | G6 | 104 |
| Kizel, Russia | F9 | 26 |
| *Kızıl, stm., Tur.* | A2 | 48 |
| Kızıltepe, Tur. | C6 | 48 |
| Kizl'ar, Russia | I7 | 26 |
| Kizyl-Arvat, Turk. | J9 | 26 |
| Kizyl-Atrek, Turk. | J8 | 26 |
| Kizyl-Su, Turk. | B12 | 48 |
| Kjustendil, Bul. | G6 | 20 |
| Kladanj, Bos. | E2 | 20 |
| Kladno, Czech Rep. | E14 | 10 |
| Klagenfurt, Aus. | I14 | 10 |
| *Klahoose Indian Reserve, B.C., Can.* | G10 | 102 |
| Klaipėda (Memel), Lith. | F4 | 22 |
| Klaksvík, Faer. Is. | D8 | 6b |
| Klamath, Ca., U.S. | C1 | 124 |
| *Klamath, stm., U.S.* | C1 | 124 |
| Klamath Falls, Or., U.S. | H4 | 122 |
| *Klamath Mountains, mts., U.S.* | B2 | 124 |
| Klangpi, Myan. | C2 | 40 |
| *Klarälven, stm., Eur.* | K13 | 6 |
| Klatovy, Czech Rep. | F13 | 10 |
| Klawer, S. Afr. | H4 | 66 |
| Klawock, Ak., U.S. | I28 | 100 |
| *Kl'az'ma, stm., Russia* | E25 | 22 |
| Kleck, Bela. | H9 | 22 |
| Kleena Kleene, B.C., Can. | F10 | 102 |
| Klemme, Ia., U.S. | G2 | 110 |
| Klemtu, B.C., Can. | E6 | 102 |
| Klerksdorp, S. Afr. | F8 | 66 |
| *Klet', mtn., Czech Rep.* | G14 | 10 |
| Kletn'a, Russia | H16 | 22 |
| Kleve, Ger. | D6 | 10 |
| Kličau̧, Bela. | H12 | 22 |
| Klickitat, Wa., U.S. | E4 | 122 |
| *Klickitat, stm., Wa., U.S.* | E4 | 122 |
| Klimavičy, Bela. | H14 | 22 |
| Klimovo, Russia | I15 | 22 |
| Klimovsk, Russia | F20 | 22 |
| Klin, Russia | E19 | 22 |
| *Klinaklini, stm., B.C., Can.* | F9 | 102 |
| Klincy, Russia | I15 | 22 |
| Klipplaat, S. Afr. | I7 | 66 |
| Klishkivtsi, Ukr. | A10 | 20 |
| Kljascicy, Bela. | F11 | 22 |
| Kłobuck, Pol. | E18 | 10 |
| Kłodzko, Pol. | E16 | 10 |
| *Klondike, hist. reg., Yk., Can.* | E25 | 100 |
| *Klondike, stm., Yk., Can.* | D26 | 100 |
| Klosterneuburg, Aus. | G16 | 10 |
| Klosters, Switz. | E12 | 13 |
| Kloten, Switz. | D10 | 13 |
| *Klotz, Lac, l., P.Q., Can.* | D18 | 96 |
| Klötze, Ger. | C11 | 10 |
| Klouto, Togo | H10 | 64 |
| *Kluane, stm., Yk., Can.* | F25 | 100 |
| *Kluane Lake, l., Yk., Can.* | F25 | 100 |
| *Kluane National Park, Yk., Can.* | F25 | 100 |
| *Kl'učevskaja Sopka, vulkan, vol., Russia* | F24 | 28 |
| Kl'uči, Russia | F24 | 28 |
| Kluczbork, Pol. | E18 | 10 |
| Klukwan, Ak., U.S. | G27 | 100 |
| Knapp, Wi., U.S. | F3 | 110 |
| Knäred, Swe. | M13 | 6 |
| Kn'ažji Gory, Russia | E18 | 22 |
| *Kneehills Creek, stm., Ab., Can.* | F21 | 102 |
| *Knee Lake, l., Mb., Can.* | C20 | 104 |
| *Knee Lake, l., Sk., Can.* | C7 | 104 |
| Knevicy, Russia | D15 | 22 |
| Kneža, Bul. | F8 | 20 |
| Knić, Yugo. | F4 | 20 |
| Knickerbocker, Tx., U.S. | H6 | 116 |
| *Knife, stm., N.D., U.S.* | D6 | 118 |
| *Knife Lake, l., On., Can.* | E23 | 104 |
| *Knight Inlet, b., B.C., Can.* | G9 | 102 |
| Knights Landing, Ca., U.S. | F4 | 124 |
| Knightstown, In., U.S. | C11 | 114 |
| *Knik Arm, b., Ak., U.S.* | F20 | 100 |
| Knin, Cro. | E11 | 18 |
| Knippa, Tx., U.S. | J7 | 116 |
| Knittelfeld, Aus. | H14 | 10 |
| Knob Noster, Mo., U.S. | D3 | 114 |
| Knokke-Heist, Bel. | F3 | 12 |
| Knox, In., U.S. | A10 | 114 |
| Knox, Pa., U.S. | F7 | 108 |
| *Knox, Cape, c., B.C., Can.* | C1 | 102 |
| Knox City, Tx., U.S. | F7 | 116 |
| *Knox Coast, Ant.* | B6 | 73 |
| Knoxville, Ga., U.S. | G3 | 112 |
| Knoxville, Ia., U.S. | I2 | 110 |
| Knoxville, Il., U.S. | J5 | 110 |
| Knoxville, Tn., U.S. | D3 | 112 |
| Knysna, S. Afr. | J6 | 66 |
| Knyszyn, Pol. | B22 | 10 |
| *Kobar Sink, depr., Eth.* | F9 | 56 |
| Kobayashi, Japan | P5 | 36 |
| Kōbe, Japan | M10 | 36 |
| København (Copenhagen), Den. | N13 | 6 |
| Koblenz, Ger. | E7 | 10 |
| Koboža, Russia | C18 | 22 |
| Kobrinskoje, Russia | B13 | 22 |
| Kobryn, Bela. | I7 | 22 |
| Kobuk, Ak., U.S. | C16 | 100 |
| Kobylin, Pol. | D17 | 10 |
| Kočani, Mac. | H6 | 20 |
| *Kočečum, stm., Russia* | D12 | 28 |
| Kočetovka, Russia | I23 | 22 |
| Kočevje, Slvn. | D9 | 18 |
| Kŏch'ang, S. Kor. | H14 | 32 |
| Koch Bihār, India | G13 | 44 |
| Kōchi, Japan | N8 | 36 |
| *Koch Island, i., N.T., Can.* | C17 | 96 |
| Kochma, Russia | E24 | 22 |
| Kodaikānal, India | G4 | 46 |
| Kodāri, Nepal | G11 | 44 |
| Kodiak, Ak., U.S. | H18 | 100 |
| *Kodiak Island, i., Ak., U.S.* | H18 | 100 |
| Kodino, Russia | J26 | 6 |
| Kodok, Sudan | M7 | 60 |
| Kodyma, Ukr. | A13 | 20 |
| Koekelare, Bel. | F2 | 12 |
| Koersel, Bel. | F7 | 12 |
| Koes, Nmb. | E4 | 66 |
| Köflach, Aus. | H15 | 10 |
| Koforidua, Ghana | H9 | 64 |
| Kōfu, Japan | L13 | 36 |
| Koga, Japan | K14 | 36 |
| *Kogaluc, stm., P.Q., Can.* | E17 | 96 |
| *Kogaluc, Baie, b., P.Q., Can.* | E17 | 96 |
| *Kogaluk, stm., Nf., Can.* | E20 | 96 |
| Kogan, Austl. | F9 | 70 |
| Køge, Den. | N13 | 6 |
| Kogoni, Mali | D6 | 64 |
| Koḥanava, Bela. | G13 | 22 |
| Kohāt, Pak. | D4 | 44 |
| Kohila, Est. | B7 | 22 |
| Kohīma, India | H16 | 44 |
| Kohler, Wi., U.S. | G8 | 110 |
| Kohtla-Järve, Est. | B10 | 22 |
| Kohŭng, S. Kor. | I15 | 32 |
| *Kohunlich, hist., Mex.* | H15 | 90 |
| Koidern, Yk., Can. | F24 | 100 |
| Koidu, S.L. | G4 | 64 |
| Koigi, Est. | C8 | 22 |
| Koimbani, Com. | k15 | 67a |
| Kojgorodok, Russia | E8 | 26 |
| Kojŏ, N. Kor. | E15 | 32 |
| *Kok (Hkok), stm., Asia* | D5 | 40 |
| Kokand, Uzb. | I12 | 26 |
| *Kokanee Glacier Provincial Park, B.C., Can.* | H17 | 102 |
| Kokčetav, Kaz. | G11 | 26 |
| Koki, Sen. | D2 | 64 |
| Kokka, Sudan | G6 | 60 |
| Kokkola (Karleby), Fin. | J18 | 6 |
| Koknese, Lat. | E8 | 22 |
| Koko, Nig. | F12 | 64 |
| Kokoda, Pap. N. Gui. | A9 | 68 |
| Kokomo, In., U.S. | B10 | 114 |
| Kokomo, Ms., U.S. | K6 | 114 |
| Kokong, Bots. | E6 | 66 |
| *Koko Nor see Qinghai Hu, l., China* | D7 | 30 |
| Kokopo, Pap. N. Gui. | k17 | 68a |
| Kokorevka, Russia | I17 | 22 |
| *Kokšaalatau, chrebet, mts., Asia* | I13 | 26 |
| Koksan, N. Kor. | E14 | 32 |
| *Koksoak, stm., P.Q., Can.* | E19 | 96 |
| Koksŏng, S. Kor. | H15 | 32 |
| Kokstad, S. Afr. | H9 | 66 |
| Kola, Russia | G23 | 6 |
| Kolahun, Lib. | G4 | 64 |
| *Kola Peninsula see Kol'skij poluostrov, pen., Russia* | D5 | 26 |
| Kolār, India | F5 | 46 |
| Kolār Gold Fields, India | F5 | 46 |
| Kolárovo, Slvk. | H18 | 10 |
| Kolbio, Kenya | B8 | 58 |
| Kolchozabad, Taj. | B3 | 44 |
| Kol'čugino, Russia | E22 | 22 |
| Kolda, Sen. | E2 | 64 |
| *Kolenté (Great Scarcies), stm., Afr.* | G3 | 64 |
| *Kolgujev, ostrov, i., Russia* | D7 | 26 |
| Kolhāpur, India | D3 | 46 |
| Kolia, C. Iv. | G6 | 64 |
| *Koliba (Corubal), stm., Afr.* | E3 | 64 |
| Koliganek, Ak., U.S. | G16 | 100 |
| *Kolimbine, stm., Afr.* | D4 | 64 |
| Kolín, Czech Rep. | E15 | 10 |
| Kolisne, Ukr. | C13 | 20 |
| Kolka, Lat. | D5 | 22 |
| *Kolkasrags, c., Lat.* | D5 | 22 |
| Kollegāl, India | F4 | 46 |
| Köln (Cologne), Ger. | E6 | 10 |
| Kolno, Pol. | B21 | 10 |
| Kolo, Niger | E11 | 64 |
| Koło, Pol. | C18 | 10 |
| Koloa, Hi., U.S. | p14 | 125a |
| Kolobovo, Russia | E24 | 22 |
| Kołobrzeg, Pol. | A15 | 10 |
| Kolodn'a, Russia | G15 | 22 |
| Kologriv, Russia | C27 | 22 |
| Koloko, Burkina | F7 | 64 |
| Kolomna, Russia | F21 | 22 |
| Kolomyya, Ukr. | H3 | 26 |
| Kolpaševo, Russia | F8 | 28 |
| Kolpino, Russia | B13 | 22 |
| Kolpny, Russia | I20 | 22 |
| *Kol'skij poluostrov (Kola Peninsula), pen., Russia* | D5 | 26 |
| Kol'ubakino, Russia | F19 | 22 |
| Kolwezi, D.R.C. | D5 | 58 |
| *Kolyma, stm., Russia* | D23 | 28 |
| *Kolymskaja nizmennost', pl., Russia* | D22 | 28 |
| Koma, Eth. | M9 | 60 |
| *Komadugu Gana, stm., Nig.* | F9 | 54 |
| *Komadugu Yobe, stm., Afr.* | F9 | 54 |
| *Komandorskije ostrova, is., Russia* | F25 | 28 |
| Komariči, Russia | I17 | 22 |
| Komárno, Slvk. | H18 | 10 |
| Komarnyky, Ukr. | F23 | 10 |
| Komárom, Hung. | H18 | 10 |
| *Komárom-Esztergom, co., Hung.* | H18 | 10 |
| Komarovo, Russia | C16 | 22 |
| *Komati (Incomáti), stm., Afr.* | E10 | 66 |
| Komatipoort, S. Afr. | E10 | 66 |
| Komatsu, Japan | K11 | 36 |
| Komatsushima, Japan | M9 | 36 |
| Kombone, Cam. | I14 | 64 |
| *Komi, state, Russia* | E8 | 26 |
| Komin Yanga, Burkina | F10 | 64 |
| Komló, Hung. | I18 | 10 |
| *Kommunizma, pik, mtn., Taj.* | J12 | 26 |
| *Komodo, Pulau, i., Indon.* | G6 | 38 |
| *Komoé, stm., Afr.* | G6 | 54 |
| Komotiní, Grc. | H9 | 20 |
| Komsomolec, Kaz. | G10 | 26 |
| *Komsomolec, ostrov, i., Russia* | A17 | 26 |
| *Komsomolec, zaliv, b., Kaz.* | H8 | 26 |
| Komsomol'sk, Russia | D23 | 22 |
| Komsomol'sk, Turk. | B17 | 48 |
| Komsomol'sk-na-Amure, Russia | G19 | 28 |
| *Komsomol'skoj Pravdy, ostrova, is., Russia* | B13 | 28 |
| Kona, Mali | D8 | 64 |
| *Kona Coast, Hi., U.S.* | r18 | 125a |
| Konakovo, Russia | E19 | 22 |
| Konakpınar, Tur. | J11 | 20 |
| *Konar, stm., Asia* | C4 | 44 |
| Konārak, India | K12 | 44 |
| Konawa, Ok., U.S. | E10 | 116 |
| Konch, India | H8 | 44 |
| *Konda, stm., Russia* | E5 | 28 |
| Kondoa, Tan. | B7 | 58 |
| Kondopoga, Russia | E4 | 26 |
| Kondratjevo, Russia | A11 | 22 |
| Kondrovo, Russia | G18 | 22 |
| Kondūz, Afg. | B3 | 44 |
| Konfara, Gui. | F5 | 64 |
| *Kông, stm., Asia* | H9 | 40 |
| Kongcheng, China | D6 | 34 |
| Kongfang, China | H5 | 34 |
| Kongju, S. Kor. | G15 | 32 |
| Konglong, China | F4 | 34 |
| Kongolo, D.R.C. | C5 | 58 |
| Kongor, Sudan | N6 | 60 |
| Kongsvinger, Nor. | K13 | 6 |
| *Kongur Shan, mtn., China* | D2 | 30 |
| Kongzhen, China | D8 | 34 |
| Konice, Czech Rep. | F16 | 10 |
| Königswinter, Ger. | E7 | 10 |
| Konin, Pol. | C18 | 10 |
| Köniz, Switz. | E7 | 13 |
| Konjic, Bos. | F1 | 20 |
| *Könkämäälven, stm., Eur.* | G17 | 6 |
| Kon'-Kolodez', Russia | I22 | 22 |
| *Konkouré, stm., Gui.* | F3 | 64 |
| Konnur, India | D3 | 46 |
| Konoša, Russia | E6 | 26 |
| Konotop, Ukr. | G4 | 26 |
| Kon'ovo, Russia | J26 | 6 |
| *Konqi, stm., China* | C4 | 30 |
| Końskie, Pol. | D20 | 10 |
| Konstantinovskij, Russia | D22 | 22 |
| Konstanz, Ger. | H9 | 10 |
| Kontagora, Nig. | F12 | 64 |
| Kontejevo, Russia | C24 | 22 |
| Kontich, Bel. | F5 | 12 |
| Kontiomäki, Fin. | I21 | 6 |
| Kontseba, Ukr. | A13 | 20 |
| Kon Tum, Viet. | G10 | 40 |
| *Kontum, Plateau du, plat., Viet.* | H10 | 40 |
| Konya, Tur. | C2 | 48 |
| Konza, Kenya | B7 | 58 |
| *Konžakovskij Kamen', gora, mtn., Russia* | F9 | 26 |
| *Koocanusa, Lake, res., N.A.* | B10 | 122 |
| Koolamarra, Austl. | C4 | 70 |
| *Koolau Range, mts., Hi., U.S.* | p15 | 125a |
| Kooloonong, Austl. | J5 | 70 |
| Koondrook, Austl. | J6 | 70 |
| Koontz Lake, In., U.S. | A10 | 114 |
| Koosharem, Ut., U.S. | F5 | 120 |
| Kooskia, Id., U.S. | D10 | 122 |
| Koossa, Gui. | G5 | 64 |
| *Kootenai (Kootenay), stm., N.A.* | I18 | 102 |
| *Kootenay (Kootenai), stm., N.A.* | H17 | 102 |
| *Kootenay Indian Reserve, B.C., Can.* | H19 | 102 |
| *Kootenay Lake, l., B.C., Can.* | H18 | 102 |
| *Kootenay National Park, B.C., Can.* | F18 | 102 |
| Kootjieskolk, S. Afr. | H5 | 66 |
| Kopargaon, India | C3 | 46 |
| Kópasker, Ice. | A5 | 6a |
| Kopejsk, Russia | F10 | 26 |
| Koper, Slvn. | D8 | 18 |
| *Kopetdag, chrebet, mts., Asia* | C15 | 48 |
| Koppal, India | E4 | 46 |
| *Kopparbergs Län, co., Swe.* | K14 | 6 |
| Koprivnica, Cro. | C11 | 18 |
| Kopt'ovo, Russia | E23 | 22 |
| Kopys', Bela. | G13 | 22 |
| *Korab (Maja e Korabit), mtn., Eur.* | H4 | 20 |
| *Korabit, Maja e (Korab), mtn., Eur.* | H4 | 20 |
| Korablino, Russia | H23 | 22 |
| *Kor'akskaja Sopka, vulkan, vol., Russia* | G23 | 28 |
| Korāput, India | C7 | 46 |
| Korba, Tun. | M5 | 18 |
| Korbach, Ger. | D8 | 10 |
| Korbous, Tun. | M5 | 18 |
| Korçë, Alb. | I4 | 20 |
| *Korčula, Otok, i., Cro.* | G11 | 18 |
| Kord Kūy, Iran | C13 | 48 |
| *Korea, North, ctry., Asia* | C12 | 30 |
| *Korea, South, ctry., Asia* | D12 | 30 |
| *Korea Bay, b., Asia* | E11 | 32 |
| *Korea Strait, strt., Asia* | I16 | 32 |
| Korekozevo, Russia | G19 | 22 |
| Korfovskij, Russia | H19 | 28 |
| Korgus, Sudan | H7 | 60 |
| Korhogo, C. Iv. | G7 | 64 |
| *Korinthiakós Kólpos (Gulf of Corinth), b., Grc.* | K6 | 20 |
| Kórinthos (Corinth), Grc. | L6 | 20 |
| *Korínthou, Dhiórix, Grc.* | L6 | 20 |
| Kōriyama, Japan | J15 | 36 |
| Korkino, Russia | G10 | 26 |
| Korla, China | C4 | 30 |
| Korneuburg, Aus. | G16 | 10 |
| Koro, Mali | D8 | 64 |
| Korogwe, Tan. | C7 | 58 |
| Koroit, Austl. | L5 | 70 |
| Koroleve, Ukr. | A7 | 20 |
| Koróni, Grc. | M5 | 20 |
| Koronowo, Pol. | B17 | 10 |
| *Körös, stm., Hung.* | I21 | 10 |
| Korosten', Ukr. | G3 | 26 |
| Korotovo, Russia | C20 | 22 |
| Korpilahti, Fin. | J19 | 6 |
| Korpo (Korppoo), Fin. | K17 | 6 |
| Korsakov, Russia | H20 | 28 |
| Korsør, Den. | N12 | 6 |
| Korsze, Pol. | A21 | 10 |
| Kortrijk (Courtrai), Bel. | G3 | 12 |
| *Koruçam Burnu, c., N. Cyp.* | D2 | 48 |
| Korumburra, Austl. | L6 | 70 |
| Koryŏng, S. Kor. | H16 | 32 |
| Kos, Grc. | M11 | 20 |
| *Kos (Cos), i., Grc.* | M11 | 20 |
| Kosa, Eth. | N9 | 60 |
| Kosa, Russia | F8 | 26 |
| Koš-Agač, Russia | G15 | 26 |
| Kosaja Gora, Russia | G20 | 22 |
| Koščagyl, Kaz. | H8 | 26 |
| Kościan, Pol. | C16 | 10 |
| Kościerzyna, Pol. | A18 | 10 |
| Kosciusko, Ms., U.S. | I7 | 114 |
| *Kosciusko, Mount, mtn., Austl.* | K8 | 70 |
| *Kosciusko National Park, Austl.* | K8 | 70 |
| *Koshikijima-rettō, is., Japan* | P4 | 36 |
| Koshkonong, Mo., U.S. | F5 | 114 |
| Košice, Slvk. | G21 | 10 |
| Kosiv, Ukr. | A9 | 20 |
| Köşk, Tur. | L12 | 20 |
| *Koskaecodde Lake, l., Nf., Can.* | D18 | 106 |
| Koski, Fin. | K18 | 6 |
| Koslan, Russia | E7 | 26 |
| Kosmynino, Russia | D23 | 22 |
| Kosŏng, N. Kor. | E16 | 32 |
| *Kosovo-Metohija, prov., Yugo.* | G5 | 20 |
| Kosovska Mitrovica, Yugo. | G4 | 20 |
| Kosse, Tx., U.S. | H10 | 116 |
| Koster, S. Afr. | E8 | 66 |
| Kosterevo, Russia | F22 | 22 |
| Kostroma, Russia | D23 | 22 |
| *Kostroma, stm., Russia* | C23 | 22 |
| Kostryzhivka, Ukr. | A9 | 20 |
| Kostrzyn, Pol. | C14 | 10 |
| Kostyantynivka, Ukr. | H5 | 26 |
| Koszalin (Köslin), Pol. | A16 | 10 |
| Kőszeg, Hung. | H16 | 10 |
| Kota, India | H6 | 44 |
| Kota Baharu, Malay. | K7 | 40 |
| Kotabaru, Indon. | F6 | 38 |
| Kotabumi, Indon. | F3 | 38 |
| Kotadabok, Indon. | O8 | 40 |
| *Kotcho Lake, l., B.C., Can.* | E8 | 96 |
| Kotel'nič, Russia | F7 | 26 |
| Kotel'nikovo, Russia | H6 | 26 |
| *Kotel'nyj, ostrov, i., Russia* | B19 | 28 |
| Köthen, Ger. | D11 | 10 |
| Kotka, Fin. | K20 | 6 |
| Kot Kapūra, India | E6 | 44 |
| Kotlas, Russia | E7 | 26 |
| Kotli, Pak. | D5 | 44 |
| *Kotlin, ostrov, i., Russia* | A12 | 22 |
| Kotly, Russia | B11 | 22 |
| Koton-Karifi, Nig. | G13 | 64 |
| Kotonkoro, Nig. | F12 | 64 |
| Kotor, Yugo. | G2 | 20 |
| Kotoriba, Cro. | C11 | 18 |
| Kotorovo, Russia | G24 | 22 |
| Kotouba, C. Iv. | G8 | 64 |
| Kotovsk, Russia | I24 | 22 |
| Kotovs'k, Ukr. | H3 | 26 |
| Kottagūdem, India | D6 | 46 |
| Kottayam, India | H4 | 46 |
| *Kotto, stm., C.A.R.* | G5 | 56 |
| *Kotuj, stm., Russia* | C12 | 28 |
| Kotzebue, Ak., U.S. | C13 | 100 |
| *Kotzebue Sound, strt., Ak., U.S.* | C13 | 100 |
| Kötzting, Ger. | F12 | 10 |
| Kou'an, China | C8 | 34 |
| Kouandé, Benin | F10 | 64 |
| *Kouchibouguac National Park, N.B., Can.* | F8 | 106 |
| Koudougou, Burkina | E8 | 64 |
| Kouéré, Burkina | F8 | 64 |
| *Koukdjuak, stm., N.T., Can.* | C18 | 96 |
| Koulamoutou, Gabon | B2 | 58 |
| Koulikoro, Mali | E6 | 64 |
| Koulouguidi, Mali | E4 | 64 |
| *Koulountou, stm., Afr.* | E3 | 64 |
| Koumbakara, Sen. | E2 | 64 |
| Koumbal, C.A.R. | M2 | 60 |
| Koumpentoum, Sen. | E2 | 64 |
| Koumra, Chad | G4 | 56 |
| Koundara, Gui. | E3 | 64 |
| Koungheul, Sen. | E2 | 64 |
| Kounradskij, Kaz. | H13 | 26 |
| Kountze, Tx., U.S. | L2 | 114 |
| Koupéla, Burkina | E9 | 64 |
| Kouroukoto, Mali | E4 | 64 |
| Kouroussa, Gui. | F5 | 54 |
| Koussanar, Sen. | E2 | 64 |
| Koussané, Mali | D4 | 64 |
| Koussane, Sen. | D3 | 64 |
| *Koussi, Emi, mtn., Chad* | E4 | 56 |
| Koussili, Mali | E4 | 64 |
| Koutia Ba, Sen. | D2 | 64 |
| Koutiala, Mali | E7 | 64 |
| Kouto, C. Iv. | G6 | 64 |
| Koutou, China | E2 | 32 |
| Kouts, In., U.S. | A9 | 114 |
| Kovarskas, Lith. | F7 | 22 |
| Kovdor, Russia | H22 | 6 |
| Kovel', Ukr. | G2 | 26 |
| Kovernino, Russia | D26 | 22 |
| Kovilpatti, India | H4 | 46 |
| Kovrov, Russia | F6 | 26 |
| Kovvur, India | D6 | 46 |
| Kowalewo Pomorskie, Pol. | B18 | 10 |
| Kowŏn, N. Kor. | D15 | 32 |
| *Koyna Reservoir, res., India* | D2 | 46 |
| Koyuk, Ak., U.S. | D14 | 100 |
| Koyukuk, Ak., U.S. | D16 | 100 |
| *Koyukuk, stm., Ak., U.S.* | D17 | 100 |
| Kozan, Tur. | C3 | 48 |
| Kozáni, Grc. | I5 | 20 |
| Kozel'sk, Russia | G18 | 22 |
| Kozhikode (Calicut), India | G3 | 46 |
| Kozlov Bereg, Russia | C10 | 22 |
| Kozlovo, Russia | E19 | 22 |
| Kpandae, Ghana | G9 | 64 |
| Kpandu, Ghana | H10 | 64 |
| *Kra, Isthmus of, Asia* | I5 | 40 |
| Krabi, Thai. | J5 | 40 |
| Krâchéh, Camb. | H9 | 40 |
| Kragerø, Nor. | L11 | 6 |
| Kragujevac, Yugo. | E4 | 20 |
| Krajenka, Pol. | B17 | 10 |
| *Krajina, reg., Cro.* | D10 | 18 |
| *Krakatoa see Rakata, Pulau, i., Indon.* | j12 | 39a |
| Krâkôr, Camb. | H8 | 40 |
| Kraków, Pol. | E19 | 10 |
| Kralendijk, Neth. Ant. | H10 | 94 |
| Kraljevo, Yugo. | F4 | 20 |
| Kralovice, Czech Rep. | F13 | 10 |
| Kramators'k, Ukr. | H5 | 26 |
| Kranj, Slvn. | C9 | 18 |
| Kranzberg, Nmb. | C2 | 66 |
| Kraskino, Russia | A18 | 32 |
| Krāslava, Lat. | F10 | 22 |
| Krasnae, Bela. | G10 | 22 |
| Krasnaja Gorbatka, Russia | F24 | 22 |
| Krasnaja Gorka, Russia | E26 | 22 |
| Krasnaja Zar'a, Russia | I20 | 22 |
| Kraśnik, Pol. | E22 | 10 |
| Krasni Okny, Ukr. | B13 | 20 |
| Krasnoarmejsk, Russia | E21 | 22 |
| Krasnodar, Russia | H5 | 26 |
| Krasnofarfornyj, Russia | B14 | 22 |
| Krasnogorsk, Russia | F20 | 22 |
| Krasnogorsk, Russia | H20 | 28 |
| Krasnoil's'k, Ukr. | A9 | 20 |
| Krasnojarsk, Russia | F10 | 28 |
| *Krasnojarskoje vodochranilišče, res., Russia* | F16 | 26 |
| Krasnoje Echo, Russia | F23 | 22 |
| Krasnoje-na-Volge, Russia | D24 | 22 |
| Krasnoje Selo, Russia | B13 | 22 |
| Krasnoje Znam'a, Turk. | C17 | 48 |
| Krasnokamsk, Russia | F9 | 26 |
| Krasnolesje, Russia | G5 | 22 |
| Krasnoslobodsk, Russia | H6 | 26 |
| Krasnoturjinsk, Russia | F10 | 26 |
| Krasnoufimsk, Russia | F9 | 26 |
| Krasnoural'sk, Russia | F10 | 26 |
| Krasnovišersk, Russia | E9 | 26 |
| Krasnovodsk, Turk. | I8 | 26 |
| *Krasnovodskij poluostrov, pen., Turk.* | A12 | 48 |
| *Krasnovodskij zaliv, b., Turk.* | B12 | 48 |
| Krasnozavodsk, Russia | E21 | 22 |
| Krasnoznamenskoje, Kaz. | G11 | 26 |
| Krasnoz'orskoje, Russia | G13 | 26 |
| Krasnyj Bogatyr', Russia | E24 | 22 |
| Krasnyj Cholm, Russia | C20 | 22 |
| Krasnyje Tkači, Russia | D22 | 22 |
| Krasnyj Kut, Russia | G7 | 26 |
| Krasnyj Luč, Russia | D13 | 22 |
| Krasnyj Okt'abr', Russia | E21 | 22 |
| Krasnyj Profintern, Russia | D23 | 22 |
| Krasnyj Rog, Russia | I16 | 22 |
| Krasnyj Tkač, Russia | F22 | 22 |
| Krasnystaw, Pol. | E23 | 10 |
| Krasnyy Luch, Ukr. | H5 | 26 |
| *Kraszna (Crasna), stm., Eur.* | A6 | 20 |
| Krebs, Ok., U.S. | E11 | 116 |
| Krečetovo, Russia | K26 | 6 |
| Krečevicy, Russia | C14 | 22 |
| Krefeld, Ger. | D6 | 10 |
| *Kremastón, Tekhnití Límni, res., Grc.* | K5 | 20 |
| Kremenchuk, Ukr. | H4 | 26 |
| *Kremenchuts'ke vodoskhovyshche, res., Ukr.* | H4 | 26 |
| Kremmling, Co., U.S. | D10 | 120 |
| Krems an der Donau, Aus. | G15 | 10 |
| Kress, Tx., U.S. | E5 | 116 |
| *Kresta, zaliv, b., Russia* | D28 | 28 |
| Krestcy, Russia | C15 | 22 |
| Kretinga, Lith. | F4 | 22 |
| Kribi, Cam. | H8 | 54 |
| Kriens, Switz. | D9 | 13 |
| *Kriljon, mys, c., Russia* | b17 | 36a |
| Křimice, Czech Rep. | F13 | 10 |
| *Krishna, stm., India* | D5 | 46 |
| Krishnagiri, India | F5 | 46 |
| Krishnanagar, India | I13 | 44 |
| *Krishnarāja Sāgara, res., India* | F4 | 46 |
| Kristdala, Swe. | M15 | 6 |
| Kristiansand, Nor. | L11 | 6 |
| Kristianstad, Swe. | M14 | 6 |
| Kristiansund, Nor. | J10 | 6 |
| Kristineberg, Swe. | I16 | 6 |
| *Kríti, prov., Grc.* | N8 | 20 |
| *Kríti (Crete), i., Grc.* | N8 | 20 |
| *Kritikón Pélagos (Sea of Crete), Grc.* | N8 | 20 |
| Kriva Palanka, Mac. | G6 | 20 |
| Krivodol, Bul. | F7 | 20 |
| Križevci, Cro. | C11 | 18 |
| *Krk, Otok, i., Cro.* | D9 | 18 |
| Krnov, Czech Rep. | E17 | 10 |
| Krobia, Pol. | D16 | 10 |
| Krokek, Swe. | L15 | 6 |
| Kroken, Nor. | I14 | 6 |
| Krokowa, Pol. | A18 | 10 |
| Krombi Pits, Bots. | B7 | 66 |
| Kroměříž, Czech Rep. | F17 | 10 |
| Kromy, Russia | I18 | 22 |
| Krŏng Kaôh Kŏng, Camb. | I7 | 40 |
| Krŏng Kêb, Camb. | I8 | 40 |
| *Kronobergs Län, co., Swe.* | M14 | 6 |
| Kronoby (Kruunupyy), Fin. | J18 | 6 |
| *Kronockaja Sopka, vulkan, vol., Russia* | G24 | 28 |
| *Kronockij zaliv, b., Russia* | G24 | 28 |
| Kronštadt, Russia | B12 | 22 |
| Kroonstad, S. Afr. | F8 | 66 |
| Kropotkin, Russia | H6 | 26 |
| Krosno, Pol. | F21 | 10 |
| Krotoszyn, Pol. | D17 | 10 |
| Krotz Springs, La., U.S. | L5 | 114 |
| Kr'učkovo, Russia | D18 | 22 |
| Krugersdorp, S. Afr. | F8 | 66 |
| Kruidfontein, S. Afr. | I5 | 66 |
| Kruisfontein, S. Afr. | J7 | 66 |
| *Krukira, Laguna de, b., Nic.* | D11 | 92 |
| Kr'ukovo, Russia | F20 | 22 |
| Kruleu̧ščyna, Bela. | F10 | 22 |
| Krumbach [Schwaben], Ger. | G10 | 10 |
| Krung Thep (Bangkok), Thai. | H6 | 40 |
| Krupka, Czech Rep. | E13 | 10 |
| Krupki, Bela. | G12 | 22 |
| Kruševac, Yugo. | F5 | 20 |
| Kruševo, Mac. | H5 | 20 |
| *Krušné hory (Erzgebirge), mts., Eur.* | B19 | 14 |
| Kruszwica, Pol. | C18 | 10 |
| Krutoje, Russia | I20 | 22 |
| *Kruzenšterna, proliv, strt., Russia* | H22 | 28 |
| *Kruzof Island, i., Ak., U.S.* | H27 | 100 |
| Kryčau̧, Bela. | H14 | 22 |
| Krydor, Sk., Can. | F7 | 104 |
| *Kryms'kyy pivostriv (Crimean Peninsula), pen., Ukr.* | H4 | 26 |
| Krynica, Pol. | F20 | 10 |
| Krynychne, Ukr. | D12 | 20 |
| Kryve Ozero, Ukr. | B14 | 20 |
| Kryvičy, Bela. | G10 | 22 |
| Kryvyy Rih (Krivoy Rog), Ukr. | H4 | 26 |
| Kryzhopil', Ukr. | A12 | 20 |
| Ksar Chellala, Alg. | C12 | 62 |
| Ksar el Barka, Maur. | B3 | 64 |
| Ksar-el-Kebir, Mor. | J6 | 16 |
| Ksar-el-Seghir, Mor. | J6 | 16 |
| Ksar Hellal, Tun. | N5 | 18 |
| Ksenjevka, Russia | G15 | 28 |
| *Ksour, Monts des, mts., Alg.* | D10 | 62 |
| Ksour Essaf, Tun. | N6 | 18 |
| Kuala Kangsar, Malay. | L6 | 40 |
| Kualakapuas, Indon. | F5 | 38 |
| Kuala Lipis, Malay. | L7 | 40 |
| Kuala Lumpur, Malay. | M6 | 40 |
| Kuala Pilah, Malay. | M7 | 40 |
| Kuala Terengganu, Malay. | L7 | 40 |
| Kuancheng, China | C6 | 32 |
| Kuantan, Malay. | M7 | 40 |
| *Kuban', stm., Russia* | H5 | 26 |
| Kubbum, Sudan | L2 | 60 |
| Kubenskoje, Russia | B22 | 22 |
| *Kubenskoje, ozero, l., Russia* | B22 | 22 |
| Kučevo, Yugo. | E5 | 20 |
| Kuchāman, India | G6 | 44 |
| Kuching, Malay. | N11 | 40 |
| Kuçovë, Alb. | I3 | 20 |
| Kudirkos Naumiestis, Lith. | G5 | 22 |
| Kudus, Indon. | j15 | 39a |
| Kudymkar, Russia | F8 | 26 |
| *Kuee Ruins, hist., Hi., U.S.* | r18 | 125a |
| Kufstein, Aus. | H12 | 10 |
| *Kugaluk, stm., N.T., Can.* | B29 | 100 |
| *Kugmallit Bay, b., N.T., Can.* | B28 | 100 |
| Kūhdasht, Iran | E9 | 48 |
| Kūhpāyeh, Iran | E12 | 48 |
| Kuidesu, China | B7 | 32 |
| Kuidou, China | J7 | 34 |
| *Kuiseb, stm., S. Afr.* | D2 | 66 |
| Kuito, Ang. | D3 | 58 |
| *Kuiu Island, i., Ak., U.S.* | H27 | 100 |
| Kujang, N. Kor. | D14 | 32 |
| Kujbyšev see Samara, Russia | G8 | 26 |
| Kujbyšev, Russia | F13 | 26 |
| Kujbyševskij, Uzb. | J11 | 26 |
| *Kujbyševskoje vodochranilišče, res., Russia* | G7 | 26 |
| Kujman', Russia | I22 | 22 |
| *Kukalaya, stm., Nic.* | D11 | 92 |
| Kukawa, Nig. | F9 | 54 |
| Kukkola, Fin. | I19 | 6 |
| Kula, Yugo. | D3 | 20 |
| Kul'ab, Taj. | J11 | 26 |
| *Kula Kangri, mtn., Bhu.* | F14 | 44 |
| Kulākh, Sau. Ar. | D2 | 47 |
| Kulautuva, Lith. | G6 | 22 |
| Kulaykilī, Sudan | L3 | 60 |
| Kuldīga, Lat. | E4 | 22 |
| Kule, Bots. | D5 | 66 |
| Kulebaki, Russia | F25 | 22 |
| Kulikovo, Russia | I22 | 22 |
| Kulim, Malay. | L6 | 40 |
| Kulm, N.D., U.S. | E9 | 118 |
| Kulmbach, Ger. | E11 | 10 |
| Kuloj, Russia | E6 | 26 |
| Kulongshan, China | B4 | 32 |
| Kulotino, Russia | C16 | 22 |
| Kul'sary, Kaz. | H8 | 26 |
| Kulti, India | I12 | 44 |
| Kulumadau, Pap. N. Gui. | A10 | 68 |
| *Kulundinskaja step', pl., Asia* | G7 | 28 |
| *Kuma, stm., Russia* | I7 | 26 |
| Kumagaya, Japan | K14 | 36 |
| Kumajri, Arm. | I6 | 26 |
| Kumamoto, Japan | O5 | 36 |
| Kumanovo, Mac. | G5 | 20 |
| Kumārapālaiyam, India | G4 | 46 |
| Kumasi, Ghana | H9 | 64 |
| Kumba, Cam. | I14 | 64 |
| Kumbakonam, India | G5 | 46 |
| Kumba Pits, Bots. | B7 | 66 |
| Kŭmch'ŏn, N. Kor. | E14 | 32 |
| Kum-Dag, Turk. | J8 | 26 |
| *Kume-jima, i., Japan* | u1 | 37b |
| Kŭmhwa, S. Kor. | E15 | 32 |
| Kumla, Swe. | L14 | 6 |
| Kumo, Nig. | F9 | 54 |
| *Kumukahi, Cape, c., Hi., U.S.* | r19 | 125a |
| Kumukuli, China | B13 | 44 |
| Kumzār, Oman | A10 | 47 |
| Kuna, Id., U.S. | G9 | 122 |
| *Kunašir, ostrov (Kunashiri-tō), i., Russia* | c21 | 36a |
| Kunchhā, Nepal | F11 | 44 |
| Kunda, Est. | B9 | 22 |
| *Kundar, stm., Asia* | E3 | 44 |
| *Kunene, prov., Nmb.* | B2 | 66 |
| *Kunene (Cunene), stm., Afr.* | E2 | 58 |
| *Kunghit Island, i., B.C., Can.* | E3 | 102 |
| Kungrad, Uzb. | I9 | 26 |
| Kungsbacka, Swe. | M13 | 6 |
| Kungur, Russia | F9 | 26 |
| Kunhegyes, Hung. | H20 | 10 |
| Kunja, Russia | E13 | 22 |
| Kunjāh, Pak. | D5 | 44 |
| Kunlong, Myan. | C5 | 40 |
| *Kunlun Shan, mts., China* | B12 | 44 |
| Kunming, China | B7 | 40 |
| Kunsan, S. Kor. | H14 | 32 |
| Kunshan, China | D9 | 34 |
| Kunszentmárton, Hung. | I20 | 10 |
| Kuntair, Gam. | E1 | 64 |

| Name | Map Ref. | Page |
|---|---|---|
| Kuntaur, Gam. | E2 | 64 |
| Kunting, China | F10 | 34 |
| Kununurra, Austl. | C5 | 68 |
| Kunwi, S. Kor. | G16 | 32 |
| Kuokegan, China | B13 | 44 |
| Kuopio, Fin. | J20 | 6 |
| *Kuopion lääni, prov., Fin.* | J20 | 6 |
| Kupang, Indon. | H7 | 38 |
| Kupanskoje, Russia | E21 | 22 |
| Kupino, Russia | G7 | 28 |
| Kupiškis, Lith. | F7 | 22 |
| Küplü, Tur. | H10 | 20 |
| *Kupreanof Island, i., Ak., U.S.* | H28 | 100 |
| Kup'yans'k, Ukr. | H5 | 26 |
| Kuqa, China | C3 | 30 |
| *Kür, stm., Asia* | B10 | 48 |
| Kurashiki, Japan | M8 | 36 |
| Kuraymah, Sudan | H6 | 60 |
| Kurayyimah, Jord. | D5 | 50 |
| Kurba, Russia | D22 | 22 |
| Kürdämir, Azer. | A10 | 48 |
| *Kür dili, spit, Azer.* | B10 | 48 |
| *Kurdistan, hist. reg., Asia* | B4 | 42 |
| Kure, Japan | M7 | 36 |
| *Kurejka, stm., Russia* | D9 | 28 |
| Kuresaare, Est. | C5 | 22 |
| Kurgan, Russia | F11 | 26 |
| Kurgan-T'ube, Taj. | J11 | 26 |
| *Kuria Muria Islands see Khurīyā Murīyā, is., Oman* | F10 | 47 |
| Kuridala, Austl. | C4 | 70 |
| Kurīgrām, Bngl. | H13 | 44 |
| *Kuril Islands see Kuril'skije ostrova, is., Russia* | H22 | 28 |
| *Kuril'skije ostrova (Kuril Islands), is., Russia* | H22 | 28 |
| *Kuril Strait see Pervyj Kuril'skij proliv, strt., Russia* | G23 | 28 |
| *Kuril Trench* | D19 | 126 |
| *Kurinwás, stm., Nic.* | E11 | 92 |
| Kurkino, Russia | H21 | 22 |
| Kurlovskij, Russia | F23 | 22 |
| Kurmuk, Sudan | L8 | 60 |
| Kurnool, India | E5 | 46 |
| Kurort Schmalkalden, Ger. | E10 | 10 |
| Kurovskoje, Russia | F21 | 22 |
| Kurow, N.Z. | F3 | 72 |
| Kuršėnai, Lith. | E5 | 22 |
| Kursk, Russia | G5 | 26 |
| *Kurššskaja kosa, spit, Eur.* | F4 | 22 |
| *Kurššskij zaliv (Kuršių marios), b., Eur.* | F3 | 22 |
| Kūrtī, Sudan | H6 | 60 |
| Kurtistown, Hi., U.S. | r18 | 125a |
| Kuru, Sudan | N4 | 60 |
| Kuruman, S. Afr. | F6 | 66 |
| *Kuruman, stm., S. Afr.* | F5 | 66 |
| *Kurumanheuwels, hills, S. Afr.* | F6 | 66 |
| Kurume, Japan | N5 | 36 |
| Kurumkan, Russia | G14 | 28 |
| *Kurun, stm., Afr.* | O8 | 60 |
| Kurunegala, Sri L. | I6 | 46 |
| *Kurzeme, hist. reg., Lat.* | E5 | 22 |
| Kusa, Russia | F9 | 26 |
| Kušalino, Russia | D19 | 22 |
| *Kusawa Lake, l., Yk., Can.* | F26 | 100 |
| Kusel, Ger. | F7 | 10 |
| Kushaka, Nig. | F13 | 64 |
| Kushiro, Japan | e19 | 36a |
| Kushnytsya, Ukr. | A7 | 20 |
| Kushtia, Bngl. | I13 | 44 |
| Kushui, China | C5 | 30 |
| Kuška, Turk. | J10 | 26 |
| *Kuška, stm., Asia* | C17 | 48 |
| *Kuskokwim, stm., Ak., U.S.* | F14 | 100 |
| *Kuskokwim Mountains, mts., Ak., U.S.* | E16 | 100 |
| Kušmurun, Kaz. | G10 | 26 |
| Küsnacht, Switz. | D10 | 13 |
| Kusŏng, N. Kor. | D13 | 32 |
| *Kussharo-ko, l., Japan* | d19 | 36a |
| Küssnacht am Rigi, Switz. | D9 | 13 |
| Kustanaj, Kaz. | G10 | 26 |
| Kustar'ovka, Russia | G25 | 22 |
| Kūstī, Sudan | K7 | 60 |
| Kušva, Russia | F9 | 26 |
| *Kut, Ko, i., Thai.* | I7 | 40 |
| Kuta, Nig. | G13 | 64 |
| Kütahya, Tur. | H13 | 4 |
| Kutaisi, Geor. | I6 | 26 |
| *Kutch, Rann of (Rann of Kachchh), reg., Asia* | H4 | 44 |
| Kutina, Cro. | D11 | 18 |
| Kutná Hora, Czech Rep. | F15 | 10 |
| Kutno, Pol. | C19 | 10 |
| *Kutse Game Reserve, Bots.* | D7 | 66 |
| Kuttura, Fin. | G20 | 6 |
| Kuttusoja, Fin. | H21 | 6 |
| Kutu, D.R.C. | B3 | 58 |
| Kutum, Sudan | J3 | 60 |
| Kuty, Ukr. | A9 | 20 |
| Kutztown, Pa., U.S. | G11 | 108 |
| Kuujjuaq, P.Q., Can. | E19 | 96 |
| Kuusamo, Fin. | I21 | 6 |
| Kuusankoski, Fin. | K20 | 6 |
| Kuvandyk, Russia | G9 | 26 |
| Kuvango, Ang. | D3 | 58 |
| Kuvšinovo, Russia | D17 | 22 |
| Kuwait see Al-Kuwayt, Kuw. | G9 | 48 |
| *Kuwait (Al-Kuwayt), ctry., Asia* | D4 | 42 |
| Kuwana, Japan | L11 | 36 |
| *Kuwayt, Jūn al- (Kuwait Bay), b., Kuw.* | G10 | 48 |
| Kuybyshev see Samara, Russia | G8 | 26 |
| Kūysanjaq, Iraq | C8 | 48 |
| *Kuyuwini, stm., Guy.* | F13 | 84 |
| Kuženkino, Russia | D16 | 22 |
| Kuzneck, Russia | G7 | 26 |
| *Kuzneckij Alatau, mts., Russia* | G9 | 28 |
| *Kvaløy, i., Nor.* | G16 | 6 |
| *Kwai see Khwae Noi, stm., Thai.* | G5 | 40 |
| Kwajok, Sudan | M4 | 60 |
| Kwakoegron, Sur. | B7 | 76 |
| *Kwando (Cuando), stm., Afr.* | E4 | 58 |
| Kwangchow see Guangzhou, China | L2 | 34 |
| Kwangju, S. Kor. | H14 | 32 |
| *Kwango (Cuango), stm., Afr.* | B3 | 58 |
| *Kwangtung see Guangdong, prov., China* | G9 | 30 |
| Kwangyang, S. Kor. | I15 | 32 |
| *Kwazulu see KwaZulu-Natal, prov., S. Afr.* | G10 | 66 |
| *KwaZulu-Natal, prov., S. Afr.* | G10 | 66 |
| Kwekwe, Zimb. | B9 | 66 |
| *Kweneng, dept., Bots.* | E7 | 66 |
| *Kwenge, stm., Afr.* | C3 | 58 |
| Kwethluk, Ak., U.S. | F14 | 100 |
| Kwidzyn, Pol. | B18 | 10 |
| Kwigillingok, Ak., U.S. | G13 | 100 |
| *Kwilu (Cuilo), stm., Afr.* | B3 | 58 |
| *Kwitaro, stm., Guy.* | F13 | 84 |
| Kwolla, Nig. | G14 | 64 |
| Kyabra, Austl. | F5 | 70 |
| Kyabram, Austl. | K6 | 70 |
| Kyaiklat, Myan. | F3 | 40 |
| Kyaikto, Myan. | F4 | 40 |
| Kyaukhnyat, Myan. | E4 | 40 |
| Kyaukpyu, Myan. | E2 | 40 |
| Kyaukse, Myan. | D4 | 40 |
| Kyauktaw, Myan. | D2 | 40 |
| Kyaunggon, Myan. | F3 | 40 |
| Kybartai, Lith. | G5 | 22 |
| Kyeikdon, Myan. | F5 | 40 |
| Kyindwe, Myan. | D2 | 40 |
| Kykotsmovi Village, Az., U.S. | I6 | 120 |
| Kyle, S.D., U.S. | H5 | 118 |
| Kyle, Sk., Can. | H6 | 104 |
| Kyle, Tx., U.S. | J9 | 116 |
| Kyle of Lochalsh, Scot., U.K. | D8 | 8 |
| *Kymen lääni, prov., Fin.* | K20 | 6 |
| Kyneton, Austl. | K6 | 70 |
| *Kyoga, Lake, l., Ug.* | A6 | 58 |
| Kyogle, Austl. | G10 | 70 |
| *Kyŏnggi-man, b., Asia* | F13 | 32 |
| Kyŏngju, S. Kor. | H17 | 32 |
| Kyŏngsan, S. Kor. | H16 | 32 |
| Kyŏngsŏng, N. Kor. | B17 | 32 |
| Kyŏngwŏn, N. Kor. | A18 | 32 |
| Kyōto, Japan | L10 | 36 |
| Kyren, Russia | G12 | 28 |
| *Kyrgyzstan, ctry., Asia* | I13 | 26 |
| Kyritz, Ger. | C12 | 10 |
| Kyštovka, Russia | F13 | 26 |
| Kyštym, Russia | F10 | 26 |
| Kyunhla, Myan. | C3 | 40 |
| Kyuquot, B.C., Can. | G7 | 102 |
| *Kyuquot Sound, strt., B.C., Can.* | G7 | 102 |
| *Kyūshū, i., Japan* | O5 | 36 |
| Kywebwe, Myan. | E4 | 40 |
| Kywong, Austl. | J7 | 70 |
| Kyyiv (Kiev), Ukr. | G4 | 26 |
| *Kyyivs'ke vodoskhovyshche, res., Ukr.* | G4 | 26 |
| Kyyjärvi, Fin. | J19 | 6 |
| Kyzyl, Russia | G10 | 28 |
| Kyzyl-Kija, Kyrg. | I12 | 26 |
| *Kyzylkum, des., Asia* | I10 | 26 |
| Kzyl-Orda, Kaz. | I11 | 26 |
| Kzyltu, Kaz. | G12 | 26 |


## L


| Name | Map Ref. | Page |
|---|---|---|
| Laa an der Thaya, Aus. | G16 | 10 |
| *La Aguja, Cabo de, c., Col.* | B5 | 84 |
| *La Alcarria, reg., Spain* | E9 | 16 |
| La Algaba, Spain | H5 | 16 |
| *La Antigua, Salina, pl., Arg.* | E5 | 80 |
| *La Araucanía, prov., Chile* | J2 | 80 |
| La Arena, Pan. | J14 | 92 |
| Laas Caanood, Som. | G10 | 56 |
| La Ascención, Mex. | E10 | 90 |
| La Asunción, Ven. | B11 | 84 |
| *La Atravesada, Loma, hill, Mex.* | C3 | 90 |
| *Laau Point, c., Hi., U.S.* | p16 | 125a |
| La Babia, Mex. | C8 | 90 |
| Labadieville, La., U.S. | M6 | 114 |
| La Baie, P.Q., Can. | D3 | 106 |
| La Banda, Arg. | D6 | 80 |
| *La Bandera, Cerro, mtn., Mex.* | E7 | 90 |
| La Bañeza, Spain | C6 | 16 |
| La Barca, Mex. | G8 | 90 |
| La Barge, Wy., U.S. | B6 | 120 |
| La Barra, Nic. | E11 | 92 |
| La Barrita, Guat. | C3 | 92 |
| La Baule-Escoublac, Fr. | E4 | 14 |
| Labé, Gui. | F3 | 64 |
| *Labe (Elbe), stm., Eur.* | B9 | 10 |
| La Belle, Fl., U.S. | M5 | 112 |
| La Belle, Mo., U.S. | B5 | 114 |
| Labelle, P.Q., Can. | A12 | 108 |
| *Laberge, Lake, l., Yk., Can.* | F27 | 100 |
| *La Biche, stm., Ab., Can.* | B22 | 102 |
| Labin, Cro. | D9 | 18 |
| Labinsk, Russia | I6 | 26 |
| La Bisbal, Spain | D15 | 16 |
| *La Blanca Grande, Laguna, l., Arg.* | J7 | 80 |
| *Labná, hist., Mex.* | G15 | 90 |
| Laboe, Ger. | A10 | 10 |
| Laborde, Arg. | G7 | 80 |
| Labouheyre, Fr. | H6 | 14 |
| Laboulaye, Arg. | H7 | 80 |
| *Labrador, reg., Nf., Can.* | F20 | 96 |
| Labrador City, Nf., Can. | F19 | 96 |
| *Labrador Sea, N.A.* | E22 | 96 |
| Lábrea, Braz. | B9 | 82 |
| *Labrieville, Réserve, P.Q., Can.* | C4 | 106 |
| Labrit, Fr. | H6 | 14 |
| La Broquerie, Mb., Can. | I18 | 104 |
| Labutta, Myan. | F3 | 40 |
| Labytnangi, Russia | D11 | 26 |
| *Lača, ozero, l., Russia* | K26 | 6 |
| *Laca Jahuira, stm., Bol.* | H8 | 82 |
| *La Cal, stm., Bol.* | G12 | 82 |
| La Calera, Chile | G3 | 80 |
| Lac-Allard, P.Q., Can. | B10 | 106 |
| La Campana, Spain | H6 | 16 |
| La Canada, Ca., U.S. | J7 | 124 |
| La Candelaria, Arg. | D6 | 80 |
| *Lacantún, stm., Mex.* | I14 | 90 |
| La Capelle [-en-Thierache], Fr. | C10 | 14 |
| Lacapelle-Marival, Fr. | H8 | 14 |
| La Carlota, Arg. | G7 | 80 |
| La Carolina, Spain | G8 | 16 |
| Lacaune, Fr. | I9 | 14 |
| *Laccadive Islands see Lakshadweep, is., India* | G2 | 46 |
| Lac du Flambeau, Wi., U.S. | E6 | 110 |
| La Ceiba, Hond. | B8 | 92 |
| La Ceiba, Ven. | C7 | 84 |
| La Center, Ky., U.S. | E8 | 114 |
| Lac-Etchemin, P.Q., Can. | F3 | 106 |
| Lacey, Wa., U.S. | C3 | 122 |
| Lac-Frontière, P.Q., Can. | F3 | 106 |
| La Chambre, Fr. | G13 | 14 |
| La Chapelle-d'Angillon, Fr. | E9 | 14 |
| La Chartre-sur-le-Loir, Fr. | E7 | 14 |
| La Châtaigneraie, Fr. | F6 | 14 |
| La Chaux-de-Fonds, Switz. | D6 | 13 |
| *Lachay, Punta, c., Peru* | D3 | 82 |
| Lachdenpochja, Russia | K22 | 6 |
| Lachen, Switz. | D10 | 13 |
| Lachhmangarh Sīkar, India | G6 | 44 |
| Lachine, P.Q., Can. | B13 | 108 |
| *Lachkaltsap Indian Reserve, B.C., Can.* | B5 | 102 |
| *Lachlan, stm., Austl.* | J6 | 70 |
| La Chorrera, Col. | H6 | 84 |
| La Chorrera, Pan. | C3 | 84 |
| *L'achovskije ostrova, is., Russia* | C20 | 28 |
| Lachute, P.Q., Can. | B12 | 108 |
| La Ciénaga, Arg. | D5 | 80 |
| La Ciotat, Fr. | I12 | 14 |
| *La Citadelle, hist., Haiti* | E8 | 94 |
| La Ciudad, Mex. | F7 | 90 |
| Lackawanna, N.Y., U.S. | E8 | 108 |
| Lac la Biche, Ab., Can. | C23 | 102 |
| Lac la Hache, B.C., Can. | F13 | 102 |
| *Lac la Ronge Provincial Park, Sk., Can.* | C10 | 104 |
| Laclede, Id., U.S. | I18 | 102 |
| Laclede, Mo., U.S. | C3 | 114 |
| La Clotilde, Arg. | D8 | 80 |
| Lac-Mégantic, P.Q., Can. | B16 | 108 |
| La Cocha, Arg. | D6 | 80 |
| La Colorada, Mex. | C4 | 90 |
| La Coma, Mex. | E10 | 90 |
| Lacombe, Ab., Can. | E21 | 102 |
| Lacombe, La., U.S. | L7 | 114 |
| Lacon, Il., U.S. | I6 | 110 |
| Lacona, Ia., U.S. | I2 | 110 |
| La Concepción, Pan. | C1 | 84 |
| La Concepción, Ven. | B7 | 84 |
| Laconia, N.H., U.S. | D15 | 108 |
| La Conner, Wa., U.S. | B3 | 122 |
| La Consulta, Arg. | G4 | 80 |
| Lacoochee, Fl., U.S. | K4 | 112 |
| La Coste, Tx., U.S. | J8 | 116 |
| *Lac qui Parle, stm., Mn., U.S.* | G11 | 118 |
| La Crescent, Mn., U.S. | G4 | 110 |
| La Crosse, In., U.S. | A10 | 114 |
| La Crosse, Ks., U.S. | M8 | 118 |
| La Crosse, Va., U.S. | C8 | 112 |
| Lacrosse, Wa., U.S. | D8 | 122 |
| La Crosse, Wi., U.S. | G4 | 110 |
| *La Crosse, stm., Wi., U.S.* | G4 | 110 |
| La Cruz, Arg. | E10 | 80 |
| La Cruz, Col. | G4 | 84 |
| La Cruz, C.R. | F9 | 92 |
| La Cruz, Ur. | G10 | 80 |
| *La Cruz, Cerro, mtn., Mex.* | I9 | 90 |
| La Cruz de Río Grande, Nic. | D10 | 92 |
| Lac Seul, On., Can. | H22 | 104 |
| *Lac Seul Indian Reserve, On., Can.* | H22 | 104 |
| La Cuesta, C.R. | I12 | 92 |
| La Cumbre, Arg. | F6 | 80 |
| La Cygne, Ks., U.S. | M13 | 118 |
| Ladainha, Braz. | D8 | 79 |
| *Ladākh Range, mts., Asia* | C7 | 44 |
| Ladário, Braz. | H13 | 82 |
| Ladd, Il., U.S. | I6 | 110 |
| Laddonia, Mo., U.S. | C5 | 114 |
| *La Désirade, i., Guad.* | F14 | 94 |
| *La Digue, i., Sey.* | B11 | 58 |
| Ladismith, S. Afr. | I5 | 66 |
| Lādīz, Iran | G16 | 48 |
| Lādnūn, India | G6 | 44 |
| Ladoga, In., U.S. | C10 | 114 |
| *Ladoga, Lake see Ladožskoje ozero, l., Russia* | E4 | 26 |
| Ladonia, Tx., U.S. | F11 | 116 |
| La Dorada, Col. | E5 | 84 |
| La Dormida, Arg. | G5 | 80 |
| Ladožskoje Ozero, Russia | A14 | 22 |
| *Ladožskoje ozero (Lake Ladoga), l., Russia* | E4 | 26 |
| Ladson, S.C., U.S. | G6 | 112 |
| *Ladue, stm., N.A.* | E24 | 100 |
| Laduškin, Russia | G3 | 22 |
| Ladva-Vetka, Russia | K24 | 6 |
| L'ady, Russia | C11 | 22 |
| *Lady Ann Strait, strt., N.T., Can.* | A16 | 96 |
| Ladybrand, S. Afr. | G8 | 66 |
| *Lady Elliot Island, i., Austl.* | E10 | 70 |
| Ladysmith, B.C., Can. | I11 | 102 |
| Ladysmith, S. Afr. | G9 | 66 |
| Ladysmith, Wi., U.S. | E4 | 110 |
| Lae, Pap. N. Gui. | m16 | 68a |
| La Encantada, Mex. | E9 | 90 |
| La Esmeralda, Mex. | D8 | 90 |
| La Esmeralda, Para. | B7 | 80 |
| La Esmeralda, Ven. | F10 | 84 |
| La Esperanza, Cuba | C3 | 94 |
| La Esperanza, Hond. | C6 | 92 |
| La Estrella, Bol. | G10 | 82 |
| La Falda, Arg. | F6 | 80 |
| La Farge, Wi., U.S. | G5 | 110 |
| Lafayette, Al., U.S. | J11 | 114 |
| Lafayette, Ca., U.S. | G3 | 124 |
| Lafayette, Co., U.S. | L2 | 118 |
| Lafayette, Ga., U.S. | E1 | 112 |
| Lafayette, In., U.S. | B10 | 114 |
| Lafayette, La., U.S. | L4 | 114 |
| Lafayette, Mn., U.S. | F1 | 110 |
| Lafayette, Tn., U.S. | F10 | 114 |
| La Fé, Cuba | D3 | 94 |
| La Fère, Fr. | C10 | 14 |
| La Feria, Tx., U.S. | M9 | 116 |
| La Ferté-Bernard, Fr. | D7 | 14 |
| La Ferté-Gaucher, Fr. | D10 | 14 |
| La Ferté-Macé, Fr. | D6 | 14 |
| La Ferté-Saint-Aubin, Fr. | E8 | 14 |
| Lafia, Nig. | G14 | 64 |
| La Flèche, Fr. | E6 | 14 |
| Lafleche, Sk., Can. | I8 | 104 |
| La Florida, Guat. | I14 | 90 |
| *Lafnitz, stm., Eur.* | H16 | 10 |
| La Follette, Tn., U.S. | C2 | 112 |
| La Fontaine, In., U.S. | B11 | 114 |
| *Lafourche, Bayou, stm., La., U.S.* | M6 | 114 |
| La Fragua, Arg. | D6 | 80 |
| La Francia, Arg. | F7 | 80 |
| La Fría, Ven. | C6 | 84 |
| *La Galite, i., Tun.* | L3 | 18 |
| La Gallareta, Arg. | E8 | 80 |
| Lagangzong, China | F14 | 44 |
| Lagarto, C.R. | G10 | 92 |
| Lagawe, Phil. | m19 | 39b |
| Lage, China | F11 | 44 |
| *Lågen, stm., Nor.* | K11 | 6 |
| *Lågen, stm., Nor.* | K12 | 6 |
| Lages, Braz. | D13 | 80 |
| Lage Zwaluwe, Neth. | E6 | 12 |
| Laghouat, Alg. | D12 | 62 |
| La Gleize, Bel. | H8 | 12 |
| La Gloria, Col. | C6 | 84 |
| Lagoa da Prata, Braz. | F6 | 79 |
| Lagoa Formosa, Braz. | E5 | 79 |
| Lagoa Santa, Braz. | E7 | 79 |
| Lagoa Vermelha, Braz. | E13 | 80 |
| Lagolândia, Braz. | C4 | 79 |
| *La Gomera, i., Spain* | o23 | 17b |
| Lagos, Nig. | H11 | 64 |
| Lagos, Port. | H3 | 16 |
| Lagos de Moreno, Mex. | G9 | 90 |
| La Gouèra, W. Sah. | J2 | 62 |
| La Goulette, Tun. | M5 | 18 |
| La Grand'Combe, Fr. | H11 | 14 |
| La Grande, Or., U.S. | E7 | 122 |
| *La Grande Deux, Réservoir, res., P.Q., Can.* | F17 | 96 |
| *La Grande Quatre, Réservoir, res., P.Q., Can.* | F18 | 96 |
| La Grange, Austl. | C4 | 68 |
| La Grange, Ga., U.S. | F1 | 112 |
| Lagrange, In., U.S. | A11 | 114 |
| La Grange, Ky., U.S. | D11 | 114 |
| La Grange, Mo., U.S. | B5 | 114 |
| La Grange, N.C., U.S. | D9 | 112 |
| La Grange, Tx., U.S. | J10 | 116 |
| Lagrange, Wy., U.S. | J3 | 118 |
| *La Gran Sabana, pl., Ven.* | E12 | 84 |
| La Grita, Ven. | C7 | 84 |
| Lagu, China | A6 | 40 |
| La Guadeloupe (Saint-Évariste), P.Q., Can. | B16 | 108 |
| *La Guajira, dept., Col.* | B6 | 84 |
| *La Guajira, Península de, pen., S.A.* | A7 | 84 |
| La Guardia, Arg. | E6 | 80 |
| La Guardia, Bol. | G10 | 82 |
| La Guerche-de-Bretagne, Fr. | E5 | 14 |
| La Guerche-sur-l'Aubois, Fr. | F9 | 14 |
| Laguna, Braz. | E14 | 80 |
| Laguna, N.M., U.S. | I9 | 120 |
| *Laguna, Ilha da, i., Braz.* | D8 | 76 |
| Laguna Beach, Ca., U.S. | K8 | 124 |
| Laguna Larga, Arg. | F7 | 80 |
| Laguna Limpia, Arg. | D9 | 80 |
| Laguna Paiva, Arg. | F8 | 80 |
| Lagunas, Peru | A4 | 82 |
| *Lagunas de Chacagua, Parque Nacional, Mex.* | I11 | 90 |
| *Lagunas de Montebello, Parque Nacional, Mex.* | A3 | 92 |
| Lagunillas, Bol. | H10 | 82 |
| Lagunillas, Ven. | C7 | 84 |
| *Lagunillás, Laguna, l., Peru* | F6 | 82 |
| *Laguntara, b., Hond.* | E10 | 92 |
| La Habana (Havana), Cuba | C3 | 94 |
| Lahaina, Hi., U.S. | q17 | 125a |
| La Harpe, Il., U.S. | J5 | 110 |
| La Harpe, Ks., U.S. | N12 | 118 |
| Lahat, Indon. | F3 | 38 |
| *LaHave, stm., N.S., Can.* | H9 | 106 |
| La Haye-du-Puits, Fr. | C5 | 14 |
| La Higuera, Chile | E3 | 80 |
| Lahij, Yemen | H4 | 47 |
| Lāhījān, Iran | C11 | 48 |
| Lahnstein, Ger. | E7 | 10 |
| Lahojsk, Bela. | G10 | 22 |
| *Lahontan Reservoir, res., Nv., U.S.* | E6 | 124 |
| Lahore, Pak. | E6 | 44 |
| La Horqueta, Col. | F6 | 84 |
| Lahr, Ger. | G7 | 10 |
| Lahri, Pak. | F3 | 44 |
| Lahti, Fin. | K19 | 6 |
| La Huaca, Peru | A1 | 82 |
| La Huacana, Mex. | H9 | 90 |
| La Huerta, N.M., U.S. | G2 | 116 |
| Lahva, Bela. | I10 | 22 |
| Laibin, China | C10 | 40 |
| Lai Chau, Viet. | C7 | 40 |
| Laifang, China | J5 | 34 |
| L'Aigle, Fr. | D7 | 14 |
| Laignes, Fr. | E11 | 14 |
| *La Independencia, Bahía de, b., Peru* | F3 | 82 |
| Laingsburg, Mi., U.S. | H11 | 110 |
| Laingsburg, S. Afr. | I5 | 66 |
| La Inmaculada, Mex. | C4 | 90 |
| Laird Hill, Tx., U.S. | J2 | 114 |
| Laishan, China | F9 | 32 |
| Laishui, China | D3 | 32 |
| Laiwu, China | G5 | 32 |
| Laiyang, China | G8 | 32 |
| *Laizhou Wan (Laichow Bay), b., China* | F7 | 32 |
| *Laja, stm., Chile* | I3 | 80 |
| *Laja, Laguna de la, l., Chile* | I3 | 80 |
| *Laja, Salto del, wtfl, Chile* | I3 | 80 |
| La Jalca, Peru | B3 | 82 |
| La Jara, Co., U.S. | G11 | 120 |
| *La Jara Canyon, val., N.M., U.S.* | H9 | 120 |
| Lajas, Cuba | C4 | 94 |
| Laje, Braz. | B9 | 79 |
| Lajeado, Braz. | E13 | 80 |
| Lajes, Braz. | E11 | 76 |
| Lajinha, Braz. | F8 | 79 |
| La Jolla, Ca., U.S. | L8 | 124 |
| Lajord, Sk., Can. | H10 | 104 |
| Lajosmizse, Hung. | H19 | 10 |
| La Joya, Peru | G6 | 82 |
| La Junta, Co., U.S. | N4 | 118 |
| Lakamané, Mali | D5 | 64 |
| Lake, Ms., U.S. | J7 | 114 |
| Lake Alfred, Fl., U.S. | K5 | 112 |
| Lake Andes, S.D., U.S. | H9 | 118 |
| Lake Arthur, La., U.S. | L4 | 114 |
| Lake Arthur, N.M., U.S. | G2 | 116 |
| Lake Benton, Mn., U.S. | G11 | 118 |
| Lake Brownwood, Tx., U.S. | H7 | 116 |
| Lake Butler, Fl., U.S. | I4 | 112 |
| Lake Cargelligo, Austl. | I7 | 70 |
| Lake Carmel, N.Y., U.S. | F13 | 108 |
| Lake Charles, La., U.S. | L3 | 114 |
| Lake City, Ar., U.S. | G6 | 114 |
| Lake City, Co., U.S. | F9 | 120 |
| Lake City, Fl., U.S. | I4 | 112 |
| Lake City, Ia., U.S. | I13 | 118 |
| Lake City, Mi., U.S. | F10 | 110 |
| Lake City, Mn., U.S. | F3 | 110 |
| Lake City, Pa., U.S. | E6 | 108 |
| Lake City, S.C., U.S. | F7 | 112 |
| Lake City, Tn., U.S. | C2 | 112 |
| Lake Cowichan, B.C., Can. | I10 | 102 |
| Lake Crystal, Mn., U.S. | F1 | 110 |
| Lake Dallas, Tx., U.S. | F9 | 116 |
| Lake Delton, Wi., U.S. | G6 | 110 |
| Lake Elsinore, Ca., U.S. | K8 | 124 |
| Lakefield, Mn., U.S. | H12 | 118 |
| Lakefield, On., Can. | F17 | 110 |
| *Lakefield National Park, Austl.* | C8 | 68 |
| Lake Forest, Fl., U.S. | N6 | 112 |
| Lake Forest, Il., U.S. | H8 | 110 |
| *Lake Fork, stm., Ut., U.S.* | D6 | 120 |
| Lake Geneva, Wi., U.S. | H7 | 110 |
| Lake George, N.Y., U.S. | D13 | 108 |
| Lake Harbor, Fl., U.S. | M6 | 112 |
| Lake Harbour, N.T., Can. | D19 | 96 |
| Lake Havasu City, Az., U.S. | J2 | 120 |
| Lake Helen, Fl., U.S. | K5 | 112 |
| Lakehurst, N.J., U.S. | G12 | 108 |
| Lake Isabella, Ca., U.S. | I7 | 124 |
| Lake Jackson, Tx., U.S. | J11 | 116 |
| Lakeland, Fl., U.S. | K5 | 112 |
| Lakeland, Ga., U.S. | H3 | 112 |
| Lake Linden, Mi., U.S. | C7 | 110 |
| Lake Louise, Ab., Can. | F18 | 102 |
| Lake Mills, Ia., U.S. | G2 | 110 |
| Lake Mills, Wi., U.S. | G7 | 110 |
| Lakemont, Pa., U.S. | G8 | 108 |
| Lake Nash, Austl. | C2 | 70 |
| Lake Norden, S.D., U.S. | G10 | 118 |
| Lake Odessa, Mi., U.S. | H10 | 110 |
| Lake Oswego, Or., U.S. | E3 | 122 |
| Lake Ozark, Mo., U.S. | D4 | 114 |
| Lake Park, Fl., U.S. | M6 | 112 |
| Lake Park, Ia., U.S. | H12 | 118 |
| Lake Park, Mn., U.S. | E11 | 118 |
| Lake Placid, Fl., U.S. | L5 | 112 |
| Lake Placid, N.Y., U.S. | C13 | 108 |
| Lake Pleasant, N.Y., U.S. | D12 | 108 |
| Lakeport, Ca., U.S. | E3 | 124 |
| Lakeport, Mi., U.S. | G13 | 110 |
| Lake Preston, S.D., U.S. | G10 | 118 |
| Lake Providence, La., U.S. | J5 | 114 |
| Lakes District, Wa., U.S. | C3 | 122 |
| Lakeshore, Ms., U.S. | L7 | 114 |
| Lakeside, Az., U.S. | J7 | 120 |
| Lakeside, Ca., U.S. | L9 | 124 |
| Lakeside, Mt., U.S. | B11 | 122 |
| Lakeside, N.S., Can. | H10 | 106 |
| Lakeside, Or., U.S. | G1 | 122 |
| Lake Stevens, Wa., U.S. | B3 | 122 |
| Laketown, Ut., U.S. | C5 | 120 |
| Lake View, Ar., U.S. | H6 | 114 |
| Lakeview, Ga., U.S. | E1 | 112 |
| Lake View, Ia., U.S. | I12 | 118 |
| Lakeview, Mi., U.S. | H10 | 110 |
| Lakeview, Mi., U.S. | G10 | 110 |
| Lake View, N.Y., U.S. | E8 | 108 |
| Lakeview, Oh., U.S. | G3 | 108 |
| Lakeview, Or., U.S. | H5 | 122 |
| Lake View, S.C., U.S. | E7 | 112 |
| Lakeview, Tx., U.S. | M3 | 114 |
| Lakeview, Tx., U.S. | E6 | 116 |
| *Lakeview Mountain, mtn., B.C., Can.* | H14 | 102 |
| Lake Village, Ar., U.S. | I5 | 114 |
| Lakeville, Mn., U.S. | F2 | 110 |
| Lake Wales, Fl., U.S. | L5 | 112 |
| Lake Wilson, Mn., U.S. | H12 | 118 |
| Lakewood, Co., U.S. | E11 | 120 |
| Lakewood, N.J., U.S. | G12 | 108 |
| Lakewood, N.Y., U.S. | E7 | 108 |
| Lakewood, Oh., U.S. | F5 | 108 |
| Lakewood, Wi., U.S. | E7 | 110 |
| Lakewood Park, N.D., U.S. | C9 | 118 |
| Lake Worth, Fl., U.S. | M6 | 112 |
| Lakhīmpur, India | G9 | 44 |
| *Lakhish, val., Asia* | E3 | 50 |
| Lakin, Ks., U.S. | N6 | 118 |
| Lakinsk, Russia | E22 | 22 |
| *Lakonikós Kólpos, b., Grc.* | M6 | 20 |
| Lakota, Ia., U.S. | H13 | 118 |
| Lakota, N.D., U.S. | C9 | 118 |
| *Lakshadweep, ter., India* | H2 | 46 |
| *Lakshadweep, is., India* | G2 | 46 |
| *Lakshadweep Sea, Asia* | H3 | 46 |
| La Lajilla, Mex. | D10 | 90 |
| *L'Albufera, l., Spain* | F11 | 16 |
| La Leonesa, Arg. | D9 | 80 |
| Lalibela, Eth. | K10 | 60 |
| La Libertad, El Sal. | D5 | 92 |
| La Libertad, Guat. | I14 | 90 |
| La Libertad, Hond. | C7 | 92 |
| La Libertad, Nic. | E9 | 92 |
| *La Libertad, dept., Peru* | B2 | 82 |
| La Ligua, Chile | G3 | 80 |
| La Lima, Hond. | B7 | 92 |
| La Línea, Spain | I6 | 16 |
| Lalitpur, India | H8 | 44 |
| Lālmanir Hāt, Bngl. | H13 | 44 |
| La Loche, Sk., Can. | B5 | 104 |
| *La Loche, stm., Sk., Can.* | B5 | 104 |
| *La Loche, Lac, l., Sk., Can.* | B5 | 104 |
| La Loupe, Fr. | D8 | 14 |
| Lalupon, Nig. | H12 | 64 |
| La Luz, Mex. | E11 | 90 |
| La Luz, Nic. | D10 | 92 |
| La Luz, N.M., U.S. | L11 | 120 |
| *Lama, ozero, l., Russia* | D16 | 26 |
| *La Macarena, Serranía de, mts., Col.* | F6 | 84 |
| La Maddalena, Italy | H4 | 18 |
| Lamadong, China | C7 | 32 |
| La Madrid, Arg. | D6 | 80 |
| La Malbaie, P.Q., Can. | E3 | 106 |
| Lamaline, Nf., Can. | F18 | 106 |
| *La Mancha, reg., Spain* | G8 | 16 |
| Lamar, Co., U.S. | M5 | 118 |
| Lamar, Mo., U.S. | E2 | 114 |
| Lamar, S.C., U.S. | E6 | 112 |
| *Lamar, stm., Wy., U.S.* | F16 | 122 |
| Lamarche, Fr. | D12 | 14 |
| La Mariscala, Ur. | H11 | 80 |
| Lamarque, Arg. | J6 | 80 |
| La Marque, Tx., U.S. | J12 | 116 |
| La Marsa, Tun. | M5 | 18 |
| Lamas, Peru | B3 | 82 |
| La Masica, Hond. | B7 | 92 |
| Lamastre, Fr. | H11 | 14 |
| Lamballe, Fr. | D4 | 14 |
| Lambaréné, Gabon | B2 | 58 |
| *Lambari, stm., Braz.* | F6 | 79 |
| Lambayeque, Peru | B2 | 82 |
| *Lambayeque, dept., Peru* | B1 | 82 |
| *Lambayeque, stm., Peru* | B2 | 82 |
| Lambert, Ms., U.S. | H6 | 114 |
| Lambert, Mt., U.S. | D3 | 118 |
| *Lambert Glacier, Ant.* | C5 | 73 |
| Lamberton, Mn., U.S. | G12 | 118 |
| Lambert's Bay, S. Afr. | I4 | 66 |
| Lambertville, N.J., U.S. | G12 | 108 |
| Lambeth, On., Can. | H14 | 110 |
| Lambomakondro, Madag. | s21 | 67b |
| Lambrama, Peru | E5 | 82 |
| *Lambton, Cape, c., N.T., Can.* | B8 | 96 |
| Lame Deer, Mt., U.S. | E19 | 122 |
| *La Media Luna, Arrecifes de, rf., Hond.* | B12 | 92 |
| La Mendieta, Arg. | C6 | 80 |
| Lamèque, N.B., Can. | E9 | 106 |
| *Lamèque, Île, i., N.B., Can.* | E9 | 106 |
| La Merced, Arg. | E6 | 80 |
| La Merced, Arg. | C6 | 80 |
| La Merced, Peru | D4 | 82 |
| La Mesa, Ca., U.S. | L8 | 124 |
| La Mesa, N.M., U.S. | L10 | 120 |
| La Mesa, Pan. | I13 | 92 |
| Lamesa, Tx., U.S. | G5 | 116 |
| Lamía, Grc. | K6 | 20 |
| *L'amin, stm., Russia* | E12 | 26 |
| *Lamine, stm., Mo., U.S.* | D4 | 114 |
| Lamming Mills, B.C., Can. | D14 | 102 |
| La Moille, Il., U.S. | I6 | 110 |
| Lamoille, Nv., U.S. | D10 | 124 |
| *Lamoille, stm., Vt., U.S.* | C14 | 108 |
| *La Moine, stm., Il., U.S.* | B6 | 114 |
| *Lamon Bay, b., Phil.* | n19 | 39b |
| Lamoni, Ia., U.S. | J2 | 110 |
| Lamont, Ab., Can. | D22 | 102 |
| Lamont, Ca., U.S. | I7 | 124 |
| Lamont, Ia., U.S. | H4 | 110 |
| Lamont, Ok., U.S. | C9 | 116 |
| La Monte, Mo., U.S. | D3 | 114 |
| *La Mosquitia, hist. reg., Hond.* | B11 | 92 |
| *La Mothe, Lac, res., P.Q., Can.* | D2 | 106 |
| La Mothe-Achard, Fr. | F5 | 14 |
| Lamotte-Beuvron, Fr. | E9 | 14 |
| La Moure, N.D., U.S. | E9 | 118 |
| Lampa, Peru | F6 | 82 |
| Lampang, Thai. | E5 | 40 |
| Lampasas, Tx., U.S. | H8 | 116 |
| *Lampasas, stm., Tx., U.S.* | H8 | 116 |
| Lampazos de Naranjo, Mex. | D9 | 90 |
| *Lampedusa, Isola di, i., Italy* | N7 | 18 |
| Lamphun, Thai. | E5 | 40 |
| Lampman, Sk., Can. | I12 | 104 |
| Lamud, Peru | B3 | 82 |
| *La Muerte, Cerro, mtn., C.R.* | H11 | 92 |
| Lana, Italy | C6 | 18 |
| *Lanai, i., Hi., U.S.* | q17 | 125a |
| Lanai City, Hi., U.S. | q17 | 125a |
| *Lanalhue, Lago, l., Chile* | I2 | 80 |
| Lanark, Il., U.S. | H6 | 110 |
| Lanark, On., Can. | E19 | 110 |
| *Lanbi Kyun, i., Myan.* | I5 | 40 |
| *Lancashire, co., Eng., U.K.* | H11 | 8 |
| Lancaster, Ca., U.S. | J7 | 124 |
| Lancaster, Eng., U.K. | G11 | 8 |
| Lancaster, Ky., U.S. | B2 | 112 |
| Lancaster, Mn., U.S. | C11 | 118 |
| Lancaster, Mo., U.S. | B4 | 114 |
| Lancaster, N.H., U.S. | C15 | 108 |
| Lancaster, N.Y., U.S. | E8 | 108 |
| Lancaster, Oh., U.S. | H4 | 108 |
| Lancaster, On., Can. | B12 | 108 |
| Lancaster, Pa., U.S. | G10 | 108 |
| Lancaster, S.C., U.S. | E6 | 112 |
| Lancaster, Tx., U.S. | G10 | 116 |
| Lancaster, Va., U.S. | B10 | 112 |
| Lancaster, Wi., U.S. | H5 | 110 |
| *Lancaster Sound, strt., N.T., Can.* | B16 | 96 |
| Lance Creek, Wy., U.S. | A12 | 120 |
| Lanchyn, Ukr. | A8 | 20 |
| Lanciano, Italy | G9 | 18 |
| Lancones, Peru | J2 | 84 |
| Lancun, China | G8 | 32 |
| Łańcut, Pol. | E22 | 10 |
| Lancy, Switz. | F5 | 13 |
| Landau, Ger. | F8 | 10 |
| Landau an der Isar, Ger. | G12 | 10 |
| Landeck, Aus. | H10 | 10 |
| Landen, Bel. | G7 | 12 |
| Lander, Wy., U.S. | B8 | 120 |
| Landerneau, Fr. | D2 | 14 |
| *Landes, dept., Fr.* | H6 | 14 |
| Landete, Spain | F10 | 16 |
| *Landing Lake, l., Mb., Can.* | C17 | 104 |
| Landis, N.C., U.S. | D6 | 112 |
| Landis, Sk., Can. | F6 | 104 |
| Landivisiau, Fr. | D2 | 14 |
| Lando, S.C., U.S. | E5 | 112 |
| Land O'Lakes, Wi., U.S. | D6 | 110 |
| Landquart, Switz. | E12 | 13 |
| Landrum, S.C., U.S. | D4 | 112 |
| Landsberg [am Lech], Ger. | G10 | 10 |
| *Land's End, c., Eng., U.K.* | K8 | 8 |
| Landshut, Ger. | G12 | 10 |
| Landskrona, Swe. | N13 | 6 |
| La Negra, Chile | B3 | 80 |
| Lanesboro, Mn., U.S. | G4 | 110 |
| Lanett, Al., U.S. | J11 | 114 |
| *Lanezi Lake, l., B.C., Can.* | D14 | 102 |
| Lang, Sk., Can. | I10 | 104 |
| *Langano, Lake, l., Eth.* | N10 | 60 |
| *Langara Island, i., B.C., Can.* | C1 | 102 |
| Langarūd, Iran | C11 | 48 |
| Langbank, Sk., Can. | H12 | 104 |
| Lang Bay, B.C., Can. | H10 | 102 |
| Langdale, Al., U.S. | G1 | 112 |
| Langdon, N.D., U.S. | C9 | 118 |
| Langeac, Fr. | G10 | 14 |
| Langeais, Fr. | E7 | 14 |
| Langenburg, Sk., Can. | H13 | 104 |
| Langenhagen, Ger. | C9 | 10 |
| Langenthal, Switz. | D8 | 13 |
| Langford, S.D., U.S. | F10 | 118 |
| Langham, Sk., Can. | F8 | 104 |
| Langholm, Scot., U.K. | F10 | 8 |
| Langley, B.C., Can. | H12 | 102 |
| Langley, Ok., U.S. | C11 | 116 |
| Langley, S.C., U.S. | F5 | 112 |
| *Langlo, stm., Austl.* | E6 | 70 |
| Langlois, Or., U.S. | H1 | 122 |
| Langnau, Switz. | E8 | 13 |
| Langogne, Fr. | H10 | 14 |
| Langon, Fr. | H6 | 14 |
| *Langøya, i., Nor.* | G14 | 6 |
| Langqiao, China | E7 | 34 |
| Langreo, Spain | B6 | 16 |
| Langres, Fr. | E12 | 14 |
| Langruth, Mb., Can. | H16 | 104 |
| Langsa, Indon. | L4 | 40 |
| Lang Son, Viet. | D9 | 40 |
| Langtian, China | J2 | 34 |
| Langue, Hond. | D7 | 92 |
| *Languedoc, hist. reg., Fr.* | I9 | 14 |
| *Langui Layo, Laguna de, l., Peru* | F6 | 82 |
| *L'Anguille, stm., Ar., U.S.* | G6 | 114 |
| Langxi, China | D8 | 34 |
| Langzhong, China | E8 | 30 |
| Lanigan, Sk., Can. | G9 | 104 |
| *Lanigan Creek, stm., Sk., Can.* | G9 | 104 |
| Länkäran, Azer. | J7 | 26 |
| Lankou, China | L4 | 34 |
| Lannemezan, Fr. | I7 | 14 |
| Lannilis, Fr. | D2 | 14 |
| Lannion, Fr. | D3 | 14 |
| L'Annonciation, P.Q., Can. | A12 | 108 |
| Lanquín, Guat. | B5 | 92 |
| L'Anse, Mi., U.S. | D7 | 110 |
| *L'Anse-aux-Meadows National Historic Park, Nf., Can.* | A18 | 106 |
| Lansford, N.D., U.S. | C6 | 118 |
| Lansing, Ia., U.S. | G4 | 110 |
| Lansing, Ks., U.S. | L13 | 118 |
| Lansing, Mi., U.S. | E2 | 108 |
| Lanslebourg, Fr. | G13 | 14 |
| Lantana, Fl., U.S. | M6 | 112 |
| Lantang, China | L3 | 34 |
| *Lantau Island see Dahau Dao, i., China* | M2 | 34 |
| Lantsch, Switz. | E12 | 13 |
| Lanusei, Italy | J4 | 18 |
| Lanxi, China | F8 | 34 |
| *Lanzarote, i., Spain* | n27 | 17b |
| Lanzhou, China | D7 | 30 |
| Laoag, Phil. | I19 | 39b |
| Lao Cai, Viet. | C7 | 40 |
| Laochang, China | B8 | 40 |
| Laoge, China | C8 | 34 |
| *Laoha, stm., China* | A7 | 32 |
| *Laois, co., Ire.* | I6 | 8 |
| Laojie, China | B5 | 40 |
| La Oliva, Spain | o27 | 17b |
| Laon, Fr. | C10 | 14 |
| Laona, Wi., U.S. | E7 | 110 |
| *La Orchila, Isla, i., Ven.* | B10 | 84 |
| La Orotava, Spain | o24 | 17b |
| La Oroya, Peru | D4 | 82 |
| *Laos (Lao), ctry., Asia* | B3 | 38 |
| Laoxinkou, China | E1 | 34 |
| Laoyingpan, China | I4 | 34 |
| Laozishan, China | B7 | 34 |
| Lapa, Braz. | C14 | 80 |
| Lapalisse, Fr. | F10 | 14 |
| La Palma, Col. | E5 | 84 |
| La Palma, El Sal. | C5 | 92 |
| La Palma, Pan. | C3 | 84 |
| La Palma, Pan. | D2 | 84 |
| *La Palma, i., Spain* | o23 | 17b |
| La Palma del Condado, Spain | H5 | 16 |
| La Paloma, Ur. | H11 | 80 |
| *La Pampa, prov., Arg.* | I5 | 80 |
| La Paragua, Ven. | D11 | 84 |
| *La Pasión, Río de, stm., Guat.* | I14 | 90 |
| La Paz, Arg. | F9 | 80 |
| La Paz, Arg. | G5 | 80 |
| La Paz, Bol. | G7 | 82 |
| La Paz, Col. | B6 | 84 |
| La Paz, Hond. | C7 | 92 |
| La Paz, Mex. | E4 | 90 |
| La Paz, Mex. | F9 | 90 |
| La Paz, Ur. | H10 | 80 |
| *La Paz, dept., Bol.* | F7 | 82 |
| *La Paz, dept., Hond.* | C7 | 92 |
| *La Paz, Bahía, b., Mex.* | E4 | 90 |

| Name | Map Ref. | Page |
|---|---|---|
| La Paz, Río de, stm., Bol. | G8 | 82 |
| La Paz Centro, Nic. | E8 | 92 |
| La Pedrera, Col. | H8 | 84 |
| Lapeer, Mi., U.S. | G12 | 110 |
| La Perla, Mex. | C7 | 90 |
| La Perouse Strait (Sōya-kaikyō), strt., Asia | b17 | 36a |
| La Pesca, Mex. | F11 | 90 |
| La Piedad de Cabadas, Mex. | G8 | 90 |
| La Pine, Or., U.S. | G4 | 122 |
| Lapin lääni, prov., Fin. | H20 | 6 |
| Lapinlahti, Fin. | J20 | 6 |
| La Pintada, Pan. | I14 | 92 |
| Lapland, hist. reg., Eur. | H18 | 6 |
| La Plata, Col. | H10 | 80 |
| La Plata, Col. | F5 | 84 |
| La Plata, Mo., U.S. | I10 | 108 |
| La Plata, Mo., U.S. | B4 | 114 |
| La Plata, stm., U.S. | H8 | 120 |
| La Plata Peak, mtn., Co., U.S. | E10 | 120 |
| La Plonge Indian Reserve, Sk., Can. | C7 | 104 |
| La Pobla de Segur, Spain | C12 | 16 |
| La Pocatière, P.Q., Can. | E3 | 106 |
| La Poile, Nf., Can. | E15 | 106 |
| La Poile Bay, b., Nf., Can. | E15 | 106 |
| Laporte, Co., U.S. | D11 | 120 |
| La Porte, In., U.S. | A10 | 114 |
| Laporte, Pa., U.S. | F10 | 108 |
| La Porte City, Ia., U.S. | H3 | 110 |
| La Potherie, Lac, l., P.Q., Can. | E18 | 96 |
| La Poza Grande, Mex. | E3 | 90 |
| Lappeenranta, Fin. | K21 | 6 |
| Lappfjärd (Lapväärtti), Fin. | J17 | 6 |
| La Presa, stm., Mex. | E4 | 90 |
| Laprida, Arg. | I7 | 80 |
| Laprida, Arg. | E6 | 80 |
| La Pryor, Tx., U.S. | K7 | 116 |
| Lâpseki, Tur. | I10 | 20 |
| Laptev Sea see Laptevykh, more, Russia | B17 | 28 |
| Laptevykh, more (Laptev Sea), Russia | B17 | 28 |
| La Puebla de Cazalla, Spain | H6 | 16 |
| La Puebla de Montalbán, Spain | F7 | 16 |
| La Puerta, Arg. | E6 | 80 |
| La Purísima, Mex. | D3 | 90 |
| Lâpuş, Rom. | B8 | 20 |
| Lapwai, Id., U.S. | D9 | 122 |
| La Quiaca, Arg. | B6 | 80 |
| L'Aquila, Italy | G8 | 18 |
| Lār, Iran | H13 | 48 |
| Lara, state, Ven. | B8 | 84 |
| Larache, Mor. | J5 | 16 |
| Laragne-Montéglin, Fr. | H12 | 14 |
| Laramate, Peru | F4 | 82 |
| Laramie, Wy., U.S. | C11 | 120 |
| Laramie, stm., U.S. | B12 | 120 |
| Laramie Mountains, mts., Wy., U.S. | B11 | 120 |
| Laranjaí, stm., Braz. | G1 | 79 |
| Laranjal, Braz. | F7 | 79 |
| Laranjeiras do Sul, Braz. | C12 | 80 |
| Laraos, Peru | E4 | 82 |
| Larap, Phil. | n20 | 39b |
| La Raya, Abra, Peru | F6 | 82 |
| L'Arbresle, Fr. | G11 | 14 |
| Larche, Col de, Eur. | H13 | 14 |
| Larchwood, Ia., U.S. | H11 | 118 |
| Lardeau, B.C., Can. | G18 | 102 |
| L'Ardoise, N.S., Can. | G13 | 106 |
| Laredo, Spain | B8 | 16 |
| Laredo, Tx., U.S. | L7 | 116 |
| Laredo Sound, strt., B.C., Can. | D6 | 102 |
| La Reforma, Mex. | E5 | 90 |
| La Réole, Fr. | H6 | 14 |
| Lares, Peru | E5 | 82 |
| La Restinga, Spain | p23 | 17b |
| Largo, Fl., U.S. | L4 | 112 |
| Largo, Cañon, val., N.M., U.S. | H9 | 120 |
| Largo, Cayo, i., Cuba | D4 | 94 |
| Largs, Scot., U.K. | F9 | 8 |
| Lari, Peru | F6 | 82 |
| Larimore, N.D., U.S. | D10 | 118 |
| Larino, Italy | H9 | 18 |
| La Rioja, Arg. | E5 | 80 |
| La Rioja, state, Spain | C9 | 16 |
| La Rioja, prov., Arg. | E5 | 80 |
| Lárisa, Grc. | J6 | 20 |
| Lárkāna, Pak. | G3 | 44 |
| Lark Harbour, Nf., Can. | C15 | 106 |
| Lárnax (Larnaca), Cyp. | D2 | 48 |
| Larned, Ks., U.S. | M8 | 118 |
| La Rochefoucauld, Fr. | G7 | 14 |
| La Rochelle, Fr. | F5 | 14 |
| La Roche-sur-Yon, Fr. | F5 | 14 |
| La Roda, Spain | F9 | 16 |
| La Romaine, P.Q., Can. | B13 | 106 |
| La Romana, Dom. Rep. | E10 | 94 |
| La Ronge, Sk., Can. | C9 | 104 |
| Larose, La., U.S. | M6 | 114 |
| La Rosita, Nic. | D10 | 92 |
| Larreynaga, Nic. | E8 | 92 |
| Larroque, Arg. | G9 | 80 |
| Larrys River, N.S., Can. | G12 | 106 |
| Larsen Bay, Ak., U.S. | H17 | 100 |
| Larsen Ice Shelf, Ant. | B12 | 73 |
| Larteh Aheneasi, Ghana | I10 | 64 |
| La Rubia, Arg. | F8 | 80 |
| La Rue, Oh., U.S. | G3 | 108 |
| Laruns, Fr. | J6 | 14 |
| Larus Lake, l., On., Can. | G20 | 104 |
| Larvik, Nor. | L12 | 6 |
| La Sabana, Arg. | D9 | 80 |
| La Sal, Ut., U.S. | F7 | 120 |
| La Salle, Col. | D12 | 120 |
| La Salle, Il., U.S. | I6 | 110 |
| La Salle, stm., Mb., Can. | I17 | 104 |
| Las Almejas, Bahía, b., Mex. | E4 | 90 |
| Las Animas, Co., U.S. | M4 | 118 |
| La Sarraz, Switz. | E6 | 13 |
| Las Arrias, Arg. | F7 | 80 |
| Las Aves, Islas, is., Ven. | A9 | 84 |
| Las Ballenas, Canal de, strt., Mex. | C3 | 90 |
| Las Bonitas, Ven. | D10 | 84 |
| Las Breñas, Arg. | D8 | 80 |
| Las Cabezas de San Juan, Spain | I6 | 16 |
| Las Cabras, Chile | H3 | 80 |
| Lascano, Ur. | G11 | 80 |
| Lascar, Volcán, vol., Chile | B5 | 80 |
| Las Catitas, Arg. | G4 | 80 |
| Lascaux, Grotte de, Fr. | G8 | 14 |
| Las Cejas, Arg. | D6 | 80 |
| Las Choapas, Mex. | I12 | 90 |
| La Scie, Nf., Can. | C18 | 106 |
| Las Cruces, N.M., U.S. | L10 | 120 |
| Las Cuevas, Mex. | C9 | 90 |
| Las Delicias, Mex. | J14 | 90 |
| La Selle, Morne, mtn., Haiti | E9 | 94 |
| La Serena, Chile | E3 | 80 |
| La Seyne, Fr. | I12 | 14 |
| Las Flores, Arg. | H4 | 80 |
| Las Flores, Arg. | F4 | 80 |
| Las Flores, Arroyo, stm., Arg. | H9 | 80 |
| Las Flores, Cerro, mtn., Mex. | I12 | 90 |
| Las Garcitas, Arg. | D9 | 80 |
| Las Guayabas, Mex. | E11 | 90 |
| Lashburn, Sk., Can. | E5 | 104 |
| Lāsh-e Joveyn, Afg. | F16 | 48 |
| Las Heras, Arg. | G4 | 80 |
| Las Hormigas, Mex. | E10 | 90 |
| La Sierra, Montaña, mts., Hond. | C7 | 92 |
| Las Iglesias, Cerro, mtn., Mex. | D6 | 90 |
| Łasin, Pol. | B19 | 10 |
| Łask, Pol. | D19 | 10 |
| L'askel'a, Russia | K22 | 6 |
| Las Lajas, Arg. | J3 | 80 |
| Las Lajas, Pan. | C2 | 84 |
| Las Lajitas, Arg. | C6 | 80 |
| Las Lomas, Peru | J2 | 84 |
| Las Lomitas, Arg. | C8 | 80 |
| Lašma, Russia | G24 | 22 |
| Las Malvinas, Arg. | H4 | 80 |
| Las Margaritas, Mex. | I14 | 90 |
| Las Marianas, Arg. | H9 | 80 |
| Las Mercedes, Ven. | C9 | 84 |
| Las Minas, Cerro, mtn., Hond. | C6 | 92 |
| Las Nieves, Mex. | D7 | 90 |
| Las Nopaleras, Cerro, mtn., Mex. | E8 | 90 |
| La Solana, Spain | G8 | 16 |
| La Soledad, Cerro, mtn., Mex. | D6 | 90 |
| Las Ovejas, Arg. | I3 | 80 |
| Las Palmas, Arg. | D9 | 80 |
| Las Palmas, Pan. | C2 | 84 |
| Las Palmas, prov., Spain | o26 | 17b |
| Las Palmas de Gran Canaria, Spain | o25 | 17b |
| La Spezia, Italy | E4 | 18 |
| Las Piedras, Ur. | H10 | 80 |
| Las Piedras, Río de, stm., Peru | E7 | 82 |
| Las Plumas, Arg. | E3 | 78 |
| Lasqueti Island, i., B.C., Can. | H10 | 102 |
| Las Rosas, Arg. | G8 | 80 |
| Las Rosas, Mex. | I13 | 90 |
| Lassance, Braz. | D6 | 79 |
| Lassay, Fr. | D6 | 14 |
| Lassen Peak, vol., Ca., U.S. | D4 | 124 |
| Lassen Volcanic National Park, Ca., U.S. | D4 | 124 |
| Las Tablas, Pan. | D2 | 84 |
| Las Tinajas, Mex. | D7 | 90 |
| Last Mountain, mtn., Sk., Can. | G10 | 104 |
| Last Mountain Lake, l., Sk., Can. | G9 | 104 |
| Las Toscas, Arg. | E9 | 80 |
| Lastoursville, Gabon | B2 | 58 |
| Las Tunas, Cuba | D6 | 94 |
| Las Tunas Grandes, Laguna, l., Arg. | I7 | 80 |
| La Suze, Fr. | E7 | 14 |
| Las Varas, Mex. | C5 | 90 |
| Las Varas, Mex. | G7 | 90 |
| Las Varillas, Arg. | F7 | 80 |
| Las Vegas, N.M., U.S. | I11 | 120 |
| Las Vegas, Nv., U.S. | H10 | 124 |
| Las Vegas, Ven. | C8 | 84 |
| La Tabatière, P.Q., Can. | B15 | 106 |
| Latacunga, Ec. | H3 | 84 |
| Latakia see Al-Lādhiqīyah, Syria | D3 | 48 |
| La Teste-de-Buch, Fr. | H5 | 14 |
| La Tetilla, Cerro, mtn., Mex. | C2 | 114 |
| Lathrop, Mo., U.S. | C2 | 114 |
| Latimer, Ia., U.S. | H2 | 110 |
| Latina, Italy | H7 | 18 |
| Latisana, Italy | D8 | 18 |
| La Toma, Arg. | G6 | 80 |
| Latornell, stm., Ab., Can. | C16 | 102 |
| La Tortuga, Isla, i., Ven. | B10 | 84 |
| Latorytsya, stm., Eur. | G22 | 10 |
| Latouche Treville, Cape, c., Austl. | C4 | 68 |
| La Tour-du-Pin, Fr. | G12 | 14 |
| Latowicz, Pol. | C21 | 10 |
| La Tremblade, Fr. | G5 | 14 |
| La Trimouille, Fr. | F8 | 14 |
| La Trinidad, Arg. | D6 | 80 |
| La Trinidad, Nic. | E8 | 92 |
| La Trinidad de Orichuna, Ven. | D8 | 84 |
| La Trinitaria, Mex. | I13 | 90 |
| La Trinité, Mart. | G14 | 94 |
| Latrobe, Austl. | M7 | 70 |
| Latrobe, Pa., U.S. | G7 | 108 |
| Latta, S.C., U.S. | E7 | 112 |
| La Tuque, P.Q., Can. | G18 | 96 |
| Lātūr, India | C4 | 46 |
| Latvia (Latvija), ctry., Eur. | D8 | 22 |
| Lauca, stm., Bol. | H7 | 82 |
| Lauchhammer, Ger. | D13 | 10 |
| Lauderdale, Ms., U.S. | J8 | 114 |
| Lauf an der Pegnitz, Ger. | F11 | 10 |
| Läufelfingen, Switz. | D8 | 13 |
| Laufen, Switz. | D8 | 13 |
| Laukuva, Lith. | F5 | 22 |
| Launceston, Austl. | M7 | 70 |
| Launceston, Eng., U.K. | K9 | 8 |
| La Unión, Chile | E2 | 78 |
| La Unión, Col. | G4 | 84 |
| La Unión, El Sal. | D7 | 92 |
| La Unión, Mex. | I9 | 90 |
| La Unión, N.M., U.S. | M10 | 120 |
| La Unión, Peru | A1 | 82 |
| La Unión, Spain | H11 | 16 |
| La Unión, Ven. | C9 | 84 |
| Laura, Austl. | B8 | 70 |
| La Urbana, Ven. | D9 | 84 |
| Laurel, De., U.S. | I11 | 108 |
| Laurel, Fl., U.S. | L4 | 112 |
| Laurel, In., U.S. | C11 | 114 |
| Laurel, Md., U.S. | H10 | 108 |
| Laurel, Ms., U.S. | K7 | 114 |
| Laurel, Mt., U.S. | E17 | 122 |
| Laurel, Ne., U.S. | I10 | 118 |
| Laurel, stm., Ky., U.S. | B2 | 112 |
| Laurel Bay, S.C., U.S. | G6 | 112 |
| Laureldale, Pa., U.S. | G11 | 108 |
| Laureles, Ur. | F11 | 80 |
| Laurel Hill, N.C., U.S. | E7 | 112 |
| Laurelville, Oh., U.S. | H4 | 108 |
| Laurens, Ia., U.S. | I13 | 118 |
| Laurens, S.C., U.S. | E4 | 112 |
| Laurentides, Les, plat., P.Q., Can. | G18 | 96 |
| Laurentides, Parc Provincial des, P.Q., Can. | E2 | 106 |
| Lauria, Italy | H10 | 18 |
| Laurie Island, i., Ant. | B12 | 73 |
| Laurier, Mb., Can. | H15 | 104 |
| Laurière, Fr. | F8 | 14 |
| Laurinburg, N.C., U.S. | E7 | 112 |
| Laurium, Mi., U.S. | C7 | 110 |
| Lausanne, Switz. | E6 | 13 |
| Laut, Pulau, i., Indon. | F6 | 38 |
| Lauta, Ger. | D14 | 10 |
| Lautaro, Chile | J2 | 80 |
| Lauterbach, Ger. | E9 | 10 |
| Lauterbrunnen, Switz. | E8 | 13 |
| Lauter [Sachsen], Ger. | E12 | 10 |
| Laut Kecil, Kepulauan, is., Indon. | F6 | 38 |
| Lauzon, P.Q., Can. | F2 | 106 |
| Lava (Łyna), stm., Eur. | G4 | 22 |
| Lava, Nosy, i., Madag. | o22 | 67b |
| Lavaca, stm., Tx., U.S. | J9 | 116 |
| Lava Hot Springs, Id., U.S. | H13 | 122 |
| Laval, Fr. | D6 | 14 |
| Laval, P.Q., Can. | B13 | 108 |
| La Vall d'Uixo, Spain | F11 | 16 |
| Lavalle, Arg. | E9 | 80 |
| Lavalle, Arg. | E6 | 80 |
| La Valley, Co., U.S. | G11 | 120 |
| Lavapié, Punta, c., Chile | I2 | 80 |
| Lávara, Grc. | H10 | 20 |
| Lavardac, Fr. | H7 | 14 |
| Lava-Tudo, stm., Braz. | E13 | 80 |
| La Vega, Dom. Rep. | E9 | 94 |
| La Vela, Cabo de, c., Col. | A6 | 84 |
| La Vela de Coro, Ven. | B8 | 84 |
| Lavelanet, Fr. | J8 | 14 |
| Lavello, Italy | H10 | 18 |
| La Venta, hist., Mex. | H12 | 90 |
| La Ventura, Mex. | E9 | 90 |
| La Verde, Arg. | D9 | 80 |
| La Vergne, Tn., U.S. | F10 | 114 |
| La Vernia, Tx., U.S. | J8 | 116 |
| Laverton, Austl. | E4 | 68 |
| La Victoria, Ven. | B9 | 84 |
| La Vila Joiosa, Spain | G11 | 16 |
| La Villa, stm., Pan. | J14 | 92 |
| Lavillette, N., Can. | E8 | 106 |
| La Viña, Arg. | C6 | 80 |
| Lavina, Mt., U.S. | D17 | 122 |
| La Virginia, Col. | E5 | 84 |
| Lavonia, Ga., U.S. | E3 | 112 |
| La Voulte-sur-Rhône, Fr. | H11 | 14 |
| Lavras, Braz. | F6 | 79 |
| Lavras do Sul, Braz. | F12 | 80 |
| Lavumisa, Swaz. | F10 | 66 |
| Lawdar, Yemen | H4 | 47 |
| Lawford Lake, l., Mb., Can. | D18 | 104 |
| Lawksawk, Myan. | D4 | 40 |
| Lawler, Ia., U.S. | G3 | 110 |
| Lawn, Nf., Can. | F18 | 106 |
| Lawn, Tx., U.S. | G7 | 116 |
| Lawn Bay, b., Nf., Can. | F18 | 106 |
| Lawndale, N.C., U.S. | D5 | 112 |
| Lawrence, In., U.S. | C10 | 114 |
| Lawrence, Ks., U.S. | M12 | 118 |
| Lawrence, Ma., U.S. | E15 | 108 |
| Lawrence, Ne., U.S. | K9 | 118 |
| Lawrenceburg, In., U.S. | C12 | 114 |
| Lawrenceburg, Ky., U.S. | D12 | 114 |
| Lawrenceburg, Tn., U.S. | G9 | 114 |
| Lawrenceville, Il., U.S. | D9 | 114 |
| Lawrenceville, Ga., U.S. | G12 | 108 |
| Lawrenceville, N.J., U.S. | C9 | 112 |
| Lawrenceville, Va., U.S. | C2 | 114 |
| Lawson, Mo., U.S. | C2 | 114 |
| Lawtey, Fl., U.S. | I4 | 112 |
| Lawton, Mi., U.S. | H10 | 110 |
| Lawton, N.D., U.S. | C9 | 118 |
| Lawton, Ok., U.S. | E8 | 116 |
| Lawz, Jabal al-, mtn., Sau. Ar. | G3 | 48 |
| Laxå, Swe. | L14 | 6 |
| Lax Kw'alaams, B.C., Can. | C4 | 102 |
| Laylá, Sau. Ar. | C5 | 47 |
| Layton, Ut., U.S. | C5 | 120 |
| Laytonville, Ca., U.S. | E2 | 124 |
| La Zarca, Mex. | E7 | 90 |
| Lázaro Cárdenas, Mex. | B2 | 90 |
| Lázaro Cárdenas, Mex. | I8 | 90 |
| Lázaro Cárdenas, Presa, res., Mex. | E7 | 90 |
| Lazdijai, Lith. | G6 | 22 |
| Lazhuilong, China | C9 | 44 |
| Lazio, prov., Italy | G7 | 18 |
| Léach, Camb. | H7 | 40 |
| Leachville, Ar., U.S. | G6 | 114 |
| Lead, S.D., U.S. | G4 | 118 |
| Leader, Sk., Can. | H5 | 104 |
| Leadore, Id., U.S. | F12 | 122 |
| Leadville, Co., U.S. | E10 | 120 |
| Leaf, stm., Mn., U.S. | E12 | 118 |
| Leaf, stm., Ms., U.S. | K8 | 114 |
| Leaf Lake, l., Sk., Can. | E12 | 104 |
| League City, Tx., U.S. | J11 | 116 |
| Leakesville, Ms., U.S. | K8 | 114 |
| Leakey, Tx., U.S. | J7 | 116 |
| Leaksville, N.C., U.S. | C7 | 112 |
| Lealman, Fl., U.S. | L4 | 112 |
| Leamington, On., Can. | H13 | 110 |
| Leán, stm., Hond. | B7 | 92 |
| Leandro N. Alem, Arg. | D11 | 80 |
| Leary, Ga., U.S. | H2 | 112 |
| Leask, Sk., Can. | E8 | 104 |
| Leatherman Peak, mtn., Id., U.S. | F12 | 122 |
| Leavenworth, In., U.S. | D10 | 114 |
| Leavenworth, Ks., U.S. | L13 | 118 |
| Leavenworth, Wa., U.S. | C5 | 122 |
| Leawood, Mo., U.S. | D2 | 114 |
| Lebak, Phil. | D7 | 38 |
| Lebam, Wa., U.S. | D2 | 122 |
| Lebanon, In., U.S. | B10 | 114 |
| Lebanon, Ks., U.S. | L9 | 118 |
| Lebanon, Ky., U.S. | E11 | 114 |
| Lebanon, Mo., U.S. | E4 | 114 |
| Lebanon, N.H., U.S. | D14 | 108 |
| Lebanon, Oh., U.S. | H2 | 108 |
| Lebanon, Or., U.S. | F3 | 122 |
| Lebanon, Pa., U.S. | G10 | 108 |
| Lebanon, S.D., U.S. | F8 | 118 |
| Lebanon, Tn., U.S. | F10 | 114 |
| Lebanon, Va., U.S. | C4 | 112 |
| Lebanon (Lubnān), ctry., Asia | C2 | 42 |
| Lebanon Junction, Ky., U.S. | E11 | 114 |
| Leb'aže, Kaz. | G13 | 26 |
| Lebec, Ca., U.S. | J7 | 124 |
| Lebed'an', Russia | H22 | 22 |
| Le Blanc, Fr. | F8 | 14 |
| Lebo, Ks., U.S. | M12 | 118 |
| Lebombo Mountains, hills, Afr. | E10 | 66 |
| Łebork, Pol. | A17 | 10 |
| Lebrija, stm., Col. | D6 | 84 |
| Lebu, Chile | I2 | 80 |
| Le Cannet, Fr. | I14 | 14 |
| Le Cateau, Fr. | B10 | 14 |
| Lecce, Italy | I13 | 18 |
| Lecco, Italy | D4 | 18 |
| Le Center, Mn., U.S. | F2 | 110 |
| Lech, stm., Eur. | G10 | 10 |
| Le Châble, Switz. | F7 | 13 |
| Le Chesne, Fr. | C11 | 14 |
| Le Cheylard, Fr. | H11 | 14 |
| Lechiguanas, Islas de las, is., Arg. | G9 | 80 |
| Lechuguilla, Cerro, mtn., Mex. | F7 | 90 |
| Le Claire, Ia., U.S. | I5 | 110 |
| Lecompte, La., U.S. | K4 | 114 |
| Le Creusot, Fr. | F11 | 14 |
| Led'anaja, gora, mtn., Russia | E26 | 28 |
| Lede, Bel. | G4 | 12 |
| Ledo, India | G16 | 44 |
| Le Doré, Lac, l., P.Q., Can. | A12 | 106 |
| Leduc, Ab., Can. | D21 | 102 |
| Lee, China | D7 | 30 |
| Lee, Ma., U.S. | E13 | 108 |
| Leech Lake, l., Mn., U.S. | C1 | 110 |
| Leech Lake, l., Sk., Can. | C12 | 104 |
| Leedey, Ok., U.S. | D7 | 116 |
| Leeds, Al., U.S. | I10 | 114 |
| Leeds, Eng., U.K. | H12 | 8 |
| Leeds, N.D., U.S. | C8 | 118 |
| Leek, Neth. | B9 | 12 |
| Leelanau Peninsula, pen., Mi., U.S. | E10 | 110 |
| Leende, Neth. | F8 | 12 |
| Leer, Ger. | B7 | 10 |
| Leesburg, Fl., U.S. | K5 | 112 |
| Leesburg, Ga., U.S. | H2 | 112 |
| Leesburg, Va., U.S. | H9 | 108 |
| Lees Summit, Mo., U.S. | D2 | 114 |
| Leesville, La., U.S. | K3 | 114 |
| Leesville, S.C., U.S. | F5 | 112 |
| Leeton, Austl. | J7 | 70 |
| Leeuwarden, Neth. | B8 | 12 |
| Leeuwin, Cape, c., Austl. | F3 | 68 |
| Lee Vining, Ca., U.S. | F5 | 124 |
| Leeward Islands, is., N.A. | F13 | 94 |
| Lefors, Tx., U.S. | D6 | 116 |
| Leftrook Lake, l., Mb., Can. | B16 | 104 |
| Legal, Ab., Can. | D21 | 102 |
| Leganés, Spain | E8 | 16 |
| Legaspi, Phil. | o20 | 39b |
| Leggett, Ca., U.S. | E2 | 124 |
| Leghorn see Livorno, Italy | F5 | 18 |
| Legion Mine, Zimb. | C9 | 66 |
| Legionowo, Pol. | C20 | 10 |
| Legnago, Italy | D6 | 18 |
| Legnano, Italy | D3 | 18 |
| Legnica (Liegnitz), Pol. | D16 | 10 |
| Le Grand, Ca., U.S. | G5 | 124 |
| Le Grand-Lucé, Fr. | E7 | 14 |
| Le Grau-du-Roi, Fr. | I11 | 14 |
| Leh, India | C7 | 44 |
| Le Havre, Fr. | C7 | 14 |
| Lehi, Ut., U.S. | D5 | 120 |
| Lehigh, Ia., U.S. | H1 | 110 |
| Lehigh, Ok., U.S. | E10 | 116 |
| Lehigh Acres, Fl., U.S. | M5 | 112 |
| Lehighton, Pa., U.S. | G11 | 108 |
| Leho, Sudan | N7 | 60 |
| Lehr, N.D., U.S. | E8 | 118 |
| Lehrte, Ger. | C9 | 10 |
| Lehtse, Est. | B8 | 22 |
| Lehututu, Bots. | D5 | 66 |
| Leiah, Pak. | E4 | 44 |
| Leibnitz, Aus. | I15 | 10 |
| Leicester, Eng., U.K. | I12 | 8 |
| Leicestershire, co., Eng., U.K. | I12 | 8 |
| Leichhardt, stm., Austl. | A3 | 70 |
| Leichhardt Range, mts., Austl. | C7 | 70 |
| Leiden, Neth. | D6 | 12 |
| Leie (Lys), stm., Eur. | B10 | 14 |
| Leigh Creek, Austl. | H3 | 70 |
| Leighton, Al., U.S. | H9 | 114 |
| Leikanger, Nor. | K10 | 6 |
| Leinan, Sk., Can. | H7 | 104 |
| Leinster, hist. reg., Ire. | H6 | 8 |
| Leipsic, Oh., U.S. | F3 | 108 |
| Leipzig, Ger. | D12 | 10 |
| Leitchfield, Ky., U.S. | E10 | 114 |
| Leitha, stm., Eur. | H16 | 10 |
| Leitrim, co., Ire. | H6 | 8 |
| Leiyang, China | I1 | 34 |
| Leizhou Bandao, pen., China | D11 | 40 |
| Leizhuang, China | D6 | 32 |
| Lek, stm., Neth. | E6 | 12 |
| Le Kreider, Alg. | C11 | 62 |
| Leksand, Swe. | K14 | 6 |
| Leksozero, ozero, l., Russia | J22 | 6 |
| Le Lamentin, Mart. | G14 | 94 |
| Leland, Il., U.S. | B8 | 114 |
| Leland, Mi., U.S. | E10 | 110 |
| Leland, Ms., U.S. | I6 | 114 |
| Leleiwi Point, c., Hi., U.S. | r18 | 125a |
| Leleque, Arg. | E2 | 78 |
| Le Limbé, Haiti | E8 | 94 |
| Leli Shan, mtn., China | D9 | 44 |
| Le Locle, Switz. | D6 | 13 |
| Le Lude, Fr. | E7 | 14 |
| Lelystad, Neth. | C7 | 12 |
| Le Maire, Estrecho de, strt., Arg. | G4 | 78 |
| Le Mans, Fr. | D7 | 14 |
| Lemay, Mo., U.S. | D6 | 114 |
| Lemay, Lac, l., P.Q., Can. | B5 | 106 |
| Lemberg, Sk., Can. | H11 | 104 |
| Lemdiyya, Alg. | B12 | 62 |
| Leme, Braz. | G5 | 79 |
| Lemesós (Limassol), Cyp. | D2 | 48 |
| Lemeta, Ak., U.S. | D21 | 100 |
| Lemgo, Ger. | C8 | 10 |
| Lemhi Pass, U.S. | F12 | 122 |
| Lemhi Range, mts., Id., U.S. | F12 | 122 |
| Lemieux Islands, is., N.T., Can. | D20 | 96 |
| Lemin, China | D10 | 40 |
| Leming, Tx., U.S. | J8 | 116 |
| Lemitar, N.M., U.S. | J10 | 120 |
| Lemmon, S.D., U.S. | E5 | 118 |
| Lemnos see Límnos, i., Grc. | J9 | 20 |
| Lemon Grove, Ca., U.S. | L8 | 124 |
| Lemont, Il., U.S. | B8 | 114 |
| Lemont, Pa., U.S. | G8 | 108 |
| Lemoore, Ca., U.S. | H6 | 124 |
| Lempa, stm., N.A. | D6 | 92 |
| Lempira, dept., Hond. | C6 | 92 |
| Lemsid, W. Sah. | G4 | 62 |
| Lena, Wi., U.S. | F7 | 110 |
| Lena, stm., Russia | C17 | 28 |
| Lençóis, Braz. | B8 | 79 |
| Lendery, Russia | J22 | 6 |
| Lenghu, China | D5 | 30 |
| Lenhovda, Swe. | M14 | 6 |
| Lenina, pik, mtn., Asia | J12 | 26 |
| Leningrad see Sankt-Peterburg, Russia | B13 | 22 |
| Leninogorsk, Kaz. | G8 | 28 |
| Leninogorsk, Russia | F8 | 26 |
| Leninsk, Russia | H7 | 26 |
| Leninsk, Uzb. | H10 | 26 |
| Leninsk-Kuzneckij, Russia | G9 | 28 |
| Lenk, Switz. | F7 | 13 |
| Lennox, Isla, i., Chile | H3 | 78 |
| Lennoxville, P.Q., Can. | B15 | 108 |
| Lenoir, N.C., U.S. | D5 | 112 |
| Lenoir City, Tn., U.S. | D2 | 112 |
| Lenore Lake, l., Sk., Can. | F9 | 104 |
| Lenox, Ga., U.S. | H3 | 112 |
| Lenox, Ia., U.S. | K13 | 118 |
| Lenox, Ma., U.S. | E13 | 108 |
| Lenox, Tn., U.S. | F7 | 114 |
| Lens, Fr. | B9 | 14 |
| Lensk, Russia | E14 | 28 |
| Lenti, Hung. | I16 | 10 |
| Lentini, Italy | L10 | 18 |
| Lentvaris, Lith. | G8 | 22 |
| Lenzburg, Switz. | D9 | 13 |
| Léo, Burkina | F8 | 64 |
| Leoben, Aus. | H15 | 10 |
| Léogâne, Haiti | E8 | 94 |
| Leola, Ar., U.S. | H4 | 114 |
| Leola, S.D., U.S. | F9 | 118 |
| Leominster, Ma., U.S. | E15 | 108 |
| Léon, Fr. | I5 | 14 |
| León, Ia., U.S. | J2 | 110 |
| León, Ks., U.S. | N11 | 118 |
| León, Mex. | G9 | 90 |
| León, Nic. | E8 | 92 |
| León, dept., Nic. | E8 | 92 |
| León, hist. reg., Spain | D6 | 16 |
| Leon, stm., Tx., U.S. | H9 | 116 |
| Leona, Punta, c., C.R. | H10 | 92 |
| Leonard, N.D., U.S. | E10 | 118 |
| Leonard, Tx., U.S. | F10 | 116 |
| Leonardtown, Md., U.S. | I10 | 108 |
| Leonardville, Ks., U.S. | L11 | 118 |
| León [de los Aldamas], Mex. | G9 | 90 |
| Leones, Arg. | G7 | 80 |
| Leonforte, Italy | L9 | 18 |
| Leongatha, Austl. | L6 | 70 |
| Leonora, Austl. | E4 | 68 |
| Leonville, La., U.S. | L5 | 114 |
| Leopold and Astrid Coast, Ant. | B5 | 73 |
| Leopoldina, Braz. | F7 | 79 |
| Leopoldo de Bulhões, Braz. | D4 | 79 |
| Léopoldville see Kinshasa, D.R.C. | B3 | 58 |
| Leoti, Ks., U.S. | M6 | 118 |
| Leova, Mol. | C12 | 20 |
| Leoville, Sk., Can. | E7 | 104 |
| Lepanto, Ar., U.S. | G6 | 114 |
| Lepanto, C.R. | H9 | 92 |
| Lepe, Spain | H4 | 16 |
| Lepel', Bela. | G11 | 22 |
| Le Pellerin, Fr. | E5 | 14 |
| Lephepe, Bots. | D7 | 66 |
| Leping, China | G6 | 34 |
| L'Épiphanie, P.Q., Can. | B13 | 108 |
| Le Pont-de-Beauvoisin, Fr. | G12 | 14 |
| Lépontine, Alpi, mts., Eur. | F13 | 14 |
| Le Port, Reu. | v17 | 67c |
| Lepreau, Point, c., N.B., Can. | G7 | 106 |
| Lepsy, Kaz. | H13 | 26 |
| Le Puy, Fr. | G10 | 14 |
| Lequeitio, Spain | I4 | 14 |
| Léraba, stm., Afr. | G7 | 64 |
| Lercara, Italy | L8 | 18 |
| Lérida, Col. | H5 | 84 |
| Lerma, stm., Mex. | G9 | 90 |
| Léros, i., Grc. | L10 | 20 |
| Le Roy, Il., U.S. | B8 | 114 |
| Le Roy, Ks., U.S. | M12 | 118 |
| Le Roy, Mn., U.S. | G3 | 110 |
| Le Roy, N.Y., U.S. | E9 | 108 |
| Lerwick, Scot., U.K. | A12 | 8 |
| Les Andelys, Fr. | C8 | 14 |
| Les Borges Blanques, Spain | D12 | 16 |
| Les Cayes, Haiti | E8 | 94 |
| Leshan, China | F7 | 30 |
| Les Haudères, Switz. | F8 | 13 |
| Lesjaskog, Nor. | J11 | 6 |
| Lesko, Pol. | F22 | 10 |
| Leskovac, Yugo. | G5 | 20 |
| Leskov Island, i., S. Geor. | J12 | 74 |
| Leslie, Ga., U.S. | G4 | 114 |
| Leslie, Mi., U.S. | H12 | 110 |
| Leslie, W.V., U.S. | I5 | 108 |
| Les Mosses, Switz. | F7 | 13 |
| Lesnoj, Russia | G23 | 22 |
| Lesogorskij, Russia | K21 | 6 |
| Lesosibirsk, Russia | F10 | 28 |
| Lesotho, ctry., Afr. | G5 | 58 |
| Lesozavodsk, Russia | H18 | 28 |
| Les Pieux, Fr. | C5 | 14 |
| Les Riceys, Fr. | E11 | 14 |
| Les Sables-d'Olonne, Fr. | F5 | 14 |
| Les Saintes, is., Guad. | G14 | 94 |
| Lessay, Fr. | C5 | 14 |
| Lessen (Lessines), Bel. | G4 | 12 |
| Lesser Antilles, is. | H14 | 94 |
| Lesser Caucasus, mts., Asia | I6 | 26 |
| Lesser Khingan Range see Xiao Hinggan Ling, mts., China | B12 | 30 |
| Lesser Slave, stm., Ab., Can. | B20 | 102 |
| Lesser Slave Lake, l., Ab., Can. | B19 | 102 |
| Lesser Sunda Islands see Tenggara, Nusa, is., Indon. | G7 | 38 |
| Lessines (Lessen), Bel. | G4 | 12 |
| Lestock, Sk., Can. | G10 | 104 |
| Le Sueur, Mn., U.S. | F2 | 110 |
| Le Sueur, stm., Mn., U.S. | F2 | 110 |
| Leškonskoje, Russia | E7 | 26 |
| Les Vans, Fr. | H11 | 14 |
| Lésvos (Lesbos), i., Grc. | J10 | 20 |
| Leszno, Pol. | D16 | 10 |
| Letcher, S.D., U.S. | H9 | 118 |
| Letenye, Hung. | I16 | 10 |
| Lethbridge, Ab., Can. | H22 | 102 |
| Lethbridge, Nf., Can. | D19 | 106 |
| Lethem, Guy. | F13 | 84 |
| Le Thillot, Fr. | E13 | 14 |
| Leti, Kepulauan, is., Indon. | G8 | 38 |
| Leticia, Col. | I8 | 84 |
| Leting, China | D6 | 32 |
| Letjiesbos, S. Afr. | I6 | 66 |
| Letlhakane, Bots. | C7 | 66 |
| Letlhakeng, Bots. | D7 | 66 |
| Letnerečenskij, Russia | I24 | 6 |
| Letpadan, Myan. | F3 | 40 |
| Letsok-aw Kyun, i., Myan. | I5 | 40 |
| Letterkenny, Ire. | G5 | 8 |
| Leu, Rom. | E8 | 20 |
| Leucadia, Ca., U.S. | K8 | 124 |
| Leuk, Switz. | F8 | 13 |
| Leuser, Gunung, mtn., Indon. | M4 | 40 |
| Leutkirch, Ger. | H10 | 10 |
| Leuven (Louvain), Bel. | G6 | 12 |
| Leuze, Bel. | G4 | 12 |
| Levack, On., Can. | D14 | 110 |
| Levádhia, Grc. | K6 | 20 |
| Levan, Ut., U.S. | E5 | 120 |
| Levanto, Italy | E4 | 18 |
| Levelland, Tx., U.S. | F4 | 116 |
| Levelock, Ak., U.S. | D5 | 72 |
| Leveque, Cape, c., Austl. | C4 | 68 |
| Levering, Mi., U.S. | E11 | 110 |
| Leverkusen, Ger. | D6 | 10 |
| Levice, Slvk. | G18 | 10 |
| Lévie, Fr. | H4 | 18 |
| Levier, Fr. | F13 | 14 |
| Le Vigan, Fr. | I10 | 14 |
| Levin, N.Z. | D5 | 72 |
| Lévis, P.Q., Can. | B4 | 112 |
| Levittown, N.Y., U.S. | G13 | 108 |
| Levittown, Pa., U.S. | G12 | 108 |
| Levkás, Grc. | K4 | 20 |
| Levkás, i., Grc. | K4 | 20 |
| Levkímmi, Grc. | J4 | 20 |
| Levroux, Fr. | F8 | 14 |
| Lev Tolstoj, Russia | H22 | 22 |
| Lewe, Myan. | E4 | 40 |
| Lewellen, Ne., U.S. | J5 | 118 |
| Lewes, De., U.S. | I11 | 108 |
| Lewes, Eng., U.K. | K14 | 8 |
| Lewis, Ia., U.S. | J12 | 118 |
| Lewis, Ks., U.S. | N8 | 118 |
| Lewis, stm., Wa., U.S. | E3 | 122 |
| Lewis, Butt of, c., Scot., U.K. | C7 | 8 |
| Lewis, Isle of, i., Scot., U.K. | C7 | 8 |
| Lewis, Mount, mtn., Nv., U.S. | D9 | 124 |
| Lewis and Clark Lake, res., U.S. | I10 | 118 |
| Lewis and Clark Range, mts., Mt., U.S. | C13 | 122 |
| Lewisburg, Ky., U.S. | F10 | 114 |
| Lewisburg, Pa., U.S. | G10 | 108 |
| Lewisburg, Tn., U.S. | G10 | 114 |
| Lewisburg, W.V., U.S. | J6 | 108 |
| Lewisport, Ky., U.S. | E10 | 114 |
| Lewis Range, mts., Mt., U.S. | B12 | 122 |
| Lewis Run, Pa., U.S. | F8 | 108 |
| Lewis Smith Lake, res., Al., U.S. | H9 | 114 |
| Lewiston, Ca., U.S. | D3 | 124 |
| Lewiston, Id., U.S. | D8 | 122 |
| Lewiston, Me., U.S. | C16 | 108 |
| Lewiston, Mi., U.S. | E11 | 110 |
| Lewiston, Mn., U.S. | G4 | 110 |
| Lewiston, N.Y., U.S. | D7 | 108 |
| Lewiston, Ut., U.S. | C5 | 120 |
| Lewiston Orchards, Id., U.S. | D9 | 122 |
| Lewistown, Il., U.S. | B6 | 114 |
| Lewistown, Mo., U.S. | B5 | 114 |
| Lewistown, Mt., U.S. | C16 | 122 |
| Lewistown, Pa., U.S. | G9 | 108 |
| Lewisville, Ar., U.S. | I3 | 114 |
| Lewisville, N.B., Can. | F9 | 106 |
| Lewisville, Tx., U.S. | F9 | 116 |
| Lewisville Lake, res., Tx., U.S. | F9 | 116 |
| Lewvan, Sk., Can. | H10 | 104 |
| Lexa, Ar., U.S. | H6 | 114 |
| Lexington, Ga., U.S. | F3 | 112 |
| Lexington, Il., U.S. | J7 | 110 |
| Lexington, Ky., U.S. | A2 | 112 |
| Lexington, Ma., U.S. | E15 | 108 |
| Lexington, Mi., U.S. | G13 | 110 |
| Lexington, Mo., U.S. | C3 | 114 |
| Lexington, Ms., U.S. | I6 | 114 |
| Lexington, N.C., U.S. | D6 | 112 |
| Lexington, Ne., U.S. | K8 | 118 |
| Lexington, Ok., U.S. | D9 | 116 |
| Lexington, Or., U.S. | E6 | 122 |
| Lexington, S.C., U.S. | F5 | 112 |
| Lexington, Tn., U.S. | G8 | 114 |
| Lexington, Tx., U.S. | I9 | 116 |
| Lexington, Va., U.S. | B7 | 112 |
| Lexington Park, Md., U.S. | I10 | 108 |
| Leyond, stm., Mb., Can. | G19 | 104 |
| Leyte, i., Phil. | C7 | 38 |
| Leyte Gulf, b., Phil. | C8 | 38 |
| Leža, Russia | C23 | 22 |
| Ležajsk, Pol. | E22 | 10 |
| Lezama, Arg. | C9 | 84 |
| Lëzna, Bela. | F13 | 22 |
| L'gov, Russia | G5 | 26 |
| Lhari, China | E6 | 30 |
| Lhasa, China | F14 | 44 |
| Lhazê, China | F12 | 44 |
| Lhokseumawe, Indon. | L4 | 40 |
| Lhorong, China | E6 | 30 |
| L'Hospitalet de Llobregat, Spain | D14 | 16 |
| Lhozhag, China | F14 | 44 |
| Lhuntsi Dzong, Bhu. | G14 | 44 |
| Li, stm., China | F9 | 30 |
| Liangcheng, China | B5 | 40 |
| Lianghe, China | D9 | 32 |
| Liangjiadian, China | G10 | 32 |
| Liangkou, China | L2 | 34 |
| Liangshan, China | A13 | 34 |
| Liangtian, China | I8 | 34 |
| Liangying, China | L5 | 34 |
| Lianhe, China | I7 | 34 |
| Lianjiang, China | L3 | 34 |
| Lianping, China | J3 | 34 |
| Lianran, China | G10 | 34 |
| Lianshan, China | I7 | 34 |
| Lianshui, China | I7 | 32 |
| Lianyungang (Xinpu), China | C11 | 30 |
| Liao, stm., China | G3 | 32 |
| Liaocheng, China | D10 | 32 |
| Liaodong Bandao (Liaotung Peninsula), pen., China | D11 | 30 |
| Liaodong Wan, b., China | I2 | 34 |
| Liaojiangshi, China | C11 | 30 |
| Liaoning, prov., China | C11 | 30 |
| Liaoyang, China | C12 | 30 |
| Liaoyuan, China | B10 | 30 |
| Liard, stm., Can. | D8 | 96 |
| Líbano, Col. | E5 | 84 |
| Libby, Mt., U.S. | B10 | 122 |
| Libenge, D.R.C. | H3 | 56 |
| Liberal, Ks., U.S. | N7 | 118 |
| Liberal, Mo., U.S. | E2 | 114 |
| Liberec, Czech Rep. | E15 | 10 |
| Liberia, C.R. | G9 | 92 |
| Liberia, ctry., Afr. | G5 | 54 |
| Libertad, Ven. | C8 | 84 |
| Libertad, Ven. | D7 | 112 |
| Libertad, Ven. | H10 | 84 |
| Libertador General Bernardo O'Higgins, prov., Chile | H3 | 80 |
| Libertador General San Martín, Arg. | B6 | 80 |
| Liberty, In., U.S. | C12 | 114 |
| Liberty, Ky., U.S. | E12 | 114 |
| Liberty, Mo., U.S. | C2 | 114 |
| Liberty, Ms., U.S. | K6 | 114 |
| Liberty, N.C., U.S. | D7 | 112 |
| Liberty, N.Y., U.S. | F12 | 108 |
| Liberty, S.C., U.S. | E4 | 112 |

Name — Map Ref. — Page

Liberty, Tx., U.S. I12 116
Liberty Center, Oh., U.S. F2 108
Liberty Hill, Tx., U.S. I9 116
Libertyville, Il., U.S. H8 110
*Lībīyah, Aṣ-Ṣaḥrā' al- (Libyan Desert), des., Afr.* D6 56
Libourne, Fr. H6 14
Libramont, Bel. I7 12
Libres, Mex. H11 90
Libreville, Gabon A1 58
Libu, China C11 40
*Libya (Lībiyā), ctry., Afr.* C4 56
*Libyan Desert see Lībīyah, Aṣ-Ṣaḥrā' al-, des., Afr.* D6 56
*Libyan Plateau see Aḍ-Diffah, plat., Afr.* B3 60
*Licancábur, Volcán, vol., S.A.* J8 82
Licantén, Chile H2 80
Licata, Italy L8 18
Lice, Tur. B6 48
Lichinga, Moz. D7 58
Lichoslavl', Russia D18 22
Lichtenfels, Ger. E11 10
Lichuan, China H5 34
Lickershamn, Swe. M16 6
Licking, Mo., U.S. E5 114
*Licking, stm., Ky., U.S.* I2 108
Lida, Bela. H8 22
Lidao, China F10 32
*Liddon Gulf, b., N.T., Can.* A10 96
Liden, Swe. J15 6
Lidesi, China B4 34
Lidgerwood, N.D., U.S. E10 118
Lidice, Pan. C3 84
Lidköping, Swe. L13 6
Lidzbark, Pol. B19 10
Lidzbark Warmiński, Pol. A20 10
*Liechtenstein, ctry., Eur.* F9 4
Liège (Luik), Bel. G8 12
*Liège, prov., Bel.* G8 12
Liegnitz see Legnica, Pol. D16 10
Lielvārde, Lat. E7 22
Lienz, Aus. I12 10
Liepāja, Lat. E4 22
Lier (Lierre), Bel. F6 12
Lierre (Lier), Bel. F6 12
Lieshout, Neth. E8 12
Liestal, Switz. D8 13
Liévin, Fr. B9 14
*Lièvre, Rivière du, stm., P.Q., Can.* B11 108
*Lièvres, Île aux, i., P.Q., Can.* E4 106
Liezen, Aus. H14 10
Liffré, Fr. D5 14
Lighthouse Point, Fl., U.S. M6 112
*Lighthouse Point, c., Mi., U.S.* E10 110
*Lighthouse Reef, rf., Belize* I16 90
*Lightning Creek, stm., Sk., Can.* I13 104
Lignières, Fr. F9 14
Lignite, N.D., U.S. C5 118
Ligny-en-Barrois, Fr. D12 14
*Ligonha, stm., Moz.* E8 58
Ligonier, In., U.S. A11 114
Ligonier, Pa., U.S. G7 108
Ligui, Mex. E4 90
*Liguria, prov., Italy* E3 18
*Ligurian Sea, Eur.* F4 18
Lihue, Hi., U.S. p14 125a
Lihula, Est. C6 22
Lijia, China F6 32
Lijiang, China F7 30
Lijiawobao, China B10 32
Likasi (Jadotville), D.R.C. D5 58
Likely, B.C., Can. E13 102
Likino-Dulevo, Russia F21 22
Liknes, Nor. L10 6
*Likoma Island, i., Mwi.* D6 58
Likou, China F6 34
*Likus, stm., Nic.* C11 92
Lilbourn, Mo., U.S. F7 114
L'Île-Rousse, Fr. J15 14
Lilienfeld, Aus. G15 10
Liling, China H2 34
Lille, Fr. B10 14
Lillebonne, Fr. C7 14
Lillehammer, Nor. K12 6
Lillers, Fr. B9 14
Lillesand, Nor. L11 6
Lillestrøm, Nor. L12 6
Lillington, N.C., U.S. D8 112
Lillooet, B.C., Can. G13 102
*Lillooet, stm., B.C., Can.* H12 102
*Lillooet Lake, l., B.C., Can.* G12 102
Lilongwe, Mwi. D6 58
Lilo Viejo, Arg. D7 80
Liloy, Phil. D7 38
Lily, Ky., U.S. B2 112
Lilydale, Austl. M7 70
Lima, Mt., U.S. F13 122
Lima, N.Y., U.S. E9 108
Lima, Oh., U.S. G2 108
Lima, Para. B10 80
Lima, Peru E3 82
*Lima, dept., Peru* E3 82
*Lima (Limia), stm., Eur.* D3 16
Limache, Chile G3 80
Limanowa, Pol. F20 10
*Limarí, stm., Chile* F3 80
*Limay, stm., Arg.* J4 80
Limay Mahuida, Arg. I5 80
Limbani, Peru F7 82
Limbaži, Lat. D7 22
Līmbdi, India I4 44
Limbe, Cam. I14 64
*Limburg, prov., Bel.* G7 12
*Limburg, prov., Neth.* F8 12
Limburg an der Lahn, Ger. E8 10
Limeira, Braz. G5 79
Limen, China H8 34
Limerick, Ire. I5 8
Limerick, Sk., Can. I8 104
*Limerick, co., Ire.* I5 8
Lime Springs, Ia., U.S. G3 110
*Limestone, stm., Mb., Can.* B20 104
*Limestone Bay, b., Mb., Can.* E16 104
*Limestone Lake, l., Mb., Can.* B18 104
*Limestone Lake, l., Sk., Can.* D11 104
*Limestone Point, pen., Mb., Can.* E16 104
*Limestone Point Lake, l., Mb., Can.* C14 104
*Limfjorden, strt., Den.* M11 6
*Limia (Lima), stm., Eur.* D3 16
Liminka, Fin. I19 6
*Limmen Bight, Austl.* B7 68
*Límnos, i., Grc.* J9 20
Limoges, Fr. G8 14
Limogne, Fr. H8 14
Limon, Co., U.S. L4 118
Limón, Hond. B9 92
*Limón, prov., C.R.* H11 92
Limoux, Fr. I9 14
*Limpopo, stm., Afr.* E11 66
Limu, China B11 40
Linachamari, Russia G22 6
Līnah, Sau. Ar. G7 48
Lin'an, China E8 34
Linares, Chile H3 80
Linares, Col. G4 84
Linares, Mex. E10 90
Linares, Spain G8 16
Lincang, China C7 40
Linch, Wy., U.S. A10 120
Lincoln, Ar., U.S. G2 114
Lincoln, Arg. H8 80
Lincoln, Ca., U.S. F4 124
Lincoln, Eng., U.K. H13 8
Lincoln, Il., U.S. B7 114
Lincoln, Ks., U.S. L9 118
Lincoln, Me., U.S. B18 108
Lincoln, Mi., U.S. F12 110
Lincoln, Mo., U.S. D3 114
Lincoln, Mt., U.S. D13 122
Lincoln, Ne., U.S. K11 118
Lincoln, N.H., U.S. C15 108
*Lincoln, Mount, mtn., Co., U.S.* E10 120
Lincoln City, Or., U.S. F1 122
Lincoln Park, Co., U.S. F11 120
Lincoln Park, Ga., U.S. G2 112
Lincoln Park, Mi., U.S. H12 110
*Lincoln Sea, N.A.* A14 86
*Lincolnshire, co., Eng., U.K.* H13 8
Lincolnton, Ga., U.S. F4 112
Lincolnton, N.C., U.S. D5 112
Lincoln Village, Ca., U.S. F4 124
Lind, Wa., U.S. D7 122
Linda, Ca., U.S. E4 124
Linda, Russia E27 22
Lindale, Ga., U.S. E1 112
Lindale, Tx., U.S. G11 116
Lindau, Ger. H9 10
*Linde, stm., Russia* D16 28
Linden, Al., U.S. J9 114
Linden, Guy. D13 84
Linden, In., U.S. B10 114
Linden, Mi., U.S. H12 110
Linden, Tn., U.S. G9 114
Linden, Tx., U.S. I2 114
Lindi, Tan. D7 58
Lindley, S. Afr. G8 66
Lindon, Co., U.S. L4 118
Lindong, China I7 34
Lindsay, Ca., U.S. H6 124
Lindsay, Ne., U.S. J10 118
Lindsay, Ok., U.S. E9 116
Lindsay, On., Can. F17 110
Lindsborg, Ks., U.S. M10 118
*Line Islands, is., Oc.* H24 126
Linesville, Pa., U.S. F6 108
Lineville, Al., U.S. I11 114
Lineville, Ia., U.S. J2 110
Linfen, China D9 30
*Linganamakki Reservoir, res., India* F3 46
Lingao, China E10 40
Lingayen, Phil. m19 39b
Lingbi, China B6 34
Lingen, Ger. C7 10
Lingfengwei, China K4 34
*Lingga, Kepulauan, is., Indon.* O8 40
*Lingga, Pulau, i., Indon.* O8 40
Linghu, China E9 34
Lingle, Wy., U.S. B12 120
Lingling, China A11 40
Linglongta, China C7 32
Lingqiu, China D2 32
Lingshan, China G8 32
Lingshui, China E11 40
Linguère, Sen. D2 64
Lingxiazhu, China F3 34
Lingyuan, China B7 32
*Linh, Ngoc, mtn., Viet.* G9 40
Linhai, China G10 34
Linhares, Braz. E8 79
Linhe, China C8 30
Linhuaiguan, China C6 34
Linjiang, China B14 32
Linjianghu, China G6 34
Linköping, Swe. L14 6
Linkou, China B13 30
Linksmakalnis, Lith. G6 22
Linkuva, Lith. E6 22
Linn, Ks., U.S. L10 118
Linn, Mo., U.S. D5 114
Linnancang, China D5 32
Linqing, China G3 32
Linqu, China G6 32
Linquan, China B4 34
Linru, China A1 34
Linruzhen, China A1 34
Lins, Braz. F4 79
Linshanhe, China E3 34
Lintao, China D7 30
Linthal, Switz. E11 13
Linton, In., U.S. C9 114
Linton, N.D., U.S. E7 118
Linville, N.C., U.S. C5 112
Linxi, China C10 30
Linxia, China D7 30
Linxiang, China F2 34
Linyanti, Nmb. B7 66
*Linyanti, stm., Afr.* B7 66
Linyi, China H6 32
Linying, China B2 34
Linz, Aus. G14 10
Linzhai, China K4 34
Linzikou, China G1 34
*Lion, Golfe du, b., Fr.* I11 14
Lipan, Tx., U.S. G8 116
*Lipari, Isola, i., Italy* K9 18
Lipcani, Mol. A10 20
Lipeck, Russia I22 22
Lipetsk see Lipeck, Russia I22 22
*Lipez, Cerro, mtn., Bol.* I8 82
Lipin Bor, Russia A20 22
Lipki, Russia H20 22
Lipno, Pol. C19 10
*Lipno, údolní nádrž, res., Czech Rep.* G14 10
Lipova, Rom. C5 20
*Lippe, stm., Ger.* D8 10
Lippstadt, Ger. D8 10
Lipscomb, Tx., U.S. C6 116
Lipton, Sk., Can. H11 104
Liptovský Mikuláš, Slvk. F19 10
*Liptrap, Cape, c., Austl.* L6 70
Lira, Ug. H7 56
Lircay, Peru E4 82
Liren, China B7 34
Lisala, D.R.C. A4 58
Lisboa (Lisbon), Port. G2 16
Lisbon, N.D., U.S. E10 118
Lisbon, N.H., U.S. C15 108
Lisbon, Oh., U.S. G6 108
Lisbon see Lisboa, Port. G2 16
Lisbon Falls, Me., U.S. D16 108
Lisburn, N. Ire., U.K. G7 8
*Lisburne, Cape, c., Ak., U.S.* B11 100
Lishe, China F10 34
Lishui, China G8 34
Lisieux, Fr. C7 14
Lisieux, Sk., Can. I9 104
Liski (Georgiu-Dež), Russia G5 26
L'Isle Jourdain, Fr. F7 14
L'Isle-sur-le-Doubs, Fr. E13 14
Lisman, Al., U.S. J8 114
Lismore, Austl. G10 70
Lismore, N.S., Can. G11 106
Lišov, Czech Rep. F14 10
Listowel, On., Can. G15 110
Lita, China H5 34
Litang, China E7 30
Litang, China G8 30
*Litang, stm., China* F7 30
Litchfield, Il., U.S. C7 114
Litchfield, Mi., U.S. H11 110
Litchfield, Mn., U.S. E1 110
Litchfield, Ne., U.S. J8 118
Litchfield Park, Az., U.S. K4 120
Litchville, N.D., U.S. E9 118
Lithgow, Austl. I9 70
*Lithinon, Ákra, c., Grc.* O8 20
Lithonia, Ga., U.S. F2 112
*Lithuania (Lietuva), ctry., Eur.* F6 22
Litian, China I3 34
Lititz, Pa., U.S. G10 108
Litoměřice, Czech Rep. E14 10
Litomyšl, Czech Rep. F16 10
Litovko, Russia H19 28
*Little, stm., Al., U.S.* H11 114
*Little, stm., Ga., U.S.* F4 112
*Little, stm., Ky., U.S.* F9 114
*Little, stm., La., U.S.* K4 114
*Little, stm., Ok., U.S.* D10 116
*Little, stm., S.C., U.S.* E5 112
*Little, stm., Tn., U.S.* D3 112
*Little, stm., U.S.* I2 114
*Little Abaco, i., Bah.* A6 94
*Little Andaman, i., India* I2 40
*Little Arkansas, stm., Ks., U.S.* M9 118
Little Bay, Nf., Can. E15 106
Little Bay Islands, Nf., Can. C18 106
*Little Bear, stm., Ut., U.S.* C5 120
*Little Belt Mountains, mts., Mt., U.S.* D15 122
*Little Bighorn, stm., U.S.* E18 122
*Little Bitterroot, stm., Mt., U.S.* C11 122
*Little Black Bear Indian Reserve, Sk., Can.* G11 104
*Little Blackfoot, stm., Mt., U.S.* D13 122
*Little Blue, stm., U.S.* L11 118
*Little Bow, stm., Ab., Can.* G21 102
*Little Buffalo, stm., Can.* D10 96
Little Bullhead, Mb., Can. G18 104
Little Catalina, Nf., Can. D20 106
*Little Cayman, i., Cay. Is.* E4 94
*Little Cedar, stm., U.S.* G3 110
*Little Churchill, stm., Mb., Can.* A19 104
Little Chute, Wi., U.S. F7 110
*Little Colorado, stm., Az., U.S.* I5 120
*Little Cottonwood, stm., Mn., U.S.* G13 118
Little Current, On., Can. E14 110
*Little Current, stm., On., Can.* F15 96
*Little Deschutes, stm., Or., U.S.* G4 122
*Little Desert, des., Austl.* K4 70
*Little Diomede Island, i., Ak., U.S.* D10 100
*Little Eau Pleine, stm., Wi., U.S.* F5 110
*Little Exuma, i., Bah.* C7 94
Little Falls, Mn., U.S. E1 110
Little Falls, N.Y., U.S. D12 108
Littlefield, Tx., U.S. F4 116
Littlefork, Mn., U.S. B2 110
*Little Fork, stm., Mn., U.S.* B2 110
Little Fort, B.C., Can. F14 102
*Little Harbour Deep, Nf., Can.* B17 106
*Little Humboldt, stm., Nv., U.S.* C8 124
*Little Inagua, i., Bah.* D8 94
*Little Juniata, stm., Pa., U.S.* G8 108
*Little Kanawha, stm., W.V., U.S.* H5 108
*Little Lake, l., La., U.S.* M6 114
*Little Limestone Lake, l., Mb., Can.* E15 104
*Little Manitou Lake, l., Sk., Can.* G9 104
*Little Mecatina, stm., Can.* F20 96
*Little Mexico, Tx., U.S.* I4 116
*Little Missouri, stm., Ar., U.S.* I3 114
*Little Missouri, stm., U.S.* D4 118
*Little Muddy, stm., Il., U.S.* E7 114
*Little Muddy, stm., N.D., U.S.* C4 118
*Little Nemaha, stm., Ne., U.S.* K11 118
*Little Nicobar, i., India* K2 40
*Little Osage, stm., U.S.* D2 114
*Little Pee Dee, stm., S.C., U.S.* F7 112
*Little Pine and Lucky Man Indian Reserve, Sk., Can.* F5 104
*Little Platte, stm., Mo., U.S.* C2 114
*Little Powder, stm., U.S.* G2 118
*Little Quill Lake, l., Sk., Can.* G10 104
*Little Rann of Kachchh, pl., India* I4 44
*Little Red, stm., Ar., U.S.* G5 114
*Little Red Deer, stm., Ab., Can.* F20 102
*Little Red River Indian Reserve, Sk., Can.* E9 104
Little River, Ks., U.S. M9 118
Little Rock, Ar., U.S. H4 114
Little Rock, Ia., U.S. H12 118
*Little Sable Point, c., Mi., U.S.* G9 110
*Little Sac, stm., Mo., U.S.* E3 114
*Little Sachigo Lake, l., On., Can.* D22 104
*Little Saint Bernard Pass see Petit-Saint-Bernard, Col du, Eur.* G13 14
*Little Salkehatchie, stm., S.C., U.S.* F6 112
*Little Salmon Lake, l., Yk., Can.* E27 100
*Little Sandy, stm., Ky., U.S.* I3 108
*Little Saskatchewan, stm., Mb., Can.* H14 104
*Little Scarcies, stm., Afr.* G4 54
*Little Sioux, stm., U.S.* I12 118
*Little Smoky, stm., Ab., Can.* B17 102
*Little Snake, stm., U.S.* C8 120
*Little Southwest Miramichi, stm., N.B., Can.* F7 106
Littlestown, Pa., U.S. H9 108
*Little Tallapoosa, stm., U.S.* F1 112
*Little Tennessee, stm., U.S.* D2 112
Littleton, Co., U.S. E11 120
Littleton, N.C., U.S. C9 112
Littleton, N.H., U.S. C15 108
Littleton, W.V., U.S. H6 108
*Little Traverse Bay, b., Mi., U.S.* E10 110
*Little Turtle, stm., On., Can.* J22 104
Little Valley, N.Y., U.S. E8 108
*Little Vermilion Lake, l., On., Can.* G21 104
*Little Wabash, stm., Il., U.S.* D8 114
*Little Washita, stm., Ok., U.S.* E8 116
*Little White, stm., S.D., U.S.* H6 118
*Little White Mountain, mtn., B.C., Can.* H15 102
*Little Wolf, stm., Wi., U.S.* F6 110
*Little Wood, stm., Id., U.S.* G11 122
*Little Zab (Zāb-e Kūchek) (Az-Zāb aṣ-Ṣaghīr), stm., Asia* D7 48
Litvínov, Czech Rep. E13 10
Liuchen, China C11 40
Liucheng, China B10 40
Liucura, Chile J3 80
Liudaogou, China B15 32
Liufangling, China E3 34
Liuguan, China F2 34
Liuhe, China A13 32
Liuhe, China C7 34
Liujia, China B9 40
Liujiadu, China C9 34
Liujiahe, China C2 34
Liuku, China B5 40
Liulongtai, China B8 32
Liuquan, China I5 32
Liurenba, China F3 34
Liushilipu, China C4 34
Liushuigou, China D1 34
Liutai, China B1 32
Liuwanglou, China I4 32
Liuyang, China G2 34
Liuyuan, China G2 32
Liuzhou, China B10 40
Liuzhuang, China B9 34
Līvāni, Lat. E9 22
Lively, On., Can. D14 110
Live Oak, Ca., U.S. E4 124
Live Oak, Fl., U.S. I4 112
Livermore, Ca., U.S. G4 124
Livermore, Ia., U.S. H1 110
Livermore, Ky., U.S. E9 114
Livermore Falls, Me., U.S. C16 108
Liverpool, Eng., U.K. H11 8
Liverpool, N.S., Can. H9 106
Liverpool, Pa., U.S. G10 108
*Liverpool, Cape, c., N.T., Can.* B17 96
*Liverpool Bay, b., N.S., Can.* H9 106
*Liverpool Bay, b., N.T., Can.* B29 100
Livingston, Al., U.S. J8 114
Livingston, Ca., U.S. G5 124
Livingston, Guat. B6 92
Livingston, Il., U.S. D7 114
Livingston, Ky., U.S. B2 112
Livingston, La., U.S. L6 114
Livingston, Mt., U.S. E15 122
Livingston, Tn., U.S. F11 114
Livingston, Tx., U.S. I12 116
Livingston, Wi., U.S. H5 110
Livingstone, Zam. A7 66
*Livingstone, Chutes de, wtfl, Afr.* B2 58
*Livingstone, Lake, res., Tx., U.S.* I11 116
*Livingstone Falls see Livingstone, Chutes de, wtfl, Afr.* B2 58
*Livingstone Mountains, mts., N.Z.* F2 72
Livingstonia, Mwi. D6 58
*Livingston Island, i., Ant.* B12 73
*Livingston Manor, N.Y., U.S.* F12 108
Livno, Bos. F12 18
Livny, Russia I20 22
Livonia, La., U.S. L5 114
Livonia, Mi., U.S. H12 110
Livonia, N.Y., U.S. E9 108
Livorno (Leghorn), Italy F5 18
Livramento do Brumado, Braz. B8 79
Lixi, China F3 34
Lixian, China E3 32
Lixing, China B4 34
Liyang, China D8 34
Liyuanbao, China J1 34
Liyujiang, China J2 34
*Lizard Head Peak, mtn., Wy., U.S.* H16 122
*Lizard Point, c., Eng., U.K.* L8 8
*Lizard Point Indian Reserve, Mb., Can.* H14 104
Lizhu, China F9 34
Ljahavičy, Bela. H9 22
Ljasnaja, Bela. I8 22
Ljuban', Bela. I10 22
Ljubča, Bela. H9 22
Ljubija, Bos. E11 18
Ljubljana, Slvn. C9 18
Ljubuški, Bos. F12 18
Ljungby, Swe. M13 6
Ljusdal, Swe. K15 6
Ljusina, Bela. I9 22
*Llaima, Volcán, vol., Chile* J3 80
*Llamara, Salar de, pl., Chile* I7 82
*Llancanelo, Laguna, l., Arg.* H4 80
Llandrindod Wells, Wales, U.K. I10 8
Llangefni, Wales, U.K. H9 8
Llangollen, Wales, U.K. I10 8
Llanidloes, Wales, U.K. I10 8
Llano, Tx., U.S. I8 116
*Llano, stm., Tx., U.S.* I8 116
*Llanos, pl., S.A.* E7 84
Llanwrtyd Wells, Wales, U.K. I10 8
Llata, Peru C3 82
Lleida, Spain D12 16
Llera de Canales, Mex. F10 90
*Lleulleu, Lago, l., Chile* J2 80
Llica, Bol. H7 82
Llico, Chile H2 80
Lliria, Spain F11 16
*Llorona, Punta, c., C.R.* I11 92
Lloydminster, Sk., Can. E4 104
*Lloyds, stm., Nf., Can.* D16 106
Llucmajor, Spain F14 16
*Llullaillaco, Volcán, vol., S.A.* C4 80
Llusco, Peru F5 82
*Lluta, stm., Chile* H7 82
*Lo (Panlong), stm., Asia* C8 40
Loa, Ut., U.S. F5 120
*Loa, stm., Chile* I7 82
Loami, Il., U.S. C7 114
Loanda, Braz. G2 79
*Loange (Luangue), stm., Afr.* C3 58
Lobanovo, Russia H21 22
Lobatse, Bots. E7 66
*Lobaye, stm., C.A.R.* H4 56
Lobelville, Tn., U.S. G9 114
Loberia, Arg. J9 80
Lobito, Ang. D2 58
Lobitos, Peru J2 84
Lobn'a, Russia E20 22
Lobos, Arg. H9 80
*Lobos, Cay, i., Bah.* C6 94
*Lobos, Isla, i., Mex.* D4 90
*Lobos, Punta, c., Chile* I6 82
*Lobos de Afuera, Islas, is., Peru* B1 82
*Lobos de Tierra, Isla, i., Peru* B1 82
Locarno, Switz. F10 13
Loches, Fr. E8 14
Lochmaben, Scot., U.K. F10 8
Lock, Austl. I1 70
Lockeport, N.S., Can. I8 106
Lockerbie, Scot., U.K. F10 8
Lockesburg, Ar., U.S. I2 114
Lockhart, Austl. J7 70
Lockhart, Tx., U.S. J9 116
Lock Haven, Pa., U.S. F9 108
Lockney, Tx., U.S. E5 116
Löcknitz, Ger. B14 10
Lockport, Il., U.S. I7 110
Lockport, La., U.S. M6 114
Lockport, Mb., Can. H18 104
Lockport, N.Y., U.S. D8 108
Lockwood, Mo., U.S. E3 114
Loc Ninh, Viet. I9 40
Locri, Italy K11 18
Locroja, Peru E4 82
Locumba, Peru G6 82
*Locumba, stm., Peru* G6 82
*Locust Fork, stm., Al., U.S.* H10 114
Locust Grove, Ok., U.S. C11 116
Lod (Lydda), Isr. E3 50
Lodejnoje Pole, Russia A16 22
Lodève, Fr. I10 14
Lodge Grass, Mt., U.S. E18 122
Lodgepole, Ab., Can. D19 102
Lodgepole, Ne., U.S. J5 118
Lodi, Ca., U.S. F4 124
Lodi, Italy D4 18
Lodi, Oh., U.S. F4 108
Lodi, Wi., U.S. G6 110
Lodja, D.R.C. B4 58
Lodwar, Kenya H8 56
Łódź, Pol. D19 10
Loei, Thai. F6 40
Loeriesfontein, S. Afr. H4 66
*Lofa, stm., Afr.* G4 54
*Lofoten, is., Nor.* G13 6
Loga, Niger E11 64
Logan, Ia., U.S. J12 118
Logan, Ks., U.S. L8 118
Logan, N.M., U.S. D3 116
Logan, Oh., U.S. H4 108
Logan, Ut., U.S. C5 120
Logan, W.V., U.S. J5 108
*Logan, stm., Ab., Can.* B23 102
*Logan, stm., Ut., U.S.* C5 120
*Logan, Mount, mtn., Yk., Can.* F24 100
Logandale, Nv., U.S. H11 124
*Logan Martin Lake, res., Al., U.S.* I10 114
*Logan Mountains, mts., Yk., Can.* E30 100
*Logan Pass, Mt., U.S.* B12 122
Logansport, In., U.S. B10 114
Logansport, La., U.S. K3 114
Loganville, Ga., U.S. F3 112
*Logone, stm., Afr.* F4 56
Logroño, Spain C9 16
Løgstør, Den. M11 6
Lohiniva, Fin. H19 6
*Lohit, stm., Asia* G16 44
Lohja, Fin. K19 6
Lohne, Ger. C8 10
Lohr, Ger. E9 10
Lohrville, Ia., U.S. I13 118
*Loi, stm., Asia* D6 40
Loi-kaw, Myan. E4 40
Loimaa, Fin. K18 6
*Loire, dept., Fr.* G11 14
*Loire, stm., Fr.* E5 14
*Loire-Atlantique, dept., Fr.* E5 14
*Loiret, dept., Fr.* D9 14
*Loir-et-Cher, dept., Fr.* E8 14
Loja, Ec. I3 84
Loja, Spain H7 16
*Loja, prov., Ec.* J3 84
Lokandu, D.R.C. B5 58
*Lokan tekojärvi, res., Fin.* H20 6
Lökbatan, Azer. A10 48
Lokka, Fin. H20 6
Løkken, Den. M11 6
Lokn'a, Russia E13 22
Loko, Nig. G13 64
Lokoja, Nig. H13 64
Lokolama, D.R.C. B3 58
Lokossa, Benin H10 64
Lokot', Russia I17 22
*Loks Land, i., N.T., Can.* D20 96
Lol, Sudan N5 60
*Lol, stm., Sudan* M4 60
Lola, Gui. H5 64
Loleta, Ca., U.S. D1 124
Lolita, Tx., U.S. K10 116
Lolo, Mt., U.S. D11 122
*Lolo Pass, U.S.* D11 122
Lolotique, El Sal. D6 92
Lom, Bul. F7 20
Lom, Russia D22 22
*Lom, stm., Afr.* G9 54
Loma, Eth. N9 60
Lomas de Zamora, Arg. H9 80
Lomax, Il., U.S. J4 110
*Lombardia, prov., Italy* D4 18
*Lomblen, Pulau, i., Indon.* G7 38
*Lombok, i., Indon.* G6 38
Lomé, Togo H10 64
Lomela, D.R.C. B4 58
Lometa, Tx., U.S. H8 116
Lomira, Wi., U.S. G7 110
Lo Miranda, Chile H3 80
Lommel, Bel. F7 12
Lomond, Ab., Can. G22 102
*Lomond, Loch, l., N.S., Can.* G13 106
*Lomond, Loch, l., Scot., U.K.* E9 8
Lomonosov, Russia B12 22
Lomonosovka, Kaz. G11 26
Lompoc, Ca., U.S. J5 124
Lom Sak, Thai. F6 40
Łomża, Pol. B22 10
Lonaconing, Md., U.S. H8 108
Loncoche, Chile D2 78
Loncopue, Arg. J3 80
Londinières, Fr. C8 14
London, Eng., U.K. J13 8
London, Ky., U.S. B2 112
London, Oh., U.S. H3 108
London, On., Can. H14 110
London, Tx., U.S. I7 116
Londonderry (Derry), N. Ire., U.K. F6 8
Londonderry, N.S., Can. G10 106
*Londonderry, Cape, c., Austl.* B5 68
Londres, Arg. D5 80
Londrina, Braz. G3 79
Lone Grove, Ok., U.S. E9 116
*Lonely Lake, l., Mb., Can.* G15 104
*Lone Mountain, mtn., Nv., U.S.* F8 124
Lone Oak, Ky., U.S. E8 114
Lone Oak, Tx., U.S. F11 116
Lone Pine, Ca., U.S. H7 124
Lone Rock, Wi., U.S. G5 110
Lone Star, Tx., U.S. J2 114
Lone Tree, Ia., U.S. I4 110
Lone Wolf, Ok., U.S. E7 116
*Longa, stm., Ang.* D2 58
*Longa, proliv, strt., Russia* C27 28
Long'an, China B10 40
Longaví, Chile H3 80
*Long Bay, b., U.S.* F8 112
Long Beach, Ca., U.S. K7 124
Long Beach, Ms., U.S. L7 114
Long Beach, N.Y., U.S. G13 108
Long Beach, Wa., U.S. D1 122
Longboat Key, Fl., U.S. L4 112
Long Branch, N.J., U.S. G13 108
*Long Branch, stm., Mo., U.S.* C4 114
*Long Cay, i., Bah.* C7 94
Longchang, China F8 30
Longchuan, China K4 34
*Longchuan (Shweli), stm., Asia* B4 40
Long Creek, Or., U.S. F6 122
*Long Creek, stm., N.A.* I11 104
Longcun, China L4 34
Longdou, China H6 34
Longeau, Fr. E12 14
Longford, Austl. L7 70
*Longford, co., Ire.* H6 8
Long Harbour, Nf., Can. E20 106
*Long Harbour, b., Nf., Can.* E18 106
Longhua, China B5 32
*Long Island, i., Austl.* D8 70
*Long Island, i., Bah.* C7 94
*Long Island, i., Nf., Can.* E19 106
*Long Island, i., N.S., Can.* H7 106
*Long Island, i., N.T., Can.* F17 96
*Long Island, i., N.Y., U.S.* G14 108
*Long Island Sound, strt., U.S.* F14 108
*Longitudinal, Valle, val., Chile* H3 80
Longjiang, China B11 30
Longjin, China G5 34
Longka, China D8 44
Longkangji, China B5 34
Longkou, China D11 30
Longkou, China I4 34
Long Lake, N.Y., U.S. D12 108
*Long Lake, l., N.D., U.S.* E7 118
Longleaf, La., U.S. K4 114
Long Leaf Park, N.C., U.S. E9 112
*Longlegged Lake, l., On., Can.* H20 104
Longli, China F8 30
Longling, China B5 40
Longmeadow, Ma., U.S. E14 108
Longmensuo, China C3 32
Longming, China C9 40
Longmont, Co., U.S. D11 120
Longnan, China K3 34
Longnawan, Indon. E5 38
Longny, Fr. M14 8
Long Pine, Ne., U.S. I8 118
*Long Point, c., Nf., Can.* D15 106
*Long Point, c., N.S., Can.* F13 106
*Long Point, pen., Mb., Can.* E16 104
*Long Point, pen., On., Can.* H15 110
Long Prairie, Mn., U.S. F13 118
*Long Prairie, stm., Mn., U.S.* E13 118
Longquan, China G8 34
Longquanguan, China E1 32
*Long Range Mountains, mts., Nf., Can.* D16 106
Longreach, Austl. D6 70
*Long Reach, b., N.B., Can.* G7 106
Long-Sault, On., Can. B12 108
Longshansuo, China E10 34
Longsheng, China B11 40
*Longs Peak, mtn., Co., U.S.* D11 120
Longtian, China J8 34
*Long Tom, stm., Or., U.S.* F2 122
Longton, Ks., U.S. N11 118
Longtoupu, China H2 34
Longueuil, P.Q., Can. B13 108
Longuyon, Fr. C12 14
Longview, Ab., Can. G20 102
Longview, N.C., U.S. D5 112
Longview, Tx., U.S. J2 114
Longview, Wa., U.S. D3 122
Longwangmiao, China G3 32
Longwood Park, N.C., U.S. E7 112
Longworth, B.C., Can. D13 102
Longwy, Fr. C12 14
Longxi, China E7 30
Long Xuyen, Viet. I8 40
Longyan, China J6 34
Longyuanba, China K3 34
Longzhou, China C9 40
Lonigo, Italy D6 18
Löningen, Ger. C7 10
Lonoke, Ar., U.S. H5 114
Lonsdale, Mn., U.S. F2 110
Lons-le-Saunier, Fr. F12 14
Lonton, Myan. B4 40
*Lontra, Ribeirão da, stm., Braz.* F2 79
Loogootee, In., U.S. D10 114
*Looking Glass, stm., Mi., U.S.* H11 110
*Lookout, Cape, c., N.C., U.S.* E10 112
*Lookout Mountain, mtn., Or., U.S.* F5 122
*Lookout Mountain, mtn., U.S.* H11 114
*Lookout Pass, U.S.* C10 122
*Lookout Ridge, mts., Ak., U.S.* B15 100
Loomis, Ne., U.S. K8 118
Loon, stm., Mb., Can. B13 104
*Loon Lake, l., Can.* C12 104
Loon op Zand, Neth. E7 12
Loop, Tx., U.S. G4 116
Lop, China B9 44
Lopar'ovo, Russia C25 22
*Lopatina, gora, mtn., Russia* G20 28
*Lopatka, mys, c., Russia* G23 28
Lop Buri, Thai. G6 40
López, Mex. D7 90
*Lopez, Cap, c., Gabon* B1 58
*Lop Nur (Lop Nor), l., China* C5 30
Łopuszno, Pol. E20 10
*Lora, stm., Ven.* C6 84
*Lora, Hāmūn-i-, l., Asia* F1 44
Lora del Río, Spain H6 16
Lorain, Oh., U.S. F4 108
Loraine, Tx., U.S. G6 116
Lorca, Spain H10 16
*Lord Howe Island, i., Austl.* F11 68
*Lord Mayor Bay, b., N.T., Can.* C14 96
Lordsburg, N.M., U.S. L8 120
Loreauville, La., U.S. L5 114
Loreley, Ger. E7 10
Lorena, Braz. G6 79
Lorenzo, Tx., U.S. F5 116
Lorenzo Geyres (Queguay), Ur. G10 80
Loreto, Arg. D10 80
Loreto, Bol. F9 82
Loreto, Braz. E9 76
Loreto, Mex. D4 90

| Name | Map Ref. | Page |
|---|---|---|
| Loreto, Mex. | F9 | 90 |
| Loreto, Para. | B10 | 80 |
| Loreto, dept., Peru | I5 | 84 |
| Loreto Mocagua, Col. | I7 | 84 |
| Lorette, Mb., Can. | I18 | 104 |
| Loretto, Ky., U.S. | E11 | 114 |
| Loretto, Tn., U.S. | G9 | 114 |
| Lorica, Col. | C5 | 84 |
| Lorient, Fr. | E3 | 14 |
| L'Orignal, On., Can. | B12 | 108 |
| Lorimor, Ia., U.S. | A2 | 114 |
| Loriol, Fr. | H11 | 14 |
| Loris, S.C., U.S. | E8 | 112 |
| Lorman, Ms., U.S. | K5 | 114 |
| Lorne, Austl. | L5 | 70 |
| Lorne, N.B., Can. | E7 | 106 |
| Lörrach, Ger. | H7 | 10 |
| Lorraine, hist. reg., Fr. | D13 | 14 |
| Lorris, Fr. | E9 | 14 |
| Losada, Col. | F5 | 84 |
| Los Alamos, Ca., U.S. | J5 | 124 |
| Los Alamos, N.M., U.S. | I10 | 120 |
| Los Aldamas, Mex. | D10 | 90 |
| Los Amates, Guat. | B5 | 92 |
| Los Americanos, Barra, i., Mex. | E11 | 90 |
| Los Andes, Chile | G3 | 80 |
| Los Angeles, Chile | J7 | 124 |
| Los Angeles, Chile | I2 | 80 |
| Los Angeles Aqueduct, Ca., U.S. | I7 | 124 |
| Los Banos, Ca., U.S. | G5 | 124 |
| Los Berros, Arg. | F4 | 80 |
| Los Blancos, Arg. | B7 | 80 |
| Los Bolones, Cerro, mtn., Mex. | I13 | 90 |
| Los Cerrillos, Arg. | F6 | 80 |
| Los Chacos, Bol. | F10 | 82 |
| Los Chiles, C.R. | F10 | 92 |
| Los Conquistadores, Arg. | F9 | 80 |
| Los Cristianos, Spain | o24 | 17b |
| Los Ebanos, Tx., U.S. | M8 | 116 |
| Los Esclavos, stm., Guat. | D4 | 92 |
| Los Frentones, Arg. | D8 | 80 |
| Los Fresnos, Tx., U.S. | M9 | 116 |
| Los Gatos, Ca., U.S. | G4 | 124 |
| Los Hermanos, Islas, is., Ven. | B10 | 84 |
| Łosice, Pol. | C22 | 10 |
| Los Juries, Arg. | E7 | 80 |
| Los Lagos, Chile | D2 | 78 |
| Los Llanos de Aridane, Spain | o23 | 17b |
| Los Lunas, N.M., U.S. | J10 | 120 |
| Los Maribios, Cordillera, mts., Nic. | E8 | 92 |
| Los Micos, Laguna de, b., Hond. | B7 | 92 |
| Los Mochis, Mex. | E5 | 90 |
| Los Molinos, Ca., U.S. | D3 | 124 |
| Lošnica, Bela. | G11 | 22 |
| Los Padillas, N.M., U.S. | J10 | 120 |
| Los Palacios, Arg. | E4 | 80 |
| Los Palacios, Cuba | C3 | 94 |
| Los Palacios y Villafranca, Spain | H6 | 16 |
| Los Pinos, stm., U.S. | G9 | 120 |
| Los Quirquinchos, Arg. | G8 | 80 |
| Los Ríos, prov., Ec. | H3 | 84 |
| Los Rodríguez, Mex. | D9 | 90 |
| Los Roques, Islas, is., Ven. | B9 | 84 |
| Los Santos, prov., Pan. | J14 | 92 |
| Los Santos de Maimona, Spain | G5 | 16 |
| Los Sauces, Chile | I2 | 80 |
| Los Sauces, Spain | o23 | 17b |
| Lossiemouth, Scot., U.K. | D10 | 8 |
| Lost, stm., U.S. | D10 | 114 |
| Lost, stm., Mn., U.S. | D12 | 118 |
| Lost, stm., U.S. | H4 | 122 |
| Lost, stm., W.V., U.S. | I8 | 108 |
| Los Taques, Ven. | B7 | 84 |
| Los Telares, Arg. | E7 | 80 |
| Los Teques, Ven. | B9 | 84 |
| Los Testigos, Islas, is., Ven. | B11 | 84 |
| Lost Hills, Ca., U.S. | I6 | 124 |
| Lostine, stm., Or., U.S. | E8 | 122 |
| Lost Nation, Ia., U.S. | I5 | 110 |
| Lost River Range, mts., Id., U.S. | F12 | 122 |
| Lost Trail Pass, U.S. | E12 | 122 |
| Losuia, Pap. N. Gui. | A10 | 68 |
| Los Vidrios, Mex. | B3 | 90 |
| Los Vilos, Chile | F3 | 80 |
| Lot, dept., Fr. | H8 | 14 |
| Lot, stm., Fr. | H7 | 14 |
| Lota, Chile | I2 | 80 |
| Lot-et-Garonne, dept., Fr. | H7 | 14 |
| Lothair, Mt., U.S. | B3 | 112 |
| Lothair, S. Afr. | F10 | 66 |
| Lothian, prov., Scot., U.K. | F10 | 8 |
| Lotsane, stm., Bots. | D8 | 66 |
| Lott, Tx., U.S. | H9 | 116 |
| Lotung, Tai. | K10 | 34 |
| Louang Namtha, Laos | D6 | 40 |
| Louangphrabang, Laos | D6 | 40 |
| Louchi, Russia | D4 | 26 |
| Loudéac, Fr. | D4 | 14 |
| Loudon, Tn., U.S. | D2 | 112 |
| Loudonville, Oh., U.S. | G4 | 108 |
| Loudun, Fr. | E7 | 14 |
| Loué, Fr. | D6 | 14 |
| Louga, Sen. | D1 | 64 |
| Louge, Arg. | I8 | 80 |
| Louhans, Fr. | F12 | 14 |
| Louin, Ms., U.S. | J7 | 114 |
| Louisa, Ky., U.S. | A4 | 112 |
| Louisa, Va., U.S. | A8 | 112 |
| Louisbourg, N.S., Can. | G14 | 106 |
| Louis Bull Indian Reserve, Ab., Can. | E21 | 102 |
| Louisburg, Ks., U.S. | M13 | 118 |
| Louisburg, N.C., U.S. | C8 | 112 |
| Louisdale, N.S., Can. | G12 | 106 |
| Louise, Ms., U.S. | J6 | 114 |
| Louise, Tx., U.S. | J10 | 116 |
| Louise, Lake, i., Ab., Can. | E21 | 102 |
| Louise Island, i., B.C., Can. | E3 | 102 |
| Louiseville, P.Q., Can. | A14 | 108 |
| Louisiade Archipelago, is., Pap. N. Gui. | B10 | 68 |
| Louisiana, Mo., U.S. | C5 | 114 |
| Louisiana, state, U.S. | E8 | 98 |
| Louis Trichardt, S. Afr. | D9 | 66 |
| Louisville, Al., U.S. | K11 | 114 |
| Louisville, Co., U.S. | F4 | 112 |
| Louisville, Ga., U.S. | D8 | 114 |
| Louisville, Il., U.S. | D8 | 114 |
| Louisville, Ky., U.S. | D11 | 114 |
| Louisville, Ms., U.S. | I7 | 114 |
| Louisville, Ne., U.S. | K11 | 118 |
| Louisville, Oh., U.S. | G5 | 108 |
| Louis-XIV, Pointe, c., P.Q., Can. | F17 | 96 |
| Loujiaying, China | A4 | 32 |
| Lount Lake, l., On., Can. | H20 | 104 |
| Loup, stm., U.S. | J10 | 118 |
| Loup City, Ne., U.S. | J9 | 118 |
| Loups Marins, Lacs des, l., P.Q., Can. | E18 | 96 |
| Lourdes, Fr. | I6 | 14 |
| Lourdes, Nf., Can. | D14 | 106 |
| Lourenço Marques see Maputo, Moz. | E11 | 66 |
| Louta, Burkina | E8 | 64 |
| Louth, co., Ire. | H7 | 8 |
| Loutre, stm., Mo., U.S. | D5 | 114 |
| Louvain (Leuven), Bel. | G6 | 12 |
| Louviers, Co., U.S. | E11 | 120 |
| Louviers, Fr. | C8 | 14 |
| Love, Sk., Can. | E10 | 104 |
| Love, Bul. | F8 | 20 |
| Lovelady, Tx., U.S. | H11 | 116 |
| Loveland, Co., U.S. | D11 | 120 |
| Loveland, Oh., U.S. | E9 | 32 |
| Lovell, Wy., U.S. | F17 | 122 |
| Lovelock, Nv., U.S. | D7 | 124 |
| Lovely, Ky., U.S. | B4 | 112 |
| Lovere, Italy | D5 | 18 |
| Loves Park, Il., U.S. | H6 | 110 |
| Lovilia, Ia., U.S. | I3 | 110 |
| Loving, N.M., U.S. | G2 | 116 |
| Loving, Tx., U.S. | F8 | 116 |
| Lovingston, Va., U.S. | B8 | 112 |
| Lovington, Il., U.S. | C8 | 114 |
| Lovington, N.M., U.S. | G3 | 116 |
| Lovosice, Czech Rep. | E14 | 10 |
| Lovozero, Russia | G24 | 6 |
| Lovozero, ozero, l., Russia | H24 | 6 |
| Lövstabruk, Swe. | K15 | 6 |
| Low, P.Q., Can. | B11 | 108 |
| Lueders, Tx., U.S. | G7 | 116 |
| Luena, Ang. | D3 | 58 |
| Luena, stm., Ang. | D4 | 58 |
| Luepa, Ven. | E12 | 84 |
| Lufeng, China | M4 | 34 |
| Lufeng, China | B7 | 40 |
| Lufkin, Tx., U.S. | K2 | 114 |
| Luga, Russia | C12 | 22 |
| Luga, stm., Russia | F0 | 22 |
| Lugano, Switz. | C4 | 18 |
| Lugano, Lago di, l., Eur. | C4 | 18 |
| Lugansk see Luhans'k, Ukr. | H5 | 26 |
| Lugenda, stm., Moz. | D7 | 58 |
| Lugnaquillia Mountain, mtn., Ire. | I7 | 8 |
| Lugo, Italy | E6 | 18 |
| Lugo, Spain | B4 | 16 |
| Lugoj, Rom. | D5 | 20 |
| Luhans'k, Ukr. | H5 | 26 |
| Lühedian, China | C3 | 34 |
| Luik (Liège), Bel. | G8 | 12 |
| Luino, Italy | C3 | 18 |
| Luishia, D.R.C. | D5 | 58 |
| Luiza, D.R.C. | C4 | 58 |
| Luiziânia, Braz. | F3 | 79 |
| Luján, Arg. | G4 | 80 |
| Luján, Arg. | G6 | 80 |
| Lujiao, China | F1 | 34 |
| Lukang, Tai. | K9 | 34 |
| Lukanga Swamp, sw., Zam. | D4 | 58 |
| Lukeville, Az., U.S. | M4 | 120 |
| Luknovo, Russia | E25 | 22 |
| Lukolela, D.R.C. | B3 | 58 |
| Lukovit, Bul. | H3 | 34 |
| Lukoyanov, Russia | C19 | 10 |
| Lukoyanov, Russia | F2 | 34 |
| Luków, Pol. | D22 | 10 |
| Lukulu, Zam. | D4 | 58 |
| Lukuś, Mn., U.S. | J5 | 110 |
| Luleå, Swe. | I18 | 6 |
| Lüleburgaz, Tur. | H11 | 20 |
| Lules, Arg. | C4 | 80 |
| Luliang, China | B7 | 40 |
| Lüliang Shan, mts., China | A11 | 32 |
| Luling, La., U.S. | J9 | 116 |
| Lumajang, Indon. | F15 | 44 |
| Lumber, stm., U.S. | E7 | 112 |
| Lumber City, Ga., U.S. | H4 | 112 |
| Lumberport, W.V., U.S. | H3 | 108 |
| Lumberton, Ms., U.S. | K7 | 114 |
| Lumberton, N.C., U.S. | E7 | 112 |
| Lumberton, Tx., U.S. | L2 | 114 |
| Lumbres, Fr. | B9 | 14 |
| Lumby, B.C., Can. | G16 | 102 |
| Lumding, India | H15 | 44 |
| Lumpkin, Ga., U.S. | G2 | 112 |
| Lumsden, Nf., Can. | C20 | 106 |
| Lumsden, Sk., Can. | H10 | 104 |
| Lumut, Malay. | L6 | 40 |
| Luna, stm., Braz. | J12 | 84 |
| Luna Pier, Mi., U.S. | I12 | 110 |
| Lūnāvāda, India | H4 | 44 |
| Lund, B.C., Can. | H10 | 102 |
| Lund, Nv., U.S. | F10 | 124 |
| Lund, Swe. | N13 | 6 |
| Lundale, W.V., U.S. | J5 | 108 |
| Lundar, Mb., Can. | H16 | 104 |
| Lundazi, Zam. | D6 | 58 |
| Lundi, stm., Zimb. | C10 | 66 |
| Lüneburg, Ger. | B10 | 10 |
| Lüneburger Heide, reg., Ger. | B10 | 10 |
| Lunel, Fr. | I11 | 14 |
| Lünen, Ger. | D7 | 10 |
| Lunenburg, N.S., Can. | H9 | 106 |
| Lunenburg, Va., U.S. | C8 | 112 |
| Lunéville, Fr. | D13 | 14 |
| Lunga, stm., Zam. | D5 | 58 |
| Lunga'nake, China | E11 | 14 |
| Lungi, S.L. | G3 | 64 |
| Lungué-Bungo, stm., Afr. | D4 | 58 |
| Luni, Bela. | I9 | 22 |
| Luninec, Bela. | I9 | 22 |
| Lunjiao, China | M2 | 34 |
| Lunna, Bela. | H7 | 22 |
| Luo, stm., China | D9 | 32 |
| Luocheng, China | D9 | 34 |
| Luoci, China | B7 | 40 |
| Luofang, China | H4 | 34 |
| Luohe, China | B3 | 34 |
| Luoheya, China | H6 | 32 |
| Luoji, China | C6 | 34 |
| Luoqiao, China | K2 | 34 |
| Luoshuihe, China | I8 | 34 |
| Luotian, China | C2 | 34 |
| Luoyang, China | E9 | 32 |
| Luoyuan, China | H8 | 34 |
| Luozi, D.R.C. | B2 | 58 |
| Lupeni, Rom. | D7 | 20 |
| Luqu, China | D7 | 32 |
| Luray, Va., U.S. | I8 | 108 |
| Lúrio, Ang. | C3 | 58 |
| Lúrio, stm., Moz. | C7 | 58 |
| Lusaka, Zam. | D5 | 58 |
| Lusambo, D.R.C. | B4 | 58 |
| Lusanga, D.R.C. | C3 | 58 |
| Luscar, Ab., Can. | D17 | 102 |
| Luseland, Sk., Can. | F5 | 104 |
| Lushnje, Alb. | I3 | 20 |
| Lushoto, Tan. | B7 | 58 |
| Lushui, China | A5 | 40 |
| Lüshun (Port Arthur), China | E9 | 32 |
| Lüsi, China | C10 | 34 |
| Lusignan, Fr. | F7 | 14 |
| Lusk, Wy., U.S. | B12 | 120 |
| Lūt, Dasht-e, des., Iran | E15 | 48 |
| Lutai, China | B4 | 34 |
| Lutai, China | J1 | 34 |
| Lutcher, La., U.S. | L6 | 114 |
| Lutesville, Mo., U.S. | E7 | 114 |
| Luther, Mi., U.S. | F10 | 110 |
| Luther, Ok., U.S. | D9 | 116 |
| Lutherstadt Eisleben, Ger. | D11 | 10 |
| Lutherstadt Wittenberg, Ger. | D12 | 10 |
| Luton, Eng., U.K. | J13 | 8 |
| Lutong, Malay. | E5 | 38 |
| Luts'k, Ukr. | C1 | 34 |
| Luttrell, Tn., U.S. | C3 | 112 |
| Lutz, Fl., U.S. | K4 | 112 |
| Lützow-Holm Bay, b., Ant. | B4 | 73 |
| Lutzputs, S. Afr. | G5 | 66 |
| Lutzville, S. Afr. | H4 | 66 |
| Luuq, Som. | H9 | 52 |
| Luverne, Al., U.S. | K10 | 114 |
| Luverne, Mn., U.S. | H11 | 118 |
| Luvuvhu, stm., S. Afr. | D10 | 66 |
| Luxana Bay, b., B.C., Can. | E3 | 102 |
| Luxembourg (Luxemburg), Lux. | I9 | 12 |
| Luxembourg, prov., Bel. | I7 | 12 |
| Luxembourg, ctry., Eur. | F9 | 4 |
| Luxeuil-les-Bains, Fr. | E13 | 14 |
| Luxi (Mangshi), China | B5 | 40 |
| Lüxia, China | I9 | 34 |
| Luxor see Al-Uqşur, Egypt | C7 | 60 |
| Lüyang, China | B9 | 32 |
| Luza, Russia | E7 | 26 |
| Luzarches, Fr. | C9 | 14 |
| Luzern, Switz. | D9 | 13 |
| Luzern, state, Switz. | D9 | 13 |
| Luzhou, China | F8 | 30 |
| Luziânia, Braz. | D5 | 79 |
| Luzon, i., Phil. | B3 | 38 |
| Luzon Strait, strt., Asia | N9 | 34 |
| L'viv (Lvov), Ukr. | H2 | 26 |
| Lvov see L'viv, Ukr. | H2 | 26 |
| L'vovskij, Russia | F20 | 22 |
| Lwówek, Pol. | C16 | 10 |
| Lybster, Scot., U.K. | C10 | 8 |
| Lyčkova, Russia | D15 | 22 |
| Lycksele, Swe. | I16 | 6 |
| Lycoming Creek, stm., Pa., U.S. | F9 | 108 |
| Lydenburg, S. Afr. | E10 | 66 |
| Lydia Mills, S.C., U.S. | E5 | 112 |
| Lyell, Mount, mtn., U.S. | F17 | 102 |
| Lyell Island, i., B.C., Can. | E3 | 102 |
| Lyerly, Ga., U.S. | E1 | 112 |
| Lyford, Tx., U.S. | M9 | 116 |
| Lykens, Pa., U.S. | G10 | 108 |
| Lykošino, Russia | C16 | 22 |
| Lyle, Mn., U.S. | G3 | 110 |
| Lyle, Wa., U.S. | E5 | 122 |
| Lyman, Ne., U.S. | J3 | 118 |
| Lyman, S.C., U.S. | E4 | 112 |
| Lyman, Ukr. | C6 | 120 |
| Lyman, Wa., U.S. | B5 | 122 |
| Lyman, Wy., U.S. | C14 | 108 |
| Lymans'ke, Ukr. | C14 | 20 |
| Lyme Regis, Eng., U.K. | K11 | 8 |
| Lynch, Ne., U.S. | I9 | 118 |
| Lynchburg, Oh., U.S. | H3 | 108 |
| Lynchburg, S.C., U.S. | E6 | 112 |
| Lynchburg, Tn., U.S. | G10 | 114 |
| Lynchburg, Va., U.S. | B7 | 112 |
| Lynches, stm., U.S. | E7 | 112 |
| Lynden, Wa., U.S. | B3 | 122 |
| Lyndhurst, Austl. | H3 | 70 |
| Lyndon, Ks., U.S. | M12 | 118 |
| Lyndon, Vt., U.S. | C14 | 108 |
| Lyndonville, Vt., U.S. | C14 | 108 |
| Lyndora, Pa., U.S. | G7 | 108 |
| Lyngdal, Nor. | L10 | 6 |
| Lyngen, Nor. | G17 | 6 |
| Lyngør, Nor. | L11 | 6 |
| Lynn, Al., U.S. | H9 | 114 |
| Lynn, In., U.S. | B12 | 114 |
| Lynn, Ma., U.S. | E16 | 108 |
| Lynn Canal, b., Ak., U.S. | G27 | 100 |
| Lynn Garden, Tn., U.S. | C4 | 112 |
| Lynn Haven, Fl., U.S. | L11 | 114 |
| Lynnville, Ia., U.S. | I3 | 110 |
| Lyntupy, Bela. | F9 | 22 |
| Lynx Lake, l., N.T., Can. | D11 | 96 |
| Lyon, Fr. | G11 | 14 |
| Lyon, Ms., U.S. | I6 | 114 |
| Lyon Inlet, b., N.T., Can. | C16 | 96 |
| Lyon Mountain, N.Y., U.S. | C13 | 108 |
| Lyonnais, Monts du, mts., Fr. | G11 | 14 |
| Lyons, Co., U.S. | D11 | 120 |
| Lyons, Ga., U.S. | G4 | 112 |
| Lyons, In., U.S. | D9 | 114 |
| Lyons, Ks., U.S. | M9 | 118 |
| Lyons, Mi., U.S. | H11 | 110 |
| Lyons, N.Y., U.S. | D10 | 108 |
| Lyons, stm., Austl. | D3 | 68 |
| Lypets'ke Druhe, Ukr. | B13 | 20 |
| Lys (Leie), stm., Eur. | B9 | 14 |
| Lys'va, Russia | F9 | 26 |
| Lysychans'k, Ukr. | H5 | 26 |
| Lytle, Tx., U.S. | J8 | 116 |
| Lytton, B.C., Can. | G13 | 102 |
| Lyubashivka, Ukr. | B14 | 20 |
| Lyubotyn, Ukr. | H5 | 26 |
| **M** | | |
| Ma, stm., Asia | D8 | 40 |
| Maalaea Bay, b., Hi., U.S. | q17 | 125a |
| Ma'alot-Tarshiḥa, Isr. | F5 | 50 |
| Ma'ān, Jord. | H5 | 50 |
| Ma'anshan, China | D7 | 34 |
| Maardu, Est. | B8 | 22 |
| Ma'arrat an-Nu'mān, Syria | D8 | 48 |
| Maas (Meuse), stm., Eur. | D5 | 10 |
| Maaseik, Neth. | F8 | 12 |
| Maasmechelen, Bel. | F8 | 12 |
| Maastricht, Neth. | G8 | 12 |
| Maave, Moz. | C12 | 66 |
| Maba, China | C7 | 34 |
| Mabank, Tx., U.S. | G10 | 116 |
| Mabel Lake, l., B.C., Can. | G16 | 102 |
| Mabeleapodi, Bots. | C6 | 66 |
| Mableton, Ga., U.S. | F2 | 112 |
| Mabton, Wa., U.S. | D6 | 122 |
| Mabrūk, Sudan | M5 | 60 |
| Mabuasehube Game Reserve, Bots. | D6 | 66 |
| Macalister, Mount, mtn., Austl. | J8 | 70 |
| Macallum Lake, l., Sk., Can. | C6 | 104 |
| MacAlpine Lake, l., N.T., Can. | C12 | 96 |
| Macao see Macau, Macao | M2 | 34 |
| Macão, Port. | F3 | 16 |
| Macapá, Braz. | C8 | 76 |
| Macará, Ec. | J3 | 84 |
| Macarani, Braz. | C8 | 79 |
| Macareo, Caño, mth., Ven. | C12 | 84 |
| Macas, Ec. | I3 | 84 |
| Macau, Braz. | E11 | 76 |
| Macau (Aomen), Macao | M2 | 34 |
| Macau, dep., Asia | G9 | 30 |
| Macaúba, Braz. | B7 | 79 |
| Macaúbas, Braz. | B7 | 79 |
| Macclenny, Fl., U.S. | I4 | 112 |
| Macclesfield, Eng., U.K. | H11 | 8 |
| Macdhui, Ben, mtn., Afr. | H8 | 66 |
| Macdonald Range, mts., B.C., Can. | H20 | 102 |
| MacDonnell Ranges, mts., Austl. | D6 | 68 |
| MacDowell Lake, l., On., Can. | F22 | 104 |
| Macduff, Scot., U.K. | D11 | 8 |
| Macdui, Ben, mtn., Scot., U.K. | D10 | 8 |
| Macedonia, hist. reg., Eur. | H6 | 20 |
| Macedonia (Makedonija), ctry., Eur. | H5 | 20 |
| Maceió, Braz. | E11 | 76 |
| Macenta, Gui. | G5 | 64 |
| Macerata, Italy | F8 | 18 |
| MacFarlane, stm., Sk., Can. | E11 | 96 |
| Macfarlane, Lake, l., Austl. | H2 | 70 |
| MacGregor, Mb., Can. | I16 | 104 |
| Machachi, Ec. | H3 | 84 |
| Machačkala, Russia | I7 | 26 |
| Machadinho, stm., Braz. | C10 | 82 |
| Machado, Braz. | F6 | 79 |
| Machado, stm., Braz. | C10 | 82 |
| Machagai, Arg. | D8 | 80 |
| Machakos, Kenya | B7 | 58 |
| Machala, Ec. | I3 | 84 |
| Machalí, Chile | H3 | 80 |
| Machaneng, Bots. | D6 | 66 |
| Machang, China | A7 | 32 |
| Machanga, China | B7 | 40 |
| Machaquilá, stm., Guat. | A5 | 92 |
| Machattie, Lake, l., Austl. | E3 | 70 |
| Machecoul, Fr. | E5 | 14 |
| Machias, Me., U.S. | C19 | 108 |
| Machias, stm., Me., U.S. | B23 | 104 |
| Machico, Port. | m21 | 17a |
| Machilipatnam (Bandar), India | D6 | 46 |
| Machiques, Ven. | B6 | 84 |
| Machupicchu, Peru | E5 | 82 |
| Machupicchu, hist., Peru | F5 | 82 |
| Machupo, stm., Bol. | E9 | 82 |
| Machynlleth, Wales, U.K. | I10 | 8 |
| Maciá, Arg. | G8 | 80 |
| Macintyre, stm., Austl. | G8 | 70 |
| Mackay, Id., U.S. | G12 | 122 |
| MacKay, stm., Ab., Can. | B2 | 104 |
| MacKay, Lake, l., Austl. | D5 | 68 |
| MacKay Lake, l., N.T., Can. | D10 | 96 |
| Mackenzie, Guy. | D13 | 84 |
| Mackenzie, stm., N.T., Can. | C6 | 96 |
| Mackenzie Bay, b., Can. | B26 | 100 |
| Mackenzie Delta, N.T., Can. | B27 | 100 |
| Mackenzie Mountains, mts., Can. | D29 | 100 |
| Mackinac, Straits of, strt., Mi., U.S. | E11 | 110 |
| Mackinac Island, i., Mi., U.S. | E11 | 110 |
| Mackinac Island, i., Mi., U.S. | E11 | 110 |
| Mackinaw, Il., U.S. | J6 | 110 |
| Mackinaw, stm., Il., U.S. | J6 | 110 |
| Mackinaw City, Mi., U.S. | E11 | 110 |
| Mackinnon Road, Kenya | B7 | 58 |
| Macklin, Sk., Can. | F5 | 104 |
| Macksville, Austl. | H10 | 70 |
| Macksville, Ks., U.S. | M9 | 118 |
| Maclean, Austl. | G10 | 70 |
| Macleod, Lake, l., Austl. | D2 | 68 |
| Maclovia Herrera, Mex. | C7 | 90 |
| Macmillan, stm., Yk., Can. | E27 | 100 |
| Macomb, Il., U.S. | J5 | 110 |
| Macomer, Italy | I3 | 18 |
| Mâcon, Fr. | F11 | 14 |
| Macon, Ga., U.S. | G3 | 112 |
| Macon, Il., U.S. | C8 | 114 |
| Macon, Mo., U.S. | C5 | 114 |
| Macon, Ms., U.S. | I8 | 114 |
| Macon, Bayou, stm., U.S. | J5 | 114 |
| Macorís, Cabo, c., Dom. Rep. | E9 | 94 |
| Macoun Lake, l., Sk., Can. | B11 | 104 |
| Macquarie, stm., Austl. | M7 | 70 |
| Macquarie, stm., Austl. | H7 | 70 |
| Macquarie Harbour, b., Austl. | N6 | 70 |
| Macquarie Island, i., Austl. | A8 | 73 |
| Mac. Robertson Land, reg., Ant. | B5 | 73 |
| Macroom, Ire. | J5 | 8 |
| MacTier, On., Can. | E16 | 110 |
| Macucuau, stm., Braz. | H12 | 84 |
| Macuelizo, Hond. | B6 | 92 |
| Macujer, Col. | G6 | 84 |
| Macunqiao, China | B5 | 34 |
| Macuro, Ven. | B12 | 84 |
| Macusani, Peru | F6 | 82 |
| Macuspana, Mex. | I13 | 90 |
| Macusse, Ang. | A5 | 66 |
| Mad, stm., Ca., U.S. | C2 | 124 |
| Mad, stm., Oh., U.S. | H2 | 108 |
| Mad, stm., Vt., U.S. | C14 | 108 |
| Madagascar (Madagasikara), ctry., Afr. | E9 | 58 |
| Madā'in Sālih, Sau. Ar. | H4 | 48 |
| Madang, Pap. N. Gui. | m16 | 68a |
| Mādārīpur, Bngl. | I14 | 44 |
| Madawaska, stm., On., Can. | E18 | 110 |
| Madadeni, Italy? | H9 | 18 |
| Maddock, N.D., U.S. | D8 | 118 |
| Madeira, i., Port. | m21 | 17a |
| Madeira, stm., S.A. | E6 | 76 |
| Madeira, Arquipélago da, is., Port. | m21 | 17a |
| Madeirinha, Paraná, mth., Braz. | I13 | 84 |
| Mädelegabel, mtn., Eur. | E17 | 14 |
| Madeleine, Iles de la, is., P.Q., Can. | E12 | 106 |
| Madeline-Centre, P.Q., Can. | C8 | 106 |
| Madera, Ca., U.S. | H5 | 124 |
| Madera, Mex. | C5 | 90 |
| Madhubani, India | G12 | 44 |
| Madhya Pradesh, state, India | I8 | 44 |
| Madibogo, S. Afr. | F7 | 66 |
| Madidi, stm., Bol. | E8 | 82 |
| Madill, Ok., U.S. | E10 | 116 |
| Madimba, D.R.C. | B3 | 58 |
| Madina do Boé, Gui.-B. | F2 | 64 |
| Madinani, C. Iv. | G6 | 64 |
| Madinat ash-Sha'b (Al-Ittihad), Yemen | H4 | 47 |
| Madingou, Congo | B2 | 58 |
| Madirobe, Madag. | p22 | 67b |
| Madison, Al., U.S. | H10 | 114 |
| Madison, Fl., U.S. | I3 | 112 |
| Madison, Ga., U.S. | F3 | 112 |
| Madison, In., U.S. | D11 | 114 |
| Madison, Ks., U.S. | M11 | 118 |
| Madison, Me., U.S. | C17 | 108 |
| Madison, Mn., U.S. | F11 | 118 |
| Madison, Mo., U.S. | C4 | 114 |
| Madison, N.C., U.S. | C7 | 112 |
| Madison, Ne., U.S. | J10 | 118 |
| Madison, Oh., U.S. | F5 | 108 |
| Madison, S.D., U.S. | G10 | 118 |
| Madison, Wi., U.S. | G6 | 110 |
| Madison, W.V., U.S. | I5 | 108 |
| Madison, stm., U.S. | E14 | 122 |
| Madison Heights, Va., U.S. | B7 | 112 |
| Madison Range, mts., Mt., U.S. | E14 | 122 |
| Madisonville, Ky., U.S. | E9 | 114 |
| Madisonville, La., U.S. | L6 | 114 |
| Madisonville, Tn., U.S. | D2 | 112 |
| Madisonville, Tx., U.S. | I11 | 116 |
| Madiun, Indon. | j15 | 39a |
| Madoc, On., Can. | F18 | 110 |
| Madoi, China | E6 | 30 |
| Madol, Sudan | M4 | 60 |
| Madona, Lat. | E9 | 22 |
| Madougou, Mali | D8 | 64 |
| Madrakah, Ra's al-, c., Oman | E10 | 47 |
| Madras see Chennai, India | F7 | 46 |
| Madras, Or., U.S. | F4 | 122 |
| Madras see Tamil Nādu, state, India | G5 | 46 |
| Madre, Laguna, b., Mex. | E10 | 90 |
| Madre, Laguna, b., Tx., U.S. | M9 | 116 |
| Madre, Sierra, mts., Phil. | m20 | 39b |
| Madre de Chiapas, Sierra, mts., N.A. | B2 | 92 |
| Madre de Dios, stm., Peru | D6 | 82 |
| Madre de Dios, dept., Peru | D8 | 82 |
| Madre de Dios, Isla, i., Chile | G1 | 78 |
| Madre del Sur, Sierra, mts., Mex. | I10 | 90 |
| Madre Occidental, Sierra, mts., Mex. | E6 | 90 |
| Madre Oriental, Sierra, mts., Mex. | F9 | 90 |
| Madre Vieja, stm., Guat. | C3 | 92 |
| Madrid, Al., U.S. | K11 | 114 |
| Madrid, Col. | E5 | 84 |
| Madrid, Ia., U.S. | I2 | 110 |
| Madrid, Ne., U.S. | K6 | 118 |
| Madrid, Spain | E8 | 16 |
| Madrid, state, Spain | E8 | 16 |
| Madridejos, Spain | F8 | 16 |
| Madriz, dept., Nic. | D8 | 92 |
| Madsen, On., Can. | H21 | 104 |
| Madura, i., Indon. | j16 | 39a |
| Madura, i., Indon. | H5 | 46 |
| Mādurai, India | G5 | 46 |
| Maebashi, Japan | K14 | 36 |
| Mae Hong Son, Thai. | C4 | 40 |
| Mae Klong, stm., Thai. | G5 | 40 |
| Maengsan, N. Kor. | D14 | 32 |
| Mae Sariang, Thai. | E4 | 40 |
| Maeser, Ut., U.S. | D7 | 120 |
| Mae Sot, Thai. | F5 | 40 |
| Maestra, Sierra, mts., Cuba | B7 | 94 |
| Maevatanana, Madag. | p22 | 67b |
| Mafeking, Mb., Can. | F13 | 104 |
| Mafeteng, Leso. | G8 | 66 |
| Maffra, Austl. | K7 | 70 |
| Mafia Island, i., Tan. | C7 | 58 |
| Mafikeng, S. Afr. | D4 | 66 |
| Mafra, Braz. | C14 | 80 |
| Magadan, Russia | F22 | 28 |
| Magadi, Kenya | B7 | 58 |
| Magaguadavic Lake, l., N.B., Can. | F7 | 106 |
| Magallanes, Phil. | o20 | 39b |
| Magallanes, Estrecho de (Strait of Magellan), strt., S.A. | G3 | 78 |
| Magangué, Col. | C5 | 84 |
| Magazine Mountain, mtn., Ar., U.S. | G3 | 114 |
| Magburaka, S.L. | G4 | 64 |
| Magdagači, Russia | G17 | 28 |
| Magdalena, Arg. | H10 | 80 |
| Magdalena, Bol. | E9 | 82 |
| Magdalena, Mex. | G8 | 90 |
| Magdalena, N.M., U.S. | J9 | 120 |
| Magdalena, Peru | E3 | 82 |
| Magdalena, dept., Col. | B5 | 84 |
| Magdalena, stm., Col. | C5 | 84 |
| Magdalena, stm., Mex. | E3 | 90 |
| Magdalena, Bahía, b., Mex. | E3 | 90 |
| Magdalena, Isla, i., Chile | E2 | 78 |
| Magdalena, Isla, i., Mex. | E3 | 90 |
| Magdalena, Punta, c., Col. | B4 | 84 |
| Magdalena de Kino, Mex. | B4 | 90 |
| Magdeburg, Ger. | C11 | 10 |
| Magee, Ms., U.S. | K7 | 114 |
| Magelang, Indon. | j15 | 39a |
| Magellan, Strait of see Magallanes, Estrecho de, strt., S.A. | G3 | 78 |
| Magenta, Italy | D3 | 18 |
| Maggia, Switz. | F10 | 13 |
| Maggiore, Lago, l., Eur. | C6 | 18 |
| Maghāghah, Egypt | C6 | 60 |
| Maghama, Maur. | D3 | 64 |
| Maghniyya, Alg. | C7 | 58 |
| Magill Lake, l., On., Can. | D20 | 104 |
| Maglaj, Bos. | E13 | 18 |
| Magnet, Mb., Can. | G15 | 104 |
| Magnitogorsk, Russia | G9 | 26 |
| Magnolia, Ar., U.S. | I3 | 114 |
| Magnolia, Ms., U.S. | K6 | 114 |
| Magnolia, N.C., U.S. | B14 | 108 |
| Magog, P.Q., Can. | B14 | 108 |
| Magozal, Mex. | G11 | 90 |
| Magpie, Mb., Can. | B9 | 106 |
| Magpie, P.Q., Can. | B9 | 106 |
| Magpie, Lac, l., P.Q., Can. | A9 | 106 |
| Magpie Ouest, stm., P.Q., Can. | A8 | 106 |
| Magrath, Ab., Can. | H22 | 102 |
| Maguarinho, Cabo, c., Braz. | D9 | 76 |
| Maguse Lake, l., N.T., Can. | D13 | 96 |
| Magway, Myan. | D3 | 40 |
| Mahābād, Iran | C8 | 48 |

| Name | Map Ref. | Page |
|---|---|---|
| Mahābaleshwar, India | D2 | 46 |
| Mahabe, Madag. | p21 | 67b |
| Mahābhārat Lek, mts., Nepal | F10 | 44 |
| Mahabo, Madag. | s22 | 67b |
| Mahabo, Madag. | r21 | 67b |
| Mahaicony Village, Guy. | D14 | 84 |
| Mahajamba, Helodranon' i, b., Madag. | o22 | 67b |
| Mahajanga, Madag. | o22 | 67b |
| Mahākālī (Sārda), stm., Asia | F9 | 44 |
| Mahakam, stm., Indon. | E6 | 38 |
| Mahalatswe, Bots. | D8 | 66 |
| Mahallāt, Iran | E11 | 48 |
| Mahanoro, Madag. | q23 | 67b |
| Mahanoy City, Pa., U.S. | G10 | 108 |
| Mahārāshtra, state, India | C3 | 46 |
| Maha Sarakham, Thai. | F7 | 40 |
| Mahasoa, Madag. | s22 | 67b |
| Mahasolo, Madag. | q22 | 67b |
| Mahates, Col. | B5 | 84 |
| Mahatsinjo, Madag. | r21 | 67b |
| Mahattat al-Hafīf, Jord. | D8 | 50 |
| Mahbūbnagar, India | D4 | 46 |
| Mahd adh-Dhahab, Sau. Ar. | C2 | 47 |
| Mahdia, Tun. | N6 | 18 |
| Mahe, India | G3 | 46 |
| Mahébourg, Mrts. | v18 | 67c |
| Mahé Island, i., Sey. | B11 | 58 |
| Mahendra Giri, mtn., India | C8 | 46 |
| Mahesāna, India | I5 | 44 |
| Mahia Peninsula, pen., N.Z. | C7 | 72 |
| Mahilëu, Bela. | H13 | 22 |
| Mahnomen, Mn., U.S. | D12 | 118 |
| Mahoba, India | H8 | 44 |
| Mahomet, Il., U.S. | B8 | 114 |
| Mahone Bay, N.S., Can. | H9 | 106 |
| Mahone Bay, b., N.S., Can. | H9 | 106 |
| Mahony Lake, l., N.T., Can. | D32 | 100 |
| Mahood Falls, B.C., Can. | F14 | 102 |
| Mahood Lake, l., B.C., Can. | F14 | 102 |
| Mahres, Tun. | C16 | 62 |
| Mahuva, India | B1 | 46 |
| Mai Aini, Erit. | J10 | 60 |
| Maicao, Col. | B6 | 84 |
| Maîche, Fr. | E13 | 14 |
| Maici, stm., Braz. | B11 | 82 |
| Maicuru, stm., Braz. | D8 | 76 |
| Maiden, N.C., U.S. | D5 | 112 |
| Maidenhead, Eng., U.K. | J13 | 8 |
| Maidstone, Eng., U.K. | J14 | 8 |
| Maidstone, Sk., Can. | E5 | 104 |
| Maiduguri, Nig. | F9 | 54 |
| Maienfeld, Switz. | D12 | 13 |
| Maigatari, Nig. | E14 | 64 |
| Maignelay, Fr. | C9 | 14 |
| Maillezais, Fr. | F6 | 14 |
| Mai Mefales, Erit. | J10 | 60 |
| Main, stm., Ger. | F9 | 10 |
| Main Channel, strt., On., Can. | E14 | 110 |
| Mai-Ndombe, Lac, l., D.R.C. | B3 | 58 |
| Maine, hist. reg., Fr. | D6 | 14 |
| Maine, state, U.S. | B13 | 98 |
| Maine, Gulf of, b., N.A. | C13 | 98 |
| Maine-et-Loire, dept., Fr. | E6 | 14 |
| Mainhardt, Ger. | F9 | 10 |
| Mainland, i., Scot., U.K. | B10 | 8 |
| Mainland, i., Scot., U.K. | A12 | 8 |
| Mainpuri, India | G8 | 44 |
| Maintenon, Fr. | D8 | 14 |
| Maintirano, Madag. | q21 | 67b |
| Main Topsail, mtn., Nf., Can. | C17 | 106 |
| Mainz, Ger. | E8 | 10 |
| Maio, i., C.V. | m17 | 64a |
| Maipo, stm., Chile | G3 | 80 |
| Maipo, Volcán, vol., S.A. | H4 | 80 |
| Maipú, Arg. | I10 | 80 |
| Maipú, Arg. | G4 | 80 |
| Maipú, Chile | G3 | 80 |
| Maiquetía, Ven. | B9 | 84 |
| Mairipotaba, Braz. | D4 | 79 |
| Maitengwe, Bots. | C8 | 66 |
| Maitengwe, stm., Afr. | C8 | 66 |
| Maitland, Austl. | J2 | 70 |
| Maitland, Austl. | I9 | 70 |
| Maitland, N.S., Can. | G10 | 106 |
| Maíz, stm., Nic. | F10 | 92 |
| Maíz, Islas del, is., Nic. | E11 | 92 |
| Maizuru, Japan | L10 | 36 |
| Maja, stm., Russia | F18 | 28 |
| Majagual, Col. | C5 | 84 |
| Majari, stm., Braz. | F12 | 84 |
| Majé, Braz. | G7 | 79 |
| Maji, Eth. | N8 | 60 |
| Majia, China | C7 | 34 |
| Majie, China | B7 | 40 |
| Majja, Russia | E18 | 28 |
| Majkain, Kaz. | G13 | 26 |
| Majkop, Russia | I6 | 26 |
| Majorca see Mallorca, i., Spain | F15 | 16 |
| Maka, Sen. | E2 | 64 |
| Makabana, Congo | B2 | 58 |
| Makalamabedi, Bots. | C6 | 66 |
| Makallé, Arg. | D9 | 80 |
| Makālu, mtn., Asia | G12 | 44 |
| Makanza, D.R.C. | A3 | 58 |
| Makaoo Indian Reserve, Ab., Can. | E4 | 104 |
| Makarjev, Russia | D26 | 22 |
| Makarov, Russia | H20 | 28 |
| Makarska, Cro. | F12 | 18 |
| Makasar, Selat (Makassar Strait), strt., Indon. | F6 | 38 |
| Makassar Strait see Makasar, Selat, strt., Indon. | F6 | 38 |
| Makat, Kaz. | H8 | 26 |
| Makawao, Hi., U.S. | q17 | 125a |
| Makeni, S.L. | G3 | 64 |
| Makeyevka see Makiyivka, Ukr. | H5 | 26 |
| Makgadikgadi, pl., Bots. | C7 | 66 |
| Makgadikgadi Pans Game Reserve, Bots. | C7 | 66 |
| Makhfar al-Quwayrah, Jord. | I4 | 50 |
| Makhfar Ramn, Jord. | I4 | 50 |
| Makhrūq, Wādī al-, val., Asia | F7 | 50 |
| Makindu, Kenya | B7 | 58 |
| Makinsk, Kaz. | G12 | 26 |
| M'akiševo, Russia | E11 | 22 |
| M'akit, Russia | E22 | 28 |
| Makiyivka, Ukr. | H5 | 26 |
| Makkah (Mecca), Sau. Ar. | D1 | 47 |
| Makó, Hung. | I20 | 10 |
| Makokou, Gabon | A2 | 58 |
| Makoua, Congo | A3 | 58 |
| Makrāna, India | G6 | 44 |
| Makran Coast, Asia | I16 | 48 |
| M'aksa, Russia | C21 | 22 |
| Maksaticha, Russia | D18 | 22 |
| Makthar, Tun. | N4 | 18 |
| Mākū, Iran | B8 | 48 |
| Makumbi, D.R.C. | C4 | 58 |
| Makung (P'enghu), Tai. | L8 | 34 |
| Makurdi, Nig. | H14 | 64 |
| Makwa Lake, l., Sk., Can. | D5 | 104 |
| Makwassie, S. Afr. | F8 | 66 |
| Mal, Maur. | C3 | 64 |
| Mala, Peru | E3 | 82 |
| Mala, stm., Peru | E3 | 82 |
| Mala, Punta, c., Pan. | D3 | 84 |
| Malabang, Phil. | D7 | 38 |
| Malabar Coast, India | F3 | 46 |
| Malabo, Eq. Gui. | J14 | 64 |
| Malacacheta, Braz. | D7 | 79 |
| Malacca, Strait of, strt., Asia | M6 | 40 |
| Malacky, Slvk. | G17 | 10 |
| Malad, stm., U.S. | C4 | 120 |
| Malad City, Id., U.S. | H13 | 122 |
| Maladzečna, Bela. | G9 | 22 |
| Málaga, Col. | D6 | 84 |
| Malaga, N.M., U.S. | G2 | 116 |
| Málaga, Spain | I7 | 16 |
| Malagash, N.S., Can. | G10 | 106 |
| Malagasy Republic see Madagascar, ctry., Afr. | E9 | 58 |
| Malagón, Spain | F8 | 16 |
| Malaimbandy, Madag. | r21 | 67b |
| Malaja Kuril'skaja Gr'ada (Habomai-Shotō), is., Russia | d21 | 36a |
| Malaja Višera, Russia | C15 | 22 |
| Malakāl, Sudan | M6 | 60 |
| Malakoff, Tx., U.S. | G10 | 116 |
| Malān, Myan. | B4 | 40 |
| Malang, Indon. | j16 | 39a |
| Malanggwā, Nepal | G11 | 44 |
| Malanje, Ang. | C3 | 58 |
| Malanville, Benin | F11 | 64 |
| Malanzán, Arg. | F5 | 80 |
| Mälaren, l., Swe. | L15 | 6 |
| Malargüe, Arg. | H4 | 80 |
| Malaspina Glacier, Ak., U.S. | G24 | 100 |
| Malaspina Strait, strt., B.C., Can. | H10 | 102 |
| Malatya, Tur. | B5 | 48 |
| Malaut, India | E6 | 44 |
| Malawi, ctry., Afr. | D6 | 58 |
| Malawi, Lake see Nyasa, Lake, l., Afr. | D6 | 58 |
| Malaybalay, Phil. | D8 | 38 |
| Malāyer, Iran | D10 | 48 |
| Malay Peninsula, pen., Asia | K6 | 40 |
| Malay Reef, rf., Austl. | A8 | 70 |
| Malaysia, ctry., Asia | E3 | 38 |
| Malazgirt, Tur. | B7 | 48 |
| Malbaie, stm., P.Q., Can. | E3 | 106 |
| Malbaie, La, b., P.Q., Can. | D9 | 106 |
| Malbork, Pol. | A19 | 10 |
| Malbrán, Arg. | E7 | 80 |
| Malcolm, Austl. | E4 | 68 |
| Malcolm Island, i., B.C., Can. | G7 | 102 |
| Malcom, Ia., U.S. | I3 | 110 |
| Maldegem, Bel. | F3 | 12 |
| Malden, Mo., U.S. | F7 | 114 |
| Maldive Islands, is., Mald. | I2 | 46 |
| Maldives, ctry., Asia | I8 | 24 |
| Maldonado, Ur. | H11 | 80 |
| Malé, Italy | C5 | 18 |
| Male', Mald. | I8 | 24 |
| Maléa, Ákra, c., Grc. | M7 | 20 |
| Mālegaon, India | B3 | 46 |
| Malek, Sudan | N6 | 60 |
| Malek Sīāh, Kūh-e, mtn., Asia | G16 | 48 |
| Malema, Moz. | D7 | 58 |
| Malen'ga, Russia | J25 | 6 |
| Māler Kotla, India | E6 | 44 |
| Malesherbes, Fr. | D9 | 14 |
| Malestroit, Fr. | E4 | 14 |
| Malha Wells, Sudan | J4 | 60 |
| Malheur, stm., Or., U.S. | G8 | 122 |
| Malheur Lake, l., Or., U.S. | G7 | 122 |
| Mali, ctry., Afr. | E6 | 54 |
| Mali, stm., Myan. | A4 | 40 |
| Maligne, stm., Ab., Can. | E17 | 102 |
| Maligne Lake, l., Ab., Can. | E17 | 102 |
| Malik, Wādī al-, val., Sudan | I6 | 60 |
| Mali Kyun, i., Myan. | H5 | 40 |
| Malin, Or., U.S. | H4 | 122 |
| Malinalco, hist., Mex. | H10 | 90 |
| Malinaltepec, Mex. | I10 | 90 |
| Malines (Mechelen), Bel. | F5 | 12 |
| Malin Head, c., Ire. | F6 | 8 |
| Maliwun, Myan. | I5 | 40 |
| Maljamar, N.M., U.S. | G3 | 116 |
| Malka, Russia | G23 | 28 |
| Malkāpur, India | B4 | 46 |
| Malkara, Tur. | I10 | 20 |
| Mallāh, Syria | C7 | 50 |
| Mallaig, Ab., Can. | C23 | 102 |
| Mallaig, Scot., U.K. | D8 | 8 |
| Mallala, Austl. | J3 | 70 |
| Mallaoua, Niger | E14 | 64 |
| Mallawī, Egypt | D6 | 60 |
| Mallery Lake, l., N.T., Can. | D13 | 96 |
| Mallet, Braz. | C13 | 80 |
| Malligasta, Arg. | E5 | 80 |
| Mallnitz, Aus. | I13 | 10 |
| Mallorca, i., Spain | F15 | 16 |
| Mallow, Ire. | I5 | 8 |
| Malmédy, Bel. | H9 | 12 |
| Malmesbury, S. Afr. | I4 | 66 |
| Malmö, Swe. | N13 | 6 |
| Malmöhus Län, co., Swe. | N13 | 6 |
| Maloarchangel'sk, Russia | I19 | 22 |
| Maloja, Switz. | F12 | 13 |
| Malojaroslavec, Russia | F19 | 22 |
| Maloje Kozino, Russia | E26 | 22 |
| Maloje Skuratovo, Russia | H20 | 22 |
| Malolos, Phil. | n19 | 39b |
| Malone, Fl., U.S. | I1 | 112 |
| Malone, N.Y., U.S. | C12 | 108 |
| Malonga, D.R.C. | D4 | 58 |
| Małopolska, reg., Pol. | E21 | 10 |
| Malošujka, Russia | E5 | 26 |
| Måløy, Nor. | K9 | 6 |
| Malpaisillo, Nic. | E8 | 92 |
| Malpas, Austl. | J4 | 70 |
| Malpelo, Isla de, i., Col. | C2 | 76 |
| Malpeque Bay, b., P.E., Can. | F10 | 106 |
| Malta, Lat. | E10 | 22 |
| Malta, Mt., U.S. | B18 | 122 |
| Malta, Oh., U.S. | H5 | 108 |
| Malta, ctry., Eur. | H10 | 4 |
| Malta, i., Malta | N9 | 18 |
| Malta Channel, strt., Eur. | M9 | 18 |
| Maltahöhe, Nmb. | E3 | 66 |
| Maltepe, Tur. | I11 | 20 |
| Maluku (Moluccas), is., Indon. | F8 | 38 |
| Maluku, Laut (Molucca Sea), Indon. | F7 | 38 |
| Malumfashi, Nig. | F13 | 64 |
| Malvern, Ar., U.S. | H4 | 114 |
| Malvern, Ia., U.S. | J12 | 118 |
| Malvern, Oh., U.S. | G5 | 108 |
| Malvinas, Arg. | E9 | 80 |
| Malwal, Sudan | M6 | 60 |
| Malý Dunaj, stm., Slvk. | H17 | 10 |
| Malyj, ostrov, i., Russia | A11 | 22 |
| Malyj An'uj, stm., Russia | D24 | 28 |
| Malyj Jenisej, stm., Russia | G11 | 28 |
| Malyj Tajmyr, ostrov, i., Russia | B13 | 28 |
| Malyj T'uters, ostrov, i., Russia | B9 | 22 |
| Malyj Uzen', stm., Eur. | H7 | 26 |
| Malyševo, Russia | D18 | 22 |
| Mamakwash Lake, l., On., Can. | G22 | 104 |
| Mamara, Peru | F5 | 82 |
| Mambaí, Braz. | C5 | 79 |
| Mamberamo, stm., Indon. | F10 | 38 |
| Mambéré, stm., C.A.R. | H4 | 56 |
| Ma-Me-O Beach, Ab., Can. | E21 | 102 |
| Mamers, Fr. | D7 | 14 |
| Mamfe, Cam. | G8 | 54 |
| Mamiá, Lago, l., Braz. | J11 | 84 |
| Mamie, N.C., U.S. | C11 | 112 |
| Mamiña, Chile | I7 | 82 |
| Mammoth, Az., U.S. | L6 | 120 |
| Mammoth, W.V., U.S. | I5 | 108 |
| Mammoth Cave National Park, Ky., U.S. | E10 | 114 |
| Mammoth Lakes, Ca., U.S. | G7 | 124 |
| Mammoth Spring, Ar., U.S. | F5 | 114 |
| Mamonovo, Russia | G2 | 22 |
| Mamoré, stm., S.A. | D9 | 82 |
| Mamori, Lago, l., Braz. | I12 | 84 |
| Mamoriá, stm., Braz. | B8 | 82 |
| Mamou, Gui. | F3 | 64 |
| Mamou, La., U.S. | L4 | 114 |
| Mamoutzou, May. | I16 | 67a |
| Mampikony, Madag. | p22 | 67b |
| Mamry, Jezioro, l., Pol. | A21 | 10 |
| Mamuchi, China | H6 | 32 |
| Ma'mūn, Sudan | K2 | 60 |
| Mamuno, Bots. | D5 | 66 |
| Mamuru, stm., Braz. | I14 | 84 |
| Man, C. Iv. | H6 | 64 |
| Man, W.V., U.S. | B5 | 112 |
| Mana, Hi., U.S. | o14 | 125a |
| Mana, stm., Fr. Gu. | B8 | 76 |
| Manabí, prov., Ec. | H2 | 84 |
| Manacacías, stm., Col. | F6 | 84 |
| Manacapuru, Braz. | I12 | 84 |
| Manacor, Spain | F15 | 16 |
| Manado, Indon. | E7 | 38 |
| Managua, Nic. | E8 | 92 |
| Managua, dept., Nic. | E8 | 92 |
| Managua, Lago de, l., Nic. | E8 | 92 |
| Manakara, Madag. | s23 | 67b |
| Manāli, India | D7 | 44 |
| Manama see Al-Manāmah, Bahr. | H11 | 48 |
| Manambato, Madag. | n23 | 67b |
| Manambolosy, Madag. | p23 | 67b |
| Mánamo, Caño, mth., Ven. | C11 | 84 |
| Mananara, Madag. | p23 | 67b |
| Mananjary, Madag. | r23 | 67b |
| Manantenina, Madag. | t22 | 67b |
| Manapiare, stm., Ven. | E9 | 84 |
| Manapire, stm., Ven. | C9 | 84 |
| Manaquiri, Lago, l., Braz. | I12 | 84 |
| Manaravolo, Madag. | s21 | 67b |
| Manas, China | C4 | 30 |
| Manās, stm., Asia | G14 | 44 |
| Manas Hu, l., China | B4 | 30 |
| Manāslu, mtn., Nepal | F11 | 44 |
| Manasquan, N.J., U.S. | G12 | 108 |
| Manassa, Co., U.S. | G11 | 120 |
| Manassas, Va., U.S. | I9 | 108 |
| Manatí, Col. | B5 | 84 |
| Manatí, P.R. | E11 | 94 |
| Manaung, Myan. | E2 | 40 |
| Manaus, Braz. | I12 | 84 |
| Manawa, Wi., U.S. | F7 | 110 |
| Manawan Lake, l., Sk., Can. | C11 | 104 |
| Manbij, Syria | C4 | 48 |
| Mancelona, Mi., U.S. | F10 | 110 |
| Mancha Real, Spain | H8 | 16 |
| Manche, dept., Fr. | C5 | 14 |
| Manchester, Ct., U.S. | F14 | 108 |
| Manchester, Eng., U.K. | H11 | 8 |
| Manchester, Ga., U.S. | G2 | 112 |
| Manchester, Ia., U.S. | H4 | 110 |
| Manchester, Ky., U.S. | B3 | 112 |
| Manchester, Ma., U.S. | E16 | 108 |
| Manchester, Mi., U.S. | H11 | 110 |
| Manchester, N.H., U.S. | E15 | 108 |
| Manchester, Oh., U.S. | I3 | 108 |
| Manchester, Tn., U.S. | G10 | 114 |
| Manchester, Vt., U.S. | D13 | 108 |
| Manchón, Guat. | C2 | 92 |
| Manchuria, hist. reg., China | B12 | 30 |
| Máncora, Peru | J2 | 84 |
| Mancos, Co., U.S. | G8 | 120 |
| Mancos, stm., U.S. | G8 | 120 |
| Mandabe, Madag. | r21 | 67b |
| Mandaguari, Braz. | G3 | 79 |
| Mandal, Nor. | L10 | 6 |
| Mandala, Puncak, mtn., Indon. | F11 | 38 |
| Mandalay, Myan. | C4 | 40 |
| Mandalgov', Mong. | B8 | 30 |
| Mandalī, Iraq | E8 | 48 |
| Mandan, N.D., U.S. | E7 | 118 |
| Mandara Mountains, mts., Afr. | F9 | 54 |
| Mandas, Italy | J4 | 18 |
| Mandeb, Bab el, strt. | H3 | 47 |
| Mandel, Afg. | E16 | 48 |
| Manderson, Wy., U.S. | F18 | 122 |
| Mandeville, Jam. | E6 | 94 |
| Mandeville, La., U.S. | L6 | 114 |
| Mandi, India | E7 | 44 |
| Mandiana, Gui. | F5 | 64 |
| Mandimba, Moz. | D7 | 58 |
| Mandioli, Pulau, i., Indon. | F8 | 38 |
| Mandioré, Lagoa, l., S.A. | H13 | 82 |
| Mandla, India | A6 | 46 |
| Mandoto, Madag. | q22 | 67b |
| Mandouri, Togo | F10 | 64 |
| Mandra, Pak. | D5 | 44 |
| Mandritsara, Madag. | o23 | 67b |
| Mandronarivo, Madag. | r21 | 67b |
| Mandsaur, India | H6 | 44 |
| Manduria, Italy | I12 | 18 |
| Māndvi, India | I3 | 44 |
| Mandya, India | F4 | 46 |
| Manfalūt, Egypt | D6 | 60 |
| Manfredonia, Italy | H10 | 18 |
| Manfredonia, Golfo di, b., Italy | H11 | 18 |
| Manga, Braz. | C7 | 79 |
| Manga, Burkina | F9 | 64 |
| Mangabeiras, Chapada das, hills, Braz. | F9 | 76 |
| Mangalagiri, India | D6 | 46 |
| Mangalore, India | F3 | 46 |
| Mangaoka, Madag. | n23 | 67b |
| Mangchang, China | F8 | 30 |
| Mange, China | D10 | 44 |
| Mange, S.L. | G3 | 64 |
| Mangham, La., U.S. | J5 | 114 |
| Manglares, Cabo, c., Col. | G3 | 84 |
| Mangochi, Mwi. | D7 | 58 |
| Mangoky, stm., Madag. | r21 | 67b |
| Mangole, Pulau, i., Indon. | F8 | 38 |
| Mangoupa, C.A.R. | O3 | 60 |
| Mangrol, India | J4 | 44 |
| Mangrove Cay, i., Bah. | B6 | 94 |
| Mangueira, Lagoa, b., Braz. | G12 | 80 |
| Mangueirinha, Braz. | C12 | 80 |
| Mangulile, Hond. | B8 | 92 |
| Mangum, Ok., U.S. | E7 | 116 |
| Mangya, China | D5 | 30 |
| Manhattan, Ks., U.S. | L11 | 118 |
| Manhattan, Mt., U.S. | E14 | 122 |
| Manhuaçu, Braz. | F7 | 79 |
| Manhuaçu, stm., Braz. | E8 | 79 |
| Manhumirim, Braz. | F8 | 79 |
| Maniago, Italy | C7 | 18 |
| Maniamba, Moz. | D7 | 58 |
| Manic Deux, Réservoir, res., P.Q., Can. | C5 | 106 |
| Manicoré, Braz. | A11 | 82 |
| Manicoré, stm., Braz. | B11 | 82 |
| Manicouagan, stm., P.Q., Can. | C5 | 106 |
| Manicouagan, Réservoir, res., P.Q., Can. | A5 | 106 |
| Manic Trois, Réservoir, res., P.Q., Can. | B5 | 106 |
| Manignan, C. Iv. | F6 | 64 |
| Manigotagan, Mb., Can. | G18 | 104 |
| Manigotagan, stm., Can. | H19 | 104 |
| Manila, Ar., U.S. | G6 | 114 |
| Manila, Phil. | n19 | 39b |
| Manila, Ut., U.S. | D7 | 120 |
| Manila Bay, b., Phil. | n19 | 39b |
| Manilla, Austl. | H9 | 70 |
| Manilla, Ia., U.S. | J12 | 118 |
| Manily, Russia | E25 | 28 |
| Manimpé, Mali | D7 | 64 |
| Manino, Russia | H17 | 22 |
| Manipur, state, India | H15 | 44 |
| Manipur, stm., Asia | C2 | 40 |
| Manisa, Tur. | K11 | 20 |
| Manissauá-Miçu, stm., Braz. | A1 | 79 |
| Manistee, Mi., U.S. | F9 | 110 |
| Manistee, stm., Mi., U.S. | F9 | 110 |
| Manistique, Mi., U.S. | E9 | 110 |
| Manistique, stm., Mi., U.S. | D9 | 110 |
| Manito, Il., U.S. | B7 | 114 |
| Manitoba, prov., Can. | D17 | 104 |
| Manitoba, Lake, l., Mb., Can. | H16 | 104 |
| Manitou, Mb., Can. | I16 | 104 |
| Manitou, stm., On., Can. | I21 | 104 |
| Manitou, stm., P.Q., Can. | B8 | 106 |
| Manitou, Lac, l., P.Q., Can. | B10 | 106 |
| Manitou, Lac, l., P.Q., Can. | B8 | 106 |
| Manitou Beach, Sk., Can. | G9 | 104 |
| Manitou Lake, l., Sk., Can. | F5 | 104 |
| Manitoulin Island, i., On., Can. | E13 | 110 |
| Manitou Springs, Co., U.S. | F12 | 120 |
| Manitowaning, On., Can. | E14 | 110 |
| Manitowish Waters, Wi., U.S. | D6 | 110 |
| Manitowoc, Wi., U.S. | F8 | 110 |
| Manitowoc, stm., Wi., U.S. | F7 | 110 |
| Maniwaki, P.Q., Can. | A11 | 108 |
| Manizales, Col. | E5 | 84 |
| Manja, Madag. | r21 | 67b |
| Manjacaze, Moz. | E11 | 66 |
| Manjakandriana, Madag. | q22 | 67b |
| Manjimup, Austl. | F3 | 68 |
| Mankato, Ks., U.S. | L9 | 118 |
| Mankato, Mn., U.S. | F2 | 110 |
| Mankayane, Swaz. | F10 | 66 |
| Mankota, Sk., Can. | I7 | 104 |
| Manlleu, Spain | C14 | 16 |
| Manly, Ia., U.S. | G2 | 110 |
| Manmād, India | B3 | 46 |
| Mannahill, Austl. | I3 | 70 |
| Mannar, Gulf of, b., Asia | H5 | 46 |
| Mannārgudi, India | G5 | 46 |
| Männedorf, Switz. | D10 | 13 |
| Mannford, Ok., U.S. | C10 | 116 |
| Mannheim, Ger. | F8 | 10 |
| Manni, China | C12 | 44 |
| Manning, Ia., U.S. | J12 | 118 |
| Manning, N.D., U.S. | D5 | 118 |
| Manning, S.C., U.S. | F6 | 112 |
| Mannington, W.V., U.S. | H6 | 108 |
| Mannum, Austl. | J3 | 70 |
| Mannville, Ab., Can. | D23 | 102 |
| Mano, stm., Afr. | H4 | 64 |
| Manoa, Bol. | C9 | 82 |
| Manoel Ribas, Braz. | C13 | 80 |
| Manokotak, Ak., U.S. | G15 | 100 |
| Manombo, Madag. | s20 | 67b |
| Manono, D.R.C. | C5 | 58 |
| Manor, Sk., Can. | I12 | 104 |
| Manor, Tx., U.S. | I9 | 116 |
| Manosque, Fr. | I12 | 14 |
| Manouane, stm., P.Q., Can. | B3 | 106 |
| Manouane, Lac, l., P.Q., Can. | B3 | 106 |
| Manouanis, stm., P.Q., Can. | A3 | 106 |
| Manouanis, Lac, l., P.Q., Can. | B3 | 106 |
| Manp'o, N. Kor. | B14 | 32 |
| Manresa, Spain | D13 | 16 |
| Mānsa, India | F6 | 44 |
| Mansa, Zam. | D5 | 58 |
| Mansel Island, i., N.T., Can. | D17 | 96 |
| Mansfield, Ar., U.S. | G2 | 114 |
| Mansfield, Austl. | K7 | 70 |
| Mansfield, Ga., U.S. | F3 | 112 |
| Mansfield, Il., U.S. | B8 | 114 |
| Mansfield, La., U.S. | J3 | 114 |
| Mansfield, Ma., U.S. | E15 | 108 |
| Mansfield, Mo., U.S. | E4 | 114 |
| Mansfield, Oh., U.S. | G4 | 108 |
| Mansfield, Pa., U.S. | F9 | 108 |
| Mansfield, Tx., U.S. | G9 | 116 |
| Mansfield, Mount, mtn., Vt., U.S. | C14 | 108 |
| Mansión, C.R. | G9 | 92 |
| Mansle, Fr. | G7 | 14 |
| Manso, stm., Braz. | F13 | 82 |
| Manson, Ia., U.S. | I13 | 118 |
| Manson, stm., B.C., Can. | B11 | 102 |
| Manson Creek, B.C., Can. | B10 | 102 |
| Mansura see Al-Manşūrah, Egypt | B6 | 60 |
| Mansura, La., U.S. | K4 | 114 |
| Manta, Ec. | H2 | 84 |
| Manta, Bahía de, b., Ec. | H2 | 84 |
| Mantagao, stm., Mb., Can. | G17 | 104 |
| Mantaro, stm., Peru | E4 | 82 |
| Manteca, Ca., U.S. | G4 | 124 |
| Mantecal, Ven. | D8 | 84 |
| Manteno, Il., U.S. | I8 | 110 |
| Manteo, N.C., U.S. | D11 | 112 |
| Mantes-la-Jolie, Fr. | D8 | 14 |
| Manti, Ut., U.S. | E5 | 120 |
| Mantiqueira, Serra da, mts., Braz. | G6 | 79 |
| Manton, Mi., U.S. | F10 | 110 |
| Mantorville, Mn., U.S. | F3 | 110 |
| Mantos Blancos, Chile | B3 | 80 |
| Mantova, Italy | D5 | 18 |
| Mantua, Cuba | C2 | 94 |
| Mantua see Mantova, Italy | D5 | 18 |
| Mantua, Oh., U.S. | F5 | 108 |
| Manturovo, Russia | C27 | 22 |
| Mäntyharju, Fin. | K20 | 6 |
| Manu, Peru | E6 | 82 |
| Manú, stm., Peru | E6 | 82 |
| Manua Islands, is., Am. Sam. | J23 | 126 |
| Manuel, Mex. | F10 | 90 |
| Manuel Antonio, Parque Nacional, C.R. | H10 | 92 |
| Manuel Benavides, Mex. | C8 | 90 |
| Manuel Derqui, Arg. | D9 | 80 |
| Manuel Urbano, Braz. | C7 | 82 |
| Manuripe (Mamuripi), stm., S.A. | D8 | 82 |
| Manuripi, stm., Bol. | E8 | 82 |
| Manus Island, i., Pap. N. Gui. | k16 | 68a |
| Manvel, N.D., U.S. | C10 | 118 |
| Many, La., U.S. | K3 | 114 |
| Manyana, Bots. | D5 | 66 |
| Manyara, Lake, l., Tan. | B7 | 58 |
| Manyberries, Ab., Can. | I4 | 104 |
| Manyč, stm., Russia | H6 | 26 |
| Many Island Lake, l., Can. | H4 | 104 |
| Manzanares, Spain | F8 | 16 |
| Manzanillo, Cuba | D6 | 94 |
| Manzanillo, Mex. | H7 | 90 |
| Manzanillo, Punta, c., Pan. | H15 | 92 |
| Manzanillo Bay, b., N.A. | E9 | 94 |
| Manzano, N.M., U.S. | J10 | 120 |
| Manzanola, Co., U.S. | M4 | 118 |
| Manzano Peak, mtn., N.M., U.S. | J10 | 120 |
| Manzhouli, China | B10 | 30 |
| Manzini, Swaz. | F10 | 66 |
| Mao, Chad | F4 | 56 |
| Mao, Dom. Rep. | E9 | 94 |
| Maó, Spain | F16 | 16 |
| Maoke, Pegunungan, mts., Indon. | F10 | 38 |
| Maoming, China | G9 | 30 |
| Maouri, Dallol, val., Niger | E11 | 64 |
| Mapari, stm., Braz. | I9 | 84 |
| Mapastepec, Mex. | J13 | 90 |
| Mapia, Kepulauan, is., Indon. | E9 | 38 |
| Mapimí, Mex. | E8 | 90 |
| Mapimí, Bolsón de, des., Mex. | D8 | 90 |
| Maping, China | D2 | 34 |
| Mapinhane, Moz. | D12 | 66 |
| Mapire, Ven. | D10 | 84 |
| Mapiri, Bol. | F7 | 82 |
| Mapiri, stm., Bol. | D8 | 82 |
| Mapixari, Ilha, i., Braz. | I10 | 84 |
| Maple, stm., Ia., U.S. | I12 | 118 |
| Maple, stm., Mi., U.S. | G11 | 110 |
| Maple, stm., Mn., U.S. | G1 | 110 |
| Maple, stm., N.D., U.S. | E10 | 118 |
| Maple, stm., U.S. | F9 | 118 |
| Maple Creek, Sk., Can. | I5 | 104 |
| Maple Lake, Mn., U.S. | E1 | 110 |
| Maple Mount, Ky., U.S. | E9 | 114 |
| Maplesville, Al., U.S. | J10 | 114 |
| Mapleton, Ia., U.S. | I12 | 118 |
| Mapleton, Mn., U.S. | G2 | 110 |
| Mapleton, Or., U.S. | F2 | 122 |
| Mapleton, Ut., U.S. | D5 | 120 |
| Mapuera, stm., Braz. | H14 | 84 |
| Mapulanguene, Moz. | E11 | 66 |
| Maputo, Moz. | E11 | 66 |
| Maputo, stm., Afr. | F11 | 66 |
| Maqna, Sau. Ar. | G3 | 48 |
| Maquela do Zombo, Ang. | C3 | 58 |
| Maquereau, Pointe au, c., P.Q., Can. | D9 | 106 |
| Maquilaú, stm., Braz. | G11 | 84 |
| Maquinchao, Arg. | E3 | 78 |
| Maquoketa, Ia., U.S. | H5 | 110 |
| Maquoketa, stm., Ia., U.S. | H5 | 110 |
| Mar, Serra do, clf, Braz. | C14 | 80 |
| Mara, Peru | F5 | 82 |
| Mara, stm., Afr. | B6 | 58 |
| Maraã, Braz. | H10 | 84 |
| Marabá, Braz. | E9 | 76 |
| Maracá, Ilha de, i., Braz. | F12 | 84 |
| Maracaí, Braz. | G3 | 79 |
| Maracaibo, Ven. | B7 | 84 |
| Maracaibo, Lago de, l., Ven. | C7 | 84 |
| Maracaju, Braz. | F1 | 79 |
| Maracaju, Serra de, hills, S.A. | F1 | 79 |
| Maracanã, stm., Braz. | C12 | 82 |
| Maracás, Braz. | B8 | 79 |
| Maracay, Ven. | B9 | 84 |
| Marādah, Libya | C4 | 56 |
| Maradi, Niger | E13 | 64 |
| Maradi, Goulbin, stm., Afr. | E13 | 64 |
| Marāgheh, Iran | C9 | 48 |
| Maragogipe, Braz. | B9 | 79 |
| Marahuaca, Cerro, mtn., Ven. | F10 | 84 |
| Maraiche Lake, l., Sk., Can. | D12 | 104 |
| Marais des Cygnes, stm., U.S. | D1 | 114 |
| Marajó, Baía de, b., Braz. | D9 | 76 |
| Marajó, Ilha de, i., Braz. | D9 | 76 |
| Marakabei, Leso. | G9 | 66 |
| Maralal, Kenya | A7 | 58 |
| Maralaleng, Bots. | E6 | 66 |
| Marampa, S.L. | G3 | 64 |
| Maramureş, co., Rom. | B8 | 20 |
| Maran, Malay. | M7 | 40 |
| Marana, Az., U.S. | L5 | 120 |
| Marand, Iran | B8 | 48 |
| Marangani, Peru | F6 | 82 |
| Maranguape, Braz. | D11 | 76 |
| Maranhão, stm., Braz. | C4 | 79 |
| Maranoa, stm., Austl. | E9 | 68 |
| Marañón, stm., Peru | D3 | 76 |
| Marapanim, Braz. | D9 | 76 |
| Marapi, stm., Braz. | G14 | 84 |
| Maras, Peru | E5 | 82 |
| Marathon, Austl. | C5 | 70 |
| Marathón, Grc. | K7 | 20 |
| Marathon, N.Y., U.S. | E10 | 108 |
| Marathon, On., Can. | B9 | 110 |
| Marathon, Tx., U.S. | I3 | 116 |
| Marathon, Wi., U.S. | F6 | 110 |
| Maraú, Braz. | C9 | 79 |
| Marau, Braz. | E12 | 80 |
| Marauiá, stm., Braz. | H10 | 84 |
| Maravilha, Braz. | D12 | 80 |
| Maravillas, Mex. | D7 | 90 |
| Marawī, Sudan | H6 | 60 |
| Marayes, Arg. | F5 | 80 |
| Marbach, Switz. | E8 | 13 |
| Marbella, Spain | I7 | 16 |
| Marble, Mn., U.S. | C2 | 110 |
| Marble, N.C., U.S. | D3 | 112 |
| Marble Bar, Austl. | D3 | 68 |
| Marble Canyon, val., Az., U.S. | H5 | 120 |
| Marble Falls, Tx., U.S. | I8 | 116 |
| Marble Hall, S. Afr. | E9 | 66 |
| Marblehead, Oh., U.S. | F4 | 108 |
| Marble Hill, Mo., U.S. | E7 | 114 |
| Marble Rock, Ia., U.S. | H3 | 110 |
| Marburg, Ger. | E8 | 10 |
| Marcala, Hond. | C6 | 92 |
| Marcali, Hung. | I17 | 10 |
| Marcaria, Italy | D5 | 18 |
| Marceau, Lac, l., P.Q., Can. | A7 | 106 |
| Marcelin, Sk., Can. | F8 | 104 |
| Marceline, Mo., U.S. | C4 | 114 |
| Marcelino Ramos, Braz. | D13 | 80 |
| Marcellus, Mi., U.S. | H10 | 110 |
| March (Morava), stm., Eur. | G16 | 10 |
| Marcha, stm., Russia | E15 | 28 |
| Marche, prov., Italy | F8 | 18 |
| Marche, hist. reg., Fr. | F8 | 14 |
| Marche-en-Famenne, Bel. | H7 | 12 |
| Marchegg, Aus. | G16 | 10 |
| Marchena, Spain | H6 | 16 |
| Mar Chiquita, Laguna, b., Arg. | I10 | 80 |
| Mar Chiquita, Laguna, l., Arg. | F7 | 80 |
| Marcigny, Fr. | F11 | 14 |
| Marcola, Or., U.S. | F3 | 122 |
| Marcona, Peru | F4 | 82 |
| Marcos Juárez, Arg. | G7 | 80 |
| Marcos Paz, Arg. | H9 | 80 |
| Marcus, Ia., U.S. | I12 | 118 |
| Marcus Baker, Mount, mtn., Ak., U.S. | F21 | 100 |
| Marcy, Mount, mtn., N.Y., U.S. | C13 | 108 |
| Mardān, Pak. | C5 | 44 |
| Mardarivka, Ukr. | B13 | 20 |
| Mar del Plata, Arg. | J10 | 80 |
| Mardin, Tur. | C6 | 48 |
| Marea de Portillo, Cuba | E6 | 94 |
| Marechal Cândido Rondon, Braz. | C11 | 80 |
| Marechal Taumaturgo, Braz. | C5 | 82 |
| Mareeba, Austl. | A6 | 70 |
| Marengo, Ia., U.S. | I3 | 110 |
| Marengo, Il., U.S. | H7 | 110 |
| Marengo, In., U.S. | D10 | 114 |
| Marenisco, Mi., U.S. | D6 | 110 |
| Marfa, Tx., U.S. | I2 | 116 |
| Margaree, N.S., Can. | F12 | 106 |
| Margaree Harbour, N.S., Can. | F12 | 106 |
| Margaret Bay, B.C., Can. | F7 | 102 |
| Margaretville, N.Y., U.S. | E12 | 108 |
| Margarita, Isla de, i., Ven. | B10 | 84 |
| Margarita Belén, Arg. | D9 | 80 |
| Margate, Eng., U.K. | J15 | 8 |
| Margate, Fl., U.S. | M6 | 112 |
| Margate, S. Afr. | H10 | 66 |
| Margate City, N.J., U.S. | H12 | 108 |
| Margecany, Slvk. | G21 | 10 |
| Margherita Peak, mtn., Afr. | A5 | 58 |
| Marghī, Afg. | C2 | 44 |
| Margilan, Uzb. | I12 | 26 |
| Margos, Peru | D3 | 82 |
| Margot Lake, l., On., Can. | F21 | 104 |
| Mārgow, Dasht-e, des., Afg. | F17 | 48 |
| Marguerite Bay, b., Ant. | B12 | 73 |
| Marhanets', Ukr. | H4 | 26 |
| María Cleofas, Isla, i., Mex. | G6 | 90 |
| María Elena, Chile | B4 | 80 |
| Maria Gail, Aus. | I13 | 10 |
| María Ignacia (Vela), Arg. | I9 | 80 |
| Maria Island, i., Austl. | N8 | 70 |
| María la Baja, Col. | C5 | 84 |
| María Madre, Isla, i., Mex. | G6 | 90 |
| María Magdalena, Isla, i., Mex. | G6 | 90 |
| Mariana, Braz. | F7 | 79 |
| Mariana Islands, is., Oc. | G18 | 126 |
| Mariana Trench | G18 | 126 |
| Mariāni, India | G16 | 44 |
| Marian Lake, l., N.T., Can. | D9 | 96 |
| Marianna, Ar., U.S. | H6 | 114 |
| Marianna, Fl., U.S. | I1 | 112 |
| Mariano I. Loza, Arg. | E9 | 80 |
| Mariano Moreno, Arg. | J3 | 80 |
| Mariánské Lázně, Czech Rep. | F12 | 10 |
| Marias, stm., Mt., U.S. | B15 | 122 |
| Marías, Islas, is., Mex. | G6 | 90 |
| Marias Pass, Mt., U.S. | B12 | 122 |
| María Teresa, Arg. | H8 | 80 |
| Mariato, Punta, c., Pan. | D2 | 84 |
| Mā'rib, Yemen | G4 | 47 |
| Maribor, Slvn. | C10 | 18 |
| Marica (Évros) (Meriç), stm., Eur. | H10 | 20 |
| Marico, stm., Afr. | E8 | 66 |
| Maricopa, Az., U.S. | K4 | 120 |
| Maricopa, Ca., U.S. | I6 | 124 |
| Maricunga, Salar de, pl., Chile | D4 | 80 |
| Marié, stm., Braz. | H9 | 84 |
| Marie Byrd Land, reg., Ant. | C10 | 73 |
| Marie-Galante, i., Guad. | G14 | 94 |
| Mariehamn, Fin. | K16 | 6 |
| Mari El see Marij El, state, Russia | F7 | 26 |
| Marie Lake, l., Ab., Can. | D4 | 104 |
| Marienbad see Mariánské Lázně, Czech Rep. | F12 | 10 |
| Marienburg see Malbork, Pol. | A19 | 10 |
| Mariental, Nmb. | E3 | 66 |
| Marienville, Pa., U.S. | F7 | 108 |
| Maries, stm., Mo., U.S. | D4 | 114 |
| Mariestad, Swe. | L13 | 6 |
| Marieta, stm., Ven. | E9 | 84 |
| Marietta, Ga., U.S. | F2 | 112 |
| Marietta, Mn., U.S. | F11 | 118 |
| Marietta, Oh., U.S. | H5 | 108 |
| Marietta, Ok., U.S. | F9 | 116 |
| Marieville, P.Q., Can. | B13 | 108 |
| Mariga, stm., Nig. | F13 | 64 |
| Marignane, Fr. | I12 | 14 |
| Marigot, Dom. | G14 | 94 |
| Marigot, Guad. | E13 | 94 |
| Mariinsk, Russia | F9 | 28 |
| Marijampole, Lith. | G6 | 22 |
| Marij El, state, Russia | F7 | 26 |
| Marikana, S. Afr. | E8 | 66 |
| Marília, Braz. | G4 | 79 |
| Marimari, stm., Braz. | J13 | 84 |
| Marimba, Ang. | C3 | 58 |
| Marín, Spain | C3 | 16 |
| Marina di Ravenna, Italy | E7 | 18 |
| Marina Fall, wtfl, Guy. | E13 | 84 |
| Mar'ina Horka, Bela. | H11 | 22 |
| Marine City, Mi., U.S. | H13 | 110 |
| Marinette, Wi., U.S. | E8 | 110 |
| Maringá, Braz. | G3 | 79 |
| Maringouin, La., U.S. | L5 | 114 |
| Marínguè, Moz. | A12 | 66 |
| Marion, Al., U.S. | J9 | 114 |
| Marion, Ar., U.S. | G6 | 114 |
| Marion, Ia., U.S. | H4 | 110 |
| Marion, Il., U.S. | E8 | 114 |
| Marion, In., U.S. | B11 | 114 |
| Marion, Ks., U.S. | M10 | 118 |
| Marion, Ky., U.S. | E8 | 114 |
| Marion, La., U.S. | J4 | 114 |
| Marion, Mi., U.S. | F10 | 110 |
| Marion, Ms., U.S. | J8 | 114 |
| Marion, N.C., U.S. | D4 | 112 |
| Marion, N.D., U.S. | E9 | 118 |
| Marion, Oh., U.S. | G3 | 108 |
| Marion, S.C., U.S. | E7 | 112 |
| Marion, S.D., U.S. | H10 | 118 |
| Marion, Va., U.S. | C5 | 112 |
| Marion, Wi., U.S. | F7 | 110 |
| Marion, Lake, res., S.C., U.S. | F6 | 112 |
| Marion Junction, Al., U.S. | J9 | 114 |
| Marion Lake, res., Ks., U.S. | M10 | 118 |
| Marion Reef, rf., Austl. | B10 | 70 |
| Marionville, Mo., U.S. | E3 | 114 |
| Mariópolis, Braz. | D12 | 80 |
| Maripa, Ven. | D10 | 84 |
| Mariposa, Ca., U.S. | G6 | 124 |
| Mariquita, Col. | E5 | 84 |
| Mariscal Estigarribia, Para. | B8 | 80 |
| Marissa, Il., U.S. | D7 | 114 |
| Maritime Alps, mts., Eur. | H14 | 14 |
| Maritime Atlas see Atlas Tellien, mts., Alg. | C11 | 62 |
| Mariupol' (Ždanov), Ukr. | H5 | 26 |
| Mariusa, Caño, mth., Ven. | C12 | 84 |
| Marīvān, Iran | D9 | 48 |
| Märjamaa, Est. | C7 | 22 |
| Marjinsko, Russia | C11 | 22 |

| Name | Map Ref. | Page |
|---|---|---|
| Marka, Som. | H9 | 56 |
| Markala, Mali | E6 | 64 |
| Markdale, On., Can. | F15 | 110 |
| Marked Tree, Ar., U.S. | G7 | 114 |
| Markesan, Wi., U.S. | G7 | 110 |
| Markham, Tx., U.S. | K10 | 116 |
| Markham, On., Can. | G16 | 110 |
| Markham, Mount, mtn., Ant. | D8 | 73 |
| Markham Bay, b., N.T., Can. | D18 | 96 |
| Markle, In., U.S. | B11 | 114 |
| Markleeville, Ca., U.S. | F6 | 124 |
| Markovo, Russia | D23 | 22 |
| Markovo, Russia | E26 | 28 |
| Marks, Ms., U.S. | H6 | 114 |
| Marks, Russia | G7 | 26 |
| Marksville, La., U.S. | K4 | 114 |
| Marktheidenfeld, Ger. | F9 | 10 |
| Marktredwitz, Ger. | E12 | 10 |
| Marka, Som. | H9 | 56 |
| Marka, Sudan | L2 | 60 |
| Marlboro, Ab., Can. | D18 | 102 |
| Marlboro, N.Y., U.S. | F13 | 108 |
| Marlborough, Eng., U.K. | J12 | 8 |
| Marlborough, Guy. | D13 | 84 |
| Marlborough, Ma., U.S. | E15 | 108 |
| Marle, Fr. | C10 | 14 |
| Marlette, Mi., U.S. | G12 | 110 |
| Marlin, Tx., U.S. | H10 | 116 |
| Marlinton, W.V., U.S. | I6 | 108 |
| Marlow, Ok., U.S. | E9 | 116 |
| Marmaduke, Ar., U.S. | F6 | 114 |
| Marmande, Fr. | H7 | 14 |
| Marmara Denizi (Sea of Marmara), Tur. | I12 | 20 |
| Marmara Ereğlisi, Tur. | I11 | 20 |
| Marmaris, Tur. | M12 | 20 |
| Marmarth, N.D., U.S. | E4 | 118 |
| Marmaton, stm., U.S. | E2 | 114 |
| Marmelos, Braz. | B11 | 82 |
| Marmelos, Rio dos, stm., Braz. | B11 | 82 |
| Marmet, W.V., U.S. | I5 | 108 |
| Marmora, On., Can. | F18 | 110 |
| Mar Muerto, Laguna, b., Mex. | I12 | 90 |
| Marnay, Fr. | E12 | 14 |
| Marne, Mi., U.S. | G10 | 110 |
| Marne, dept., Fr. | D11 | 14 |
| Marne, stm., Fr. | C10 | 14 |
| Marne au Rhin, Canal de la, Fr. | D13 | 14 |
| Maroa, Il., U.S. | B8 | 114 |
| Maroa, Ven. | F9 | 84 |
| Maroala, Madag. | o22 | 67b |
| Maroantsetra, Madag. | o23 | 67b |
| Maroelaboom, Nmb. | B4 | 66 |
| Marolambo, Madag. | r23 | 67b |
| Maromme, Fr. | C8 | 14 |
| Maromokotro, mtn., Madag. | o23 | 67b |
| Marondera, Zimb. | B10 | 66 |
| Maroni, stm., S.A. | C8 | 76 |
| Maros (Mureş), stm., Eur. | C4 | 20 |
| Maroseranana, Madag. | q23 | 67b |
| Maroua, Cam. | F9 | 54 |
| Marovato, Madag. | o23 | 67b |
| Marovoay, Madag. | p22 | 67b |
| Marquand, Mo., U.S. | E6 | 114 |
| Marquesas Islands see Marquises, Îles, is., Fr. Poly. | I26 | 126 |
| Marquesas Keys, is., Fl., U.S. | O4 | 112 |
| Marquette, Ks., U.S. | M10 | 118 |
| Marquette, Mi., U.S. | D8 | 110 |
| Marquise, Fr. | B8 | 14 |
| Marquises, Îles (Marquesas Islands), is., Fr. Poly. | I26 | 126 |
| Marrah, Jabal, mtn., Sudan | K3 | 60 |
| Marrakech, Mor. | E6 | 62 |
| Marrawah, Austl. | M6 | 70 |
| Marree, Austl. | G3 | 70 |
| Marrero, La., U.S. | M6 | 114 |
| Marromeu, Moz. | B12 | 66 |
| Mars, Pa., U.S. | G6 | 108 |
| Marsá al-Burayqah, Libya | B4 | 56 |
| Marsabit, Kenya | H8 | 56 |
| Marsala, Italy | L7 | 18 |
| Marsā Matrūḥ, Egypt | B4 | 60 |
| Marsden, Austl. | I7 | 70 |
| Marseille, Fr. | I12 | 14 |
| Marseille-en-Beauvaisis, Fr. | C8 | 14 |
| Marseilles, Il., U.S. | I7 | 110 |
| Marshall, Ar., U.S. | G4 | 114 |
| Marshall, Il., U.S. | C9 | 114 |
| Marshall, Lib. | H4 | 64 |
| Marshall, Mi., U.S. | H11 | 110 |
| Marshall, Mn., U.S. | G12 | 118 |
| Marshall, Mo., U.S. | C4 | 114 |
| Marshall, N.C., U.S. | D4 | 112 |
| Marshall, Tx., U.S. | J2 | 114 |
| Marshall, Va., U.S. | I9 | 108 |
| Marshall, N.C., U.S. | D4 | 112 |
| Marshall Islands, ctry., Oc. | H20 | 126 |
| Marshalltown, Ia., U.S. | H3 | 110 |
| Marshallville, Ga., U.S. | G3 | 112 |
| Marshfield, Mo., U.S. | E4 | 114 |
| Marshfield, Wi., U.S. | F5 | 110 |
| Marsh Harbour, Bah. | A6 | 94 |
| Mars Hill, N.C., U.S. | D4 | 112 |
| Marsh Island, i., La., U.S. | M5 | 114 |
| Marsh Lake, l., Yk., Can. | F27 | 100 |
| Marsh Peak, mtn., Ut., U.S. | D7 | 120 |
| Marshville, N.C., U.S. | E6 | 112 |
| Marsing, Id., U.S. | G9 | 122 |
| Mart, Tx., U.S. | H10 | 116 |
| Martaban, Myan. | F4 | 40 |
| Martaban, Gulf of, b., Myan. | F4 | 40 |
| Martapura, Indon. | F5 | 38 |
| Marten Mountain, mtn., Ab., Can. | B20 | 102 |
| Marne R. Gómez, Presa, res., Mex. | D10 | 90 |
| Martha's Vineyard, i., Ma., U.S. | F16 | 108 |
| Martí, Cuba | D6 | 94 |
| Martigny, Switz. | F7 | 13 |
| Martigues, Fr. | I12 | 14 |
| Martil, Mor. | E7 | 62 |
| Martin, Ky., U.S. | B4 | 112 |
| Martin, Mi., U.S. | H10 | 110 |
| Martin, N.D., U.S. | D7 | 118 |
| Martin, S.D., U.S. | H6 | 118 |
| Martin, Slvk. | F18 | 10 |
| Martin, Tn., U.S. | F8 | 114 |
| Martina Franca, Italy | I12 | 18 |
| Martindale, Tn., U.S. | J9 | 116 |
| Martinez, Ca., U.S. | F3 | 124 |
| Martinez, Ga., U.S. | F4 | 112 |
| Martínez de la Torre, Mex. | G11 | 90 |
| Martinho Campos, Braz. | E6 | 79 |
| Martinique, dep., N.A. | G14 | 94 |
| Martinique Passage, strt., N.A. | | |
| Martin Lake, res., Al., U.S. | J11 | 114 |
| Martinniemi, Fin. | I19 | 6 |
| Martinsberg, Aus. | G15 | 10 |
| Martinsburg, Pa., U.S. | G8 | 108 |
| Martinsburg, W.V., U.S. | H9 | 108 |
| Martins Ferry, Oh., U.S. | G6 | 108 |
| Martinsville, Il., U.S. | C9 | 114 |
| Martinsville, In., U.S. | C10 | 114 |
| Martinsville, Va., U.S. | C7 | 112 |
| Martisovo, Russia | E14 | 22 |
| Martos, Spain | H8 | 16 |
| Martre, Lac la, l., N.T., Can. | K10 | 116 |
| Martti, Fin. | H21 | 6 |
| Maru, Nig. | E13 | 64 |
| Marugame, Japan | M8 | 36 |
| Marula, Ang. | C9 | 66 |
| Marunga, Ang. | A5 | 66 |
| Marungu, mts., D.R.C. | C5 | 58 |
| Maʻrūṭ, Afg. | E2 | 44 |
| Marvejols, Fr. | H10 | 14 |
| Marvell, Ar., U.S. | H6 | 114 |
| Marvine, Mount, mtn., Ut., U.S. | F5 | 120 |
| Marwayne, Ab., Can. | E4 | 104 |
| Mary, Turk. | J10 | 26 |
| Maryborough, Austl. | E10 | 70 |
| Maryborough, Austl. | K5 | 70 |
| Marydale, S. Afr. | G6 | 66 |
| Maryfield, Sk., Can. | I13 | 104 |
| Mary Kathleen, Austl. | C3 | 70 |
| Maryland, state, U.S. | D11 | 108 |
| Maryneal, Tx., U.S. | G6 | 116 |
| Marys, stm., Nv., U.S. | C10 | 124 |
| Marystown, Nf., Can. | E18 | 106 |
| Marysvale, Ut., U.S. | F4 | 120 |
| Marysville, B.C., Can. | H19 | 102 |
| Marysville, Ca., U.S. | E4 | 124 |
| Marysville, Ks., U.S. | L11 | 118 |
| Marysville, Mi., U.S. | H13 | 110 |
| Marysville, N.B., Can. | G7 | 106 |
| Marysville, Oh., U.S. | G3 | 108 |
| Marysville, Pa., U.S. | G10 | 108 |
| Marysville, Wa., U.S. | B3 | 122 |
| Maryville, Mo., U.S. | B2 | 114 |
| Maryville, Tn., U.S. | D3 | 112 |
| Marzagão, Braz. | D4 | 79 |
| Marzo, Punta, c., Col. | D4 | 84 |
| Marzūq, Sahrāʾ, des., Libya | D3 | 56 |
| Masachapa, Nic. | F8 | 92 |
| Masada see Meẕada, Horvot, hist., Isr. | F4 | 50 |
| Masagua, Guat. | C4 | 92 |
| Masai Steppe, plat., Tan. | B7 | 58 |
| Masaka, Ug. | B6 | 58 |
| Masallı, Azer. | B10 | 48 |
| Masan, S. Kor. | H16 | 32 |
| Masasi, Tan. | D7 | 58 |
| Masatepe, Nic. | F8 | 92 |
| Masaya, Nic. | F8 | 92 |
| Masaya, dept., Nic. | E8 | 92 |
| Masbate, Phil. | C7 | 38 |
| Mascarene Islands, is., Afr. | F11 | 58 |
| Mascasín, Arg. | F5 | 80 |
| Mascota, Mex. | G7 | 90 |
| Mascoutah, Il., U.S. | D7 | 114 |
| Masefield, Sk., Can. | I7 | 104 |
| Maseru, Leso. | G8 | 66 |
| Mashaba Mountains, mts., Zimb. | B10 | 66 |
| Mashābih, i., Sau. Ar. | I4 | 48 |
| Mashar, Sudan | M4 | 60 |
| Mashhad, Iran | C15 | 48 |
| Mashīz, Iran | G14 | 48 |
| Māshkēl, Hāmūn-i, l., Asia | G17 | 48 |
| Māshkēl, Rūd-i (Māshkīd), stm., Asia | G17 | 48 |
| Mashra'ur-Raqq, Sudan | M5 | 60 |
| Masi Manimba, D.R.C. | B3 | 58 |
| Maşīrah, Khalīj, b., Oman | E11 | 47 |
| Maşīrah, Jazīrat, i., Oman | C10 | 47 |
| Masjed-e Soleymān, Iran | F10 | 48 |
| Mask, Lough, l., Ire. | H4 | 8 |
| Maska, Nig. | F13 | 64 |
| Maskanah, Syria | C5 | 48 |
| Maskin, Oman | C10 | 47 |
| Maskwa, stm., Ab., Can. | H19 | 104 |
| Masoala, Madag. | o24 | 67b |
| Masoala, Cap, c., Madag. | o24 | 67b |
| Masoala, Presqu'île de, pen., Madag. | o24 | 67b |
| Masoarivo, Madag. | q21 | 67b |
| Masomeloka, Madag. | r23 | 67b |
| Mason, Mi., U.S. | H11 | 110 |
| Mason, Oh., U.S. | H2 | 108 |
| Mason, Tn., U.S. | G7 | 114 |
| Mason, Tx., U.S. | I7 | 116 |
| Mason, W.V., U.S. | H4 | 108 |
| Mason City, Ia., U.S. | G2 | 110 |
| Mason City, Il., U.S. | B7 | 114 |
| Mason City, Ne., U.S. | J8 | 118 |
| Masqaṭ (Muscat), Oman | C11 | 47 |
| Massa, Italy | E5 | 18 |
| Massachusetts, state, U.S. | D12 | 98 |
| Massachusetts Bay, b., Ma., U.S. | E16 | 108 |
| Massafra, Italy | I12 | 18 |
| Massa Marittima, Italy | F5 | 18 |
| Massangena, Moz. | C11 | 66 |
| Massarosa, Italy | F5 | 18 |
| Massena, N.Y., U.S. | C12 | 108 |
| Massenya, Chad | F4 | 56 |
| Masset, B.C., Can. | C2 | 102 |
| Masset Inlet, b., B.C., Can. | D2 | 102 |
| Masseube, Fr. | I7 | 14 |
| Massillon, On., Can. | D13 | 110 |
| Massillon, Oh., U.S. | G5 | 108 |
| Massina, reg., Mali | D7 | 64 |
| Massinga, Moz. | D12 | 66 |
| Massive, Mount, mtn., Co., U.S. | E10 | 120 |
| Maştağa, Azer. | I8 | 26 |
| Masterton, Tx., U.S. | D5 | 116 |
| Masterton, N.Z. | D5 | 72 |
| Mastok, Bela. | H13 | 22 |
| Mastung, Pak. | F2 | 44 |
| Mastūrah, Sau. Ar. | C1 | 47 |
| Masty, Bela. | H7 | 22 |
| Masuda, Japan | M6 | 36 |
| Masvingo, Zimb. | C10 | 66 |
| Matachewan, On., Can. | C15 | 110 |
| Matacuni, stm., Ven. | F10 | 84 |
| Mata de São João, Braz. | B9 | 79 |
| Matadi, D.R.C. | C2 | 58 |
| Matador, Tx., U.S. | E6 | 116 |
| Matagalpa, Nic. | E9 | 92 |
| Matagalpa, dept., Nic. | E9 | 92 |
| Matagorda, P.Q., Can. | G17 | 96 |
| Matagorda, Tx., U.S. | K11 | 116 |
| Matagorda Bay, b., Tx., U.S. | K10 | 116 |
| Matagorda Island, i., Tx., U.S. | K10 | 116 |
| Matale, Sri L. | I6 | 46 |
| Matam, Sen. | D3 | 64 |
| Matamata, Cerro, mtn., C.R. | H11 | 92 |
| Matamoras, Pa., U.S. | F12 | 108 |
| Matamoros, Mex. | E11 | 90 |
| Matamoros, Mex. | E8 | 90 |
| Matane, P.Q., Can. | D6 | 106 |
| Matanzas, Cuba | C4 | 94 |
| Matanzas, Mex. | G9 | 90 |
| Matapalo, Cabo, c., C.R. | I11 | 92 |
| Matape, stm., Mex. | C4 | 90 |
| Matapédia, P.Q., Can. | E7 | 106 |
| Matapédia, Lac, l., P.Q., Can. | D6 | 106 |
| Mataquito, stm., Chile | H3 | 80 |
| Matará, Peru | B2 | 82 |
| Matara, Sri L. | J6 | 46 |
| Mataram, Indon. | G6 | 38 |
| Mataránga, Peru | G5 | 82 |
| Matatiele, S. Afr. | H9 | 66 |
| Mataurá, stm., Braz. | B11 | 82 |
| Mateare, Nic. | E8 | 92 |
| Matehuala, Mex. | F9 | 90 |
| Matera, Italy | I11 | 18 |
| Mátészalka, Hung. | H22 | 10 |
| Mateur, Tun. | L4 | 18 |
| Matewan, W.V., U.S. | I15 | 104 |
| Mather, Mb., Can. | I15 | 104 |
| Mather, Pa., U.S. | H6 | 108 |
| Matheson Island, Mb., Can. | G18 | 104 |
| Mathews, Va., U.S. | B10 | 112 |
| Mathis, Tx., U.S. | K9 | 116 |
| Mathura, India | G7 | 44 |
| Matiacoali, Burkina | E10 | 64 |
| Matías Barbosa, Braz. | F7 | 79 |
| Matías Romero, Mex. | I12 | 90 |
| Matícora, stm., Ven. | B7 | 84 |
| Matiguás, Nic. | E9 | 92 |
| Matipó, Braz. | F7 | 79 |
| Matiyure, stm., Ven. | D8 | 84 |
| Matlamanyane, Bots. | B7 | 66 |
| M'atlevo, Russia | G18 | 22 |
| Matmata, Tun. | D15 | 62 |
| Mato, stm., Ven. | D10 | 84 |
| Matočkin Šar, proliv, strt., Russia | C8 | 26 |
| Mato Grosso, state, Braz. | D13 | 82 |
| Mato Grosso, Planalto do, plat., Braz. | G7 | 76 |
| Matonipi, stm., P.Q., Can. | A4 | 106 |
| Matopo Hills, hills, Zimb. | C9 | 66 |
| Matos, stm., Bol. | F9 | 82 |
| Matosinhos, Port. | D3 | 16 |
| Matou, Tai. | L9 | 34 |
| Matoury, Fr. Gu. | C8 | 76 |
| Matouying, China | D6 | 32 |
| Mato Verde, Braz. | C7 | 79 |
| Matozinhos, Braz. | E6 | 79 |
| Matrah, Oman | C11 | 47 |
| Matrei in Osttirol, Aus. | H12 | 10 |
| Matru, S.L. | H3 | 64 |
| Matsapha, Swaz. | F10 | 66 |
| Matsudo, Japan | L14 | 36 |
| Matsue, Japan | L8 | 36 |
| Matsumae, Japan | F15 | 36 |
| Matsumoto, Japan | K12 | 36 |
| Matsu Tao, i., Tai. | I8 | 34 |
| Matsuyama, Japan | M7 | 36 |
| Mattagami, stm., On., Can. | F16 | 96 |
| Mattagami Heights, On., Can. | B14 | 110 |
| Mattawa, On., Can. | D17 | 110 |
| Mattawa, Wa., U.S. | D6 | 122 |
| Mattawamkeag, Me., U.S. | B18 | 108 |
| Matterhorn, Aus. | H16 | 10 |
| Matterhorn, mtn., Nv., U.S. | C10 | 124 |
| Mattersburg, Aus. | H16 | 10 |
| Matthews Ridge, Guy. | D12 | 84 |
| Mattituck, N.Y., U.S. | D10 | 108 |
| Mattoon, Il., U.S. | C8 | 114 |
| Mattoon, Wi., U.S. | E6 | 110 |
| Mattydale, N.Y., U.S. | D10 | 108 |
| Matubara, Moz. | E11 | 66 |
| Matucana, Peru | D3 | 82 |
| Matuku, i., Fiji | q19 | 125a |
| Maturín, Ven. | C11 | 84 |
| Maturuca, Russia | B20 | 22 |
| Matutína, Braz. | E6 | 79 |
| Maúa, Moz. | D7 | 58 |
| Maubeuge, Fr. | B10 | 14 |
| Maud, Ok., U.S. | D10 | 116 |
| Maud, Tx., U.S. | I2 | 114 |
| Maude, Austl. | J6 | 70 |
| Maués, Braz. | I14 | 84 |
| Maués, stm., Braz. | I14 | 84 |
| Maui, i., Hi., U.S. | q17 | 125a |
| Mauldin, S.C., U.S. | E4 | 112 |
| Maule, prov., Chile | H2 | 80 |
| Maule, stm., Chile | H2 | 80 |
| Maule, Laguna del, l., Chile | I3 | 80 |
| Mauléon, Fr. | F6 | 14 |
| Maumee, Oh., U.S. | F3 | 108 |
| Maumee, stm., U.S. | F2 | 108 |
| Maumere, Indon. | G7 | 38 |
| Maun, Bots. | C6 | 66 |
| Maʻuna Rea, vol., Hi., U.S. | r18 | 125a |
| Maunaloa, Hi., U.S. | p16 | 125a |
| Mauna Loa, vol., Hi., U.S. | r18 | 125a |
| Maunath Bhanjan, India | H10 | 44 |
| Maunatlala, Bots. | D8 | 66 |
| Maungdaw, Myan. | D2 | 40 |
| Maunoir, Lac, l., N.T., Can. | C32 | 100 |
| Maupin, Or., U.S. | E4 | 122 |
| Mau Rānīpur, India | H8 | 44 |
| Maure-de-Bretagne, Fr. | E5 | 14 |
| Maurepas, Lake, l., La., U.S. | L6 | 114 |
| Mauri, stm., Bol. | G7 | 82 |
| Mauriac, Fr. | G9 | 14 |
| Mauritania (Mauritanie), ctry., Afr. | D4 | 54 |
| Mauritius, ctry., Afr. | F11 | 58 |
| Mauritius, i., Mrts. | v18 | 67c |
| Mauron, Fr. | D4 | 14 |
| Maury Channel, strt., N.T., Can. | A13 | 96 |
| Mauston, Wi., U.S. | G5 | 110 |
| Mauterndorf, Aus. | H13 | 10 |
| Mauthausen, Aus. | G14 | 10 |
| Mauvezin, Fr. | I7 | 14 |
| Mavaca, stm., Ven. | F10 | 84 |
| Maverick, Az., U.S. | K7 | 120 |
| Mavinga, Ang. | E4 | 58 |
| Mawchi, Myan. | E4 | 40 |
| Maw-daung Pass, Asia | I5 | 40 |
| Mawdesley Lake, l., Mb., Can. | D14 | 104 |
| Mawkhi, Myan. | F5 | 40 |
| Mawlaik, Myan. | C3 | 40 |
| Mawlamyine (Moulmein), Myan. | F4 | 40 |
| Maw Taung, mtn., Asia | I5 | 40 |
| Max, N.D., U.S. | D5 | 118 |
| Maxcanú, Mex. | G15 | 90 |
| Maxixe, Moz. | D12 | 66 |
| Maxton, N.C., U.S. | E7 | 112 |
| Maxwell, Ca., U.S. | E3 | 124 |
| Maxwell, Ia., U.S. | I2 | 110 |
| Maxwell, Ne., U.S. | J6 | 118 |
| Maxwell, N.M., U.S. | C2 | 116 |
| Maxwell Bay, b., N.T., Can. | B15 | 96 |
| May, Tx., U.S. | H8 | 116 |
| May, stm., Ak., U.S. | F20 | 100 |
| May, Cape, pen., N.J., U.S. | I12 | 108 |
| May, Mount, mtn., Ab., Can. | C15 | 102 |
| Mayagua, i., Bah. | C8 | 94 |
| Mayaguana, i., Bah. | C8 | 94 |
| Mayaguana Passage, strt., Bah. | C8 | 94 |
| Mayagüez, P.R. | E11 | 94 |
| Mayaky, Ukr. | C14 | 20 |
| Mayales, Punta, c., Nic. | F9 | 92 |
| Mayapan, hist., Mex. | G15 | 90 |
| Mayari, Cuba | D7 | 94 |
| Maya Mountains, mts., N.A. | I15 | 90 |
| Maybeury, W.V., U.S. | B5 | 112 |
| Maybole, Scot., U.K. | F9 | 8 |
| Mayen, Ger. | M13 | 8 |
| Mayenne, Fr. | D6 | 14 |
| Mayenne, dept., Fr. | D6 | 14 |
| Mayer, Az., U.S. | J4 | 120 |
| Mayersville, Ms., U.S. | J6 | 114 |
| Mayerthorpe, Ab., Can. | D19 | 102 |
| Mayfield, Ky., U.S. | E8 | 114 |
| Mayfield, Ut., U.S. | E5 | 120 |
| Mayflower, Ar., U.S. | H4 | 114 |
| May Inlet, b., N.T., Can. | A12 | 96 |
| May Jirgui, Niger | E14 | 64 |
| Maymont, Sk., Can. | F7 | 104 |
| Maymyo, Myan. | C4 | 40 |
| Maynard, Ia., U.S. | H4 | 110 |
| Maynardville, Tn., U.S. | C3 | 112 |
| Mayne, stm., Austl. | D4 | 70 |
| Mayo, Fl., U.S. | I3 | 112 |
| Mayo, Yk., Can. | E27 | 100 |
| Mayo, co., Ire. | H4 | 8 |
| Mayo, stm., Col. | G4 | 84 |
| Mayo, stm., Mex. | D5 | 90 |
| Mayo, stm., Peru | B3 | 82 |
| Mayo Lake, l., Yk., Can. | E27 | 100 |
| Mayodan, N.C., U.S. | C7 | 112 |
| Mayon Volcano, vol., Phil. | o20 | 39b |
| Mayor Buratovich, Arg. | J7 | 80 |
| Mayor Pablo Lagerenza, Para. | H11 | 82 |
| Mayotte, dep., Afr. | D9 | 58 |
| May Pen, Jam. | F6 | 94 |
| Mayrhofen, Aus. | H11 | 10 |
| Mays Landing, N.J., U.S. | H12 | 108 |
| Maysville, Ky., U.S. | I3 | 108 |
| Maysville, Mo., U.S. | C2 | 114 |
| Maysville, N.C., U.S. | E9 | 112 |
| Maysville, Ok., U.S. | E9 | 116 |
| Mayumba, Gabon | B2 | 58 |
| Māyūram, India | G5 | 46 |
| Mayville, Mi., U.S. | G12 | 110 |
| Mayville, N.D., U.S. | E10 | 118 |
| Mayville, N.Y., U.S. | E7 | 108 |
| Mayville, Wi., U.S. | G7 | 110 |
| Maywood, Ne., U.S. | K7 | 118 |
| Maza, Arg. | I7 | 80 |
| Mazabuka, Zam. | E5 | 58 |
| Mazagan see El-Jadida, Mor. | D6 | 62 |
| Mazagão, Braz. | D8 | 76 |
| Mazamet, Fr. | I9 | 14 |
| Mazán, stm., Peru | I6 | 84 |
| Mazār, Jabal, mtn., Asia | A6 | 50 |
| Mazara del Vallo, Italy | L7 | 18 |
| Mazar-e Sharīf, Afg. | B2 | 44 |
| Mazaruni, stm., Guy. | E13 | 84 |
| Mazatenango, Guat. | C3 | 92 |
| Mazatlán, Mex. | F6 | 90 |
| Mazatzal Peak, mtn., Az., U.S. | J5 | 120 |
| Mažeikiai, Lith. | D5 | 22 |
| Mazenod, Sk., Can. | I8 | 104 |
| Mazeppa, Mn., U.S. | F3 | 110 |
| Mazhuang, China | D5 | 34 |
| Mazirbe, Lat. | C7 | 22 |
| Mazoe, stm., Afr. | E6 | 58 |
| Mazomanie, Wi., U.S. | G6 | 110 |
| Mazsalaca, Lat. | D8 | 22 |
| Mazunga, Zimb. | C9 | 66 |
| Mazury, reg., Pol. | B20 | 10 |
| Mazyr, Bela. | G3 | 26 |
| Mbabane, Swaz. | F10 | 66 |
| Mbacké, Sen. | D2 | 64 |
| Mbaga, C.A.R. | O3 | 60 |
| Mbaïki, C.A.R. | H4 | 56 |
| Mbakaou, Cam. | G5 | 56 |
| Mbala, Ug. | A3 | 58 |
| Mbale, Ug. | B5 | 58 |
| Mbalmayo, Cam. | H5 | 54 |
| Mbamba Bay, Tan. | D6 | 58 |
| Mbandaka (Coquilhatville), D.R.C. | A3 | 58 |
| Mbanga, Cam. | I14 | 64 |
| M'banza Congo, Ang. | C2 | 58 |
| Mbanza-Ngungu, D.R.C. | C2 | 58 |
| Mbarara, Ug. | B5 | 58 |
| Mbari, stm., C.A.R. | G5 | 56 |
| Mbashe, stm., S. Afr. | H8 | 66 |
| M'bengué, C. Iv. | F7 | 64 |
| Mbeya, Tan. | C6 | 58 |
| Mbinda, Congo | B2 | 58 |
| Mbini, Eq. Gui. | H5 | 54 |
| Mbomou (Bomu), stm., Afr. | H5 | 56 |
| Mbora, Sudan | N5 | 60 |
| Mborio, Sudan | N5 | 60 |
| Mbour, Sen. | C1 | 64 |
| Mbout, Sudan | D3 | 64 |
| Mbuji-Mayi (Bakwanga), D.R.C. | C4 | 58 |
| Mburucuyá, Arg. | C9 | 80 |
| McAdam, N.B., Can. | G6 | 106 |
| McAdoo, Tx., U.S. | G11 | 108 |
| McAlester, Ok., U.S. | E11 | 116 |
| McAllen, Tx., U.S. | M8 | 116 |
| McArthur, Oh., U.S. | H4 | 108 |
| McAuley, Mb., Can. | H13 | 104 |
| McBain, Mi., U.S. | F11 | 110 |
| McBee, S.C., U.S. | E6 | 112 |
| McBeth Fjord, N.T., Can. | C19 | 96 |
| McBride, B.C., Can. | D14 | 102 |
| McCall, Id., U.S. | F9 | 122 |
| McCall Creek, Ms., U.S. | K6 | 114 |
| McCallum, Nf., Can. | E17 | 106 |
| McCamey, Tx., U.S. | H4 | 116 |
| McCammon, Id., U.S. | H13 | 122 |
| McCanna, N.D., U.S. | C8 | 118 |
| McCaysville, Ga., U.S. | E2 | 112 |
| McClarty Lake, l., Mb., Can. | D14 | 104 |
| McCleary, Wa., U.S. | C2 | 122 |
| McClellanville, S.C., U.S. | F7 | 112 |
| McClintock, Mount, mtn., Ant. | D8 | 73 |
| McCloud, Ca., U.S. | C3 | 124 |
| McClure, Il., U.S. | E7 | 114 |
| McClusky, N.D., U.S. | D7 | 118 |
| McColl, S.C., U.S. | E7 | 112 |
| McComas, W.V., U.S. | B5 | 112 |
| McComb, Ms., U.S. | K6 | 114 |
| McComb, Oh., U.S. | F3 | 108 |
| McConaughy, Lake, res., Ne., U.S. | J6 | 118 |
| McConnell Range, mts., N.T., Can. | E33 | 100 |
| McConnellsburg, Pa., U.S. | H9 | 108 |
| McConnellsville, Oh., U.S. | H5 | 108 |
| McCook, Ne., U.S. | K7 | 118 |
| McCormick, S.C., U.S. | F4 | 112 |
| McCoy Lake, l., On., Can. | F22 | 104 |
| McCreary, Mb., Can. | H15 | 104 |
| McCrory, Ar., U.S. | G5 | 114 |
| McCune, Ks., U.S. | N13 | 118 |
| McCurtain, Ok., U.S. | D12 | 116 |
| McCusker, stm., Sk., Can. | B5 | 104 |
| McDade, Tx., U.S. | I9 | 116 |
| McDavid, Fl., U.S. | L9 | 114 |
| McDermitt, Nv., U.S. | C8 | 124 |
| McDermott, Oh., U.S. | I3 | 108 |
| McDonald, Ks., U.S. | L6 | 118 |
| McDonough, Ga., U.S. | F2 | 112 |
| Mcensk, Russia | H19 | 22 |
| McEwen, Tn., U.S. | F9 | 114 |
| McFadden, Wy., U.S. | C10 | 120 |
| McFarland, Ca., U.S. | I6 | 124 |
| McFarland, Wi., U.S. | B5 | 112 |
| McGehee, Ar., U.S. | I5 | 114 |
| McGill, Nv., U.S. | E11 | 124 |
| McGrath, Ak., U.S. | E17 | 100 |
| McGraw, N.Y., U.S. | E10 | 108 |
| McGregor, Ia., U.S. | G4 | 110 |
| McGregor, Tx., U.S. | H9 | 116 |
| McGregor, stm., B.C., Can. | C13 | 102 |
| McGregor Lake, l., Ab., Can. | G22 | 102 |
| McGregor Range, mts., Austl. | F5 | 70 |
| McHenry, Il., U.S. | H7 | 110 |
| McHenry, Ms., U.S. | L7 | 114 |
| Mchinji, Mwi. | D6 | 58 |
| McInnes Lake, l., On., Can. | F21 | 104 |
| McIntosh, Al., U.S. | K8 | 114 |
| McIntosh, Mn., U.S. | D12 | 118 |
| McIntosh, S.D., U.S. | F6 | 118 |
| McIntosh Lake, l., Sk., Can. | B18 | 104 |
| McIntyre Bay, b., B.C., Can. | C3 | 102 |
| McKeand, stm., N.T., Can. | D19 | 96 |
| McKee, Ky., U.S. | B3 | 112 |
| McKeesport, Pa., U.S. | G7 | 108 |
| McKenzie, Al., U.S. | K10 | 114 |
| McKenzie, Tn., U.S. | F8 | 114 |
| McKenzie Bridge, Or., U.S. | F3 | 122 |
| McKenzie Island, On., Can. | G21 | 104 |
| McKenzie Lake, l., Sk., Can. | C12 | 104 |
| McKinley, Mount, mtn., Ak., U.S. | E19 | 100 |
| McKinleyville, Ca., U.S. | D1 | 124 |
| McKinney, Tx., U.S. | F10 | 116 |
| McKnight Lake, l., Mb., Can. | B13 | 104 |
| McLain, Ms., U.S. | K8 | 114 |
| McLaughlin, S.D., U.S. | F7 | 118 |
| McLaughlin, stm., Mb., Can. | E18 | 104 |
| McLaurin, Ms., U.S. | K7 | 114 |
| McLean, Il., U.S. | B7 | 114 |
| McLean, Sk., Can. | H10 | 104 |
| McLean, Tx., U.S. | E7 | 116 |
| McLean Lake, l., Sk., Can. | B5 | 104 |
| McLeansboro, Il., U.S. | D8 | 114 |
| McLennan, Ab., Can. | B18 | 102 |
| McLeod, stm., Ab., Can. | D19 | 102 |
| McLeod Bay, b., N.T., Can. | D10 | 96 |
| McLeod Lake, B.C., Can. | C11 | 102 |
| McLoughlin, Mount, mtn., Or., U.S. | H3 | 122 |
| McLoughlin Bay, b., N.T., Can. | C13 | 96 |
| McLouth, Ks., U.S. | L12 | 118 |
| McLure, B.C., Can. | F14 | 102 |
| M'Clure Strait, strt., N.T., Can. | B9 | 96 |
| McMahon, Sk., Can. | H7 | 104 |
| McMillan, Lake, res., N.M., U.S. | G2 | 116 |
| McMinnville, Or., U.S. | E2 | 122 |
| McMinnville, Tn., U.S. | G11 | 114 |
| McMurdo, sci., Ant. | C8 | 73 |
| McMurdo Sound, strt., Ant. | C8 | 73 |
| McNary, Az., U.S. | J7 | 120 |
| McNeil, Ar., U.S. | I3 | 114 |
| McNeil, Mount, mtn., B.C., Can. | C4 | 102 |
| McNeill, Ms., U.S. | L7 | 114 |
| McPhail, stm., Mb., Can. | F19 | 104 |
| McPherson, Ks., U.S. | M10 | 118 |
| McPherson Range, mts., Austl. | G10 | 70 |
| McQueeney, Tx., U.S. | J8 | 116 |
| McRae, Ar., U.S. | G5 | 114 |
| McRae, Ga., U.S. | G4 | 112 |
| McRoberts, Ky., U.S. | B4 | 112 |
| McVeigh, Ky., U.S. | B4 | 112 |
| McVille, N.D., U.S. | D9 | 118 |
| McWilliams, Al., U.S. | K9 | 114 |
| M'Daourouch, Alg. | M2 | 18 |
| Meacham, Sk., Can. | F9 | 104 |
| Mead, Ne., U.S. | J11 | 118 |
| Mead, Lake, res., U.S. | H2 | 120 |
| Meade, Ks., U.S. | N7 | 118 |
| Meade, stm., Ak., U.S. | A18 | 100 |
| Meade Peak, mtn., Co., U.S. | E10 | 120 |
| Meaden Peak, mtn., Co., U.S. | D9 | 120 |
| Meadow, Tx., U.S. | F4 | 116 |
| Meadow, Ut., U.S. | F4 | 120 |
| Meadow Lake, Sk., Can. | D6 | 104 |
| Meadow Lake Provincial Park, rec., Sk., Can. | D5 | 104 |
| Meadowview, Va., U.S. | C5 | 112 |
| Meadville, Mo., U.S. | C3 | 114 |
| Meadville, Ms., U.S. | K6 | 114 |
| Meadville, Pa., U.S. | F6 | 108 |
| Meaford, On., Can. | F15 | 110 |
| Meaghers Grant, N.S., Can. | H10 | 106 |
| Méan, Bel. | H8 | 12 |
| Meana, Turk. | C16 | 48 |
| Meandarra, Austl. | F8 | 70 |
| Meander River, Ab., Can. | E9 | 96 |
| Meath, co., Ire. | H6 | 8 |
| Meath, hist. reg., Ire. | H6 | 8 |
| Meaux, Fr. | D10 | 14 |
| Mebane, N.C., U.S. | C7 | 112 |
| Mecaya, stm., Col. | H4 | 84 |
| Mecca see Makkah, Sau. Ar. | D1 | 47 |
| Mechanic Falls, Me., U.S. | C18 | 108 |
| Mechanicsburg, Oh., U.S. | G3 | 108 |
| Mechanicville, Ga., U.S. | I4 | 110 |
| Mechanicsville, Va., U.S. | B9 | 112 |
| Mechelen (Malines), Bel. | F6 | 12 |
| Mechita, Arg. | H8 | 80 |
| Mechra Safsaf, Mor. | K9 | 16 |
| Mechriyya, Alg. | D10 | 62 |
| Mechroha, Alg. | M2 | 18 |
| Mecklenburg, hist. reg., Ger. | B12 | 10 |
| Mecklenburger Bucht, b., Ger. | A11 | 10 |
| Mecklenburg-Vorpommern, state, Ger. | B12 | 10 |
| Meda, Port. | E4 | 16 |
| Medan, Indon. | M5 | 40 |
| Medanos, Arg. | I5 | 80 |
| Médanos, Punta, c., Arg. | I9 | 80 |
| Medaryville, In., U.S. | A10 | 114 |
| Meddouha, Al., U.S. | D3 | 112 |
| Mede, Italy | E3 | 18 |
| Medeiros Neto, Braz. | D9 | 79 |
| Medellín, Col. | D4 | 84 |
| Medemblik, Neth. | C8 | 12 |
| Médenine, Tun. | D16 | 62 |
| Mederdra, Maur. | C2 | 64 |
| Medford, Ok., U.S. | C9 | 116 |
| Medford, Or., U.S. | H3 | 122 |
| Medford, Wi., U.S. | E5 | 110 |
| Medgidia, Rom. | E12 | 20 |
| Mediapolis, Ia., U.S. | I4 | 110 |
| Mediaş, Rom. | C8 | 20 |
| Medical Lake, Wa., U.S. | C8 | 122 |
| Medicina, Italy | E6 | 18 |
| Medicine Bow, Wy., U.S. | C10 | 120 |
| Medicine Bow, stm., Wy., U.S. | B10 | 120 |
| Medicine Bow Mountains, mts., U.S. | C10 | 120 |
| Medicine Bow Peak, mtn., Wy., U.S. | C10 | 120 |
| Medicine Hat, Ab., Can. | H4 | 104 |
| Medicine Lake, Mt., U.S. | C3 | 118 |
| Medicine Lodge, Ks., U.S. | N9 | 118 |
| Medicine Lodge, stm., U.S. | B8 | 116 |
| Medina, Braz. | D8 | 79 |
| Medina, N.D., U.S. | E8 | 118 |
| Medina, N.Y., U.S. | D8 | 108 |
| Medina, Oh., U.S. | F5 | 108 |
| Medina see Al-Madinah, Sau. Ar. | B1 | 47 |
| Medina, Tx., U.S. | J7 | 116 |
| Medina, stm., Tx., U.S. | J8 | 116 |
| Medina del Campo, Spain | D7 | 16 |
| Medininái, Lith. | G8 | 22 |
| Medinīpur, India | I12 | 44 |
| Medio, Punta, c., Chile | D3 | 80 |
| Mediterranean Sea | E9 | 52 |
| Medjerda, Monts de la, mts., Afr. | M3 | 18 |
| Mednogorsk, Russia | G9 | 26 |
| Mednoje, Russia | E18 | 22 |
| Mednyj, ostrov, i., Russia | G25 | 28 |
| Médoc, reg., Fr. | G6 | 14 |
| Medora, In., U.S. | D10 | 114 |
| Medora, N.D., U.S. | E4 | 118 |
| Médouneu, Gabon | A2 | 58 |
| Medstead, Sk., Can. | E6 | 104 |
| Meductic, N.B., Can. | F6 | 106 |
| Medveđa, Yugo. | G5 | 20 |
| Medvedevskoje, Russia | C18 | 22 |
| Medvedica, stm., Russia | G6 | 26 |
| Medvežjegorsk, Russia | E4 | 26 |
| Medvežʹi ostrova, is., Russia | C24 | 28 |
| Medway, stm., N.S., Can. | H9 | 106 |
| Medyn', Russia | G18 | 22 |
| Meekatharra, Austl. | E3 | 68 |
| Meeker, Co., U.S. | D9 | 120 |
| Meeks Bay, Ca., U.S. | E5 | 124 |
| Meelpaeg Lake, res., Nf., Can. | D17 | 106 |
| Meer, Bel. | F6 | 12 |
| Meerane, Ger. | E12 | 10 |
| Meerut, India | F7 | 44 |
| Meeteetse, Wy., U.S. | F17 | 122 |
| Mega, Eth. | H8 | 56 |
| Mégantic, Lac, l., P.Q., Can. | B16 | 108 |
| Mégara, Grc. | K7 | 20 |
| Megargel, Tx., U.S. | F8 | 116 |
| Meghālaya, state, India | H14 | 44 |
| Meghna, stm., Bngl. | H14 | 44 |
| Mehadia, Rom. | E6 | 20 |
| Mehar, Pak. | G2 | 44 |
| Mehdia, Alg. | C11 | 62 |
| Mehedinţi, co., Rom. | E6 | 20 |
| Meherrin, stm., U.S. | C9 | 112 |
| Mehrān, Iran | E9 | 48 |
| Meia Ponte, Rio de, stm., Braz. | D2 | 79 |
| Meigs, Ga., U.S. | H2 | 112 |
| Meiktila, Myan. | D3 | 40 |
| Meilie, China | I6 | 34 |
| Meiners Oaks, Ca., U.S. | J6 | 124 |
| Meiningen, Ger. | E10 | 10 |
| Meiringen, Switz. | E9 | 13 |
| Meissen, Ger. | D13 | 10 |
| Meixian, China | K5 | 34 |
| Meiyino, Sudan | N8 | 60 |
| Meizhai, China | I4 | 34 |
| Mejerda, Oued (Oued Medjerda), stm., Afr. | M4 | 18 |
| Mejez el Bab, Tun. | M4 | 18 |
| Mejicanos, El Sal. | D5 | 92 |
| Mejillones, Chile | B3 | 80 |
| Mejillones, Península, pen., Austl. | B3 | 80 |
| Mejillones del Sur, Bahía de, b., Chile | B3 | 80 |
| Mékambo, Gabon | A2 | 58 |
| Mekele, Eth. | K10 | 60 |
| Meknès, Mor. | D8 | 62 |
| Mekong, stm., Asia | H8 | 40 |
| Mekoryuk, Ak., U.S. | F11 | 100 |
| Mékrou, stm., Afr. | F7 | 54 |
| Melado, stm., Chile | H3 | 80 |
| Melaka, Malay. | M7 | 40 |
| Melanesia, is., Oc. | I19 | 126 |
| Melbourne, Austl. | K6 | 70 |
| Melbourne, Fl., U.S. | K6 | 112 |
| Melbourne, Ia., U.S. | I2 | 110 |
| Melbourne Island, i., N.T., Can. | C12 | 96 |
| Melby House, Scot., U.K. | A12 | 8 |
| Melcher, Ia., U.S. | I2 | 110 |
| Melchor Múzquiz, Mex. | D9 | 90 |
| Meldorf, Ger. | A9 | 10 |
| Meldrum Bay, On., Can. | E12 | 110 |
| Meldrum Creek, B.C., Can. | E12 | 102 |
| Melechovo, Russia | E24 | 22 |
| Melegnano, Italy | D4 | 18 |
| Melekess, Russia | F24 | 22 |
| Meleuz, Russia | G9 | 26 |
| Mélèzes, Rivière aux, stm., P.Q., Can. | E18 | 96 |
| Melfi, Chad | F4 | 56 |
| Melfi, Italy | H10 | 18 |
| Melfort, Sk., Can. | F10 | 104 |
| Melgaço, Port. | C3 | 16 |
| Melgar, Col. | E5 | 84 |
| Melghir, Chott, l., Alg. | C14 | 62 |
| Melhus, Nor. | J12 | 6 |
| Meli, stm., Afr. | G4 | 64 |
| Meliane, Oued, stm., Tun. | M5 | 18 |
| Melilla, Sp. N. Afr. | C9 | 62 |
| Melincué, Arg. | G8 | 80 |
| Melipilla, Chile | G3 | 80 |
| Melita, Mb., Can. | I13 | 104 |
| Melitopol', Ukr. | F15 | 4 |
| Mellègue, Oued, stm., Afr. | M3 | 18 |
| Mellen, Wi., U.S. | D5 | 110 |
| Mellette, S.D., U.S. | F9 | 118 |
| Melnytsya-Podilʹsʹka, Ukr. | A10 | 20 |
| Melo, stm., Para. | I12 | 82 |
| Melong, Cam. | I14 | 64 |
| Melos see Milos, i., Grc. | M8 | 20 |
| Melrose, Fl., U.S. | F13 | 118 |
| Melrose, N.M., U.S. | E3 | 116 |
| Melrose, Mt., U.S. | D18 | 122 |
| Melrose, Wi., U.S. | F5 | 110 |
| Melton Mowbray, Eng., U.K. | I13 | 8 |
| Melúa, Mol. | D3 | 80 |
| Melun, Fr. | D9 | 14 |
| Melut, Myan. | D2 | 40 |
| Melvern, Ks., U.S. | M12 | 118 |
| Melville, Sk., Can. | H12 | 104 |
| Melville, Détroit de see Viscount Melville Sound, strt., N.T., Can. | B11 | 96 |
| Melville, Lake, l., Nf., Can. | F21 | 96 |
| Melville Bugt, b., Grnld. | B13 | 86 |

| Name | Map Ref. | Page |
|---|---|---|
| Melville Hills, hills, N.T., Can. | B33 | 100 |
| Melville Island, i., Austl. | B6 | 68 |
| Melville Island, i., N.T., Can. | B8 | 86 |
| Melville Peninsula, pen., N.T., Can. | C16 | 96 |
| Melville Sound, strt., N.T., Can. | C11 | 96 |
| Melvin, Il., U.S. | J7 | 110 |
| Melvin, Ky., U.S. | B4 | 112 |
| Melvin, Tx., U.S. | H7 | 116 |
| Melvin, Lough, l., Eur. | G5 | 8 |
| Melvin Lake, l., Mb., Can. | A14 | 104 |
| Melyana, Alg. | B12 | 62 |
| Melzo, Italy | D4 | 18 |
| Memel, S. Afr. | F9 | 66 |
| Memel see Nemunas, stm., Eur. | F6 | 22 |
| Memmingen, Ger. | H10 | 10 |
| Memo, stm., Ven. | C9 | 84 |
| Mémôt, Camb. | I9 | 40 |
| Mempawah, Indon. | N10 | 40 |
| Memphis, Il., U.S. | L4 | 112 |
| Memphis, Mi., U.S. | H13 | 110 |
| Memphis, Mo., U.S. | B4 | 114 |
| Memphis, Tn., U.S. | G6 | 114 |
| Memphis, Tx., U.S. | E6 | 116 |
| Memphremagog, Lake, l., N.A. | B14 | 108 |
| Mena, Ar., U.S. | H2 | 114 |
| Menahga, Mn., U.S. | E12 | 118 |
| Ménaka, Mali | D11 | 64 |
| Menaldum, Neth. | B8 | 12 |
| Menan, Id., U.S. | G14 | 122 |
| Menard, Tx., U.S. | I7 | 116 |
| Menasha, Wi., U.S. | F7 | 110 |
| Menawashei, Sudan | K3 | 60 |
| Mendawai, stm., Indon. | F5 | 38 |
| Mende, Fr. | H10 | 14 |
| Mendenhall, Ms., U.S. | K7 | 114 |
| Méndez, Mex. | E10 | 90 |
| Mendi, Eth. | M8 | 60 |
| Mendi, Pap. N. Gui. | G11 | 38 |
| Mendocino, Ca., U.S. | E2 | 124 |
| Mendocino, Cape, c., Ca., U.S. | D1 | 124 |
| Mendon, Il., U.S. | B5 | 114 |
| Mendon, Mi., U.S. | H10 | 110 |
| Mendota, Ca., U.S. | H5 | 124 |
| Mendota, Il., U.S. | I6 | 110 |
| Mendoza, Arg. | G4 | 80 |
| Mendoza, Peru | B3 | 82 |
| Mendoza, prov., Arg. | H4 | 80 |
| Mendoza, stm., Arg. | G4 | 80 |
| Ménéac, Fr. | D4 | 14 |
| Mene de Mauroa, Ven. | B7 | 84 |
| Mene Grande, Ven. | C7 | 84 |
| Menemen, Tur. | K11 | 20 |
| Menen (Menin), Bel. | G3 | 12 |
| Menfi, Italy | L7 | 18 |
| Mengcheng, China | E10 | 30 |
| Menggala, Indon. | F4 | 38 |
| Menggu, China | A7 | 40 |
| Mengla, China | C6 | 40 |
| Menghai, China | C6 | 40 |
| Mengzhi, China | B5 | 40 |
| Mengzi, China | C7 | 40 |
| Menihek Lakes, l., Nf., Can. | F19 | 96 |
| Menindee, Austl. | I5 | 70 |
| Menindee Lake, l., Austl. | I5 | 70 |
| Menlo Park, Ca., U.S. | G3 | 124 |
| Menno, S.D., U.S. | H10 | 118 |
| Meno, Ok., U.S. | C8 | 116 |
| Menominee, Mi., U.S. | E8 | 110 |
| Menominee, stm., U.S. | E8 | 110 |
| Menomonee Falls, Wi., U.S. | G7 | 110 |
| Menomonie, Wi., U.S. | F4 | 110 |
| Menongue, Ang. | D3 | 58 |
| Menorca, i., Spain | F16 | 16 |
| Mens, Fr. | H12 | 14 |
| Mentasta Mountains, mts., Ak., U.S. | E23 | 100 |
| Mentawai, Kepulauan, is., Indon. | F2 | 38 |
| Mentawai, Selat, strt., Indon. | F3 | 38 |
| Menton, Fr. | I14 | 14 |
| Mentone, Tx., U.S. | H3 | 116 |
| Mentor, Oh., U.S. | F5 | 108 |
| Menzel Bourguiba, Tun. | L4 | 18 |
| Menzel Bou Zelfa, Tun. | M5 | 18 |
| Menzel Djemil, Tun. | L4 | 18 |
| Menzel Temime, Tun. | M5 | 18 |
| Menzies, Austl. | E4 | 68 |
| Menzies, Mount, mtn., Ant. | C5 | 73 |
| Meoqui, Mex. | C7 | 90 |
| Meota, Sk., Can. | E6 | 104 |
| Meppel, Neth. | C9 | 12 |
| Meppen, Ger. | C7 | 10 |
| Meqerghane, Sebkha, pl., Alg. | G11 | 62 |
| Mequon, Wi., U.S. | G8 | 110 |
| Mer, Fr. | E8 | 14 |
| Meramec, stm., Mo., U.S. | D5 | 114 |
| Merano (Meran), Italy | C6 | 18 |
| Merasheen, Nf., Can. | E19 | 106 |
| Merasheen Island, i., Nf., Can. | E19 | 106 |
| Merate, Italy | D4 | 18 |
| Merauke, Indon. | G11 | 38 |
| Mercaderes, Col. | G4 | 84 |
| Mercâra, India | F3 | 46 |
| Merced, Ca., U.S. | G5 | 124 |
| Merced, stm., Ca., U.S. | G5 | 124 |
| Mercedario, Cerro, mtn., Arg. | F3 | 80 |
| Mercedes, Arg. | H9 | 80 |
| Mercedes, Arg. | G6 | 80 |
| Mercedes, Tx., U.S. | M9 | 116 |
| Mercedes, Ur. | G9 | 80 |
| Mercer, Mo., U.S. | B3 | 114 |
| Mercer, Wi., U.S. | D5 | 110 |
| Mercersburg, Pa., U.S. | H9 | 108 |
| Merchants Bay, b., N.T., Can. | C20 | 96 |
| Merchtem, Bel. | G5 | 12 |
| Mercoal, Ab., Can. | D17 | 102 |
| Mercury, Nv., U.S. | H10 | 124 |
| Mercy, Cape, c., N.T., Can. | D20 | 96 |
| Mercy Bay, b., N.T., Can. | B9 | 96 |
| Meredith, N.H., U.S. | D15 | 108 |
| Meredith, Lake, res., Tx., U.S. | D5 | 116 |
| Meredosia, Il., U.S. | C6 | 114 |
| Mereeg, Som. | H10 | 56 |
| Merenkurkku (Norra Kvarken), strt., Eur. | J17 | 6 |
| Merevari, stm., Ven. | E10 | 84 |
| Merewa, Eth. | N9 | 60 |
| Mergui (Myeik), Myan. | H5 | 40 |
| Mergui Archipelago, is., Myan. | H5 | 40 |
| Meriç (Marica) (Évros), stm., Eur. | H10 | 20 |
| Mérida, Mex. | G15 | 90 |
| Mérida, Spain | G5 | 16 |
| Mérida, Ven. | C7 | 84 |
| Mérida, state, Ven. | C7 | 84 |
| Mérida, Cordillera de, mts., Ven. | C7 | 84 |
| Meriden, Ct., U.S. | F14 | 108 |
| Meridian, Ga., U.S. | H5 | 112 |
| Meridian, Id., U.S. | G9 | 122 |
| Meridian, Ms., U.S. | J8 | 114 |
| Meridian, Tx., U.S. | H9 | 116 |
| Meridianville, Al., U.S. | H10 | 114 |
| Mérignac, Fr. | H6 | 14 |
| Merigold, Ms., U.S. | I6 | 114 |
| Merimbula, Austl. | K8 | 70 |
| Merín, Laguna (Lagoa Mirim), b., S.A. | G12 | 80 |
| Merino, Co., U.S. | K4 | 118 |
| Merinos, Ur. | G10 | 80 |
| Merkel, Tx., U.S. | G6 | 116 |
| Merkendorf, Ger. | F10 | 10 |
| Merkinė, Lith. | G7 | 22 |
| Merkulaviču, Bela. | I13 | 22 |
| Merlin, On., Can. | H13 | 110 |
| Merlin, Or., U.S. | H2 | 122 |
| Merlo, Arg. | G6 | 80 |
| Merna, Ne., U.S. | J8 | 118 |
| Mernye, Hung. | I17 | 10 |
| Meron, Hare, mtn., Isr. | C4 | 50 |
| Merredin, Austl. | F3 | 68 |
| Merrick, On., Can. | C11 | 108 |
| Merrill, Ia., U.S. | I11 | 118 |
| Merrill, Mi., U.S. | G11 | 110 |
| Merrill, Or., U.S. | H4 | 122 |
| Merrill, Wi., U.S. | F5 | 110 |
| Merrillville, In., U.S. | A9 | 114 |
| Merrimack, stm., U.S. | D15 | 108 |
| Merritt, B.C., Can. | G14 | 102 |
| Merritt Island, Fl., U.S. | K6 | 112 |
| Merriwa, Austl. | I9 | 70 |
| Mer Rouge, La., U.S. | J5 | 114 |
| Merryville, La., U.S. | L3 | 114 |
| Mersch, Lux. | I9 | 12 |
| Merseburg, Ger. | D11 | 10 |
| Mersey, stm., Austl. | M7 | 70 |
| Mersey, stm., N.S., Can. | H9 | 106 |
| Mersing, Malay. | M7 | 40 |
| Mörsrags, Lat. | C7 | 22 |
| Merthyr Tydfil, Wales, U.K. | J10 | 8 |
| Mértola, Port. | H4 | 16 |
| Mertzon, Tx., U.S. | H6 | 116 |
| Méru, Fr. | C9 | 14 |
| Meru, Kenya | A7 | 58 |
| Meru, Mount, mtn., Tan. | B7 | 58 |
| Mervin, Sk., Can. | E6 | 104 |
| Méry, Bela. | F10 | 22 |
| Méry, Fr. | D10 | 14 |
| Merzig, Ger. | F6 | 10 |
| Mesa, Az., U.S. | K5 | 120 |
| Mesa, stm., Spain | D10 | 16 |
| Mesabi Range, hills, Mn., U.S. | C3 | 110 |
| Mesagne, Italy | I12 | 18 |
| Mesa Mountain, mtn., Co., U.S. | G10 | 120 |
| Mesa Verde National Park, Co., U.S. | G8 | 120 |
| Mescalero, N.M., U.S. | K11 | 120 |
| Meschede, Ger. | D8 | 10 |
| Meščovsk, Russia | G18 | 22 |
| Mesfinto, Eth. | K9 | 60 |
| Mesgouez, Lac, l., P.Q., Can. | F17 | 96 |
| Meshgīn Shahr, Iran | B9 | 48 |
| Mesick, Mi., U.S. | F10 | 110 |
| Mesilinka, stm., B.C., Can. | A10 | 102 |
| Mesilla, N.M., U.S. | L10 | 120 |
| Meslay-du-Maine, Fr. | E6 | 14 |
| Mesocco, Switz. | F11 | 13 |
| Mesolóngion, Grc. | K5 | 20 |
| Mesopotamia, hist. reg., Asia | D8 | 48 |
| Mesquita, Braz. | E7 | 79 |
| Mesquite, Nv., U.S. | H11 | 124 |
| Mesquite, Tx., U.S. | G10 | 116 |
| Messalo, stm., Moz. | D7 | 58 |
| Messina, Italy | K10 | 18 |
| Messina, S. Afr. | D10 | 66 |
| Messina, Stretto di, strt., Italy | K10 | 18 |
| Messini, Grc. | L6 | 20 |
| Messíniakós Kólpos, b., Grc. | M6 | 20 |
| Messix Peak, mtn., Ut., U.S. | C4 | 120 |
| Messojacha, stm., Russia | D13 | 26 |
| Mestá, Grc. | K9 | 20 |
| Mesta (Néstos), stm., Eur. | H7 | 20 |
| Mestghanem, Alg. | C11 | 62 |
| Mestre, Italy | D7 | 18 |
| Meszah Peak, mtn., B.C., Can. | G29 | 100 |
| Meta, dept., Col. | F6 | 84 |
| Meta, stm., S.A. | D9 | 84 |
| Meta Incognita Peninsula, pen., N.T., Can. | D19 | 96 |
| Metairie, La., U.S. | M6 | 114 |
| Metaline Falls, Wa., U.S. | B8 | 122 |
| Metamora, Il., U.S. | J6 | 110 |
| Metán, Arg. | C6 | 80 |
| Metapán, El Sal. | C5 | 92 |
| Meteghan, N.S., Can. | H7 | 106 |
| Metema, Eth. | K9 | 60 |
| Meteor Crater, crat., Az., U.S. | I5 | 120 |
| Methóni, Grc. | M5 | 20 |
| Methow, stm., Wa., U.S. | B6 | 122 |
| Metiskow, Ab., Can. | F4 | 104 |
| Metković, Cro. | F12 | 18 |
| Metlakatla, Ak., U.S. | I29 | 100 |
| Metlakatla, B.C., Can. | C4 | 102 |
| Metlaoui, Tun. | C15 | 62 |
| Metlatonoc, Mex. | I10 | 90 |
| Meto, Bayou, stm., Ar., U.S. | H5 | 114 |
| Metolius, stm., Or., U.S. | F4 | 122 |
| Metropolis, Il., U.S. | E8 | 114 |
| Metropolitan, Mi., U.S. | D8 | 110 |
| Metsematluku, Bots. | E7 | 66 |
| Metter, Ga., U.S. | G4 | 112 |
| Mettuppālaiyam, India | G4 | 46 |
| Mettūr, India | G4 | 46 |
| Metu, Eth. | M8 | 60 |
| Metulla, Isr. | B5 | 50 |
| Metz, Fr. | C13 | 14 |
| Meulan, Fr. | C8 | 14 |
| Meureudu, Indon. | L4 | 40 |
| Meurthe, stm., Fr. | D13 | 14 |
| Meurthe-et-Moselle, dept., Fr. | D13 | 14 |
| Meuse, dept., Fr. | C12 | 14 |
| Meuse (Maas), stm., Eur. | E5 | 10 |
| Meuselwitz, Ger. | E12 | 10 |
| Mexia, Tx., U.S. | H10 | 116 |
| Mexiana, Ilha, i., Braz. | D9 | 76 |
| Mexicali, Mex. | A2 | 90 |
| Mexican Hat, Ut., U.S. | G7 | 120 |
| Mexico, Me., U.S. | C16 | 108 |
| Mexico, Mo., U.S. | C5 | 114 |
| Mexico, N.Y., U.S. | D10 | 108 |
| México, state, Mex. | H10 | 90 |
| Mexico, Gulf of, b., N.A. | F9 | 90 |
| Mexico Beach, Fl., U.S. | J1 | 112 |
| Mexico City see Ciudad de México, Mex. | H10 | 90 |
| Meximieux, Fr. | G12 | 14 |
| Meycauayan, Phil. | n19 | 39b |
| Meyers Chuck, Ak., U.S. | I28 | 100 |
| Meyersdale, Pa., U.S. | H7 | 108 |
| Meyísti, i., Grc. | H13 | 4 |
| Meymac, Fr. | G9 | 14 |
| Meymaneh, Afg. | C1 | 44 |
| Meymeh, stm., Asia | E9 | 48 |
| Meyrargues, Fr. | I12 | 14 |
| Meyronne, Sk., Can. | I8 | 104 |
| Mezada, Horvot (Masada), hist., Isr. | F4 | 50 |
| Mezapa, Hond. | B7 | 92 |
| Mezcala, Mex. | I10 | 90 |
| Mezcalapa, stm., Mex. | I13 | 90 |
| Mezen', Russia | D6 | 26 |
| Mezen', stm., Russia | D6 | 26 |
| Meziadin Lake, l., B.C., Can. | A5 | 102 |
| Mézin, Fr. | H7 | 14 |
| Mezinovskij, Russia | F23 | 22 |
| Mezőberény, Hung. | I21 | 10 |
| Mezőcsát, Hung. | H20 | 10 |
| Mezőkovácsháza, Hung. | I20 | 10 |
| Mezőkövesd, Hung. | H20 | 10 |
| Mezőtúr, Hung. | H20 | 10 |
| Mezquital, Mex. | F7 | 90 |
| Mezquital, stm., Mex. | E7 | 90 |
| Mglin, Russia | H15 | 22 |
| M'Goun, Irhil, mtn., Mor. | E7 | 62 |
| Mhow, India | I6 | 44 |
| Miahuatlán de Porfirio Díaz, Mex. | I11 | 90 |
| Miajadas, Spain | F6 | 16 |
| Miami, Az., U.S. | K6 | 120 |
| Miami, Fl., U.S. | N6 | 112 |
| Miami, Ok., U.S. | C12 | 116 |
| Miami, Tx., U.S. | D6 | 116 |
| Miami Beach, Fl., U.S. | N6 | 112 |
| Miami Canal, Fl., U.S. | M6 | 112 |
| Miamisburg, Oh., U.S. | H2 | 108 |
| Miami Springs, Fl., U.S. | N6 | 112 |
| Miāndowāb, Iran | C9 | 48 |
| Miandrivazo, Madag. | q21 | 67b |
| Miāneh, Iran | C9 | 48 |
| Miangas, Pulau, i., Indon. | D8 | 38 |
| Mianhu, China | L5 | 34 |
| Miānwāli, Pak. | D4 | 44 |
| Mianyang, China | E7 | 30 |
| Mianyang, China | E2 | 34 |
| Miaoli, Tai. | K9 | 34 |
| Miarinavaratra, Madag. | r22 | 67b |
| Miass, Russia | G10 | 26 |
| Miastko, Pol. | A17 | 10 |
| Micanopy, Fl., U.S. | J4 | 112 |
| Micaúne, Moz. | B13 | 66 |
| Michajlov, Russia | G22 | 22 |
| Michajlovka, Russia | G6 | 26 |
| Michaud, Point, c., N.S., Can. | G13 | 106 |
| Michel, B.C., Can. | H20 | 102 |
| Miches, Dom. Rep. | E10 | 94 |
| Michigamme, stm., Mi., U.S. | D7 | 110 |
| Michigan, N.D., U.S. | C9 | 118 |
| Michigan, state, U.S. | C9 | 96 |
| Michigan, Lake, l., U.S. | F8 | 110 |
| Michigan Center, Mi., U.S. | H11 | 110 |
| Michigan City, In., U.S. | A10 | 114 |
| Michipicoten Island, i., On., Can. | C10 | 110 |
| Michnevo, Russia | F20 | 22 |
| Michoacán, state, Mex. | H9 | 90 |
| Mico, stm., Nic. | E10 | 92 |
| Mico, Montañas del, mts., Guat. | B5 | 92 |
| Micronesia, ctry., Oc. | G19 | 126 |
| Micronesia, Federated States of, ctry., Oc. | H19 | 126 |
| Mičurinsk, Russia | I23 | 22 |
| Midale, Sk., Can. | I11 | 104 |
| Midar, Mor. | C9 | 62 |
| Mid-Atlantic Ridge | F9 | 128 |
| Middelburg, Neth. | E4 | 12 |
| Middelburg, S. Afr. | H7 | 66 |
| Middelburg, S. Afr. | E9 | 66 |
| Middelfart, Den. | N11 | 6 |
| Middelharnis, Neth. | E5 | 12 |
| Middelwater, S. Afr. | D10 | 66 |
| Middenmeer, Neth. | C7 | 12 |
| Middle, stm., Ia., U.S. | A2 | 114 |
| Middle America Trench | H10 | 86 |
| Middle Andaman, i., India | H2 | 46 |
| Middle-Bay, P.Q., Can. | A16 | 106 |
| Middle Brook, Nf., Can. | D19 | 106 |
| Middle Caicos, i., T./C. Is. | D9 | 94 |
| Middle Channel, mth., N.T., Can. | B27 | 100 |
| Middle Fabius, stm., Mo., U.S. | C4 | 114 |
| Middlefield, Oh., U.S. | F5 | 108 |
| Middle Loup, stm., Ne., U.S. | J8 | 118 |
| Middle Musquodoboit, N.S., Can. | G10 | 106 |
| Middleport, Oh., U.S. | H4 | 108 |
| Middleport, N.Y., U.S. | D8 | 108 |
| Middlesboro, Ky., U.S. | C3 | 112 |
| Middlesex, Belize | I15 | 90 |
| Middlesex, N.J., U.S. | D2 | 110 |
| Middleton, N.S., Can. | H8 | 106 |
| Middleton, Wi., U.S. | G6 | 110 |
| Middleton Island, i., Ak., U.S. | G21 | 100 |
| Middletown, Ct., U.S. | F14 | 108 |
| Middletown, De., U.S. | H11 | 108 |
| Middletown, Il., U.S. | B7 | 114 |
| Middletown, In., U.S. | H4 | 108 |
| Middletown, Md., U.S. | H9 | 108 |
| Middletown, N.Y., U.S. | F12 | 108 |
| Middletown, Oh., U.S. | H2 | 108 |
| Middletown, Pa., U.S. | G10 | 108 |
| Middletown, R.I., U.S. | F15 | 108 |
| Middletown, Va., U.S. | H8 | 108 |
| Middleville, Mi., U.S. | H10 | 110 |
| Midelt, Mor. | D8 | 62 |
| Midgic, N.B., Can. | G9 | 106 |
| Midi, Canal du, Fr. | I9 | 14 |
| Midi de Bigorre, Pic du, mtn., Fr. | J7 | 14 |
| Midland, Ca., U.S. | K11 | 124 |
| Midland, On., Can. | F16 | 110 |
| Midland, Mi., U.S. | G11 | 110 |
| Midland, N.C., U.S. | D6 | 112 |
| Midland, S.D., U.S. | G6 | 118 |
| Midland, Tx., U.S. | H4 | 116 |
| Midlothian, Tx., U.S. | G10 | 116 |
| Midnapore, Ab., Can. | G20 | 102 |
| Midongy Sud, Madag. | s22 | 67b |
| Miduzhen, China | B6 | 40 |
| Midvale, Ut., U.S. | F9 | 122 |
| Midville, Ga., U.S. | G4 | 112 |
| Midway, B.C., Can. | H16 | 102 |
| Midway, Ky., U.S. | I2 | 108 |
| Midway, Ky., U.S. | H11 | 116 |
| Midway, Ut., U.S. | D5 | 120 |
| Midway Islands, dep., Oc. | F22 | 126 |
| Midway Park, N.C., U.S. | E9 | 112 |
| Midwest, Wy., U.S. | A10 | 120 |
| Midwest City, Ok., U.S. | D9 | 116 |
| Midyat, Tur. | C6 | 48 |
| Midžor (Midžur), mtn., Eur. | F6 | 20 |
| Miechów, Pol. | E20 | 10 |
| Międzychód, Pol. | C15 | 10 |
| Międzyrzec Podlaski, Pol. | C22 | 10 |
| Międzyrzecz, Pol. | C15 | 10 |
| Miélan, Fr. | I7 | 14 |
| Mielec, Pol. | E21 | 10 |
| Mier, Mex. | D10 | 90 |
| Miercurea-Ciuc, Rom. | C10 | 20 |
| Mieres, Spain | B6 | 16 |
| Mier y Noriega, Mex. | F9 | 90 |
| Mifflinburg, Pa., U.S. | G9 | 108 |
| Migdal, Isr. | C5 | 50 |
| Miguel Alemán, Presa, res., Mex. | H11 | 90 |
| Miguel Auza, Mex. | E8 | 90 |
| Miguel de la Borda, Pan. | H14 | 92 |
| Miguel Hidalgo, Presa, res., Mex. | D5 | 90 |
| Miguelópolis, Braz. | F4 | 79 |
| Miguel Riglos, Arg. | I7 | 80 |
| Mihailovci, Bela. | H10 | 22 |
| Mihara, Japan | M8 | 36 |
| Mijdahah, Yemen | G6 | 47 |
| Mikašèviču, Bela. | I10 | 22 |
| Mikhrot Shelomo Hamelekh (Timna') (King Solomon's Mines), hist., Isr. | I3 | 50 |
| Mikkeli, Fin. | K20 | 6 |
| Mikkelin lääni, prov., Fin. | J20 | 6 |
| Mikkwa, stm., Ab., Can. | E10 | 96 |
| Mikołajki, Pol. | B21 | 10 |
| Mikołów, Pol. | E18 | 10 |
| Mikonos, Grc. | L9 | 20 |
| Mikun', Russia | E8 | 26 |
| Milaca, Mn., U.S. | G10 | 118 |
| Milagro, Ec. | I3 | 84 |
| Milan see Milano, Italy | D4 | 18 |
| Milan, Ga., U.S. | G3 | 112 |
| Milan, In., U.S. | C11 | 114 |
| Milan, Mn., U.S. | F12 | 118 |
| Milan, Mo., U.S. | B3 | 114 |
| Milan, N.M., U.S. | I9 | 120 |
| Milan, Tn., U.S. | G8 | 114 |
| Milano (Milan), Italy | D4 | 18 |
| Milanoa, Madag. | r23 | 67b |
| Milano, Tx., U.S. | I10 | 116 |
| Milazzo, Italy | K10 | 18 |
| Milbank, S.D., U.S. | F11 | 118 |
| Milbanke Sound, strt., B.C., Can. | E6 | 102 |
| Milburn, Ok., U.S. | E10 | 116 |
| Milden, Sk., Can. | G7 | 104 |
| Mildmay, On., Can. | F14 | 110 |
| Mildred, Pa., U.S. | F10 | 108 |
| Mildura, Austl. | J5 | 70 |
| Mile, China | B7 | 40 |
| Miles, Austl. | F6 | 70 |
| Miles, Tx., U.S. | H6 | 116 |
| Miles City, Mt., U.S. | D20 | 122 |
| Mile Seven Hundred Thirty Three, Yk., Can. | F29 | 100 |
| Milestone, Sk., Can. | H10 | 104 |
| Milevsko, Czech Rep. | F14 | 10 |
| Milford, Ct., U.S. | F13 | 108 |
| Milford, De., U.S. | I11 | 108 |
| Milford, Il., U.S. | J8 | 110 |
| Milford, In., U.S. | A11 | 114 |
| Milford, Ia., U.S. | H12 | 118 |
| Milford, Me., U.S. | C18 | 108 |
| Milford, Ma., U.S. | E15 | 108 |
| Milford, Mi., U.S. | H12 | 110 |
| Milford, N.H., U.S. | E15 | 108 |
| Milford, Ne., U.S. | K11 | 118 |
| Milford, Oh., U.S. | H2 | 108 |
| Milford, Pa., U.S. | F12 | 108 |
| Milford, Ut., U.S. | F3 | 120 |
| Milford Center, Oh., U.S. | B3 | 108 |
| Milford Haven, Wales, U.K. | J7 | 8 |
| Milford Station, N.S., Can. | G10 | 106 |
| Milh, Bahr al-, l., Iraq | E7 | 48 |
| Milicz, Pol. | D17 | 10 |
| Milk, stm., N.A. | B19 | 122 |
| Mil'kovo, Russia | G23 | 28 |
| Milk River Ridge Reservoir, res., Ab., Can. | H22 | 102 |
| Millau, Fr. | H10 | 14 |
| Millboro, Va., U.S. | B7 | 112 |
| Millbrook, N.Y., U.S. | F13 | 108 |
| Millbrook, On., Can. | F17 | 110 |
| Mill City, Or., U.S. | F3 | 122 |
| Millcreek, Pa., U.S. | E6 | 108 |
| Millcreek, Ut., U.S. | D5 | 120 |
| Mill Creek, W.V., U.S. | I7 | 108 |
| Milledgeville, Ga., U.S. | F3 | 112 |
| Milledgeville, Il., U.S. | I6 | 110 |
| Mille Lacs, Lac des, l., On., Can. | D2 | 110 |
| Mille Lacs Lake, l., Mn., U.S. | E2 | 118 |
| Millen, Ga., U.S. | G5 | 112 |
| Miller, Mo., U.S. | D3 | 114 |
| Miller, S.D., U.S. | G9 | 118 |
| Miller Mountain, mtn., Nv., U.S. | F7 | 124 |
| Millersburg, Mi., U.S. | E11 | 110 |
| Millersburg, Oh., U.S. | G5 | 108 |
| Millersburg, Pa., U.S. | G10 | 108 |
| Millersport, Oh., U.S. | H4 | 108 |
| Millers Ferry, Al., U.S. | J10 | 114 |
| Millerton, N.Y., U.S. | F13 | 108 |
| Millerton Lake, res., Ca., U.S. | D17 | 106 |
| Millerton Junction, Nf., Can. | C17 | 106 |
| Millet, Ab., Can. | D21 | 102 |
| Millett, Tx., U.S. | K7 | 116 |
| Millevaches, Plateau de, plat., Fr. | G9 | 14 |
| Mill Hall, Pa., U.S. | F9 | 108 |
| Millicent, Austl. | K4 | 70 |
| Milligan, Fl., U.S. | L10 | 114 |
| Milligan, Ne., U.S. | K10 | 118 |
| Millington, Tn., U.S. | G2 | 114 |
| Millinocket, Me., U.S. | B18 | 108 |
| Mill Island, i., N.T., Can. | D17 | 96 |
| Millmerran, Austl. | F9 | 70 |
| Millport, Al., U.S. | I8 | 114 |
| Millry, Al., U.S. | K8 | 114 |
| Mills, Wy., U.S. | B10 | 120 |
| Milis Lake, l., N.T., Can. | D9 | 96 |
| Millstatt, Aus. | I13 | 10 |
| Millstream Chichester National Park, Austl. | D3 | 68 |
| Milltown, In., U.S. | D10 | 114 |
| Milltown, Mt., U.S. | D12 | 122 |
| Milltown, Wi., U.S. | E3 | 110 |
| Mill Valley, Ca., U.S. | G3 | 124 |
| Millville, N.J., U.S. | H11 | 108 |
| Millville, Va., U.S. | H8 | 108 |
| Millwood Lake, res., Ar., U.S. | I2 | 114 |
| Milne Bay, b., Pap. N. Gui. | B10 | 68 |
| Milner, Co., U.S. | E10 | 118 |
| Milnor, N.D., U.S. | E10 | 118 |
| Milo, Ab., Can. | G22 | 102 |
| Milo, Me., U.S. | C18 | 108 |
| Milos, Grc. | M8 | 20 |
| Milos, i., Grc. | M8 | 20 |
| Miloslavskoje, Russia | H22 | 22 |
| Milpitas, Ca., U.S. | G4 | 124 |
| Milroy, In., U.S. | C11 | 114 |
| Milroy, Pa., U.S. | G9 | 108 |
| Miltenberg, Ger. | F9 | 10 |
| Milton, De., U.S. | I11 | 108 |
| Milton, Fl., U.S. | L9 | 114 |
| Milton, In., U.S. | J3 | 110 |
| Milton, N.D., U.S. | C9 | 118 |
| Milton, N.Z. | G2 | 72 |
| Milton, On., Can. | G16 | 110 |
| Milton, Pa., U.S. | F10 | 108 |
| Milton, Vt., U.S. | C13 | 108 |
| Milton, Wi., U.S. | H7 | 110 |
| Milton, W.V., U.S. | I4 | 108 |
| Milton-Freewater, Or., U.S. | E7 | 122 |
| Miltonvale, Ks., U.S. | L10 | 118 |
| Milverton, On., Can. | G15 | 110 |
| Milwaukee, Wi., U.S. | G8 | 110 |
| Milwaukee, stm., Wi., U.S. | G7 | 110 |
| Milwaukie, Or., U.S. | E3 | 122 |
| Mim, Ghana | H8 | 64 |
| Mimbres, stm., N.M., U.S. | L9 | 120 |
| Mimoso, Braz. | G14 | 82 |
| Mimoso do Sul, Braz. | F8 | 79 |
| Mims, Fl., U.S. | K6 | 112 |
| Min, stm., China | E7 | 30 |
| Min, stm., China | I7 | 34 |
| Mina, Nv., U.S. | F7 | 124 |
| Mināb, Iran | H14 | 48 |
| Mina El Limón, Nic. | E8 | 92 |
| Minago, stm., Mb., Can. | D16 | 104 |
| Minahasa, pen., Indon. | E7 | 38 |
| Mina Pirquitas, Arg. | B5 | 80 |
| Minas, Cuba | D6 | 94 |
| Minas, Ur. | H11 | 80 |
| Minas, Sierra de las, mts., Guat. | B5 | 92 |
| Minas Basin, b., N.S., Can. | G9 | 106 |
| Minas Channel, strt., N.S., Can. | G9 | 106 |
| Minas de Barroterán, Mex. | D9 | 90 |
| Minas de Corrales, Ur. | F11 | 80 |
| Minas de Matahambre, Cuba | C3 | 94 |
| Minas de Oro, Hond. | C7 | 92 |
| Minas Gerais, state, Braz. | E6 | 79 |
| Minas Novas, Braz. | D7 | 79 |
| Minatare, Ne., U.S. | J4 | 118 |
| Minatitlán, Mex. | I12 | 90 |
| Minbu, Myan. | D3 | 40 |
| Minco, Ok., U.S. | D9 | 116 |
| Mindanao, i., Phil. | D8 | 38 |
| Mindelo, C.V. | k16 | 64a |
| Mindemoya, On., Can. | E13 | 110 |
| Minden, Ger. | C8 | 10 |
| Minden, La., U.S. | J3 | 114 |
| Minden, Ne., U.S. | K9 | 118 |
| Minden, Nv., U.S. | F6 | 124 |
| Minden, On., Can. | F17 | 110 |
| Minden City, Mi., U.S. | G13 | 110 |
| Mindenmines, Mo., U.S. | E2 | 114 |
| Mindon, Myan. | E3 | 40 |
| Mindoro, i., Phil. | C7 | 38 |
| Mindoro Strait, strt., Phil. | C7 | 38 |
| Mine Centre, On., Can. | B3 | 110 |
| Mineral, Wa., U.S. | D3 | 122 |
| Mineral de Cucharas, Mex. | F7 | 90 |
| Mineral'nye Vody, Russia | I6 | 26 |
| Mineral Point, Wi., U.S. | H5 | 110 |
| Mineral Springs, Ar., U.S. | I3 | 114 |
| Mineral Wells, Tx., U.S. | G8 | 116 |
| Minersville, Pa., U.S. | G10 | 108 |
| Minersville, Ut., U.S. | F3 | 120 |
| Minerva, Oh., U.S. | G5 | 108 |
| Minervino Murge, Italy | H11 | 18 |
| Mineville, N.Y., U.S. | C13 | 108 |
| Minfeng, China | D3 | 30 |
| Mingan, P.Q., Can. | B9 | 106 |
| Mingan, stm., P.Q., Can. | B10 | 106 |
| Mingan, Îles de, is., P.Q., Can. | B10 | 106 |
| Mingan Archipelago National Park, P.Q., Can. | B10 | 106 |
| Mingela, Austl. | B7 | 70 |
| Minggang, China | C3 | 34 |
| Mingo Junction, Oh., U.S. | G6 | 108 |
| Minhang, China | D10 | 34 |
| Minhla, Myan. | D3 | 40 |
| Minho, hist. reg., Port. | D3 | 16 |
| Minho (Miño), stm., Eur. | D3 | 16 |
| Minhou, China | I7 | 34 |
| Minicoy Island, i., India | H2 | 46 |
| Minier, Il., U.S. | B7 | 114 |
| Minīn, Syria | A6 | 50 |
| Ministikwan Lake, l., Sk., Can. | D5 | 104 |
| Minitonas, Mb., Can. | F13 | 104 |
| Minjar, Russia | F9 | 26 |
| Min'kovo, Russia | B26 | 22 |
| Minle, China | D7 | 30 |
| Minna, Nig. | G13 | 64 |
| Minneapolis, Ks., U.S. | L10 | 118 |
| Minneapolis, Mn., U.S. | F2 | 118 |
| Minnedosa, Mb., Can. | H15 | 104 |
| Minnehaha, Wa., U.S. | E3 | 122 |
| Minneola, Ks., U.S. | N7 | 118 |
| Minneota, Mn., U.S. | G12 | 118 |
| Minnesota, state, U.S. | D8 | 98 |
| Minnesota, stm., Mn., U.S. | F2 | 118 |
| Minnesota Lake, Mn., U.S. | G2 | 118 |
| Minnetonka, Mn., U.S. | F2 | 118 |
| Minnewanka, Lake, l., Ab., Can. | F19 | 102 |
| Minnie Lake, l., On., Can. | H15 | 104 |
| Mino, Japan | L11 | 36 |
| Miño (Minho), stm., Eur. | D3 | 16 |
| Minocqua, Wi., U.S. | E6 | 110 |
| Minonk, Il., U.S. | J6 | 110 |
| Minong, Wi., U.S. | D4 | 110 |
| Minot, N.D., U.S. | C6 | 118 |
| Minsk, Bela. | H10 | 22 |
| Minsk Mazowiecki, Pol. | C21 | 10 |
| Minster, Oh., U.S. | G2 | 108 |
| Mintaka Pass, Asia | B6 | 44 |
| Minto, Ak., U.S. | D20 | 100 |
| Minto, Mb., Can. | I14 | 104 |
| Minto, N.B., Can. | F7 | 106 |
| Minto, N.D., U.S. | C10 | 118 |
| Minto, Yk., Can. | E26 | 100 |
| Mintó, Lac, l., P.Q., Can. | E17 | 96 |
| Minto Inlet, b., N.T., Can. | B9 | 96 |
| Minton, Sk., Can. | I10 | 104 |
| Minturn, Co., U.S. | E10 | 120 |
| Minturno, Italy | H8 | 18 |
| Minusinsk, Russia | G10 | 28 |
| Minxian, China | E7 | 30 |
| Minya see Al-Minyā, Egypt | C6 | 60 |
| Minya Konka see Gongga Shan, mtn., China | F7 | 30 |
| Mio, Mi., U.S. | F11 | 110 |
| Mir, Bela. | H9 | 22 |
| Mira, Port. | E3 | 16 |
| Mira, stm., Col. | G3 | 84 |
| Mira, stm., N.S., Can. | G13 | 106 |
| Mira Bay, b., N.S., Can. | F14 | 106 |
| Miracema do Tocantins, Braz. | E9 | 76 |
| Mirador, Braz. | E10 | 76 |
| Miradouro, Braz. | F7 | 79 |
| Miraflores, Arg. | E6 | 80 |
| Miraflores, Col. | F5 | 84 |
| Miraflores, Col. | G6 | 84 |
| Miraflores, Esclusas de, Pan. | I15 | 92 |
| Mīrah, Wādī al-, val., Asia | B11 | 60 |
| Miraj, India | D3 | 46 |
| Miramar, Arg. | J10 | 80 |
| Miramar, Arg. | F7 | 80 |
| Miramar, C.R. | G10 | 92 |
| Miramas, Fr. | I12 | 14 |
| Miramichi Bay, b., N.B., Can. | E9 | 106 |
| Miranda, Braz. | I13 | 82 |
| Miranda, Ca., U.S. | D2 | 124 |
| Miranda, Col. | F4 | 84 |
| Miranda, state, Ven. | B9 | 84 |
| Miranda, stm., Braz. | H13 | 82 |
| Miranda de Ebro, Spain | C9 | 16 |
| Miranda do Douro, Port. | D5 | 16 |
| Mirande, Fr. | I7 | 14 |
| Mirandela, Port. | D4 | 16 |
| Mirando City, Tx., U.S. | L7 | 116 |
| Mirandola, Italy | E6 | 18 |
| Mirante do Paranapanema, Braz. | G3 | 79 |
| Mirapuxi, stm., Braz. | B3 | 79 |
| Mira Taglio, Italy | D7 | 18 |
| Miravalles, Volcán, vol., C.R. | G9 | 92 |
| Mirbāt, Oman | F9 | 47 |
| Mirebeau-sur-Bèze, Fr. | E12 | 14 |
| Mirecourt, Fr. | D13 | 14 |
| Miri, Malay. | E5 | 38 |
| Miriam Vale, Austl. | E9 | 70 |
| Mirim, Lagoa (Laguna Merín), b., S.A. | G12 | 80 |
| Miriñay, stm., Arg. | E10 | 80 |
| Miritiparaná, stm., Col. | H7 | 84 |
| Mirjāveh, Iran | G16 | 48 |
| Mirnyj, Russia | E14 | 28 |
| Mirnyj, sci., Ant. | B6 | 73 |
| Mirond Lake, l., Sk., Can. | C12 | 104 |
| Mirow, Ger. | B12 | 10 |
| Mirpur, Pak. | D5 | 44 |
| Mīrpur Khās, Pak. | H3 | 44 |
| Mirria, Niger | E14 | 64 |
| Mirror, Ab., Can. | E21 | 102 |
| Mirzāpur, India | H10 | 44 |
| Mirzā, Bi'r, well, Egypt | F4 | 60 |
| Misāhah, Bi'r, well, Egypt | H4 | 60 |
| Miscou Centre, N.B., Can. | E9 | 106 |
| Miscou Island, i., N.B., Can. | E9 | 106 |
| Miscou Point, c., N.B., Can. | E9 | 106 |
| Misenheimer, N.C., U.S. | D6 | 112 |
| Mishagua, stm., Peru | D5 | 82 |
| Mishan, China | B13 | 30 |
| Mishawaka, In., U.S. | A10 | 114 |
| Mishbīh, Jabal, mtn., Egypt | J3 | 48 |
| Mishicot, Wi., U.S. | F8 | 110 |
| Misikan, China | C13 | 44 |
| Misilmeri, Italy | K8 | 18 |
| Misiones, prov., Arg. | D11 | 80 |
| Misiones, dept., Para. | D10 | 80 |
| Misión San Francisco de Laishí, Arg. | D9 | 80 |
| Misión San Vicente, Mex. | B1 | 90 |
| Miskī, Sudan | J3 | 60 |
| Miskito Channel, strt., Nic. | C11 | 92 |
| Miskitos, Cayos, is., Nic. | C12 | 92 |
| Miskolc, Hung. | G20 | 10 |
| Mislata, Spain | A10 | 62 |
| Misool, Pulau, i., Indon. | F9 | 38 |
| Misquamaebin Lake, l., On., Can. | E23 | 104 |
| Misrātah, Libya | B4 | 56 |
| Missinaibi, stm., On., Can. | F16 | 96 |
| Missinaibi Lake, l., On., Can. | B12 | 110 |
| Mission, S.D., U.S. | H7 | 118 |
| Mission, Tx., U.S. | M8 | 116 |
| Mission City, B.C., Can. | H12 | 102 |
| Mississauga, On., Can. | G16 | 110 |
| Mississinewa, stm., In., U.S. | B11 | 114 |
| Mississippi, state, U.S. | E9 | 98 |
| Mississippi, stm., U.S. | E8 | 98 |
| Mississippi Delta, La., U.S. | M7 | 114 |
| Mississippi Sound, strt., U.S. | L8 | 114 |
| Mississippi State, Ms., U.S. | I8 | 114 |
| Missoula, Mt., U.S. | D12 | 122 |
| Missouri, state, U.S. | D8 | 98 |
| Missouri, stm., U.S. | C9 | 98 |
| Missouri Valley, Ia., U.S. | J12 | 118 |
| Mistaken Point, c., Nf., Can. | F20 | 106 |
| Mistanipisipou, stm., P.Q., Can. | A11 | 106 |
| Mistassibi, stm., P.Q., Can. | G18 | 96 |
| Mistassibi Nord-Est, stm., P.Q., Can. | B2 | 106 |
| Mistassini, stm., P.Q., Can. | F18 | 96 |
| Mistassini, Lac, l., P.Q., Can. | F18 | 96 |
| Mistatim, Sk., Can. | F11 | 104 |
| Mistawasis Indian Reserve, Sk., Can. | E8 | 104 |
| Misterbianco, Italy | L9 | 18 |
| Misteri, Sudan | K2 | 60 |
| Misti, Volcán, vol., Peru | G6 | 82 |
| Mistikan, stm., P.Q., Can. | B23 | 104 |
| Mistretta, Italy | L9 | 18 |
| Mita, Punta, c., Mex. | G7 | 90 |
| Mitchell, Austl. | F7 | 70 |
| Mitchell, In., U.S. | D10 | 114 |
| Mitchell, Ne., U.S. | J4 | 118 |
| Mitchell, On., Can. | G14 | 110 |
| Mitchell, Or., U.S. | F6 | 122 |
| Mitchell, S.D., U.S. | H9 | 118 |
| Mitchell, stm., Austl. | H7 | 70 |
| Mitchell, Lake, l., Al., U.S. | J10 | 114 |
| Mitchell, Mount, mtn., N.C., U.S. | D4 | 112 |
| Mitchell Lake, l., B.C., Can. | E14 | 102 |
| Mitchellville, Ia., U.S. | J2 | 118 |
| Mitilíni, Grc. | J10 | 20 |

| Name | Map Ref. | Page |
|---|---|---|
| Mitis, Lac, l., P.Q., Can. | D6 | 106 |
| Mitishto, stm., Mb., Can. | D15 | 104 |
| Mitla, hist., Mex. | I11 | 90 |
| Mito, Japan | K15 | 36 |
| Mitsamiouli, Com. | k15 | 67a |
| Mitsinjo, Madag. | p21 | 67b |
| Mitsio, Nosy, i., Madag. | n23 | 67b |
| Mitsiwa (Massawa), Erit. | J10 | 60 |
| Mittellandkanal, Ger. | C9 | 10 |
| Mittenwald, Ger. | H11 | 10 |
| Mittersill, Aus. | H12 | 10 |
| Mitú, Col. | G7 | 84 |
| Mitumba, Monts, mts., D.R.C. | B5 | 58 |
| Mitwaba, D.R.C. | C5 | 58 |
| Mitzic, Gabon | A2 | 58 |
| Miura, Japan | L14 | 36 |
| Mixco Viejo, hist., Guat. | C4 | 92 |
| Miyake-jima, i., Japan | M14 | 36 |
| Miyako, Japan | H16 | 36 |
| Miyakonojō, Japan | P6 | 36 |
| Miyazaki, Japan | P6 | 36 |
| Miyazu, Japan | L10 | 36 |
| Miyun, China | C4 | 32 |
| Mizan Teferi, Eth. | N8 | 60 |
| Mizdah, Libya | B3 | 56 |
| Mize, Ms., U.S. | K7 | 114 |
| Mizen Head, c., Ire. | J4 | 8 |
| Mizhhir'ya, Ukr. | A7 | 20 |
| Mizoram, state, India | I15 | 44 |
| Mizpé Ramon, Isr. | G3 | 50 |
| Mizque, Bol. | G9 | 82 |
| Mizque, stm., Bol. | H9 | 82 |
| Mjadzel, Bela. | G9 | 22 |
| Mjøsa, l., Nor. | K12 | 6 |
| Mladá Boleslav, Czech Rep. | E14 | 10 |
| Mladenovac, Yugo. | E4 | 20 |
| Mlanje Peak see Sapitwa, mtn., Mwi. | E7 | 58 |
| Mława, Pol. | B20 | 10 |
| Mmabatho, S. Afr. | E7 | 66 |
| Mmadinare, Bots. | C8 | 66 |
| Mo, Nor. | H14 | 6 |
| Mo, stm., Afr. | G10 | 64 |
| Moa, stm., Afr. | G4 | 54 |
| Moa, stm., Braz. | B5 | 82 |
| Moab, Ut., U.S. | F7 | 120 |
| Moaco, stm., Braz. | C7 | 82 |
| Moa Island, i., Austl. | B8 | 68 |
| Moama, Austl. | K6 | 70 |
| Moanda, Gabon | B2 | 58 |
| Moar Lake, l., Can. | F19 | 104 |
| Mobara, Japan | L15 | 36 |
| Mobaye, C.A.R. | H5 | 56 |
| Mobeetie, Tx., U.S. | D6 | 116 |
| Moberly, Mo., U.S. | C4 | 114 |
| Moberly, stm., B.C., Can. | A13 | 102 |
| Moberly Lake, B.C., Can. | B13 | 102 |
| Moberly Lake, l., B.C., Can. | B13 | 102 |
| Mobile, Al., U.S. | L8 | 114 |
| Mobile, Az., U.S. | K4 | 120 |
| Mobile, stm., Al., U.S. | L8 | 114 |
| Mobile Bay, b., Al., U.S. | L8 | 114 |
| Mobridge, S.D., U.S. | F7 | 118 |
| Moca, Dom. Rep. | E9 | 94 |
| Mocal, stm., N.A. | C6 | 92 |
| Moçambique, Moz. | E8 | 58 |
| Mocanal, Spain | p23 | 17b |
| Mocha see al-Makhā', Yemen | H3 | 47 |
| Mocha, Isla, i., Chile | J2 | 80 |
| Moche, stm., Peru | C2 | 82 |
| Moche, hist., Peru | C2 | 82 |
| Mochudi, Bots. | E8 | 66 |
| Mocímboa da Praia, Moz. | D8 | 58 |
| Mocksville, N.C., U.S. | D6 | 112 |
| Moclips, Wa., U.S. | C1 | 122 |
| Môco, Serra do, mtn., Ang. | D3 | 58 |
| Mocoa, Col. | G4 | 84 |
| Mococa, Braz. | F5 | 79 |
| Mocoduene, Moz. | D12 | 66 |
| Mocoretá, Arg. | F10 | 80 |
| Mocorito, Mex. | E6 | 90 |
| Moctezuma, Mex. | C5 | 90 |
| Moctezuma, stm., Mex. | C5 | 90 |
| Moctezuma, stm., Mex. | G10 | 90 |
| Mocuba, Moz. | E7 | 58 |
| Modane, Fr. | G13 | 14 |
| Modderrivier, S. Afr. | G7 | 66 |
| Modena, Italy | E5 | 18 |
| Modesto, Ca., U.S. | G5 | 124 |
| Modica, Italy | M9 | 18 |
| Mödling, Aus. | G16 | 10 |
| Moe, Austl. | L7 | 70 |
| Moeda, Braz. | F6 | 79 |
| Moema, Braz. | E6 | 79 |
| Moengo, Sur. | B8 | 76 |
| Moenkopi, Az., U.S. | H5 | 120 |
| Moffit, N.D., U.S. | E7 | 118 |
| Moga, India | E6 | 44 |
| Mogadiscio see Muqdisho, Som. | H10 | 56 |
| Mogadishu see Muqdisho, Som. | H10 | 56 |
| Mogán, Spain | p25 | 17b |
| Mogapinyana, Bots. | D8 | 66 |
| Mogaung, Myan. | B4 | 40 |
| Mogincual, Moz. | E8 | 58 |
| Mogliano Veneto, Italy | D7 | 18 |
| Mogoča, Russia | G15 | 28 |
| Mogogh, Sudan | M6 | 60 |
| Mogok, Myan. | C4 | 40 |
| Mogollon Rim, clf., Az., U.S. | J6 | 120 |
| Mogotes, Col. | D6 | 84 |
| Mogotón, mtn., N.A. | D8 | 92 |
| Moguer, Spain | H5 | 16 |
| Mogzon, Russia | G14 | 28 |
| Mohács, Hung. | J18 | 10 |
| Mohall, N.D., U.S. | C6 | 118 |
| Mohammedia (Fedala), Mor. | D7 | 62 |
| Mohave, Lake, res., U.S. | I11 | 124 |
| Mohawk, Mi., U.S. | C7 | 110 |
| Mohawk, N.Y., U.S. | E12 | 108 |
| Mohe, China | A11 | 30 |
| Moho, Peru | G6 | 82 |
| Mohon Peak, mtn., Az., U.S. | J4 | 120 |
| Mohyliv-Podil's'kyy, Ukr. | A13 | 20 |
| Moinești, Rom. | C10 | 20 |
| Moiporá, Braz. | D3 | 79 |
| Mõisaküla, Est. | C8 | 22 |
| Moisés Ville, Arg. | F8 | 80 |
| Moisie, P.Q., Can. | B7 | 106 |
| Moisie, stm., P.Q., Can. | F19 | 96 |
| Moisie, Baie de la, b., P.Q., Can. | B8 | 106 |
| Moissac, Fr. | H8 | 14 |
| Moitaco, Ven. | C10 | 84 |
| Mojácar, Spain | H9 | 16 |
| Mojados, Spain | D7 | 16 |
| Mojana, Brazo, mth., Col. | C5 | 84 |
| Mojave, Ca., U.S. | I7 | 124 |
| Mojave Desert, des., Ca., U.S. | J8 | 124 |
| Mojiguaçú, stm., Braz. | F5 | 79 |
| Mojimirim, Braz. | F5 | 79 |
| Mojkovac, Russia | D12 | 28 |
| Mojo, Eth. | M10 | 60 |
| Mojynty, Russia | H12 | 26 |
| Mokāma, India | H11 | 44 |
| Mokelumne, stm., Ca., U.S. | F4 | 124 |
| Mokine, Tun. | N5 | 18 |
| Mokp'o, S. Kor. | I14 | 32 |
| Mokrisset, Mor. | K6 | 16 |
| Mokša, stm., Russia | G24 | 22 |
| Mokwa, Nig. | G6 | 64 |
| Mol, Bel. | F7 | 12 |
| Mola di Bari, Italy | H12 | 18 |
| Molalla, Or., U.S. | E3 | 122 |
| Molanosa, Sk., Can. | D9 | 104 |
| Moldau see Vltava, stm., Czech Rep. | F14 | 10 |
| Moldavia, hist. reg., Rom. | B11 | 20 |
| Moldavia see Moldova, ctry., Eur. | F13 | 4 |
| Molde, Nor. | J10 | 6 |
| Moldova, ctry., Eur. | F13 | 4 |
| Moldoveanu, Vârful, mtn., Rom. | D8 | 20 |
| Môle, Cap du, c., Haiti | E8 | 94 |
| Molega Lake, l., N.S., Can. | H9 | 106 |
| Molepolole, Bots. | E7 | 66 |
| Molétai, Lith. | F8 | 22 |
| Molfetta, Italy | H11 | 18 |
| Molina, Chile | H3 | 80 |
| Molina de Segura, Spain | G10 | 16 |
| Moline, Il., U.S. | I5 | 110 |
| Moline, Ks., U.S. | N11 | 118 |
| Molino, Fl., U.S. | L9 | 114 |
| Molinos, Arg. | C5 | 80 |
| Molins de Rei, Spain | D14 | 16 |
| Molise, prov., Italy | H9 | 18 |
| Mollendo, Peru | G5 | 82 |
| Mollepata, Peru | E5 | 82 |
| Mölln, Ger. | B10 | 10 |
| Mölndal, Swe. | M13 | 6 |
| Moločnoje, Russia | B22 | 22 |
| Mologa, stm., Russia | C19 | 22 |
| Molokai, i., Hi., U.S. | p16 | 125a |
| Molong, Austl. | I8 | 70 |
| Molopo, stm., Afr. | F5 | 66 |
| Molotov see Perm', Russia | F9 | 26 |
| Molou, Chad | K1 | 60 |
| Molsheim, Fr. | D14 | 14 |
| Molson Lake, l., Mb., Can. | D18 | 104 |
| Molteno, S. Afr. | H8 | 66 |
| Moluccas see Maluku, is., Indon. | F8 | 38 |
| Molucca Sea see Maluku, Laut, Indon. | F7 | 38 |
| Moma, Moz. | E7 | 58 |
| Moma, stm., Russia | D20 | 28 |
| Momanga, Nmb. | B5 | 66 |
| Mombachito, Cerro, mtn., Nic. | E9 | 92 |
| Mombacho, Volcán, vol., Nic. | E8 | 92 |
| Mombasa, Kenya | B7 | 58 |
| Mombetsu, Japan | c18 | 36a |
| Momence, Il., U.S. | I8 | 110 |
| Momotombo, Volcán, vol., Nic. | E8 | 92 |
| Mompós, Col. | C5 | 84 |
| Mona, Ut., U.S. | E5 | 120 |
| Mona, Canal de la, strt., N.A. | E11 | 94 |
| Mona, Isla de, i., P.R. | E11 | 94 |
| Mona, Punta, c., C.R. | H12 | 92 |
| Monaca, Pa., U.S. | G6 | 108 |
| Monaco, ctry., Eur. | G9 | 4 |
| Monadnock Mountain, mtn., N.H., U.S. | E14 | 108 |
| Monagas, state, Ven. | C11 | 84 |
| Monaghan, co., Ire. | G6 | 8 |
| Monagrillo, Pan. | D2 | 84 |
| Monahans, Tx., U.S. | H4 | 116 |
| Monango, N.D., U.S. | E9 | 118 |
| Monarch, Mt., U.S. | E5 | 112 |
| Monarch Mountain, mtn., B.C., Can. | F9 | 102 |
| Monarch Pass, Co., U.S. | F10 | 120 |
| Monashee Mountains, mts., B.C., Can. | F16 | 102 |
| Monashee Provincial Park, B.C., Can. | G16 | 102 |
| Monastir, Tun. | N5 | 18 |
| Monastir see Bitola, Mac. | H5 | 20 |
| Monastyrščina, Russia | G14 | 22 |
| Moncalieri, Italy | D2 | 18 |
| Monção, Braz. | D9 | 76 |
| Monçegorsk, Russia | D4 | 26 |
| Mönchengladbach, Ger. | D6 | 10 |
| Moncks Corner, S.C., U.S. | F6 | 112 |
| Monclova, Mex. | D4 | 90 |
| Moncontour, Fr. | D4 | 14 |
| Moncton, N.B., Can. | F6 | 106 |
| Mondaí, Braz. | D12 | 80 |
| Monday, stm., Para. | C11 | 80 |
| Mondoro, Mali | D9 | 64 |
| Mondoubleau, Fr. | E7 | 14 |
| Mondovi, Wi., U.S. | F4 | 110 |
| Mondovì, Italy | H8 | 18 |
| Mondragone, Italy | H8 | 18 |
| Monero, N.M., U.S. | H10 | 120 |
| Moneron, ostrov, i., Russia | a16 | 36a |
| Monessen, Pa., U.S. | G7 | 108 |
| Monesterio, Spain | G5 | 16 |
| Monett, Mo., U.S. | F3 | 114 |
| Monette, Ar., U.S. | G6 | 114 |
| Monfalcone, Italy | D8 | 18 |
| Monflanquin, Fr. | H7 | 14 |
| Monforte, Port. | F4 | 16 |
| Monforte de Lemos, Spain | C4 | 16 |
| Mongaguá, Braz. | H5 | 79 |
| Mongala, Sudan | G7 | 56 |
| Mong Cai, Viet. | D9 | 40 |
| Monger, Îles, is., P.Q., Can. | A15 | 106 |
| Mongers Lake, l., Austl. | E3 | 68 |
| Möng Hsat, Myan. | D5 | 40 |
| Möng Mit, Myan. | C4 | 40 |
| Mongo, Chad | F4 | 56 |
| Mongo, stm., Afr. | G4 | 64 |
| Mongol Altajn nuruu, mts., Asia | H16 | 26 |
| Mongolia (Mongol Ard Uls), ctry., Asia | B8 | 30 |
| Mongororo, Chad | K2 | 60 |
| Möng Pai, Myan. | E4 | 40 |
| Mongu, Zam. | E4 | 58 |
| Möng Yawng, Myan. | D5 | 40 |
| Monheim, Ger. | G10 | 10 |
| Monico, Wi., U.S. | E6 | 110 |
| Monida Pass, U.S. | F13 | 122 |
| Monino, Russia | F21 | 22 |
| Moniquirá, Col. | E6 | 84 |
| Monistrol-sur-Loire, Fr. | G11 | 14 |
| Monitor Range, mts., Nv., U.S. | F9 | 124 |
| Monitor Valley, val., Nv., U.S. | F9 | 124 |
| Monkey River, Belize | A6 | 92 |
| Mońki, Pol. | B22 | 10 |
| Monkira, Austl. | E4 | 70 |
| Monmouth, Il., U.S. | J5 | 110 |
| Monmouth, Or., U.S. | F2 | 122 |
| Monmouth Mountain, mtn., B.C., Can. | F11 | 102 |
| Mono, stm., Afr. | G7 | 54 |
| Mono, Caño, stm., Col. | E8 | 84 |
| Mono, Punta, c., Nic. | F11 | 92 |
| Mono Lake, l., Ca., U.S. | F7 | 124 |
| Monona, Ia., U.S. | B10 | 114 |
| Monona, Wi., U.S. | G6 | 110 |
| Monongahela, stm., U.S. | H7 | 108 |
| Monopoli, Italy | I12 | 18 |
| Monòver, Spain | G11 | 16 |
| Monreale, Italy | K8 | 18 |
| Monroe, Ga., U.S. | F3 | 112 |
| Monroe, Ia., U.S. | H4 | 110 |
| Monroe, La., U.S. | J4 | 114 |
| Monroe, Mi., U.S. | I12 | 110 |
| Monroe, N.C., U.S. | E6 | 112 |
| Monroe, Ne., U.S. | J10 | 118 |
| Monroe, N.Y., U.S. | F12 | 108 |
| Monroe, Or., U.S. | F2 | 122 |
| Monroe, Ut., U.S. | F4 | 120 |
| Monroe, Va., U.S. | B7 | 112 |
| Monroe, Wa., U.S. | C4 | 122 |
| Monroe, Wi., U.S. | H6 | 110 |
| Monroe City, Mo., U.S. | C5 | 114 |
| Monroe Lake, res., In., U.S. | C10 | 114 |
| Monroeville, Al., U.S. | K9 | 114 |
| Monroeville, In., U.S. | B12 | 114 |
| Monroeville, Oh., U.S. | F4 | 108 |
| Monroeville, Pa., U.S. | G7 | 108 |
| Monrovia, Lib. | H4 | 64 |
| Mons (Bergen), Bel. | H4 | 12 |
| Monséfu, Peru | B2 | 82 |
| Monselice, Italy | D6 | 18 |
| Monson, Me., U.S. | B17 | 108 |
| Montabaur, Ger. | E7 | 10 |
| Montagnana, Italy | D6 | 18 |
| Montagu, S. Afr. | I5 | 66 |
| Montague, Ca., U.S. | C3 | 124 |
| Montague, Mi., U.S. | G9 | 110 |
| Montague, P.E., Can. | F11 | 106 |
| Montague, Tx., U.S. | F9 | 116 |
| Montague, Isla, i., Mex. | B2 | 90 |
| Montague Island, i., Ak., U.S. | F21 | 100 |
| Montagu Island, i., S. Geor. | A2 | 73 |
| Montaigu, Fr. | F5 | 14 |
| Montalbán, Spain | E10 | 16 |
| Montalcino, Italy | F6 | 18 |
| Montalegre, Port. | D4 | 16 |
| Montana, Bul. | F7 | 20 |
| Montana, Switz. | F7 | 13 |
| Montana, state, U.S. | B4 | 98 |
| Montana Indian Reserve, Ab., Can. | E21 | 102 |
| Montargis, Fr. | D9 | 14 |
| Montauban, Fr. | H8 | 14 |
| Montauk, N.Y., U.S. | F15 | 108 |
| Montauk Point, c., N.Y., U.S. | F15 | 108 |
| Montbard, Fr. | E11 | 14 |
| Montbarrey, Fr. | E12 | 14 |
| Montbéliard, Fr. | E13 | 14 |
| Mont Blanc, Tunnel du, Eur. | G6 | 13 |
| Montbrison, Fr. | G11 | 14 |
| Montbron, Fr. | F7 | 14 |
| Montceau-[les-Mines], Fr. | F11 | 14 |
| Montcevelles, Lac, l., P.Q., Can. | A13 | 106 |
| Montchanin, Fr. | F11 | 14 |
| Montclair, Ca., U.S. | J8 | 124 |
| Montclair, N.J., U.S. | G12 | 108 |
| Mont-de-Marsan, Fr. | I6 | 14 |
| Montdidier, Fr. | C9 | 14 |
| Monte, Laguna del, l., Arg. | I7 | 80 |
| Monteagle, Tn., U.S. | G11 | 114 |
| Monte Albán, hist., Mex. | I11 | 90 |
| Monte Alegre, Braz. | D8 | 76 |
| Monte Alegre de Goiás, Braz. | B5 | 79 |
| Monte Alegre de Minas, Braz. | E4 | 79 |
| Monte Azul, Braz. | C7 | 79 |
| Monte Azul Paulista, Braz. | F4 | 79 |
| Montebello, P.Q., Can. | B12 | 108 |
| Monte Bello Islands, is., Austl. | D3 | 68 |
| Monte Buey, Arg. | G7 | 80 |
| Montecarlo, Arg. | D11 | 80 |
| Monte Caseros, Arg. | F10 | 80 |
| Montecassino, Abbazia di, Italy | H8 | 18 |
| Montecatini-Terme, Italy | F5 | 18 |
| Montecillos, Cordillera de, mts., Hond. | C7 | 92 |
| Montecito, Ca., U.S. | J6 | 124 |
| Monte Comán, Arg. | H5 | 80 |
| Monte Creek, B.C., Can. | G15 | 102 |
| Monte Cristi, Dom. Rep. | E9 | 94 |
| Montecristi, Ec. | D1 | 84 |
| Monte Cristo, Bol. | F11 | 82 |
| Monte Escobedo, Mex. | F8 | 90 |
| Montego Bay, Jam. | E6 | 94 |
| Monte Grande, Chile | F3 | 80 |
| Montegut, La., U.S. | M6 | 114 |
| Monteith, Mount, mtn., B.C., Can. | B12 | 102 |
| Montelíbano, Col. | C5 | 84 |
| Montélimar, Fr. | H11 | 14 |
| Montelindo, stm., Para. | B9 | 80 |
| Montellano, Spain | H6 | 16 |
| Montello, Nv., U.S. | C11 | 124 |
| Montello, Wi., U.S. | G6 | 110 |
| Monte Maíz, Arg. | G7 | 80 |
| Montemorelos, Mex. | E10 | 90 |
| Montemor-o-Novo, Port. | G3 | 16 |
| Montemor-o-Velho, Port. | E3 | 16 |
| Montendre, Fr. | G6 | 14 |
| Montenegro, Braz. | D12 | 80 |
| Montenegro see Crna Gora, state, Yugo. | G2 | 20 |
| Monte Pascoal, Parque Nacional de, Braz. | D9 | 79 |
| Monte Patria, Chile | F3 | 80 |
| Montepuez, Moz. | D7 | 58 |
| Montepulciano, Italy | F6 | 18 |
| Monte Quemado, Arg. | C7 | 80 |
| Montereau-Faut-Yonne, Fr. | D9 | 14 |
| Monterey, Ca., U.S. | H4 | 124 |
| Monterey, Va., U.S. | I7 | 108 |
| Monterey Bay, b., Ca., U.S. | H4 | 124 |
| Montería, Col. | C5 | 84 |
| Montero, Bol. | G10 | 82 |
| Monteros, Arg. | D6 | 80 |
| Monterotondo, Italy | G7 | 18 |
| Monterrey, Mex. | E9 | 90 |
| Montesano, Wa., U.S. | D2 | 122 |
| Monte Sant'Angelo, Italy | H10 | 18 |
| Montesarchio, Italy | H9 | 18 |
| Montes Claros, Braz. | D7 | 79 |
| Montevallo, Al., U.S. | I10 | 114 |
| Montevarchi, Italy | F6 | 18 |
| Montevideo, Ur. | H10 | 80 |
| Monte Vista, Co., U.S. | G10 | 120 |
| Montezuma, Ga., U.S. | G2 | 112 |
| Montezuma, In., U.S. | C9 | 114 |
| Montezuma, Ia., U.S. | H4 | 110 |
| Montezuma, Ks., U.S. | N7 | 118 |
| Montfort, Fr. | D5 | 14 |
| Montfort, Wi., U.S. | H5 | 110 |
| Montgomery, Al., U.S. | J10 | 114 |
| Montgomery, La., U.S. | K4 | 114 |
| Montgomery, Mn., U.S. | F2 | 110 |
| Montgomery, Pa., U.S. | F10 | 108 |
| Montgomery, Tx., U.S. | I11 | 116 |
| Montgomery, W.V., U.S. | I5 | 108 |
| Montgomery City, Mo., U.S. | C5 | 114 |
| Monthermé, Fr. | C11 | 14 |
| Monthois, Fr. | C11 | 14 |
| Monticello, Fl., U.S. | I3 | 112 |
| Monticello, Ga., U.S. | F3 | 112 |
| Monticello, Ia., U.S. | H4 | 110 |
| Monticello, Il., U.S. | B8 | 114 |
| Monticello, In., U.S. | B10 | 114 |
| Monticello, Ky., U.S. | F12 | 114 |
| Monticello, Me., U.S. | E2 | 110 |
| Monticello, Mo., U.S. | B5 | 114 |
| Monticello, Ms., U.S. | K6 | 114 |
| Monticello, N.Y., U.S. | F12 | 108 |
| Monticello, Wi., U.S. | H6 | 110 |
| Montichiari, Italy | D5 | 18 |
| Montignac, Fr. | G8 | 14 |
| Montigny-le-Roi, Fr. | D12 | 14 |
| Montigny-sur-Aube, Fr. | E11 | 14 |
| Montijo, Pan. | D2 | 84 |
| Montijo, Port. | G3 | 16 |
| Montijo, Spain | G5 | 16 |
| Montilla, Spain | H7 | 16 |
| Montividiu, Braz. | C7 | 79 |
| Montivilliers, Fr. | C7 | 14 |
| Mont-Joli, P.Q., Can. | D5 | 106 |
| Mont-Laurier, P.Q., Can. | G17 | 96 |
| Mont-Louis, P.Q., Can. | C5 | 106 |
| Montluçon, Fr. | F9 | 14 |
| Montluel, Fr. | F12 | 14 |
| Montmagny, P.Q., Can. | F3 | 106 |
| Montmédy, Fr. | C12 | 14 |
| Montmirail, Fr. | D10 | 14 |
| Montmorency see Beauport, P.Q., Can. | F2 | 106 |
| Montmorency, stm., P.Q., Can. | E2 | 106 |
| Montmorillon, Fr. | F7 | 14 |
| Monto, Austl. | E9 | 70 |
| Montoro, Spain | G7 | 16 |
| Montour Falls, N.Y., U.S. | E10 | 108 |
| Montoursville, Pa., U.S. | F10 | 108 |
| Montpelier, Id., U.S. | H14 | 122 |
| Montpelier, In., U.S. | B11 | 114 |
| Montpelier, Ms., U.S. | I8 | 114 |
| Montpelier, Oh., U.S. | F2 | 108 |
| Montpelier, Vt., U.S. | C14 | 108 |
| Montpellier, Fr. | I10 | 14 |
| Montpon-Ménesterol, Fr. | G7 | 14 |
| Montréal, P.Q., Can. | B13 | 108 |
| Montreal, Wi., U.S. | D5 | 110 |
| Montreal, stm., Sk., Can. | D9 | 104 |
| Montreal Lake, Sk., Can. | D9 | 104 |
| Montreal Lake, l., Sk., Can. | D9 | 104 |
| Montreal Lake Indian Reserve, Sk., Can. | D9 | 104 |
| Montreuil, Fr. | B8 | 14 |
| Montreux, Switz. | F6 | 13 |
| Montrevel-[en-Bresse], Fr. | F12 | 14 |
| Montrose, Ia., U.S. | J4 | 110 |
| Montrose, Mi., U.S. | G12 | 110 |
| Montrose, Pa., U.S. | F11 | 108 |
| Montrose, Scot., U.K. | E11 | 8 |
| Montrose, S.D., U.S. | H10 | 118 |
| Montross, Va., U.S. | I10 | 108 |
| Monts, Pointe des, c., P.Q., Can. | C6 | 106 |
| Mont-Sainte-Anne, Parc du, P.Q., Can. | E3 | 106 |
| Mont-Saint-Michel see Le Mont-Saint-Michel, Fr. | D5 | 14 |
| Montserrat, dep., N.A. | F13 | 94 |
| Montvale, Va., U.S. | B7 | 112 |
| Monument, Or., U.S. | F6 | 122 |
| Monument Peak, mtn., Id., U.S. | H11 | 122 |
| Monument Valley, val., U.S. | G6 | 120 |
| Monywa, Myan. | C3 | 40 |
| Monza, Italy | D4 | 18 |
| Monze, Zam. | E5 | 58 |
| Monzón, Peru | C3 | 82 |
| Monzón, Spain | D12 | 16 |
| Moodie Island, i., N.T., Can. | D19 | 96 |
| Moody, Tx., U.S. | H9 | 116 |
| Mooirivier, S. Afr. | G9 | 66 |
| Mookane, Bots. | E7 | 66 |
| Moolawatana, Austl. | G3 | 70 |
| Moonie, stm., Austl. | F8 | 70 |
| Moonta, Austl. | J2 | 70 |
| Moora, Austl. | F3 | 68 |
| Moorcroft, Wy., U.S. | G12 | 122 |
| Moore, Id., U.S. | G12 | 122 |
| Moore, Mt., U.S. | D16 | 122 |
| Moore, Ok., U.S. | D9 | 116 |
| Moore, Tx., U.S. | J7 | 116 |
| Moore, Lake, l., Austl. | E3 | 68 |
| Moore Haven, Fl., U.S. | M5 | 112 |
| Mooreland, Ok., U.S. | C7 | 116 |
| Mooresville, In., U.S. | C10 | 114 |
| Mooresville, N.C., U.S. | D6 | 112 |
| Moorhead, Mn., U.S. | E11 | 118 |
| Moorhead, Ms., U.S. | I6 | 114 |
| Mooringsport, La., U.S. | J3 | 114 |
| Moornanyah Lake, l., Austl. | I4 | 70 |
| Mooreesburg, S. Afr. | I4 | 66 |
| Moosburg, Ger. | G11 | 10 |
| Moosehead Lake, l., Me., U.S. | B17 | 108 |
| Moose Heights, B.C., Can. | D12 | 102 |
| Moose Jaw, Sk., Can. | G17 | 104 |
| Moose Jaw, stm., Sk., Can. | H9 | 104 |
| Moose Lake, Mb., Can. | E14 | 104 |
| Moose Lake, Mn., U.S. | D3 | 110 |
| Moose Lake, l., Mb., Can. | E15 | 104 |
| Mooselookmeguntic Lake, l., Me., U.S. | C16 | 108 |
| Moose Mountain, mtn., Sk., Can. | I12 | 104 |
| Moose Mountain Creek, stm., Sk., Can. | H11 | 104 |
| Moose Mountain Provincial Park, Sk., Can. | I12 | 104 |
| Moose Pass, Ak., U.S. | F20 | 100 |
| Moosic, Sk., Can. | H13 | 104 |
| Moosomin Indian Reserve, Sk., Can. | E6 | 104 |
| Moosonee, On., Can. | F16 | 96 |
| Mopane, S. Afr. | D9 | 66 |
| Mopeia, Moz. | E7 | 58 |
| Mopipi, Bots. | C7 | 66 |
| Mopti, Mali | D4 | 64 |
| Moquegua, Peru | G6 | 82 |
| Moquegua, dept., Peru | G6 | 82 |
| Mór, Hung. | H18 | 10 |
| Mora, Mn., U.S. | E2 | 110 |
| Mora, N.M., U.S. | H11 | 120 |
| Mora, Spain | F8 | 16 |
| Mora, Swe. | K14 | 6 |
| Mora, stm., N.M., U.S. | H11 | 120 |
| Morādābād, India | F8 | 44 |
| Morada Nova de Minas, Braz. | E6 | 79 |
| Moradel, Montaña de, mtn., Hond. | B8 | 92 |
| Mora de Rubielos, Spain | E11 | 16 |
| Morafenobe, Madag. | p21 | 67b |
| Morahalom, Hung. | I19 | 10 |
| Mor'akovskij Zaton, Russia | F14 | 26 |
| Moraleda, Canal, strt., Chile | E2 | 78 |
| Morales, Guat. | B3 | 92 |
| Morales, Peru | B3 | 82 |
| Morales, Laguna, b., Mex. | F11 | 90 |
| Moran, Ks., U.S. | N12 | 118 |
| Moran, Mi., U.S. | E11 | 110 |
| Moran, Tx., U.S. | G7 | 116 |
| Morant Cays, is., Jam. | F6 | 94 |
| Morant Point, c., Jam. | F6 | 94 |
| Moratalla, Spain | G10 | 16 |
| Morava, hist. reg., Czech Rep. | F17 | 10 |
| Morava (March), stm., Eur. | G16 | 10 |
| Moravia, C.R. | H11 | 92 |
| Moravia, Ia., U.S. | J3 | 110 |
| Moravia, N.Y., U.S. | E10 | 108 |
| Moravia see Morava, hist. reg., Czech Rep. | F17 | 10 |
| Morawhanna, Guy. | C13 | 84 |
| Moraya, Bol. | I9 | 82 |
| Moray Firth, est., Scot., U.K. | D10 | 8 |
| Morazán, Guat. | C4 | 92 |
| Morazán, Hond. | B7 | 92 |
| Morbegno, Italy | C4 | 18 |
| Morbi, India | E4 | 44 |
| Morbihan, dept., Fr. | E6 | 14 |
| Morcenx, Fr. | H6 | 14 |
| Morden, Mb., Can. | I16 | 104 |
| Mordovia, state, Russia | G6 | 26 |
| Mordovo, Russia | I23 | 22 |
| Mordves, Russia | G21 | 22 |
| Mordvinia see Mordovia, state, Russia | G6 | 26 |
| Moreau, stm., S.D., U.S. | F6 | 118 |
| Moree, Austl. | G8 | 70 |
| Morée, Fr. | E8 | 14 |
| Morehead, Ky., U.S. | I3 | 108 |
| Morehead City, N.C., U.S. | E10 | 112 |
| Morehouse, Mo., U.S. | F7 | 114 |
| Moreland, Ga., U.S. | F2 | 112 |
| Moreland, Ky., U.S. | E12 | 114 |
| Morelia, Mex. | H9 | 90 |
| Morell, P.E., Can. | F11 | 106 |
| Morelos, Mex. | D6 | 90 |
| Morelos, state, Mex. | H10 | 90 |
| Morena, India | G8 | 44 |
| Morena, Sierra, mts., Spain | G6 | 16 |
| Morenci, Az., U.S. | K7 | 120 |
| Morenci, Mi., U.S. | I11 | 110 |
| Moreno, Bahía, b., Chile | B3 | 80 |
| Møre og Romsdal, co., Nor. | J10 | 6 |
| Moresby Island, i., B.C., Can. | E3 | 102 |
| Mores Island, i., Bah. | A6 | 94 |
| Moreșnet, Bel. | G8 | 12 |
| Moreton Island, i., Austl. | F10 | 70 |
| Moreuil, Fr. | C9 | 14 |
| Morez, Fr. | F13 | 14 |
| Morgan, Ga., U.S. | H2 | 112 |
| Morgan, Mn., U.S. | G13 | 118 |
| Morgan, Tx., U.S. | G9 | 116 |
| Morgan, Ut., U.S. | C5 | 120 |
| Morgan, stm., Al., U.S. | H10 | 114 |
| Morgan City, La., U.S. | M5 | 114 |
| Morganfield, Ky., U.S. | E9 | 114 |
| Morgan Hill, Ca., U.S. | G4 | 124 |
| Morganito, Ven. | E9 | 84 |
| Morgantown, In., U.S. | C10 | 114 |
| Morgantown, Ky., U.S. | E10 | 114 |
| Morgantown, Ms., U.S. | K5 | 114 |
| Morgantown, W.V., U.S. | H7 | 108 |
| Morganza, La., U.S. | L5 | 114 |
| Morgenzon, S. Afr. | F9 | 66 |
| Morghāb (Murgab), stm., Asia | B16 | 48 |
| Morhange, Fr. | D13 | 14 |
| Moriah, Mount, mtn., Nv., U.S. | E11 | 124 |
| Moriarty, N.M., U.S. | J10 | 120 |
| Moribaya, Gui. | G5 | 64 |
| Morice, stm., B.C., Can. | C7 | 102 |
| Morice Lake, l., B.C., Can. | C7 | 102 |
| Morichal Largo, stm., Ven. | C11 | 84 |
| Moriki, Nig. | E13 | 64 |
| Moringen, Ger. | D9 | 10 |
| Morino, Russia | D13 | 22 |
| Morinville, Ab., Can. | D21 | 102 |
| Morioka, Japan | H16 | 36 |
| Morkill, stm., B.C., Can. | D14 | 102 |
| Morkoka, stm., Russia | D14 | 28 |
| Morlaix, Fr. | D3 | 14 |
| Morley, Mi., U.S. | G10 | 110 |
| Mormal', Bela. | I12 | 22 |
| Morney, Austl. | F5 | 70 |
| Morning Sun, Ia., U.S. | I4 | 110 |
| Mornington, Austl. | L6 | 70 |
| Mornington, Isla, i., Chile | F1 | 78 |
| Mornington Island, i., Austl. | A3 | 70 |
| Moro, Or., U.S. | E5 | 122 |
| Moro, stm., Afr. | H4 | 64 |
| Morobe, Pap. N. Gui. | m16 | 68a |
| Morocco, In., U.S. | B9 | 114 |
| Morocco (Al-Magreb), ctry., Afr. | B5 | 54 |
| Morococala, Bol. | H8 | 82 |
| Morococha, Peru | D3 | 82 |
| Morogoro, Tan. | C7 | 58 |
| Moro Gulf, b., Phil. | D7 | 38 |
| Moroleón, Mex. | G9 | 90 |
| Morombe, Madag. | r20 | 67b |
| Morón, Arg. | H9 | 80 |
| Morón, Cuba | C5 | 94 |
| Mörön, Mong. | B7 | 30 |
| Morona, stm., S.A. | C3 | 84 |
| Morona-Santiago, prov., Ec. | I3 | 84 |
| Morondava, Madag. | r21 | 67b |
| Morón de la Frontera, Spain | H6 | 16 |
| Moroni, Com. | k15 | 67a |
| Moroni, Ut., U.S. | E5 | 120 |
| Morotai, i., Indon. | E8 | 38 |
| Morozovsk, Russia | H6 | 26 |
| Morrill, Ne., U.S. | J4 | 118 |
| Morrilton, Ar., U.S. | G4 | 114 |
| Morrin, Ab., Can. | F22 | 102 |
| Morrinhos, Braz. | D4 | 79 |
| Morrinsville, N.Z. | B5 | 72 |
| Morris, Il., U.S. | I7 | 110 |
| Morris, Mb., Can. | I17 | 104 |
| Morris, Mn., U.S. | F12 | 118 |
| Morris, Ok., U.S. | D11 | 116 |
| Morris Jesup, Kap, c., Grnld. | A16 | 86 |
| Morrison, Arg. | G7 | 80 |
| Morrison, Il., U.S. | I6 | 110 |
| Morrison, Tn., U.S. | G11 | 114 |
| Morristown, Mn., U.S. | F2 | 110 |
| Morristown, N.J., U.S. | G12 | 108 |
| Morristown, N.Y., U.S. | E11 | 108 |
| Morristown, Tn., U.S. | C3 | 112 |
| Morristown, Vt., U.S. | C14 | 108 |
| Morrito, Nic. | E8 | 92 |
| Morro, Ven. | I2 | 84 |
| Morro Bay, Ca., U.S. | I5 | 124 |
| Morro do Chapéu, Braz. | F10 | 76 |
| Morropón, Peru | A1 | 82 |
| Morrosquillo, Golfo de, b., Col. | C5 | 84 |
| Morrow, La., U.S. | L4 | 114 |
| Morrumbene, Moz. | D12 | 66 |
| Moršansk, Russia | H24 | 22 |
| Morse, La., U.S. | L4 | 114 |
| Morse, Sk., Can. | H7 | 104 |
| Morse, Tx., U.S. | C5 | 116 |
| Morson, On., Can. | I20 | 104 |
| Mortagne, Fr. | D7 | 14 |
| Mortagne-sur-Sèvre, Fr. | E6 | 14 |
| Mortain, Fr. | D6 | 14 |
| Mortara, Italy | D3 | 18 |
| Morteau, Fr. | E13 | 14 |
| Morteros, Arg. | F7 | 80 |
| Mortes, Rio das, stm., Braz. | B3 | 79 |
| Mortesoro, Sudan | L8 | 60 |
| Mortlach, Sk., Can. | H8 | 104 |
| Mortlake, Austl. | L5 | 70 |
| Morton, Il., U.S. | J6 | 110 |
| Morton, Mn., U.S. | G13 | 118 |
| Morton, Ms., U.S. | J7 | 114 |
| Morton, Tx., U.S. | F4 | 116 |
| Morton, Wa., U.S. | D3 | 122 |
| Mortons Gap, Ky., U.S. | E9 | 114 |
| Moruya, Austl. | J9 | 70 |
| Morven, Austl. | F7 | 70 |
| Morven, Ga., U.S. | I3 | 112 |
| Morven, N.C., U.S. | E6 | 112 |
| Morwell, Austl. | L7 | 70 |
| Morženga, Russia | B23 | 22 |
| Mosal'sk, Russia | G17 | 22 |
| Moščnyj, ostrov, i., Russia | A10 | 22 |
| Moscow, Id., U.S. | D9 | 122 |
| Moscow see Moskva, Russia | F20 | 22 |
| Mosel (Moselle), stm., Eur. | C13 | 14 |
| Moselle, Ms., U.S. | K7 | 114 |
| Moselle, dept., Fr. | D13 | 14 |
| Moselle (Mosel), stm., Eur. | D13 | 14 |
| Mosers River, N.S., Can. | H11 | 106 |
| Moses Lake, Wa., U.S. | C6 | 122 |
| Moses Point, Ak., U.S. | D13 | 100 |
| Mosetse, Bots. | C8 | 66 |
| Moshanpu, China | F1 | 34 |
| Moshaweng, stm., S. Afr. | F6 | 66 |
| Mosheim, Tn., U.S. | C4 | 112 |
| Moshi, Tan. | B7 | 58 |
| Mosina, Pol. | C16 | 10 |
| Mosinee, Wi., U.S. | F6 | 110 |
| Mosjøen, Nor. | H13 | 6 |
| Moskva (Moscow), Russia | F20 | 22 |
| Moskva, stm., Russia | F21 | 22 |
| Moskvy, kanal imeni, Russia | E20 | 22 |
| Mošok, Russia | F24 | 22 |
| Mosolovo, Russia | G23 | 22 |
| Mosomane, Bots. | E8 | 66 |
| Mosonmagyaróvár, Hung. | H17 | 10 |
| Mosopa, Bots. | E7 | 66 |
| Mosquera, Col. | F3 | 84 |
| Mosquera, N.M., U.S. | D3 | 116 |
| Mosquito, Punta, c., Pan. | C4 | 84 |
| Mosquito, Riacho, stm., Para. | B9 | 80 |
| Mosquito Creek Lake, res., Oh., U.S. | F6 | 108 |
| Mosquito Indian Reserve, Sk., Can. | F6 | 104 |
| Mosquitos, Costa de, hist. reg., Nic. | D11 | 92 |
| Mosquitos, Golfo de los, b., Pan. | H13 | 92 |
| Moss, Nor. | L12 | 6 |
| Mossaka, Congo | B3 | 58 |
| Mossâmedes, Braz. | D3 | 79 |
| Mossbank, Sk., Can. | I9 | 104 |
| Mosselbaai, S. Afr. | J6 | 66 |
| Mossendjo, Congo | B2 | 58 |
| Mossleigh, Ab., Can. | G21 | 102 |
| Mossoró, Braz. | E11 | 76 |
| Moss Point, Ms., U.S. | L8 | 114 |
| Moss Vale, Austl. | J9 | 70 |
| Mossy, stm., Mb., Can. | G15 | 104 |
| Mossy, stm., Sk., Can. | D11 | 104 |
| Most, Czech Rep. | E13 | 10 |
| Mosta, Russia | E25 | 22 |
| Mostar, Bos. | F12 | 18 |
| Mostardas, Braz. | F13 | 80 |
| Mostoos Hills, hills, Sk., Can. | C5 | 104 |
| Mostys'ka, Ukr. | F23 | 10 |
| Mosul see Al-Mawsil, Iraq | C7 | 48 |
| Mota, Eth. | L9 | 60 |
| Motagua, stm., N.A. | B6 | 92 |
| Motala, Swe. | L14 | 6 |
| Motatán, Ven. | C7 | 84 |
| Motherwell, Scot., U.K. | F9 | 8 |
| Motīhāri, India | G11 | 44 |
| Motloutse, Bots. | C8 | 66 |
| Motozintla de Mendoza, Mex. | J13 | 90 |
| Motril, Spain | I8 | 16 |
| Motru, Rom. | E7 | 20 |
| Mott, N.D., U.S. | E5 | 118 |
| Motueka, N.Z. | D4 | 72 |
| Motul [de Felipe Carrillo Puerto], Mex. | G15 | 90 |
| Motupe, Peru | B2 | 82 |
| Mouaskar, Alg. | C11 | 62 |
| Mouchoir Passage, strt., N.A. | D9 | 94 |
| Moudjéria, Maur. | C3 | 64 |
| Moudon, Switz. | E6 | 13 |
| Mouila, Gabon | B2 | 58 |
| Mouit, Maur. | C3 | 64 |
| Mouka, C.A.R. | N1 | 60 |
| Moulamein, Austl. | J6 | 70 |
| Moulay-Idriss, Mor. | C8 | 62 |
| Moulins, Fr. | F10 | 14 |
| Moulins-la-Marche, Fr. | D7 | 14 |
| Moulmein see Mawlamyine, Myan. | F4 | 40 |
| Moulmeingyun, Myan. | F3 | 40 |
| Moulouya, Oued, stm., Mor. | C9 | 62 |
| Moultrie, Ga., U.S. | H3 | 112 |
| Moulton, Al., U.S. | H9 | 114 |
| Moulton, Tx., U.S. | J9 | 116 |
| Moultrie, Lake, res., S.C., U.S. | F6 | 112 |
| Mound Bayou, Ms., U.S. | I6 | 114 |
| Mound City, Il., U.S. | E7 | 114 |
| Mound City, Ks., U.S. | M13 | 118 |
| Mound City, Mo., U.S. | B1 | 114 |
| Mound City, S.D., U.S. | F7 | 118 |
| Moundou, Chad | G8 | 56 |
| Moundridge, Ks., U.S. | M10 | 118 |
| Mounds, Ok., U.S. | D10 | 116 |
| Moundsville, W.V., U.S. | H6 | 108 |
| Moundville, Al., U.S. | J9 | 114 |
| Mountainair, N.M., U.S. | J10 | 120 |
| Mountain Brook, Al., U.S. | I10 | 114 |
| Mountain City, Ga., U.S. | E3 | 112 |
| Mountain City, Nv., U.S. | C10 | 124 |
| Mountain City, Tn., U.S. | C5 | 112 |
| Mountain Creek, Al., U.S. | J10 | 114 |
| Mountain Grove, Mo., U.S. | E5 | 114 |
| Mountain Home, Ar., U.S. | F4 | 114 |
| Mountain Home, Id., U.S. | G10 | 122 |
| Mountain Iron, Mn., U.S. | C3 | 110 |

| Name | Map Ref. | Page |
|---|---|---|
| Mountain Lake, Mn., U.S. | H13 | 118 |
| Mountain Nile (Baḥr al-Jabal), stm., Sudan | M6 | 60 |
| Mountain Park, Ab., Can. | E17 | 102 |
| Mountain Pine, Ar., U.S. | H3 | 114 |
| Mountain Point, Ak., U.S. | I29 | 100 |
| Mountain View, Ar., U.S. | G4 | 114 |
| Mountain View, Ca., U.S. | G3 | 124 |
| Mountain View, Mo., U.S. | F5 | 114 |
| Mountain View, Ok., U.S. | D8 | 116 |
| Mountain View, Wy., U.S. | C6 | 120 |
| Mountain View, Wy., U.S. | B10 | 120 |
| Mountain Village, Ak., U.S. | E13 | 100 |
| Mount Airy, Md., U.S. | H9 | 108 |
| Mount Airy, N.C., U.S. | C6 | 112 |
| Mount Alida, S. Afr. | G10 | 66 |
| Mount Angel, Or., U.S. | E3 | 122 |
| Mount Assiniboine Provincial Park, B.C., Can. | G19 | 102 |
| Mount Ayr, Ia., U.S. | K13 | 118 |
| Mount Barker, Austl. | F3 | 68 |
| Mount Barker, Austl. | J3 | 70 |
| Mount Brydges, On., Can. | H14 | 110 |
| Mount Calm, Tx., U.S. | H10 | 116 |
| Mount Carleton Provincial Park, N.B., Can. | E7 | 106 |
| Mount Carmel, Il., U.S. | D9 | 114 |
| Mount Carmel, Nf., Can. | E20 | 106 |
| Mount Carmel, Pa., U.S. | G10 | 108 |
| Mount Carroll, Il., U.S. | H6 | 110 |
| Mount Clare, W.V., U.S. | H6 | 108 |
| Mount Clemens, Mi., U.S. | H13 | 110 |
| Mount Currie Indian Reserve, B.C., Can. | G12 | 102 |
| Mount Desert Island, i., Me., U.S. | C18 | 108 |
| Mount Dora, Fl., U.S. | K5 | 112 |
| Mount Edgecumbe, Ak., U.S. | H27 | 100 |
| Mount Enterprise, Tx., U.S. | K2 | 114 |
| Mount Forest, On., Can. | G15 | 110 |
| Mount Gambier, Austl. | K4 | 70 |
| Mount Garnet, Austl. | A6 | 70 |
| Mount Gay, W.V., U.S. | J4 | 108 |
| Mount Gilead, N.C., U.S. | D6 | 112 |
| Mount Gilead, Oh., U.S. | G4 | 108 |
| Mount Hagen, Pap. N. Gui. | G11 | 38 |
| Mount Holly, N.C., U.S. | D5 | 112 |
| Mount Holly Springs, Pa., U.S. | G9 | 108 |
| Mount Hope, Austl. | J1 | 70 |
| Mount Hope, Ks., U.S. | N10 | 118 |
| Mount Hope, W.V., U.S. | J5 | 108 |
| Mount Horeb, Wi., U.S. | G6 | 110 |
| Mount Ida, Ar., U.S. | H3 | 114 |
| Mount Isa, Austl. | C3 | 70 |
| Mount Jackson, Va., U.S. | I8 | 108 |
| Mount Jewett, Pa., U.S. | F8 | 108 |
| Mount Juliet, Tn., U.S. | F10 | 114 |
| Mount Kisco, N.Y., U.S. | F13 | 108 |
| Mount Lebanon, Pa., U.S. | G6 | 108 |
| Mount Magnet, Austl. | E3 | 68 |
| Mount Manara, Austl. | I5 | 70 |
| Mount Morgan, Austl. | D9 | 70 |
| Mount Morris, Il., U.S. | H6 | 110 |
| Mount Morris, Mi., U.S. | G12 | 110 |
| Mount Morris, N.Y., U.S. | E9 | 108 |
| Mount Mulligan, Austl. | A6 | 70 |
| Mount Olive, Il., U.S. | C7 | 114 |
| Mount Olive, Ms., U.S. | K7 | 114 |
| Mount Olive, N.C., U.S. | D8 | 112 |
| Mount Olivet, Ky., U.S. | I2 | 108 |
| Mount Orab, Oh., U.S. | H3 | 108 |
| Mount Perry, Austl. | E9 | 70 |
| Mount Pleasant, Ia., U.S. | J4 | 110 |
| Mount Pleasant, Mi., U.S. | G11 | 110 |
| Mount Pleasant, N.C., U.S. | D6 | 112 |
| Mount Pleasant, On., Can. | G15 | 110 |
| Mount Pleasant, Pa., U.S. | G7 | 108 |
| Mount Pleasant, S.C., U.S. | G7 | 112 |
| Mount Pleasant, Tn., U.S. | G9 | 114 |
| Mount Pleasant, Tx., U.S. | F12 | 116 |
| Mount Pleasant, Ut., U.S. | E5 | 120 |
| Mount Pulaski, Il., U.S. | B7 | 114 |
| Mount Rainier National Park, Wa., U.S. | D4 | 122 |
| Mount Revelstoke National Park, B.C., Can. | F16 | 102 |
| Mount Robson Provincial Park, B.C., Can. | E15 | 102 |
| Mount Savage, Md., U.S. | H8 | 108 |
| Mount Seymour Provincial Park, B.C., Can. | H12 | 102 |
| Mount Shasta, Ca., U.S. | C3 | 124 |
| Mount Sterling, Il., U.S. | C6 | 114 |
| Mount Sterling, Ky., U.S. | A3 | 112 |
| Mount Sterling, Oh., U.S. | H3 | 108 |
| Mount Stewart, P.E., Can. | F11 | 106 |
| Mount Stewart, S. Afr. | I7 | 66 |
| Mount Surprise, Austl. | B6 | 70 |
| Mount Uniacke, N.S., Can. | H10 | 106 |
| Mount Union, Pa., U.S. | G9 | 108 |
| Mount Vernon, Al., U.S. | K8 | 114 |
| Mount Vernon, Ga., U.S. | G4 | 112 |
| Mount Vernon, Ia., U.S. | I4 | 110 |
| Mount Vernon, Il., U.S. | D8 | 114 |
| Mount Vernon, In., U.S. | E9 | 114 |
| Mount Vernon, Ky., U.S. | B2 | 112 |
| Mount Vernon, Mo., U.S. | E3 | 114 |
| Mount Vernon, Oh., U.S. | G4 | 108 |
| Mount Vernon, Or., U.S. | F6 | 122 |
| Mount Vernon, S.D., U.S. | H9 | 118 |
| Mount Vernon, Tx., U.S. | F11 | 116 |
| Mount Vernon, Wa., U.S. | B3 | 122 |
| Mount Victory, Oh., U.S. | G3 | 108 |
| Mount Wolf, Pa., U.S. | G10 | 108 |
| Moura, Austl. | E8 | 70 |
| Moura, Braz. | H12 | 84 |
| Moura, Port. | G4 | 16 |
| Mourdi, Dépression du, depr., Chad | E5 | 56 |
| Mourdiah, Mali | D6 | 64 |
| Mourne Mountains, mts., N. Ire., U.K. | G7 | 8 |
| Moussoro, Chad | F4 | 56 |
| Moutier, Switz. | D7 | 13 |
| Moûtiers, Fr. | G13 | 14 |
| Mouzon, Fr. | C12 | 14 |
| Moville, Ia., U.S. | I11 | 118 |
| Moville, Ire. | F6 | 8 |
| Moweaqua, Il., U.S. | C7 | 114 |
| Moya, Com. | I16 | 67a |
| Moya, Peru | E4 | 82 |
| Moyahua, Mex. | G8 | 90 |
| Moyamba, S.L. | G3 | 64 |
| Moyen Atlas, mts., Mor. | D8 | 62 |
| Moyeuvre-Grande, Fr. | C13 | 14 |
| Moyie, B.C., Can. | H19 | 102 |
| Moyie Springs, Id., U.S. | B9 | 122 |
| Moyobamba, Peru | B3 | 82 |
| Moyogalpa, Nic. | F9 | 92 |
| Moyuta, Volcán, vol., Guat. | C4 | 92 |
| Možajsk, Russia | F19 | 22 |
| Mozambique (Moçambique), ctry., Afr. | E7 | 58 |
| Mozambique Channel, strt., Afr. | E8 | 58 |
| Mozarlândia, Braz. | C3 | 79 |
| Mozdok, Russia | I6 | 26 |
| Možga, Russia | F8 | 26 |
| Mphoengs, Zimb. | C8 | 66 |
| Mpika, Zam. | D6 | 58 |
| Mpraeso, Ghana | H9 | 64 |
| Mpumalanga, prov., S. Afr. | E10 | 66 |
| Mpwapwa, Tan. | C7 | 58 |
| Mqanduli, S. Afr. | H9 | 66 |
| Mrągowo, Pol. | B21 | 10 |
| M'Ramani, Com. | I16 | 67a |
| Mrkopalj, Cro. | D9 | 18 |
| M'Saken, Tun. | N5 | 18 |
| Mscislaŭ, Bela. | G14 | 22 |
| M'Sila, Alg. | C13 | 62 |
| Mšinskaja, Russia | B12 | 22 |
| Msta, Russia | D17 | 22 |
| Msta, stm., Russia | C14 | 22 |
| Mstera, Russia | E24 | 22 |
| Mszczonów, Pol. | D20 | 10 |
| Mtamvuna, stm., S. Afr. | H9 | 66 |
| Mtwara, Tan. | D8 | 58 |
| Mu, Cerro, mtn., S.A. | C6 | 84 |
| Muanda, D.R.C. | C2 | 58 |
| Muang Hôngsa, Laos | E6 | 40 |
| Muang Huang, Laos | E7 | 40 |
| Muang Khammouan, Laos | F8 | 40 |
| Muang Khi, Laos | E6 | 40 |
| Muang Không, Laos | G8 | 40 |
| Muang Khôngxédôn, Laos | G8 | 40 |
| Muang Long, Laos | D6 | 40 |
| Muang Ngoy, Laos | D7 | 40 |
| Muang Ou Nua, Laos | C6 | 40 |
| Muang Ou Tai, Laos | C6 | 40 |
| Muang Pak-Lay, Laos | E6 | 40 |
| Muang Pakxan, Laos | E7 | 40 |
| Muang Phiang, Laos | E6 | 40 |
| Muang Phoun, Laos | E7 | 40 |
| Muang Sing, Laos | D6 | 40 |
| Muang Souy, Laos | E7 | 40 |
| Muang Thadua, Laos | E6 | 40 |
| Muang Vangviang, Laos | E7 | 40 |
| Muang Vapi, Laos | G8 | 40 |
| Muang Xaignabouri, Laos | E6 | 40 |
| Muang Xay, Laos | D6 | 40 |
| Muang Xépôn, Laos | F9 | 40 |
| Muang Xon, Laos | D7 | 40 |
| Muang You, Laos | E7 | 40 |
| Muar (Bandar Maharani), Malay. | M7 | 40 |
| Muarasiberut, Indon. | F2 | 38 |
| Mucajaí, stm., Braz. | F12 | 84 |
| Muchanovo, Russia | E21 | 22 |
| Muchinga Mountains, mts., Zam. | D6 | 58 |
| Muchtolovo, Russia | F26 | 22 |
| Muckadilla, Austl. | F8 | 70 |
| Mučkapskij, Russia | J25 | 22 |
| Muconda, Ang. | D4 | 58 |
| Mucuchíes, Ven. | C7 | 84 |
| Mucugê, Braz. | B8 | 79 |
| Mucuim, stm., Braz. | B9 | 82 |
| Muçum, Braz. | E13 | 80 |
| Mucupia, Moz. | B13 | 66 |
| Mucupina, Monte, mtn., Hond. | B8 | 92 |
| Mucur, Tur. | B3 | 48 |
| Mucuri, Braz. | E9 | 79 |
| Mucuri, stm., Braz. | E9 | 79 |
| Mucusso, Ang. | B5 | 66 |
| Mud, stm., Ky., U.S. | E10 | 114 |
| Mud, stm., W.V., U.S. | I4 | 108 |
| Mudan, stm., China | B12 | 30 |
| Mudanjiang, China | C12 | 30 |
| Muddy, stm., Nv., U.S. | H11 | 124 |
| Mudgee, Austl. | I8 | 70 |
| Mudjatik, stm., Sk., Can. | B7 | 104 |
| Mudjuga, Russia | J26 | 6 |
| Mudon, Myan. | F4 | 40 |
| Mudu, China | D9 | 34 |
| Muelle de los Bueyes, Nic. | E10 | 92 |
| Muenster, Tx., U.S. | F9 | 116 |
| Muerto, stm., Arg. | B7 | 80 |
| Mufulira, Zam. | D5 | 58 |
| Mu Gia, Deo, Asia | F8 | 40 |
| Muğla, Tur. | L12 | 20 |
| Mugron, Fr. | I6 | 14 |
| Muḥammad, Ra's, c., Egypt | D8 | 60 |
| Muḥammad Qawl, Sudan | G9 | 60 |
| Mühlacker, Ger. | G8 | 10 |
| Mühldorf, Ger. | G12 | 10 |
| Mühlhausen, Ger. | D10 | 10 |
| Mühlig-Hofmann Mountains, mts., Ant. | C3 | 73 |
| Muhu, i., Est. | C6 | 22 |
| Muhu väin, strt., Est. | C6 | 22 |
| Muiron Islands, is., Austl. | D2 | 68 |
| Muisne, Ec. | G2 | 84 |
| Mujang-ni, S. Kor. | H14 | 32 |
| Mujezerskij, Russia | J22 | 6 |
| Mujnak, Uzb. | I9 | 26 |
| Muju, S. Kor. | G15 | 32 |
| Mukacheve, Ukr. | H2 | 26 |
| Mukah, Malay. | E5 | 38 |
| Mukdahan, Thai. | F8 | 40 |
| Mukden see Shenyang, China | B11 | 32 |
| Mukilteo, Wa., U.S. | C3 | 122 |
| Mukry, Turk. | J11 | 26 |
| Muktsar, India | E6 | 44 |
| Mukutawa, stm., Mb., Can. | E18 | 104 |
| Mukwonago, Wi., U.S. | H7 | 110 |
| Mula, Spain | G10 | 16 |
| Mulanje, Mwi. | E7 | 58 |
| Mulas, Punta de, c., Cuba | D7 | 94 |
| Mulatos, Mex. | C5 | 90 |
| Mulberry, Ar., U.S. | G2 | 114 |
| Mulberry, Fl., U.S. | L5 | 112 |
| Mulberry, In., U.S. | B10 | 114 |
| Mulberry, stm., Ar., U.S. | G3 | 114 |
| Mulberry Fork, stm., Al., U.S. | I9 | 114 |
| Mulchatna, stm., Ak., U.S. | F17 | 100 |
| Mulchén, Chile | I2 | 80 |
| Mulde, stm., Ger. | D12 | 10 |
| Muldoon, Tx., U.S. | J9 | 116 |
| Muldraugh, Ky., U.S. | E11 | 114 |
| Muldrow, Ok., U.S. | G2 | 114 |
| Mule, Lac la, l., P.Q., Can. | A8 | 106 |
| Mulegé, Mex. | D3 | 90 |
| Mulegns, Switz. | E12 | 13 |
| Muleshoe, Tx., U.S. | E4 | 116 |
| Mulgowie, Austl. | F10 | 70 |
| Mulgrave, N.S., Can. | G12 | 106 |
| Mulhacén, mtn., Spain | H8 | 16 |
| Mulhall, Ok., U.S. | C9 | 116 |
| Mulhouse, Fr. | E14 | 14 |
| Mull, Island of, i., Scot., U.K. | E7 | 8 |
| Mullan, Id., U.S. | C10 | 122 |
| Mullen, Ne., U.S. | I6 | 118 |
| Mullengudgery, Austl. | H7 | 70 |
| Mullens, W.V., U.S. | B5 | 112 |
| Muller, Pegunungan, mts., Indon. | E5 | 38 |
| Mullett Lake, l., Mi., U.S. | E11 | 110 |
| Mullewa, Austl. | E3 | 68 |
| Mullica, stm., N.J., U.S. | H12 | 108 |
| Mulligan, stm., Austl. | D3 | 70 |
| Mullin, Tx., U.S. | H8 | 116 |
| Mullingar, Ire. | H6 | 8 |
| Mullins, S.C., U.S. | E7 | 112 |
| Mullinville, Ks., U.S. | N8 | 118 |
| Mullumbimby, Austl. | G10 | 70 |
| Multān, Pak. | E4 | 44 |
| Mulvane, Ks., U.S. | N10 | 118 |
| Mulyah Mountain, mtn., Austl. | H6 | 70 |
| Mumbai (Bombay), India | C2 | 46 |
| Mumbwa, Zam. | D5 | 58 |
| Mumford, Tx., U.S. | I10 | 116 |
| Mumu, Sudan | K2 | 60 |
| Mumungwe, Bots. | C8 | 66 |
| Mun, stm., Thai. | G8 | 40 |
| Muna, Mex. | G15 | 90 |
| Munā, Sau. Ar. | D1 | 47 |
| Muna, stm., Russia | D15 | 28 |
| Münchberg, Ger. | E11 | 10 |
| München (Munich), Ger. | G11 | 10 |
| München-Gladbach see Mönchengladbach, Ger. | D6 | 10 |
| Münchenstein, Switz. | C8 | 13 |
| Munchique, Cerro, mtn., Col. | F4 | 84 |
| Munch'ŏn, N. Kor. | D15 | 32 |
| Muncie, In., U.S. | B11 | 114 |
| Muncy, Pa., U.S. | F10 | 108 |
| Mundare, Ab., Can. | D22 | 102 |
| Munday, Tx., U.S. | F7 | 116 |
| Mundelein, Il., U.S. | H7 | 110 |
| Münden, Ger. | D9 | 10 |
| Mundo Novo, Braz. | A8 | 79 |
| Mundubbera, Austl. | E9 | 70 |
| Munene, Zimb. | C10 | 66 |
| Munford, Tn., U.S. | G7 | 114 |
| Munfordville, Ky., U.S. | E11 | 114 |
| Mungallala, Austl. | F7 | 70 |
| Mungbere, D.R.C. | H6 | 56 |
| Munger, India | H12 | 44 |
| Mungindi, Austl. | G8 | 70 |
| Munhango, Ang. | D3 | 58 |
| Munich see München, Ger. | G11 | 10 |
| Munising, Mi., U.S. | D9 | 110 |
| Muniz Freire, Braz. | F8 | 79 |
| Munku-Sardyk, gora, mtn., Asia | G12 | 28 |
| Munro Lake, l., Mb., Can. | D19 | 104 |
| Munsan, S. Kor. | F14 | 32 |
| Münsingen, Switz. | E8 | 13 |
| Munson, Ab., Can. | F22 | 102 |
| Munsons Corners, N.Y., U.S. | E10 | 108 |
| Munster, Ger. | C10 | 10 |
| Münster, Ger. | D7 | 10 |
| Munster, Fr. | D14 | 14 |
| Munster, hist. reg., Ire. | I5 | 8 |
| Munuscong Lake, l., N.A. | D11 | 110 |
| Muong Saiapoun, Laos | E6 | 40 |
| Muonio, Fin. | H18 | 6 |
| Muqayshiṭ, i., U.A.E. | B8 | 47 |
| Muqdisho (Mogadishu), Som. | H10 | 56 |
| Muqi, China | B12 | 32 |
| Muqui, Braz. | F8 | 79 |
| Mur (Mura), stm., Eur. | I15 | 10 |
| Mura (Mur), stm., Eur. | I16 | 10 |
| Muradiye, Tur. | B7 | 48 |
| Murakami, Japan | I14 | 36 |
| Muraši, Russia | F7 | 26 |
| Murat, stm., Tur. | B5 | 48 |
| Muravjovo, Russia | E17 | 22 |
| Murča, Port. | D4 | 16 |
| Mūrcheh Khvort, Iran | E11 | 48 |
| Murchison, Austl. | K6 | 70 |
| Murchison, Tx., U.S. | G11 | 116 |
| Murchison, stm., Austl. | E3 | 68 |
| Murchison, Mount, mtn., N.Z. | E3 | 72 |
| Murchison Falls see Kabalega Falls, wtfl, Ug. | H7 | 56 |
| Murcia, Spain | H10 | 16 |
| Murcia, state, Spain | G10 | 16 |
| Murciélago, Islas, is., C.R. | G9 | 92 |
| Murdo, S.D., U.S. | H7 | 118 |
| Mureck, Aus. | I15 | 10 |
| Mureș, co., Rom. | C8 | 20 |
| Mureș (Maros), stm., Eur. | C5 | 20 |
| Muret, Fr. | I8 | 14 |
| Murfreesboro, Ar., U.S. | H3 | 114 |
| Murfreesboro, N.C., U.S. | C9 | 112 |
| Murfreesboro, Tn., U.S. | G10 | 114 |
| Murgab, Taj. | J12 | 26 |
| Murgab (Morghāb), stm., Asia | B16 | 48 |
| Murgha Kibzai, Pak. | E3 | 44 |
| Murgon, Austl. | F9 | 70 |
| Muri, Switz. | E7 | 13 |
| Muriaé, Braz. | F7 | 79 |
| Muriaé, stm., Braz. | F8 | 79 |
| Muriel Lake, l., Ab., Can. | C24 | 102 |
| Müritz, l., Ger. | B12 | 10 |
| Murmansk, Russia | D4 | 26 |
| Murmino, Russia | G23 | 22 |
| Murnei, Sudan | K2 | 60 |
| Murom, Russia | F25 | 22 |
| Muroran, Japan | e15 | 36a |
| Muroto, Japan | N9 | 36 |
| Murphy, Id., U.S. | G9 | 122 |
| Murphy, N.C., U.S. | D2 | 112 |
| Murphy Lake, l., B.C., Can. | E13 | 102 |
| Murphys, Ca., U.S. | F5 | 124 |
| Murphysboro, Il., U.S. | E7 | 114 |
| Murray, Ia., U.S. | I2 | 110 |
| Murray, Ky., U.S. | F8 | 114 |
| Murray, Ut., U.S. | D5 | 120 |
| Murray, stm., Austl. | J3 | 70 |
| Murray, stm., B.C., Can. | B13 | 102 |
| Murray, Lake, l., Pap. N. Gui. | G11 | 38 |
| Murray, Lake, res., S.C., U.S. | E5 | 112 |
| Murray, Mount, mtn., Yk., Can. | F30 | 100 |
| Murray Bay see La Malbaie, P.Q., Can. | E3 | 106 |
| Murray Bridge, Austl. | J3 | 70 |
| Murray City, Oh., U.S. | H4 | 108 |
| Murray Harbour, P.E., Can. | F11 | 106 |
| Murray Head, c., P.E., Can. | F11 | 106 |
| Murray Maxwell Bay, b., N.T., Can. | B16 | 96 |
| Murray River, P.E., Can. | F11 | 106 |
| Murraysburg, S. Afr. | H6 | 66 |
| Murrayville, Il., U.S. | C6 | 114 |
| Murree, Pak. | D5 | 44 |
| Murrhardt, Ger. | G9 | 10 |
| Murrí, stm., Col. | D4 | 84 |
| Murrumbidgee, stm., Austl. | J6 | 70 |
| Murrumburrah, Austl. | J8 | 70 |
| Murrurundi, Austl. | H9 | 70 |
| Murska Sobota, Slvn. | C11 | 18 |
| Murtajāpur, India | B4 | 46 |
| Murten, Switz. | E7 | 13 |
| Murtle Lake, l., B.C., Can. | E15 | 102 |
| Murtoa, Austl. | K5 | 70 |
| Murtosa, Port. | E3 | 16 |
| Muru, stm., Braz. | C6 | 82 |
| Murud, Gunong, mtn., Malay. | E6 | 38 |
| Murupara, N.Z. | C6 | 72 |
| Murutinga, Braz. | I13 | 84 |
| Murwāra, India | I9 | 44 |
| Murwillumbah, Austl. | G10 | 70 |
| Mürzzuschlag, Aus. | H15 | 10 |
| Muş, Tur. | B6 | 48 |
| Mūsā, Jabal (Mount Sinai), mtn., Egypt | C7 | 60 |
| Musaid, Libya | B3 | 60 |
| Musala, mtn., Bul. | G7 | 20 |
| Musan, N. Kor. | A17 | 32 |
| Musandam Peninsula, pen., Oman | A10 | 47 |
| Mūsā Qal'eh, Afg. | D1 | 44 |
| Musay'īd, Qatar | D11 | 56 |
| Muscat see Masqaṭ, Oman | C11 | 47 |
| Muscatatuck, stm., In., U.S. | D10 | 114 |
| Muscatine, Ia., U.S. | I4 | 110 |
| Mus-Chaja, gora, mtn., Russia | E20 | 28 |
| Muscle Shoals, Al., U.S. | H9 | 114 |
| Musclow, Mount, mtn., B.C., Can. | D7 | 102 |
| Musclow Lake, l., On., Can. | G20 | 104 |
| Muscoda, Wi., U.S. | G5 | 110 |
| Muscowpetung Indian Reserve, Sk., Can. | H10 | 104 |
| Müsgebi, Tur. | L11 | 20 |
| Musgrave, Austl. | B8 | 68 |
| Musgravetown, Nf., Can. | D20 | 106 |
| Mushandike Sanctuary, Zimb. | C10 | 66 |
| Mushie, D.R.C. | B3 | 58 |
| Mushin, Nig. | H11 | 64 |
| Muskeg, stm., Ab., Can. | D16 | 102 |
| Muskeg Lake Indian Reserve, Sk., Can. | F8 | 104 |
| Muskegon, Mi., U.S. | G9 | 110 |
| Muskegon, stm., Mi., U.S. | D1 | 108 |
| Muskegon Heights, Mi., U.S. | G9 | 110 |
| Muskingum, stm., Oh., U.S. | H5 | 108 |
| Muskoday Indian Reserve, Sk., Can. | E9 | 104 |
| Muskogee, Ok., U.S. | D11 | 116 |
| Muskowekwan Indian Reserve, Sk., Can. | G10 | 104 |
| Muskrat Dam Lake, l., On., Can. | E23 | 104 |
| Muskwa, stm., B.C., Can. | E8 | 96 |
| Muskwa Lake, l., Ab., Can. | A20 | 102 |
| Muslimbāgh, Pak. | E2 | 44 |
| Musoma, Tan. | B6 | 58 |
| Musquanousse, Lac, l., P.Q., Can. | B12 | 106 |
| Musquaro, Lac, l., P.Q., Can. | B12 | 106 |
| Musquodoboit Harbour, N.S., Can. | H10 | 106 |
| Musselshell, stm., Mt., U.S. | C18 | 122 |
| Mussomeli, Italy | L8 | 18 |
| Mussuma, Ang. | D4 | 58 |
| Mustafakemalpaşa, Tur. | I12 | 20 |
| Mustang Island, i., Tx., U.S. | L10 | 116 |
| Mustinka, stm., Mn., U.S. | F11 | 118 |
| Mustla, Est. | C8 | 22 |
| Mustvee, Est. | C9 | 22 |
| Muswellbrook, Austl. | I9 | 70 |
| Mūt, Egypt | E5 | 60 |
| Mut, Tur. | C2 | 48 |
| Mutá, Ponta do, c., Braz. | B9 | 79 |
| Mutambara, Zimb. | B11 | 66 |
| Mutare, Zimb. | B11 | 66 |
| Mutlu (Rezovska), stm., Eur. | H11 | 20 |
| Mutsamudu, Com. | I16 | 67a |
| Mutsu, Japan | F16 | 36 |
| Mutsu-wan, b., Japan | F15 | 36 |
| Muttaburra, Austl. | D6 | 70 |
| Muttenz, Switz. | C8 | 13 |
| Mutuípe, Braz. | B9 | 79 |
| Mutum, Braz. | E8 | 79 |
| Mutum, stm., Braz. | J8 | 84 |
| Mutunópolis, Braz. | B4 | 79 |
| Muxima, Ang. | C2 | 58 |
| Muymano, stm., S.A. | D7 | 82 |
| Muy Muy, Nic. | E9 | 92 |
| Muyua Island, i., Pap. N. Gui. | A10 | 68 |
| Muyumba, D.R.C. | C5 | 58 |
| Muzaffarābād, Pak. | C5 | 44 |
| Muzaffarnagar, India | F7 | 44 |
| Muzaffarpur, India | G11 | 44 |
| Muzat, stm., China | C3 | 30 |
| Muztag, mtn., China | B9 | 44 |
| Muztag, mtn., China | B12 | 44 |
| Mvolo, Sudan | N5 | 60 |
| Mvuma, Zimb. | B10 | 66 |
| Mwali (Mohéli), i., Com. | I15 | 67a |
| Mwanza, Tan. | B6 | 58 |
| Mweka, D.R.C. | B4 | 58 |
| Mwenezi, Zimb. | C10 | 66 |
| Mweru, Lake, l., Afr. | C5 | 58 |
| Mwinilunga, Zam. | D4 | 58 |
| Myaing, Myan. | D3 | 40 |
| Myanaung, Myan. | E3 | 40 |
| Myanmar (Burma), ctry., Asia | A2 | 38 |
| Myaungmya, Myan. | F3 | 40 |
| Myebon, Myan. | D2 | 40 |
| Myerstown, Pa., U.S. | G10 | 108 |
| Myingyan, Myan. | D3 | 40 |
| Myitkyinā, Myan. | E4 | 40 |
| Myittha, Myan. | D4 | 40 |
| Myjava, Slvk. | G17 | 10 |
| Mykolayiv, Ukr. | H4 | 26 |
| Mykolayivka, Ukr. | C13 | 20 |
| Myllymäki, Fin. | J19 | 6 |
| Mymensingh, Bngl. | H14 | 44 |
| Mynämäki, Fin. | K18 | 6 |
| Mynfontein, S. Afr. | H6 | 66 |
| Myrnam, Ab., Can. | D23 | 102 |
| Myrskylä (Mörskom), Fin. | K19 | 6 |
| Myrtle Beach, S.C., U.S. | F8 | 112 |
| Myrtle Creek, Or., U.S. | G2 | 122 |
| Myrtle Grove, Fl., U.S. | L9 | 114 |
| Myrtle Point, Or., U.S. | G1 | 122 |
| Myrtletowne, Ca., U.S. | D1 | 124 |
| Myski, Russia | G9 | 28 |
| Myškino, Russia | D21 | 22 |
| Myślenice, Pol. | F19 | 10 |
| Mysłowice, Pol. | E19 | 10 |
| Mysore, India | F4 | 46 |
| Mystic, Ct., U.S. | F15 | 108 |
| Mystic, Ia., U.S. | J3 | 110 |
| Myszków, Pol. | E19 | 10 |
| Myt, Russia | E25 | 22 |
| My Tho, Viet. | I9 | 40 |
| Mytišči, Russia | F20 | 22 |
| Myton, Ut., U.S. | D6 | 120 |
| Mzimba, Mwi. | D6 | 58 |
| Mzimvubu, stm., S. Afr. | H9 | 66 |
| Mzuzu, Mwi. | D6 | 58 |
| **N** | | |
| Na (Tengtiao), stm., Asia | C7 | 40 |
| Naalehu, Hi., U.S. | r18 | 125a |
| Naas, Ire. | H7 | 8 |
| Nabā, Jabal an- (Mount Nebo), mtn., Jord. | E5 | 50 |
| Nabalat Al-Ḥajanah, Sudan | K5 | 60 |
| Nabburg, Ger. | F12 | 10 |
| Naberežnyje Čelny, Russia | F8 | 26 |
| Nabesna, Ak., U.S. | E23 | 100 |
| Nabeul, Tun. | M5 | 18 |
| Nābha, India | E7 | 44 |
| Nabileque, stm., Braz. | I13 | 82 |
| Nabī Shu'ayb, Jabal an-, mtn., Yemen | G3 | 47 |
| Nabisipi, stm., P.Q., Can. | B11 | 106 |
| Nabogame, Mex. | D6 | 90 |
| Naboomspruit, S. Afr. | E9 | 66 |
| Nabq, Egypt | C8 | 60 |
| Nābulus, W.B. | D4 | 50 |
| Nacala-Velha, Moz. | D8 | 58 |
| Nacaome, Hond. | D7 | 92 |
| Naches, stm., Wa., U.S. | D4 | 122 |
| Náchod, Czech Rep. | E16 | 10 |
| Nachodka, Russia | I18 | 28 |
| Nachvak Fiord, Nf., Can. | E20 | 96 |
| Nacimiento, Chile | I2 | 80 |
| Naco, Az., U.S. | M7 | 120 |
| Naco, Mex. | B5 | 90 |
| Nacogdoches, Tx., U.S. | K2 | 114 |
| Nácori Chico, Mex. | C5 | 90 |
| Nacozari de García, Mex. | B5 | 90 |
| Ñacunday, Para. | D11 | 80 |
| Nadaleen Mountain, mtn., Yk., Can. | D28 | 100 |
| Naden Harbour, b., B.C., Can. | C2 | 102 |
| Nadiād, India | I5 | 44 |
| Nădlac, Rom. | C4 | 20 |
| Nador, Mor. | C9 | 62 |
| Nadvirna, Ukr. | A8 | 20 |
| Nadvoicy, Russia | J24 | 6 |
| Nadym, Russia | D12 | 26 |
| Nadym, stm., Russia | D12 | 26 |
| Nafadji, Sen. | E4 | 64 |
| Näfels, Switz. | D11 | 13 |
| Nafī, Sau. Ar. | I7 | 48 |
| Naga, Phil. | o20 | 39b |
| Nâga, Kreb en, clf, Afr. | I7 | 62 |
| Naga Hills, mts., Asia | B3 | 40 |
| Nāgāland, state, India | H16 | 44 |
| Nagano, Japan | K13 | 36 |
| Nagaoka, Japan | J13 | 36 |
| Nagaon, India | G15 | 44 |
| Nāgappattinam, India | G5 | 46 |
| Nāgārjuna Sāgar, res., India | D5 | 46 |
| Nagarote, Nic. | E8 | 92 |
| Nagar Pārkar, Pak. | H4 | 44 |
| Nagasaki, Japan | O4 | 36 |
| Nāgaur, India | G5 | 44 |
| Nagda, India | I6 | 44 |
| Nāgercoil, India | H4 | 46 |
| Nagīna, India | F8 | 44 |
| Nagold, Ger. | G8 | 10 |
| Nagorno-Karabakh, hist. reg., Azer. | A9 | 48 |
| Nagornyj, Russia | F16 | 28 |
| Nagoya, Japan | L11 | 36 |
| Nāgpur, India | J8 | 44 |
| Nagqu, China | E5 | 30 |
| Nagua, Dom. Rep. | E10 | 94 |
| Nagyatád, Hung. | I17 | 10 |
| Nagybajom, Hung. | I17 | 10 |
| Nagyecsed, Hung. | H22 | 10 |
| Nagykálló, Hung. | H21 | 10 |
| Nagykanizsa, Hung. | I17 | 10 |
| Nagykőrös, Hung. | H19 | 10 |
| Naha, Japan | u2 | 37b |
| Nāhan, India | E7 | 44 |
| Nahang (Nihing), stm., Asia | H17 | 48 |
| Nahanni National Park, N.T., Can. | F31 | 100 |
| Nahariyya, Isr. | B4 | 50 |
| Nahāvand, Iran | D10 | 48 |
| Nahe, China | B11 | 30 |
| Nahirne, Ukr. | D12 | 20 |
| Nahma, Mi., U.S. | E9 | 110 |
| Nahualate, stm., Guat. | C3 | 92 |
| Nahuel Huapí, Lago, l., Arg. | E2 | 78 |
| Nahunta, Ga., U.S. | H5 | 112 |
| Naica, Mex. | D7 | 90 |
| Naicam, Sk., Can. | F10 | 104 |
| Naikoon Provincial Park, B.C., Can. | D3 | 102 |
| Nailin, China | B7 | 32 |
| Nā'īn, Iran | E12 | 48 |
| Nain, Nf., Can. | E20 | 96 |
| Naini Tāl, India | F8 | 44 |
| Nairn, La., U.S. | M7 | 114 |
| Nairobi, Kenya | B7 | 58 |
| Naissaar, i., Est. | B7 | 22 |
| Naivasha, Kenya | B7 | 58 |
| Najafābād, Iran | E11 | 48 |
| Najasa, stm., Cuba | D6 | 94 |
| Nájera, Spain | C9 | 16 |
| Naj'Ḥammādī, Egypt | D7 | 60 |
| Najībābād, India | F8 | 44 |
| Najin, N. Kor. | A18 | 32 |
| Najstenjarvi, Russia | J23 | 6 |
| Naju, S. Kor. | H14 | 32 |
| Nakadōri-shima, i., Japan | O4 | 36 |
| Nakaminato, Japan | K15 | 36 |
| Nakano-shima, i., Japan | r4 | 37b |
| Nakape, Sudan | O5 | 60 |
| Nakatsu, Japan | N6 | 36 |
| Nakfa, Erit. | I10 | 60 |
| Nakhon Nayok, Thai. | G6 | 40 |
| Nakhon Pathom, Thai. | H6 | 40 |
| Nakhon Phanom, Thai. | F8 | 40 |
| Nakhon Ratchasima, Thai. | G7 | 40 |
| Nakhon Sawan, Thai. | G6 | 40 |
| Nakhon Si Thammarat, Thai. | J5 | 40 |
| Nakina, On., Can. | F15 | 96 |
| Nakło nad Notecią, Pol. | B17 | 10 |
| Naknek, Ak., U.S. | G16 | 100 |
| Nakskov, Den. | N12 | 6 |
| Nakuru, Kenya | B7 | 58 |
| Nakusp, B.C., Can. | G17 | 102 |
| Nalajch, Mong. | B8 | 30 |
| Nālanda, India | H11 | 44 |
| Nal'čik, Russia | I6 | 26 |
| Nalgonda, India | D5 | 46 |
| Nālūt, Libya | E16 | 62 |
| Nam, stm., Asia | D5 | 40 |
| Namaacha, Moz. | E11 | 66 |
| Namak, Daryācheh-ye, l., Iran | D11 | 48 |
| Namakan Lake, l., N.A. | B3 | 110 |
| Namaksār, Kowl-e, l., Asia | D18 | 48 |
| Namangan, Uzb. | I12 | 26 |
| Namapa, Moz. | D7 | 58 |
| Namatanai, Pap. N. Gui. | k17 | 68a |
| Nambour, Austl. | F10 | 70 |
| Nambucca Heads, Austl. | H10 | 70 |
| Nam Can, Viet. | J8 | 40 |
| Nam Co, l., China | E14 | 44 |
| Nam Dinh, Viet. | D9 | 40 |
| Namekagon, stm., Wi., U.S. | D3 | 110 |
| Namen (Namur), Bel. | H6 | 12 |
| Namew Lake, l., Can. | D13 | 104 |
| Namhkam, Myan. | C4 | 40 |
| Namib Desert, des., Nmb. | D2 | 66 |
| Namibe, Ang. | E2 | 58 |
| Namibia, ctry., Afr. | F3 | 58 |
| Namjagbarwa Feng, mtn., China | F16 | 44 |
| Namoi, stm., Austl. | H8 | 70 |
| Namounou, Burkina | F10 | 64 |
| Nampa, Ab., Can. | A17 | 102 |
| Nampa, Id., U.S. | G9 | 122 |
| Nampawng, Myan. | C4 | 40 |
| Namp'o, N. Kor. | E13 | 32 |
| Nampula, Moz. | E7 | 58 |
| Namsang, Myan. | D4 | 40 |
| Namsos, Nor. | I12 | 6 |
| Namtu, Myan. | A2 | 38 |
| Namu, B.C., Can. | F7 | 102 |
| Namur (Namen), Bel. | H6 | 12 |
| Namur, prov., Bel. | H6 | 12 |
| Namutoni, Nmb. | B3 | 66 |
| Namwŏn, S. Kor. | H15 | 32 |
| Namyang, N. Kor. | A17 | 32 |
| Namyit Island, i., Asia | C5 | 38 |
| Namysłów, Pol. | D17 | 10 |
| Nan, Thai. | E6 | 40 |
| Nan, stm., Thai. | F6 | 40 |
| Nanaimo, B.C., Can. | H11 | 102 |
| Nanam, N. Kor. | B17 | 32 |
| Nanango, Austl. | F10 | 70 |
| Nanao, Japan | J11 | 36 |
| Nanay, stm., Peru | I6 | 84 |
| Nanchang, China | G4 | 34 |
| Nancheng, China | H5 | 34 |
| Nanchong, China | E8 | 30 |
| Nancowry Island, i., India | K2 | 40 |
| Nancun, China | G8 | 32 |
| Nancy, Fr. | D13 | 14 |
| Nanda Devi, mtn., India | E8 | 44 |
| Nandaime, Nic. | F8 | 92 |
| Nānded, India | C4 | 46 |
| Nanding, stm., Asia | C5 | 40 |
| N'andoma, Russia | E6 | 26 |
| Nandu, stm., China | E11 | 40 |
| Nandurbār, India | J6 | 44 |
| Nandyāl, India | E5 | 46 |
| Nanga Parbat, mtn., Pak. | C6 | 44 |
| Nangin, Myan. | I5 | 40 |
| Nangnim, N. Kor. | C15 | 32 |
| Nangola, Mali | E6 | 64 |
| Nang Rong, Thai. | G7 | 40 |
| Nanika Lake, l., B.C., Can. | D7 | 102 |
| Nanjangūd, India | F4 | 46 |
| Nanjiang, China | C9 | 34 |
| Nanjing (Nanking), China | C7 | 34 |
| Nankang, China | J3 | 34 |
| Nanking see Nanjing, China | C7 | 34 |
| Nankou, China | I6 | 34 |
| Nan Ling, mts., China | J2 | 34 |
| Nanlinqiao, China | F3 | 34 |
| Nannine, Austl. | E3 | 68 |
| Nanning, China | C10 | 40 |
| Nanowin, stm., Mb., Can. | E18 | 104 |
| Nanpi, China | E4 | 32 |
| Nanping, China | I7 | 34 |
| Nanpu, China | D6 | 32 |
| Nansa, stm., Spain | B7 | 16 |
| Nansei-shotō (Ryukyu Islands), is., Japan | s4 | 37b |
| Nanshan see Qilian Shan, mts., China | D6 | 30 |
| Nanshan Island, i., Asia | C6 | 38 |
| Nant, Fr. | H10 | 14 |
| Nantais, Lac, l., P.Q., Can. | D18 | 96 |
| Nantang, China | I4 | 34 |
| Nantes, Fr. | E5 | 14 |
| Nanticoke, Pa., U.S. | F10 | 108 |
| Nanticoke, stm., U.S. | I11 | 108 |
| Nanton, Ab., Can. | G21 | 102 |
| Nantong, China | C9 | 34 |
| Nant'ou, Tai. | L9 | 34 |
| Nantua, Fr. | F12 | 14 |
| Nantucket, Ma., U.S. | F16 | 108 |
| Nantucket Island, i., Ma., U.S. | F16 | 108 |
| Nantucket Sound, strt., Ma., U.S. | F16 | 108 |
| Nanty Glo, Pa., U.S. | G8 | 108 |
| Nanuque, Braz. | D8 | 79 |
| Nanwan, China | C2 | 34 |
| Nanxiang, China | D10 | 34 |
| Nanxiong, China | J3 | 34 |
| Nanyang, China | B1 | 34 |
| Nanzhao, China | B1 | 34 |
| Naococane, Lac, l., P.Q., Can. | F18 | 96 |
| Não-me-Toque, Braz. | E12 | 80 |
| Naosap Lake, l., Mb., Can. | D13 | 104 |
| Náousa, Grc. | I6 | 20 |
| Napa, Ca., U.S. | F3 | 124 |
| Napakiak, Ak., U.S. | F14 | 100 |
| Napanee, On., Can. | F19 | 110 |
| Napaskiak, Ak., U.S. | F14 | 100 |
| Napè, Laos | E8 | 40 |
| Napenay, Arg. | D8 | 80 |
| Naperville, Il., U.S. | I7 | 110 |
| Napetipi, stm., Can. | A15 | 106 |
| Napier, N.Z. | C6 | 72 |
| Napier, S. Afr. | J4 | 66 |
| Napier Mountains, mts., Ant. | B4 | 73 |
| Napinka, Mb., Can. | I14 | 104 |
| Naples, Fl., U.S. | M5 | 112 |
| Naples, Id., U.S. | B9 | 122 |
| Naples see Napoli, Italy | I9 | 18 |
| Naples, N.Y., U.S. | E9 | 108 |
| Naples, Tx., U.S. | I2 | 114 |
| Napo, prov., Ec. | H4 | 84 |
| Napo, stm., S.A. | I6 | 84 |
| Napoleon, N.D., U.S. | E8 | 118 |
| Napoleon, Oh., U.S. | F2 | 108 |
| Napoleonville, La., U.S. | M5 | 114 |
| Napoli (Naples), Italy | I9 | 18 |
| Nappanee, In., U.S. | A10 | 114 |
| Naqādah, Egypt | E7 | 60 |
| Naqadeh, Iran | C8 | 48 |
| Nara, Japan | M10 | 36 |
| Nara, Mali | D6 | 64 |
| Naracoorte, Austl. | K4 | 70 |
| Naradhan, Austl. | I7 | 70 |
| Naramata, B.C., Can. | H15 | 102 |
| Naranjal, Ec. | I3 | 84 |
| Naranjito, Hond. | C6 | 92 |
| Naranjo, C.R. | G10 | 92 |
| Naranjo, stm., Guat. | C3 | 92 |
| Narasapur, India | D6 | 46 |
| Narasaraopet, India | D6 | 46 |
| Narathiwat, Thai. | K6 | 40 |
| Nara Visa, N.M., U.S. | D3 | 116 |
| Nārāyanganj, Bngl. | I14 | 44 |
| Nārāyaṇi (Gandak), stm., Asia | G11 | 44 |
| Nārāyanpet, India | D4 | 46 |
| Narbonne, Fr. | I10 | 14 |
| Narcosli Creek, stm., B.C., Can. | E12 | 102 |
| Nardò, Italy | I13 | 18 |
| Nare, stm., Col. | D5 | 84 |
| Nares Strait, strt., N.A. | A13 | 86 |
| Narew, stm., Eur. | C21 | 10 |
| Narinda, Baie de, b., Madag. | o22 | 67b |
| Nariño, dept., Col. | G3 | 84 |
| Narita, Japan | L15 | 36 |
| Nar'jan-Mar, Russia | D8 | 26 |
| Narmada, stm., India | J5 | 44 |
| Nārnaul, India | F7 | 44 |
| Narni, Italy | G7 | 18 |
| Naro, Italy | L8 | 18 |
| Narodnaja, gora, mtn., Russia | D10 | 26 |
| Naro-Fominsk, Russia | F19 | 22 |
| Narol, Pol. | E23 | 10 |
| Narooma, Austl. | K9 | 70 |
| Narrabri, Austl. | H8 | 70 |
| Narran, stm., Austl. | G7 | 70 |
| Narrandera, Austl. | J7 | 70 |
| Narraway, stm., Can. | C14 | 102 |
| Narrogin, Austl. | F3 | 68 |
| Narromine, Austl. | I8 | 70 |
| Narrows, Va., U.S. | B6 | 112 |
| Narsimhapur, India | I8 | 44 |
| Narsīpatnam, India | D7 | 46 |
| Narva, Est. | B11 | 22 |
| Narva, stm., Eur. | B10 | 22 |
| Narva laht (Narvskij zaliv), b., Eur. | B10 | 22 |
| Narvik, Nor. | G15 | 6 |
| Narvskij zaliv (Narva laht), b., Eur. | B10 | 22 |

| Name | Map Ref. | Page |
|---|---|---|
| Narvskoje vodochranilišče, res., Eur. | B11 | 22 |
| Naryn, Kyrg. | I13 | 26 |
| Naryn, stm., Asia | I12 | 26 |
| Naryškino, Russia | I18 | 22 |
| Na San, Thai. | J5 | 40 |
| Nasarawa, Nig. | G13 | 64 |
| Naschel, Arg. | G6 | 80 |
| Nash, Tx., U.S. | I2 | 114 |
| Nāshik, India | C2 | 46 |
| Nashua, Ia., U.S. | H3 | 110 |
| Nashua, Mt., U.S. | B19 | 122 |
| Nashua, N.H., U.S. | E15 | 108 |
| Nashville, Ar., U.S. | I3 | 114 |
| Nashville, Ga., U.S. | H3 | 112 |
| Nashville, Il., U.S. | D7 | 114 |
| Nashville, In., U.S. | C10 | 114 |
| Nashville, Mi., U.S. | H10 | 110 |
| Nashville, N.C., U.S. | D9 | 112 |
| Nashville, Tn., U.S. | F10 | 114 |
| Nashwaak, stm., N.B., Can. | F7 | 106 |
| Nashwaaksis, N.B., Can. | G7 | 106 |
| Nashwauk, Mn., U.S. | C2 | 110 |
| Nasielsk, Pol. | C20 | 10 |
| Näsijärvi, l., Fin. | K18 | 6 |
| Nāsir, Sudan | M7 | 60 |
| Nāsir, Buhayrat, res., Afr. | D7 | 56 |
| Naslābād, India | G6 | 44 |
| Naslābād, Pak. | F3 | 44 |
| Naskaupi, stm., Nf., Can. | F20 | 96 |
| Nass, stm., B.C., Can. | B5 | 102 |
| Nassau, Bah. | B6 | 94 |
| Nassau, N.Y., U.S. | E13 | 108 |
| Nassawadox, Va., U.S. | C11 | 112 |
| Nasser, Lake see Nāsir, Buhayrat, res., Afr. | D7 | 56 |
| Nassereith, Aus. | H10 | 13 |
| Nässjö, Swe. | M14 | 6 |
| Nastapoca, stm., P.Q., Can. | E17 | 96 |
| Nastapoka Islands, is., N.T., Can. | E17 | 96 |
| Nasva, Russia | E13 | 22 |
| Nata, Bots. | C4 | 66 |
| Natá, Pan. | C2 | 84 |
| Nata, stm., Afr. | B8 | 66 |
| Natagaima, Col. | F5 | 84 |
| Natal, B.C., Can. | H20 | 102 |
| Natal, Braz. | E11 | 76 |
| Natal, Indon. | E2 | 38 |
| Natal see KwaZulu-Natal, prov., S. Afr. | G10 | 66 |
| Natalia, Tx., U.S. | J8 | 116 |
| Natalkuz Lake, l., B.C., Can. | D9 | 102 |
| Natash, Wādī, val., Egypt | I2 | 48 |
| Natashquan, P.Q., Can. | B12 | 106 |
| Natashquan, stm., Can. | F20 | 96 |
| Natashquan, Pointe de, c., P.Q., Can. | B12 | 106 |
| Natashquan Est, stm., P.Q., Can. | A12 | 106 |
| Natchez, Ms., U.S. | K5 | 114 |
| Natchitoches, La., U.S. | K3 | 114 |
| Natimuk, Austl. | K4 | 70 |
| Nation, stm., B.C., Can. | B11 | 102 |
| National City, Ca., U.S. | L8 | 124 |
| Natipi, Lac, l., P.Q., Can. | A2 | 106 |
| Natitingou, Benin | F10 | 64 |
| Native Bay, b., N.T., Can. | D16 | 96 |
| Nativity, Church of the, W.B. | E4 | 50 |
| Natl, Jord. | E5 | 50 |
| Natoma, Ks., U.S. | L8 | 118 |
| Natong, China | C9 | 40 |
| Natron, Lake, l., Afr. | B7 | 58 |
| Natuna Besar, i., Indon. | L10 | 40 |
| Natuna Besar, Kepulauan, is., Indon. | L10 | 40 |
| Naturaliste, Cape, c., Austl. | F3 | 68 |
| Naturaliste Channel, strt., Austl. | E2 | 68 |
| Naturita, Co., U.S. | F8 | 120 |
| Nau, Cap de la, c., Spain | G12 | 16 |
| Nauders, Aus. | I10 | 10 |
| Nauen, Ger. | C12 | 10 |
| Naugatuck, Ct., U.S. | F13 | 108 |
| Naughton, On., Can. | D14 | 110 |
| Naujamiestis, Lith. | F7 | 22 |
| Naujoji Akmenė, Lith. | E5 | 22 |
| Naumburg, Ger. | D11 | 10 |
| Naungpale, Myan. | E4 | 40 |
| Nauru, ctry., Oc. | I20 | 126 |
| Nauta, Peru | J6 | 84 |
| Nautla, Mex. | G11 | 90 |
| Nauvoo, Il., U.S. | J4 | 110 |
| Nava, Mex. | C9 | 90 |
| Navadwip, India | H13 | 44 |
| Navael'nja, Bela. | H8 | 22 |
| Navahermosa, Spain | F7 | 16 |
| Navahrudak, Bela. | H8 | 22 |
| Navajo, N.M., U.S. | I7 | 120 |
| Navajo, stm., U.S. | G10 | 120 |
| Navajo Mountain, mtn., Ut., U.S. | G6 | 120 |
| Navajo Reservoir, res., U.S. | H9 | 120 |
| Navalmoral de la Mata, Spain | F6 | 16 |
| Navapolack, Bela. | F11 | 22 |
| Navarin, mys, c., Russia | E27 | 28 |
| Navarino, Isla, i., Chile | H3 | 78 |
| Navarra, prov., Spain | C10 | 16 |
| Navarro, Arg. | H9 | 80 |
| Navašino, Russia | F25 | 22 |
| Navasota, Tx., U.S. | I10 | 116 |
| Navasota, stm., Tx., U.S. | H10 | 116 |
| Navassa, N.C., U.S. | E8 | 112 |
| Navassa Island, i., N.A. | E7 | 94 |
| Navia, Arg. | H5 | 80 |
| Navidad, Chile | G3 | 80 |
| Navidad, stm., Tx., U.S. | J10 | 116 |
| Naviraí, Braz. | G1 | 79 |
| Navl'a, Russia | I17 | 22 |
| Năvodari, Rom. | E12 | 20 |
| Navoi, Uzb. | I11 | 26 |
| Navojoa, Mex. | D5 | 90 |
| Navoloki, Russia | D24 | 22 |
| Návpaktos, Grc. | K5 | 20 |
| Návplion, Grc. | L6 | 20 |
| Navsāri, India | H13 | 44 |
| Nawabganj, Bngl. | H13 | 44 |
| Nawābshāh, Pak. | G2 | 44 |
| Nāwah, Afg. | D2 | 44 |
| Nawalgarh, India | G6 | 44 |
| Naxçıvan, Azer. | J7 | 26 |
| Naxçıvan Muxtar Respublikasi, state, Azer. | B8 | 48 |
| Náxos, Grc. | L9 | 20 |
| Náxos, i., Grc. | L9 | 20 |
| Nayarit, state, Mex. | F7 | 90 |
| Nāy Band, Iran | E14 | 48 |
| Naylor, Mo., U.S. | F6 | 114 |
| Nayoro, Japan | c17 | 36a |
| Nazaré, Braz. | B9 | 79 |
| Nazaré, Port. | F2 | 16 |
| Nazaré da Mata, Braz. | E11 | 76 |
| Nazareth see Nazeret, Isr. | C4 | 50 |
| Nazareth, Pa., U.S. | G11 | 108 |
| Nazário, Braz. | D3 | 79 |
| Nazarovo, Russia | F10 | 28 |
| Nazas, Mex. | E7 | 90 |
| Nazas, stm., Mex. | E7 | 90 |
| Nazca, Peru | F4 | 82 |
| Naze, Japan | s4 | 37b |
| N'azepetrovsk, Russia | F9 | 26 |
| Nazerat (Nazareth), Isr. | C4 | 50 |
| Nazerat 'Illit, Isr. | C4 | 50 |
| Nazija, Russia | B14 | 22 |
| Nazilli, Tur. | L12 | 20 |
| Nazko, stm., B.C., Can. | E11 | 102 |
| Nazret, Eth. | M10 | 60 |
| Nazyvajevsk, Russia | F12 | 26 |
| Ndalatando, Ang. | C2 | 58 |
| Ndali, Benin | G11 | 64 |
| Ndélé, C.A.R. | G5 | 56 |
| Ndende, Gabon | B2 | 58 |
| N'Djamena, Chad | F4 | 56 |
| Ndjolé, Gabon | B2 | 58 |
| Ndola, Zam. | D5 | 58 |
| Neagh, Lough, l., N. Ire., U.K. | G7 | 8 |
| Neah Bay, Wa., U.S. | B1 | 122 |
| Neamt, co., Rom. | C10 | 20 |
| Néa Páfos (Paphos), Cyp. | D2 | 48 |
| Near Islands, is., Ak., U.S. | j1 | 101a |
| Nebaj, Guat. | B3 | 92 |
| Nebit-Dag, Turk. | J8 | 26 |
| Neblina, Pico da, mtn., S.A. | | |
| Nebo, Il., U.S. | C6 | 114 |
| Nebo, Mount, mtn., Ut., U.S. | E5 | 120 |
| Nebolči, Russia | B16 | 22 |
| Nebraska, state, U.S. | C6 | 98 |
| Nebraska City, Ne., U.S. | K12 | 118 |
| Necedah, Wi., U.S. | F5 | 110 |
| Nechako, stm., B.C., Can. | C5 | 102 |
| Nechako Plateau, plat., B.C., Can. | C10 | 102 |
| Nechako Range, mts., B.C., Can. | D10 | 102 |
| Nechako Reservoir, res., B.C., Can. | D9 | 102 |
| Neche, N.D., U.S. | C10 | 118 |
| Neches, stm., Tx., U.S. | L2 | 114 |
| Nechí, Col. | C5 | 84 |
| Nechí, stm., Col. | D5 | 84 |
| Nechmeya, Alg. | M2 | 18 |
| Neckar, stm., Ger. | F9 | 10 |
| Neckarsulm, Ger. | F9 | 10 |
| Necochea, Arg. | J9 | 80 |
| Nederland, Tx., U.S. | M3 | 114 |
| Neder Rijn, mth., Neth. | H14 | 44 |
| Nédong, China | F5 | 30 |
| Nédroma, Alg. | B11 | 62 |
| Neebish Island, i., Mi., U.S. | D11 | 110 |
| Needle Mountain, mtn., Wy., U.S. | F16 | 122 |
| Needles, Ca., U.S. | J11 | 124 |
| Needville, Tx., U.S. | J11 | 116 |
| Neembucú, dept., Para. | D9 | 80 |
| Neenah, Wi., U.S. | F7 | 110 |
| Neepawa, Mb., Can. | H15 | 104 |
| Nefta, Tun. | D14 | 62 |
| Neftza, Tun. | M4 | 18 |
| Negage, Ang. | C3 | 58 |
| Negaunee, Mi., U.S. | D8 | 110 |
| Negele, Eth. | G8 | 56 |
| Negev Desert see HaNegev, reg., Isr. | G3 | 50 |
| Negombo, Sri L. | I5 | 46 |
| Negotin, Yugo. | E6 | 20 |
| Negra, Laguna, l., Ur. | H12 | 80 |
| Negra, Punta, c., Belize | A6 | 92 |
| Negra, Punta, c., Peru | B1 | 82 |
| Negreira, Spain | C3 | 16 |
| Negreşti, Rom. | C11 | 20 |
| Negrine, Alg. | C14 | 62 |
| Negritos, Peru | J2 | 84 |
| Negro, stm., Arg. | E4 | 78 |
| Negro, stm., Bol. | D9 | 82 |
| Negro, stm., Bol. | F10 | 82 |
| Negro, stm., Braz. | C13 | 80 |
| Negro, stm., Braz. | A6 | 82 |
| Negro, stm., Braz. | H13 | 82 |
| Negro, stm., Col. | C10 | 84 |
| Negro, stm., N.A. | E7 | 92 |
| Negro, stm., Para. | C10 | 80 |
| Negro, stm., S.A. | G10 | 80 |
| Negro, stm., S.A. | H13 | 84 |
| Negros, i., Phil. | C7 | 38 |
| Neguac, N.B., Can. | E8 | 106 |
| Nehalem, Or., U.S. | E2 | 122 |
| Nehalem, stm., Or., U.S. | E2 | 122 |
| Neharělae, Bela. | H10 | 22 |
| Nehawka, Ne., U.S. | K12 | 118 |
| Nehbandān, Iran | F16 | 48 |
| Neiba, Dom. Rep. | E9 | 94 |
| Neidpath, Sk., Can. | H7 | 104 |
| Neiges, Piton des, mtn., Reu. | v17 | 67c |
| Neihart, Mt., U.S. | D15 | 122 |
| Neijiang, China | F8 | 30 |
| Neilburg, Sk., Can. | F5 | 104 |
| Neillsville, Wi., U.S. | F5 | 110 |
| Nei Monggol Zizhiqu (Inner Mongolia), prov., China | C10 | 30 |
| Neira, Col. | E5 | 84 |
| Neisse (Nysa Łużycka), stm., Eur. | D14 | 10 |
| Neiva, Col. | F5 | 84 |
| Neixpa, stm., Mex. | H8 | 90 |
| Neja, Russia | C26 | 22 |
| Nejapa de Madero, Mex. | I12 | 90 |
| Nejdek, Czech Rep. | E12 | 10 |
| Nejo, Eth. | M8 | 60 |
| Nekemte, Eth. | M9 | 60 |
| Nekoosa, Wi., U.S. | F6 | 110 |
| Nekrasovskoje, Russia | D23 | 22 |
| Neksø, Den. | N14 | 6 |
| Nelidovo, Russia | E15 | 22 |
| Neligh, Ne., U.S. | I9 | 118 |
| Nellikuppam, India | G5 | 46 |
| Nellore, India | E5 | 46 |
| Nel'ma, Russia | H19 | 28 |
| Nelson, B.C., Can. | H17 | 102 |
| Nelson, N.Z. | D4 | 72 |
| Nelson, stm., Mb., Can. | B21 | 104 |
| Nelson, Cape, c., Austl. | L4 | 70 |
| Nelson House, Mb., Can. | C16 | 104 |
| Nelsonville, Oh., U.S. | H4 | 108 |
| Nelspruit, S. Afr. | E10 | 66 |
| Néma, Maur. | C6 | 64 |
| Nemadji, stm., U.S. | D3 | 110 |
| Nemaha, Ne., U.S. | K12 | 118 |
| Neman, Russia | F5 | 22 |
| Neman (Nemunas), stm., Eur. | F5 | 22 |
| Nemeiben Lake, l., Sk., Can. | C9 | 104 |
| Nemenčine, Lith. | G8 | 22 |
| Nemours, Fr. | D9 | 14 |
| Nemuna, Bjeshkët e, mts., Eur. | G3 | 20 |
| Nemunas (Neman), stm., Eur. | F5 | 22 |
| Nemuro, Japan | d20 | 36a |
| Nemuro Strait, strt., Asia | c20 | 36a |
| Nen, stm., China | B11 | 30 |
| Nenagh, Ire. | I5 | 8 |
| Nenana, Ak., U.S. | D20 | 100 |
| Nenana, stm., Ak., U.S. | D20 | 100 |
| Nenaševo, Russia | G20 | 22 |
| Nentón, stm., N.A. | B3 | 92 |
| Neodesha, Ks., U.S. | N12 | 118 |
| Neoga, Il., U.S. | C8 | 114 |
| Neola, Ia., U.S. | J12 | 118 |
| Neola, Ut., U.S. | D6 | 120 |
| Neopit, Wi., U.S. | F7 | 110 |
| Neosho, Mo., U.S. | F2 | 114 |
| Neosho, stm., U.S. | F1 | 114 |
| Nepa, stm., Russia | F13 | 28 |
| Nepal (Nepāl), ctry., Asia | D11 | 42 |
| Nepālganj, Nepal | F9 | 44 |
| Nepeña, Peru | C2 | 82 |
| Nephi, Ut., U.S. | E5 | 120 |
| Nepisiguit, stm., N.B., Can. | E8 | 106 |
| Nepisiguit Bay, b., N.B., Can. | E8 | 106 |
| Neptune, N.J., U.S. | G12 | 108 |
| Neptune Beach, Fl., U.S. | I5 | 112 |
| Nera, stm., Eur. | E5 | 20 |
| Nerča, stm., Russia | G15 | 28 |
| Nerchinsk, Russia | G15 | 28 |
| Nerčinskij Zavod, Russia | G15 | 28 |
| Nerechta, Russia | D23 | 22 |
| Nereta, Lat. | E8 | 22 |
| Nerja, Spain | I8 | 16 |
| Nerl', Russia | E23 | 22 |
| Nerl', stm., Russia | E23 | 22 |
| Nerópolis, Braz. | D4 | 79 |
| Nerussa, stm., Russia | I17 | 22 |
| Nerva, Spain | H5 | 16 |
| Nesher, Isr. | C4 | 50 |
| Nesle, Fr. | C9 | 14 |
| Ness, Loch, l., Scot., U.K. | D9 | 8 |
| Ness City, Ks., U.S. | M8 | 118 |
| Nesselrode, Mount, mtn., N.A. | G27 | 100 |
| Nesselwang, Ger. | H10 | 10 |
| Nesslau, Switz. | D11 | 13 |
| Nesterov, Russia | G5 | 22 |
| Néstos (Mesta), stm., Eur. | H8 | 20 |
| Nestoyita, Ukr. | B13 | 20 |
| Nes Ziyyona, Isr. | E3 | 50 |
| Netanya, Isr. | D3 | 50 |
| Netherdale, Austl. | C8 | 70 |
| Netherlands (Nederland), ctry., Eur. | E9 | 4 |
| Netherlands Antilles (Nederlandse Antillen), dep., N.A. | H10 | 94 |
| Netrakona, Bngl. | H14 | 44 |
| Nettilling Fiord, N.T., Can. | C19 | 96 |
| Nettilling Lake, l., N.T., Can. | C18 | 96 |
| Nettleton, Ms., U.S. | H8 | 114 |
| Nettuno, Italy | H7 | 18 |
| Neubrandenburg, Ger. | B13 | 10 |
| Neuburg an der Donau, Ger. | G11 | 10 |
| Neuchâtel, Switz. | E6 | 13 |
| Neuchâtel, state, Switz. | D6 | 13 |
| Neuchâtel, Lac de, l., Switz. | E6 | 13 |
| Neudorf, Sk., Can. | H12 | 104 |
| Neuenhagen, Ger. | C13 | 10 |
| Neuf-Brisach, Fr. | D14 | 14 |
| Neufchâteau, Bel. | I7 | 12 |
| Neufchâteau, Fr. | D12 | 14 |
| Neufchâtel-en-Bray, Fr. | C8 | 14 |
| Neuhausen, Switz. | C10 | 13 |
| Neu-Isenburg, Ger. | E8 | 10 |
| Neumarkt [im Hausruckkreis], Aus. | G13 | 10 |
| Neumarkt in der Oberpfalz, Ger. | F11 | 10 |
| Neumarkt in Steiermark, Aus. | H14 | 10 |
| Neumarkt-Sankt Veit, Ger. | G12 | 10 |
| Neumünster, Ger. | A9 | 10 |
| Neunburg vorm Wald, Ger. | F12 | 10 |
| Neunkirchen/Saar, Ger. | F7 | 10 |
| Neuquén, Arg. | J4 | 80 |
| Neuquén, prov., Arg. | J4 | 80 |
| Neuquén, stm., Arg. | J4 | 80 |
| Neurara, Chile | C4 | 80 |
| Neuruppin, Ger. | C12 | 10 |
| Neuschwanstein, Schloss, Ger. | C14 | 13 |
| Neuse, stm., N.C., U.S. | E10 | 112 |
| Neusiedl am See, Aus. | H16 | 10 |
| Neusiedler See, l., Eur. | H16 | 10 |
| Neustadt [an der Aisch], Ger. | F10 | 10 |
| Neustadt an der Waldnaab, Ger. | F12 | 10 |
| Neustadt an der Weinstrasse, Ger. | F8 | 10 |
| Neustadt bei Coburg, Ger. | E11 | 10 |
| Neustadt in Holstein, Ger. | A10 | 10 |
| Neustrelitz, Ger. | B13 | 10 |
| Neu-Ulm, Ger. | G10 | 10 |
| Neuville-sur-Saône, Fr. | G11 | 14 |
| Neuwied, Ger. | E7 | 10 |
| Neva, stm., Russia | B13 | 22 |
| Nevada, Ia., U.S. | H2 | 110 |
| Nevada, Mo., U.S. | E2 | 114 |
| Nevada, Oh., U.S. | G3 | 108 |
| Nevada, state, U.S. | D3 | 98 |
| Nevada, Sierra, mts., Ca., U.S. | F6 | 124 |
| Nevada, Sierra, mts., Spain | H8 | 16 |
| Nevada City, Ca., U.S. | E4 | 124 |
| Nevado, Cerro, mtn., Arg. | H4 | 80 |
| Nevado, Cerro, mtn., Col. | F5 | 84 |
| Nevado de Colima, Parque Nacional de, Mex. | H8 | 90 |
| Nevado de Toluca, Parque Nacional, Mex. | H9 | 90 |
| Nevel', Russia | E12 | 22 |
| Nevel'sk, Russia | H20 | 28 |
| Never, Russia | G16 | 28 |
| Nevers, Fr. | E10 | 14 |
| Nevertire, Austl. | H7 | 70 |
| Nevesinje, Bos. | F2 | 20 |
| Nevinnomyssk, Russia | I6 | 26 |
| Nevis, i., St. K./N. | F13 | 94 |
| Nevis, Ben, mtn., Scot., U.K. | E9 | 8 |
| Nevjansk, Russia | F10 | 26 |
| Nevşehir, Tur. | C3 | 48 |
| New, stm., Belize | H15 | 90 |
| New, stm., Guy. | F14 | 84 |
| New, stm., N.A. | L10 | 124 |
| Newala, Tan. | E7 | 58 |
| New Albany, In., U.S. | D11 | 114 |
| New Albany, Ms., U.S. | H7 | 114 |
| New Albany, Oh., U.S. | G4 | 110 |
| New Alfa, Sudan | J8 | 60 |
| New Amsterdam, Guy. | D14 | 84 |
| Newark, De., U.S. | H11 | 108 |
| Newark, N.J., U.S. | G12 | 108 |
| Newark, N.Y., U.S. | D9 | 108 |
| Newark, Oh., U.S. | G4 | 108 |
| Newark-on-Trent, Eng., U.K. | H12 | 8 |
| Newark Valley, N.Y., U.S. | E10 | 108 |
| New Athens, Il., U.S. | D7 | 114 |
| New Augusta, Ms., U.S. | K7 | 114 |
| Newaygo, Mi., U.S. | G10 | 110 |
| New Baden, Il., U.S. | D7 | 114 |
| New Baltimore, Mi., U.S. | H13 | 110 |
| New Bedford, Ma., U.S. | F16 | 108 |
| Newberg, Or., U.S. | E3 | 122 |
| New Berlin, Il., U.S. | C7 | 114 |
| New Berlin, N.Y., U.S. | E11 | 108 |
| New Berlin, Wi., U.S. | H7 | 110 |
| New Bern, N.C., U.S. | D9 | 112 |
| Newbern, Al., U.S. | J9 | 114 |
| Newbern, Tn., U.S. | F7 | 114 |
| Newberry, Fl., U.S. | J4 | 112 |
| Newberry, Mi., U.S. | D10 | 110 |
| Newberry, S.C., U.S. | E5 | 112 |
| New Bethlehem, Pa., U.S. | F7 | 108 |
| New Bight, Bah. | B7 | 94 |
| New Bloomfield, Pa., U.S. | G9 | 108 |
| New Boston, Il., U.S. | I5 | 110 |
| New Boston, Oh., U.S. | I4 | 108 |
| New Braunfels, Tx., U.S. | J8 | 116 |
| New Bremen, Oh., U.S. | G2 | 108 |
| New Britain, Ct., U.S. | F14 | 108 |
| New Britain, i., Pap. N. Gui. | m17 | 68a |
| New Brockton, Al., U.S. | K11 | 114 |
| Newbrook, Ab., Can. | C22 | 102 |
| New Brunswick, N.J., U.S. | G12 | 108 |
| New Brunswick, prov., Can. | G19 | 96 |
| New Buffalo, Mi., U.S. | I9 | 110 |
| Newburg, Mo., U.S. | E5 | 114 |
| Newburgh, In., U.S. | I9 | 114 |
| Newburgh, N.Y., U.S. | F12 | 108 |
| Newburgh, On., Can. | F19 | 110 |
| Newbury, Eng., U.K. | J12 | 8 |
| Newbury, Vt., U.S. | C14 | 108 |
| Newburyport, Ma., U.S. | E16 | 108 |
| New Caledonia, dep., Oc. | K20 | 126 |
| New-Carlisle, P.Q., Can. | D8 | 106 |
| Newcastle, Austl. | I9 | 70 |
| Newcastle, Co., U.S. | E9 | 120 |
| New Castle, De., U.S. | H11 | 108 |
| New Castle, In., U.S. | C11 | 114 |
| New Castle, Ky., U.S. | D11 | 114 |
| Newcastle, N.B., Can. | E8 | 106 |
| New Castle, Oh., U.S. | I1 | 108 |
| New Castle, Ok., U.S. | D9 | 116 |
| Newcastle, On., Can. | G17 | 110 |
| New Castle, Pa., U.S. | F6 | 108 |
| Newcastle, S. Afr. | F9 | 66 |
| New Castle, Va., U.S. | B6 | 112 |
| Newcastle, Wy., U.S. | H3 | 118 |
| Newcastle Mine, Ab., Can. | F22 | 102 |
| Newcastle-under-Lyme, Eng., U.K. | H11 | 8 |
| Newcastle upon Tyne, Eng., U.K. | G12 | 8 |
| Newcastle Waters, Austl. | C6 | 68 |
| New City, N.Y., U.S. | F13 | 108 |
| Newcomerstown, Oh., U.S. | G5 | 108 |
| New Concord, Oh., U.S. | H5 | 108 |
| New Cumberland, W.V., U.S. | G6 | 108 |
| New Dayton, Ab., Can. | H22 | 102 |
| New Delhi, India | F7 | 44 |
| New Denver, B.C., Can. | H17 | 102 |
| New Edinburg, Ar., U.S. | I4 | 114 |
| New Effington, S.D., U.S. | F11 | 118 |
| New Egypt, N.J., U.S. | G12 | 108 |
| Newell, Ia., U.S. | I12 | 118 |
| Newell, S.D., U.S. | G4 | 118 |
| Newell, W.V., U.S. | G6 | 108 |
| Newell, Lake, l., Ab., Can. | G23 | 102 |
| New Ellenton, S.C., U.S. | F5 | 112 |
| Newellton, La., U.S. | J5 | 114 |
| New England, N.D., U.S. | E5 | 118 |
| New England Range, mts., Austl. | H9 | 70 |
| Newfane, Vt., U.S. | E14 | 108 |
| New Florence, Mo., U.S. | D5 | 114 |
| New Florence, Pa., U.S. | G7 | 108 |
| Newfound Gap, U.S. | D3 | 112 |
| Newfoundland, prov., Can. | F21 | 96 |
| Newfoundland, i., Nf., Can. | D17 | 106 |
| New Franklin, Mo., U.S. | C4 | 114 |
| New Freedom, Pa., U.S. | H10 | 108 |
| New Galloway, Scot., U.K. | F9 | 8 |
| New Georgia, i., Sol. Is. | A11 | 68 |
| New Germany, N.S., Can. | H9 | 106 |
| New Glarus, Wi., U.S. | H6 | 110 |
| New Glasgow, N.S., Can. | G11 | 106 |
| New Guinea, i. | m15 | 68a |
| Newgulf, Tx., U.S. | J11 | 116 |
| Newhalem, Wa., U.S. | B4 | 122 |
| Newhall, Ca., U.S. | J7 | 124 |
| New Hamburg, On., Can. | G15 | 110 |
| New Hampshire, state, U.S. | C12 | 98 |
| New Hampton, Ia., U.S. | G3 | 110 |
| New Hanover, i., Pap. N. Gui. | k17 | 68a |
| New Harmony, In., U.S. | D9 | 114 |
| New Hartford, Ct., U.S. | F14 | 108 |
| New Hartford, Ia., U.S. | H3 | 110 |
| New Haven, Ct., U.S. | F14 | 108 |
| New Haven, Il., U.S. | E8 | 114 |
| New Haven, In., U.S. | A11 | 114 |
| New Haven, Ky., U.S. | E11 | 114 |
| New Haven, Mo., U.S. | D5 | 114 |
| New Hazelton, B.C., Can. | B7 | 102 |
| New Hebrides see Vanuatu, ctry., Oc. | J20 | 126 |
| New Hebrides Trench | K21 | 126 |
| Newhebron, Ms., U.S. | K7 | 114 |
| New Holland, Oh., U.S. | H3 | 108 |
| New Holland, Pa., U.S. | G10 | 108 |
| New Holstein, Wi., U.S. | G7 | 110 |
| New Hope, Al., U.S. | H10 | 114 |
| New Iberia, La., U.S. | L5 | 114 |
| New Ireland, i., Pap. N. Gui. | k17 | 68a |
| New Jersey, state, U.S. | C12 | 98 |
| New Johnsonville, Tn., U.S. | F9 | 114 |
| New Kensington, Pa., U.S. | G7 | 108 |
| New Kent, Va., U.S. | B10 | 112 |
| Newkirk, Ok., U.S. | C9 | 116 |
| New Kowloon see Xinjiulong, China | M3 | 34 |
| Newland, N.C., U.S. | C5 | 112 |
| Newlands, Austl. | C7 | 70 |
| New Leipzig, N.D., U.S. | E6 | 118 |
| New Lexington, Oh., U.S. | H4 | 108 |
| New Liskeard, On., Can. | C16 | 110 |
| New London, Ct., U.S. | F14 | 108 |
| New London, Ia., U.S. | I4 | 110 |
| New London, Mn., U.S. | F1 | 110 |
| New London, Mo., U.S. | C5 | 114 |
| New London, N.H., U.S. | D15 | 108 |
| New London, Oh., U.S. | F4 | 108 |
| New London, Tx., U.S. | J2 | 114 |
| New London, Wi., U.S. | F7 | 110 |
| New Madrid, Mo., U.S. | F7 | 114 |
| Newman, Austl. | D3 | 68 |
| Newman, Ca., U.S. | G4 | 124 |
| Newman, Il., U.S. | C9 | 114 |
| Newman Grove, Ne., U.S. | J10 | 118 |
| New Market, Al., U.S. | H10 | 114 |
| Newmarket, Eng., U.K. | I14 | 8 |
| New Market, Ia., U.S. | K13 | 118 |
| Newmarket, On., Can. | F16 | 110 |
| New Market, Va., U.S. | I8 | 108 |
| New Martinsville, W.V., U.S. | H6 | 108 |
| New Meadows, Id., U.S. | F9 | 122 |
| New Mexico, state, U.S. | E5 | 98 |
| New Milford, Ct., U.S. | F13 | 108 |
| New Milford, Pa., U.S. | F11 | 108 |
| Newnan, Ga., U.S. | F2 | 112 |
| New Norfolk, Austl. | N7 | 70 |
| New Norway, Ab., Can. | E22 | 102 |
| New Orleans, La., U.S. | M6 | 114 |
| New Oxford, Pa., U.S. | H9 | 108 |
| New Paltz, N.Y., U.S. | F12 | 108 |
| New Paris, Oh., U.S. | H2 | 108 |
| New Philadelphia, Oh., U.S. | G5 | 108 |
| New Pine Creek, Or., U.S. | I5 | 122 |
| New Plymouth, Id., U.S. | G9 | 122 |
| New Plymouth, N.Z. | C5 | 72 |
| Newport, Ar., U.S. | C5 | 114 |
| Newport, In., U.S. | C9 | 114 |
| Newport, Ky., U.S. | H2 | 108 |
| Newport, N.C., U.S. | E10 | 112 |
| Newport, N.H., U.S. | D14 | 108 |
| Newport, Or., U.S. | F1 | 122 |
| Newport, Pa., U.S. | G9 | 108 |
| Newport, P.Q., Can. | D9 | 106 |
| Newport, R.I., U.S. | F15 | 108 |
| Newport, Tn., U.S. | D3 | 112 |
| Newport, Vt., U.S. | C14 | 108 |
| Newport, Wa., U.S. | B8 | 122 |
| Newport, Wales, U.K. | I9 | 8 |
| Newport Beach, Ca., U.S. | K8 | 124 |
| Newport News, Va., U.S. | C10 | 112 |
| Newport [-on-Tay], Scot., U.K. | E11 | 8 |
| New Port Richey, Fl., U.S. | K4 | 112 |
| New Prague, Mn., U.S. | F2 | 110 |
| New Providence, Tn., U.S. | F9 | 114 |
| New Richland, Mn., U.S. | G2 | 110 |
| New Richmond, Oh., U.S. | I2 | 108 |
| New-Richmond, P.Q., Can. | D8 | 106 |
| New Richmond, Wi., U.S. | E3 | 110 |
| New Road, N.S., Can. | H10 | 106 |
| New Roads, La., U.S. | L5 | 114 |
| New Rochelle, N.Y., U.S. | G13 | 108 |
| New Rockford, N.D., U.S. | D8 | 118 |
| New Ross, Ire. | I7 | 8 |
| New Ross, N.S., Can. | H9 | 106 |
| Newry, N. Ire., U.K. | G7 | 8 |
| Newry, S.C., U.S. | E4 | 112 |
| New Salem, N.D., U.S. | E6 | 118 |
| New Schwabenland, reg., Ant. | C2 | 73 |
| New Sharon, Ia., U.S. | I3 | 110 |
| New Siberian Islands see Novosibirskoje ostrova, is., Russia | B20 | 28 |
| New Smyrna Beach, Fl., U.S. | J6 | 112 |
| New South Wales, state, Austl. | F9 | 68 |
| New Stuyahok, Ak., U.S. | G16 | 100 |
| New Tazewell, Tn., U.S. | C3 | 112 |
| New Thunderchild Indian Reserve, Sk., Can. | E6 | 104 |
| Newtok, Ak., U.S. | F12 | 100 |
| Newton, Ga., U.S. | H2 | 112 |
| Newton, Ia., U.S. | I2 | 110 |
| Newton, Il., U.S. | C9 | 114 |
| Newton, Ks., U.S. | M10 | 118 |
| Newton, Ma., U.S. | E15 | 108 |
| Newton, Ms., U.S. | J7 | 114 |
| Newton, N.C., U.S. | D5 | 112 |
| Newton, N.J., U.S. | F12 | 108 |
| Newton, Tx., U.S. | L3 | 114 |
| Newton Abbot, Eng., U.K. | K10 | 8 |
| Newton Falls, N.Y., U.S. | C12 | 108 |
| Newton Stewart, Scot., U.K. | G9 | 8 |
| New Town, N.D., U.S. | D5 | 118 |
| Newtown, Nf., Can. | C20 | 106 |
| Newtownabbey, N. Ire., U.K. | G8 | 8 |
| New Ulm, Mn., U.S. | G13 | 118 |
| New Ulm, Tx., U.S. | J10 | 116 |
| New Vienna, Oh., U.S. | H3 | 108 |
| New Vineyard, Me., U.S. | C16 | 108 |
| New Washington, Oh., U.S. | G4 | 108 |
| New Waterford, N.S., Can. | F13 | 106 |
| New Waverly, Tx., U.S. | I11 | 116 |
| New Westminster, B.C., Can. | H12 | 102 |
| New Whiteland, In., U.S. | C10 | 114 |
| New Wilmington, Pa., U.S. | F6 | 108 |
| New World Island, i., Nf. | C19 | 106 |
| New York, state, U.S. | C11 | 98 |
| New York, N.Y., U.S. | G13 | 108 |
| New York Mills, Mn., U.S. | E12 | 118 |
| New York State Barge Canal, N.Y., U.S. | D8 | 108 |
| New Zealand, ctry., Oc. | D4 | 72 |
| Ney Lake, l., Can. | D22 | 104 |
| Neyriz, Iran | G13 | 48 |
| Neyshābūr, Iran | C15 | 48 |
| Nezahualcóyotl, Mex. | H10 | 90 |
| Nezahualcóyotl, Presa, res., Mex. | I13 | 90 |
| Neznanovo, Russia | G23 | 22 |
| Nezperce, Id., U.S. | D9 | 122 |
| Ngami, Lake, l., Bots. | C6 | 66 |
| Ngamiland, dept., Bots. | B6 | 66 |
| Ngamo, Zimb. | B8 | 66 |
| Nganga Ringco, l., China | E10 | 44 |
| Ngangla Kangri, mts., China | D10 | 44 |
| Ngaoundéré, Cam. | G9 | 54 |
| Ngezi Recreational Park, Zimb. | B10 | 66 |
| Ngoko, stm., Afr. | A3 | 58 |
| Ngolo, C.A.R. | M2 | 60 |
| Ngoring Hu, l., China | E6 | 30 |
| Ngotwane, stm., Afr. | E5 | 66 |
| Nguigmi, Niger | F9 | 54 |
| Nguru, Nig. | F9 | 54 |
| Nhamundá, Braz. | I14 | 84 |
| Nhamundá, stm., Braz. | H14 | 84 |
| Nhandeara, Braz. | F3 | 79 |
| Nha Trang, Viet. | H10 | 40 |
| Nhill, Austl. | K4 | 70 |
| Niafounké, Mali | D7 | 64 |
| Niagara, Wi., U.S. | E7 | 110 |
| Niagara Falls, N.Y., U.S. | D7 | 108 |
| Niagara Falls, On., Can. | F17 | 110 |
| Niagara-on-the-Lake, On., Can. | G16 | 110 |
| Niamey, Niger | E11 | 64 |
| Niangara, D.R.C. | H6 | 56 |
| Niangola, Burkina | F7 | 64 |
| Niangua, stm., Mo., U.S. | E4 | 114 |
| Niantic, Ct., U.S. | F14 | 108 |
| Niaro, Sudan | L6 | 60 |
| Nias, Pulau, i., Indon. | N4 | 40 |
| Nica, Russia | F10 | 26 |
| Nicaragua, ctry., N.A. | F9 | 92 |
| Nicaragua, Lago de, l., Nic. | F9 | 92 |
| Nicastro, Italy | K11 | 18 |
| Nice, Fr. | I14 | 14 |
| Niceville, Fl., U.S. | L10 | 114 |
| Nichinan, Japan | P6 | 36 |
| Nicholas Channel, strt., N.A. | C4 | 94 |
| Nicholasville, Ky., U.S. | B2 | 112 |
| Nicholls, Ga., U.S. | H4 | 112 |
| Nicholl's Town, Bah. | B5 | 94 |
| Nicholson, Ms., U.S. | L7 | 114 |
| Nicholson, stm., Austl. | A2 | 70 |
| Nickerie, dept., Sur. | E14 | 84 |
| Nickerson, Ks., U.S. | M9 | 118 |
| Nicobar Islands, is., India | J2 | 40 |
| Nicola, stm., B.C., Can. | G14 | 102 |
| Nicola Lake, l., B.C., Can. | G14 | 102 |
| Nicola Mameet Indian Reserve, B.C., Can. | G14 | 102 |
| Nicolet, P.Q., Can. | A14 | 108 |
| Nicolet, Lake, l., Mi., U.S. | D11 | 110 |
| Nicollet, Mn., U.S. | F1 | 110 |
| Nicosia (Levkosía), Cyp. | D2 | 48 |
| Nicosia, Italy | L9 | 18 |
| Nicosia (Levkosía), N. Cyp. | D2 | 48 |
| Nicotera, Italy | K10 | 18 |
| Nicoya, C.R. | G9 | 92 |
| Nicoya, Golfo de, b., C.R. | H10 | 92 |
| Nicoya, Península de, pen., C.R. | H9 | 92 |
| Nictheroy see Niterói, Braz. | H10 | 76 |
| Nida, Lith. | F4 | 22 |
| Nidzica, Pol. | B20 | 10 |
| Niederbronn-les-Bains, Fr. | D14 | 14 |
| Niederösterreich, state, Aus. | G15 | 10 |
| Niedersachsen, state, Ger. | C8 | 10 |
| Niedu, China | J3 | 34 |
| Niekerkshoop, S. Afr. | G6 | 66 |
| Niellé, C.I. | F7 | 64 |
| Niemodlin, Pol. | E17 | 10 |
| Niéna, Mali | F6 | 64 |
| Nienburg, Ger. | C9 | 10 |
| Niers, stm., Eur. | E9 | 12 |
| Niesky, Ger. | D14 | 10 |
| Nieszawa, Pol. | C18 | 10 |
| Nieu Bethesda, S. Afr. | H7 | 66 |
| Nieuw Amsterdam, Sur. | B7 | 76 |
| Nieuwegein, Neth. | D7 | 12 |
| Nieuweschans, Neth. | B11 | 12 |
| Nieuwe Tonge, Neth. | E5 | 12 |
| Nieuw Nickerie, Sur. | E14 | 84 |
| Nieuwolda, Neth. | B10 | 12 |
| Nieuwoudtville, S. Afr. | H4 | 66 |
| Nieuwpoort (Nieuport), Bel. | F2 | 12 |
| Nieuw-Schoonebeek, Neth. | C10 | 12 |
| Nieva, stm., Peru | J4 | 84 |
| Nièvre, dept., Fr. | E10 | 14 |
| Niga, Mali | E7 | 64 |
| Niğde, Tur. | C3 | 48 |
| Nigel, i., B.C., Can. | G7 | 102 |
| Niger, ctry., Afr. | E8 | 54 |
| Niger, stm., Afr. | G8 | 54 |
| Nigeria, ctry., Afr. | F8 | 54 |
| Nigrita, Grc. | I7 | 20 |
| Nihing (Nahang), stm., Asia | H17 | 48 |
| Nihuil, Embalse del, res., Arg. | H4 | 80 |
| Niharha, Japan | J14 | 36 |
| Niihama, Japan | N8 | 36 |
| Niihau, i., Hi., U.S. | p13 | 125a |
| Nii-jima, i., Japan | M14 | 36 |
| Nijil, Jord. | G5 | 50 |
| Nijkerk, Neth. | D8 | 12 |
| Nijmegen, Neth. | E8 | 12 |
| Nijvel (Nivelles), Bel. | G5 | 12 |
| Nijverdal, Neth. | D9 | 12 |
| Nikel', Russia | G22 | 6 |
| Nikip Lake, l., On., Can. | F23 | 104 |
| Nikki, Benin | G11 | 64 |
| Nikkō, Japan | K14 | 36 |
| Nikolajevsk-na-Amure, Russia | G20 | 28 |
| Nikol'sk, Russia | G7 | 26 |
| Nikol'sk, Russia | F7 | 26 |
| Nikolski, Ak., U.S. | J10 | 100 |
| Nikol'skij, Russia | K4 | 6 |
| Nikopol', Ukr. | H4 | 26 |
| Nikshahr, Iran | H16 | 48 |
| Nikšić, Yugo. | G2 | 20 |
| Nikulino, Russia | C27 | 22 |
| Nile (Nahr an-Nīl), stm., Afr. | C7 | 56 |
| Niles, Il., U.S. | H8 | 110 |
| Niles, Mi., U.S. | I9 | 110 |
| Niles, Oh., U.S. | F6 | 108 |
| Nilkitkwa, stm., B.C., Can. | B8 | 102 |
| Nimach, India | H6 | 44 |
| Nimba, Mont, mtn., Afr. | G5 | 54 |
| Nimba Range, mts., Afr. | G5 | 54 |
| Nîmes, Fr. | I11 | 14 |
| Nimmitabel, Austl. | K8 | 70 |
| Nimpkish Lake, l., B.C., Can. | G8 | 102 |
| Nimule, Sudan | H7 | 56 |
| Nindigully, Austl. | G8 | 70 |
| Nindirí, Nic. | G8 | 92 |
| Nine Degree Channel, strt., India | H2 | 46 |
| Ninette, Mb., Can. | I15 | 104 |
| Ninety Mile Beach, Austl. | L7 | 70 |
| Ninety Six, S.C., U.S. | E4 | 112 |
| Ninga, Mb., Can. | I15 | 104 |
| Ningari, Mali | D8 | 64 |
| Ningbo, China | F10 | 34 |
| Ningcheng (Tianyi), China | B7 | 32 |
| Ningdu, China | I4 | 34 |
| Ninghai, China | F10 | 34 |
| Ningi, Nig. | F14 | 64 |
| Ningming, China | C9 | 40 |
| Ningnan, China | E8 | 30 |
| Ningshan, China | E8 | 30 |
| Ningxia see Yinchuan, China | D8 | 30 |
| Ningwu, China | D9 | 32 |
| Ningxia Huizu Zizhiqu (Ningxia Hui), prov., China | D1 | 34 |
| Ningxiang, China | G1 | 34 |
| Ninh Binh, Viet. | D9 | 40 |
| Ninhue, Chile | I2 | 80 |
| Ninilchik, Ak., U.S. | F19 | 100 |
| Ninnescah, stm., Ks., U.S. | N10 | 118 |
| Nioaque, Braz. | I14 | 84 |
| Niobrara, stm., U.S. | I9 | 118 |
| Niono, Mali | F6 | 64 |
| Nioro du Sahel, Mali | D5 | 64 |
| Niort, Fr. | F6 | 14 |
| Nipani, India | D3 | 46 |
| Nipawin, Sk., Can. | E10 | 104 |
| Nipawin Provincial Park, Sk., Can. | D10 | 104 |
| Nipe, Bahía de, b., Cuba | D7 | 94 |
| Nipekamew, stm., Sk., Can. | D9 | 104 |
| Nipekamew Lake, l., Sk., Can. | D9 | 104 |
| Nipigon, On., Can. | A7 | 110 |
| Nipigon, stm., On., Can. | G15 | 96 |
| Nipin, stm., Sk., Can. | C6 | 104 |
| Nipisi Lake, l., Ab., Can. | B20 | 102 |
| Nipissing, Lake, l., On., Can. | D16 | 110 |
| Nipisis, Lac, l., P.Q., Can. | A7 | 106 |
| Nipisso, Lac, l., P.Q., Can. | B8 | 106 |

| Name | Map Ref. | Page |
|---|---|---|
| Nipomo, Ca., U.S. | I5 | 124 |
| Nippers Harbour, Nf., Can. | C18 | 106 |
| Niquelândia, Braz. | C4 | 79 |
| Niquero, Cuba | D6 | 94 |
| Niquivil, Arg. | F4 | 80 |
| Nirgua, Ven. | B8 | 84 |
| Nirmal, India | C5 | 46 |
| Niš, Yugo. | F5 | 20 |
| Nisāb, Sau. Ar. | G8 | 48 |
| Niscemi, Italy | L9 | 18 |
| Nishio, Japan | M12 | 36 |
| *Niska Lake, l., Sk., Can.* | C6 | 104 |
| *Nisling, stm., Yk., Can.* | E25 | 100 |
| *Nisqually, stm., Wa., U.S.* | D3 | 122 |
| Nisswa, Mn., U.S. | D1 | 110 |
| *Nistru (Dnister), stm., Eur.* | H3 | 26 |
| *Nisutlin, stm., Yk., Can.* | F28 | 100 |
| Niterói, Braz. | G7 | 79 |
| Nithi River, B.C., Can. | C9 | 102 |
| *Nitinat Lake, l., B.C., Can.* | I10 | 102 |
| Nitra, Slvk. | G18 | 10 |
| Nitro, W.V., U.S. | I5 | 108 |
| Niubu, China | D6 | 34 |
| *Niue, dep., Oc.* | K23 | 126 |
| *Niut, Gunung, mtn., Indon.* | N10 | 40 |
| Niutuo, China | D4 | 32 |
| Niuzhuang, China | C10 | 32 |
| *Nive, stm., Austl.* | E7 | 70 |
| Nivelles (Nijvel), Bel. | G5 | 12 |
| *Nivernais, hist. reg., Fr.* | E10 | 14 |
| Niverville, Mb., Can. | I17 | 104 |
| Nivskij, Russia | H23 | 6 |
| Nixa, Mo., U.S. | E3 | 114 |
| Nixon, Nv., U.S. | E6 | 124 |
| Nixon, Tx., U.S. | J9 | 116 |
| Nizāmābād, India | C5 | 46 |
| *Nizām Sāgar, res., India* | C4 | 46 |
| Nizhyn, Ukr. | G4 | 26 |
| Nizip, Tur. | C4 | 48 |
| *Nízke Tatry, mts., Slvk.* | G19 | 10 |
| Nižn'aja Pojma, Russia | F11 | 28 |
| *Nižn'aja Tunguska, stm., Russia* | E10 | 28 |
| Nižn'aja Tura, Russia | F9 | 26 |
| Nižneudinsk, Russia | G11 | 28 |
| Nižnevartovsk, Russia | E13 | 26 |
| Nižnij Novgorod (Gor'kij), Russia | E27 | 22 |
| Nižnij P'andž, Taj. | J11 | 26 |
| Nižnij Tagil, Russia | F9 | 26 |
| Nizwā, Oman | C10 | 47 |
| Nizzana, Isr. | G2 | 50 |
| Njasviž, Bela. | H9 | 22 |
| *Njazidja (Grande Comore), i., Com.* | k15 | 67a |
| Njombe, Tan. | C6 | 58 |
| Nkhata Bay, Mwi. | D6 | 58 |
| Nkhotakota, Mwi. | D6 | 58 |
| Nkongsamba, Cam. | H8 | 54 |
| Nkurenkuru, Nmb. | A4 | 66 |
| *Nmai, stm., Myan.* | B4 | 40 |
| Noākhāli, Bngl. | I14 | 44 |
| Noatak, Ak., U.S. | C13 | 100 |
| Nobeoka, Japan | O6 | 36 |
| Noble, Il., U.S. | D8 | 114 |
| Noble, Ok., U.S. | D9 | 116 |
| Noblesville, In., U.S. | B10 | 114 |
| Noboribetsu, Japan | e16 | 36a |
| Nobres, Braz. | F13 | 82 |
| Nobsa, Col. | E6 | 84 |
| Nocatee, Fl., U.S. | L5 | 112 |
| Nocera [Inferiore], Italy | I9 | 18 |
| Noci, Italy | I12 | 18 |
| Nockatunga, Austl. | F5 | 70 |
| Nocona, Tx., U.S. | F9 | 116 |
| Nocupétaro, Mex. | H9 | 90 |
| *Nodaway, stm., U.S.* | B1 | 114 |
| Noel, Mo., U.S. | F2 | 114 |
| Noetinger, Arg. | G7 | 80 |
| Nogales, Az., U.S. | M6 | 120 |
| Nogales, Chile | G3 | 80 |
| Nogales, Mex. | B4 | 90 |
| Nogara, Eth. | K9 | 60 |
| Nogaro, Fr. | I6 | 14 |
| Nōgata, Japan | N5 | 36 |
| Nogent-le-Rotrou, Fr. | D7 | 14 |
| Noginsk, Russia | F21 | 22 |
| *Nogoa, stm., Austl.* | D7 | 70 |
| Nogoyá, Arg. | G9 | 80 |
| *Nógrád, co., Hung.* | H19 | 10 |
| *Noirmoutier, Île de, i., Fr.* | E4 | 14 |
| Nokaneng, Bots. | B6 | 66 |
| Nokomis, Fl., U.S. | L4 | 112 |
| Nokomis, Il., U.S. | C7 | 114 |
| Nokomis, Sk., Can. | G9 | 104 |
| *Nokomis Lake, l., Sk., Can.* | B11 | 104 |
| Nola, Italy | I9 | 18 |
| *Nolichucky, stm., U.S.* | C3 | 112 |
| *Nolin, stm., Ky., U.S.* | E10 | 114 |
| *Nolin Lake, res., Ky., U.S.* | E10 | 114 |
| Nolinsk, Russia | F7 | 26 |
| Nombre de Dios, Mex. | F7 | 90 |
| Nombre de Dios, Pan. | C3 | 84 |
| *Nombre de Dios, Cordillera, mts., Hond.* | B8 | 92 |
| Nome, Ak., U.S. | D12 | 100 |
| Nomgon, Mong. | C8 | 30 |
| Nominingue, P.Q., Can. | A11 | 108 |
| *Nonacho Lake, l., N.T., Can.* | D11 | 96 |
| Nondalton, Ak., U.S. | F17 | 100 |
| Nondweni, S. Afr. | G10 | 66 |
| Nong'an, China | C12 | 30 |
| Nong Khai, Thai. | F7 | 40 |
| Nongoma, S. Afr. | F10 | 66 |
| Nono, Eth. | M9 | 60 |
| Nonoai, Braz. | D12 | 80 |
| Nonoava, Mex. | D6 | 90 |
| Nonogasta, Arg. | E5 | 80 |
| Nonsan, S. Kor. | G15 | 32 |
| Nonthaburi, Thai. | H6 | 40 |
| Nontron, Fr. | G7 | 14 |
| *Nooksack, stm., Wa., U.S.* | B3 | 122 |
| Noonan, N.D., U.S. | C4 | 118 |
| *Noord-Brabant, prov., Neth.* | E6 | 12 |
| *Noord-Holland, prov., Neth.* | C6 | 12 |
| Noordoewer, Nmb. | G3 | 66 |
| *Noordoostpolder, reg., Neth.* | C8 | 12 |
| Noordwijk aan Zee, Neth. | D5 | 12 |
| *Noordzeekanaal, Neth.* | D5 | 12 |
| Noorvik, Ak., U.S. | C14 | 100 |
| *Nootka Island, i., B.C., Can.* | H8 | 102 |
| *Nootka Sound, strt., B.C., Can.* | H8 | 102 |
| Nóqui, Ang. | C2 | 58 |
| *Norah, i., Erit.* | E9 | 56 |
| Noralee, B.C., Can. | D8 | 102 |
| Nora Springs, Ia., U.S. | G2 | 110 |
| Norberto de la Riestra, Arg. | H9 | 80 |
| Norborne, Mo., U.S. | C3 | 114 |
| Norcatur, Ks., U.S. | L7 | 118 |
| Norcia, Italy | G8 | 18 |
| Norcross, Ga., U.S. | F2 | 112 |
| *Nord, dept., Fr.* | B10 | 14 |
| *Nord, Grand lac du, l., P.Q., Can.* | B6 | 106 |
| *Nord, Petit lac du, l., P.Q., Can.* | B6 | 106 |
| *Nordaustlandet, i., Nor.* | B3 | 24 |
| Nordegg, Ab., Can. | E18 | 102 |
| *Nordegg, stm., Ab., Can.* | E19 | 102 |
| Norden, Ger. | B7 | 10 |
| Nordenham, Ger. | B8 | 10 |
| *Nordenšel'da, archipelag, is., Russia* | B11 | 28 |
| *Nordenskiold, stm., Yk., Can.* | F26 | 100 |
| Norderstedt, Ger. | B10 | 10 |
| Nordhausen, Ger. | D10 | 10 |
| Nordheim, Tx., U.S. | K9 | 116 |
| Nordhorn, Ger. | C7 | 10 |
| *Nordkapp, c., Nor.* | F19 | 6 |
| *Nordland, co., Nor.* | H14 | 6 |
| Nördlingen, Ger. | G10 | 10 |
| *Nordostrundingen, c., Grnld.* | A18 | 86 |
| *Nord-Ostsee-Kanal, Ger.* | A9 | 10 |
| Nordreisa, Nor. | G17 | 6 |
| *Nordrhein-Westfalen, state, Ger.* | D7 | 10 |
| *Nord-Trøndelag, co., Nor.* | I12 | 6 |
| Nore, Nor. | K11 | 6 |
| Norfolk, Ne., U.S. | I10 | 118 |
| Norfolk, Va., U.S. | C10 | 112 |
| *Norfolk, co., Eng., U.K.* | I15 | 8 |
| *Norfolk Island, dep., Oc.* | K20 | 126 |
| *Norfork Lake, res., U.S.* | F4 | 114 |
| Noril'sk, Russia | D9 | 28 |
| Norlina, N.C., U.S. | C8 | 112 |
| Normal, Al., U.S. | H10 | 114 |
| Normal, Il., U.S. | J7 | 110 |
| Norman, Ar., U.S. | H3 | 114 |
| Norman, Ok., U.S. | D9 | 116 |
| *Norman, stm., Austl.* | B4 | 70 |
| *Norman, Lake, res., N.C., U.S.* | D6 | 112 |
| *Normandie, hist. reg., Fr.* | D6 | 14 |
| *Normandie, Collines de, hills, Fr.* | D6 | 14 |
| *Normandy see Normandie, hist. reg., Fr.* | D6 | 14 |
| Normangee, Tx., U.S. | H10 | 116 |
| Norman Park, Ga., U.S. | H3 | 112 |
| Normanton, Austl. | A4 | 70 |
| Norman Wells, N.T., Can. | D31 | 100 |
| Norogachi, Mex. | D6 | 90 |
| Norphlet, Ar., U.S. | I4 | 114 |
| Norquay, Sk., Can. | G12 | 104 |
| *Norra Kvarken (Merenkurkku), strt., Eur.* | J17 | 6 |
| *Norrbottens Län, co., Swe.* | H16 | 6 |
| Norridgewock, Me., U.S. | C17 | 108 |
| Norris, Tn., U.S. | C2 | 112 |
| Norris Arm, Nf., Can. | C18 | 106 |
| Norris City, Il., U.S. | E8 | 114 |
| *Norris Lake, res., Tn., U.S.* | C3 | 112 |
| Norris Point, Nf., Can. | C16 | 106 |
| Norristown, Pa., U.S. | G11 | 108 |
| Norrköping, Swe. | L15 | 6 |
| Norrtälje, Swe. | L16 | 6 |
| Norseman, Austl. | F4 | 68 |
| Norsk, Russia | G17 | 28 |
| *Norte, Canal do, strt., Braz.* | C8 | 76 |
| *Norte, Serra do, plat., Braz.* | D12 | 82 |
| *Norte de Santander, state, Col.* | J8 | 94 |
| *Norte de Santander, dept., Col.* | C6 | 84 |
| Nortelândia, Braz. | F13 | 82 |
| North, S.C., U.S. | F5 | 112 |
| *North, stm., Al., U.S.* | I9 | 114 |
| *North, stm., Ia., U.S.* | I2 | 110 |
| *North, stm., Nf., Can.* | E20 | 96 |
| *North, Cape, c., N.S., Can.* | E13 | 106 |
| North Adams, Ma., U.S. | E13 | 108 |
| North Albany, Or., U.S. | F2 | 122 |
| Northam, Austl. | F3 | 68 |
| *North America* | E9 | 86 |
| Northampton, Austl. | E2 | 68 |
| Northampton, Eng., U.K. | I13 | 8 |
| Northampton, Ma., U.S. | E14 | 108 |
| Northampton, Pa., U.S. | G11 | 108 |
| *Northamptonshire, co., Eng., U.K.* | I13 | 8 |
| *North Andaman, i., India* | H2 | 40 |
| *North Anna, stm., Va., U.S.* | B9 | 112 |
| North Anson, Me., U.S. | C17 | 108 |
| North Asheboro, N.C., U.S. | D7 | 112 |
| North Atlanta, Ga., U.S. | F2 | 112 |
| North Augusta, S.C., U.S. | F5 | 112 |
| *North Aulatsivik Island, i., Nf., Can.* | E20 | 96 |
| North Baltimore, Oh., U.S. | F3 | 108 |
| North Battleford, Sk., Can. | F6 | 104 |
| North Bay, On., Can. | D16 | 110 |
| North Bend, B.C., Can. | H13 | 102 |
| North Bend, Ne., U.S. | J11 | 118 |
| North Bend, Or., U.S. | G1 | 122 |
| North Bennington, Vt., U.S. | E13 | 108 |
| North Berwick, Me., U.S. | D16 | 108 |
| North Berwick, Scot., U.K. | E11 | 8 |
| North Bourke, Austl. | H6 | 70 |
| North Branch, Mi., U.S. | G12 | 110 |
| North Branch, Mn., U.S. | E3 | 110 |
| *North Caicos, i., T./C. Is.* | D9 | 94 |
| *North Canadian, stm., Ok., U.S.* | D10 | 116 |
| North Canton, Ga., U.S. | E2 | 112 |
| North Canton, Oh., U.S. | G5 | 108 |
| *North Cape see Nordkapp, c., Nor.* | F19 | 6 |
| *North Cape, c., N.Z.* | A4 | 72 |
| *North Cape, c., P.E., Can.* | E9 | 106 |
| *North Caribou Lake, l., On., Can.* | F14 | 96 |
| *North Carolina, state, U.S.* | D11 | 98 |
| *North Cascades National Park, Wa., U.S.* | B4 | 122 |
| *North Channel, strt., On., Can.* | D12 | 110 |
| *North Channel, strt., U.K.* | F8 | 8 |
| North Charleston, S.C., U.S. | G7 | 112 |
| North Chicago, Il., U.S. | H8 | 110 |
| North College Hill, Oh., U.S. | H2 | 108 |
| North Collins, N.Y., U.S. | E8 | 108 |
| North Conway, N.H., U.S. | C15 | 108 |
| North Creek, N.Y., U.S. | D13 | 108 |
| North Crossett, Ar., U.S. | I5 | 114 |
| *North Dakota, state, U.S.* | B6 | 98 |
| North East, Md., U.S. | H11 | 108 |
| North East, Pa., U.S. | E7 | 108 |
| *North-East, dept., Bots.* | C8 | 66 |
| *North East Point, c., Bah.* | D8 | 94 |
| *North East Point, c., Bah.* | C8 | 94 |
| *Northeast Providence Channel, strt., Bah.* | B6 | 94 |
| Northeim, Ger. | D10 | 10 |
| North English, Ia., U.S. | I3 | 110 |
| *Northern, prov., S. Afr.* | D9 | 66 |
| Northern Arm, Nf., Can. | C18 | 106 |
| *Northern Cape, prov., S. Afr.* | G5 | 66 |
| *Northern Dvina see Severnaja Dvina, stm., Russia* | E6 | 26 |
| *Northern Indian Lake, l., Mb., Can.* | E13 | 96 |
| *Northern Ireland, ter., U.K.* | G7 | 8 |
| *Northern Mariana Islands, dep., Oc.* | G19 | 126 |
| *Northern Territory, ter., Austl.* | C6 | 68 |
| *North Fabius, stm., U.S.* | B4 | 114 |
| Northfield, Ma., U.S. | E14 | 108 |
| Northfield, Mn., U.S. | F2 | 110 |
| Northfield, Vt., U.S. | C14 | 108 |
| *North Flinders Range, mts., Austl.* | H3 | 70 |
| North Fond du Lac, Wi., U.S. | G7 | 110 |
| *North Foreland, c., Eng., U.K.* | J15 | 8 |
| North Fork, Ca., U.S. | G6 | 124 |
| *North Fork, stm., U.S.* | F4 | 114 |
| North Fort Myers, Fl., U.S. | M5 | 112 |
| North Freedom, Wi., U.S. | G6 | 110 |
| *North Frisian Islands, is., Eur.* | A8 | 10 |
| Northglenn, Co., U.S. | E12 | 120 |
| North Gulfport, Ms., U.S. | L7 | 114 |
| North Henderson, N.C., U.S. | C8 | 112 |
| *North Henik Lake, l., N.T., Can.* | D13 | 96 |
| North Hero, Vt., U.S. | C13 | 108 |
| North Highlands, Ca., U.S. | F4 | 124 |
| *North Island, i., N.Z.* | B4 | 72 |
| North Judson, In., U.S. | A10 | 114 |
| North Kenai, Ak., U.S. | F19 | 100 |
| North Kingsville, Oh., U.S. | F6 | 108 |
| *North Knife Lake, l., Mb., Can.* | E13 | 96 |
| North La Junta, Co., U.S. | N4 | 118 |
| North Lakhimpur, India | G16 | 44 |
| North Las Vegas, Nv., U.S. | H10 | 124 |
| *North La Veta Pass, Co., U.S.* | G11 | 120 |
| North Liberty, In., U.S. | A10 | 114 |
| North Little Rock, Ar., U.S. | H4 | 114 |
| North Logan, Ut., U.S. | C5 | 120 |
| *North Loon Mountain, mtn., Id., U.S.* | E10 | 122 |
| North Loup, Ne., U.S. | J9 | 118 |
| *North Loup, stm., Ne., U.S.* | J9 | 118 |
| *North Macmillan, stm., Yk., Can.* | E28 | 100 |
| *North Magnetic Pole* | B9 | 86 |
| *North Mamm Peak, mtn., Co., U.S.* | E9 | 120 |
| North Manchester, In., U.S. | A11 | 114 |
| *North Manitou Island, i., Mi., U.S.* | E9 | 110 |
| North Mankato, Mn., U.S. | F1 | 110 |
| North Miami, Fl., U.S. | N6 | 112 |
| North Miami Beach, Fl., U.S. | N6 | 112 |
| *North Moose Lake, l., Mb., Can.* | D14 | 104 |
| North Muskegon, Mi., U.S. | G9 | 110 |
| North Myrtle Beach, S.C., U.S. | F8 | 112 |
| *North Nahanni, stm., N.T., Can.* | E32 | 100 |
| *North New River Canal, Fl., U.S.* | M6 | 112 |
| North Newton, Ks., U.S. | M10 | 118 |
| North Ogden, Ut., U.S. | C5 | 120 |
| Northome, Mn., U.S. | C1 | 110 |
| *North Ossetia see Severnaja Osetija, state, Russia* | I6 | 26 |
| *North Palisade, mtn., Ca., U.S.* | G7 | 124 |
| North Palm Beach, Fl., U.S. | M6 | 112 |
| North Park, Il., U.S. | H6 | 110 |
| North Platte, Ne., U.S. | J7 | 118 |
| *North Platte, stm., U.S.* | C6 | 98 |
| North Pole, Ak., U.S. | D21 | 100 |
| *North Pole* | A4 | 86 |
| Northport, Al., U.S. | I9 | 114 |
| Northport, Mi., U.S. | E10 | 110 |
| Northport, Wa., U.S. | B8 | 122 |
| North Portal, Sk., Can. | I12 | 104 |
| North Powder, Or., U.S. | E8 | 122 |
| *North Ram, stm., Ab., Can.* | E18 | 102 |
| *North Rhine-Westphalia see Nordrhein-Westfalen, state, Ger.* | D7 | 10 |
| North Richland Hills, Tx., U.S. | G9 | 116 |
| North Rim, Az., U.S. | H4 | 120 |
| North Rustico, P.E., Can. | F10 | 106 |
| North Salt Lake, Ut., U.S. | D5 | 120 |
| *North Santiam, stm., Or., U.S.* | F3 | 122 |
| *North Saskatchewan, stm., Can.* | F10 | 96 |
| *North Sea, Eur.* | D8 | 4 |
| *North Shoal Lake, l., Mb., Can.* | H17 | 104 |
| *North Siberian Lowland see Severo-Sibirskaja nizmennost', pl., Russia* | C18 | 26 |
| *North Solitary Island, i., Austl.* | G10 | 70 |
| *North Spicer Island, i., N.T., Can.* | C17 | 96 |
| *North Spirit Lake, l., On., Can.* | F22 | 104 |
| *North Spot, i., Belize* | A6 | 92 |
| *North Stradbroke Island, i., Austl.* | F10 | 70 |
| North Sydney, N.S., Can. | F13 | 106 |
| *North Taranaki Bight, N.Z.* | C5 | 72 |
| North Terre Haute, In., U.S. | C9 | 114 |
| *North Thompson, stm., B.C., Can.* | G14 | 102 |
| North Troy, Vt., U.S. | C14 | 108 |
| North Tunica, Ms., U.S. | H6 | 114 |
| *North Twin Lake, l., Nf., Can.* | C18 | 106 |
| *North Uist, i., Scot., U.K.* | D6 | 8 |
| *Northumberland, co., Eng., U.K.* | F11 | 8 |
| *Northumberland Isles, is., Austl.* | C9 | 70 |
| *Northumberland Strait, strt., Can.* | F9 | 106 |
| North Vancouver, B.C., Can. | H11 | 102 |
| North Vernon, In., U.S. | C11 | 114 |
| Northville, N.Y., U.S. | D12 | 108 |
| *North Wabasca Lake, l., Ab., Can.* | A21 | 102 |
| *North-West, prov., S. Afr.* | F7 | 66 |
| *North West Cape, c., Austl.* | D2 | 68 |
| *Northwest Gander, stm., Nf., Can.* | D18 | 106 |
| *Northwest Miramichi, stm., N.B., Can.* | E7 | 106 |
| *Northwest Providence Channel, strt., Bah.* | A5 | 94 |
| North West River, Nf., Can. | F20 | 96 |
| *Northwest Territories, prov., Can.* | C12 | 96 |
| North Wilkesboro, N.C., U.S. | C5 | 112 |
| North Windham, Me., U.S. | D16 | 108 |
| Northwood, Ia., U.S. | G2 | 110 |
| Northwood, N.D., U.S. | D10 | 118 |
| *North Yamhill, stm., Or., U.S.* | E2 | 122 |
| North York, On., Can. | G16 | 110 |
| *North Yorkshire, co., Eng., U.K.* | G12 | 8 |
| North Zulch, Tx., U.S. | I10 | 116 |
| Norton, Ks., U.S. | L8 | 118 |
| Norton, N.B., Can. | G8 | 106 |
| Norton, Va., U.S. | C4 | 112 |
| Norton Shores, Mi., U.S. | G9 | 110 |
| *Norton Sound, strt., Ak., U.S.* | E12 | 100 |
| Nortonville, Ks., U.S. | L12 | 118 |
| Nortorf, Ger. | A9 | 10 |
| *Norvegia, Cape, c., Ant.* | C2 | 73 |
| Norwalk, Ct., U.S. | F13 | 108 |
| Norwalk, Ia., U.S. | I2 | 110 |
| Norwalk, Oh., U.S. | F4 | 108 |
| Norway, Ia., U.S. | I4 | 110 |
| Norway, Me., U.S. | C16 | 108 |
| Norway, Mi., U.S. | E8 | 110 |
| *Norway (Norge), ctry., Eur.* | C10 | 4 |
| *Norway Bay, b., N.T., Can.* | B12 | 96 |
| Norway House, Mb., Can. | E17 | 104 |
| *Norwegian Sea, Eur.* | C1 | 24 |
| Norwich, Ct., U.S. | F14 | 108 |
| Norwich, Eng., U.K. | I15 | 8 |
| Norwich, Ks., U.S. | N10 | 118 |
| Norwich, N.Y., U.S. | E11 | 108 |
| Norwich, On., Can. | H15 | 110 |
| Norwood, Co., U.S. | F8 | 120 |
| Norwood, Ma., U.S. | E15 | 108 |
| Norwood, Mn., U.S. | F2 | 110 |
| Norwood, N.C., U.S. | D6 | 112 |
| Norwood, N.Y., U.S. | C12 | 108 |
| Norwood, Oh., U.S. | H2 | 108 |
| Norwood, On., Can. | F18 | 110 |
| Norwoodville, Ia., U.S. | I2 | 110 |
| *Nose Creek, stm., Ab., Can.* | C15 | 102 |
| Noshiro, Japan | G15 | 36 |
| *Nosop (Nossob), stm., Afr.* | E5 | 66 |
| Nossa Senhora do Livramento, Braz. | F13 | 82 |
| *Nossob (Nosop), stm., Afr.* | E5 | 66 |
| Nosy Varika, Madag. | r23 | 67b |
| Notasulga, Al., U.S. | J11 | 114 |
| Notch Hill, B.C., Can. | G15 | 102 |
| *Notch Peak, mtn., Ut., U.S.* | E3 | 120 |
| *Noteć, stm., Pol.* | C15 | 10 |
| *Notigi Lake, l., Mb., Can.* | C15 | 104 |
| *Notikewin, stm., Ab., Can.* | E9 | 96 |
| *Nótion Aiyaíon, prov., Grc.* | L9 | 20 |
| Noto, Italy | M10 | 18 |
| Notodden, Nor. | L11 | 6 |
| *Noto-hantō, pen., Japan* | J11 | 36 |
| *Notozero, ozero, l., Russia* | H23 | 6 |
| Notre-Dame, N.B., Can. | F9 | 106 |
| *Notre-Dame, Monts, mts., P.Q., Can.* | D5 | 106 |
| *Notre Dame Bay, b., Nf., Can.* | C18 | 106 |
| Notre-Dame-de-Lourdes, Mb., Can. | I16 | 104 |
| Notre-Dame-du-Laus, P.Q., Can. | A11 | 108 |
| Notrees, Tx., U.S. | H4 | 116 |
| *Nottawasaga Bay, b., On., Can.* | F15 | 110 |
| *Nottaway, stm., P.Q., Can.* | F17 | 96 |
| Nottingham, Eng., U.K. | I12 | 8 |
| *Nottingham Island, i., N.T., Can.* | D17 | 96 |
| *Nottinghamshire, co., Eng., U.K.* | H12 | 8 |
| Nottoway, Va., U.S. | B8 | 112 |
| *Nottoway, stm., Va., U.S.* | C10 | 112 |
| *Notukeu Creek, stm., Sk., Can.* | I7 | 104 |
| Nouâdhibou, Maur. | J2 | 62 |
| *Nouâdhibou, Râs, c., Afr.* | J2 | 62 |
| Nouakchott, Maur. | B2 | 64 |
| Nouâmghâr, Maur. | B1 | 64 |
| Nouméa, N. Cal. | K20 | 126 |
| Nouna, Burkina | E8 | 64 |
| Noupoort, S. Afr. | H7 | 66 |
| *Nouveau-Québec, Cratère du, crat., P.Q., Can.* | D18 | 96 |
| Nouvelle, P.Q., Can. | D7 | 106 |
| *Nouvelle, stm., P.Q., Can.* | D7 | 106 |
| *Nouvelle-France, Cap de, c., P.Q., Can.* | D18 | 96 |
| Nova América, Braz. | C4 | 79 |
| Nova Andradina, Braz. | G2 | 79 |
| Nova Caipemba, Ang. | C2 | 58 |
| Nova Era, Braz. | E7 | 79 |
| Nova Esperança, Braz. | G2 | 79 |
| Nova Friburgo, Braz. | G7 | 79 |
| Nova Gradiška, Cro. | D12 | 18 |
| Nova Granada, Braz. | F4 | 79 |
| Nova Iguaçu, Braz. | G7 | 79 |
| Nova Ivanivka, Ukr. | D13 | 20 |
| Novaja Kazanka, Kaz. | H7 | 26 |
| Novaja Ladoga, Russia | A15 | 22 |
| *Novaja Sibir', ostrov, i., Russia* | B21 | 28 |
| *Novaja Zemľa, is., Russia* | C9 | 26 |
| Nova Kakhovka, Ukr. | H4 | 26 |
| Nova Lamego, Gui.-B. | E2 | 64 |
| Nova Lima, Braz. | E7 | 79 |
| Nova Mambone, Moz. | C12 | 66 |
| Nova Olinda do Norte, Braz. | I13 | 84 |
| Nova Ponte, Braz. | E5 | 79 |
| Nova Prata, Braz. | E13 | 80 |
| Novara, Italy | D3 | 18 |
| Nova Roma, Braz. | B5 | 79 |
| *Nova Scotia, prov., Can.* | G20 | 96 |
| Nova Sofala, Moz. | C12 | 66 |
| Novato, Ca., U.S. | F3 | 124 |
| Nova Varoš, Yugo. | F3 | 20 |
| Nova Venécia, Braz. | E8 | 79 |
| Nova Vida, Braz. | D10 | 82 |
| *Nova Vida, Cachoeira, wtfl, Braz.* | C10 | 82 |
| Nova Zagora, Bul. | G10 | 20 |
| Novelda, Spain | G11 | 16 |
| Nové Zámky, Slvk. | H18 | 10 |
| Novgorod, Russia | C14 | 22 |
| Novi Bečej, Yugo. | D4 | 20 |
| Novice, Tx., U.S. | H7 | 116 |
| Novigrad, Cro. | E10 | 18 |
| Novi Ligure, Italy | E3 | 18 |
| Novinger, Mo., U.S. | B4 | 114 |
| Novi Pazar, Bul. | F11 | 20 |
| Novi Pazar, Yugo. | F4 | 20 |
| Novi Sad, Yugo. | D3 | 20 |
| Novki, Russia | E24 | 22 |
| Novl'anka, Russia | F24 | 22 |
| Novlenskoje, Russia | B22 | 22 |
| *Novo, stm., Braz.* | A6 | 82 |
| Nôvo Acôrdo, Braz. | B5 | 79 |
| Novoaltajsk, Russia | G8 | 28 |
| Novoanninskij, Russia | G6 | 26 |
| Novo Aripuanã, Braz. | J12 | 84 |
| Novo Brasil, Braz. | D3 | 79 |
| Novočerkassk, Russia | H6 | 26 |
| Novo Cruzeiro, Braz. | D8 | 79 |
| Novodugino, Russia | F17 | 22 |
| Novodvinsk, Russia | E6 | 26 |
| Novo Hamburgo, Braz. | E13 | 80 |
| Novo Horizonte, Braz. | F4 | 79 |
| Novohrad-Volyns'kyy, Ukr. | G3 | 26 |
| Novoizborsk, Russia | D10 | 22 |
| Novoje Leušino, Russia | E23 | 22 |
| Novokaširsk, Russia | G21 | 22 |
| Novokazalinsk, Kaz. | H10 | 26 |
| Novokujbyševsk, Russia | G7 | 26 |
| Novokuzneck, Russia | G9 | 28 |
| Novol'vovsk, Russia | H21 | 22 |
| Novo Mesto, Slvn. | D10 | 18 |
| Novomoskovsk, Russia | G21 | 22 |
| Novomoskovs'k, Ukr. | H5 | 26 |
| Novopetrovskoje, Russia | F19 | 22 |
| Novopiscovo, Russia | D24 | 22 |
| Novorossijsk, Russia | I5 | 26 |
| Novorybnoje, Russia | C13 | 28 |
| Novoržev, Russia | D12 | 22 |
| Novošachtinsk, Russia | H5 | 26 |
| Novoselytsya, Ukr. | A10 | 20 |
| Novosibirsk, Russia | F8 | 28 |
| *Novosibirskije ostrova, is., Russia* | B20 | 28 |
| *Novosibirskoje vodochranilišče, res., Russia* | G14 | 26 |
| Novosil', Russia | I20 | 22 |
| Novosil's'ke, Ukr. | D12 | 20 |
| Novosokol'niki, Russia | E13 | 22 |
| Novos'olki, Russia | G22 | 22 |
| Novotroick, Russia | G9 | 26 |
| Novouzensk, Russia | G7 | 26 |
| Novov'atsk, Russia | F7 | 26 |
| Novov'azniki, Russia | E25 | 22 |
| Novovolyns'k, Ukr. | G2 | 26 |
| Novozavidovskij, Russia | E19 | 22 |
| Novozybkov, Russia | I14 | 22 |
| Novska, Cro. | D11 | 18 |
| Nový Bohumín, Czech Rep. | F18 | 10 |
| Nový Jičín, Czech Rep. | F18 | 10 |
| Novyj Nekouz, Russia | D21 | 22 |
| Novyj Ropsk, Russia | I15 | 22 |
| Nowa Ruda, Pol. | E16 | 10 |
| Nowa Sól (Neusalz), Pol. | D15 | 10 |
| Nowata, Ok., U.S. | C11 | 116 |
| *Nowitna, stm., Ak., U.S.* | D17 | 100 |
| Nowogród, Pol. | H4 | 22 |
| Nowogrodziec, Pol. | D15 | 10 |
| *Nowood, stm., Wy., U.S.* | F18 | 122 |
| Nowra, Austl. | J9 | 70 |
| *Nowshāk, mtn., Asia* | B4 | 44 |
| Nowshera, Pak. | C4 | 44 |
| Nowy Dwór Mazowiecki, Pol. | C20 | 10 |
| Nowy Sącz, Pol. | F20 | 10 |
| Nowy Targ, Pol. | F20 | 10 |
| Noxapater, Ms., U.S. | J7 | 114 |
| Noxen, Pa., U.S. | F10 | 108 |
| Noxon, Mt., U.S. | B10 | 122 |
| *Noxubee, stm., U.S.* | I8 | 114 |
| Noyon, Fr. | C10 | 14 |
| N'Riquinha, Ang. | E4 | 58 |
| Nsanje, Mwi. | E7 | 58 |
| Nsawam, Ghana | I9 | 64 |
| Nsukka, Nig. | H13 | 64 |
| Ntakat, Maur. | C4 | 64 |
| *Ntem, stm., Afr.* | H9 | 54 |
| N'Tsaoueni, Com. | k15 | 67a |
| *Ntwetwe Pan, pl., Bots.* | C7 | 66 |
| *Nuanetsi, stm., Afr.* | C10 | 66 |
| Nuanli, China | C6 | 40 |
| *Nūbah, Jibāl an-, mts., Sudan* | L6 | 60 |
| *Nubian Desert, des., Sudan* | G8 | 60 |
| *Ñuble, stm., Chile* | I3 | 80 |
| Nucet, Rom. | C6 | 20 |
| *Nuchatlitz Inlet, b., B.C., Can.* | H8 | 102 |
| N'uchča, Russia | E7 | 26 |
| Nucla, Co., U.S. | F8 | 120 |
| *Nucuray, stm., Peru* | J5 | 84 |
| *Nueces, stm., Tx., U.S.* | L9 | 116 |
| *Nueltin Lake, l., Can.* | D13 | 96 |
| Nuestra Señora de Talavera, Arg. | C7 | 80 |
| *Nueva, Isla, i., Chile* | H3 | 78 |
| Nueva Antioquia, Col. | D8 | 84 |
| *Nueva Asunción, dept., Para.* | I11 | 82 |
| Nueva Ciudad Guerrero, Mex. | D10 | 90 |
| Nueva Concepción, El Sal. | C5 | 92 |
| *Nueva Esparta, state, Ven.* | B10 | 84 |
| Nueva Francia, Arg. | E8 | 80 |
| Nueva Galia, Arg. | H6 | 80 |
| Nueva Germania, Para. | B10 | 80 |
| Nueva Gerona, Cuba | D3 | 94 |
| Nueva Helvecia, Ur. | H10 | 80 |
| Nueva Imperial, Chile | J2 | 80 |
| Nueva Italia de Ruiz, Mex. | H8 | 90 |
| Nueva Ocotepeque, Hond. | C5 | 92 |
| Nueva Palmira, Ur. | G9 | 80 |
| Nueva Rosita, Mex. | D9 | 90 |
| Nueva San Salvador, El Sal. | D5 | 92 |
| *Nueva Segovia, dept., Nic.* | D8 | 92 |
| Nueva Venecia, Guat. | B3 | 92 |
| *Nueve, Canal Numero, Arg.* | I9 | 80 |
| Nueve de Julio, Arg. | H8 | 80 |
| Nuevitas, Cuba | D6 | 94 |
| *Nuevo, Bajo, Col.* | G5 | 94 |
| *Nuevo, Cayo, i., Mex.* | G13 | 90 |
| Nuevo Berlín, Ur. | G9 | 80 |
| Nuevo Casas Grandes, Mex. | B6 | 90 |
| Nuevo Chagres, Pan. | H14 | 92 |
| Nuevo Delicias, Mex. | D8 | 90 |
| Nuevo Laredo, Mex. | D10 | 90 |
| *Nuevo León, state, Mex.* | D9 | 90 |
| Nuevo Progreso, Mex. | H13 | 90 |
| Nuevo Rocafuerte, Ec. | H5 | 84 |
| Nuia, Est. | C8 | 22 |
| Nuits-Saint-Georges, Fr. | E11 | 14 |
| *N'uja, stm., Russia* | E14 | 28 |
| *N'uk, ozero, l., Russia* | I22 | 6 |
| *Nukey Bluff, clf, Austl.* | I1 | 70 |
| Nukus, Uzb. | I9 | 26 |
| Nulato, Ak., U.S. | D15 | 100 |
| Nullagine, Austl. | D4 | 68 |
| *Nullarbor National Park, Austl.* | F6 | 68 |
| *Nullarbor Plain, pl., Austl.* | F5 | 68 |
| *Numabin Bay, b., Sk., Can.* | B11 | 104 |
| Numazu, Japan | L13 | 36 |
| Numurkah, Austl. | K6 | 70 |
| Nunapitchuk, Ak., U.S. | F13 | 100 |
| Nunda, N.Y., U.S. | E9 | 108 |
| *Nungesser Lake, l., On., Can.* | G21 | 104 |
| *Nunivak Island, i., Ak., U.S.* | F11 | 100 |
| Nunjiang, China | B12 | 30 |
| Nunkini, Mex. | G14 | 90 |
| Nunnelly, Tn., U.S. | G9 | 114 |
| *Nuomin, stm., China* | B11 | 30 |
| *Nuon, stm., Afr.* | H5 | 64 |
| Nuoro, Italy | I4 | 18 |
| Nuqui, Col. | E4 | 84 |
| *Nura, stm., Kaz.* | G12 | 26 |
| N'urba, Russia | E15 | 28 |
| Nürburgring, Ger. | H10 | 12 |
| Nurek, Taj. | A3 | 44 |
| Nuremberg see Nürnberg, Ger. | F11 | 10 |
| Nürnberg (Nuremberg), Ger. | F11 | 10 |
| Nurri, Italy | J4 | 18 |
| *Nurri, Mount, hill, Austl.* | H7 | 70 |
| Nursery, Tx., U.S. | K9 | 116 |
| Nürtingen, Ger. | G9 | 10 |
| Nüsah, Yemen | G5 | 47 |
| Nusaybin, Tur. | C6 | 48 |
| *Nu Shan, mts., China* | F6 | 30 |
| Nushki, Pak. | F2 | 44 |
| *Nut Lake Indian Reserve, Sk., Can.* | F11 | 104 |
| Nutrioso, Az., U.S. | K7 | 120 |
| *Nuttby Mountain, hill, N.S., Can.* | G10 | 106 |
| Nutter Fort, W.V., U.S. | H6 | 108 |
| Nuwaybi' al-Muzayyinah, Egypt | C8 | 60 |
| Nuwerus, S. Afr. | H4 | 66 |
| Nxainxai, Bots. | B5 | 66 |
| *Nxai Pan National Park, Bots.* | B7 | 66 |
| Nxaunxau, Bots. | B5 | 66 |
| Nyaake, Lib. | I6 | 64 |
| Nyabing, Austl. | F3 | 68 |
| Nyack, N.Y., U.S. | F13 | 108 |
| Nyah West, Austl. | J5 | 70 |
| *Nyainqêntanglha Shan, mts., China* | E13 | 44 |
| Nyakrom, Ghana | I9 | 64 |
| Nyala, Sudan | K3 | 60 |
| Nyamandhlovu, Zimb. | B9 | 66 |
| Nyamina, Mali | E6 | 64 |
| Nyamlell, Sudan | M4 | 60 |
| Nyanza, Rw. | B5 | 58 |
| *Nyasa, Lake (Lake Malawi), l., Afr.* | D6 | 58 |
| *Nyasaland see Malawi, ctry., Afr.* | D6 | 58 |
| Nyaunglebin, Myan. | F4 | 40 |
| Nybergsund, Nor. | K13 | 6 |
| Nyiel, Sudan | N6 | 60 |
| Nyíradony, Hung. | H21 | 10 |
| Nyírbátor, Hung. | H22 | 10 |
| Nyíregyháza, Hung. | H21 | 10 |
| Nykøbing, Den. | M11 | 6 |
| Nykøbing, Den. | N12 | 6 |
| Nyköping, Swe. | L15 | 6 |
| Nylstroom, S. Afr. | E9 | 66 |
| Nymburk, Czech Rep. | E15 | 10 |
| Nynäshamn, Swe. | L15 | 6 |
| Nyngan, Austl. | H7 | 70 |
| Nyon, Switz. | F5 | 13 |
| *Nyong, stm., Cam.* | H9 | 54 |
| Nýrsko, Czech Rep. | F13 | 10 |
| Nysa, Pol. | E17 | 10 |
| *Nysa Łużycka (Neisse), stm., Eur.* | D14 | 10 |
| Nyssa, Or., U.S. | G9 | 122 |
| Nytva, Russia | F9 | 26 |
| Nyzhankovychi, Ukr. | F22 | 10 |
| Nzébéla, Gui. | G5 | 64 |
| Nzérékoré, Gui. | H5 | 64 |
| N'zeto, Ang. | C2 | 58 |
| *Nzi, stm., C. Iv.* | H7 | 64 |
| *Nzwani (Anjouan), i., Com.* | I16 | 67a |
| **O** | | |
| Oacoma, S.D., U.S. | H8 | 118 |
| *Oahe, Lake, res., U.S.* | F7 | 118 |
| *Oahu, i., Hi., U.S.* | p15 | 125a |
| *Oak, stm., Mb., Can.* | I14 | 104 |
| Oakbank, Austl. | I4 | 70 |
| Oak Bay, B.C., Can. | I11 | 102 |
| Oak Bluffs, Ma., U.S. | F16 | 108 |
| Oakboro, N.C., U.S. | D6 | 112 |
| Oakburn, Mb., Can. | H14 | 104 |
| Oak City, N.C., U.S. | D9 | 112 |
| Oak City, Ut., U.S. | E4 | 120 |
| Oak Creek, Co., U.S. | D10 | 120 |
| *Oak Creek, stm., Az., U.S.* | J5 | 120 |
| Oakdale, Ca., U.S. | G5 | 124 |
| Oakdale, La., U.S. | L4 | 114 |
| Oakdale, Ne., U.S. | I10 | 118 |
| Oakdale, Tn., U.S. | D2 | 112 |
| Oakes, N.D., U.S. | E9 | 118 |
| Oakesdale, Wa., U.S. | C8 | 122 |
| Oakey, Austl. | F9 | 70 |
| Oakfield, Me., U.S. | A18 | 108 |
| Oakfield, N.Y., U.S. | D8 | 108 |
| Oakfield, Wi., U.S. | G7 | 110 |
| Oak Grove, La., U.S. | J5 | 114 |
| Oak Harbor, Wa., U.S. | B3 | 122 |
| Oak Hill, Fl., U.S. | K6 | 112 |
| Oak Hill, Mi., U.S. | F9 | 110 |
| Oak Hill, Oh., U.S. | I4 | 108 |
| Oak Hill, W.V., U.S. | J5 | 108 |
| Oakhurst, Ca., U.S. | G6 | 124 |
| Oakhurst, Tx., U.S. | I11 | 116 |
| *Oak Island, i., N.S., Can.* | H9 | 106 |
| Oak Knolls, Ca., U.S. | J5 | 124 |
| Oak Lake, Mb., Can. | I14 | 104 |
| *Oak Lake, l., Mb., Can.* | I14 | 104 |
| *Oak Lake, l., On., Can.* | H21 | 104 |
| Oakland, Ca., U.S. | G3 | 124 |
| Oakland, Ia., U.S. | J12 | 118 |
| Oakland, Il., U.S. | C8 | 114 |
| Oakland, Md., U.S. | H7 | 108 |
| Oakland, Me., U.S. | C17 | 108 |
| Oakland, Ms., U.S. | H7 | 114 |
| Oakland, Ne., U.S. | J11 | 118 |
| Oakland, Or., U.S. | G2 | 122 |
| Oakland City, In., U.S. | D9 | 114 |
| Oakland Park, Fl., U.S. | M6 | 112 |
| Oak Lawn, Il., U.S. | I8 | 110 |
| Oaklawn, Ks., U.S. | N10 | 118 |
| Oakley, Id., U.S. | H12 | 122 |
| Oakley, Ks., U.S. | L7 | 118 |
| Oakman, Al., U.S. | I9 | 114 |
| Oak Park, Il., U.S. | I8 | 110 |
| Oak Point, Mb., Can. | H16 | 104 |
| Oakridge, Or., U.S. | G3 | 122 |
| Oak Ridge, Tn., U.S. | C2 | 112 |
| Oaktown, In., U.S. | D9 | 114 |
| Oak View, Ca., U.S. | J6 | 124 |
| Oakville, Mb., Can. | I17 | 104 |
| Oakville, On., Can. | G16 | 110 |
| Oakwood, Oh., U.S. | F2 | 108 |
| Oakwood, Tx., U.S. | H11 | 116 |
| Oamaru, N.Z. | F3 | 72 |
| Oancea, Rom. | D12 | 20 |
| Oatlands, Austl. | N7 | 70 |
| Oatman, Az., U.S. | I2 | 120 |
| *Oaxaca, state, Mex.* | I11 | 90 |
| Oaxaca [de Juárez], Mex. | I11 | 90 |
| *Ob', stm., Russia* | D11 | 26 |
| Obal', Bela. | F12 | 22 |
| Obama, Japan | L10 | 36 |
| Oban, Austl. | C3 | 70 |
| Oban, Nig. | I14 | 64 |
| Oban, Scot., U.K. | E8 | 8 |
| O Barco de Valdeorras, Spain | C5 | 16 |
| Obed, Ab., Can. | D17 | 102 |
| *Obed, stm., Tn., U.S.* | C2 | 112 |
| Obeliai, Lith. | F8 | 22 |
| Oberá, Arg. | D11 | 80 |
| Oberdrauburg, Aus. | I12 | 10 |
| Obergurgl, Aus. | I11 | 10 |
| Oberhausen, Ger. | D6 | 10 |
| Oberlin, Ks., U.S. | L7 | 118 |
| Oberlin, La., U.S. | L4 | 114 |
| Oberlin, Oh., U.S. | F4 | 108 |
| Obernai, Fr. | D14 | 14 |
| Obernburg am Main, Ger. | F9 | 10 |
| Oberon, Austl. | I8 | 70 |
| *Oberösterreich, state, Aus.* | G13 | 10 |
| Oberpullendorf, Aus. | H16 | 10 |
| Obertyn, Ukr. | A9 | 20 |
| Oberursel, Ger. | E8 | 10 |
| Obervellach, Aus. | I13 | 10 |
| Oberwart, Aus. | H16 | 10 |
| Obi, Nig. | G14 | 64 |
| *Obi, Kepulauan, is., Indon.* | F8 | 38 |
| Obiaruku, Nig. | I13 | 64 |
| Óbidos, Braz. | D7 | 76 |
| Obihiro, Japan | e18 | 36a |
| *Obilatu, Pulau, i., Indon.* | F8 | 38 |
| Obing, Ger. | G12 | 10 |
| Obion, Tn., U.S. | F7 | 114 |

Name — Map Ref. — Page

Obion, stm., Tn., U.S. F7 114
Oblong, Il., U.S. C9 114
Oblučje, Russia H18 28
Obninsk, Russia F19 22
Obock, Dji. F9 56
Oborniki, Pol. C16 10
Oboz'orskij, Russia J27 6
O'Brien, Or., U.S. H2 122
Obščij Syrt, mtn., Eur. G8 26
Observatory Inlet, b., B.C., Can. B5 102
Obskaja guba, b., Russia D12 26
Obuasi, Ghana H9 64
Obuchova, Russia E15 22
Obžericha, Russia D25 22
Ocala, Fl., U.S. J4 112
Ocallí, Peru B2 82
Ocamo, stm., Ven. F10 84
Ocampo, Mex. C5 90
Ocampo, Mex. D8 90
Ocaña, Col. C6 84
Occidental, Cordillera, mts., Col. E4 84
Occidental, Cordillera, mts., Peru C3 82
Oceana, W.V., U.S. B5 112
Ocean Cape, c., Ak., U.S. G25 100
Ocean City, Md., U.S. I11 108
Ocean City, N.J., U.S. H12 108
Ocean Falls, B.C., Can. E7 102
Oceano, Ca., U.S. I5 124
Ocean Park, Wa., U.S. D1 122
Oceanside, Ca., U.S. K8 124
Ocean Springs, Ms., U.S. L8 114
Ocha, Russia G20 28
Ochapowace Indian Reserve, Sk., Can. H12 104
Ocheyedan, Ia., U.S. H12 118
O'Chiese Indian Reserve, Ab., Can. E19 102
Ochlocknee, Ga., U.S. I2 112
Ochlockonee, stm., U.S. I2 112
Ocho Rios, Jam. E6 94
Ochota, stm., Russia F20 28
Ochotsk, Russia F20 28
Ochre River, Mb., Can. G15 104
Ochsenfurt, Ger. F10 10
Ochvat, Russia E15 22
Ocilla, Ga., U.S. H3 112
Ocmulgee, stm., Ga., U.S. H3 112
Ocniţa, Mol. A11 20
Ocoa, Bahía de, b., Dom. Rep. E9 94
Ocoee, Fl., U.S. K5 112
Ocoee (Toccoa), stm., U.S. D2 112
Ocoña, Peru G5 82
Ocoña, stm., Peru G5 82
Oconee, stm., Ga., U.S. G4 112
Ocongate, Peru E6 82
Oconomowoc, Wi., U.S. G7 110
Oconto, Wi., U.S. F8 110
Oconto, stm., Wi., U.S. F7 110
Oconto Falls, Wi., U.S. F7 110
Ocós, Guat. C2 92
Ocosingo, Mex. I13 90
Ocotal, Nic. D8 92
Ocotepeque, dept., Hond. C5 92
Ocotlán, Mex. G8 90
Ocotlán de Morelos, Mex. I11 90
Ocozocoautla [de Espinosa], Mex. I13 90
Ocracoke, N.C., U.S. D11 112
Ocracoke Island, i., N.C., U.S. D11 112
Ocros, Peru D3 82
Ocú, Pan. J14 92
Ocumare del Tuy, Ven. B9 84
Ocuri, Bol. H9 82
Ocussi, Indon. A4 68
Oda, Ghana I9 64
Oda, Jabal, mtn., Sudan G9 60
Odanakumadona, Bots. C7 66
Ōdate, Japan G15 36
Odawara, Japan L14 36
Odda, Nor. K10 6
Odebolt, Ia., U.S. I12 118
Odei, stm., Mb., Can. B17 104
Odell, Il., U.S. I7 110
Odell, Ne., U.S. K11 118
Odell, Tx., U.S. E7 116
Odem, Tx., U.S. L9 116
Ödemiş, Tur. K11 20
Odendaalsrus, S. Afr. F8 66
Odense, Den. N12 6
Oder (Odra), stm., Eur. C14 10
Oderberg, Ger. C14 10
Oderzo, Italy D7 18
Odesa (Odessa), Ukr. H4 26
Odessa, Mo., U.S. D3 114
Odessa, On., Can. F19 110
Odessa, Tx., U.S. H4 116
Odessa see Odesa, Ukr. H4 26
Odessa, Wa., U.S. C7 122
Odesskoje, Russia G12 26
Odiakwe, Bots. C7 66
Odīb, Wādī, val., Sudan F9 60
Odienné, C. Iv. G6 64
Odin, Mount, mtn., B.C., Can. G16 102
Odincovo, Russia F20 22
Odojev, Russia H19 22
Odon, In., U.S. D10 114
O'Donnell, Tx., U.S. G5 116
Odorheiu Secuiesc, Rom. C9 20
Odum, Ga., U.S. H4 112
Odzi, Zimb. B11 66
Oebisfelde, Ger. C11 10
Oeiras, Braz. E10 76
Oelde, Ger. D8 10
Oelsnitz, Ger. E12 10
Oelwein, Ia., U.S. H4 110
Oesterdam, Neth. F5 12
Oettingen in Bayern, Ger. G10 10
Oetz, Aus. H10 10
O'Fallon, Mo., U.S. D6 114
Ofaqim, Isr. F3 50
Offa, Nig. G12 64
Offaly, co., Ire. H6 8
Offenbach, Ger. E8 10
Offenburg, Ger. G7 10
Oficina Alemania, Chile C4 80
Oficina Alianza, Chile I7 82
Oficina Chile, Chile C4 80
Oficina Pedro de Valdivia, Chile B4 80
Oficina Victoria, Chile I7 82
Ōfunato, Japan H16 36
Oga, Japan H14 36
Ogaden, reg., Afr. G9 56
Ōgaki, Japan L11 36
Ogallala, Ne., U.S. J6 118
Ogbomosho, Nig. G12 64
Ogden, Ia., U.S. H1 110
Ogden, Ks., U.S. L11 118
Ogden, Ut., U.S. C5 120
Ogden, Mount, mtn., N.A. G28 100
Ogdensburg, N.Y., U.S. C11 108
Ogeechee, stm., Ga., U.S. G5 112
Ogema, Sk., Can. I10 104
Ogilvie, Mn., U.S. E2 110
Ogilvie, stm., Yk., Can. D25 100
Ogilvie Mountains, mts., Yk., Can. D25 100
Oglesby, Il., U.S. I6 110
Oglesby, Tx., U.S. H9 116
Oglethorpe, Ga., U.S. G2 112
Oglio, stm., Italy D5 18
Ogmore, Austl. D8 70
Ognon, stm., Fr. E12 14
Ogoja, Nig. H14 64
Ogoki, stm., On., Can. F15 96
Ogooué, stm., Afr. B1 58
Ogr, Sudan K4 60
Ogre, Lat. E7 22
O Grove, Spain C3 16
Ogulin, Cro. D10 18
Ogunquit, Me., U.S. D16 108
Ogurčinskij, ostrov, i., Turk. B12 48
Oğuzeli, Tur. C4 48
Ogwashi-Uku, Nig. H13 64
Ohanet, Alg. F15 62
Ōhara, Japan L15 36
O'Higgins, Lago (Lago San Martín), l., S.A. F2 78
Ohio, Il., U.S. I6 110
Ohio, state, U.S. C10 98
Ohio, stm., U.S. D9 98
Ohio City, Oh., U.S. G2 108
Ohře, stm., Eur. E13 10
Ohrid, Mac. H4 20
Ohrid, Lake, l., Eur. H4 20
Öhringen, Ger. F9 10
Ohuira, Bahía, b., Mex. E5 90
Oiapoque, Braz. C8 76
Oiapoque (Oyapock), stm., S.A. C8 76
Oies, Île aux, i., P.Q., Can. E3 106
Oil Center, N.M., U.S. G3 116
Oil City, La., U.S. J3 114
Oil City, Pa., U.S. F7 108
Oil Creek, stm., Pa., U.S. F7 108
Oildale, Ca., U.S. I6 124
Oilton, Ok., U.S. C10 116
Oilton, Tx., U.S. L8 116
Oil Trough, Ar., U.S. G5 114
Oise, dept., Fr. C9 14
Oise, stm., Eur. C9 14
Oisemont, Fr. C8 14
Ōita, Japan N6 36
Ojai, Ca., U.S. J6 124
Ojat', stm., Russia A16 22
Ojinaga, Mex. C7 90
Ojocaliente, Mex. F8 90
Ojo del Carrizo, Mex. C7 90
Ojo de Liebre, Laguna, b., Mex. D2 90
Ojos del Salado, Nevado, mtn., S.A. D4 80
Ojos Negros, Mex. B1 90
Oju, Nig. H14 64
Oka, stm., Russia E26 22
Oka, stm., Russia G12 28
Okahandja, Nmb. C3 66
Okanagan (Okanogan), stm., N.A. H15 102
Okanagan Centre, B.C., Can. G15 102
Okanagan Falls, B.C., Can. H15 102
Okanagan Indian Reserve, B.C., Can. G15 102
Okanagan Lake, l., B.C., Can. G15 102
Okanagan Landing, B.C., Can. G15 102
Okanagan Mountain Provincial Park, B.C., Can. H15 102
Okanagan Range (Okanogan Range), mts., N.A. H14 102
Okanogan, Wa., U.S. B6 122
Okanogan (Okanagan), stm., N.A. I15 102
Okaputa, Nmb. C3 66
Okāra, Pak. E5 44
Okarche, Ok., U.S. D9 116
Okaukuejo, Nmb. B2 66
Okavango (Cubango), stm., Afr. E3 58
Okavango Delta, Bots. B6 66
Okawville, Il., U.S. D7 114
Okaya, Japan K13 36
Okayama, Japan M8 36
Okazaki, Japan M12 36
Okeechobee, Fl., U.S. L6 112
Okeechobee, Lake, l., Fl., U.S. M6 112
Okeene, Ok., U.S. C8 116
Okefenokee Swamp, sw., U.S. I4 112
Okeigbo, Nig. H12 64
Okemah, Ok., U.S. D10 116
Okemos, Mi., U.S. H11 110
Okene, Nig. H13 64
Oke-Ode, Nig. G12 64
Okhotsk, Sea of, Asia c19 36a
Okhtyrka, Ukr. G4 26
Okiep, S. Afr. G3 66
Okinawa, Japan u2 37b
Okinawa-jima, i., Japan u2 37b
Okinawa-shotō, is., Japan u2 37b
Okino-Daitō-jima, i., Japan G13 30
Okino-Erabu-shima, i., Japan t3 37b
Okino-Tori-shima (Parece Vela), i., Japan G14 30
Oki-shotō, is., Japan K8 36
Okladnevo, Russia C16 22
Oklahoma, state, U.S. D7 98
Oklahoma City, Ok., U.S. D9 116
Oklawaha, Fl., U.S. J5 112
Oklee, Mn., U.S. D12 118
Okmulgee, Ok., U.S. D10 116
Okolona, Ar., U.S. I3 114
Okolona, Ky., U.S. D11 114
Okolona, Ms., U.S. H8 114
Okombahe, Nmb. C2 66
Okotoks, Ab., Can. G21 102
Okpara, stm., Afr. H11 64
Okrika, Nig. I13 64
Okt'abr', Russia D20 22
Okt'abr'skij, Russia D23 22
Okt'abr'skij, Russia C27 22
Okt'abr'skij, Russia G21 22
Okt'abr'skij, Russia G8 26
Okt'abr'skoje, Russia I22 22
Okt'abr'skoj Revol'ucii, ostrov, i., Russia B17 26
Okulovka, Russia C16 22
Okushiri-tō, i., Japan e14 36a
Okuta, Nig. G11 64
Okwa (Chapman's), stm., Afr. D5 66
Okwoga, Nig. H13 64
Ola, Ar., U.S. G3 114
Olá, Pan. I14 92
Ólafsfjörður, Ice. A4 6a
Olancha, Ca., U.S. H7 124
Olancha Peak, mtn., Ca., U.S. H7 124
Olanchito, Hond. B8 92
Olancho, dept., Hond. C9 92
Öland, i., Swe. M15 6
Olanta, S.C., U.S. F7 112
Olar, S.C., U.S. F5 112
Olary, Austl. I4 70
Olascoaga, Arg. H8 80
Olathe, Co., U.S. F9 120
Olathe, Ks., U.S. M13 118
Olavarría, Arg. I8 80
Oława, Pol. E17 10
Olbia, Italy I4 18
Olca, Volcán, vol., S.A. I7 82
Olcott, N.Y., U.S. D8 108
Old Bahama Channel, strt., N.A. C5 94
Old Crow, Yk., Can. C25 100
Old Crow, stm., N.A. B24 100
Olden, Tx., U.S. G8 116
Oldenburg, hist. reg., Ger. B8 10
Oldenburg [in Holstein], Ger. A10 10
Oldenzaal, Neth. D10 12
Old Faithful Geyser, well, Wy., U.S. F15 122
Old Forge, N.Y., U.S. D12 108
Old Forge, Pa., U.S. F11 108
Old Fort Mountain, mtn., B.C., Can. B8 102
Oldham, S.D., U.S. G10 118
Old Harbor, Ak., U.S. H18 100
Old Hickory Lake, res., Tn., U.S. F10 114
Oldman, stm., Ab., Can. H23 102
Old Man Mountain, mtn., Nf., Can. C16 106
Oldmeldrum, Scot., U.K. D11 8
Old Orchard Beach, Me., U.S. D16 108
Old Perlican, Nf., Can. D20 106
Olds, Ab., Can. F20 102
Old Saybrook, Ct., U.S. F14 108
Old Tate, Bots. C8 66
Old Town, Me., U.S. C18 108
Old Trap, N.C., U.S. C10 112
Old Wives Lake, l., Sk., Can. H8 104
Olean, N.Y., U.S. E8 108
O'Leary, P.E., Can. F9 106
Olecko, Pol. A22 10
Oleksandriya, Ukr. H4 26
Olen, Bel. F6 12
Ølen, Nor. L9 6
Olenegorsk, Russia D4 26
Olenij, ostrov, i., Russia C13 26
Olenino, Russia E16 22
Olen'ok, stm., Russia C16 28
Olen'okskij zaliv, b., Russia C16 28
Oléron, Île d', i., Fr. G5 14
Oleśnica, Pol. D17 10
Olesno, Pol. E18 10
Ol'ga, Russia I19 28
Ölgij, Mong. B4 30
Olhão, Port. H4 16
Ol'hopil', Ukr. A13 20
Oli, stm., Afr. G12 64
Olifants (Rio dos Elefantes), stm., Afr. E10 66
Ólimbos, mtn., Cyp. D2 48
Ólimbos, Óros (Mount Olympus), mtn., Grc. I6 20
Olímpia, Braz. F4 79
Olin, Ia., U.S. I4 110
Olinalá, Mex. I10 90
Olinda, Braz. E12 76
Olio, Austl. C5 70
Oliva, Arg. G7 80
Oliva, Spain G11 16
Oliva de la Frontera, Spain G5 16
Olivares, Cerro de, mtn., S.A. F4 80
Olive Branch, Ms., U.S. H7 114
Olive Hill, Ky., U.S. I3 108
Olivehurst, Ca., U.S. E4 124
Oliveira, Braz. F6 79
Oliveira dos Brejinhos, Braz. B7 79
Olivenza, Spain G4 16
Oliver, B.C., Can. H15 102
Oliver Lake, l., Sk., Can. B11 104
Oliver Springs, Tn., U.S. C2 112
Olivet, Mi., U.S. H11 110
Olivet, S.D., U.S. H10 118
Olivia, Mn., U.S. G13 118
Olla, La., U.S. K4 114
Ollagüe, Chile I7 82
Ollagüe, Volcán, vol., S.A. I7 82
Ollantaitambo, Peru E5 82
Olmos, Peru A2 82
Olney, Il., U.S. D8 114
Olney, Tx., U.S. F8 116
Ol'okma, stm., Russia F16 28
Ol'okminsk, Russia E16 28
Olomane, stm., P.Q., Can. A13 106
Olomega, Laguna, l., El Sal. D6 92
Olomouc, Czech Rep. F17 10
Olonec, Russia E4 26
Olongapo, Phil. n19 39b
Oloron-Sainte-Marie, Fr. I6 14
Olot, Spain C14 16
Olov'annaja, Russia G15 28
Olpe, Ger. D7 10
Olpe, Ks., U.S. M11 118
Olsztyn (Allenstein), Pol. B20 10
Olsztynek, Pol. B20 10
Olt, co., Rom. E8 20
Olt, stm., Rom. E8 20
Olta, Arg. F5 80
Olten, Switz. D8 13
Olteniţa, Rom. E10 20
Olton, Tx., U.S. E4 116
Oltu, Tur. A6 48
Oluan Pi, c., Tai. N9 34
Olukonda, Nmb. B3 66
Olustee, Fl., U.S. I4 112
Olustee, Ok., U.S. E7 116
Ol'utorskij, mys, c., Russia F26 28
Ol'utorskij zaliv, b., Russia F26 28
Olvera, Spain I6 16
Olympia, Wa., U.S. C3 122
Olympic Mountains, mts., Wa., U.S. C2 122
Olympic National Park, Wa., U.S. C2 122
Olympus, Mount see Ólimbos, Óros, mtn., Grc. I6 20
Olympus, Mount, mtn., Wa., U.S. C2 122
Om', stm., Russia F7 28
Omagh, N. Ire., U.K. G6 8
Omaguas, Peru J6 84
Omaha, Ne., U.S. J12 118
Omaha, Tx., U.S. I2 114
Omaheke, prov., Nmb. C4 66
Omak, Wa., U.S. B6 122
Oman ('Umān), ctry., Asia E6 42
Oman, Gulf of, b., Asia B10 47
Omar, W.V., U.S. B5 112
Omarama, N.Z. F2 72
Omaruru, Nmb. C2 66
Omatako, stm., Nmb. B5 66
Omate, Peru G6 82
Ombombo, Nmb. B1 66
Omboué, Gabon B1 58
Omčak, Russia E21 28
Omdurman see Umm Durmān, Sudan J7 60
Omega, Ga., U.S. H3 112
Omegna, Italy D3 18
Omemee, On., Can. F17 110
Omeo, Austl. K7 70
Ometepe, Isla de, i., Nic. F9 92
Ometepec, Mex. I10 90
Om Hajer, Erit. J9 60
Omineca, stm., B.C., Can. B10 102
Omineca Mountains, mts., B.C., Can. B9 102
Ōmiya, Japan L14 36
Ommaney, Cape, c., Ak., U.S. H27 100
Ommanney Bay, b., N.T., Can. B12 96
Omo, stm., Afr. G8 56
Omoa, Bahía de, b., N.A. B6 92
Omoloj, stm., Russia C18 28
Omolon, stm., Russia D23 28
Omro, Wi., U.S. F7 110
Omsk, Russia F6 28
Omsukčan, Russia E23 28
Omu-Aran, Nig. G12 64
Ōmuta, Japan N5 36
Omutninsk, Russia F8 26
On, Viet. D9 40
Onabas, Mex. C5 90
Onaga, Ks., U.S. L11 118
Onamia, Mn., U.S. D2 110
Onancock, Va., U.S. B11 112
Onarga, Il., U.S. J7 110
Onatchiway, Lac, l., P.Q., Can. C2 106
Onawa, Ia., U.S. I11 118
Onaway, Mi., U.S. E11 110
Oncativo, Arg. F7 80
Once, Canal Numero, Arg. I9 80
Onda, Spain F11 16
Ondangwa, Nmb. A3 66
Ondas, Rio de, stm., Braz. B6 79
Onderdijk, Neth. C7 12
Ondjiva, Ang. E3 58
Ondo, Nig. H12 64
Öndörchaan, Mong. B9 30
Ondozero, ozero, l., Russia J23 6
One Arrow Indian Reserve, Sk., Can. F8 104
Oneco, Fl., U.S. L4 112
Onega, Russia E5 26
Onega, stm., Russia J26 6
Onega, Lake see Onežskoje ozero, l., Russia E5 26
One Hundred and Two, stm., Mo., U.S. C2 114
One Hundred Fifty Mile House, B.C., Can. E13 102
One Hundred Mile House, B.C., Can. F13 102
Oneida, Il., U.S. I5 110
Oneida, Ky., U.S. B3 112
Oneida, N.Y., U.S. D11 108
Oneida, Tn., U.S. C2 112
Oneida Lake, l., N.Y., U.S. D11 108
O'Neill, Ne., U.S. I9 118
Onekama, Mi., U.S. F9 110
Onekotan, ostrov, i., Russia H22 28
Oneonta, Al., U.S. I10 114
Oneonta, N.Y., U.S. E11 108
Oneşti, Rom. C10 20
Onežskaja guba, b., Russia I25 6
Onežskij poluostrov, pen., Russia I25 6
Onežskoje ozero, l., Russia E5 26
Ongjin, N. Kor. F13 32
Ongole, India E6 46
Onida, S.D., U.S. G7 118
Onistagane, Lac, l., P.Q., Can. B2 106
Onitsha, Nig. H13 64
Ōno, Japan L11 36
Onoda, Japan N6 36
Onomichi, Japan M8 36
Onon, stm., Asia A9 30
Onoto, Ven. C10 84
Onoway, Ab., Can. D20 102
Onseepkans, S. Afr. G4 66
Onset, Ma., U.S. F16 108
Onslow, Austl. D3 68
Onslow Bay, b., N.C., U.S. E9 112
Ontario, Ca., U.S. J8 124
Ontario, Oh., U.S. G4 108
Ontario, Or., U.S. F9 122
Ontario, prov., Can. F15 96
Ontario, Lake, l., N.A. G18 110
Ontinyent (Onteniente), Spain G11 16
Ontonagon, Mi., U.S. D6 110
Ontonagon, stm., Mi., U.S. D6 110
Onverwacht, Sur. B7 76
Ŏnyang, S. Kor. G15 32
Oodnadatta, Austl. E7 68
Ooldea, Austl. F6 68
Oolitic, In., U.S. D10 114
Oologah, Ok., U.S. C11 116
Oologah Lake, res., Ok., U.S. C11 116
Oona River, B.C., Can. D4 102
Oostburg, Wi., U.S. G8 110
Oostelijk Flevoland, reg., Neth. C8 12
Oostende (Ostende), Bel. F2 12
Oosterend, Neth. B6 12
Oosterhout, Neth. E6 12
Oosterschelde, b., Neth. E4 12
Oosterscheldedam, Neth. E4 12
Oosterwolde, Neth. C9 12
Oostflakkee, Neth. E5 12
Oost-Vlaanderen, prov., Bel. G4 12
Oostvleteren, Bel. G2 12
Ootsa Lake, B.C., Can. D8 102
Ootsa Lake, l., B.C., Can. D8 102
Ootsi, Bots. E7 66
Opala, D.R.C. B4 58
Opalaca, Cordillera, mts., Hond. C6 92
Oparino, Russia F7 26
Opasquia, On., Can. E21 104
Opasquia Lake, l., On., Can. E21 104
Opatów, Pol. E21 10
Opava, Czech Rep. F17 10
Opava, stm., Eur. E17 10
Opelika, Al., U.S. J11 114
Opelousas, La., U.S. L4 114
Opheim, Mt., U.S. B19 122
Ophir, Or., U.S. H1 122
Opihikao, Hi., U.S. r19 125a
Opinaca, stm., P.Q., Can. F17 96
Opiscotéo, Lac, l., P.Q., Can. F19 96
Opobo, Nig. I13 64
Opočka, Russia E11 22
Opoczno, Pol. D20 10
Opole (Oppeln), Pol. E17 10
Opononono Lake, l., Nmb. B2 66
Oporto see Porto, Port. D3 16
Opotiki, N.Z. B6 72
Opp, Al., U.S. K10 114
Oppland, co., Nor. K11 6
Opportunity, Mt., U.S. D13 122
Opportunity, Wa., U.S. C8 122
Opsa, Bela. F9 22
Optic Lake, Mb., Can. D13 104
Opuwo, Nmb. B1 66
Oquawka, Il., U.S. J5 110
Ora, Italy C6 18
Oracle, Az., U.S. L6 120
Oradea, Rom. B5 20
Orai, India H8 44
Oran see Wahran, Alg. A6 54
Oran, Mo., U.S. E7 114
Orange, Austl. I8 70
Orange, Fr. H11 14
Orange, Ma., U.S. E14 108
Orange, Tx., U.S. L3 114
Orange, Va., U.S. I8 108
Orange (Oranje), stm., Afr. G4 66
Orange, Cabo, c., Braz. C8 76
Orangeburg, S.C., U.S. F6 112
Orange City, Fl., U.S. K5 112
Orange City, Ia., U.S. H11 118
Orange Cove, Ca., U.S. H6 124
Orange Grove, Tx., U.S. L9 116
Orange Lake, Fl., U.S. J4 112
Orange Park, Fl., U.S. I5 112
Orangeville, On., Can. G15 110
Orangeville, Ut., U.S. E5 120
Orange Walk, Belize H15 90
Oranienburg, Ger. C13 10
Oranjefontein, S. Afr. D8 66
Oranjemund, Nmb. G3 66
Oranjerivier, S. Afr. G7 66
Oranjestad, Aruba H9 94
Or 'Aqiva, Isr. C3 50
Orarak, Sudan N7 60
Orăştie, Rom. D7 20
Oravais (Oravainen), Fin. J18 6
Orbe, Switz. E6 13
Orbetello, Italy G6 18
Orbisonia, Pa., U.S. G9 108
Orbost, Austl. K8 70
Orcadas, sci., Ant. B1 73
Orcera, Spain G9 16
Orchard, Ne., U.S. I9 118
Orchard City, Co., U.S. F9 120
Orchard Homes, Mt., U.S. D11 122
Orchard Mesa, Co., U.S. E8 120
Orchard Park, N.Y., U.S. E8 108
Orchard Valley, Wy., U.S. C12 120
Orchies, Fr. B10 14
Orchon, stm., Mong. B7 30
Ord, Ne., U.S. J9 118
Ord, stm., Austl. C5 68
Ord, Mount, mtn., Austl. C5 68
Orderville, Ut., U.S. G4 120
Ordoqui, Arg. H8 80
Ordu, Tur. G15 4
Ordway, Co., U.S. M4 118
Ore, Nig. H12 64
Örebro, Swe. L14 6
Orechovo-Zujevo, Russia F21 22
Ore City, Tx., U.S. J2 114
Oredež, Russia C13 22
Oregon, Il., U.S. H6 110
Oregon, Mo., U.S. C1 114
Oregon, Oh., U.S. F3 108
Oregon, state, U.S. C2 98
Oregon City, Or., U.S. E3 122
Orel, Russia I19 22
Orellana, Peru B4 82
Orem, Ut., U.S. D5 120
Orenburg, Russia G9 26
Orenčik, Tur. J13 20
Orense, Arg. J9 80
Orestes Pereyra, Mex. D7 90
Orestiás, Grc. H10 20
Orfanoú, Kólpos, b., Grc. I7 20
Orfordville, Wi., U.S. H6 110
Organ Needle, mtn., N.M., U.S. L10 120
Orgelet, Fr. F12 14
Orgtrud, Russia E23 22
Orgūn, Afg. D3 44
Orhanlar, Tur. J11 20
Orhei, Mol. B12 20
Orica, Hond. C8 92
Orichuna, stm., Ven. D8 84
Orick, Ca., U.S. C1 124
Orient, Ia., U.S. J13 118
Oriental, N.C., U.S. D10 112
Oriental, Cordillera, mts., Col. E6 84
Oriental, Cordillera, mts., Peru C4 82
Oriente, Arg. J8 80
Orillia, On., Can. F16 110
Orinduik, Guy. E12 84
Orinoco, stm., S.A. C11 84
Orinoco, Delta del, Ven. C12 84
Oriola (Orihuela), Spain G11 16
Orion, Il., U.S. I5 110
Oripää, Fin. K18 6
Oriskany, N.Y., U.S. D11 108
Orissa, state, India B7 46
Orissaare, Est. C6 22
Oristano, Italy J3 18
Orituco, stm., Ven. C9 84
Oriximiná, Braz. D7 76
Orizaba, Mex. H11 90
Orizaba, Pico de (Volcán Citlaltépetl), vol., Mex. H11 90
Orizona, Braz. D4 79
Orkney, S. Afr. F8 66
Orkney, Sk., Can. I7 104
Orkney, prov., Scot., U.K. B10 8
Orkney Islands, is., Scot., U.K. B10 8
Orland, Ca., U.S. E3 124
Orlândia, Braz. F5 79
Orlando, Fl., U.S. K5 112
Orléanais, hist. reg., Fr. E8 14
Orleans, Ca., U.S. C2 124
Orléans, Fr. E8 14
Orleans, In., U.S. D10 114
Orleans, Ma., U.S. F17 108
Orleans, Ne., U.S. K8 118
Orléans, On., Can. B11 108
Orleans, Vt., U.S. C14 108
Orléans, Île d', i., P.Q., Can. F3 106
Orlová, Czech Rep. F18 10
Ormāra, Pak. I18 48
Ormiston, Sk., Can. I9 104
Ormoc, Phil. C7 38
Ormond Beach, Fl., U.S. J5 112
Ornans, Fr. E13 14
Orne, dept., Fr. D7 14
Orne, stm., Fr. D6 14
Örnsköldsvik, Swe. J16 6
Oro, N. Kor. C15 32
Orocué, Col. E7 84
Orocuina, Hond. D8 92
Orodara, Burkina F7 64
Orofino, Id., U.S. D9 122
Oro Grande, Ca., U.S. J8 124
Oromocto, N.B., Can. G7 106
Oromocto Lake, l., N.B., Can. G7 106
Oron, Nig. I14 64
Orono, Me., U.S. C18 108
Orono, On., Can. G17 110
Oronoque, stm., Guy. F14 84
Orosháza, Hung. I20 10
Orosí, Volcán, vol., C.R. G9 92
Oroville, Ca., U.S. E4 124
Oroville, Wa., U.S. B6 122
Oroville, Lake, res., Ca., U.S. E4 124
Orrick, Mo., U.S. C2 114
Orrin, N.D., U.S. C7 118
Orr Lake, l., Mb., Can. B17 104
Orroroo, Austl. I3 70
Orrs Island, Me., U.S. D17 108
Orrville, Al., U.S. J9 114
Orrville, Oh., U.S. G5 108
Orša, Bela. G13 22
Orsières, Switz. F7 13
Orsk, Russia G9 26
Orta Nova, Italy H10 18
Ortega, Col. F5 84
Ortegal, Cabo, c., Spain B4 16
Orteguaza, stm., Col. G5 84
Orthez, Fr. I6 14
Orthon, stm., Bol. D8 82
Orting, Wa., U.S. C3 122
Ortisei, Italy C6 18
Ortiz, Mex. C4 90
Ortiz, Ven. C9 84
Ortles (Otler), mtn., Italy E14 13
Ortona, Italy G9 18
Ortonville, Mn., U.S. F11 118
Orūmīyeh (Reẓā'īyeh), Iran C8 48
Oruro, Bol. G8 82
Oruro, dept., Bol. H8 82
Orvieto, Italy G7 18
Orwell, Oh., U.S. F6 108
Orxon, stm., China B10 30
Or Yehuda, Isr. D3 50
Orzinuovi, Italy D4 18
Orzola, Spain n27 17b
Orzysz, Pol. B21 10
Oš, Kyrg. I12 26
Osa, Península de, pen., C.R. I11 92
Osage, Ia., U.S. G3 110
Osage, Wy., U.S. H3 118
Osage, stm., Mo., U.S. D4 114
Osage Beach, Mo., U.S. D4 114
Osage City, Ks., U.S. M12 118
Ōsaka, Japan M10 36
Ōsaka-wan, b., Japan M10 36
Osakis, Mn., U.S. F12 118
Osan, S. Kor. F15 32
Osawatomie, Ks., U.S. M13 118
Osborne, Ks., U.S. L9 118
Osburn, Id., U.S. C10 122
Oscar Peak, mtn., B.C., Can. C5 102
Osceola, Ar., U.S. G7 114
Osceola, Ia., U.S. I2 110
Osceola, Mo., U.S. D3 114
Osceola, Ne., U.S. J10 118
Osceola, Wi., U.S. E3 110
Osceola Mills, Pa., U.S. G8 108
Oschatz, Ger. D13 10
Oschersleben, Ger. C11 10
Oscoda, Mi., U.S. F12 110
Osgood, In., U.S. C11 114
O'Shanassy, stm., Austl. B3 70
Oshawa, On., Can. G17 110
Oshigambo, Nmb. A3 66
Ō-shima, i., Japan M14 36
Ō-shima, i., Japan f14 36a
Oshkosh, Ne., U.S. J5 118
Oshkosh, Wi., U.S. F7 110
Oshnovīyeh, Iran D8 48
Oshogbo, Nig. H12 64
Oshwe, D.R.C. B3 58
Osi, Nig. G12 64
Osich'ŏn-ni, N. Kor. B16 32
Osijek, Cro. D2 20
Osilinka, stm., B.C., Can. A10 102
Osimo, Italy F8 18
Osinniki, Russia G9 28
Osire, Nmb. C3 66
Oskaloosa, Ia., U.S. I3 110
Oskaloosa, Ks., U.S. L12 118
Oskarshamn, Swe. M15 6
Oskū, Iran C9 48
Oslo, Nor. L12 6
Osmānābād, India C4 46
Osmaniye, Tur. C4 48
Osmond, Ne., U.S. I10 118
Osmore, stm., Peru G6 82
Osnabrück, Ger. C8 10
Osório Fonseca, Braz. I13 84
Osorno, Chile E2 78
Osoyoos, B.C., Can. H15 102
Osoyoos Indian Reserve, B.C., Can. H15 102
Osoyoos Lake, l., N.A. H15 102
Ospino, Ven. C8 84
Ospwagan Lake, l., Mb., Can. C16 104
Ossa, Mount, mtn., Austl. M7 70
Ossabaw Island, i., Ga., U.S. H5 112
Osse, stm., Nig. H12 64
Osseo, Wi., U.S. F4 110
Ossian, Ia., U.S. G4 110
Ossian, In., U.S. B11 114
Ossining, N.Y., U.S. F13 108
Ossipee, N.H., U.S. D15 108
Ossora, Russia F24 28
Ošta, Russia K24 6
Ostaškov, Russia D16 22
Ostende (Oostende), Bel. F2 12
Osterburg, Ger. C11 10
Östergötlands Län, co., Swe. L14 6
Osterholz-Scharmbeck, Ger. B8 10
Osterode, Ger. D10 10
Östersund, Swe. J14 6
Osterwieck, Ger. D10 10
Østfold, co., Nor. L12 6
Ostfriesische Inseln, is., Ger. B7 10
Ostfriesland, hist. reg., Ger. B7 10
Ost'or, Russia G15 22
Ostrava, Czech Rep. F18 10
Ostróda, Pol. B19 10
Ostrogožsk, Russia G5 26
Ostrołęka, Pol. B21 10
Ostrov, Czech Rep. E12 10
Ostrov, Russia D11 22
Ostrov, i., Slvk. H17 10
Ostrovskoje, Russia D25 22
Ostrowiec Świętokrzyski, Pol. E21 10
Ostrów Mazowiecka, Pol. C21 10
Ostrów Wielkopolski, Pol. D17 10
Ostrzeszów, Pol. D17 10
Ostúa, stm., N.A. C5 92
Ostuni, Italy I12 18
Ōsumi-kaikyō, strt., Japan Q5 36
Ōsumi-shotō, is., Japan q5 37b
Osuna, Spain H6 16
Osvaldo Cruz, Braz. F3 79
Oswego, Il., U.S. I7 110
Oswego, Ks., U.S. N12 118
Oswego, N.Y., U.S. D10 108
Oswego, stm., N.Y., U.S. D10 108
Oświęcim, Pol. E19 10
Osyka, Ms., U.S. K6 114
Otaci, Mol. A11 20
Otaki, N.Z. D5 72
Otanmäki, Fin. I20 6
Otaru, Japan d16 36a
Otava, Fin. K20 6
Otava, stm., Czech Rep. F13 10
Otavalo, Ec. G3 84
Otavi, Nmb. B3 66
Otepää, Est. C9 22
Oteros, stm., Mex. D5 90
Othello, Wa., U.S. D6 122
Óthiris, Óros, mts., Grc. J6 20
Oti, stm., Afr. G7 54
Otinapa, Mex. E7 90

| Name | Map Ref. | Page |
|---|---|---|

Otis, Co., U.S. — K5 118
Otis, Ks., U.S. — M8 118
Otish, Monts, mts., P.Q., Can. — F18 96
Otjimbingue, Nmb. — D3 66
Otjiwarongo, Nmb. — C3 66
Otočac, Cro. — E10 18
Otoque, Isla, i., Pan. — I15 92
Otoro, stm., Hond. — C6 92
Otoskwin, stm., On., Can. — F14 96
Otra, stm., Nor. — L10 6
Otradnyj, Russia — G8 26
Otranto, Italy — I13 18
Otranto, Strait of, strt., Eur. — I2 20
Otsego, Mi., U.S. — H10 110
Otselic, stm., N.Y., U.S. — E11 108
Ōtsu, Japan — K11 36
Otta, Nor. — K11 6
Ottawa, Il., U.S. — I7 110
Ottawa, Ks., U.S. — M12 118
Ottawa, Oh., U.S. — F2 108
Ottawa, Wi., U.S. — B11 108
Ottawa, stm., Can. — G17 96
Ottawa Islands, is., N.T., Can. — E16 96
Otterburne, Mb., Can. — I17 104
Otter Creek, Fl., U.S. — J4 112
Otter Lake, Mi., U.S. — G12 110
Otter Lake, l., Sk., Can. — C10 104
Otter Tail, stm., Mn., U.S. — E11 118
Otterville, Mo., U.S. — D3 114
Ottoville, Oh., U.S. — G2 108
Ottumwa, Ia., U.S. — I3 110
Ottweiler, Ger. — F7 10
Otu, Nig. — G11 64
Otumpa, Arg. — D7 80
Otuquis, Bañados de, sw., Bol. — H12 82
Oturkpo, Nig. — H14 64
Otway, Cape, c., Austl. — L5 70
Otwock, Pol. — C21 10
Otyniya, Ukr. — A8 20
Öztztaler Alpen, mts., Eur. — C5 18
Ou, stm., China — J2 34
Ou, stm., Laos — D7 40
Ouachita, stm., U.S. — K5 114
Ouachita, Lake, res., Ar., U.S. — H3 114
Ouachita Mountains, mts., U.S. — H2 114
Ouadâne, Maur. — J5 62
Ouadda, C.A.R. — M2 60
Ouagadougou, Burkina — E9 64
Ouahigouya, Burkina — E9 64
Ouaka, stm., C.A.R. — G5 56
Oualâta, Maur. — C6 64
Oualé, stm., Afr. — F10 64
Oualidia, Mor. — D6 62
Ouallam, Niger — D11 64
Ouallene, Alg. — H11 62
Ouanda Djallé, C.A.R. — M2 60
Ouaninou, C. Iv. — G6 64
Ouan Taredert, Alg. — G15 62
Ouarâne, reg., Maur. — A4 64
Ouarkziz, Jbel, mts., Afr. — F6 62
Ouarzazate, Mor. — E7 62
Ouassolou, stm., Afr. — F5 64
Ouatcha, Niger — E14 64
Oubangui (Ubangi), stm., Afr. — H8 52
Oud-Beijerland, Neth. — E5 12
Ouddorp, Neth. — F4 12
Oudenaarde (Audenarde), Bel. — G4 12
Oude Pekela, Neth. — B10 12
Oudtshoorn, S. Afr. — I6 66
Oudyoumoudi, Burkina — D9 64
Oued Cheham, Alg. — M2 18
Oued Meliz, Tun. — M3 18
Oued Tlelat, Alg. — J11 16
Oued Zarga, Tun. — M4 18
Oued-Zem, Mor. — D7 62
Ouémé, stm., Benin — H11 64
Ouenza, Alg. — N3 18
Ouessant, Île d' (Ushant), i., Fr. — D1 14
Ouesso, Congo — A3 58
Ouest, Pointe de l', P.Q., Can. — C9 106
Ouezzane, Mor. — C8 62
Ouham, stm., Afr. — G4 56
Ouidah, Benin — H11 64
Ouistreham, Fr. — C6 14
Oujda, Mor. — C10 62
Oulainen, Fin. — I19 6
Oulu, Fin. — I19 6
Oulujärvi, l., Fin. — I20 6
Oulujoki, stm., Fin. — I20 6
Oulun lääni, prov., Fin. — I20 6
Oum-Chalouba, Chad — E5 56
Oum El Bouagui, Alg. — C14 62
Oum er Rbia, Oued, stm., Mor. — D7 62
Ounara, Mor. — E6 62
Ounianga Kébir, Chad — E5 56
Ouray, Co., U.S. — F9 120
Ouray, Mount, mtn., Co., U.S. — F10 120
Ourense, Spain — C4 16
Ourinhos, Braz. — G4 79
Ouro, Paraná do, stm., Braz. — C6 82
Ouro Fino, Braz. — G5 79
Ouro Preto, Braz. — F7 79
Ouro Prêto, stm., Braz. — D9 82
Oursi, Burkina — D9 64
Ourthe, stm., Bel. — H8 12
Ōu-sammyaku, mts., Japan — I15 36
Ouse, stm., Eng., U.K. — H12 8
Outaouais, Rivière des see Ottawa, stm., Can. — G17 96
Outardes, Baie aux, b., P.Q., Can. — C5 106
Outardes, Rivière aux, stm., P.Q., Can. — C5 106
Outardes Quatre, Réservoir, res., P.Q., Can. — C4 106
Outardes Trois, Barrage, P.Q., Can. — C5 106
Outer Hebrides, is., Scot., U.K. — D6 8
Outer Island, i., Wi., U.S. — C5 110
Outjo, Nmb. — C3 66
Outlook, Mt., U.S. — C3 118
Outlook, Sk., Can. — G7 104
Ouvidor, Braz. — E5 79
Ouyen, Austl. — J5 70
Ouzouer-le-Marché, Fr. — E8 14
Ouzzal, Oued i-n-, val., Alg. — J12 62
Ovalle, Chile — F3 80
Ovamboland, hist. reg., Nmb. — A3 66
Ovana, Cerro, mtn., Ven. — E9 84
Ovejas, Col. — C5 84
Overbrook, Ks., U.S. — M12 118
Overflakkee, i., Neth. — E5 12
Overflowing, stm., Can. — E13 104
Overhalla, Nor. — I12 6
Overijssel, prov., Neth. — D9 12
Overland Park, Ks., U.S. — M13 118
Overpelt, Bel. — F7 12
Overton, Ne., U.S. — K8 118
Overton, Nv., U.S. — H11 124

Overton, Tx., U.S. — G12 116
Övertorneå, Swe. — H18 6
Ovett, Ms., U.S. — K7 114
Ovid, N.Y., U.S. — E10 108
Ovid, Mi., U.S. — G11 110
Oviedo, Spain — B6 16
Ovino, Russia — B16 22
Ovruch, Russia — H16 22
Ovstug, Russia — H16 22
Owando, Congo — B3 58
Owasso, Ok., U.S. — C11 116
Owatonna, Mn., U.S. — F2 110
Owbeh, Afg. — D17 48
Owego, N.Y., U.S. — E10 108
Owen, Wi., U.S. — F5 110
Owensboro, Ky., U.S. — E9 114
Owens Lake, l., Ca., U.S. — H8 124
Owen Sound, On., Can. — F15 110
Owen Stanley Range, mts., Pap. N. Gui. — m16 68a
Owensville, In., U.S. — D9 114
Owensville, Mo., U.S. — D5 114
Owenton, Ky., U.S. — D12 114
Owerri, Nig. — I13 64
Owikeno Lake, l., B.C., Can. — F7 102
Owingsville, Ky., U.S. — I3 108
Owl, stm., Ab., Can. — B23 102
Owl, stm., Mb., Can. — E14 96
Owl Creek Mountains, mts., Wy., U.S. — G17 122
Owo, Nig. — H12 64
Owosso, Mi., U.S. — H11 110
Owyhee, Nv., U.S. — C9 124
Owyhee, stm., U.S. — G8 122
Owyhee, Lake, res., Or., U.S. — G8 122
Oxapampa, Peru — D4 82
Oxbow, Sk., Can. — I12 104
Oxford, Al., U.S. — I11 114
Oxford, Eng., U.K. — J12 8
Oxford, In., U.S. — B9 114
Oxford, Ks., U.S. — N13 118
Oxford, Md., U.S. — I10 108
Oxford, Me., U.S. — C16 108
Oxford, Mi., U.S. — H12 110
Oxford, Ms., U.S. — H7 114
Oxford, N.C., U.S. — C8 112
Oxford, Ne., U.S. — K8 118
Oxford, N.S., Can. — G10 106
Oxford, N.Y., U.S. — E11 108
Oxford, Oh., U.S. — H2 108
Oxford, Pa., U.S. — H11 108
Oxford, Wi., U.S. — G6 110
Oxford House, Mb., Can. — D19 104
Oxford House Indian Reserve, Mb., Can. — D19 104
Oxford Junction, Ia., U.S. — I5 110
Oxfordshire, co., Eng., U.K. — J12 8
Oxkutzcab, Mex. — G15 90
Oxley, Austl. — J6 70
Oxnard, Ca., U.S. — J6 124
Oyama, B.C., Can. — G15 102
Oyama, Japan — K14 36
Oyem, Gabon — A2 58
Oyen, Ab., Can. — G4 104
Oyo, Nig. — H11 64
Oyón, Peru — D3 82
Oyonnax, Fr. — F12 14
Oyotún, Peru — B2 82
Ozamiz, Phil. — D7 38
Ozark, Al., U.S. — K11 114
Ozark, Ar., U.S. — G3 114
Ozark, Mo., U.S. — E3 114
Ozark Plateau, plat., U.S. — F3 114
Ozarks, Lake of the, res., Mo., U.S. — D4 114
Ózd, Hung. — G20 10
Ożerelje, Russia — G21 22
Ozernovskij, Russia — G23 28
Ozery, Russia — G21 22
Ozieri, Italy — I4 18
Ozimek, Pol. — E18 10
Ozona, Tx., U.S. — I5 116
Ozorków, Pol. — D19 10
Oz'ornyj, Russia — D23 22
Ozubulu, Nig. — I13 64
Ozuluama, Mex. — G11 90

**P**

Paarl, S. Afr. — I4 66
Paauilo, Hi., U.S. — q18 125a
Pabellones, Ensenada, b., Mex. — E6 90
Pabianice, Pol. — D19 10
Pablo, Mt., U.S. — C11 122
Pābna, Bngl. — H13 44
Pabradė, Lith. — F8 22
Pacaás Novos, stm., Braz. — D9 82
Pacaás Novos, Serra dos, mts., Braz. — D10 82
Pacaembu, Braz. — F3 79
Pacaltsdorp, S. Afr. — I6 66
Pacarán, Peru — E3 82
Pacaraos, Peru — D3 82
Pacasmayo, Peru — B2 82
Pace, Fl., U.S. — L9 114
Pace, Ms., U.S. — I6 114
Pachacamac, hist., Peru — E3 82
Pachino, Italy — M10 18
Pachitea, stm., Peru — C4 82
Pachiza, Peru — B3 82
Pacharmarhi, India — I8 44
Pacho, Col. — E5 84
Pachuca (de Soto), Mex. — G10 90
Pacific, B.C., Can. — C5 102
Pacific, Mo., U.S. — D6 114
Pacifica, Ca., U.S. — G3 124
Pacific Grove, Ca., U.S. — H4 124
Pacific Ocean — J24 126
Pacific Ranges, mts., B.C., Can. — F8 102
Pacific Rim National Park, B.C., Can. — I9 102
Pacllón, Peru — D3 82
Pacohuaras, stm., Bol. — D5 82
Pacora, Col. — C3 84
Pacuare, stm., C.R. — G11 92
Pacui, stm., Braz. — D6 79
Pacuneiro, stm., Braz. — B2 79
Padang, Indon. — O6 40
Padangendau, Indon. — O6 40
Padangpanjang, Indon. — O5 40
Padangsidempuan, Indon. — N5 40
Padcaya, Bol. — I9 82
Paddle Prairie, Ab., Can. — E9 96
Paden City, W.V., U.S. — H6 108
Paderborn, Ger. — D8 10
Padilla, Bol. — H9 82
Padloping Island, i., N.T., Can. — C20 96
Padova, Italy — D6 18
Padre Bernardo, Braz. — C4 79

Padre Island, i., Tx., U.S. — L9 116
Padre Paraíso, Braz. — D8 79
Padsville, Bela. — F10 22
Padua see Padova, Italy — D6 18
Paducah, Ky., U.S. — E8 114
Paducah, Tx., U.S. — E6 116
Paektu-san, mtn., Asia — A16 32
Páez, stm., Col. — F4 84
Pag, Cro. — E10 18
Pag, Otok, i., Cro. — E10 18
Pagadian, Phil. — D7 38
Pagai Selatan, Pulau, i., Indon. — F3 38
Pagai Utara, Pulau, i., Indon. — F3 38
Pagan, Myan. — D3 40
Pagancillo, Arg. — E4 80
Pagégiai, Lith. — E5 22
Pageland, S.C., U.S. — E6 112
Pagoda Peak, mtn., Co., U.S. — D9 120
Pagoda Point, c., Myan. — G3 40
Pagon, Bukit, mtn., Asia — E6 38
Pagosa Springs, Co., U.S. — G9 120
Pagouda, Togo — G10 64
Pahala, Hi., U.S. — r18 125a
Pahang, stm., Malay. — M7 40
Pāhara, Laguna, b., Nic. — C11 92
Pahoa, Hi., U.S. — r19 125a
Pahokee, Fl., U.S. — M6 112
Pahost, Bela. — H12 22
Pahraničny, Bela. — H6 22
Pahrump, Nv., U.S. — H10 124
Pahvant Range, mts., Ut., U.S. — F4 120
Pai, stm., Asia — E5 40
Paico, Peru — E5 82
Paide, Est. — C8 22
Paige, Tx., U.S. — I9 116
Paignton, Eng., U.K. — K10 8
Paiján, Peru — B2 82
Päijänne, l., Fin. — K19 6
Paila, stm., Bol. — H7 82
Pailin, Camb. — H7 40
Pailitas, Col. — C5 84
Paimpol, Fr. — D3 14
Painesdale, Mi., U.S. — D7 110
Painesville, Oh., U.S. — F5 108
Paint, stm., Mi., U.S. — D7 110
Painted Desert, des., Az., U.S. — I5 120
Painted Rock Reservoir, res., Az., U.S. — K4 120
Paint Lake, l., Mb., Can. — C17 104
Paint Rock, Tx., U.S. — H7 116
Paint Rock, stm., Al., U.S. — H10 114
Paintsville, Ky., U.S. — B4 112
Paisley, Or., U.S. — H5 122
Paisley, Scot., U.K. — F9 8
Paita, Peru — A1 82
Paita, Bahía de, b., Peru — A1 82
Paizhou, China — E2 34
Pajala, Swe. — H18 6
Pajan, Ec. — H2 84
Pájara, Spain — o26 17b
Pajjer, gora, mtn., Russia — D10 26
Pak Ban, Laos — D7 40
Pakch'ŏn, N. Kor. — D14 32
Pakeng, Sudan — N6 60
Pakhoi see Beihai, China — G8 30
Pakistan (Pākistān), ctry., Asia — C9 42
Pakokku, Myan. — D3 40
Pakouabo, C. Iv. — H7 64
Pakowki Lake, l., Ab., Can. — I4 104
Păkpattan, Pak. — E5 44
Pak Phanang, Thai. — J6 40
Pak Phraek, Thai. — J6 40
Pakrac, Cro. — D12 18
Pakruojis, Lith. — E6 22
Paks, Hung. — I18 10
P'akupur, stm., Russia — E7 26
Pakwash Lake, l., On., Can. — H21 104
Pakxé, Laos — G8 40
Pala, Chad — G3 56
Palacca Point, c., Bah. — q18 125a
Palacios, Tx., U.S. — K10 116
Palacios, stm., Bol. — G10 82
Palagonia, Italy — L9 18
Palagruža, Otoci, is., Cro. — G11 18
Palaimós, Spain — D15 16
Palamau, Bngl. — H11 44
Palanga, Lith. — F4 22
Palangkaraya, Indon. — F5 38
Palani, India — G4 46
Palānpur, India — H5 44
Palapye, Bots. — D8 66
Palatka, Fl., U.S. — J5 112
Palatka, Russia — E22 28
Palau, ctry., Oc. — H17 126
Palau, i., Phil. — H5 40
Palauk, Myan. — H5 40
Palawan, i., Phil. — D6 38
Pălayankottai, India — H4 46
Palca, Bol. — G8 82
Palca, Peru — D4 82
Palcamayo, Peru — D4 82
Pal'co, Russia — H17 22
Paldiski, Est. — B7 22
Palech, Russia — E24 22
Palena, Italy — H9 18
Palembang, Indon. — F3 38
Palena, stm., U.S. — B12 112
Palencia, Spain — C7 16
Palenque, Mex. — I14 90
Palenque, hist., Mex. — I13 90
Palenque, Punta, c., Dom. Rep. — E9 94
Palermo, Col. — F5 84
Palermo, Italy — K8 18
Palermo, Ur. — G11 80
Palestina, Braz. — F4 79
Palestine, Ar., U.S. — H6 114
Palestine, Il., U.S. — C9 114
Palestine, Tx., U.S. — H11 116
Palestine, hist. reg., Asia — D4 50
Palestine, Lake, res., Tx., U.S. — G11 116
Palestrina, Italy — H7 18
Paletwa, Myan. — D2 40
Pālghāt, India — G4 46
Pāli, India — H5 44
Palin, Guat. — C4 92
Palisade, Ne., U.S. — K6 118
Palisade, Nv., U.S. — D9 124
Palisades Reservoir, res., U.S. — G14 122
Paliseul, Bel. — I7 12
Pālitāna, India — I4 44
Palivere, Est. — C6 22
Palizada, Mex. — H13 90
Palk Bay, b., Asia — H5 46
Palk Strait, strt., Asia — H5 46

Palla Bianca (Weisskugel), mtn., Eur. — E14 13
Pallasca, Peru — C2 82
Palling, B.C., Can. — C9 102
Palliser, Cape, c., N.Z. — D5 72
Palma, Braz. — F7 79
Palma, Moz. — D8 58
Pal'ma, Russia — J24 6
Palma [de Mallorca], Spain — F15 16
Palma del Río, Spain — H6 16
Palma di Montechiaro, Italy — L8 18
Palmar Camp, Belize — I15 90
Palmar de los Sepúlveda, Mex. — B5 84
Palmar de Varela, Col. — B5 84
Palmares, C.R. — G10 92
Palmares, Braz. — E11 76
Palmares do Sul, Braz. — F13 80
Palmarito, Ven. — D7 84
Palmar Sur, C.R. — I11 92
Palmas, Braz. — F9 76
Palmas, Braz. — D12 80
Palmas Bellas, Pan. — C2 84
Palmas de Monte Alto, Braz. — C7 79
Palma Soriano, Cuba — D6 94
Palm Bay, Fl., U.S. — K6 112
Palm Beach, Fl., U.S. — M6 112
Palmdale, Ca., U.S. — J7 124
Palm Desert, Ca., U.S. — K9 124
Palmeira, Braz. — C13 80
Palmeira, C.V. — k17 64a
Palmeira das Missões, Braz. — D12 80
Palmeira d'Oeste, Braz. — F3 79
Palmeiras, Braz. — B8 79
Palmeiras, stm., Braz. — C3 79
Palmeiras, stm., Braz. — D4 79
Palmelo, Braz. — D4 79
Palmer, Ak., U.S. — F20 100
Palmer, Ma., U.S. — E14 108
Palmer, Ms., U.S. — K7 114
Palmer, Ne., U.S. — J9 118
Palmer, Tn., U.S. — G11 114
Palmer, Tx., U.S. — G10 116
Palmer, sci., Ant. — B12 73
Palmer Lake, Co., U.S. — F12 120
Palmer Land, reg., Ant. — C12 73
Palmerston, N.Z. — F3 72
Palmerston, On., Can. — G15 110
Palmerston, Cape, c., Austl. — C7 70
Palmerston North, N.Z. — D5 72
Palmerton, Pa., U.S. — G11 108
Palmetto, Fl., U.S. — L4 112
Palmetto, Ga., U.S. — F2 112
Palmetto, La., U.S. — L5 114
Palmi, Italy — K10 18
Palminópolis, Braz. — D3 79
Palmira, Arg. — G4 80
Palmira, Col. — F4 84
Palmira, Ec. — I3 84
Palmitas, Ur. — G10 80
Palmitos, Braz. — D12 80
Palm Springs, Ca., U.S. — K9 124
Palmyra, Il., U.S. — C7 114
Palmyra, Mo., U.S. — C5 114
Palmyra, N.Y., U.S. — D9 108
Palmyra, Pa., U.S. — G10 108
Palmyra see Tudmur, Syria — E4 50
Palmyra, Va., U.S. — B8 112
Palmyra Atoll, atoll, Oc. — H23 126
Palo Alto, Ca., U.S. — G3 124
Palo Flechado Pass, N.M., U.S. — H11 120
Paloich, Sudan — L7 60
Palomar Mountain, mtn., Ca., U.S. — K9 124
Palomas Viejo, Mex. — B6 90
Palo Negro, Ven. — B9 84
Palo Pinto, Tx., U.S. — G8 116
Palopo, Indon. — F7 38
Palora, stm., Braz. — H3 84
Palos, see Palos de la Frontera, Spain — H5 16
Palos, Cabo de, c., Spain — H11 16
Palo Santo, Arg. — B8 80
Palos de la Frontera, Spain — H5 16
Palouse, Wa., U.S. — D8 122
Palouse, stm., U.S. — D7 122
Palo Verde, Ca., U.S. — K11 124
Palo Verde, Parque Nacional, C.R. — G9 92
Palpa, Peru — F4 82
Palpalá, Arg. — C6 80
Palu, Indon. — F6 38
Palwal, India — F7 44
Pama, Burkina — F10 64
Pamban Island, i., India — H5 46
Pambeguina, Nig. — F14 64
Pamekasan, Indon. — j16 39a
Pamiers, Fr. — I8 14
Pamir, mts., Asia — B5 44
Pamlico, stm., N.C., U.S. — D9 108
Pamlico Sound, strt., N.C., U.S. — D11 112
Pampa, Tx., U.S. — D6 116
Pampa, stm., Braz. — D8 79
Pampa Almirón, Arg. — D9 80
Pampa del Chañar, Arg. — F4 80
Pampa del Infierno, Arg. — D8 80
Pampa de los Guanacos, Arg. — D8 80
Pampa Grande, Bol. — H9 82
Pampas, Peru — E4 82
Pampas, stm., Braz. — E5 82
Pampero, stm., Braz. — F3 80
Pamplico, S.C., U.S. — E7 112
Pamplona, Col. — C6 84
Pamplona (Iruña), Spain — C10 16
Pampoenpoort, S. Afr. — H6 66
Pamunkey, stm., Va., U.S. — B9 112
Pana, Il., U.S. — C7 114
Panabá, Mex. — G15 90
Panaca, Nv., U.S. — G11 124
Panacea, Fl., U.S. — I2 112
Panaji (Panjim), India — E2 46
Panamá, Il., U.S. — C7 114
Panama (Panamá), ctry., N.A. — G8 88
Panamá, Bahía de, b., Pan. — C3 84
Panamá, Canal de, Pan. — H15 92
Panamá, Golfo de, b., Pan. — C3 84
Panamá, Istmo de, Pan. — C3 84
Panamá Vieja, hist., Pan. — H15 92
Panambi, Braz. — E12 80
Panamint Range, mts., Ca., U.S. — H8 124
Panão, Peru — D3 82
Panay, i., Phil. — C7 38
Panay Gulf, b., Phil. — D7 38
Pancake Range, mts., Nv., U.S. — F10 124
Pancas, Braz. — E8 79
Pančevo, Yugo. — E4 20
Pandamatenga, Bots. — B7 66
Pandan, Phil. — C7 38
Pan de Azúcar, Ur. — G2 79
Pandélys, Lith. — E8 22
Pandharpur, India — D3 46

Pāndhurna, India — B5 46
Pando, dept., Bol. — D8 82
P'andž (Panj), stm., Asia — A4 44
Panevėžys, Lith. — F7 22
Panfang, China — H4 34
Panfilov, Kaz. — I14 26
Pangala, Congo — B2 58
Pangalanes, Canal des, Madag. — q23 67b
Pangani, Tan. — C7 58
Pangburn, Ar., U.S. — H5 114
Pangfou see Bengbu, China — E10 30
Pangi, D.R.C. — B5 58
Pangkalanbuun, Indon. — F5 38
Pangkalpinang, Indon. — F4 38
Pangman, Sk., Can. — H10 104
Pangnirtung, N.T., Can. — C19 96
Pangong Tso, l., Asia — D8 44
Panguitch, Ut., U.S. — G4 120
Panguna, Pap. N. Gui. — m15 68a
Panino, Russia — E17 22
Pānipat, India — F7 44
Panj (P'andž), stm., Asia — B4 44
Panjāb, Afg. — C2 44
Panjgūr, Pak. — H18 48
Panjim see Panaji, India — E2 46
Pankshin, Nig. — G14 64
Paniong (Lo), stm., Asia — C8 40
Panna, India — H9 44
Pannawonica, Austl. — D3 68
Panola, Al., U.S. — K10 114
Panora, Ia., U.S. — J13 118
Panorama, Braz. — F3 79
Pansik, Rápido, wtfl, N.A. — C9 92
Pantelleria, Isola di, i., Italy — M7 18
Pantha, Myan. — C3 40
Pánuco, Mex. — G10 90
Pánuco, stm., Mex. — G10 90
Panuke Lake, l., N.S., Can. — B8 106
Panxian, China — H3 32
Panyam, Nig. — G14 64
Panyang, Sudan — L5 60
Panyu, China — M2 34
Panzós, Guat. — C4 92
Pao, stm., Ven. — C8 84
Paola, Italy — J11 18
Paola, Ks., U.S. — M13 118
Paoli, In., U.S. — D10 114
Paonia, Co., U.S. — F9 120
Paotow see Baotou, China — C9 30
Paozi, China — A10 32
Pápa, Hung. — H17 10
Papagaio, stm., Braz. — I11 84
Papagayo, Golfo de, b., C.R. — G9 92
Papaikou, Hi., U.S. — r18 125a
Papantla [de Olarte], Mex. — G11 90
Papenburg, Ger. — B7 10
Papillion, Ne., U.S. — J11 118
Papineau-Labelle, Réserve, P.Q., Can. — B11 108
Papua, Gulf of, b., Pap. N. Gui. — m15 68a
Papua New Guinea, ctry., Oc. — m15 68a
Papudo, Chile — F3 80
Papun, Myan. — E4 40
Papunáua, stm., Col. — G7 84
Papuri, stm., S.A. — G7 84
Paquera, C.R. — H10 92
Pará, state, Braz. — B13 82
Pará, stm., Braz. — D9 76
Pará, stm., Braz. — E6 79
Paraburdoo, Austl. — D3 68
Paracari, stm., Braz. — A13 82
Paracas, Bahía de, b., Peru — E3 82
Paracas, Península de, pen., Peru — E3 82
Paracatu, Braz. — D5 79
Paracel Islands see Xisha Qundao, is., China — B5 38
Parachilna, Austl. — H3 70
Parachute, Co., U.S. — E8 120
Paraćin, Yugo. — F5 20
Parád, Hung. — H20 10
Parada, Punta, c., Peru — F4 82
Paradas, Spain — H6 16
Paradise, Guy. — D14 84
Paradise, Ca., U.S. — E4 124
Paradise, Mo., U.S. — C2 114
Paradise, Nv., U.S. — H10 124
Paradise Hill, Sk., Can. — E5 104
Paradise Valley, Az., U.S. — K5 120
Paradise Valley, Nv., U.S. — C8 124
Parado, Indon. — D14 82
Paragonah, Ut., U.S. — F4 120
Paragould, Ar., U.S. — F6 114
Paragua, stm., Bol. — E11 82
Paragua, stm., Ven. — D11 84
Paraguaçu Paulista, Braz. — G3 79
Paraguaná, Península de, pen., Ven. — B8 84
Paraguarí, Para. — C10 80
Paraguarí, dept., Para. — D10 80
Paraguay, ctry., S.A. — G9 74
Paraguay (Paraguai), stm., S.A. — G9 74
Paraíba do Sul, stm., Braz. — F7 79
Paraíso, Braz. — F7 79
Paraíso, C.R. — H11 92
Paraíso, Pan. — H13 90
Paraíso do Norte, Braz. — D7 79
Paraisópolis, Braz. — G6 79
Paraitinga, stm., Braz. — G6 79
Parakou, Benin — G11 64
Paramakudi, India — H5 46
Paramaribo, Sur. — B7 76
Paramirim, Braz. — B7 79
Paramonga, Peru — D3 82
Paramušir, ostrov, i., Russia — G23 28
Paran, Nahal (Wādī al-Jirāfī), val. — H3 50
Paraná, Arg. — F8 80
Paraná, state, Braz. — C13 80
Paraná, stm., Braz. — B5 79
Paraná, stm., S.A. — C14 80
Paranaguá, Braz. — C14 80
Paranaíba, Braz. — E3 79
Paranaíba, stm., Braz. — E3 79
Paranaíta, stm., Braz. — C13 82
Paranam, Sur. — B7 76
Paranapanema, stm., Braz. — G3 79
Paranapiacaba, Serra do, mts., Braz. — C14 80
Paranavaí, Braz. — G2 79
Paranhos, Braz. — G1 79
Paraopeba, Braz. — E6 79
Parapara, Ven. — C9 84
Parapeti, stm., Bol. — H10 82
Paras, Peru — E4 82
Paratinga, Braz. — B7 79
Parauari, stm., Braz. — J13 84
Paraúna, Braz. — D3 79
Paray-le-Monial, Fr. — F11 14
Pārbati, stm., India — H7 44
Parbhani, India — H13 44
Parchim, Ger. — C4 46
Parchment, Mi., U.S. — H10 110
Parczew, Pol. — D22 10
Pardeeville, Wi., U.S. — G3 50
Pardes Hanna-Karkur, Isr. — C6 79
Pardo, stm., Braz. — F4 79
Pardo, stm., Braz. — G4 79
Pardo, stm., Braz. — C9 79
Pardo, stm., Braz. — F2 79
Pardubice, Czech Rep. — E15 10
Parečča, Bela. — H7 22
Parecis, stm., Braz. — E13 82
Parecis, Chapada dos, mts., Braz. — F12 82
Paredón, Mex. — E9 90
Paren', stm., Russia — E24 28
Parent, P.Q., Can. — G18 96
Parepare, Indon. — F6 38
Parera, Arg. — H6 80
Parfino, Russia — D14 22
Paria, stm., U.S. — H5 120
Paria, Gulf of, b. — B11 84
Paria, Península de, pen., Ven. — B11 84
Pariaguán, Ven. — C10 84
Pariaman, Indon. — O6 40
Pariamanu, stm., Peru — E6 82
Paricutín, vol., Mex. — H8 90
Farida, Isla, i., Pan. — I12 92
Parika, Guy. — D13 84
Parima, stm., S.A. — H9 84
Parima, Sierra, mts., S.A. — F10 84
Pariñas, Punta, c., Peru — J2 84
Parintins, Braz. — I14 84
Pariquera-Açu, Braz. — C15 80
Paris, Ar., U.S. — G3 114
Paris, Fr. — D9 14
Paris, Il., U.S. — C9 114
Paris, Ky., U.S. — I2 108
Paris, Me., U.S. — C16 108
Paris, Mo., U.S. — C4 114
Paris, On., Can. — G15 110
Paris, Tn., U.S. — F8 114
Paris, Tx., U.S. — F11 116
Parismina, C.R. — G11 92
Parismina, stm., C.R. — G11 92
Parit Buntar, Malay. — L6 40
Park, stm., N.D., U.S. — C10 118
Parkano, Fin. — J18 6
Park City, Ks., U.S. — N10 118
Park City, Mt., U.S. — E17 122
Park City, Ut., U.S. — D5 120
Parkdale, Or., U.S. — E4 122
Parkdale, P.E., Can. — F10 106
Parker, Az., U.S. — J2 120
Parker, Co., U.S. — L3 118
Parker, Fl., U.S. — L3 118
Parker, S.D., U.S. — H10 118
Parker, Cape, c., N.T., Can. — A17 96
Parker City, In., U.S. — B11 114
Parkersburg, Ia., U.S. — H3 110
Parkersburg, Il., U.S. — E9 114
Parkersburg, W.V., U.S. — H5 108
Parkers Prairie, Mn., U.S. — E12 118
Parkes, Austl. — I8 70
Park Falls, Wi., U.S. — E5 110
Park Forest, Il., U.S. — I8 110
Parkhill, On., Can. — G14 110
Parkin, Ar., U.S. — G6 114
Parkland, Wa., U.S. — C3 122
Park Range, mts., Co., U.S. — D10 120
Park Rapids, Mn., U.S. — E12 118
Park River, N.D., U.S. — C10 118
Parkrose, Or., U.S. — E4 122
Parksley, Va., U.S. — B11 112
Parkston, S.D., U.S. — H10 118
Parksville, B.C., Can. — H10 102
Parkville, Mo., U.S. — C2 114
Parkwater, Wa., U.S. — C8 122
Parla, Spain — E8 16
Parlākimidi, India — C8 46
Parle, Lac qui, l., Mn., U.S. — F11 118
Parli, India — C4 46
Parma, Id., U.S. — G9 122
Parma, Italy — E5 18
Parma, Mo., U.S. — E7 114
Parma, Oh., U.S. — F5 108
Parnaguá, Braz. — F10 76
Parnaíba, Braz. — D10 76
Parnaíba, stm., Braz. — D10 76
Parnassós, mtn., Grc. — K6 20
Pärnu, Est. — C7 22
Pärnu-Jaagupi, Est. — C7 22
Paro, Bhu. — G13 44
Paromaj, Russia — G20 28
Paroo, stm., Austl. — H5 70
Páros, i., Grc. — L9 20
Parowan, Ut., U.S. — G4 120
Parpaillon, mts., Fr. — H13 14
Parpan, Switz. — I3 80
Parral, Chile — D2 80
Parral see Hidalgo del Parral, Mex. — D7 90
Parral, stm., Mex. — D7 90
Parramatta, Austl. — I9 114
Parras de la Fuente, Mex. — E8 90
Parrish, Al., U.S. — I9 114
Parrish, Fl., U.S. — L4 112
Parrita, C.R. — H10 92
Parrsboro, N.S., Can. — H10 92
Parry, Cape, c., N.T., Can. — B8 96
Parry, Mount, mtn., B.C., Can. — E6 102
Parry Bay, b., N.T., Can. — C16 96
Parry Channel, strt., N.T., Can. — B9 96
Parry Peninsula, pen., N.T., Can. — B32 100
Parry Sound, On., Can. — E15 110
Parsberg, Ger. — F11 10
Parseierspitze, mtn., Aus. — D13 13
Parshall, N.D., U.S. — C5 118
Parsnip, stm., B.C., Can. — C12 102
Parsons, Ks., U.S. — N12 118
Parsons, Tn., U.S. — G8 114
Parsons, W.V., U.S. — H7 108
Parson's Pond, Nf., Can. — B16 106
Parsons Pond, l., Nf., Can. — B16 106
Pārsti — C8 22
Partanna, Italy — L7 18
Parthenay, Fr. — F6 14
Partinico, Italy — K8 18
Partizansk, Russia — I18 28

Partridge Crop Lake, l., Mb., Can. — C17 104
Partridge Point, c., Nf., Can. — B17 106
Paru, stm., Braz. — D8 76
Parú, stm., Ven. — E10 84
Paru de Oeste, stm., Braz. — D7 76
Paruro, Peru — E6 82
Pārvatīpuram, India — C7 46
Paryang, China — E10 44
Paryčy, Bela. — I12 22
Pasaco, Guat. — D4 92
Pasadena, Ca., U.S. — J7 124
Pasadena, Nf., Can. — C16 106
Pasadena, Tx., U.S. — J11 116
Pasado, Cabo, c., Ec. — H2 84
Pasaje, Ec. — I3 84
Pasaje, stm., Arg. — C6 80
Pa Sak, stm., Thai. — G6 40
Pasawng, Myan. — E4 40
Pascagoula, Ms., U.S. — L8 114
Pascagoula, stm., Ms., U.S. — L8 114
Pașcani, Rom. — B10 20
Pasco, Wa., U.S. — D6 122
Pasco, dept., Peru — D4 82
Pascoag, R.I., U.S. — F15 108
Pascua, Isla de (Easter Island), i., Chile — G4 74
Pas-de-Calais, dept., Fr. — B9 14
Pasewalk, Ger. — B14 10
Pasig, Phil. — n19 39b
P'asina, stm., Russia — C9 28
Pasinler, Tur. — B6 48
P'asino, ozero, l., Russia — D9 28
P'asinskij zaliv, b., Russia — C14 26
Pasir Puteh, Malay. — L7 40
Pasley Bay, b., N.T., Can. — B13 96
Pasmore, stm., Austl. — H3 70
Pasni, Pak. — I17 48
Paso del Cerro, Ur. — F11 80
Paso de los Libres, Arg. — E10 80
Paso de los Toros, Ur. — G10 80
Paso de Patria, Para. — D9 80
Paso Hondo, Mex. — J13 90
Pasorapa, Bol. — H9 82
Paso Robles, Ca., U.S. — I5 124
Pasqua Indian Reserve, Sk., Can. — H10 104
Pasquia Hills, hills, Sk., Can. — E12 104
Pasquotank, stm., N.C., U.S. — C10 112
Pasrūr, Pak. — D6 44
Passadumkeag, Me., U.S. — B18 108
Passage Point, c., N.T., Can. — B9 96
Passaic, N.J., U.S. — G12 108
Passamaquoddy Bay, b., N.A. — G7 106
Passau, Ger. — G13 10
Passero, Capo, c., Italy — M10 18
Pass Island, Nf., Can. — E17 106
Pašškij Perevoz, Russia — A15 22
Passo Fundo, Braz. — E12 80
Passos, Braz. — F5 79
Pastavy, Bela. — F9 22
Pastaza, prov., Ec. — H4 84
Pastaza, stm., S.A. — J4 84
Pastecho, stm., Ab., Can. — B20 102
Pasteur, Lac, l., P.Q., Can. — B7 106
Pasto, Col. — G4 84
Pastora Peak, mtn., Az., U.S. — H7 120
Pasuruan, Indon. — j16 39a
Pasvalys, Lith. — E7 22
Pásztó, Hung. — H19 10
Patacamaya, Bol. — G8 82
Patagonia, Az., U.S. — M6 120
Patagonia, reg., Arg. — F3 78
Pātan, India — I5 44
Patargān, Daqq-e, sw., Asia — E16 48
Pătârlagele, Rom. — D10 20
Pataz, Peru — B3 82
Patchewollock, Austl. — J5 70
Patchogue, N.Y., U.S. — G13 108
Patea, N.Z. — C5 72
Pategi, Nig. — G12 64
Pate Island, i., Kenya — B8 58
Patensie, S. Afr. — I7 66
Paterna, Spain — F11 16
Paternion, Aus. — I13 10
Paternò, Italy — L9 18
Pateros, Wa., U.S. — B6 122
Paterson, N.J., U.S. — G12 108
Paterson, S. Afr. — I7 66
Pathānkot, India — D6 44
Pathein (Bassein), Myan. — F3 40
Pathfinder Reservoir, res., Wy., U.S. — B10 120
Pathiong, Sudan — N6 60
Patía, Col. — G3 84
Patía, stm., Col. — G3 84
Patiāla, India — E7 44
P'atigorsk, Russia — I6 26
Pativilca, Peru — D3 82
Pativilca, stm., Peru — D3 82
Pātkai Range, mts., Asia — G16 44
Patna, India — H11 44
Pato Branco, Braz. — D12 80
Patoka, Il., U.S. — D7 114
Patoka, stm., In., U.S. — D9 114
Patos, Braz. — E11 76
Patos, Lagoa dos, b., Braz. — F13 80
Patos, Río de los, stm., Arg. — F4 80
Patos, Rio dos, stm., Braz. — E13 82
Patos de Minas, Braz. — E5 79
P'atovskij, Russia — G19 22
Patquía, Arg. — E5 80
Pātrai, Grc. — K5 20
Patraïkós Kólpos, b., Grc. — K5 20
Patras see Pátrai, Grc. — K5 20
Patrocínio, Braz. — E4 79
Patrocínio Paulista, Braz. — F5 79
Pattada, Italy — I4 18
Pattani, Thai. — K6 40
Patten, Me., U.S. — B18 108
Patterson, Ca., U.S. — G4 124
Patterson, La., U.S. — H4 112
Patterson, La., U.S. — M5 114
Patterson, Mount, mtn., Yk., Can. — D27 100
Patti, Italy — K9 18
Pattison, Ms., U.S. — K6 114
Patton, Pa., U.S. — G8 108
Pattonsburg, Mo., U.S. — B2 114
Pattullo, Mount, mtn., B.C., Can. — H30 100
Patuca, stm., Hond. — B10 92
Patuca, Punta, c., Hond. — B10 92
Patul, Cerro, mtn., Ec. — I3 84
Patulul, Guat. — C3 92
Patuxent, stm., Md., U.S. — I10 108
Pátzcuaro, Mex. — H9 90
Patzicía, Guat. — C4 92
Patzún, Guat. — C4 92
Pau, Fr. — I6 14
Pau Brasil, Braz. — C9 79
Paucarbamba, Peru — E4 82
Paucarpata, Peru — G6 82
Paucartambo, Peru — E6 82
Pauini, Braz. — B8 82
Pauini, stm., Braz. — H11 84

Pauk, Myan. — D3 40
Paul, Id., U.S. — H12 122
Paul, Lac à, l., P.Q., Can. — C3 106
Paulaya, stm., Hond. — B9 92
Paulden, Ms., U.S. — J7 114
Paulhan, Fr. — I10 14
Paulicéia, Braz. — F3 79
Paulina Peak, mtn., Or., U.S. — G4 122
Pauline, Mount, mtn., Can. — D15 102
Paulistana, Braz. — E10 76
Paulistas, Braz. — E7 79
Paullina, Ia., U.S. — I12 118
Paull Lake, l., Sk., Can. — B10 104
Paulo Afonso, Braz. — E11 76
Paulo de Faria, Braz. — F4 79
Pauloff Harbor (Pavlof Harbor), Ak., U.S. — I13 100
Paulpietersburg, S. Afr. — F10 66
Pauls Valley, Ok., U.S. — E9 116
Paungbyin, Myan. — B3 40
Paungde, Myan. — E3 40
Pausa, Peru — F5 82
Paute, Ec. — I3 84
Paute, stm., Ec. — I3 84
Pauto, stm., Col. — E7 84
Pāveh, Iran — D9 48
Pavelca, Russia — H22 22
Pavia, Italy — D4 18
Pavilion, B.C., Can. — G13 102
Pavillion, Wy., U.S. — A8 120
Pavilly, Fr. — C7 14
Pāvilosta, Lat. — E4 22
Pavlikeni, Bul. — F9 20
Pavlodar, Kaz. — G7 28
Pavlovo, Russia — F26 22
Pavlovsk, Russia — B13 22
Pavlovskij Posad, Russia — F21 22
Pavo, Ga., U.S. — H2 112
Pavón, Col. — F6 84
Paw Creek, N.C., U.S. — D6 112
Pawhuska, Ok., U.S. — C10 116
Pawnee, Il., U.S. — C7 114
Pawnee, Ok., U.S. — C10 116
Pawnee, stm., Ks., U.S. — M8 118
Pawnee City, Ne., U.S. — K11 118
Pawnee Rock, Ks., U.S. — M9 118
Paw Paw, Il., U.S. — I7 110
Paw Paw, Mi., U.S. — H10 110
Paw Paw, W.V., U.S. — H8 108
Paw Paw Lake, Mi., U.S. — H9 110
Pawtucket, R.I., U.S. — F15 108
Paxton, Il., U.S. — J7 110
Paxton, Ne., U.S. — J6 118
Paya, Hond. — B9 92
Payakumbuh, Indon. — O6 40
Payas, Cerro, mtn., Hond. — B9 92
Payerne, Switz. — E6 13
Payette, Id., U.S. — F9 122
Payette, stm., Id., U.S. — G9 122
Payne, Oh., U.S. — F2 108
Payne, Lac, l., P.Q., Can. — E18 96
Payne Bay, b., Can. — D19 96
Paynesville, Mn., U.S. — F13 118
Paynton, Sk., Can. — E6 104
Paysandú, Ur. — G9 80
Payson, Az., U.S. — J5 120
Payson, Il., U.S. — C5 114
Payson, Ut., U.S. — D5 120
Payún, Cerro, mtn., Arg. — I4 80
Paz, stm., N.A. — D4 92
Pazardžik, Bul. — G8 20
Pazarköy, Tur. — J11 20
Paz de Aríporo, Col. — E7 84
Paz de Río, Col. — E6 84
Pazin, Cro. — D8 18
Pazňa, Bol. — H8 82
Pea, stm., U.S. — K10 114
Peabody, Ks., U.S. — M10 118
Peabody, Ma., U.S. — E16 108
Peace, stm., Can. — E10 96
Peace, stm., U.S. — L5 112
Peace Canyon Dam, B.C., Can. — B13 102
Peace River, Ab., Can. — A17 102
Peach Creek, W.V., U.S. — J5 108
Peachland, B.C., Can. — H15 102
Peach Orchard, Ga., U.S. — F4 112
Peach Springs, Az., U.S. — H3 120
Peacock Hills, hills, N.T., Can. — C11 96
Peak Hill, Austl. — E3 68
Peak Hill, Austl. — I7 66
Peale, Mount, mtn., Ut., U.S. — F7 120
Pearce, Az., U.S. — M7 120
Pearceburg, Va., U.S. — B6 112
Pearl, Il., U.S. — C6 114
Pearl, Ms., U.S. — J6 114
Pearl, stm., U.S. — L7 114
Pearland, Tx., U.S. — J11 116
Pearl Harbor, b., Hi., U.S. — p16 125a
Pearl Peak, mtn., Nv., U.S. — D10 124
Pearl River, La., U.S. — L7 114
Pearl River, N.Y., U.S. — F12 108
Pearsall, Tx., U.S. — K7 116
Pearse Island, i., B.C., Can. — C4 102
Pearsoll Peak, mtn., Or., U.S. — H2 122
Pearson, Ga., U.S. — H4 112
Pearson Lake, l., Mb., Can. — B17 104
Pearston, S. Afr. — I7 66
Peary Land, reg., Grnld. — A16 86
Pebane, Moz. — E7 58
Pebas, Peru — I7 84
Peç, Yugo. — G4 20
Pecan Bayou, stm., Tx., U.S. — H7 116
Pecan Gap, Tx., U.S. — F11 116
Peçanha, Braz. — E7 79
Pecatonica, Il., U.S. — H6 110
Pecatonica, stm., U.S. — H6 110
Pečenga, Russia — D4 26
Pechenizhyn, Ukr. — A8 20
Pechora see Pečora, stm., Russia — D8 26
Pecica, Rom. — C5 20
Peck, Mi., U.S. — G13 110
Pečora, Russia — D9 26
Pečora, stm., Russia — D8 26
Pečorskaja guba, b., Russia — D8 26
Pečorskoje more, Russia — D8 26
Pečory, Russia — D10 22
Pecos, N.M., U.S. — I11 120
Pecos, stm., U.S. — J5 116
Pécs, Hung. — I18 10
Pedasí, Pan. — D2 84
Peddāpuram, India — C7 46
Pedder, Lake, res., Austl. — N7 70
Pedernales, Arg. — H9 80
Pedernales, Dom. Rep. — E9 94
Pedernales, Ven. — C11 84
Pedernales, stm., Tx., U.S. — I7 116
Pedernales, Salar de, pl., Chile — D4 80
Pedra Azul, Braz. — D8 79
Pedra Grande, Recifes da, rf., Braz. — D9 79
Pedra Lume, C.V. — k17 64a
Pedras, Braz. — I14 84

Pedras Negras, Braz. — E10 82
Pedraza, Col. — B5 84
Pedregal, Pan. — C1 84
Pedregal, Ven. — B7 84
Pedregulho, Braz. — F5 79
Pedreiras, Braz. — D10 76
Pedriceña, Mex. — E8 90
Pedro Afonso, Braz. — E9 76
Pedro Cays, is., Jam. — F6 94
Pedrógão Grande, Port. — F3 16
Pedro Gomes, Braz. — E1 79
Pedro II, Braz. — D10 76
Pedro II, Ilha, i., S.A. — H3 84
Pedro Juan Caballero, Para. — B11 80
Pedro Leopoldo, Braz. — E6 79
Pedro Luro, Arg. — J7 80
Pedro Muñoz, Spain — F9 16
Pedro Osório, Braz. — F12 80
Pedro R. Fernández, Arg. — E9 80
Peebinga, Austl. — J4 70
Peebles, Oh., U.S. — I3 108
Pee Dee, stm., U.S. — D6 112
Peekskill, N.Y., U.S. — F13 108
Peel, I. of Man — G9 8
Peel, stm., Can. — C27 100
Peel Channel, mth., N.T., Can. — C27 100
Peel Point, c., N.T., Can. — B10 96
Peel Sound, strt., N.T., Can. — B13 96
Peene, stm., Ger. — B13 10
Peepeekisis Indian Reserve, Sk., Can. — H11 104
Peerless, Mt., U.S. — B20 122
Peers, Ab., Can. — D18 102
Peesane, Sk., Can. — F11 104
Peetz, Co., U.S. — K4 118
Pegasus Bay, b., N.Z. — E4 72
Pegnitz, Ger. — F11 10
Pegnitz, stm., Ger. — F11 10
Pego, Spain — G11 16
Pegu see Bago, Myan. — F4 40
Peguis Indian Reserve, Mb., Can. — G17 104
Pegu Yoma, mts., Myan. — E3 40
Pehčevo, Mac. — H6 20
Pehuajó, Arg. — H8 80
Peigan Indian Reserve, Ab., Can. — H21 102
Peikang, Tai. — L9 34
Peine, Ger. — C10 10
Peipus, Lake see Čudskoje ozero, l., Eur. — C10 22
Peissenberg, Ger. — H11 10
Peixe, Braz. — B4 79
Peixe, Rio do, stm., Braz. — G3 79
Peixe, Rio do, stm., Braz. — C3 79
Peixian, China — E10 30
Peiziyan, China — H3 32
Pekalongan, Indon. — j14 39a
Pekanbaru, Indon. — N6 40
Pekin, Il., U.S. — J6 110
Pekin, In., U.S. — D10 114
Peking see Beijing, China — D4 32
Peklino, Russia — H16 22
Pelabuhan Kelang, Malay. — M6 40
Pelagie, Isole, is., Italy — N7 18
Pelahatchie, Ms., U.S. — J7 114
Pełczyce, Pol. — B15 10
Pelechuco, Bol. — F7 82
Pelée, Montagne, mtn., Mart. — G14 94
Pelee, Point, c., On., Can. — I13 110
Pelega, Vârful, mtn., Rom. — D6 20
Pelham, Al., U.S. — I10 114
Pelham, Ga., U.S. — H2 112
Pelican Bay, b., Mb., Can. — F14 104
Pelican Lake, l., Ab., Can. — B21 102
Pelican Lake, l., Mb., Can. — E18 104
Pelican Lake, l., Mb., Can. — F14 104
Pelican Lake, l., Sk., Can. — I15 104
Pelican Lake, l., Sk., Can. — H8 104
Pelican Lake, l., Sk., Can. — C11 104
Pelican Mountain, mtn., Ab., Can. — B21 102
Pelican Narrows, Sk., Can. — C12 104
Pelican Rapids, Mb., Can. — F14 104
Pelican Rapids, Mn., U.S. — E11 118
Pelileo, Ec. — H3 84
Pelister, mtn., Mac. — H5 20
Pelkosenniemi, Fin. — H20 6
Pella, Ia., U.S. — I3 110
Pell City, Al., U.S. — I10 114
Pellegrini, Arg. — I7 80
Pellegrini, Lago, l., Arg. — J4 80
Pelletier Lake, l., Mb., Can. — B17 104
Pello, Fin. — H19 6
Pellston, Mi., U.S. — E11 110
Pelly, stm., Yk., Can. — E26 100
Pelly Bay, b., N.T., Can. — C14 96
Pelly Crossing, Yk., Can. — E26 100
Pelly Lake, l., N.T., Can. — C12 96
Pelly Mountains, mts., Yk., Can. — F28 100
Pelón, Cerro, mtn., Mex. — G9 90
Peloncillo Mountains, mts., U.S. — L7 120
Pelopónnesos see Pelopónnisos, pen., Grc. — L6 20
Pelopónnisos, prov., Grc. — L6 20
Pelopónnisos (Peloponnesus), pen., Grc. — L6 20
Pelotas, Braz. — F12 80
Pelotas, stm., Braz. — D13 80
Pel'ušn'a, Russia — C15 22
Pemadumcook Lake, l., Me., U.S. — C18 108
Pemalang, Indon. — j14 39a
Pematangsiantar, Indon. — M5 40
Pemba, Moz. — D8 58
Pemba, i., Tan. — C7 58
Pemberton, Austl. — F3 68
Pemberton, B.C., Can. — G12 102
Pembina, N.D., U.S. — C10 118
Pembina, stm., N.A. — I16 104
Pembine, Wi., U.S. — E8 110
Pembroke, Ga., U.S. — G5 112
Pembroke, Ky., U.S. — F9 114
Pembroke, Me., U.S. — C19 108
Pembroke, N.C., U.S. — C7 112
Pembroke, Va., U.S. — B6 112
Pembroke, Wales, U.K. — J9 8
Pembroke, On., Can. — G10 110
Pembroke, Cape, c., N.T., Can. — D16 96
Pembroke Pines, Fl., U.S. — M6 112
Pemigewasset, stm., N.H., U.S. — D15 108
Pemmican Portage, Sk., Can. — E12 104
Pemuco, Chile — I2 80
Pemynoos Indian Reserve, B.C., Can. — G13 102
Peña Barroza, Bol. — J8 82
Peña Blanca, Pan. — I13 92

Penafiel, Port. — D3 16
Peña Gorda, Cerro, mtn., Mex. — G7 90
Penápolis, Braz. — F3 79
Peñaranda de Bracamonte, Spain — E6 16
Pen Argyl, Pa., U.S. — G11 108
Peñarroya-Pueblonuevo, Spain — G6 16
Peñas, Golfo de, b., Chile — F2 78
Peñasco, Rio, stm., N.M., U.S. — L11 120
Pencahue, Chile — H3 80
Pence, Wi., U.S. — D5 110
Pendembu, S.L. — G3 64
Pender, Ne., U.S. — I11 118
Pendjari, stm., Afr. — F7 54
Pendleton, In., U.S. — C11 114
Pendleton, Or., U.S. — E7 122
Pendleton, S.C., U.S. — E4 112
Pend Oreille, Lake, l., Id., U.S. — B9 122
Pend Oreille, stm., N.A. — B8 122
Penedo, Braz. — F11 76
Penedono, Port. — E4 16
Penetanguishene, On., Can. — F16 110
Penfield, Il., U.S. — J8 110
Penganga, stm., India — C5 46
P'enghu Ch'üntao (Pescadores), is., Tai. — L8 34
P'enghu Shuitao, strt., Tai. — L8 34
Pengkou, China — J5 34
Penglai (Dengzhou), China — F8 32
Pengshui, China — F8 30
Penguin, Austl. — M7 70
Pengxian, China — E7 30
Penha, Braz. — D14 80
Penhold, Ab., Can. — E21 102
Penibética, Cordillera, mts., Spain — H8 16
Peniche, Port. — F2 16
Penitas, Tx., U.S. — M8 116
Penjamillo [de Degollado], Mex. — G9 90
Pennant Point, c., N.S., Can. — H10 106
Pennant Station, Sk., Can. — H6 104
Pennask Lake, l., B.C., Can. — G14 102
Pennask Mountain, mtn., B.C., Can. — H14 102
Penne, Italy — G8 18
Penn Hills, Pa., U.S. — G7 108
Pennines, mts., Eng., U.K. — G11 8
Pennines, Alpes, mts., Eur. — G8 13
Pennington Gap, Va., U.S. — C3 112
Pennsboro, W.V., U.S. — H6 108
Penns Grove, N.J., U.S. — H11 108
Pennsylvania, state, U.S. — C11 98
Penny, B.C., Can. — D13 102
Penny Ice Cap, N.T., Can. — C19 96
Penny Strait, strt., N.T., Can. — A13 96
Peno, Russia — E15 22
Penobscot, stm., Me., U.S. — B18 108
Penobscot Bay, b., Me., U.S. — C18 108
Penola, Austl. — K4 70
Peñón Blanco, Mex. — E7 90
Penong, Austl. — F6 68
Penonomé, Pan. — C2 84
Penrith, Austl. — I9 70
Pensacola, Fl., U.S. — L9 114
Pensacola Bay, b., Fl., U.S. — L9 114
Pensacola Mountains, mts., Ant. — D1 73
Pensaukee, stm., Wi., U.S. — F7 110
Pense, Sk., Can. — H9 104
Pensilvania, Col. — E5 84
Pentagon Mountain, mtn., Mt., U.S. — C12 122
Pentecôte, stm., P.Q., Can. — B6 106
Pentecôte, Lac, l., P.Q., Can. — B6 106
Penticton, B.C., Can. — H15 102
Penticton Indian Reserve, B.C., Can. — H15 102
Pentland, Austl. — C6 70
Pentland Firth, strt., Scot., U.K. — C10 8
Pentwater, Mi., U.S. — G9 110
Penwegon, Myan. — E4 40
Penwell, Tx., U.S. — H4 116
Penza, Russia — G7 26
Penzance, Eng., U.K. — K8 8
Penzberg, Ger. — H11 10
Penžina, stm., Russia — E25 28
Penžinskaja guba, b., Russia — E24 28
Peñ'aki, Russia — E25 22
Peoria, Az., U.S. — K4 120
Peoria, Il., U.S. — J6 110
Peoria Heights, Il., U.S. — J6 110
Peotone, Il., U.S. — I8 110
Pepaw, stm., Sk., Can. — F12 104
Pepel, Sudan — N7 60
Pepin, Wi., U.S. — F3 110
Pepin, Lake, l., U.S. — F3 110
Pequot Lakes, Mn., U.S. — E1 118
Perabumulih, Indon. — F3 38
Perak, stm., Malay. — L6 40
Perales, Chile — H3 80
Peralta, N.M., U.S. — J10 120
Pérdeberg, S. Afr. — G7 66
Perdido, Al., U.S. — K9 114
Perdido, stm., Braz. — I13 82
Perdido, Monte, mtn., Spain — C12 16
Perdido, stm., U.S. — L9 114
Perdizes, Braz. — E5 79
Perdu, Lac, l., P.Q., Can. — B3 106
Perdue, Sk., Can. — E6 104
Perechyn, Ukr. — G22 10
Perehonivka, Ukr. — A14 20
Pereira, Col. — E5 84
Pereira Barreto, Braz. — F3 79
Pere Marquette, stm., Mi., U.S. — G10 110
Peremyšl', Russia — G19 22
Perené, stm., Peru — E4 82
Pereslavl'-Zalesskij, Russia — E21 22
Peresypkino Pervoje, Russia — I25 22
Pérez, Arg. — G8 80
Perg, Aus. — G14 10
Pergamino, Arg. — G8 80
Pergine Valsugana, Italy — C6 18
Pergola, Italy — F7 18
Perham, Mn., U.S. — E12 118
Péribonca, stm., P.Q., Can. — G19 102
Péribonca, Lac, l., P.Q., Can. — C2 106
Péribonka, Can. — G19 102

Perico, Arg. — C6 80
Pericos, Mex. — E6 90
Peridot, Az., U.S. — K6 120
Périers, Fr. — C5 14
Périgord, hist. reg., Fr. — G7 14
Périgueux, Fr. — G7 14
Perija, Serranía De, mts., S.A. — B6 84
Periyakulam, India — G4 46
Perkasie, Pa., U.S. — G11 108
Perkins, Ok., U.S. — D9 116
Perkinston, Ms., U.S. — L7 114
Perleberg, Ger. — B11 10
Perm', Russia — F9 26
Pernatty Lagoon, l., Austl. — H2 70
Pernik, Bul. — G7 20
Péronne, Fr. — C9 14
Perote, Mex. — H11 90
Perow, B.C., Can. — C8 102
Perpignan, Fr. — J9 14
Perrault Falls, On., Can. — H21 104
Perrin, Tx., U.S. — F8 116
Perrine, Fl., U.S. — N6 112
Perris, Ca., U.S. — K8 124
Perro, Laguna del, l., N.M., U.S. — J11 120
Perros, Bahía de, b., Cuba — C5 94
Perry, Fl., U.S. — I3 112
Perry, Ga., U.S. — G3 112
Perry, Ia., U.S. — I1 110
Perry, Ks., U.S. — L12 118
Perry, Mi., U.S. — H11 110
Perry, Mo., U.S. — C5 114
Perry, N.Y., U.S. — E8 108
Perry, Ok., U.S. — C9 116
Perry, Ut., U.S. — C4 120
Perry Lake, res., Ks., U.S. — L12 118
Perrysburg, Oh., U.S. — F3 108
Perryton, Tx., U.S. — C6 116
Perryville, Ak., U.S. — I15 100
Perryville, Ar., U.S. — G4 114
Perryville, Ky., U.S. — B2 112
Perryville, Mo., U.S. — E7 114
Peršamajski, Bela. — H8 22
Perseverancia, Bol. — F10 82
Persia see Iran, ctry., Asia — C5 42
Persian Gulf (Arabian Gulf), b., Asia — H11 48
Pertek, Tur. — B5 48
Perth, Austl. — F3 68
Perth, On., Can. — F19 110
Perth, Scot., U.K. — E10 8
Perth Amboy, N.J., U.S. — G12 108
Perth-Andover, N.B., Can. — F6 106
Pertokrar, Erit. — I9 60
Peru, Il., U.S. — I6 110
Peru, In., U.S. — B10 114
Peru, Ne., U.S. — K12 118
Peru, N.Y., U.S. — C13 108
Peru (Perú), ctry., S.A. — E3 76
Peruaçu, stm., Braz. — C6 79
Perugia, Italy — F7 18
Perugorría, Arg. — E9 80
Peruíbe, Braz. — C15 80
Perúpe, stm., Braz. — D9 79
Pervomajsk, Russia — I18 22
Pervomajskij, Russia — H23 22
Pervomays'k, Ukr. — H4 26
Pervoural'sk, Russia — F9 26
Pervyj Kuril'skij proliv, strt., Russia — G23 28
Pes', Russia — C17 22
Pesaro, Italy — F7 18
Pesca, Col. — E6 84
Pescadores see P'enghu Ch'üntao, is., Tai. — L8 34
Pescadores, Punta, c., Mex. — F5 90
Pescadores, Punta, c., Peru — G5 82
Pesčanoje, Russia — J24 6
Pescara, Italy — G9 18
Pescia, Italy — F6 18
Pesé, Pan. — D2 84
Peshawar, Pak. — C4 44
Peshtigo, Wi., U.S. — E8 110
Peshtigo, stm., Wi., U.S. — E7 110
Peski, Russia — F21 22
Pesmes, Fr. — E12 14
Pesočenskij, Russia — G19 22
Pesočnoje, Russia — C22 22
Pesočnyj, Russia — A13 22
Peso da Régua, Port. — D4 16
Pespire, Hond. — D7 92
Pesqueira, Braz. — E11 76
Pessac, Fr. — H6 14
Pest, co., Hung. — H19 10
Pest'aki, Russia — E25 22
Peštera, Bul. — G8 20
Pestovo, Russia — C18 22
Petacalco, Bahía, b., Mex. — I8 90
Petah Tiqwa, Isr. — D3 50
Petal, Ms., U.S. — K7 114
Petalcingo, Mex. — I13 90
Petalión, Kólpos, b., Grc. — L8 20
Petaluma, Ca., U.S. — F3 124
Pétange, Lux. — I8 12
Petare, Ven. — B9 84
Petatlán, Mex. — I9 90
Petawawa, On., Can. — E18 110
Petén, dept., Guat. — A5 92
Petén Itzá, Lago, l., Guat. — I15 90
Petenwell Lake, res., Wi., U.S. — F6 110
Peterborough, Austl. — I3 70
Peterborough, Eng., U.K. — I13 8
Peterborough, On., Can. — F17 110
Peterculter, Scot., U.K. — D11 8
Peterhead, Scot., U.K. — D12 8
Peter Lake, l., N.T., Can. — D14 96
Peter Lougheed Provincial Park, Ab., Can. — G19 102
Peterman, Al., U.S. — K9 114
Peters, stm., Can. — C6 104
Petersburg, Ak., U.S. — H28 100
Petersburg, Il., U.S. — B7 114
Petersburg, In., U.S. — D9 114
Petersburg, Mi., U.S. — I12 110
Petersburg, Tn., U.S. — G10 114
Petersburg, Va., U.S. — B5 112
Petersburg, W.V., U.S. — I7 108
Peterson, Al., U.S. — I12 114
Pétervására, Hung. — G20 10
Petilia Policastro, Italy — J11 18
Pétionville, Haiti — E8 94
Petit Bois Island, i., U.S. — L8 114
Petitcodiac, N.B., Can. — G8 106
Petitcodiac, stm., N.B., Can. — F9 106

Petite Rivière Noire, Piton de la, mtn., Mrts. — v18 67c
Petit Forte, Nf., Can. — E19 106
Petit-Goâve, Haiti — E8 94
Petit Jean, stm., Ar., U.S. — G3 114
Petit Mécatina, Île du, i., P.Q., Can. — B14 106
Petitot, stm., Can. — E8 96
Petit-Saint-Bernard, Col du, Eur. — G13 14
Petitsikapau Lake, l., Nf., Can. — F19 96
Petlād, India — I5 44
Petlalcingo, Mex. — H11 90
Petorca, Chile — G3 80
Petoskey, Mi., U.S. — E11 110
Petownikip Lake, l., On., Can. — F22 104
Petra, hist., Jord. — H4 50
Petra Velikogo, zaliv, b., Russia — I18 22
Petre, Point, c., On., Can. — G18 110
Petrified Forest National Park, Az., U.S. — J7 120
Petrila, Rom. — D7 20
Petrinja, Cro. — D11 18
Petrodvorec, Russia — B12 22
Petrólea, Col. — C6 84
Petrolia, On., Can. — H13 110
Petrolia, Tx., U.S. — E8 116
Petrolina, Braz. — E10 76
Petrolina de Goiás, Braz. — D4 79
Petropavlovsk, Kaz. — G12 28
Petropavlovsk-Kamčatskij, Russia — G23 28
Petrópolis, Braz. — G7 79
Petros, Tn., U.S. — C2 112
Petrovsk, Russia — G7 26
Petrovskoje, Russia — I23 22
Petrovsk-Zabajkal'skij, Russia — G13 28
Petrozavodsk, Russia — E4 26
Petrusburg, S. Afr. — G7 66
Petrus Steyn, S. Afr. — F9 66
Petrusville, S. Afr. — H7 66
Petrykau, Bela. — I11 22
Petten, Neth. — C6 12
Pettus, Tx., U.S. — K9 116
Petty Harbour, Nf., Can. — E21 106
Petuchovo, Russia — F11 26
Petuški, Russia — F22 22
Peuerbach, Aus. — G13 10
Pevek, Russia — D26 28
Peykjahlíd, Ice. — B5 6a
Pézenas, Fr. — I10 14
Pezinok, Slvk. — G17 10
Pfäffikon, Switz. — D10 13
Pfarrkirchen, Ger. — G12 10
Pforzheim, Ger. — G8 10
Pfronten, Ger. — H10 10
Pfungstadt, Ger. — F8 10
Pha-an, Myan. — F4 40
Phagwara, India — E6 44
Phala, Bots. — D8 66
Phalaborwa, S. Afr. — D10 66
Phalodi, India — G5 44
Phalsbourg, Fr. — D14 14
Phaltan, India — D3 46
Phan, Thai. — E5 40
Phangan, Ko, i., Thai. — J6 40
Phangnga, Thai. — J5 40
Phanom Dongrak, Thiu Khao, mts., Asia — G7 40
Phan Rang, Viet. — I10 40
Phan Thiet, Viet. — I10 40
Phariāro, Pak. — G3 44
Pharr, Tx., U.S. — M8 116
Phatthalung, Thai. — K6 40
Phayao, Thai. — E5 40
Pheasant Creek, stm., Sk., Can. — G11 104
Pheba, Ms., U.S. — I8 114
Phelps, N.Y., U.S. — E9 108
Phelps, Wi., U.S. — D6 110
Phenix City, Al., U.S. — G1 112
Phepane, stm., S. Afr. — E6 66
Phetchabun, Thai. — F6 40
Phetchabun, Thiu Khao, mts., Thai. — F6 40
Phetchaburi, Thai. — H5 40
Phichit, Thai. — F6 40
Philadelphia, Ms., U.S. — J7 114
Philadelphia, N.Y., U.S. — C11 108
Philadelphia, Pa., U.S. — G11 108
Philadelphia, Tn., U.S. — D2 112
Phil Campbell, Al., U.S. — H9 114
Philip, S.D., U.S. — G5 118
Philipp, Ms., U.S. — I6 114
Philippeville, Bel. — H6 12
Philippi, W.V., U.S. — H6 108
Philippi, Lake, l., Austl. — E3 70
Philippines (Pilipinas), ctry., Asia — C7 38
Philippine Sea — G17 126
Philippine Trench — H16 126
Philippolis, S. Afr. — H7 66
Philipsburg, Neth. Ant. — F13 94
Philipsburg, Mt., U.S. — D13 122
Philipsburg, Pa., U.S. — G8 108
Philipstown, S. Afr. — H7 66
Phillip Island, i., Austl. — L6 70
Phillips, Me., U.S. — C16 108
Phillips, Wi., U.S. — E5 110
Phillipsburg, Ga., U.S. — H3 112
Phillipsburg, Ks., U.S. — L9 118
Phillipsburg, N.J., U.S. — G11 108
Philmont, N.Y., U.S. — E13 108
Philo, Il., U.S. — B8 114
Philo, Oh., U.S. — H5 108
Philomath, Or., U.S. — F2 122
Philpots Island, i., N.T., Can. — B17 96
Phimai, Thai. — G7 40
Phitsanulok, Thai. — F6 40
Phnom Penh see Phnum Pénh, Camb. — I8 40
Phnum Pénh, Camb. — I8 40
Phoenix, Az., U.S. — K4 120
Phoenix Islands, is., Kir. — I22 126
Phoenixville, Pa., U.S. — G11 108
Phon, Thai. — G7 40
Phôngsali, Laos — D7 40
Phra Nakhon Si Ayutthaya, Thai. — G6 40
Phrae, Thai. — E6 40
Phuket, Thai. — K5 40
Phuket, Ko, i., Thai. — J5 40
Phu Ly, Viet. — D8 40
Phumĭ Béng, Camb. — H8 40
Phumĭ Chhŭk, Camb. — I8 40
Phumĭ Kâmpóng Kông, Camb. — I7 40
Phumĭ Kâmpóng Srálau, Camb. — H8 40
Phumĭ Sâmraông, Camb. — H9 40
Phumĭ Srê Rônéam, Camb. — I8 40
Phuoc Binh, Viet. — I9 40
Phu Quoc, Dao, i., Viet. — I8 40
Phu Tho, Viet. — D8 40
Phutthaisong, Thai. — G7 40

| Name | Map Ref. | Page |
|---|---|---|
| Phu Yen, Viet. | D8 | 40 |
| Piacenza, Italy | D4 | 18 |
| Piacouadie, Lac, l., P.Q., Can. | A3 | 106 |
| Pialba, Austl. | E10 | 70 |
| Piana, Fr. | I23 | 15a |
| Pianoro, Italy | E6 | 18 |
| Piapot, Sk., Can. | I5 | 104 |
| Piapot Indian Reserve, Sk., Can. | H10 | 104 |
| Piaseczno, Pol. | C21 | 10 |
| Piashti, Lac, l., P.Q., Can. | B11 | 106 |
| Piatã, Braz. | B8 | 79 |
| Piatra-Neamţ, Rom. | C10 | 20 |
| Piauí, stm., Braz. | D8 | 79 |
| Piaus, stm., Braz. | B4 | 79 |
| Piave, stm., Italy | D7 | 18 |
| Piaxtla, stm., Mex. | E7 | 90 |
| Piazza Armerina, Italy | L9 | 18 |
| Pibor, stm., Afr. | G7 | 56 |
| Pibor Post, Sudan | N7 | 40 |
| Pica, Chile | I7 | 82 |
| Picacho, Az., U.S. | L5 | 120 |
| Picardie, hist. reg., Fr. | C9 | 14 |
| Picayune, Ms., U.S. | L7 | 114 |
| Piccadilly, Nf. | D15 | 106 |
| Pichana, stm., Peru | I7 | 84 |
| Pichanal, Arg. | B6 | 80 |
| Picher, Ok., U.S. | C12 | 116 |
| Pichidegua, Chile | H2 | 80 |
| Pichilemu, Chile | H2 | 80 |
| Pichimá, Col. | E4 | 84 |
| Pichi-Mahuida, Arg. | J6 | 80 |
| Pichincha, prov., Ec. | H3 | 84 |
| Pichis, stm., Peru | D4 | 82 |
| Pichucalco, Mex. | I13 | 90 |
| Pickardville, Ab., Can. | C21 | 102 |
| Pickens, Ms., U.S. | J7 | 114 |
| Pickens, S.C., U.S. | E4 | 112 |
| Pickens, W.V., U.S. | I6 | 108 |
| Pickensville, Al., U.S. | I8 | 114 |
| Pickerel Lake, l., Mb., Can. | F15 | 104 |
| Pickering, On., Can. | G16 | 110 |
| Pickford, Mi., U.S. | D11 | 110 |
| Pickle Crow, On., Can. | F14 | 96 |
| Pickstown, S.D., U.S. | H9 | 118 |
| Picton, Tx., U.S. | F11 | 116 |
| Pickwick Lake, res., U.S. | H8 | 114 |
| Pico, i., Port. | k19 | 62a |
| Pico, Ponta do, mtn., Port. | k19 | 62a |
| Pico de Orizaba, Parque Nacional, Mex. | H11 | 90 |
| Picos, Braz. | E10 | 76 |
| Picota, Peru | B3 | 82 |
| Picton, Austl. | J9 | 70 |
| Picton, N.Z. | D5 | 72 |
| Picton, On., Can. | F18 | 110 |
| Picton, Isla, i., Chile | H3 | 78 |
| Pictou, N.S., Can. | G11 | 106 |
| Pictou Island, i., N.S., Can. | G11 | 106 |
| Picture Butte, Ab., Can. | H22 | 102 |
| Pidálion, Akrotírion, c., Cyp. | D3 | 48 |
| Pidurutalagala, mtn., Sri L. | I6 | 46 |
| Piedecuesta, Col. | D6 | 84 |
| Piedicroce, Fr. | I24 | 15a |
| Piedmont, Al., U.S. | I11 | 114 |
| Piedmont, S.C., U.S. | E6 | 114 |
| Piedmont, S.C., U.S. | E4 | 112 |
| Piedra, C.R. | H11 | 92 |
| Piedra Roja, Pan. | I13 | 92 |
| Piedras, Punta, c., Arg. | H10 | 80 |
| Piedras, Punta, c., Ven. | B12 | 84 |
| Piedras Blancas, Arg. | F9 | 80 |
| Piedras Coloradas, Ur. | G10 | 80 |
| Piedras Negras, Guat. | I14 | 90 |
| Piedras Negras, Mex. | C9 | 90 |
| Piedras Negras, hist., Guat. | I14 | 90 |
| Piedra Sola, Ur. | G10 | 80 |
| Pieksämäki, Fin. | J20 | 6 |
| Pielavesi, Fin. | J20 | 6 |
| Pielinen, l., Fin. | J21 | 6 |
| Piemonte, prov., Italy | E2 | 18 |
| Piendamó, Col. | F4 | 84 |
| Pienza, Italy | F6 | 18 |
| Pierce, Co., U.S. | D12 | 120 |
| Pierce, Id., U.S. | D10 | 122 |
| Pierce, Ne., U.S. | I10 | 118 |
| Pierce City, Mo., U.S. | F2 | 114 |
| Pierce Lake, l., Sk., Can. | D22 | 104 |
| Pierce Lake, l., Sk., Can. | D5 | 104 |
| Pierceton, In., U.S. | A11 | 114 |
| Pierpont, S.D., U.S. | F10 | 118 |
| Pierre, S.D., U.S. | G7 | 118 |
| Pierre, Bayou, stm., La., U.S. | K3 | 114 |
| Pierre Part, La., U.S. | M5 | 114 |
| Pierson, Fl., U.S. | J5 | 112 |
| Pierz, Mn., U.S. | E1 | 110 |
| Piešt'any, Slvk. | G17 | 10 |
| Pietermaritzburg, S. Afr. | G10 | 66 |
| Pietersburg, S. Afr. | D9 | 66 |
| Pietrasanta, Italy | F5 | 18 |
| Piet Retief, S. Afr. | F10 | 66 |
| Pigeon, Mi., U.S. | G12 | 110 |
| Pigeon, stm., Mb., Can. | F18 | 104 |
| Pigeon, stm., Mi., U.S. | E11 | 110 |
| Pigeon, stm., U.S. | D3 | 112 |
| Pigeon, stm., U.S. | C7 | 112 |
| Pigeon Forge, Tn., U.S. | D3 | 112 |
| Pigeon Lake, l., Ab., Can. | D20 | 102 |
| Pigg, stm., Va., U.S. | C7 | 112 |
| Piggott, Ar., U.S. | F6 | 114 |
| Piggs Peak, Swaz. | E10 | 66 |
| Pigna, Italy | F2 | 18 |
| Pigüé, Arg. | I7 | 80 |
| Pihtipudas, Fin. | J19 | 6 |
| P'ihyŏn, N. Kor. | C12 | 32 |
| Pijijiapan, Mex. | J13 | 90 |
| Pijol, Pico, mtn., Hond. | B7 | 92 |
| Pikal'ovo, Russia | B17 | 22 |
| Pikangikum, On., Can. | G20 | 104 |
| Pikangikum Lake, l., On., Can. | G20 | 104 |
| Pike, stm., Wi., U.S. | E8 | 110 |
| Pikes Peak, mtn., Co., U.S. | F11 | 120 |
| Pikesville, Md., U.S. | H10 | 108 |
| Piketberg, S. Afr. | I4 | 66 |
| Piketon, Oh., U.S. | H3 | 108 |
| Pikeville, Ky., U.S. | B4 | 112 |
| Pikeville, Tn., U.S. | G11 | 114 |
| Pikwitonei, Mb., Can. | C17 | 104 |
| Piła, Arg. | I9 | 80 |
| Piła (Schneidemühl), Pol. | B16 | 10 |
| Pilar, Austl. | J4 | 70 |
| Pilar, Arg. | F7 | 80 |
| Pilar, Arg. | F8 | 80 |
| Pilar, Para. | D9 | 80 |
| Pilar de Goiás, Braz. | C4 | 79 |
| Pilar do Sul, Braz. | G5 | 79 |
| Pilawa, Pol. | D21 | 10 |
| Pilaya, stm., Bol. | I9 | 82 |
| Pilcomayo, stm., S.A. | B8 | 80 |
| Pilcomayo, Brazo Norte, stm., Para. | C9 | 80 |
| Pilcomayo, Brazo Sur, stm., Para. | C9 | 80 |
| Pilger, Ne., U.S. | I10 | 118 |
| Pilibhit, India | F8 | 44 |
| Pilica, stm., Pol. | D20 | 10 |
| Pillaro, Ec. | H3 | 84 |
| Pilley's Island, Nf., Can. | C18 | 106 |
| Pilot, mtn., Austl. | K8 | 70 |
| Pilot Butte, Sk., Can. | H10 | 104 |
| Pilot Grove, Mo., U.S. | D4 | 114 |
| Pilot Knob, Mo., U.S. | E6 | 114 |
| Pilot Mound, Mb., Can. | I16 | 104 |
| Pilot Mountain, N.C., U.S. | C6 | 112 |
| Pilot Peak, mtn., Nv., U.S. | F8 | 124 |
| Pilot Point, Tx., U.S. | F10 | 116 |
| Pilot Rock, Or., U.S. | E7 | 122 |
| Pilot Station, Ak., U.S. | F13 | 100 |
| Pilottown, La., U.S. | M7 | 114 |
| Pilpah Range, mts., Austl. | C3 | 70 |
| Pilsen see Plzeň, Czech Rep. | F13 | 10 |
| Piltene, Lat. | D4 | 22 |
| Pim, stm., Russia | E6 | 28 |
| Pima, Az., U.S. | L7 | 120 |
| Pimba, Austl. | G2 | 70 |
| Pimenta Bueno, stm., Braz. | E8 | 82 |
| Pimental, Peru | B2 | 82 |
| Pina, Spain | D11 | 16 |
| Pinalón, Cerro, mtn., Guat. | B5 | 92 |
| Pinang see George Town, Malay. | | |
| Pinang, Pulau, i., Malay. | L6 | 40 |
| Pınarbaşı, Tur. | B4 | 48 |
| Pınarhisar, Tur. | H11 | 20 |
| Pinas, Arg. | F6 | 80 |
| Piñas, Ec. | I3 | 84 |
| Piñas, Cerro, mtn., Hond. | B9 | 92 |
| Pincher Creek, Ab., Can. | H21 | 102 |
| Pinchi Lake, l., B.C., Can. | C10 | 102 |
| Pinckney, Mi., U.S. | H12 | 110 |
| Pinckneyville, Il., U.S. | D7 | 114 |
| Pinconning, Mi., U.S. | G12 | 110 |
| Pińczów, Pol. | E20 | 10 |
| Pindaíba, Ribeirão, stm., Braz. | C3 | 79 |
| Pindamonhangaba, Braz. | G5 | 79 |
| Pindhos Óros (Pindus Mountains), mts., Grc. | J5 | 20 |
| Pinduši, Russia | J24 | 6 |
| Pindus Mountains see Pindhos Óros, mts., Grc. | J5 | 20 |
| Pine, stm., B.C., Can. | A13 | 102 |
| Pine, stm., Mi., U.S. | G14 | 104 |
| Pine, stm., Mi., U.S. | F12 | 110 |
| Pine, stm., Wi., U.S. | E7 | 110 |
| Pine Apple, Al., U.S. | K10 | 114 |
| Pine Barrens, reg., N.J., U.S. | H12 | 108 |
| Pine Bluff, Ar., U.S. | H4 | 114 |
| Pine Bluffs, Wy., U.S. | J3 | 118 |
| Pine Bush, N.Y., U.S. | F12 | 108 |
| Pine Castle, Fl., U.S. | K5 | 112 |
| Pine City, Mn., U.S. | E3 | 110 |
| Pine Creek, Austl. | B6 | 68 |
| Pine Creek, stm., Ab., Can. | C22 | 102 |
| Pine Creek Indian Reserve, Mb., Can. | F14 | 104 |
| Pine Creek Lake, res., Ok., U.S. | E11 | 116 |
| Pinedale, Ca., U.S. | H6 | 124 |
| Pinedale, Wy., U.S. | B7 | 120 |
| Pine Falls, Mb., Can. | H18 | 104 |
| Pinega, stm., Russia | E7 | 26 |
| Pine Grove, Pa., U.S. | G10 | 108 |
| Pine Grove, W.V., U.S. | H6 | 108 |
| Pine Hill, Al., U.S. | K9 | 114 |
| Pine Hills, Fl., U.S. | K5 | 112 |
| Pinehouse Lake, l., Sk., Can. | C8 | 104 |
| Pinehouse Lake, l., Sk., Can. | C8 | 104 |
| Pinehurst, Ga., U.S. | G3 | 112 |
| Pinehurst, Id., U.S. | E9 | 122 |
| Pinehurst, N.C., U.S. | D6 | 112 |
| Pinehurst Lake, l., Ab., Can. | C23 | 102 |
| Pine Island, Mn., U.S. | F3 | 110 |
| Pine Island, i., Fl., U.S. | M4 | 112 |
| Pine Island Bay, b., Ant. | C11 | 73 |
| Pineland, Tx., U.S. | K3 | 114 |
| Pinellas Park, Fl., U.S. | L4 | 112 |
| Pine Mountain, mtn., Wy., U.S. | | |
| Pine Pass, B.C., Can. | B12 | 102 |
| Pine Point, N.T., Can. | D10 | 96 |
| Pine Portage Dam, On., Can. | G15 | 96 |
| Pine Prairie, La., U.S. | L4 | 114 |
| Pine Ridge, S.D., U.S. | H5 | 118 |
| Pine River, Mn., U.S. | G14 | 104 |
| Pinerolo, Italy | D2 | 18 |
| Pinetop, Az., U.S. | J7 | 120 |
| Pinetops, N.C., U.S. | D9 | 112 |
| Pinetown, S. Afr. | G10 | 66 |
| Pine Valley, val., Ut., U.S. | F3 | 120 |
| Pineville, Ky., U.S. | C3 | 112 |
| Pineville, La., U.S. | K4 | 114 |
| Pineville, Mo., U.S. | F2 | 114 |
| Pineville, N.C., U.S. | D5 | 112 |
| Pineville, W.V., U.S. | B5 | 112 |
| Pinewood, S.C., U.S. | F6 | 112 |
| Piney, Fr. | D11 | 14 |
| Piney, stm., Tn., U.S. | G9 | 114 |
| Piney Woods, Ms., U.S. | J7 | 114 |
| Ping, stm., Thai. | F5 | 40 |
| Ping'anbu, China | B4 | 32 |
| Pingdingshan, China | B2 | 34 |
| Pingdu, China | G7 | 32 |
| Pinghu, China | E10 | 34 |
| Pingjiang, China | G2 | 34 |
| Pingliang, China | D8 | 32 |
| Pingquan, China | C5 | 32 |
| Pingshui, China | F9 | 34 |
| Ping'tung, Tai. | M9 | 34 |
| Pingwu, China | E7 | 30 |
| Pingxiang, China | H2 | 34 |
| Pingxiang, China | C9 | 40 |
| Pingyao, China | D9 | 30 |
| Pingyi, China | H5 | 32 |
| Pinhal Novo, Port. | G3 | 16 |
| Pinheiro, Braz. | D9 | 76 |
| Pinheiro Machado, Braz. | F12 | 80 |
| Pinhel, Port. | E4 | 16 |
| Pinhuã, stm., Braz. | B7 | 82 |
| Pini, Pulau, i., Indon. | N5 | 40 |
| Pinillos, Col. | C5 | 84 |
| Piniós, stm., Grc. | J6 | 20 |
| Pinjarra, Austl. | F3 | 68 |
| Pinlebu, Myan. | B3 | 40 |
| Pinnacle Buttes, mtn., Wy., U.S. | G16 | 122 |
| Pinnaroo, Austl. | J4 | 70 |
| Pinneberg, Ger. | B9 | 10 |
| Pinos, Mex. | F9 | 90 |
| Pinos Puente, Spain | H8 | 16 |
| Pinrang, Indon. | F6 | 38 |
| Pinsk, Bela. | I9 | 22 |
| Pinson, Al., U.S. | I10 | 114 |
| Pintado, stm., Braz. | B4 | 79 |
| Pintados, Chile | I7 | 82 |
| Pintados, Salar de, pl., Chile | I7 | 82 |
| Pinto Butte, mtn., Sk., Can. | I7 | 104 |
| Pinto Creek, stm., Sk., Can. | D17 | 102 |
| Pintoyacu, stm., Ec. | H4 | 84 |
| Pintoyacu, stm., Peru | I5 | 84 |
| Pin'ug, Russia | E7 | 26 |
| Pioche, Nv., U.S. | G11 | 124 |
| Piombino, Italy | G5 | 18 |
| Pioneer, Oh., U.S. | F2 | 108 |
| Pioneer Mine, B.C., Can. | G10 | 104 |
| Pioner, ostrov, i., Russia | B16 | 28 |
| Pionerskij, Russia | G3 | 22 |
| Pionki, Pol. | D21 | 10 |
| Piorini, stm., Braz. | I11 | 84 |
| Piorini, Lago, l., Braz. | I11 | 84 |
| Piotrków Trybunalski, Pol. | D19 | 10 |
| Pipanaco, Salar de, pl., Arg. | D5 | 80 |
| Pipestone, Mn., U.S. | G11 | 118 |
| Pipestone, stm., On., Can. | D5 | 96 |
| Pipestone Creek, stm., Can. | I13 | 104 |
| Pipinas, Arg. | H10 | 80 |
| Pipmuacan, Réservoir, res., P.Q., Can. | C3 | 106 |
| Piqua, Oh., U.S. | G2 | 108 |
| Piquiri, stm., Braz. | C12 | 80 |
| Piquiri, stm., Braz. | G14 | 82 |
| Piquiri, stm., Braz. | G14 | 82 |
| Pira, Benin | G10 | 64 |
| Piracanjuba, stm., Braz. | D4 | 79 |
| Piracicaba, Braz. | G5 | 79 |
| Piracicaba, stm., Braz. | D3 | 79 |
| Piraçununga, Braz. | F5 | 79 |
| Piraeus see Piraiévs, Grc. | | |
| Piraí do Sul, Braz. | C14 | 80 |
| Piraiévs (Piraeus), Grc. | L7 | 20 |
| Piraju, Braz. | G4 | 79 |
| Pirajuba, Braz. | E4 | 79 |
| Pirajuí, Braz. | F4 | 79 |
| Piran, Slvn. | D8 | 18 |
| Pirané, Arg. | C9 | 80 |
| Piranga, Braz. | F7 | 79 |
| Piranhas, Braz. | D3 | 79 |
| Pīrān Shahr, Iran | C8 | 48 |
| Pirapó, stm., Braz. | G2 | 79 |
| Pirapora, Braz. | D7 | 79 |
| Piraputanga, Braz. | F1 | 79 |
| Piraquara, Braz. | C14 | 80 |
| Pirarajá, Ur. | G11 | 80 |
| Piratinga, stm., Braz. | C5 | 79 |
| Piratini, Braz. | F12 | 80 |
| Piratini, stm., Braz. | E11 | 80 |
| Piratuba, Braz. | D13 | 80 |
| Piratucu, stm., Braz. | I14 | 84 |
| Piraúba, Lac, l., P.Q., Can. | B2 | 106 |
| Piray, stm., Bol. | I11 | 82 |
| Pirenópolis, Braz. | C4 | 79 |
| Pires do Rio, Braz. | D4 | 79 |
| Pírgos, Grc. | L5 | 20 |
| Piripiri, Braz. | D10 | 76 |
| Piribebuy, Para. | C10 | 80 |
| Píritu, Ven. | B8 | 84 |
| Píritu, Ven. | C9 | 84 |
| Pirmasens, Ger. | F7 | 10 |
| Pirna, Ger. | E13 | 10 |
| Pirot, Yugo. | F6 | 20 |
| Pirovano, Arg. | I7 | 80 |
| Pir Panjāl Range, mts., Asia | D6 | 44 |
| Pirtleville, Az., U.S. | M7 | 120 |
| Pisa, Italy | F5 | 18 |
| Pisagua, Chile | H6 | 82 |
| Pisco, Peru | E3 | 82 |
| Pisco, stm., Peru | E4 | 82 |
| Piscov, Russia | D23 | 22 |
| Písek, Czech Rep. | F14 | 10 |
| Pisgah Forest, N.C., U.S. | D4 | 112 |
| Pishan, China | B8 | 44 |
| Pishchana, Ukr. | A13 | 20 |
| Pishchanka, Ukr. | A12 | 20 |
| Pishin, Pak. | E2 | 44 |
| Pishīn Lora (Lowrah), stm., Asia | G18 | 48 |
| Pisinemo, Az., U.S. | L4 | 120 |
| Pismo Beach, Ca., U.S. | I5 | 124 |
| Pisqui, stm., Peru | B4 | 82 |
| Pisticci, Italy | I11 | 18 |
| Pistoia, Italy | F5 | 18 |
| Pistolet Bay, b., Nf., Can. | A18 | 106 |
| Pisz, Pol. | B21 | 10 |
| Pit, stm., Ca., U.S. | D3 | 124 |
| Pital, Col. | F5 | 84 |
| Pitalito, Col. | G4 | 84 |
| Pitanga, Braz. | C13 | 80 |
| Pitangueiras, Braz. | F4 | 79 |
| Pitangui, Braz. | E6 | 79 |
| Pitcairn, dep., Oc. | K27 | 126 |
| Piteå, Swe. | I17 | 6 |
| Pitelino, Russia | G24 | 22 |
| Piteşti, Rom. | E8 | 20 |
| Pithapuram, India | D7 | 46 |
| Pithiviers, Fr. | C9 | 14 |
| Pitigliano, Italy | G6 | 18 |
| Pitiquito, Mex. | B3 | 90 |
| Pitk'aranta, Russia | K22 | 6 |
| Pitt Island, i., B.C., Can. | D5 | 102 |
| Pitt Lake, l., B.C., Can. | H12 | 102 |
| Pittsboro, Ms., U.S. | I7 | 114 |
| Pittsboro, N.C., U.S. | D7 | 112 |
| Pittsburg, Ks., U.S. | N13 | 118 |
| Pittsburg, Tx., U.S. | I2 | 114 |
| Pittsburgh, Pa., U.S. | G7 | 108 |
| Pittsfield, Il., U.S. | C6 | 114 |
| Pittsfield, Me., U.S. | C17 | 108 |
| Pittsfield, N.H., U.S. | D15 | 108 |
| Pittsford, Mi., U.S. | I11 | 110 |
| Pittston, Pa., U.S. | F11 | 108 |
| Pittsview, Al., U.S. | J11 | 114 |
| Pittsworth, Austl. | F9 | 70 |
| Pituil, Arg. | E5 | 80 |
| Pitumarca, Peru | F6 | 82 |
| Pium, Braz. | F9 | 76 |
| Piura, Peru | A1 | 82 |
| Piura, dept., Peru | A1 | 82 |
| Piura, stm., Peru | A1 | 82 |
| Pivan', Russia | G19 | 28 |
| Pivdennyy Buh, stm., Ukr. | H4 | 26 |
| Pivijay, Col. | B5 | 84 |
| Pixley, Ca., U.S. | I6 | 124 |
| Pizzo, Italy | K11 | 18 |
| Pjaršai, Bela. | G9 | 22 |
| Placentia, Nf., Can. | E20 | 106 |
| Placentia Bay, b., Nf., Can. | E19 | 106 |
| Placerville, Ca., U.S. | F5 | 124 |
| Placetas, Cuba | C5 | 94 |
| Plácido de Castro, Braz. | D8 | 82 |
| Plácido Rosas, Ur. | G12 | 80 |
| Plain City, Oh., U.S. | G3 | 108 |
| Plain City, Ut., U.S. | C4 | 120 |
| Plain Dealing, La., U.S. | J3 | 114 |
| Plainfield, Ct., U.S. | F15 | 108 |
| Plainfield, Il., U.S. | C10 | 114 |
| Plainfield, Wi., U.S. | F6 | 110 |
| Plains, Ga., U.S. | G2 | 112 |
| Plains, Ks., U.S. | N7 | 118 |
| Plains, Mt., U.S. | C11 | 122 |
| Plains, Tx., U.S. | F4 | 116 |
| Plainview, Ne., U.S. | I10 | 118 |
| Plainview, Tx., U.S. | E5 | 116 |
| Plainville, In., U.S. | D9 | 114 |
| Plainville, Ks., U.S. | L8 | 118 |
| Plainwell, Mi., U.S. | H10 | 110 |
| Plaisance, Baie de, b., P.Q., Can. | E12 | 106 |
| Plaistow, N.H., U.S. | E15 | 108 |
| Plakhtiyvka, Ukr. | C13 | 20 |
| Planada, Ca., U.S. | G5 | 124 |
| Planaltina, Braz. | C5 | 79 |
| Planalto, Braz. | D12 | 80 |
| Planeta Rica, Col. | C5 | 84 |
| Plankinton, S.D., U.S. | H9 | 118 |
| Plano, Il., U.S. | I7 | 110 |
| Plano, Tx., U.S. | F10 | 116 |
| Plantagenet, On., Can. | B11 | 108 |
| Plantation, Fl., U.S. | M6 | 112 |
| Plant City, Fl., U.S. | K4 | 112 |
| Plantersville, Al., U.S. | J10 | 114 |
| Plantersville, Ms., U.S. | H8 | 114 |
| Plantsite, Az., U.S. | K7 | 120 |
| Plaquemine, La., U.S. | L5 | 114 |
| Plasencia, Spain | E5 | 16 |
| Plaster Rock, N.B., Can. | F6 | 106 |
| Plast, Russia | G10 | 26 |
| Plata, Isla de la, i., Ec. | H1 | 84 |
| Plata, Río de la, est., S.A. | H10 | 80 |
| Plato, Col. | C5 | 84 |
| Platonovka, Russia | I24 | 22 |
| Platta, Switz. | E10 | 13 |
| Platte, S.D., U.S. | H9 | 118 |
| Platte, stm., Ne., U.S. | D11 | 110 |
| Platte, stm., Wi., U.S. | H5 | 110 |
| Platte, stm., U.S. | J10 | 118 |
| Platte Center, Ne., U.S. | J10 | 118 |
| Platte City, Mo., U.S. | C2 | 114 |
| Platteville, Co., U.S. | D12 | 120 |
| Platteville, Wi., U.S. | H5 | 110 |
| Plattling, Ger. | G12 | 10 |
| Plattsburg, Mo., U.S. | C2 | 114 |
| Plattsburgh, N.Y., U.S. | C13 | 108 |
| Plattsmouth, Ne., U.S. | J12 | 118 |
| Platveld, Nmb. | B3 | 66 |
| Plau, Ger. | B12 | 10 |
| Plauen, Ger. | E12 | 10 |
| Plav, Yugo. | G3 | 20 |
| Plavinas, Lat. | E8 | 22 |
| Plavsk, Russia | H20 | 22 |
| Playa Azul, Mex. | I8 | 90 |
| Playa Bonita, C.R. | H10 | 92 |
| Playa del Carmen, Mex. | G16 | 90 |
| Playa Noriega, Laguna, l., Mex. | C4 | 90 |
| Playas, Lake, l., N.M., U.S. | M8 | 120 |
| Playa Vicente, Mex. | I12 | 90 |
| Play Cu, Viet. | H9 | 40 |
| Playgreen Lake, l., Mb., Can. | D16 | 104 |
| Plaza, N.D., U.S. | C6 | 118 |
| Plaza de Caisán, Pan. | I12 | 92 |
| Plaza Huincul, Arg. | J4 | 80 |
| Pleasant, Lake, res., Az., U.S. | K4 | 120 |
| Pleasant, Mount, hill, N.B., Can. | G7 | 106 |
| Pleasant Bay, N.S., Can. | F13 | 106 |
| Pleasantdale, Sk., Can. | F10 | 104 |
| Pleasant Gap, Pa., U.S. | G9 | 108 |
| Pleasant Garden, N.C., U.S. | D6 | 112 |
| Pleasant Grove, Ut., U.S. | D5 | 120 |
| Pleasant Hill, La., U.S. | K3 | 114 |
| Pleasant Hill, Mo., U.S. | D2 | 114 |
| Pleasanton, Ks., U.S. | M13 | 118 |
| Pleasant Plains, Il., U.S. | C7 | 114 |
| Pleasantville, Ia., U.S. | I2 | 110 |
| Pleasantville, N.J., U.S. | H12 | 108 |
| Pleasantville, Pa., U.S. | F7 | 108 |
| Plechanovo, Russia | G20 | 22 |
| Pleiku see Play Cu, Viet. | H9 | 40 |
| Pléneuf, Fr. | D4 | 14 |
| Plenty, Bay of, b., N.Z. | B6 | 72 |
| Plentywood, Mt., U.S. | C2 | 118 |
| Pleseck, Russia | E6 | 26 |
| Pleščanicy, Bela. | G10 | 22 |
| Plessisville, P.Q., Can. | A15 | 108 |
| Plétipi, Lac, l., P.Q., Can. | F18 | 96 |
| Pleven, Bul. | F8 | 20 |
| Plevna, Mt., U.S. | E3 | 118 |
| Pljevlja, Yugo. | F3 | 20 |
| Plock, Pol. | C19 | 10 |
| Ploemeur, Fr. | E4 | 14 |
| Plöen, Ger. | A10 | 10 |
| Plonge, Lac la, l., Sk., Can. | C7 | 104 |
| Płońsk, Pol. | C20 | 10 |
| Ploskoje, Russia | I21 | 22 |
| Plottier, Arg. | J4 | 80 |
| Plouay, Fr. | E3 | 14 |
| Ploudalmézeau, Fr. | D2 | 14 |
| Plouguenast, Fr. | D4 | 14 |
| Plouha, Fr. | D4 | 14 |
| Plovdiv, Bul. | G8 | 20 |
| Plover, stm., Wi., U.S. | F6 | 110 |
| Plumas, Mb., Can. | H15 | 104 |
| Plummer, Id., U.S. | C9 | 122 |
| Plumtree, Zimb. | C8 | 66 |
| Plunge, Lith. | F4 | 22 |
| Plymouth, Eng., U.K. | K9 | 8 |
| Plymouth, In., U.S. | A10 | 114 |
| Plymouth, Ma., U.S. | F16 | 108 |
| Plymouth, Monts. | F13 | 94 |
| Plymouth, N.C., U.S. | D10 | 112 |
| Plymouth, N.H., U.S. | D15 | 108 |
| Plymouth, Oh., U.S. | F4 | 108 |
| Plymouth, Pa., U.S. | F11 | 108 |
| Plymouth, Wi., U.S. | G8 | 110 |
| Plzeň, Czech Rep. | F13 | 10 |
| Po, stm., Italy | E7 | 18 |
| Pô, Burkina | F9 | 64 |
| Poás, Volcán, vol., C.R. | G10 | 92 |
| Pobé, Benin | H11 | 64 |
| Pobeda, gora, mtn., Russia | D21 | 28 |
| Pobeda Ice Island, i., Ant. | B6 | 73 |
| Pobedino, Russia | H20 | 28 |
| Pobedy, pik, mtn., Asia | F6 | 114 |
| Pocahontas, Ar., U.S. | F6 | 114 |
| Pocahontas, Ia., U.S. | I13 | 118 |
| Pocahontas, Il., U.S. | D7 | 114 |
| Pocatalico, stm., W.V., U.S. | I5 | 108 |
| Pocatello, Id., U.S. | H13 | 122 |
| Počep, Russia | H16 | 22 |
| Pöchlarn, Aus. | G15 | 10 |
| Pochinok, Russia | G15 | 22 |
| Pochutla, Mex. | J11 | 90 |
| Pocito, Salar, pl., Arg. | C5 | 80 |
| Pocoata, Bol. | H8 | 82 |
| Pocões, Braz. | C8 | 79 |
| Pocola, Ok., U.S. | G2 | 114 |
| Pocomoke City, Md., U.S. | J11 | 108 |
| Pocomoke, stm., Md., U.S. | I11 | 108 |
| Pocona, Bol. | G9 | 82 |
| Poconé, Braz. | G7 | 82 |
| Pocono Mountains, hills, Pa., U.S. | F11 | 108 |
| Pocono Summit, Pa., U.S. | F11 | 108 |
| Poços de Caldas, Braz. | F5 | 79 |
| Pocri, Pan. | I14 | 92 |
| Poção, Braz. | D12 | 80 |
| Podborov'je, Russia | B13 | 22 |
| Podčer'je, Russia | E9 | 26 |
| Poděbrady, Czech Rep. | E15 | 10 |
| Podgorica, Yugo. | G3 | 20 |
| Podkamennaja Tunguska, stm., Russia | E11 | 28 |
| Podol'sk, Russia | F20 | 22 |
| Podor, Maur. | C2 | 64 |
| Podoz'orskij, Russia | D23 | 22 |
| Podporož'je, Russia | E4 | 26 |
| Podravska Slatina, Cro. | D1 | 20 |
| Podu Turcului, Rom. | C11 | 20 |
| Pofadder, S. Afr. | G4 | 66 |
| Pogan, China | G5 | 34 |
| Pogar, Russia | I16 | 22 |
| Poggibonsi, Italy | F6 | 18 |
| Pogoanele, Rom. | E11 | 20 |
| Pogoreloje Gorodišče, Russia | E17 | 22 |
| Pograničnyj, Russia | I18 | 28 |
| P'ohang, S. Kor. | G17 | 32 |
| Pohjois-Karjalan lääni, prov., Fin. | J21 | 6 |
| Poinsett, Cape, c., Ant. | B6 | 73 |
| Point, Tx., U.S. | G11 | 116 |
| Point Arena, Ca., U.S. | F2 | 124 |
| Point Au Fer Island, i., La., U.S. | M5 | 114 |
| Point Comfort, Tx., U.S. | K10 | 116 |
| Pointe-à-la-Frégate, P.Q., Can. | C9 | 106 |
| Pointe-à-la-Garde, P.Q., Can. | D7 | 106 |
| Pointe à la Hache, La., U.S. | M6 | 114 |
| Pointe-à-Maurier, P.Q., Can. | B14 | 106 |
| Pointe-à-Pitre, Guad. | F14 | 94 |
| Point Edward, On., Can. | G13 | 110 |
| Pointe-Noire, Congo | B2 | 58 |
| Point Fortin, Trin. | I14 | 94 |
| Point Hope, Ak., U.S. | B11 | 100 |
| Point Imperial, mtn., Az., U.S. | H5 | 120 |
| Point Lake, l., N.T., Can. | C10 | 96 |
| Point Leamington, Nf., Can. | C18 | 106 |
| Point Marion, Pa., U.S. | H7 | 108 |
| Point Pelee National Park, On., Can. | I13 | 110 |
| Point Pleasant, N.J., U.S. | G12 | 108 |
| Point Pleasant, W.V., U.S. | I4 | 108 |
| Point Sapin, N.B., Can. | F9 | 106 |
| Poisson Blanc, Réservoir du, res., P.Q., Can. | A11 | 108 |
| Poissy, Fr. | D9 | 14 |
| Poitiers, Fr. | F7 | 14 |
| Poix, Fr. | C8 | 14 |
| Pojarkovo, Russia | H17 | 28 |
| Pojo, Bol. | G9 | 82 |
| Pojoaque Valley, N.M., U.S. | I10 | 120 |
| Pojuca, Braz. | B9 | 79 |
| Pojuca, stm., Braz. | B9 | 79 |
| Pokhara, Nepal | F10 | 44 |
| Pokrov, Russia | F22 | 22 |
| Pokrovsk, Russia | E17 | 28 |
| Pokrovskoje, Russia | I19 | 22 |
| Pola, stm., Russia | D14 | 22 |
| Polacca, Az., U.S. | I6 | 120 |
| Polack, Bela. | F11 | 22 |
| Pola de Lena, Spain | B6 | 16 |
| Polán, Iran | I16 | 48 |
| Polanco, Ur. | G11 | 80 |
| Poland (Polska), ctry., Eur. | E14 | 4 |
| Polatsk, Bela. | A16 | 10 |
| Polcura, Chile | I3 | 80 |
| Pol-e Khomrī, Afg. | C3 | 44 |
| Polesye, reg., Eur. | G3 | 26 |
| Polevskoj, Russia | F10 | 26 |
| Polgár, Hung. | H21 | 10 |
| Pólgyo, S. Kor. | I15 | 32 |
| Police, Pol. | B14 | 10 |
| Poligny, Fr. | F12 | 14 |
| Pólis, Cyp. | D2 | 48 |
| Polistena, Italy | K11 | 18 |
| Políyiros, Grc. | I7 | 20 |
| Polk, Ne., U.S. | J10 | 118 |
| Polk, Pa., U.S. | F7 | 108 |
| Polkton, N.C., U.S. | D6 | 112 |
| Polla, Italy | I10 | 18 |
| Pollāchi, India | G4 | 46 |
| Pöllau, Aus. | H15 | 10 |
| Pollock, La., U.S. | K4 | 114 |
| Pollock, S.D., U.S. | F7 | 118 |
| Polo, Bol. | H9 | 82 |
| Polo, Il., U.S. | I6 | 110 |
| Polochic, stm., Guat. | B5 | 92 |
| Polonio, Cabo, c., Ur. | H12 | 80 |
| Polonnaruwa, Sri L. | I6 | 46 |
| Polotn'anyj, Russia | G19 | 22 |
| Polson, Mt., U.S. | C11 | 122 |
| Poltava, Ukr. | H4 | 26 |
| Poltimore, P.Q., Can. | B11 | 108 |
| Põltsamaa, Est. | C8 | 22 |
| Poluj, stm., Russia | D11 | 26 |
| Polunočnoje, Russia | E10 | 26 |
| Polynesia, is., Oc. | I24 | 126 |
| Polysajevo, Russia | G15 | 26 |
| Pomabamba, Peru | C3 | 82 |
| Pomacanchi, Peru | F6 | 82 |
| Pomata, Peru | G7 | 82 |
| Pombal, Port. | F3 | 16 |
| Pombal, Braz. | E11 | 76 |
| Pomene, Moz. | D12 | 66 |
| Pomerania, hist. reg., Eur. | A16 | 10 |
| Pomeranian Bay, b., Eur. | A14 | 10 |
| Pomerode, Braz. | D14 | 80 |
| Pomeroon, stm., Guy. | D13 | 84 |
| Pomeroy, Ia., U.S. | I13 | 118 |
| Pomeroy, Oh., U.S. | H4 | 108 |
| Pomeroy, Wa., U.S. | D8 | 122 |
| Pomme de Terre, stm., Mn., U.S. | F11 | 118 |
| Pomme de Terre, stm., Mo., U.S. | E3 | 114 |
| Pomona, Ca., U.S. | J8 | 124 |
| Pomona Park, Fl., U.S. | J5 | 112 |
| Pompano Beach, Fl., U.S. | M6 | 112 |
| Pompei, hist., Italy | I9 | 18 |
| Pompéia, Braz. | G3 | 79 |
| Pompéu, Braz. | E6 | 79 |
| Pompton Lakes, N.J., U.S. | F12 | 108 |
| Pomquet, N.S., Can. | G12 | 106 |
| Ponask Lake, l., On., Can. | D22 | 104 |
| Ponass Lakes, l., Sk., Can. | F11 | 104 |
| Ponca, Ne., U.S. | I11 | 118 |
| Ponca City, Ok., U.S. | C9 | 116 |
| Ponce, P.R. | E11 | 94 |
| Ponce de Leon, Fl., U.S. | L11 | 114 |
| Ponchatoula, La., U.S. | L6 | 114 |
| Poncheville, Lac, l., P.Q., Can. | F17 | 96 |
| Pondcreek, Ok., U.S. | C9 | 116 |
| Pondicherry, India | G5 | 46 |
| Pondicherry, ter., India | G5 | 46 |
| Pond Inlet, N.T., Can. | B17 | 96 |
| Pond Inlet, N.T., Can. | B17 | 96 |
| Pondoland, hist. reg., S. Afr. | H9 | 66 |
| Ponferrada, Spain | C5 | 16 |
| Ponhook Lake, l., N.S., Can. | H9 | 106 |
| Ponnūru Nidubrolu, India | D6 | 46 |
| Ponoj, stm., Russia | D5 | 26 |
| Ponoka, Ab., Can. | E21 | 102 |
| Ponorogo, Indon. | j15 | 39a |
| Pons, Fr. | G6 | 14 |
| Ponta do Sol, Port. | m20 | 17a |
| Ponta Grossa, Braz. | C13 | 80 |
| Pontalina, Braz. | D4 | 79 |
| Ponta Porã, Braz. | G1 | 79 |
| Pontarlier, Fr. | F13 | 14 |
| Pontassieve, Italy | F6 | 18 |
| Pont-Audemer, Fr. | C7 | 14 |
| Pont-Aven, Fr. | E3 | 14 |
| Pont Canavese, Italy | D2 | 18 |
| Pontchartrain, Lake, l., La., U.S. | L6 | 114 |
| Pont-d'Ain, Fr. | F12 | 14 |
| Pont-de-Vaux, Fr. | F11 | 14 |
| Ponte Alta do Bom Jesus, Braz. | B5 | 79 |
| Ponte Branca, Braz. | D2 | 79 |
| Pontedera, Italy | F5 | 18 |
| Ponteix, Sk., Can. | I7 | 104 |
| Ponte Nova, Braz. | F7 | 79 |
| Ponte Serrada, Braz. | D13 | 80 |
| Pontevedra, Spain | C3 | 16 |
| Ponte Vedra Beach, Fl., U.S. | I5 | 112 |
| Pontiac, Il., U.S. | J7 | 110 |
| Pontiac, Mi., U.S. | H12 | 110 |
| Pontianak, Indon. | F4 | 38 |
| Pontivy, Fr. | D4 | 14 |
| Pont-l'Abbé, Fr. | E2 | 14 |
| Pont-l'Évêque, Fr. | C7 | 14 |
| Pontoise, Fr. | C9 | 14 |
| Pontotoc, Ms., U.S. | H8 | 114 |
| Pontotoc, Tx., U.S. | I8 | 116 |
| Pontremoli, Italy | E4 | 18 |
| Pontresina, Switz. | F12 | 13 |
| Ponts, Spain | D13 | 16 |
| Pont-sur-Yonne, Fr. | D10 | 14 |
| Pontypridd, Wales, U.K. | J10 | 8 |
| Pony, Mt., U.S. | E14 | 122 |
| Ponyri, Russia | I19 | 22 |
| Ponziane, Isole, is., Italy | I7 | 18 |
| Poole, Eng., U.K. | K12 | 8 |
| Pooler, Ga., U.S. | G5 | 112 |
| Pooley Island, i., B.C., Can. | E6 | 102 |
| Pool's Cove, Nf., Can. | E18 | 106 |
| Poolville, Tx., U.S. | G9 | 116 |
| Poona see Pune, India | C2 | 46 |
| Poopo, Bol. | H8 | 82 |
| Poopó, Lago, l., Bol. | H8 | 82 |
| Poor Man Indian Reserve, Sk., Can. | G10 | 104 |
| Popa, Isla, i., Pan. | H12 | 92 |
| Popayán, Col. | F4 | 84 |
| Pope, Ms., U.S. | H7 | 114 |
| Poperinge, Bel. | G2 | 12 |
| Popham Bay, b., N.T., Can. | D19 | 96 |
| Popigaj, stm., Russia | C14 | 28 |
| Popilit Lake, l., Austl. | I4 | 70 |
| Poplar, Mt., U.S. | C2 | 118 |
| Poplar, Wi., U.S. | D4 | 110 |
| Poplar, stm., Can. | F18 | 104 |
| Poplar, stm., U.S. | D11 | 118 |
| Poplar Bluff, Mo., U.S. | F6 | 114 |
| Poplar Hill, On., Can. | F14 | 104 |
| Poplar Point, Mb., Can. | H17 | 104 |
| Poplarville, Ms., U.S. | L7 | 114 |
| Popocatépetl, Volcán, vol., Mex. | H10 | 90 |
| Popokabaka, D.R.C. | C3 | 58 |
| Popoli, Italy | G8 | 18 |
| Popondetta, Pap. N. Gui. | m16 | 68a |
| Popovo, Bul. | F10 | 20 |
| Poppel, Bel. | F7 | 12 |
| Poppi, Italy | F6 | 18 |
| Popple, stm., Wi., U.S. | E7 | 110 |
| Poprad, Slvk. | F20 | 10 |
| Poprad, stm., Eur. | F20 | 10 |
| Pöptong, N. Kor. | E15 | 32 |
| Poptún, Guat. | A5 | 92 |
| Poquoson, Va., U.S. | B10 | 112 |
| Porangatu, Braz. | B4 | 79 |
| Porazava, Bela. | I7 | 22 |
| Porbandar, India | J3 | 44 |
| Porce, stm., Col. | D5 | 84 |
| Porcher Island, i., B.C., Can. | D4 | 102 |
| Porciúncula, Braz. | F7 | 79 |
| Porco, Bol. | H9 | 82 |
| Porcos, Rio dos, stm., Braz. | B6 | 79 |
| Porcuna, Spain | H7 | 16 |
| Porcupine, stm., N.A. | C23 | 100 |
| Porcupine Hills, hills, Can. | F13 | 104 |
| Pordenone, Italy | D7 | 18 |
| Porecatu, Braz. | G3 | 79 |
| Poreče Rybnoje, Russia | D22 | 22 |
| Pori, Fin. | K17 | 6 |
| Porlamar, Ven. | B11 | 84 |
| Poroma, Bol. | H9 | 82 |
| Poronajsk, Russia | H20 | 28 |
| Poroshkove, Ukr. | G22 | 10 |
| Porosozero, Russia | J23 | 6 |
| Porpoise Bay, b., Ant. | B7 | 73 |
| Porrentruy, Switz. | D7 | 13 |
| Portachuelo, Bol. | G10 | 82 |
| Port Adelaide, Austl. | J3 | 70 |
| Portadown, N. Ire., U.K. | G7 | 8 |
| Portage, Mi., U.S. | H10 | 110 |
| Portage, Ut., U.S. | C4 | 120 |
| Portage, Wi., U.S. | G6 | 110 |
| Portage, stm., Oh., U.S. | F3 | 108 |
| Portage Bay, b., Mb., Can. | G16 | 104 |
| Portage la Prairie, Mb., Can. | I16 | 104 |
| Portageville, Mo., U.S. | F7 | 114 |
| Portal, Ga., U.S. | G5 | 112 |
| Portal, N.D., U.S. | C5 | 118 |
| Port Alberni, B.C., Can. | H10 | 102 |
| Portal del Infierno, wtfl, Hond. | C9 | 92 |
| Portales, N.M., U.S. | E3 | 116 |
| Port Alfred (Kowie), S. Afr. | I8 | 66 |
| Port Alice, B.C., Can. | G7 | 102 |
| Port Allegany, Pa., U.S. | F8 | 108 |
| Port Allen, La., U.S. | L5 | 114 |
| Port Angeles, Wa., U.S. | B2 | 122 |
| Port Anson, Nf., Can. | C18 | 106 |
| Port Antonio, Jam. | E6 | 94 |
| Port Aransas, Tx., U.S. | L9 | 116 |
| Port Arthur, Austl. | N7 | 70 |
| Port Arthur see Lüshun, China | E9 | 32 |
| Port Arthur see Thunder Bay, On., Can. | B6 | 110 |
| Port Arthur, Tx., U.S. | M3 | 114 |
| Port Augusta, Austl. | I2 | 70 |
| Port au Port Bay, b., Nf., Can. | D15 | 106 |
| Port au Port Peninsula, pen., Nf., Can. | D14 | 106 |
| Port-au-Prince, Haiti | E8 | 94 |
| Port-au-Prince, Baie de, b., Haiti | E8 | 94 |
| Port-aux-Basques see Channel-Port-aux-Basques, Nf., Can. | E14 | 106 |
| Port Barre, La., U.S. | L5 | 114 |
| Port-Bergé, Madag. | o22 | 67b |

Port-Pusa


| Name | Map Ref. | Page |
|---|---|---|
| Port Blair, India | I2 | 40 |
| Port Blandford, Nf., Can. | D19 | 106 |
| Port Borden, P.E., Can. | F10 | 106 |
| Port-Bouët, C. Iv. | I8 | 64 |
| Port Broughton, Austl. | I2 | 70 |
| Port Byron, Il., U.S. | I5 | 110 |
| Port Canning, India | I13 | 44 |
| Port-Cartier, P.Q., Can. | B7 | 106 |
| *Port-Cartier Sept-Îles, Réserve, P.Q., Can.* | B6 | 106 |
| Port Chalmers, N.Z. | F3 | 72 |
| Port Charlotte, Fl., U.S. | M4 | 112 |
| Port Chester, N.Y., U.S. | F13 | 108 |
| Port Clements, B.C., Can. | D2 | 102 |
| Port Clinton, Oh., U.S. | F4 | 108 |
| Port Clyde, Me., U.S. | D17 | 108 |
| Port Colborne, On., Can. | H16 | 110 |
| Port Coquitlam, B.C., Can. | H12 | 102 |
| Port Credit, On., Can. | G16 | 110 |
| *Port-Daniel, Réserve, P.Q., Can.* | D9 | 106 |
| Port-de-Paix, Haiti | E8 | 94 |
| Port Dickson, Malay. | M6 | 40 |
| Port Dover, On., Can. | H15 | 110 |
| *Porte Crayon, Mount, mtn., W.V., U.S.* | I7 | 108 |
| Port Edward, B.C., Can. | C4 | 102 |
| Port Edward, S. Afr. | H10 | 66 |
| Port Edwards, Wi., U.S. | F6 | 110 |
| Portegolpe, C.R. | G9 | 92 |
| Porteirinha, Braz. | C7 | 79 |
| Portel, Braz. | D8 | 76 |
| Port Elgin, N.B., Can. | F9 | 106 |
| Port Elgin, On., Can. | F14 | 110 |
| Port Elizabeth, S. Afr. | I7 | 66 |
| Port-en-Bessin, Fr. | C6 | 14 |
| Porter, Ok., U.S. | D11 | 116 |
| Porter, Tx., U.S. | I11 | 116 |
| *Porter Lake, l., Sk., Can.* | B7 | 104 |
| Porterville, Ca., U.S. | H6 | 124 |
| Porterville, Ms., U.S. | J8 | 114 |
| Port Essington, B.C., Can. | C5 | 102 |
| *Portete, Bahía, b., Col.* | A6 | 84 |
| Port Fairy, Austl. | L5 | 70 |
| Port Gamble, Wa., U.S. | C3 | 122 |
| Port Gentil, Gabon | B1 | 58 |
| Port Germein, Austl. | I3 | 70 |
| Port Gibson, Ms., U.S. | K6 | 114 |
| Port Graham, Ak., U.S. | G19 | 100 |
| Port Greville, N.S., Can. | G9 | 106 |
| Port Harcourt, Nig. | I13 | 64 |
| Port Hardy, B.C., Can. | G7 | 102 |
| Port Hawkesbury, N.S., Can. | G12 | 106 |
| Port Hedland, Austl. | D3 | 68 |
| Port Henry, N.Y., U.S. | C13 | 108 |
| Port Hill, P.E., Can. | F10 | 106 |
| Port Hood, N.S., Can. | F12 | 106 |
| Port Hope, Mi., U.S. | G13 | 110 |
| Port Hope, On., Can. | G17 | 110 |
| Port Howe, Bah. | B7 | 94 |
| Port Huron, Mi., U.S. | H13 | 110 |
| Port-İliç, Azer. | B10 | 48 |
| Portimão, Port. | H3 | 16 |
| Port Isabel, Tx., U.S. | M9 | 116 |
| Port Jervis, N.Y., U.S. | F12 | 108 |
| Port Kembla, Austl. | J9 | 70 |
| Portland, Ar., U.S. | I5 | 114 |
| Portland, Austl. | I9 | 70 |
| Portland, Austl. | L4 | 70 |
| Portland, In., U.S. | B12 | 114 |
| Portland, Me., U.S. | D16 | 108 |
| Portland, Mi., U.S. | H11 | 110 |
| Portland, N.D., U.S. | D10 | 118 |
| Portland, Or., U.S. | E3 | 122 |
| Portland, Tn., U.S. | F10 | 114 |
| Portland, Tx., U.S. | L9 | 116 |
| *Portland, Bill of, c., Eng., U.K.* | K11 | 8 |
| *Portland, Cape, c., Austl.* | M7 | 70 |
| *Portland Bay, b., Austl.* | L4 | 70 |
| *Portland Bight, Jam.* | F6 | 94 |
| *Portland Canal, b., N.A.* | B4 | 102 |
| *Portland Creek Pond, l., Nf., Can.* | B16 | 106 |
| *Portland Inlet, b., B.C., Can.* | C4 | 102 |
| *Portland Point, c., Jam.* | F6 | 94 |
| Port Laoise, Ire. | H6 | 8 |
| Port Lavaca, Tx., U.S. | K10 | 116 |
| Port Leyden, N.Y., U.S. | D11 | 108 |
| Port Lincoln, Austl. | J1 | 70 |
| Port Lions, Ak., U.S. | H18 | 100 |
| Port Loko, S.L. | G3 | 64 |
| Port-Louis, Fr. | E3 | 14 |
| Port Louis, Mrts. | v18 | 67c |
| Port Macquarie, Austl. | H10 | 70 |
| Port Maitland, N.S., Can. | I7 | 106 |
| Port Maria, Jam. | E6 | 94 |
| Port McNeill, B.C., Can. | G7 | 102 |
| Port McNicoll, On., Can. | F16 | 110 |
| Port Mellon, B.C., Can. | H11 | 102 |
| Port-Menier, P.Q., Can. | C9 | 106 |
| Port Moody, B.C., Can. | H12 | 102 |
| Port Moresby, Pap. N. Gui. | m16 | 68a |
| Port Morien, N.S., Can. | F14 | 106 |
| Port Mouton, N.S., Can. | I9 | 106 |
| Port Neches, Tx., U.S. | M3 | 114 |
| Port Nelson, Mb., Can. | A22 | 104 |
| *Portneuf, stm., Id., U.S.* | H13 | 122 |
| *Portneuf, stm., P.Q., Can.* | D4 | 106 |
| *Portneuf, Lac, l., P.Q., Can.* | C3 | 106 |
| Portneuf-sur-Mer, P.Q., Can. | D4 | 106 |
| Port Neville, B.C., Can. | G8 | 102 |
| Port Nolloth, S. Afr. | G3 | 66 |
| Port Norris, N.J., U.S. | H11 | 108 |
| Porto, Port. | D3 | 16 |
| Porto Acre, Braz. | C8 | 82 |
| Porto Alegre, Braz. | F13 | 80 |
| Porto Amboim, Ang. | D2 | 58 |
| Porto Belo, Braz. | D14 | 80 |
| Portobelo, Pan. | C3 | 84 |
| Port O'Connor, Tx., U.S. | K10 | 116 |
| Porto de Moz, Braz. | D8 | 76 |
| Porto de Pedras, Braz. | E11 | 76 |
| Porto Empedocle, Italy | L8 | 18 |
| Porto Esperança, Braz. | H13 | 82 |
| Porto Esperidião, Braz. | F12 | 82 |
| Porto Farina, Tun. | L5 | 18 |
| Porto Feliz, Braz. | G5 | 79 |
| Porto Ferreira, Braz. | F5 | 79 |
| Port of Spain, Trin. | I14 | 94 |
| Portogruaro, Italy | D7 | 18 |
| Porto Inglês, C.V. | m17 | 64a |
| Portola, Ca., U.S. | E5 | 124 |
| Porto Lucena, Braz. | D11 | 80 |
| Pörtom (Pirttikylä), Fin. | J17 | 6 |
| Porto Mendes, Braz. | C11 | 80 |
| Porto Murtinho, Braz. | I13 | 82 |
| Porto Nacional, Braz. | F9 | 76 |
| Porto-Novo, Benin | H11 | 64 |
| Port Orange, Fl., U.S. | J6 | 112 |
| Port Orchard, Wa., U.S. | C3 | 122 |
| Porto Recanati, Italy | F8 | 18 |
| Port Orford, Or., U.S. | H1 | 122 |
| Porto San Giorgio, Italy | F8 | 18 |
| *Porto Santo, i., Port.* | I21 | 17a |
| Porto São José, Braz. | G2 | 79 |
| Porto Seguro, Braz. | D9 | 79 |
| Porto-Séguro, Togo | H10 | 64 |
| Porto Torres, Italy | I3 | 18 |
| Porto União, Braz. | D13 | 80 |
| Porto Válter, Braz. | C5 | 82 |
| Porto-Vecchio, Fr. | m24 | 15a |
| Porto Velho, Braz. | C10 | 82 |
| Portoviejo, Ec. | H2 | 84 |
| Port Perry, On., Can. | F17 | 110 |
| *Port Phillip Bay, b., Austl.* | L6 | 70 |
| Port Pirie, Austl. | I3 | 70 |
| Port Rexton, Nf., Can. | D20 | 106 |
| Port Richey, Fl., U.S. | K4 | 112 |
| Port Rowan, On., Can. | H15 | 110 |
| Port Royal, Pa., U.S. | G9 | 108 |
| Port Royal, S.C., U.S. | G6 | 112 |
| *Port Royal National Historic Park, N.S., Can.* | H8 | 106 |
| Port Said see Būr Sa'īd, Egypt | B7 | 60 |
| Port Saint Joe, Fl., U.S. | J1 | 112 |
| Port Saint Johns, S. Afr. | H9 | 66 |
| Port Saint Lucie, Fl., U.S. | L6 | 112 |
| Port-Saint-Servan, P.Q., Can. | A15 | 106 |
| Port Sanilac, Mi., U.S. | G13 | 110 |
| Port Saunders, Nf., Can. | B16 | 106 |
| Portsea, Austl. | L6 | 70 |
| Port Shepstone, S. Afr. | H10 | 66 |
| Portsmouth, Eng., U.K. | K12 | 8 |
| Portsmouth, N.H., U.S. | D16 | 108 |
| Portsmouth, Oh., U.S. | I4 | 108 |
| Portsmouth, Va., U.S. | C10 | 112 |
| Portsoy, Scot., U.K. | D11 | 8 |
| Port Stanley, On., Can. | H14 | 110 |
| Port Sudan see Būr Sūdān, Sudan | H9 | 60 |
| Port Sulphur, La., U.S. | M7 | 114 |
| Port Talbot, Wales, U.K. | J10 | 8 |
| Port Taufiq see Būr Tawfīq, Egypt | G2 | 48 |
| *Porttipahdan tekojärvi, res., Fin.* | G20 | 6 |
| Port Townsend, Wa., U.S. | B3 | 122 |
| *Portugal, ctry., Eur.* | H6 | 4 |
| *Portugal, Cachoeira, wtfl, Braz.* | C9 | 82 |
| Portugal Cove South, Nf., Can. | F20 | 106 |
| Portugalete, Spain | B8 | 16 |
| *Portuguesa, state, Ven.* | C8 | 84 |
| *Portuguesa, stm., Ven.* | C9 | 84 |
| *Portuguese Guinea see Guinea-Bissau, ctry., Afr.* | F3 | 54 |
| Port Union, Nf., Can. | D20 | 106 |
| Port-Vendres, Fr. | J10 | 14 |
| Portville, N.Y., U.S. | E8 | 108 |
| Port Wakefield, Ak., U.S. | G18 | 100 |
| Port Wakefield, Austl. | J3 | 70 |
| Port Washington, Wi., U.S. | G8 | 110 |
| Port Wentworth, Ga., U.S. | G5 | 112 |
| Port Wing, Wi., U.S. | D4 | 110 |
| Porum, Ok., U.S. | D11 | 116 |
| Porvenir, Chile | G2 | 78 |
| Porvenir, Mex. | B7 | 90 |
| Porzuna, Spain | F7 | 16 |
| Posada, Italy | I4 | 18 |
| Posadas, Arg. | D11 | 80 |
| Posadas, Spain | H6 | 16 |
| Poschiavo, Switz. | F13 | 13 |
| Pošechon'e, Russia | C22 | 22 |
| Posen, Mi., U.S. | E12 | 110 |
| Posen see Poznań, Pol. | C16 | 10 |
| Positano, Italy | I9 | 18 |
| Posjet, Russia | I18 | 28 |
| Posse, Braz. | C5 | 79 |
| *Possession Islands, is., Ant.* | C8 | 73 |
| Pössneck, Ger. | E11 | 10 |
| *Possum Kingdom Lake, res., Tx., U.S.* | G8 | 116 |
| Post, Tx., U.S. | F5 | 116 |
| Poste-de-la-Baleine, P.Q., Can. | E17 | 96 |
| Postelle, Tn., U.S. | D2 | 112 |
| Poste Ramartina, Madag. | q21 | 67b |
| Post Falls, Id., U.S. | C9 | 122 |
| Postojna, Slvn. | D9 | 18 |
| P'ostraja Dresva, Russia | E23 | 28 |
| Postrevalle, Bol. | H10 | 82 |
| Postville, Ia., U.S. | G4 | 110 |
| Pótam, Mex. | D4 | 90 |
| *Potaro, stm., Guy.* | E13 | 84 |
| Potaro Landing, Guy. | E13 | 84 |
| Poté, Braz. | D8 | 79 |
| Poteau, Ok., U.S. | G2 | 114 |
| *Poteau, stm., U.S.* | G2 | 114 |
| Poteet, Tx., U.S. | J8 | 116 |
| Potenza, Italy | I10 | 18 |
| Potes, Spain | B7 | 16 |
| Potgietersrus, S. Afr. | E9 | 66 |
| Poth, Tx., U.S. | J8 | 116 |
| *Potholes Reservoir, res., Wa., U.S.* | C6 | 122 |
| Poti, Geor. | I6 | 26 |
| *Poti, stm., Braz.* | E10 | 76 |
| Potiraguá, Braz. | C9 | 79 |
| Potirendaba, Braz. | F4 | 79 |
| Potiskum, Nig. | F9 | 54 |
| Potlatch, Id., U.S. | D9 | 122 |
| Potomac, Il., U.S. | B9 | 114 |
| *Potomac, stm., U.S.* | I10 | 108 |
| Potomac Heights, Md., U.S. | I9 | 108 |
| Potosí, Bol. | H9 | 82 |
| Potosi, Mo., U.S. | E6 | 114 |
| *Potosí, dept., Bol.* | I8 | 82 |
| Potrerillos, Chile | D4 | 80 |
| Potrerillos, Hond. | B7 | 92 |
| Potrerillos Arriba, Pan. | I12 | 92 |
| Potrero, C.R. | G9 | 92 |
| Potrero Grande, C.R. | H11 | 92 |
| *Potro, Cerro del, mtn., S.A.* | E4 | 80 |
| Potsdam, Ger. | C13 | 10 |
| Potsdam, N.Y., U.S. | C12 | 108 |
| Potter, Ne., U.S. | J4 | 118 |
| Potterville, Mi., U.S. | H11 | 110 |
| Potts Camp, Ms., U.S. | H7 | 114 |
| Pottstown, Pa., U.S. | G11 | 108 |
| Pottsville, Pa., U.S. | G10 | 108 |
| Potwin, Ks., U.S. | N10 | 118 |
| P'otzu, Tai. | L9 | 34 |
| Pouancé, Fr. | E5 | 14 |
| Pouce-Coupe, B.C., Can. | B14 | 102 |
| *Pouce Coupé, stm., Can.* | A15 | 102 |
| Pouch Cove, Nf., Can. | E21 | 106 |
| Poughkeepsie, N.Y., U.S. | F13 | 108 |
| Poulan, Ga., U.S. | H3 | 112 |
| *Poulin-de-Courval, Lac, l., P.Q., Can.* | D3 | 106 |
| Poulsbo, Wa., U.S. | C3 | 122 |
| Poultney, Vt., U.S. | D13 | 108 |
| Poŭn, S. Kor. | G15 | 32 |
| Pound, Va., U.S. | B4 | 112 |
| *Poundmaker Indian Reserve, Sk., Can.* | F5 | 104 |
| Pouso Alegre, Braz. | G6 | 79 |
| Pouso Redondo, Braz. | D14 | 80 |
| Pouthisat, Camb. | H7 | 40 |
| Považská Bystrica, Slvk. | F18 | 10 |
| Povenec, Russia | J24 | 6 |
| Póvoa de Varzim, Port. | D3 | 16 |
| Povorino, Russia | G6 | 26 |
| Povungnituk, P.Q., Can. | D17 | 96 |
| *Povungnituk, Rivière de, stm., P.Q., Can.* | D18 | 96 |
| Powassan, On., Can. | D16 | 110 |
| Poway, Ca., U.S. | L8 | 124 |
| *Powder, stm., Or., U.S.* | F8 | 122 |
| *Powder, stm., U.S.* | B5 | 98 |
| Powderly, Ky., U.S. | E9 | 114 |
| Powderly, Tx., U.S. | F11 | 116 |
| Powell, Wy., U.S. | F17 | 122 |
| *Powell, stm., U.S.* | C3 | 112 |
| *Powell, Lake, res., U.S.* | G6 | 120 |
| *Powell, Mount, mtn., Co., U.S.* | E10 | 120 |
| Powellhurst, Or., U.S. | E3 | 122 |
| *Powell Lake, l., B.C., Can.* | G10 | 102 |
| Powell River, B.C., Can. | H10 | 102 |
| Powellton, W.V., U.S. | I5 | 108 |
| Powers, Mi., U.S. | E8 | 110 |
| Powers, Or., U.S. | H1 | 122 |
| Powers Lake, N.D., U.S. | C5 | 118 |
| Powhatan, La., U.S. | K3 | 114 |
| Powhatan, Va., U.S. | B9 | 112 |
| Powhatan Point, Oh., U.S. | H6 | 108 |
| *Powys, co., Wales, U.K.* | I10 | 8 |
| Poxoréo, Braz. | C1 | 79 |
| *Poyang Hu, l., China* | F5 | 34 |
| Poyen, Ar., U.S. | H4 | 114 |
| *Poygan, Lake, l., Wi., U.S.* | F7 | 110 |
| Poynette, Wi., U.S. | G6 | 110 |
| Požarevac, Yugo. | E5 | 20 |
| Poza Rica, Mex. | G11 | 90 |
| Poznań, Pol. | C16 | 10 |
| Pozo Almonte, Chile | I7 | 82 |
| Pozoblanco, Spain | G7 | 16 |
| Pozo Colorado, Para. | B9 | 80 |
| Pozo del Molle, Arg. | G7 | 80 |
| Pozo del Tigre, Arg. | C8 | 80 |
| Pozo Hondo, Arg. | D6 | 80 |
| Pozo Negro, Spain | o27 | 17b |
| Pozuelo de Alarcón, Spain | E8 | 16 |
| Pozuelos, Ven. | B10 | 84 |
| *Pozuelos, Laguna, l., Arg.* | B6 | 80 |
| Pozuzo, Peru | D4 | 82 |
| *Pozuzo, stm., Peru* | C4 | 82 |
| Pozzallo, Italy | M9 | 18 |
| Pozzuoli, Italy | I9 | 18 |
| Prachin Buri, Thai. | G6 | 40 |
| Prachuap Khiri Khan, Thai. | I5 | 40 |
| Pradera, Col. | F4 | 84 |
| Prades, Fr. | J9 | 14 |
| Prado, Braz. | D9 | 79 |
| Prados, Braz. | F6 | 79 |
| Prague see Praha, Czech Rep. | E14 | 10 |
| Prague, Ne., U.S. | J11 | 118 |
| Prague, Ok., U.S. | D10 | 116 |
| Praha (Prague), Czech Rep. | E14 | 10 |
| *Prahova, co., Rom.* | D10 | 20 |
| Praia, C.V. | m17 | 64a |
| Praia Grande, Braz. | E14 | 80 |
| Prainha Nova, Braz. | B11 | 82 |
| *Prairie, stm., Mn., U.S.* | C2 | 110 |
| *Prairie, stm., Wi., U.S.* | E6 | 110 |
| Prairie City, Ia., U.S. | I2 | 110 |
| Prairie City, Il., U.S. | J5 | 110 |
| Prairie City, Or., U.S. | F7 | 122 |
| Prairie du Chien, Wi., U.S. | G4 | 110 |
| Prairie du Sac, Wi., U.S. | G6 | 110 |
| Prairie Grove, Ar., U.S. | G2 | 114 |
| Prairie River, Sk., Can. | F11 | 104 |
| *Prairies, Lake of the, res., Can.* | G13 | 104 |
| Prairie View, Tx., U.S. | I11 | 116 |
| Prairie Village, Ks., U.S. | M13 | 118 |
| Prampram, Ghana | I10 | 64 |
| Pran Buri, Thai. | H5 | 40 |
| *Praslin, Lac, l., P.Q., Can.* | B4 | 106 |
| *Praslin Island, i., Sey.* | B11 | 58 |
| Prata, Braz. | E4 | 79 |
| *Prata, Rio da, stm., Braz.* | D5 | 79 |
| *Prata, Rio da, stm., Braz.* | E4 | 79 |
| Pratāpgarh, India | H6 | 44 |
| Pratápolis, Braz. | F5 | 79 |
| *Pratas Island see Tungsha Tao, i., Tai.* | G10 | 30 |
| Pratinha, Braz. | E5 | 79 |
| Prato, Italy | F6 | 18 |
| Pratt, Ks., U.S. | N9 | 118 |
| Prattsburg, N.Y., U.S. | E9 | 108 |
| Prattville, Al., U.S. | J10 | 114 |
| *Pratudão, stm., Braz.* | B6 | 79 |
| Pravdinsk, Russia | G4 | 22 |
| Pravdinsk, Russia | E26 | 22 |
| Pravdinskij, Russia | E20 | 22 |
| Praya, Indon. | G6 | 38 |
| Pr'aža, Russia | K23 | 6 |
| Prečistoje, Russia | F15 | 22 |
| Prečistoje, Russia | C23 | 22 |
| Preda, Switz. | E12 | 13 |
| Predazzo, Italy | C6 | 18 |
| Predeal, Rom. | D9 | 20 |
| Predeşti, Rom. | E7 | 20 |
| Predlitz [-Turrach], Aus. | H13 | 10 |
| Preeceville, Sk., Can. | G12 | 104 |
| Pré-en-Pail, Fr. | D6 | 14 |
| Preetz, Ger. | A10 | 10 |
| Pregarten, Aus. | G14 | 10 |
| *Pregol'a, stm., Russia* | G4 | 22 |
| Pregonero, Ven. | C7 | 84 |
| Preiļi, Lith. | F4 | 22 |
| Preiļi, Lat. | E9 | 22 |
| Prelate, Sk., Can. | H5 | 104 |
| Premnitz, Ger. | C12 | 10 |
| Premont, Tx., U.S. | L8 | 116 |
| Prentice, Wi., U.S. | E5 | 110 |
| Prentiss, Ms., U.S. | K7 | 114 |
| Prenzlau, Ger. | B13 | 10 |
| *Preparis Island, i., Myan.* | G2 | 40 |
| *Preparis North Channel, strt., Myan.* | G3 | 40 |
| *Preparis South Channel, strt., Myan.* | G3 | 40 |
| Přerov, Czech Rep. | F17 | 10 |
| Prescott, Ar., U.S. | I3 | 114 |
| Prescott, Az., U.S. | J4 | 120 |
| Prescott, On., Can. | C11 | 108 |
| Prescott, Wi., U.S. | F3 | 110 |
| *Prescott Island, i., N.T., Can.* | B13 | 96 |
| Preševo, Yugo. | G5 | 20 |
| Presho, S.D., U.S. | H7 | 118 |
| Presidencia de la Plaza, Arg. | D9 | 80 |
| Presidencia Roca, Arg. | D9 | 80 |
| Presidencia Roque Sáenz Peña, Arg. | D8 | 80 |
| Presidente Epitácio, Braz. | F2 | 79 |
| Presidente Getúlio, Braz. | D14 | 80 |
| *Presidente Hayes, dept., Para.* | C9 | 80 |
| Presidente Olegário, Braz. | E5 | 79 |
| Presidente Prudente, Braz. | G3 | 79 |
| Presidente Venceslau, Braz. | F3 | 79 |
| Presidio, Tx., U.S. | J2 | 116 |
| *Presidio, stm., Mex.* | F7 | 90 |
| Prešov, Slvk. | F21 | 10 |
| *Prespa, Lake, l., Eur.* | I4 | 20 |
| *Presque Isle, pen., Pa., U.S.* | E6 | 108 |
| Preston, Eng., U.K. | H11 | 8 |
| Preston, Ga., U.S. | G2 | 112 |
| Preston, Ia., U.S. | H5 | 110 |
| Preston, Id., U.S. | H14 | 122 |
| Preston, Ks., U.S. | N9 | 118 |
| Preston, Mn., U.S. | G3 | 110 |
| Prestonsburg, Ky., U.S. | B4 | 112 |
| Prestville, Ab., Can. | B16 | 102 |
| Prestwick, Scot., U.K. | F9 | 8 |
| *Preto, stm., Braz.* | B4 | 79 |
| *Preto, stm., Braz.* | D5 | 79 |
| *Preto, stm., Braz.* | E3 | 79 |
| *Preto, stm., Braz.* | F4 | 79 |
| *Preto, stm., Braz.* | C10 | 82 |
| *Preto, stm., Braz.* | H10 | 84 |
| *Preto do Igapó-açu, stm., Braz.* | J12 | 84 |
| Pretoria, S. Afr. | E9 | 66 |
| Pretty Prairie, Ks., U.S. | N9 | 118 |
| Préveza, Grc. | K4 | 20 |
| Prey Vêng, Camb. | I8 | 40 |
| *Pribilof Islands, is., Ak., U.S.* | H9 | 100 |
| Priboj, Yugo. | F3 | 20 |
| Příbram, Czech Rep. | F14 | 10 |
| Price, Tx., U.S. | J2 | 114 |
| Price, Ut., U.S. | E6 | 120 |
| *Price, stm., Ut., U.S.* | E6 | 120 |
| *Price Island, i., B.C., Can.* | E6 | 102 |
| Prichard, Al., U.S. | L8 | 114 |
| Priddy, Tx., U.S. | H8 | 116 |
| Priego de Córdoba, Spain | H7 | 16 |
| Priekule, Lat. | E4 | 22 |
| Priekule, Lith. | F4 | 22 |
| Prienai, Lith. | G6 | 22 |
| Prieska, S. Afr. | G6 | 66 |
| *Priest, stm., Id., U.S.* | B9 | 122 |
| *Priest Lake, l., Id., U.S.* | B9 | 122 |
| *Priestley, Mount, mtn., B.C., Can.* | B6 | 102 |
| Priest River, Id., U.S. | B9 | 122 |
| Prievidza, Slvk. | G18 | 10 |
| Prijedor, Bos. | E11 | 18 |
| Prijutovo, Russia | G8 | 26 |
| *Prikaspijskaja nizmennost', pl.* | H7 | 26 |
| Prilep, Mac. | H5 | 20 |
| Priluki, Ukr. | G4 | 26 |
| Primeiro de Maio, Braz. | G3 | 79 |
| Primera, Tx., U.S. | M9 | 116 |
| *Primero, stm., Arg.* | F7 | 80 |
| Primghar, Ia., U.S. | H12 | 118 |
| Primorje [Warnicken], Russia | G3 | 22 |
| Primorsk, Russia | G3 | 22 |
| Primorsk, Russia | A11 | 22 |
| *Primrose Lake, l., Can.* | D5 | 104 |
| Prince Albert, S. Afr. | I6 | 66 |
| Prince Albert, Sk., Can. | E9 | 104 |
| *Prince Albert Mountains, mts., Ant.* | C8 | 73 |
| *Prince Albert National Park, Sk., Can.* | D8 | 104 |
| *Prince Albert Sound, strt., N.T., Can.* | B9 | 96 |
| *Prince Charles Island, i., N.T., Can.* | C17 | 96 |
| *Prince Charles Mountains, mts., Ant.* | C5 | 73 |
| *Prince Edward Island, prov., Can.* | G20 | 96 |
| *Prince Edward Island National Park, P.E., Can.* | F10 | 106 |
| *Prince Edward Islands, is., S. Afr.* | M7 | 126 |
| Prince Frederick, Md., U.S. | I10 | 108 |
| Prince George, B.C., Can. | D12 | 102 |
| Prince George, Va., U.S. | B9 | 112 |
| *Prince Leopold Island, i., N.T., Can.* | B15 | 96 |
| *Prince of Wales, Cape, c., Ak., U.S.* | D10 | 100 |
| *Prince of Wales Island, i., Ak., U.S.* | I28 | 100 |
| *Prince of Wales Island, i., Austl.* | B8 | 68 |
| *Prince of Wales Island, i., N.T., Can.* | B13 | 96 |
| *Prince of Wales Strait, strt., N.T., Can.* | B9 | 96 |
| *Prince Olav Coast, Ant.* | B4 | 73 |
| *Prince Patrick Island, i., N.T., Can.* | B8 | 86 |
| *Prince Regent Inlet, b., N.T., Can.* | B14 | 96 |
| Prince Rupert, B.C., Can. | C4 | 102 |
| Princess Anne, Md., U.S. | I11 | 108 |
| *Princess Astrid Coast, Ant.* | C3 | 73 |
| *Princess Martha Coast, Ant.* | C2 | 73 |
| *Princess Ragnhild Coast, Ant.* | C3 | 73 |
| *Princess Royal Channel, strt., B.C., Can.* | D6 | 102 |
| *Princess Royal Island, i., B.C., Can.* | E6 | 102 |
| Princes Town, Trin. | I14 | 94 |
| Princeton, B.C., Can. | H14 | 102 |
| Princeton, Ca., U.S. | E3 | 124 |
| Princeton, Il., U.S. | I6 | 110 |
| Princeton, In., U.S. | D9 | 114 |
| Princeton, Ky., U.S. | E9 | 114 |
| Princeton, Me., U.S. | B19 | 108 |
| Princeton, Mi., U.S. | D8 | 110 |
| Princeton, Mn., U.S. | E2 | 110 |
| Princeton, Mo., U.S. | B3 | 114 |
| Princeton, N.C., U.S. | D8 | 112 |
| Princeton, Nf., Can. | D20 | 106 |
| Princeton, N.J., U.S. | G12 | 108 |
| Princeton, Wi., U.S. | G6 | 110 |
| Princeton, W.V., U.S. | B5 | 112 |
| Princeville, Il., U.S. | J6 | 110 |
| Princeville, N.C., U.S. | D9 | 112 |
| Princeville, P.Q., Can. | A15 | 108 |
| *Prince William Sound, strt., Ak., U.S.* | F21 | 100 |
| *Príncipe, i., S. Tom./P.* | A1 | 58 |
| *Principe Channel, strt., B.C., Can.* | D4 | 102 |
| Príncipe da Beira, Braz. | E9 | 82 |
| Prineville, Or., U.S. | F5 | 122 |
| Prinzapolka, Nic. | D11 | 92 |
| *Prinzapolka, stm., Nic.* | D11 | 92 |
| *Prior, Cabo, c., Spain* | B3 | 16 |
| Prioz'orsk, Russia | K22 | 6 |
| *Pripet Marshes see Polesje, reg., Eur.* | G3 | 26 |
| Priština, Yugo. | G5 | 20 |
| Pritchett, Co., U.S. | N5 | 118 |
| Pritzwalk, Ger. | B12 | 10 |
| Privas, Fr. | H11 | 14 |
| Priverno, Italy | H8 | 18 |
| Privolžsk, Russia | D24 | 22 |
| *Privolžskaja vozvyšennost', plat., Russia* | G7 | 26 |
| Privolžskij, Russia | G7 | 26 |
| Prizren, Yugo. | G4 | 20 |
| Prizzi, Italy | L8 | 18 |
| Prnjavor, Bos. | E12 | 18 |
| Probolinggo, Indon. | j16 | 39a |
| Probstzella, Ger. | E11 | 10 |
| Procter, B.C., Can. | H18 | 102 |
| Proctor, Mn., U.S. | D3 | 110 |
| Proctor, Vt., U.S. | D13 | 108 |
| Proddatūr, India | E5 | 46 |
| Progreso, Mex. | G15 | 90 |
| Progreso, Ur. | H10 | 80 |
| Project City, Ca., U.S. | D3 | 124 |
| Prokopjevsk, Russia | G9 | 28 |
| Prokuplje, Yugo. | F5 | 20 |
| Proletarij, Russia | C14 | 22 |
| Proletarskij, Russia | F20 | 22 |
| Prome (Pyè), Myan. | E3 | 40 |
| Promissão, Braz. | F4 | 79 |
| Promontogno, Switz. | F12 | 13 |
| Pronsk, Russia | G22 | 22 |
| *Prophet, stm., B.C., Can.* | E8 | 96 |
| Prophetstown, Il., U.S. | I6 | 110 |
| Propriá, Braz. | F11 | 76 |
| Propriano, Fr. | m23 | 15a |
| Proserpine, Austl. | C8 | 70 |
| Prospect, Oh., U.S. | G3 | 108 |
| Prosser, Wa., U.S. | D6 | 122 |
| Prostějov, Czech Rep. | F17 | 10 |
| Proston, Austl. | F9 | 70 |
| Protection, Ks., U.S. | N8 | 118 |
| Protem, S. Afr. | J5 | 66 |
| Protville, Tun. | M5 | 18 |
| Provadija, Bul. | F11 | 20 |
| Provencal, La., U.S. | K3 | 114 |
| *Provence, hist. reg., Fr.* | I13 | 14 |
| Providence, Ky., U.S. | E9 | 114 |
| Providence, R.I., U.S. | F15 | 108 |
| Providence, Ut., U.S. | C5 | 120 |
| *Providence, Cape, c., N.Z.* | F1 | 72 |
| *Providence Island, i., Sey.* | C10 | 58 |
| *Providencia, Isla de, i., Col.* | D8 | 94 |
| *Providenciales, i., T./C. Is.* | D8 | 94 |
| Providenija, Russia | E29 | 28 |
| Provincetown, Ma., U.S. | E16 | 108 |
| Provins, Fr. | D10 | 14 |
| Provo, Ut., U.S. | D5 | 120 |
| *Provo, stm., Ut., U.S.* | D5 | 120 |
| Provost, Ab., Can. | F4 | 104 |
| Prudentópolis, Braz. | C13 | 80 |
| *Prudhoe Bay, b., Ak., U.S.* | A20 | 100 |
| *Prudhoe Island, i., Austl.* | C8 | 70 |
| Prudnik, Pol. | E17 | 10 |
| Prüm, Ger. | E6 | 10 |
| Pruszków, Pol. | C20 | 10 |
| *Prut, stm., Eur.* | D12 | 20 |
| Prutz, Aus. | H10 | 10 |
| Pružany, Bela. | I7 | 22 |
| *Prydz Bay, b., Ant.* | B5 | 73 |
| Pryor, Ok., U.S. | C11 | 116 |
| *Prypjac', stm., Eur.* | G3 | 26 |
| Przasnysz, Pol. | B20 | 10 |
| Przedbórz, Pol. | D19 | 10 |
| Przemyśl, Pol. | F22 | 10 |
| Przeworsk, Pol. | E22 | 10 |
| Pskov, Russia | D11 | 22 |
| *Pskovskoje ozero, l., Eur.* | C11 | 22 |
| Pszczyna, Pol. | F18 | 10 |
| *Ptarmigan, Cape, c., N.T., Can.* | B9 | 96 |
| Ptolemaïs, Grc. | I5 | 20 |
| Ptuj, Slvn. | C10 | 18 |
| Puán, Arg. | I7 | 80 |
| Puan, S. Kor. | H14 | 32 |
| Pubnico, N.S., Can. | I8 | 106 |
| Pucallpa, Peru | C4 | 82 |
| Pucara, Bol. | H9 | 82 |
| Pucarani, Bol. | G7 | 82 |
| *Puccha, stm., Peru* | C3 | 82 |
| Pučež, Russia | E26 | 22 |
| Pucheng, China | H7 | 34 |
| Pucheta, Arg. | E10 | 80 |
| Puck, Pol. | A18 | 10 |
| *Pudding, stm., Or., U.S.* | E3 | 122 |
| *Pudops Dam, Nf., Can.* | D17 | 106 |
| Pudož, Russia | E5 | 26 |
| *Puduari, stm., Braz.* | I12 | 84 |
| Puduhe, China | B7 | 40 |
| Pudukkottai, India | G5 | 46 |
| *Puebla, state, Mex.* | H10 | 90 |
| Puebla [de Zaragoza], Mex. | H10 | 90 |
| Pueblo, Co., U.S. | F12 | 120 |
| Pueblo Libertador, Arg. | F9 | 80 |
| Pueblo Nuevo, Col. | C5 | 84 |
| Pueblo Nuevo, Nic. | D8 | 92 |
| Pueblo Nuevo, Ven. | B8 | 84 |
| Pueblo Nuevo Tiquisate, Guat. | C3 | 92 |
| Pueblo of Acoma, N.M., U.S. | I9 | 120 |
| Puebloviejo, Ec. | H3 | 84 |
| *Pueblo Viejo, Laguna, b., Mex.* | F11 | 90 |
| Pueblo Yaqui, Mex. | D4 | 90 |
| Puelches, Arg. | J6 | 80 |
| Puente Alto, Chile | G3 | 80 |
| Puente Genil, Spain | H7 | 16 |
| *Puerco, stm., U.S.* | I7 | 120 |
| *Puerco, Rio, stm., N.M., U.S.* | J10 | 120 |
| Puerto Acosta, Bol. | F7 | 82 |
| Puerto Adela, Para. | C11 | 80 |
| Puerto Aisén, Chile | F2 | 78 |
| Puerto Alegre, Bol. | E11 | 82 |
| Puerto Ángel, Mex. | J11 | 90 |
| Puerto Arista, Mex. | J13 | 90 |
| Puerto Armuelles, Pan. | C1 | 84 |
| Puerto Asís, Col. | G4 | 84 |
| Puerto Ayacucho, Ven. | E9 | 84 |
| Puerto Bahía Negra, Para. | I12 | 82 |
| Puerto Baquerizo Moreno, Ec. | j14 | 84a |
| Puerto Barrios, Guat. | B6 | 92 |
| Puerto Bermejo, Arg. | D9 | 80 |
| Puerto Bermúdez, Peru | D4 | 82 |
| Puerto Berrío, Col. | D5 | 84 |
| Puerto Bolívar, Ec. | I3 | 84 |
| Puerto Boyacá, Col. | E5 | 84 |
| Puerto Busch, Bol. | I13 | 82 |
| Puerto Cabello, Ven. | B8 | 84 |
| Puerto Cabezas, Nic. | C11 | 92 |
| Puerto Carreño, Col. | D9 | 84 |
| Puerto Casado, Para. | B10 | 80 |
| Puerto Castilla, Hond. | A8 | 92 |
| Puerto Chicama, Peru | B2 | 82 |
| Puerto Colombia, Col. | B5 | 84 |
| Puerto Cortés, Hond. | B7 | 92 |
| Puerto Cumarebo, Ven. | B8 | 84 |
| Puerto de Eten, Peru | B2 | 82 |
| Puerto de la Cruz, Spain | o24 | 17b |
| Puerto Delicia, Arg. | D11 | 80 |
| Puerto de Lomas, Peru | F4 | 82 |
| Puerto Delón, Hond. | C9 | 92 |
| Puerto del Rosario, Spain | o27 | 17b |
| Puerto El Triunfo, El Sal. | D6 | 92 |
| Puerto Escondido, Mex. | J11 | 90 |
| Puerto Esperanza, Arg. | D11 | 80 |
| Puerto Fonciere, Para. | B10 | 80 |
| Puerto Francisco de Orellana, Ec. | H4 | 84 |
| Puerto Guaraní, Para. | I13 | 82 |
| Puerto Heath, Bol. | E7 | 82 |
| Puerto Iguazú, Arg. | C11 | 80 |
| Puerto Inírida, Col. | F9 | 84 |
| Puerto Jiménez, C.R. | I11 | 92 |
| Puerto Juárez, Mex. | G16 | 90 |
| Puerto la Cruz, Ven. | B10 | 84 |
| Puerto Leda, Para. | I12 | 82 |
| Puerto Leguízamo, Col. | H5 | 84 |
| Puerto Lempira, Hond. | B11 | 92 |
| Puerto Libertad, Arg. | C11 | 80 |
| Puerto Libertad, Mex. | C3 | 90 |
| Puerto Limón, Col. | F6 | 84 |
| Puerto Limón, C.R. | G11 | 92 |
| Puertollano, Spain | G7 | 16 |
| Puerto López, Col. | E6 | 84 |
| Puerto Madero, Mex. | C2 | 92 |
| Puerto Maldonado, Peru | E7 | 82 |
| Puerto Manatí, Cuba | D6 | 94 |
| Puerto Mihanovich, Para. | I13 | 82 |
| Puerto Montt, Chile | E2 | 78 |
| Puerto Morazán, Nic. | E7 | 92 |
| Puerto Morelos, Mex. | G16 | 90 |
| Puerto Nariño, Col. | E9 | 84 |
| Puerto Natales, Chile | G2 | 78 |
| Puerto Padre, Cuba | D6 | 94 |
| Puerto Páez, Ven. | D9 | 84 |
| Puerto Peñasco, Mex. | B3 | 90 |
| Puerto Pilón, Pan. | H15 | 92 |
| Puerto Pinasco, Para. | B10 | 80 |
| Puerto Piray, Arg. | D11 | 80 |
| Puerto Píritu, Ven. | B10 | 84 |
| Puerto Plata, Dom. Rep. | E9 | 94 |
| Puerto Portillo, Peru | C5 | 82 |
| Puerto Princesa, Phil. | D6 | 38 |
| Puerto Real, Spain | I5 | 16 |
| Puerto Rico, Arg. | D11 | 80 |
| Puerto Rico, Bol. | D8 | 82 |
| Puerto Rico, Col. | G5 | 84 |
| *Puerto Rico, dep., N.A.* | E11 | 94 |
| *Puerto Rico Trench* | G13 | 86 |
| Puerto Rondón, Col. | D7 | 84 |
| Puerto Saavedra, Chile | J2 | 80 |
| Puerto Salgar, Col. | E5 | 84 |
| Puerto Sandino, Nic. | E8 | 92 |
| Puerto San José, Guat. | D4 | 92 |
| Puerto San Julián, Arg. | F3 | 78 |
| Puerto Santa Cruz, Arg. | G3 | 78 |
| Puerto Sastre, Para. | B10 | 80 |
| Puerto Siles, Bol. | E9 | 82 |
| Puerto Suárez, Bol. | H13 | 82 |
| Puerto Supe, Peru | D3 | 82 |
| Puerto Tejada, Col. | F4 | 84 |
| Puerto Tolosa, Col. | H5 | 84 |
| Puerto Umbría, Col. | G4 | 84 |
| Puerto Vallarta, Mex. | G7 | 90 |
| Puerto Varas, Chile | E2 | 78 |
| Puerto Victoria, Arg. | D11 | 80 |
| Puerto Victoria, Peru | C4 | 82 |
| Puerto Viejo, C.R. | G11 | 92 |
| Puerto Viejo, C.R. | H12 | 92 |
| Puerto Villamil, Ec. | j13 | 84a |
| Puerto Villamizar, Col. | C6 | 84 |
| Puerto Villarroel, Bol. | G9 | 82 |
| Puerto Wilches, Col. | D6 | 84 |
| Puerto Ybapobó, Para. | B10 | 80 |
| *Pueyrredón, Lago (Lago Cochrane), l., S.A.* | F2 | 78 |
| Pugačov, Russia | G7 | 26 |
| *Puget Sound, strt., Wa., U.S.* | C3 | 122 |
| Puget-Théniers, Fr. | I13 | 14 |
| *Puglia, prov., Italy* | I11 | 18 |
| Pugwash, N.S., Can. | G10 | 106 |
| Puhaviĉy, Bela. | H11 | 22 |
| Puica, Peru | F5 | 82 |
| Puigcerdà, Spain | C13 | 16 |
| *Puigmal, mtn., Eur.* | C14 | 16 |
| *Puinahua, Canal de, mth., Peru* | A4 | 82 |
| Pujehun, S.L. | H4 | 64 |
| Pujiang, China | F8 | 34 |
| Pujilí, Ec. | H3 | 84 |
| Pukch'ang, N. Kor. | D14 | 32 |
| Pukch'ŏng, N. Kor. | C16 | 32 |
| *Pukeashun Mountain, mtn., B.C., Can.* | F15 | 102 |
| Pukekohe, N.Z. | B5 | 72 |
| *Pukhan-gang, stm., Asia* | F15 | 32 |
| Pukou, China | C7 | 34 |
| Puksoozero, Russia | J27 | 6 |
| Pula, Cro. | E8 | 18 |
| Pulacayo, Bol. | I8 | 82 |
| *Púlar, Cerro, mtn., Chile* | C4 | 80 |
| Pulaski, N.Y., U.S. | D10 | 108 |
| Pulaski, Tn., U.S. | G10 | 114 |
| Pulaski, Va., U.S. | B6 | 112 |
| Pulaski, Wi., U.S. | F7 | 110 |
| Puławy, Pol. | D21 | 10 |
| Pulgaon, India | B5 | 46 |
| Puli, Tai. | L9 | 34 |
| Puliyangudi, India | H4 | 46 |
| Pullman, Wa., U.S. | D8 | 122 |
| Púllo, Peru | F5 | 82 |
| Pully, Switz. | E6 | 13 |
| *Pulog, Mount, mtn., Phil.* | m19 | 39b |
| Pulsano, Italy | I12 | 18 |
| Pułtusk, Pol. | C21 | 10 |
| *Puná, Isla, i., Ec.* | I2 | 84 |
| Punakha, Bhu. | G13 | 44 |
| Punata, Bol. | G9 | 82 |
| Pūnch, India | D6 | 44 |
| Punchaw, B.C., Can. | D11 | 102 |
| Punduga, Russia | A23 | 22 |
| Pune (Poona), India | C2 | 46 |
| *Púngoè, stm., Afr.* | B11 | 66 |
| P'ungsan, N. Kor. | C16 | 32 |
| Punia, D.R.C. | B5 | 58 |
| *Punilla, Sierra de la, mts., Arg.* | E4 | 80 |
| Puning, China | L5 | 34 |
| Punitaqui, Chile | F3 | 80 |
| *Punjab, state, India* | E6 | 44 |
| Punnichy, Sk., Can. | G10 | 104 |
| Puno, Peru | F6 | 82 |
| *Puno, dept., Peru* | F8 | 82 |
| *Punta, Cerro de, mtn., P.R.* | E11 | 94 |
| Punta Alta, Arg. | J7 | 80 |
| Punta Arenas, Chile | G2 | 78 |
| *Punta Banda, Cabo, c., Mex.* | B1 | 90 |
| Punta Cardón, Ven. | B7 | 84 |
| Punta Colnett, Mex. | B1 | 90 |
| Punta de Bombón, Peru | G6 | 82 |
| Punta de Díaz, Chile | E3 | 80 |
| Punta de Piedras, Chile | D3 | 80 |
| Punta del Este, Ur. | H11 | 80 |
| Punta de los Llanos, Arg. | F5 | 80 |
| Punta de Mata, Ven. | C11 | 84 |
| Punta de Piedras, Ven. | B10 | 84 |
| Punta Gorda, Belize | I15 | 90 |
| Punta Gorda, Fl., U.S. | M4 | 112 |
| Punta Gorda, Nic. | F11 | 92 |
| *Punta Gorda, stm., Nic.* | F11 | 92 |
| *Punta Gorda, Bahía de, b., Nic.* | F11 | 92 |
| *Punta Negra, Salar de, pl., Chile* | C4 | 80 |
| Punta Prieta, Mex. | C2 | 90 |
| Puntarenas, C.R. | H10 | 92 |
| *Puntarenas, prov., C.R.* | I11 | 92 |
| Puntas del Sauce, Ur. | G10 | 80 |
| Punto Fijo, Ven. | B7 | 84 |
| *Puntzi Lake, l., B.C., Can.* | E10 | 102 |
| Punxsutawney, Pa., U.S. | G8 | 108 |
| Puolanka, Fin. | I20 | 6 |
| Puqi, China | F9 | 30 |
| Puquio, Peru | F4 | 82 |
| *Pur, stm., Russia* | D7 | 28 |
| *Puracé, Volcán, vol., Col.* | F4 | 84 |
| Purcell, Ok., U.S. | D9 | 116 |
| *Purcell Mountains, mts., N.A.* | G18 | 102 |
| Purcellville, Va., U.S. | H9 | 108 |
| Purdy, Mo., U.S. | F3 | 114 |
| *Purgatoire, stm., Co., U.S.* | N4 | 118 |
| Puri, India | K11 | 44 |
| Purificación, Col. | F5 | 84 |
| Purificación, Mex. | H7 | 90 |
| *Purificación, stm., Mex.* | E10 | 90 |
| *Purikari neem, c., Est.* | B8 | 22 |
| Purmerend, Neth. | C6 | 12 |
| Pūrnia, India | H12 | 44 |
| Purros, Nmb. | B1 | 66 |
| *Puruí, stm., Braz.* | H8 | 84 |
| Puruliya, India | I12 | 44 |
| *Puruni, stm., Guy.* | D13 | 84 |
| *Purus (Purús), stm., S.A.* | D6 | 76 |
| Purvis, Ms., U.S. | K7 | 114 |
| Purwakarta, Indon. | j13 | 39a |
| Purwokerto, Indon. | j14 | 39a |
| Pusan, S. Kor. | H17 | 32 |

| Name | Map Ref. | Page |
|---|---|---|
| Pushkar, India | G6 | 44 |
| Pushthrough, Nf., Can. | E17 | 106 |
| Puskiakiwenin Indian Reserve, Ab., Can. | E4 | 104 |
| Puškin, Russia | B13 | 22 |
| Puškino, Russia | E20 | 22 |
| Puskinskije Gory, Russia | D11 | 22 |
| Puskwaskau, stm., Ab., Can. | B17 | 102 |
| Püspökladány, Hung. | H21 | 10 |
| Püssi, Est. | B10 | 22 |
| Pustoška, Russia | E12 | 22 |
| Putaendo, Chile | G3 | 80 |
| Putao, Myan. | G17 | 44 |
| Put'atino, Russia | G24 | 22 |
| Putian, China | J8 | 34 |
| Putina, Peru | F7 | 82 |
| Puting, Tanjung, c., Indon. | F5 | 38 |
| Putnam, Ct., U.S. | F15 | 108 |
| Putnam, Tx., U.S. | G7 | 116 |
| Putney, Ga., U.S. | H2 | 112 |
| Putney, Vt., U.S. | E14 | 108 |
| Putorana, plato, plat., Russia | D17 | 26 |
| Putre, Chile | H7 | 82 |
| Puttalam, Sri L. | H5 | 46 |
| Puttgarden, Ger. | A11 | 10 |
| Putú, Chile | H2 | 80 |
| Putumayo, ter., Col. | G4 | 84 |
| Putumayo (Içá), stm., S.A. | I7 | 84 |
| Putuo, China | F11 | 34 |
| Putyla, Ukr. | A9 | 20 |
| Pu'uhonua o Honaunau National Historical Park, Hi., U.S. | r18 | 125a |
| Puukohola National Historic Site, hist., Hi., U.S. | q18 | 125a |
| Puula, l., Fin. | K20 | 6 |
| Puumala, Fin. | K21 | 6 |
| Puurmani, Est. | C9 | 22 |
| Puxi, China | J8 | 34 |
| Puxico, Mo., U.S. | F6 | 114 |
| Puyallup, Wa., U.S. | C3 | 122 |
| Puyallup, stm., Wa., U.S. | D3 | 122 |
| Puyang, China | H2 | 32 |
| Puyango (Tumbes), stm., S.A. | I3 | 84 |
| Puy-de-Dôme, dept., Fr. | G10 | 14 |
| Puylaurens, Fr. | I9 | 14 |
| Puyo, Ec. | H4 | 84 |
| Puyô, S. Kor. | G14 | 32 |
| Pweto, D.R.C. | C5 | 58 |
| Pyapon, Myan. | F3 | 40 |
| Pyaye, Myan. | F3 | 40 |
| Pye Islands, is., Ak., U.S. | G19 | 100 |
| Pyhäjoki, Fin. | I19 | 6 |
| Pyhäjärvi, l., Fin. | J21 | 6 |
| Pyinmana, Myan. | E4 | 40 |
| Pymatuning Reservoir, res., U.S. | F6 | 108 |
| Pyŏktong, N. Kor. | C13 | 32 |
| Pyŏlch'ang-ni, N. Kor. | D14 | 32 |
| P'yŏngch'ang, S. Kor. | F16 | 32 |
| P'yŏngsan, N. Kor. | E14 | 32 |
| P'yŏngt'aek, S. Kor. | F15 | 32 |
| P'yŏngyang, N. Kor. | D13 | 32 |
| Pyote, Tx., U.S. | H3 | 116 |
| Pyramid Lake, l., Nv., U.S. | D6 | 124 |
| Pyrenees, mts., Eur. | C13 | 16 |
| Pyrénées-Atlantiques, dept., Fr. | I6 | 14 |
| Pyrénées-Orientales, dept., Fr. | J9 | 14 |
| Pyrzyce, Pol. | B14 | 10 |
| Pytalovo, Russia | D10 | 22 |
| Pyu, Myan. | E4 | 40 |
| Pyuntaza, Myan. | F4 | 40 |

**Q**

| Name | Map Ref. | Page |
|---|---|---|
| Qacentina (Constantine), Alg. | B14 | 62 |
| Qā'emshahr, Iran | C12 | 48 |
| Qā'en, Iran | E15 | 48 |
| Qaidam Pendi, China | B16 | 44 |
| Qalāt, Afg. | D2 | 44 |
| Qal'at ash-Shaqīf (Beaufort Castle), hist., Leb. | B5 | 50 |
| Qal'at Bīshah, Sau. Ar. | D3 | 47 |
| Qal'at Ṣāliḥ, Iraq | F9 | 48 |
| Qal'at Sukkar, Iraq | F9 | 48 |
| Qal'eh-ye Now, Afg. | C2 | 44 |
| Qallābāt, Sudan | K9 | 60 |
| Qalqīlya, W.B. | D3 | 50 |
| Qamar, Ghubbat al-, b., Yemen | F8 | 47 |
| Qamdo, China | E6 | 30 |
| Qānā, Leb. | B4 | 50 |
| Qanā, Sau. Ar. | H6 | 48 |
| Qandahār, Afg. | E1 | 44 |
| Qandala, Som. | F10 | 56 |
| Qantur, Sudan | M3 | 60 |
| Qārah, Sau. Ar. | G6 | 48 |
| Qardho, Som. | G10 | 56 |
| Qarqan, stm., China | D4 | 30 |
| Qārūn, Birkat, l., Egypt | C6 | 60 |
| Qāsh, Nahr al- (Gash), stm., Afr. | E8 | 56 |
| Qaşr al-Farāfirah, Egypt | D4 | 60 |
| Qasr el-Boukhari, Alg. | C12 | 62 |
| Qaşr-e Shīrīn, Iran | D7 | 48 |
| Qa'tabah, Yemen | H4 | 47 |
| Qaţanā, Syria | B6 | 50 |
| Qatar (Qaṭar), ctry., Asia | D5 | 42 |
| Qattara Depression see Qaṭṭārah, Munkhafaḍ al-, depr., Egypt | B4 | 60 |
| Qaṭṭārah, Munkhafaḍ al- (Qattara Depression), depr., Egypt | B4 | 60 |
| Qazimämmäd, Azer. | I7 | 26 |
| Qazvīn, Iran | C11 | 48 |
| Qesari, Ḥorbat (Caesarea), hist., Isr. | C3 | 50 |
| Qeshm, Iran | H14 | 48 |
| Qeshm, Jazīreh-ye, i., Iran | H13 | 48 |
| Qetura, Isr. | I4 | 50 |
| Qezel Owzan, stm., Iran | C10 | 48 |
| Qianfang, China | G5 | 34 |
| Qianqi, China | H9 | 34 |
| Qianyang, China | F9 | 30 |
| Qiaogou, China | C4 | 34 |
| Qiddîsah Kātrīnâ, Dayr al- (Monastery of Saint Catherine), Egypt | G3 | 48 |
| Qidong, China | D10 | 34 |
| Qidu, China | E6 | 34 |
| Qiemo, China | A11 | 44 |
| Qift (Coptos), Egypt | D7 | 60 |
| Qijiang, China | F8 | 30 |
| Qijiawan, China | E3 | 34 |
| Qila Lādgasht, Pak. | H17 | 48 |
| Qilian Shan, China | D6 | 30 |
| Qilian Shan, mts., China | D6 | 30 |
| Qimen, China | J2 | 34 |
| Qinā, Egypt | D7 | 60 |
| Qinā, Wādī, val., Egypt | H2 | 48 |
| Qingchengzi, China | C11 | 32 |
| Qingdao (Tsingtao), China | G8 | 32 |
| Qinghai (Tsinghai), prov., China | D6 | 30 |
| Qinghai Hu, l., China | D7 | 30 |
| Qinghezhen, China | F5 | 32 |

| Name | Map Ref. | Page |
|---|---|---|
| Qingjiang, China | G4 | 34 |
| Qingjiang, China | B8 | 34 |
| Qinglong, China | K1 | 34 |
| Qinglong, China | B8 | 40 |
| Qingpu, China | D10 | 34 |
| Qingshan, China | E3 | 34 |
| Qingshui, stm., China | D8 | 30 |
| Qingshui, stm., China | F8 | 30 |
| Qingtang, China | K2 | 34 |
| Qingyang, China | D8 | 30 |
| Qingyangzhen, China | D9 | 34 |
| Qingyuan, China | G8 | 30 |
| Qingyuan, China | L2 | 34 |
| Qingzhou, China | L5 | 34 |
| Qinhuangdao (Chinwangtao), China | D7 | 32 |
| Qin Ling, mts., China | E8 | 30 |
| Qinzhou, China | D10 | 40 |
| Qionglai, China | E7 | 30 |
| Qiongzhong, China | E10 | 40 |
| Qiongzhou Haixia, strt., China | D11 | 40 |
| Qipanshan, China | A5 | 32 |
| Qiqian, China | A11 | 30 |
| Qiqihar (Tsitsihar), China | B11 | 30 |
| Qiryat Ata, Isr. | C4 | 50 |
| Qiryat Bialik, Isr. | C4 | 50 |
| Qiryat Gat, Isr. | E3 | 50 |
| Qiryat Mal'akhi, Isr. | E3 | 50 |
| Qiryat Motzkin, Isr. | C4 | 50 |
| Qiryat Ono, Isr. | D3 | 50 |
| Qiryat Shemona, Isr. | B5 | 50 |
| Qishn, Yemen | G7 | 47 |
| Qishon, stm., Asia | C4 | 50 |
| Qishuyan, China | D9 | 34 |
| Qitai, China | C4 | 30 |
| Qiyang, China | A11 | 40 |
| Qnadsa, Alg. | C6 | 62 |
| Qogir Feng (K2), mtn., Asia | C7 | 44 |
| Qom, Iran | D11 | 48 |
| Qomsheh, Iran | E11 | 48 |
| Qondūz, Afg. | J11 | 26 |
| Qondūz, stm., Afg. | B3 | 44 |
| Qonggyai, China | F5 | 30 |
| Qorveh, Iran | D9 | 48 |
| Quabbin Reservoir, res., Ma., U.S. | E14 | 108 |
| Quadra Island, i., B.C., Can. | G9 | 102 |
| Quadros, Lagoa dos, b., Braz. | E13 | 80 |
| Quakenbrück, Ger. | C7 | 10 |
| Quakertown, Pa., U.S. | G11 | 108 |
| Qualicum Beach, B.C., Can. | H10 | 102 |
| Quanah, Tx., U.S. | E7 | 116 |
| Quangang, China | J8 | 34 |
| Quang Ngai, Viet. | G10 | 40 |
| Quang Trach, Viet. | F9 | 40 |
| Quantico, Va., U.S. | I9 | 108 |
| Quanzhou (Chuanchou), China | K7 | 34 |
| Qu'Appelle, Sk., Can. | H11 | 104 |
| Qu'Appelle, stm., Can. | H13 | 104 |
| Qu'Appelle Dam, Sk., Can. | G8 | 104 |
| Quaraí, Braz. | F10 | 80 |
| Quaraí, stm., S.A. | F10 | 80 |
| Quarryville, Pa., U.S. | H10 | 108 |
| Quartu Sant'Elena, Italy | J4 | 18 |
| Quartz Hill, Ca., U.S. | J7 | 124 |
| Quartz Lake, l., N.T., Can. | B16 | 96 |
| Quartz Mountain, mtn., Or., U.S. | G3 | 122 |
| Quartzsite, Az., U.S. | K2 | 120 |
| Quatsino Sound, strt., B.C., Can. | G7 | 102 |
| Qūchān, Iran | C15 | 48 |
| Queanbeyan, Austl. | J8 | 70 |
| Québec, P.Q., Can. | F2 | 106 |
| Québec, prov., Can. | F18 | 96 |
| Quebeck, Tn., U.S. | G11 | 114 |
| Quebra-Anzol, stm., Braz. | E5 | 79 |
| Quebracho, Ur. | F10 | 80 |
| Quedas, Moz. | B11 | 66 |
| Quedlinburg, Ger. | D11 | 10 |
| Queen Alexandra Range, mts., Ant. | D8 | 73 |
| Queen Bess, Mount, mtn., B.C., Can. | F10 | 102 |
| Queen Charlotte, B.C., Can. | D2 | 102 |
| Queen Charlotte Islands, is., B.C., Can. | D2 | 102 |
| Queen Charlotte Mountains, mts., B.C., Can. | D2 | 102 |
| Queen Charlotte Sound, strt., B.C., Can. | F5 | 102 |
| Queen Charlotte Strait, strt., B.C., Can. | G7 | 102 |
| Queen City, Mo., U.S. | B4 | 114 |
| Queen City, Tx., U.S. | I2 | 114 |
| Queen Elizabeth Islands, is., N.T., Can. | B9 | 86 |
| Queen Mary Coast, Ant. | B6 | 73 |
| Queen Maud Gulf, b., N.T., Can. | C12 | 96 |
| Queen Maud Land, reg., Ant. | C3 | 73 |
| Queen Maud Mountains, mts., Ant. | D9 | 73 |
| Queens Channel, strt., N.T., Can. | A13 | 96 |
| Queenscliff, Austl. | L6 | 70 |
| Queensland, state, Austl. | D9 | 68 |
| Queensport, N.S., Can. | G12 | 106 |
| Queens Sound, strt., B.C., Can. | F6 | 102 |
| Queenstown, Austl. | N6 | 70 |
| Queenstown, Guy. | D13 | 84 |
| Queenstown, N.Z. | F2 | 72 |
| Queenstown, S. Afr. | H8 | 66 |
| Queguay Grande, stm., Ur. | G10 | 80 |
| Queimadas, Braz. | G7 | 79 |
| Quelimane, Moz. | A13 | 66 |
| Quemado, N.M., U.S. | J8 | 120 |
| Quemado, Tx., U.S. | K6 | 116 |
| Quemado, Punta de, c., Cuba | D7 | 94 |
| Quemado de Güines, Cuba | C4 | 94 |
| Quemoy see Chinmen Tao, i., Tai. | K7 | 34 |
| Quemú Quemú, Arg. | I7 | 80 |
| Quepos, C.R. | H10 | 92 |
| Quercy, hist. reg., Fr. | H8 | 14 |
| Querecotillo, Peru | A1 | 82 |
| Querétaro, Mex. | G9 | 90 |
| Querétaro, state, Mex. | G10 | 90 |
| Querobabi, Mex. | B4 | 90 |
| Quesada, C.R. | G10 | 92 |
| Quesada, Spain | H8 | 16 |
| Queshan, China | C3 | 34 |
| Quesnel, B.C., Can. | E12 | 102 |
| Quesnel, stm., B.C., Can. | E12 | 102 |
| Quesnel Lake, l., B.C., Can. | E13 | 102 |
| Questa, N.M., U.S. | H11 | 120 |
| Quetta, Pak. | E2 | 44 |
| Quettehou, Fr. | C5 | 14 |
| Quetzaltenango, Guat. | C3 | 92 |
| Quetzaltenango, dept., Guat. | C3 | 92 |
| Quevedo, Ec. | H3 | 84 |
| Quezaltepeque, El Sal. | D5 | 92 |
| Quezaltepeque, Guat. | C5 | 92 |

| Name | Map Ref. | Page |
|---|---|---|
| Quezon City, Phil. | n19 | 39b |
| Qufu, China | H5 | 32 |
| Quibdó, Col | E4 | 84 |
| Quiberon, Fr. | E3 | 14 |
| Quibor, Ven. | C8 | 84 |
| Quiches, Peru | C3 | 82 |
| Quilindy, Para. | C10 | 80 |
| Quila, Mex. | D6 | 90 |
| Quilalí, Nic. | D8 | 92 |
| Quilcene, Wa., U.S. | C3 | 122 |
| Quilimarí, Chile | G3 | 80 |
| Quilino, Arg. | E6 | 80 |
| Quillabamba, Peru | E5 | 82 |
| Quillacollo, Bol. | G8 | 82 |
| Quillagua, Chile | I7 | 82 |
| Quillan, Fr. | J9 | 14 |
| Quill Lake, Sk., Can. | F10 | 104 |
| Quillota, Chile | G3 | 80 |
| Quilon, India | H4 | 46 |
| Quilpie, Austl. | F6 | 70 |
| Quilpué, Chile | G3 | 80 |
| Quimarí, Alto de, mtn., Col. | D4 | 84 |
| Quimbaya, Col. | E5 | 84 |
| Quimby, Ia., U.S. | I12 | 118 |
| Quime, Bol. | G8 | 82 |
| Quimilí, Arg. | D7 | 80 |
| Quimper, Fr. | D2 | 14 |
| Quimperlé, Fr. | E3 | 14 |
| Quinault, stm., Wa., U.S. | C2 | 122 |
| Quince Mil, Peru | E6 | 82 |
| Quinches, Peru | E3 | 82 |
| Quincy, Ca., U.S. | I2 | 112 |
| Quincy, Fl., U.S. | I2 | 112 |
| Quincy, Il., U.S. | C5 | 114 |
| Quincy, Ma., U.S. | E15 | 108 |
| Quincy, Mi., U.S. | I11 | 110 |
| Quincy, Wa., U.S. | C6 | 122 |
| Quindío, dept., Col. | E5 | 84 |
| Quines, Arg. | G6 | 80 |
| Quinga, Moz. | E8 | 58 |
| Quinhagak, Ak., U.S. | G14 | 100 |
| Qui Nhon, Viet. | H10 | 40 |
| Quinlan, Tx., U.S. | G10 | 116 |
| Quinn, stm., Nv., U.S. | C7 | 124 |
| Quintanar de la Orden, Spain | F8 | 16 |
| Quintana Roo, state, Mex. | H15 | 90 |
| Quinte, Bay of, b., On., Can. | F18 | 110 |
| Quinter, Ks., U.S. | L7 | 118 |
| Quintero, Chile | G3 | 80 |
| Quintette Mountain, mtn., B.C., Can. | C14 | 102 |
| Quintin, Fr. | D4 | 14 |
| Quinton, Ok., U.S. | D11 | 116 |
| Quinton, Sk., Can. | G10 | 104 |
| Quiriguá, hist., Guat. | B5 | 92 |
| Quirihue, Chile | I2 | 80 |
| Quirindi, Austl. | H9 | 70 |
| Quirinópolis, Braz. | E3 | 79 |
| Quiriquire, Ven. | C11 | 84 |
| Quiroga, Mex. | H9 | 90 |
| Quiroga, Spain | C4 | 16 |
| Quirós, Arg. | E6 | 80 |
| Quirpon Island, i., Nf., Can. | A18 | 106 |
| Quissanga, Moz. | D8 | 58 |
| Quitaque, Tx., U.S. | E5 | 116 |
| Quitilipi, Arg. | D8 | 80 |
| Quitman, Ga., U.S. | I3 | 112 |
| Quitman, Ms., U.S. | J8 | 114 |
| Quitman, Tx., U.S. | G11 | 116 |
| Quito, Ec. | H3 | 84 |
| Quivilla, Peru | C3 | 82 |
| Quixadá, Braz. | D11 | 76 |
| Quixeramobim, Braz. | D7 | 84 |
| Quixito, stm., Braz. | J7 | 84 |
| Qujiang, China | K2 | 34 |
| Qujing, China | B7 | 40 |
| Qulin, Mo., U.S. | F6 | 114 |
| Qumar, stm., China | D5 | 30 |
| Qumarlêb, China | E6 | 30 |
| Quoich, stm., N.T., Can. | D14 | 96 |
| Quorn, Austl. | I3 | 70 |
| Qurayyāt, Oman | C11 | 47 |
| Qurdūd, Sudan | L5 | 60 |
| Qūş, Egypt | E7 | 60 |
| Quthing, Leso. | H8 | 66 |
| Quxi, China | L5 | 34 |
| Quxian, China | G7 | 34 |
| Quyon, P.Q., Can. | B10 | 108 |
| Quyquyó, Para. | D10 | 80 |
| Quzhou, China | G2 | 32 |

**R**

| Name | Map Ref. | Page |
|---|---|---|
| Raab (Rába), stm., Eur. | H15 | 10 |
| Raahe, Fin. | I19 | 6 |
| Raalte, Neth. | D9 | 12 |
| Ra'ananna, Isr. | D3 | 50 |
| Raasiku, Est. | B8 | 22 |
| Raba, Indon. | G6 | 38 |
| Rába (Raab), stm., Eur. | H17 | 10 |
| Rabak, Sudan | K7 | 60 |
| Rabat (Victoria), Malta | M9 | 18 |
| Rabat, Mor. | C7 | 62 |
| Rabaul, Pap. N. Gui. | k17 | 68a |
| Rabbit Ears Pass, Co., U.S. | D10 | 120 |
| Rābigh, Sau. Ar. | C1 | 47 |
| Rabinal, Guat. | B4 | 92 |
| Rabka, Pol. | F19 | 10 |
| Rabkavi Banhatti, India | I3 | 44 |
| Rábnița (Rybnica), Mol. | B13 | 20 |
| Raboôsaostrovsk, Russia | I24 | 6 |
| Rabyānah, Ṣaḥrā', des., Libya | D5 | 56 |
| Raccoon, stm., Ia., U.S. | A3 | 114 |
| Race, Cape, c., Nf., Can. | F20 | 106 |
| Raceland, La., U.S. | M6 | 114 |
| Race Point, c., Ma., U.S. | E16 | 108 |
| Rach'a, Russia | A13 | 22 |
| Rach Gia, Viet. | I8 | 40 |
| Raciborz (Ratibor), Pol. | E18 | 10 |
| Racine, Wi., U.S. | H8 | 110 |
| Răckeve, Hung. | H18 | 10 |
| Radaškovičy, Bela. | G10 | 22 |
| Rădăuti, Rom. | B9 | 20 |
| Radcliff, Ky., U.S. | E11 | 114 |
| Radeberg, Ger. | D13 | 10 |
| Radebeul, Ger. | D13 | 10 |
| Rades, Tun. | B16 | 62 |
| Radford, Va., U.S. | B6 | 112 |
| Radisson, Sk., Can. | E7 | 104 |
| Radium Hot Springs, B.C., Can. | G18 | 102 |
| Radofinnikovo, Russia | B13 | 22 |
| Radolfzell, Ger. | H8 | 10 |
| Radom, Pol. | D21 | 10 |
| Radomsko, Pol. | D19 | 10 |
| Rådøy, i., Nor. | F9 | 6 |
| Radoviš, Mac. | H6 | 20 |
| Radun', Bela. | G8 | 22 |
| Radvilškis, Lith. | F6 | 22 |
| Radville, Sk., Can. | I10 | 104 |
| Radwá, Jabal, mtn., Sau. Ar. | E10 | 60 |
| Radway, Ab., Can. | C22 | 102 |
| Rae, stm., N.T., Can. | C9 | 96 |
| Rãe Bareli, India | G9 | 44 |
| Rãe Isthmus, N.T., Can. | C15 | 96 |

| Name | Map Ref. | Page |
|---|---|---|
| Rae Strait, strt., N.T., Can. | C13 | 95 |
| Raetihi, N.Z. | C5 | 72 |
| Rafaela, Arg. | F8 | 80 |
| Rafah, Gaza | F2 | 50 |
| Raffadali, Italy | L8 | 18 |
| Rafḥā', Sau. Ar. | G7 | 48 |
| Rafsanjān, Iran | F14 | 48 |
| Raft, stm., Iran | H12 | 122 |
| Raft River Mountains, mts., Ut., U.S. | C3 | 120 |
| Raga, Sudan | M3 | 60 |
| Ragged Island, i., Bah. | C7 | 94 |
| Ragged Island Range, is., Bah. | C7 | 94 |
| Ragland, Al., U.S. | I10 | 114 |
| Ragusa, Italy | M9 | 18 |
| Raguva, Lith. | F7 | 22 |
| Rahaçou, Bela. | H13 | 22 |
| Rahad, stm., Afr. | L2 | 60 |
| Rahad al-Bardī, Sudan | L2 | 60 |
| Rahīmyār Khān, Pak. | F4 | 44 |
| Rāichūr, India | D4 | 46 |
| Raiford, Fl., U.S. | I4 | 112 |
| Raiganj, India | H13 | 44 |
| Raigarh, India | J10 | 44 |
| Railton, Austl. | M7 | 70 |
| Rainbow Falls, wtfl, B.C., Can. | E15 | 102 |
| Rainelle, W.V., U.S. | J6 | 108 |
| Rainier, Mount, mtn., Wa., U.S. | D4 | 122 |
| Rainy, stm., Mn., U.S. | E11 | 110 |
| Rainy, stm., N.A. | J20 | 104 |
| Rainy Lake, l., N.A. | B1 | 110 |
| Rainy River, On., Can. | B1 | 110 |
| Raipur, India | J9 | 44 |
| Ra'īs, Sau. Ar. | C1 | 47 |
| Raisin, stm., Mi., U.S. | I12 | 110 |
| Raitī, Nic. | C9 | 92 |
| Rājahmundry, India | D6 | 46 |
| Rājãj, Sudan | L3 | 60 |
| Rajang, stm., Malay. | E5 | 38 |
| Rājapālaiyam, India | H4 | 46 |
| Rājasthān, state, India | G5 | 44 |
| Rajčichinsk, Russia | H17 | 23 |
| Rajka, Hung. | G17 | 10 |
| Rājkot, India | I4 | 44 |
| Rājpipla, India | B2 | 46 |
| Rājshāhi, Bngl. | H13 | 44 |
| Rakamaz, Hung. | G21 | 10 |
| Rakaposhi, mtn., Pak. | B6 | 44 |
| Rakata, Pulau, i., Indon. | j12 | 39a |
| Rakhiv, Ukr. | A8 | 20 |
| Rakops, Bots. | C7 | 66 |
| Rakovník, Czech Rep. | E13 | 10 |
| Rakvere, Est. | B9 | 22 |
| Raleigh, Ms., U.S. | J8 | 114 |
| Raleigh, N.C., U.S. | D8 | 112 |
| Raleigh, Nf., Can. | A18 | 106 |
| Ralls, Tx., U.S. | F5 | 116 |
| Ralston, Ne., U.S. | J11 | 118 |
| Ralston, Pa., U.S. | F10 | 108 |
| Ram, stm., Ab., Can. | E19 | 102 |
| Rama, Isr. | C4 | 50 |
| Rama, Nic. | E10 | 92 |
| Rama, stm., Nic. | F10 | 92 |
| Ramacca, Italy | L9 | 18 |
| Ramah, N.M., U.S. | I8 | 120 |
| Rām Allāh, W.B. | E4 | 50 |
| Ramanāthapuram, India | H5 | 46 |
| Ramasucha, Russia | I16 | 22 |
| Ramat Gan, Isr. | D3 | 50 |
| Ramat HaSharon, Isr. | D3 | 50 |
| Ramat Yisha, Isr. | D3 | 50 |
| Ramathlabama, Bots. | E7 | 66 |
| Rambervillers, Fr. | D13 | 14 |
| Rambouillet, Fr. | D8 | 14 |
| Ramea, Nf., Can. | E16 | 106 |
| Ramea Islands, is., Nf., Can. | E16 | 106 |
| Ramenskoje, Russia | F21 | 22 |
| Ramer, Al., U.S. | J10 | 114 |
| Rameški, Russia | D19 | 22 |
| Rāmeswaram, India | H5 | 46 |
| Rāmhormoz, Iran | F10 | 48 |
| Ramingstein, Aus. | H13 | 10 |
| Ramiriquí, Col. | E6 | 84 |
| Ramla, Isr. | E3 | 50 |
| Ramiu, stm., Afr. | F9 | 56 |
| Ramm, Jabal, mtn., Jord. | I4 | 50 |
| Rāmnicu Sărat, Rom. | D11 | 20 |
| Rāmnicu Vâlcea, Rom. | D8 | 20 |
| Ramona, Ca., U.S. | K9 | 124 |
| Ramona, Ok., U.S. | C11 | 116 |
| Ramona, S.D., U.S. | G10 | 118 |
| Ramos, Mex. | E9 | 90 |
| Ramos, stm., Mex. | C5 | 90 |
| Ramot, Golan | C5 | 50 |
| Ramotswa, Bots. | E7 | 66 |
| Rampart, Ak., U.S. | D19 | 100 |
| Ramparts, stm., N.T., Can. | D29 | 100 |
| Rāmpur, India | F8 | 44 |
| Rāmpur Hāt, India | H12 | 44 |
| Ramseur, N.C., U.S. | D7 | 112 |
| Ramsey, Il., U.S. | C7 | 114 |
| Ramsey, I. of Man | G9 | 8 |
| Rāmshīr, Iran | F10 | 48 |
| Ramu, stm., Pap. N. Gui. | m16 | 68a |
| Ramygala, Turk. | F7 | 22 |
| Rānaghāt, India | I13 | 44 |
| Ranburne, Al., U.S. | I11 | 114 |
| Rancagua, Chile | H3 | 80 |
| Rance, stm., Fr. | D5 | 14 |
| Rancevo, Russia | E17 | 22 |
| Rancharia, Braz. | G3 | 79 |
| Ranchería, Yk., Can. | F29 | 100 |
| Ranchería, stm., Col. | B6 | 84 |
| Ranches of Taos, N.M., U.S. | H11 | 120 |
| Ranchester, Wy., U.S. | F18 | 122 |
| Rānchī, India | I11 | 44 |
| Ranchillos, Arg. | D6 | 80 |
| Ranch Lake, l., Sk., Can. | F10 | 104 |
| Rancho Cordova, Ca., U.S. | F4 | 124 |
| Rancul, Arg. | H6 | 80 |
| Randers, Den. | M12 | 6 |
| Randleman, N.C., U.S. | D7 | 112 |
| Randolph, Az., U.S. | L5 | 120 |
| Randolph, Ne., U.S. | I10 | 118 |
| Randolph, Ut., U.S. | C5 | 120 |
| Randolph, Vt., U.S. | D14 | 108 |
| Random Island, i., Nf., Can. | D20 | 106 |
| Random Lake, Wi., U.S. | G8 | 110 |
| Rânea, Swe. | I18 | 6 |
| Rāngāmāti, Bngl. | I15 | 44 |
| Range Indian Reserve, B.C., Can. | H15 | 102 |
| Rangeley, Me., U.S. | C16 | 108 |
| Rangely, Co., U.S. | D8 | 120 |
| Ranger, Tx., U.S. | G8 | 116 |
| Rangoon see Yangon, Myan. | B2 | 38 |
| Rangpur, Bngl. | H13 | 44 |
| Ranguana Cay, i., Belize | A6 | 92 |
| Ranguana Entrance, strt., Belize | A6 | 92 |
| Rānībennur, India | E3 | 46 |

| Name | Map Ref. | Page |
|---|---|---|
| Rāniganj, India | I12 | 44 |
| Rānikhet, India | F8 | 44 |
| Ranken, Austl. | C2 | 70 |
| Ranken Store, Austl. | B2 | 70 |
| Rankin, Il., U.S. | B9 | 114 |
| Rankin, Tx., U.S. | H5 | 116 |
| Rankin Inlet, N.T., Can. | D14 | 96 |
| Ranlo, N.C., U.S. | D5 | 112 |
| Rann of Kutch, reg., Asia | H3 | 44 |
| Ranohira, Madag. | s21 | 67b |
| Ranomafana, Madag. | t22 | 67b |
| Ranong, Thai. | J5 | 40 |
| Ranopiso, Madag. | t22 | 67b |
| Ranotsara Nord, Madag. | s22 | 67b |
| Ransom, Ks., U.S. | M8 | 118 |
| Ranson, W.V., U.S. | H9 | 108 |
| Rantauprapat, Indon. | F7 | 38 |
| Rantoul, Il., U.S. | B8 | 114 |
| Raoping, China | L6 | 34 |
| Raoul, Ga., U.S. | E3 | 112 |
| Rapa, Ponta do, c., Braz. | D14 | 80 |
| Rapallo, Italy | E4 | 18 |
| Rapel, stm., Chile | G3 | 80 |
| Rapelli, Arg. | D6 | 80 |
| Rapid, stm., Mn., U.S. | B11 | 110 |
| Rapidan, stm., Va., U.S. | I9 | 108 |
| Rapid City, Mb., Can. | H14 | 104 |
| Rapid City, Mi., U.S. | F10 | 110 |
| Rapid City, S.D., U.S. | G4 | 118 |
| Rapid River, Mi., U.S. | E9 | 110 |
| Rapina, Est. | C10 | 22 |
| Rapla, Est. | B7 | 22 |
| Rappahannock, stm., Va., U.S. | B10 | 112 |
| Rapperswil, Switz. | D10 | 13 |
| Rāptī, stm., Asia | G10 | 44 |
| Rapulo, stm., Bol. | F8 | 82 |
| Rarotonga, i., Cook Is. | H10 | 84 |
| Ra's al-'Ayn, Syria | C6 | 48 |
| Ra's an-Naqb, Egypt | I3 | 50 |
| Ra's an-Naqb, Jord. | H4 | 50 |
| Rāscani, Mol. | B11 | 20 |
| Rascov, Mol. | B12 | 20 |
| Ras Dashen Terara, mtn., Eth. | K10 | 60 |
| Raseiniai, Lith. | F6 | 22 |
| Râs el Aïoun, Alg. | N3 | 18 |
| Râs el Ma, Alg. | C10 | 62 |
| Rashād, Sudan | L6 | 60 |
| Rashīd, Egypt | B6 | 60 |
| Rasht, Iran | C10 | 48 |
| Rāsipuram, India | G5 | 46 |
| Raška, Yugo. | F4 | 20 |
| Rasony, Bela. | L5 | 18 |
| Rass Jebel, Tun. | A16 | 62 |
| Rasskazovo, Russia | I24 | 22 |
| Rassuā, ostrov, i., Russia | H22 | 28 |
| Ra's Tannūrah, Sau. Ar. | H11 | 48 |
| Rastatt, Ger. | G8 | 10 |
| Rastede, Ger. | B8 | 10 |
| Rasūl, Pak. | D5 | 44 |
| Rat, stm., Ab., Can. | H18 | 104 |
| Rat, stm., Mb., Can. | B15 | 104 |
| Ratamka, Bela. | H10 | 22 |
| Ratangarh, India | F6 | 44 |
| Rätansbyn, Swe. | J14 | 6 |
| Rāth, India | H8 | 44 |
| Rathbun Lake, res., Ia., U.S. | J2 | 110 |
| Rathdrum, Id., U.S. | C9 | 122 |
| Rathenow, Ger. | C12 | 10 |
| Rathwell, Mb., Can. | I16 | 104 |
| Rat Islands, is., Ak., U.S. | k4 | 101a |
| Rat Lake, l., Mb., Can. | B15 | 104 |
| Ratnāgiri, India | D2 | 46 |
| Ratnapura, Sri L. | I6 | 46 |
| Raton, N.M., U.S. | C2 | 116 |
| Raton Pass, N.M., U.S. | O3 | 118 |
| Rattlesnake, Mt., U.S. | D12 | 122 |
| Rattling Brook, Nf., Can. | C17 | 106 |
| Ratz, Mount, mtn., B.C., Can. | H28 | 100 |
| Ratzeburg, Ger. | B10 | 10 |
| Raub, Malay. | M6 | 40 |
| Rauch, Arg. | I9 | 80 |
| Raul Soares, Braz. | F7 | 79 |
| Rauma, Fin. | K17 | 6 |
| Raurkela, India | I11 | 44 |
| Rävar, Iran | F14 | 48 |
| Ravelo, Bol. | H9 | 82 |
| Raven, Va., U.S. | B5 | 112 |
| Ravenna, Italy | E7 | 18 |
| Ravenna, Ky., U.S. | B3 | 112 |
| Ravenna, Mi., U.S. | G10 | 110 |
| Ravenna, Ne., U.S. | J9 | 118 |
| Ravenna, Oh., U.S. | F5 | 108 |
| Ravensburg, Ger. | H9 | 10 |
| Ravenscrag, Sk., Can. | I5 | 104 |
| Ravensthorpe, Austl. | F4 | 68 |
| Ravenswood, W.V., U.S. | I5 | 108 |
| Rāvi, stm., Asia | E5 | 44 |
| Ravnina, Turk. | C17 | 48 |
| Rāwalpindi, Pak. | D5 | 44 |
| Rawa Mazowiecka, Pol. | D20 | 10 |
| Rawāndūz, Iraq | C8 | 48 |
| Rawdon, P.Q., Can. | D16 | 110 |
| Rawicz, Pol. | D15 | 10 |
| Rawlins, Wy., U.S. | C5 | 120 |
| Rawlinna, Austl. | E4 | 68 |
| Rawson, Arg. | E3 | 78 |
| Rawson, Arg. | H8 | 80 |
| Raxaul, India | G11 | 44 |
| Ray, Cape, c., Nf., Can. | E14 | 106 |
| Raya, Bukit, mtn., Indon. | F5 | 38 |
| Rāyadurg, India | E4 | 46 |
| Raymond, Il., U.S. | C7 | 114 |
| Raymond, Ms., U.S. | J6 | 114 |
| Raymond Terrace, Austl. | I9 | 70 |
| Raymondville, Tx., U.S. | M9 | 116 |
| Raymore, Sk., Can. | G10 | 104 |
| Rayne, La., U.S. | L4 | 114 |
| Rayón, Mex. | C4 | 90 |
| Rayones, Mex. | E9 | 90 |
| Rayong, Thai. | H6 | 40 |
| Raytown, Mo., U.S. | C2 | 114 |
| Rayville, La., U.S. | J5 | 114 |
| Razan, Iran | D10 | 48 |
| Razan, Russia | G22 | 22 |
| Razancevo, Russia | E22 | 22 |
| Razdan, Arm. | A8 | 48 |
| Razdil'na, Mol. | C14 | 20 |
| Razeni, Mol. | C12 | 20 |
| Razgrad, Bul. | F10 | 20 |
| Razorback Mountain, mtn., B.C., Can. | F10 | 102 |
| Razsk, Russia | H23 | 22 |
| Ré, Île de, i., Fr. | F5 | 14 |
| Reading, Eng., U.K. | J13 | 8 |
| Reading, Ks., U.S. | M12 | 118 |

| Name | Map Ref. | Page |
|---|---|---|
| Reading, Mi., U.S. | I11 | 110 |
| Reading, Oh., U.S. | H2 | 108 |
| Reading, Pa., U.S. | G11 | 108 |
| Readlyn, Ia., U.S. | H3 | 110 |
| Readstown, Wi., U.S. | F4 | 110 |
| Real, Cordillera, mts., S.A. | H9 | 82 |
| Real, Estero, stm., Nic. | E7 | 92 |
| Real del Padre, Arg. | H5 | 80 |
| Realicó, Arg. | H6 | 80 |
| Realitos, Tx., U.S. | L8 | 116 |
| Reardan, Wa., U.S. | C8 | 122 |
| Reata, Mex. | D9 | 90 |
| Reay, Scot., U.K. | C10 | 8 |
| Reboly, Russia | J22 | 6 |
| Rebouças, Braz. | C13 | 80 |
| Rebun-tō, i., Japan | b16 | 36a |
| Recalde, Arg. | I8 | 80 |
| Recanati, Italy | F8 | 18 |
| Recane, Russia | E14 | 22 |
| Recherche, Archipelago of the, is., Austl. | F4 | 68 |
| Recife, Braz. | E12 | 76 |
| Recinto, Chile | I3 | 80 |
| Recklinghausen, Ger. | D7 | 10 |
| Reconquista, Arg. | E9 | 80 |
| Recreio, Braz. | F7 | 79 |
| Recreo, Arg. | E6 | 80 |
| Rector, Ar., U.S. | F6 | 114 |
| Recuay, Peru | C3 | 82 |
| Rèčyca, Bela. | I13 | 22 |
| Red (Hong) (Yuan), stm., Asia | C8 | 40 |
| Red, stm., Ky., U.S. | B3 | 112 |
| Red, stm., N.A. | B7 | 98 |
| Red, stm., N.M., U.S. | H11 | 120 |
| Red, stm., Tn., U.S. | E8 | 98 |
| Red, stm., Wi., U.S. | E7 | 110 |
| Redange, Lux. | I8 | 12 |
| Red Bank, N.J., U.S. | G12 | 108 |
| Red Bank, Tn., U.S. | G11 | 114 |
| Red Banks, Ms., U.S. | H8 | 114 |
| Red Bay, Al., U.S. | H8 | 114 |
| Redbay, Fl., U.S. | L11 | 114 |
| Red Bay, Nf., Can. | A17 | 106 |
| Redberry Lake, l., Sk., Can. | F7 | 104 |
| Red Bluff, Ca., U.S. | D3 | 124 |
| Red Bluff Reservoir, res., U.S. | B8 | 90 |
| Red Boiling Springs, Tn., U.S. | F11 | 114 |
| Red Bud, Il., U.S. | D7 | 114 |
| Red Cedar, stm., Mi., U.S. | H11 | 110 |
| Red Cedar, stm., Wi., U.S. | E4 | 110 |
| Redcliff, Ab., Can. | H4 | 104 |
| Red Cliff, Co., U.S. | E10 | 120 |
| Redcliffe, Austl. | F10 | 70 |
| Red Cliffs, Austl. | J5 | 70 |
| Red Cloud, Ne., U.S. | K9 | 118 |
| Red Cross Lake, l., Mb., Can. | C22 | 104 |
| Red Deer, Ab., Can. | E21 | 102 |
| Red Deer, stm., Can. | F12 | 104 |
| Red Deer Lake, l., Ab., Can. | E21 | 102 |
| Red Deer Lake, l., Mb., Can. | F13 | 104 |
| Red Devil, Ak., U.S. | F16 | 100 |
| Redding, Ca., U.S. | D3 | 124 |
| Redeye, stm., Mn., U.S. | E12 | 118 |
| Redfield, Ia., U.S. | J13 | 118 |
| Redfield, S.D., U.S. | G9 | 118 |
| Redford, Tx., U.S. | J2 | 116 |
| Red Hook, N.Y., U.S. | F13 | 108 |
| Red Indian Lake, l., Nf., Can. | D17 | 106 |
| Red Island, i., Nf., Can. | E19 | 106 |
| Redkino, Russia | E19 | 22 |
| Redlake, Mn., U.S. | D12 | 118 |
| Red Lake, On., Can. | G21 | 104 |
| Red Lake, l., Az., U.S. | G20 | 104 |
| Red Lake, l., Mn., U.S. | C11 | 118 |
| Red Lake Falls, Mn., U.S. | D11 | 118 |
| Red Lake Road, On., Can. | I21 | 104 |
| Redlands, Ca., U.S. | J8 | 124 |
| Redlands, Co., U.S. | E8 | 120 |
| Redlands, S. Afr. | G6 | 66 |
| Red Level, Al., U.S. | K10 | 114 |
| Red Lick, Ms., U.S. | K6 | 114 |
| Red Lion, Pa., U.S. | H10 | 108 |
| Red Lodge, Mt., U.S. | E16 | 122 |
| Redmond, Or., U.S. | F4 | 122 |
| Redmond, Ut., U.S. | E5 | 120 |
| Redmond, Wa., U.S. | C3 | 122 |
| Red Mountain, mtn., Ca., U.S. | C2 | 124 |
| Red Mountain Pass, Co., U.S. | G9 | 120 |
| Red Oak, Ia., U.S. | J12 | 118 |
| Red Oak, Ok., U.S. | E11 | 116 |
| Redon, Fr. | E4 | 14 |
| Redonda, Antig. | F13 | 94 |
| Redondo Islands, is., B.C., Can. | G10 | 102 |
| Redondo, Port. | G4 | 16 |
| Redondo Beach, Ca., U.S. | K7 | 124 |
| Red Pass, B.C., Can. | E16 | 102 |
| Red Pheasant Indian Reserve, Sk., Can. | F6 | 104 |
| Red Rock, B.C., Can. | D12 | 102 |
| Red Rock, On., Can. | B7 | 110 |
| Red Rock, stm., Mt., U.S. | F13 | 122 |
| Red Rock Lake, res., Ia., U.S. | I2 | 110 |
| Red Sea | D8 | 56 |
| Red Springs, N.C., U.S. | E7 | 112 |
| Redstone, Co., U.S. | E11 | 102 |
| Redstone, stm., N.T., Can. | E32 | 100 |
| Red Sucker Lake, l., Mb., Can. | C22 | 104 |
| Redvers, Sk., Can. | I13 | 104 |
| Redwater, Ab., Can. | D21 | 102 |
| Redwater, stm., Mt., U.S. | D2 | 118 |
| Redwillow, stm., Can. | B15 | 102 |
| Red Wing, Mn., U.S. | F3 | 110 |
| Redwood, stm., Mn., U.S. | G12 | 118 |
| Redwood City, Ca., U.S. | G3 | 124 |
| Redwood Falls, Mn., U.S. | G12 | 118 |
| Redwood National Park, Ca., U.S. | C1 | 124 |
| Redwood Valley, Ca., U.S. | E2 | 124 |
| Ree, Lough, l., Ire. | H5 | 8 |
| Reed City, Mi., U.S. | G10 | 110 |
| Reeder, N.D., U.S. | E5 | 118 |
| Reed Lake, l., Mb., Can. | D14 | 104 |
| Reedley, Ca., U.S. | H7 | 124 |
| Reedsburg, Wi., U.S. | G5 | 110 |
| Reeds Peak, mtn., N.M., U.S. | K9 | 120 |
| Reedsport, Or., U.S. | G1 | 122 |
| Reedsville, Wi., U.S. | F8 | 110 |
| Reefton, N.Z. | E3 | 72 |
| Reelfoot Lake, l., Tn., U.S. | F7 | 114 |
| Reese, stm., Nv., U.S. | D8 | 124 |
| Reesville, Oh., U.S. | I8 | 114 |
| Reform, Al., U.S. | I8 | 114 |
| Refuge Cove, B.C., Can. | G10 | 102 |
| Refugio, Tx., U.S. | K9 | 116 |
| Regaïa, Mor. | J6 | 6 |

| Name | Map Ref. | Page |
|---|---|---|
| Regência, Braz. | E9 | 79 |
| Regensburg, Ger. | F12 | 10 |
| Regent, N.D., U.S. | E5 | 118 |
| Reggâne, Alg. | G11 | 62 |
| Reggello, Italy | F6 | 18 |
| Reggio di Calabria, Italy | K10 | 18 |
| Reggio nell'Emilia, Italy | E5 | 18 |
| Reghin, Rom. | C8 | 20 |
| Régina, Fr. Gu. | C8 | 76 |
| Regina, Sk., Can. | H10 | 104 |
| Regina Beach, Sk., Can. | H9 | 104 |
| Región Metropolitana, prov., Chile | G3 | 80 |
| Registro, Braz. | C15 | 80 |
| Registro do Araguaia, Braz. | C3 | 79 |
| Regnéville, Fr. | C5 | 14 |
| Reguengos de Monsaraz, Port. | G4 | 16 |
| Rehau, Ger. | E12 | 10 |
| Rehoboth, Nmb. | D3 | 66 |
| Rehoboth Beach, De., U.S. | I11 | 108 |
| Reḥovot, Isr. | E3 | 50 |
| Reichenau, Switz. | E11 | 13 |
| Reichenbach, Ger. | E12 | 10 |
| Reid Lake, res., Sk., Can. | H6 | 104 |
| Reidsville, Ga., U.S. | G4 | 112 |
| Reidsville, N.C., U.S. | C7 | 112 |
| Reigate, Eng., U.K. | J13 | 8 |
| Reigoldswil, Switz. | D8 | 13 |
| Reims, Fr. | C11 | 14 |
| Reinach, Switz. | D9 | 13 |
| Reinach, Switz. | C8 | 13 |
| Reinbeck, Ia., U.S. | H3 | 110 |
| Reindeer, stm., Sk., Can. | C11 | 104 |
| Reindeer Island, i., Mb., Can. | F17 | 104 |
| Reindeer Lake, l., Can. | E12 | 96 |
| Reindeer Station, N.T., Can. | B27 | 100 |
| Reinga, Cape, c., N.Z. | A4 | 72 |
| Reinosa, Spain | B7 | 16 |
| Reisdorf, Lux. | E9 | 12 |
| Reisterstown, Md., U.S. | H10 | 108 |
| Reitz, S. Afr. | F9 | 66 |
| Reliance, N.T., Can. | D11 | 96 |
| Reliance, Wy., U.S. | C7 | 120 |
| Remada, Tun. | D16 | 62 |
| Remagen, Ger. | E7 | 10 |
| Remanso, Braz. | E10 | 76 |
| Rembang, Indon. | j15 | 39a |
| Remecó, Arg. | I7 | 80 |
| Remedios, Col. | D5 | 84 |
| Remedios, Pan. | C2 | 84 |
| Remedios, Punta, c., El Sal. | D5 | 92 |
| Remer, Mn., U.S. | C2 | 110 |
| Remeshk, Iran | H15 | 48 |
| Remington, In., U.S. | B9 | 114 |
| Remington, Va., U.S. | I9 | 108 |
| Remiremont, Fr. | D13 | 14 |
| Remoulins, Fr. | I11 | 14 |
| Remsen, Ia., U.S. | I12 | 118 |
| Remus, Mi., U.S. | G10 | 110 |
| Renaix (Ronse), Bel. | G4 | 12 |
| Renata, B.C., Can. | H16 | 102 |
| Rencēni, Lat. | D8 | 22 |
| Rencontre East, Nf., Can. | E18 | 106 |
| Rende, Italy | J11 | 18 |
| Rend Lake, res., Il., U.S. | E8 | 114 |
| Rendsburg, Ger. | A9 | 10 |
| Renens, Switz. | E6 | 13 |
| Renews, Nf., Can. | F21 | 106 |
| Renfrew, On., Can. | E19 | 110 |
| Rengat, Indon. | O7 | 40 |
| Rengo, Chile | H3 | 80 |
| Reng Tläng, mtn., Asia | J15 | 44 |
| Renhua, China | J2 | 34 |
| Reni, Ukr. | D12 | 20 |
| Renick, W.V., U.S. | J6 | 108 |
| Renmark, Austl. | J4 | 70 |
| Rennell, i., Sol. Is. | B12 | 68 |
| Rennell Sound, strt., B.C., Can. | D2 | 102 |
| Rennes, Fr. | D5 | 14 |
| Rennick Glacier, Ant. | C8 | 73 |
| Rennie, Mb., Can. | I19 | 104 |
| Reno, Nv., U.S. | E6 | 124 |
| Reno, stm., Italy | E6 | 18 |
| Renous, N.B., Can. | F8 | 106 |
| Renous, stm., N.B., Can. | F7 | 106 |
| Renovo, Pa., U.S. | F9 | 108 |
| Renshou, China | H6 | 34 |
| Rensselaer, In., U.S. | B9 | 114 |
| Rensselaer, N.Y., U.S. | E13 | 108 |
| Rentería, Spain | B10 | 16 |
| Renton, Wa., U.S. | C3 | 122 |
| Renville, Mn., U.S. | G12 | 118 |
| Renwick, Ia., U.S. | H1 | 110 |
| Renwick, stm., Eur. | I16 | 14 |
| Repetek, Turk. | J10 | 26 |
| Repino, Russia | A12 | 22 |
| Repton, Al., U.S. | K9 | 114 |
| Republic, Ks., U.S. | L10 | 118 |
| Republic, Mi., U.S. | D8 | 110 |
| Republic, Wa., U.S. | B7 | 122 |
| Republican, stm., U.S. | L10 | 118 |
| Repulse Bay, N.T., Can. | C15 | 96 |
| Repulse Bay, b., Austl. | C8 | 70 |
| Requena, Peru | A5 | 82 |
| Requena, Spain | F10 | 16 |
| Réquista, Fr. | H9 | 14 |
| Reschenpass, Eur. | F17 | 14 |
| Resen, Mac. | H5 | 20 |
| Reserva, Braz. | C13 | 80 |
| Reserve, La., U.S. | L6 | 114 |
| Reserve, N.M., U.S. | K8 | 120 |
| Rešetnikovo, Russia | E19 | 22 |
| Resistência, Arg. | D9 | 80 |
| Resița, Rom. | D5 | 20 |
| Rešma, Russia | D25 | 22 |
| Resolute, N.T., Can. | B14 | 96 |
| Resolution Island, i., N.T., Can. | D20 | 96 |
| Resolution Island, i., N.Z. | F1 | 72 |
| Resplendor, Braz. | E8 | 79 |
| Restigouche (Restigouche), stm., Can. | E6 | 106 |
| Restín, Punta, c., Peru | J2 | 84 |
| Restinga Sêca, Braz. | E12 | 80 |
| Reston, Mb., Can. | I13 | 104 |
| Restrepo, Col. | E6 | 84 |
| Restrepo, Col. | F4 | 84 |
| Retalhuleu, Guat. | C3 | 92 |
| Retalhuleu, dept., Guat. | C3 | 92 |
| Retamosa, Ur. | G11 | 80 |
| Rethel, Fr. | C11 | 14 |
| Rethímnon, Grc. | N8 | 20 |
| Réunion (Réunion), dep., Afr. | F11 | 58 |
| Reus, Spain | D13 | 16 |
| Reuss, stm., Switz. | D9 | 13 |
| Reuterstadt Stavenhagen, Ger. | B12 | 10 |
| Reutlingen, Ger. | G9 | 10 |
| Rev'akino, Russia | G20 | 22 |
| Revda, Russia | F9 | 26 |
| Revelstoke, B.C., Can. | G16 | 102 |
| Revelstoke, Lake, res., B.C., Can. | F16 | 102 |
| Reventazón, Braz. | F9 | 82 |
| Reventazón, stm., C.R. | G11 | 92 |
| Revigny-sur-Ornain, Fr. | D11 | 14 |
| Revillagigedo, Islas, is., Mex. | H4 | 90 |
| Revillagigedo Island, i., Ak., U.S. | I29 | 100 |
| Revillo, S.D., U.S. | F11 | 118 |
| Revin, Fr. | C11 | 14 |
| Revol'ucii, pik, mtn., Taj. | A5 | 44 |
| Revúe, stm., Afr. | B11 | 66 |
| Rewa, India | H9 | 44 |
| Rewa, stm., Guy. | F13 | 84 |
| Rewari, India | F7 | 44 |
| Rexburg, Id., U.S. | G14 | 122 |
| Rexford, Ks., U.S. | L7 | 118 |
| Rexford, Mt., U.S. | B10 | 122 |
| Rexton, N.B., Can. | F9 | 106 |
| Rey, Isla del, i., Pan. | C3 | 84 |
| Rey, Laguna del, l., Mex. | D8 | 90 |
| Reyes, Pt. | F8 | 82 |
| Reyes, Point, c., Ca., U.S. | I8 | 124 |
| Reyhanlı, Tur. | C4 | 48 |
| Reykjanes, pen., Ice. | C2 | 6a |
| Reykjavík, Ice. | B3 | 6a |
| Reyno, Ar., U.S. | F6 | 114 |
| Reynolds, Ga., U.S. | G2 | 112 |
| Reynolds, N.D., U.S. | D10 | 118 |
| Reynoldsville, Pa., U.S. | F8 | 108 |
| Reynosa, Mex. | D10 | 90 |
| Rež, Russia | F10 | 26 |
| Reza, gora (Küh-e Rīzeh), mtn., Asia | C15 | 48 |
| Rezé, Fr. | E5 | 14 |
| Rēzekne, Lat. | E10 | 22 |
| Rezina, Mol. | B12 | 20 |
| Rezovska (Mutlu), stm., Eur. | G11 | 20 |
| Rhaetian Alps, mts., Eur. | F16 | 14 |
| Rhame, N.D., U.S. | E4 | 118 |
| Rheda-Wiedenbrück, Ger. | D8 | 10 |
| Rheims see Reims, Fr. | C11 | 14 |
| Rhein, Sk., Can. | G12 | 104 |
| Rhein see Rhine, stm., Eur. | D6 | 10 |
| Rheine, Ger. | C7 | 10 |
| Rheinland-Pfalz, state, Ger. | E6 | 10 |
| Rhine, Ga., U.S. | H3 | 112 |
| Rhine (Rhein) (Rhin), stm., Eur. | D6 | 10 |
| Rhinebeck, N.Y., U.S. | F13 | 108 |
| Rhinelander, Wi., U.S. | E5 | 110 |
| Rhir, Cap, c., Mor. | E6 | 62 |
| Rho, Italy | D4 | 18 |
| Rhode Island, state, U.S. | C12 | 98 |
| Rhode Island Sound, strt., U.S. | F15 | 108 |
| Rhodes see Ródhos, i., Grc. | M12 | 20 |
| Rhodesia see Zimbabwe, ctry., Afr. | E5 | 58 |
| Rhodope Mountains (Rodopi) (Orosirá Rodhópis), mts., Eur. | H8 | 20 |
| Rigi, mtn., Switz. | D10 | 13 |
| Rhön, dept., Fr. | G11 | 14 |
| Rhön, mts., Ger. | E9 | 10 |
| Rhône, dept., Fr. | G11 | 14 |
| Rhône, stm., Eur. | H11 | 14 |
| Rhône au Rhin, Canal du, Fr. | H7 | 10 |
| Rhourde-el-Baguel, Alg. | E14 | 62 |
| Riaba, Eq. Gui. | J14 | 64 |
| Riachão, Braz. | E9 | 76 |
| Riacho de Santana, Braz. | B7 | 79 |
| Rialma, Braz. | C4 | 79 |
| Rianápolis, Braz. | C4 | 79 |
| Riangnom, Sudan | M6 | 60 |
| Riaño, Spain | C6 | 16 |
| Riau, Kepulauan, is., Indon. | N8 | 40 |
| Ribas do Rio Pardo, Braz. | F2 | 79 |
| Ribauè, Braz. | D14 | 14 |
| Ribeira, Braz. | C14 | 80 |
| Ribeira do Iguape, stm., Braz. | C14 | 80 |
| Ribeira Grande, C.V. | k16 | 64a |
| Ribeirão do Pinhal, Braz. | F5 | 79 |
| Ribeirão Prêto, Braz. | F5 | 79 |
| Ribeirão Vermelho, Braz. | F6 | 79 |
| Ribeirãozinho, Braz. | D2 | 79 |
| Ribemont, Fr. | C10 | 14 |
| Ribera, Italy | L8 | 18 |
| Riberalta, Bol. | D8 | 82 |
| Rib Lake, Wi., U.S. | E5 | 110 |
| Ribnica, Slvn. | D9 | 18 |
| Ribnitz-Damgarten, Ger. | A12 | 10 |
| Ribstone Creek, stm., Ab., Can. | F3 | 104 |
| Ricardo Flores Magón, Mex. | C6 | 90 |
| Ricaurte, Col. | G4 | 84 |
| Riccia, Italy | H9 | 18 |
| Riccione, Italy | F7 | 18 |
| Rice, Tx., U.S. | G10 | 116 |
| Riceville, Ia., U.S. | G3 | 110 |
| Riceville, Tn., U.S. | D2 | 112 |
| Richan, On., Can. | I22 | 104 |
| Richard Collinson Inlet, b., N.T., Can. | B10 | 96 |
| Richards, Tx., U.S. | I11 | 116 |
| Richard's Bay, S. Afr. | G11 | 66 |
| Richard's Bay, S. Afr. | G11 | 66 |
| Richard's Harbour, Nf., Can. | E17 | 106 |
| Richards Island, i., N.T., Can. | B27 | 100 |
| Richardson, Tx., U.S. | G10 | 116 |
| Richardson, stm., Can. | D5 | 96 |
| Richardson Mountains, mts., Can. | C26 | 100 |
| Richardton, N.D., U.S. | E6 | 118 |
| Riche, Pointe, c., Nf., Can. | B16 | 106 |
| Richelieu, Fr. | E7 | 14 |
| Richer, Mb., Can. | I18 | 104 |
| Richey, Mt., U.S. | D2 | 118 |
| Richfield, Id., U.S. | G11 | 122 |
| Richfield, Pa., U.S. | G9 | 108 |
| Richfield, Ut., U.S. | F7 | 120 |
| Richfield Springs, N.Y., U.S. | E12 | 108 |
| Richford, Vt., U.S. | C2 | 108 |
| Rich Hill, Mo., U.S. | D2 | 114 |
| Richibucto, N.B., Can. | F9 | 106 |
| Richisau, Switz. | D10 | 13 |
| Richland, Ga., U.S. | G2 | 112 |
| Richland, Mi., U.S. | H10 | 110 |
| Richland, Tx., U.S. | G10 | 116 |
| Richland Center, Wi., U.S. | G5 | 110 |
| Richlands, N.C., U.S. | C9 | 112 |
| Richlands, Va., U.S. | B5 | 112 |
| Richland Springs, Tx., U.S. | H8 | 116 |
| Richmond, Austl. | C5 | 70 |
| Richmond, Austl. | C5 | 70 |
| Richmond, B.C., Can. | H11 | 102 |
| Richmond, Ca., U.S. | G3 | 124 |
| Richmond, Ca., U.S. | C12 | 114 |
| Richmond, In., U.S. | E12 | 114 |
| Richmond, Ky., U.S. | A2 | 112 |
| Richmond, Mi., U.S. | H13 | 110 |
| Richmond, Mo., U.S. | C3 | 114 |
| Richmond, N.Z. | D4 | 72 |
| Richmond, P.Q., Can. | B11 | 108 |
| Richmond, P.Q., Can. | B14 | 108 |
| Richmond, S. Afr. | H6 | 66 |
| Richmond, S. Afr. | G10 | 66 |
| Richmond, Tx., U.S. | J11 | 116 |
| Richmond, Ut., U.S. | C5 | 120 |
| Richmond, Va., U.S. | B9 | 112 |
| Richmond, Vt., U.S. | C14 | 108 |
| Richmond Heights, Fl., U.S. | N6 | 112 |
| Richmond Highlands, Wa., U.S. | C3 | 122 |
| Richmond Hill, Ga., U.S. | H5 | 112 |
| Richmond Hill, On., Can. | G16 | 110 |
| Richmondville, N.Y., U.S. | E12 | 108 |
| Rich Square, N.C., U.S. | C9 | 112 |
| Richton, Ms., U.S. | K8 | 114 |
| Richwood, Oh., U.S. | G3 | 108 |
| Richwood, W.V., U.S. | I6 | 108 |
| Rico, Co., U.S. | G10 | 120 |
| Riddle, Or., U.S. | H2 | 122 |
| Riddle Mountain, mtn., Or., U.S. | G7 | 122 |
| Ridgecrest, Ca., U.S. | I8 | 124 |
| Ridgedale, Sk., Can. | E10 | 104 |
| Ridge Farm, Il., U.S. | C9 | 114 |
| Ridgefield, Ct., U.S. | F13 | 108 |
| Ridgeland, Ms., U.S. | J6 | 114 |
| Ridgeland, S.C., U.S. | G6 | 112 |
| Ridgely, Tn., U.S. | F7 | 114 |
| Ridgetown, On., Can. | H14 | 110 |
| Ridgeville, Mb., Can. | I17 | 104 |
| Ridgeville, S.C., U.S. | F6 | 112 |
| Ridgeway, Mo., U.S. | B3 | 114 |
| Ridgeway, Wi., U.S. | G6 | 110 |
| Ridgway, Co., U.S. | F9 | 120 |
| Ridgway, Il., U.S. | E8 | 114 |
| Ridgway, Pa., U.S. | F8 | 108 |
| Riding Mountain, mtn., Mb., Can. | H15 | 104 |
| Riding Mountain National Park, mtn., Can. | H14 | 104 |
| Ried im Innkreis, Aus. | G13 | 10 |
| Riegelwood, N.C., U.S. | E8 | 112 |
| Rienzi, Ms., U.S. | H8 | 114 |
| Riesa, Ger. | D13 | 10 |
| Riesco, Isla, i., Chile | G2 | 78 |
| Riesi, Italy | L9 | 18 |
| Rietavas, Lith. | F4 | 22 |
| Rietfontein, Nmb. | C5 | 66 |
| Rieti, Italy | G7 | 18 |
| Rif, mts., Mor. | C8 | 62 |
| Riffe Lake, res., Wa., U.S. | D3 | 122 |
| Rifle, Co., U.S. | E9 | 120 |
| Rifle, stm., Mi., U.S. | F11 | 110 |
| Rift Valley, val., Afr. | I9 | 52 |
| Rīga, Lat. | E7 | 22 |
| Rīga, Gulf of (Rīgas jūras līcis) (Riia laht), b., Eur. | D6 | 22 |
| Rigacikun, Nig. | F13 | 64 |
| Rīgān, Iran | G15 | 48 |
| Rigby, Id., U.S. | G14 | 122 |
| Rigestān, reg., Afg. | E1 | 44 |
| Riggins, Id., U.S. | E9 | 122 |
| Rigi, mtn., Switz. | D10 | 13 |
| Rigo, Pap. N. Gui. | A9 | 68 |
| Rīiser-Larsen Peninsula, pen., Ant. | B4 | 73 |
| Rijeka, Cro. | D9 | 18 |
| Rijssen, Neth. | D5 | 12 |
| Rijswijk, Neth. | D5 | 12 |
| Riley, Ks., U.S. | L11 | 118 |
| Rillito, Az., U.S. | L5 | 120 |
| Rima, stm., Nig. | E12 | 64 |
| Rímac, stm., Peru | D3 | 82 |
| Rimachi, Laguna, l., Peru | J4 | 84 |
| Rimavská Sobota, Slvk. | G20 | 10 |
| Rimbey, Ab., Can. | E20 | 102 |
| Rimersburg, Pa., U.S. | F7 | 108 |
| Rimi, Nig. | E13 | 64 |
| Rimini, Italy | E7 | 18 |
| Rimouski, P.Q., Can. | D5 | 106 |
| Rimouski, stm., P.Q., Can. | D5 | 106 |
| Rimouski, Réserve, P.Q., Can. | D5 | 106 |
| Rinard, Il., U.S. | E9 | 114 |
| Rincón, C.R. | I11 | 92 |
| Rincon, Ga., U.S. | G5 | 112 |
| Rincon, N.M., U.S. | L9 | 120 |
| Rinconada, Arg. | B5 | 80 |
| Rincón de la Vieja, Parque Nacional, C.R. | G9 | 92 |
| Rincón del Bonete, Lago Artificial de, res., Ur. | G11 | 80 |
| Rincón del Ocote, Cerro, mtn., Hond. | D7 | 92 |
| Rincón de Romos, Mex. | F8 | 90 |
| Rindal, Nor. | J11 | 6 |
| Ringebu, Nor. | K12 | 6 |
| Ringgold, Ga., U.S. | E1 | 112 |
| Ringgold, La., U.S. | J3 | 114 |
| Ringim, Nig. | E14 | 64 |
| Ringling, Ok., U.S. | E9 | 116 |
| Ringsted, Ia., U.S. | H13 | 118 |
| Rinjani, Gunung, mtn., Indon. | G6 | 38 |
| Rinteln, Ger. | C9 | 10 |
| Rio, Wi., U.S. | G6 | 110 |
| Rio Azul, Braz. | C13 | 80 |
| Riobamba, Ec. | H3 | 84 |
| Río Blanco, Chile | G3 | 80 |
| Rio Branco, Braz. | C8 | 82 |
| Río Branco, Ur. | G12 | 80 |
| Río Bravo, Mex. | E10 | 90 |
| Rio Brilhante, Braz. | F1 | 79 |
| Río Caribe, Ven. | B11 | 84 |
| Río Casca, Braz. | F7 | 79 |
| Río Ceballos, Arg. | F6 | 80 |
| Río Chico, Ven. | B10 | 84 |
| Rio Claro, Braz. | G5 | 79 |
| Rio Claro, Trin. | I14 | 94 |
| Río Colorado, Arg. | J6 | 80 |
| Río Cuarto, Arg. | G6 | 80 |
| Rio de Contas, Braz. | B8 | 79 |
| Rio de Janeiro, Braz. | G7 | 79 |
| Rio de Janeiro, state, Braz. | G7 | 79 |
| Río de Jesús, Pan. | J13 | 92 |
| Río Dell, Ca., U.S. | D1 | 124 |
| Río de Oro, Col. | C6 | 84 |
| Rio do Prado, Braz. | D8 | 79 |
| Rio do Sul, Braz. | D14 | 80 |
| Río Espera, Braz. | F7 | 79 |
| Río Gallegos, Arg. | G3 | 78 |
| Río Grande, Braz. | F12 | 80 |
| Río Grande, Mex. | F8 | 90 |
| Río Grande, Nic. | E9 | 92 |
| Rio Grande see Grande, Rio, stm., N.A. | F7 | 98 |
| Rio Grande City, Tx., U.S. | M8 | 116 |
| Rio Grande do Sul, state, Braz. | E11 | 80 |
| Ríohacha, Col. | B6 | 84 |
| Río Hato, Pan. | C2 | 84 |
| Río Hondo, Arg. | M9 | 116 |
| Rioja, Nig. | B3 | 82 |
| Río Lagartos, Mex. | G15 | 90 |
| Riolândia, Braz. | E4 | 79 |
| Rio Largo, Braz. | E11 | 76 |
| Riom, Fr. | G10 | 14 |
| Río Mulatos, Bol. | H8 | 82 |
| Riondel, B.C., Can. | H18 | 102 |
| Rio Negro, Braz. | D14 | 80 |
| Río Negro, Col. | D5 | 84 |
| Rionegro, Col. | D6 | 84 |
| Río Negro, prov., Arg. | J6 | 80 |
| Río Negro, Pantanal do, sw., Braz. | H13 | 82 |
| Rionero in Vulture, Italy | I10 | 18 |
| Rio Novo do Sul, Braz. | F8 | 79 |
| Rio Pardo, Braz. | E12 | 80 |
| Rio Pardo de Minas, Braz. | C7 | 79 |
| Rio Piedras, Arg. | C6 | 80 |
| Río Pilcomayo, Parque Nacional, Arg. | C9 | 80 |
| Rio Piracicaba, Braz. | E7 | 79 |
| Rio Pomba, Braz. | F7 | 79 |
| Rio Preto, Braz. | G7 | 79 |
| Rio Rancho, N.M., U.S. | I10 | 120 |
| Río San Juan, dept., Nic. | F10 | 92 |
| Río Segundo, Arg. | F7 | 80 |
| Riosucio, Col. | E5 | 84 |
| Riosucio, Col. | D4 | 84 |
| Río Tercero, Arg. | G6 | 80 |
| Río Tinto, Braz. | E11 | 76 |
| Rio Verde, Braz. | D3 | 79 |
| Rioverde, Mex. | G10 | 90 |
| Rio Verde de Mato Grosso, Braz. | E1 | 79 |
| Rio Vermelho, Braz. | E7 | 79 |
| Rio Vista, Ca., U.S. | F4 | 124 |
| Rioz, Fr. | E13 | 14 |
| Riozinho, stm., Braz. | I9 | 84 |
| Ripley, Ms., U.S. | H8 | 114 |
| Ripley, N.Y., U.S. | E7 | 108 |
| Ripley, Oh., U.S. | I3 | 108 |
| Ripley, Tn., U.S. | G7 | 114 |
| Ripley, W.V., U.S. | I5 | 108 |
| Ripoll, Spain | C14 | 16 |
| Ripon, Ca., U.S. | G4 | 124 |
| Ripon, Eng., U.K. | G12 | 8 |
| Ripon, P.Q., Can. | B11 | 108 |
| Ripon, Wi., U.S. | G7 | 110 |
| Riposto, Italy | L10 | 18 |
| Ririe, Id., U.S. | G14 | 122 |
| Risaralda, dept., Col. | E4 | 84 |
| Riscle, Fr. | I6 | 14 |
| Risco, Ilha do, i., Braz. | I13 | 84 |
| Rishin-tō, i., Japan | b16 | 36a |
| Rishmayyā, Leb. | A5 | 50 |
| Rishon LeZiyyon, Isr. | E3 | 50 |
| Rising Star, Tx., U.S. | G8 | 116 |
| Rising Sun, In., U.S. | D12 | 114 |
| Rising Sun, Md., U.S. | H10 | 108 |
| Risingsun, Oh., U.S. | F3 | 108 |
| Rison, Ar., U.S. | I4 | 114 |
| Risør, Nor. | L11 | 6 |
| Rissani, Mor. | E8 | 62 |
| Risti, Est. | C7 | 22 |
| Ristigouche (Restigouche), stm., Can. | E6 | 106 |
| Ritter, Mount, mtn., Ca., U.S. | G6 | 124 |
| Rittman, Oh., U.S. | G5 | 108 |
| Ritzville, Wa., U.S. | C7 | 122 |
| Riva, Italy | D5 | 18 |
| Rivadavia, Arg. | H7 | 80 |
| Rivadavia, Arg. | G4 | 80 |
| Rivadavia, Arg. | F4 | 80 |
| Rivadavia, Chile | E3 | 80 |
| Rivanna, stm., Va., U.S. | B8 | 112 |
| Rivas, Nic. | F9 | 92 |
| Rivas, dept., Nic. | F8 | 92 |
| Rive-de-Gier, Fr. | G11 | 14 |
| Rivera, Arg. | I7 | 80 |
| Rivera, Col. | F5 | 84 |
| Rivera, Ur. | F11 | 80 |
| Riverbank, Ca., U.S. | G5 | 124 |
| River Cess, Lib. | I5 | 64 |
| Riverdale, Ca., U.S. | H6 | 124 |
| Riverdale, N.D., U.S. | D6 | 118 |
| River Falls, Wi., U.S. | F3 | 110 |
| River Hébert, N.S., Can. | G9 | 106 |
| Riverhead, N.Y., U.S. | G14 | 108 |
| Riverhurst, Sk., Can. | H6 | 104 |
| Riverina, reg., Austl. | J6 | 70 |
| River John, N.S., Can. | G10 | 106 |
| Rivermont, N.C., U.S. | D9 | 112 |
| River of Ponds, Nf., Can. | B16 | 106 |
| River Road, In., U.S. | F2 | 122 |
| Rivers, Mb., Can. | H14 | 104 |
| Rivers, Lake of the, l., Sk., Can. | I9 | 104 |
| Riverside, S. Afr. | J5 | 66 |
| Riverside, Ca., U.S. | K8 | 124 |
| Riverside, Ia., U.S. | I4 | 110 |
| Riverside, Tx., U.S. | I11 | 116 |
| Rivers Inlet, B.C., Can. | F7 | 102 |
| Rivers Inlet, b., B.C., Can. | F7 | 102 |
| Riverton, Il., U.S. | C7 | 114 |
| Riverton, Mb., Can. | H18 | 104 |
| Riverton, N.J., U.S. | K9 | 118 |
| Riverton, N.Z. | G2 | 72 |
| Riverton, Ut., U.S. | D5 | 120 |
| Riverton, Va., U.S. | I8 | 108 |
| Riverton, Wy., U.S. | A5 | 120 |
| Riverton Heights, Wa., U.S. | C3 | 122 |
| River View, Al., U.S. | J11 | 114 |
| Riverview, Fl., U.S. | L4 | 112 |
| Riverview, Ks., U.S. | N10 | 118 |
| Rives, Tn., U.S. | F7 | 114 |
| Rivesaltes, Fr. | J9 | 14 |
| Rivesville, W.V., U.S. | H6 | 108 |
| Riviera, Az., U.S. | I2 | 120 |
| Riviera, Tx., U.S. | L9 | 116 |
| Riviera Beach, Fl., U.S. | M6 | 112 |
| Rivière-à-Claude, P.Q., Can. | C8 | 106 |
| Rivière-au-Tonnerre, P.Q., Can. | B9 | 106 |
| Rivière-Bleue, P.Q., Can. | E4 | 106 |
| Rivière-de-la-Chaloupe, P.Q., Can. | C11 | 106 |
| Rivière-du-Loup, P.Q., Can. | D4 | 106 |
| Rivière-Matane, P.Q., Can. | D6 | 106 |
| Rivière-Pentecôte, P.Q., Can. | C6 | 106 |
| Rivière-Verte, N.B., Can. | E5 | 106 |
| Riviersonderend, S. Afr. | J4 | 66 |
| Rivne, Ukr. | G3 | 26 |
| Rivoli, Italy | D2 | 18 |
| Riyadh see Ar-Riyāḍ, Sau. Ar. | B5 | 47 |
| Rize, Tur. | G16 | 4 |
| Rizhao, China | H7 | 32 |
| Roa, Nor. | K12 | 6 |
| Roachdale, In., U.S. | C10 | 114 |
| Road Town, Br. Vir. Is. | E12 | 94 |
| Roan Cliffs, clf, U.S. | E7 | 120 |
| Roan Mountain, Tn., U.S. | C4 | 112 |
| Roanne, Fr. | F11 | 14 |
| Roanoke, Al., U.S. | I11 | 114 |
| Roanoke, Il., U.S. | B8 | 114 |
| Roanoke, Va., U.S. | B7 | 112 |
| Roanoke, stm., U.S. | C9 | 112 |
| Roanoke Island, i., N.C., U.S. | C11 | 112 |
| Roanoke Rapids, N.C., U.S. | C9 | 112 |
| Roan Plateau, plat., U.S. | E6 | 120 |
| Roaring Spring, Pa., U.S. | G8 | 108 |
| Roaring Springs, Tx., U.S. | E5 | 116 |
| Roatán, Hond. | A8 | 92 |
| Roatán, Isla de, i., Hond. | A8 | 92 |
| Robāṭ Karīm, Iran | D11 | 48 |
| Robā Oued Yahia, Tun. | M4 | 18 |
| Robbins, N.C., U.S. | D7 | 112 |
| Robbins, Tn., U.S. | C2 | 112 |
| Robbins Island, i., Austl. | M6 | 70 |
| Robbinsville, N.C., U.S. | D3 | 112 |
| Röbel, Ger. | B12 | 10 |
| Robeline, La., U.S. | K3 | 114 |
| Robersonville, N.C., U.S. | D9 | 112 |
| Roberta, Ga., U.S. | G2 | 112 |
| Roberta Mills, N.C., U.S. | D6 | 112 |
| Robert Lee, Tx., U.S. | H6 | 116 |
| Roberts, Id., U.S. | G13 | 122 |
| Roberts, Mt., U.S. | E16 | 122 |
| Robert's Arm, Nf., Can. | D18 | 106 |
| Roberts Creek Mountain, mtn., Nv., U.S. | E9 | 124 |
| Robertsdale, Al., U.S. | L9 | 114 |
| Robertsdale, Pa., U.S. | G8 | 108 |
| Robertsfield, Lib. | H4 | 64 |
| Robert S. Kerr Lake, res., Ok., U.S. | D11 | 116 |
| Robertson, S. Afr. | I4 | 66 |
| Robertson, Lac, l., P.Q., Can. | A14 | 106 |
| Roberts Peak, mtn., B.C., Can. | E14 | 102 |
| Robertsport, Lib. | H4 | 64 |
| Roberval, P.Q., Can. | G18 | 96 |
| Robesonia, Pa., U.S. | H10 | 108 |
| Robins, Ia., U.S. | H4 | 110 |
| Robinson, stm., Austl. | C7 | 70 |
| Robinson, Tx., U.S. | H9 | 116 |
| Róbinson Crusoe, Isla, i., Chile | H7 | 74 |
| Robinson Range, mts., Austl. | E3 | 68 |
| Robinsons, Nf., Can. | D15 | 106 |
| Robinvale, Austl. | J5 | 70 |
| Roblin, Mb., Can. | G13 | 104 |
| Roboré, Bol. | H12 | 82 |
| Robson, Mount, mtn., B.C., Can. | D15 | 102 |
| Robstown, Tx., U.S. | L9 | 116 |
| Roby, Tx., U.S. | G6 | 116 |
| Roca, Cabo da, c., Port. | G2 | 16 |
| Rocafuerte, Ec. | H2 | 84 |
| Rocanville, Sk., Can. | H13 | 104 |
| Roca Partida, Isla, i., Mex. | H3 | 90 |
| Roca Partida, Punta, c., Mex. | H12 | 90 |
| Rocas, Atol das, atoll, Braz. | D12 | 76 |
| Roccastrada, Italy | F6 | 18 |
| Rocciamelone, mtn., Italy | D2 | 18 |
| Rocha, Ur. | H11 | 80 |
| Rochedinho, Braz. | F1 | 79 |
| Rochedo, Braz. | E1 | 79 |
| Rochefort, Bel. | H7 | 12 |
| Rochefort, Fr. | G6 | 14 |
| Rochelle, Ga., U.S. | H3 | 112 |
| Rochelle, Il., U.S. | I6 | 110 |
| Rochelle, Tx., U.S. | H7 | 116 |
| Roche-Percée, Sk., Can. | I12 | 104 |
| Rochester, Austl. | K6 | 70 |
| Rochester, In., U.S. | A10 | 114 |
| Rochester, Mi., U.S. | H12 | 110 |
| Rochester, Mn., U.S. | F3 | 110 |
| Rochester, N.H., U.S. | D9 | 108 |
| Rochester, N.Y., U.S. | F7 | 116 |
| Rochester, Tx., U.S. | F6 | 116 |
| Rochlitz, Ger. | D12 | 10 |
| Rock, stm., Mi., U.S. | D8 | 110 |
| Rock, stm., U.S. | I6 | 110 |
| Rockall, i., Scot., U.K. | D5 | 4 |
| Rock Bay, B.C., Can. | G9 | 102 |
| Rockcastle, stm., Ky., U.S. | B2 | 112 |
| Rock Creek, B.C., Can. | H16 | 102 |
| Rock Creek Butte, mtn., Or., U.S. | F7 | 122 |
| Rockdale, Il., U.S. | I7 | 110 |
| Rockdale, Tx., U.S. | I10 | 116 |
| Rockefeller Plateau, plat., Ant. | D10 | 73 |
| Rockenhausen, Ger. | F7 | 10 |
| Rock Falls, Il., U.S. | I6 | 110 |
| Rockford, Al., U.S. | J10 | 114 |
| Rockford, Il., U.S. | G3 | 110 |
| Rockford, Il., U.S. | H6 | 110 |
| Rockford, Mi., U.S. | G10 | 110 |
| Rockford, Oh., U.S. | G2 | 108 |
| Rockford, Tn., U.S. | D3 | 112 |
| Rockglen, Sk., Can. | I9 | 104 |
| Rock Hall, Md., U.S. | H10 | 108 |
| Rock Hill, S.C., U.S. | D5 | 112 |
| Rockingham, N.C., U.S. | E7 | 112 |
| Rockingham Bay, b., Austl. | B7 | 70 |
| Rocklake, N.D., U.S. | C8 | 118 |
| Rock Lake, l., Mb., Can. | I15 | 104 |
| Rockland, Id., U.S. | H13 | 122 |
| Rockland, Ma., U.S. | E16 | 108 |
| Rockland, Me., U.S. | C17 | 108 |
| Rockland, Mi., U.S. | D6 | 110 |
| Rockland, On., Can. | B11 | 108 |
| Rocklands Reservoir, res., Austl. | K5 | 70 |
| Rockledge, Fl., U.S. | K6 | 112 |
| Rocklin, Ca., U.S. | F4 | 124 |
| Rockmart, Ga., U.S. | E1 | 112 |
| Rockport, Ca., U.S. | E2 | 124 |
| Rockport, In., U.S. | E10 | 114 |
| Rockport, Ky., U.S. | E10 | 114 |
| Rock Port, Mo., U.S. | B1 | 114 |
| Rockport, Tx., U.S. | K10 | 116 |
| Rock Rapids, Ia., U.S. | H11 | 118 |
| Rock River, Wy., U.S. | C11 | 120 |
| Rock Sound, Bah. | B6 | 94 |
| Rockspring, Tx., U.S. | H6 | 116 |
| Rock Springs, Wy., U.S. | C3 | 120 |
| Rockton, Il., U.S. | H6 | 110 |
| Rock Valley, Ia., U.S. | H11 | 118 |
| Rockville, Ct., U.S. | F13 | 108 |
| Rockville, In., U.S. | C9 | 114 |
| Rockville, Md., U.S. | H9 | 108 |
| Rockwall, Tx., U.S. | G10 | 116 |
| Rockwell, Ia., U.S. | H2 | 110 |
| Rockwell City, Ia., U.S. | I13 | 118 |
| Rockwood, Me., U.S. | B17 | 108 |
| Rockwood, Pa., U.S. | H7 | 108 |
| Rockwood, Tn., U.S. | D2 | 112 |
| Rocky, Ok., U.S. | D7 | 116 |
| Rocky, stm., Ab., Can. | D17 | 102 |
| Rocky, stm., N.C., U.S. | D7 | 112 |
| Rockyford, Ab., Can. | F21 | 102 |
| Rocky Ford, Co., U.S. | M4 | 118 |
| Rocky Harbour, Nf., Can. | C16 | 106 |
| Rocky Lake, l., Mb., Can. | D13 | 104 |
| Rocky Mount, N.C., U.S. | C9 | 112 |
| Rocky Mount (Staunton), stm., U.S. | C9 | 112 |
| Rocky Mount, Va., U.S. | C7 | 112 |
| Rocky Mountain, mtn., Mt., U.S. | C13 | 122 |
| Rocky Mountain House, Ab., Can. | E20 | 102 |
| Rocky Mountain National Park, U.S. | K2 | 118 |
| Rocky Mountains, mts., N.A. | E8 | 86 |
| Roda, Va., U.S. | C4 | 112 |
| Rodalben, Ger. | F7 | 10 |
| Rødby, Den. | N12 | 6 |
| Roddickton, Nf., Can. | B17 | 106 |
| Rodeo, Arg. | F4 | 80 |
| Rodeo, Mex. | E7 | 90 |
| Rodeo, N.M., U.S. | M7 | 120 |
| Roderick Island, i., B.C., Can. | E6 | 102 |
| Rodewisch, Ger. | E12 | 10 |
| Rodez, Fr. | H9 | 14 |
| Ródhos (Rhodes), Grc. | M12 | 20 |
| Ródhos (Rhodes), i., Grc. | M12 | 20 |
| Rodi Garganico, Italy | H10 | 18 |
| Roding, Ger. | F12 | 10 |
| Rodney, Ms., U.S. | K5 | 114 |
| Rodney, On., Can. | H14 | 110 |
| Rodniki, Russia | D24 | 22 |
| Rodrigues, i., Mrts. | K7 | 24 |
| Roebourne, Austl. | D3 | 68 |
| Roeland Park, Ks., U.S. | L13 | 118 |
| Roelofarendsveen, Neth. | D6 | 12 |
| Roer (Rur), stm., Eur. | F9 | 12 |
| Roermond, Neth. | F9 | 12 |
| Roes Welcome Sound, strt., N.T., Can. | D15 | 96 |
| Roff, Ok., U.S. | E10 | 116 |
| Rogačèvo, Russia | E20 | 22 |
| Rogagua, Laguna, l., Bol. | E8 | 82 |
| Rogaguado, Laguna, l., Bol. | E8 | 82 |
| Rogaland, co., Nor. | L10 | 6 |
| Rogatica, Bos. | F3 | 20 |
| Rogers, Ar., U.S. | F2 | 114 |
| Rogers, Tx., U.S. | I9 | 116 |
| Rogers, Mount, mtn., Va., U.S. | C5 | 112 |
| Rogers City, Mi., U.S. | E12 | 110 |
| Rogers Lake, l., Ca., U.S. | J8 | 124 |
| Rogers Pass, B.C., Can. | F17 | 102 |
| Rogersville, Al., U.S. | H9 | 114 |
| Rogersville, N.B., Can. | F8 | 106 |
| Rogersville, Tn., U.S. | C3 | 112 |
| Rogliano, Fr. | J16 | 14 |
| Rogoźno, Pol. | C17 | 10 |
| Rogue, stm., Mi., U.S. | G10 | 110 |
| Rogue, stm., Or., U.S. | H1 | 122 |
| Rogue River, Or., U.S. | H2 | 122 |
| Rohtak, India | F7 | 44 |
| Rohunta, Laguna, b., Hond. | B11 | 92 |
| Roi Et, Thai. | F7 | 40 |
| Roisel, Fr. | C10 | 14 |
| Roja, Lat. | D5 | 22 |
| Rojas, Arg. | H8 | 80 |
| Rojo, Cabo, c., Mex. | G11 | 90 |
| Rojo, Cabo, c., P.R. | F11 | 94 |
| Rokeby National Park, Austl. | B8 | 68 |
| Rokiškis, Lith. | F8 | 22 |
| Rokycany, Czech Rep. | F13 | 10 |
| Roland, Ia., U.S. | H4 | 114 |
| Roland, Mb., Can. | I17 | 104 |
| Rolândia, Braz. | G3 | 79 |
| Røldal, Nor. | L10 | 6 |
| Roldán, Arg. | G8 | 80 |
| Roldanillo, Col. | E4 | 84 |
| Rolette, N.D., U.S. | C8 | 118 |
| Rolfe, Ia., U.S. | I13 | 118 |
| Roll, Az., U.S. | L3 | 120 |
| Rolla, B.C., Can. | B14 | 102 |
| Rolla, Ks., U.S. | N6 | 118 |
| Rolla, Mo., U.S. | E5 | 114 |
| Rolla, N.D., U.S. | C8 | 118 |
| Rolle, Switz. | F5 | 13 |
| Rolleston, Austl. | E8 | 70 |
| Rolling Fork, Ms., U.S. | J6 | 114 |
| Rolling Fork, stm., Ky., U.S. | E11 | 114 |
| Rolling River Indian Reserve, Mb., Can. | H15 | 104 |
| Rollingstone, Austl. | B7 | 70 |
| Roma, Austl. | F8 | 70 |
| Roma (Rome), Italy | H7 | 18 |
| Roma, Tx., U.S. | M7 | 116 |
| Romagna, hist. reg., Italy | H18 | 14 |
| Romaine, stm., Can. | F20 | 96 |
| Roman, Rom. | C10 | 20 |
| Romania (România), ctry., Eur. | F13 | 4 |
| Romankivtsi, Ukr. | A11 | 20 |
| Roman-Kosh, hora, mtn., Ukr. | I4 | 26 |
| Romano, Cayo, i., Cuba | C6 | 94 |
| Romanshorn, Switz. | C11 | 13 |
| Romans [-sur-Isère], Fr. | G12 | 14 |
| Rome, Ga., U.S. | E1 | 112 |
| Rome, Il., U.S. | J6 | 110 |
| Rome see Roma, Italy | H7 | 18 |
| Rome, Ms., U.S. | I6 | 114 |
| Rome, N.Y., U.S. | D11 | 108 |
| Romeo, Mi., U.S. | H12 | 110 |
| Rometan, Uzb. | B18 | 48 |
| Romilly-sur-Seine, Fr. | D10 | 14 |
| Rommani, Mor. | C7 | 62 |
| Romney, W.V., U.S. | H8 | 108 |
| Romny, Ukr. | G4 | 26 |
| Romont, Switz. | E6 | 13 |
| Romorantin-Lanthenay, Fr. | E8 | 14 |
| Ron, Mui, c., Viet. | E9 | 40 |
| Ronan, Mt., U.S. | C11 | 122 |
| Roncador, Serra do, plat., Braz. | F8 | 76 |
| Ronceverte, W.V., U.S. | B6 | 112 |
| Ronchamp, Fr. | E13 | 14 |
| Ronda, Spain | H6 | 16 |
| Rønde, Den. | M12 | 6 |
| Rondon, Braz. | G2 | 79 |
| Rondônia, state, Braz. | D10 | 82 |
| Rondonópolis, Braz. | D1 | 79 |
| Ronge, Lac la, l., Sk., Can. | C9 | 104 |
| Rongshui, China | B10 | 40 |
| Rõngu, Est. | C9 | 22 |
| Rønne, Den. | N14 | 6 |
| Ronneby, Swe. | M14 | 6 |
| Ronne Entrance, b., Ant. | C12 | 73 |
| Ronne Ice Shelf, Ant. | C8 | 73 |
| Ronse (Renaix), Bel. | G4 | 12 |
| Ronuro, stm., Braz. | B1 | 79 |
| Roodhouse, Il., U.S. | C6 | 114 |
| Rooibokklaagte, stm., Nmb. | C5 | 66 |
| Roorkee, India | F7 | 44 |
| Roosendaal, Neth. | E5 | 12 |
| Roosevelt, Az., U.S. | K5 | 120 |
| Roosevelt, Ok., U.S. | E7 | 116 |
| Roosevelt, Ut., U.S. | C12 | 118 |
| Roosevelt, stm., Braz. | B11 | 82 |
| Roosevelt Campobello International Park, N.B., Can. | H7 | 106 |
| Roosevelt Island, i., Ant. | C9 | 73 |
| Root, stm., Mn., U.S. | G4 | 110 |
| Root, stm., N.T., Can. | E32 | 100 |
| Root, stm., Wi., U.S. | H8 | 110 |
| Root Lake, l., Mb., Can. | D13 | 104 |
| Roper, N.C., U.S. | D10 | 112 |
| Roper, stm., Austl. | B6 | 68 |
| Ropesville, Tx., U.S. | F4 | 116 |
| Roque Pérez, Arg. | H9 | 80 |
| Roraima, state, Braz. | C11 | 84 |
| Roraima, Mount, mtn., S.A. | E12 | 84 |
| Rorey Lake, l., N.T., Can. | C30 | 100 |
| Rorketon, Mb., Can. | G15 | 104 |
| Røros, Nor. | J12 | 6 |
| Rorschach, Switz. | D12 | 13 |
| Rørvik, Nor. | I12 | 6 |
| Rosa, Lake, l., Bah. | D8 | 94 |
| Rosa, Monte, mtn., Eur. | G8 | 13 |
| Rošal', Russia | F22 | 22 |
| Rosalia, Wa., U.S. | C8 | 122 |
| Rosamond, Ca., U.S. | J7 | 124 |
| Rosamorada, Mex. | F7 | 90 |
| Rosário, Arg. | G8 | 80 |
| Rosário, Braz. | D10 | 76 |
| Rosario, Mex. | F7 | 90 |

| Name | Map Ref. | Page |
|---|---|---|

Rosario, Mex. . . . . . . . . D5 90
Rosario, Para. . . . . . . . . C10 80
Rosario, Ur. . . . . . . . . . H10 80
Rosario, Ven. . . . . . . . . B6 84
Rosario, stm., Arg. . . . . . C6 80
Rosario, Bahía, b., Mex. . . C2 90
Rosario, Islas del, is., Col. . B13 84
Rosario de Arriba, Arg. . . . B2 90
Rosario de la Frontera, Arg. C6 80
Rosario de Lerma, Arg. . . . C6 80
Rosário del Tala, Arg. . . . G9 80
Rosário Oeste, Braz. . . . . F11 80
Rosário do Sul, Braz. . . . . F13 82
Rosarno, Italy . . . . . . . . K10 18
Roščino, Russia . . . . . . . A12 22
Roscoe, S.D., U.S. . . . . . F8 118
Roscoe, Tx., U.S. . . . . . . G6 116
Roscoe, stm., N.T., Can. . . B34 100
Roscommon, Ire. . . . . . . . H5 8
Roscommon, Mi., U.S. . . . . F11 110
Roscommon, co., Ire. . . . . H5 8
Roscrea, Ire. . . . . . . . . I6 8
Rose, Mount, mtn., Nv.,
U.S. . . . . . . . . . . . . E6 124
Roseau, Dom. . . . . . . . . G14 94
Roseau, Mn., U.S. . . . . . . C12 118
Roseau, stm., N.A. . . . . . B11 118
Roseberry Lakes, l., On.,
Can. . . . . . . . . . . . . F22 104
Rosebery, Austl. . . . . . . . M6 70
Rose-Blanche, Nf., Can. . . . E15 106
Roseboro, N.C., U.S. . . . . E8 112
Rosebud, Mt., U.S. . . . . . D19 122
Rosebud, S.D., U.S. . . . . . H7 118
Rosebud, Tx., U.S. . . . . . H10 116
Rosebud, stm., Ab., Can. . . F21 102
Roseburg, Or., U.S. . . . . . G2 122
Rosebush, Mi., U.S. . . . . . G11 110
Rose City, Mi., U.S. . . . . . F11 110
Rosedale, Ab., Can. . . . . . F22 102
Rosedale, Austl. . . . . . . . E9 70
Rosedale, In., U.S. . . . . . C9 114
Rosedale, La., U.S. . . . . . L5 114
Rosedale, Ms., U.S. . . . . . I5 114
Rosehall, Guy. . . . . . . . . D14 84
Rosehearty, Scot., U.K. . . . D11 8
Rose-Hill, Mrts. . . . . . . . v18 67c
Rose Hill, N.C., U.S. . . . . E8 112
Rose Hill, Va., U.S. . . . . . C3 112
Rose Lake, B.C., Can. . . . . C8 102
Roseland, La., U.S. . . . . . L6 114
Rosemary, Ab., Can. . . . . . G22 102
Rosenberg, Tx., U.S. . . . . J11 116
Rosendal, Nor. . . . . . . . . L10 6
Rosenheim, Ger. . . . . . . . H12 10
Rosepine, La., U.S. . . . . . L3 114
Rose Point, c., B.C., Can. . . C3 102
Rosetown, Sk., Can. . . . . . G6 104
Rosetta see Rashīd, Egypt . B6 60
Rose Valley, Sk., Can. . . . . F11 104
Roseville, Ca., U.S. . . . . . F4 124
Roseville, Il., U.S. . . . . . . J5 110
Roseville, Mi., U.S. . . . . . H13 110
Roseville, Mn., U.S. . . . . . E2 110
Roseville, Oh., U.S. . . . . . H4 108
Rosewood, Austl. . . . . . . F10 70
Rosh Ha'Ayin, Isr. . . . . . D3 50
Rosholt, S.D., U.S. . . . . . F11 118
Rosholt, Wi., U.S. . . . . . . F6 110
Rosh Pinna, Isr. . . . . . . . C5 50
Rosiclare, Il., U.S. . . . . . . E8 114
Rosignano Marittimo, Italy . F5 18
Rosignol, Guy. . . . . . . . . D14 84
Roşiori de Vede, Rom. . . . . E9 20
Roskilde, Den. . . . . . . . . N13 6
Rosl'akovo, Russia . . . . . . G23 6
Rosl'atino, Russia . . . . . . B27 22
Roslavl', Russia . . . . . . . H15 22
Roslyn, Wa., U.S. . . . . . . C5 122
Rosman, N.C., U.S. . . . . . D4 112
Rosporden, Fr. . . . . . . . . E3 14
Ross, Austl. . . . . . . . . . N7 70
Ross, N.Z. . . . . . . . . . . E3 72
Ross, stm., Yk., Can. . . . . E29 100
Rossano, Italy . . . . . . . . J11 18
Rossburn, Mb., Can. . . . . . H14 104
Rossell y Rius, Ur. . . . . . G11 80
Rossford, Oh., U.S. . . . . . F3 108
Ross Ice Shelf, Ant. . . . . . D9 73
Rossignol, Lake, l., N.S.,
Can. . . . . . . . . . . . . H8 106
Ross Island, i., Ant. . . . . . C8 73
Ross Lake, l., Mb., Can. . . . D17 104
Rossiter, Pa., U.S. . . . . . . G8 108
Ross Lake, res., N.A. . . . . B4 122
Rossland, B.C., Can. . . . . . H17 102
Rosslare, Ire. . . . . . . . . I7 8
Rosslau, Ger. . . . . . . . . D12 10
Rosso, Maur. . . . . . . . . . C2 64
Ross-on-Wye, Eng., U.K. . . J11 8
Rossoš', Russia . . . . . . . G5 26
Ross R. Barnett Reservoir,
res., Ms., U.S. . . . . . . . J6 114
Ross River, Yk., Can. . . . . F28 100
Ross Sea, Ant. . . . . . . . . C9 73
Rossville, Ga., U.S. . . . . . E11 112
Rossville, Il., U.S. . . . . . . B9 114
Rossville, Ks., U.S. . . . . . L12 118
Rosthern, Sk., Can. . . . . . F8 104
Rostock, Ger. . . . . . . . . A12 10
Rostov, Russia . . . . . . . . D22 22
Rostov-na-Donu, Russia . . . H5 26
Roswell, Ga., U.S. . . . . . . F2 116
Roswell, N.M., U.S. . . . . . K11 120
Rota, Spain . . . . . . . . . . I5 16
Rotan, Tx., U.S. . . . . . . . G6 116
Rotenburg, Ger. . . . . . . . B9 10
Rotenburg, Ger. . . . . . . . D9 10
Roth, Ger. . . . . . . . . . . F11 10
Rothaargebirge, mts., Ger. . D8 10
Rothenburg ob der Tauber,
Ger. . . . . . . . . . . . . F10 10
Rothesay, N.B., Can. . . . . . G7 106
Rothsay, Mn., U.S. . . . . . . E11 118
Rothschild, Wi., U.S. . . . . . F6 110
Rothwell, N.B., Can. . . . . . F7 106
Roti, Pulau, i., Indon. . . . . H7 38
Roto, Austl. . . . . . . . . . I6 70
Rotondella, Italy . . . . . . . I11 18
Rotorua, N.Z. . . . . . . . . . C6 72
Rott am Inn, Ger. . . . . . . H12 10
Rottenmann, Aus. . . . . . . H14 10
Rotterdam, Neth. . . . . . . . E5 12
Rotterdam, N.Y., U.S. . . . . E13 108
Rottweil, Ger. . . . . . . . . G8 10
Roubaix, Fr. . . . . . . . . . B10 14
Roudnice, Czech Rep. . . . . E14 10
Rouen, Fr. . . . . . . . . . . C8 14
Rougé, Fr. . . . . . . . . . . E5 14
Rougemont, Fr. . . . . . . . . E13 14
Rough, stm., Ky., U.S. . . . . E10 114
Rough River Lake, res.,
Ky., U.S. . . . . . . . . . . E10 114
Rouillac, Fr. . . . . . . . . . G6 14
Rouleau, Sk., Can. . . . . . . H10 104
Roulette, Pa., U.S. . . . . . . F8 108
Round Harbour, Nf., Can. . . C18 106
Round Head, Nf., Can. . . . . E9 70
Round Lake, Mn., U.S. . . . . H12 118
Round Lake, l., Nf., Can. . . . A17 106
Round Lake, l., Sk., Can. . . . H12 104

Round Mountain, Nv., U.S. . F8 124
Round Mountain, mtn.,
Austl. . . . . . . . . . . . . H10 70
Round Pond, l., Nf., Can. . . D17 106
Round Rock, Tx., U.S. . . . . I9 116
Roundup, Mt., U.S. . . . . . D17 122
Rousay Point, N.Y., U.S. . . . U.S.
Roussillon, hist. reg., Fr. . . J9 14
Rowan Lake, l., On., Can. . . I21 104
Rowena, Tx., U.S. . . . . . . H6 116
Rowland, N.C., U.S. . . . . . E7 112
Rowlesburg, W.V., U.S. . . . H7 108
Rowley, stm., N.T., Can. . . . B17 96
Rowley Island, l., N.T., Can. . C17 96
Rowley Shoals, rf., Austl. . . C3 68
Roxas, Phil. . . . . . . . . . C7 38
Roxboro, N.C., U.S. . . . . . C8 112
Roxburgh, N.Z. . . . . . . . . F2 72
Roxie, Ms., U.S. . . . . . . . K5 114
Roxton, Tx., U.S. . . . . . . F11 116
Roy, N.M., U.S. . . . . . . . D2 116
Roy, Ut., U.S. . . . . . . . . C4 120
Roy, Wa., U.S. . . . . . . . . C3 122
Royal, Ia., U.S. . . . . . . . H12 118
Royal Canal, Ire. . . . . . . . H6 8
Royal Center, In., U.S. . . . B10 114
Royal City, Wa., U.S. . . . . D6 122
Royale, Isle, i., Mi., U.S. . . B7 110
Royal Gorge, val., Co., U.S. . F11 120
Royal Leamington Spa,
Eng., U.K. . . . . . . . . . I12 8
Royal Oak, Mi., U.S. . . . . . H12 110
Royalton, Mn., U.S. . . . . . E1 110
Royal Tunbridge Wells,
Eng., U.K. . . . . . . . . . J14 8
Royan, Fr. . . . . . . . . . . G5 14
Roye, Fr. . . . . . . . . . . . C9 14
Roylyanka, Ukr. . . . . . . . C13 20
Royse City, Tx., U.S. . . . . . G10 116
Royston, Ga., U.S. . . . . . . E3 112
Rožaj, Yugo. . . . . . . . . . G4 20
Roždestvo, Russia . . . . . . D16 22
Rožňava, Slvk. . . . . . . . . G20 10
Roznov, Rom. . . . . . . . . . C10 20
Roztocze, hills, Eur. . . . . . E22 10
Rtiščevo, Russia . . . . . . . G6 26
Ruacaná, Nmb. . . . . . . . . A2 66
Ruacana Falls, wtfl, Afr. . . . A2 66
Ruapehu, Rep., N.Z. . . . . . C5 72
Ruapehu, Mount, mtn., N.Z. L21 126
Rub' al Khali see Ar-Rub' al-
Khālī, des., Asia . . . . . . D7 47
Rubcovsk, Russia . . . . . . . G8 28
Rubiataba, Braz. . . . . . . . C4 79
Rubim, Braz. . . . . . . . . . D8 79
Rubino, C. Iv. . . . . . . . . H7 64
Rubio, Ven. . . . . . . . . . . D6 84
Rubizhne, Ukr. . . . . . . . . H5 26
Ruboani, Sudan . . . . . . . . M6 60
Ruby, Ak., U.S. . . . . . . . . D17 100
Ruby, stm., Mt., U.S. . . . . . E13 122
Ruby Dome, mtn., Nv., U.S. . D10 124
Ruby Mountains, mts., Nv.,
U.S. . . . . . . . . . . . . D10 124
Ruby Valley, val., Nv., U.S. . D10 124
Rucava, Lat. . . . . . . . . . E4 22
Rudall, Austl. . . . . . . . . . I2 70
Rudall River National Park,
Austl. . . . . . . . . . . . . D4 68
Ruda Śląska, Pol. . . . . . . . E18 10
Rüdersdorf, Ger. . . . . . . . C13 10
Rüdiškes, Lith. . . . . . . . . G7 22
Rudn'a, Russia . . . . . . . . G14 22
Rudnyj, Kaz. . . . . . . . . . G10 28
Rudnytsya, Ukr. . . . . . . . . A12 20
Rudo, Bos. . . . . . . . . . . F3 20
Rudolf, Lake (Lake
Turkana), l., Afr. . . . . . . H8 56
Rudolstadt, Ger. . . . . . . . E11 10
Rudong, China . . . . . . . . C10 34
Rūdsar, Iran . . . . . . . . . C11 48
Rudyard, Mi., U.S. . . . . . . D11 110
Rudyard, Mt., U.S. . . . . . . B15 122
Rudzensk, Bela. . . . . . . . H10 22
Rue, Fr. . . . . . . . . . . . . B8 14
Ruen, mtn., Eur. . . . . . . . G6 20
Rufā'ah, Sudan . . . . . . . . J7 60
Ruffieux, Fr. . . . . . . . . . G12 14
Ruffin, S.C., U.S. . . . . . . F6 112
Rufino, Arg. . . . . . . . . . H7 80
Rufisque, Sen. . . . . . . . . D1 64
Rufus, Or., U.S. . . . . . . . E5 122
Rugao, China . . . . . . . . . C9 34
Rugby, Eng., U.K. . . . . . . I12 8
Rugby, N.D., U.S. . . . . . . C8 118
Rügen, i., Ger. . . . . . . . . A13 10
Rugged Mountain, mtn.,
B.C., Can. . . . . . . . . . G8 102
Ruhr, stm., Ger. . . . . . . . F10 12
Rui'an, China . . . . . . . . . D9 34
Ruidoso, N.M., U.S. . . . . . K11 120
Ruidoso, Río, stm., N.M.,
U.S. . . . . . . . . . . . . K11 120
Ruidoso Downs, N.M., U.S. . K11 120
Ruijin, China . . . . . . . . . J5 34
Ruivo, Pico, mtn., Port. . . . m21 17a
Ruiz, Mex. . . . . . . . . . . M7 90
Ruiz de Montoya, Arg. . . . . D11 80
Rūjiena, Lat. . . . . . . . . . D8 22
Rukwa, Lake, l., Tan. . . . . . C6 58
Rule, Tx., U.S. . . . . . . . . F7 116
Ruleville, Ms., U.S. . . . . . I6 114
Rulo, Ne., U.S. . . . . . . . . K12 118
Ruma, Yugo. . . . . . . . . . D3 20
Rumbek, Sudan . . . . . . . . N5 60
Rumbek, Bel. . . . . . . . . . G3 12
Rum Cay, i., Bah. . . . . . . . C7 94
Rumford, Me., U.S. . . . . . . C16 108
Rumia, Pol. . . . . . . . . . . A18 10
Rumigny, Fr. . . . . . . . . . C11 14
Rum Jungle, Austl. . . . . . . B6 68
Rummānah, Egypt . . . . . . B7 60
Rumoi, Japan . . . . . . . . . d16 36a
Runan, China . . . . . . . . . B3 34
Runanga, N.Z. . . . . . . . . E3 72
Rundu, Nmb. . . . . . . . . . A4 66
Runge, Tx., U.S. . . . . . . . K9 116
Rungwa, Tan. . . . . . . . . . C6 58
Rungwa, stm., Tan. . . . . . . C6 58
Ruo, stm., China . . . . . . . C6 30
Ruoqiang, China . . . . . . . D4 30
Ruoxi, China . . . . . . . . . F4 34
Rupea, Rom. . . . . . . . . . C9 20
Rupert, Id., U.S. . . . . . . . H12 122
Rupert, W.V., U.S. . . . . . . J6 108
Rupert, Rivière de, stm.,
Que., Can. . . . . . . . . . F17 96
Rupununi, stm., Guy. . . . . . F13 84
Ruqqād, Wādī ar-, val., Asia C5 50
Rur (Roer), stm., Eur. . . . . F9 12

Rural Hall, N.C., U.S. . . . . C6 112
Rural Retreat, Va., U.S. . . . C5 112
Rurrenabaque, Bol. . . . . . F8 82
Rurstausee, res., Ger. . . . . G9 12
Rušan, Taj. . . . . . . . . . . B4 44
Rusape, Zimb. . . . . . . . . B11 66
Ruşayriş, Khazzān ar-, res.,
Afr. . . . . . . . . . . . . . L8 60
Ruse, Bul. . . . . . . . . . . F9 20
Rush, stm., N.D., U.S. . . . . D10 118
Rush, stm., Wi., U.S. . . . . . F3 110
Rush Center, Ks., U.S. . . . . M8 118
Rush City, Mn., U.S. . . . . . E3 110
Rushford, Mn., U.S. . . . . . G4 110
Rushmore, Mn., U.S. . . . . . H12 118
Rush Springs, Ok., U.S. . . . E9 116
Rushville, Il., U.S. . . . . . . B6 114
Rushville, In., U.S. . . . . . . C11 114
Rushville, Ne., U.S. . . . . . I5 118
Rusk, Tx., U.S. . . . . . . . . H11 116
Ruskin, Fl., U.S. . . . . . . . L4 112
Russas, Braz. . . . . . . . . . D11 76
Russell, Ont., Can. . . . . . . J2 110
Russell, Ks., U.S. . . . . . . M9 118
Russell, Ky., U.S. . . . . . . I4 108
Russell, Ky., U.S. . . . . . . H13 104
Russell, Mn., U.S. . . . . . . G12 118
Russell, On., Can. . . . . . . B11 108
Russell, Pa., U.S. . . . . . . F7 108
Russell, Cape, c., N.T.,
Can. . . . . . . . . . . . . A9 96
Russell Island, i., N.T., Can. B13 96
Russell Lake, l., Mb., Can. . . B13 104
Russells Point, Oh., U.S. . . . G3 108
Russell Springs, Ky., U.S. . . E11 114
Russellville, Al., U.S. . . . . . H9 114
Russellville, Ar., U.S. . . . . . G3 114
Russellville, Ky., U.S. . . . . F10 114
Russellville, Mo., U.S. . . . . D4 114
Rüsselsheim, Ger. . . . . . . E8 10
Russia, ctry., Eur. . . . . . . E14 26
Russian, stm., Ca., U.S. . . . F2 124
Russiaville, In., U.S. . . . . . B10 114
Russkij, ostrov, i., Russia . . B17 26
Rust, Aus. . . . . . . . . . . H16 10
Rustavi, Geor. . . . . . . . . I7 26
Rustburg, Va., U.S. . . . . . . B7 112
Rustenburg, S. Afr. . . . . . . E8 66
Ruston, La., U.S. . . . . . . . J4 114
Rute, Spain . . . . . . . . . . H7 16
Ruteng, Indon. . . . . . . . . G7 38
Rutenga, Zimb. . . . . . . . . C10 66
Ruth, Ms., U.S. . . . . . . . . K6 114
Ruth, Nv., U.S. . . . . . . . . E11 124
Rutherford, Tn., U.S. . . . . . F8 114
Rutherfordton, N.C., U.S. . . D5 112
Ruthton, Mn., U.S. . . . . . . G11 118
Ruthven, Ia., U.S. . . . . . . H13 118
Rūti, Switz. . . . . . . . . . . D10 13
Rutland, B.C., Can. . . . . . . H15 102
Rutland, N.D., U.S. . . . . . . E10 118
Rutland, Vt., U.S. . . . . . . . D14 108
Rutledge, Ga., U.S. . . . . . F3 112
Rutledge, Tn., U.S. . . . . . . C3 112
Rutog, China . . . . . . . . . D4 44
Rutshuru, D.R.C. . . . . . . . B5 58
Rutter, Ont., U.S. . . . . . . . D15 110
Ruvuma (Rovuma), stm.,
Afr. . . . . . . . . . . . . . D7 58
Ruy Barbosa, Braz. . . . . . B8 79
Ruza, Russia . . . . . . . . . F19 22
Ružajevka, Russia . . . . . . G6 26
Ružany, Bela. . . . . . . . . . I7 22
Ružomberok, Slvk. . . . . . . F19 10
Ryan, Ok., U.S. . . . . . . . . E9 116
Ryan, stm., B.C., Can. . . . . G11 102
Sacupana, Ven. . . . . . . . . C12 84
Sada, i., Japan . . . . . . . . B5 15
Ṣa'dah, Yemen . . . . . . . . F3 47
Saddle Lake Indian
Reserve, Ab., Can. . . . . D23 102
Saddle Mountain, mtn., Co.,
U.S. . . . . . . . . . . . . F11 120
Sadiola, Mali . . . . . . . . . E4 64
Sadiya, India . . . . . . . . . G16 44
Sadler Lake, l., Sk., Can. . . C11 104
Sado, i., Japan . . . . . . . . I13 36
Sadrinsk, Russia . . . . . . . F10 26
Sädvaluspen, Swe. . . . . . . H15 6
Saegertown, Pa., U.S. . . . . F6 108
Safed see Zefat, Isr. . . . . . C5 50
Safājah, Jazīrat, i., Egypt . . H2 43
Safford, Az., U.S. . . . . . . L7 120
Safi, Mor. . . . . . . . . . . . D6 62
Safonovo, Russia . . . . . . . F4 30
Saga, China . . . . . . . . . . F4 30
Saga, Japan . . . . . . . . . . N5 36
Sagaing, Myan. . . . . . . . . D3 43
Sagamihara, Japan . . . . . . L14 36
Sagami-nada, b., Japan . . . L14 36
Saganthit Kyun, i., Myan. . . I5 40
Sāgar, India . . . . . . . . . . H8 44
Sagavanirktok, stm., Ak.,
U.S. . . . . . . . . . . . . B20 100
Sagerton, Tx., U.S. . . . . . . F7 116
Saginaw, stm., Mi., U.S. . . . G12 110
Saginaw Bay, b., Mi., U.S. . . G12 110
Sagleipie, Lib. . . . . . . . . H5 64
Saglek Bay, b., Nf., Can. . . . E16 96
Sagonar, Russia . . . . . . . G16 28
Sagua de Tánamo, Cuba . . D7 94
Sagua la Grande, Cuba . . . C4 94
Saguenay, stm., P.Q., Can. . D3 106
Sagunt, Spain . . . . . . . . . F11 16
Sa'gya, China . . . . . . . . . F13 44
Ṣaḥāb, Jord. . . . . . . . . . E6 50
Sahaba, Sudan . . . . . . . . H6 60
Sahagún, Col. . . . . . . . . . C5 84
Sahara, des., Afr. . . . . . . . F7 52
Sahāranpur, India . . . . . . . F7 44
Sahbuz, Azer. . . . . . . . . . B8 48
Ṣāhibganj, India . . . . . . . H12 44
Şahin, Tur. . . . . . . . . . . H10 20
Şāhīwāl, Pak. . . . . . . . . . E5 44
Sahuaripa, Mex. . . . . . . . C5 90
Sahuayo de José María
Morelos, Mex. . . . . . . . G8 90
Sai Buri, Thai. . . . . . . . . K6 40
Saïda, Alg. . . . . . . . . . . C11 62
Saïdia, Mor. . . . . . . . . . . C9 62
Saidpur, Bngl. . . . . . . . . H13 44
Saidu, Pak. . . . . . . . . . . C5 44
Saignelégier, Switz. . . . . . D7 13
Saigon see Thanh Pho Ho
Chi Minh, Viet. . . . . . . . I9 40
Saijō, Japan . . . . . . . . . . E8 36
Saiki, Japan . . . . . . . . . . O6 36
Saimaa, l., Fin. . . . . . . . . K20 6
Saint Alban's, Nf., Can. . . . E18 106
Saint Albans, Eng., U.K. . . . J13 8
Saint Albans, Vt., U.S. . . . . C14 108
Saint Albans, W.V., U.S. . . . I5 108

Sabina, Oh., U.S. . . . . . . H3 108
Sabinal, Tx., U.S. . . . . . . J7 116
Sabinal, Cayo, i., Cuba . . . D6 94
Sabiñánigo, Spain . . . . . . C11 16
Sabinas, stm., Mex. . . . . . D9 90
Sabinas, stm., Mex. . . . . . D10 90
Sabinas Hidalgo, Mex. . . . . D9 90
Sabine, Mount, mtn., Ant. . . C8 73
Sabine, stm., U.S. . . . . . . E8 94
Sabine Lake, l., U.S. . . . . . M3 114
Sabine Pass, b., U.S. . . . . M3 114
Sabine Peninsula, pen.,
N.T., Can. . . . . . . . . . A11 96
Sabinópolis, Braz. . . . . . . E7 79
Sabinosa, Spain . . . . . . . p22 17b
Sabirabad, Azer. . . . . . . . A10 43
Sable, Cape, c., N.S., Can. . I8 106
Sable, Cape, pen., Fl., U.S. . N5 112
Sable, Île de, i., N. Cal. . . . C11 63
Sable, Rivière du, stm.,
Can. . . . . . . . . . . . . E19 96
Sable Island, i., N.S., Can. . I14 106
Sable-sur-Sarthe, Fr. . . . . E6 14
Sabogal, stm., C.R. . . . . . G10 92
Sabonkafi, Niger . . . . . . . D14 64
Sabou, Burkina . . . . . . . . E8 64
Sabres, Fr. . . . . . . . . . . H6 14
Sabrina Coast, Ant. . . . . . B7 73
Sabula, Ia., U.S. . . . . . . . H5 110
Ṣabyā, Sau. Ar. . . . . . . . . F3 47
Sabzevār, Iran . . . . . . . . C14 43
Sac, stm., Mo., U.S. . . . . . E3 114
Sacaba, Bol. . . . . . . . . . G8 82
Sacaca, Bol. . . . . . . . . . H8 82
Sacajawea Peak, mtn., Or.,
U.S. . . . . . . . . . . . . E8 122
Sacanche, Peru . . . . . . . . B3 82
Sacarilunga, stm., Braz. . . . E13 82
Sacaton, Az., U.S. . . . . . . K5 120
Sac City, Ia., U.S. . . . . . . I13 113
Săcele, Rom. . . . . . . . . . D9 20
Sachachi, Switz. . . . . . . . D6 13
Sachayoj, Arg. . . . . . . . . D8 80
Sachigo, stm., On., Can. . . . F14 96
Sachigo Lake, l., On., Can. . E22 104
Šachovskaja, Russia . . . . . E18 22
Šachrisabz, Uzb. . . . . . . . J11 25
Sachsen, state, Ger. . . . . . E13 10
Sachsen-Anhalt, state, Ger. . C11 10
Sachs Harbour, N.T., Can. . . H6 25
Sachunja, Russia . . . . . . . F7 26
Šack, Russia . . . . . . . . . G24 22
Sackets Harbor, N.Y., U.S. . D10 108
Sackville, N.B., Can. . . . . . G9 106
Saco, Me., U.S. . . . . . . . . D16 108
Saco, Mt., U.S. . . . . . . . . B18 122
Saco, stm., U.S. . . . . . . . D16 108
Sacramento, Braz. . . . . . . E5 79
Sacramento, Ca., U.S. . . . . F4 124
Sacramento, stm., Ca., U.S. . F4 124
Sacramento, stm., N.M.,
U.S. . . . . . . . . . . . . L11 120
Sacramento, Pampa del, pl.,
Peru . . . . . . . . . . . . . C4 82
Sacramento Mountains,
mts., N.M., U.S. . . . . . . L11 120
Sacramento Valley, val.,
Ca., U.S. . . . . . . . . . . D3 124
Sacre, stm., Braz. . . . . . . E12 82
Sacred Heart, Mn., U.S. . . . G12 118
Sa Dec, Viet. . . . . . . . . . I8 40
Sadêng, China . . . . . . . . . F4 30
Sadiola, Mali . . . . . . . . . E4 64

Saint-Albert, Ab., Can. . . . . D21 102
Saint-Alexandre-de-
Kamouraska, P.Q., Can. . . E4 106
Saint-Amand-Montrond, Fr. . F9 14
Sainte-Amélie, Mb., Can. . . H15 104
Saint-Amour, Fr. . . . . . . . F12 14
Saint-André, Reu. . . . . . . v17 67c
Saint-André, Cap, c.,
Madag. . . . . . . . . . . . p21 67b
Sainte-Anne-de-
Madawaska, N.B., Can. . . E5 106
Sainte-Anne-des-Chênes,
Mb., Can. . . . . . . . . . I18 104
Sainte-Anne-des-Monts,
P.Q., Can. . . . . . . . . . C7 106
Sainte-Anne-de-Beaupré,
P.Q., Can. . . . . . . . . . E3 106
Saint-Anne's, Eng., U.K. . . H10 8
Saint Ann's Bay, Jam. . . . . E6 94
Saint Anns Bay, b., N.S.,
Can. . . . . . . . . . . . . F13 106
Saint-Anselme, P.Q., Can. . . F3 106
Saint-Ansgar, Ia., U.S. . . . . G3 110
Saint-Anthony, Id., U.S. . . . G14 122
Saint-Anthony, N.B., Can. . . F9 106
Saint-Anthony, Nf., Can. . . . A18 106
Saint-Arnaud, Austl. . . . . . K5 70
Saint-Augustin, Fl., U.S. . . . J5 112
Saint-Augustin, Guy. . . . . . F13 84
Saint-Augustin Nord-Ouest,
stm., P.Q., Can. . . . . . . A14 106
Saint-Augustin-Saguenay,
P.Q., Can. . . . . . . . . . A15 106
Saint-Avold, Fr. . . . . . . . . C13 14
Saint-Barbe, Nf., Can. . . . . A17 106
Saint-Barthélemy, i., Guad. . F13 94
Saint-Basile, N.B., Can. . . . E5 106
Saint-Béat, Fr. . . . . . . . . J7 14
Saint-Blaise, Switz. . . . . . D6 13
Saint-Bonnet, Fr. . . . . . . . H13 14
Saint-Bonnet-de-Joux, Fr. . . F11 14
Saint Brendan's, Nf., Can. . D20 106
Saint Bride, Mount, mtn.,
Ab., Can. . . . . . . . . . . F19 102
Saint-Bride's, Nf., Can. . . . F19 106
Saint-Brieuc, Fr. . . . . . . . D4 14
Saint-Brieux, Sk., Can. . . . F10 104
Saint-Calais, Fr. . . . . . . . E7 14
Saint Catharines, Ont., Can. G16 110
Saint Catherines Island, i.,
Ga., U.S. . . . . . . . . . . H5 112
Saint-Cergue, Switz. . . . . . F5 13
Saint-Chamond, Fr. . . . . . G11 14
Saint-Charles, Ar., U.S. . . . H5 114
Saint Charles, Il., U.S. . . . . I7 110
Saint Charles, Mi., U.S. . . . G11 110
Saint Charles, Mn., U.S. . . . G3 110
Saint Charles, Mo., U.S. . . . D6 114
Saint Charles Mesa, Co.,
U.S. . . . . . . . . . . . . M3 118
Saint Christopher (Saint
Kitts), i., St. K./N. . . . . . F13 94
Saint Christopher-Nevis see
Saint Kitts and Nevis,
ctry., N.A. . . . . . . . . . F13 94
Saint Clair, Mi., U.S. . . . . . H13 110
Saint Clair, Mo., U.S. . . . . . D6 114
Saint Clair, Pa., U.S. . . . . . F11 108
Saint Clair, Lake, l., N.A. . . . H13 110
Saint Clair Shores, Mi., U.S. H13 110
Saint-Clairsville, Oh., U.S. . . G8 108
Saint-Claude, Fr. . . . . . . . F12 14
Saint-Claude, Mb., Can. . . . I16 104
Saint-Cloud, Fl., U.S. . . . . K5 112
Saint-Cloud, Mn., U.S. . . . . E1 110
Sainte-Croix, Switz. . . . . . E6 13
Saint Croix, i., V.I.U.S. . . . . F12 94
Saint Croix, stm., U.S. . . . . G6 106
Saint Croix Falls, Wi., U.S. . . E3 110
Saint Cyr Range, mts., Yk.,
Can. . . . . . . . . . . . . F28 100
Saint-David, Fr. . . . . . . . . M6 120
Saint David, Il., U.S. . . . . . J5 110
Saint David's, Wales, U.K. . . . .
Saint David's Head, c.,
Wales, U.K. . . . . . . . . J8 8
Saint-Denis, Fr. . . . . . . . . D9 14
Saint-Denis, Reu. . . . . . . . v17 67c
Saint-Dié, Fr. . . . . . . . . . D13 14
Saint-Dizier, Fr. . . . . . . . . D11 14
Saint Edward, Ne., U.S. . . . J10 118
Saint Eleanor's, P.E., Can. . F10 106
Saint Elias, Cape, c., Ak.,
U.S. . . . . . . . . . . . . G22 100
Saint Elias, Mount, mtn.,
N.A. . . . . . . . . . . . . G24 100
Saint Elias Mountains, mts.,
N.A. . . . . . . . . . . . . G24 100
Saint-Élie, P.Q., Can. . . . . C8 76
Saint Elmo, Il., U.S. . . . . . D8 114
Saint-Éloi, P.Q., Can. . . . . D4 106
Saint-Étienne, Fr. . . . . . . . G11 14
Saint-Eustache, P.Q., Can. . B13 108
Saint-Fabien, P.Q., Can. . . . D5 106
Saint-Félicien, P.Q., Can. . . G18 96
Sainte-Félicité, P.Q., Can. . . D6 106
Saint-Félix-de-Valois, P.Q.,
Can. . . . . . . . . . . . . A13 108
Saint-Florent, Fr. . . . . . . . I24 15a
Saint-Flour, Fr. . . . . . . . . G10 14
Sainte-Foy, P.Q., Can. . . . . F2 106
Sainte-Foy-la-Grande, Fr. . . H7 14
Saint Francis, Ks., U.S. . . . L6 118
Saint Francis, S.D., U.S. . . . H7 118
Saint Francis, Wi., U.S. . . . H8 110
Saint Francis, stm., N.A. . . . E4 106
Saint Francis, Cape, c., Nf.,
Can. . . . . . . . . . . . . E21 106
Saint Francisville, Il., U.S. . . B12 114
Saint Francisville, La., U.S. . L5 114
Saint-François, Lac, l., P.Q.,
Can. . . . . . . . . . . . . B15 108
Sainte-Genevieve, Mo., U.S. E6 114
Saint George, Austl. . . . . . G8 70
Saint George, N.B., Can. . . . G7 106
Saint George, On., Can. . . . G15 110
Saint George, S.C., U.S. . . . F6 112
Saint George, Ut., U.S. . . . . G3 120
Saint George, Cape, c., Nf.,
Can. . . . . . . . . . . . . D14 106
Saint George Island, Ak.,
U.S. . . . . . . . . . . . . H10 100

Saint George Island, i., Fl.,
U.S. . . . . . . . . . . . . J2 112
Saint-Georges, P.Q., Fr. Gu. C8 76
Saint George's, Gren. . . . . H14 94
Saint George's, Nf., Can. . . D15 106
Saint George's, P.Q., Can. . . A16 108
Saint George's Bay, b., Nf.,
Can. . . . . . . . . . . . . D14 106
Saint Georges Bay, b.,
N.S., Can. . . . . . . . . . G12 106
Saint George's Channel,
strt., Eur. . . . . . . . . . . J7 8
Saint Georges Head, c.,
Austl. . . . . . . . . . . . . J9 70
Saint-Germain, Fr. . . . . . . D9 14
Saint-Germain-du-Bois, Fr. . F12 14
Saint-Géry, Fr. . . . . . . . . H8 14
Saint-Gilles (Sint-Gillis), Bel. G5 12
Saint-Gingolph, Switz. . . . . F6 13
Saint-Girons, Fr. . . . . . . . J8 14
Saint Gregory, Mount, mtn.,
Nf., Can. . . . . . . . . . . C15 106
Saint-Guénolé, Fr. . . . . . . E3 14
Saint Helena, Fl., U.S. . . . . F3 124
Saint Helena, dep., Afr. . . . J6 52
Saint Helena Sound, strt.,
S.C., U.S. . . . . . . . . . G6 112
Saint Helens, Austl. . . . . . M8 70
Saint Helens, Or., U.S. . . . . E3 122
Saint Helens, Mount, vol.,
Wa., U.S. . . . . . . . . . . D3 122
Saint-Hilaire-du-Harcouët,
Fr. . . . . . . . . . . . . . D5 14
Saint-Hippolyte, Fr. . . . . . E13 14
Saint-Hippolyte-du-Fort, Fr. . I10 14
Saint-Hyacinthe, P.Q., Can. . B14 108
Saint Ignace, Mi., U.S. . . . . E11 110
Saint Ignace, N.B., Can. . . . F8 106
Saint Ignace Island, i., On.,
Can. . . . . . . . . . . . . B8 110
Saint Ignatius, Guy. . . . . . F13 84
Saint Ignatius, Mt., U.S. . . . C11 122
Saint-Imier, Switz. . . . . . . D7 13
Saint-Isidore, N.B., Can. . . . E8 106
Saint James, Mi., U.S. . . . . E10 110
Saint James, Mn., U.S. . . . . H13 118
Saint James, N.Y., U.S. . . . G13 108
Saint James, Cape, c.,
B.C., Can. . . . . . . . . . F3 102
Saint-Jean, stm., P.Q., Can. . B9 106
Saint-Jean-Baptiste, Mb.,
Can. . . . . . . . . . . . . I17 104
Saint-Jean-d'Angély, Fr. . . . G6 14
Saint-Jean-de-Losne, Fr. . . E12 14
Saint-Jean-de-Luz, Fr. . . . . I5 14
Saint-Jean-Pied-de-Port, Fr. I5 14
Saint-Jean-Port-Joli, Fr. . . . . .
Saint-Jean-sur-Richelieu,
P.Q., Can. . . . . . . . . . B13 108
Saint-Jérôme, P.Q., Can. . . B12 108
Saint Jo, Tx., U.S. . . . . . . F9 116
Saint John, Ks., U.S. . . . . . M9 118
Saint John, N.B., Can. . . . . G7 106
Saint John, N.D., U.S. . . . . C8 118
Saint John, stm., N.A. . . . . C8 122
Saint John, i., V.I.U.S. . . . . E12 94
Saint John, stm., N.A. . . . . G7 106
Saint John, Cape, c., Nf.,
Can. . . . . . . . . . . . . B18 106
Saint John, Lake, l., Nf.,
Can. . . . . . . . . . . . . D19 106
Saint John Bay, b., Nf.,
Can. . . . . . . . . . . . . B16 106
Saint John Island, i., Nf.,
Can. . . . . . . . . . . . . B16 106
Saint John's, Antig. . . . . . F14 94
Saint Johns, Az., U.S. . . . . J7 120
Saint Johns, Mi., U.S. . . . . G11 110
Saint John's, Nf., Can. . . . . E21 106
Saint Johns, Fl., U.S. . . . . I5 112
Saint Johnsbury, Vt., U.S. . . C14 108
Saint Joseph, Il., U.S. . . . . B8 114
Saint Joseph, La., U.S. . . . K5 114
Saint Joseph, Mn., U.S. . . . H9 114
Saint Joseph, Mo., U.S. . . . C2 114
Saint Joseph, N.B., Can. . . . G9 106
Saint Joseph, Tn., U.S. . . . I11 114
Saint Joseph, Lake, l., On.,
Can. . . . . . . . . . . . . F14 96
Saint-Joseph-d'Alma see
Alma, P.Q., Can. . . . . . . D2 106
Saint-Joseph-de-Beauce,
P.Q., Can. . . . . . . . . . F3 106
Saint Joseph Island, i., On.,
Can. . . . . . . . . . . . . D12 110
Saint-Jovite, P.Q., Can. . . . A12 108
Saint-Julien-en-Born, Fr. . . H5 14
Saint-Julien-en-Genevois,
Fr. . . . . . . . . . . . . . F13 14
Sainte-Julienne, P.Q., Can. . B13 108
Saint-Junien, Fr. . . . . . . . G7 14
Saint-Just-en-Chaussée, Fr. C9 14
Saint Kilda, i., Scot., U.K. . . D5 8
Saint Kitts see
Christopher, i., St. K./N. . . F13 94
Saint Kitts and Nevis, ctry.,
N.A. . . . . . . . . . . . . F13 94
Saint-Lambert, P.Q., Can. . . B13 108
Saint Landry, La., U.S. . . . . L4 114
Saint-Laurent, Mb., Can. . . H17 104
Saint-Laurent-du-Maroni,
Gu. . . . . . . . . . . . . . B8 76
Saint Lawrence, Austl. . . . . D8 70
Saint Lawrence, Nf., Can. . . F18 106
Saint Lawrence, stm., N.A. . G19 96
Saint Lawrence, Cape, c.,
N.S., Can. . . . . . . . . . E12 106
Saint Lawrence, Gulf of, b.,
N.A. . . . . . . . . . . . . D11 96
Saint Lawrence Island, i.,
Ak., U.S. . . . . . . . . . . E9 100
Saint-Lazare, Mb., Can. . . . H13 104
Saint-Léonard, N.B., Can. . . E6 106
Saint-Léonard-d'Aston,
P.Q., Can. . . . . . . . . . A14 108
Saint-Lô, Fr. . . . . . . . . . C5 14
Saint-Louis, Fr. . . . . . . . . G11 110
Saint Louis, Mo., U.S. . . . . D6 114
Saint-Louis, Reu. . . . . . . . v17 67c
Saint-Louis, Sen. . . . . . . . C1 64
Saint-Louis, stm., U.S. . . . . D3 110
Saint-Louis, Lac, l., P.Q. . . . . .
Saint-Louis-de-Kent, N.B.,
Can. . . . . . . . . . . . . F9 106
Saint-Loup-sur-Semouse,
Fr. . . . . . . . . . . . . . E13 14
Saint Lucia, ctry., N.A. . . . . H14 94
Saint Lucia Channel, strt.,
N.A. . . . . . . . . . . . . G14 94
Sainte-Lucie, Mrtn. . . . . . . m24 15a
Saint Lucie Canal, Fl., U.S. . L6 112

| Name | Map Ref. | Page |
|---|---|---|
| Saint-Malo, Fr. | D4 | 14 |
| *Saint-Malo, Golfe de, b., Fr.* | D4 | 14 |
| Saint-Marc, Haiti | E8 | 94 |
| *Saint-Marc, Canal de, strt., Haiti* | E8 | 94 |
| *Saint Margaret Bay, b., Nf., Can.* | A17 | 106 |
| *Saint Margarets Bay, b., N.S., Can.* | H9 | 106 |
| *Sainte-Marguerite, stm., P.Q., Can.* | B7 | 106 |
| *Sainte-Marguerite, Baie, b., P.Q., Can.* | B7 | 106 |
| *Sainte-Marie, Cap, c., Madag.* | t21 | 67b |
| Sainte-Marie-aux-Mines, Fr. | D14 | 14 |
| Saint Maries, Id., U.S. | C9 | 122 |
| Saint Marks, Fl., U.S. | I2 | 112 |
| Sainte-Marthe-de-Gaspé, P.Q., Can. | C7 | 106 |
| *Saint-Martin (Sint Maarten), i., N.A.* | E13 | 94 |
| *Saint Martin, Lake, l., Mb., Can.* | G16 | 104 |
| Saint Martins, N.B., Can. | G8 | 106 |
| Saint Martinville, La., U.S. | L5 | 114 |
| Saint Mary, Mo., U.S. | E7 | 114 |
| *Saint Mary, stm., B.C., Can.* | H18 | 102 |
| *Saint Mary, stm., N.A.* | H21 | 102 |
| *Saint Mary Peak, mtn., Austl.* | H3 | 70 |
| *Saint Mary Reservoir, res., Ab., Can.* | H21 | 102 |
| Saint Marys, Ak., U.S. | E13 | 100 |
| Saint Marys, Austl. | M8 | 70 |
| Saint Marys, Ga., U.S. | I5 | 112 |
| Saint Marys, Ks., U.S. | L11 | 118 |
| Saint Mary's, Nf., Can. | F20 | 106 |
| Saint Marys, Oh., U.S. | G2 | 108 |
| Saint Mary's, On., Can. | G14 | 110 |
| Saint Marys, Pa., U.S. | F8 | 108 |
| Saint Marys, W.V., U.S. | H5 | 108 |
| *Saint Marys, stm., N.A.* | D11 | 110 |
| *Saint Marys, stm., N.S., Can.* | G11 | 106 |
| *Saint Marys, stm., U.S.* | G2 | 108 |
| *Saint Marys, stm., U.S.* | I5 | 112 |
| *Saint Mary's, Cape, c., Nf., Can.* | F19 | 106 |
| *Saint Marys, Cape, c., N.S., Can.* | H7 | 106 |
| *Saint Mary's Bay, b., Nf., Can.* | F20 | 106 |
| *Saint Marys Bay, b., N.S., Can.* | H7 | 106 |
| Saint-Mathieu, Fr. | G7 | 14 |
| *Saint Matthew Island, i., Ak., U.S.* | F8 | 100 |
| Saint Matthews, Ky., U.S. | D11 | 114 |
| Saint Matthews, S.C., U.S. | F6 | 112 |
| Saint-Maur [-des-Fossés], Fr. | D9 | 14 |
| *Saint-Maurice, stm., P.Q., Can.* | G18 | 96 |
| Sainte-Maxime, Fr. | I13 | 14 |
| Saint-Méen-le-Grand, Fr. | D4 | 14 |
| Saint Meinrad, In., U.S. | D10 | 114 |
| Sainte-Menehould, Fr. | C11 | 14 |
| Sainte-Mère-Église, Fr. | C5 | 14 |
| Saint Michael, Ak., U.S. | E13 | 100 |
| Saint Michaels, Md., U.S. | I10 | 108 |
| Saint-Mihiel, Fr. | D12 | 14 |
| Saint-Moritz see Sankt Moritz, Switz. | F16 | 14 |
| Saint-Nazaire, Fr. | E4 | 14 |
| Saint Nazianz, Wi., U.S. | F8 | 110 |
| Saint-Nicolas see Sint-Niklaas, Bel. | F5 | 12 |
| Saint-Omer, Fr. | B9 | 14 |
| *Saintonge, hist. reg., Fr.* | G6 | 14 |
| Saint-Pacôme, P.Q., Can. | E4 | 106 |
| Saint-Pamphile, P.Q., Can. | F4 | 106 |
| Saint Paris, Oh., U.S. | G3 | 108 |
| Saint-Pascal, P.Q., Can. | E4 | 106 |
| Saint Paul, Ab., Can. | D23 | 102 |
| Saint-Paul, Fr. | H13 | 14 |
| Saint Paul, In., U.S. | C11 | 114 |
| Saint Paul, Ks., U.S. | N12 | 118 |
| Saint Paul, Mn., U.S. | F2 | 110 |
| Saint Paul, Ne., U.S. | J9 | 118 |
| Saint-Paul, Reu. | v17 | 67c |
| Saint Paul, Va., U.S. | C4 | 112 |
| *Saint-Paul, stm., Can.* | F21 | 96 |
| *Saint Paul, stm., Lib.* | H4 | 64 |
| *Saint-Paul, Île, i., Afr.* | L11 | 126 |
| Saint Paul Island, Ak., U.S. | H9 | 100 |
| *Saint Paul Island, i., N.S., Can.* | E13 | 106 |
| Saint Pauls, N.C., U.S. | E8 | 112 |
| *Saint Pauls Inlet, b., Nf., Can.* | C16 | 106 |
| Saint Peter, Mn., U.S. | F2 | 110 |
| *Saint Peter Island, i., Austl.* | F6 | 68 |
| Saint Peter Port, Guernsey | C4 | 14 |
| Saint Peters, N.S., Can. | G13 | 106 |
| Saint Peters Bay, P.E., Can. | F11 | 106 |
| Saint Petersburg, Fl., U.S. | L4 | 112 |
| Saint Petersburg see Sankt-Peterburg, Russia | B13 | 22 |
| Saint-Pierre, Mart. | G14 | 94 |
| Saint-Pierre, Reu. | v17 | 67c |
| Saint-Pierre, St. P./M. | F17 | 106 |
| *Saint-Pierre, Lac, l., P.Q., Can.* | B5 | 106 |
| *Saint Pierre and Miquelon (Saint-Pierre-et-Miquelon), dep., N.A.* | F17 | 106 |
| Saint-Pierre-Église, Fr. | C5 | 14 |
| *Saint Pierre Island, i., Sey.* | C10 | 58 |
| Saint Pierre-Jolys, Mb., Can. | I18 | 104 |
| Saint-Pol-de-Léon, Fr. | D3 | 14 |
| Saint-Pol-sur-Ternoise, Fr. | B9 | 14 |
| Saint-Pons, Fr. | I9 | 14 |
| Saint-Prosper-de-Dorchester, P.Q., Can. | F3 | 106 |
| Saint-Quentin, Fr. | C10 | 14 |
| Saint-Quentin, N.B., Can. | E6 | 106 |
| Saint-Raphaël, Fr. | I13 | 14 |
| Saint Regis, Mt., U.S. | C10 | 122 |
| *Saint Regis, stm., N.A.* | C12 | 108 |
| Saint Regis Falls, N.Y., U.S. | C12 | 108 |
| Saint-Rémi-d'Amherst, P.Q., Can. | A12 | 108 |
| Saint-Rémy-de-Provence, Fr. | I11 | 14 |
| Saint Robert, Mo., U.S. | E4 | 114 |
| Saint-Romuald, P.Q., Can. | F2 | 106 |
| Sainte-Rose-du-Lac, Mb., Can. | G15 | 104 |
| Saintes, Fr. | G6 | 14 |
| Saint-Seine-l'Abbaye, Fr. | E11 | 14 |
| Saint Shotts, Nf., Can. | F20 | 106 |
| Saint-Siméon, P.Q., Can. | E4 | 106 |
| Saint Simons Island, Ga., U.S. | H5 | 112 |
| *Saint Simons Island, i., Ga., U.S.* | H5 | 112 |
| Saintes-Maries-de-la-Mer, Fr. | I11 | 14 |
| Saint Stephen, N.B., Can. | G6 | 106 |
| Saint Stephen, S.C., U.S. | F7 | 112 |
| Sainte-Thérèse, P.Q., Can. | B13 | 108 |
| Saint Thomas, N.D., U.S. | C10 | 118 |
| Saint Thomas, On., Can. | H14 | 110 |
| *Saint Thomas, i., V.I.U.S.* | E12 | 94 |
| Saint-Tite-des-Caps, P.Q., Can. | E3 | 106 |
| Saint-Trond see Sint-Truiden, Bel. | G7 | 12 |
| Saint-Tropez, Fr. | I13 | 14 |
| Saint-Urbain-de-Charlevoix, P.Q., Can. | E3 | 106 |
| Saint-Valéry-en-Caux, Fr. | C7 | 14 |
| Saint-Valéry-sur-Somme, Fr. | B8 | 14 |
| Saint-Vallier-de-Thiey, Fr. | I13 | 14 |
| Saint Vincent, Mn., U.S. | C10 | 118 |
| *Saint Vincent, i., St. Vin.* | H14 | 94 |
| *Saint Vincent, Cape see São Vicente, Cabo de, c., Port.* | H2 | 16 |
| *Saint Vincent, Gulf, b., Austl.* | J3 | 70 |
| *Saint Vincent and the Grenadines, ctry., N.A.* | H14 | 94 |
| Saint-Vincent-de-Tyrosse, Fr. | I5 | 14 |
| *Saint Vincent Passage, strt., N.A.* | H14 | 94 |
| Saint Vincent's, Nf., Can. | F20 | 106 |
| Saint-Vith (Sankt Vith), Bel. | H9 | 12 |
| Saint Walburg, Sk., Can. | E5 | 104 |
| Saint-Yvon, P.Q., Can. | C9 | 106 |
| Sai Yok, Thai. | G5 | 40 |
| Sajama, Bol. | H7 | 82 |
| *Sajama, Nevado, mtn., Bol.* | H7 | 82 |
| *Sajano-Sušenskoje vodochranilišče, res., Russia* | G16 | 26 |
| Şajat, Turk. | B17 | 48 |
| Šajmak', Taj. | B6 | 44 |
| Sajnšand, Mong. | C9 | 30 |
| *Sajó (Slaná), stm., Eur.* | G20 | 10 |
| Sajószentpéter, Hung. | G20 | 10 |
| Sa Kaeo, Thai. | H7 | 40 |
| Sakai, Japan | M10 | 36 |
| Sakaiminato, Japan | L8 | 36 |
| Sakākah, Sau. Ar. | G6 | 48 |
| *Sakakawea, Lake, res., N.D., U.S.* | D5 | 118 |
| *Sakami, stm., P.Q., Can.* | F17 | 96 |
| *Sakami, Lac, l., P.Q., Can.* | F17 | 96 |
| Sakania, D.R.C. | D5 | 58 |
| Sakaraha, Madag. | s21 | 67b |
| Sakarya, Tur. | G14 | 4 |
| *Sakarya, stm., Tur.* | G14 | 4 |
| Sakata, Japan | I14 | 36 |
| Sakchu, N. Kor. | C13 | 32 |
| Sakété, Benin | H11 | 64 |
| *Sakhalin see Sachalin, ostrov, i., Russia* | G20 | 28 |
| *Şakhrīyāt, Jabal aş-, mtn., Jord.* | F6 | 50 |
| Şakht Sar, Iran | C11 | 48 |
| Šakiai, Lith. | G6 | 22 |
| Sakiet Sidi Youssef, Tun. | M3 | 18 |
| Sakon Nakhon, Thai. | F8 | 40 |
| Sakrand, Pak. | G3 | 44 |
| Sakrivier, S. Afr. | H5 | 66 |
| Saks, Al., U.S. | I11 | 114 |
| *Sakwaso Lake, l., On., Can.* | E23 | 104 |
| *Sal, i., C.V.* | k17 | 64a |
| *Sal, stm., Russia* | H6 | 26 |
| *Sal, Cay, i., Bah.* | C4 | 94 |
| *Sal, Punta, c., Hond.* | B7 | 92 |
| Sala, Swe. | L15 | 6 |
| Salaberry-de-Valleyfield, P.Q., Can. | B12 | 108 |
| Salacgrīva, Lat. | D7 | 22 |
| *Salada, Laguna, l., Mex.* | A2 | 90 |
| Saladas, Arg. | E9 | 80 |
| Saladillo, Arg. | H9 | 80 |
| *Saladillo, stm., Arg.* | G7 | 80 |
| *Saladillo, stm., Arg.* | E7 | 80 |
| *Saladillo Dulce, Arroyo, stm., Arg.* | F8 | 80 |
| Salado, Arg. | E5 | 80 |
| *Salado, stm., Arg.* | H5 | 80 |
| *Salado, stm., Arg.* | F8 | 80 |
| *Salado, stm., Arg.* | H9 | 80 |
| *Salado, stm., Arg.* | E5 | 80 |
| *Salado, stm., Cuba* | D6 | 94 |
| *Salado, stm., Mex.* | D10 | 90 |
| *Salado, Rio, stm., N.M., U.S.* | J9 | 120 |
| *Şălaj, co., Rom.* | B7 | 20 |
| Šalakuša, Russia | J27 | 6 |
| Salala, Chile | F3 | 80 |
| Salala, Lib. | H4 | 64 |
| Şalālah, Oman | F9 | 47 |
| Salamá, Guat. | B4 | 92 |
| Salamá, Hond. | C8 | 92 |
| Salamanca, Chile | F3 | 80 |
| Salamanca, Mex. | G9 | 90 |
| Salamanca, N.Y., U.S. | E8 | 108 |
| Salamanca, Peru | F5 | 82 |
| Salamanca, Spain | E6 | 16 |
| *Salamat, Bahr, stm., Chad* | F4 | 56 |
| Salamina, Col. | E5 | 84 |
| Salamís, Grc. | L7 | 20 |
| *Salamís, i., Grc.* | L7 | 20 |
| *Salamonie, stm., In., U.S.* | B11 | 114 |
| Salantai, Lith. | E4 | 22 |
| Salaquí, Col. | D4 | 84 |
| *Salaquí, stm., Col.* | D4 | 84 |
| Salas, Peru | B2 | 82 |
| Salatiga, Indon. | j15 | 39a |
| Salavat, Russia | G9 | 26 |
| Salaverry, Peru | C2 | 82 |
| Salavina, Arg. | E7 | 80 |
| *Sala y Gómez, Isla, i., Chile* | G4 | 74 |
| Salcajá, Guat. | C3 | 92 |
| *Salccantay, Nevado, mtn., Peru* | E5 | 82 |
| Şalcedo, Dom. Rep. | E9 | 94 |
| Šalčininkai, Lith. | G8 | 22 |
| *Saldaña, stm., Col.* | F5 | 84 |
| Saldanha, S. Afr. | I3 | 66 |
| Saldungaray, Arg. | J8 | 80 |
| Saldus, Lat. | E5 | 22 |
| Sale, Austl. | L7 | 70 |
| Salé, Mor. | C7 | 62 |
| *Salebabu, Pulau, i., Indon.* | E8 | 38 |
| Salechard, Russia | D5 | 28 |
| Sale Creek, Tn., U.S. | G11 | 114 |
| Salem, Ar., U.S. | F5 | 114 |
| Salem, Ia., U.S. | J4 | 110 |
| Salem, Il., U.S. | D8 | 114 |
| Salem, In., U.S. | D10 | 114 |
| Salem, India | G5 | 46 |
| Salem, Ky., U.S. | E8 | 114 |
| Salem, Ma., U.S. | E16 | 108 |
| Salem, Mo., U.S. | E5 | 114 |
| Salem, N.H., U.S. | E15 | 108 |
| Salem, N.J., U.S. | H11 | 108 |
| Salem, N.Y., U.S. | D13 | 108 |
| Salem, Oh., U.S. | G6 | 108 |
| Salem, Or., U.S. | F2 | 122 |
| Salem, S.D., U.S. | H10 | 118 |
| Salem, Ut., U.S. | D5 | 120 |
| Salem, Va., U.S. | B6 | 112 |
| Salem, W.V., U.S. | H6 | 108 |
| Salemi, Italy | L7 | 18 |
| *Salentina, Penisola, pen., Italy* | I13 | 18 |
| Salerno, Italy | I9 | 18 |
| *Salerno, Golfo di, b., Italy* | I9 | 18 |
| Salgar, Col. | E5 | 84 |
| Salgótarján, Hung. | G19 | 10 |
| Sali, Alg. | G10 | 62 |
| *Salí, stm., Arg.* | D6 | 80 |
| Salida, Co., U.S. | F11 | 120 |
| Salies-de-Béarn, Fr. | I6 | 14 |
| Salihli, Tur. | K12 | 20 |
| Salihorsk, Bela. | I10 | 22 |
| Salim, Sudan | K5 | 60 |
| Salima, Mwi. | D6 | 58 |
| Salimani, Com. | k15 | 67a |
| Salina, Ks., U.S. | M10 | 118 |
| Salina, Ok., U.S. | C11 | 116 |
| Salina, Ut., U.S. | F5 | 120 |
| Salina Cruz, Mex. | I12 | 90 |
| *Salina Point, c., Bah.* | C7 | 94 |
| Salinas, Braz. | D7 | 79 |
| Salinas, Ca., U.S. | H4 | 124 |
| Salinas, Ec. | I2 | 84 |
| *Salinas, stm., Braz.* | D7 | 79 |
| *Salinas, stm., Ca., U.S.* | H4 | 124 |
| *Salinas, Pampa de las, pl., Arg.* | G5 | 80 |
| Salinas de Garci Mendoza, Bol. | H8 | 82 |
| Salinas de Hidalgo, Mex. | F9 | 90 |
| Saline, La., U.S. | J4 | 114 |
| Saline, Mi., U.S. | H12 | 110 |
| *Saline, stm., Ar., U.S.* | I4 | 114 |
| *Saline, stm., Il., U.S.* | E8 | 114 |
| *Saline, stm., Ks., U.S.* | M10 | 118 |
| *Saline Bayou, stm., La., U.S.* | J3 | 114 |
| Salingyi, Myan. | D3 | 40 |
| Salisbury, Austl. | J3 | 70 |
| Salisbury, Eng., U.K. | J12 | 8 |
| Salisbury, Md., U.S. | I11 | 108 |
| Salisbury, Mo., U.S. | C4 | 114 |
| Salisbury, N.C., U.S. | D6 | 112 |
| Salisbury, Pa., U.S. | H7 | 108 |
| Salisbury see Harare, Zimb. | A10 | 66 |
| *Salisbury Island, i., N.T., Can.* | D17 | 96 |
| *Salisbury Plain, pl., Eng., U.K.* | J12 | 8 |
| *Salish Mountains, mts., Mt., U.S.* | B11 | 122 |
| Salitpa, Al., U.S. | K8 | 114 |
| *Salkehatchie, stm., S.C., U.S.* | F5 | 112 |
| Şalkhad, Syria | D7 | 50 |
| Sallanches, Fr. | G13 | 14 |
| Salliqueló, Arg. | I7 | 80 |
| Sallisaw, Ok., U.S. | D12 | 116 |
| Salluit, P.Q., Can. | D17 | 96 |
| *Sallūm, Khalīj as-, b., Afr.* | B3 | 60 |
| Salmās, Iran | B8 | 48 |
| Salmi, Russia | K22 | 6 |
| Salmo, B.C., Can. | H17 | 102 |
| Salmon, Id., U.S. | E12 | 122 |
| *Salmon, stm., B.C., Can.* | C11 | 102 |
| *Salmon, stm., Id., U.S.* | E9 | 122 |
| *Salmon, stm., N.A.* | C12 | 108 |
| *Salmon, stm., N.B., Can.* | F8 | 106 |
| *Salmon, stm., N.Y., U.S.* | D11 | 108 |
| *Salmon, stm., Or., U.S.* | E4 | 122 |
| Salmon Arm, B.C., Can. | G15 | 102 |
| Salmon-Bay, P.Q., Can. | A16 | 106 |
| *Salmon Mountain, mtn., N.A.* | B15 | 108 |
| *Salmon Mountains, mts., Ca., U.S.* | C2 | 124 |
| *Salmon River Mountains, mts., Id., U.S.* | E10 | 122 |
| Salmon Valley, B.C., Can. | C12 | 102 |
| Salo, Fin. | K18 | 6 |
| Salò, Italy | D5 | 18 |
| *Salobra, stm., Braz.* | I13 | 82 |
| Salome, Az., U.S. | K3 | 120 |
| Salon-de-Provence, Fr. | I12 | 14 |
| Salonika see Thessaloníki, Grc. | I6 | 20 |
| Salonta, Rom. | C5 | 20 |
| *Saloum, stm., Sen.* | D2 | 64 |
| Sal Rei, C.V. | k17 | 64a |
| Salsacate, Arg. | F6 | 80 |
| *Salsilgo, Qawz, dunes, Afr.* | L2 | 60 |
| *Salsipuedes, Canal, strt., Mex.* | C3 | 90 |
| *Salsipuedes, Punta, c., C.R.* | I11 | 92 |
| *Salsipuedes, Punta, c., Mex.* | A1 | 90 |
| Sal'sk, Russia | H6 | 26 |
| Salsomaggiore Terme, Italy | E4 | 18 |
| *Salt, stm., Az., U.S.* | K5 | 120 |
| *Salt, stm., Ky., U.S.* | D11 | 114 |
| *Salt, stm., Mo., U.S.* | C5 | 114 |
| *Salt, stm., U.S.* | G14 | 122 |
| Salta, Arg. | C6 | 80 |
| *Salta, prov., Arg.* | C5 | 80 |
| Saltcoats, Sk., Can. | G12 | 104 |
| Saltillo, Mex. | E9 | 90 |
| Saltillo, Ms., U.S. | H8 | 114 |
| Saltillo, Tn., U.S. | G8 | 114 |
| Salt Lake City, Ut., U.S. | D5 | 120 |
| Salto, Arg. | H8 | 80 |
| Salto, Ur. | F10 | 80 |
| Salto da Divisa, Braz. | D9 | 79 |
| Salto de las Rosas, Arg. | H4 | 80 |
| Salto del Guairá, Para. | C11 | 80 |
| Salto Grande, Braz. | G4 | 79 |
| Salton City, Ca., U.S. | K10 | 124 |
| *Salton Sea, l., Ca., U.S.* | K10 | 124 |
| Saltville, Va., U.S. | C5 | 112 |
| Saluda, S.C., U.S. | E5 | 112 |
| Saluda, Va., U.S. | B10 | 112 |
| *Saluda, stm., S.C., U.S.* | E5 | 112 |
| Sālūr, India | C7 | 46 |
| Saluzzo, Italy | E2 | 18 |
| Salvador, Braz. | B9 | 79 |
| *Salvador, El see El Salvador, ctry., N.A.* | D6 | 92 |
| *Salvador, Lake, l., La., U.S.* | M6 | 114 |
| Salvador Mazza, Arg. | B7 | 80 |
| Salvage, Nf., Can. | D20 | 106 |
| Salvaterra de Magos, Port. | F3 | 16 |
| Salvatierra, Mex. | G9 | 90 |
| *Salwā, Dawḥat, b., Asia* | I11 | 48 |
| Salwā Baḥrī, Egypt | E7 | 60 |
| *Salween (Nu) (Thanlwin), stm., Asia* | D5 | 40 |
| Salyan, Azer. | J7 | 26 |
| Salyān, Nepal | F10 | 44 |
| Salyer, Ca., U.S. | D2 | 124 |
| Salyersville, Ky., U.S. | B3 | 112 |
| *Salzach, stm., Eur.* | G12 | 10 |
| Salzburg, Aus. | H13 | 10 |
| *Salzburg, state, Aus.* | H13 | 10 |
| Salzgitter, Ger. | C10 | 10 |
| *Salzkammergut, reg., Aus.* | H13 | 10 |
| Salzwedel, Ger. | C11 | 10 |
| Samā, Jord. | D6 | 50 |
| *Sama, stm., Peru* | G6 | 82 |
| Samacá, Col. | E6 | 84 |
| Samaipata, Bol. | H10 | 82 |
| *Samalá, stm., Guat.* | C3 | 92 |
| Sāmalkot, India | D7 | 46 |
| Samālūt, Egypt | C6 | 60 |
| *Samambaia, stm., Braz.* | G2 | 79 |
| Samaná, Dom. Rep. | E10 | 94 |
| *Samaná, Bahía de, b., Dom. Rep.* | E10 | 94 |
| *Samaná, Cabo, c., Dom. Rep.* | E10 | 94 |
| *Samana Cay, i., Bah.* | C8 | 94 |
| Samandağı, Tur. | C3 | 48 |
| Samaniego, Col. | G4 | 84 |
| Samar, Isr. | I4 | 50 |
| Samara (Kujbyšev), Russia | G8 | 26 |
| *Samara, stm., Russia* | G8 | 26 |
| Samarai, Pap. N. Gui. | n17 | 68a |
| Samaria, Id., U.S. | H13 | 122 |
| Samariapo, Ven. | E9 | 84 |
| Samarinda, Indon. | F6 | 38 |
| Samarkand, Uzb. | J11 | 26 |
| Sāmarrā', Iraq | D7 | 48 |
| Samastīpur, India | H11 | 44 |
| Samaúna, Braz. | B11 | 82 |
| Şamaxı, Azer. | A10 | 48 |
| Sambalpur, India | J10 | 44 |
| Sambas, Indon. | N10 | 40 |
| Sambava, Madag. | o24 | 67b |
| Sambawizi, Zimb. | B8 | 66 |
| Sambhal, India | F8 | 44 |
| Sāmbhar, India | G6 | 44 |
| Sambir, Ukr. | F23 | 10 |
| Sâmbor, Camb. | H8 | 40 |
| *Samborombón, stm., Arg.* | H10 | 80 |
| *Samborombón, Bahía, b., Arg.* | I10 | 80 |
| Samborondón, Ec. | H3 | 84 |
| *Sambre, stm., Eur.* | B11 | 14 |
| *Sambú, stm., Pan.* | C3 | 84 |
| Sambusu, Nmb. | A4 | 66 |
| Samch'ŏk, S. Kor. | F17 | 32 |
| Samch'ŏnp'o, S. Kor. | I16 | 32 |
| Samedan, Switz. | E12 | 13 |
| Samho, N. Kor. | D15 | 32 |
| *Samiria, stm., Peru* | J5 | 84 |
| *Samnaungruppe, mts., Eur.* | D13 | 13 |
| Samnye, S. Kor. | H15 | 32 |
| *Samoa Islands, is., Oc.* | J22 | 126 |
| Samo Alto, Chile | F3 | 80 |
| Samoded, Russia | E6 | 26 |
| Sámos, Grc. | L11 | 20 |
| *Sámos, i., Grc.* | L10 | 20 |
| Samoset, Fl., U.S. | L4 | 112 |
| *Samosir, Pulau, i., Indon.* | M5 | 40 |
| *Samothrace see Samothráki, i., Grc.* | I9 | 20 |
| *Samothráki (Samothrace), i., Grc.* | I9 | 20 |
| S'amozero, Russia | K23 | 6 |
| Sampacho, Arg. | G6 | 80 |
| Sampit, Indon. | F5 | 38 |
| Sampués, Col. | C5 | 84 |
| Sampur, Russia | I24 | 22 |
| *Sam Rayburn Reservoir, res., Tx., U.S.* | K2 | 114 |
| Samre, Eth. | K10 | 60 |
| Samreboi, Ghana | I8 | 64 |
| Samson, Al., U.S. | K10 | 114 |
| *Samson Indian Reserve, Ab., Can.* | E21 | 102 |
| Samsun, Tur. | G15 | 4 |
| Samtown, La., U.S. | K4 | 114 |
| Samuhú, Arg. | D8 | 80 |
| *Samui, Ko, i., Thai.* | J6 | 40 |
| Samut Prakan, Thai. | H6 | 40 |
| Samut Sakhon, Thai. | H6 | 40 |
| Samut Songkhram, Thai. | H6 | 40 |
| S'amža, Russia | A24 | 22 |
| San, Mali | E7 | 64 |
| *San (Xan), stm., Asia* | H9 | 40 |
| *San, stm., Eur.* | E22 | 10 |
| Saña, Peru | B2 | 82 |
| Şan'ā', Yemen | G4 | 47 |
| *Sanaba, stm., Afr.* | D4 | 64 |
| *Sanaga, stm., Cam.* | J14 | 64 |
| San Agustín, Arg. | J9 | 80 |
| San Agustín, Arg. | F6 | 80 |
| San Agustín, Col. | G4 | 84 |
| San Agustín de Valle Fértil, Arg. | F5 | 80 |
| San Alejo, El Sal. | D7 | 92 |
| *Sanalona, Presa, res., Mex.* | E6 | 90 |
| *San Ambrosio, Isla, i., Chile* | B1 | 78 |
| *Sanana, Pulau, i., Indon.* | F8 | 38 |
| Sanandaj, Iran | D9 | 48 |
| Sanandita, Bol. | I10 | 82 |
| San Andreas, Ca., U.S. | F5 | 124 |
| San Andrés, Col. | H4 | 94 |
| San Andrés, Mex. | D2 | 90 |
| San Andrés, Pan. | I12 | 92 |
| *San Andrés, Isla de, i., Col.* | H4 | 94 |
| San Andrés de Giles, Arg. | H9 | 80 |
| *San Andres Mountains, mts., N.M., U.S.* | L10 | 120 |
| San Andrés Sajcabajá, Guat. | B4 | 92 |
| San Andrés Tuxtla, Mex. | H12 | 90 |
| *San Andrés y Providencia, ter., Col.* | H4 | 94 |
| Sananduva, Braz. | D13 | 80 |
| San Angelo, Tx., U.S. | H6 | 116 |
| San Anselmo, Ca., U.S. | G3 | 124 |
| San Antero, Col. | C5 | 84 |
| San Antonio, Arg. | E6 | 80 |
| San Antonio, Belize | A5 | 92 |
| San Antonio, Chile | D3 | 80 |
| San Antonio, Chile | G3 | 80 |
| San Antonio, Col. | F5 | 84 |
| San Antonio, C.R. | G9 | 92 |
| San Antonio, N.M., U.S. | I10 | 120 |
| San Antonio, Peru | B3 | 82 |
| San Antonio, Tx., U.S. | J8 | 116 |
| San Antonio, Ur. | F10 | 80 |
| *San Antonio, stm., Mex.* | B2 | 90 |
| *San Antonio, stm., Tx., U.S.* | K9 | 116 |
| *San Antonio, Cabo, c., Arg.* | I10 | 80 |
| *San Antonio, Cabo de, c., Cuba* | D2 | 94 |
| *San Antonio, Mount, mtn., Ca., U.S.* | J8 | 124 |
| *San Antonio, Punta, c., Mex.* | C2 | 90 |
| *San Antonio, Punta, c., Mex.* | D4 | 90 |
| *San Antonio, Rio, stm., U.S.* | H10 | 120 |
| *San Antonio Bay, b., Tx., U.S.* | K10 | 116 |
| San Antonio de Areco, Arg. | H9 | 80 |
| San Antonio de los Baños, Cuba | C3 | 94 |
| San Antonio de los Cobres, Arg. | C5 | 80 |
| San Antonio del Táchira, Ven. | D6 | 84 |
| San Antonio de Tamanaco, Ven. | C9 | 84 |
| San Antonio El Bravo, Mex. | B7 | 90 |
| *San Antonio Mountain, mtn., N.M., U.S.* | H10 | 120 |
| San Antonio Suchitepéquez, Guat. | C3 | 92 |
| Sanatorium, Ms., U.S. | K7 | 114 |
| San Augustine, Tx., U.S. | K2 | 114 |
| *San Augustin Pass, N.M., U.S.* | L10 | 120 |
| San Bartolomé, Spain | n27 | 17b |
| San Benedetto del Tronto, Italy | G8 | 18 |
| *San Benedicto, Isla, i., Mex.* | H4 | 90 |
| San Benito, Bol. | G9 | 82 |
| San Benito, Guat. | I15 | 90 |
| San Benito, Peru | B2 | 82 |
| San Benito, Tx., U.S. | M9 | 116 |
| *San Benito, stm., Ca., U.S.* | H4 | 124 |
| San Bernardino, Ca., U.S. | J8 | 124 |
| San Bernardino, Switz. | F11 | 13 |
| *San Bernardino Mountains, mts., Ca., U.S.* | J9 | 124 |
| San Bernardo, Arg. | D8 | 80 |
| San Bernardo, Chile | G3 | 80 |
| San Bernardo, Mex. | E7 | 90 |
| *San Bernardo, Isla, i., Nic.* | F9 | 92 |
| *San Bernardo, Islas de, is., Col.* | C4 | 84 |
| San Bernardo del Viento, Col. | C5 | 84 |
| San Blas, Mex. | G7 | 90 |
| San Blas, Mex. | D5 | 90 |
| *San Blas, Cape, c., Fl., U.S.* | J1 | 112 |
| *San Blas, Golfo de, b., Pan.* | C3 | 84 |
| *San Blas, Serranía De, mts., Pan.* | C3 | 84 |
| San Blas de los Sauces, Arg. | E5 | 80 |
| San Borja, Bol. | F8 | 82 |
| Sanborn, Ia., U.S. | H12 | 118 |
| Sanborn, Mn., U.S. | G12 | 118 |
| Sanborn, N.D., U.S. | E9 | 118 |
| San Bruno, Ca., U.S. | G3 | 124 |
| San Buenaventura, Bol. | F8 | 82 |
| San Buenaventura, Mex. | D9 | 90 |
| Sancang, China | C9 | 34 |
| San Carlos, Arg. | D11 | 80 |
| San Carlos, Arg. | G4 | 80 |
| San Carlos, Arg. | C6 | 80 |
| San Carlos, Az., U.S. | K6 | 120 |
| San Carlos, Ca., U.S. | G3 | 124 |
| San Carlos, Chile | I3 | 80 |
| San Carlos, Mex. | C9 | 90 |
| San Carlos, Mex. | E10 | 90 |
| San Carlos, Nic. | F10 | 92 |
| San Carlos, Pan. | C3 | 84 |
| San Carlos, Para. | B10 | 80 |
| San Carlos, Phil. | C7 | 38 |
| San Carlos, Phil. | n19 | 39b |
| San Carlos, Ur. | H11 | 80 |
| San Carlos, Ven. | C8 | 84 |
| *San Carlos, stm., C.R.* | G10 | 92 |
| *San Carlos, stm., Ven.* | C8 | 84 |
| *San Carlos, Riacho, stm., Para.* | B9 | 80 |
| San Carlos Centro, Arg. | F8 | 80 |
| San Carlos de Bariloche, Arg. | E2 | 78 |
| San Carlos de Bolívar, Arg. | I8 | 80 |
| San Carlos de Guaroa, Col. | F6 | 84 |
| San Carlos del Zulia, Ven. | C7 | 84 |
| San Carlos de Río Negro, Ven. | G9 | 84 |
| San Cataldo, Italy | L8 | 18 |
| San Cayetano, Arg. | J9 | 80 |
| Sancerre, Fr. | E9 | 14 |
| Sánchez, Dom. Rep. | E10 | 94 |
| Sanch'ŏng, S. Kor. | H15 | 32 |
| San Ciro de Acosta, Mex. | G10 | 90 |
| San Clemente, Ca., U.S. | K8 | 124 |
| San Clemente, Spain | F9 | 16 |
| *San Clemente, Cerro, mtn., Chile* | F2 | 78 |
| *San Clemente Island, i., Ca., U.S.* | L7 | 124 |
| San Cosme, Arg. | D9 | 80 |
| San Cristóbal, Arg. | F8 | 80 |
| San Cristóbal, Dom. Rep. | E9 | 94 |
| San Cristóbal, Ven. | D6 | 84 |
| *San Cristóbal, Bahía, b., Mex.* | D2 | 90 |
| *San Cristóbal, Isla, i., Ec.* | j14 | 84a |
| *San Cristóbal, Volcán, vol., Nic.* | E7 | 92 |
| San Cristóbal de la Laguna, Spain | o24 | 17b |
| San Cristóbal de las Casas, Mex. | I13 | 90 |
| San Cristóbal Totonicapán, Guat. | C3 | 92 |
| San Cristóbal Verapaz, Guat. | B4 | 92 |
| Sancti Spíritus, Cuba | D5 | 94 |
| *Sancy, Puy de, mtn., Fr.* | G9 | 14 |
| *Sand, stm., Ab., Can.* | D3 | 104 |
| San Damián, Peru | E3 | 82 |
| Sandaré, Mali | D4 | 64 |
| Sand Coulee, Mt., U.S. | C14 | 122 |
| Sanders, Az., U.S. | I7 | 120 |
| Sanderson, Tx., U.S. | I4 | 116 |
| Sandersville, Ga., U.S. | G4 | 112 |
| Sandersville, Ms., U.S. | K7 | 114 |
| *Sandfly Lake, l., Sk., Can.* | C8 | 104 |
| Sand Fork, W.V., U.S. | I6 | 108 |
| Sandgate, Austl. | F10 | 70 |
| *Sand Hill, stm., Mn., U.S.* | D11 | 118 |
| *Sand Hills, hills, Ne., U.S.* | J6 | 118 |
| Sandia, Peru | F7 | 82 |
| *Sandia Crest, mtn., N.M., U.S.* | I10 | 120 |
| San Diego, Ca., U.S. | L8 | 124 |
| San Diego, Tx., U.S. | L8 | 116 |
| *San Diego, stm., Ca., U.S.* | L9 | 124 |
| *San Diego, Cabo, c., Arg.* | G3 | 78 |
| *San Diego Aqueduct, Ca., U.S.* | K8 | 124 |
| San Diego de la Unión, Mex. | G9 | 90 |
| San Dionisio, Nic. | E9 | 92 |
| *Sand Lake, l., On., Can.* | H20 | 104 |
| Sandoa, D.R.C. | C4 | 58 |
| Sandomierz, Pol. | E21 | 10 |
| Sandoná, Col. | G4 | 84 |
| San Donà di Piave, Italy | D7 | 18 |
| Sandoval, Il., U.S. | D7 | 114 |
| Sandovalina, Braz. | G3 | 79 |
| Sandovo, Russia | C19 | 22 |
| Sandoway, Myan. | E3 | 40 |
| Sandpoint, Id., U.S. | B9 | 122 |
| Sandringham, Eng., U.K. | I13 | 8 |
| Sandspit, B.C., Can. | D3 | 102 |
| Sand Springs, Ok., U.S. | C10 | 116 |
| Sand Springs, Tx., U.S. | G5 | 116 |
| Sandston, Va., U.S. | B9 | 112 |
| Sandstone, Austl. | E3 | 68 |
| Sandstone, Mn., U.S. | D3 | 110 |
| *Sandu Ao, b., China* | I8 | 34 |
| Sandusky, Mi., U.S. | G13 | 110 |
| Sandusky, Oh., U.S. | F4 | 108 |
| *Sandusky, stm., Oh., U.S.* | F3 | 108 |
| Sandvika, Nor. | L12 | 6 |
| Sandviken, Swe. | K15 | 6 |
| Sandwich, Il., U.S. | I7 | 110 |
| Sandwich, Ma., U.S. | F16 | 108 |
| *Sandwich Bay, b., Nf., Can.* | F21 | 96 |
| Sandwick, B.C., Can. | H10 | 102 |
| *Sandwīp Island, i., Bngl.* | I14 | 44 |
| Sandy, Or., U.S. | E3 | 122 |
| Sandy, Ut., U.S. | D5 | 120 |
| *Sandy, stm., Me., U.S.* | C17 | 108 |
| *Sandy Bay, b., Nic.* | C11 | 92 |
| *Sandy Bay Indian Reserve, Mb., Can.* | H16 | 104 |
| *Sandy Cape, c., Austl.* | E10 | 70 |
| Sandy Hook, Ky., U.S. | A3 | 112 |
| Sandy Hook, Ms., U.S. | K7 | 114 |
| *Sandy Hook, spit, N.J., U.S.* | G12 | 108 |
| Sandykači, Turk. | J10 | 26 |
| *Sandy Lake, l., Nf., Can.* | C17 | 106 |
| *Sandy Lake, l., On., Can.* | E22 | 104 |
| Sandy Point Town, St. K./N. | F13 | 94 |
| Sandy Springs, Ga., U.S. | F2 | 112 |
| San Elizario, Tx., U.S. | M10 | 120 |
| San Enrique, Arg. | H8 | 80 |
| San Estanislao, Para. | C10 | 80 |
| San Esteban, Hond. | B9 | 92 |
| *San Esteban, Isla, i., Mex.* | C3 | 90 |
| San Felipe, Chile | G3 | 80 |
| San Felipe, Col. | G9 | 84 |
| San Felipe, Mex. | B2 | 90 |
| San Felipe, Mex. | G9 | 90 |
| San Felipe, Phil. | n19 | 39b |
| San Felipe, Ven. | B8 | 84 |
| *San Felipe, Castillo de, hist., Guat.* | B5 | 92 |
| *San Felipe, Cayos de, is., Cuba* | D3 | 94 |
| San Felipe de Vichayal, Peru | A1 | 82 |
| San Felipe Nuevo Mercurio, Mex. | E8 | 90 |
| San Felipe Pueblo, N.M., U.S. | I10 | 120 |
| *San Félix, stm., Pan.* | I13 | 92 |
| *San Félix, Isla, i., Chile* | G6 | 74 |
| San Fernando, Ca., U.S. | J7 | 124 |
| San Fernando, Chile | H3 | 80 |
| San Fernando, Mex. | E10 | 90 |
| San Fernando, Phil. | m19 | 39b |
| San Fernando, Phil. | n19 | 39b |
| San Fernando, Spain | I5 | 16 |
| San Fernando, Trin. | I14 | 94 |
| San Fernando, Ven. | D9 | 84 |
| San Fernando de Atabapo, Ven. | E9 | 84 |
| San Fernando del Valle de Catamarca, Arg. | E6 | 80 |
| Sanford, Co., U.S. | G11 | 120 |
| Sanford, Fl., U.S. | K5 | 112 |
| Sanford, Me., U.S. | D16 | 108 |
| Sanford, Mi., U.S. | G11 | 110 |
| Sanford, N.C., U.S. | D7 | 112 |
| Sanford, Tx., U.S. | D5 | 116 |
| *Sanford, Mount, mtn., Ak., U.S.* | E22 | 100 |
| San Francisco, Arg. | F7 | 80 |
| San Francisco, Ca., U.S. | G3 | 124 |
| San Francisco, Col. | G4 | 84 |
| San Francisco, C.R. | H9 | 92 |
| San Francisco, El Sal. | D6 | 92 |
| San Francisco, Pan. | I14 | 92 |
| *San Francisco, stm., Arg.* | B6 | 80 |
| *San Francisco, stm., U.S.* | K8 | 120 |
| *San Francisco, Paso de, S.A.* | D4 | 80 |
| *San Francisco Bay, b., Ca., U.S.* | G3 | 124 |
| San Francisco de Borja, Mex. | D6 | 90 |
| San Francisco de la Paz, Hond. | C8 | 92 |
| San Francisco del Chañar, Arg. | E7 | 80 |
| San Francisco del Monte de Oro, Arg. | G5 | 80 |
| San Francisco del Oro, Mex. | D7 | 90 |
| San Francisco del Rincón, Mex. | G9 | 90 |
| San Francisco de Macoris, Dom. Rep. | E9 | 94 |
| San Francisco de Mostazal, Chile | G3 | 80 |
| San Francisco Libre, Nic. | E8 | 92 |
| *San Franco, Cerro, mtn., Hond.* | B7 | 92 |
| San Gabriel, Ec. | G4 | 84 |
| *San Gabriel, stm., Tx., U.S.* | I9 | 116 |
| San Gabriel Chilac, Mex. | H11 | 90 |
| *San Gabriel Mountains, mts., Ca., U.S.* | J7 | 124 |
| Sangamner, India | C3 | 46 |
| *Sangamon, stm., Il., U.S.* | B6 | 114 |
| Sanga Puitã, Braz. | G1 | 79 |
| *Sangay, vol., Ec.* | H3 | 84 |
| *Sangayán, Isla, i., Peru* | E3 | 82 |
| Sangchungshih, Tai. | J10 | 34 |
| Sang-e Māsheh, Afg. | D2 | 44 |
| Sanger, Ca., U.S. | H6 | 124 |
| Sanger, Tx., U.S. | F9 | 116 |
| Sângera, Mol. | B12 | 20 |
| Sangerhausen, Ger. | D11 | 10 |
| San Germán, Cuba | D6 | 94 |
| San Germán, P.R. | E11 | 94 |
| Sangerville, Me., U.S. | B17 | 108 |
| *Sanggan, stm., China* | C9 | 30 |
| *Sangha, stm., Afr.* | A3 | 58 |
| *Sangihe, Kepulauan, is., Indon.* | E8 | 38 |
| *Sangihe, Pulau, i., Indon.* | E8 | 38 |
| San Gil, Col. | D6 | 84 |
| San Gimignano, Italy | F6 | 18 |
| San Giovanni in Fiore, Italy | J11 | 18 |
| San Giovanni in Persiceto, Italy | E6 | 18 |
| San Giovanni Rotondo, Italy | H10 | 18 |
| San Giovanni Valdarno, Italy | F6 | 18 |
| Sangju, S. Kor. | G16 | 32 |
| Sāngli, India | D3 | 46 |
| Sangolquí, Ec. | H3 | 84 |
| *San Gorgonio Mountain, mtn., Ca., U.S.* | J9 | 124 |
| *San Gottardo, Passo del, Switz.* | E10 | 13 |
| *Sangre de Cristo Mountains, mts., U.S.* | G11 | 120 |
| San Gregorio, Arg. | H7 | 80 |
| San Gregorio, Ur. | G11 | 80 |
| Sangre Grande, Trin. | I14 | 94 |
| Sangrūr, India | E6 | 44 |
| Sanguandian, China | D7 | 34 |
| Sangudo, Ab., Can. | D20 | 102 |
| *Sangue, Rio do, stm., Braz.* | D12 | 82 |
| Sanhecun, China | A17 | 32 |
| *San Hipólito, Punta, c., Mex.* | D3 | 90 |
| *Sanibel Island, i., Fl., U.S.* | M4 | 112 |
| San Ignacio, Arg. | D11 | 80 |
| San Ignacio, C.R. | H10 | 92 |
| San Ignacio, Hond. | C7 | 92 |
| San Ignacio, Mex. | D3 | 90 |
| San Ignacio, Mex. | F9 | 90 |
| San Ignacio, Para. | D10 | 80 |
| *San Ignacio, Isla, i., Mex.* | E5 | 90 |
| *San Ignacio, Laguna, l., Mex.* | D3 | 90 |
| San Ignacio de Moxo, Bol. | F9 | 82 |
| San Ignacio de Velasco, Bol. | G11 | 82 |
| *San Ildefonso, Cerro, mtn., Hond.* | B6 | 92 |
| San Isidro, Arg. | H9 | 80 |
| San Isidro, Arg. | E6 | 80 |
| San Isidro, C.R. | H11 | 92 |
| San Isidro, Nic. | E8 | 92 |
| San Isidro, Tx., U.S. | M8 | 116 |
| San Jacinto, Ca., U.S. | K9 | 124 |
| San Jacinto, Col. | C5 | 84 |
| *San Jacinto, West Fork, stm., Tx., U.S.* | I11 | 116 |
| San Javier, Arg. | D11 | 80 |
| San Javier, Arg. | F9 | 80 |
| San Javier, Bol. | F9 | 82 |
| San Javier, Bol. | G10 | 82 |
| San Javier, Ur. | G9 | 80 |
| *San Javier, stm., Arg.* | E9 | 80 |

Name — Map Ref. — Page

San Javier de Loncomilla, Chile H3 80
Sanjāwi, Pak. E3 44
San Jerónimo, Guat. B4 92
San Jerónimo Norte, Arg. F8 80
Sanjō, Japan J13 36
San Joaquín, Bol. E9 82
San Joaquín, Para. C10 80
San Joaquín, stm., Bol. E10 82
San Joaquin, stm., Ca., U.S. G4 124
San Joaquin Valley, val., Ca., U.S. H5 124
San Jon, N.M., U.S. D3 116
San Jorge, Arg. F8 80
San Jorge, El Sal. D6 92
San Jorge, Nic. F9 92
San Jorge, stm., Col. C5 84
San Jorge, Bahía, b., Mex. B3 90
San Jorge, Golfo, b., Arg. F3 78
San José, Arg. D11 80
San Jose, Ca., U.S. G4 124
San José, C.R. H10 92
San Jose, Il., U.S. B7 114
San Jose, N.M., U.S. I11 120
San José, Para. C10 80
San Jose, Phil. n19 39b
San José, prov., C.R. H11 92
San Jose, stm., B.C., Can. F13 102
San José, Isla, i., Mex. E4 90
San José, Isla, i., Pan. C3 84
San Jose, Rio, stm., N.M., U.S. J9 120
San José Batuc, Mex. C5 90
San José Buena Vista, Guat. D4 92
San José de Bácum, Mex. D4 90
San José de Chiquitos, Bol. G11 82
San José de Copán, Hond. C6 92
San José de Feliciano, Arg. F9 80
San José de Guanipa, Ven. C10 84
San José de Guaribe, Ven. C10 84
San José de Jáchal, Arg. F4 80
San José de la Esquina, Arg. G8 80
San José de las Lajas, Cuba C3 94
San José de las Raíces, Mex. E9 90
San José del Cabo, Mex. F5 90
San José del Guaviare, Col. F6 84
San José de los Molinos, Peru E4 82
San José de Mayo, Ur. H10 80
San José de Ocuné, Col. E7 84
San José de Sisa, Peru B3 82
San José de Tiznados, Ven. C9 84
San Jose Island, i., Tx., U.S. K10 116
San Juan, Arg. F4 80
San Juan, Guat. B6 92
San Juan, Peru F4 82
San Juan, P.R. E11 94
San Juan, prov., Arg. F4 80
San Juan, stm., Arg. G5 80
San Juan, stm., Col. E4 84
San Juan, stm., Mex. E10 90
San Juan, stm., N.A. G10 92
San Juan, stm., Peru E4 82
San Juan, stm., S.A. G3 84
San Juan, stm., U.S. G6 120
San Juan, stm., Ven. B11 84
San Juan, Pico, mtn., Cuba D4 94
San Juan Bautista, Ca., U.S. H4 124
San Juan Bautista, Para. D10 80
San Juan Cotzal, Guat. B3 92
San Juan de Abajo, Mex. G7 90
San Juan de Colón, Ven. C6 84
San Juan de Guadalupe, Mex. E8 90
San Juan de la Maguana, Dom. Rep. E9 94
San Juan del César, Col. B6 84
San Juan del Norte, Nic. G11 92
San Juan del Oro, stm., Bol. I9 82
San Juan de los Cayos, Ven. B8 84
San Juan de los Morros, Ven. C9 84
San Juan del Río, Mex. E7 90
San Juan del Río, Mex. G9 90
San Juan del Sur, Nic. F9 92
San Juan de Micay, stm., Col. F4 84
San Juan de Payara, Ven. D9 84
San Juan Evangelista, Mex. I12 90
San Juanico, Mex. D3 90
San Juanillo, C.R. G9 92
San Juan Islands, is., Wa., U.S. B3 122
San Juanito, Isla, i., Mex. G6 90
San Juan Mountains, mts., Co., U.S. G9 120
San Juan Nepomuceno, Col. C5 84
San Juan Nepomuceno, Para. D11 80
San Juan Sacatepéquez, Guat. C4 92
San Juan Teotihuacán, Mex. H10 90
San Justo, Arg. F8 80
Sankarani, stm., Afr. F5 64
Sankosh, stm., Asia G14 44
Sankt Aegyd am Neuwalde, Aus. H15 10
Sankt Anton [am Arlberg], Aus. H10 10
Sankt Gallen, Aus. H14 10
Sankt Gallen, Switz. D11 13
Sankt Gallen, state, Switz. D11 13
Sankt Gilgen, Aus. H13 10
Sankt Goar, Ger. E7 10
Sankt Goarshausen, Ger. E7 10
Sankt Ingbert, Ger. F7 10
Sankt Johann im Pongau, Aus. H13 10
Sankt Johann in Tirol, Aus. H12 10
Sankt Moritz, Switz. E12 13
Sankt Niklaus, Switz. F8 13
Sankt Paul [im Lavanttal], Aus. I14 10
Sankt-Peterburg (Saint Petersburg), Russia B13 22
Sankt Peter-Ording, Ger. A8 10
Sankt Pölten, Aus. G15 10
Sankt Valentin, Aus. G14 10
Sankt Veit an der Glan, Aus. I14 10
Sankt Vith (Saint-Vith), Bel. H9 12
Sankt Wendel, Ger. F7 10
San Lázaro, Para. B10 80
San Lázaro, Cabo, c., Mex. E3 90
San Leandro, Ca., U.S. G3 124
Sanlicheng, China D3 34
Şanlıurfa, Tur. C5 48
San Lope, Col. D7 84
San Lorenzo, Arg. E9 80
San Lorenzo, Arg. G8 80
San Lorenzo, Bol. I9 82
San Lorenzo, Ec. G3 84
San Lorenzo, Hond. D7 92
San Lorenzo, Mex. E8 90
San Lorenzo, Nic. E9 92
San Lorenzo, Ven. C7 84
San Lorenzo, stm., Mex. E6 90
San Lorenzo, Bahía de, b., Hond. D7 92
San Lorenzo, Cabo, c., Ec. H2 84
San Lorenzo, Isla, i., Mex. C3 90
San Lorenzo, Isla, i., Peru E3 82
San Lorenzo de El Escorial, Spain E7 16
Sanlúcar de Barrameda, Spain I5 16
Sanlúcar la Mayor, Spain H5 16
San Lucas, Bol. I9 82
San Lucas, Ec. I3 84
San Lucas, Mex. F5 90
San Lucas, Cabo, c., Mex. F5 90
San Luis, Arg. G5 80
San Luis, Az., U.S. L5 120
San Luis, Co., U.S. G11 120
San Luis, Cuba D7 94
San Luis, Guat. A5 92
San Luis, Ven. B8 84
San Luis, prov., Arg. H5 80
San Luis, Laguna, l., Bol. E9 82
San Luis, Sierra de, mts., Arg. G6 80
San Luis de la Paz, Mex. G9 90
San Luis del Cordero, Mex. E7 90
San Luis del Palmar, Arg. D9 80
San Luis Gonzaga, Mex. E4 90
San Luis Gonzaga, Bahía, b., Mex. C2 90
San Luis Jilotepeque, Guat. C5 92
San Luis Obispo, Ca., U.S. I5 124
San Luis Peak, mtn., Co., U.S. G10 120
San Luis Potosí, Mex. F9 90
San Luis Potosí, state, Mex. F9 90
San Luis Reservoir, res., Ca., U.S. G4 124
San Luis Río Colorado, Mex. A2 90
San Luis Valley, val., Co., U.S. G10 120
Sanluri, Italy J3 18
San Manuel, Arg. I9 80
San Manuel, Az., U.S. L6 120
San Marcial, stm., Mex. C4 90
San Marcos, Chile F3 80
San Marcos, Col. C5 84
San Marcos, C.R. H10 92
San Marcos, El Sal. D5 92
San Marcos, Guat. C3 92
San Marcos, Hond. C6 92
San Marcos, Hond. B6 92
San Marcos, Mex. I10 90
San Marcos, Tx., U.S. J9 116
San Marcos, dept., Guat. B3 92
San Marcos, stm., Tx., U.S. J9 116
San Marcos, Isla, i., Mex. D3 90
San Marcos de Colón, Hond. D8 92
San Marino, S. Mar. F7 18
San Marino, ctry., Eur. G10 4
San Martín, Arg. E6 80
San Martín, Arg. G4 80
San Martín, Col. F6 84
San Martín, dept., Peru B3 82
San Martín, stm., Bol. D8 82
San Martín, stm., Bol. E10 82
San Martín, Lago (Lago O'Higgins), l., S.A. F2 78
San Martín de los Andes, Arg. E2 78
San Martín Texmelucan, Mex. H10 90
San Mateo, Ca., U.S. G3 124
San Mateo, Fl., U.S. J5 112
San Mateo, N.M., U.S. I9 120
San Mateo, Ven. C10 84
San Mateo Ixtatán, Guat. B3 92
San Matías, Bol. G12 82
San Matías, Golfo, b., Arg. E4 78
Sanmenxia, China E9 30
San Miguel, Arg. E10 80
San Miguel, Bol. G11 82
San Miguel, Ca., U.S. I5 124
San Miguel, Ec. H3 84
San Miguel, El Sal. D6 92
San Miguel, Mex. C9 90
San Miguel, Pan. C3 84
San Miguel, Peru E5 82
San Miguel, Spain o24 17b
San Miguel, stm., Bol. F10 82
San Miguel, stm., Co., U.S. F8 120
San Miguel (Cuilco), stm., N.A. B2 92
San Miguel, stm., S.A. H11 82
San Miguel, Cerro, hill, Bol. H11 82
San Miguel, Golfo de, b., Pan. C3 84
San Miguel, Volcán de, vol., El Sal. D6 92
San Miguel de Allende, Mex. G9 90
San Miguel de Cruces, Mex. E7 90
San Miguel del Monte, Arg. H9 80
San Miguel de Pallaques, Peru B2 82
San Miguel de Salcedo, Ec. H3 84
San Miguel de Tucumán, Arg. D6 80
San Miguel el Alto, Mex. G8 90
San Miguelito, Nic. F10 92
San Miguel Ixtahuacán, Guat. B3 92
San Miniato, Italy F5 18
Sannār, Sudan K7 60
Sannicandro Garganico, Italy H10 18
San Nicolás, Hond. B6 92
San Nicolás, Peru F4 82
San Nicolás, Spain p25 17b
San Nicolás, stm., Mex. H7 90
San Nicolás de los Arroyos, Arg. G8 80
San Nicolás de los Garza, Mex. E9 90
San Nicolas Island, i., Ca., U.S. K6 124
Sânnicolau Mare, Rom. C4 20
Sannikova, proliv, strt., Russia C20 28
Sanniquellie, Lib. H5 64
Sano, Japan K14 36
Sañogasta, Arg. E5 80
Sanok, Pol. F22 10
San Onofre, Col. C5 84
San Pablo, Col. G4 84
San Pablo, Phil. n19 39b
San Pablo, stm., Bol. F10 82
San Pablo, stm., Pan. I13 92
San Pablo Bay, b., Ca., U.S. F3 124
San Pedro, Arg. G9 80
San Pedro, Arg. C6 80
San Pedro, Arg. D6 80
San Pedro, Chile A4 80
San Pedro, Chile C6 80
San Pédro, C. Iv. I6 64
San Pedro, Col. C5 84
San Pedro, C.R. H10 92
San Pedro, Para. C10 80
San Pedro, Tx., U.S. L9 116
San Pedro, Ven. C7 84
San Pedro, dept., Para. C10 80
San Pedro, stm., Mex. B5 90
San Pedro, stm., N.A. I14 90
San Pedro, stm., N.A. L6 120
San Pedro, Punta, c., Chile C3 80
San Pedro, Volcán, vol., Chile A4 80
San Pedro Ayampuc, Guat. C4 92
San Pedro Carchá, Guat. B4 92
San Pedro Channel, strt., Ca., U.S. K7 124
San Pedro de Atacama, Chile B4 80
San Pedro de Buena Vista, Bol. H9 82
San Pedro de Curahuara, Bol. G7 82
San Pedro de la Cueva, Mex. C5 90
San Pedro de las Colonias, Mex. E8 90
San Pedro del Gallo, Mex. E7 90
San Pedro de Lloc, Peru B2 82
San Pedro del Norte, Nic. D10 92
San Pedro del Paraná, Para. D10 80
San Pedro de Macorís, Dom. Rep. E10 94
San Pedro Peaks, mts., N.M., U.S. H10 120
San Pedro Pinula, Guat. C5 92
San Pedro Pochutla, Mex. J11 90
San Pedro Sacatepéquez, Guat. C3 92
San Pedro Sula, Hond. B6 92
San Pedro Tabasco, Mex. I14 90
San Pelayo, Col. C5 84
San Pitch, stm., Ut., U.S. E5 120
Sanpoil, stm., Wa., U.S. B7 122
San Quintín, Cabo, c., Mex. B1 90
San Rafael, Arg. H4 80
San Rafael, Ca., U.S. G3 124
San Rafael, Chile H3 80
San Rafael, Mex. E9 90
San Rafael, N.M., U.S. I9 120
San Rafael, Ven. B7 84
San Rafael, stm., Bol. H12 82
San Rafael, stm., Ut., U.S. F5 120
San Rafael del Norte, Nic. D8 92
San Rafael del Sur, Nic. F8 92
San Rafael Desert, des., Ut., U.S. F6 120
San Rafael Oriente, El Sal. D6 92
San Rafael Swell, plat., Ut., U.S. F6 120
San Rafael Tasajera, El Sal. D6 92
San Ramón, Arg. D6 80
San Ramón, Bol. E9 82
San Ramón, C.R. G10 92
San Ramón, Hond. C10 92
San Ramón, Peru D4 82
San Ramón, Ur. H11 80
San Ramón de la Nueva Orán, Arg. B6 80
Sanrao, China L5 34
San Remo, Italy F2 18
San Román, stm., Guat. A4 92
San Román, Cabo, c., Ven. A7 84
San Roque, Arg. E9 80
San Roque, Arg. F4 80
San Roque, Spain I6 16
San Roque, Punta, c., Mex. D2 90
San Rosendo, Chile I2 80
San Saba, Tx., U.S. H8 116
San Saba, stm., Tx., U.S. I7 116
San Salvador, Arg. E10 80
San Salvador, Arg. F9 80
San Salvador, El Sal. D5 92
San Salvador (Watling Island), i., Bah. B7 94
San Salvador, Volcán de, vol., El Sal. D5 92
San Salvador de Jujuy, Arg. C6 80
Sansanné-Mango, Togo F10 64
San Sebastián, El Sal. D6 92
San Sebastián, Guat. C3 92
San Sebastián, Hond. C6 92
San Sebastián de la Gomera, Spain o23 17b
San Sebastián de Yalí, Nic. D8 92
Sansepolcro, Italy F7 18
San Severo, Italy H10 18
Sanshui, China L1 34
San Simon, Az., U.S. L7 120
San Simon, stm., Az., U.S. L7 120
San Simón, stm., Bol. E10 82
Sanso, Mali F6 64
San Solano, Arg. F6 80
Sans-Souci, hist., Haiti E8 94
Santa, Peru C2 82
Santa, stm., Peru C2 82
Santa, Isla del, i., Peru C2 82
Santa Adélia, Braz. F4 79
Santa Albertina, Braz. F3 79
Santa Ana, Arg. D11 80
Santa Ana, Bol. E9 82
Santa Ana, Bol. H12 82
Santa Ana, Ca., U.S. K8 124
Santa Ana, Col. C5 84
Santa Ana, Ec. H2 84
Santa Ana, El Sal. D5 92
Santa Ana, Mex. E9 90
Santa Ana, Mex. B4 90
Santa Ana, Ven. C10 84
Santa Ana, Volcán de, vol., El Sal. D5 92
Santa Ana del Alto Beni, Bol. F8 82
Santa Anna, Tx., U.S. H7 116
Santa Barbara, Ca., U.S. J6 124
Santa Bárbara, Chile I2 80
Santa Bárbara, Col. E5 84
Santa Bárbara, Hond. C6 92
Santa Bárbara, Mex. D7 90
Santa Bárbara, Ven. F9 84
Santa Bárbara, Ven. D7 84
Santa Bárbara, dept., Hond. B6 92
Santa Bárbara, stm., Bol. G11 82
Santa Barbara Channel, strt., Ca., U.S. J5 124
Santa Bárbara do Sul, Braz. E12 80
Santa Catalina, Arg. A5 80
Santa Catalina, Gulf of, b., Ca., U.S. L7 124
Santa Catalina, Isla, i., Mex. E4 90
Santa Catalina Island, i., Ca., U.S. K7 124
Santa Catalina o Calovébora, Pan. I13 92
Santa Catarina, Mex. E9 90
Santa Catarina, state, Braz. D13 80
Santa Catarina, Ilha de, i., Braz. D14 80
Santa Cecília, Braz. D13 80
Santa Clara, Ca., U.S. G4 124
Santa Clara, Col. I8 84
Santa Clara, Cuba C5 94
Santa Clara, Mex. C6 90
Santa Clara, Ut., U.S. G3 120
Santa Clara, stm., Ut., U.S. G3 120
Santa Clara de Olimar, Ur. G11 80
Santa Clotilde, Peru I6 84
Santa Coloma de Farners, Spain D14 16
Santa Comba Dão, Port. E3 16
Santa Cruz, Braz. E8 79
Santa Cruz, Ca., U.S. H3 124
Santa Cruz, Chile H3 80
Santa Cruz, C.R. G9 92
Santa Cruz, Peru B2 82
Santa Cruz, Phil. n19 39b
Santa Cruz, Phil. o20 39b
Santa Cruz, Port. m21 17a
Santa Cruz, Ven. C7 84
Santa Cruz, dept., Bol. G11 82
Santa Cruz, stm., Arg. G2 78
Santa Cruz, stm., N.A. L5 120
Santa Cruz, Isla, i., Ec. j13 84a
Santa Cruz, Sierra de, mts., Guat. B5 92
Santa Cruz Cabrália, Braz. D9 79
Santa Cruz de Goiás, Braz. D4 79
Santa Cruz de la Palma, Spain o23 17b
Santa Cruz de la Sierra, Bol. G10 82
Santa Cruz del Quiché, Guat. B3 92
Santa Cruz del Sur, Cuba D5 94
Santa Cruz de Tenerife, Spain o24 17b
Santa Cruz de Tenerife, prov., Spain o23 17b
Santa Cruz do Rio Pardo, Braz. G4 79
Santa Cruz do Sul, Braz. E12 80
Santa Cruz Island, i., Ca., U.S. J6 124
Santa Cruz Islands, is., Sol. Is. J20 126
Santa Elena, Arg. F9 80
Santa Elena, Ec. I2 84
Santa Elena, El Sal. D6 92
Santa Elena, Mex. D8 90
Santa Elena, stm., Bol. G8 82
Santa Elena, Bahía de, b., Ec. I2 84
Santa Elena, Cabo, c., C.R. G9 92
Santa Elena, Golfo de, b., C.R. G9 92
Santa Elena, Punta, c., Ec. I2 84
Santa Elena de Uairén, Ven. E12 84
Santa Eulalia, Guat. B3 92
Santa Eulària del Riu, Spain G13 16
Santa Fe, Arg. F8 80
Santa Fé, Braz. C3 79
Santa Fé, Braz. G3 79
Santa Fe, Hond. B8 92
Santa Fe, N.M., U.S. I11 120
Santa Fé, Pan. I13 92
Santa Fe, Spain H8 16
Santa Fe, prov., Arg. F8 80
Santa Fe, stm., N.M., U.S. I10 120
Santa Fe Baldy, mtn., N.M., U.S. I11 120
Santa Fe de Bogotá, Col. E5 84
Santa Fé do Sul, Braz. F3 79
Santa Filomena, Braz. E9 76
Santa Helena de Goiás, Braz. D3 79
Santai, China E8 30
Santa Inês, Braz. B9 79
Santa Inés, Bahía, b., Mex. D4 90
Santa Inés, Isla, i., Chile G2 78
Santa Isabel, Arg. I5 80
Santa Isabel, Arg. G8 80
Santa Isabel, Ec. I3 84
Santa Isabel, i., Sol. Is. I19 126
Santa Isabel, stm., Guat. B5 92
Santa Isabel de Sihuas, Peru G5 82
Santa Juliana, Braz. E5 79
Santa Lucía, Arg. E9 80
Santa Lucía, Arg. F4 80
Santa Lucía, Cuba D6 94
Santa Lucía, Ur. H10 80
Santa Lucía, Ven. C8 84
Santa Lucía Cotzumalguapa, Guat. C3 92
Santa Lucia Range, mts., Ca., U.S. H4 124
Santa Luzia, i., C.V. E2 54
Santa Magdalena, Arg. H7 80
Santa Margarita, Ca., U.S. I5 124
Santa Margarita, Isla, i., Mex. E4 90
Santa Margherita Ligure, Italy E4 18
Santa María, Arg. D5 80
Santa Maria, Braz. E12 80
Santa Maria, Ca., U.S. J5 124
Santa María, C.R. H11 92
Santa Maria, C.V. k17 64a
Santa María, Pan. I14 92
Santa Maria, Switz. F11 13
Santa Maria, Switz. E13 13
Santa Maria, stm., Braz. F11 80
Santa María, stm., Braz. A11 80
Santa María, stm., Mex. B6 90
Santa María, stm., Mex. G10 90
Santa María, stm., Pan. I14 92
Santa María, Bahía, b., Mex. E5 90
Santa María, Cabo, c., Ur. H11 80
Santa Maria, Cabo de, c., Ang. D2 58
Santa Maria, Cape, c., Bah. C7 94
Santa María, Isla, i., Chile I2 80
Santa María, Isla, i., Ec. j13 84a
Santa María, Laguna, l., Mex. B6 90
Santa María, Volcán, vol., Guat. C3 92
Santa María Asunción Tlaxiaco, Mex. I11 90
Santa Maria Capua Vetere, Italy H9 18
Santa María Colotepec, Mex. J11 90
Santa Maria da Vitória, Braz. B6 79
Santa María de Huazamota, Mex. F7 90
Santa María de Ipire, Ven. C10 84
Santa Maria de Itabira, Braz. E7 79
Santa María del Oro, Mex. E7 90
Santa María del Río, Mex. G9 90
Santa María de Mohovano, Mex. D8 90
Santa Maria di Leuca, Capo, c., Italy J13 18
Santa Maria do Suaçuí, Braz. E7 79
Santa Maria Madalena, Braz. F7 79
Santa-Maria-Siché, Fr. m23 15a
Santa Marinella, Italy G6 18
Santa Marta, Col. B5 84
Santa Marta, Guat. D3 92
Santa Marta, Cerro, mtn., Mex. H12 90
Santa Marta, Ciénaga Grande, b., Col. B5 84
Santa Marta Grande, Cabo de, c., Braz. E14 80
Santa Monica, Ca., U.S. J7 124
Santa Monica Bay, b., Ca., U.S. K7 124
Santana, Braz. B6 79
Santana, Port. m21 17a
Santana, stm., Braz. E3 79
Santana, Coxilha de, hills, S.A. F11 80
Santana da Boa Vista, Braz. F12 80
Santana do Livramento, Braz. F11 80
Santander, Col. F4 84
Santander, Spain B8 16
Santander, dept., Col. D6 84
Santander Jiménez, Mex. E10 90
Santanilla, Islas, is., Hond. F3 94
Sant Antoni de Portmany, Spain G13 16
Santa Paula, Ca., U.S. J6 124
Santaquin, Ut., U.S. E5 120
Santarém, Braz. D8 76
Santarém, Port. F3 16
Santaren Channel, strt., Bah. C5 94
Santa Rita, Col. G6 84
Santa Rita, Hond. B7 92
Santa Rita, Mex. C4 90
Santa Rita, Ven. B7 84
Santa Rita de Catuna, Arg. F5 80
Santa Rita do Araguaia, Braz. D2 79
Santa Rita do Weil, Braz. I8 84
Santa Rosa, Arg. I6 80
Santa Rosa, Arg. B6 80
Santa Rosa, Bol. F8 82
Santa Rosa, Bol. D8 82
Santa Rosa, Bol. G10 82
Santa Rosa, Braz. C5 79
Santa Rosa, Braz. D11 80
Santa Rosa, Ca., U.S. F3 124
Santa Rosa, Col. F8 84
Santa Rosa, C.R. G9 92
Santa Rosa, Ec. I3 84
Santa Rosa, N.M., U.S. E2 116
Santa Rosa, Para. D10 80
Santa Rosa, Para. I11 82
Santa Rosa, Tx., U.S. M9 116
Santa Rosa, Ven. C8 84
Santa Rosa, dept., Guat. C4 92
Santa Rosa, Parque Nacional, C.R. G9 92
Santa Rosa Beach, Fl., U.S. L10 114
Santa Rosa de Aguán, Hond. B9 92
Santa Rosa de Amanadona, Ven. G9 84
Santa Rosa de Cabal, Col. E5 84
Santa Rosa [de Copán], Hond. C6 92
Santa Rosa del Conlara, Arg. G6 80
Santa Rosa de Leales, Arg. D6 80
Santa Rosa de Lima, El Sal. D7 92
Santa Rosa del Palmar, Bol. G10 82
Santa Rosa de Osos, Col. D5 84
Santa Rosa de Río Primero, Arg. F7 80
Santa Rosa de Sucumbíos, Ec. G4 84
Santa Rosa de Viterbo, Col. E6 84
Santa Rosa Island, i., Ca., U.S. K5 124
Santa Rosa Island, i., Fl., U.S. L10 114
Santa Rosalía, Mex. D3 90
Santa Rosalía, Ven. C8 84
Santa Rosa Range, mts., Nv., U.S. C8 124
Šantarskije ostrova, is., Russia F19 28
Santa Sylvina, Arg. D8 80
Santa Teresa, Braz. E8 79
Santa Teresa, Mex. E11 90
Santa Teresa, stm., Braz. B4 79
Santa Teresa, Embalse de, res., Spain E6 16
Santa Tereza de Goiás, Braz. B4 79
Santa Uxia, Spain C2 16
Santa Vitória, Braz. E3 79
Santa Vitória do Palmar, Braz. G12 80
Santa Ynez, stm., Ca., U.S. J5 124
Sant Carles de la Ràpita, Spain E12 16
Santee, Ca., U.S. L9 124
Santee, stm., S.C., U.S. F7 112
Sant Feliu de Guíxols, Spain D15 16
Santhià, Italy D3 18
Santiago, Bol. H12 82
Santiago, Braz. E11 80
Santiago, Chile G3 80
Santiago, Mex. F5 90
Santiago, Pan. C2 84
Santiago, Para. D10 80
Santiago, Peru F4 82
Santiago, i., C.V. m17 64a
Santiago, stm., Mex. E7 90
Santiago, stm., S.A. I4 84
Santiago, Cerro, mtn., Pan. I13 92
Santiago, Isla, i., Ec. j13 84a
Santiago, Serranía de, mts., Bol. H12 82
Santiago Atitlán, Guat. C3 92
Santiago Choapan, Mex. I12 90
Santiago de Cao, Peru B2 82
Santiago de Chocorvos, Peru E4 82
Santiago de Chuco, Peru C2 82
Santiago de Compostela, Spain C3 16
Santiago de Cuba, Cuba D7 94
Santiago de Huari, Bol. H8 82
Santiago de Huata, Bol. G7 82
Santiago del Estero, Arg. D6 80
Santiago del Estero, prov., Arg. E7 80
Santiago de los Caballeros, Dom. Rep. E9 94
Santiago de Machaca, Bol. G7 82
Santiago de Méndez, Ec. I3 84
Santiago Ixcuintla, Mex. G7 90
Santiago Jamiltepec, Mex. I11 90
Santiago Larre, Arg. H9 80
Santiago Papasquiaro, Mex. E7 90
Santiaguillo, Laguna, l., Mex. E7 90
Santiam Pass, Or., U.S. F4 122
San Timoteo, Ven. C7 84
Säntis, mtn., Switz. D11 13
Sant Jordi, Golf de, b., Spain E13 16
Santo, Tx., U.S. G8 116
Santo Amaro, Braz. B9 79
Santo Anastácio, Braz. F3 79
Santo André, Braz. G5 79
Santo Ângelo, Braz. E11 80
Santo Antão, i., C.V. k16 64a
Santo António, S. Tom./P. A1 58
Santo Antônio, stm., Braz. E6 79
Santo Antônio da Patrulha, Braz. E13 80
Santo Antônio de Jesus, Braz. B9 79
Santo Antônio de Pádua, Braz. F7 79
Santo Antônio do Amparo, Braz. F6 79
Santo Antônio do Içá, Braz. I9 84
Santo Antônio do Leverger, Braz. F13 82
Santo Antônio do Rio Verde, Braz. D5 79
Santo Antônio do Sudoeste, Braz. D12 80
Santo Augusto, Braz. D12 80
Santo Corazón, Bol. G12 82
Santo Domingo, Dom. Rep. E10 94
Santo Domingo, Mex. E3 90
Santo Domingo, Nic. E9 92
Santo Domingo, stm., Mex. A3 92
Santo Domingo de los Colorados, Ec. H3 84
Santo Domingo Pueblo, N.M., U.S. I10 120
Santo Domingo Tehuantepec, Mex. I12 90
Santo Domingo Zanatepec, Mex. I12 90
Santo Estêvão, Braz. B9 79
San Tomé, Ven. C10 84
Santoña, Spain B8 16
Santo Onofre, stm., Braz. B7 79
Santorini see Thíra, i., Grc. M9 20
Santos, Braz. G5 79
Santos Dumont, Braz. F7 79
Santos Tomás del Norte, Nic. D8 92
Santo Tomás, Col. B5 84
Santo Tomás, Mex. B1 90
Santo Tomás, Nic. E9 92
Santo Tomás, Peru B3 82
Santo Tomás, Peru F5 82
Santo Tomás, stm., Peru F5 82
Santo Tomás, Punta, c., Mex. B1 90
Santo Tomé, Arg. E10 80
Santo Tomé, Arg. F8 80
Santuario de Quillacas, Bol. H8 82
Santunying, China C6 32
San Ubaldo, Nic. F9 92
San Vicente, Arg. E6 80
San Vicente, El Sal. D6 92
San Vicente, Volcán de, vol., El Sal. D6 92
San Vicente de Cañete, Peru E3 82
San Vicente de Chucurí, Col. D6 84
San Vicente del Caguán, Col. F5 84
San Vicente de Tagua-Tagua, Chile H3 80
San Vincenzo, Italy F5 18
San Vito, C.R. I12 92
San Vito, Italy J4 18
San Vito dei Normanni, Italy I12 18
San Ygnacio, Tx., U.S. L7 116
Sanyuan, China E8 30
Sanza Pombo, Ang. C3 58
Sanzha, China B2 32
São Benedito, stm., Braz. C13 82
São Bento, Braz. D10 76
São Bento do Sul, Braz. D14 80
São Borja, Braz. E10 80
São Caetano do Sul, Braz. G5 79
São Carlos, Braz. G5 79
São Cristóvão, Braz. F11 76
São Domingos, Braz. B5 79
São Domingos, Braz. D12 80
São Domingos, Gui.-B. E1 64
São Domingos, stm., Braz. B5 79
São Domingos, stm., Braz. E2 79
São Domingos, stm., Braz. E9 82
São Felipe, Braz. C8 79
São Filipe, C.V. m16 64a
São Francisco, Braz. C6 79
São Francisco, stm., Braz. E11 76
São Francisco, stm., Braz. C8 79
São Francisco, Baía de, b., Braz. D14 80
São Francisco, Ilha de, i., Braz. D14 80
São Francisco de Assis, Braz. E11 80
São Francisco de Goiás, Braz. C4 79
São Francisco de Paula, Braz. E13 80
São Francisco do Sul, Braz. D14 80
São Gabriel, Braz. F11 80
São Gabriel da Palha, Braz. E8 79
São Gabriel de Goiás, Braz. C5 79
São Gonçalo do Abaeté, Braz. E6 79
São Gonçalo do Sapucaí, Braz. F6 79
São Gonçalo dos Campos, Braz. B9 79
Sao Hill, Tan. C7 58
São Jerônimo, Braz. E13 80
São Jerônimo, Serra de, plat., Braz. D1 79
São Jerônimo da Serra, Braz. G3 79
São João, stm., Braz. B3 79
São João da Barra, Braz. F8 79
São João da Boa Vista, Braz. F5 79
São João D'Aliança, Braz. C5 79
São João da Madeira, Port. E3 16
São João da Ponte, Braz. C6 79
São João del-Rei, Braz. F6 79
São João do Araguaia, Braz. E9 76
São João do Paraíso, Braz. C7 79
São João Evangelista, Braz. E7 79
São Joaquim, Braz. E14 80
São Joaquim, Parque Nacional de, Braz. E14 80
São Joaquim da Barra, Braz. F5 79
São José, Braz. D14 80
São José, stm., Braz. E8 79
São José de Anauá, Braz. G12 84
São José do Cedro, Braz. D12 80
São José do Norte, Braz. G12 80
São José do Rio Preto, Braz. F4 79
São José dos Campos, Braz. G6 79
São José dos Pinhais, Braz. C14 80
São Leopoldo, Braz. E13 80
São Lourenço, Braz. G6 79
São Lourenço, Pantanal de, sw., Braz. G13 82
São Lourenço do Oeste, Braz. D12 80
São Lourenço do Sul, Braz. F13 80
São Luís, Braz. D10 76
São Luís de Montes Belos, Braz. D3 79

| Name | Map Ref. | Page |
|---|---|---|

| Name | Map Ref. | Page |
|---|---|---|
| São Luís Gonzaga, Braz. | E11 | 80 |
| São Manuel, Braz. | G4 | 79 |
| São Manuel, stm., Braz. | C13 | 82 |
| São Marcos, stm., Braz. | D5 | 79 |
| São Mateus, Braz. | E9 | 79 |
| São Mateus, Braço Norte, stm., Braz. | E8 | 79 |
| São Mateus do Sul, Braz. | C13 | 80 |
| São Miguel, i., Port. | m21 | 62a |
| São Miguel, stm., Braz. | D8 | 79 |
| São Miguel do Araguaia, Braz. | B3 | 79 |
| São Miguel d'Oeste, Braz. | D12 | 80 |
| Saona, Isla, i., Dom. Rep. | E10 | 94 |
| Saône, stm., Fr. | F11 | 14 |
| Saône-et-Loire, dept., Fr. | F11 | 14 |
| São Nicolau, i., C.V. | k16 | 64a |
| São Paulo, Braz. | G5 | 79 |
| São Paulo, state, Braz. | G4 | 79 |
| São Paulo de Olivença, Braz. | I8 | 84 |
| São Pedro, Braz. | E3 | 79 |
| São Pedro, stm., Braz. | D8 | 79 |
| São Pedro do Sul, Braz. | E11 | 80 |
| São Pedro do Sul, Port. | E3 | 16 |
| São Raimundo Nonato, Braz. | E10 | 76 |
| São Romão, Braz. | D6 | 79 |
| São Roque, Braz. | G5 | 79 |
| São Roque, Cabo de, c., Braz. | E11 | 76 |
| São Sebastião, Braz. | G6 | 79 |
| São Sebastião, Ilha de, i., Braz. | G6 | 79 |
| São Sebastião, Ponta, c., Moz. | D12 | 66 |
| São Sebastião do Maranhão, Braz. | E7 | 79 |
| São Sebastião do Paraíso, Braz. | F5 | 79 |
| São Sebastião do Rio Claro, Braz. | C3 | 79 |
| São Sepé, Braz. | F12 | 80 |
| São Simão, Braz. | E3 | 79 |
| São Simão, Braz. | F5 | 79 |
| São Tiago, Braz. | F6 | 79 |
| São Timóteo, Braz. | B7 | 79 |
| São Tomé, S. Tom./P. | A1 | 58 |
| São Tomé, i., S. Tom./P. | A1 | 58 |
| São Tomé, Braz. | C13 | 82 |
| São Tomé, Cabo de, c., Braz. | F8 | 79 |
| Sao Tome and Principe (São Tomé e Príncipe), ctry., Afr. | A1 | 58 |
| Saoura, Oued, val., Alg. | F10 | 62 |
| São Vicente, Braz. | G5 | 79 |
| São Vicente, i., C.V. | k16 | 64a |
| São Vicente, Cabo de (Cape Saint Vincent), c., Port. | H2 | 16 |
| São Vicente de Minas, Braz. | F6 | 79 |
| Sapé, Braz. | E11 | 76 |
| Sapele, Nig. | I12 | 64 |
| Sapello, stm., N.M., U.S. | I11 | 120 |
| Sapelo Island, i., Ga., U.S. | H5 | 112 |
| Saphane, Tur. | J13 | 20 |
| Šapitwa, mtn., Mwi. | E7 | 58 |
| Šapki, Russia | B14 | 22 |
| Sa Pobla, Spain | F15 | 16 |
| Sapodilla Cays, i., Belize | A6 | 92 |
| Saponé, Burkina | G4 | 64 |
| Saposoa, Peru | B3 | 82 |
| Sapožok, Russia | H23 | 22 |
| Sapporo, Japan | d16 | 36a |
| Sapri, Italy | I10 | 18 |
| Saptakośi, stm., Nepal | G12 | 44 |
| Sapulpa, Ok., U.S. | D10 | 116 |
| Sāqiat al-'Abd, Sudan | G6 | 60 |
| Saqqez, Iran | C9 | 48 |
| Saquena, Peru | A5 | 82 |
| Saquisilí, Ec. | H3 | 84 |
| Sarāb, Iran | C9 | 48 |
| Saraburi, Thai. | G6 | 40 |
| Saracura, stm., Braz. | B8 | 79 |
| Saragosa, Tx., U.S. | H3 | 116 |
| Saragossa see Zaragoza, Spain | D11 | 16 |
| Sarai, Ec. | I3 | 84 |
| Saraj, Russia | H24 | 22 |
| Sarajevo, Bos. | F2 | 20 |
| Sarakhs, Iran | C16 | 48 |
| Saraland, Al., U.S. | L8 | 114 |
| Saran', Russia | H12 | 26 |
| Saranac, Mi., U.S. | H10 | 110 |
| Saranac, N.Y., U.S. | C13 | 108 |
| Saranac Lake, N.Y., U.S. | C12 | 108 |
| Sarandi, Braz. | D12 | 80 |
| Sarandí del Yi, Ur. | G11 | 80 |
| Sarandí Grande, Ur. | G10 | 80 |
| Saransk, Russia | G7 | 26 |
| Sarapiquí, stm., C.R. | G11 | 92 |
| Sarapul, Russia | F8 | 26 |
| Sarare, Ven. | C8 | 84 |
| Sara Sara, Nevado, mtn., Peru | F5 | 82 |
| Sarasota, Fl., U.S. | L4 | 112 |
| Šarašova, Bela. | I7 | 22 |
| Sarata, Ukr. | C13 | 20 |
| Saratoga, Tx., U.S. | G3 | 124 |
| Saratoga, Tx., U.S. | I12 | 116 |
| Saratoga, Wy., U.S. | C10 | 120 |
| Saratoga Springs, N.Y., U.S. | D13 | 108 |
| Saratov, Russia | G7 | 26 |
| Saratovskoje vodochranilišče, res., Russia | G7 | 26 |
| Sararurco, mtn., Ec. | H4 | 84 |
| Saravan, Laos | G9 | 40 |
| Sarawak, hist. reg., Malay. | E5 | 38 |
| Saraya, Gui. | F4 | 64 |
| Saraykóy, Tur. | L12 | 20 |
| Sarbāz, Iran | H16 | 48 |
| Sárbogárd, Hung. | I18 | 10 |
| Sarcee Indian Reserve, Ab., Can. | G20 | 102 |
| Sarcoxie, Mo., U.S. | E2 | 114 |
| Sárda (Mahākālī), stm., Asia | F6 | 44 |
| Sardārshahr, India | F5 | 44 |
| Sardegna, prov., Italy | I4 | 18 |
| Sardegna (Sardinia), i., Italy | I4 | 18 |
| Sardinal, C.R. | G9 | 92 |
| Sardinata, Col. | C6 | 84 |
| Sardinia see Sardegna, i., Italy | I4 | 18 |
| Sardis, Al., U.S. | J10 | 114 |
| Sardis, Ga., U.S. | G5 | 112 |
| Sardis, Ms., U.S. | H7 | 114 |
| Sardis, Tn., U.S. | G8 | 114 |
| Sardis Lake, res., Ms., U.S. | H7 | 114 |
| Sar-e Pol, Afg. | B1 | 44 |
| Sarepta, La., U.S. | J3 | 114 |
| Sargans, Switz. | D11 | 13 |
| Sargasso Sea | B8 | 74 |
| Sargent, Ga., U.S. | F2 | 112 |
| Sargent, Ne., U.S. | J8 | 118 |
| Sargodha, Pak. | D5 | 44 |
| Sarh, Chad | C4 | 56 |
| Sārī, Iran | C12 | 48 |
| Saric, Mex. | B4 | 90 |
| Sārif, Yemen | F7 | 47 |
| Sarıkamış, Tur. | A7 | 48 |
| Sarina, Austl. | C8 | 70 |
| Sariñena, Spain | D11 | 16 |
| Sarīr, Libya | D2 | 60 |
| Sarita, Tx., U.S. | B9 | 116 |
| Sariwŏn, N. Kor. | E13 | 32 |
| Sarja, Russia | F7 | 26 |
| Sark, i., Guernsey | L11 | 8 |
| Sarkad, Hung. | I21 | 10 |
| Šarkaŭščyna, Bela. | F10 | 22 |
| Şarköy, Tur. | B4 | 48 |
| Šarkoŭščyna, Bela. | F10 | 22 |
| Şarkışla, Tur. | I11 | 20 |
| Šarlauk, Turk. | B13 | 48 |
| Sarles, N.D., U.S. | C9 | 118 |
| Sármellék, Hung. | I17 | 10 |
| Sarmiento de Gamboa, Cerro, mtn., Chile | G2 | 78 |
| Särna, Swe. | K13 | 6 |
| Sarnen, Switz. | E9 | 13 |
| Sarnia, On., Can. | H13 | 110 |
| Sarno, Italy | I9 | 18 |
| Saron, S. Afr. | I4 | 66 |
| Saronikós Kólpos, b., Grc. | L7 | 20 |
| Saronno, Italy | D4 | 18 |
| Sárospatak, Hung. | G21 | 10 |
| Sarpsborg, Nor. | L12 | 6 |
| Sarralbe, Fr. | C14 | 14 |
| Sarrebourg, Fr. | D14 | 14 |
| Sarreguemines, Fr. | C14 | 14 |
| Sarre-Union, Fr. | D14 | 14 |
| Sarro, Mali | E7 | 64 |
| Sarstoon (Sarstún), stm., N.A. | B5 | 92 |
| Sarstún (Sarstoon), stm., N.A. | B5 | 92 |
| Sartang, stm., Russia | D18 | 28 |
| Sartell, Mn., U.S. | E1 | 110 |
| Sartène, Fr. | H3 | 18 |
| Sarthe, dept., Fr. | D7 | 14 |
| Sartilly, Fr. | D5 | 14 |
| Saruhanlı, Tur. | K11 | 20 |
| Sarūr, Oman | C11 | 47 |
| Sárvár, Hung. | H16 | 10 |
| Sarvestān, Iran | G12 | 48 |
| Saryg-Sep, Russia | G17 | 26 |
| Sarykol'skij chrebet, mts., Asia | A6 | 44 |
| Saryozek, Kaz. | I13 | 26 |
| Sarysu, stm., Kaz. | H11 | 26 |
| Sary-Taš, Kyrg. | J12 | 26 |
| Sarzana, Italy | E4 | 18 |
| Sasaginnigak Lake, l., Mb., Can. | G19 | 104 |
| Sasakwa, Ok., U.S. | E10 | 116 |
| Sāsarām, India | H11 | 44 |
| Sásd, Hung. | I18 | 10 |
| Sasebo, Japan | N4 | 36 |
| Saskatchewan, prov., Can. | F11 | 96 |
| Saskatchewan, stm., Can. | E13 | 104 |
| Saskatoon, Sk., Can. | F8 | 104 |
| Saslaya, mtn., Nic. | H2 | 94 |
| Sasnovy Bor, Bela. | I12 | 22 |
| Sasolburg, S. Afr. | F8 | 66 |
| Sasovo, Russia | G24 | 22 |
| Saspamco, Tx., U.S. | J8 | 116 |
| Sassafras, Ky., U.S. | B3 | 112 |
| Sassafras Mountain, mtn., U.S. | D4 | 112 |
| Sassandra, C. Iv. | I6 | 64 |
| Sassandra, stm., C. Iv. | I6 | 64 |
| Sassari, Italy | I3 | 18 |
| Sassoferrato, Italy | F7 | 18 |
| Sasso Marconi, Italy | E6 | 18 |
| S'as'stroj, Russia | A15 | 22 |
| Sassuolo, Italy | E5 | 18 |
| Sastown, Lib. | I6 | 64 |
| Sastre, Arg. | F8 | 80 |
| Sasyk, ozero, l., Ukr. | D13 | 20 |
| Satah Mountain, mtn., B.C., Can. | E10 | 102 |
| Šatalovo, Russia | G15 | 22 |
| Sata-misaki, c., Japan | Q5 | 36 |
| Satanta, Ks., U.S. | N7 | 118 |
| Sātāra, India | D2 | 46 |
| Satara, S. Afr. | E10 | 66 |
| Satélite, Mex. | B6 | 90 |
| Satellite Beach, Fl., U.S. | K6 | 112 |
| Satipo, Peru | D4 | 82 |
| Satīt (Tekezē), stm., Afr. | J9 | 60 |
| Satka, Russia | F9 | 26 |
| Satna, India | H9 | 44 |
| Sátoraljaújhely, Hung. | G21 | 10 |
| Sātpura Range, mts., India | J7 | 44 |
| Satsuma, Fl., U.S. | J5 | 112 |
| Satsunan-shotō, is., Japan | r4 | 37b |
| Sattahip, Myan. | H6 | 40 |
| Satthwa, Myan. | F3 | 40 |
| Satu Mare, Rom. | B6 | 20 |
| Satu Mare, co., Rom. | B6 | 20 |
| Satun, Thai. | K6 | 40 |
| Šatura, Russia | F22 | 22 |
| Saturnino M. Laspiur, Arg. | F7 | 80 |
| Saturtorf, Ger. | F22 | 22 |
| Sauce, Arg. | F9 | 80 |
| Sauce, Peru | B3 | 82 |
| Sauce, Ven. | H10 | 80 |
| Sauce Corto, Arroyo, stm., Arg. | I8 | 80 |
| Saucier, Ms., U.S. | L7 | 114 |
| Saucillo, Mex. | C7 | 90 |
| Sauda, Nor. | L10 | 6 |
| Saudi Arabia (Al-'Arabiyah as-Su'ūdīyah), ctry., Asia | D4 | 42 |
| Sauer (Sûre), stm., Eur. | I10 | 12 |
| Saueruiná, stm., Braz. | E12 | 82 |
| Sauê-Uiná, stm., Braz. | E12 | 82 |
| Saugatuck, Mi., U.S. | H9 | 110 |
| Saugerties, N.Y., U.S. | E13 | 108 |
| Saugstad, Mount, mtn., B.C., Can. | E8 | 102 |
| Saujil, Arg. | E5 | 80 |
| Sauk, stm., Mn., U.S. | E1 | 110 |
| Sauk Centre, Mn., U.S. | F13 | 118 |
| Sauk City, Wi., U.S. | G6 | 110 |
| Sauk Rapids, Mn., U.S. | E1 | 110 |
| Saukville, Wi., U.S. | G8 | 110 |
| Saül, Fr. Gu. | C8 | 76 |
| Saulgau, Ger. | G9 | 10 |
| Saulieu, Fr. | E11 | 14 |
| Saulkrasti, Lat. | D7 | 22 |
| Sault-au-Mouton, P.Q., Can. | D4 | 106 |
| Sault aux Cochons, Rivière du, stm., P.Q., Can. | D4 | 106 |
| Saulteaux, stm., Ab., Can. | C20 | 102 |
| Saulteaux Indian Reserve, Sk., Can. | E6 | 104 |
| Sault Sainte Marie, On., Can. | D11 | 110 |
| Sault Sainte Marie, Mi., U.S. | D11 | 110 |
| Saumarez Reef, rf., Austl. | C10 | 70 |
| Saumons, Rivière aux, stm., P.Q., Can. | C11 | 106 |
| Saumur, Fr. | E6 | 14 |
| Saunders Island, i., S. Geor. | J12 | 74 |
| Sauquoit, N.Y., U.S. | D11 | 108 |
| Saurimo, Ang. | C4 | 58 |
| Sausalito, Ca., U.S. | F2 | 124 |
| Sauveterre-de-Béarn, Fr. | I6 | 14 |
| Sauvo, Fin. | K18 | 6 |
| Sava, Italy | I12 | 18 |
| Sava, stm., Eur. | E11 | 4 |
| Savage, Md., U.S. | H10 | 108 |
| Savage, Mt., U.S. | D3 | 118 |
| Savai'i, i., W. Sam. | J22 | 126 |
| Savalou, Benin | H10 | 64 |
| Savane, stm., P.Q., Can. | A2 | 106 |
| Savanna, Il., U.S. | H5 | 110 |
| Savanna, Ok., U.S. | E11 | 116 |
| Savannah, Ga., U.S. | G5 | 112 |
| Savannah, Mo., U.S. | C2 | 114 |
| Savannah, Tn., U.S. | G8 | 114 |
| Savannah, stm., U.S. | G5 | 112 |
| Savannah Haven, Pa., U.S. | G10 | 108 |
| Savannah-la-Mar, Jam. | E5 | 94 |
| Savé, Benin | G11 | 64 |
| Save (Sabi), stm., Afr. | C12 | 66 |
| Sāveh, Iran | D11 | 48 |
| Savelli, Italy | J11 | 18 |
| Saverne, Fr. | D14 | 14 |
| Savigliano, Italy | E2 | 18 |
| Savino, Russia | E24 | 22 |
| Savinskij, Russia | J27 | 6 |
| Šavnik, Yugo. | G3 | 20 |
| Savognin, Switz. | E12 | 13 |
| Savoie, dept., Fr. | G13 | 14 |
| Savona, B.C., Can. | G14 | 102 |
| Savona, Italy | E3 | 18 |
| Savoonga, Ak., U.S. | E9 | 100 |
| Savoy, Tx., U.S. | F10 | 116 |
| Savran', Ukr. | A14 | 20 |
| Savu Sea see Sawu, Laut, Indon. | G7 | 38 |
| Sawahlunto, Indon. | O6 | 40 |
| Sawāi Mādhopur, India | H7 | 44 |
| Sawākin, Sudan | H9 | 60 |
| Sawatch Range, mts., Co., U.S. | E10 | 120 |
| Sawdā', Jabal, mtn., Sau. Ar. | E3 | 47 |
| Sawdā', Jabal as-, hills, Libya | C4 | 56 |
| Sawdā', Qurnat as-, mtn., Leb. | D4 | 48 |
| Sawdirī, Sudan | J5 | 60 |
| Sawhāj, Egypt | D6 | 60 |
| Sawknah, Libya | C4 | 56 |
| Sawqirah, Ghubbat, b., Oman | E10 | 47 |
| Sawu, Laut (Savu Sea), Indon. | G7 | 38 |
| Sawu, Pulau, i., Indon. | H7 | 38 |
| Sawyer, Mi., U.S. | I9 | 110 |
| Sawyer, N.D., U.S. | C6 | 118 |
| Sawyers Hill, hill, Nf., Can. | E20 | 106 |
| Saxby, stm., Austl. | B4 | 70 |
| Saxis, Va., U.S. | B11 | 112 |
| Saxon, Switz. | F7 | 13 |
| Saxon, Wi., U.S. | D5 | 110 |
| Saxony see Sachsen, state, Ger. | C9 | 10 |
| Saxton, Pa., U.S. | G8 | 108 |
| Say, Niger | E11 | 64 |
| Sayán, Peru | D3 | 82 |
| Sayan Mountains (Sajany), mts., Asia | G11 | 28 |
| Sayaxché, Guat. | I14 | 90 |
| Saybrook, Il., U.S. | B8 | 114 |
| Saydā (Sidon), Leb. | A4 | 50 |
| Sayhūt, Yemen | G7 | 47 |
| Sayil, hist., Mex. | G15 | 90 |
| Saylorville Lake, res., Ia., U.S. | I2 | 110 |
| Saylūn, Khirbat (Shiloh), hist., W.B. | D4 | 50 |
| Sayre, Ok., U.S. | D7 | 116 |
| Sayre, Pa., U.S. | F10 | 108 |
| Sayreville, N.J., U.S. | G12 | 108 |
| Sayula, Mex. | H8 | 90 |
| Sayward, B.C., Can. | G9 | 102 |
| Saywūn, Yemen | G6 | 47 |
| Sazonovo, Russia | B18 | 22 |
| Sazud, Taj. | B5 | 44 |
| Sba, Alg. | F10 | 62 |
| Sbeïtla, Tun. | N4 | 18 |
| Sbiba, Tun. | N4 | 18 |
| Scafell Pikes, mtn., Eng., U.K. | G10 | 8 |
| Scalea, Italy | J10 | 18 |
| Scammon, Ks., U.S. | N13 | 118 |
| Scandia, Ks., U.S. | L10 | 118 |
| Scanlon, Mn., U.S. | D3 | 110 |
| Scapa, Ab., Can. | F23 | 102 |
| Scapa Flow, b., Scot., U.K. | C10 | 8 |
| Scapegoat Mountain, mtn., Mt., U.S. | C13 | 122 |
| Ščapino, Russia | F23 | 28 |
| Scappoose, Or., U.S. | E3 | 122 |
| Scarborough, Eng., U.K. | G13 | 8 |
| Scarborough, On., Can. | G16 | 110 |
| Scarborough, Trin. | I14 | 94 |
| Scatarie Island, i., N.S., Can. | G14 | 106 |
| Scawfell Island, i., Austl. | C8 | 70 |
| Ščelkovo, Russia | F21 | 22 |
| Sceptre, Sk., Can. | H5 | 104 |
| Ščerbinka, Russia | F20 | 22 |
| Schaarbeek (Schaerbeek), Bel. | G5 | 12 |
| Schaffhausen, Switz. | C10 | 13 |
| Schaffhausen, state, Switz. | C10 | 13 |
| Schaller, Ia., U.S. | I12 | 118 |
| Schärding, Aus. | G13 | 10 |
| Schefferville, P.Q., Can. | F19 | 96 |
| Scheibbs, Aus. | G15 | 10 |
| Scheinfeld, Ger. | F10 | 10 |
| Schelde (Escaut), stm., Eur. | G5 | 12 |
| Schenectady, N.Y., U.S. | E13 | 108 |
| Schertz, Tx., U.S. | J8 | 116 |
| Schesslitz, Ger. | F11 | 10 |
| Scheveningen, Neth. | D5 | 12 |
| Schiedam, Neth. | E5 | 12 |
| Schiermonnikoog, Neth. | B9 | 12 |
| Schiermonnikoog, i., Neth. | B9 | 12 |
| Schio, Italy | D6 | 18 |
| Schipbeek, stm., Eur. | D9 | 12 |
| Schkeuditz, Ger. | D12 | 10 |
| Schladming, Aus. | H13 | 10 |
| Schlater, Ms., U.S. | I6 | 114 |
| Schleiz, Ger. | E11 | 10 |
| Schleswig, Ia., U.S. | I12 | 118 |
| Schleswig-Holstein, state, Ger. | A9 | 10 |
| Schliersee, Ger. | H11 | 10 |
| Schlitz, Ger. | E9 | 10 |
| Schlüchtern, Ger. | E9 | 10 |
| Schmidmühlen, Ger. | F11 | 10 |
| Schmölln, Ger. | E12 | 10 |
| Schneverdingen, Ger. | B9 | 10 |
| Schodn'a, Russia | F20 | 22 |
| Schofield, Wi., U.S. | F6 | 110 |
| Schoharie, N.Y., U.S. | E12 | 108 |
| Schönebeck, Ger. | C11 | 10 |
| Schongau, Ger. | H10 | 10 |
| Schoolcraft, Mi., U.S. | H10 | 110 |
| Schopfheim, Ger. | H7 | 10 |
| Schöppenstedt, Ger. | C11 | 10 |
| Schorndorf, Ger. | G9 | 10 |
| Schouten Islands, is., Austl. | N8 | 70 |
| Schouwen, i., Neth. | E4 | 12 |
| Schramberg, Ger. | G8 | 10 |
| Schreiber, On., Can. | C5 | 110 |
| Schriever, La., U.S. | M6 | 114 |
| Schrofenstein, mtn., Nmb. | F4 | 66 |
| Schulenburg, Tx., U.S. | J10 | 116 |
| Schultz Lake, l., N.T., Can. | D13 | 96 |
| Schumacher, On., Can. | B14 | 110 |
| Schüpfheim, Switz. | E9 | 13 |
| Schuyler, Ne., U.S. | J10 | 118 |
| Schuyler, Va., U.S. | B8 | 112 |
| Schuylkill, stm., Pa., U.S. | G11 | 108 |
| Schuylkill Haven, Pa., U.S. | G10 | 108 |
| Schwabach, Ger. | F11 | 10 |
| Schwaben, hist. reg., Ger. | G10 | 10 |
| Schwäbische Alb, mts., Ger. | G9 | 10 |
| Schwäbisch Gmünd, Ger. | G9 | 10 |
| Schwäbisch Hall, Ger. | F9 | 10 |
| Schwäbmünchen, Ger. | G10 | 10 |
| Schwanden, Switz. | D11 | 13 |
| Schwandorf, Ger. | F12 | 10 |
| Schwaner, Pegunungan, mts., Indon. | F5 | 38 |
| Schwarzach im Pongau, Aus. | H13 | 10 |
| Schwarzenburg, Switz. | E7 | 13 |
| Schwarzwald (Black Forest), mts., Ger. | G8 | 10 |
| Schwaz, Aus. | H11 | 10 |
| Schwedt, Ger. | B14 | 10 |
| Schweinfurt, Ger. | E10 | 10 |
| Schweizer Nationalpark, Switz. | E13 | 13 |
| Schwerin, Ger. | B11 | 10 |
| Schwyz, Switz. | D10 | 13 |
| Schwyz, state, Switz. | D10 | 13 |
| Sciacca, Italy | L8 | 18 |
| Scicli, Italy | M9 | 18 |
| Scilla, Italy | K10 | 18 |
| Scilly, Isles of, is., Eng., U.K. | L7 | 8 |
| Scio, Oh., U.S. | G5 | 108 |
| Scio, Or., U.S. | F3 | 122 |
| Scioto, stm., Oh., U.S. | I3 | 108 |
| Scipio, Ut., U.S. | E4 | 120 |
| Scobey, Mt., U.S. | B20 | 122 |
| Scone, Austl. | I9 | 70 |
| Scooba, Ms., U.S. | J8 | 114 |
| Scordia, Italy | L9 | 18 |
| Scotia, Ne., U.S. | J9 | 118 |
| Scotia, N.Y., U.S. | E13 | 108 |
| Scotia Sea | A1 | 73 |
| Scotland, On., Can. | G15 | 110 |
| Scotland, S.D., U.S. | H10 | 118 |
| Scotland, Tx., U.S. | F8 | 116 |
| Scotland, ter., U.K. | D9 | 8 |
| Scotland Neck, N.C., U.S. | C9 | 112 |
| Scotlandville, La., U.S. | L5 | 114 |
| Scotstown, N.S., Can. | G11 | 106 |
| Scott, Ms., U.S. | I5 | 114 |
| Scott, Sk., Can. | F6 | 104 |
| Scott, stm., Ca., U.S. | C3 | 124 |
| Scott, Cape, c., B.C., Can. | G6 | 102 |
| Scott, Mount, mtn., Or., U.S. | H3 | 122 |
| Scott Base, sci., Ant. | C8 | 73 |
| Scott City, Ks., U.S. | M7 | 118 |
| Scott City, Mo., U.S. | E7 | 114 |
| Scottburgh, S. Afr. | H10 | 66 |
| Scottdale, Pa., U.S. | F5 | 108 |
| Scott Islands, is., B.C., Can. | G6 | 102 |
| Scott Mountain, mtn., Id., U.S. | F10 | 122 |
| Scottsbluff, Ne., U.S. | J4 | 118 |
| Scottsboro, Al., U.S. | H10 | 114 |
| Scottsburg, In., U.S. | D11 | 114 |
| Scottsdale, Austl. | M7 | 70 |
| Scottsdale, Az., U.S. | K5 | 120 |
| Scotts Hill, Tn., U.S. | G8 | 114 |
| Scottsville, Ky., U.S. | F10 | 114 |
| Scottville, Mi., U.S. | G9 | 110 |
| Scout Lake, Sk., Can. | I8 | 104 |
| Scranton, Ks., U.S. | M7 | 118 |
| Scranton, N.D., U.S. | E4 | 118 |
| Scranton, Pa., U.S. | F11 | 108 |
| Screven, Ga., U.S. | H4 | 112 |
| Scribner, Ne., U.S. | J11 | 118 |
| Ščučʹje, Kaz. | G12 | 26 |
| Ščučyn, Bela. | H7 | 22 |
| Scuol (Schuls), Switz. | E13 | 13 |
| Scurry, Tx., U.S. | G10 | 116 |
| Scutari, Lake, l., Eur. | G3 | 20 |
| Seabird Island Indian Reserve, B.C., Can. | H13 | 102 |
| Šeksna, Russia | B21 | 22 |
| Seaboard, N.C., U.S. | C9 | 112 |
| Seadrift, Tx., U.S. | K10 | 116 |
| Seaford, De., U.S. | I11 | 108 |
| Seaforth, On., Can. | G14 | 110 |
| Seager Wheeler Lake, l., Sk., Can. | D11 | 104 |
| Seagraves, Tx., U.S. | G4 | 116 |
| Seahorse Point, c., N.T., Can. | D16 | 96 |
| Sea Islands, is., U.S. | I5 | 112 |
| Sea Isle City, N.J., U.S. | H12 | 108 |
| Seal, stm., Mb., Can. | E13 | 96 |
| Sea Lake, Austl. | J5 | 70 |
| Seal Cays, is., T./C. Is. | D9 | 94 |
| Seal Cove, Nf., Can. | C17 | 106 |
| Seal Cove, N.B., Can. | H7 | 106 |
| Seale, Al., U.S. | J11 | 114 |
| Sealevel, N.C., U.S. | D9 | 112 |
| Seal Island, i., N.S., Can. | I7 | 106 |
| Seal Lake, l., Nf., Can. | F20 | 96 |
| Sealy, Tx., U.S. | J10 | 116 |
| Seara, Braz. | D12 | 80 |
| Searchlight, Nv., U.S. | I11 | 124 |
| Searcy, Ar., U.S. | G5 | 114 |
| Searsport, Me., U.S. | C18 | 108 |
| Seaside, Ca., U.S. | H4 | 124 |
| Seaside, Or., U.S. | E2 | 122 |
| Seaside Park, N.J., U.S. | H12 | 108 |
| Seattle, Wa., U.S. | C3 | 122 |
| Seattle, Mount, mtn., N.A. | F25 | 100 |
| Sébaco, Nic. | E8 | 92 |
| Sebago Lake, l., Me., U.S. | C16 | 108 |
| Sebakwe Recreational Area, Zimb. | B10 | 66 |
| Šebalino, Russia | G15 | 26 |
| Sebastián Vizcaíno, Bahía, b., Mex. | C2 | 90 |
| Sebastopol, Ca., U.S. | F3 | 124 |
| Sebastopol, Ms., U.S. | J7 | 114 |
| Sebderat, Erit. | J9 | 60 |
| Sebeka, Mn., U.S. | E12 | 118 |
| Sebeş, Rom. | D7 | 20 |
| Sebes Körös (Crişul Repede), stm., Eur. | B5 | 20 |
| Sebewaing, Mi., U.S. | G12 | 110 |
| Sebez, Russia | E11 | 22 |
| Şebinkarahisar, Tur. | A5 | 48 |
| Sebiş, Rom. | C6 | 20 |
| Sebnitz, Ger. | E14 | 10 |
| Sebree, Ky., U.S. | E9 | 114 |
| Sebring, Fl., U.S. | L5 | 112 |
| Secas, Islas, is., Pan. | J12 | 92 |
| Sechelt, B.C., Can. | H11 | 102 |
| Sechura, Peru | A1 | 82 |
| Sechura, Desierto de, des., Peru | A1 | 82 |
| Seclantás, Arg. | C5 | 80 |
| Seco, stm., Arg. | B7 | 80 |
| Sečovce, Slvk. | G21 | 10 |
| Section, Al., U.S. | H11 | 114 |
| Sécure, stm., Bol. | F9 | 82 |
| Security, Co., U.S. | M3 | 118 |
| Seda, China | E7 | 30 |
| Seda, Lat. | D8 | 22 |
| Seda, Lith. | E5 | 22 |
| Sedalia, Ab., Can. | G4 | 104 |
| Sedalia, Mo., U.S. | D3 | 114 |
| Sedan, Fr. | C11 | 14 |
| Sedan, Ks., U.S. | N11 | 118 |
| Sedano, Spain | C8 | 16 |
| Sedel'nikovo, Russia | F13 | 26 |
| Sedgefield, N.C., U.S. | D6 | 112 |
| Sedgewick, Ab., Can. | E23 | 102 |
| Sedgwick, Co., U.S. | K5 | 118 |
| Sedgwick, Ks., U.S. | N10 | 118 |
| Sedgwick, Mount, mtn., N.M., U.S. | I8 | 120 |
| Sedini, Italy | I3 | 18 |
| Sedlčany, Czech Rep. | F14 | 10 |
| Sedom (Sodom), hist., Isr. | F4 | 50 |
| Sedona, Az., U.S. | J5 | 120 |
| Sedot Yam, Isr. | D3 | 50 |
| Sedova, pik, mtn., Russia | C8 | 26 |
| Sedrata, Alg. | M2 | 18 |
| Sedro Woolley, Wa., U.S. | B3 | 122 |
| Šeduva, Lith. | F6 | 22 |
| Seeberg, Switz. | D8 | 13 |
| Seeber Lake, l., On., Can. | E21 | 104 |
| Seefeld in Tirol, Aus. | H11 | 10 |
| Seehausen, Ger. | C11 | 10 |
| Seeheim, Nmb. | F3 | 66 |
| Seeis, Nmb. | D3 | 66 |
| Seekaskootch Indian Reserve, Sk., Can. | E5 | 104 |
| Seeley Lake, Mt., U.S. | C12 | 122 |
| Seelow, Ger. | C14 | 10 |
| Seelyville, In., U.S. | C9 | 114 |
| Seengen, Switz. | D9 | 13 |
| Sées, Fr. | D7 | 14 |
| Seesen, Ger. | D10 | 10 |
| Sefadu, S.L. | G4 | 64 |
| Sefar, hist., Alg. | H15 | 62 |
| Sefare, Bots. | D8 | 66 |
| Sefid Ābeh, Iran | F16 | 48 |
| Sefrou, Mor. | D8 | 62 |
| Segamat, Malay. | M7 | 40 |
| Seganga, Zam. | E4 | 58 |
| Segarcea, Rom. | E7 | 20 |
| Segbana, Benin | F11 | 64 |
| Segbwema, S.L. | G4 | 64 |
| Segeža, Russia | E4 | 26 |
| Segni, Italy | H8 | 18 |
| Segorbe, Spain | F11 | 16 |
| Ségou, Mali | E6 | 64 |
| Segovia, Col. | D5 | 84 |
| Segovia, Spain | E7 | 16 |
| Segozero, ozero, l., Russia | J23 | 6 |
| Segre, stm., Eur. | D12 | 16 |
| Séguédine, Niger | D9 | 54 |
| Séguéla, C. Iv. | H6 | 64 |
| Segui, Arg. | F8 | 80 |
| Seguin, Tx., U.S. | J9 | 116 |
| Segundo, Co., U.S. | N3 | 118 |
| Segura, Port. | F5 | 16 |
| Segura, stm., Spain | G11 | 16 |
| Sehithwa, Bots. | C6 | 66 |
| Seia, Port. | E4 | 16 |
| Seibert, Co., U.S. | L5 | 118 |
| Seiling, Ok., U.S. | C8 | 116 |
| Seilo, Sudan | K2 | 60 |
| Sein, Île de, i., Fr. | D2 | 14 |
| Seinäjoki, Fin. | J18 | 6 |
| Seine, stm., Fr. | C7 | 14 |
| Seine, stm., On., Can. | I18 | 104 |
| Seine, Baie de la, b., Fr. | C6 | 14 |
| Seine-et-Marne, dept., Fr. | D10 | 14 |
| Seine-Maritime, dept., Fr. | C8 | 14 |
| Sejm, stm., Eur. | G4 | 26 |
| Sejmčan, Russia | E22 | 28 |
| Seke, Eth. | M10 | 60 |
| Seki, Japan | L11 | 36 |
| Seki, Tur. | M13 | 20 |
| Sekoma, Bots. | E6 | 66 |
| Sekondi-Takoradi, Ghana | I9 | 64 |
| Sekota, Eth. | K10 | 60 |
| Selah, Wa., U.S. | C5 | 122 |
| Selaru, Pulau, i., Indon. | G9 | 38 |
| Selatan, Tanjung, c., Indon. | F5 | 38 |
| Selawik, Ak., U.S. | C14 | 100 |
| Selayar, Pulau, i., Indon. | G7 | 38 |
| Selb, Ger. | E12 | 10 |
| Selbu, Nor. | J12 | 6 |
| Selby, S.D., U.S. | F7 | 118 |
| Selbyville, De., U.S. | I11 | 108 |
| Sel'co, Russia | H17 | 22 |
| Selden, Ks., U.S. | L7 | 118 |
| Seldovia, Ak., U.S. | G19 | 100 |
| Selebi Phikwe, Bots. | D8 | 66 |
| Selemdža, stm., Russia | G19 | 26 |
| Selenga (Selenge), stm., Asia | B7 | 30 |
| Selennjach, stm., Russia | D20 | 28 |
| Sélestat, Fr. | D14 | 14 |
| Selezn'ovo, Russia | A11 | 22 |
| Selfridge, N.D., U.S. | E7 | 118 |
| Sélibaby, Maur. | D3 | 64 |
| Selichova, zaliv, b., Russia | F23 | 28 |
| Seliger, ozero, l., Russia | D16 | 22 |
| Seligman, Az., U.S. | J3 | 120 |
| Seligman, Mo., U.S. | F3 | 114 |
| Selinsgrove, Pa., U.S. | G10 | 108 |
| Seližarovo, Russia | E16 | 22 |
| Selje, Nor. | J9 | 6 |
| Seljord, Nor. | L11 | 6 |
| Selkirk, Mb., Can. | H18 | 104 |
| Selkirk, Scot., U.K. | F11 | 8 |
| Selkirk Mountains, mts., N.A. | F16 | 102 |
| Seller Lake, l., Mb., Can. | C20 | 104 |
| Sellers, S.C., U.S. | E8 | 112 |
| Sellersburg, In., U.S. | D11 | 114 |
| Sellersville, Pa., U.S. | G11 | 108 |
| Sells, Az., U.S. | M5 | 120 |
| Selma, Al., U.S. | J9 | 114 |
| Selma, Ca., U.S. | H6 | 124 |
| Selma, In., U.S. | D7 | 110 |
| Selma, N.C., U.S. | D8 | 112 |
| Selma, Or., U.S. | H2 | 122 |
| Selmer, Tn., U.S. | G8 | 114 |
| Selmont, Al., U.S. | J9 | 114 |
| Selous, Mount, mtn., Yk., Can. | E28 | 100 |
| Selva, Arg. | D7 | 80 |
| Selvas, for., Braz. | E6 | 76 |
| Selwyn, Austl. | C4 | 70 |
| Selwyn, Mount, mtn., B.C., Can. | B11 | 102 |
| Selwyn Mountains, mts., Can. | D28 | 100 |
| Selwyn Range, mts., Austl. | C4 | 70 |
| Seman, stm., Alb. | I3 | 20 |
| Semans, Sk., Can. | G10 | 104 |
| Semarang, Indon. | j15 | 39a |
| Semenivka, Ukr. | I15 | 22 |
| Semeru, Gunung, mtn., Indon. | k16 | 39a |
| Semežava, Bela. | I9 | 22 |
| Semibratovo, Russia | D22 | 22 |
| Seminary, Ms., U.S. | K7 | 114 |
| Seminoe Reservoir, res., Wy., U.S. | B10 | 120 |
| Seminole, Ok., U.S. | D10 | 116 |
| Seminole, Tx., U.S. | G4 | 116 |
| Seminole, Lake, res., U.S. | I2 | 112 |
| Semipalatinsk, Kaz. | G8 | 28 |
| Semmens Lake, l., Mb. | C20 | 104 |
| Semnān, Iran | D12 | 48 |
| Semois, stm., Eur. | I7 | 12 |
| Semonaicha, Kaz. | G14 | 26 |
| Sem'onov, Russia | F6 | 26 |
| Semple Lake, l., Mb., Can. | C19 | 104 |
| Semporna, Malay. | E6 | 38 |
| Semuliki, stm., Afr. | A5 | 58 |
| Semur-en-Auxois, Fr. | E11 | 14 |
| Sena, Bol. | D8 | 82 |
| Sena, Moz. | E7 | 58 |
| Senador Canedo, Braz. | D4 | 79 |
| Senador Firmino, Braz. | F7 | 79 |
| Senador Pompeu, Braz. | E11 | 76 |
| Senahú, Guat. | B5 | 92 |
| Sena Madureira, Braz. | C7 | 82 |
| Senanga, Zam. | E4 | 58 |
| Senate, Sk., Can. | I5 | 104 |
| Senath, Mo., U.S. | F6 | 114 |
| Senatobia, Ms., U.S. | H7 | 114 |
| Sendafa, Eth. | M10 | 60 |
| Sendai, Japan | I15 | 36 |
| Šëndo, China | E15 | 44 |
| Seneca, Il., U.S. | I7 | 110 |
| Seneca, Ks., U.S. | L11 | 118 |
| Seneca, Mo., U.S. | E2 | 114 |
| Seneca, Or., U.S. | F7 | 122 |
| Seneca, S.C., U.S. | E4 | 112 |
| Seneca Falls, N.Y., U.S. | E10 | 108 |
| Seneca Lake, l., N.Y., U.S. | E10 | 108 |
| Senegal (Sénégal), ctry., Afr. | F4 | 54 |
| Sénégal, stm., Afr. | F4 | 54 |
| Senekal, S. Afr. | G8 | 66 |
| Senftenberg, Ger. | D14 | 10 |
| Sengés, Braz. | H4 | 79 |
| Senhor do Bonfim, Braz. | F10 | 76 |
| Senica, Slvk. | G17 | 10 |
| Senigallia, Italy | F8 | 18 |
| Senise, Italy | I11 | 18 |
| Senj, Cro. | E9 | 18 |
| Šenja, i., Nor. | G15 | 6 |
| Šenkursk, Russia | E6 | 26 |
| Senlac, Sk., Can. | F5 | 104 |
| Senlis, Fr. | C9 | 14 |
| Senmonorom, Camb. | H9 | 40 |
| Sennori, Italy | I3 | 18 |
| Sennoia, Ga., U.S. | F2 | 112 |
| Senqu see Orange, stm., Afr. | G4 | 66 |
| Sens, Fr. | D10 | 14 |
| Senta, Yugo. | D4 | 20 |
| Sentinel, Ok., U.S. | D7 | 116 |
| Sentinel Peak, mtn., B.C., Can. | C13 | 102 |
| Seo de Urgel, Spain | C13 | 16 |
| Seoni, India | I8 | 44 |
| Seoul see Sŏul, S. Kor. | F14 | 32 |
| Sepatini, stm., Braz. | B9 | 82 |
| Sepetiba, Baía de, b., Braz. | G7 | 79 |
| Sepik, stm., Pap. N. Gui. | k15 | 68a |
| Sępólno Krajeńskie, Pol. | B17 | 10 |
| Sępopa, Bots. | B6 | 66 |
| Sepotí, stm., Braz. | B11 | 82 |
| Sepotuba, stm., Braz. | F13 | 82 |
| Sept-Îles (Seven Islands), P.Q., Can. | B7 | 106 |
| Sepulga, stm., Al., U.S. | K10 | 114 |
| Sequatchie, stm., Tn., U.S. | D11 | 112 |
| Sequeros, Spain | E5 | 16 |
| Sequim, Wa., U.S. | B2 | 122 |
| Sequoia National Park, Ca., U.S. | H7 | 124 |
| Serabad, Uzb. | B2 | 44 |
| Serachs, Turk. | C16 | 48 |
| Serafimovič, Russia | H6 | 26 |
| Seraidi, Alg. | M2 | 18 |
| Seraing, Bel. | G7 | 12 |
| Seram (Ceram), i., Indon. | F8 | 38 |
| Seram, Laut (Ceram Sea), Indon. | F8 | 38 |
| Serang, Indon. | j13 | 39a |
| Serbia see Srbija, state, Yugo. | F4 | 20 |
| Serdobsk, Russia | G6 | 26 |
| Serebr'anyje Prudy, Russia | G21 | 22 |
| Sered', Slvk. | G17 | 10 |
| Seredejskij, Russia | G18 | 22 |
| Seredina-Buda, Ukr. | I17 | 22 |
| Seredžius, Lith. | F6 | 22 |
| Seremban, Malay. | M6 | 40 |
| Serengeti Plain, pl., Tan. | B6 | 58 |
| Serenje, Zam. | D5 | 58 |
| Seret (Siret), stm., Eur. | A9 | 20 |
| Sergeant Bluff, Ia., U.S. | I11 | 118 |
| Sergeja Kirova, ostrova, is., Russia | B15 | 28 |
| Sergejevka, Russia | I18 | 28 |
| Sergijev Posad, Russia | E21 | 22 |
| Seria, Bru. | E5 | 38 |
| Serian, Malay. | N11 | 40 |
| Sérifos, i., Grc. | L8 | 20 |
| Sérigny, stm., P.Q., Can. | E19 | 96 |
| Serkhe, Cerro, mtn., Bol. | G7 | 82 |
| Şerlovaja Gora, Russia | G15 | 28 |
| Sermata, Pulau, i., Indon. | G8 | 38 |
| Serodino, Arg. | G8 | 80 |
| Serov, Russia | F10 | 26 |
| Serowe, Bots. | D8 | 66 |
| Serpa, Port. | H4 | 16 |
| Serpent, Rivière au, stm., P.Q., Can. | C2 | 106 |
| Serpents Mouth, strt. | C12 | 84 |
| Serpuchov, Russia | G20 | 22 |
| Serra de Outes, Spain | C3 | 16 |
| Serra do Navio, Braz. | C8 | 76 |
| Serra do Salitre, Braz. | E5 | 79 |
| Serrai, Grc. | H7 | 20 |
| Serrana, Braz. | F5 | 79 |
| Serrânia, Braz. | F5 | 79 |
| Serranópolis, Braz. | D3 | 79 |
| Serrezuela, Arg. | F6 | 80 |
| Serrinha, Braz. | F11 | 76 |
| Serro, Braz. | E7 | 79 |
| Sersale, Italy | J11 | 18 |
| Sertânia, Braz. | E11 | 76 |
| Seruíni, stm., Braz. | C8 | 82 |
| Serule, Bots. | C8 | 66 |
| Sêrxü, China | E6 | 30 |
| Sesfontein, Nmb. | B1 | 66 |
| Sesheke, Zam. | E4 | 58 |
| Sessa Aurunca, Italy | H8 | 18 |
| Sestao, Spain | B9 | 16 |
| Sestri Levante, Italy | E4 | 18 |
| Sestroreck, Russia | A12 | 22 |
| Sešupė, stm., Eur. | F5 | 22 |
| Setana, Japan | e14 | 36a |
| Sète, Fr. | I10 | 14 |
| Sete Barras, Braz. | C15 | 80 |
| Sete de Setembro, stm., Braz. | B2 | 79 |

| Name | Map Ref. | Page |
|---|---|---|
| Sete Lagoas, Braz. | E6 | 79 |
| Sete Quedas, Parque Nacional de, Braz. | C11 | 80 |
| Seth Ward, Tx., U.S. | E5 | 116 |
| Set Net, Punta, c., Nic. | E11 | 92 |
| Seto, Japan | L12 | 36 |
| Seto-naikai, Japan | M7 | 36 |
| Seton Lake, l., B.C., Can. | G12 | 102 |
| Seton Portage, B.C., Can. | G12 | 102 |
| Settat, Mor. | D7 | 62 |
| Setté Cama, Gabon | B1 | 58 |
| Sette-Daban, chrebet, mts., Russia | E19 | 28 |
| Settee Lake, l., Mb., Can. | A18 | 104 |
| Setting Lake, l., Mb., Can. | C16 | 104 |
| Setúbal, Port. | G3 | 16 |
| Setúbal, Baía de, b., Port. | G3 | 16 |
| Seui, Italy | J4 | 18 |
| Seul, Lac, l., On., Can. | H22 | 104 |
| Seurre, Fr. | E12 | 14 |
| Sevan, Arm. | A8 | 48 |
| Sevan, ozero, l., Arm. | I7 | 26 |
| Sévaré, Mali | D7 | 64 |
| Sevastopol', Ukr. | I4 | 26 |
| Seven Islands see Sept-Îles, P.Q., Can. | B7 | 106 |
| Seven Persons, Ab., Can. | I4 | 104 |
| Seven Sisters Peaks, mts., B.C., Can. | C6 | 102 |
| Seventy Mile House, B.C., Can. | F13 | 102 |
| Severn, stm., On., Can. | E15 | 96 |
| Severn, stm., U.K. | J11 | 8 |
| Severnaja Dvina, stm., Russia | E6 | 26 |
| Severnaja Osetija, state, Russia | I6 | 26 |
| Severnaja Sos'va, stm., Russia | E4 | 28 |
| Severnaja Zeml'a, is., Russia | B17 | 26 |
| Severna Park, Md., U.S. | H10 | 108 |
| Severn Lake, l., On., Can. | E24 | 104 |
| Severnyje uvaly, hills, Russia | B27 | 22 |
| Severodvinsk, Russia | E5 | 26 |
| Severo-Dvinskij kanal, Russia | B21 | 22 |
| Severomorsk, Russia | D4 | 26 |
| Severo-Sibirskaja nizmennost', pl., Russia | C18 | 26 |
| Severoural'sk, Russia | E9 | 26 |
| Severo-Zadonsk, Russia | G21 | 22 |
| Severy, Ks., U.S. | N11 | 118 |
| Sevier, stm., Ut., U.S. | E4 | 120 |
| Sevier Desert, des., Ut., U.S. | E4 | 120 |
| Sevier Lake, l., Ut., U.S. | F3 | 120 |
| Sevierville, Tn., U.S. | D3 | 112 |
| Sevilla, Col. | E5 | 84 |
| Sevilla (Seville), Spain | H6 | 16 |
| Sevilla, Isla, i., Pan. | I12 | 92 |
| Seville, Fl., U.S. | J5 | 112 |
| Seville, Oh., U.S. | F5 | 108 |
| Seville see Sevilla, Spain | H6 | 16 |
| Şevketiye, Tur. | I11 | 20 |
| Ševsk, Russia | I17 | 22 |
| Sewanee, Tn., U.S. | G11 | 114 |
| Seward, Ak., U.S. | F20 | 100 |
| Seward, Ne., U.S. | K10 | 118 |
| Seward, Pa., U.S. | G7 | 108 |
| Seward Glacier, N.A. | F24 | 100 |
| Seward Peninsula, pen., Ak., U.S. | D13 | 100 |
| Sewell, Chile | H3 | 80 |
| Sexsmith, Ab., Can. | B16 | 102 |
| Sextin, stm., Mex. | E7 | 90 |
| Seybaplaya, Mex. | H14 | 90 |
| Seychelles, ctry., Afr. | B11 | 58 |
| Seyðisfjörður, Ice. | B6 | 6a |
| Seylac, Som. | F9 | 56 |
| Seymour, Austl. | K6 | 70 |
| Seymour, Ct., U.S. | F13 | 108 |
| Seymour, Ia., U.S. | J2 | 110 |
| Seymour, In., U.S. | D11 | 114 |
| Seymour, Mo., U.S. | E4 | 114 |
| Seymour, S. Afr. | I8 | 66 |
| Seymour, Tx., U.S. | F7 | 116 |
| Seymour, Wi., U.S. | F7 | 110 |
| Seymour, stm., B.C., Can. | F8 | 102 |
| Seymour Inlet, b., B.C., Can. | F7 | 102 |
| Seymourville, La., U.S. | L5 | 114 |
| Seyssel, Fr. | G12 | 14 |
| Sezela, S. Afr. | H10 | 66 |
| Sfântu Gheorghe, Rom. | D9 | 20 |
| Sfântu Gheorghe, Ostrovul, i., Rom. | D13 | 20 |
| Sfax, Tun. | C16 | 62 |
| Sfizef, Alg. | C10 | 62 |
| 's-Gravenbrakel see Braine-le-Comte, Bel. | G5 | 12 |
| 's-Gravenhage (The Hague), Neth. | D5 | 12 |
| Shaanxi (Shensi), prov., China | D8 | 30 |
| Shabeelle (Shebele), stm., Afr. | H9 | 56 |
| Shabwah, Yemen | G5 | 47 |
| Shache (Yarkand), China | A7 | 44 |
| Shackan Indian Reserve, B.C., Can. | G13 | 102 |
| Shackleton Ice Shelf, Ant. | B6 | 73 |
| Shādegān, Iran | F10 | 48 |
| Shady Cove, Or., U.S. | H3 | 122 |
| Shady Grove, Fl., U.S. | I3 | 112 |
| Shadyside, Oh., U.S. | H6 | 108 |
| Shafer Butte, mtn., Id., U.S. | G9 | 122 |
| Shafter, Ca., U.S. | I6 | 124 |
| Shagamu, Nig. | H11 | 64 |
| Shageluk, Ak., U.S. | E15 | 100 |
| Shag Rocks, S. Geor. | G8 | 78 |
| Shāhābād, India | E7 | 44 |
| Shāhābād, India | D4 | 46 |
| Shah Alam, Malay. | M6 | 40 |
| Shahdād, Namakzār-e, pl., Iran | F15 | 48 |
| Shahdol, India | I9 | 44 |
| Shahe, China | I6 | 32 |
| Shāhjahānpur, India | G8 | 44 |
| Shāh Jūy, Afg. | D2 | 44 |
| Shāhpur, Pak. | F3 | 44 |
| Shāhpura, India | H6 | 44 |
| Shahrak, Afg. | C1 | 44 |
| Shahr-e Bābak, Iran | F13 | 48 |
| Shahr-e Kord, Iran | E11 | 48 |
| Shā'ib al-Banāt, Jabal, mtn., Egypt | H2 | 48 |
| Shaikou, China | H6 | 34 |
| Shakawe, Bots. | B5 | 66 |
| Shaker Heights, Oh., U.S. | F5 | 108 |
| Shaki, Nig. | G11 | 64 |
| Shākir, Jazīrat, i., Egypt | H2 | 48 |
| Shakopee, Mn., U.S. | F2 | 110 |
| Shaktoolik, Ak., U.S. | D14 | 100 |
| Shala, Lake, l., Eth. | N10 | 60 |
| Shalalth, B.C., Can. | G12 | 102 |
| Shalatayn, Bi'r, well, Egypt | J3 | 48 |
| Shaler Mountains, mts., N.T., Can. | B10 | 96 |
| Shaleshanto, Bots. | B6 | 66 |
| Shallotte, N.C., U.S. | F8 | 112 |
| Shallowater, Tx., U.S. | F5 | 116 |
| Shām, Bādiyat ash- (Syrian Desert), des., Asia | E6 | 48 |
| Shām, Jabal ash-, mtn., Oman | C10 | 47 |
| Shamattawa, Mb., Can. | C22 | 104 |
| Shambe, Sudan | N6 | 60 |
| Shambu, Eth. | M9 | 60 |
| Shamīl, Iran | H14 | 48 |
| Shāmli, India | F7 | 44 |
| Shamokin, Pa., U.S. | G10 | 108 |
| Shamrock, Fl., U.S. | J3 | 112 |
| Shamrock, Tx., U.S. | D6 | 116 |
| Shamva, Zimb. | E6 | 58 |
| Shanany, ozero, l., Ukr. | D13 | 20 |
| Shanbiao, China | H1 | 32 |
| Shandī, Sudan | I7 | 60 |
| Shandong (Shantung), prov., China | D10 | 30 |
| Shandong Bandao (Shantung Peninsula), pen., China | F8 | 32 |
| Shangani, Zimb. | B9 | 66 |
| Shangani, stm., Zimb. | B9 | 66 |
| Shangcheng, China | D4 | 34 |
| Shangfu, China | G3 | 34 |
| Shanggu, China | C6 | 32 |
| Shanghai, China | D10 | 34 |
| Shanghai Shi, China | E11 | 30 |
| Shangjiaodao, China | F8 | 34 |
| Shangping, China | K3 | 34 |
| Shangqing, China | G6 | 34 |
| Shangqiu (Zhuji), China | A4 | 34 |
| Shangrao, China | G6 | 34 |
| Shangshui, China | B3 | 34 |
| Shangxian, China | E8 | 30 |
| Shangxingzhen, China | D8 | 34 |
| Shangyuan, China | B8 | 32 |
| Shangzhi, China | B12 | 30 |
| Shanhaiguan, China | C7 | 32 |
| Shankou, China | G3 | 34 |
| Shannon, Ga., U.S. | E1 | 112 |
| Shannon, Il., U.S. | H6 | 110 |
| Shannon, Ms., U.S. | H8 | 114 |
| Shannon, S. Afr. | G8 | 66 |
| Shannon, stm., Ire. | I4 | 8 |
| Shannontown, S.C., U.S. | F6 | 112 |
| Shanpo, China | E3 | 34 |
| Shansi see Shanxi, prov., China | D9 | 30 |
| Shāntipur, India | I13 | 44 |
| Shantou (Swatow), China | L5 | 34 |
| Shanxi (Shansi), prov., China | D9 | 30 |
| Shanxian, China | I4 | 32 |
| Shanxu, China | C9 | 40 |
| Shanyin, China | D9 | 30 |
| Shaodian, China | B3 | 34 |
| Shaoguan, China | K2 | 34 |
| Shaowu, China | H6 | 34 |
| Shaoxing, China | E9 | 34 |
| Shaoyang, China | F9 | 30 |
| Shaqqā, Syria | C7 | 50 |
| Shaqrā', Sau. Ar. | I8 | 48 |
| Shaqrā', Yemen | H4 | 47 |
| Sharafkhāneh, Iran | B8 | 48 |
| Sharbatāt, Ra's ash-, c., Oman | F10 | 47 |
| Sharbot Lake, On., Can. | F19 | 110 |
| Share, Nig. | G12 | 64 |
| Shark Bay, b., Austl. | E2 | 68 |
| Sharktooth Mountain, mtn., B.C., Can. | G31 | 100 |
| Sharm ash-Shaykh, Egypt | D8 | 60 |
| Sharon, N.D., U.S. | D10 | 118 |
| Sharon, Pa., U.S. | F6 | 108 |
| Sharon, Tn., U.S. | F8 | 114 |
| Sharon, Wi., U.S. | H7 | 110 |
| Sharon Springs, Ks., U.S. | M6 | 118 |
| Sharpe, Lake, res., S.D., U.S. | G8 | 118 |
| Sharpe Lake, l., Mb., Can. | D21 | 104 |
| Sharqī, Al-Jabal ash- (Anti-Lebanon), mts., Asia | A6 | 50 |
| Sharqīyah, Aş-Şaḥrā' ash- (Arabian Desert), des., Egypt | D7 | 60 |
| Shasha, Eth. | N8 | 60 |
| Shashe, stm., Afr. | C9 | 66 |
| Shashemene, Eth. | N10 | 60 |
| Shashi, China | E9 | 30 |
| Shasta, Ca., U.S. | D3 | 124 |
| Shasta, stm., Ca., U.S. | C3 | 124 |
| Shasta, Mount, vol., Ca., U.S. | C3 | 124 |
| Shasta Lake, res., Ca., U.S. | D3 | 124 |
| Shatawī, Sudan | J7 | 60 |
| Shattuck, Ok., U.S. | C7 | 116 |
| Shatuji, China | H3 | 32 |
| Shaunavon, Sk., Can. | I6 | 104 |
| Shaw, Ms., U.S. | I6 | 114 |
| Shawano, Wi., U.S. | F7 | 110 |
| Shawinigan, P.Q., Can. | G18 | 96 |
| Shawnee, Ks., U.S. | L13 | 118 |
| Shawnee, Oh., U.S. | H4 | 108 |
| Shawnee, Ok., U.S. | D10 | 116 |
| Shawneetown, Il., U.S. | E8 | 114 |
| Shawo, China | G3 | 34 |
| Shawville, P.Q., Can. | B10 | 108 |
| Shaybārā, i., Sau. Ar. | I4 | 48 |
| Shay Gap, Austl. | D4 | 68 |
| Shaykh, Jabal ash- (Mount Hermon), mtn., Asia | B5 | 50 |
| Shaykh 'Uthmān, Yemen | H4 | 47 |
| Shayuan, China | H9 | 34 |
| Shebele (Shabeelle), stm., Afr. | G9 | 56 |
| Shebelē Wenz, stm., Afr. | H3 | 42 |
| Sheberghān, Afg. | B1 | 44 |
| Sheboygan, Wi., U.S. | G8 | 110 |
| Sheboygan, stm., Wi., U.S. | G8 | 110 |
| Sheboygan Falls, Wi., U.S. | G8 | 110 |
| Shechem see Nābulus, W.B. | D4 | 50 |
| Shediac, N.B., Can. | F9 | 106 |
| Shedin Peak, mtn., B.C., Can. | B7 | 102 |
| Sheenjek, stm., Ak., U.S. | C23 | 100 |
| Sheep, stm., Ab., Can. | G20 | 102 |
| Sheep Creek, stm., Ab., Can. | D15 | 102 |
| Sheep Mountain, mtn., Wy., U.S. | G15 | 122 |
| Sheet Harbour, N.S., Can. | H11 | 106 |
| Shefar'am, Isr. | C4 | 50 |
| Sheffield, Al., U.S. | H9 | 114 |
| Sheffield, Eng., U.K. | H12 | 8 |
| Sheffield, Ia., U.S. | H2 | 110 |
| Sheffield, Il., U.S. | I6 | 110 |
| Sheffield, N.Z. | E4 | 72 |
| Sheffield, Pa., U.S. | F7 | 108 |
| Sheffield, Tx., U.S. | I5 | 116 |
| Sheffield Lake, l., Nf., Can. | C17 | 106 |
| Shegaon, India | B4 | 46 |
| Sheho, Sk., Can. | G11 | 104 |
| Sheikh Hasan, Eth. | K8 | 60 |
| Shekatika, P.Q., Can. | A15 | 106 |
| Shekhūpura, Pak. | E5 | 44 |
| Shelagyote Peak, mtn., B.C., Can. | B7 | 102 |
| Shelbina, Mo., U.S. | C4 | 114 |
| Shelburn, In., U.S. | C9 | 114 |
| Shelburne, N.S., Can. | I8 | 106 |
| Shelburne, On., Can. | F15 | 110 |
| Shelburne Falls, Ma., U.S. | E14 | 108 |
| Shelby, Ia., U.S. | J12 | 118 |
| Shelby, Mi., U.S. | G9 | 110 |
| Shelby, Ms., U.S. | I6 | 114 |
| Shelby, Mt., U.S. | B14 | 122 |
| Shelby, N.C., U.S. | D5 | 112 |
| Shelby, Ne., U.S. | J10 | 118 |
| Shelby, Oh., U.S. | G4 | 108 |
| Shelbyville, Il., U.S. | C8 | 114 |
| Shelbyville, In., U.S. | C11 | 114 |
| Shelbyville, Ky., U.S. | D11 | 114 |
| Shelbyville, Mo., U.S. | C4 | 114 |
| Shelbyville, Tn., U.S. | G10 | 114 |
| Shelbyville, Lake, res., Il., U.S. | C8 | 114 |
| Sheldon, Ia., U.S. | H12 | 118 |
| Sheldon, Mo., U.S. | E2 | 114 |
| Shelikof Strait, strt., Ak., U.S. | H17 | 100 |
| Shell, stm., Mb., Can. | G13 | 104 |
| Shellbrook, Sk., Can. | E8 | 104 |
| Shell Brook, stm., Sk., Can. | E8 | 104 |
| Shelley, B.C., Can. | C12 | 102 |
| Shelley, Id., U.S. | G13 | 122 |
| Shellharbour, Austl. | J9 | 70 |
| Shell Lake, Sk., Can. | E7 | 104 |
| Shell Lake, Wi., U.S. | E4 | 110 |
| Shellman, Ga., U.S. | H2 | 112 |
| Shellmouth Dam, Mb., Can. | H13 | 104 |
| Shell Rock, Ia., U.S. | H3 | 110 |
| Shell Rock, stm., U.S. | G2 | 110 |
| Shellsburg, Ia., U.S. | H4 | 110 |
| Shelton, Ct., U.S. | F13 | 108 |
| Shelton, Ne., U.S. | K9 | 118 |
| Shelton, Wa., U.S. | C2 | 122 |
| Shemogue, N.B., Can. | F9 | 106 |
| Shemya Station, Ak., U.S. | j2 | 101a |
| Shenandoah, Ia., U.S. | K12 | 118 |
| Shenandoah, Pa., U.S. | G10 | 108 |
| Shenandoah, Va., U.S. | I8 | 108 |
| Shenandoah, stm., U.S. | H9 | 108 |
| Shenandoah National Park, Va., U.S. | I8 | 108 |
| Shendam, Nig. | G14 | 64 |
| Shengang, China | H5 | 34 |
| Shengtian, China | H2 | 34 |
| Shengze, China | E9 | 34 |
| Shenqiu, China | B4 | 34 |
| Shensi see Shaanxi, prov., China | D8 | 30 |
| Shenyang (Mukden), China | B11 | 32 |
| Shenzhen, China | M3 | 34 |
| Sheopur, India | H7 | 44 |
| Shepard, Ab., Can. | G21 | 102 |
| Shepetivka, Ukr. | G3 | 26 |
| Shepherd, Mi., U.S. | G11 | 110 |
| Shepherd, Tx., U.S. | L1 | 114 |
| Shepherdstown, W.V., U.S. | H9 | 108 |
| Shepherdsville, Ky., U.S. | E11 | 114 |
| Sheppard Peak, mtn., B.C., Can. | H28 | 100 |
| Shepparton, Austl. | K6 | 70 |
| Sheqi, China | B1 | 34 |
| Sherab, Sudan | L3 | 60 |
| Sherada, Eth. | N9 | 60 |
| Sherard, Cape, c., N.T., Can. | B16 | 96 |
| Sherbro Island, i., S.L. | H3 | 64 |
| Sherbrooke, N.S., Can. | G12 | 106 |
| Sherbrooke, P.Q., Can. | B15 | 108 |
| Sherbrooke Lake, l., N.S., Can. | H9 | 106 |
| Sherburn, Mn., U.S. | H13 | 118 |
| Sherburne, N.Y., U.S. | E11 | 108 |
| Sheridan, Ar., U.S. | H4 | 114 |
| Sheridan, In., U.S. | B10 | 114 |
| Sheridan, Mt., U.S. | E13 | 122 |
| Sheridan, Or., U.S. | E2 | 122 |
| Sheridan, Tx., U.S. | J10 | 116 |
| Sheridan, Wy., U.S. | F19 | 122 |
| Sherman, Ms., U.S. | H8 | 114 |
| Sherman, N.Y., U.S. | E7 | 108 |
| Sherman, Tx., U.S. | F10 | 116 |
| Sherman Mills, Me., U.S. | B18 | 108 |
| Sherman Station, Me., U.S. | B18 | 108 |
| Sherpur, Bngl. | H14 | 44 |
| Sherrard, Il., U.S. | I5 | 110 |
| Sherridon, Mb., Can. | C13 | 104 |
| Sherrill, N.Y., U.S. | D11 | 108 |
| Shertallai, India | H4 | 46 |
| 's-Hertogenbosch, Neth. | E7 | 12 |
| Sherwood, Ar., U.S. | H4 | 114 |
| Sherwood, N.D., U.S. | C6 | 118 |
| Sherwood, Oh., U.S. | F2 | 108 |
| Sherwood, P.E., Can. | F10 | 106 |
| Sherwood, Tn., U.S. | G11 | 114 |
| Sherwood Park, Ab., Can. | D21 | 102 |
| Sherwood Shores, Tx., U.S. | I8 | 116 |
| Sheshea, stm., Peru | C5 | 82 |
| Shetland, prov., Scot., U.K. | A12 | 8 |
| Shetland Islands, is., Scot., U.K. | A12 | 8 |
| Shevchenkove, Ukr. | D13 | 20 |
| Shewa Gimira, Eth. | N8 | 60 |
| Shexian, China | F7 | 34 |
| Sheyenne, N.D., U.S. | D8 | 118 |
| Sheyenne, stm., N.D., U.S. | E10 | 118 |
| Sheykhābād, Afg. | C3 | 44 |
| Shḥīm, Leb. | A4 | 50 |
| Shiba, China | C7 | 34 |
| Shibām, Yemen | G6 | 47 |
| Shibarni, Sudan | J3 | 60 |
| Shibata, Japan | J14 | 36 |
| Shibetsu, Japan | c17 | 36a |
| Shibīn al-Kawm, Egypt | B6 | 60 |
| Shicheng, China | I5 | 34 |
| Shickley, Ne., U.S. | K10 | 118 |
| Shickshinny, Pa., U.S. | F10 | 108 |
| Shidao, China | G10 | 32 |
| Shidler, Ok., U.S. | C10 | 116 |
| Shields, stm., Mt., U.S. | E15 | 122 |
| Shifodian, China | C4 | 34 |
| Shigaib, Sudan | J2 | 60 |
| Shigezhuang, China | E4 | 32 |
| Shihan, Wādī, val., Asia | E8 | 47 |
| Shihe, China | D9 | 32 |
| Shijiazhuang, China | E2 | 32 |
| Shijing, China | K7 | 34 |
| Shikārpur, Pak. | G3 | 44 |
| Shikohābād, India | G8 | 44 |
| Shikoku, i., Japan | N8 | 36 |
| Shiliguri, India | G13 | 44 |
| Shillelagh, Ire. | I7 | 8 |
| Shillington, Pa., U.S. | G11 | 108 |
| Shillong, India | H14 | 44 |
| Shilo, Canadian Forces Base, mil., Mb., Can. | I15 | 104 |
| Shiloh, Oh., U.S. | H2 | 108 |
| Shiloh see Saylūn, Khirbat, hist., W.B. | D4 | 50 |
| Shilong, China | L2 | 34 |
| Shimabara, Japan | O5 | 36 |
| Shimada, Japan | M13 | 36 |
| Shimbiris, mtn., Som. | F10 | 56 |
| Shimen, China | D6 | 32 |
| Shimian, China | F7 | 30 |
| Shimiaozi, China | C11 | 32 |
| Shimizu, Japan | L13 | 36 |
| Shimla, India | E7 | 44 |
| Shimodate, Japan | K14 | 36 |
| Shimoga, India | F3 | 46 |
| Shimokita-hantō, pen., Japan | F16 | 36 |
| Shimonoseki, Japan | N5 | 36 |
| Shināş, Oman | B10 | 47 |
| Shīndand, Afg. | E17 | 48 |
| Shiner, Tx., U.S. | J9 | 116 |
| Shingbwiyang, Myan. | A4 | 40 |
| Shinglehouse, Pa., U.S. | F8 | 108 |
| Shingū, Japan | M9 | 36 |
| Shingū, Japan | N10 | 36 |
| Shingwidzi (Singuédeze), stm., Afr. | D10 | 66 |
| Shinjō, Japan | I15 | 36 |
| Shinkolobwe, D.R.C. | D5 | 58 |
| Shinnston, W.V., U.S. | H6 | 108 |
| Shinyanga, Tan. | B6 | 58 |
| Shiocton, Wi., U.S. | F7 | 110 |
| Shiogama, Japan | I16 | 36 |
| Shiojiri, Japan | K12 | 36 |
| Shiono-misaki, c., Japan | N10 | 36 |
| Ship Cove, Nf., Can. | E19 | 106 |
| Shiping, China | C7 | 40 |
| Shipman, Va., U.S. | B8 | 112 |
| Shippegan, N.B., Can. | E9 | 106 |
| Shippensburg, Pa., U.S. | G9 | 108 |
| Shiprock, N.M., U.S. | H8 | 120 |
| Ship Rock, mtn., N.M., U.S. | H8 | 120 |
| Shipshaw, stm., P.Q., Can. | D2 | 106 |
| Shipu, China | F10 | 34 |
| Shirakami-misaki, c., Japan | f15 | 36a |
| Shiraoi, Japan | e16 | 36a |
| Shīrāz, Iran | G12 | 48 |
| Shire, stm., Afr. | E6 | 58 |
| Shiretoko-misaki, c., Japan | c20 | 36a |
| Shirley, In., U.S. | C11 | 114 |
| Shiroishi, Japan | I15 | 36 |
| Shirpur, India | B3 | 46 |
| Shīrvān, Iran | C14 | 48 |
| Shishmaref, Ak., U.S. | C11 | 100 |
| Shitan, China | L2 | 34 |
| Shively, Ky., U.S. | D11 | 114 |
| Shivpuri, India | H7 | 44 |
| Shivwits Plateau, plat., Az., U.S. | H3 | 120 |
| Shixia, China | C2 | 32 |
| Shizheng, China | K4 | 34 |
| Shizuoka, Japan | M13 | 36 |
| Shkodër, Alb. | G3 | 20 |
| Shoal Harbour, Nf., Can. | D20 | 106 |
| Shoal Lake, Mb., Can. | H14 | 104 |
| Shoal Lake, l., Can. | I19 | 104 |
| Shoals, In., U.S. | D10 | 114 |
| Shoalwater Bay, b., Austl. | D9 | 70 |
| Shōdo-shima, i., Japan | M9 | 36 |
| Shoe Cove, Nf., Can. | C18 | 106 |
| Shoreacres, B.C., Can. | H17 | 102 |
| Shorewood, Wi., U.S. | G8 | 110 |
| Shortsville, N.Y., U.S. | E9 | 108 |
| Shoshone, Id., U.S. | H11 | 122 |
| Shoshone, stm., Wy., U.S. | F17 | 122 |
| Shoshone Basin, Wy., U.S. | H17 | 122 |
| Shoshone Mountains, mts., Nv., U.S. | F8 | 124 |
| Shoshong, Bots. | D8 | 66 |
| Shoshoni, Wy., U.S. | A8 | 120 |
| Shostka, Ukr. | G4 | 26 |
| Shouning, China | H8 | 34 |
| Shouxian, China | C5 | 34 |
| Show Low, Az., U.S. | J6 | 120 |
| Shreve, Oh., U.S. | G4 | 108 |
| Shreveport, La., U.S. | J3 | 114 |
| Shrewsbury, Eng., U.K. | I11 | 8 |
| Shrewsbury, Ma., U.S. | E15 | 108 |
| Shri Dūngargarh, India | F6 | 44 |
| Shrīrangapattana, India | F4 | 46 |
| Shropshire, co., Eng., U.K. | I11 | 8 |
| Shuajingsi, China | E7 | 30 |
| Shuangcheng, China | B12 | 30 |
| Shuanghe, China | D5 | 34 |
| Shuangjiangqiao, China | B5 | 40 |
| Shuangliao, China | C11 | 30 |
| Shuangmiaozi, China | A10 | 32 |
| Shuangyashan, China | B13 | 30 |
| Shubenacadie, stm., N.S., Can. | G10 | 106 |
| Shubrā al-Khaymah, Egypt | B6 | 60 |
| Shubuta, Ms., U.S. | K8 | 114 |
| Shuhong, China | G9 | 34 |
| Shuijing, China | A5 | 40 |
| Shuikouguan, China | C9 | 40 |
| Shuitouwei, China | I4 | 34 |
| Shuksan, Mount, mtn., Wa., U.S. | B4 | 122 |
| Shulaps Peak, mtn., B.C., Can. | G12 | 102 |
| Shule, stm., China | C6 | 30 |
| Shullsburg, Wi., U.S. | H5 | 110 |
| Shunchang, China | I6 | 34 |
| Shunde, China | M2 | 34 |
| Shungnak, Ak., U.S. | C16 | 100 |
| Shuqualak, Ms., U.S. | J8 | 114 |
| Shurugwi, Zimb. | B10 | 66 |
| Shūsh, Iran | E10 | 48 |
| Shūshtar, Iran | E10 | 48 |
| Shuswap, stm., B.C., Can. | G16 | 102 |
| Shuswap Lake, l., B.C., Can. | G15 | 102 |
| Shuwak, Sudan | J8 | 60 |
| Shwebo, Myan. | C3 | 40 |
| Shweli (Longchuan), stm., Asia | C4 | 40 |
| Shyok, stm., Asia | C7 | 44 |
| Shyryayeve, Ukr. | B14 | 20 |
| Siālkot, Pak. | D6 | 44 |
| Siam see Thailand, ctry., Asia | B3 | 38 |
| Siam, Gulf of see Thailand, Gulf of, b., Asia | I6 | 40 |
| Sian see Xi'an, China | E8 | 30 |
| Si'an, China | E8 | 34 |
| Siapa, stm., Ven. | G10 | 84 |
| Siasconset, Ma., U.S. | F17 | 108 |
| Šiaškotan, ostrov, i., Russia | H22 | 28 |
| Šiauliai, Lith. | F6 | 22 |
| Sibā'ī, Jabal as-, mtn., Egypt | I3 | 48 |
| Sibaj, Russia | G9 | 26 |
| Sibasa, S. Afr. | D10 | 66 |
| Sibbald, Ab., Can. | G4 | 104 |
| Šibenik, Cro. | F10 | 18 |
| Siberia see Sibir', reg., Russia | D14 | 28 |
| Siberut, Pulau, i., Indon. | F2 | 38 |
| Sibi, Pak. | F2 | 44 |
| Sibir' (Siberia), reg., Russia | D14 | 28 |
| Sibir'akova, ostrov, i., Russia | C13 | 26 |
| Sibiti, Congo | B2 | 58 |
| Sibiu, Rom. | D8 | 20 |
| Sibiu, co., Rom. | D8 | 20 |
| Sibley, Ia., U.S. | H12 | 118 |
| Sibley, La., U.S. | J3 | 114 |
| Sibley, Ms., U.S. | K5 | 114 |
| Sibley Peninsula, pen., On., Can. | B7 | 110 |
| Sibolga, Indon. | N5 | 40 |
| Sibsāgar, India | G16 | 44 |
| Sibuyan Island, i., Phil. | C7 | 38 |
| Sibuyan Sea, Phil. | C7 | 38 |
| Sicamous, B.C., Can. | G15 | 102 |
| Siccus, stm., Austl. | H3 | 70 |
| Sichote-Alin', mts., Russia | H19 | 28 |
| Sichuan (Szechwan), prov., China | E7 | 30 |
| Sichuanzhai, China | C6 | 40 |
| Sicilia, prov., Italy | L9 | 18 |
| Sicilia (Sicily), i., Italy | L9 | 18 |
| Sicily see Sicilia, i., Italy | L9 | 18 |
| Sicily, Strait of, strt. | L6 | 18 |
| Sicily Island, La., U.S. | K5 | 114 |
| Sico Tinto, stm., Hond. | B9 | 92 |
| Sicuani, Peru | F6 | 82 |
| Šid, Yugo. | D3 | 20 |
| Siddhapur, India | I5 | 44 |
| Siddipet, India | C5 | 46 |
| Sidéradougou, Burkina | F7 | 64 |
| Sideròpolis, Braz. | E14 | 80 |
| Sídheros, Ákra, c., Grc. | N10 | 20 |
| Sidhi, India | H9 | 44 |
| Sīdī 'Abd ar-Raḥmān, Egypt | B5 | 60 |
| Sidi Aïssa, Alg. | C12 | 62 |
| Sidi Ali Ben Nasrallah, Tun. | N4 | 18 |
| Sīdī Barrānī, Egypt | B3 | 60 |
| Sidi bel Abbès, Alg. | C10 | 62 |
| Sidi Bennour, Mor. | D6 | 62 |
| Sidi Bou Zid, Tun. | C15 | 62 |
| Sidi Daoud, Tun. | L5 | 18 |
| Sīdī Ḥunaysh, Egypt | B4 | 60 |
| Sidi Ifni, Mor. | F5 | 62 |
| Sidi Kacem, Mor. | C8 | 62 |
| Sidikalang, Indon. | M5 | 40 |
| Sidi Moussa, Oued, val., Alg. | G13 | 62 |
| Sidi Okba, Alg. | C13 | 62 |
| Sidi Slimane, Mor. | C8 | 62 |
| Sidi Smail, Mor. | D6 | 62 |
| Sidley, Mount, mtn., Ant. | C10 | 73 |
| Sidmouth, Eng., U.K. | K10 | 8 |
| Sidnaw, Mi., U.S. | D7 | 110 |
| Sidney, B.C., Can. | I11 | 102 |
| Sidney, Ia., U.S. | K12 | 118 |
| Sidney, Il., U.S. | B8 | 114 |
| Sidney, Mt., U.S. | D3 | 118 |
| Sidney, Ne., U.S. | J5 | 118 |
| Sidney, N.Y., U.S. | E11 | 108 |
| Sidney, Oh., U.S. | G2 | 108 |
| Sidney Lanier, Lake, res., Ga., U.S. | E3 | 112 |
| Sido, Mali | F6 | 64 |
| Sidon see Şaydā, Leb. | A4 | 50 |
| Sidon, Ms., U.S. | I6 | 114 |
| Sidra, Gulf of see Surt, Khalīj, b., Libya | B4 | 56 |
| Sidrolândia, Braz. | F1 | 79 |
| Siedlce, Pol. | C22 | 10 |
| Siegburg, Ger. | E7 | 10 |
| Siegen, Ger. | E8 | 10 |
| Siemianowice Śląskie, Pol. | E19 | 10 |
| Siemiatycze, Pol. | C22 | 10 |
| Siĕmréab, Camb. | H7 | 40 |
| Siena, Italy | F6 | 18 |
| Sieradz, Pol. | D18 | 10 |
| Sierck-les-Bains, Fr. | C13 | 14 |
| Sierpc, Pol. | C19 | 10 |
| Sierra Blanca, Tx., U.S. | M11 | 120 |
| Sierra Blanca Peak, mtn., N.M., U.S. | K11 | 120 |
| Sierra Chica, Arg. | I8 | 80 |
| Sierra Colorada, Arg. | E3 | 78 |
| Sierra de Agua, Belize | I15 | 90 |
| Sierra Gorda, Chile | B4 | 80 |
| Sierra Leone, ctry., Afr. | G4 | 54 |
| Sierra Nevada, Parque Nacional, Ven. | C7 | 84 |
| Sierras Bayas, Arg. | I8 | 80 |
| Sierra Vista, Az., U.S. | M6 | 120 |
| Sierre, Switz. | F8 | 13 |
| Siesta Key, Fl., U.S. | L4 | 112 |
| Siete Puntas, stm., Para. | B9 | 80 |
| Sífnos, i., Grc. | M8 | 20 |
| Sifton, Mb., Can. | G14 | 104 |
| Sig, Alg. | J11 | 16 |
| Sig, Russia | I24 | 6 |
| Sigean, Fr. | I9 | 14 |
| Sighetu Marmației, Rom. | B7 | 20 |
| Sighișoara, Rom. | C8 | 20 |
| Sigli, Indon. | L3 | 40 |
| Siglufjörður, Ice. | A4 | 6a |
| Sigmaringen, Ger. | G9 | 10 |
| Signal Hill National Historic Park, Nf., Can. | E21 | 106 |
| Signal Mountain, Tn., U.S. | G11 | 114 |
| Signal Peak, mtn., Ut., U.S. | G3 | 120 |
| Signy, sci., Ant. | B1 | 73 |
| Signy-l'Abbaye, Fr. | C11 | 14 |
| Sigourney, Ia., U.S. | I3 | 110 |
| Sigre, stm., Hond. | B10 | 92 |
| Sígsig, Ec. | I3 | 84 |
| Siguanea, Ensenada de la, b., Cuba | D3 | 94 |
| Siguatepeque, Hond. | C7 | 92 |
| Sigüenza, Spain | D9 | 16 |
| Siguiri, Gui. | F5 | 64 |
| Sigulda, Lat. | D7 | 22 |
| Sigurd, Ut., U.S. | F5 | 120 |
| Sihanoukville see Kâmpóng Saôm, Camb. | I7 | 40 |
| Sihu, China | I5 | 32 |
| Sihuas, Peru | C3 | 82 |
| Sihuas, stm., Peru | G5 | 82 |
| Siirt, Tur. | C6 | 48 |
| Sijiazi, China | B8 | 32 |
| Sikandarābād, India | F7 | 44 |
| Sikanni Chief, stm., B.C., Can. | E8 | 96 |
| Sīkar, India | G6 | 44 |
| Sikasso, Mali | F7 | 64 |
| Sikensi, C. Iv. | I7 | 64 |
| Sikeston, Mo., U.S. | F7 | 114 |
| Sikkim, state, India | G13 | 44 |
| Şikosi, Nmb. | A6 | 66 |
| Šikotan, ostrov (Shikotan-tō), i., Russia | d21 | 36a |
| Şilacayoapan, Mex. | I10 | 90 |
| Šilalė, Lith. | F5 | 22 |
| Silandro, Italy | C5 | 18 |
| Silao, Mex. | G9 | 90 |
| Silas, Al., U.S. | K8 | 114 |
| Sīlat az-Zahr, W.B. | D4 | 50 |
| Silay, Phil. | C7 | 38 |
| Silchar, India | H15 | 44 |
| Şile, Tur. | H13 | 20 |
| Šiler City, N.C., U.S. | D7 | 112 |
| Silesia, hist. reg., Pol. | D16 | 10 |
| Silet, Alg. | I13 | 62 |
| Siletz, Or., U.S. | F2 | 122 |
| Siletz, stm., Or., U.S. | F2 | 122 |
| Silgaḍhī, Nepal | F9 | 44 |
| Silhouette, i., Sey. | B11 | 58 |
| Siliana, Tun. | M4 | 18 |
| Silifke, Tur. | C2 | 48 |
| Siling Co, l., China | E13 | 44 |
| Silistra, Bul. | E11 | 20 |
| Şilivri, Tur. | H12 | 20 |
| Šilka, Russia | G15 | 28 |
| Šilka, stm., Russia | G15 | 28 |
| Sillamäe, Est. | B10 | 22 |
| Sillem Island, i., N.T., Can. | B18 | 96 |
| Sillian, Aus. | I12 | 10 |
| Sillustani, hist., Peru | F6 | 82 |
| Şiloam Springs, Ar., U.S. | F2 | 114 |
| Šilovo, Russia | G23 | 22 |
| Silsbee, Tx., U.S. | L2 | 114 |
| Silsby Lake, l., Mb., Can. | C19 | 104 |
| Silton, Sk., Can. | H10 | 104 |
| Şiluko, Nig. | H12 | 64 |
| Šilutė, Lith. | F4 | 22 |
| Silvan (Miyafarkin), Tur. | B6 | 48 |
| Silvânia, Braz. | D4 | 79 |
| Silvaplana, Switz. | F12 | 13 |
| Silver, Tx., U.S. | G6 | 116 |
| Silver Bank Passage, strt., N.A. | D9 | 94 |
| Silver Bay, Mn., U.S. | C4 | 110 |
| Silver Bell, Az., U.S. | L5 | 120 |
| Silver City, N.C., U.S. | D7 | 112 |
| Silver City, N.M., U.S. | L8 | 120 |
| Silver Creek, Ms., U.S. | K7 | 114 |
| Silver Creek, Ne., U.S. | J10 | 118 |
| Silver Creek, N.Y., U.S. | E7 | 108 |
| Silverdale, Wa., U.S. | C3 | 122 |
| Silver Lake, Ks., U.S. | L12 | 118 |
| Silver Lake, Mn., U.S. | F1 | 110 |
| Silver Lake, Or., U.S. | G4 | 122 |
| Silver Lake, Wi., U.S. | H7 | 110 |
| Silver Spring, Md., U.S. | I9 | 108 |
| Silver Star Mountain, mtn., Wa., U.S. | B5 | 122 |
| Silver Star Provincial Park, B.C., Can. | G15 | 102 |
| Silverthrone Mountain, mtn., B.C., Can. | F8 | 102 |
| Silvertip Mountain, mtn., Mt., U.S. | C12 | 122 |
| Silverton, B.C., Can. | H17 | 102 |
| Silverton, Co., U.S. | G9 | 120 |
| Silverton, Or., U.S. | E3 | 122 |
| Silverton, Tx., U.S. | E5 | 116 |
| Silvi, Italy | G9 | 18 |
| Silvia, Col. | F4 | 84 |
| Silvretta Gruppe, mts., Eur. | E13 | 13 |
| Sima, Com. | I16 | 67a |
| Şima, Russia | E22 | 22 |
| Šimanovsk, Russia | G17 | 28 |
| Simao, China | G7 | 30 |
| Simav, Tur. | J12 | 20 |
| Simcoe, On., Can. | H15 | 110 |
| Simcoe, Lake, l., On., Can. | F16 | 110 |
| Simeria, Rom. | D7 | 20 |
| Simeulue, Pulau, i., Indon. | M4 | 40 |
| Simferopol', Ukr. | I4 | 26 |
| Sími, i., Grc. | M11 | 20 |
| Simikoṭ, Nepal | F9 | 44 |
| Similkameen, stm., N.A. | H14 | 102 |
| Simiri, Niger | D11 | 64 |
| Simití, Col. | D6 | 84 |
| Simi Valley, Ca., U.S. | J7 | 124 |
| Simla, Co., U.S. | L3 | 118 |
| Simmern, Ger. | F7 | 10 |
| Simmesport, La., U.S. | L5 | 114 |
| Simmie, Sk., Can. | I6 | 104 |
| Simms, Mt., U.S. | C14 | 122 |
| Simnas, Lith. | G6 | 22 |
| Simoca, Arg. | D6 | 80 |
| Simojovel, Mex. | I13 | 90 |
| Simonette, stm., Ab., Can. | C17 | 102 |
| Simonhouse Lake, l., Mb., Can. | D13 | 104 |
| Simon's Town, S. Afr. | J4 | 66 |
| Şimoom Sound, B.C., Can. | G8 | 102 |
| Šimorskoje, Russia | F25 | 22 |
| Simpang-kiri, stm., Indon. | M4 | 40 |
| Simplon Pass, Switz. | F9 | 13 |
| Simplon Tunnel, Eur. | F9 | 13 |
| Simpson, La., U.S. | K3 | 114 |
| Simpson Desert, des., Austl. | D7 | 68 |
| Simpson Desert National Park, Austl. | E3 | 70 |
| Simpson Lake, l., N.T., Can. | B31 | 100 |
| Simpson Peak, mtn., B.C., Can. | G29 | 100 |
| Simpson Peninsula, pen., N.T., Can. | C15 | 96 |
| Simpson Strait, strt., N.T., Can. | C13 | 96 |
| Simpsonville, S.C., U.S. | E4 | 112 |
| Şimsbury, Ct., U.S. | F14 | 108 |
| Šimsk, Russia | C13 | 22 |
| Simušir, ostrov, i., Russia | H22 | 28 |
| Sīnā', Shibh Jazīrat (Sinai Peninsula), pen., Egypt | C7 | 60 |
| Sinai, Mount see Mūsā, Jabal, mtn., Egypt | C7 | 60 |
| Sinaia, Rom. | D9 | 20 |
| Sinai Peninsula see Sīnā', Shibh Jazīrat, pen., Egypt | C7 | 60 |
| Sin'aja, stm., Russia | E16 | 28 |
| Sinaloa, state, Mex. | F6 | 90 |
| Sinaloa, stm., Mex. | E5 | 90 |
| Sinalunga, Italy | F6 | 18 |
| Sinamaica, Ven. | B7 | 84 |
| Sinan, China | F8 | 30 |
| Sinanju, N. Kor. | D13 | 32 |
| Sīnāwin, Libya | E16 | 62 |
| Sinbo, Myan. | B4 | 40 |
| Sincé, Col. | C5 | 84 |
| Sincelejo, Col. | C5 | 84 |
| Sinch'ang, N. Kor. | C16 | 32 |
| Sinch'ŏn, N. Kor. | E13 | 32 |
| Sinclair, Wy., U.S. | C9 | 120 |
| Sinclair, Lake, res., Ga., U.S. | F3 | 112 |
| Sinclair Mills, B.C., Can. | C13 | 102 |
| Sindara, Gabon | B2 | 58 |
| Sindelfingen, Ger. | G9 | 10 |
| Sindi, Est. | C7 | 22 |
| Sındırgı, Tur. | J12 | 20 |
| Sindri, India | I12 | 44 |
| Sine, val., Sen. | D2 | 64 |
| Sinekçi, Tur. | I11 | 20 |
| Sinendé, Benin | F11 | 64 |
| Sinez'orki, Russia | H17 | 22 |
| Singapore, Sing. | N7 | 40 |
| Singapore, ctry., Asia | E3 | 38 |
| Singapore Strait, strt., Asia | N8 | 40 |
| Singaraja, Indon. | G6 | 38 |
| Sing Buri, Thai. | G6 | 40 |
| Singen [Hohentwiel], Ger. | H8 | 10 |
| Singer, La., U.S. | L3 | 114 |
| Singida, Tan. | B6 | 58 |
| Singkaling Hkāmti, Myan. | A3 | 40 |
| Singkang, Indon. | F7 | 38 |
| Singkawang, Indon. | N10 | 40 |
| Singkep, Pulau, i., Indon. | O8 | 40 |
| Singleton, Austl. | I9 | 70 |
| Singuédeze (Shingwidzi), stm., Afr. | D10 | 66 |
| Sinhŭng, N. Kor. | C15 | 32 |
| Sinj, Cro. | F11 | 18 |
| Sinjah, Sudan | K7 | 60 |
| Sinjai, Indon. | G7 | 38 |
| Sinjauka, Bela. | I9 | 22 |
| Sinkāt, Sudan | H9 | 60 |
| Sinkiang see Xinjiang Uygur Zizhiqu, prov., China | C3 | 30 |
| Sinmak, N. Kor. | E14 | 32 |
| Sinnai, Italy | J4 | 18 |
| Sinnamahoning, Pa., U.S. | F8 | 108 |
| Sinnamary, Fr. Gu. | B8 | 76 |
| Sinnar, India | C3 | 46 |
| Sinnes, Nor. | L10 | 6 |
| Sinnūris, Egypt | C6 | 60 |
| Sinop, Tur. | G15 | 4 |
| Sinp'o, N. Kor. | C16 | 32 |
| Sinsheim, Ger. | C15 | 14 |
| Sint-Amandsberg, Bel. | F4 | 12 |
| Sintang, Indon. | E5 | 38 |
| Sint Annaland, Neth. | E5 | 12 |
| Sint Annaparochie, Neth. | B8 | 12 |
| Sint Eustatius, i., Neth. Ant. | F13 | 94 |
| Sint Maarten (Saint-Martin), i., N.A. | E13 | 94 |
| Sint-Michiels, Bel. | F3 | 12 |

| Name | Map Ref. | Page |
|---|---|---|
| Sint-Niklaas (Saint-Nicolas), Bel. | F5 | 12 |
| Sinton, Tx., U.S. | K9 | 116 |
| Sintra, Port. | G2 | 16 |
| Sint-Truiden (Saint-Trond), Bel. | G7 | 12 |
| Sinú, stm., Col. | C5 | 84 |
| Sinuiju, N. Kor. | C12 | 32 |
| Siocon, Phil. | D7 | 38 |
| Siófok, Hung. | I18 | 10 |
| Sion (Sitten), Switz. | F7 | 13 |
| Sioux Center, Ia., U.S. | H11 | 118 |
| Sioux City, Ia., U.S. | I11 | 118 |
| Sioux Falls, S.D., U.S. | H11 | 118 |
| Sioux Lookout, On., Can. | H23 | 104 |
| Sioux Narrows, On., Can. | I20 | 104 |
| Sioux Rapids, Ia., U.S. | I12 | 118 |
| Sipaliwini, stm., Sur. | F14 | 84 |
| Sipapo, stm., Ven. | E9 | 84 |
| Siparia, Trin. | I14 | 94 |
| Siping, China | C11 | 30 |
| Sipiwesk, Mb., Can. | C17 | 104 |
| Sipiwesk Lake, l., Mb., Can. | C17 | 104 |
| Siple, Mount, mtn., Ant. | C10 | 73 |
| Sipsey, stm., Al., U.S. | I9 | 114 |
| Sipu, China | C1 | 32 |
| Sipunskij, mys, c., Russia | G24 | 28 |
| Siqueira Campos, Braz. | G4 | 79 |
| Siquia, stm., Nic. | E10 | 92 |
| Siquirres, C.R. | G11 | 92 |
| Siquisique, Ven. | B8 | 84 |
| Si Racha, Thai. | H6 | 40 |
| Siracusa, Para. | I11 | 82 |
| Siracusa (Syracuse), Italy | L10 | 18 |
| Sirājganj, Bngl. | H13 | 44 |
| Sir Alexander, Mount, mtn., B.C., Can. | D14 | 102 |
| Sirasso, C. Iv. | G6 | 64 |
| Sirba, stm., Afr. | E10 | 64 |
| Sirdar, B.C., Can. | H18 | 102 |
| Sir Douglas, Mount, mtn., Can. | G19 | 102 |
| Sire, Eth. | M9 | 60 |
| Sir Edward Pellew Group, is., Austl. | C7 | 68 |
| Šireqa, Russia | A24 | 22 |
| Siret (Seret), stm., Eur. | D11 | 20 |
| Sirevåg, Nor. | L9 | 6 |
| Sir Francis Drake, Mount, mtn., B.C., Can. | G10 | 102 |
| Sirhān, Wādī as-, val., Sau. Ar. | F5 | 48 |
| Siriya-zaki, c., Japan | F16 | 36 |
| Sir James MacBrien, Mount, mtn., N.T., Can. | E31 | 100 |
| Sīrjān, Iran | G13 | 48 |
| Sir Joseph Banks Group, is., Austl. | J2 | 70 |
| Sirocina, Bela. | F12 | 22 |
| Sirohi, India | H5 | 44 |
| Sironj, India | H7 | 44 |
| Šíros, i., Grc. | L8 | 20 |
| Sir Sandford, Mount, mtn., B.C., Can. | F17 | 102 |
| Sirsi, India | E3 | 46 |
| Sirte, Gulf of see Surt, Khalīj, b., Libya | B4 | 56 |
| Sirupa, stm., Mex. | C5 | 90 |
| Širvān (Diyālā), stm., Asia | E8 | 48 |
| Širvintos, Lith. | F7 | 22 |
| Sir Wilfrid Laurier, Mount, mtn., B.C., Can. | E15 | 102 |
| Sís, stm., Guat. | C3 | 92 |
| Sisak, Cro. | D11 | 18 |
| Si Sa Ket, Thai. | G8 | 40 |
| Sishen, S. Afr. | F6 | 66 |
| Sishui, China | H5 | 32 |
| Sisib Lake, l., Mb., Can. | F15 | 104 |
| Sisipuk Lake, l., Can. | C13 | 104 |
| Siskiyou Mountains, mts., U.S. | C2 | 124 |
| Siskiyou Pass, U.S. | H3 | 122 |
| Sisquoc, stm., Ca., U.S. | J6 | 124 |
| Sissach, Switz. | D8 | 13 |
| Sissili, stm., Afr. | F9 | 64 |
| Sisson Branch Reservoir, res., N.B., Can. | E6 | 106 |
| Sissonne, Fr. | C10 | 14 |
| Sissonville, W.V., U.S. | I5 | 108 |
| Sīstān, reg., Asia | F17 | 48 |
| Sister Bay, Wi., U.S. | E8 | 110 |
| Sisters, Or., U.S. | F4 | 122 |
| Sistersville, W.V., U.S. | H6 | 108 |
| Sitabamba, Peru | C3 | 82 |
| Sitakili, Mali | E4 | 64 |
| Sītāmarhi, India | H11 | 44 |
| Sitampiky, Madag. | p22 | 67b |
| Sītāpur, India | G9 | 44 |
| Siteki, Swaz. | F10 | 66 |
| Sitidgi Lake, l., N.T., Can. | B38 | 100 |
| Sítio D'Abádia, Braz. | C5 | 79 |
| Sitka, Ak., U.S. | H27 | 100 |
| Sitona, Erit. | J9 | 60 |
| Sitrah, Bahr. | H11 | 48 |
| Sittard, Neth. | F8 | 12 |
| Sittoung, stm., Myan. | F4 | 40 |
| Sittwe (Akyab), Myan. | D2 | 40 |
| Siuna, Nic. | D10 | 92 |
| Siuri, India | I12 | 44 |
| Sivakāsi, India | H4 | 46 |
| Sivas, Tur. | B4 | 48 |
| Sivé, Maur. | D3 | 64 |
| Siveluč, vulkan, vol., Russia | F24 | 28 |
| Siverek, Tur. | C5 | 48 |
| Siverskij, Russia | B13 | 22 |
| Sivers'kyy Donets', stm., Eur. | H5 | 26 |
| Siwah, Egypt | C3 | 60 |
| Siwān, India | G11 | 44 |
| Sixaola, stm., N.A. | H12 | 92 |
| Sixitou, China | H8 | 34 |
| Siyāl, Jazā'ir, is., Egypt | J4 | 48 |
| Siyeteb, Sudan | H8 | 60 |
| Sizun, Fr. | D2 | 14 |
| Sjælland, i., Den. | N12 | 6 |
| Sjenica, Yugo. | F4 | 20 |
| Skærbæk, Den. | N11 | 6 |
| Skaftung, Den. | J17 | 6 |
| Skagen, Den. | M12 | 6 |
| Skagerrak, strt., Eur. | M11 | 6 |
| Skagit, stm., N.A. | B4 | 122 |
| Skagway, Ak., U.S. | G27 | 100 |
| Skaidi, Nor. | F19 | 6 |
| Skaistkalne, Lat. | E7 | 22 |
| Skalino, Russia | C23 | 22 |
| Skalistyj Golec, gora, mtn., Russia | F15 | 28 |
| Skandeborg, Den. | M11 | 6 |
| Skaraborgs Län, co., Swe. | L13 | 6 |
| Skarð, Ice. | B4 | 6a |
| Skärdu, Pak. | C6 | 44 |
| Skarżysko-Kamienna, Pol. | D20 | 10 |
| Skawina, Pol. | F19 | 10 |
| Skeena, stm., B.C., Can. | C5 | 102 |
| Skeena Crossing, B.C., Can. | B7 | 102 |
| Skeena Mountains, mts., B.C., Can. | A7 | 102 |
| Skei, Nor. | K10 | 6 |
| Skeleton Coast, Nmb. | B1 | 66 |
| Skellefteå, Swe. | I17 | 6 |
| Skellytown, Tx., U.S. | D5 | 116 |
| Skene, Swe. | M13 | 6 |
| Skiatook, Ok., U.S. | C10 | 116 |
| Skidal', Bela. | H7 | 22 |
| Skidegate, B.C., Can. | D2 | 102 |
| Skidegate Inlet, b., B.C., Can. | D3 | 102 |
| Skidmore, Tx., U.S. | K9 | 116 |
| Skien, Nor. | L11 | 6 |
| Skierniewice, Pol. | D20 | 10 |
| Skihist Mountain, mtn., B.C., Can. | G13 | 102 |
| Skikda (Philippeville), Alg. | B14 | 62 |
| Skilak Lake, l., Ak., U.S. | F19 | 100 |
| Skillet Fork, stm., Il., U.S. | D8 | 114 |
| Skipton, Austl. | K5 | 70 |
| Skiros, Grc. | K8 | 20 |
| Skive, Den. | M11 | 6 |
| Šklou, Bela. | G13 | 22 |
| Skokie, Il., U.S. | H8 | 110 |
| Skopin, Russia | H22 | 22 |
| Skopje, Mac. | H5 | 20 |
| Skövde, Swe. | L13 | 6 |
| Skovorodino, Russia | G16 | 28 |
| Skowhegan, Me., U.S. | C17 | 108 |
| Skownan, Mb., Can. | G15 | 104 |
| Skrīveri, Lat. | E8 | 22 |
| Skrudaliena, Lat. | F9 | 22 |
| Skrunda, Lat. | E5 | 22 |
| Skukuza, S. Afr. | E10 | 66 |
| Skull Valley, Az., U.S. | J4 | 120 |
| Skuna, stm., Ms., U.S. | I7 | 114 |
| Skunk, stm., Ia., U.S. | J4 | 110 |
| Skuodas, Lith. | E4 | 22 |
| Skuratovskij, Russia | G20 | 22 |
| Skye, Island of, i., Scot., U.K. | D7 | 8 |
| Skykomish, stm., Wa., U.S. | C4 | 122 |
| Skyland, N.C., U.S. | D4 | 112 |
| Skyring, Seno, strt., Chile | G2 | 78 |
| Slagoviśśi, Russia | H18 | 22 |
| Slamet, Gunung, mtn., Indon. | j14 | 39a |
| Slancy, Russia | B11 | 22 |
| Slaný, Czech Rep. | E14 | 10 |
| Slater, Ia., U.S. | I2 | 110 |
| Slater, Mo., U.S. | C3 | 114 |
| Slatina, Rom. | E8 | 20 |
| Slaton, Tx., U.S. | F5 | 116 |
| Slaughter, La., U.S. | L5 | 114 |
| Slauharad, Bela. | H13 | 22 |
| Slav'ansk-na-Kubani, Russia | H5 | 26 |
| Slave, stm., Can. | D10 | 96 |
| Slave Coast, Afr. | I11 | 64 |
| Slave Lake, Ab., Can. | B20 | 102 |
| Slavgorod, Russia | G7 | 28 |
| Slavkov u Brna, Czech Rep. | F16 | 10 |
| Slavonia, hist. reg., Cro. | D12 | 18 |
| Slavonska Požega, Cro. | D12 | 18 |
| Slavonski Brod, Cro. | D13 | 18 |
| Slavsk, Russia | F4 | 22 |
| Sławno, Pol. | A16 | 10 |
| Slayton, Mn., U.S. | H12 | 118 |
| Sled Lake, l., Sk., Can. | D7 | 104 |
| Sledzjuki, Bela. | H13 | 22 |
| Sleepy Eye, Mn., U.S. | G13 | 118 |
| Slidell, La., U.S. | L7 | 114 |
| Sliedrecht, Neth. | E6 | 12 |
| Sligo, Ire. | G5 | 8 |
| Sligo, Pa., U.S. | F7 | 108 |
| Sligo, co., Ire. | G5 | 8 |
| Slinger, Wi., U.S. | G7 | 110 |
| Slippery Rock, Pa., U.S. | F6 | 108 |
| Sliven, Bul. | G10 | 20 |
| Slivnica, Bul. | G7 | 20 |
| Sloan, Ia., U.S. | I11 | 118 |
| Sloan, Nv., U.S. | I10 | 124 |
| Slobidka, Ukr. | B13 | 20 |
| Slobodskoj, Russia | F8 | 26 |
| Slobozia, Mol. | C13 | 20 |
| Slobozia, Rom. | E11 | 20 |
| Slobozia, Rom. | F9 | 20 |
| Slocan, B.C., Can. | H17 | 102 |
| Slocan Lake, l., B.C., Can. | H17 | 102 |
| Slonim, Bela. | H8 | 22 |
| Slosh Indian Reserve, B.C., Can. | G12 | 102 |
| Slovakia, ctry., Eur. | F11 | 4 |
| Slovenia (Slovenija), ctry., Eur. | C9 | 18 |
| Slovenj Gradec, Slvn. | C10 | 18 |
| Slovenska Bistrica, Slvn. | C10 | 18 |
| Slov'yans'k, Ukr. | H5 | 26 |
| Sl'ud'anka, Russia | G12 | 28 |
| Slunj, Cro. | D10 | 18 |
| Słupca, Pol. | C17 | 10 |
| Słupsk (Stolp), Pol. | A17 | 10 |
| Slurry, S. Afr. | E7 | 66 |
| Smackover, Ar., U.S. | I4 | 114 |
| Smalininkai, Lith. | F5 | 22 |
| Smallwood Reservoir, res., Nf., Can. | F20 | 96 |
| Smara, W. Sah. | G5 | 62 |
| Smarhon', Bela. | G9 | 22 |
| Smeaton, Sk., Can. | E10 | 104 |
| Smederevo, Yugo. | E4 | 20 |
| Smethport, Pa., U.S. | F8 | 108 |
| Smidovič, Russia | H18 | 28 |
| Šmidta, ostrov, i., Russia | A16 | 26 |
| Smila, Ukr. | H4 | 26 |
| Smilavičy, Bela. | H11 | 22 |
| Smiley, Sk., Can. | G5 | 104 |
| Smiley, Tx., U.S. | J9 | 116 |
| Smiltene, Lat. | D8 | 22 |
| Smirnovo, Kaz. | G12 | 26 |
| Smir-Restinga, Mor. | J6 | 16 |
| Smith, stm., B.C., Can. | B20 | 102 |
| Smith, stm., Ca., U.S. | C1 | 124 |
| Smith, stm., Mt., U.S. | C14 | 122 |
| Smith, stm., Or., U.S. | G2 | 122 |
| Smith, stm., U.S. | C6 | 112 |
| Smith Arm, b., N.T., Can. | C33 | 100 |
| Smith Center, Ks., U.S. | L9 | 118 |
| Smithers, B.C., Can. | C7 | 102 |
| Smithfield, N.C., U.S. | I5 | 108 |
| Smithfield, S. Afr. | H8 | 66 |
| Smithfield, Ut., U.S. | C5 | 120 |
| Smithfield, Va., U.S. | C10 | 112 |
| Smith Island, i., Ant. | B12 | 73 |
| Smithland, Ky., U.S. | E8 | 114 |
| Smith Mountain Lake, res., Va., U.S. | B7 | 112 |
| Smith Point, c., N.S., Can. | G10 | 106 |
| Smith River, Ca., U.S. | C1 | 124 |
| Smiths, Al., U.S. | J11 | 114 |
| Smiths Falls, On., Can. | F19 | 110 |
| Smith Sound, strt., B.C., Can. | F7 | 102 |
| Smithton, Austl. | M6 | 70 |
| Smithton, Mo., U.S. | D3 | 114 |
| Smithton, Pa., U.S. | H2 | 112 |
| Smithville, Ga., U.S. | H2 | 112 |
| Smithville, Mo., U.S. | C2 | 114 |
| Smithville, Tn., U.S. | G11 | 114 |
| Smithville, Tx., U.S. | I9 | 116 |
| Smokey, Cape, c., N.S., Can. | F13 | 106 |
| Smokey Dome, mtn., Id., U.S. | G11 | 122 |
| Smoky, stm., Ab., Can. | B17 | 102 |
| Smoky Cape, c., Austl. | H10 | 70 |
| Smoky Hill, stm., U.S. | M10 | 118 |
| Smoky Lake, Ab., Can. | C22 | 102 |
| Smolensk, Russia | G15 | 22 |
| Smoljan, Bul. | H8 | 20 |
| Smoot, Wy., U.S. | B6 | 120 |
| Smoothstone, stm., Sk., Can. | C8 | 104 |
| Smoothstone Lake, l., Sk., Can. | D8 | 104 |
| Smyrna, De., U.S. | H11 | 108 |
| Smyrna, Ga., U.S. | F2 | 112 |
| Smyrna, Tn., U.S. | G10 | 114 |
| Smyrna see İzmir, Tur. | K11 | 20 |
| Smythe, Mount, mtn., B.C., Can. | E8 | 96 |
| Snag, Yk., Can. | E24 | 100 |
| Snake, stm., Mn., U.S. | E2 | 110 |
| Snake, stm., Ne., U.S. | I6 | 118 |
| Snake, stm., U.S. | D7 | 122 |
| Snake, stm., Yk., Can. | D28 | 100 |
| Snake Indian, stm., Ab., Can. | D16 | 102 |
| Snake River Plain, pl., Id., U.S. | G12 | 122 |
| Snake Valley, val., U.S. | E12 | 124 |
| Snares Islands, is., N.Z. | M20 | 126 |
| Sneads, Fl., U.S. | I2 | 112 |
| Sneedville, Tn., U.S. | C3 | 112 |
| Sneek, Neth. | B8 | 12 |
| Snelling, Ca., U.S. | G5 | 124 |
| Snežná, mtn., Eur. | E15 | 10 |
| Śniardwy, Jezioro, l., Pol. | B21 | 10 |
| Snina, Slvk. | G22 | 10 |
| Snipe Lake, l., Ab., Can. | B18 | 102 |
| Snohomish, Wa., U.S. | C3 | 122 |
| Snoqualmie Pass, U.S. | C4 | 122 |
| Snøtinden, mtn., Nor. | H14 | 6 |
| Snover, Mi., U.S. | G13 | 110 |
| Snowbird Lake, l., N.T., Can. | D12 | 96 |
| Snowden, Sk., Can. | E10 | 104 |
| Snowdon, mtn., Wales, U.K. | H9 | 8 |
| Snowdoun, Al., U.S. | J10 | 114 |
| Snowdrift, N.T., Can. | D10 | 96 |
| Snowflake, Az., U.S. | J6 | 120 |
| Snow Hill, Md., U.S. | I11 | 108 |
| Snow Hill, N.C., U.S. | D9 | 112 |
| Snow Lake, Mb., Can. | D14 | 104 |
| Snowmass Mountain, mtn., Co., U.S. | E9 | 120 |
| Snow Peak, mtn., Wa., U.S. | B7 | 122 |
| Snowy, stm., Austl. | K8 | 70 |
| Snowy Mountains, mts., Austl. | K8 | 70 |
| Snowyside Peak, mtn., Id., U.S. | G11 | 122 |
| Snyatyn, Ukr. | A9 | 20 |
| Snyder, Ok., U.S. | E8 | 116 |
| Snyder, Tx., U.S. | G6 | 116 |
| Soacha, Col. | E5 | 84 |
| Soahany, Madag. | q21 | 67b |
| Soalala, Madag. | p21 | 67b |
| Soamanonga, Madag. | s21 | 67b |
| Soanindrariny, Madag. | q22 | 67b |
| Soap Lake, Wa., U.S. | C6 | 122 |
| Soatá, Col. | D6 | 84 |
| Soavinandriana, Madag. | q22 | 67b |
| Sobaek-sanmaek, mts., S. Kor. | G15 | 32 |
| Sobat, stm., Sudan | M7 | 60 |
| Sobernheim, Ger. | F7 | 10 |
| Sobinka, Russia | F23 | 22 |
| Soboko, C.A.R. | N3 | 60 |
| Sobolivka, Ukr. | A13 | 20 |
| Sobradinho, Braz. | E12 | 80 |
| Sobrado, Port. | D3 | 16 |
| Sobral, Braz. | D10 | 76 |
| Socaire, Chile | B5 | 80 |
| Soc Giang, Viet. | C9 | 40 |
| Sochaczew, Pol. | C20 | 10 |
| Sochi see Soči, Russia | I5 | 26 |
| Sŏch'ŏn, S. Kor. | G14 | 32 |
| Soči, Russia | I5 | 26 |
| Social Circle, Ga., U.S. | F3 | 112 |
| Société, Archipel de la (Society Islands), is., Fr. Poly. | J24 | 126 |
| Society Hill, S.C., U.S. | E7 | 112 |
| Soco, stm., Dom. Rep. | E9 | 94 |
| Socoltenango, Mex. | I13 | 90 |
| Socompa, Paso, S.A. | C4 | 80 |
| Socorro, Col. | D6 | 84 |
| Socorro, N.M., U.S. | J10 | 120 |
| Socorro, Tx., U.S. | M10 | 120 |
| Socorro, Isla, i., Mex. | H4 | 90 |
| Socota, Peru | B2 | 82 |
| Socotra see Suquţrā, i., Yemen | G5 | 42 |
| Soc Trang, Viet. | J8 | 40 |
| Socuéllamos, Spain | F9 | 16 |
| Soda Creek, B.C., Can. | E12 | 102 |
| Soda Lake, l., Ca., U.S. | I9 | 124 |
| Soda Springs, Id., U.S. | H14 | 122 |
| Soddy-Daisy, Tn., U.S. | G11 | 114 |
| Söderhamn, Swe. | K15 | 6 |
| Söderköping, Swe. | L15 | 6 |
| Södermanlands Län, co., Swe. | L15 | 6 |
| Södertälje, Swe. | L15 | 6 |
| Sodo, Eth. | N9 | 60 |
| Sodus, N.Y., U.S. | D9 | 108 |
| Soe, Indon. | G7 | 38 |
| Soekmekaar, S. Afr. | D9 | 66 |
| Soela väin, strt., Est. | C5 | 22 |
| Soest, Ger. | D8 | 10 |
| Sofia see Sofija, Bul. | G7 | 20 |
| Sofia, stm., Madag. | o22 | 67b |
| Sofija (Sofia), Bul. | G7 | 20 |
| Sofrino, Russia | E20 | 22 |
| Sogakofe, Ghana | H10 | 64 |
| Sogamoso, Col. | E6 | 84 |
| Sogamoso, stm., Col. | D6 | 84 |
| Sognefjorden, Nor. | K9 | 6 |
| Søgne, Nor. | L10 | 6 |
| Sogn og Fjordane, co., Nor. | K10 | 6 |
| Sogo Nur, l., China | C7 | 30 |
| Sögütalan, Tur. | I12 | 20 |
| Sogxian, China | E5 | 30 |
| Soin, Burkina | E6 | 64 |
| Sointula, B.C., Can. | G7 | 102 |
| Soissons, Fr. | C10 | 14 |
| Sojat, India | H5 | 44 |
| Sokal'skogo, proliv, strt., Russia | B12 | 28 |
| Sokch'o, S. Kor. | E16 | 32 |
| Sok, Tur. | L11 | 20 |
| Sokodé, Togo | G10 | 64 |
| Sokol, Russia | F6 | 26 |
| Sokólka, Pol. | B23 | 10 |
| Sokolov, Czech Rep. | E12 | 10 |
| Sokolovo, Russia | I17 | 22 |
| Sokołów Podlaski, Pol. | C22 | 10 |
| Sokoto, Nig. | E12 | 64 |
| Sokyryany, Ukr. | A11 | 20 |
| Sol, Costa del, Spain | I7 | 16 |
| Solacolu, Rom. | E10 | 20 |
| Solāpur, India | D3 | 46 |
| Solano, Phil. | m19 | 39b |
| Solano, Phil. | B3 | 38 |
| Solcava, Slvn. | C9 | 18 |
| Solca, Arg. | F5 | 80 |
| Sol'cy, Russia | C13 | 22 |
| Sol de Julio, Arg. | E7 | 80 |
| Soldiers Grove, Wi., U.S. | G5 | 110 |
| Soldotna, Ak., U.S. | F19 | 100 |
| Soledad, Ca., U.S. | H4 | 124 |
| Soledad, Col. | B5 | 84 |
| Soledad, Ven. | C11 | 84 |
| Soledad Diez Gutiérrez, Mex. | F9 | 90 |
| Soledade, Braz. | E12 | 80 |
| Solen, N.D., U.S. | E7 | 118 |
| Solentiname, Archipiélago de, is., Nic. | F9 | 92 |
| Solenzara, Fr. | m24 | 15a |
| Soligalič, Russia | B25 | 22 |
| Solikamsk, Russia | F9 | 26 |
| Soli, Italy | H8 | 18 |
| Sol'-Ileck, Russia | G8 | 26 |
| Soliman, Tun. | M5 | 18 |
| Solimões see Amazon, stm., S.A. | D7 | 76 |
| Solingen, Ger. | D7 | 10 |
| Solís, Ur. | H11 | 80 |
| Sollefteå, Swe. | J15 | 6 |
| Söller, Spain | F14 | 16 |
| Solnečnogorsk, Russia | E19 | 22 |
| Sologne, reg., Fr. | E9 | 14 |
| Solok, Indon. | O6 | 40 |
| Sololá, Guat. | C3 | 92 |
| Sololá, dept., Guat. | C3 | 92 |
| Solomon, Az., U.S. | L7 | 120 |
| Solomon, Ks., U.S. | M10 | 118 |
| Solomon, stm., Ks., U.S. | L10 | 118 |
| Solomon Islands, ctry., Oc. | I19 | 126 |
| Solomon Sea, Oc. | I19 | 126 |
| Solomon's Pools see Sulaymān, Birak, hist., W.B. | E4 | 50 |
| Solon, China | B11 | 30 |
| Solon, Ia., U.S. | I4 | 110 |
| Solon, Me., U.S. | C17 | 108 |
| Solon Springs, Wi., U.S. | D4 | 110 |
| Solopaca, Italy | H9 | 18 |
| Solotča, Russia | G22 | 22 |
| Solothurn, Switz. | D8 | 13 |
| Solothurn, state, Switz. | D7 | 13 |
| Solotvyn, Ukr. | A8 | 20 |
| Solotvyna, Ukr. | B7 | 20 |
| Soloveckije ostrova, is., Russia | I24 | 6 |
| Solovjevsk, Russia | H15 | 28 |
| Solovjova, Russia | A13 | 22 |
| Solovjova, Russia | H21 | 26 |
| Solovskoje, Russia | G14 | 28 |
| Sol'vyčegodsk, Russia | E7 | 26 |
| Solway Firth, est., U.K. | G10 | 8 |
| Solwezi, Zam. | D5 | 58 |
| Soly, Bela. | G9 | 22 |
| Sŏma, Japan | J15 | 36 |
| Soma, Tur. | J11 | 20 |
| Somalia (Somaliya), ctry., Afr. | G10 | 56 |
| Somali Republic see Somalia, ctry., Afr. | G10 | 56 |
| Sombor, Yugo. | D3 | 20 |
| Sombrerete, Mex. | F8 | 90 |
| Sombrero, i., St. K./N. | E13 | 94 |
| Sombrero Channel, strt., India | K2 | 40 |
| Sombrio, Braz. | E14 | 80 |
| Sombrio, Lagoa do, b., Braz. | E14 | 80 |
| Sŏmerałva, Est. | D9 | 22 |
| Somers, Mt., U.S. | B11 | 122 |
| Somerset, Austl. | M6 | 70 |
| Somerset, Ky., U.S. | B2 | 112 |
| Somerset, Ma., U.S. | F15 | 108 |
| Somerset, Mb., Can. | I16 | 104 |
| Somerset, Oh., U.S. | H4 | 108 |
| Somerset, Pa., U.S. | G7 | 108 |
| Somerset, Tx., U.S. | J8 | 116 |
| Somerset, co., Eng., U.K. | J11 | 8 |
| Somerset East, S. Afr. | H7 | 66 |
| Somerset Island, i., N.T., Can. | B14 | 96 |
| Somerset West, S. Afr. | J4 | 66 |
| Somers Point, N.J., U.S. | H12 | 108 |
| Somersworth, N.H., U.S. | D16 | 108 |
| Somerton, Az., U.S. | L2 | 120 |
| Somerville, N.J., U.S. | G12 | 108 |
| Somerville, Tn., U.S. | G7 | 114 |
| Somerville, Tx., U.S. | I10 | 116 |
| Somerville Lake, res., Tx., U.S. | I10 | 116 |
| Someş (Szamos), stm., Eur. | B7 | 20 |
| Somino, Russia | B17 | 22 |
| Somme, dept., Fr. | C9 | 14 |
| Somme, stm., Fr. | C9 | 14 |
| Sömmerda, Ger. | D11 | 10 |
| Somogy, co., Hung. | I17 | 10 |
| Somotillo, Nic. | D8 | 92 |
| Somoto, Nic. | D8 | 92 |
| Somport, Puerto de, Eur. | C11 | 16 |
| Sompuis, Fr. | D11 | 14 |
| Son, stm., India | H10 | 44 |
| Soná, Pan. | C2 | 84 |
| Sonaguera, Hond. | B8 | 92 |
| Sonapur, India | B7 | 46 |
| Sŏnbong-ni, N. Kor. | C13 | 32 |
| Sŏnch'ŏn, N. Kor. | D12 | 32 |
| Sondags, stm., S. Afr. | H7 | 66 |
| Sønderborg, Den. | N11 | 6 |
| Sondershausen, Ger. | D10 | 10 |
| Sondrio, Italy | C4 | 18 |
| Sonepur, India | B7 | 46 |
| Song Cau, Viet. | H10 | 40 |
| Songea, Tan. | D7 | 58 |
| Songhua, stm., China | B13 | 30 |
| Songhua Hu, res., China | C12 | 30 |
| Songhwa, N. Kor. | E13 | 32 |
| Songjiang, China | D10 | 34 |
| Songjianghen, China | A14 | 30 |
| Songkhla, Thai. | K6 | 40 |
| Sŏngju, S. Kor. | H16 | 32 |
| Songlinba, China | K4 | 34 |
| Songnim, N. Kor. | E13 | 32 |
| Songuj, Russia | G23 | 6 |
| Songxi, China | H7 | 34 |
| Sonid, stm., China | C9 | 30 |
| Sonipat, India | F7 | 44 |
| Sonmiani, Pak. | H2 | 44 |
| Son La, Viet. | D7 | 40 |
| Sonneberg, Ger. | E11 | 10 |
| Sonningdale, Sk., Can. | F7 | 104 |
| Sono, Rio do, stm., Braz. | D6 | 79 |
| Sonoma, Ca., U.S. | F3 | 124 |
| Sonora, Tx., U.S. | I6 | 116 |
| Sonora, stm., Mex. | C4 | 90 |
| Sonora, state, Mex. | B3 | 90 |
| Sonoran Desert, des., N.A. | M4 | 112 |
| Sonoyta, Mex. | B3 | 90 |
| Sonqor, Iran | D9 | 48 |
| Sŏnsan, S. Kor. | G16 | 32 |
| Sonseca, Spain | F8 | 16 |
| Sonskyn, S. Afr. | H8 | 66 |
| Sonson, Col. | E5 | 84 |
| Sonsonate, El Sal. | D5 | 92 |
| Sontag, Ms., U.S. | K6 | 114 |
| Son Tay, Viet. | D8 | 40 |
| Sonthofen, Ger. | H10 | 10 |
| Soo see Sault Sainte Marie, Mex. | | |
| Sochow see Suzhou, China | D9 | 34 |
| Sooke, B.C., Can. | I11 | 102 |
| Sopchoppy, Fl., U.S. | I2 | 112 |
| Soperton, Ga., U.S. | G4 | 112 |
| Sop Hao, Laos | D8 | 40 |
| Sophia, W.V., U.S. | B5 | 112 |
| Sopot, Pol. | A18 | 10 |
| Sopron, Hung. | H16 | 10 |
| Sopur, India | C6 | 44 |
| Sora, Italy | H8 | 18 |
| Soral, Italy | H8 | 18 |
| Sorata, Bol. | F7 | 82 |
| Soraya, Peru | F5 | 82 |
| Sorel, P.Q., Can. | A13 | 108 |
| Sorell, Austl. | N7 | 70 |
| Sorell, Cape, c., Austl. | N6 | 70 |
| Soria, Spain | D9 | 16 |
| Soriano, Ur. | G9 | 80 |
| Sørli, Nor. | I13 | 6 |
| Soroca, Mol. | A12 | 20 |
| Sorocaba, Braz. | G5 | 79 |
| Soročinsk, Russia | G8 | 26 |
| Sorong, Indon. | F9 | 38 |
| Soroti, Ug. | H7 | 56 |
| Sørøya, i., Nor. | F18 | 6 |
| Sorrento, Italy | I9 | 18 |
| Sorrento, La., U.S. | L6 | 114 |
| Sorris Sorris, Nmb. | C2 | 66 |
| Sør Rondane Mountains, mts., Ant. | C3 | 73 |
| Sorsele, Swe. | I15 | 6 |
| Sorsogon, Phil. | o21 | 39b |
| Sortavala, Russia | E4 | 26 |
| Sortland, Nor. | G14 | 6 |
| Sør-Trøndelag, co., Nor. | J12 | 6 |
| Sörve neem, c., Est. | D5 | 22 |
| Sŏsan, S. Kor. | G14 | 32 |
| Sosneado, Cerro, mtn., Arg. | H4 | 80 |
| Sosnogorsk, Russia | E8 | 26 |
| Sosnovec, Russia | I24 | 6 |
| Sosnovka, Russia | H15 | 28 |
| Sosnovo, Russia | A13 | 22 |
| Sosnovo-Oz'orskoje, Russia | G14 | 28 |
| Sosnovskoje, Russia | F26 | 22 |
| Sosnovyj Bor, Russia | B12 | 22 |
| Sosnowiec, Pol. | E19 | 10 |
| Soso, Ms., U.S. | K7 | 114 |
| Sos'va, Russia | F10 | 26 |
| Sotkamo, Fin. | I21 | 6 |
| Soto la Marina, Mex. | F10 | 90 |
| Soto la Marina, Barra, i., Mex. | E11 | 90 |
| Sotomayor, Bol. | H9 | 82 |
| Sotteville, Fr. | C8 | 14 |
| Souderton, Pa., U.S. | G11 | 108 |
| Soufrière, mtn., Guad. | F14 | 94 |
| Soufrière, mtn., St. Vin. | H14 | 94 |
| Souguer, Alg. | C11 | 62 |
| Souhegan, stm., N.H., U.S. | E15 | 108 |
| Souilly, Fr. | C12 | 14 |
| Souk-Ahras, Alg. | B14 | 62 |
| Souk-Khemis-du-Sahel, Mor. | J6 | 16 |
| Souk-el-Arba-des-Beni-Hassan, Mor. | J6 | 16 |
| Sŏul (Seoul), S. Kor. | F14 | 32 |
| Soulougou, Burkina | E10 | 64 |
| Sounding Creek, stm., Ab., Can. | G4 | 104 |
| Sounding Lake, l., Ab., Can. | F4 | 104 |
| Soúnion, Ákra, c., Grc. | L8 | 20 |
| Souris, P.E., Can. | F11 | 106 |
| Souris, stm., N.A. | B17 | 118 |
| Sourou, stm., Afr. | E8 | 64 |
| Sousa, Braz. | E11 | 76 |
| Sousânia, Braz. | D4 | 79 |
| Sousel, Port. | F4 | 16 |
| Sousse, Tun. | N5 | 18 |
| South Africa (Suid-Afrika), ctry., Afr. | F8 | 66 |
| South America | F8 | 74 |
| Southampton, Eng., U.K. | K12 | 8 |
| Southampton, N.S., Can. | G9 | 106 |
| Southampton, N.Y., U.S. | F14 | 108 |
| Southampton, On., Can. | F14 | 110 |
| Southampton, Cape, c., N.T., Can. | D16 | 96 |
| Southampton Island, i., N.T., Can. | D16 | 96 |
| South Andaman, i., India | I2 | 40 |
| South Anna, stm., Va., U.S. | B9 | 112 |
| South Aulatsivik Island, i., Nf., Can. | E20 | 96 |
| South Australia, state, Austl. | F7 | 68 |
| Southaven, Ms., U.S. | H6 | 114 |
| South Bald Mountain, mtn., Co., U.S. | D11 | 120 |
| South Baldy, mtn., N.M., U.S. | K9 | 120 |
| Southbank, B.C., Can. | C9 | 102 |
| South Bay, Fl., U.S. | M6 | 112 |
| South Bay, b., On., Can. | B15 | 104 |
| South Bay, b., N.T., Can. | D16 | 96 |
| South Baymouth, On., Can. | E13 | 110 |
| South Beloit, Il., U.S. | H7 | 110 |
| South Bend, In., U.S. | A10 | 114 |
| South Bend, Wa., U.S. | D2 | 122 |
| South Bentinck Arm, b., B.C., Can. | E8 | 102 |
| South Boston, Va., U.S. | C8 | 112 |
| South Branch, Nf., Can. | E14 | 106 |
| South Brookfield, N.S., Can. | H9 | 106 |
| South Bruny Island, i., Austl. | N7 | 70 |
| South Burlington, Vt., U.S. | C13 | 108 |
| South Carolina, state, U.S. | D5 | 98 |
| South Charleston, W.V., U.S. | I5 | 108 |
| South China Sea, Asia | M7 | 34 |
| South Coffeyville, Ok., U.S. | C11 | 116 |
| South Dakota, state, U.S. | C6 | 98 |
| South East, Bots. | E7 | 66 |
| South East Cape, c., Austl. | N7 | 70 |
| Southend, Sk., Can. | E11 | 104 |
| Southend-on-Sea, Eng., U.K. | J14 | 8 |
| Southern, dept., Bots. | E7 | 66 |
| Southern Alps, mts., N.Z. | E3 | 72 |
| Southern Cross, Austl. | F3 | 68 |
| Southern Ghats, mts., India | H4 | 46 |
| Southern Indian Lake, l., Mb., Can. | E13 | 96 |
| Southern Pines, N.C., U.S. | D7 | 112 |
| South Esk, stm., Austl. | M7 | 70 |
| Southery, Sk., Can. | H10 | 104 |
| South Fabius, stm., Mo., U.S. | C5 | 114 |
| Southfield, Mi., U.S. | H12 | 110 |
| South Foreland, c., Eng., U.K. | J15 | 8 |
| South Fork, Co., U.S. | G10 | 120 |
| South Fort George, B.C., Can. | D12 | 102 |
| South Fulton, Tn., U.S. | F8 | 114 |
| Southgate, Mi., U.S. | H12 | 110 |
| South Georgia, i., S. Geor. | J11 | 74 |
| South Glamorgan, co., Wales, U.K. | J10 | 8 |
| South Hadley, Ma., U.S. | E14 | 108 |
| South Hątia Island, i., Bngl. | I14 | 44 |
| South Haven, Ks., U.S. | N10 | 118 |
| South Haven, Mi., U.S. | H9 | 110 |
| South Heart, stm., Ab., Can. | B18 | 102 |
| South Henderson, N.C., U.S. | C8 | 112 |
| South Henik Lake, l., N.T., Can. | D13 | 96 |
| South Hero, Vt., U.S. | C13 | 108 |
| South Hill, Va., U.S. | C8 | 112 |
| South Holston Lake, res., U.S. | C4 | 112 |
| South Houston, Tx., U.S. | J11 | 116 |
| South Indian Lake, Mb., Can. | B16 | 104 |
| Southington, Ct., U.S. | F14 | 108 |
| South International Falls, Mn., U.S. | B2 | 110 |
| South Island, i., N.Z. | E2 | 72 |
| South Kenosha, Wi., U.S. | H8 | 110 |
| South Lake Tahoe, Ca., U.S. | F6 | 124 |
| Southland, Tx., U.S. | F5 | 116 |
| Southlawn, Il., U.S. | C7 | 114 |
| South Loup, stm., Ne., U.S. | J8 | 118 |
| South Lyon, Mi., U.S. | H12 | 110 |
| South Macmillan, stm., Yk., Can. | E28 | 100 |
| South Magnetic Pole | B7 | 73 |
| South Medford, Or., U.S. | H3 | 122 |
| South Miami, Fl., U.S. | N6 | 112 |
| South Mills, N.C., U.S. | C10 | 112 |
| South Milwaukee, Wi., U.S. | H8 | 110 |
| South Molton, Eng., U.K. | J10 | 8 |
| South Moose Lake, l., Mb., Can. | E14 | 104 |
| South Mountain, mtn., Id., U.S. | H9 | 122 |
| South Nahanni, stm., N.T., Can. | D7 | 96 |
| South Nation, stm., On., Can. | B11 | 108 |
| South Naknek, Ak., U.S. | G16 | 100 |
| South Negril Point, c., Jam. | E5 | 94 |
| South Ogden, Ut., U.S. | C5 | 120 |
| South Orkney Islands, is., Ant. | B1 | 73 |
| South Paris, Me., U.S. | C16 | 108 |
| South Pass, Wy., U.S. | H17 | 122 |
| South Pekin, Il., U.S. | J6 | 110 |
| South Pittsburg, Tn., U.S. | G11 | 114 |
| South Platte, stm., U.S. | C6 | 98 |
| South Pole, Ant. | D4 | 73 |
| South Porcupine, On., Can. | B14 | 110 |
| Southport, Austl. | F10 | 70 |
| Southport, Eng., U.K. | H10 | 8 |
| Southport, Fl., U.S. | L11 | 114 |
| Southport, In., U.S. | C10 | 114 |
| Southport, N.C., U.S. | E8 | 112 |
| Southport, N.Y., U.S. | E10 | 108 |
| South Portland, Me., U.S. | D16 | 108 |
| South Range, Mi., U.S. | C7 | 110 |
| South River, On., Can. | E16 | 110 |
| South Rockwood, Mi., U.S. | H12 | 110 |
| South Sandwich Islands, is., S. Geor. | A2 | 73 |
| South Saskatchewan, stm., Can. | F8 | 104 |
| South Shetland Islands, is., Ant. | B1 | 73 |
| South Sioux City, Ne., U.S. | I11 | 118 |
| South Slocan, B.C., Can. | H17 | 102 |
| South Spicer Island, i., N.T., Can. | C17 | 96 |
| South Superior, Wy., U.S. | C8 | 120 |
| South Taranaki Bight, N.Z. | C5 | 72 |
| South Thompson, stm., B.C., Can. | G14 | 102 |
| South Torrington, Wy., U.S. | I3 | 118 |
| South Tucson, Az., U.S. | L6 | 120 |
| South Twillingate Island, i., Nf., Can. | C19 | 106 |
| South Uist, i., Scot., U.K. | D6 | 8 |
| South Wabasca Lake, l., Ab., Can. | B21 | 102 |
| South West Africa see Namibia, ctry., Afr. | F3 | 58 |
| South West Cape, c., Austl. | N7 | 70 |
| South West City, Mo., U.S. | F2 | 114 |
| Southwest Harbor, Me., U.S. | C18 | 108 |
| Southwest Miramichi, stm., N.B., Can. | F7 | 106 |
| Southwest National Park, Austl. | N7 | 70 |
| Southwest Point, c., Bah. | B6 | 94 |
| South Whitley, In., U.S. | A11 | 114 |
| South Williamson, Ky., U.S. | B4 | 112 |
| South Windham, Me., U.S. | D16 | 108 |
| South Yamhill, stm., Or., U.S. | E2 | 122 |
| Soutpan, S. Afr. | G8 | 66 |
| Souvigny, Fr. | F10 | 14 |
| Sovata, Rom. | H20 | 22 |
| Sovetsk, Russia | F7 | 26 |
| Sovetsk, Russia | F4 | 22 |
| Sovetskaja Gavan', Russia | H20 | 28 |
| Sovetskij, Russia | A11 | 22 |
| Soweto, S. Afr. | F8 | 66 |
| Soyapango, El Sal. | D5 | 92 |
| Soyo, Ang. | C2 | 58 |
| Spa, Bel. | G8 | 12 |
| Spain (España), ctry., Eur. | G7 | 4 |
| Spakenburg, Neth. | D8 | 12 |
| Spalding, Eng., U.K. | I13 | 8 |
| Spalding, Ne., U.S. | J9 | 118 |
| Spalding, Sk., Can. | F10 | 104 |
| Spaniard's Bay, Nf., Can. | E20 | 106 |
| Spanish, stm., On., Can. | D13 | 110 |
| Spanish Fork, Ut., U.S. | D5 | 120 |
| Spanish North Africa, dep., Afr. | J6 | 16 |
| Spanish Peak, mtn., Or., U.S. | F6 | 122 |
| Spanish Sahara see Western Sahara, dep., Afr. | D4 | 54 |
| Spanish Town, Jam. | F6 | 94 |
| Sparkman, Ar., U.S. | I3 | 114 |
| Sparks, Ga., U.S. | H3 | 112 |
| Sparks, Nv., U.S. | E6 | 124 |
| Sparland, Il., U.S. | I6 | 110 |
| Sparlingville, Mi., U.S. | H13 | 110 |

| Name | Map Ref. | Page |
|---|---|---|

Sparrows Point, Md., U.S. — H10 108
Sparta, Ga., U.S. — F4 112
Sparta see Spárti, Grc. — L6 20
Sparta, Il., U.S. — D7 114
Sparta, Ky., U.S. — D12 114
Sparta, Mi., U.S. — G10 110
Sparta, N.C., U.S. — C5 112
Sparta, N.J., U.S. — F12 108
Sparta, Tn., U.S. — G11 114
Sparta, Wi., U.S. — G5 110
Spartanburg, S.C., U.S. — E5 112
Spárti (Sparta), Grc. — L6 20
Spartivento, Capo, c., Italy — K3 18
Spartivento, Capo, c., Italy — L11 18
Spas-Demensk, Russia — G17 22
Spas-Klepiki, Russia — F23 22
Spassk-Dal'nij, Russia — I18 28
Spátha, Ákra, c., Grc. — N7 20
Spear, Cape, c., Nf., Can. — E21 106
Spearfish, S.D., U.S. — G4 118
Spearman, Tx., U.S. — C5 116
Spearville, Ks., U.S. — N8 118
Spectrum Range, mts., B.C., Can. — H29 100
Spednic Lake, l., N.A. — G6 106
Speedway, In., U.S. — C10 114
Speightstown, Barb. — H15 94
Spello, Italy — G7 18
Spenard, Ak., U.S. — F20 100
Spence Bay, N.T., Can. — C14 96
Spencer, Ia., U.S. — H12 118
Spencer, In., U.S. — C10 114
Spencer, Ma., U.S. — E15 108
Spencer, N.C., U.S. — D6 112
Spencer, Ne., U.S. — I9 118
Spencer, S.D., U.S. — H10 118
Spencer, Tn., U.S. — G11 114
Spencer, Wi., U.S. — F5 110
Spencer, W.V., U.S. — I5 108
Spencer, Cape, c., Austl. — J2 70
Spencer, Cape, c., N.B., Can. — G8 106
Spencer Gulf, b., Austl. — J2 70
Spencerville, Oh., U.S. — G2 108
Spences Bridge, B.C., Can. — G13 102
Spenser Mountains, mts., N.Z. — E4 72
Sperryville, Va., U.S. — I8 108
Speyer, Ger. — F8 10
Speyside, Trin. — E4 18
Spezia see La Spezia, Italy — E4 18
Spicer, Mn., U.S. — F13 118
Spickard, Mo., U.S. — B3 114
Spiez, Switz. — E8 13
Spijkenisse, Neth. — F5 12
Spillimacheen, stm., B.C., Can. — F18 102
Spillville, Ia., U.S. — G4 110
Spinazzola, Italy — I11 18
Spincourt, Fr. — C12 14
Spindale, N.C., U.S. — D5 112
Spirit Lake, Ia., U.S. — H12 118
Spirit Lake, Id., U.S. — C9 122
Spirit River, Ab., Can. — B16 102
Spiritwood, Sk., Can. — E7 104
Spiro, Ok., U.S. — G2 114
Spirovo, Russia — D17 22
Spišská Nová Ves, Slvk. — G20 10
Spitsbergen, i., Nor. — B2 24
Spittal an der Drau, Aus. — I13 10
Spitz, Aus. — G15 10
Split, Cro. — F11 18
Split, Cape, c., N.S., Can. — G9 106
Split Lake, l., Mb., Can. — B18 104
Spluga, Passo della (Splügenpass), Eur. — E11 13
Splügen, Switz. — E11 13
Spofford, Tx., U.S. — J6 116
Spogi, Lat. — E9 22
Spokane, Wa., U.S. — C8 122
Spokane, stm., U.S. — C7 122
Spoleto, Italy — G7 18
Spoon, stm., Il., U.S. — B6 114
Spooner, Wi., U.S. — E4 110
Spornoje, Russia — E22 28
Spotsylvania, Va., U.S. — I9 108
Sprague, Mb., Can. — I19 104
Sprague, Wa., U.S. — C8 122
Sprague, stm., Or., U.S. — H4 122
Spratly Islands, is., Asia — D5 38
Spray, Or., U.S. — F6 122
Spray Lakes Reservoir, res., Ab., Can. — G19 102
Spremberg, Ger. — D14 10
Spring, stm., Ar., U.S. — F5 114
Spring, stm., U.S. — E3 114
Springbok, S. Afr. — F3 66
Spring City, Tn., U.S. — D2 112
Spring City, Ut., U.S. — E5 120
Springdale, Ar., U.S. — F2 114
Springdale, Nf., Can. — C17 106
Springdale, S.C., U.S. — F5 112
Springdale, Ut., U.S. — G4 120
Springdale, Wa., U.S. — B8 122
Spring Dale, W.V., U.S. — B6 112
Springe, Ger. — C9 10
Springer, N.M., U.S. — C2 116
Springerville, Az., U.S. — J7 120
Springfield, Co., U.S. — N5 118
Springfield, Fl., U.S. — L11 114
Springfield, Ga., U.S. — G5 112
Springfield, Il., U.S. — C7 114
Springfield, Ky., U.S. — E11 114
Springfield, Ma., U.S. — E14 108
Springfield, Mn., U.S. — G13 118
Springfield, Mo., U.S. — E3 114
Springfield, Oh., U.S. — H3 108
Springfield, Or., U.S. — F2 122
Springfield, S.C., U.S. — F5 112
Springfield, S.D., U.S. — I10 118
Springfield, Tn., U.S. — F10 114
Springfield, Vt., U.S. — D14 108
Springfontein, S. Afr. — H7 66
Spring Garden, Guy. — D13 84
Spring Glen, Ut., U.S. — E6 120
Spring Green, Wi., U.S. — G5 110
Spring Grove, Mn., U.S. — G4 110
Spring Grove, Pa., U.S. — H10 108
Springhill, La., U.S. — I3 114
Springhill, N.S., Can. — G9 106
Spring Hope, N.C., U.S. — D8 112
Springhouse, B.C., Can. — F12 102
Spring Lake, N.C., U.S. — D8 112
Spring Mountains, mts., Nv., U.S. — H10 124
Springs, S. Afr. — F9 66
Springsure, Austl. — E8 70
Springtown, Tx., U.S. — G9 116
Springvale, Austl. — D4 70
Springvale, Me., U.S. — D16 108
Spring Valley, Ca., U.S. — L9 124
Spring Valley, Il., U.S. — I6 110
Spring Valley, Mn., U.S. — G3 110
Spring Valley, N.Y., U.S. — F12 108
Spring Valley, Wi., U.S. — F3 110
Springview, Ne., U.S. — I8 118
Springville, Al., U.S. — I10 114
Springville, Ca., U.S. — H7 124
Springville, N.Y., U.S. — E8 108
Springville, Ut., U.S. — D5 120
Sproat Lake, l., B.C., Can. — H9 102

Spruce, stm., Sk., Can. — E9 104
Spruce Brook, Nf., Can. — D15 106
Spruce Grove, Ab., Can. — D21 102
Spruce Knob, mtn., W.V., U.S. — I7 108
Spruce Lake, Sk., Can. — E5 104
Spruce Mountain, mtn., Az., U.S. — J4 120
Spruce Mountain, mtn., Nv., U.S. — D11 124
Spruce Pine, Al., U.S. — H9 114
Spruce Pine, N.C., U.S. — D4 112
Spruce Woods Provincial Park, Mb., Can. — I15 104
Spur, Tx., U.S. — F6 116
Spurfield, Ab., Can. — B20 102
Spurger, Tx., U.S. — L2 114
Spuzzum, B.C., Can. — H13 102
Spy Hill, Sk., Can. — H13 104
Squally Channel, strt., B.C., Can. — D5 102
Squamish, B.C., Can. — H11 102
Squamish, stm., B.C., Can. — G11 102
Squatec, P.Q., Can. — E5 106
Squaw Cap Mountain, mtn., N.B., Can. — E7 106
Squaw Peak, mtn., Mt., U.S. — C11 122
Squaw Rapids, Sk., Can. — E11 104
Squaw Rapids Dam, Sk., Can. — E11 104
Squilax, B.C., Can. — G15 102
Squinzano, Italy — I13 18
Squire, W.V., U.S. — B5 112
Srbija (Serbia), state, Yugo. — F4 20
Srbobran, Yugo. — D3 20
Sredinnyj chrebet, mts., Russia — F24 28
Sredna Gora, mts., Bul. — G8 20
Srednee Kujto, ozero, l., Russia — I22 6
Srednekolymsk, Russia — D22 28
Srednerusskaja vozvyšennost', plat., Russia — G5 26
Srednesibirskoje ploskogorje, plat., Russia — D13 28
Śrem, Pol. — C17 10
Srê Moăt, Camb. — H9 40
Sremska Mitrovica, Yugo. — E3 20
Sremski Karlovci, Yugo. — D3 20
Sretensk, Russia — G15 28
Sri Jayawardenepura (Kotte), Sri L. — I5 46
Srīkākulam, India — C7 46
Sri Kālahasti, India — F5 46
Sri Lanka, ctry., Asia — H11 42
Srīnagar, India — C6 44
Srīrampur, India — C3 46
Srīrangam, India — G5 46
Srīvilliputtūr, India — H4 46
Środa Wielkopolski, Pol. — C17 10
Staaten, stm., Austl. — C8 68
Staaten River National Park, Austl. — C8 68
Stacyville, Ia., U.S. — G3 110
Stade, Ger. — B9 10
Staden, Bel. — G3 12
Stadl-Paura, Aus. — G13 10
Stadskanaal, Neth. — B10 12
Staffelstein, Ger. — E11 10
Stafford, Eng., U.K. — I11 8
Stafford, Ks., U.S. — N9 118
Stafford, Va., U.S. — I9 108
Staffordshire, co., Eng., U.K. — I11 8
Stafford Springs, Ct., U.S. — F14 108
Staicele, Lat. — D7 22
Staines, Eng., U.K. — J13 8
Stakhanov, Ukr. — H5 26
Stalden, Switz. — F8 13
Stalheim, Nor. — K10 6
Stalingrad see Volgograd, Russia — H6 26
Stalowa Wola, Pol. — E22 10
Stambaugh, Mi., U.S. — D7 110
Stamford, Austl. — C5 70
Stamford, Ct., U.S. — F13 108
Stamford, N.Y., U.S. — E12 108
Stamford, Tx., U.S. — G7 116
Stamford, Lake, res., Tx., U.S. — F7 116
Stamps, Ar., U.S. — I3 114
Stanaford, W.V., U.S. — J5 108
Stanardsville, Va., U.S. — I8 108
Stanberry, Mo., U.S. — B2 114
Standard, Ab., Can. — F22 102
Standard, Ak., U.S. — D20 100
Standerton, S. Afr. — F9 66
Standish, Mi., U.S. — G12 110
Stanfield, Or., U.S. — E6 122
Stanford, Ky., U.S. — B2 112
Stanford, Mt., U.S. — C15 122
Stanhope, Ia., U.S. — H2 110
Stanislaus, stm., Ca., U.S. — G5 124
Stanley, Falk. Is. — G5 78
Stanley, N.B., Can. — F7 106
Stanley, N.C., U.S. — D5 112
Stanley, N.D., U.S. — C5 118
Stanley, Wi., U.S. — F5 110
Stanley Reservoir, res., India — G4 46
Stanleyville see Kisangani, D.R.C. — A5 58
Stanovoj chrebet, mts., Russia — F17 28
Stanovoje nagorje (Stanovoy Mountains), mts., Russia — F14 28
Stans, Switz. — E9 13
Stanthorpe, Austl. — G9 70
Stanton, Ia., U.S. — J12 118
Stanton, Ky., U.S. — B3 112
Stanton, Mi., U.S. — G10 110
Stanton, N.D., U.S. — D6 118
Stanton, Ne., U.S. — J10 118
Stanton, Tn., U.S. — G7 114
Stanton, Tx., U.S. — G5 116
Stantonsburg, N.C., U.S. — D9 112
Stanwood, Wa., U.S. — B3 122
Stapleton, Al., U.S. — L9 114
Stapleton, Ne., U.S. — J7 118
Star, Ms., U.S. — J6 114
Star, N.C., U.S. — D7 112
Stará Boleslav, Czech Rep. — E14 10
Starachowice, Pol. — D21 10
Staraja Russa, Russia — C14 22
Staraja Toropa, Russia — E14 22
Staraja Vičuga, Russia — D24 22
Stara Pazova, Yugo. — E4 20
Stara Planina (Balkan Mountains), mts., Eur. — G8 20
Stara Ushytsya, Ukr. — A11 20
Stara Zagora, Bul. — G9 20
Starbuck, Mb., Can. — I17 104
Starbuck, Mn., U.S. — F12 118
Starbuck, Wa., U.S. — D7 122
Star City, Ar., U.S. — I5 114
Star City, In., U.S. — B10 114
Star City, Sk., Can. — F10 104

Stargard Szczeciński (Stargard in Pommern), Pol. — B15 10
Stargo, Az., U.S. — K7 120
Starica, Russia — E17 22
Stari Popyljuchy, Ukr. — A12 20
Starke, Fl., U.S. — J4 112
Starkville, Ms., U.S. — I8 114
Starnberg, Ger. — G11 10
Starnberger See, l., Ger. — H11 10
Starobin, Bela. — I10 22
Starodub, Russia — I15 22
Starogard Gdański, Pol. — B18 10
Staroje Sjalo, Bela. — F12 22
Staroje Ustje, Russia — H24 22
Starokozache, Ukr. — C13 20
Staroseslavino, Russia — H23 22
Starožilovo, Russia — G22 22
Staryj Oskol, Russia — G5 26
Staryj Sambir, Ukr. — F22 10
Staryy Oskol, Russia — G5 26
Stassfurt, Ger. — D11 10
Staszów, Pol. — E21 10
State Center, Ia., U.S. — H2 110
State College, Pa., U.S. — G9 108
State Line, Ms., U.S. — K8 114
Statenville, Ga., U.S. — I3 112
State Road, N.C., U.S. — C6 112
Statesboro, Ga., U.S. — G5 112
Statesville, N.C., U.S. — D6 112
Staunton, Il., U.S. — C7 114
Staunton, Va., U.S. — I7 108
Stavanger, Nor. — L9 6
Stave Lake, l., B.C., Can. — H12 102
Stavely, Ab., Can. — G21 102
Stavne, Ukr. — G22 10
Stavropol', Russia — H6 26
Stawell, Austl. — K5 70
Stawell, stm., Austl. — C5 70
Stawiszyn, Pol. — D18 10
Stayner, On., Can. — F15 110
Stayton, Or., U.S. — F3 122
Steamboat Mountain, mtn., Wy., U.S. — C8 120
Steamboat Springs, Co., U.S. — D10 120
Stearns, Ky., U.S. — C2 112
Stebbins, Ak., U.S. — E13 100
Steckborn, Switz. — C10 13
Steele, Mo., U.S. — F7 114
Steele, N.D., U.S. — E8 118
Steeleville, Il., U.S. — D7 114
Steelville, Mo., U.S. — E5 114
Steepbank, stm., Ab., Can. — B3 104
Steephill Lake, l., Sk., Can. — C11 104
Steep Rock, Mb., Can. — G16 104
Stefanie, Lake see Chew Bahir, l., Afr. — H8 56
Stefansson Island, i., N.T., Can. — B11 96
Steffisburg, Switz. — E8 13
Steiermark, state, Aus. — H15 10
Stein, Switz. — C8 13
Steinach, Aus. — H11 10
Steinbach, Mb., Can. — I18 104
Steinhausen, Nmb. — C4 66
Steinkjer, Nor. — I12 6
Steksovo, Russia — F26 22
Stella, Ne., U.S. — K12 118
Stellaquo Indian Reserve, B.C., Can. — C10 102
Stellarton, N.S., Can. — G11 106
Stellenbosch, S. Afr. — I4 66
Stenay, Fr. — C12 14
Stendal, Ger. — C11 10
Stende, Lat. — D5 22
Stephen, Mn., U.S. — C11 118
Stephens, Ar., U.S. — I3 114
Stephens, Port, b., Austl. — I10 70
Stephens City, Va., U.S. — H8 108
Stephens Island, i., B.C., Can. — C4 102
Stephens Lake, res., Mb., Can. — B19 104
Stephenson, Mi., U.S. — E8 110
Stephenville, Nf., Can. — D15 106
Stephenville, Tx., U.S. — G8 116
Stephenville Crossing, Nf., Can. — D15 106
Stepn'ak, Kaz. — G12 26
Stereá Ellás, prov., Grc. — K7 20
Sterkstroom, S. Afr. — H8 66
Sterling, Ak., U.S. — F19 100
Sterling, Co., U.S. — K4 118
Sterling, Il., U.S. — I6 110
Sterling, Ks., U.S. — M9 118
Sterling, Mi., U.S. — F11 110
Sterling, Ok., U.S. — K11 118
Sterling City, Tx., U.S. — H6 116
Sterlington, La., U.S. — J4 114
Sterlitamak, Russia — G9 26
Stettin see Szczecin, Pol. — B14 10
Stettler, Ab., Can. — E22 102
Steubenville, Oh., U.S. — G6 108
Stevenson, Al., U.S. — H11 114
Stevenson, Wa., U.S. — E4 122
Stevenson Lake, l., Mb., Can. — E18 104
Stevens Pass, U.S. — C4 122
Stevens Point, Wi., U.S. — F6 110
Stevens Village, Ak., U.S. — C20 100
Stevensville, Mi., U.S. — H9 110
Stevensville, Mt., U.S. — D11 122
Stewardson, Il., U.S. — C8 114
Stewart, B.C., Can. — B5 102
Stewart, Mn., U.S. — F1 110
Stewart, stm., Yk., Can. — E25 100
Stewart Island, i., N.Z. — G1 72
Stewarton, Scot., U.K. — F9 8
Stewartstown, Pa., U.S. — H10 108
Stewartsville, Mo., U.S. — C2 114
Stewart Valley, Sk., Can. — H7 104
Stewartville, Mn., U.S. — G3 110
Stewiacke, N.S., Can. — G10 106
Steynsburg, S. Afr. — H7 66
Steyr, Aus. — G14 10
Steytlerville, S. Afr. — I7 66
Stickney, S.D., U.S. — H9 118
Stif, Alg. — B13 62
Stigler, Ok., U.S. — D11 116
Stikine, stm., N.A. — H29 100
Stikine Ranges, mts., B.C., Can. — G29 100
Stilbaai, S. Afr. — J5 66
Stilfontein, S. Afr. — F8 66
Stilis, Grc. — K6 20
Still, Az., U.S. — C13 62
Stillhouse Hollow Lake, res., Tx., U.S. — H9 116
Stillmore, Ga., U.S. — G4 112
Stillwater, Mn., U.S. — E3 110
Stillwater, Ok., U.S. — C9 116
Stillwater, stm., Mt., U.S. — E16 122
Stillwell, Ok., U.S. — G2 114
Stimson, Mount, mtn., Mt., U.S. — B12 122
Stinking Water Creek, stm., Ne., U.S. — K6 118
Stinnett, Tx., U.S. — D5 116

Štip, Mac. — H6 20
Stirling, Ab., Can. — H22 102
Stirling, On., Can. — F18 110
Stirling, Scot., U.K. — E10 8
Stirling City, Ca., U.S. — E4 124
Stirrat, W.V., U.S. — B4 112
Stittsville, On., Can. — E20 110
Stockach, Ger. — H9 10
Stockbridge, Ga., U.S. — F2 112
Stockbridge, Mi., U.S. — H11 110
Stockdale, Tx., U.S. — J9 116
Stockerau, Aus. — G16 10
Stockett, Mt., U.S. — C14 122
Stockholm, Swe. — L16 6
Stockton, Al., U.S. — L9 114
Stockton, Ca., U.S. — G4 124
Stockton, Il., U.S. — H5 110
Stockton, Ks., U.S. — L8 118
Stockton, Mo., U.S. — E3 114
Stockton, Ut., U.S. — D4 120
Stockton [-on-Tees], Eng., U.K. — G12 8
Stockton Plateau, plat., Tx., U.S. — I4 116
Stockton Reservoir, res., Mo., U.S. — E3 114
Stockton Springs, Me., U.S. — C18 108
Stockville, Ne., U.S. — K7 118
Stodolišče, Russia — G15 22
Stœng Trêng, Camb. — H8 40
Stoke-on-Trent, Eng., U.K. — H11 8
Stokes, Bos. — F12 18
Stolberg, Ger. — E6 10
Stolbovcoj, ostrov, i., Russia — C19 28
Stolp see Słupsk, Pol. — A17 10
Stoneboro, Pa., U.S. — F6 108
Stonefort, Il., U.S. — E8 114
Stone Harbor, N.J., U.S. — H12 108
Stonehenge, Austl. — E5 70
Stone Indian Reserve, B.C., Can. — F11 102
Stone Mountain, Ga., U.S. — F2 112
Stoner, B.C., Can. — D12 102
Stoneville, N.C., U.S. — C7 112
Stonewall, Mb., Can. — H17 104
Stonewall, Ms., U.S. — J8 114
Stonewall, Ok., U.S. — E10 116
Stoney Creek, On., Can. — G16 110
Stonington, Il., U.S. — C7 114
Stonington, Me., U.S. — C18 108
Stony, stm., Mn., U.S. — C4 110
Stony Creek Indian Reserve, B.C., Can. — D10 102
Stony Indian Reserve, Ab., Can. — D20 102
Stony Plain, Ab., Can. — D20 102
Stony Plain Indian Reserve, Ab., Can. — D21 102
Stony Point, Mi., U.S. — I12 110
Stony Point, N.C., U.S. — D5 112
Stony Rapids, Sk., Can. — E11 96
Storby, Fin. — K16 6
Storkerson Bay, b., N.T., Can. — B8 96
Storkerson Peninsula, pen., N.T., Can. — B11 96
Storlien, Swe. — J13 6
Storm Bay, b., Austl. — N7 70
Storm Lake, Ia., U.S. — I12 118
Stormsrivier, S. Afr. — I6 66
Stornoway, Scot., U.K. — C7 8
Storozhynets', Ukr. — A9 20
Storrs, Ct., U.S. — F14 108
Storthoaks, Sk., Can. — I13 104
Story, Wy., U.S. — F19 122
Story City, Ia., U.S. — H2 110
Stoȗbcy, Bela. — H9 22
Stoughton, Ma., U.S. — E15 108
Stoughton, Sk., Can. — I11 104
Stoughton, Wi., U.S. — H6 110
Stout Lake, l., On., Can. — F20 104
Stover, Mo., U.S. — D4 114
Stow, Oh., U.S. — F5 108
Stowe, Vt., U.S. — C14 108
Stowell, Tx., U.S. — M2 114
Stoyoma Mountain, mtn., B.C., Can. — H13 102
Stradella, Italy — D4 18
Stradzečy, Bela. — J6 22
Strahan, Austl. — N6 70
Strakonice, Czech Rep. — F13 10
Stralsund, Ger. — A13 10
Strand, S. Afr. — J4 66
Strangford Lough, l., N. Ire., U.K. — G8 8
Stranraer, Scot., U.K. — G8 8
Strasbourg, Fr. — D14 14
Strasbourg, Sk., Can. — G10 104
Strasburg, Co., U.S. — L3 118
Strasburg, N.D., U.S. — E7 118
Strasburg, Oh., U.S. — G5 108
Strasburg, Pa., U.S. — H10 108
Strasburg, Va., U.S. — I8 108
Stratford, Ct., U.S. — F13 108
Stratford, Ia., U.S. — H2 110
Stratford, N.Z. — C5 72
Stratford, Ok., U.S. — E10 116
Stratford, On., Can. — G15 110
Stratford, Tx., U.S. — C4 116
Stratford, Wi., U.S. — F5 110
Stratford-upon-Avon, Eng., U.K. — I12 8
Strathalbyn, Austl. — J3 70
Strathclair, Mb., Can. — H14 104
Strathclyde, prov., Scot., U.K. — F8 8
Strathcona Provincial Park, B.C., Can. — H9 102
Strathmore, Ab., Can. — F21 102
Strathmore, Ca., U.S. — H6 124
Strathroy, On., Can. — H14 110
Stratton, Co., U.S. — L5 118
Stratton, Me., U.S. — B16 108
Stratton, Ne., U.S. — K6 118
Straubing, Ger. — G12 10
Strausberg, Ger. — C13 10
Strawberry, stm., Ar., U.S. — F5 114
Strawberry, stm., Ut., U.S. — D6 120
Strawberry Point, Ia., U.S. — H4 110
Strawn, Tx., U.S. — G8 116
Streatham, B.C., Can. — D8 102
Streator, Il., U.S. — I7 110
Streeter, N.D., U.S. — E8 118
Streetman, Tx., U.S. — H10 116
Streetsboro, Oh., U.S. — F5 108
Streetsville, On., Can. — G16 110
Strel'na, Russia — B13 22
Strenči, Lat. — D8 22
Stresa, Italy — D3 18
Strešyn, Bela. — I13 22
Streymoy, i., Faer. Is. — D8 6b
Strickland, stm., Pap. N. Gui. — m15 68a
Strimón (Struma), stm., Eur. — I7 20
Strobel, Arg. — G8 80

Süregoncf Point, c., Ak., U.S. — H15 100
Szremboli, Isola, i., Italy — K10 18
Streme, Ab., Can. — E22 102
Stremeferry, Scot., U.K. — D8 8
Stremness, Scot., U.K. — C10 8
Strömsburg, Ne., U.S. — J10 118
Strömsund, Swe. — J14 6
Strong, Ar., U.S. — I4 114
Strong, stm., Ms., U.S. — J7 114
Strong City, Ks., U.S. — M11 118
Stronghurst, Il., U.S. — J5 110
Stroud, Austl. — I9 70
Stroud, Ok., U.S. — D10 116
Stroudsburg, Pa., U.S. — G11 108
Struer, Den. — M11 6
Struga, Mac. — H4 20
Strugi-Krasnyje, Russia — C12 22
Struum, Wi., U.S. — F4 110
Struthers, Oh., U.S. — F6 108
Stryker, Oh., U.S. — F2 108
Stryy, Ukr. — H2 26
Strzegom, Pol. — E16 10
Strzelce Opolskie, Pol. — E18 10
Strzelecki Creek, stm., Austl. — G4 70
Strzelecki Desert, des., Austl. — F4 70
Strzelin, Pol. — E17 10
Stuart, Fl., U.S. — L6 112
Stuart, Ia., U.S. — J13 118
Stuart, Ne., U.S. — I8 118
Stuart, Va., U.S. — C6 112
Stuart, stm., B.C., Can. — C10 102
Stuart Lake, l., B.C., Can. — C10 102
Stuarts Draft, Va., U.S. — A7 112
Studen Kladenec, Jazovir, res., Bul. — H9 20
Stuie, B.C., Can. — E8 102
Stull, On., Can. — D22 104
Stull Lake, l., Mb., Can. — D22 104
Stupart, stm., Mb., Can. — C21 104
Stupino, Russia — G21 22
Sturgeon, Mo., U.S. — C4 114
Sturgeon, stm., Mi., U.S. — E11 110
Sturgeon Bay, Wi., U.S. — F8 110
Sturgeon Bay, b., Mb., Can. — F17 104
Sturgeon Falls, On., Can. — D16 110
Sturgeon Lake, l., Ab., Can. — B17 102
Sturgeon Lake, l., On., Can. — C24 104
Sturgeon Lake Indian Reserve, B.C., Can. — D10 102
Sturgeon Lake Indian Reserve, Ab., Can. — B17 102
Sturgeon Landing, Sk., Can. — D13 104
Sturgis, Ky., U.S. — E9 114
Sturgis, Mi., U.S. — I10 110
Sturgis, Ms., U.S. — I7 114
Sturgis, S.D., U.S. — G4 118
Sturgis, Sk., Can. — G12 104
Sturtevant, Wi., U.S. — H8 110
Sturt National Park, Austl. — G4 70
Sturt Stony Desert, des., Austl. — G4 70
Stutterheim, S. Afr. — I8 66
Stuttgart, Ar., U.S. — H5 114
Stuttgart, Ger. — G9 10
Stykkishólmur, Ice. — B2 6a
Styx, stm., Al., U.S. — L9 114
Su, Kaz. — I12 26
Suaçuí Grande, stm., Braz. — E7 79
Suaita, Col. — D5 84
Su'ao, China — H9 34
Suapure, stm., Ven. — D9 84
Suaqui Grande, Mex. — C5 90
Subačius, Lith. — F7 22
Subansiri, stm., Asia — F14 44
Subate, Lat. — E8 22
Subiaco, Italy — H8 18
Sublette, Ks., U.S. — N7 118
Subotica, Yugo. — C3 20
Suca, Eth. — N10 60
Sucarnoochee, stm., U.S. — J8 114
Suceava, Rom. — B10 20
Suceava, co., Rom. — B9 20
Sucha [Beskidzka], Pol. — F19 10
Süchbaatar, Mong. — A8 30
Suchiapa, stm., Mex. — I13 90
Süchil, Mex. — F8 90
Suchitepéquez, dept., Guat. — D3 92
Suchitoto, El Sal. — D5 92
Suchodol'skij, Russia — H21 22
Suchona, stm., Russia — E6 26
Suchoteka, Russia — I24 22
Suchou see Suzhou, China — E11 30
Suchumi, Geor. — I6 26
Sucio, stm., Col. — D4 84
Sucker Creek Indian Reserve, Ab., Can. — B18 102
Sucre, Bol. — H9 82
Sucre, Col. — C5 84
Sucre, Ec. — H2 84
Sucre, state, Ven. — B11 84
Sucre, dept., Col. — C5 84
Sucúa, Ec. — I3 84
Sucuaro, Col. — E8 84
Sucunduri, stm., Braz. — B12 82
Sucuriú, stm., Braz. — F3 79
Sud, Canal du, strt., Haiti — E8 94
Suda, stm., Russia — B20 22
Sudan, Tx., U.S. — E4 116
Sudan (As-Sūdān), ctry., Afr. — E7 56
Sudan, reg., Afr. — F9 54
Sudañez, Bol. — H9 82
Sudbury, On., Can. — D14 110
Suddie, Guy. — D13 84
Sudeten see Sudety, mts., Eur. — E16 10
Sudety, mts., Eur. — E16 10
Sudislavl', Russia — D24 22
Sudogda, Russia — F23 22
Süd-Orkney-Inseln, is., S. — B1 73
Sud-Ouest, Pointe du, c., — C10 106
Súdpol, Ant. — D4 73
Süd-Shetland-Inseln, is., S. — B1 73
Sudureyri, Faer. Is. — E8 6b
Sudoroy, i., Faer. Is. — E8 6b
Sue, stm., Sudan — N5 60
Sueca, Spain — F11 16
Suez see As-Suways, Egypt — C7 60
Suez, Gulf of see Suways, Khalīj as- b., Egypt — C7 60
Suez Canal see Suways, Qanāt as-, Egypt — C7 60
Sufaynah, Sau. Ar. — C2 47
Suffield, Ab., Can. — H3 104
Suffield, Canadian Forces Base, mil., Ab., Can. — H3 104
Suffolk, Va., U.S. — C10 112
Suffolk, co., Eng., U.K. — I15 8

Sufu see Kashi, China — D2 30
Sugar, stm., N.H., U.S. — D14 108
Sugar, stm., U.S. — H6 110
Sugar City, Id., U.S. — G14 122
Sugarcreek, Pa., U.S. — F7 108
Sugar Grove, Va., U.S. — C5 112
Sugar Hill, Ga., U.S. — E2 112
Sugar Island, i., Mi., U.S. — D11 110
Sugar Land, Tx., U.S. — J11 116
Sugarloaf Mountain, mtn., Me., U.S. — B16 108
Sugarloaf Point, c., Austl. — I10 70
Suggi Lake, l., Sk., Can. — D12 104
Sugoj, stm., Russia — E23 28
Şuhār, Oman — B10 47
Suhl, Ger. — E10 10
Suhr, Switz. — D9 13
Suiá-Miçú, stm., Braz. — A2 79
Suichuan, China — I3 34
Suide, China — D9 30
Suifenhe, China — C13 30
Suihua, China — B12 30
Suining, China — E8 30
Suipacha, Arg. — H9 80
Suiping, China — B3 34
Suippes, Fr. — C11 14
Suixian, China — D2 34
Suiyangdian, China — C1 34
Suizhong, China — C8 32
Suizhou, China — E2 34
Šuja, Russia — K24 6
Šuja, Russia — E24 22
Sujāngarh, India — G6 44
Sujiatun, China — C11 32
Sukabumi, Indon. — j13 39a
Sukagawa, Japan — j15 36
Sukch'ŏn, N. Kor. — D13 32
Sukhothai, Thai. — F5 40
Sukkozero, Russia — E4 26
Sukkur, Pak. — G3 44
Sukumo, Japan — O7 36
Sukunka, stm., B.C., Can. — B13 102
Sul, Baía, b., Braz. — D14 80
Sul, Canal do, strt., Braz. — D9 76
Sula, Kepulauan, is., Indon. — F8 38
Sulaco, stm., Hond. — B7 92
Sulaimān Range, mts., Pak. — F3 44
Sulawesi (Celebes), i., Indon. — F7 38
Sulaymān, Birak (Solomon's Pools), hist., W.B. — E4 50
Sulechów, Pol. — C15 10
Sulejówek, Pol. — C21 10
Sulima, S.L. — H4 64
Sulingen, Ger. — C8 10
Suliteima, mtn., Eur. — H15 6
Sullana, Peru — A1 82
Sulligent, Al., U.S. — I8 114
Sullivan, Il., U.S. — C8 114
Sullivan, In., U.S. — D9 114
Sullivan, Mo., U.S. — D5 114
Sullivan Lake, l., Ab., Can. — E23 102
Sully, Fr. — E9 14
Sulmona, Italy — G8 18
Sulphur, La., U.S. — L3 114
Sulphur, Ok., U.S. — E10 116
Sulphur, Yk., U.S. — E25 100
Sulphur, stm., U.S. — I2 114
Sulphur Springs, Tx., U.S. — F11 116
Sulphur Springs Valley, val., Az., U.S. — M7 120
Sultan, Wa., U.S. — C4 122
Sultānpur, India — G10 44
Sulu Archipelago, is., Phil. — D7 38
Sulu Sea, Asia — D6 38
Suluk, stm., Al., U.S. — L9 114
Sulūq, Libya — B5 56
Sulzbach-Rosenberg, Ger. — F11 10
Sumampa, Arg. — E7 80
Sumas, Wa., U.S. — A3 122
Sumatra see Sumatera, i., Indon. — F3 38
Sumatra, i., Indon. — F3 38
Sumayh, Sudan — K6 60
Sumba, Faer. Is. — E8 6b
Sumba, i., Indon. — G7 38
Sumbawa, i., Indon. — G6 38
Sumbawa Besar, Indon. — G6 38
Sumbawanga, Tan. — C6 58
Sumbay, Peru — F6 82
Sumbe, Ang. — D2 58
Sümber, Mong. — B8 30
Sumbilla, Spain — B10 16
Sumbuya, S.L. — H4 64
Sümeg, Hung. — H17 10
Sumen, Bul. — F10 20
Sumenep, Indon. — j16 39a
Sumerl'a, Russia — F7 26
Sumiha, Bela. — I12 22
Sumisu-jima, i., Japan — E15 30
Sumiswald, Switz. — D8 13
Summerfield, Fl., U.S. — J4 112
Summerfield, N.C., U.S. — C7 112
Summerford, Nf., Can. — C19 106
Summerland, B.C., Can. — H15 102
Summerside, P.E., Can. — F12 106
Summersville, Mo., U.S. — E5 114
Summersville, W.V., U.S. — I6 108
Summerton, S.C., U.S. — F6 112
Summertown, Tn., U.S. — G9 114
Summerville, Ga., U.S. — E1 112
Summerville, S.C., U.S. — F6 112
Summit, Ms., U.S. — K6 114
Summit, S.D., U.S. — F10 118
Summit Lake, B.C., Can. — C12 102
Summit Mountain, mtn., Nv., U.S. — E9 124
Summit Peak, mtn., Co., U.S. — G10 120
Sumner, Ia., U.S. — H3 110
Sumner, Ms., U.S. — I6 114
Sumner, Wa., U.S. — C3 122
Sumoto, Japan — M9 36
Šumperk, Czech Rep. — F16 10
Sumprabum, Myan. — A4 40
Sumqayıt, Azer. — I7 26
Sumrall, Ms., U.S. — K7 114
Šumšu, ostrov, i., Russia — G23 28
Sumter, S.C., U.S. — F6 112
Sumy, Ukr. — F17 22
Sumzom, China — F7 30
Sun, stm., Mt., U.S. — C14 122
Suna, stm., Russia — J23 6
Sunbright, Tn., U.S. — C2 112
Sunburst, Mt., U.S. — B14 122
Sunbury, Austl. — K6 70
Sunbury, Oh., U.S. — G3 108
Sunbury, Pa., U.S. — G10 108
Sunchales, Arg. — F8 80
Sunch'ang, S. Kor. — H15 32
Sunchild Indian Reserve, Ab., Can. — E19 102
Suncho Corral, Arg. — D7 80
Sunch'ŏn, N. Kor. — D13 32
Sunch'ŏn, S. Kor. — I15 32
Sun City, Az., U.S. — K4 120
Suncook, stm., N.H., U.S. — D15 108
Sunda, Selat, strt., Indon. — G4 38
Sundance, Wy., U.S. — G3 118

| Name | Map Ref. | Page |
|---|---|---|
| Sundarbans, reg., Asia | J13 | 44 |
| Sunda Strait see Sunda, Selat, strt., Indon. | G4 | 38 |
| Sundown, Tx., U.S. | F4 | 116 |
| Sundre, Ab., Can. | F20 | 102 |
| Sundridge, On., Can. | E16 | 110 |
| Sundsvall, Swe. | J15 | 6 |
| Sunflower, Ms., U.S. | I6 | 114 |
| Sunflower, Mount, mtn., Ks., U.S. | L5 | 118 |
| Sungaipenuh, Indon. | F3 | 38 |
| Sungai Petani, Malay. | L6 | 40 |
| Sunjiabu, China | E7 | 34 |
| Sunjikäy, Sudan | K5 | 60 |
| Sunland Park, N.M., U.S. | L10 | 120 |
| Sunnybrae, N.S., Can. | G11 | 106 |
| Sunnynook, Ab., Can. | F23 | 102 |
| Sunnyside, Nf., Can. | E20 | 106 |
| Sunnyside, Ut., U.S. | E6 | 120 |
| Sunnyside, Wa., U.S. | D5 | 122 |
| Sunnyslope, Ab., Can. | F21 | 102 |
| Sunnyvale, Ca., U.S. | G3 | 124 |
| Sun Prairie, Wi., U.S. | G6 | 110 |
| Sunray, Tx., U.S. | C5 | 116 |
| Sunrise, Wy., U.S. | B12 | 120 |
| Sunrise Manor, Nv., U.S. | H10 | 124 |
| Sunset, La., U.S. | L4 | 114 |
| Sunset, Tx., U.S. | F9 | 116 |
| Sunset Country, reg., Austl. | J4 | 70 |
| Sunset Heights, Tx., U.S. | H4 | 116 |
| Sunset Prairie, B.C. Can. | B14 | 102 |
| Sunshine, Austl. | K6 | 70 |
| Suntrana, Ak., U.S. | E20 | 100 |
| Suntu, Eth. | M9 | 60 |
| Sun Valley, Id., U.S. | G11 | 122 |
| Sunwapta, stm., Ab., Can. | E17 | 102 |
| Sunyani, Ghana | H8 | 64 |
| Sunzom, China | F6 | 30 |
| Suojarvi, Russia | J23 | 6 |
| Suonenjoki, Fin. | J20 | 6 |
| Supamo, stm., Ven. | D11 | 84 |
| Supaul, India | H9 | 82 |
| Supe, Eth. | M8 | 60 |
| Superior, Az., U.S. | K5 | 120 |
| Superior, Mt., U.S. | C11 | 122 |
| Superior, Ne., U.S. | K9 | 118 |
| Superior, Wi., U.S. | D3 | 110 |
| Superior, Laguna, l., Mex. | I12 | 90 |
| Superior, Lake, l., N.A. | C8 | 110 |
| Suphan Buri, Thai. | G6 | 40 |
| Suponevo, Russia | H17 | 22 |
| Sup'ung-chosuji, res., Asia | C13 | 32 |
| Sūq ash-Shuyūkh, Iraq | E9 | 48 |
| Suq'at al-Jamal, Sudan | K4 | 60 |
| Suqian, China | B7 | 34 |
| Sūq Suwayq, Sau. Ar. | I5 | 48 |
| Suqutrā (Socotra), i., Yemen | G5 | 42 |
| Sūr (Tyre), Leb. | B4 | 50 |
| Sūr, Oman | C11 | 47 |
| Sura, stm., Russia | G7 | 26 |
| Surabaya, Indon. | j16 | 39a |
| Surakarta, Indon. | j15 | 39a |
| Sūrat, India | J5 | 44 |
| Surat Thani (Ban Don), Thai. | J5 | 40 |
| Suraż, Bela. | F13 | 22 |
| Suraž, Russia | H15 | 22 |
| Surdulica, Yugo. | G6 | 20 |
| Süre (Sauer), stm., Eur. | I9 | 12 |
| Surendranagar, India | I4 | 44 |
| Suretka, C.R. | H12 | 92 |
| Surf City, N.J., U.S. | H12 | 108 |
| Surfers Paradise, Austl. | G10 | 70 |
| Surgoinsville, Tn., U.S. | C4 | 112 |
| Surgut, Russia | E6 | 28 |
| Suriāpet, India | D5 | 46 |
| Surigao, Phil. | D8 | 38 |
| Surin, Thai. | G7 | 40 |
| Suriname, ctry., S.A. | C7 | 76 |
| Suring, Wi., U.S. | F7 | 110 |
| Sürmaq, Iran | F12 | 48 |
| Surprise, Az., U.S. | K4 | 120 |
| Surprise Valley, val., U.S. | C5 | 124 |
| Surrency, Ga., U.S. | H4 | 112 |
| Surrey, N.D., U.S. | C6 | 118 |
| Surrey, co., Eng., U.K. | J13 | 8 |
| Surry, Va., U.S. | B10 | 112 |
| Sursee, Switz. | D9 | 13 |
| Surt, Libya | B4 | 56 |
| Surt, Khalīj, b., Libya | B4 | 56 |
| Surtsey, i., Ice. | C3 | 6a |
| Sürüç, Tur. | C5 | 48 |
| Surumu, stm., Braz. | F12 | 84 |
| Susa, Italy | D2 | 18 |
| Susaki, Japan | N8 | 36 |
| Susanino, Russia | C24 | 22 |
| Susanville, Ca., U.S. | D5 | 124 |
| Şuşch, Switz. | E13 | 13 |
| Sušenskoje, Russia | G16 | 26 |
| Sušice, Czech Rep. | F13 | 10 |
| Susitna, Ak., U.S. | F19 | 100 |
| Susitna, stm., Ak., U.S. | E19 | 100 |
| Susoh, Indon. | M4 | 40 |
| Susquehanna, Pa., U.S. | F11 | 108 |
| Susquehanna, stm., U.S. | H10 | 108 |
| Susques, Arg. | B5 | 80 |
| Sussex, N.B., Can. | G8 | 106 |
| Sussex, N.J., U.S. | F12 | 108 |
| Sussex, Va., U.S. | C9 | 112 |
| Susuman, Russia | E21 | 28 |
| Susurluk, Tur. | J12 | 20 |
| Susuzmüsellim, Tur. | H11 | 20 |
| Sutherland, Ia., U.S. | I13 | 118 |
| Sutherland, Ne., U.S. | J6 | 118 |
| Sutherland, S. Afr. | I5 | 66 |
| Sutherland, stm., B.C. Can. | C9 | 102 |
| Sutherlin, Or., U.S. | G2 | 122 |
| Sutlej (Satluj) (Langqên), stm., Asia | F4 | 44 |
| Sutter, Ca., U.S. | E4 | 124 |
| Sutter Creek, Ca., U.S. | F5 | 124 |
| Sutton, Ak., U.S. | F20 | 100 |
| Sutton, Ne., U.S. | K10 | 118 |
| Sutton, W.V., U.S. | I6 | 108 |
| Sutton in Ashfield, Eng., U.K. | H12 | 8 |
| Suttons Bay, Mi., U.S. | F10 | 110 |
| Sutton West, On., Can. | E16 | 110 |
| Suttor, stm., Austl. | C7 | 70 |
| Suurbraak, S. Afr. | J5 | 66 |
| Suure-Jaani, Est. | J21 | 126 |
| Suva, Fiji | J21 | 126 |
| Suvainiškis, Lith. | E8 | 22 |
| Suvorov, Russia | G2 | 42 |
| Suvorove, Ukr. | D12 | 20 |
| Suwa, Erit. | G2 | 47 |
| Suwa, Japan | K13 | 36 |
| Suwałki, Pol. | A22 | 10 |
| Suwannee, stm., U.S. | J3 | 112 |
| Suwannee Lake, l., Mb., Can. | B14 | 104 |
| Suwanose-jima, i., Japan | r4 | 37b |
| Suwayh, Jord. | D5 | 50 |
| Suways, Khalīj as- (Gulf of Suez), b., Egypt | C7 | 60 |
| Suways, Qanāt as- (Suez Canal), Egypt | C7 | 60 |
| Suwŏn, S. Kor. | F15 | 32 |
| Suxi, China | B5 | 34 |
| Suxian, China | B5 | 34 |
| Suyo, Peru | J2 | 84 |
| Suzak, Kaz. | I11 | 26 |
| Suzdal', Russia | E23 | 22 |
| Suzhou (Soochow), China | D9 | 34 |
| Suzigou, China | C11 | 32 |
| Suzuka, Japan | M11 | 36 |
| Svalbard, is., Nor. | B2 | 24 |
| Svalyava, Ukr. | A6 | 20 |
| Svappavaara, Swe. | H17 | 6 |
| Svataj, Russia | D22 | 28 |
| Sv'atoj Nos, mys, c., Russia | G26 | 28 |
| Sv'atoj Nos, mys, c., Russia | C22 | 28 |
| Svay Riĕng, Camb. | I8 | 40 |
| Svėdasai, Lith. | F8 | 22 |
| Svelgen, Nor. | K9 | 6 |
| Svelvik, Nor. | L12 | 6 |
| Sven', Russia | H17 | 22 |
| Svenčionėliai, Lith. | F9 | 22 |
| Svenčionys, Lith. | F9 | 22 |
| Sverdlovsk see Jekaterinburg, Russia | F10 | 26 |
| Sverdlovs'k, Ukr. | H5 | 26 |
| Sverdrup, ostrov, i., Russia | C13 | 26 |
| Svetlahorsk, Bela. | I12 | 22 |
| Svetlograd, Russia | H6 | 26 |
| Svetlogorsk, Russia | G3 | 22 |
| Svetlyj, Russia | G3 | 22 |
| Svetogorsk, Russia | K21 | 6 |
| Svilajnac, Yugo. | E20 | 20 |
| Svilengrad, Bul. | H10 | 20 |
| Svindal, Nor. | L10 | 6 |
| Svir, Bela. | G9 | 22 |
| Svir', stm., Russia | A16 | 22 |
| Svirica, Russia | A15 | 22 |
| Svirsk, Russia | G12 | 28 |
| Svir'stroj, Russia | A16 | 22 |
| Svislač, Bela. | H7 | 22 |
| Svištov, Bul. | F9 | 20 |
| Svobodnyj, Russia | G17 | 28 |
| Svolvær, Nor. | G14 | 6 |
| Swain Reefs, rf., Austl. | C10 | 70 |
| Swainsboro, Ga., U.S. | G4 | 112 |
| Swakop, stm., Nmb. | D2 | 66 |
| Swakopmund, Nmb. | D2 | 66 |
| Swan, stm., Ab., Can. | B19 | 102 |
| Swan, stm., Can. | F14 | 104 |
| Swan, stm., Mn., U.S. | C2 | 110 |
| Swan, stm., Mt., U.S. | C12 | 122 |
| Swanee see Suwannee, stm., U.S. | J3 | 112 |
| Swan Hill, Austl. | J5 | 70 |
| Swan Hills, Ab., Can. | C19 | 102 |
| Swan Hills, hills, Ab., Can. | C19 | 102 |
| Swan Islands see Santanilla, Islas, is., Hond. | F3 | 94 |
| Swan Lake, Mb., Can. | I16 | 104 |
| Swan Lake, Mt., U.S. | C12 | 122 |
| Swan Lake, l., Mb., Can. | F14 | 104 |
| Swan Lake, l., On., Can. | D23 | 104 |
| Swannanoa, N.C., U.S. | D4 | 112 |
| Swanquarter, N.C., U.S. | D10 | 112 |
| Swan Range, mts., Mt., U.S. | C12 | 122 |
| Swan River, Mb., Can. | F13 | 104 |
| Swansboro, N.C., U.S. | E9 | 112 |
| Swansea, Austl. | N8 | 70 |
| Swansea, S.C., U.S. | F5 | 112 |
| Swansea, Wales, U.K. | J10 | 8 |
| Swanton, Oh., U.S. | F3 | 108 |
| Swanton, Vt., U.S. | C13 | 108 |
| Swanville, Mn., U.S. | E1 | 110 |
| Swartz Creek, Mi., U.S. | H12 | 110 |
| Swarzędz, Pol. | C17 | 10 |
| Swasey Peak, mtn., Ut., U.S. | E3 | 120 |
| Swatow see Shantou, China | L5 | 34 |
| Swaziland, ctry., Afr. | G6 | 58 |
| Swea City, Ia., U.S. | H13 | 118 |
| Sweden (Sverige), ctry., Eur. | C11 | 4 |
| Swedish Knoll, mtn., Ut., U.S. | E5 | 120 |
| Swedru, Ghana | I9 | 64 |
| Sweeny, Tx., U.S. | J11 | 116 |
| Sweet Briar, Va., U.S. | B7 | 112 |
| Sweet Grass Indian Reserve, Sk., Can. | F6 | 104 |
| Sweet Home, Or., U.S. | F3 | 122 |
| Sweet Springs, Mo., U.S. | D3 | 114 |
| Sweetwater, Tn., U.S. | D2 | 112 |
| Sweetwater, Tx., U.S. | G6 | 116 |
| Sweetwater, stm., Wy., U.S. | H18 | 122 |
| Swellendam, S. Afr. | J5 | 66 |
| Swepsonville, N.C., U.S. | C7 | 112 |
| Świdnica (Schweidnitz), Pol. | E16 | 10 |
| Świdnik, Pol. | D22 | 10 |
| Świdwin, Pol. | B15 | 10 |
| Świebodzice, Pol. | E16 | 10 |
| Świebodzin, Pol. | C15 | 10 |
| Świecie, Pol. | B18 | 10 |
| Swift Current, Sk., Can. | H7 | 104 |
| Swift Current Creek, stm., Sk., Can. | H7 | 104 |
| Swifton, Ar., U.S. | G5 | 114 |
| Swilly, Lough, b., Ire. | F6 | 8 |
| Swinburne, Cape, c., N.T., Can. | B13 | 96 |
| Swindle Island, i., B.C., Can. | E6 | 102 |
| Swindon, Eng., U.K. | J12 | 8 |
| Świnoujście (Swinemünde), Pol. | B14 | 10 |
| Switzerland, ctry., Eur. | F9 | 4 |
| Swords Range, mts., Austl. | C4 | 70 |
| Sycamore, Il., U.S. | H7 | 110 |
| Sycamore, Oh., U.S. | G3 | 108 |
| Sycan, stm., Or., U.S. | H4 | 122 |
| Syčovka, Russia | F17 | 22 |
| Sydenham, On., Can. | F19 | 110 |
| Sydney, Austl. | I9 | 70 |
| Sydney, N.S., Can. | F13 | 106 |
| Sydney Lake, l., On., Can. | H20 | 104 |
| Sydney Mines, N.S., Can. | F13 | 106 |
| Syke, Ger. | C8 | 10 |
| Sykesville, Md., U.S. | H10 | 108 |
| Sykesville, Pa., U.S. | F8 | 108 |
| Syktyvkar, Russia | E8 | 26 |
| Sylacauga, Al., U.S. | I10 | 114 |
| Sylhet, Bngl. | H14 | 44 |
| Sylt, i., Ger. | A8 | 10 |
| Sylva, N.C., U.S. | D3 | 112 |
| Sylvan Grove, Ks., U.S. | L9 | 118 |
| Sylvania, Ga., U.S. | G5 | 112 |
| Sylvania, Oh., U.S. | F3 | 108 |
| Sylvan Lake, Ab., Can. | E20 | 102 |
| Sylvan Lake, l., Ab., Can. | E20 | 102 |
| Sylvester, Ga., U.S. | H3 | 112 |
| Sylvester, Tx., U.S. | G6 | 116 |
| Sylvester, Mount, hill, Nf., Can. | D18 | 106 |
| Sylvia, Ks., U.S. | N9 | 118 |
| Symsonville, N.C., U.S. | I11 | 26 |
| Synevir, Ukr. | A7 | 20 |
| Syntul, Russia | F24 | 22 |
| Syracuse, In., U.S. | A11 | 114 |
| Syracuse see Siracusa, Italy | N6 | 118 |
| Syracuse, Ks., U.S. | K11 | 118 |
| Syracuse, N.Y., U.S. | D10 | 108 |
| Syrdarja, Uzb. | I11 | 26 |
| Syr Darya (Syrdar'ja), stm., Asia | H10 | 26 |
| Syria (Sūrīyah), ctry., Asia | B2 | 42 |
| Syriam, Myan. | F4 | 40 |
| Syrskij, Russia | I22 | 22 |
| Sysert', Russia | F10 | 26 |
| Syzran', Russia | G7 | 26 |
| Szabolcs-Szatmár-Bereg, co., Hung. | G22 | 10 |
| Szamos (Somes), stm., Eur. | B6 | 20 |
| Szamotuły, Pol. | C16 | 10 |
| Szarvas, Hung. | I20 | 10 |
| Szczeciński, Zalew, b., Eur. | B14 | 10 |
| Szczecin (Stettin), Pol. | B14 | 10 |
| Szczecinek (Neustettin), Pol. | B16 | 10 |
| Szczuczyn, Pol. | B22 | 10 |
| Szczytno, Pol. | B21 | 10 |
| Szechwan see Sichuan, prov., China | E7 | 30 |
| Szécsény, Hung. | G19 | 10 |
| Szeged, Hung. | I20 | 10 |
| Szeghalom, Hung. | H21 | 10 |
| Székesfehérvár, Hung. | H18 | 10 |
| Szekszárd, Hung. | I18 | 10 |
| Szentendre, Hung. | H19 | 10 |
| Szentes, Hung. | I20 | 10 |
| Szentgotthárd, Hung. | I16 | 10 |
| Szerencs, Hung. | G21 | 10 |
| Szob, Hung. | H18 | 10 |
| Szolnok, Hung. | H20 | 10 |
| Szombathely, Hung. | H16 | 10 |
| Szprotawa, Pol. | D15 | 10 |
| Szubin, Pol. | B17 | 10 |

**T**

| Tabacal, Arg. | B6 | 80 |
| Tabaco, Phil. | o20 | 39b |
| Tabacundo, Ec. | G3 | 84 |
| Tabalosos, Peru | B3 | 82 |
| Tabarka, Tun. | M3 | 18 |
| Tabas, Iran | E14 | 48 |
| Tabasará, stm., Pan. | I13 | 92 |
| Tabas Masīnā, Iran | E16 | 48 |
| Tabatinga, stm., Braz. | D7 | 79 |
| Tabelbala, Alg. | C6 | 54 |
| Tabla, Niger | E11 | 64 |
| Table Bay, b., S. Afr. | I4 | 66 |
| Table Mountain, mtn., Nf., Can. | E14 | 106 |
| Table Rock, Ne., U.S. | K11 | 118 |
| Table Rock Lake, res., U.S. | F3 | 114 |
| Tablogo, Togo | H10 | 64 |
| Taboco, stm., Braz. | I14 | 82 |
| Taboga, Pan. | I15 | 92 |
| Tábor, Czech Rep. | F14 | 10 |
| Tabor, Ia., U.S. | K12 | 118 |
| Tabor, S.D., U.S. | I10 | 118 |
| Tabora, Tan. | C6 | 58 |
| Tabor City, N.C., U.S. | E8 | 112 |
| Tabou, C. Iv. | I6 | 64 |
| Tabrīz, Iran | B9 | 48 |
| Tabūk, Sau. Ar. | G4 | 48 |
| Tacámbaro de Codallos, Mex. | H9 | 90 |
| Tacaná, Guat. | B2 | 92 |
| Tacaná, Volcán, vol., N.A. | B2 | 92 |
| Tacañitas, Arg. | E7 | 80 |
| Tache, Lac, l., N.T., Can. | D8 | 96 |
| Tacheng, China | B3 | 30 |
| Tachiataš, Uzb. | I9 | 26 |
| Tachie, stm., B.C. Can. | C10 | 102 |
| Tachikawa, Japan | L14 | 36 |
| Táchira, state, Ven. | D6 | 84 |
| Tachov, Czech Rep. | F12 | 10 |
| Tachtamygda, Russia | G16 | 28 |
| Taciuá, Lago, stm., Braz. | J12 | 84 |
| Tacna, Az., U.S. | L3 | 120 |
| Tacna, Peru | H6 | 82 |
| Tacna, dept., Peru | G6 | 82 |
| Tacoma, Wa., U.S. | C3 | 122 |
| Taco Pozo, Arg. | C7 | 80 |
| Tacotalpa, stm., Mex. | I13 | 90 |
| Tacuarembó, Ur. | F11 | 80 |
| Tacuarembó, stm., Ur. | F11 | 80 |
| Tacuarí, stm., Ur. | G11 | 80 |
| Tacuatí, Para. | B10 | 80 |
| Tacuaré, Cachoeira, wtfl, Braz. | A14 | 82 |
| Tacutu (Takutu), stm., S.A. | F12 | 84 |
| Tademaït, Plateau du, plat., Alg. | F12 | 62 |
| Tādepallegūdem, India | D6 | 46 |
| Tadia, Ciénaga de, l., Col. | D4 | 84 |
| Tadjemout, Alg. | H12 | 62 |
| Tadjoura, Dji. | F9 | 56 |
| Tadoule Lake, l., Mb., Can. | E13 | 96 |
| Tadoussac, P.Q., Can. | D4 | 106 |
| Tādpatri, India | D3 | 46 |
| Tadzhikistan see Tajikistan, ctry., Asia | J12 | 26 |
| T'aebaek-sanmaek, mts., Asia | F16 | 32 |
| Taech'ŏn, S. Kor. | G14 | 32 |
| Taedong, N. Kor. | D13 | 32 |
| Taegu, S. Kor. | H16 | 32 |
| Taegwan, N. Kor. | C13 | 32 |
| T'aein, N. Kor. | H14 | 32 |
| Taejŏn, S. Kor. | G15 | 32 |
| Ta'erwan, China | D2 | 34 |
| Tafalla, Spain | C10 | 16 |
| Tafas, Syria | C6 | 50 |
| Tafassâsset, Oued, val., Afr. | D8 | 54 |
| Tafiré, C. Iv. | G7 | 64 |
| Tafí Viejo, Arg. | D6 | 80 |
| Tafraoute, Mor. | F6 | 62 |
| Taft, Ca., U.S. | I6 | 124 |
| Taft, Ok., U.S. | D11 | 116 |
| Taft, Tx., U.S. | L9 | 116 |
| Taganrog, Russia | H5 | 26 |
| Tagawa, Japan | N5 | 36 |
| Tagaytay, Phil. | n19 | 39b |
| Taghit, Alg. | E9 | 62 |
| Tagish, Lake, l., Can. | G27 | 100 |
| Taguatinga, Braz. | B5 | 79 |
| Taguke, China | D13 | 44 |
| Tagula Island, i., Pap. N. Gui. | B10 | 68 |
| Tagus (Tejo) (Tajo), stm., Eur. | G4 | 4 |
| Tah, Sebkha, l., Afr. | G4 | 62 |
| Tahakopa, N.Z. | G2 | 72 |
| Tahala, Mor. | C8 | 62 |
| Tahanaoute, Mor. | E2 | 62 |
| Tahart, Alg. | I13 | 62 |
| Tahat, mtn., Alg. | I13 | 62 |
| Tāhlāb, stm., Asia | G17 | 48 |
| Tahlab, i., Ms., U.S. | I5 | 114 |
| Tahchitle, Isla, i., Mex. | E5 | 90 |
| Talchuano, Chile | H3 | 80 |
| Talco, Tx., U.S. | F11 | 116 |
| Taldom, Russia | E20 | 22 |
| Taldykorgan, Kaz. | H13 | 26 |
| Talent, Or., U.S. | H3 | 122 |
| Tāleshi, Iran | C10 | 48 |
| Talgar, Kaz. | I13 | 26 |
| Taliabu, Pulau, i., Indon. | F7 | 38 |
| Talica, Russia | F10 | 26 |
| Talickij Čamlyk, Russia | I23 | 22 |
| Talihina, Ok., U.S. | E11 | 116 |
| Talisay, Phil. | o20 | 39b |
| Tall 'Afar, Iraq | C7 | 48 |
| Tallahassee, Fl., U.S. | I3 | 112 |
| Tallahatchie, stm., Ms., U.S. | I6 | 114 |
| Tallangatta, Austl. | K7 | 70 |
| Tallapoosa, Ga., U.S. | F1 | 112 |
| Tallapoosa, stm., U.S. | J10 | 114 |
| Tallassee, Al., U.S. | J11 | 114 |
| Tallinn, Est. | B7 | 22 |
| Tall Kalakh, Syria | D4 | 48 |
| Tallmadge, Oh., U.S. | F5 | 108 |
| Tallulah, La., U.S. | J5 | 114 |
| Talman, stm., I., N.T., Can. | B10 | 96 |
| Talmage, Ne., U.S. | K11 | 118 |
| Tal'menka, Russia | G14 | 26 |
| Talo, mtn., Eth. | L9 | 60 |
| Taloga, Ok., U.S. | C8 | 116 |
| Talpa, Tx., U.S. | H7 | 116 |
| Talsi, Lat. | D5 | 22 |
| Taltal, Chile | C3 | 80 |

| Tahoka, Tx., U.S. | F5 | 116 |
| Tahoua, Niger | D12 | 64 |
| Tahquamenon, stm., Mi., U.S. | D10 | 110 |
| Tahsis, B.C., Can. | H8 | 102 |
| Tahtā, Egypt | D6 | 60 |
| Tahtsa Lake, l., B.C., Can. | D7 | 102 |
| Tahtsa Peak, mtn., B.C., Can. | D7 | 102 |
| Tahuamanu, stm., S.A. | D7 | 82 |
| Tahuna, Indon. | E8 | 38 |
| Tai'an, China | G5 | 32 |
| Taibai Shan, mtn., China | D2 | 32 |
| T'aichung, Tai. | K9 | 34 |
| Taif see Aṭ-Ṭā'if, Sau. Ar. | D2 | 47 |
| Taihang Shan, mts., China | D9 | 30 |
| Taihape, N.Z. | C5 | 72 |
| Taihe, China | B4 | 34 |
| Tai Hu, l., China | D9 | 34 |
| Taijiang, China | A10 | 40 |
| Taikkyi, Myan. | F3 | 40 |
| Tailai, China | B11 | 30 |
| Tailem Bend, Austl. | J3 | 70 |
| T'ainan, Tai. | L9 | 34 |
| Taínaron, Ákra, c., Grc. | M6 | 20 |
| Taining, China | I5 | 34 |
| Tiodoeiras, Braz. | C7 | 79 |
| T'aipei, Tai. | J10 | 34 |
| Taipeihsien, Tai. | J10 | 34 |
| Taiping, China | M2 | 34 |
| Taiping, Malay. | L6 | 40 |
| Taishun, China | H8 | 34 |
| Taitao, Península de, pen., Chile | F1 | 78 |
| Taitouying, China | C7 | 32 |
| T'aitung, Tai. | M9 | 34 |
| Taiwan (T'aiwan), ctry., Asia | G11 | 30 |
| Taiwan Strait, strt., Asia | K8 | 34 |
| Taixian, China | C9 | 34 |
| Taixing, China | C9 | 34 |
| Taiyiba, Isr. | D4 | 50 |
| Taiyuan, China | D9 | 30 |
| Taizhou, China | C8 | 34 |
| Ta'izz, Yemen | H4 | 47 |
| Tajerouine, Tun. | N3 | 18 |
| Tajga, Russia | F9 | 28 |
| Tajgonos, mys, c., Russia | E24 | 28 |
| Tajikistan, ctry., Asia | J12 | 26 |
| Tajimi, Japan | L12 | 36 |
| Tajique, N.M., U.S. | J10 | 120 |
| Tajitos, Mex. | B3 | 90 |
| Tajmura, stm., Russia | E17 | 26 |
| Tajmyr, ozero, l., Russia | C18 | 26 |
| Tajmyr, poluostrov, pen., Russia | B18 | 26 |
| Tajšet, Russia | F11 | 28 |
| Tajumulco, Volcán, vol., Guat. | B3 | 92 |
| Tak, Thai. | F5 | 40 |
| Takāb, Iran | C9 | 48 |
| Takachu, Bots. | D5 | 66 |
| Takahashi, Japan | M8 | 36 |
| Takahe, Mount, mtn., Ant. | C11 | 73 |
| Takaka, N.Z. | D4 | 72 |
| Takakkaw Falls, wtfl, B.C., Can. | F18 | 102 |
| Takamatsu, Japan | M9 | 36 |
| Takaoka, Japan | K12 | 36 |
| Takapuna, N.Z. | B5 | 72 |
| Takasaki, Japan | K14 | 36 |
| Takatsuki, Japan | M10 | 36 |
| Takayama, Japan | K12 | 36 |
| Takefu, Japan | L11 | 36 |
| Takenake, China | C9 | 44 |
| Takengon, Indon. | L4 | 40 |
| Take-shima, i., Japan | q5 | 37b |
| Take-shima (Tok-to), is., Asia | J6 | 36 |
| Takêv, Camb. | I8 | 40 |
| Takhli, Thai. | G6 | 40 |
| Takijuki Lake, l., N.T., Can. | C10 | 96 |
| Takikawa, Japan | d16 | 36a |
| Takla Lake, l., B.C., Can. | B9 | 102 |
| Takla Landing, B.C., Can. | B9 | 102 |
| Taklimakan Shamo, des., China | D3 | 30 |
| Takrouna, Tun. | M5 | 18 |
| Taku, stm., N.A. | G28 | 100 |
| Takua Pa, Thai. | J5 | 40 |
| Taku Glacier, Ak., U.S. | G27 | 100 |
| Takum, Nig. | H14 | 64 |
| Takuti (Tacutu), stm., S.A. | F13 | 84 |
| Takysie Lake, B.C., Can. | D9 | 102 |
| Tala, Ur. | G8 | 80 |
| Tala, Ur. | H11 | 80 |
| Talačyn, Bela. | G12 | 22 |
| Talagang, Pak. | D5 | 44 |
| Talagante, Chile | G3 | 80 |
| Talamanca, Cordillera de, mts., C.R. | H11 | 92 |
| Talara, Peru | J2 | 84 |
| Talas, Kyrg. | I12 | 26 |
| Talasea, Pap. N. Gui. | m17 | 68a |
| Talata Mafara, Nig. | E13 | 64 |
| Talaud, Kepulauan, is., Indon. | E8 | 38 |
| Talavera de la Reina, Spain | F7 | 16 |
| Talawdī, Sudan | L6 | 60 |
| Talbot Lake, l., Mb., Can. | D15 | 104 |
| Talbotton, Ga., U.S. | G2 | 112 |
| Talbragar, stm., Austl. | I8 | 70 |

| Taltapin Lake, l., B.C., Can. | C9 | 102 |
| Taltson, stm., N.T., Can. | D10 | 96 |
| Talwood, Austl. | G8 | 70 |
| Tama, Arg. | F5 | 80 |
| Tama, Ia., U.S. | I2 | 110 |
| Tamacuarí, Pico, mtn., S.A. | G10 | 84 |
| Tamadjert, Alg. | H14 | 62 |
| Tamale, Ghana | G9 | 64 |
| Tamana, Japan | O5 | 36 |
| Tamaná, Cerro, mtn., Col. | E4 | 84 |
| Tamanaco, stm., Ven. | C10 | 84 |
| Tamaniquá, Braz. | I10 | 84 |
| Tamano, Japan | M8 | 36 |
| Tamanrasset, Alg. | I13 | 62 |
| Tamapatz, Mex. | G10 | 90 |
| Tamaqua, Pa., U.S. | G11 | 108 |
| Tamar, stm., Austl. | M7 | 70 |
| Támara, Col. | E6 | 84 |
| Tamarac, stm., Mn., U.S. | C10 | 118 |
| Tamaroa, Il., U.S. | D7 | 114 |
| Tamarugal, Pampa del, pl., Chile | I7 | 82 |
| Tamási, Hung. | I18 | 10 |
| Tamaské, Niger | D12 | 64 |
| Tamaulipas, state, Mex. | F10 | 90 |
| Tamaya, stm., Peru | C4 | 82 |
| Tamazula, Mex. | E6 | 90 |
| Tamazula de Gordiano, Mex. | H8 | 90 |
| Tamazulapan del Progreso, Mex. | I11 | 90 |
| Tamazunchale, Mex. | G10 | 90 |
| Tambacounda, Sen. | E3 | 64 |
| Tamba Dabatou, Gui. | F4 | 64 |
| Tämbaram, India | F6 | 46 |
| Tambelan, Kepulauan, is., Indon. | N9 | 40 |
| Tamberías, Arg. | F4 | 80 |
| Tambo, Austl. | E7 | 70 |
| Tambo, Peru | E4 | 82 |
| Tambo, stm., Austl. | K7 | 70 |
| Tambo, stm., Peru | G6 | 82 |
| Tamboara, Braz. | G2 | 79 |
| Tambo Grande, Peru | A1 | 82 |
| Tambohorano, Madag. | p20 | 67b |
| Tambopata, stm., S.A. | E7 | 82 |
| Tambor, C.R. | H9 | 92 |
| Tamboritha, Mount, mtn., Austl. | K7 | 70 |
| Tamboryacu, stm., Peru | H5 | 84 |
| Tambov, Russia | I24 | 22 |
| Tambura, Sudan | N4 | 60 |
| Tamchaket, Maur. | C4 | 64 |
| Tame, Col. | D7 | 84 |
| Tamega, stm., Eur. | E6 | 90 |
| Tameghza, Tun. | C14 | 62 |
| Tamel Aike, Arg. | F2 | 78 |
| Tamelelt, Mor. | E7 | 62 |
| Tamenghest, Alg. | I13 | 62 |
| Tamenghest, Oued, val., Alg. | I11 | 62 |
| Tamiahua, Mex. | G11 | 90 |
| Tamiahua, Laguna de, b., Mex. | G11 | 90 |
| Tamiami Canal, Fl., U.S. | N5 | 112 |
| Tamil Nādu, state, India | G5 | 46 |
| Tamiš (Timiş), stm., Eur. | D4 | 20 |
| Tamitatoala, stm., Braz. | B2 | 79 |
| Tam Ky, Viet. | G10 | 40 |
| Tamms, Il., U.S. | E7 | 114 |
| Tampa, Fl., U.S. | L4 | 112 |
| Tampa Bay, b., Fl., U.S. | L4 | 112 |
| Tampaón, stm., Mex. | G10 | 90 |
| Tampere, Fin. | K18 | 6 |
| Tampico, Il., U.S. | I6 | 110 |
| Tampico, Mex. | F11 | 90 |
| Tampin, Malay. | M7 | 40 |
| Tam Quan, Viet. | G10 | 40 |
| Tamri, Mor. | E6 | 62 |
| Tamsagbulag, Mong. | B10 | 30 |
| Tamsalu, Est. | B9 | 22 |
| Tamshiyacu, Peru | J6 | 84 |
| Tamsweg, Aus. | H13 | 10 |
| Tamworth, Austl. | H9 | 70 |
| Tamyang, S. Kor. | H14 | 32 |
| Tana, Chile | H7 | 82 |
| Tana (Teno), stm., Eur. | F20 | 6 |
| Tana, Lake, l., Eth. | K9 | 60 |
| Tanabe, Japan | N10 | 36 |
| Tanabi, Braz. | F4 | 79 |
| Tanacross, Ak., U.S. | E23 | 100 |
| Tanafjorden, b., Nor. | G8 | 90 |
| Tanahbala, Pulau, i., Indon. | O5 | 40 |
| Tanahmasa, Pulau, i., Indon. | O5 | 40 |
| Tanami Desert, des., Austl. | C5 | 68 |
| Tan An, Viet. | I9 | 40 |
| Tanana, Ak., U.S. | D18 | 100 |
| Tanana, stm., Ak., U.S. | D19 | 100 |
| Tananarive see Antananarivo, Madag. | q22 | 67b |
| Tancheng, China | I6 | 32 |
| Tanch'ŏn, N. Kor. | C16 | 32 |
| Tancítaro, Pico de, mtn., Mex. | H8 | 90 |
| Tānda, India | G10 | 44 |
| Tandil, Arg. | I9 | 80 |
| Tandou Lake, l., Austl. | I5 | 70 |
| Tane, Chile | G15 | 62 |
| Taneatua, N.Z. | C6 | 72 |
| Tanega-shima, i., Japan | q6 | 37b |
| Tanen Taunggyi, mts., Asia | E4 | 40 |
| Tanetown, Md., U.S. | H9 | 108 |
| Tanezrouft, des., Afr. | D6 | 54 |
| Tanga, Tan. | C7 | 58 |
| Tangail, Bngl. | H13 | 44 |
| Tanganyika, Lake, l., Afr. | C5 | 58 |
| Tangarana, stm., Peru | I5 | 84 |
| Tangcun, China | J2 | 34 |
| Tanger (Tangier), Mor. | C8 | 62 |
| Tanggula Shan, mts., China | D13 | 44 |
| Tangier see Tanger, Mor. | C8 | 62 |
| Tangier, N.S., Can. | H11 | 106 |
| Tangipahoa, stm., La., U.S. | K6 | 114 |
| Tangjiaguo, China | J2 | 34 |
| Tangjin, S. Kor. | G14 | 32 |
| Tangra Yumco, l., China | B5 | 32 |
| Tangshan, China | D10 | 30 |
| Tanguiéta, Benin | F10 | 64 |
| Tangxian, China | F9 | 32 |
| Tanimbar, Kepulauan, is., Indon. | G9 | 38 |
| Taninges, Fr. | F13 | 14 |
| Tanjiajing, China | H7 | 32 |
| Tanjungbalai, Indon. | M5 | 40 |
| Tanjungpandan, Indon. | N8 | 40 |
| Tanjungselor, Indon. | N5 | 40 |

| Tannu-Ola, chrebet, mts., Asia | G10 | 28 |
| Tannūrah, Ra's, c., Sau. Ar. | H11 | 48 |
| Tano, stm., Afr. | I8 | 64 |
| Tânout, Niger | D14 | 64 |
| Tanquinho, Braz. | A9 | 79 |
| Tanshui, Tai. | J10 | 34 |
| Tánsin, Isla de, i., Hond. | B11 | 92 |
| Tánsin, Laguna de b., Hond. | B11 | 92 |
| Tantā, Egypt | B6 | 60 |
| Tan-Tan, Mor. | F5 | 62 |
| Tantoyuca, Mex. | G10 | 90 |
| Tanuku, India | D6 | 46 |
| Tanyang, S. Kor. | G16 | 32 |
| Tanzania, ctry., Afr. | C6 | 58 |
| Tao, China | E7 | 30 |
| Taochong, China | D7 | 34 |
| Tao'er, stm., China | B11 | 30 |
| Taolekapa, China | D11 | 44 |
| Taoling, China | J8 | 34 |
| Taormina, Italy | L10 | 18 |
| Taos, Mo., U.S. | D4 | 114 |
| Taos, N.M., U.S. | H11 | 120 |
| Taos Pueblo, N.M., U.S. | H11 | 120 |
| Taoudenni, Mali | I8 | 62 |
| Taounate, Mor. | C8 | 62 |
| Taoura, Alg. | M3 | 18 |
| Taourirt, Mor. | C9 | 62 |
| Taoussa, Mali | C9 | 64 |
| Taoyuan, China | J6 | 34 |
| Tapa, Est. | B8 | 22 |
| Tapachula, Mex. | J13 | 90 |
| Tapah, Malay. | L6 | 40 |
| Tapaje, stm., Col. | F3 | 84 |
| Tapajós, stm., Braz. | D7 | 76 |
| Tapalqué, Arg. | I8 | 80 |
| Tapanahony, stm., Sur. | C7 | 76 |
| Tapauá, Braz. | A10 | 82 |
| Tapauá, stm., Braz. | A9 | 82 |
| Tapejara, Braz. | E12 | 80 |
| Tapera, Braz. | E12 | 80 |
| Taperas, Bol. | G11 | 82 |
| Taperoá, Braz. | B9 | 79 |
| Tapes, Braz. | F13 | 80 |
| Taphan Hin, Thai. | F6 | 40 |
| Tāpi, stm., India | B2 | 46 |
| Tapiche, stm., Peru | A5 | 82 |
| Taping (Daying), stm., Asia | B4 | 40 |
| Tapirai, Braz. | G3 | 79 |
| Tāplejung, Nepal | G12 | 44 |
| Tapoa, stm., Afr. | E11 | 64 |
| Tapolca, Hung. | I17 | 10 |
| Tappahannock, Va., U.S. | B10 | 112 |
| Tappen, N.D., U.S. | E8 | 118 |
| Tappi-zaki, c., Japan | F15 | 36 |
| Tappo, Ghana | F8 | 64 |
| Tapurucuara, Braz. | H10 | 84 |
| Taqtâu' Ḥayyā, Sudan | H9 | 60 |
| Taquara, Braz. | E13 | 80 |
| Taquaras, Ponta das, c., Braz. | D2 | 79 |
| Taquari, Braz. | E13 | 80 |
| Taquari, Braz. | E13 | 80 |
| Taquari, stm., Braz. | H13 | 82 |
| Taquari, Pantanal do, sw., Braz. | H13 | 82 |
| Taquaritinga, Braz. | F4 | 79 |
| Taquarivaí, Braz. | G3 | 79 |
| Taquarucu, stm., Braz. | D9 | 112 |
| Tara, stm., Russia | F6 | 28 |
| Tara, Russia | F6 | 28 |
| Taraba, stm., Afr. | G9 | 54 |
| Tarabine, Oued ti-n-, val., Afr. | J14 | 62 |
| Tarabuco, Bol. | C1 | 82 |
| Tarābulus (Tripoli), Leb. | D3 | 48 |
| Tarābulus (Tripoli), Libya | B3 | 56 |
| Tarābulus (Tripolitania), hist. reg., Libya | B3 | 56 |
| Taraclia, Mol. | D12 | 20 |
| Tarago, Austl. | J8 | 70 |
| Taragua, Indon. | H8 | 84 |
| Tarakan, Indon. | E6 | 38 |
| Taranaki, Mount see Egmont, Mount, vol., N.Z. | C4 | 72 |
| Tarancón, Spain | E8 | 16 |
| Taranto, Italy | I12 | 18 |
| Taranto, Golfo di, b., Italy | I12 | 18 |
| Tarapacá, Braz. | I8 | 84 |
| Tarapoto, Peru | B3 | 82 |
| Taraquá, Braz. | G8 | 84 |
| Tarare, Fr. | G11 | 14 |
| Tarariras, Ur. | H10 | 80 |
| Tarāsa Dwip, i., India | J2 | 40 |
| Tarascon, Fr. | J8 | 14 |
| Tarascon, Fr. | I11 | 14 |
| Tarat, Alg. | G15 | 62 |
| Tarata, Bol. | G8 | 82 |
| Tarata, Peru | G6 | 82 |
| Tarauacá, Braz. | C4 | 82 |
| Tarauacá, stm., Braz. | B6 | 82 |
| Tarawa, atoll, Kir. | H21 | 126 |
| Tarawera, N.Z. | C6 | 72 |
| Tarazona, Spain | C9 | 16 |
| Tarazona de la Mancha, Spain | F10 | 16 |
| Tarbagataj, chrebet, mts., Asia | H8 | 28 |
| Tarbes, Fr. | I7 | 14 |
| Tarboro, N.C., U.S. | D9 | 112 |
| Tarbū, Libya | C4 | 56 |
| Tarcento, Italy | C8 | 18 |
| Tarcoola, Austl. | F6 | 68 |
| Tardajos, Spain | C8 | 16 |
| Tardoki-Jani, gora, mtn., Russia | H19 | 28 |
| Täreendö, Swe. | H18 | 6 |
| Tarentum, Pa., U.S. | G7 | 108 |
| Tarfâ, Ra's at-, c., Sau. Ar. | F3 | 47 |
| Tarfâ, Wādī at-, val., Egypt | G4 | 62 |
| Tarfaya, Mor. | G4 | 62 |
| Targhee Pass, U.S. | F14 | 122 |
| Târgovişte, Bul. | F10 | 20 |
| Târgovişte, Rom. | D9 | 20 |
| Târgu Cărbuneşti, Rom. | E7 | 20 |
| Tarquist, Mor. | C8 | 62 |
| Târgu Jiu, Rom. | D7 | 20 |
| Târgu-Neamţ, Rom. | B10 | 20 |
| Târgu Ocna, Rom. | C10 | 20 |
| Târguşor, Rom. | E12 | 20 |
| Tarhjicht, Mor. | F7 | 62 |
| Tari, Pap. N. Gui. | G11 | 38 |
| Taríba, Ven. | D6 | 84 |
| Tarifa, Spain | I6 | 16 |
| Tarifa, Punta de, c., Spain | I6 | 16 |
| Tarija, Bol. | I9 | 82 |
| Tarim, Yemen | F6 | 47 |
| Tarim, stm., China | C3 | 30 |
| Tarim Pendi, China | F10 | 38 |
| Taritatu, stm., Indon. | F10 | 38 |
| Tarka, Niger | D13 | 64 |
| Tarkastad, S. Afr. | H8 | 66 |
| Tarkio, Mo., U.S. | B1 | 114 |
| Tarkio, stm., U.S. | K12 | 118 |

| Name | Map Ref. | Page |
|---|---|---|
| Tarkwa, Ghana | I9 | 64 |
| Tarlac, Phil. | n19 | 39b |
| Tarm, Den. | N11 | 6 |
| Tarma, Peru | D4 | 82 |
| Tarn, dept., Fr. | I9 | 14 |
| Tärnaby, Swe. | I14 | 6 |
| Tårnäveni, Rom. | C8 | 20 |
| Tarnobrzeg, Pol. | E21 | 10 |
| Tarnów, Pol. | E21 | 10 |
| Tarnowskie Góry, Pol. | E18 | 10 |
| Taroom, Austl. | E8 | 70 |
| Taroudant, Mor. | E6 | 62 |
| Tarpon Springs, Fl., U.S. | K4 | 112 |
| Tarqui, Peru | H5 | 84 |
| Tarra, stm., Ven. | C6 | 84 |
| Tarrafal, Mor. | k16 | 64a |
| Tarrafal, C.V. | m17 | 64a |
| Tarragona, Spain | D13 | 16 |
| Tarraleah, Austl. | n13 | 69 |
| Tårrega, Spain | D13 | 16 |
| Tarsus, Tur. | C3 | 48 |
| Tartagal, Arg. | B7 | 80 |
| Tartagal, Arg. | E9 | 80 |
| Tartu, Est. | C9 | 22 |
| Tartūs, Syria | D3 | 48 |
| Tarumirim, Braz. | E8 | 79 |
| Tarusa, Russia | G20 | 22 |
| Tarutung, Indon. | M5 | 40 |
| Tarutyne, Ukr. | C13 | 20 |
| Tarvisio, Italy | C8 | 18 |
| Tarvo, stm., S.A. | F11 | 82 |
| Tarzan, Tx., U.S. | G5 | 116 |
| Tašauz, Turk. | I9 | 26 |
| Tasejeva, stm., Russia | F16 | 26 |
| Tasejevo, Russia | F16 | 26 |
| Taseko, stm., B.C., Can. | F11 | 102 |
| Taseko Lakes, l., B.C., Can. | F11 | 102 |
| Taseko Mountain, mtn., B.C., Can. | F11 | 102 |
| Tashi Gang Dzong, Bhu. | G14 | 44 |
| Tashk, Daryācheh-ye, l., Iran | G12 | 48 |
| Tashkent see Taškent, Uzb. | I11 | 26 |
| Tasikmalaya, Indon. | j14 | 39a |
| Taškent, Uzb. | I11 | 26 |
| Taškepri, Turk. | J10 | 26 |
| Tasman Bay, b., N.Z. | D4 | 72 |
| Tasmania, state, Austl. | H9 | 68 |
| Tasmania, i., Austl. | N7 | 70 |
| Tasman Peninsula, pen., Austl. | N7 | 70 |
| Tasman Sea, Oc. | L19 | 126 |
| Tâşnad, Rom. | B6 | 20 |
| Tassara, Niger | C12 | 64 |
| Tassialouc, Lac, l., P.Q., Can. | E18 | 96 |
| Taštagol, Russia | G9 | 28 |
| Tastiota, Mex. | C4 | 90 |
| Tata, Hung. | H18 | 10 |
| Tatabánya, Hung. | H18 | 10 |
| T'at'a, vulkan, vol., Russia | c21 | 36a |
| Tataouine, Tun. | D16 | 62 |
| Tatarbunary, Ukr. | D13 | 20 |
| Tatarija, state, Russia | F8 | 26 |
| Tataria, Bela. | H11 | 22 |
| Tatarlar, Tur. | H10 | 20 |
| Tatarsk, Russia | F7 | 28 |
| Tatarskij proliv, strt., Russia | H20 | 28 |
| Tatarstan see Tatarija, state, Russia | F8 | 26 |
| Tatar Strait see Tatarskij proliv, strt., Russia | H20 | 28 |
| Tate, Ga., U.S. | E2 | 112 |
| Tate, stm., Austl. | A4 | 70 |
| Tathlina Lake, l., N.T., Can. | D9 | 96 |
| Tatitlek, Ak., U.S. | F21 | 100 |
| Tatla Lake, B.C., Can. | F10 | 102 |
| Tatla Lake, l., B.C., Can. | F10 | 102 |
| Tatlayoko Lake, B.C., Can. | F10 | 102 |
| Tatlayoko Lake, l., B.C., Can. | F10 | 102 |
| Tatlow, Mount, mtn., B.C., Can. | F11 | 102 |
| Tatnam, Cape, c., Mb., Can. | E14 | 96 |
| Tatrang, China | A11 | 44 |
| Tatta, Pak. | H2 | 44 |
| Tatuk Lake, l., B.C., Can. | D10 | 102 |
| Tatum, N.M., U.S. | F3 | 116 |
| Tatum, Tx., U.S. | J2 | 114 |
| Tatvan, Tur. | B7 | 48 |
| Taubaté, Braz. | G6 | 79 |
| Tauberbischofsheim, Ger. | F9 | 10 |
| Taučik, Kaz. | I8 | 26 |
| Tauini, stm., Braz. | G13 | 84 |
| Taulabé, Hond. | C7 | 92 |
| Taumarunui, N.Z. | C5 | 72 |
| Taum Sauk Mountain, mtn., Mo., U.S. | E6 | 114 |
| Taunay, Braz. | I13 | 82 |
| Taung, S. Afr. | F7 | 66 |
| Taungdwingyi, Myan. | D3 | 40 |
| Taunggyi, Myan. | D4 | 40 |
| Taungup, Myan. | E3 | 40 |
| Taunton, Eng., U.K. | J10 | 8 |
| Taunton, Ma., U.S. | F15 | 108 |
| Taupo, N.Z. | C6 | 72 |
| Taupo, Lake, l., N.Z. | C5 | 72 |
| Tauragė, Lith. | F5 | 22 |
| Tauranga, N.Z. | B6 | 72 |
| Taurianova, Italy | K11 | 18 |
| Tauripampa, Peru | E3 | 82 |
| Taurisma, Peru | F5 | 82 |
| Tauroa Point, c., N.Z. | A4 | 72 |
| Taurus Mountains see Toros Dağları, mts., Tur. | H14 | 4 |
| Tauste, Spain | D10 | 16 |
| Tavai, Para. | D11 | 80 |
| Tavananasa, Switz. | E11 | 13 |
| Tavares, Fl., U.S. | K5 | 112 |
| Tavda, Russia | F11 | 26 |
| Tavda, stm., Russia | F10 | 26 |
| Tavernes de la Valldigna, Spain | F11 | 16 |
| Tavernier, Fl., U.S. | N6 | 112 |
| Tavira, Port. | H4 | 16 |
| Tavistock, On., Can. | G15 | 110 |
| Tavolžan, Kaz. | G13 | 26 |
| Tavor, Har (Mount Tabor), mtn., Isr. | C4 | 50 |
| Tavoy see Dawei, Myan. | G5 | 40 |
| Tavşanlı, Tur. | J13 | 20 |
| Tawakoni, Lake, res., Tx., U.S. | G10 | 116 |
| Tawas City, Mi., U.S. | F12 | 110 |
| Tawilah, Juzur, is., Egypt | H2 | 48 |
| Tawkar, Sudan | H9 | 60 |
| Taxco de Alarcón, Mex. | H10 | 90 |
| Taxisco, Guat. | C4 | 92 |
| Taxkorgan, China | D2 | 30 |
| Tay, stm., Scot., U.K. | E10 | 8 |
| Tay, stm., Yk., Can. | E28 | 100 |
| Tayabamba, Peru | C3 | 82 |
| Taylor, Ar., U.S. | I3 | 114 |
| Taylor, Az., U.S. | J6 | 120 |
| Taylor, B.C., Can. | A14 | 102 |
| Taylor, Ne., U.S. | J8 | 118 |
| Taylor, Tx., U.S. | I9 | 116 |
| Taylor, Mount, mtn., N.M., U.S. | I9 | 120 |
| Taylors, S.C., U.S. | E4 | 112 |
| Taylorsville, In., U.S. | C11 | 114 |
| Taylorsville, Ky., U.S. | D11 | 114 |
| Taylorsville, Ms., U.S. | K7 | 114 |
| Taylorsville, N.C., U.S. | D5 | 112 |
| Taylorville, Il., U.S. | C7 | 114 |
| Taymā', Sau. Ar. | H5 | 48 |
| Taymouth, N.B., Can. | F7 | 106 |
| Taymyr Peninsula see Tajmyr, poluostrov, pen., Russia | B12 | 28 |
| Tay Ninh, Viet. | I9 | 40 |
| Tayoltita, Mex. | E7 | 90 |
| Tayside, prov., Scot., U.K. | E10 | 8 |
| Taytay, Phil. | C6 | 38 |
| Tayyārah, Sudan | K6 | 60 |
| Taza, Mor. | C6 | 62 |
| Tazenakht, Mor. | E7 | 62 |
| Tazin, stm., Can. | D10 | 96 |
| Tazin Lake, l., Sk., Can. | E11 | 96 |
| Tazovskaja guba, b., Russia | D7 | 28 |
| Tazovskij poluostrov, pen., Russia | D13 | 26 |
| Tazrouk, Alg. | I14 | 62 |
| Tazumal, Vol., El Sal. | D5 | 92 |
| Tazungdām, Myan. | F17 | 44 |
| Tbessa, Alg. | C15 | 62 |
| Tbilisi, Geor. | I6 | 26 |
| Tchamba, Togo | G10 | 64 |
| Tchaourou, Benin | G11 | 64 |
| Tchefuncta, stm., La., U.S. | L6 | 114 |
| Tchentlo Lake, l., B.C., Can. | B9 | 102 |
| Tchériba, Burkina | E8 | 64 |
| Tchesinkut Lake, l., B.C., Can. | C9 | 102 |
| Tchetti, Benin | H10 | 64 |
| Tchibanga, Gabon | B2 | 58 |
| Tchin-Tabáradene, Niger | D12 | 64 |
| Tchula, Ms., U.S. | I6 | 114 |
| Tczew, Pol. | A18 | 10 |
| Teá, stm., Braz. | H10 | 84 |
| Teaca, Rom. | C8 | 20 |
| Teacapan, Mex. | F7 | 90 |
| Teague, Tx., U.S. | H10 | 116 |
| Te Anau, Lake, l., N.Z. | F1 | 72 |
| Teapa, Mex. | I13 | 90 |
| Te Awamutu, N.Z. | C5 | 72 |
| Teba, Spain | I7 | 16 |
| Tebicuary, stm., Para. | D10 | 80 |
| Tebicuary-Mí, stm., Para. | D10 | 80 |
| Tebingtinggi, Indon. | M5 | 40 |
| Tebingtinggi, Pulau, i., Indon. | N7 | 40 |
| Téboursouk, Tun. | M4 | 18 |
| Tébourba, Tun. | M4 | 18 |
| Tecalitlán, Mex. | H8 | 90 |
| Tecamachalco, Mex. | H11 | 90 |
| Tecate, Mex. | A1 | 90 |
| Teche, Bayou, stm., La., U.S. | L5 | 114 |
| Techirghiol, Rom. | E12 | 20 |
| Techlé, W. Sah. | J3 | 62 |
| Tecklenburg, Ger. | C7 | 10 |
| Tecomán, Mex. | H8 | 90 |
| Tecopa, Ca., U.S. | I9 | 124 |
| Tecpan de Galeana, Mex. | I9 | 90 |
| Tecpán Guatemala, Guat. | C3 | 92 |
| Tecuala, Mex. | F7 | 90 |
| Tecuamburro, Volcán, vol., Guat. | C4 | 92 |
| Tecuci, Rom. | D11 | 20 |
| Tecumseh, Mi., U.S. | H12 | 110 |
| Tecumseh, Ne., U.S. | K11 | 118 |
| Tecumseh, Ok., U.S. | D10 | 116 |
| Tedžen, Turk. | J10 | 26 |
| Tedžen (Harīrūd), stm., Asia | C16 | 48 |
| Teec Nos Pos, Az., U.S. | H7 | 120 |
| Teeli, Russia | G16 | 26 |
| Tees, stm., Eng., U.K. | G12 | 8 |
| Teesside see Middlesbrough, Eng., U.K. | G12 | 8 |
| Teeswater, On., Can. | F14 | 110 |
| Tefé, Braz. | I10 | 84 |
| Tefé, stm., Braz. | D5 | 76 |
| Tefé, Lago, l., Braz. | I10 | 84 |
| Tegal, Indon. | j14 | 39a |
| Tegelen, Neth. | F9 | 12 |
| Tegernsee, Ger. | H11 | 10 |
| Tegina, Nig. | F13 | 64 |
| Tegucigalpa, Hond. | C7 | 92 |
| Teguise, Spain | n27 | 17b |
| Tehachapi, Ca., U.S. | I7 | 124 |
| Tehachapi Pass, Ca., U.S. | I7 | 124 |
| Tehamiyam, Sudan | H9 | 60 |
| Tehek Lake, l., N.T., Can. | D13 | 96 |
| Téhini, C. Iv. | G8 | 64 |
| Tehrān, Iran | D11 | 48 |
| Tehrathum, Nepal | G12 | 44 |
| Tehuacán, Mex. | H11 | 90 |
| Tehuantepec, Golfo de, b., Mex. | J12 | 90 |
| Tehuantepec, Istmo de, Mex. | I12 | 90 |
| Teide, Pico del, mtn., Spain | o24 | 17b |
| Teixeira Pinto, Gui.-B. | E2 | 64 |
| Teixeira Soares, Braz. | C13 | 80 |
| Tejamén, Mex. | E7 | 90 |
| Tejkovo, Russia | E23 | 22 |
| Tejo see Tagus, stm., Eur. | F3 | 16 |
| Tejupan, Punta, c., Mex. | H8 | 90 |
| Tejupilco de Hidalgo, Mex. | H9 | 90 |
| Tekamah, Ne., U.S. | J11 | 118 |
| Tekapo, Lake, l., N.Z. | E3 | 72 |
| Tekax, Mex. | G15 | 90 |
| Tekeli, Kaz. | I13 | 26 |
| Tekezē, stm., Afr. | F8 | 56 |
| Tekirdağ, Tur. | I11 | 20 |
| Tekoa, Wa., U.S. | C8 | 122 |
| Te Kuiti, N.Z. | C5 | 72 |
| Tela, Hond. | B7 | 92 |
| Tela, Bahía de, b., Hond. | B7 | 92 |
| Télagh, Alg. | C10 | 62 |
| Tel Aviv-Yafo, Isr. | D3 | 50 |
| Telde, Spain | o25 | 17b |
| Telefomin, Pap. N. Gui. | G11 | 38a |
| Telegraph Cove, B.C., Can. | G8 | 102 |
| Telegraph Creek, B.C., Can. | H29 | 100 |
| Telemark, co., Nor. | L11 | 6 |
| Telén, Arg. | I6 | 80 |
| Teleorman, co., Rom. | F8 | 20 |
| Telertheba, Djebel, mtn., Alg. | H14 | 62 |
| Telescope Peak, mtn., Ca., U.S. | H8 | 124 |
| Telfs, Aus. | H11 | 10 |
| Telica, Volcán, vol., Nic. | E8 | 92 |
| Telkwa, B.C., Can. | C7 | 102 |
| Telkwa, stm., B.C., Can. | C7 | 102 |
| Tell City, In., U.S. | E10 | 114 |
| Teller, Ak., U.S. | D11 | 100 |
| Tellicherry, India | F3 | 46 |
| Tellico, stm., U.S. | D2 | 112 |
| Tellico Plains, Tn., U.S. | D2 | 112 |
| Tello, Col. | F5 | 84 |
| Telluride, Co., U.S. | G9 | 120 |
| Tel Megiddo (Armageddon), hist., Isr. | C4 | 50 |
| Tel Mond, Isr. | D3 | 50 |
| Telok Anson, Malay. | L6 | 40 |
| Teloloapan, Mex. | H10 | 90 |
| Telpaneca, Nic. | D8 | 92 |
| Telšiai, Lith. | F5 | 22 |
| Telti, Italy | I4 | 18 |
| Teltow, Ger. | C13 | 10 |
| Tema, Ghana | I10 | 64 |
| Temagami, Lake, l., On., Can. | C15 | 110 |
| Temax, Mex. | G15 | 90 |
| Tembenčí, stm., Russia | D11 | 28 |
| Temblador, Ven. | C11 | 84 |
| Tembleque, Spain | F8 | 16 |
| Temecula, Ca., U.S. | K8 | 124 |
| Temera, Mor. | D7 | 62 |
| Témiscamie, Lac, l., P.Q., Can. | A1 | 106 |
| Témiscouata, Lac, l., P.Q., Can. | E5 | 106 |
| Temora, Austl. | J7 | 70 |
| Temosachic, Mex. | C6 | 90 |
| Tempe, Az., U.S. | K5 | 120 |
| Temperance, Mi., U.S. | I12 | 110 |
| Tempio Pausania, Italy | I4 | 18 |
| Tempisque, stm., C.R. | G9 | 92 |
| Temple, Ok., U.S. | E8 | 116 |
| Temple, Tx., U.S. | H9 | 116 |
| Templeton, stm., Austl. | C3 | 70 |
| Templin, Ger. | B13 | 10 |
| Tempoal, stm., Mex. | G10 | 90 |
| Tempoal de Sánchez, Mex. | G10 | 90 |
| Tempy, Austl. | E20 | 70 |
| Temr'uk, Russia | H5 | 26 |
| Temuco, Chile | J2 | 80 |
| Tenabo, Mex. | G14 | 90 |
| Tenaha, Tx., U.S. | K2 | 114 |
| Tenakee Springs, Ak., U.S. | H27 | 100 |
| Tenāli, India | D6 | 46 |
| Tenasserim, Myan. | H5 | 40 |
| Tendaho, Eth. | F9 | 56 |
| Tende, Col de, Eur. | H14 | 14 |
| Ten Degree Channel, strt., India | J2 | 40 |
| Tenente Marques, stm., Braz. | D11 | 82 |
| Tenente Portela, Braz. | D12 | 80 |
| Ténéré, des., Niger | E9 | 54 |
| Tenerife, i., Spain | o24 | 17b |
| Ténès, Alg. | B11 | 62 |
| Teng'aopu, China | B10 | 32 |
| Tengchong, China | B5 | 40 |
| Tengger, Nusa (Lesser Sunda Islands), is., Indon. | G7 | 38 |
| Tengiz, ozero, l., Kaz. | G11 | 26 |
| Tengtiao, China | H4 | 34 |
| Tengtiao (He), stm., Asia | C7 | 40 |
| Tengxian, China | H5 | 32 |
| Teniente Rodolfo Marsh, sci., Ant. | B1 | 73 |
| Tenino, Wa., U.S. | D3 | 122 |
| Tenkāsi, India | H4 | 46 |
| Tenke, D.R.C. | D5 | 58 |
| Tenkiller Ferry Lake, res., Ok., U.S. | D11 | 116 |
| Tenkodogo, Burkina | F9 | 64 |
| Ten Mile Lake, l., Nf., Can. | A17 | 106 |
| Tennant Creek, Austl. | C6 | 68 |
| Tennessee, state, U.S. | G9 | 98 |
| Tennessee, stm., U.S. | E7 | 98 |
| Tennille, Ga., U.S. | G4 | 112 |
| Teno, Chile | H3 | 80 |
| Teno (Tana), stm., Eur. | F20 | 6 |
| Tenosique, Mex. | I14 | 90 |
| Tenryū, Japan | M12 | 36 |
| Tensas, stm., La., U.S. | K5 | 114 |
| Tensed, Id., U.S. | C9 | 122 |
| Ten Sleep, Wy., U.S. | F18 | 122 |
| Tenterfield, Austl. | G10 | 70 |
| Ten Thousand Islands, is., Fl., U.S. | N5 | 112 |
| Teocaltiche, Mex. | G8 | 90 |
| Teodelina, Arg. | H8 | 80 |
| Teófilo Otoni, Braz. | D8 | 79 |
| Teo Lakes, l., Sk., Can. | G5 | 104 |
| Teotihuacán, hist., Mex. | H10 | 90 |
| Teotitlán, Mex. | H11 | 90 |
| Tepalcatepec, Mex. | H8 | 90 |
| Tepeaca, Mex. | H11 | 90 |
| Tepehuanes, Mex. | E7 | 90 |
| Tepehuanes, stm., Mex. | E7 | 90 |
| Tepeji de Ocampo, Mex. | H10 | 90 |
| Tepelenë, Alb. | I4 | 20 |
| Tepi, Eth. | N8 | 60 |
| Tepic, Mex. | G7 | 90 |
| Teplice, Czech Rep. | E13 | 10 |
| Teplovo, Russia | F25 | 22 |
| Tepoca, Bahía, b., Mex. | B3 | 90 |
| Tepoca, Punta, c., Mex. | B3 | 90 |
| Tepopa, Cabo, c., Mex. | C3 | 90 |
| Téra, Niger | D10 | 64 |
| Tera, stm., Spain | D6 | 16 |
| Teramo, Italy | G8 | 18 |
| Terang, Austl. | L5 | 70 |
| Terborg, Neth. | E9 | 12 |
| Terbuny, Russia | I21 | 22 |
| Terceira, i., Port. | k21 | 82a |
| Tercero, stm., Arg. | G7 | 80 |
| Tereida, Sudan | L8 | 60 |
| Terek, stm., Russia | I7 | 26 |
| Terence Bay, N.S., Can. | H10 | 106 |
| Terenino, Russia | G16 | 22 |
| Terenos, Braz. | F1 | 79 |
| Teresina, Braz. | E10 | 76 |
| Teresópolis, Braz. | G7 | 79 |
| Terespol, Russia | C23 | 10 |
| Teresva, Ukr. | A7 | 20 |
| Terhorne, Neth. | B8 | 12 |
| Teribe, stm., N.A. | H12 | 92 |
| Terlingua, Tx., U.S. | J3 | 116 |
| Termas de Río Hondo, Arg. | D6 | 80 |
| Termez (Dyje), stm., Eur. | G15 | 10 |
| Termini Imerese, Italy | L8 | 18 |
| Términos, Laguna de, b., Mex. | H14 | 90 |
| Termoli, Italy | G10 | 18 |
| Ternate, Indon. | E8 | 38 |
| Ternej, Russia | H19 | 28 |
| Terneuzen, Neth. | F4 | 12 |
| Terni, Italy | G7 | 18 |
| Ternivka, Ukr. | H3 | 26 |
| Ternopil', Ukr. | H2 | 26 |
| Teror, Spain | o25 | 17b |
| Terpenija, mys, c., Russia | H20 | 28 |
| Terpenija, zaliv, b., Russia | H20 | 28 |
| Terra Alta, W.V., U.S. | H7 | 108 |
| Terra Bella, Ca., U.S. | I6 | 124 |
| Terrace, B.C., Can. | C6 | 102 |
| Terrace Bay, On., Can. | B8 | 110 |
| Terracina, Italy | H8 | 18 |
| Terra Nova, Braz. | I3 | 84 |
| Terra Nova, stm., Nf., Can. | D19 | 106 |
| Terra Nova National Park, Nf., Can. | D20 | 106 |
| Terra Rica, Braz. | G2 | 79 |
| Terra Roxa, Braz. | G3 | 79 |
| Terra Santa, Braz. | I14 | 84 |
| Terrassa, Spain | D14 | 16 |
| Terrebonne Bay, b., La., U.S. | M6 | 114 |
| Terre Haute, In., U.S. | C9 | 114 |
| Terrell, Tx., U.S. | G10 | 116 |
| Terrell Hills, Tx., U.S. | J8 | 116 |
| Terrenceville, Nf., Can. | E19 | 106 |
| Terror Point, c., B.C., Can. | D5 | 102 |
| Terry, Ms., U.S. | J6 | 114 |
| Terry, Mt., U.S. | J6 | 114 |
| Terry Peak, mtn., S.D., U.S. | G4 | 118 |
| Terschelling, i., Neth. | B7 | 12 |
| Teruel, Col. | F5 | 84 |
| Teruel, Spain | E10 | 16 |
| Terzaghi Dam, B.C., Can. | G12 | 102 |
| Teša, Russia | F25 | 22 |
| Tešanj, Bos. | E2 | 20 |
| Tesalia, Col. | F5 | 84 |
| Tes-Chem (Tesijn), stm., Asia | A5 | 30 |
| Teseney, Erit. | J9 | 60 |
| Tesijn (Tes-Chem), stm., Asia | B6 | 30 |
| Teslić, Bos. | E1 | 20 |
| Teslin, Yk., Can. | F28 | 100 |
| Teslin, stm., Can. | F27 | 100 |
| Teslin Lake, l., Can. | F28 | 100 |
| Tesouras, stm., Braz. | C3 | 79 |
| Tesouro, Braz. | D2 | 79 |
| Tessala, Monts du, mts., Alg. | J11 | 16 |
| Tessalit, Mali | A10 | 64 |
| Tessaoua, Niger | E13 | 64 |
| Tessenderlo, Bel. | F7 | 12 |
| Tessy-sur-Vire, Fr. | D5 | 14 |
| Testour, Tun. | M4 | 18 |
| Tesuque, N.M., U.S. | I11 | 120 |
| Tetachuck Lake, l., B.C., Can. | D9 | 102 |
| Tetagouche, stm., N.B., Can. | E8 | 106 |
| Tete, Moz. | E6 | 58 |
| Tête-à-la-Baleine, P.Q., Can. | B14 | 106 |
| Tête-Jaune-Cache, B.C., Can. | E15 | 102 |
| Tétépisca, Lac, l., P.Q., Can. | A4 | 106 |
| Teterow, Ger. | B12 | 10 |
| Tetlin, Ak., U.S. | E23 | 100 |
| Tetlin Lake, l., Ak., U.S. | E23 | 100 |
| Teton, stm., U.S. | C14 | 122 |
| Teton, Id., U.S. | G14 | 122 |
| Teton Range, mts., Wy., U.S. | G15 | 122 |
| Tétouan, Mor. | C8 | 62 |
| Tetovo, Mac. | G4 | 20 |
| Teuco, stm., Arg. | C8 | 80 |
| Teulada, Italy | K3 | 18 |
| Teulada, Capo, c., Italy | K3 | 18 |
| Teúl de González Ortega, Mex. | G8 | 90 |
| Teuli, Bela. | I7 | 22 |
| Teulon, Mb., Can. | H17 | 104 |
| Teutopolis, Il., U.S. | C8 | 114 |
| Teuva, Fin. | J17 | 6 |
| Tevere (Tiber), stm., Italy | G7 | 18 |
| Teverya (Tiberias), Isr. | C5 | 50 |
| Texada Island, i., B.C., Can. | H10 | 102 |
| Texarkana, Ar., U.S. | I2 | 114 |
| Texarkana, Tx., U.S. | I2 | 114 |
| Texas, Austl. | G9 | 70 |
| Texas, state, U.S. | E7 | 98 |
| Texas City, Tx., U.S. | J12 | 116 |
| Texel, i., Neth. | B6 | 12 |
| Texhoma, Ok., U.S. | C5 | 116 |
| Texico, N.M., U.S. | E3 | 116 |
| Texline, Tx., U.S. | C3 | 116 |
| Texoma, Lake, res., U.S. | F10 | 116 |
| Teyateyaneng, Leso. | G8 | 66 |
| Teywarah, Afg. | D1 | 44 |
| Teziutlán, Mex. | H11 | 90 |
| Tezpur, India | G15 | 44 |
| Tezzeron Lake, l., B.C., Can. | C10 | 102 |
| Tha-anne, stm., N.T., Can. | D13 | 96 |
| Thabana-Ntlenyana, mtn., Leso. | G9 | 66 |
| Thabazimbi, S. Afr. | E9 | 66 |
| Thai Binh, Viet. | D9 | 40 |
| Thailand (Prathet Thai), ctry., Asia | B3 | 38 |
| Thailand, Gulf of, b., Asia | I6 | 40 |
| Thai Nguyen, Viet. | D8 | 40 |
| Thal, Pak. | D4 | 44 |
| Thala, Tun. | N3 | 18 |
| Thalfang, Ger. | F6 | 10 |
| Thalia, Tx., U.S. | F7 | 116 |
| Thalwil, Switz. | D10 | 13 |
| Thamar, Jabal, mtn., Yemen | H4 | 47 |
| Thames, N.Z. | B5 | 72 |
| Thames, stm., Eng., U.K. | J12 | 8 |
| Thamesford, On., Can. | G14 | 110 |
| Thamesville, On., Can. | H14 | 110 |
| Thāna, India | C2 | 46 |
| Thanbyuzayat, Myan. | G4 | 40 |
| Thanh Binh, Viet. | G10 | 40 |
| Thanh Hoa, Viet. | E8 | 40 |
| Thanh Pho Ho Chi Minh (Saigon), Viet. | I9 | 40 |
| Thanjāvūr, India | G5 | 46 |
| Thann, Fr. | E14 | 14 |
| Thar Desert (Great Indian Desert), des., Asia | F4 | 44 |
| Thargomindah, Austl. | G5 | 70 |
| Thar Nhom, Sudan | N6 | 60 |
| Tharrawaddy, Myan. | F3 | 40 |
| Thásos, i., Grc. | I8 | 20 |
| Thatcher, Az., U.S. | L7 | 120 |
| Thaton, Myan. | F4 | 40 |
| Thaungdut, Myan. | B3 | 40 |
| Thaungyin, stm., Asia | F5 | 40 |
| Thaya (Dyje), stm., Eur. | G15 | 10 |
| Thayer, Mo., U.S. | F5 | 114 |
| Thayetmyo, Myan. | E3 | 40 |
| Thazi, Myan. | D4 | 40 |
| Thealka, Ky., U.S. | B4 | 112 |
| Thebes see Thívai, Grc. | K7 | 20 |
| Thebes, Il., U.S. | E7 | 114 |
| Thebes, hist., Egypt | E7 | 60 |
| Thedford, Ne., U.S. | J7 | 118 |
| The Dalles, Or., U.S. | E4 | 122 |
| The English Companys islands, is., Austl. | B7 | 68 |
| The Fens, reg., Eng., U.K. | I14 | 8 |
| The Fishing Lakes, l., Sk., Can. | H11 | 104 |
| The Fiat Tops, mts., Co., U.S. | D9 | 120 |
| The Hague see 's-Gravenhage, Neth. | E5 | 12 |
| The Key Indian Reserve, Sk., Can. | G12 | 104 |
| The Little Minch, strt., Scot., U.K. | D7 | 8 |
| The Lynd, Austl. | B6 | 70 |
| The Minch, strt., Scot., U.K. | C8 | 8 |
| Thenia, Alg. | B12 | 62 |
| Theniet el Hadd, Alg. | C12 | 62 |
| Theodore, Al., U.S. | L8 | 114 |
| Theodore, Austl. | E9 | 70 |
| Theodore, Sk., Can. | G12 | 104 |
| Theodore Roosevelt Lake, res., Az., U.S. | K5 | 120 |
| Théologos, Grc. | I8 | 20 |
| The Pas, Mb., Can. | E13 | 104 |
| The Rajah, mtn., Ab., Can. | D16 | 102 |
| The Rand see Witwatersrand, reg., S. Afr. | E8 | 66 |
| Theresa, N.Y., U.S. | C11 | 108 |
| Thermaïkós Kólpos, b., Grc. | I6 | 20 |
| Thermopílai (Thermopylae), hist., Grc. | K6 | 20 |
| Thermopolis, Wy., U.S. | A8 | 120 |
| Thermopylae see Thermopílai, hist., Grc. | K6 | 20 |
| The Rock, Austl. | J7 | 70 |
| Thesiger Bay, b., N.T., Can. | B6 | 96 |
| The Sound, strt., Eur. | N13 | 6 |
| Thessalia, hist. reg., Grc. | J6 | 20 |
| Thessalia, prov., Grc. | J6 | 20 |
| Thessalon, On., Can. | D12 | 110 |
| Thessaloníki (Salonika), Grc. | I6 | 20 |
| Thetford-Mines, P.Q., Can. | A15 | 108 |
| The Valley, Anguilla | E13 | 94 |
| Thibaudeau, Mb., Can. | A20 | 104 |
| Thibodaux, La., U.S. | M6 | 114 |
| Thicket Portage, Mb., Can. | C17 | 104 |
| Thief, stm., Mn., U.S. | C11 | 118 |
| Thief River Falls, Mn., U.S. | C11 | 118 |
| Thielsen, Mount, mtn., Or., U.S. | G3 | 122 |
| Thiene, Italy | D6 | 18 |
| Thiers, Fr. | G10 | 14 |
| Thiès, Sen. | D1 | 64 |
| Thiesi, Italy | I3 | 18 |
| Thika, Kenya | B7 | 58 |
| Thimphu, Bhu. | G13 | 44 |
| Thingvellir, Ice. | B3 | 6a |
| Thingvellir National Park, Ice. | B3 | 6a |
| Thionville, Fr. | C13 | 14 |
| Thíra (Santorini), i., Grc. | M9 | 20 |
| Thiruvārūr, India | G5 | 46 |
| Thistle Island, i., Austl. | J2 | 70 |
| Thívai (Thebes), Grc. | K7 | 20 |
| Thlewiaza, stm., N.T., Can. | D13 | 96 |
| Thoa, stm., N.T., Can. | D11 | 96 |
| Thonoyandou, S. Afr. | D10 | 66 |
| Thoi Binh, Viet. | J8 | 40 |
| Thomas, Ok., U.S. | D8 | 116 |
| Thomas, W.V., U.S. | H7 | 108 |
| Thomasboro, Il., U.S. | B8 | 114 |
| Thomaston, Al., U.S. | J9 | 114 |
| Thomaston, Ct., U.S. | F13 | 108 |
| Thomaston, Ga., U.S. | G2 | 112 |
| Thomaston, Me., U.S. | C17 | 108 |
| Thomasville, Al., U.S. | K9 | 114 |
| Thomasville, Ga., U.S. | I3 | 112 |
| Thomasville, N.C., U.S. | D6 | 112 |
| Thom Lake, l., Mb., Can. | C18 | 104 |
| Thomlinson, Mount, mtn., B.C., Can. | B7 | 102 |
| Thompson, Mb., Can. | C17 | 104 |
| Thompson, stm., B.C., Can. | G13 | 102 |
| Thompson Falls, Mt., U.S. | C10 | 122 |
| Thompson Pass, Ak., U.S. | F22 | 100 |
| Thompsonville, Mi., U.S. | F10 | 110 |
| Thomsen, stm., N.T., Can. | B9 | 96 |
| Thomson, Ga., U.S. | F4 | 112 |
| Thomson, Il., U.S. | B6 | 114 |
| Thomson, stm., Austl. | E5 | 70 |
| Thomson Lake, res., Sk., Can. | I8 | 104 |
| Thon Buri, Thai. | H6 | 40 |
| Thongwa, Myan. | F4 | 40 |
| Thonon-les-Bains, Fr. | F13 | 14 |
| Thonotosassa, Fl., U.S. | K4 | 112 |
| Thonze, Myan. | F3 | 40 |
| Thorburn, N.S., Can. | G11 | 106 |
| Thoreau, N.M., U.S. | I8 | 120 |
| Thorhild, Ab., Can. | C21 | 102 |
| Thorial, Sudan | M5 | 60 |
| Thornapple, stm., Wi., U.S. | F5 | 110 |
| Thornbury, On., Can. | F15 | 110 |
| Thorndale, Tx., U.S. | I9 | 116 |
| Thorne, stm., Ca., U.S. | D23 | 104 |
| Thornton, Ar., U.S. | I4 | 114 |
| Thornton, Co., U.S. | E12 | 120 |
| Thornton, Tx., U.S. | H10 | 116 |
| Thorntonville, Tx., U.S. | H4 | 116 |
| Thorp, Wi., U.S. | F5 | 110 |
| Thorsby, Ab., Can. | D20 | 102 |
| Thorsby, Al., U.S. | J10 | 114 |
| Thorsteinson Lake, l., Mb., Can. | A17 | 104 |
| Thouars, Fr. | F6 | 14 |
| Thousand Lake Mountain, mtn., Ut., U.S. | F5 | 120 |
| Thousand Oaks, Ca., U.S. | J7 | 124 |
| Thrace, hist. reg., Eur. | H10 | 20 |
| Thrakikón Pélagos, Grc. | I8 | 20 |
| Three Fingered Jack, mtn., Or., U.S. | F4 | 122 |
| Three Forks, Mt., U.S. | E14 | 122 |
| Three Hills, Ab., Can. | F21 | 102 |
| Three Hummock Island, i., Austl. | M6 | 70 |
| Three Lakes, Wi., U.S. | E6 | 110 |
| Three Mile Plains, N.S., Can. | H9 | 106 |
| Three Oaks, Mi., U.S. | I9 | 110 |
| Three Pagodas Pass, Asia | G5 | 40 |
| Threepoint Lake, l., Mb., Can. | C16 | 104 |
| Three Rivers, Mi., U.S. | I10 | 110 |
| Three Rivers, Tx., U.S. | K8 | 116 |
| Three Sisters, S. Afr. | H6 | 66 |
| Three Sisters, mtn., Or., U.S. | F4 | 122 |
| Three Springs, Austl. | E3 | 68 |
| Throat, stm., Mn., U.S. | G21 | 104 |
| Throckmorton, Tx., U.S. | F7 | 116 |
| Thu Dau Mot, Viet. | I9 | 40 |
| Thule, Grnld. | B13 | 86 |
| Thun, Switz. | E8 | 13 |
| Thunder Bay, On., Can. | B6 | 110 |
| Thunder Bay, b., Mi., U.S. | F12 | 110 |
| Thunder Bay, stm., Mi., U.S. | F12 | 110 |
| Thunder Bay, b., Mi., U.S. | E12 | 110 |
| Thunderbolt, Ga., U.S. | G5 | 112 |
| Thunder Creek, stm., Sk., Can. | H8 | 104 |
| Thunder Hills, hills, Sk., Can. | C8 | 104 |
| Thunersee, l., Switz. | E8 | 13 |
| Thung Song, Thai. | J5 | 40 |
| Thur, stm., Switz. | C10 | 13 |
| Thurgau, state, Switz. | C11 | 13 |
| Thüringen, state, Ger. | D11 | 10 |
| Thüringer Wald, mts., Ger. | E10 | 10 |
| Thurmont, Md., U.S. | H9 | 108 |
| Thursday Island, Austl. | B8 | 68 |
| Thurso, Scot., U.K. | C10 | 8 |
| Thurston Island, i., Ant. | C11 | 73 |
| Thwaites Iceberg Tongue, Ant. | C11 | 73 |
| Thyolo, Mwi. | E7 | 58 |
| Tía Juana, Ven. | B7 | 84 |
| Tianchang, China | C8 | 34 |
| Tiandong, China | C9 | 40 |
| Tianfanjie, China | F5 | 34 |
| Tianjiazhen, China | F4 | 34 |
| Tianjin (Tientsin), China | D5 | 32 |
| Tianjin Shi, China | D10 | 30 |
| Tianjun, China | D6 | 30 |
| Tianlin, China | B9 | 40 |
| Tianmen, China | E2 | 34 |
| Tianshui, China | E8 | 30 |
| Tiantai, China | F10 | 34 |
| Tiantou, China | I4 | 34 |
| Tianxiyang, China | I7 | 34 |
| Tianzhu, China | D7 | 30 |
| Tianzhuang, China | J2 | 34 |
| Tibají, Braz. | C13 | 80 |
| Tibají, stm., Braz. | B13 | 80 |
| Tibasti, Sarīr, des., Libya | D4 | 56 |
| Tibbie, Al., U.S. | K8 | 114 |
| Tibe, Eth. | M9 | 60 |
| Tiber see Tevere, stm., Italy | G7 | 18 |
| Tibesti, mts., Chad | D4 | 56 |
| Tibet see Xizang Zizhiqu, prov., China | E3 | 30 |
| Tibiri, Niger | E13 | 64 |
| Tibooburra, Austl. | G5 | 70 |
| Tiburón, Cabo, c. | C4 | 84 |
| Tiburón, Isla, i., Mex. | C3 | 90 |
| Tiča, Jazovir, res., Bul. | F10 | 20 |
| Tice, Fl., U.S. | M5 | 112 |
| Tichît, Maur. | B5 | 64 |
| Tichmenevo, Russia | C21 | 22 |
| Tichoreck, Russia | H6 | 26 |
| Tichvin, Russia | B16 | 22 |
| Ticino, state, Switz. | F10 | 13 |
| Ticino, stm., Eur. | D3 | 18 |
| Tickfaw, La., U.S. | L6 | 114 |
| Tickfaw, stm., La., U.S. | L6 | 114 |
| Ticonderoga, N.Y., U.S. | D13 | 108 |
| Ticul, Mex. | G15 | 90 |
| Tide Lake, l., Ab., Can. | H3 | 104 |
| Tidikelt, pl., Alg. | G11 | 62 |
| Tidioute, Pa., U.S. | F7 | 108 |
| Tidjikja, Maur. | B4 | 64 |
| Tidore, Indon. | E8 | 38 |
| Tiekou, China | K7 | 20 |
| Tieli, China | B12 | 30 |
| Tieling, China | A11 | 32 |
| Tielt, Bel. | F3 | 12 |
| Tielutou, China | H4 | 34 |
| Tiémé, C. Iv. | G6 | 64 |
| T'ienchung, Tai. | L9 | 34 |
| Tien Shan, mts., Asia | C3 | 30 |
| Tientsin see Tianjin, China | D5 | 32 |
| Tie Plant, Ms., U.S. | I7 | 114 |
| Tierra Amarilla, Chile | D3 | 80 |
| Tierra Amarilla, N.M., U.S. | H10 | 120 |
| Tierra Blanca, Mex. | H11 | 90 |
| Tierra del Fuego, i., S.A. | G3 | 78 |
| Tierralta, Col. | C4 | 84 |
| Tieshanguan, China | L2 | 34 |
| Tietê, Braz. | G5 | 79 |
| Tietê, stm., Braz. | F3 | 79 |
| Tif, Alg. | G11 | 62 |
| Tiffany Mountain, mtn., Wa., U.S. | B6 | 122 |
| Tiffin, Oh., U.S. | F3 | 108 |
| Tifton, Ga., U.S. | H3 | 112 |
| Tiftona, Tn., U.S. | D1 | 112 |
| Tighennif, Alg. | C11 | 62 |
| Tighina (Bender), Mol. | F13 | 4 |
| Tigil', Russia | F23 | 28 |
| Tiglid, Mor. | F5 | 62 |
| Tignall, Ga., U.S. | F4 | 112 |
| Tignish, P.E., Can. | F9 | 106 |
| Tigre, Col. | J5 | 84 |
| Tigre, stm., Peru | J5 | 84 |
| Tigre, stm., Ven. | C11 | 84 |
| Tigre, Cerro, mtn., C.R. | I11 | 92 |
| Tigris (Dicle) (Dijlah), stm., Asia | F9 | 48 |
| Tiguabos, Cuba | D7 | 94 |
| Tiguentourine, Alg. | G15 | 62 |
| Tihāmah, pl., Asia | H4 | 48 |
| Tihuatlán, Mex. | G11 | 90 |
| Tijamuchi, stm., Bol. | F3 | 82 |
| Tijesno, Cro. | F10 | 18 |
| Tijuana, Mex. | A1 | 90 |
| Tijucas, Braz. | D14 | 80 |
| Tijucas do Sul, Braz. | C14 | 80 |
| Tijuco, stm., Braz. | E4 | 79 |
| Tikal, hist., Guat. | I15 | 90 |
| Tiko, Cam. | I14 | 64 |
| Tikrīt, Iraq | D7 | 48 |
| Tikša, Russia | I23 | 6 |
| Tikšeozero, ozero, l., Russia | H22 | 6 |
| Tilarán, C.R. | G10 | 92 |
| Tilbalakan, Laguna, b., Hond. | B10 | 92 |
| Tilburg, Neth. | E7 | 12 |
| Tilbury, On., Can. | H13 | 110 |
| Tilcara, Arg. | B6 | 80 |
| Tilden, Il., U.S. | D7 | 114 |
| Tilden, Ne., U.S. | I10 | 118 |
| Tilden, Tx., U.S. | K8 | 116 |
| Tilemsès, Niger | D11 | 64 |
| Tilemsi, Vallée du, val., Mali | B10 | 64 |
| Tilhar, India | G8 | 44 |
| Tilimsen, Alg. | C10 | 62 |
| Tilisarao, Arg. | G6 | 80 |
| Tillaberi, Niger | D10 | 64 |
| Tillamook, Or., U.S. | E2 | 122 |
| Tillanchāng Dwip, i., India | J2 | 40 |
| Tilley, Ab., Can. | G23 | 102 |
| Tillia, Niger | C12 | 64 |
| Tillmans Corner, Al., U.S. | L8 | 114 |
| Tillson, N.Y., U.S. | F12 | 108 |
| Tillsonburg, On., Can. | H15 | 110 |
| Tilpa, Austl. | H6 | 70 |
| Tilrhemt, Alg. | D12 | 62 |
| Tilton, Il., U.S. | B9 | 114 |
| Tilton, N.H., U.S. | D15 | 108 |
| Tiltonsville, Oh., U.S. | G6 | 108 |
| Timā, Egypt | D6 | 60 |
| Timaná, Col. | F4 | 84 |
| Timane, stm., Para. | I12 | 82 |
| Timanskij kr'až, mtn., Russia | D7 | 26 |
| Timaru, N.Z. | F3 | 72 |
| Timbedgha, Maur. | C5 | 64 |
| Timber Lake, S.D., U.S. | F6 | 118 |
| Timbío, Col. | F4 | 84 |
| Timbó, Braz. | D14 | 80 |
| Timboon, Austl. | L5 | 70 |
| Timbuktu see Tombouctou, Mali | B9 | 64 |
| Timétrine, Mali | B9 | 64 |
| Timeu Creek, stm., Ab., Can. | C20 | 102 |
| Timgad, hist., Alg. | C14 | 62 |
| Timimoun, Alg. | F11 | 62 |
| Timiris, Râs, c., Maur. | B2 | 64 |
| Timirjazevskij, Russia | F14 | 26 |
| Timmendorfer Strand, Ger. | A10 | 10 |
| Timmins, On., Can. | B14 | 110 |

| Name | Map Ref. | Page |
|---|---|---|

Timmonsville, S.C., U.S. — E7 112
Timms Hill, hill, Wi., U.S. — E5 110
Timor, i., Indon. — G8 38
Timor Sea — J16 126
Timotes, Ven. — C7 84
Timoudi, Alg. — F10 62
Timpson, Tx., U.S. — K2 114
Tims Ford Lake, res., Tn., U.S. — G10 114
Tinaca Point, c., Phil. — D8 38
Tinaco, Ven. — C8 84
Ṭīnah, Khalīj aṭ-, b., Egypt — F2 48
Tinaja, Punta, c., Peru — G5 82
Ti-n-Amzi, val., Afr. — B12 64
Tinaquillo, Ven. — C8 84
Tindivanam, India — F5 46
Tindouf, Alg. — G6 62
Tindouf, Hamada de, reg., Afr. — F6 62
Tindouf, Sebkha de, pl., Alg. — G7 62
Tineo, Spain — B5 16
Tinga, mtn., Afr. — M2 60
Tingha, Austl. — G9 70
Tinghert, Hamādat [Plateau du Tinghert], plat., Afr. — F15 62
Tinghert, Plateau du (Hamādat Tinghert), plat., Afr. — F15 62
Tingo de Saposoa, Peru — B3 82
Tingo María, Peru — C4 82
Tingri, China — F12 44
Tingsjiao, China — F3 34
Tingvoll, Nor. — J11 6
Tinharé, Ilha de, i., Braz. — B9 79
Tinh Bien, Viet. — I8 40
Tinkisso, stm., Gui. — F5 64
Tinniswood, Mount, mtn., B.C., Can. — G11 102
Tinnoset, Nor. — L11 6
Tinogasta, Arg. — E5 80
Tínos, Grc. — L9 20
Tínos, i., Grc. — L9 20
Tinquipaya, Bol. — H9 82
Tinrhir, Mor. — E8 62
Tinsley, Ms., U.S. — J6 114
Tinsukia, India — G16 44
Tintagel, B.C., Can. — C9 102
Tinte, Cerro, mtn., S.A. — J8 82
Tintina, Arg. — D7 80
Ti-n-Zaouatene, Alg. — B11 64
Tio, Erit. — G2 47
Tioga, N.D., U.S. — C5 118
Tioga, Pa., U.S. — F9 108
Tioga, stm., U.S. — F9 108
Tiojala, Fin. — K18 6
Tioman, Pulau, i., Malay. — M8 40
Tionesta, Pa., U.S. — F7 108
Tionesta Creek, stm., Pa., U.S. — F7 108
Tior, Sudan — N6 60
Tioro, Selat, strt., Indon. — F7 38
Tioughnioga, stm., N.Y., U.S. — E10 108
Tipitapa, Nic. — E8 92
Tippecanoe, stm., In., U.S. — A10 114
Tipperary, Ire. — I5 8
Tipperary, co., Ire. — I5 8
Tipton, Ca., U.S. — H6 124
Tipton, In., U.S. — I4 110
Tipton, In., U.S. — B10 114
Tipton, Mo., U.S. — D4 114
Tipton, Ok., U.S. — E7 116
Tiptonville, Tn., U.S. — F7 114
Tip Top Mountain, mtn., On., Can. — B10 110
Tiputini, stm., Ec. — H4 84
Tīra, Isr. — D3 50
Tiradentes, Braz. — F6 79
Tīrān, i., Sau. Ar. — H3 48
Tīrān, Maḍīq, strt. — D8 60
Tiran, Strait of see Tīrān, Maḍīq, strt. — D8 60
Tiranë, Alb. — H3 20
Tirano, Italy — C5 18
Tiraque, Bol. — G9 82
Tiraspol, Mol. — F13 4
Tirat Karmel, Isr. — C3 50
Tirat Zevi, Isr. — D5 50
Tirich Mīr, mtn., Pak. — B4 44
Tirilye, Tur. — I12 20
Tiriro, Gui. — F5 64
Tírnavos, Grc. — J6 20
Tirol, state, Aus. — H10 10
Tiros, Braz. — E6 79
Tiroungoulou, C.A.R. — M2 60
Tirschenreuth, Ger. — F12 10
Tiruchchirāppalli, India — G5 46
Tiruchengodu, India — G4 46
Tirulai, Lith. — F6 22
Tirunelveli, India — H4 46
Tirupati, India — F5 46
Tiruppattūr, India — F5 46
Tiruppur, India — G4 46
Tiruvannāmalai, India — F5 46
Tiruvottiyūr, India — F6 46
Tisa (Tisza) (Tysa), stm., Eur. — C4 20
Tisdale, Sk., Can. — F10 104
Tishomingo, Ms., U.S. — H8 114
Tishomingo, Ok., U.S. — E10 116
Tisisat Falls, wtfl, Eth. — L9 60
Tišiyah, Syria — D6 50
Tiskilwa, Il., U.S. — I6 110
Tisma, Nic. — E8 92
Tissemsilt, Alg. — C11 62
Tīsta, stm., Asia — G13 44
Tisza (Tisza) (Tysa), stm., Eur. — C4 20
Tiszaföldvár, Hung. — I20 10
Tiszafüred, Hung. — H20 10
Tiszavasvári, Hung. — H21 10
Tit, Alg. — I13 62
Titaf, Alg. — G10 62
Titicaca, Lago, l., S.A. — F7 82
Titonka, Ia., U.S. — G1 110
Titov Veles, Mac. — H5 20
Titov vrh, mtn., Mac. — G4 20
Titran, Nor. — J11 6
Tittabawassee, stm., Mi., U.S. — G11 110
Tittmoning, Ger. — G12 10
Title, Port. — H6 56
Titusville, Fl., U.S. — K6 112
Titusville, Pa., U.S. — F7 108
Tivoli, Italy — H7 18
Tivoli, Tx., U.S. — K10 116
Tizi-Ouzou, Alg. — B13 62
Tiznados, stm., Ven. — C9 84
Tiznit, Mor. — F6 62
Tjolotjo, Zimb. — B8 66
Tlacolula, Mex. — H12 90
Tlacotepec, Mex. — I10 90
Tlahualilo de Zaragoza, Mex. — D8 90
Tlalixtaquilla, Mex. — I10 90
Tlalnepantla, Mex. — H10 90
Tlaltenango de Sánchez Román, Mex. — G8 90
Tlapacoyan, Mex. — I10 90
Tlapeng, Bots. — D5 66
Tlaquepaque, Mex. — G8 90

Tlaxcala [de Xicoténcatl], Mex. — H10 90
Tłuszcz, Pol. — C21 10
Toabré, stm., Pan. — I14 92
Toachi, stm., Ec. — H3 84
Toahayaná, Mex. — D6 90
Toamasina, Madag. — q21 67b
Toano, Va., U.S. — B10 112
Toast, N.C., U.S. — C6 112
Toay, Arg. — I6 80
Toba, Japan — M11 36
Toba, Mali — F6 64
Toba, Danau, l., Indon. — M5 40
Tobacco, stm., Mi., U.S. — G11 110
Tobacco Plains Indian Reserve, B.C., Can. — H19 102
Tobago, i., Trin. — I14 94
Toba Inlet, b., B.C., Can. — G10 102
Toba Kākar Range, mts., Pak. — E3 44
Tobas, Arg. — E7 80
Toba Tek Singh, Pak. — E5 44
Tobejuba, Isla, i., Ven. — C12 84
Tobelo, Indon. — E8 38
Tobercurry, Ire. — G5 8
Tobermory, Austl. — F5 70
Tobermory, On., Can. — E14 110
Tobias, Ne., U.S. — K10 118
Tobin Lake, l., Sk., Can. — E11 104
Tobique, stm., N.B., Can. — E6 106
Tobol, Kaz. — G10 26
Tobol, stm., Asia — F11 26
Tobol'sk, Russia — F11 26
Tobruk see Ṭubruq, Libya — A2 60
Tobyhanna, Pa., U.S. — F11 108
Tocantinia, Braz. — E9 76
Tocantinópolis, Braz. — E9 76
Tocantins, stm., Braz. — D9 76
Tocantins, stm., Braz. — A13 82
Tocantinzinho, stm., Braz. — C4 79
Toccoa, Ga., U.S. — E3 112
Toccoa (Ocoee), stm., U.S. — E2 112
Tochcala Lake, l., B.C., Can. — C9 102
Tochigi, Japan — K14 36
Tochtamyš, Taj. — B6 44
Toco, Chile — B4 80
Tocoa, Hond. — B8 92
Tocoʻnao, Chile — B4 80
Tocopilla, Chile — B3 80
Tocuco, stm., Ven. — C6 84
Tocumwal, Austl. — J6 70
Tocuyo, stm., Ven. — B8 84
Tocuyo de la Costa, Ven. — B8 84
Todd, Italy — G7 18
Todos Santos, Bol. — G9 82
Todos Santos, Mex. — F4 90
Todos Santos, Bahía, b., Mex. — B1 90
Todtnau, Ger. — H7 10
T'oejŏ, N. Kor. — D15 32
Tofield, Ab., Can. — D22 102
Tofino, B.C., Can. — H9 102
Togiak, Ak., U.S. — G14 100
Togian, Kepulauan, is., Indon. — F7 38
Togo, ctry., Afr. — G7 54
Toguchin, Russia — F14 26
Togwotee Pass, Wy., U.S. — G15 122
Toinya, Sudan — N5 60
Toiyabe Range, mts., Nv., U.S. — E8 124
Tokanui, N.Z. — G2 72
Tokara-rettō, is., Japan — r4 37b
Tokar'ovka, Russia — J24 22
Tokat, Tur. — A4 48
Tokelau, dep., Oc. — I22 126
Tokmak, Kyrg. — I13 26
Toko Range, mts., Austl. — D3 70
Tokoroa, N.Z. — C5 72
Toksook Bay, Ak., U.S. — F12 100
Toksovo, Russia — A13 22
Tokuno-shima, i., Japan — s3 37b
Tokushima, Japan — M9 36
Tokuyama, Japan — M6 36
Tōkyō, Japan — L14 36
Tokyo Bay see Tōkyō-wan, b., Japan — L14 36
Tōkyō-wan, b., Japan — L14 36
Tokzār, Afg. — C2 44
Tolé, Pan. — I13 92
Toledo, Bol. — H8 82
Toledo, Col. — D6 84
Toledo, Il., U.S. — I3 110
Toledo, Il., U.S. — C8 114
Toledo, Ia., U.S. — H3 110
Toledo, Oh., U.S. — F2 108
Toledo, Or., U.S. — F2 122
Toledo, Spain — F7 16
Toledo Bend Reservoir, res., U.S. — K3 114
Tolentino, Italy — F8 18
Tolga, Alg. — C13 62
Toliara, Madag. — s20 67b
Tolima, dept., Col. — F5 84
Tolima, Nevado del, mtn., Col. — E5 84
Toljatti, Russia — G7 26
Tolleson, Az., U.S. — K4 120
Tolloche, Arg. — C7 80
Tolmačovo, Russia — C12 22
Tolmezzo, Italy — C8 18
Tolna, Hung. — I18 10
Tolna, co., Hung. — I18 10
Tolo, Teluk, b., Indon. — F7 38
Tolongoma, Madag. — r22 67b
Tolono, Il., U.S. — C8 114
Tolosa, Spain — B9 16
Tolstoj, mys, c., Russia — F23 28
Toltén, Chile — D2 78
Tolú, Col. — C5 84
Toluca, Il., U.S. — I6 110
Toluca, Nevado de, vol., Mex. — H10 90
Toluca [de Lerdo], Mex. — H10 90
Tolwa, Sudan — N7 60
Tom', stm., Russia — F9 28
Tomah, Wi., U.S. — G5 110
Tomahawk, Wi., U.S. — F6 110
Tomakomai, Japan — e16 36a
Tomar, Port. — F3 16
Tomás Barrón (Eucaliptus), Bol. — G8 82
Tomás Gomensoro, Ur. — F10 80
Tomashpil', Ukr. — A12 20
Tomaszów Lubelski, Pol. — E23 10
Tomaszów Mazowiecki, Pol. — D20 10
Tomatlán, Mex. — H7 90
Tomave, Bol. — I8 82
Tomazina, Braz. — G4 79
Tombador, Serra do, plat., Braz. — D13 82
Tomball, Tx., U.S. — I11 116
Tombe, Sudan — O6 60
Tombigbee, stm., U.S. — K8 114
Tombos, Braz. — F7 79
Tombouctou (Timbuktu), Mali — C8 64
Tombstone, Ariz., U.S. — M6 120
Tombstone Mountain, mtn., Yk., Can. — D25 100

Tombua, Ang. — E2 58
Tomé, Chile — I2 80
Tomelloso, Spain — F8 16
Tomini, Teluk, b., Indon. — F7 38
Tominian, Mali — E7 64
Tommot, Russia — F17 28
Tomo, stm., Col. — E8 84
Tompkins, Nf., Can. — E14 106
Tompkins, Sk., Can. — H6 104
Tompkinsville, Ky., U.S. — F11 114
Tom Price, Austl. — D3 68
Tomra, Nor. — J10 6
Toms, stm., N.J., U.S. — G12 108
Tomsk, Russia — F8 28
Toms River, N.J., U.S. — H12 108
Tonalá, Mex. — I13 90
Tonantins, Braz. — I9 84
Tonantins, stm., Braz. — I8 84
Tonasket, Wa., U.S. — B6 122
Tonawanda, N.Y., U.S. — D8 108
Tonbridge, Eng., U.K. — J14 8
Tondano, Indon. — E7 38
Tønder, Den. — N11 6
Tondoro, Nmb. — A4 66
Tonekābon, Iran — C11 48
Tonga, Sudan — M6 60
Tonga, ctry., Oc. — K22 126
Tongaat, S. Afr. — G10 66
Tonganoxie, Ks., U.S. — L12 118
Tongcheng, China — D5 34
Tongchengzha, China — D7 34
Tongchuan, China — D8 30
Tonggou, China — B13 32
Tongguan, China — E9 30
Tongguan, China — G1 34
Tonghai, China — B7 40
Tonghe, China — C1 34
Tonghua, China — B13 32
Tongjosŏn-man, b., N. Kor. — D16 32
Tongli, China — D9 34
Tongliao, China — C11 30
Tongling, China — E6 34
Tongmu, China — H2 34
Tongnae, S. Kor. — H17 32
Tongo, Austl. — B13 22
Tongobory, Madag. — s21 67b
Tongoy, Chile — E3 80
Tongren, China — F8 30
Tongsa Dzong, Bhu. — G14 44
Tongshi, China — H5 32
Tongtai, China — C9 34
Tongtian, stm., China — D17 44
Tongue, Scot., U.K. — C9 8
Tongue, stm., N.D., U.S. — C10 118
Tongue, stm., U.S. — E19 122
Tongxian, China — D4 32
Tongyu, China — C11 30
Tongzhaipu, China — C1 34
Tongzi, China — F8 30
Tonica, Il., U.S. — I6 110
Tonj, Sudan — N5 60
Tonk, India — G6 44
Tonkawa, Ok., U.S. — C9 116
Tonkin, Gulf of, b., Asia — D10 40
Tônlé Sab, Bœng, l., Camb. — H8 40
Tonle Sap see Tônlé Sab, Bœng, l., Camb. — H8 40
Tonneins, Fr. — H7 14
Tonnerre, Fr. — E10 14
Tönning, Ger. — A8 10
Tōno, Japan — H16 36
Tonopah, Nv., U.S. — F8 124
Tonosí, Pan. — D2 92
Tonota, Bots. — C8 66
Tønsberg, Nor. — L12 6
Toobeah, Austl. — G8 70
Tooele, Ut., U.S. — D4 120
Toompine, Austl. — F6 70
Toomsboro, Ga., U.S. — G3 112
Toosey Indian Reserve, B.C., Can. — F12 102
Tootsi, Est. — C7 22
Toowoomba, Austl. — F9 70
Topawa, Az., U.S. — M5 120
Topeka, Ks., U.S. — L12 118
Topia, Mex. — E6 90
Topki, Russia — F9 28
Topko, gora, mtn., Russia — F19 28
Topley, B.C., Can. — C8 102
Toplița, Rom. — C9 20
T'oploje, Russia — H20 22
Topol'čany, Slvk. — G18 10
Topolobampo, Mex. — E5 90
Topolog, Rom. — E12 20
Topozero, ozero, l., Russia — I22 6
Toppenish, Wa., U.S. — D5 122
Topsham, Me., U.S. — D17 108
Tor, Eth. — N7 60
Toraya, Peru — F5 82
Torbat-e Ḥeydarīyeh, Iran — D15 48
Torbat-e Jām, Iran — D16 48
Torbay see Torquay, Eng., U.K. — K10 8
Torbay, Nf., Can. — E21 106
Torbejevo, Russia — G26 22
Torbino, Russia — C15 22
Torbrook, N.S., Can. — H9 106
Torch, stm., Sk., Can. — E11 104
Torch Lake, l., Mi., U.S. — E10 110
Tordesillas, Spain — D6 16
Töre, Swe. — I18 6
Torez, Ukr. — H5 26
Torgau, Ger. — D13 10
Torino (Turin), Italy — D2 18
Toriparu, Braz. — D2 79
Torit, Sudan — H7 56
Torneälven (Tornionjoki), stm., Eur. — H18 6
Torngat Mountains, mts., Can. — F10 106
Tornillo, Tx., U.S. — M10 120
Tornio, Fin. — I19 6
Tornionjoki (Torneälven), stm., Eur. — H18 6
Tornquist, Arg. — J7 80
Toro, Cerro, mtn., Mex. — H7 90
Toro, Cerro, mtn., S.A. — E2 78
Törökszentmiklós, Hung. — H20 10
Torola, stm., N.A. — D6 92
Toron, Nevado, mtn., S.A. — H7 82
Toronto, Ks., U.S. — N12 118
Toronto, On., Can. — G16 110
Toronto, Oh., U.S. — G6 108
Toronto, S.D., U.S. — G11 118
Toropec, Russia — E14 22
Tororo, Ug. — A6 58
Toros Dağları, mts., Tur. — H14 4
Torošino, Russia — D11 22
Torotoro, Bol. — H9 82
Torpy, stm., B.C., Can. — D14 102
Torquay, Eng., U.K. — K10 8
Torquay, Sk., Can. — I11 104
Torrance, Ca., U.S. — K7 124
Torrance Lake, l., Mb., Can. — A16 104
Torre del Campo, Spain — H8 16
Torredonjimeno, Spain — H8 16

Torrejón de Ardoz, Spain — E8 16
Torrelavega, Spain — B7 16
Torremaggiore, Italy — H10 18
Torremolinos, Spain — I7 16
Torrens, Lake, l., Austl. — H2 70
Torrens Creek, Austl. — C6 70
Torrent, Arg. — E10 80
Torrent, Spain — F11 16
Torreón, Mex. — E8 90
Torreperojil, Spain — G8 16
Torres, Braz. — E14 80
Torres de Alcalá, Mor. — J7 16
Torres Strait, strt., Oc. — B8 68
Torrevella, Spain — H11 16
Torridon, Scot., U.K. — D8 8
Torriglia, Italy — E4 18
Torrijos, Spain — F7 16
Torrington, Ct., U.S. — F13 108
Torrington, Wy., U.S. — I3 118
Torrinha, Braz. — G4 79
Torrox, Spain — I8 16
Tors Cove, Nf., Can. — E21 106
Tórshavn, Faer. Is. — D8 6
Tortola, i., Br. Vir. Is. — E12 94
Tórtolas, Cerro de las, mtn., S.A. — E4 80
Tortoli, Italy — J4 18
Tortona, Italy — E3 18
Tortosa, Spain — E12 16
Tortue, Île de la, i., Haiti — D8 94
Tortuguero, Parque Nacional, C.R. — G11 92
Toruń, Pol. — B18 10
Torunos, Ven. — C7 84
Torup, Swe. — M13 6
Tõrva, Est. — C8 22
Toržok, Russia — F4 26
T'osan, N. Kor. — E14 32
Tosa-shimizu, Japan — O7 36
Tosa-wan, b., Japan — N8 36
Toscana (Tuscany), prov., Italy — F5 18
Toscano, stm., Mex. — B3 90
Tosno, Russia — B13 22
T'osovo-Netyl'skij, Russia — C14 22
T'osovskij, Russia — C13 22
Tostado, Arg. — E8 80
Tōstamaa, Est. — C7 22
Tostón, Spain — o26 17b
Totagatic, stm., Wi., U.S. — D4 110
Totana, Spain — H10 16
Toteng, Bots. — C6 66
Tôtes, Fr. — C8 14
Tot'ma, Russia — B25 22
Totness, Sur. — E14 84
Totonicapán, Guat. — C3 92
Totonicapán, dept., Guat. — B3 92
Totora, Bol. — G9 82
Totora, Bol. — G7 82
Totoras, Arg. — G8 80
Totos, Peru — E4 82
Tototlán, Mex. — G8 90
Touba, C. Iv. — G6 64
Toubkal, Jebel, mtn., Mor. — E7 62
Touchwood Hills, hills, Sk., Can. — G10 104
Touchwood Lake, l., Ab., Can. — C23 102
Touchwood Lake, l., Mb., Can. — D19 104
Toudaogou, China — A17 32
Tougan, Burkina — E8 64
Touggourt, Alg. — D13 62
Toukoto, Mali — E5 64
Toul, Fr. — D12 14
Touliu, Tai. — L9 34
Toulnustouc, stm., P.Q., Can. — C5 106
Toulon, Fr. — I12 14
Toulon, Il., U.S. — I6 110
Toulouse, Fr. — I8 14
Tounan, Tai. — L9 34
Toungoo, Myan. — E4 40
Touques, stm., Fr. — C7 14
Touraine, P.Q., Can. — B11 108
Tourakom, Laos — E7 40
Tourcoing, Fr. — B10 14
Tournai (Doornik), Bel. — G3 12
Tourndo, Oued, val., Afr. — I16 62
Tournus, Fr. — F11 14
Tou Rout, Viet. — E7 14
Tousside, Pic, mtn., Chad — D4 56
Toustain, Alg. — M3 18
Toutle, stm., Wa., U.S. — D3 122
Toutouhe, China — D5 34
Touwsrivier, S. Afr. — I5 66
Tovar, Ven. — C7 84
Tovarkovskij, Russia — H21 22
Tow, Tx., U.S. — I8 116
Towanda, Ks., U.S. — N11 118
Towanda, Pa., U.S. — F10 108
Tower, Mn., U.S. — C3 110
Tower City, N.D., U.S. — E10 118
Tower City, Pa., U.S. — G10 108
Tower Hill, Il., U.S. — C8 114
Town and Country, Wa., U.S. — C8 122
Towner, N.D., U.S. — C7 118
Townsend, Mt., U.S. — D14 122
Townsend, Mount, mtn., Can. — K8 70
Townshend Island, i., Austl. — B7 70
Townsville, Austl. — B7 70
Towrzī, Afg. — E1 44
Towson, Md., U.S. — H10 108
Toxkan, stm., China — C2 30
Toyah, Tx., U.S. — H3 116
Toyama, Japan — K12 36
Toyama-wan, b., Japan — K12 36
Toyohashi, Japan — M12 36
Toyokawa, Japan — M11 36
Toyonaka, Japan — M10 36
Toyooka, Japan — L9 36
Toyota, Japan — L12 36
Tozeur, Tun. — D6 62
Toro, Tun. — D6 62
Trabuja, Braz. — G4 79
Trabzon, Tur. — G15 4
Tracadie, N.B., Can. — E9 106
Tracy, Mn., U.S. — G12 110
Tracy, P.Q., Can. — A13 108
Tracy City, Tn., U.S. — G11 114
Trade Lake, l., Sk., Can. — C11 104
Tradewater, stm., Ky., U.S. — E9 114
Traer, Ia., U.S. — H3 110
Trafalgar, Cabo, c., Spain — I5 16
Traiguén, Chile — J2 80
Trail, B.C., Can. — H17 102
Traíra (Taraira), stm., S.A. — I10 84
Traíras, Braz. — C4 79
Trakai, Lith. — G7 22
Trakt, Russia — D9 22
Tralee, Ire. — I4 8
Trammel, Va., U.S. — B4 112
Tramore, Ire. — I6 8
Tramping Lake, l., Sk., Can. — F6 104
Trancas, Arg. — D6 80

Trancoso, Port. — E4 16
Tranebjerg, Den. — N12 6
Trang, Thai. — K5 40
Trangahy, Madag. — q21 67b
Trangie, Austl. — I7 70
Trani, Italy — H11 18
Transantarctic Mountains, mts., Ant. — D9 73
Transkei, hist. reg., S. Afr. — H9 66
Transylvania, hist. reg., Rom. — C7 20
Transylvanian Alps see Carpații Meridionali, mts., Rom. — D8 20
Trapani, Italy — K7 18
Traralgon, Austl. — L7 70
Trasacco, Italy — H8 18
Trasimeno, Lago, l., Italy — F7 18
Trás-os-Montes, hist. reg., Port. — D4 16
Trat, Thai. — H7 40
Traun, Aus. — G14 10
Traun, stm., Aus. — G14 10
Traunstein, Ger. — H12 10
Travellers Lake, l., Austl. — I5 70
Traverse, Lake, l., U.S. — F11 118
Traverse Bay, b., Mb., Can. — H18 104
Traverse City, Mi., U.S. — F10 110
Travers Reservoir, res., Ab., Can. — G22 102
Travis, Lake, res., Tx., U.S. — I8 116
Travnik, Bos. — E12 18
Trbovlje, Slvn. — C10 18
Trebinje, Bos. — G2 20
Trebišov, Slvk. — G21 10
Treble Mountain, mtn., B.C., Can. — B5 102
Treblinka, Pol. — C22 10
Trecate, Italy — D3 18
Treene, stm., Ger. — A9 10
Tregosse Islets, is., Austl. — C8 70
Tréguier, Fr. — D3 14
Treherne, Mb., Can. — I16 104
Treinta y Tres, Ur. — G11 80
Trélazé, Fr. — E6 14
Trelew, Arg. — E3 78
Trelleborg, Swe. — N13 6
Tremblant, Mont, mtn., P.Q., Can. — A12 108
Trembleur Lake, l., B.C., Can. — C9 102
Tremedal, Braz. — C8 79
Tremont, Il., U.S. — J6 110
Tremont, Pa., U.S. — G10 108
Tremonton, Ut., U.S. — C4 120
Trempealeau, Wi., U.S. — F4 110
Trempealeau, stm., Wi., U.S. — F4 110
Trenčín, Slvk. — G18 10
Trenque Lauquen, Arg. — H7 80
Trent see Trento, Italy — C6 18
Trent, stm., Eng., U.K. — H13 8
Trente et un Milles, Lac des, l., P.Q., Can. — A11 108
Trentino-Alto Adige, prov., Italy — C6 18
Trento, Italy — C6 18
Trenton, Fl., U.S. — J4 112
Trenton, Ga., U.S. — E1 112
Trenton, Ky., U.S. — F9 114
Trenton, Mo., U.S. — B3 114
Trenton, Ne., U.S. — K6 118
Trenton, N.C., U.S. — D9 112
Trenton, N.J., U.S. — G11 108
Trenton, N.S., Can. — G11 106
Trenton, On., Can. — F18 110
Trenton, Tn., U.S. — F7 114
Trenton, Tx., U.S. — F10 116
Trentwood, Wa., U.S. — C8 122
Trepassey, Nf., Can. — F20 106
Trepassey Bay, b., Nf., Can. — F20 106
Tres Algarrobos, Arg. — H7 80
Tres Árboles, Arg. — G10 80
Tres Arroyos, Arg. — J8 80
Três Corações, Braz. — F6 79
Três Coroas, Braz. — E13 80
Tres de Maio, Braz. — D11 80
Três Esquinas, Col. — G5 84
Três Fronteiras, Braz. — F3 79
Tres Isletas, Arg. — D8 80
Três Lagoas, Braz. — F2 79
Tres Lomas, Arg. — I7 80
Três Marias, Represa de, res., Braz. — E6 79
Tres Montosas, mtn., N.M., U.S. — J9 120
Tres Palos, Laguna, b., Mex. — I10 90
Três Passos, Braz. — D11 80
Tres Picos, Cerro, mtn., Arg. — J8 80
Três Pontas, Braz. — F6 79
Tres Puntas, Cabo, c., Arg. — F3 78
Tres Puntas, Cabo, c., Guat. — B6 92
Três Ranchos, Braz. — E5 79
Três Rios, Braz. — G7 79
Três Ríos, C.R. — H11 92
Tres Vírgenes, Volcán de las, vol., Mex. — D3 90
Tres Zapotes, hist., Mex. — H12 90
Treuchtlingen, Ger. — G11 10
Treuenbrietzen, Ger. — C12 10
Treviglio, Italy — D4 18
Treviso, Italy — D7 18
Trevorton, Pa., U.S. — G10 108
Trévoux, Fr. — F11 14
Trezevant, Tn., U.S. — F8 114
Triabunna, Austl. — N7 70
Triánda, Grc. — M12 20
Triangle, Va., U.S. — I9 108
Triángulos, Arrecifes, rf., Mex. — G13 90
Tribugá, Ensenada de, b., Col. — E4 84
Tribune, Ks., U.S. — M6 118
Tribune, Sk., Can. — I11 104
Tribune Channel, strt., B.C., Can. — G8 102
Trichardt, S. Afr. — F9 66
Trichūr, India — G4 46
Trier, Ger. — F6 10
Trieste, Italy — D8 18
Trigal, Bol. — H9 82
Triglav, mtn., Slvn. — C8 18
Triguos, Spain — H5 16
Trikala, Grc. — J5 20
Trikhonís, Límni, l., Grc. — K5 20
Trikora, Puncak, mtn., Indon. — F10 38
Trilby, Fl., U.S. — K4 112
Trimont, Mn., U.S. — H13 110
Trin, Switz. — E11 13
Trincheras, Mex. — B4 90
Trincomalee, Sri L. — H6 46
Trindade, Braz. — D4 79

Trindade, i., Braz. — G12 74
Třinec, Czech Rep. — F18 10
Trinidad, Bol. — F9 82
Trinidad, Co., U.S. — N3 118
Trinidad, Col. — E7 84
Trinidad, Cuba — D5 94
Trinidad, Hond. — C6 92
Trinidad, Tx., U.S. — G10 116
Trinidad, Ur. — G10 80
Trinidad, i., Trin. — I14 94
Trinidad, Isla, i., Arg. — J8 80
Trinidad and Tobago, ctry., N.A. — I14 94
Trinity, Nf., Can. — D20 106
Trinity, Tx., U.S. — I11 116
Trinity, stm., Ca., U.S. — D2 124
Trinity, stm., Tx., U.S. — I12 116
Trinity Bay, b., Nf., Can. — E20 106
Trinity Bay, b., Tx., U.S. — J12 116
Trinkat Island, i., India — J2 40
Trino, Italy — D3 18
Tripoli see Ṭarābulus, Leb. — D3 48
Tripoli see Ṭarābulus, Libya — B3 56
Tripolis, Grc. — L6 20
Tripolis, hist., Tur. — L13 20
Tripp, S.D., U.S. — H10 118
Tripura, state, India — H14 44
Triquet, Lac, l., P.Q., Can. — B14 106
Tristan da Cunha Group, is., St. Hel. — L5 52
Tristão, Îles, is., Afr. — F2 64
Triste, Golfo de, b., Ven. — B8 84
Trivandrum, India — H4 46
Trochu, Ab., Can. — F21 102
Trogir, Cro. — F11 18
Troia, Italy — H10 18
Troick, Russia — G10 26
Troicko-Pečorsk, Russia — E9 26
Troina, Italy — L9 18
Troisdorf, Ger. — E7 10
Trois-Pistoles, P.Q., Can. — D6 106
Trois-Rivières, P.Q., Can. — A14 108
Trojan, Bul. — G8 20
Trojekurovo, Russia — H22 22
Trollhättan, Swe. — L13 6
Trombetas, stm., Braz. — H14 84
Tromelin, Île, i., Afr. — E10 58
Trompsburg, S. Afr. — H7 66
Troms, co., Nor. — G16 6
Tromsø, Nor. — G16 6
Trona, Ca., U.S. — I8 124
Tronador, Monte, mtn., S.A. — E2 78
Troncoso, Mex. — F8 90
Trondheim, Nor. — J12 6
Troon, Scot., U.K. — F9 8
Tropas, Rio das, stm., Braz. — B13 82
Tropea, Italy — K10 18
Trophy Mountain, mtn., B.C., Can. — F15 102
Tropic, Ut., U.S. — G4 120
Tropojë, Alb. — G4 20
Troškūnai, Lith. — F7 22
Trosna, Russia — H18 22
Trostjanec', Ukr. — A13 20
Trotwood, Oh., U.S. — H2 108
Trou-du-Nord, Haiti — C6 94
Troup, Tx., U.S. — G11 116
Trout, stm., N.T., Can. — D8 96
Trout Creek, Mi., U.S. — D6 110
Trout Creek Pass, Co., U.S. — F11 120
Trout Lake, l., B.C., Can. — G17 102
Trout Lake, l., N.T., Can. — D8 96
Trout Lake, l., On., Can. — H21 104
Trout River, Nf., Can. — C15 106
Troutville, Va., U.S. — B7 112
Trouville [-sur-Mer], Fr. — C7 14
Trowbridge, Eng., U.K. — J11 8
Troy, Al., U.S. — K11 114
Troy, Id., U.S. — D9 122
Troy, Il., U.S. — E10 114
Troy, In., U.S. — D10 114
Troy, Ks., U.S. — L12 118
Troy, Mo., U.S. — D6 114
Troy, Mt., U.S. — B10 122
Troy, N.C., U.S. — D7 112
Troy, N.H., U.S. — E14 108
Troy, N.Y., U.S. — E13 108
Troy, Oh., U.S. — G2 108
Troy, Pa., U.S. — F10 108
Troy, Tn., U.S. — F7 114
Troy, hist., Tur. — J10 20
Troyes, Fr. — D11 14
Troyits'ke, Ukr. — A14 20
Troy Peak, mtn., Nv., U.S. — F10 124
Trstenik, Yugo. — F5 20
Truax, Sk., Can. — I10 104
Trubčevsk, Russia — I16 22
Truchas Peak, mtn., N.M., U.S. — H11 120
Truckee, Ca., U.S. — E5 124
Truckee, stm., U.S. — E6 124
Trujillo, Col. — E4 84
Trujillo, Hond. — B8 92
Trujillo, Peru — C2 82
Trujillo, Spain — F6 16
Trujillo, Ven. — C7 84
Trujillo, state, Ven. — C7 84
Truman, Mn., U.S. — H13 110
Trumann, Ar., U.S. — G6 114
Trumansburg, N.Y., U.S. — E10 108
Trundle, Austl. — I7 70
Truro, N.S., Can. — G10 106
Truscott, Tx., U.S. — F7 116
Truth or Consequences (Hot Springs), N.M., U.S. — K9 120
Trutnov, Czech Rep. — E15 10
Trybuny, Ukr. — A14 20
Tryon, N.C., U.S. — D4 112
Tryon, Ne., U.S. — J7 118
Trzcianka, Pol. — B16 10
Trzebiatów, Pol. — B14 10
Trzebinia, Pol. — E19 10
Tsarabaria, Madag. — n23 67b
Tsaratanana, Madag. — p22 67b
Tsaratanana, Massif du, mtn., Madag. — o23 67b
Tsau, Bots. — C6 66
Tsaukaib, Nmb. — F2 66
Tsavo, Kenya — B7 58
Tsaydaychuz Peak, mtn., B.C., Can. — D8 102
Tsayta Lake, l., B.C., Can. — B9 102
Tsebrykove, Ukr. — B14 20
Tsévié, Togo — H10 64
Tshabong, Bots. — F6 66
Tshela, D.R.C. — B2 58
Tshesebe, Bots. — C8 66
Tshidilamolomo, S. Afr. — E7 66
Tshikapa, D.R.C. — C4 58
Tshofa, D.R.C. — C5 58
Tshukudu, Bots. — D6 66

| Name | Map Ref. | Page |
|---|---|---|
| Tshwaane, Bots. | D6 | 66 |
| Tsiafajavona, mtn., Madag. | q22 | 67b |
| Tsianaloka, Madag. | q21 | 67b |
| Tsihombe, Madag. | t21 | 67b |
| Tsilmamo, Eth. | N8 | 60 |
| Tsimilofo, Madag. | t21 | 67b |
| Tsimpsean Indian Reserve, B.C., Can. | C4 | 102 |
| Tsineng, S. Afr. | F6 | 66 |
| Tsingtao see Qingdao, China | G8 | 32 |
| Tsinjomitondraka, Madag. | o22 | 67b |
| Tsiribihina, stm., Madag. | q21 | 67b |
| Tsiroanomandidy, Madag. | q22 | 67b |
| Tsitondroina, Madag. | r22 | 67b |
| Tsitsutl Peak, mtn., B.C., Can. | E9 | 102 |
| Tsivory, Madag. | t22 | 67b |
| Tsobis, Nmb. | B3 | 66 |
| Tsomo, stm., S. Afr. | H8 | 66 |
| Tsoying, Tai. | M9 | 34 |
| Tsu, Japan | M11 | 36 |
| Tsuchiura, Japan | K15 | 36 |
| Tsugaru-kaikyō, strt., Japan | f15 | 36a |
| Tsumeb, Nmb. | B3 | 66 |
| Tsumis Park, Nmb. | D3 | 66 |
| Tsumkwe, Nmb. | B5 | 66 |
| Tsuni see Zunyi, China | F8 | 30 |
| Tsuruga, Japan | L11 | 36 |
| Tsuruoka, Japan | I14 | 36 |
| Tsushima, is., Japan | M4 | 36 |
| Tsushima-kaikyō (Eastern Channel), strt., Japan | N4 | 36 |
| Tsuyama, Japan | L9 | 36 |
| Tua Chau, Viet. | D7 | 40 |
| Tual, Indon. | G9 | 38 |
| Tuam, Ire. | H5 | 8 |
| Tuamotu, Îles, is., Fr. Poly. | J26 | 126 |
| Tuanfeng, China | E3 | 34 |
| Tuanlin, China | D7 | 32 |
| Tuanwang, China | G8 | 32 |
| Tuapse, Russia | I5 | 26 |
| Tubac, Az., U.S. | M5 | 120 |
| Tuba City, Az., U.S. | H5 | 120 |
| Tubarão, Braz. | E14 | 80 |
| Tübingen, Ger. | G9 | 10 |
| Ṭubruq (Tobruk), Libya | A2 | 60 |
| Tucacas, Ven. | B8 | 84 |
| Tucacas, Punta, c., Ven. | B8 | 84 |
| Tucano, Braz. | F11 | 76 |
| Tucava, stm., Bol. | H12 | 82 |
| Tuchengzi, China | C12 | 32 |
| Tuchola, Pol. | B17 | 10 |
| Tuckerman, Ar., U.S. | G5 | 114 |
| Tuckerton, N.J., U.S. | H12 | 108 |
| Tučkovo, Russia | F19 | 22 |
| Tucson, Az., U.S. | L6 | 120 |
| Tucumã, mth., Braz. | J9 | 84 |
| Tucumán, prov., Arg. | D6 | 80 |
| Tucumcari, N.M., U.S. | D3 | 116 |
| Tucunuco, Arg. | F4 | 80 |
| Tucupido, Ven. | C10 | 84 |
| Tucupita, Ven. | C11 | 84 |
| Tucuruí, Braz. | D9 | 76 |
| Tudcum, Arg. | F4 | 80 |
| Tudela, Spain | C10 | 16 |
| Tudmur (Palmyra), Syria | D5 | 48 |
| Tudu, Est. | B9 | 22 |
| Tugaske, Sk., Can. | H8 | 104 |
| Tug Fork, stm., U.S. | A4 | 112 |
| Tugidak Island, i., Ak., U.S. | H17 | 100 |
| Tuichi, stm., Bol. | F8 | 82 |
| Tuineje, Spain | o26 | 17b |
| Tujmazy, Russia | G8 | 26 |
| T'ukalinsk, Russia | F12 | 26 |
| Tukangbesi, Kepulauan, is., Indon. | G7 | 38 |
| Tuktoyaktuk, N.T., Can. | B28 | 100 |
| Tuktoyaktuk Peninsula, pen., N.T., Can. | B29 | 100 |
| Tukums, Lat. | D6 | 22 |
| Tula, Mex. | F10 | 90 |
| Tula, Russia | G20 | 22 |
| Tulancingo, Mex. | G10 | 90 |
| Tulare, Ca., U.S. | H6 | 124 |
| Tulare, S.D., U.S. | G9 | 118 |
| Tularosa, N.M., U.S. | K10 | 120 |
| Tularosa, stm., N.M., U.S. | K8 | 120 |
| Tularosa Valley, N.M., U.S. | L10 | 120 |
| Tulbagh, S. Afr. | I4 | 66 |
| Tulcán, Ec. | G4 | 84 |
| Tulcea, Rom. | D12 | 20 |
| Tulcea, co., Rom. | D12 | 20 |
| Tule, stm., Ca., U.S. | H6 | 124 |
| Tule, stm., Nic. | F10 | 92 |
| Tulelake, Ca., U.S. | C4 | 124 |
| Tulemalu Lake, l., N.T., Can. | D13 | 96 |
| Tule Valley, val., Ut., U.S. | E3 | 120 |
| T'ul'gan, Russia | G9 | 26 |
| Tuli, Zimb. | C9 | 66 |
| Tulia, Tx., U.S. | E5 | 116 |
| Tuling, China | J7 | 34 |
| Ṭūlkarm, W.B. | D4 | 50 |
| Tullahoma, Tn., U.S. | G10 | 114 |
| Tullamore, Austl. | I7 | 70 |
| Tullamore, Ire. | H6 | 8 |
| Tulle, Fr. | G8 | 14 |
| Tullibigeal, Austl. | I7 | 70 |
| Tulln, Aus. | G16 | 10 |
| Tullos, La., U.S. | K4 | 114 |
| Tullus, Sudan | L3 | 60 |
| Tully, Austl. | A6 | 70 |
| Tuloma, stm., Russia | G23 | 6 |
| Tulsa, Ok., U.S. | C11 | 116 |
| Tulsequah, B.C., Can. | E6 | 96 |
| Tuluá, Col. | E4 | 84 |
| Tuluksak, Ak., U.S. | F14 | 100 |
| Tulum, Mex. | G16 | 90 |
| Tulum, hist., Mex. | G16 | 90 |
| Tulumayo, stm., Peru | D4 | 82 |
| Tulun, Russia | G12 | 28 |
| Tulungagung, Indon. | k15 | 39a |
| Tuma, Russia | F23 | 22 |
| Tuma, stm., Nic. | D10 | 92 |
| Tumaco, Col. | G3 | 84 |
| Tumaco, Rada de, b., Col. | G3 | 84 |
| Tumatumari, Guy. | E13 | 84 |
| Tumba, Lac, l., D.R.C. | B3 | 58 |
| Tumbarumba, Austl. | J8 | 70 |
| Tumbes, Peru | I2 | 84 |
| Tumbes, dept., Peru | F2 | 84 |
| Tumbes (Puyango), stm., S.A. | I2 | 84 |
| Tumble Mountain, mtn., Mt., U.S. | E15 | 122 |
| Tumbler Ridge, B.C., Can. | B14 | 102 |
| Tumbotino, Russia | F26 | 22 |
| Tumby Bay, Austl. | J2 | 70 |
| Tumča, stm., Eur. | H21 | 6 |
| Tumen, China | A17 | 32 |
| T'umen', Russia | F11 | 26 |
| Tumen (Tuman-gang), stm., Asia | A18 | 32 |
| Tumeremo, Ven. | D12 | 84 |
| Tumiritinga, Braz. | E8 | 79 |
| Tumkūr, India | F4 | 46 |
| Tumos, stm., Nmb. | D2 | 66 |
| Tumpat, Malay. | K7 | 40 |
| Tumsar, India | B5 | 46 |
| Tumuc-Humac Mountains, mts., S.A. | C7 | 76 |
| Tumut, Austl. | J8 | 70 |
| Tumwater, Wa., U.S. | C3 | 122 |
| Tunago Lake, l., N.T., Can. | C32 | 100 |
| Tunari, Cerro, mtn., Bol. | G8 | 82 |
| Tunas de Zaza, Cuba | D5 | 94 |
| Tunaydah, Egypt | E5 | 60 |
| Tunçbilek, Tur. | J13 | 20 |
| Tunduru, Tan. | D7 | 58 |
| Tundža, stm., Eur. | G10 | 20 |
| T'ung, stm., Russia | E16 | 28 |
| Tungabhadra Reservoir, res., India | E4 | 46 |
| Tungaru, Sudan | L6 | 60 |
| Tungkang, Tai. | M9 | 34 |
| Tungla, Nic. | D10 | 92 |
| Tungsha Tao (Pratas Island), i., Tai. | G10 | 30 |
| Tungshih, Tai. | K9 | 34 |
| Tungsten, N.T., Can. | F30 | 100 |
| Tungurahua, prov., Ec. | H3 | 84 |
| Tuni, India | D7 | 46 |
| Tunia, stm., Col. | G6 | 84 |
| Tunica, Ms., U.S. | H6 | 114 |
| Tunis, Tun. | M5 | 18 |
| Tunis, Golfe de, b., Tun. | L5 | 18 |
| Tunisia (Tunisie), ctry., Afr. | B8 | 54 |
| Tunja, Col. | E6 | 84 |
| Tunkás, Mex. | G15 | 90 |
| Tunkhannock, Pa., U.S. | F11 | 108 |
| Tunnel Hill, Ga., U.S. | E1 | 112 |
| Tunnelton, W.V., U.S. | H7 | 108 |
| Tuntutuliak, Ak., U.S. | F13 | 100 |
| Tununak, Ak., U.S. | F12 | 100 |
| Tunungayualok Island, i., Nf., Can. | E20 | 96 |
| Tunuyán, Arg. | G4 | 80 |
| Tunuyán, stm., Arg. | G5 | 80 |
| Tunxi, China | F7 | 34 |
| Tuo, stm., China | E7 | 30 |
| Tuocheng, China | K4 | 34 |
| Tuokusidawan Ling, mtn., China | B11 | 44 |
| Tuolumne, Ca., U.S. | G5 | 124 |
| Tuolumne, stm., Ca., U.S. | G5 | 124 |
| Tupã, Braz. | F3 | 79 |
| Tupaciguara, Braz. | E4 | 79 |
| Tupana, stm., Braz. | J12 | 84 |
| Tupanciretã, Braz. | E12 | 80 |
| Tuparro, stm., Col. | E8 | 84 |
| Tupelo, Ms., U.S. | H8 | 114 |
| Tupelo, Ok., U.S. | E10 | 116 |
| Tupinambarana, Ilha, i., Braz. | I14 | 84 |
| Tupi Paulista, Braz. | F3 | 79 |
| Tupiraçaba, Braz. | C4 | 79 |
| Tupiza, Bol. | I9 | 82 |
| Tupper, B.C., Can. | B14 | 102 |
| Tupper Lake, N.Y., U.S. | C12 | 108 |
| Tupungato, Arg. | G4 | 80 |
| Tupungato, Cerro, mtn., S.A. | G4 | 80 |
| Túquerres, Col. | G4 | 84 |
| Tura, India | H14 | 44 |
| Tura, stm., Russia | F10 | 26 |
| Turabah, Sau. Ar. | D2 | 47 |
| Ṭurayf, Sau. Ar. | F5 | 48 |
| Turbaco, Col. | B5 | 84 |
| Turbacz, mtn., Pol. | F20 | 10 |
| Turbat, Pak. | I17 | 48 |
| Turbo, Col. | C4 | 84 |
| Turda, Rom. | C7 | 20 |
| Turdej, Russia | H21 | 22 |
| Turek, Pol. | C18 | 10 |
| Turfan see Turpan, China | C4 | 30 |
| Turfan Depression see Turpan Pendi, depr., China | C4 | 30 |
| Turgaj, Kaz. | H10 | 26 |
| Turgaj, stm., Kaz. | H10 | 26 |
| Turgajskaja ložbina, val., Kaz. | G10 | 26 |
| Turgajskoje plato, plat., Kaz. | G10 | 26 |
| Turginovo, Russia | E19 | 22 |
| Turgoš, Russia | B18 | 22 |
| Turgutlu, Tur. | K11 | 20 |
| Türi, Est. | C8 | 22 |
| Turia, stm., Spain | F11 | 16 |
| Turimiquire, Cerro, mtn., Ven. | B11 | 84 |
| Turin, Ab., Can. | H22 | 102 |
| Turin see Torino, Italy | D2 | 18 |
| Turinsk, Russia | F10 | 26 |
| Turka, Ukr. | F23 | 10 |
| Turkestan, Kaz. | I11 | 26 |
| Túrkeve, Hung. | H20 | 10 |
| Turkey, Tx., U.S. | E6 | 116 |
| Turkey (Türkiye), ctry., Asia | H15 | 4 |
| Turkey, stm., Ia., U.S. | H4 | 110 |
| Turkey Creek, stm., Ne., U.S. | K10 | 118 |
| Turkish Republic of Northern Cyprus see Cyprus, North, ctry., Asia | H14 | 4 |
| Turkmenistan, ctry., Asia | I9 | 26 |
| Turkmeniya see Turkmenistan, ctry., Asia | I9 | 26 |
| Turks and Caicos Islands, dep., N.A. | D9 | 94 |
| Turks Island Passage, strt., T./C. Is. | D9 | 94 |
| Turks Islands, is., T./C. Is. | D9 | 94 |
| Turku (Åbo), Fin. | K18 | 6 |
| Turley, Ok., U.S. | C11 | 116 |
| Turlock, Ca., U.S. | G5 | 124 |
| Turmalina, Braz. | D7 | 79 |
| Turnagain, stm., B.C., Can. | G31 | 100 |
| Turnagain Arm, b., Ak., U.S. | F20 | 100 |
| Turneffe Islands, is., Belize | I16 | 90 |
| Turner, Mt., U.S. | B17 | 122 |
| Turner, Or., U.S. | F3 | 122 |
| Turners Falls, Ma., U.S. | E14 | 108 |
| Turner Valley, Ab., Can. | G20 | 102 |
| Turnhout, Bel. | F6 | 12 |
| Türnitz, Aus. | H15 | 10 |
| Turnor Lake, l., Sk., Can. | B6 | 104 |
| Turnu Măgurele, Rom. | F8 | 20 |
| Turon, Ks., U.S. | N9 | 118 |
| Turpan, China | C4 | 30 |
| Turpan Pendi, depr., China | C4 | 30 |
| Turquino, Pico, mtn., Cuba | E6 | 94 |
| Turrell, Ar., U.S. | G6 | 114 |
| Turrialba, C.R. | H11 | 92 |
| Turrialba, Volcán, vol., C.R. | G11 | 92 |
| Turriff, Scot., U.K. | D11 | 8 |
| Turrubares, Cerro, mtn., C.R. | H10 | 92 |
| Turtle, stm., Mb., Can. | G15 | 104 |
| Turtle, stm., On., Can. | I22 | 104 |
| Turtle Creek, N.B., Can. | G9 | 106 |
| Turtle-Flambeau Flowage, res., Wi., U.S. | D5 | 110 |
| Turtleford, Sk., Can. | E6 | 104 |
| Turtle Lake, N.D., U.S. | D7 | 118 |
| Turtle Lake, Wi., U.S. | E3 | 110 |
| Turtle Lake, l., Sk., Can. | E6 | 104 |
| Turtle Mountain, hill, Mb., Can. | I14 | 104 |
| Turtle Mountain Provincial Park, Mb., Can. | I14 | 104 |
| Turu, stm., Russia | D12 | 28 |
| Turuchan, stm., Russia | D9 | 28 |
| Turun-Porin lääni, prov., Fin. | K18 | 6 |
| Turvo, Braz. | E14 | 80 |
| Turvo, stm., Braz. | D3 | 79 |
| Turvo, stm., Braz. | F4 | 79 |
| Tusas, Rio, stm., N.M., U.S. | H10 | 120 |
| Tuscaloosa, Al., U.S. | I9 | 114 |
| Tuscany see Toscana, prov., Italy | F5 | 18 |
| Tuscarora Mountain, mtn., Pa., U.S. | G9 | 108 |
| Tuscarora Mountains, mts., Nv., U.S. | D9 | 124 |
| Tuscola, Il., U.S. | C8 | 114 |
| Tuscola, Tx., U.S. | G7 | 116 |
| Tuscumbia, Al., U.S. | H9 | 114 |
| Tuscumbia, Mo., U.S. | D4 | 114 |
| Tuskegee, Al., U.S. | J11 | 114 |
| Tustumena Lake, l., Ak., U.S. | F19 | 100 |
| Tutajev, Russia | D22 | 22 |
| Tutang, China | F5 | 34 |
| Tuticorin, India | H5 | 46 |
| Tutóia, Braz. | D10 | 76 |
| Tutrakan, Bul. | E10 | 20 |
| Tuttle, N.D., U.S. | D8 | 118 |
| Tuttle, Ok., U.S. | D9 | 116 |
| Tuttle Creek Lake, res., Ks., U.S. | L11 | 118 |
| Tutupaca, Volcán, vol., Peru | G6 | 82 |
| Tutwiler, Ms., U.S. | H6 | 114 |
| Tuva, state, Russia | G16 | 26 |
| Tuvalu, ctry., Oc. | I21 | 126 |
| Ṭuwayq, Jabal, mts., Sau. Ar. | D4 | 47 |
| Tuxford, Sk., Can. | H9 | 104 |
| Tuxpan, Mex. | G7 | 90 |
| Tuxpan, Mex. | G11 | 90 |
| Tuxtepec, Mex. | H11 | 90 |
| Tuxtla Gutiérrez, Mex. | I13 | 90 |
| Tuy, stm., Ven. | B9 | 84 |
| Tuy An, Viet. | H10 | 40 |
| Tuyen Quang, Viet. | D8 | 40 |
| Tuy Hoa, Viet. | H10 | 40 |
| Tuz Gölü, l., Tur. | H14 | 4 |
| Ṭūz Khurmātū, Iraq | D8 | 48 |
| Tuzla, Bos. | E2 | 20 |
| Tuzly, Ukr. | D14 | 20 |
| Tver' (Kalinin), Russia | E18 | 22 |
| Tweed, On., Can. | F18 | 110 |
| Tweed Heads, Austl. | G10 | 70 |
| Tweedsmuir Provincial Park, B.C., Can. | D8 | 102 |
| Twee Rivieren, S. Afr. | F5 | 66 |
| Twelve Mile Lake, l., Sk., Can. | I8 | 104 |
| Twentynine Palms, Ca., U.S. | J9 | 124 |
| Twillingate, Nf., Can. | C19 | 106 |
| Twin Bridges, Mt., U.S. | E13 | 122 |
| Twin City, Ga., U.S. | G4 | 112 |
| Twin Falls, Id., U.S. | H11 | 122 |
| Twin Lakes, Ga., U.S. | I3 | 112 |
| Twin Lakes, Wi., U.S. | H7 | 110 |
| Twinsburg, Oh., U.S. | F5 | 108 |
| Twin Valley, Mn., U.S. | D11 | 118 |
| Twisp, Wa., U.S. | B5 | 122 |
| Twitya, stm., N.T., Can. | D30 | 100 |
| Twofold Bay, b., Austl. | K8 | 70 |
| Two Harbors, Mn., U.S. | C4 | 110 |
| Two Hills, Ab., Can. | D23 | 102 |
| Two Medicine, stm., Mt., U.S. | B13 | 122 |
| Two River Lake, l., On., Can. | E23 | 104 |
| Two Rivers, Wi., U.S. | F8 | 110 |
| Tyachiv, Ukr. | A7 | 20 |
| Tybee Island, Ga., U.S. | G6 | 112 |
| Tychy, Pol. | E18 | 10 |
| Tye, Tx., U.S. | G7 | 116 |
| Tygh Valley, Or., U.S. | E4 | 122 |
| Tyler, Mn., U.S. | G11 | 118 |
| Tyler, Tx., U.S. | G11 | 116 |
| Tylertown, Ms., U.S. | K6 | 114 |
| Tym, stm., Russia | E8 | 28 |
| Tyndall, S.D., U.S. | I10 | 118 |
| Tyndinskij, Russia | F16 | 28 |
| Tyne, stm., Eng., U.K. | G11 | 8 |
| Tynemouth, Eng., U.K. | F12 | 8 |
| Týn nad Vltavou, Czech Rep. | F14 | 10 |
| Tyonek, Ak., U.S. | F19 | 100 |
| Tyre see Ṣūr, Leb. | B4 | 50 |
| Tyrma, Russia | G18 | 28 |
| Tyrone, Ok., U.S. | C5 | 116 |
| Tyrone, Pa., U.S. | G8 | 108 |
| Tyrrell, Lake, l., Austl. | J5 | 70 |
| Tyrrhenian Sea (Mare Tirreno), Eur. | I7 | 18 |
| Tysa (Tisa) (Tisza), stm., Eur. | A8 | 20 |
| Tytuvėnai, Lith. | F6 | 22 |
| Ty Ty, Ga., U.S. | H3 | 112 |
| Tzaneen, S. Afr. | D10 | 66 |
| Tzucacab, Mex. | G15 | 90 |

## U

| Name | Map Ref. | Page |
|---|---|---|
| Uatumã, stm., Braz. | I13 | 84 |
| Uaupés (Vaupés), stm., S.A. | G9 | 84 |
| Uaxactún, hist., Guat. | I15 | 90 |
| Ubá, Braz. | F7 | 79 |
| Ubaitaba, Braz. | C9 | 79 |
| Ubangi (Oubangui), stm., Afr. | H10 | 54 |
| Ubatã, Braz. | C9 | 79 |
| Ubaté, Col. | E6 | 84 |
| Ubatuba, Braz. | G6 | 79 |
| Ubayyiḍ, Wādī al-, val., Asia | B11 | 60 |
| Ube, Japan | N6 | 36 |
| Úbeda, Spain | G8 | 16 |
| Uberaba, Braz. | E5 | 79 |
| Uberaba, stm., Braz. | E4 | 79 |
| Uberaba, Lagoa, l., S.A. | G13 | 82 |
| Uberlândia, Braz. | E4 | 79 |
| Ubiaja, Nig. | H13 | 64 |
| Ubly, Mi., U.S. | G13 | 110 |
| Ubon Ratchathani, Thai. | G8 | 40 |
| Ubundu, D.R.C. | B5 | 58 |
| Ucacha, Arg. | G7 | 80 |
| Uč-Adži, Turk. | B17 | 48 |
| Ucar, Azer. | A9 | 48 |
| Ucayali, dept., Peru | C4 | 82 |
| Ucayali, stm., Peru | A4 | 82 |
| Uchi Lake, On., Can. | G22 | 104 |
| Uchiura-wan, b., Japan | e15 | 36a |
| Uchiza, Peru | C3 | 82 |
| Uchoa, Braz. | F4 | 79 |
| Ucholovo, Russia | H23 | 22 |
| Uchta, Russia | E8 | 26 |
| Uchtoma, Russia | A21 | 22 |
| Uckermark, reg., Ger. | B13 | 10 |
| Ucluelet, B.C., Can. | I9 | 102 |
| Ucon, Id., U.S. | G14 | 122 |
| Uda, stm., Russia | G18 | 28 |
| Udagamandalam, India | G4 | 46 |
| Udaipur, India | H5 | 44 |
| Udall, Ks., U.S. | N10 | 118 |
| Udamalpet, India | G4 | 46 |
| Udaquiola, Arg. | I9 | 80 |
| Udaypur, Nepal | G12 | 44 |
| Udbina, Cro. | E10 | 18 |
| Uddevalla, Swe. | L12 | 6 |
| Udgīr, India | C4 | 46 |
| Udine, Italy | C8 | 18 |
| Udmurtia see Udmurtija, state, Russia | F8 | 26 |
| Udmurtija, state, Russia | F8 | 26 |
| Udoml'a, Russia | D18 | 22 |
| Udon Thani, Thai. | F7 | 40 |
| Udskaja guba, b., Russia | G19 | 28 |
| Udupi, India | F3 | 46 |
| Ueckermünde, Ger. | B14 | 10 |
| Ueda, Japan | K13 | 36 |
| Uelzen, Ger. | C10 | 10 |
| Ueno, Japan | M11 | 36 |
| Uetersen, Ger. | B9 | 10 |
| Ufa, Russia | G9 | 26 |
| Uffenheim, Ger. | F10 | 10 |
| Ufra, Turk. | A12 | 48 |
| Ugab, stm., Nmb. | C1 | 66 |
| Ugāle, Lat. | D5 | 22 |
| Uganda, ctry., Afr. | A6 | 58 |
| Ughaybish, Sudan | L6 | 60 |
| Ugie, S. Afr. | H9 | 66 |
| Uglegorsk, Russia | H20 | 28 |
| Uglič, Russia | D21 | 22 |
| Uglovka, Russia | C16 | 22 |
| Ugodskij Zavod, Russia | F19 | 22 |
| Ugoma, mtn., D.R.C. | B5 | 58 |
| Ugra, Russia | G17 | 22 |
| Uh (Uzh), stm., Eur. | G22 | 10 |
| Uha-dong, N. Kor. | C13 | 32 |
| Uherské Hradiště, Czech Rep. | F17 | 10 |
| Uherský Brod, Czech Rep. | F17 | 10 |
| Uhlenhorst, Nmb. | D3 | 66 |
| Uhlman Lake, l., Mb., Can. | B16 | 104 |
| Uhrichsville, Oh., U.S. | G5 | 108 |
| Uíge, Ang. | C3 | 58 |
| Ŭijŏngbu, S. Kor. | F15 | 32 |
| Ŭiju, N. Kor. | C12 | 32 |
| Uil, stm., Kaz. | H8 | 26 |
| Uinebona, stm., Ven. | E11 | 84 |
| Uinta, stm., Ut., U.S. | D6 | 120 |
| Uinta Mountains, mts., Ut., U.S. | D6 | 120 |
| Ŭisŏng, S. Kor. | G16 | 32 |
| Uitenhage, S. Afr. | I7 | 66 |
| Uithoorn, Neth. | D6 | 12 |
| Uj, stm., Asia | G10 | 26 |
| Ujandina, stm., Russia | D20 | 28 |
| Ujar, Russia | F16 | 26 |
| Ujarrás, hist., C.R. | H11 | 92 |
| Ujemskij, Russia | I27 | 6 |
| Újfehértó, Hung. | H21 | 10 |
| Uji-guntō, is., Japan | p4 | 37b |
| Ujiji, Tan. | B5 | 58 |
| Ujjain, India | I6 | 44 |
| 'Ujmān, U.A.E. | B9 | 47 |
| Ujungkulon National Park, Indon. | j12 | 39a |
| Ujungpandang, Indon. | G6 | 38 |
| Ukiah, Ca., U.S. | E2 | 124 |
| Ukiah, Or., U.S. | E7 | 122 |
| Ukmergė, Lith. | F7 | 22 |
| Ukraine, ctry., Eur. | F14 | 4 |
| Ula, Bela. | F12 | 22 |
| Ulaanbaatar, Mong. | B8 | 30 |
| Ulaangom, Mong. | B5 | 30 |
| Ulan, Austl. | I8 | 70 |
| Ulan Bator see Ulaanbaatar, Mong. | B8 | 30 |
| Ulang, stm., Nic. | C11 | 92 |
| Ulan-Ude, Russia | G13 | 28 |
| Ułazów, Pol. | E23 | 10 |
| Ulchin, S. Kor. | G17 | 32 |
| Ulcinj, Yugo. | H3 | 20 |
| Ulco, S. Afr. | G7 | 66 |
| Ulcumayo, Peru | D4 | 82 |
| Uldz, stm., Asia | H14 | 28 |
| Ulen, Mn., U.S. | D11 | 118 |
| Ulhāsnagar, India | C2 | 46 |
| Uliastaj, Mong. | B6 | 30 |
| Uljanovka, Russia | B13 | 22 |
| Uljanovsk, Russia | G7 | 26 |
| Ulladulla, Austl. | J9 | 70 |
| Ullapool, Scot., U.K. | D8 | 8 |
| Ullin, Il., U.S. | E7 | 114 |
| Ulm, Ger. | G10 | 10 |
| Ulm, Mt., U.S. | C14 | 122 |
| Ulmarra, Austl. | G10 | 70 |
| Ulongué, Moz. | D6 | 58 |
| Ulrum, Neth. | B9 | 12 |
| Ulsan, S. Kor. | H17 | 32 |
| Ulster, hist. reg., Eur. | G6 | 8 |
| Ultraoriental, Cordillera (Serra do Divisor), mts., S.A. | C5 | 82 |
| Ulu, Russia | E17 | 28 |
| Ulúa, stm., Hond. | B6 | 92 |
| Ulubey, Tur. | K13 | 20 |
| Ulukışla, Tur. | C3 | 48 |
| Ulungur, stm., China | B4 | 30 |
| Ulungur Hu, l., China | B4 | 30 |
| Uluru National Park, Austl. | E6 | 68 |
| Ulverstone, Austl. | M7 | 70 |
| Ul'yanovka, Ukr. | A14 | 20 |
| Ulysses, Ks., U.S. | N6 | 118 |
| Ulysses, Ne., U.S. | J10 | 118 |
| Ulzë, Alb. | H3 | 20 |
| Umán, Mex. | G15 | 90 |
| Uman', Ukr. | H4 | 26 |
| Umari, stm., Braz. | B9 | 82 |
| Umarkot, Pak. | H3 | 44 |
| Umatilla, Fl., U.S. | K5 | 112 |
| Umatilla, Or., U.S. | E6 | 122 |
| Umatilla, stm., Or., U.S. | E6 | 122 |
| Umbertide, Italy | F7 | 18 |
| Umboi Island, i., Pap. N. Gui. | m16 | 68a |
| Umbrail, Pass, Eur. | E13 | 13 |
| Umbria, prov., Italy | G7 | 18 |
| Umbuzero, ozero, l., Russia | H24 | 6 |
| Umeå, Swe. | J17 | 6 |
| Umfreville Lake, l., On., Can. | H20 | 104 |
| Umfuli, stm., Zimb. | A9 | 66 |
| Umhlanga Rocks, S. Afr. | G10 | 66 |
| Umkomaas, S. Afr. | H10 | 66 |
| Umm al-Birak, Sau. Ar. | C1 | 47 |
| Umm al-Qaywayn, U.A.E. | B9 | 47 |
| Umm al-Qiṭṭayn, Jord. | D7 | 50 |
| Umm Badr, Sudan | J4 | 60 |
| Umm Dabbī, Sudan | J6 | 60 |
| Umm Dhibbān, Sudan | J5 | 60 |
| Umm Digulgulaya, Sudan | L3 | 60 |
| Umm Durmān (Omdurman), Sudan | J7 | 60 |
| Umm el Fahm, Isr. | C4 | 50 |
| Umm Jamālah, Sudan | L5 | 60 |
| Umm Kaddādah, Sudan | K4 | 60 |
| Umm Kuwaykah, Sudan | K7 | 60 |
| Umm Lajj, Sau. Ar. | I4 | 48 |
| Umm Mirdi, Sudan | H7 | 60 |
| Umm Qantur, Sudan | J6 | 60 |
| Umm Qaṣr, Iraq | F9 | 48 |
| Umm Quṣayr, Jord. | E5 | 50 |
| Umm Ruwābah, Sudan | K6 | 60 |
| Umm Sayyālah, Sudan | J6 | 60 |
| Umm Shalīl, Sudan | L2 | 60 |
| Umm Shuṭūr, Sudan | N7 | 60 |
| Umm Walad, Syria | C6 | 50 |
| Um'ot, Russia | I25 | 22 |
| Um'ot, Russia | G25 | 22 |
| Umpqua, stm., Or., U.S. | G2 | 122 |
| Umred, India | B5 | 46 |
| Umreth, India | I5 | 44 |
| Ŭmsŏng, S. Kor. | G15 | 32 |
| Umtata, S. Afr. | H9 | 66 |
| Umtentweni, S. Afr. | H10 | 66 |
| Umuahia, Nig. | I13 | 64 |
| Umuarama, Braz. | G2 | 79 |
| Umzinto, S. Afr. | H10 | 66 |
| Una, Braz. | C9 | 79 |
| Unadilla, Ga., U.S. | G3 | 112 |
| Unadilla, N.Y., U.S. | E11 | 108 |
| Unadilla, stm., N.Y., U.S. | E11 | 108 |
| Unaí, Braz. | D5 | 79 |
| Unalakleet, Ak., U.S. | E14 | 100 |
| Unalaska, Ak., U.S. | J11 | 100 |
| Unare, stm., Ven. | C10 | 84 |
| 'Unayzah, Sau. Ar. | H7 | 48 |
| 'Unayzah, Jabal, mtn., Asia | E5 | 48 |
| 'Unayzah, Jabal, mtn., Jord. | G5 | 50 |
| Uncia, Bol. | H8 | 82 |
| Uncompahgre, stm., Co., U.S. | F9 | 120 |
| Uncompahgre Peak, mtn., Co., U.S. | F9 | 120 |
| Uncompahgre Plateau, plat., Co., U.S. | F8 | 120 |
| Underwood, N.D., U.S. | D6 | 118 |
| Undva nina, c., Est. | C4 | 22 |
| Uneča, Russia | I15 | 22 |
| Uneiuxi, stm., Braz. | H10 | 84 |
| Ungarie, Austl. | I7 | 70 |
| Ungava, Péninsule d', pen., P.Q., Can. | E18 | 96 |
| Ungava Bay, b., Can. | E19 | 96 |
| Unggi, N. Kor. | A18 | 32 |
| União, Braz. | D10 | 76 |
| União da Vitória, Braz. | D13 | 80 |
| União dos Palmares, Braz. | E11 | 76 |
| Unicoi, Tn., U.S. | C4 | 112 |
| Unimak Island, i., Ak., U.S. | I12 | 100 |
| Unimak Pass, strt., Ak., U.S. | I12 | 100 |
| Unini, stm., Braz. | H12 | 84 |
| Unión, Arg. | H6 | 80 |
| Unión, C.R. | I11 | 92 |
| Union, Ia., U.S. | H2 | 110 |
| Union, La., U.S. | L6 | 114 |
| Union, Mo., U.S. | D5 | 114 |
| Union, Ms., U.S. | J7 | 114 |
| Union, N.J., U.S. | G12 | 108 |
| Union, Or., U.S. | E8 | 122 |
| Unión, Para. | C10 | 80 |
| Union, S.C., U.S. | E5 | 112 |
| Union, Wa., U.S. | C2 | 122 |
| Union, W.V., U.S. | B6 | 112 |
| Union Bay, B.C., Can. | H10 | 102 |
| Union City, Ga., U.S. | F2 | 112 |
| Union City, In., U.S. | B11 | 114 |
| Union City, Mi., U.S. | H10 | 110 |
| Union City, Oh., U.S. | G2 | 108 |
| Union City, Pa., U.S. | F7 | 108 |
| Union City, Tn., U.S. | F7 | 114 |
| Unión de Reyes, Cuba | C4 | 94 |
| Unión de Tula, Mex. | H7 | 90 |
| Union Gap, Wa., U.S. | D5 | 122 |
| Union Grove, Wi., U.S. | H7 | 110 |
| Union Park, Fl., U.S. | K5 | 112 |
| Union Point, Ga., U.S. | F3 | 112 |
| Union Springs, Al., U.S. | J11 | 114 |
| Union Springs, N.Y., U.S. | E10 | 108 |
| Uniontown, Al., U.S. | J9 | 114 |
| Uniontown, Ky., U.S. | E9 | 114 |
| Uniontown, Pa., U.S. | H7 | 108 |
| Unionville, Mi., U.S. | G12 | 110 |
| Unionville, Mo., U.S. | B3 | 114 |
| Unipouheos Indian Reserve, Ab., Can. | E4 | 104 |
| United, Pa., U.S. | G7 | 108 |
| United Arab Emirates (Al-Imārāt al-'Arabīyah al-Muttaḥidah), ctry., Asia | E5 | 42 |
| United Arab Republic see Egypt, ctry., Afr. | C7 | 56 |
| United Kingdom, ctry., Eur. | E7 | 4 |
| United States, ctry., N.A. | D7 | 98 |
| Unity, Sk., Can. | F5 | 104 |
| Universal City, Tx., U.S. | J8 | 116 |
| University, Ms., U.S. | H7 | 114 |
| University City, Mo., U.S. | D6 | 114 |
| University Park, N.M., U.S. | L10 | 120 |
| University Park, Tx., U.S. | G10 | 116 |
| Unjha, India | I5 | 44 |
| Uno, Canal Numero, Arg. | I10 | 80 |
| Ŭnp'a, N. Kor. | E13 | 32 |
| Unquillo, Arg. | F6 | 80 |
| Ŭnsan, N. Kor. | D14 | 32 |
| Unterterzen, Switz. | D11 | 13 |
| Unterwalden, state, Switz. | E9 | 13 |
| Unuli Horog, China | C14 | 44 |
| Unža, Russia | C27 | 22 |
| Unža, stm., Russia | D26 | 22 |
| Uozu, Japan | K12 | 36 |
| Upala, C.R. | G9 | 92 |
| Upano, stm., Ec. | I3 | 84 |
| Upata, Ven. | C11 | 84 |
| Upemba, Lac, l., D.R.C. | C5 | 58 |
| Upham, N.D., U.S. | C7 | 118 |
| Upía, stm., Col. | E6 | 84 |
| Upington, S. Afr. | G5 | 66 |
| Upire, stm., Ven. | B8 | 84 |
| Upland, Ne., U.S. | K9 | 118 |
| Upleta, India | J4 | 44 |
| Upolu, i., W. Sam. | J22 | 126 |
| Upolu Point, c., Hi., U.S. | q18 | 125a |
| Upper Arlington, Oh., U.S. | G3 | 108 |
| Upper Arrow Lake, l., B.C., Can. | G17 | 102 |
| Upper Blackville, N.B., Can. | F8 | 106 |
| Upper Darby, Pa., U.S. | H11 | 108 |
| Upper Demerara-Berbice, prov., Guy. | D13 | 84 |
| Upper Fraser, B.C., Can. | C13 | 102 |
| Upper Goose Lake, l., On., Can. | G22 | 104 |
| Upper Hat Creek, B.C., Can. | G13 | 102 |
| Upper Humber, stm., Nf., Can. | C16 | 106 |
| Upper Iowa, stm., U.S. | G4 | 110 |
| Upper Island Cove, Nf., Can. | E20 | 106 |
| Upper Klamath Lake, l., Or., U.S. | H4 | 122 |
| Upper Lake, Ca., U.S. | E3 | 124 |
| Upper Liard, Yk., Can. | F30 | 100 |
| Upper Manitou Lake, l., On., Can. | I22 | 104 |
| Upper Musquodoboit, N.S., Can. | G11 | 106 |
| Upper Red Lake, l., Mn., U.S. | C13 | 118 |
| Upper Sandusky, Oh., U.S. | G3 | 108 |
| Upper Sheila, N.B., Can. | E9 | 106 |
| Upper Takutu-Upper Essequibo, prov., Guy. | F13 | 84 |
| Upper Windigo Lake, l., On., Can. | F23 | 104 |
| Uppsala, Swe. | L15 | 6 |
| Upsala see Uppsala, Swe. | L15 | 6 |
| Upstart, Cape, c., Austl. | B7 | 70 |
| Upton, Ky., U.S. | E11 | 114 |
| Upton, Wy., U.S. | G3 | 118 |
| Uquía, Cerro, mtn., Ven. | E11 | 84 |
| Urabá, Golfo de, b., Col. | C4 | 84 |
| Uracoa, Ven. | C11 | 84 |
| Uraj, Russia | E10 | 26 |
| Ural, stm. | H8 | 26 |
| Uralla, Austl. | H9 | 70 |
| Ural Mountains see Ural'skije gory, mts., Russia | E9 | 26 |
| Ural'sk, Kaz. | G8 | 26 |
| Ural'skije gory (Ural Mountains), mts., Russia | E9 | 26 |
| Urana, Austl. | J7 | 70 |
| Urandangi, Austl. | C3 | 70 |
| Urandi, Braz. | C7 | 79 |
| Urangan, Austl. | E10 | 70 |
| Urania, La., U.S. | K4 | 114 |
| Uranium City, Sk., Can. | E11 | 96 |
| Urariá, Paraná, mth., Braz. | I14 | 84 |
| Uraricaá, stm., Braz. | F11 | 84 |
| Uraricoera, Braz. | F12 | 84 |
| Uraricoera, stm., Braz. | F12 | 84 |
| Ura-T'ube, Taj. | J11 | 26 |
| Uravan, Co., U.S. | F8 | 120 |
| Urawa, Japan | L14 | 36 |
| Urbana, Ar., U.S. | I4 | 114 |
| Urbana, Il., U.S. | B8 | 114 |
| Urbana, Mo., U.S. | E3 | 114 |
| Urbana, Oh., U.S. | G3 | 108 |
| Urbandale, Ia., U.S. | A3 | 114 |
| Urbania, Italy | F7 | 18 |
| Urbino, Italy | F7 | 18 |
| Urcos, Peru | E6 | 82 |
| Urdinarrain, Arg. | G9 | 80 |
| Uré, Col. | D5 | 84 |
| Urėčča, Bela. | I10 | 22 |
| Urén, stm., C.R. | H11 | 92 |
| Ureña, Ven. | D6 | 84 |
| Ures, Mex. | C4 | 90 |
| Urgenč, Uzb. | I10 | 26 |
| Ürgüp, Tur. | B3 | 48 |
| Uri, state, Switz. | E10 | 13 |
| Uriah, Al., U.S. | K9 | 114 |
| Uriah, Mount, mtn., N.Z. | E3 | 72 |
| Uribante, stm., Ven. | D7 | 84 |
| Uribe, Col. | F5 | 84 |
| Uribia, Col. | B6 | 84 |
| Urich, Mo., U.S. | D2 | 114 |
| Urique, Mex. | D6 | 90 |
| Urique, stm., Mex. | D6 | 90 |
| Urituyacu, stm., Peru | J5 | 84 |
| Urla, Tur. | K10 | 20 |
| Urmia see Orūmīyeh, Iran | C8 | 48 |
| Uroševac, Yugo. | G5 | 20 |
| Urrao, Col. | D4 | 84 |
| Ursa, Il., U.S. | B5 | 114 |
| Uršel'skij, Russia | F23 | 22 |
| Urtigueira, Braz. | C13 | 80 |
| Uru, stm., Braz. | C4 | 79 |
| Uruaçu, Braz. | C4 | 79 |
| Uruana, Braz. | C4 | 79 |
| Uruapan del Progreso, Mex. | H8 | 90 |
| Urubamba, Peru | E5 | 82 |
| Urubamba, stm., Peru | D5 | 82 |
| Urubaxi, stm., Braz. | H10 | 84 |
| Urubu, stm., Braz. | I13 | 84 |
| Urucará, Braz. | I14 | 84 |
| Urucu, stm., Braz. | J10 | 84 |
| Uruçuca, Braz. | C9 | 79 |
| Urucuia, stm., Braz. | D6 | 79 |
| Urucurituba, Braz. | I14 | 84 |
| Uruguaiana, Braz. | E10 | 80 |
| Uruguay, ctry., S.A. | C5 | 78 |
| Uruguay (Uruguai), stm., S.A. | G9 | 80 |
| Urumchi see Ürümqi, China | C4 | 30 |
| Ürümqi, China | C4 | 30 |
| Urundel, Arg. | B6 | 80 |
| Urup, ostrov, i., Russia | H22 | 28 |
| Urupá, stm., Braz. | D10 | 82 |
| Urupadi, stm., Braz. | J14 | 84 |
| Urupês, Braz. | F4 | 79 |
| Ur'upinsk, Russia | G6 | 26 |
| Urussanga, Braz. | E14 | 80 |
| Urutaí, Braz. | D4 | 79 |
| Urutaú, Arg. | C7 | 80 |
| Uržum, Russia | F8 | 26 |
| Usa, Japan | N6 | 36 |
| Usa, stm., Russia | D9 | 26 |
| Ušačy, Bela. | F11 | 22 |
| Uşak, Tur. | K13 | 20 |
| Ušaki, Russia | B13 | 22 |
| Usakos, Nmb. | D2 | 66 |
| Usedom, i., Eur. | A14 | 10 |
| 'Usfān, Sau. Ar. | D1 | 47 |
| Ushant see Ouessant, Île d', i., Fr. | D1 | 14 |
| 'Ushayrah, Sau. Ar. | D2 | 47 |
| Ushuaia, Arg. | G3 | 78 |
| Usingen, Ger. | E8 | 10 |
| Usk, B.C., Can. | C6 | 102 |
| Usk, Wa., U.S. | B8 | 122 |
| Uslar, Ger. | D9 | 10 |
| Usman', Russia | I22 | 22 |
| Usolje-Sibirskoje, Russia | G12 | 28 |
| Usoro, Nig. | I13 | 64 |
| Uspallata, Arg. | G4 | 80 |
| Uspanapa, stm., Mex. | I12 | 90 |
| Ussuri (Wusuli), stm., Asia | B13 | 30 |
| Ussurijsk, Russia | I18 | 28 |
| Ustaritz, Fr. | I5 | 14 |
| Ust'-Barguzin, Russia | G13 | 28 |
| Ust'-Chorna, Ukr. | A7 | 20 |
| Ust'-Cil'ma, Russia | D8 | 26 |
| Ust'-Dolyssy, Russia | E12 | 22 |
| Uster, Switz. | D10 | 13 |
| Ust'-Ilimskoje vodochranilišče, res., Russia | F18 | 26 |
| Ústí nad Labem, Czech Rep. | E14 | 10 |
| Ústí nad Orlicí, Czech Rep. | F16 | 10 |
| Ust'-Išim, Russia | F12 | 26 |
| Ustje, Russia | D22 | 22 |
| Ustka, Pol. | A16 | 10 |
| Ust'-Kamčatsk, Russia | F24 | 28 |
| Ust'-Kamenogorsk, Kaz. | H8 | 28 |
| Ust'-Katav, Russia | G9 | 26 |
| Ust'-Koksa, Russia | G15 | 26 |
| Ust'-Kut, Russia | F13 | 28 |
| Ust'-Luga, Russia | B11 | 22 |
| Ust'-Nera, Russia | E20 | 28 |
| Uštobe, Kaz. | H13 | 26 |
| Ust'-Omčug, Russia | E21 | 28 |
| Ust'-Ordynskij, Russia | G12 | 28 |
| Ust'uckoje, Russia | C18 | 22 |
| Ust'urt, plato, plat., Asia | I9 | 26 |
| Ust'-Usa, Russia | D9 | 26 |
| Ust'užna, Russia | C19 | 22 |
| Usu, China | C3 | 30 |
| Usulután, El Sal. | D6 | 92 |
| Usumacinta, stm., N.A. | I14 | 90 |
| Ušumun, Russia | G17 | 28 |
| Utah, state, U.S. | D4 | 98 |
| Utah Lake, l., Ut., U.S. | D5 | 120 |
| Utapi, Nmb. | A2 | 66 |
| Utashinai, Japan | d17 | 36a |
| Ute, Ia., U.S. | I12 | 118 |
| Utembo, stm., Ang. | E4 | 58 |
| Utena, Lith. | F8 | 22 |
| Utete, Tan. | C7 | 58 |
| Uthai Thani, Thai. | G6 | 40 |
| Utiariti, Braz. | E12 | 82 |
| Utica, Ks., U.S. | M7 | 118 |
| Utica, Mi., U.S. | H12 | 110 |
| Utica, Ms., U.S. | J6 | 114 |
| Utica, Ne., U.S. | K10 | 118 |
| Utica, N.Y., U.S. | D11 | 108 |
| Utica, Oh., U.S. | G4 | 108 |
| Utiel, Spain | F10 | 16 |

| Name | Map Ref. | Page |
|---|---|---|
| Utikoomak Lake Indian Reserve, Ab., Can. | B19 | 102 |
| Utikuma Lake, l., Ab., Can. | B19 | 102 |
| Utila, Hond. | A8 | 92 |
| Utila, Isla de, i., Hond. | A8 | 92 |
| Utinga, stm., Braz. | B8 | 79 |
| Utique, Tun. | L5 | 18 |
| Uto, Japan | O5 | 36 |
| Utopia, Tx., U.S. | J7 | 116 |
| Utorgoš, Russia | C13 | 22 |
| Utrecht, Neth. | D7 | 12 |
| Utrecht, S. Afr. | F10 | 66 |
| Utrecht, prov., Neth. | D7 | 12 |
| Utrera, Spain | H6 | 16 |
| Utsunomiya, Japan | K14 | 36 |
| Uttaradit, Thai. | F6 | 40 |
| Uttar Pradesh, state, India | G9 | 44 |
| Utuado, P.R. | E11 | 94 |
| Uudenmaan lääni, prov., Fin. | K19 | 6 |
| Uusikaupunki (Nystad), Fin. | K17 | 6 |
| Uvá, Braz. | C3 | 79 |
| Uvá, stm., Col. | F8 | 84 |
| Uvalda, Ga., U.S. | F3 | 112 |
| Uvalde, Tx., U.S. | J7 | 116 |
| Uvarovičy, Bela. | I13 | 22 |
| Uvarovka, Russia | F18 | 22 |
| Uvarovo, Russia | J25 | 22 |
| Uvat, Russia | F11 | 26 |
| Uvinza, Tan. | C6 | 58 |
| Uvira, D.R.C. | B5 | 58 |
| Uvs nuur, l., Asia | A5 | 30 |
| Uwajima, Japan | N7 | 36 |
| Uwayl, Sudan | M4 | 60 |
| 'Uwaynāt, Jabal al-, mtn., Afr. | D5 | 56 |
| Uxbridge, On., Can. | F16 | 110 |
| Uxmal, hist., Mex. | G15 | 90 |
| Uyuni, Bol. | I8 | 82 |
| Uyuni, Salar de, pl., Bol. | I8 | 82 |
| Uzava, Lat. | D4 | 22 |
| Uzbekistan, ctry., Asia | I10 | 26 |
| Uzboj, stm., Turk. | B13 | 48 |
| Uzda, Bela. | H10 | 22 |
| Uzdin, Yugo. | D4 | 20 |
| Uzhhorod, Ukr. | H2 | 26 |
| Užice, Yugo. | F3 | 20 |
| Uzlovaja, Russia | H21 | 22 |
| Uzunköprü, Tur. | H10 | 20 |
| Užur, Russia | F9 | 28 |
| Užventis, Lith. | F5 | 22 |

## V

| Name | Map Ref. | Page |
|---|---|---|
| Vääksy, Fin. | K19 | 6 |
| Vaala, Fin. | I20 | 6 |
| Vaalserberg, mtn., Neth. | G9 | 12 |
| Vaalwater, S. Afr. | D9 | 66 |
| Vaanta (Vanda), Fin. | K19 | 6 |
| Vaasa (Vasa), Fin. | J17 | 6 |
| Vaasan lääni, prov., Fin. | J18 | 6 |
| Vabalninkas, Lith. | F7 | 22 |
| Vabkent, Uzb. | A18 | 48 |
| Vác, Hung. | H19 | 10 |
| Vaca, Bol. | H10 | 82 |
| Vača, Russia | F25 | 22 |
| Vacacaí, stm., Braz. | F11 | 80 |
| Vacaria, Braz. | E13 | 80 |
| Vacaria, stm., Braz. | D7 | 79 |
| Vacaria, Serra da, hills, Braz. | F1 | 79 |
| Vacaville, Ca., U.S. | F4 | 124 |
| Vaccarès, Étang de, b., Fr. | I11 | 14 |
| Vach, stm., Russia | E7 | 28 |
| Vache, Île à, i., Haiti | E8 | 94 |
| Vachš, stm., Taj. | J11 | 26 |
| Vacoas, Mrts. | v18 | 67c |
| Vadino, Russia | F16 | 22 |
| Vadodara, India | I5 | 44 |
| Vado Ligure, Italy | E3 | 18 |
| Vaduz, Liech. | E16 | 14 |
| Vaga, stm., Russia | E8 | 26 |
| Vågåmo, Nor. | K11 | 6 |
| Vágar, i., Faer. Is. | D8 | 6b |
| Váh, stm., Slvk. | G17 | 10 |
| Vaiden, Ms., U.S. | I7 | 114 |
| Vaihingen, Ger. | G8 | 10 |
| Väike-Maarja, Est. | B9 | 22 |
| Vail, Co., U.S. | E10 | 120 |
| Vail, Ia., U.S. | I12 | 118 |
| Vailly-sur-Aisne, Fr. | C10 | 14 |
| Vainode, Lat. | E4 | 22 |
| Vajgač, ostrov, i., Russia | C9 | 26 |
| Valais (Wallis), state, Switz. | F7 | 13 |
| Valašské Meziříčí, Czech Rep. | F17 | 10 |
| Valatie, N.Y., U.S. | E13 | 108 |
| Vâlcea, co., Rom. | E8 | 20 |
| Valcheta, Arg. | E3 | 78 |
| Valdagno, Italy | D6 | 18 |
| Valdaj Hills see Valdajskaja vozvyšennost', hills, Russia | D15 | 22 |
| Valdaj, Russia | D16 | 22 |
| Valdajskaja vozvyšennost', hills, Russia | D16 | 22 |
| Valdelândia, Braz. | C3 | 79 |
| Valdemārpils, Lat. | D5 | 22 |
| Valdepeñas, Spain | G8 | 16 |
| Valders, Wi., U.S. | F8 | 110 |
| Valdés, Península, pen., Arg. | E4 | 78 |
| Val-des-Bois, P.Q., Can. | B11 | 108 |
| Valdez, Ec. | D5 | 84 |
| Valdez, Ak., U.S. | F21 | 100 |
| Val-d'Isère, Fr. | G13 | 14 |
| Valdivia, Chile | D2 | 78 |
| Valdivia, Col. | D5 | 84 |
| Valdobbiadene, Italy | D7 | 18 |
| Val-d'Oise, dept., Fr. | C9 | 14 |
| Valdosta, Ga., U.S. | I3 | 112 |
| Vale, Or., U.S. | G8 | 122 |
| Valemount, B.C., Can. | E15 | 102 |
| Valença, Braz. | B9 | 79 |
| Valença, Port. | C3 | 16 |
| Valençay, Fr. | E8 | 14 |
| Valence, Fr. | H11 | 14 |
| Valencia, Hond. | C9 | 92 |
| Valencia, Spain | F11 | 16 |
| Valencia, Ven. | B8 | 84 |
| València, prov., Spain | F11 | 16 |
| València, Golfo de (g.), Spain | F11 | 16 |
| Valencia, Lago de, l., Ven. | B9 | 84 |
| Valencia de Alcántara, Spain | F4 | 16 |
| Valenciennes, Fr. | B10 | 14 |
| Valentine, Ne., U.S. | I7 | 118 |
| Valentine, Tx., U.S. | I2 | 116 |
| Valenza, Italy | D3 | 18 |
| Valera, Ven. | C7 | 84 |
| Valga, Est. | D9 | 22 |
| Valiente, Península, pen., Pan. | C2 | 84 |
| Valiente, Punta, c., Pan. | H13 | 92 |
| Valier, Mt., U.S. | B13 | 122 |
| Valjevo, Yugo. | E3 | 20 |
| Valka, Lat. | D9 | 22 |
| Valkininkas, Lith. | G7 | 22 |
| Valladolid, Ec. | J3 | 84 |
| Valladolid, Mex. | G15 | 90 |
| Valladolid, Spain | D7 | 16 |
| Valldal, Nor. | J10 | 6 |
| Valle, Lat. | E7 | 22 |
| Valle, Spain | B7 | 16 |
| Valle, dept., Hond. | D7 | 92 |
| Vallecitos, N.M., U.S. | H10 | 120 |
| Valle d'Aosta, prov., Italy | D2 | 18 |
| Valle de Guanape, Ven. | C10 | 84 |
| Valle de la Pascua, Ven. | C9 | 84 |
| Valle de Olivos, Mex. | D6 | 90 |
| Valle de Santiago, Mex. | G9 | 90 |
| Valle de Zaragoza, Mex. | E7 | 90 |
| Valle Edén, Ur. | F10 | 80 |
| Vallegrande, Bol. | H9 | 82 |
| Valle Hermoso, Arg. | F6 | 80 |
| Valle Hermoso, Mex. | E11 | 90 |
| Vallehermoso, Spain | o23 | 17b |
| Vallejo, Ca., U.S. | F3 | 124 |
| Vallenar, Chile | E3 | 80 |
| Valles Caldera, crat., N.M., U.S. | I10 | 120 |
| Valletta, Malta | N9 | 18 |
| Valley, Al., U.S. | J11 | 114 |
| Valley, Ne., U.S. | J11 | 118 |
| Valley, stm., Mb., Can. | G14 | 104 |
| Valley Bend, W.V., U.S. | I7 | 108 |
| Valley Center, Ks., U.S. | N10 | 118 |
| Valley City, N.D., U.S. | E10 | 118 |
| Valley Falls, Ks., U.S. | L12 | 118 |
| Valley Head, Al., U.S. | H11 | 114 |
| Valley Head, W.V., U.S. | I6 | 108 |
| Valley Mills, Tx., U.S. | H9 | 116 |
| Valley of the Kings, hist., Egypt | E7 | 60 |
| Valley Springs, S.D., U.S. | H11 | 118 |
| Valley Station, Ky., U.S. | D11 | 114 |
| Valleyview, Ab., Can. | B17 | 102 |
| Valley View, Tx., U.S. | F9 | 116 |
| Valliant, Ok., U.S. | E11 | 116 |
| Vallimanca, Arroyo, stm., Arg. | H8 | 80 |
| Vallorbe, Switz. | E5 | 13 |
| Valls, Spain | D13 | 16 |
| Val-Marie, Sk., Can. | I7 | 104 |
| Valmaseda, Spain | B8 | 16 |
| Valmiera, Lat. | D8 | 22 |
| Valognes, Fr. | C5 | 14 |
| Valongo, Port. | D3 | 16 |
| Valožyn, Bela. | G9 | 22 |
| Valpaços, Port. | D4 | 16 |
| Valparaíso, Braz. | F3 | 79 |
| Valparaíso, Chile | G3 | 80 |
| Valparaiso, Fl., U.S. | L10 | 114 |
| Valparaiso, In., U.S. | A9 | 114 |
| Valparaiso, Ne., U.S. | J11 | 118 |
| Valparaíso, prov., Chile | G3 | 80 |
| Valréas, Fr. | H11 | 14 |
| Valsbaai, b., S. Afr. | J4 | 66 |
| Valsetz, Or., U.S. | F2 | 122 |
| Valtimo, Fin. | J21 | 6 |
| Valverde del Camino, Spain | H5 | 16 |
| Van, Tur. | B7 | 48 |
| Van, Tx., U.S. | G11 | 116 |
| Van Alstyne, Tx., U.S. | F10 | 116 |
| Vananda, B.C., Can. | H10 | 102 |
| Van Buren, In., U.S. | G2 | 114 |
| Van Buren, Mo., U.S. | F5 | 114 |
| Vanč, Taj. | J12 | 26 |
| Vanceboro, Me., U.S. | B19 | 108 |
| Vanceburg, Ky., U.S. | I3 | 108 |
| Vancleave, Ms., U.S. | L8 | 114 |
| Vancouver, B.C., Can. | H11 | 102 |
| Vancouver, Wa., U.S. | E3 | 122 |
| Vancouver, Cape, c., Ak., U.S. | F12 | 100 |
| Vancouver, Cape, c., Austl. | G3 | 68 |
| Vancouver, Mount, mtn., N.A. | F25 | 100 |
| Vancouver Island, i., B.C., Can. | H9 | 102 |
| Vancouver Island Ranges, mts., B.C., Can. | H9 | 102 |
| Vandalia, Il., U.S. | D7 | 114 |
| Vandalia, Mo., U.S. | C5 | 114 |
| Vandalia, Oh., U.S. | H2 | 108 |
| Vandeckerckhove Lake, l., Mb., Can. | A13 | 104 |
| Vanderbijlpark, S. Afr. | F8 | 66 |
| Vanderbilt, Mi., U.S. | E11 | 110 |
| Vanderbilt, Tx., U.S. | K10 | 116 |
| Vandergrift, Pa., U.S. | G7 | 108 |
| Vanderhoof, B.C., Can. | C10 | 102 |
| Vanderlin Island, i., Austl. | C7 | 68 |
| Vandervoort, Ar., U.S. | H2 | 114 |
| Van Diemen Gulf, b., Austl. | B6 | 68 |
| Vändra, Est. | C8 | 22 |
| Vanegas, Mex. | F9 | 90 |
| Vänern, l., Swe. | L13 | 6 |
| Vänersborg, Swe. | L13 | 6 |
| Vangaindrano, Madag. | s22 | 67b |
| Van Gölü, l., Tur. | B7 | 48 |
| Vangsnes, Nor. | K10 | 6 |
| Vanguard, Sk., Can. | I7 | 104 |
| Van Horn, Tx., U.S. | H2 | 116 |
| Van Horne, Ia., U.S. | H3 | 110 |
| Vanier, On., Can. | B11 | 108 |
| Vanimo, Pap. N. Gui. | F11 | 38 |
| Vanino, Russia | H20 | 28 |
| Vänkleek Hill, On., Can. | B12 | 108 |
| Van Lear, Ky., U.S. | B4 | 112 |
| Vanndale, Ar., U.S. | G6 | 114 |
| Van Ninh, Viet. | H10 | 40 |
| Van Rees, Pegunungan, mts., Indon. | F10 | 38 |
| Vanrhynsdorp, S. Afr. | H4 | 66 |
| Vansant, Va., U.S. | B4 | 112 |
| Vansittart Island, i., N.T., Can. | C16 | 96 |
| Vansjoe, Russia | C19 | 22 |
| Vandesrus, S. Afr. | G3 | 66 |
| Vanua Levu, i., Fiji | J21 | 126 |
| Vanua, ctry., Oc. | J21 | 126 |
| Van Vleck, Tx., U.S. | J11 | 116 |
| Vanzylsrus, S. Afr. | F6 | 66 |
| Var, dept., Fr. | I13 | 14 |
| Var, stm., Fr. | I13 | 14 |
| Varaklāni, Lat. | E9 | 22 |
| Varallo, Italy | D3 | 18 |
| Varanasi (Benares), India | H10 | 44 |
| Varangerfjorden, Nor. | G22 | 6 |
| Varangerhalvøya, pen., Nor. | F21 | 6 |
| Varazdin, Cro. | C11 | 18 |
| Varazze, Italy | E3 | 18 |
| Varberg, Swe. | M13 | 6 |
| Vardaman, Ms., U.S. | I7 | 114 |
| Vardar (Axiós), stm., Eur. | H6 | 20 |
| Varde, Nor. | F22 | 6 |
| Varegovo, Russia | D22 | 22 |
| Varel, Ger. | B8 | 10 |
| Varena, Lith. | G7 | 22 |
| Vareš, Bos. | E2 | 20 |
| Varese, Italy | D3 | 18 |
| Vârfurile, Rom. | C6 | 20 |
| Varginha, Braz. | F6 | 79 |
| Varjão, Braz. | D4 | 79 |
| Varkaus, Fin. | J20 | 6 |
| Varna, Bul. | F11 | 20 |
| Varnsdorf, Czech Rep. | E14 | 10 |
| Värnamo, Swe. | M14 | 6 |
| Varnville, S.C., U.S. | G5 | 112 |
| Várpalota, Hung. | H18 | 10 |
| Värska, Est. | D10 | 22 |
| Várzea, Rio da, stm., Braz. | D12 | 80 |
| Várzea Grande, Braz. | F13 | 82 |
| Varzeão, Braz. | C14 | 80 |
| Vas, co., Hung. | H16 | 10 |
| Vasalemma, Est. | B7 | 22 |
| Vašhkivci, Ukr. | A11 | 20 |
| Vasilevo, Russia | D18 | 22 |
| Vasiliká, Grc. | I7 | 20 |
| Vasiljevskij Moch, Russia | D18 | 22 |
| Vasiljevskoje, Russia | E24 | 22 |
| Vaskelovo, Russia | A13 | 22 |
| Vaslui, Rom. | C11 | 20 |
| Vaslui, co., Rom. | C11 | 20 |
| Vass, N.C., U.S. | D7 | 112 |
| Vassar, Mi., U.S. | G12 | 110 |
| Västerås, Swe. | L15 | 6 |
| Västerbottens Län, co., Swe. | I15 | 6 |
| Västernorrlands Län, co., Swe. | J15 | 6 |
| Västervik, Swe. | M15 | 6 |
| Västmanlands Län, co., Swe. | L15 | 6 |
| Vasto, Italy | G9 | 18 |
| Vas'ugan, stm., Russia | F13 | 26 |
| Vas'uganje, sw., Russia | F7 | 28 |
| Vasvár, Hung. | H16 | 10 |
| Vatan, Fr. | E8 | 14 |
| Vatican City see Città del Vaticano, ctry., Eur. | H7 | 18 |
| V'atka, stm., Russia | F8 | 26 |
| Vatnajökull, Ice. | B5 | 6a |
| Vatneyri, Ice. | B2 | 6a |
| Vatomandry, Madag. | q23 | 67b |
| Vatra Dornei, Rom. | B9 | 20 |
| V'atskie Pol'any, Russia | F8 | 26 |
| V'attern, l., Swe. | L14 | 6 |
| Vaucluse, dept., Fr. | I12 | 14 |
| Vaucouleurs, Fr. | D12 | 14 |
| Vaud, state, Switz. | E6 | 13 |
| Vaughan, On., Can. | G16 | 110 |
| Vaughn, N.M., U.S. | J11 | 120 |
| Vaukavysk, Bela. | H7 | 22 |
| Vaupés, ter., Col. | G7 | 84 |
| Vaupés (Uaupés), stm., S.A. | G7 | 84 |
| Vauréal, Chute, wtfl, P.Q., Can. | C11 | 106 |
| Vauvert, Fr. | I11 | 14 |
| Vauxhall, Ab., Can. | G22 | 102 |
| Vavatenina, Madag. | p23 | 67b |
| Vavoua, C. Iv. | H6 | 64 |
| Växjö, Swe. | M14 | 6 |
| Vazante, Braz. | E5 | 79 |
| Vazante Grande, stm., Braz. | H13 | 82 |
| V'azemskij, Russia | H18 | 22 |
| V'az'ma, Russia | F17 | 22 |
| V'azniki, Russia | E25 | 22 |
| Veazie, Me., U.S. | C18 | 108 |
| Veblen, S.D., U.S. | F10 | 118 |
| Vecht, stm., Eur. | C9 | 12 |
| Vechta, Ger. | C8 | 10 |
| Vecsés, Hung. | H19 | 10 |
| Vedea, Rom. | E9 | 20 |
| Vedea, stm., Rom. | E8 | 20 |
| Vedia, Arg. | H8 | 80 |
| Veedersburg, In., U.S. | B9 | 114 |
| Veendam, Neth. | B10 | 12 |
| Veenendaal, Neth. | D8 | 12 |
| Vega, Tx., U.S. | D4 | 116 |
| Veghel, Neth. | E8 | 12 |
| Vegreville, Ab., Can. | D22 | 102 |
| Veguita, N.M., U.S. | J10 | 120 |
| Veinticinco de Mayo, Arg. | H8 | 80 |
| Veinticinco de Mayo, Arg. | H10 | 80 |
| Veintiocho de Mayo, Ec. | I3 | 84 |
| Veintisiete de Abril, C.R. | G9 | 92 |
| Vejer de la Frontera, Spain | I6 | 16 |
| Vejle, Den. | N11 | 6 |
| Velardeña, Mex. | E8 | 90 |
| Velas, Cabo, c., C.R. | G9 | 92 |
| Velázquez, Ur. | H11 | 80 |
| Velddrif, S. Afr. | I4 | 66 |
| Velden, Ger. | G12 | 10 |
| Veldhoven, Neth. | F7 | 12 |
| Velet'ma, Russia | F25 | 22 |
| Velez, Col. | E5 | 84 |
| Velez de la Gomera, Peñón de, i., Sp. N. Afr. | J7 | 16 |
| Velez-Málaga, Spain | I7 | 16 |
| Vel'gija, Russia | C16 | 22 |
| Velhas, Rio das, stm., Braz. | D6 | 79 |
| Velika, stm., Russia | E26 | 28 |
| Velika Morava, stm., Yugo. | E5 | 20 |
| Velika Plana, Yugo. | E5 | 20 |
| Velikije Luki, Russia | E13 | 22 |
| Velikij Ust'ug, Russia | E7 | 26 |
| Velikodvorskij, Russia | F23 | 22 |
| Veliko Gradište, Yugo. | E5 | 20 |
| Velikoje, Russia | D22 | 22 |
| Veliko Târnovo, Bul. | F9 | 20 |
| Velingara, Sen. | F4 | 54 |
| Veliž, Russia | F14 | 22 |
| Velletri, Italy | H7 | 18 |
| Vellore, India | F5 | 46 |
| Velma, Ok., U.S. | E9 | 116 |
| Velp, Neth. | D8 | 12 |
| Vel'sk, Russia | E6 | 26 |
| Velten, Ger. | C13 | 10 |
| Velva, N.D., U.S. | C7 | 118 |
| Velykyj Bereznyj, Ukr. | A11 | 20 |
| Velyka Mykhaylivka, Ukr. | B13 | 20 |
| Velyki Luchky, Ukr. | A6 | 20 |
| Velykyy Bychkiv, Ukr. | B8 | 20 |
| Velykoploske, Ukr. | B13 | 20 |
| Venadillo, Col. | E5 | 84 |
| Venado, Isla del, i., Nic. | F11 | 92 |
| Venado Tuerto, Arg. | G8 | 80 |
| Venâncio Aires, Braz. | E12 | 80 |
| Venceslau Braz, Braz. | G4 | 79 |
| Vendas Novas, Port. | G3 | 16 |
| Vendée, dept., Fr. | E5 | 14 |
| Vendôme, Fr. | E8 | 14 |
| Venecia, C.R. | G10 | 92 |
| Veneto, prov., Italy | D7 | 18 |
| Venev, Russia | G21 | 22 |
| Venezia (Venice), Italy | D7 | 18 |
| Venezuela, ctry., S.A. | B5 | 76 |
| Venezuela, Golfo de, b., S.A. | B7 | 84 |
| Vengerovo, Russia | F13 | 26 |
| Veniaminof, Mount, mtn., Ak., U.S. | H15 | 100 |
| Venice, Fl., U.S. | L4 | 112 |
| Venice see Venezia, Italy | D7 | 18 |
| Venice, La., U.S. | M7 | 114 |
| Venice, Gulf of, b., Eur. | D8 | 18 |
| Vénissieux, Fr. | G11 | 14 |
| Venlo, Neth. | F9 | 12 |
| Venosa, Italy | I10 | 18 |
| Vent, Aus. | I10 | 10 |
| Ventanas, Ec. | H3 | 84 |
| Ventersdorp, S. Afr. | F8 | 66 |
| Venterstad, S. Afr. | H7 | 66 |
| Ventimiglia, Italy | F2 | 18 |
| Ventspils, Lat. | D4 | 22 |
| Ventuari, stm., Ven. | E9 | 84 |
| Ventura, Ca., U.S. | J6 | 124 |
| Venus, Fl., U.S. | L5 | 112 |
| Venustiano Carranza, Mex. | H8 | 90 |
| Venustiano Carranza, Bahía, b., Mex. | H16 | 90 |
| Venustiano Carranza, Presa, res., Mex. | D9 | 90 |
| Vera, Arg. | E8 | 80 |
| Vera, Spain | H10 | 16 |
| Veracruz [Llave], Mex. | H12 | 90 |
| Veracruz, state, Mex. | H11 | 90 |
| Veraguas, prov., Pan. | I13 | 92 |
| Veramejki, Bela. | H14 | 22 |
| Veranópolis, Braz. | E13 | 80 |
| Vērāval, India | J4 | 44 |
| Verbania, Italy | D3 | 18 |
| Verbilki, Russia | E20 | 22 |
| Verbkovskij, Russia | F25 | 22 |
| Vercelli, Italy | D3 | 18 |
| Vercel [-Villedieu-le-Camp], Fr. | E13 | 14 |
| Verchnaja Salda, Russia | F10 | 26 |
| Verchn'aja Tajmyra, stm., Russia | C11 | 28 |
| Verchn'aja Troica, Russia | D20 | 22 |
| Verchn'aja Tura, Russia | F9 | 26 |
| Verchnedneprovskij, Russia | G16 | 22 |
| Verchnemulomskoje vodochranilišče, res., Russia | G22 | 6 |
| Verchnevil'ujsk, Russia | E16 | 28 |
| Verchnij Baskunčak, Russia | H7 | 26 |
| Verchnij Ufalej, Russia | F10 | 26 |
| Verchojansk, Russia | D18 | 28 |
| Verchojanskij chrebet, mts., Russia | D17 | 28 |
| Verchoturje, Russia | F10 | 26 |
| Verchovje, Russia | I20 | 22 |
| Verchadero, Ur. | F11 | 80 |
| Vercors, reg., Fr. | H12 | 14 |
| Verda, Ky., U.S. | B3 | 112 |
| Verde, stm., Az., U.S. | K5 | 120 |
| Verde, stm., Braz. | C4 | 79 |
| Verde, stm., Braz. | D5 | 79 |
| Verde, stm., Braz. | D7 | 79 |
| Verde, stm., Braz. | E4 | 79 |
| Verde, stm., Braz. | E13 | 82 |
| Verde, stm., Braz. | E4 | 79 |
| Verde, stm., Mex. | G8 | 90 |
| Verde, stm., Para. | B9 | 80 |
| Verde, stm., S.A. | F11 | 82 |
| Verde, Arroyo, stm., Bol. | C7 | 94 |
| Verde, Cape, c., Bah. | C7 | 94 |
| Verde Grande, stm., Braz. | C7 | 79 |
| Verden, Ger. | C9 | 10 |
| Verden, Ok., U.S. | D8 | 116 |
| Verde Pequeno, stm., Braz. | C7 | 79 |
| Verdi, Nv., U.S. | E6 | 124 |
| Verdigre, Ne., U.S. | I9 | 118 |
| Verdigris, stm., U.S. | C11 | 116 |
| Verdinho, stm., Braz. | D3 | 79 |
| Verdon, Ne., U.S. | K12 | 118 |
| Verdun, Fr. | C12 | 14 |
| Verdun, P.Q., Can. | B13 | 108 |
| Verdun-sur-le-Doubs, Fr. | F12 | 14 |
| Verdun-sur-Meuse, Fr. | C12 | 14 |
| Vereeniging, S. Afr. | F8 | 66 |
| Veregin, Sk., Can. | G12 | 104 |
| Vereščagino, Russia | F8 | 26 |
| Vergara, Ur. | G12 | 80 |
| Vergennes, Vt., U.S. | C13 | 108 |
| Verhnjadzvinsk, Bela. | E10 | 22 |
| Verín, Spain | D4 | 16 |
| Veriora, Est. | C10 | 22 |
| Verkhovyna, Ukr. | A8 | 20 |
| Verkhoyansk see Verchojansk, Russia | D18 | 28 |
| Vermejo, stm., N.M., U.S. | H12 | 120 |
| Vermelho, stm., Braz. | C3 | 79 |
| Vermette Lake, l., Sk., Can. | C5 | 104 |
| Vermilion, Ab., Can. | D24 | 102 |
| Vermilion, Oh., U.S. | E4 | 108 |
| Vermilion, stm., Ab., Can. | D24 | 102 |
| Vermilion, stm., U.S. | I7 | 110 |
| Vermilion, stm., La., U.S. | M4 | 114 |
| Vermilion, stm., Mn., U.S. | C3 | 110 |
| Vermilion Bay, On., Can. | H21 | 104 |
| Vermilion Bay, b., La., U.S. | M4 | 114 |
| Vermilion Lake, l., Mn., U.S. | C3 | 110 |
| Vermilion Lake, l., On., Can. | H22 | 104 |
| Vermilion Pass, Can. | F18 | 102 |
| Vermillion, S.D., U.S. | I11 | 118 |
| Vermillion, stm., S.D., U.S. | I11 | 118 |
| Vermont, Il., U.S. | B6 | 114 |
| Vermont, state, U.S. | C12 | 98 |
| Vernal, Ut., U.S. | D7 | 120 |
| Verndale, Mn., U.S. | E12 | 118 |
| Verneuil, Fr. | D7 | 14 |
| Vernon, On., Can. | B11 | 108 |
| Vernon, B.C., Can. | G15 | 102 |
| Vernon, Ct., U.S. | F14 | 108 |
| Vernon, Fl., U.S. | L11 | 114 |
| Vernon, Fr. | C8 | 14 |
| Vernon, In., U.S. | D11 | 114 |
| Vernon, Tx., U.S. | E7 | 116 |
| Vernonia, Or., U.S. | E2 | 122 |
| Vernon River, P.E.I., Can. | F11 | 106 |
| Verny, Fr. | C13 | 14 |
| Véroia, Grc. | I6 | 20 |
| Verona, Ms., U.S. | H8 | 114 |
| Verona, N.D., U.S. | E8 | 118 |
| Verona, Italy | D5 | 18 |
| Verona, Wi., U.S. | H6 | 110 |
| Verret, Lake, l., La., U.S. | M5 | 114 |
| Verrettes, Haiti | E8 | 94 |
| Versailles, Fr. | C8 | 14 |
| Versailles, Il., U.S. | C6 | 114 |
| Versailles, In., U.S. | C11 | 114 |
| Versailles, Ky., U.S. | D12 | 114 |
| Versailles, Mo., U.S. | D4 | 114 |
| Versailles, Oh., U.S. | G1 | 108 |
| Versino-Darasunskij, Russia | G15 | 28 |
| Verte, Île, i., P.Q., Can. | D4 | 106 |
| Vertientes, Cuba | D5 | 94 |
| Vertou, Fr. | E5 | 14 |
| Verviers, Bel. | C10 | 14 |
| Vervins, Fr. | C10 | 14 |
| Vescovato, Fr. | K24 | 15a |
| Vesele, Ukr. | C16 | 20 |
| Veškajma, Russia | G7 | 26 |
| Vesoul, Fr. | E13 | 14 |
| Vespasiano, Braz. | E7 | 79 |
| Vesta, C.R. | H11 | 92 |
| Vest-Agder, co., Nor. | L10 | 6 |
| Vestavia Hills, Al., U.S. | I10 | 114 |
| Vesterålen, is., Nor. | G14 | 6 |
| Vestfjorden, Nor. | H14 | 6 |
| Vestfold, co., Nor. | L12 | 6 |
| Vestmannaeyjar, Ice. | C3 | 6a |
| Vesuvio, vol., Italy | I9 | 18 |
| Vesuvius see Vesuvio, vol., Italy | I9 | 18 |
| Veszprém, Hung. | H17 | 10 |
| Veszprém, co., Hung. | H17 | 10 |
| Vésztő, Hung. | I21 | 10 |
| Vetlanda, Swe. | M14 | 6 |
| Vetluga, Russia | F7 | 26 |
| Vetralla, Italy | G7 | 18 |
| Vetrișoaia, Rom. | C12 | 20 |
| Vetschau, Ger. | D14 | 10 |
| Vetryna, Bela. | F11 | 22 |
| Veurne (Furnes), Bel. | F2 | 12 |
| Vevay, In., U.S. | D11 | 114 |
| Vevey, Switz. | F6 | 13 |
| Vézelise, Fr. | D13 | 14 |
| Viacha, Bol. | G7 | 82 |
| Viadana, Italy | E5 | 18 |
| Viadutos, Braz. | D12 | 80 |
| Viale, Arg. | F8 | 80 |
| Viamão, Braz. | F13 | 80 |
| Viamonte, Arg. | G7 | 80 |
| Viana, Braz. | D9 | 76 |
| Viana do Alentejo, Port. | G3 | 16 |
| Viana do Castelo, Port. | D3 | 16 |
| Viangchan (Vientiane), Laos | F7 | 40 |
| Viangphoukha, Laos | D6 | 40 |
| Viareggio, Italy | F5 | 18 |
| Vibank, Sk., Can. | H11 | 104 |
| Viborg, Den. | M11 | 6 |
| Viborg, S.D., U.S. | H10 | 118 |
| Vibo Valentia, Italy | K11 | 18 |
| Vibraye, Fr. | D7 | 14 |
| Viburnum, Mo., U.S. | E5 | 114 |
| Vic (Vich), Spain | D14 | 16 |
| Vicam, Mex. | D4 | 90 |
| Vicco, Ky., U.S. | B3 | 112 |
| Vic-en-Bigorre, Fr. | I7 | 14 |
| Vicente Guerrero, Mex. | H9 | 90 |
| Vicente López, Arg. | H9 | 80 |
| Vicente Noble, Dom. Rep. | E9 | 94 |
| Vicenza, Italy | D6 | 18 |
| Vich see Vic, Spain | D14 | 16 |
| Vichada, dept., Col. | E8 | 84 |
| Vichada, stm., Col. | E8 | 84 |
| Vichadero, Ur. | F11 | 80 |
| Vichuquén, Chile | H2 | 80 |
| Vichy, Fr. | F10 | 14 |
| Vici, Ok., U.S. | C7 | 116 |
| Vicksburg, Mi., U.S. | H10 | 110 |
| Vicksburg, Ms., U.S. | J6 | 114 |
| Vico, Fr. | I23 | 15a |
| Viçosa, Braz. | F7 | 79 |
| Victor, Ia., U.S. | I3 | 110 |
| Victor, Id., U.S. | G14 | 122 |
| Victor, Mt., U.S. | D11 | 122 |
| Victor, Lac, l., P.Q., Can. | B12 | 106 |
| Victor Harbor, Austl. | J3 | 70 |
| Victoria, Arg. | G8 | 80 |
| Victoria, B.C., Can. | I11 | 102 |
| Victoria, Chile | I2 | 80 |
| Victoria, Gren. | H14 | 94 |
| Victoria (Xianggang), China | M3 | 34 |
| Victoria, Ks., U.S. | M8 | 118 |
| Victoria, Malay. | D6 | 38 |
| Victoria, P.E.I., Can. | F10 | 106 |
| Victoria, Sey. | B11 | 58 |
| Victoria, Tx., U.S. | K9 | 116 |
| Victoria, Va., U.S. | C8 | 112 |
| Victoria, state, Austl. | C6 | 68 |
| Victoria, stm., Austl. | C6 | 68 |
| Victoria, Lake, l., Afr. | B6 | 58 |
| Victoria, Lake, l., Austl. | I4 | 70 |
| Victoria, Mount, mtn., Myan. | D2 | 40 |
| Victoria, Mount, mtn., Pap. N. Gui. | A9 | 68 |
| Victoria Beach, Mb., Can. | H18 | 104 |
| Victoria Falls, Zimb. | A7 | 66 |
| Victoria Falls, wtfl, Afr. | A7 | 66 |
| Victoria Harbour, On., Can. | F16 | 110 |
| Victoria Island, i., N.T., Can. | B10 | 96 |
| Victoria Lake, res., Nf., Can. | D16 | 106 |
| Victoria Land, reg., Ant. | C8 | 73 |
| Victoria Nile, stm., Ug. | H7 | 56 |
| Victoria Peak, mtn., B.C., Can. | G8 | 102 |
| Victoria Peak, mtn., Belize | I15 | 90 |
| Victoria River Downs, Austl. | C6 | 68 |
| Victoria Strait, strt., N.T., Can. | C12 | 96 |
| Victoriaville, P.Q., Can. | A15 | 108 |
| Victoria West, S. Afr. | H6 | 66 |
| Victorica, Arg. | I6 | 80 |
| Victorino, Ven. | F9 | 84 |
| Victorville, Ca., U.S. | J8 | 124 |
| Vičuga, Russia | D24 | 22 |
| Vicuña, Chile | F3 | 80 |
| Vicuña Mackenna, Arg. | G6 | 80 |
| Vidalia, Ga., U.S. | G4 | 112 |
| Vidalia, La., U.S. | K5 | 114 |
| Vidauban, Fr. | I13 | 14 |
| Videira, Braz. | D13 | 80 |
| Vidigueira, Port. | G3 | 16 |
| Vidin, Bul. | F6 | 20 |
| Vidisha, India | I7 | 44 |
| Vidlica, Russia | K23 | 6 |
| Vidor, Tx., U.S. | L2 | 114 |
| Vidzeme, hist. reg., Lat. | D8 | 22 |
| Vidzy, Bela. | F9 | 22 |
| Viechtach, Ger. | F12 | 10 |
| Viedma, Arg. | E4 | 78 |
| Viedma, Lago, l., Arg. | F2 | 78 |
| Viejo, Cerro, mtn., Peru | J3 | 84 |
| Viekšniai, Lith. | E5 | 22 |
| Vielha, Spain | C12 | 16 |
| Vienna see Wien, Aus. | G3 | 10 |
| Vienna, Ga., U.S. | G3 | 112 |
| Vienna, Il., U.S. | E7 | 114 |
| Vienna, Md., U.S. | I11 | 108 |
| Vienna, Mo., U.S. | D5 | 114 |
| Vienna, S.D., U.S. | G10 | 118 |
| Vienna, W.V., U.S. | H5 | 108 |
| Vienne, Fr. | G11 | 14 |
| Vienne, dept., Fr. | F7 | 14 |
| Vienne, stm., Fr. | E7 | 14 |
| Vientiane see Viangchan, Laos | F7 | 40 |
| Vieques, P.R. | E13 | 94 |
| Vieques, Isla de, i., P.R. | E12 | 94 |
| Viernheim, Ger. | F8 | 10 |
| Vierwaldstättersee, l., Switz. | D9 | 13 |
| Vierzon, Fr. | E9 | 14 |
| Vieste, Italy | H11 | 18 |
| Vietnam, ctry., Asia | B4 | 38 |
| Viet Tri, Viet. | D8 | 40 |
| Vieux-Fort, P.Q., Can. | A16 | 106 |
| Vieux Fort, St. Luc. | H14 | 94 |
| Vievis, Lith. | G7 | 22 |
| Vieytes, Arg. | H10 | 80 |
| Vigan, Phil. | m19 | 39b |
| Vigeland, Nor. | L10 | 6 |
| Vigevano, Italy | D3 | 18 |
| Vigneulles-lès-Hattonchâtel, Fr. | D12 | 14 |
| Vignola, Italy | E6 | 18 |
| Vigo, Spain | C3 | 16 |
| Vihowa, Pak. | E4 | 44 |
| Viitasaari, Fin. | J19 | 6 |
| Vijāpur, India | I5 | 44 |
| Vijayawāda, India | D6 | 46 |
| Vijošë (Aóös), stm., Eur. | I4 | 20 |
| Viking, Ab., Can. | D23 | 102 |
| Vikna, i., Nor. | I10 | 6 |
| Vikramasingapuram, India | H4 | 46 |
| Vila da Ribeira Brava, C.V. | k16 | 64a |
| Vila do Bispo, Port. | H3 | 16 |
| Vila Fontes, Moz. | A12 | 66 |
| Vilafranca del Penedès, Spain | D13 | 16 |
| Vila Gomes da Costa, Moz. | D11 | 66 |
| Vilaka, Lat. | D10 | 22 |
| Vilama, Laguna de, l., Arg. | B5 | 80 |
| Vila Machado, Moz. | B12 | 66 |
| Vilanculos, Moz. | C12 | 66 |
| Viļāni, Lat. | E9 | 22 |
| Vila Nova de Foz Côa, Port. | D4 | 16 |
| Vila Nova de Gaia, Port. | D3 | 16 |
| Vilanova i la Geltrú, Spain | D13 | 16 |
| Vila Novo de Ourém, Port. | F3 | 16 |
| Vila Paiva de Andrada, Moz. | B12 | 66 |
| Vila Real, Port. | D4 | 16 |
| Vila Real de Santo António, Port. | H4 | 16 |
| Vilar Formoso, Port. | E5 | 16 |
| Vila Velha, Braz. | F8 | 79 |
| Vila Velha de Ródão, Port. | F4 | 16 |
| Vil'che, Ukr. | F22 | 10 |
| Vilejka, Bela. | G9 | 22 |
| Vilela, Arg. | D7 | 80 |
| Vilhelmina, Swe. | I15 | 6 |
| Vilhena, Braz. | E11 | 82 |
| Viljandi, Est. | C8 | 22 |
| Vilkaviškis, Lith. | G6 | 22 |
| Vil'kickogo, ostrov, i., Russia | C13 | 26 |
| Vil'kickogo, proliv, strt., Russia | B18 | 26 |
| Vilkija, Lith. | F6 | 22 |
| Villa Abecia, Bol. | I9 | 82 |
| Villa Aberastain, Arg. | F4 | 80 |
| Villa Alemana, Chile | G3 | 80 |
| Villa Ángela, Arg. | D8 | 80 |
| Villa Atamisqui, Arg. | E7 | 80 |
| Villa Atuel, Arg. | H5 | 80 |
| Villa Bella, Bol. | D9 | 82 |
| Villa Berthet, Arg. | D8 | 80 |
| Villa Bruzual, Ven. | C8 | 84 |
| Villa Cañás, Arg. | H8 | 80 |
| Villacañas, Spain | F8 | 16 |
| Villa Carlos Paz, Arg. | F6 | 80 |
| Villacarrillo, Spain | G8 | 16 |
| Villa Castelli, Arg. | E4 | 80 |
| Villach, Aus. | I13 | 10 |
| Villacidro, Italy | J3 | 18 |
| Villa Comaltitlán, Mex. | B2 | 92 |
| Villa Concepción del Tío, Arg. | F7 | 80 |
| Villa Constitución, Arg. | G8 | 80 |
| Villada, Spain | C7 | 16 |
| Villa de Arista, Mex. | F9 | 90 |
| Villa de Arriaga, Mex. | G9 | 90 |
| Villa de Cos, Mex. | F8 | 90 |
| Villa de Cura, Ven. | B9 | 84 |
| Villa del Carmen, Arg. | G6 | 80 |
| Villa del Rosario, Arg. | F7 | 80 |
| Villa del Rosario, Arg. | F10 | 80 |
| Villa de María, Arg. | E7 | 80 |
| Villa de Nova Sintra, C.V. | k16 | 64a |
| Villa de San Antonio, Hond. | C7 | 92 |
| Villa de San Francisco, Hond. | C8 | 92 |
| Villa de Soto, Arg. | F6 | 80 |
| Villadiego, Spain | C7 | 16 |
| Villa Dolores, Arg. | F6 | 80 |
| Villa Elisa, Arg. | G9 | 80 |
| Villa Flores, Mex. | I13 | 90 |
| Villa Florida, Para. | C10 | 80 |
| Villafranca de los Barros, Spain | G5 | 16 |
| Villafranca di Verona, Italy | D5 | 18 |
| Village, Ok., U.S. | D9 | 116 |
| Villa General Roca, Arg. | G5 | 80 |
| Villagrán, Mex. | E10 | 90 |
| Villa Grove, Il., U.S. | C8 | 114 |
| Villaguay, Arg. | F9 | 80 |
| Villa Guerrero, Mex. | H10 | 90 |
| Villa Guillermina, Arg. | E8 | 80 |
| Villa Hayes, Para. | C10 | 80 |
| Villahermosa, Mex. | I13 | 90 |
| Villa Hernandarias, Arg. | F9 | 80 |
| Villa Hidalgo, Mex. | G8 | 90 |
| Villa Huidobro, Arg. | H6 | 80 |
| Villaines-la-Juhel, Fr. | D6 | 14 |
| Villa Insurgentes, Mex. | E4 | 90 |
| Villa Iris, Arg. | J7 | 80 |
| Villa Krause, Arg. | F4 | 80 |
| Villa Larca, Arg. | G6 | 80 |
| Villaldama, Mex. | D9 | 90 |
| Villalonga, Arg. | J7 | 80 |
| Villa Mainero, Mex. | E10 | 90 |
| Villa María, Arg. | F7 | 80 |
| Villa María Grande, Arg. | F9 | 80 |
| Villamartín, Bol. | I8 | 82 |
| Villa Matoque, Arg. | C7 | 80 |
| Villa Mazán, Arg. | E5 | 80 |
| Villa Media Agua, Arg. | F4 | 80 |
| Villamil, Ec. | I2 | 84 |
| Villa Mercedes, Arg. | G6 | 80 |
| Villamontes, Bol. | I10 | 82 |
| Villa Nueva, Arg. | G7 | 80 |
| Villa Nueva, Col. | B6 | 84 |
| Villanueva, Guat. | C4 | 92 |
| Villa Nueva, Hond. | B6 | 92 |
| Villanueva, Mex. | F8 | 90 |
| Villa Nueva, Nic. | E8 | 92 |
| Villanueva, N.M., U.S. | I11 | 120 |
| Villanueva de Córdoba, Spain | G7 | 16 |
| Villanueva de la Serana, Spain | F6 | 16 |
| Villanueva del Río y Minas, Spain | H6 | 16 |
| Villa Ocampo, Arg. | E8 | 80 |
| Villa Ocampo, Mex. | E7 | 90 |
| Villa Ojo de Agua, Arg. | E7 | 80 |
| Villa Oliva, Para. | D10 | 80 |
| Villa Oropeza, Bol. | H9 | 82 |
| Villapinzón, Col. | E5 | 84 |
| Villa Quinteros, Arg. | D6 | 80 |
| Villa Ramírez, Arg. | F9 | 80 |
| Villarcayo, Spain | C8 | 16 |
| Villa Regina, Arg. | J5 | 80 |
| Villa Reynolds, Arg. | G6 | 80 |
| Villa Rica, Ga., U.S. | F2 | 112 |

| Name | Map Ref. | Page |
|---|---|---|
| Villa Rivero, Bol. | G9 | 82 |
| Villarrica, Chile | D2 | 78 |
| Villarrica, Col. | F5 | 84 |
| Villarrica, Para. | C10 | 80 |
| Villarrobledo, Spain | F9 | 16 |
| Villas, N.J., U.S. | H12 | 108 |
| Villa Sandino, Nic. | E10 | 92 |
| Villa San José, Arg. | G9 | 80 |
| Villa San Martín, Arg. | E6 | 80 |
| Villa Santa, Montaña, mtn., Hond. | C8 | 92 |
| Villa Santo Domingo, Mex. | F9 | 90 |
| Villasayas, Spain | D9 | 16 |
| Villa Serrano, Bol. | H9 | 82 |
| Villasimius, Italy | J4 | 18 |
| Villasor, Italy | J3 | 18 |
| Villa Tunari, Bol. | G9 | 82 |
| Villa Unión, Arg. | E4 | 80 |
| Villa Unión, Arg. | E7 | 80 |
| Villa Unión, Mex. | C9 | 90 |
| Villa Unión, Mex. | F6 | 90 |
| Villa Valeria, Arg. | H6 | 80 |
| Villaviciosa, Spain | B6 | 16 |
| Villaviciosa, Col. | B6 | 84 |
| Villa Viscarra, Bol. | G9 | 82 |
| Villazón, Bol. | J9 | 82 |
| Villa Zorraquín, Arg. | F9 | 80 |
| Villé, Fr. | D14 | 14 |
| Villedieu, Fr. | D5 | 14 |
| Villefort, Fr. | H10 | 14 |
| Villefranche, Fr. | G11 | 14 |
| Villena, Spain | G11 | 16 |
| Villeneuve-d'Aveyron, Fr. | H9 | 14 |
| Villeneuve-Saint-Georges, Fr. | D9 | 14 |
| Villeneuve-sur-Lot, Fr. | H7 | 14 |
| Ville Platte, La., U.S. | L4 | 114 |
| Villers-Bocage, Fr. | C9 | 14 |
| Villers-Bocage, Fr. | C6 | 14 |
| Villersexel, Fr. | E13 | 14 |
| Villerupt, Fr. | C12 | 14 |
| Ville-Saint-Georges see Saint-Georges, P.Q., Can. | A16 | 108 |
| Villeta, Col. | E5 | 84 |
| Villeurbanne, Fr. | G11 | 14 |
| Villiers, S. Afr. | F9 | 66 |
| Villingen-Schwenningen, Ger. | G8 | 10 |
| Villisca, Ia., U.S. | K13 | 118 |
| Vilna, Ab., Can. | C23 | 102 |
| Vilnius, Lith. | G8 | 22 |
| Vilshofen, Ger. | G13 | 10 |
| Vil'uj, Russia | E16 | 28 |
| Vil'ujsk, Russia | E16 | 28 |
| Vil'ujskoje vodochranilišče, res., Russia | E20 | 26 |
| Vimianzo, Spain | B2 | 16 |
| Vimoutiers, Fr. | D7 | 14 |
| Vimperk, Czech Rep. | F13 | 10 |
| Vina, stm., Cam. | G9 | 54 |
| Viña del Mar, Chile | G3 | 80 |
| Vinalhaven, Me., U.S. | C18 | 108 |
| Vinaròs, Spain | E12 | 16 |
| Vincennes, In., U.S. | D9 | 114 |
| Vincennes Bay, b., Ant. | B6 | 73 |
| Vincent, Al., U.S. | I10 | 114 |
| Vinces, Ec. | H3 | 84 |
| Vinchina, Arg. | E4 | 80 |
| Vinchos, Peru | E4 | 82 |
| Vindhya Range, mts., India | I7 | 44 |
| Vinegar Hill, mtn., Or., U.S. | F7 | 122 |
| Vine Grove, Ky., U.S. | E11 | 114 |
| Vinemont, Al., U.S. | H10 | 114 |
| Vineland, N.J., U.S. | H11 | 108 |
| Vineyard Haven, Ma., U.S. | F16 | 108 |
| Ving Ngün, Myan. | C5 | 40 |
| Vinh, Viet. | E8 | 40 |
| Vinh Long, Viet. | I8 | 40 |
| Vinita, Ok., U.S. | C11 | 116 |
| Vinkovci, Cro. | D2 | 20 |
| Vinnytsya, Ukr. | H3 | 26 |
| Vinson Massif, mtn., Ant. | C12 | 73 |
| Vinton, Ia., U.S. | H3 | 110 |
| Vinton, La., U.S. | L3 | 114 |
| Vinton, Va., U.S. | B7 | 112 |
| Viny, Russia | C15 | 22 |
| Viola, Il., U.S. | I5 | 110 |
| Viola, Wi., U.S. | G5 | 110 |
| Violín, Isla, i., C.R. | I11 | 92 |
| Vipiteno, Italy | C6 | 18 |
| Vipos, Arg. | D6 | 80 |
| Virac, Phil. | C7 | 38 |
| Virac, Phil. | m19 | 39b |
| Viradouro, Braz. | F4 | 79 |
| Virago Sound, strt., B.C., Can. | C2 | 102 |
| Viramgām, India | I5 | 44 |
| Viranşehir, Tur. | C5 | 48 |
| Virbalis, Lith. | G5 | 22 |
| Virden, Il., U.S. | C7 | 114 |
| Virden, Mb., Can. | I14 | 104 |
| Virden, N.M., U.S. | L7 | 120 |
| Vire, Fr. | D6 | 14 |
| Virelles, Bel. | H5 | 12 |
| Virgem da Lapa, Braz. | D7 | 79 |
| Virgil, Ks., U.S. | N11 | 118 |
| Virgilina, Va., U.S. | C8 | 112 |
| Virgin, stm., U.S. | H2 | 120 |
| Virgin Gorda, i., Br. Vir. Is. | E12 | 94 |
| Virginia, Il., U.S. | C6 | 114 |
| Virginia, Mn., U.S. | C3 | 110 |
| Virginia, S. Afr. | G8 | 66 |
| Virginia, state, U.S. | D11 | 98 |
| Virginia Beach, Va., U.S. | C11 | 112 |
| Virginia City, Mt., U.S. | E14 | 122 |
| Virginia City, Nv., U.S. | E6 | 124 |
| Virginia Falls, wtfl, N.T., Can. | F32 | 100 |
| Virginiatown, On., Can. | B16 | 110 |
| Virgin Islands, dep, N.A. | E12 | 94 |
| Virgínópolis, Braz. | E7 | 79 |
| Virgolândia, Braz. | E7 | 79 |
| Viróchey, Camb. | H9 | 40 |
| Virojoki, Fin. | K20 | 6 |
| Viroqua, Wi., U.S. | G5 | 110 |
| Virovitica, Cro. | D12 | 18 |
| Virrat, Fin. | J18 | 6 |
| Virtaniemi, Fin. | G21 | 6 |
| Virtsu, Est. | C6 | 22 |
| Virú, Peru | C2 | 82 |
| Virudunagar, India | H4 | 46 |
| Virungu, D.R.C. | C5 | 58 |
| Viru-Nigula, Est. | B9 | 22 |
| Vis, Cro. | F11 | 18 |
| Vis (Fish), stm., Nmb. | E3 | 66 |
| Vis, Otok, i., Cro. | F11 | 18 |
| Visalia, Ca., U.S. | H6 | 124 |
| Visayan Sea, Phil. | C7 | 38 |
| Visby, Swe. | M16 | 6 |
| Viscount, Sk., Can. | G9 | 104 |
| Viscount Melville Sound, strt., N.T., Can. | B11 | 96 |
| Visé (Wezet), Bel. | G8 | 12 |
| Višegrad, Bos. | F3 | 20 |
| Viseu, Port. | E4 | 16 |
| Vishākhapatnam, India | D7 | 46 |
| Vislinskij zaliv, b., Eur. | A19 | 10 |
| Visnagar, India | I5 | 44 |
| Viso, Monte, mtn., Italy | E2 | 18 |
| Visoko, Bos. | F2 | 20 |
| Visokoi Island, i., S. Geor. | A2 | 73 |
| Visp, Switz. | F8 | 13 |

| Visselhövede, Ger. | C9 | 10 |
|---|---|---|
| Vista, Ca., U.S. | K8 | 124 |
| Vista Alegre, Arg. | J4 | 80 |
| Vista Flores, Arg. | G4 | 80 |
| Vistula see Wisła, stm., Pol. | A18 | 10 |
| Vita, Mb., Can. | I18 | 104 |
| Vita, stm., Col. | E8 | 84 |
| Vitarte, Peru | E3 | 82 |
| Viterbo, Italy | G7 | 18 |
| Vitichi, Bol. | I9 | 82 |
| Viti Levu, i., Fiji | J21 | 126 |
| Vitim, stm., Russia | F14 | 28 |
| Vítor, Peru | G6 | 82 |
| Vítor, stm., Peru | G5 | 82 |
| Vitória, Braz. | F8 | 79 |
| Vitoria (Gasteiz), Spain | C9 | 16 |
| Vitória da Conquista, Braz. | C8 | 79 |
| Vitré, Fr. | D5 | 14 |
| Vitry-le-François, Fr. | D11 | 14 |
| Vittangi, Swe. | H17 | 6 |
| Vitteaux, Fr. | E11 | 14 |
| Vittel, Fr. | D12 | 14 |
| Vittoria, Italy | M9 | 18 |
| Vittorio Veneto, Italy | D7 | 18 |
| Viver, Spain | F11 | 16 |
| Vivi, stm., Russia | D17 | 26 |
| Vivian, La., U.S. | J3 | 114 |
| Vivoratá, Arg. | I10 | 80 |
| Vivorillo, Cayos, is., Hond. | B11 | 92 |
| Vizcaíno, Desierto de, des., Mex. | D3 | 90 |
| Vize, Tur. | H11 | 20 |
| Vize, ostrov, i., Russia | B13 | 26 |
| Vizianagaram, India | C7 | 46 |
| Vizzini, Italy | L9 | 18 |
| Vlaardingen, Neth. | E5 | 12 |
| Vladikavkaz, Russia | I6 | 26 |
| Vladimir, Russia | E23 | 22 |
| Vladimirskij Tupik, Russia | F16 | 22 |
| Vladivostok, Russia | I18 | 28 |
| Vlasenica, Bos. | E2 | 20 |
| Vlasotince, Yugo. | G6 | 20 |
| Vlieland, i., Neth. | B7 | 12 |
| Vlissingen (Flushing), Neth. | F4 | 12 |
| Vloně see Vlorë, Alb. | I3 | 20 |
| Vlorë, Alb. | I3 | 20 |
| Vlorës, Gji i, b., Alb. | I3 | 20 |
| Vltava, stm., Czech Rep. | F14 | 10 |
| Vnukovo, Russia | F20 | 22 |
| Voca, Tx., U.S. | H7 | 116 |
| Vochtoga, Russia | C24 | 22 |
| Vodlozero, ozero, l., Russia | J25 | 6 |
| Vodňany, Czech Rep. | F14 | 10 |
| Vogelsberg, mts., Ger. | E9 | 10 |
| Voghera, Italy | E4 | 18 |
| Vohenstrauss, Ger. | F12 | 10 |
| Vohibinany, Madag. | q23 | 67b |
| Vohilava, Madag. | r23 | 67b |
| Vohimarina, Madag. | n24 | 67b |
| Vohipeno, Madag. | s22 | 67b |
| Võhma, Est. | C7 | 22 |
| Void, Fr. | D12 | 14 |
| Voinjama, Lib. | G5 | 64 |
| Voiron, Fr. | G12 | 14 |
| Voitsberg, Aus. | H15 | 10 |
| Voj-Vož, Russia | E8 | 26 |
| Volcán, Arg. | B6 | 80 |
| Volcán, Pan. | C1 | 84 |
| Volcano, Hi., U.S. | r18 | 125a |
| Volchov, Russia | B15 | 22 |
| Volchov, stm., Russia | B15 | 22 |
| Volga, Ia., U.S. | H4 | 110 |
| Volga, Russia | D21 | 22 |
| Volga, S.D., U.S. | G11 | 118 |
| Volga, stm., Russia | H7 | 26 |
| Volgino, Russia | C16 | 22 |
| Volgo-Baltijskij kanal, Russia | L26 | 6 |
| Volgodonsk, Russia | H6 | 26 |
| Volgograd (Stalingrad), Russia | H6 | 26 |
| Volgogradskoje vodochranilišče, res., Russia | H7 | 26 |
| Volintiri, Mol. | C13 | 20 |
| Volkach, Ger. | F10 | 10 |
| Völkermarkt, Aus. | I14 | 10 |
| Völklingen, Ger. | F6 | 10 |
| Volksrust, S. Afr. | F9 | 66 |
| Volockaja, Russia | A25 | 22 |
| Volodarsk, Russia | E26 | 22 |
| Volodarskoje, Kaz. | G11 | 26 |
| Vologda, Russia | B22 | 22 |
| Vologda, stm., Russia | B22 | 22 |
| Volokolamsk, Russia | E18 | 22 |
| Vólos, Grc. | J6 | 20 |
| Volosovo, Russia | B12 | 22 |
| Volot, Russia | D14 | 22 |
| Volovets', Ukr. | A7 | 20 |
| Volovo, Russia | H21 | 22 |
| Vol'sk, Russia | G7 | 26 |
| Volta, stm., Ghana | H10 | 64 |
| Volta, Lake, res., Ghana | H9 | 64 |
| Volta Blanche (White Volta), stm., Afr. | F6 | 54 |
| Volta Noire (Black Volta), stm., Afr. | F6 | 54 |
| Volta Redonda, Braz. | G6 | 79 |
| Volta Rouge, stm., Afr. | F9 | 64 |
| Volterra, Italy | F5 | 18 |
| Voltri, Italy | E3 | 18 |
| Volyně, Czech Rep. | F13 | 10 |
| Volžsk, Russia | F7 | 26 |
| Volžskij, Russia | H6 | 26 |
| Vonda, Sk., Can. | G11 | 104 |
| Vondrozo, Madag. | s22 | 67b |
| Vopnafjördur, Ice. | B6 | 6a |
| Voranava, Bela. | G8 | 22 |
| Vorarlberg, state, Aus. | H9 | 10 |
| Vorau, Aus. | H15 | 10 |
| Vorden, Neth. | D9 | 12 |
| Vorder-Grauspitz, mtn., Eur. | B13 | 13 |
| Vorderrhein, stm., Switz. | E10 | 13 |
| Vordingborg, Den. | N12 | 6 |
| Vóreion Aiyaíon, prov., Grc. | K9 | 20 |
| Vorga, Russia | H15 | 22 |
| Vóriai Sporádhes, is., Grc. | J7 | 20 |
| Vorkuta, Russia | D10 | 26 |
| Vormsi, i., Est. | B6 | 22 |
| Vorob'jovo, Russia | B23 | 22 |
| Vorokhta, Ukr. | A8 | 20 |
| Voronov, Mol. | B13 | 20 |
| Voronež, Russia | G5 | 26 |
| Voroshilovgrad see Luhans'k, Ukr. | H5 | 26 |
| Vorsma, Russia | F26 | 22 |
| Võrtsjärv, l., Est. | C9 | 22 |
| Võru, Est. | D10 | 22 |
| Voskresenskoje, Russia | F21 | 22 |
| Voskresenskoje, Russia | B20 | 22 |
| Voskresenskoje, Russia | D20 | 22 |
| Voss, Nor. | K10 | 6 |
| Vostočno-Sibirskoje more (East Siberian Sea), Russia | C23 | 28 |

| Vostočnyj Sajan, mts., Russia | G11 | 26 |
|---|---|---|
| Votkinsk, Russia | F8 | 26 |
| Votuporanga, Braz. | F4 | 79 |
| Voulou, C.A.R. | M2 | 60 |
| Vouziers, Fr. | C11 | 14 |
| Voves, Fr. | D8 | 14 |
| Voyageurs National Park, Mn., U.S. | B3 | 110 |
| Vože, ozero, l., Russia | K26 | 6 |
| Vožega, Russia | A23 | 22 |
| Voznesens'k, Ukr. | H4 | 26 |
| Voznesenskoje, Russia | G25 | 22 |
| Vraca, Bul. | F7 | 20 |
| Vrådal, Nor. | L11 | 6 |
| Vrancea, co., Rom. | D10 | 20 |
| Vrangel'a, ostrov, i., Russia | C28 | 28 |
| Vranje, Yugo. | G5 | 20 |
| Vrbas, Yugo. | D3 | 20 |
| Vrede, S. Afr. | F9 | 66 |
| Vredenburg, S. Afr. | I3 | 66 |
| Vredendal, S. Afr. | K9 | 114 |
| Vredendal, S. Afr. | H4 | 66 |
| Vreed en Hoop, Guy. | D13 | 84 |
| Vrin, Switz. | E11 | 13 |
| Vrindāvan, India | F7 | 44 |
| Vrondádhes, Grc. | K10 | 20 |
| Vršac, Yugo. | D5 | 20 |
| Vryburg, S. Afr. | F7 | 66 |
| Vryheid, S. Afr. | F10 | 66 |
| Vsetín, Czech Rep. | F17 | 10 |
| Vsevidof, Mount, mtn., Ak., U.S. | J10 | 100 |
| Vtoryje Levyje Lamki, Russia | H24 | 22 |
| Vukovar, Cro. | D3 | 20 |
| Vulcan, Ab., Can. | G21 | 102 |
| Vulcan, Mi., U.S. | E8 | 110 |
| Vulcan, Rom. | D7 | 20 |
| Vučjanešti, Mol. | D12 | 20 |
| Vung Tau, Viet. | I9 | 40 |
| Vuohijärvi, Fin. | K20 | 6 |
| Vuoksenniska, Fin. | K21 | 6 |
| Vuotso, Fin. | G20 | 6 |
| Vuyyūru, India | D6 | 46 |
| Vyborg, Russia | A11 | 22 |
| Vyborgskij zaliv, b., Russia | A11 | 22 |
| Vyčegda, stm., Russia | E7 | 26 |
| Vygoniči, Russia | H17 | 22 |
| Vygozero, ozero, l., Russia | J24 | 6 |
| Vyksa, Russia | F25 | 22 |
| Vylkove, Ukr. | D13 | 20 |
| Vynohradiv, Ukr. | A7 | 20 |
| Vypolzovo, Russia | D16 | 22 |
| Vyrica, Russia | B13 | 22 |
| Vyša, Russia | H25 | 22 |
| Vyšgorodok, Russia | D11 | 22 |
| Vyškov, Czech Rep. | F17 | 10 |
| Vyškov, Russia | I14 | 22 |
| Vyšnij Voloček, Russia | D17 | 22 |
| Vysock, Russia | A11 | 22 |
| Vysokaje, Bela. | I6 | 22 |
| Vysoké Tatry, mts., Eur. | F20 | 10 |
| Vysokiniči, Russia | G19 | 22 |
| Vysokogornyj, Russia | G19 | 28 |
| Vysokoje, Russia | E17 | 22 |
| Vysokovsk, Russia | E19 | 22 |
| Vyšší Brod, Czech Rep. | G14 | 10 |
| Vytegra, Russia | E5 | 26 |
| Vyzhnytsya, Ukr. | A9 | 20 |

## W

| Wa, Ghana | F8 | 64 |
|---|---|---|
| Waal, stm., Neth. | E7 | 12 |
| Waao, China | B8 | 40 |
| Wabag, Pap. N. Gui. | G11 | 38 |
| Wabamun, Ab., Can. | D20 | 102 |
| Wabamun Indian Reserve, Ab., Can. | D20 | 102 |
| Wabamun Lake, l., Ab., Can. | D20 | 102 |
| Wabana, Nf., Can. | E21 | 106 |
| Wabasca, Ab., Can. | A21 | 102 |
| Wabasca, stm., Ab., Can. | E9 | 96 |
| Wabasca Indian Reserve, Ab., Can. | B21 | 102 |
| Wabash, In., U.S. | B11 | 114 |
| Wabash, stm., U.S. | E9 | 114 |
| Wabasha, Mn., U.S. | F3 | 110 |
| Wabasso, Fl., U.S. | L6 | 112 |
| Wabasso, Mn., U.S. | G12 | 118 |
| Wabeno, Wi., U.S. | E7 | 110 |
| Wabigoon Lake, l., On., Can. | I22 | 104 |
| Wabowden, Mb., Can. | D16 | 104 |
| Wąbrzeźno, Pol. | B18 | 10 |
| W.A.C. Bennett Dam, B.C., Can. | A12 | 102 |
| Waccamaw, stm., U.S. | F8 | 112 |
| Wachapreague, Va., U.S. | B11 | 112 |
| Wachusett, B.C., Can. | C8 | 102 |
| Waco, Tx., U.S. | H9 | 116 |
| Waconda Lake, res., Ks., U.S. | L9 | 118 |
| Waconia, Mn., U.S. | F2 | 110 |
| Wacouno, stm., P.Q., Can. | A8 | 106 |
| Wad Al-Haddād, Sudan | K7 | 60 |
| Wad Bandah, Sudan | K4 | 60 |
| Wad Ban Naqa, Sudan | I7 | 60 |
| Waddenzee, Neth. | B7 | 12 |
| Waddington, N.Y., U.S. | C11 | 108 |
| Waddington, Mount, mtn., B.C., Can. | F9 | 102 |
| Wade, Mount, mtn., Ant. | D9 | 73 |
| Wadena, Mn., U.S. | E12 | 118 |
| Wadena, Sk., Can. | G11 | 104 |
| Wadesboro, N.C., U.S. | E6 | 112 |
| Wad Ḥāmid, Sudan | I7 | 60 |
| Wadham Islands, is., Nf., Can. | C20 | 106 |
| Wadhams, B.C., Can. | F7 | 102 |
| Wādī as-Sīr, Jord. | E5 | 50 |
| Wādī Ḥalfā', Sudan | G6 | 60 |
| Wadley, Al., U.S. | I11 | 114 |
| Wadley, Ga., U.S. | G4 | 112 |
| Wad Medanī, Sudan | J7 | 60 |
| Wadowice, Pol. | F19 | 10 |
| Wadsworth, Nv., U.S. | E6 | 124 |
| Wadsworth, Oh., U.S. | F5 | 108 |
| Waegwan, S. Kor. | H16 | 32 |
| Waelder, Tx., U.S. | J9 | 116 |
| Wafang, China | B6 | 32 |
| Wafrah, Kuw. | G10 | 48 |
| Wageningen, Neth. | E8 | 12 |
| Wageningen, Sur. | E14 | 84 |
| Wager Bay, b., N.T., Can. | C15 | 96 |
| Wagga Wagga, Austl. | J7 | 70 |
| Wagin, Austl. | F3 | 68 |
| Waging am See, Ger. | H12 | 10 |
| Wagner, S.D., U.S. | H9 | 118 |
| Wagoner, Ok., U.S. | D11 | 116 |
| Wagon Mound, N.M., U.S. | C2 | 116 |
| Wagrowiec, Pol. | C17 | 10 |
| Waha, Libya | C4 | 56 |
| Wāh Cantonment, Pak. | D5 | 44 |
| Wahiawa, Hi., U.S. | p15 | 125a |
| Wahoo, Ne., U.S. | J11 | 118 |
| Wahpeton, N.D., U.S. | E11 | 118 |
| Wahran (Oran), Alg. | C10 | 62 |
| Wahroonga, Hi., U.S. | p15 | 125a |
| Waialae, Hi., U.S. | p15 | 125a |
| Waianae, Hi., U.S. | p15 | 125a |

| Waiau, N.Z. | E4 | 72 |
|---|---|---|
| Waiblingen, Ger. | G9 | 10 |
| Waidhofen an der Thaya, Aus. | G15 | 10 |
| Waidhofen an der Ybbs, Aus. | H14 | 10 |
| Waigeo, Pulau, i., Indon. | F9 | 38 |
| Waihi, N.Z. | C5 | 72 |
| Waikato, stm., N.Z. | C5 | 72 |
| Waikerie, Austl. | J3 | 70 |
| Wailuku, Hi., U.S. | q17 | 125a |
| Waimate, N.Z. | F3 | 72 |
| Waimea, Hi., U.S. | p15 | 125a |
| Wainganga, stm., India | C6 | 46 |
| Waingapu, Indon. | G7 | 38 |
| Waini, stm., Guy. | D13 | 84 |
| Wainwright, Ab., Can. | E24 | 102 |
| Wainwright, Ak., U.S. | A14 | 100 |
| Waipara, N.Z. | E4 | 72 |
| Waipukurau, N.Z. | C6 | 72 |
| Wairoa, N.Z. | C6 | 72 |
| Waitara, N.Z. | C5 | 72 |
| Waite Park, Mn., U.S. | E1 | 110 |
| Waitsburg, Wa., U.S. | D7 | 122 |
| Waiuku, N.Z. | B5 | 72 |
| Wajima, Japan | J11 | 36 |
| Waka, Eth. | N9 | 60 |
| Waka, Tx., U.S. | C5 | 116 |
| Wakarusa, In., U.S. | A10 | 114 |
| Wakarusa, stm., Ks., U.S. | M12 | 118 |
| Wakaw, Sk., Can. | F9 | 104 |
| Wakaw Lake, l., Sk., Can. | F9 | 104 |
| Wakayama, Japan | M10 | 36 |
| Wakefield, Ks., U.S. | L10 | 118 |
| Wakefield, Ne., U.S. | I11 | 118 |
| Wakefield, R.I., U.S. | F15 | 108 |
| Wakefield, Va., U.S. | C10 | 112 |
| Wake Forest, N.C., U.S. | D8 | 112 |
| Wake Island, dep., Oc. | G20 | 126 |
| Wakema, Myan. | F3 | 40 |
| Wakeman, stm., B.C., Can. | F8 | 102 |
| Wake Village, Tx., U.S. | I2 | 114 |
| Wakita, Ok., U.S. | C9 | 116 |
| Wakkanai, Japan | b16 | 36a |
| Wakonda, S.D., U.S. | H10 | 118 |
| Waku Kundo, Ang. | D3 | 58 |
| Walachia, hist. reg., Rom. | E8 | 20 |
| Wałbrzych (Waldenburg), Pol. | E16 | 10 |
| Walcha, Austl. | H9 | 70 |
| Walcheren, i., Neth. | E4 | 12 |
| Walcott, B.C., Can. | C8 | 102 |
| Walcott, I5 | I5 | 110 |
| Walcott, N.D., U.S. | E11 | 118 |
| Wałcz, Pol. | B16 | 10 |
| Wald, Switz. | D10 | 13 |
| Waldbillig, Lux. | I9 | 12 |
| Waldeck, Ger. | D9 | 10 |
| Walden, Co., U.S. | D10 | 120 |
| Walden Ridge, mtn., Tn., U.S. | G11 | 114 |
| Waldheim, Sk., Can. | F8 | 104 |
| Waldkirchen, Ger. | G13 | 10 |
| Waldmünchen, Ger. | F12 | 10 |
| Waldo, Ar., U.S. | I3 | 114 |
| Waldo, B.C., Can. | H19 | 102 |
| Waldoboro, Me., U.S. | C17 | 108 |
| Waldport, Or., U.S. | F1 | 122 |
| Waldron, Ar., U.S. | H2 | 114 |
| Waldron, In., U.S. | C11 | 114 |
| Waldron, Mi., U.S. | I11 | 110 |
| Waldron, Sk., Can. | H12 | 104 |
| Waldshut-Tiengen, Ger. | H8 | 10 |
| Waidviertel, reg., Aus. | G15 | 10 |
| Walenstadt, Switz. | D11 | 13 |
| Wales, Ak., U.S. | D10 | 100 |
| Wales, ter., U.K. | I10 | 8 |
| Wales Island, i., B.C., Can. | C4 | 102 |
| Wales Island, i., N.T., Can. | C15 | 96 |
| Walgett, Austl. | G8 | 70 |
| Walgreen Coast, Ant. | C11 | 73 |
| Walhachin, B.C., Can. | G14 | 102 |
| Walhalla, N.D., U.S. | C10 | 118 |
| Walhalla, S.C., U.S. | E3 | 112 |
| Walker, Ia., U.S. | H4 | 110 |
| Walker, Mn., U.S. | C11 | 110 |
| Walker, stm., Nv., U.S. | E7 | 124 |
| Walker, Lac, l., P.Q., Can. | B6 | 106 |
| Walker Lake, l., Mb., Can. | D18 | 104 |
| Walker Lake, l., Nv., U.S. | F7 | 124 |
| Walkersville, Md., U.S. | H9 | 108 |
| Walkerton, In., U.S. | A10 | 114 |
| Walkerton, On., Can. | F14 | 110 |
| Walkertown, N.C., U.S. | C6 | 112 |
| Walkerville, Mt., U.S. | D13 | 122 |
| Wall, S.D., U.S. | H5 | 118 |
| Wallace, Id., U.S. | C10 | 122 |
| Wallace, N.C., U.S. | E9 | 112 |
| Wallace, Ne., U.S. | K6 | 118 |
| Wallaceburg, On., Can. | H13 | 110 |
| Wallangarra, Austl. | G9 | 70 |
| Walla Walla, Wa., U.S. | D7 | 122 |
| Waller, Tx., U.S. | I11 | 116 |
| Wallingford, Ct., U.S. | F14 | 108 |
| Wallingford, Vt., U.S. | D14 | 108 |
| Wallis, Tx., U.S. | J10 | 116 |
| Wallis and Futuna, dep., Oc. | J22 | 126 |
| Wallisellen, Switz. | D10 | 13 |
| Wall Lake, Ia., U.S. | I12 | 118 |
| Wallowa, Or., U.S. | E8 | 122 |
| Wallowa, stm., Or., U.S. | E8 | 122 |
| Wallowa Mountains, mts., Or., U.S. | E8 | 122 |
| Walls, Ms., U.S. | H6 | 114 |
| Wallula, Lake, res., U.S. | D7 | 122 |
| Walnut, Ia., U.S. | A1 | 114 |
| Walnut, Il., U.S. | I8 | 110 |
| Walnut, Oh., U.S. | A5 | 114 |
| Walnut, Pa., U.S. | F7 | 108 |
| Walnut, stm., Ks., U.S. | N10 | 118 |
| Walnut Cove, N.C., U.S. | C6 | 112 |
| Walnut Grove, Al., U.S. | G12 | 118 |
| Walnut Ridge, Ar., U.S. | F6 | 114 |
| Walnut Springs, Tx., U.S. | G9 | 116 |
| Walpeup, Austl. | J5 | 70 |
| Walpole, Co., U.S. | D14 | 108 |
| Walsenburg, Co., U.S. | G12 | 120 |
| Walsh, Co., U.S. | I4 | 104 |
| Walsh, Co., U.S. | N5 | 118 |
| Walsrode, Ger. | C9 | 10 |
| Walterboro, S.C., U.S. | G6 | 112 |
| Walter F. George Lake, res., U.S. | H1 | 112 |
| Walters, Ok., U.S. | A11 | 114 |
| Waltershausen, Ger. | E10 | 10 |
| Waltersville, Ms., U.S. | J6 | 114 |
| Walthall, Ms., U.S. | I7 | 114 |
| Waltham, Ma., U.S. | E15 | 108 |
| Walthill, Ne., U.S. | I11 | 118 |
| Walton, In., U.S. | B10 | 114 |
| Walton, Ky., U.S. | I2 | 114 |
| Walton, N.Y., U.S. | C9 | 106 |
| Walton, N.Y., U.S. | E11 | 108 |
| Walvis Bay, Nmb. | D2 | 66 |
| Walworth, Wi., U.S. | H7 | 110 |
| Wamba, Nig. | G14 | 64 |
| Wamba, stm., Afr. | C3 | 58 |

| Wamego, Ks., U.S. | L11 | 118 |
|---|---|---|
| Wampsville, N.Y., U.S. | D11 | 108 |
| Wampú, Hond. | B9 | 92 |
| Wampú, stm., Hond. | B9 | 92 |
| Wampum, Pa., U.S. | G6 | 108 |
| Wamsutter, Wy., U.S. | I18 | 122 |
| Wanaaring, Austl. | G6 | 70 |
| Wanaka, N.Z. | F2 | 72 |
| Wanan, China | F3 | 110 |
| Wanapitei Lake, l., On., Can. | m19 | 39b |
| Wanbi, Austl. | J4 | 70 |
| Wanblee, S.D., U.S. | H6 | 118 |
| Wanchese, N.C., U.S. | D11 | 112 |
| Wandering, stm., Ab., Can. | B22 | 102 |
| Wando, S. Kor. | I14 | 32 |
| Wandoan, Austl. | F8 | 70 |
| Wanette, Ok., U.S. | E9 | 116 |
| Wanfoxia, China | C6 | 30 |
| Wangal, stm., Can. | K7 | 70 |
| Wanganui, N.Z. | C5 | 72 |
| Wangaratta, Austl. | J7 | 70 |
| Wangary, Austl. | J1 | 70 |
| Wangdü Phodrang, Bhu. | G13 | 44 |
| Wanghu, China | D1 | 32 |
| Wanghuzhuang, China | E5 | 32 |
| Wangjiang, China | E5 | 34 |
| Wangqan Yang, b., China | E11 | 30 |
| Wangsi, China | E4 | 32 |
| Wangtuan, China | F10 | 32 |
| Wangzhong, China | H4 | 32 |
| Wangzhuangbu, China | D1 | 32 |
| Wanham, Ab., Can. | B16 | 102 |
| Wani, India | B5 | 46 |
| Wanigela, Pap. N. Gui. | A9 | 68 |
| Wanipigow, stm., Can. | G19 | 104 |
| Wänkäner, India | I4 | 44 |
| Wanli, China | D9 | 34 |
| Wanneroo, Austl. | F3 | 68 |
| Wanxian, China | E8 | 30 |
| Wanzai, China | G3 | 34 |
| Wanzleben, Ger. | C11 | 10 |
| Wapakoneta, Oh., U.S. | G2 | 108 |
| Wapanucka, Oh., U.S. | E10 | 116 |
| Wapato, Wa., U.S. | D5 | 122 |
| Wapawekka Hills, hills, Sk., Can. | D10 | 104 |
| Wapella, Sk., Can. | H12 | 104 |
| Wapello, Ia., U.S. | I4 | 110 |
| Wapesi Lake, l., On., Can. | H22 | 104 |
| Wapisu Lake, l., Mb., Can. | C15 | 104 |
| Wapiti, stm., Can. | B15 | 102 |
| Wappingers Falls, N.Y., U.S. | F13 | 108 |
| Wapsipinicon, stm., U.S. | I5 | 110 |
| Wapus Lake, l., Sk., Can. | B12 | 104 |
| Waqqāş, Jord. | C5 | 50 |
| War, W.V., U.S. | B5 | 112 |
| Warangal, India | C5 | 46 |
| Waratah, Austl. | M6 | 70 |
| Warbreccan, Austl. | E5 | 70 |
| Warburg, Ger. | D9 | 10 |
| Warburton, Austl. | K6 | 70 |
| Warburton, stm., Austl. | E7 | 68 |
| Warburton Bay, b., N.T., Can. | D10 | 96 |
| Warburton Creek, stm., Austl. | E7 | 68 |
| Ward, stm., Austl. | E7 | 70 |
| Ward Cove, Ak., U.S. | B3 | 102 |
| Warden, Wa., U.S. | D6 | 122 |
| Wardha, India | B5 | 46 |
| Wardha, stm., India | C5 | 46 |
| Wardlow, Ab., Can. | G23 | 102 |
| Wardner, B.C., Can. | H19 | 102 |
| Ware, Ma., U.S. | E14 | 108 |
| Ware, stm., U.S. | E14 | 108 |
| Waregem, Bel. | G3 | 12 |
| Wareham, Eng., U.K. | K11 | 8 |
| Wareham, Ma., U.S. | F16 | 108 |
| Waremme (Borgworm), Bel. | G7 | 12 |
| Waren, Ger. | B12 | 10 |
| Warendorf, Ger. | D7 | 10 |
| Ware Shoals, S.C., U.S. | E4 | 112 |
| Wargla, Alg. | E13 | 62 |
| Warialda, Austl. | G9 | 70 |
| Warin Chamrap, Thai. | G8 | 40 |
| Werkworth, On., Can. | F18 | 110 |
| Werman, Sk., Can. | F8 | 104 |
| Warmbad, Nmb. | G4 | 66 |
| Warmbad, S. Afr. | E9 | 66 |
| Warminster, Eng., U.K. | J11 | 8 |
| Warminster, Pa., U.S. | G11 | 108 |
| Warm Springs, Mt., U.S. | D13 | 122 |
| Warm Springs, Or., U.S. | F4 | 122 |
| Warm Springs, Va., U.S. | A7 | 112 |
| Warm Springs, stm., Or., U.S. | E4 | 122 |
| Warner, Ab., Can. | H22 | 102 |
| Warner, N.H., U.S. | D15 | 108 |
| Warner, Ok., U.S. | D11 | 116 |
| Warner Lakes, l., Or., U.S. | H6 | 122 |
| Warner Mountains, mts., U.S. | C5 | 124 |
| Warner Peak, mtn., Or., U.S. | H6 | 122 |
| Warner Robins, Ga., U.S. | G3 | 112 |
| Warnes, Arg. | H8 | 80 |
| Warnes, Bol. | G10 | 82 |
| Warpath, stm., Man., Can. | F16 | 104 |
| Warracknabeal, Austl. | K5 | 70 |
| Warr Acres, Ok., U.S. | D9 | 116 |
| Warragul, Austl. | L6 | 70 |
| Warrego, stm., Austl. | G7 | 70 |
| Warrego Range, mts., Austl. | E7 | 70 |
| Warren, Ar., U.S. | I4 | 114 |
| Warren, Austl. | H7 | 70 |
| Warren, Il., U.S. | H6 | 110 |
| Warren, Mi., U.S. | H12 | 110 |
| Warren, Mn., U.S. | C11 | 118 |
| Warren, Oh., U.S. | F6 | 108 |
| Warren, Pa., U.S. | F7 | 108 |
| Warren Point, c., N.T., Can. | B28 | 100 |
| Warrens, Wi., U.S. | F5 | 110 |
| Warrensburg, Mo., U.S. | D3 | 114 |
| Warrensburg, N.Y., U.S. | D13 | 108 |
| Warrenton, Ga., U.S. | F4 | 112 |
| Warrenton, Mo., U.S. | D5 | 114 |
| Warrenton, N.C., U.S. | C8 | 112 |
| Warrenton, Or., U.S. | D2 | 122 |
| Warrenton, S. Afr. | G7 | 66 |
| Warrenton, Va., U.S. | I9 | 108 |
| Warri, Nig. | I12 | 64 |
| Warrington, Fl., U.S. | L9 | 114 |
| Warrior, Al., U.S. | I10 | 114 |
| Warrnambool, Austl. | L5 | 70 |
| Warroad, Mn., U.S. | C12 | 118 |
| Warsaw, Il., U.S. | J4 | 110 |
| Warsaw, In., U.S. | A11 | 114 |
| Warsaw, Ky., U.S. | I2 | 114 |
| Warsaw, Mo., U.S. | D3 | 114 |
| Warsaw, N.C., U.S. | E8 | 112 |
| Warsaw, N.Y., U.S. | D8 | 108 |
| Warsaw, Oh., U.S. | G4 | 108 |
| Warsaw see Warszawa, Pol. | C21 | 10 |
| Warspite, Ab., Can. | C22 | 102 |
| Warszawa (Warsaw), Pol. | C21 | 10 |
| Warta, stm., Pol. | C15 | 10 |
| Wartburg, hist., Ger. | E10 | 10 |
| Wartrace, Tn., U.S. | G10 | 114 |

| Warud, India | B5 | 46 |
|---|---|---|
| Warunta, Laguna de, l., Hond. | B10 | 92 |
| Warwick, Austl. | G10 | 70 |
| Warwick, Eng., U.K. | I12 | 8 |
| Warwick, P.Q., Can. | B15 | 108 |
| Warwick, R.I., U.S. | F15 | 108 |
| Warwick Channel, strt., Austl. | B7 | 68 |
| Warwickshire, co., Eng., U.K. | I12 | 8 |
| Wasaga Beach, On., Can. | F15 | 110 |
| Wasagu, Nig. | F12 | 64 |
| Wasatch Plateau, plat., Ut., U.S. | E5 | 120 |
| Wasatch Range, mts., Ut., U.S. | D5 | 120 |
| Wascana Creek, stm., Sk., Can. | H10 | 104 |
| Wasco, Ca., U.S. | I6 | 124 |
| Wasco, Or., U.S. | E5 | 122 |
| Waseca, Mn., U.S. | F2 | 110 |
| Wasekamio Lake, l., Sk., Can. | B6 | 104 |
| Washademoak Lake, l., N.B., Can. | G8 | 106 |
| Washburn, Il., U.S. | J6 | 110 |
| Washburn, N.D., U.S. | D6 | 118 |
| Washburn, Wi., U.S. | D5 | 110 |
| Washburn Lake, l., N.T., Can. | B11 | 96 |
| Washicoutai, P.Q., Can. | B13 | 106 |
| Washington, D.C., U.S. | I9 | 108 |
| Washington, Ga., U.S. | F4 | 112 |
| Washington, Ia., U.S. | I4 | 110 |
| Washington, Il., U.S. | J6 | 110 |
| Washington, In., U.S. | D9 | 114 |
| Washington, Ks., U.S. | L10 | 118 |
| Washington, Ky., U.S. | I3 | 98 |
| Washington, La., U.S. | L4 | 114 |
| Washington, Mo., U.S. | D5 | 114 |
| Washington, N.C., U.S. | D9 | 112 |
| Washington, Pa., U.S. | G6 | 108 |
| Washington, Tx., U.S. | I10 | 116 |
| Washington, Ut., U.S. | G3 | 120 |
| Washington, Va., U.S. | I8 | 108 |
| Washington, state, U.S. | B2 | 98 |
| Washington, Mount, mtn., N.H., U.S. | C15 | 108 |
| Washington Court House, Oh., U.S. | H3 | 108 |
| Washington Island, Wi., U.S. | E9 | 110 |
| Washington Island, i., Wi., U.S. | E9 | 110 |
| Washington Terrace, Ut., U.S. | C5 | 120 |
| Washita, stm., U.S. | E10 | 116 |
| Washow Bay, b., Mb., Can. | G18 | 104 |
| Washtucna, Wa., U.S. | D7 | 122 |
| Wasilla, Ak., U.S. | F20 | 100 |
| Waskada, Mb., Can. | I14 | 104 |
| Waskaganish, P.Q., Can. | F17 | 96 |
| Waskahigan, stm., Ab., Can. | C17 | 102 |
| Waskaiowaka Lake, l., Mb., Can. | B18 | 104 |
| Waskatenau, Ab., Can. | C22 | 102 |
| Waskesiu Lake, l., Sk., Can. | E8 | 104 |
| Waskom, Tx., U.S. | J2 | 114 |
| Waspam, Nic. | C11 | 92 |
| Waspuk, stm., Nic. | C10 | 92 |
| Wassen, Switz. | E10 | 13 |
| Wassenaar, Neth. | D5 | 12 |
| Wasseralfingen, Ger. | G10 | 10 |
| Wasserbillig, Lux. | I10 | 12 |
| Wasserburg am Inn, Ger. | G12 | 10 |
| Wass Lake, l., Mb., Can. | E19 | 104 |
| Wassou, Gui. | F3 | 64 |
| Wassy, Fr. | D11 | 14 |
| Watampone, Indon. | F7 | 38 |
| Watapi Lake, l., Sk., Can. | C5 | 104 |
| Waterberg, Nmb. | C3 | 66 |
| Waterberg Plateau Park, Nmb. | C3 | 66 |
| Waterbury, Ct., U.S. | F13 | 108 |
| Waterbury, Vt., U.S. | C14 | 108 |
| Waterdown, On., Can. | G16 | 110 |
| Wateree, stm., S.C., U.S. | E6 | 112 |
| Wateree Lake, res., S.C., U.S. | E6 | 112 |
| Waterford, Ca., U.S. | G5 | 124 |
| Waterford, Ire. | I6 | 8 |
| Waterford, On., Can. | H15 | 110 |
| Waterford, Pa., U.S. | F7 | 108 |
| Waterford, Wi., U.S. | H7 | 110 |
| Waterford, co., Ire. | I6 | 8 |
| Waterhen, Sk., Can. | D6 | 104 |
| Waterhen Lake, l., Mb., Can. | F15 | 104 |
| Waterloo, Al., U.S. | H8 | 114 |
| Waterloo, Bel. | G5 | 12 |
| Waterloo, Ia., U.S. | H3 | 110 |
| Waterloo, Il., U.S. | D6 | 114 |
| Waterloo, N.Y., U.S. | E10 | 108 |
| Waterloo, On., Can. | G15 | 110 |
| Waterloo, P.Q., Can. | B14 | 108 |
| Waterloo, Wi., U.S. | G7 | 110 |
| Waterman, Il., U.S. | I7 | 110 |
| Waterproof, La., U.S. | K5 | 114 |
| Watersmeet, Mi., U.S. | D6 | 110 |
| Waterton, stm., Austl. | H21 | 102 |
| Waterton-Glacier International Peace Park, N.A. | B12 | 122 |
| Waterton Lakes National Park, Ab., Can. | H21 | 102 |
| Watertown, N.Y., U.S. | D11 | 108 |
| Watertown, S.D., U.S. | G10 | 118 |
| Watertown, Wi., U.S. | G7 | 110 |
| Water Valley, Ms., U.S. | H7 | 114 |
| Waterville, Me., U.S. | C17 | 108 |
| Waterville, Mn., U.S. | F2 | 110 |
| Waterville, N.S., Can. | G9 | 106 |
| Waterville, N.Y., U.S. | F3 | 108 |
| Watervliet, N.Y., U.S. | E13 | 108 |
| Watford, Eng., U.K. | J12 | 8 |
| Watford City, N.D., U.S. | D4 | 118 |
| Wathaman, stm., Sk., Can. | A11 | 104 |
| Wathaman Lake, l., Sk., Can. | | |
| Wathena, Ks., U.S. | L13 | 118 |
| Watino, Ab., Can. | B17 | 102 |
| Watkins Glen, N.Y., U.S. | E10 | 108 |
| Watkinsville, Ga., U.S. | F3 | 112 |
| Watling Island see San Salvador, i., Bah. | B7 | 94 |
| Watonga, Ok., U.S. | D8 | 116 |
| Watonwan, stm., Mn., U.S. | G13 | 118 |
| Watrous, N.M., U.S. | I12 | 120 |
| Watrous, Sk., Can. | G9 | 104 |
| Watseka, Il., U.S. | J8 | 110 |
| Watson, Sk., Can. | F10 | 104 |
| Watson Lake, Yk., Can. | F30 | 100 |
| Watsontown, Pa., U.S. | F10 | 108 |
| Watsonville, Ca., U.S. | H4 | 124 |
| Wattens, Aus. | H11 | 9 |
| Wattenwil, Switz. | E8 | 13 |

## Watt-Wils

Name — Map Ref. — Page


Watts Bar Lake, res., Tn., U.S. D2 112
Watts Mills, S.C., U.S. E4 112
Wattwil, Switz. D11 13
Watubela, Kepulauan, is., Indon. F9 38
Watzmann, mtn., Ger. H12 10
Waubay, S.D., U.S. F10 118
Wauchope, Austl. H10 70
Wauchula, Fl., U.S. L5 112
Wauconda, Wa., U.S. B6 122
Waugh, Mb., Can. I19 104
Waugh Mountain, mtn., Id., U.S. E11 122
Waukaringa, Austl. I3 70
Waukegan, Il., U.S. H8 110
Waukesha, Wi., U.S. G7 110
Waukomis, Ok., U.S. C9 116
Waukon, Ia., U.S. G4 110
Waunakee, Wi., U.S. G6 110
Wauneta, Ne., U.S. K6 118
Waupaca, Wi., U.S. F6 110
Waupun, Wi., U.S. G7 110
Waurika, Ok., U.S. E9 116
Wausa, Ne., U.S. I10 118
Wausau, Wi., U.S. F6 110
Wausaukee, Wi., U.S. E8 110
Wauseon, Oh., U.S. F2 108
Wautoma, Wi., U.S. F6 110
Wauwatosa, Wi., U.S. G7 110
Wauzeka, Wi., U.S. G5 110
Wave Hill, Austl. C6 68
Waveland, Ms., U.S. L7 114
Waverly, Al., U.S. J11 114
Waverly, Ia., U.S. H3 110
Waverly, Il., U.S. C7 114
Waverly, Ks., U.S. M12 118
Waverly, Mn., U.S. E2 110
Waverly, Mo., U.S. C3 114
Waverly, Ne., U.S. K11 118
Waverly, N.Y., U.S. E10 108
Waverly, Oh., U.S. H4 108
Waverly, Tn., U.S. F9 114
Waverly, Va., U.S. B9 112
Waverly Hall, Ga., U.S. G2 112
Wavre (Waver), Bel. G6 12
Wāw, Sudan N4 60
Wawa, On., Can. C11 110
Wawa, Sudan G6 60
Wawa, stm., Nic. C11 92
Wāw al-Kabīr, Libya C4 56
Wawanesa, Mb., Can. I15 104
Wawota, Sk., Can. I12 104
Waxahachie, Tx., U.S. G10 116
Waxhaw, N.C., U.S. E6 112
Wayabula, Indon. E8 38
Waycross, Ga., U.S. H4 112
Wayland, Ia., U.S. I4 110
Wayland, Ky., U.S. B4 112
Wayland, Mi., U.S. H10 110
Wayland, N.Y., U.S. E9 108
Waylyn, S.C., U.S. G7 112
Wayne, Ab., Can. F22 102
Wayne, Mi., U.S. H12 110
Wayne, Ne., U.S. I10 118
Wayne, N.J., U.S. G12 108
Wayne, Ok., U.S. E9 116
Wayne, W.V., U.S. I4 108
Wayne City, Il., U.S. D8 114
Waynesboro, Ga., U.S. F4 112
Waynesboro, Ms., U.S. K8 114
Waynesboro, Pa., U.S. H9 108
Waynesboro, Tn., U.S. G9 114
Waynesboro, Va., U.S. A8 112
Waynesburg, Oh., U.S. G5 108
Waynesburg, Pa., U.S. H6 108
Waynesville, Il., U.S. B7 114
Waynesville, Mo., U.S. E4 114
Waynesville, N.C., U.S. D4 112
Waynoka, Ok., U.S. C8 116
Wāzah Khwāh, Afg. D3 44
Wāzin, Libya E16 62
Wazīrābād, Pak. D6 44
We, Pulau, i., Indon. L3 40
Weagamow Lake, l., On., Can. F23 104
Weatherford, Ok., U.S. D8 116
Weatherford, Tx., U.S. G9 116
Weatherly, Pa., U.S. G11 108
Weaubleau, Mo., U.S. E3 114
Weaver, Al., U.S. I11 114
Weaver Lake, l., Mb., Can. F18 104
Weaverville, Ca., U.S. D3 124
Weaverville, N.C., U.S. D4 112
Webb, Ms., U.S. I6 114
Webb, Sk., Can. H6 104
Webb City, Mo., U.S. E2 114
Webber Lake, l., Mb., Can. D20 104
Webbwood, On., Can. D14 110
Weber, stm., Ut., U.S. D5 120
Weber, Mount, mtn., B.C., Can. B6 102
Weber City, Va., U.S. C4 112
Weberi Bekera, Eth. M10 60
Webster, Ab., Can. B16 102
Webster, Fl., U.S. K4 112
Webster, Ma., U.S. E15 108
Webster, S.D., U.S. F10 118
Webster, Wi., U.S. E3 110
Webster City, Ia., U.S. H2 110
Webster Springs, W.V., U.S. I6 108
Weda, Indon. E8 38
Weddell Sea, Ant. B1 73
Wedderburn, Austl. K5 70
Wedge Mountain, mtn., B.C., Can. G12 102
Wedgeport, N.S., Can. I8 106
Wedowee, Al., U.S. I11 114
Wedweil, Sudan M4 60
Wedza, Zimb. B10 66
Weed, Ca., U.S. C3 124
Weedsport, N.Y., U.S. D10 108
Weedville, Pa., U.S. F8 108
Weems, Va., U.S. B10 112
Weenen, S. Afr. G10 66
Weeping Water, Ne., U.S. K11 118
Weert, Neth. F8 12
Weesp, Neth. D7 12
Wee Waa, Austl. H8 70
Węgrów, Pol. C22 10
Wei, stm., China E8 30
Weiden in der Oberpfalz, Ger. F12 10
Weifang, China G7 32
Weihai, China F10 32
Weilburg, Ger. E8 10
Weilheim, Ger. H11 10
Weimar, Ger. E11 10
Weimar, Tx., U.S. J10 116
Weinan, China E8 30
Weiner, Ar., U.S. G6 114
Weinfelden, Switz. C11 13
Weinheim, Ger. F8 10
Weipa, Austl. B8 68
Weippe, Id., U.S. D10 122
Weir, Ks., U.S. N13 118
Weir, Ms., U.S. I7 114
Weir, stm., Austl. F9 70
Weir, stm., Mb., Can. B21 104
Weir River, Mb., Can. B20 104
Weirsdale, Fl., U.S. K5 112
Weirton, W.V., U.S. G6 108
Weisburd, Arg. D7 80
Weiser, Id., U.S. F9 122
Weiser, stm., Id., U.S. F9 122
Weishan (Xiazhen), China I5 32
Weishancheng, China C2 34
Weisner Mountain, mtn., Al., U.S. H11 114
Weissenburg, Switz. E7 13
Weissenburg in Bayern, Ger. F10 10
Weissenfels, Ger. D11 10
Weisshorn, mtn., Switz. F8 13
Weisskugel (Palla Bianca), mtn., Eur. E14 13
Weiss Lake, res., U.S. E1 112
Weitou, China K7 34
Weitra, Aus. G14 10
Weiz, Aus. H15 10
Weizhen, China F2 32
Weizhou Wan, b., Asia K7 34
Wejherowo, Pol. A18 10
Wekusko Lake, l., Mb., Can. D15 104
Welaka, Fl., U.S. J5 112
Welch, Ok., U.S. C11 116
Welch, Tx., U.S. G4 116
Welch, W.V., U.S. B5 112
Welcome, Mn., U.S. H13 118
Welcome, S.C., U.S. E4 112
Weldon, Il., U.S. B8 114
Weldon, N.C., U.S. C9 112
Weldon, Sk., Can. E9 104
Weldon, stm., U.S. B3 114
Weldona, Co., U.S. K4 118
Weleetka, Ok., U.S. D10 116
Welkite, Eth. M9 60
Welkom, S. Afr. F8 66
Welland, On., Can. H16 110
Welland, stm., On., Can. G16 110
Wellborn, Fl., U.S. I4 112
Wellborn, Tx., U.S. I10 116
Wellesley Islands, is., Austl. A3 70
Wellesley Lake, l., Yk., Can. E25 100
Wellfleet, Ma., U.S. F16 108
Wellington, Austl. I8 70
Wellington, Co., U.S. D11 120
Wellington, Eng., U.K. I11 8
Wellington, Ks., U.S. N10 118
Wellington, Mo., U.S. C3 114
Wellington, N.Z. D5 72
Wellington, Oh., U.S. F4 108
Wellington, On., Can. G18 110
Wellington, S. Afr. I4 66
Wellington, Tx., U.S. E6 116
Wellington, Ut., U.S. E6 120
Wellington, Isla, i., Chile F2 78
Wellington Bay, b., N.T., Can. C11 96
Wellington Channel, strt., N.T., Can. A14 96
Wellington Station, P.E., Can. F9 106
Wellman, Ia., U.S. I4 110
Wellman, Tx., U.S. F4 116
Wells, B.C., Can. D13 102
Wells, Mi., U.S. E8 110
Wells, Mn., U.S. G2 110
Wells, Nv., U.S. C11 124
Wells, N.Y., U.S. D12 108
Wells, Tx., U.S. K2 114
Wellsboro, Pa., U.S. F9 108
Wellsburg, Ia., U.S. H3 110
Wellsburg, W.V., U.S. G6 108
Wellsford, N.Z. B5 72
Wells Gray Provincial Park, B.C., Can. E15 102
Wells Lake, l., Mb., Can. A13 104
Wells-next-the-Sea, Eng., U.K. I14 8
Wellston, Oh., U.S. H4 108
Wellston, Ok., U.S. D9 116
Wellsville, Ks., U.S. M12 118
Wellsville, Mo., U.S. C5 114
Wellsville, N.Y., U.S. E9 108
Wellsville, Oh., U.S. G6 108
Wellsville, Ut., U.S. C5 120
Wellton, Az., U.S. L2 120
Wels, Aus. G14 10
Welsford, N.B., Can. G7 106
Welsh, La., U.S. L4 114
Welwitschia, Nmb. C2 66
Wembley, Ab., Can. B15 102
Wenatchee, Wa., U.S. C5 122
Wenatchee, stm., Wa., U.S. C5 122
Wenatchee Mountains, mts., Wa., U.S. C5 122
Wenchow see Wenzhou, China G9 34
Wendell, Id., U.S. H11 122
Wendell, N.C., U.S. D8 112
Wenden, Az., U.S. K3 120
Wendeng, China F10 32
Wendo, Eth. N10 60
Wendover, Ut., U.S. D2 120
Wengyang, China G9 34
Wengyuan, China K3 34
Wenling, China G10 34
Wenlock, stm., Austl. B8 68
Wenona, Il., U.S. I6 110
Wenshan, China C8 40
Wentworth, Austl. J4 70
Wentworth, N.C., U.S. C7 112
Wentworth, S.D., U.S. H11 118
Wenzhou, China G9 34
Werda, Bots. E6 66
Werdau, Ger. E12 10
Werder, Ger. C12 10
Were Ilu, Eth. L10 60
Wernigerode, Ger. D10 10
Werra, stm., Ger. E10 10
Werribee, Austl. K6 70
Werris Creek, Austl. H9 70
Wertheim, Ger. F9 10
Wertingen, Ger. G10 10
Wesel, Ger. D6 10
Weser, stm., Ger. B8 10
Weskan, Ks., U.S. M6 118
Weslaco, Tx., U.S. M9 116
Wesley, Ia., U.S. G2 110
Wesleyville, Nf., Can. C20 106
Wesleyville, Pa., U.S. E6 108
Wessel, Cape, c., Austl. B7 68
Wessel Islands, is., Austl. B7 68
Wessington, S.D., U.S. G9 118
Wessington Springs, S.D., U.S. G9 118
Wesson, Ms., U.S. K6 114
West, Ms., U.S. I7 114
West, Tx., U.S. H9 116
West, stm., Vt., U.S. D14 108
West Alexandria, Oh., U.S. H2 108
West Allis, Wi., U.S. G7 110
Westbank, B.C., Can. H15 102
West Bank, hist. reg., W.B. E4 50
Westbay, Fl., U.S. L11 114
West Bay, N.S., Can. G12 106
West Bay, b., Tx., U.S. J12 116
West Bend, Ia., U.S. I13 118
West Bend, Wi., U.S. G7 110
West Bengal, state, India I12 44
West Blocton, Al., U.S. I9 114
Westbourne, Mb., Can. H16 104
West Branch, Ia., U.S. I4 110
West Branch, Mi., U.S. F11 110
Westbridge, B.C., Can. H16 102
Westbrook, Me., U.S. D16 108
Westbrook, Mn., U.S. G12 118
Westbrook, Tx., U.S. G5 116
West Burlington, Ia., U.S. J4 110
West Butte, mtn., Mt., U.S. B14 122
Westby, Mt., U.S. C3 118
Westby, Wi., U.S. G5 110
West Caicos, i., T./C. Is. D8 94
West Carlisle, Tx., U.S. F5 116
West Channel, mth., N.T., Can. B27 100
West Chester, Pa., U.S. H11 108
Westchester Station, N.S., Can. G10 106
Westcliffe, Co., U.S. F11 120
West Columbia, S.C., U.S. F5 112
West Columbia, Tx., U.S. J11 116
West Concord, Mn., U.S. F3 110
West Des Moines, Ia., U.S. I2 110
West Elk Mountains, mts., Co., U.S. F9 120
West Elk Peak, mtn., Co., U.S. F9 120
West End, Ar., U.S. H4 114
West End, Bah. A5 94
West End, N.C., U.S. D7 112
Westerlo, Bel. F6 12
Westerly, R.I., U.S. F15 108
Western, Ne., U.S. K10 118
Western, stm., Austl. D5 70
Western Australia, state, Austl. E4 68
Western Cape, prov., S. Afr. I5 66
Western Channel, strt., Asia I16 32
Western Desert see Gharbīyah, Aş-Şahrā' al-, des., Egypt D4 60
Western Ghāts, mts., India D2 46
Western Isles, prov., Scot., U.K. D6 8
Westernport, Md., U.S. H7 108
Western Sahara, dep., Afr. D4 54
Western Samoa, ctry., Oc. J22 126
Western Shore, N.S., Can. H9 106
Westerschelde, est., Neth. F4 12
Westerstede, Ger. B7 10
Westerville, Oh., U.S. G4 108
West Falkland, i., Falk. Is. G4 78
West Fargo, N.D., U.S. E11 118
Westfield, Il., U.S. C8 114
Westfield, In., U.S. B10 114
Westfield, Ma., U.S. E14 108
Westfield, N.J., U.S. G12 108
Westfield, N.Y., U.S. E7 108
Westfield, Pa., U.S. F9 108
Westfield, Wi., U.S. G6 110
West Fiord, N.T., Can. A14 96
West Fork, Ar., U.S. G2 114
West Frankfort, Il., U.S. E8 114
Westgate, Austl. F7 70
West Glacier, Mt., U.S. B12 122
West Glamorgan, co., Wales, U.K. J10 8
West Hamlin, W.V., U.S. I4 108
West Hartford, Ct., U.S. F14 108
Westhaven, Ca., U.S. C1 124
West Haven, Ct., U.S. F14 108
West Helena, Ar., U.S. H6 114
Westhoff, Tx., U.S. J9 116
Westhope, N.D., U.S. C6 118
West Ice Shelf, Ant. B5 73
West Indies, is. E9 94
West Jefferson, N.C., U.S. C5 112
West Jefferson, Oh., U.S. H3 108
West Jordan, Ut., U.S. D5 120
West Kettle, stm., B.C., Can. H15 102
West Kingston, R.I., U.S. F15 108
West Lafayette, In., U.S. B10 114
West Lafayette, Oh., U.S. G5 108
Westlake, La., U.S. L3 114
West Laramie, Wy., U.S. C11 120
West Lebanon, In., U.S. B9 114
West Liberty, Ia., U.S. I4 110
West Liberty, Ky., U.S. B3 112
West Liberty, Oh., U.S. G3 108
Westlock, Ab., Can. C21 102
West Lorne, On., Can. H14 110
Westmeath, co., Ire. H6 8
West Melbourne, Fl., U.S. K6 112
West Memphis, Ar., U.S. G6 114
West Mifflin, Pa., U.S. G7 108
Westminster, Co., U.S. E11 120
Westminster, Md., U.S. H10 108
Westminster, S.C., U.S. E3 112
West Monroe, La., U.S. J4 114
Westmont, Pa., U.S. G8 108
Westmoreland, Ks., U.S. L11 118
Westmoreland, Tn., U.S. F10 114
Westmorland, Ca., U.S. K10 124
West Nicholson, Zimb. C9 66
West Nishnabotna, stm., Ia., U.S. K12 118
Weston, Co., U.S. G12 120
Weston, Id., U.S. H14 122
Weston, Mo., U.S. C2 114
Weston, Ne., U.S. J11 118
Weston, Oh., U.S. F3 108
Weston, Or., U.S. E7 122
Weston, W.V., U.S. H6 108
Weston-super-Mare, Eng., U.K. J11 8
West Orange, Tx., U.S. L3 114
Westover, Tn., U.S. G8 114
Westover, W.V., U.S. H7 108
West Palm Beach, Fl., U.S. M6 112
West Paris, Me., U.S. C16 108
West Pensacola, Fl., U.S. L9 114
Westphalia, Ks., U.S. M12 118
West Plains, Mo., U.S. F5 114
West Point, Ca., U.S. F5 124
West Point, Ga., U.S. G1 112
West Point, Ia., U.S. J4 110
West Point, Ky., U.S. E11 114
West Point, Ms., U.S. I8 114
West Point, Ne., U.S. J11 118
West Point, N.Y., U.S. F13 108
West Point, Va., U.S. B10 112
West Point, c., Austl. J2 70
West Point, c., P.E., Can. F9 106
West Point Lake, res., U.S. F1 112
Westport, Ct., U.S. F13 108
Westport, In., U.S. C11 114
Westport, Nf., Can. C17 106
Westport, N.S., Can. H7 106
Westport, N.Z. D3 72
Westport, On., Can. F19 110
Westport, Or., U.S. D2 122
Westport, Wa., U.S. D1 122
West Portsmouth, Oh., U.S. I3 108
West Prairie, stm., Ab., Can. B18 102
West Quoddy Head, c., Me., U.S. C20 108
West Richland, Wa., U.S. D6 122
West Road, stm., B.C., Can. D11 102
West Rutland, Vt., U.S. D13 108
West Sacramento, Ca., U.S. F4 124
West Saint Marys, stm., N.S., Can. G11 106
West Saint Modeste, Nf., Can. A17 106
West Salem, Il., U.S. D8 114
West Salem, Oh., U.S. G4 108
West Salem, Wi., U.S. G4 110
West Shoal Lake, l., Mb., Can. H17 104
West Siberian Plain see Zapadno-Sibirskaja ravnina, pl., Russia E13 26
West Slope, Or., U.S. E3 122
West Spanish Peak, mtn., Co., U.S. G12 120
West Sussex, co., Eng., U.K. K13 8
West Terre Haute, In., U.S. C9 114
West Union, Ia., U.S. H4 110
West Union, Oh., U.S. I3 108
West Union, W.V., U.S. H6 108
West Unity, Oh., U.S. F2 108
West Valley, Mt., U.S. D12 122
West Valley City, Ut., U.S. D5 120
West Vancouver, B.C., Can. H11 102
Westville, In., U.S. A10 114
Westville, N.S., Can. G11 106
Westville, Ok., U.S. G2 114
West Virginia, state, U.S. D10 98
West-Vlaanderen, prov., Bel. F2 12
West Warwick, R.I., U.S. F15 108
West Webster, N.Y., U.S. D9 108
Westwego, La., U.S. M6 114
Westwold, B.C., Can. G15 102
Westwood, Ca., U.S. D4 124
Westwood Lakes, Fl., U.S. N6 112
West Wyalong, Austl. I7 70
West Yellowstone, Mt., U.S. F14 122
Wetar, Pulau, i., Indon. G8 38
Wetaskiwin, Ab., Can. E21 102
Wete, Tan. C7 58
Wethersfield, Ct., U.S. F14 108
Wetiko Hills, hills, Can. D22 104
Wetmore, Ks., U.S. L12 118
Wet Mountains, mts., Co., U.S. F11 120
Wetteren, Bel. F4 12
Wetumka, Ok., U.S. D10 116
Wetumpka, Al., U.S. J10 114
Wetzikon, Switz. D10 13
Wetzlar, Ger. E8 10
Wewahitchka, Fl., U.S. I1 112
Wewak, Pap. N. Gui. k15 68a
Wewoka, Ok., U.S. D10 116
Wexford, Ire. I7 8
Wexford, co., Ire. I7 8
Weyakwin Lake, l., Sk., Can. D8 104
Weyauwega, Wi., U.S. F7 110
Weyburn, Sk., Can. I11 104
Weymouth, Eng., U.K. K11 8
Weymouth, Ma., U.S. E16 108
Weymouth, N.S., Can. H7 106
Whakatane, N.Z. B6 72
Whangarei, N.Z. A5 72
Wharton, Tx., U.S. J10 116
Wharton, W.V., U.S. J5 108
Wharton Lake, l., N.T., Can. D13 96
Whataroa, N.Z. E3 72
What Cheer, Ia., U.S. I3 110
Whatley, Al., U.S. K9 114
Whatshan Lake, l., B.C., Can. G16 102
Wheatland, Ca., U.S. E4 124
Wheatland, Ia., U.S. I5 110
Wheatland, Wy., U.S. B12 120
Wheatley, Ar., U.S. H5 114
Wheatley, On., Can. H13 110
Wheaton, Il., U.S. A8 114
Wheaton, Md., U.S. H9 108
Wheaton, Mn., U.S. F11 118
Wheat Ridge, Co., U.S. E11 120
Wheeler, Ms., U.S. H8 114
Wheeler, Tx., U.S. D6 116
Wheeler, stm., P.Q., Can. E19 96
Wheeler, stm., Sk., Can. A9 104
Wheeler Lake, res., Al., U.S. H9 114
Wheeler Peak, mtn., Ca., U.S. F6 124
Wheeler Peak, mtn., N.M., U.S. H11 120
Wheeler Peak, mtn., Nv., U.S. F11 124
Wheeling, W.V., U.S. G6 108
Wheelwright, Arg. G8 80
Wheelwright, Ky., U.S. B4 112
Whidbey Island, i., Wa., U.S. B3 122
Whigham, Ga., U.S. I2 112
Whitakers, N.C., U.S. C9 112
Whitbourne, Nf., Can. E20 106
Whitby, On., Can. G17 110
Whitchurch-Stouffville, On., Can. G16 110
White, Ga., U.S. E2 112
White, S.D., U.S. G11 118
White, stm., Az., U.S. K6 120
White, stm., B.C., Can. G19 102
White, stm., In., U.S. D9 114
White, stm., N.A. E24 100
White, stm., Nv., U.S. G11 124
White, stm., U.S. H5 114
White, stm., U.S. H7 118
White, stm., U.S. D7 120
White, stm., Vt., U.S. D14 108
White, stm., Wi., U.S. D5 110
White Bay, b., Nf., Can. B17 106
White Bear Indian Reserve, Sk., Can. I12 104
White Bear Lake, Mn., U.S. E2 110
Whitebear Lake, l., Sk., Can. G6 104
White Bluff, Tn., U.S. F9 114
White Butte, mtn., N.D., U.S. E4 118
Whitecap Lake, l., Mb., Can. B19 104
White Castle, La., U.S. L5 114
White City, Ks., U.S. M11 118
White Cliffs, Austl. H5 70
White Cloud, Mi., U.S. G10 110
Whitecourt, Ab., Can. C19 102
White Deer, Tx., U.S. D5 116
White Earth, stm., N.D., U.S. C5 118
Whiteface, Tx., U.S. F4 116
Whiteface, stm., Mn., U.S. C3 110
Whiteface Mountain, mtn., N.Y., U.S. C13 108
Whitefield, N.H., U.S. C15 108
Whitefish, Mt., U.S. B11 122
Whitefish, stm., Mi., U.S. E8 110
Whitefish Bay, Wi., U.S. G8 110
Whitefish Bay, b., N.A. D11 110
Whitefish Bay, b., On., Can. I20 104
Whitefish Lake, l., Ab., Can. C23 102
Whitefish Lake, l., Mb., Can. C21 104
Whitefish Lake, l., N.T., Can. D11 96
White Fish Lake Indian Reserve, Ab., Can. C23 102
Whitefish Point, Mi., U.S. D11 110
Whitefish Point, c., Mi., U.S. D10 110
White Fox, Sk., Can. E10 104
White Fox, stm., Sk., Can. E10 104
White Gull Creek, stm., Sk., Can. E10 104
White Hall, Ar., U.S. H4 114
White Hall, Il., U.S. C6 114
Whitehall, Mi., U.S. G9 110
Whitehall, Mt., U.S. E13 122
Whitehall, N.Y., U.S. D13 108
Whitehall, Wi., U.S. F4 110
White Haven, Pa., U.S. F11 108
Whitehorse, Yk., Can. F27 100
White House, Tn., U.S. F10 114
Whitehouse, Tx., U.S. G11 116
White Island, i., N.T., Can. C16 96
White Lake, S.D., U.S. H9 118
White Lake, Wi., U.S. E7 110
White Lake, l., La., U.S. M4 114
Whitelaw, Ab., Can. A16 102
Whitemark, Austl. M8 70
White Mountain, Ak., U.S. D13 100
White Mountain Peak, mtn., Ca., U.S. G7 124
White Mountains, mts., N.H., U.S. C15 108
White Mountains, mts., U.S. G7 124
Whitemouth, Mb., Can. I19 104
Whitemouth, stm., Mb., Can. I19 104
Whitemouth Lake, l., Mb., Can. I19 104
Whitemud, stm., Mb., Can. H15 104
White Nile (Al-Baḥr al-Abyaḍ), stm., Sudan L7 60
White Oak, Tx., U.S. J2 114
White Pass, N.A. G27 100
White Pigeon, Mi., U.S. I10 110
White Pine, Mi., U.S. D6 110
White Pine, Tn., U.S. C3 112
White Plains, N.C., U.S. C6 112
White Plains, N.Y., U.S. F13 108
Whiteriver, Az., U.S. K7 120
White River, On., Can. B10 110
White River, S.D., U.S. H7 118
White River Junction, Vt., U.S. D14 108
White Rock, B.C., Can. H12 102
Whiterocks, stm., Ut., U.S. D7 120
White Russia see Belarus, ctry., Eur. H11 26
Whitesail Lake, l., B.C., Can. D7 102
White Salmon, Wa., U.S. E4 122
White Salmon, stm., Wa., U.S. E4 122
Whitesand, stm., Sk., Can. G12 104
Whitesboro, Tx., U.S. F10 116
Whitesburg, Ky., U.S. B4 112
White Sea see Beloje more, Russia D5 26
White Settlement, Tx., U.S. G9 116
Whiteshell Provincial Park, Mb., Can. I19 104
White Springs, Fl., U.S. I4 112
White Stone Lake, l., Mb., Can. B17 104
White Sulphur Springs, Mt., U.S. D15 122
White Sulphur Springs, W.V., U.S. B6 112
Whitesville, Ky., U.S. E10 114
Whitesville, W.V., U.S. J5 108
Whiteswan Lakes, l., Sk., Can. D9 104
Whiteville, N.C., U.S. E8 112
Whiteville, Tn., U.S. G7 114
White Volta (Volta Blanche), stm., Afr. F6 54
Whitewater, Ks., U.S. N10 118
Whitewater, Mt., U.S. B18 122
Whitewater, Wi., U.S. H7 110
Whitewater, stm., Mo., U.S. E7 114
Whitewater, stm., U.S. C11 114
Whitewater Baldy, mtn., N.M., U.S. K8 120
Whitewater Lake, l., Mb., Can. I14 104
Whitewood, Austl. C5 70
Whitewood, S.D., U.S. G4 118
Whitewood, Sk., Can. H12 104
Whitewright, Tx., U.S. F10 116
Whithorn, Scot., U.K. G9 8
Whiting, Ia., U.S. I11 118
Whiting, Ks., U.S. L12 118
Whiting, Wi., U.S. F6 110
Whitley City, Ky., U.S. C2 112
Whitman, Ma., U.S. E16 108
Whitmire, S.C., U.S. E5 112
Whitney, On., Can. E17 110
Whitney, Tx., U.S. H9 116
Whitney, Lake, res., Tx., U.S. H9 116
Whitney, Mount, mtn., Ca., U.S. H7 124
Whitney Point, N.Y., U.S. E11 108
Whitsunday Island, i., Austl. C8 70
Whittemore, Ia., U.S. H13 118
Whittemore, Mi., U.S. F12 110
Whittier, Ak., U.S. F20 100
Whittier, N.C., U.S. D3 112
Whittle, Cap, c., P.Q., Can. B13 106
Whittlesea, Austl. K6 70
Whittlesea, S. Afr. I8 66
Whitwell, Tn., U.S. G11 114
Wholdaia Lake, l., N.T., Can. D12 96
Whyalla, Austl. I2 70
Whycocomagh, N.S., Can. G12 106
Wiarton, On., Can. F14 110
Wiau Lake, l., Ab., Can. B23 102
Wiawso, Ghana H8 64
Wibaux, Mt., U.S. E3 118
Wichita, Ks., U.S. N10 118
Wichita, stm., Tx., U.S. E8 116
Wichita Falls, Tx., U.S. F8 116
Wichita Mountains, mts., Ok., U.S. E8 116
Wick, Scot., U.K. C10 8
Wickenburg, Az., U.S. K4 120
Wickett, Tx., U.S. H4 116
Wickham, Cape, c., Austl. L5 70
Wickliffe, Ky., U.S. F7 114
Wicklow, co., Ire. I7 8
Wicklow Mountains, mts., Ire. H7 8
Widen, W.V., U.S. I6 108
Widerøe, Mount, mtn., Ant. C3 73
Wiehl, Ger. E7 10
Wiek, Ger. A13 10
Wieliczka, Pol. F20 10
Wielkopolska, reg., Pol. D17 10
Wieluń, Pol. D18 10
Wien (Vienna), Aus. G16 10
Wiener Neustadt, Aus. H16 10
Wienerwald, mts., Aus. G16 10
Wieprz, stm., Pol. E22 10
Wierden, Neth. D10 12
Wiergate, Tx., U.S. K3 114
Wiesbaden, Ger. E8 10
Wieselburg, Aus. G15 10
Wiesloch, Ger. F8 10
Wietze, Ger. C9 10
Wigan, Eng., U.K. H11 8
Wiggins, Co., U.S. K3 118
Wiggins, Ms., U.S. L7 114
Wigtown, Scot., U.K. G9 8
Wijalpurā, Nepal G11 44
Wil, Switz. D11 13
Wilber, Ne., U.S. K11 118
Wilberforce Falls, wtfl, N.T., Can. C11 96
Wilbur, Wa., U.S. C7 122
Wilburton, Ok., U.S. E11 116
Wilcannia, Austl. H5 70
Wilcox, Ne., U.S. K8 118
Wilcox, Pa., U.S. F8 108
Wilcox, Sk., Can. H10 104
Wildcat Hill, hill, Sk., Can. E12 104
Wilder, Id., U.S. G9 122
Wildersville, Tn., U.S. G8 114
Wildhaus, Switz. D11 13
Wildhay, stm., Ab., Can. D17 102
Wildnest Lake, l., Sk., Can. C12 104
Wildon, Aus. I15 10
Wild Rice, stm., Mn., U.S. D11 118
Wild Rice, stm., N.D., U.S. E10 118
Wildrose, N.D., U.S. C4 118
Wild Rose, Wi., U.S. F6 110
Wildwood, Ab., Can. D19 102
Wildwood, N.J., U.S. I12 108
Wilhelm, Mount, mtn., Pap. N. Gui. m15 68a
Wilhelmina Gebergte, mts., Sur. F14 84
Wilhelminakanaal, Neth. E7 12
Wilhelmina Peak see Trikora, Puncak, mtn., Indon. F10 38
Wilhelmshaven, Ger. B8 10
Wilhelmstal, Nmb. C3 66
Wilkerson Pass, Co., U.S. E11 120
Wilkes-Barre, Pa., U.S. F11 108
Wilkesboro, N.C., U.S. C5 112
Wilkes Land, reg., Ant. C7 73
Wilkie, Sk., Can. F6 104
Will, Mount, mtn., B.C., Can. H30 100
Willacoochee, Ga., U.S. H3 112
Willamette, stm., Or., U.S. E3 122
Willamina, Or., U.S. E2 122
Willandra Billabong Creek, stm., Austl. I6 70
Willapa, stm., Wa., U.S. D2 122
Willapa Bay, b., Wa., U.S. D1 122
Willard, Mo., U.S. E3 114
Willard, N.M., U.S. J10 120
Willard, Oh., U.S. F4 108
Willard, Ut., U.S. C4 120
Willard, Punta, c., Mex. C3 90
Willcox, Az., U.S. L7 120
Willcox Playa, l., Az., U.S. L7 120
Willemstad, Neth. Ant. H10 94
William Bill Dannelly Reservoir, res., Al., U.S. J9 114
William Lake, l., Mb., Can. E15 104
Williams, Az., U.S. I4 120
Williams, Ca., U.S. E3 124
Williams, Ia., U.S. H2 110
Williams, Mn., U.S. C13 118
Williams, stm., Austl. C4 70
Williams Bay, Wi., U.S. H7 110
Williamsburg, Ia., U.S. I3 110
Williamsburg, Ky., U.S. C2 112
Williamsburg, Pa., U.S. G8 108
Williamsburg, Va., U.S. B10 112
Williams Lake, B.C., Can. E12 102
Williams Lake Indian Reserve, B.C., Can. E12 102
Williamson, N.Y., U.S. D9 108
Williamson, W.V., U.S. B4 112
Williamson, Mount, mtn., Ca., U.S. H7 124
Williamsport, In., U.S. B9 114
Williamsport, Nf., Can. B17 106
Williamsport, Pa., U.S. F9 108
Williamston, Mi., U.S. H11 110
Williamston, N.C., U.S. D9 112
Williamston, S.C., U.S. E4 112
Williamstown, Ky., U.S. I2 108
Williamstown, Ma., U.S. E13 108
Williamstown, N.J., U.S. H12 108
Williamstown, Vt., U.S. C14 108
Williamstown, W.V., U.S. H5 108
Williamsville, Il., U.S. C7 114
Willimantic, Ct., U.S. F14 108
Willingboro, N.J., U.S. G12 108
Willingdon, Ab., Can. D22 102
Willingdon, Mount, mtn., Ab., Can. F18 102
Willis, Tx., U.S. I11 116
Willisau, Switz. D9 13
Willis Group, is., Austl. C10 68
Willis Island, i., Nf., Can. D20 106
Williston, Fl., U.S. J4 112
Williston, N.D., U.S. C4 118
Williston, S. Afr. H5 66
Williston, S.C., U.S. F5 112
Williston Lake, res., B.C., Can. A10 102
Willisville, Il., U.S. E7 114
Willits, Ca., U.S. E2 124
Willmar, Mn., U.S. F12 118
Willmore Wilderness Provincial Park, Ab., Can. D15 102
Willoughby, Oh., U.S. F5 108
Willoughby, Cape, c., Austl. J3 70
Willow, Ak., U.S. F19 100
Willow, stm., Ab., Can. B20 102
Willow, stm., B.C., Can. E12 102
Willow, stm., Mn., U.S. D2 110
Willow, stm., Wi., U.S. E3 110
Willowbrook, Sk., Can. G12 104
Willow Bunch, Sk., Can. I9 104
Willow Bunch Lake, l., Sk., Can. I9 104
Willow City, N.D., U.S. C7 118
Willow Creek, Ca., U.S. D2 124
Willow Creek, Mt., U.S. E14 122
Willow Creek, stm., Ab., Can. G20 102
Willowick, Oh., U.S. F5 108
Willow Lake, S.D., U.S. G10 118
Willow Lake, l., N.T., Can. D9 96
Willowlake, stm., N.T., Can. D8 96
Willowmore, S. Afr. I6 66
Willow River, B.C., Can. C12 102
Willows, Ca., U.S. E3 124
Willow Springs, Mo., U.S. F5 114
Wills, Lake, l., Austl. D5 68
Willshire, Oh., U.S. G2 108
Wills Point, Tx., U.S. G10 116
Willunga, Austl. J3 70
Wilmar, Ar., U.S. I5 114
Wilmer, Al., U.S. L8 114
Wilmer, Tx., U.S. G10 116
Wilmette, Il., U.S. H8 110
Wilmington, Austl. I3 70
Wilmington, De., U.S. H11 108
Wilmington, Il., U.S. I7 110
Wilmington, N.C., U.S. E9 112
Wilmington, Oh., U.S. H3 108
Wilmington, Vt., U.S. E14 108
Wilmore, Ky., U.S. B2 112
Wilmot, Ar., U.S. I5 114
Wilmot, S.D., U.S. F11 118
Wilsall, Mt., U.S. E15 122
Wilson, Ar., U.S. G6 114
Wilson, Austl. I3 70
Wilson, Ks., U.S. M9 118
Wilson, La., U.S. L5 114

| Name | Map Ref. | Page |
|---|---|---|
| Wilson, N.C., U.S. | D9 | 112 |
| Wilson, N.Y., U.S. | D8 | 108 |
| Wilson, Ok., U.S. | E9 | 116 |
| Wilson, Tx., U.S. | F5 | 116 |
| Wilson, stm., Austl. | A4 | 70 |
| Wilson, stm., Or., U.S. | E2 | 122 |
| Wilson, Cape, c., N.T., Can. | C16 | 96 |
| Wilson, Mount, mtn., Ca., U.S. | J7 | 124 |
| Wilson, Mount, mtn., Co., U.S. | G9 | 120 |
| Wilson, Mount, mtn., Nv., U.S. | F11 | 124 |
| Wilson Lake, res., Al., U.S. | H9 | 114 |
| Wilson Lake, res., Ks., U.S. | M9 | 118 |
| Wilsons Beach, N.B., Can. | H7 | 106 |
| Wilsons Promontory, c., Austl. | L7 | 70 |
| Wilsonville, Ne., U.S. | K7 | 118 |
| Wilton, Me., U.S. | C16 | 108 |
| Wilton, N.D., U.S. | D7 | 118 |
| Wilton, N.H., U.S. | E15 | 108 |
| Wilton, Wi., U.S. | G5 | 110 |
| Wiltshire, co., Eng., U.K. | J12 | 8 |
| Wiluna, Austl. | E4 | 68 |
| Wimapedi, stm., Mb., Can. | C15 | 104 |
| Wimauma, Fl., U.S. | L4 | 112 |
| Wimberley, Tx., U.S. | I8 | 116 |
| Wimbledon, N.D., U.S. | D9 | 118 |
| Winagami Lake, l., Ab., Can. | B18 | 102 |
| Winamac, In., U.S. | A10 | 114 |
| Winburg, S. Afr. | G8 | 66 |
| Winchendon, Ma., U.S. | E14 | 108 |
| Winchester, Eng., U.K. | J12 | 8 |
| Winchester, Id., U.S. | D9 | 122 |
| Winchester, Il., U.S. | C6 | 114 |
| Winchester, In., U.S. | B12 | 114 |
| Winchester, Ky., U.S. | B2 | 112 |
| Winchester, N.H., U.S. | E14 | 108 |
| Winchester, On., Can. | B11 | 108 |
| Winchester, Tn., U.S. | G10 | 114 |
| Winchester, Va., U.S. | H8 | 112 |
| Wind, stm., Wy., U.S. | G17 | 122 |
| Wind, stm., Yk., Can. | D27 | 100 |
| Windber, Pa., U.S. | G8 | 108 |
| Wind Cave National Park, S.D., U.S. | H4 | 118 |
| Windermere, B.C., Can. | G19 | 102 |
| Windfall, Ab., Can. | C18 | 102 |
| Windhoek, Nmb. | D3 | 66 |
| Windigo, stm., On., Can. | E23 | 104 |
| Windigo Lake, l., On., Can. | F23 | 104 |
| Windischgarsten, Aus. | H14 | 10 |
| Wind Lake, Wi., U.S. | H7 | 110 |
| Windom, Mn., U.S. | H12 | 118 |
| Windom Peak, mtn., Co., U.S. | G9 | 120 |
| Windorah, Austl. | E5 | 70 |
| Window Rock, Az., U.S. | I7 | 120 |
| Wind River Peak, mtn., Wy., U.S. | H16 | 122 |
| Wind River Range, mts., Wy., U.S. | G16 | 122 |
| Windsor, Austl. | I9 | 70 |
| Windsor, Ca., U.S. | F3 | 124 |
| Windsor, Co., U.S. | D12 | 120 |
| Windsor, Ct., U.S. | F14 | 108 |
| Windsor, Eng., U.K. | J13 | 8 |
| Windsor, Il., U.S. | C8 | 114 |
| Windsor, Mo., U.S. | D3 | 114 |
| Windsor, N.C., U.S. | D10 | 112 |
| Windsor, Nf., Can. | D18 | 106 |
| Windsor, N.S., Can. | H9 | 106 |
| Windsor, On., Can. | H12 | 110 |
| Windsor, P.Q., Can. | B14 | 108 |
| Windsor, Va., U.S. | C10 | 112 |
| Windsor Forest, Ga., U.S. | H5 | 112 |
| Windsor Locks, Ct., U.S. | F14 | 108 |
| Windthorst, Tx., U.S. | F8 | 116 |
| Windward Islands, is., N.A. | H14 | 94 |
| Windward Passage, strt., N.A. | E7 | 94 |
| Windy Lake, l., On., Can. | D12 | 104 |
| Windy Peak, mtn., Co., U.S. | F10 | 120 |
| Windy Peak, mtn., Wa., U.S. | B6 | 122 |
| Winefred, stm., Ab., Can. | C4 | 104 |
| Winefred Lake, l., Ab., Can. | B24 | 102 |
| Winejok, Sudan | M4 | 60 |
| Winfield, Ab., Can. | E20 | 102 |
| Winfield, Al., U.S. | I9 | 114 |
| Winfield, Ia., U.S. | I4 | 110 |
| Winfield, Ks., U.S. | N11 | 118 |
| Winfield, Mo., U.S. | D6 | 114 |
| Winfield, W.V., U.S. | I5 | 108 |
| Wing, N.D., U.S. | D7 | 118 |
| Wingate, N.C., U.S. | E6 | 112 |
| Wingene, Bel. | F3 | 12 |
| Wingham, Austl. | H10 | 70 |
| Wingham, On., Can. | G8 | 110 |
| Wingo, Ky., U.S. | F8 | 114 |
| Winifred, Mt., U.S. | C16 | 122 |
| Winifreda, Arg. | I6 | 80 |
| Winisk, On., Can. | E15 | 96 |
| Winisk, stm., On., Can. | F15 | 96 |
| Winisk Lake, l., On., Can. | F15 | 96 |
| Wink, Tx., U.S. | H3 | 116 |
| Winkana, Myan. | G5 | 40 |
| Winkelman, Az., U.S. | L6 | 120 |
| Winkler, Mb., Can. | I17 | 104 |
| Winlaw, B.C., Can. | H17 | 102 |
| Winlock, Wa., U.S. | D3 | 122 |
| Winneba, Ghana | I9 | 64 |
| Winnebago, Il., U.S. | H6 | 110 |
| Winnebago, Mn., U.S. | G1 | 110 |
| Winnebago, Ne., U.S. | I11 | 118 |
| Winnebago, stm., Ia., U.S. | G2 | 110 |
| Winnebago, Lake, l., Wi., U.S. | F7 | 110 |
| Winneconne, Wi., U.S. | F7 | 110 |
| Winnemucca, Nv., U.S. | D8 | 124 |
| Winner, S.D., U.S. | H8 | 118 |
| Winnetka, Il., U.S. | H8 | 110 |
| Winnett, Mt., U.S. | C17 | 122 |
| Winnfield, La., U.S. | K4 | 114 |
| Winnibigoshish, Lake, l., Mn., U.S. | C1 | 110 |
| Winnie, Tx., U.S. | M2 | 114 |
| Winnipeg, Mb., Can. | I17 | 104 |
| Winnipeg, stm., Can. | H18 | 104 |
| Winnipeg, Lake, l., Can. | F17 | 104 |
| Winnipeg Beach, Mb., Can. | H18 | 104 |
| Winnipegosis, Austl. | G15 | 104 |
| Winnipegosis, Lake, l., Mb., Can. | F14 | 104 |
| Winnipesaukee, Lake, l., N.H., U.S. | D5 | 108 |
| Winnsboro, La., U.S. | J5 | 114 |
| Winnsboro, S.C., U.S. | E5 | 112 |
| Winnsboro, Tx., U.S. | G11 | 116 |
| Winnsboro Mills, S.C., U.S. | E5 | 112 |
| Winona, Ks., U.S. | L6 | 118 |
| Winona, Mn., U.S. | D7 | 110 |
| Winona, Mn., U.S. | F4 | 110 |
| Winona, Ms., U.S. | I7 | 114 |
| Winona Lake, In., U.S. | A11 | 114 |
| Winooski, Vt., U.S. | C13 | 108 |
| Winooski, stm., Vt., U.S. | C14 | 108 |
| Winschoten, Neth. | B11 | 12 |

| Winside, Ne., U.S. | I10 | 118 |
| Winslow, Az., U.S. | I6 | 120 |
| Winslow, Me., U.S. | C17 | 108 |
| Winsted, Ct., U.S. | F13 | 108 |
| Winsted, Mn., U.S. | F1 | 110 |
| Winston, Or., U.S. | H3 | 122 |
| Winston-Salem, N.C., U.S. | C6 | 112 |
| Wintego Lake, l., Sk., Can. | C12 | 104 |
| Winter, Wi., U.S. | E4 | 110 |
| Winter Garden, Fl., U.S. | K5 | 112 |
| Winter Harbor, Me., U.S. | C18 | 108 |
| Winter Harbour, B.C., Can. | G6 | 102 |
| Winterhaven, Ca., U.S. | L11 | 124 |
| Winter Haven, Fl., U.S. | K5 | 112 |
| Wintering Lake, l., Mb., Can. | C17 | 104 |
| Winter Island, i., N.T., Can. | C16 | 96 |
| Winter Park, Fl., U.S. | K5 | 112 |
| Winter Park, N.C., U.S. | E9 | 112 |
| Winterport, Me., U.S. | C18 | 108 |
| Winters, Ca., U.S. | F4 | 124 |
| Winters, Tx., U.S. | H7 | 116 |
| Winterset, Ia., U.S. | I1 | 110 |
| Winterthur, Switz. | C10 | 13 |
| Winterton, Nf., Can. | E20 | 106 |
| Winterville, Ga., U.S. | F3 | 112 |
| Winterville, Me., U.S. | I5 | 114 |
| Winterville, Ms., U.S. | D9 | 113 |
| Winterville, N.C., U.S. | D9 | 112 |
| Winthrop, Ia., U.S. | H4 | 110 |
| Winthrop, Me., U.S. | C17 | 108 |
| Winthrop, Mn., U.S. | F1 | 110 |
| Winthrop Harbor, Il., U.S. | H8 | 110 |
| Winton, Austl. | D5 | 70 |
| Winton, N.C., U.S. | C10 | 112 |
| Winton, N.Z. | G2 | 72 |
| Wipperfürth, Ger. | D7 | 10 |
| Wirātanagar, Nepal | G12 | 44 |
| Wirganj, Nepal | G11 | 44 |
| Wirral, pen., Eng., U.K. | H10 | 8 |
| Wirraminna, Austl. | H2 | 70 |
| Wiscasset, Me., U.S. | C17 | 108 |
| Wisconsin, state, U.S. | C9 | 98 |
| Wisconsin, stm., Wi., U.S. | G5 | 110 |
| Wisconsin, Lake, res., Wi., U.S. | G6 | 110 |
| Wisconsin Dells, Wi., U.S. | G5 | 110 |
| Wisconsin Rapids, Wi., U.S. | F6 | 110 |
| Wisdom, Mt., U.S. | E12 | 122 |
| Wise, Va., U.S. | C4 | 112 |
| Wishart, Sk., Can. | G10 | 104 |
| Wishek, N.D., U.S. | E8 | 118 |
| Wishram, Wa., U.S. | E5 | 122 |
| Wisła, stm., Pol. | A18 | 10 |
| Wismar, Ger. | B11 | 10 |
| Wismar, Guy. | D13 | 84 |
| Wisner, La., U.S. | K5 | 114 |
| Wisner, Ne., U.S. | J11 | 118 |
| Wissembourg, Fr. | C14 | 14 |
| Wisznice, Pol. | D23 | 10 |
| Witbank, S. Afr. | E9 | 66 |
| Witbooisvlei, Nmb. | E4 | 66 |
| Witchekan Lake, l., Sk., Can. | E7 | 104 |
| Withlacoochee, stm., U.S. | I3 | 112 |
| Witjira National Park, Austl. | E7 | 68 |
| Witless Bay, Nf., Can. | E21 | 106 |
| Witrivier, S. Afr. | E10 | 66 |
| Witt, Il., U.S. | C7 | 114 |
| Wittenberg, Ger. | D12 | 10 |
| Wittenberg, Wi., U.S. | F6 | 110 |
| Wittenberge, Ger. | B11 | 10 |
| Wittenoom, Austl. | D3 | 68 |
| Wittingen, Ger. | C10 | 10 |
| Wittlich, Ger. | F6 | 10 |
| Wittmund, Ger. | B7 | 10 |
| Wittstock, Ger. | B12 | 10 |
| Witu, Kenya | B8 | 58 |
| Witwatersrand, reg., S. Afr. | E8 | 66 |
| Witzputz, Nmb. | F3 | 66 |
| Wiwa Creek, stm., Sk., Can. | H7 | 104 |
| Wiżajny, Pol. | A22 | 10 |
| Włocławek, Pol. | C19 | 10 |
| Wörgl, Aus. | H12 | 10 |
| Work Channel, strt., B.C., Can. | C4 | 102 |
| Workington, Eng., U.K. | G10 | 8 |
| Worksop, Eng., U.K. | H12 | 8 |
| Workum, Neth. | C7 | 12 |
| Worland, Wy., U.S. | F18 | 122 |
| Wormerveer, Neth. | D6 | 12 |
| Worms, Ger. | F8 | 10 |
| Wortham, Tx., U.S. | H10 | 116 |
| Worthing, Eng., U.K. | K13 | 8 |
| Worthington, In., U.S. | C10 | 114 |
| Worthington, Mn., U.S. | H12 | 118 |
| Worthington, Oh., U.S. | G3 | 108 |
| Worthington Peak, mtn., Nv., U.S. | C10 | 124 |
| Woudrichem, Neth. | E7 | 12 |
| Wounded Knee, S.D., U.S. | H5 | 118 |
| Wounta, Nic. | D11 | 92 |
| Wounta, Laguna de, b., Nic. | D11 | 92 |
| Wouw, Neth. | E5 | 12 |
| Wowan, Austl. | D9 | 70 |
| Woy Woy, Austl. | I9 | 70 |
| Wrangel Island see Vrangel'a, ostrov, i., Russia | C28 | 100 |
| Wrangell, Ak., U.S. | H28 | 100 |
| Wrangell, Cape, c., Ak., U.S. | E22 | 100 |
| Wrangell Island, i., Ak., U.S. | H28 | 100 |
| Wrangell Mountains, mts., Ak., U.S. | F23 | 100 |
| Wrath, Cape, c., Scot., U.K. | C8 | 8 |
| Wray, Co., U.S. | K5 | 118 |
| Wreck Reef, rf., Austl. | D11 | 70 |
| Wrens, Ga., U.S. | F4 | 112 |
| Wrentham, Ab., Can. | H22 | 102 |
| Wrexham, Wales, U.K. | H10 | 8 |
| Wright, Mount, mtn., Mt., U.S. | C13 | 122 |
| Wright City, Mo., U.S. | D5 | 114 |
| Wright City, Ok., U.S. | E11 | 116 |
| Wright Patman Lake, res., Tx., U.S. | I2 | 114 |
| Wrightson, Mount, mtn., Az., U.S. | M6 | 120 |
| Wrightstown, Wi., U.S. | G4 | 112 |
| Wrightsville, Ga., U.S. | G4 | 112 |
| Wrightsville Beach, N.C., U.S. | E9 | 112 |
| Wrightwood, Ca., U.S. | J8 | 124 |
| Wrigley, N.T., Can. | E33 | 100 |
| Wrigley, Tn., U.S. | G9 | 114 |
| Wrocław (Breslau), Pol. | D17 | 10 |
| Wrong Lake, l., Mb., Can. | F18 | 104 |
| Wrottesley, Cape, c., N.T., Can. | B8 | 96 |
| Wroxton, Sk., Can. | G13 | 104 |
| Września, Pol. | C17 | 10 |
| Wschowa, Pol. | D15 | 10 |
| Wuchang, China | D11 | 40 |
| Wuchuan, China | D1 | 34 |
| Wudian, China | D1 | 34 |
| Wudinna, Austl. | I1 | 70 |
| Wudu, China | E7 | 30 |

| Wood, S.D., U.S. | H7 | 118 |
| Wood, stm., B.C., Can. | E16 | 102 |
| Wood, stm., Sk., Can. | I8 | 104 |
| Wood, stm., Sk., Can. | I8 | 104 |
| Wood, stm., Wy., U.S. | G16 | 122 |
| Wood, Mount, mtn., Yk., Can. | F24 | 100 |
| Woodall Mountain, hill, Ms., U.S. | H8 | 114 |
| Wood Bay, b., N.T., Can. | B30 | 100 |
| Woodbine, Ga., U.S. | H5 | 112 |
| Woodbine, Ia., U.S. | J12 | 118 |
| Woodbine, Ky., U.S. | C2 | 112 |
| Woodbridge, Va., U.S. | I9 | 108 |
| Woodburn, Or., U.S. | E3 | 122 |
| Woodbury, Ct., U.S. | F13 | 108 |
| Woodbury, Ga., U.S. | G2 | 112 |
| Woodbury, N.J., U.S. | H11 | 108 |
| Woodbury, Tn., U.S. | G10 | 114 |
| Woodenbong, Austl. | G10 | 70 |
| Woodfibre, B.C., Can. | H11 | 102 |
| Wood Islands, P.E., Can. | G11 | 106 |
| Woodlake, Ca., U.S. | H6 | 124 |
| Woodlake, Ne., U.S. | I7 | 118 |
| Woodland, Ca., U.S. | F4 | 124 |
| Woodland, Me., U.S. | G2 | 112 |
| Woodland, Me., U.S. | B19 | 108 |
| Woodland, N.C., U.S. | C10 | 112 |
| Woodland Park, Co., U.S. | F11 | 120 |
| Woodlawn, Ky., U.S. | E8 | 114 |
| Wood Mountain, mtn., Sk., Can. | I8 | 104 |
| Wood Mountain Indian Reserve, Sk., Can. | I8 | 104 |
| Woodridge, Mb., Can. | I18 | 104 |
| Wood River, Il., U.S. | D6 | 114 |
| Wood River, Ne., U.S. | K9 | 118 |
| Woodroffe, stm., Austl. | C2 | 70 |
| Woodroffe, Mount, mtn., Austl. | E6 | 68 |
| Woodrow, N.C., U.S. | D9 | 112 |
| Woodruff, Az., U.S. | J6 | 120 |
| Woodruff, S.C., U.S. | E4 | 112 |
| Woodruff, Wi., U.S. | E6 | 110 |
| Woods, Lake of the, l., N.A. | B13 | 118 |
| Woods, Lake of the, l., N.A. | B13 | 118 |
| Woodsboro, Tx., U.S. | K9 | 116 |
| Woodsfield, Oh., U.S. | H5 | 108 |
| Woods Hole, Ma., U.S. | F16 | 108 |
| Woodside, Austl. | L7 | 70 |
| Woodson, Tx., U.S. | F7 | 116 |
| Woodstock, Il., U.S. | H7 | 110 |
| Woodstock, N.B., Can. | F6 | 106 |
| Woodstock, N.Y., U.S. | E12 | 108 |
| Woodstock, Oh., U.S. | G15 | 110 |
| Woodstock, Va., U.S. | I8 | 108 |
| Woodstock, Vt., U.S. | D14 | 108 |
| Woodville, Al., U.S. | H10 | 114 |
| Woodville, Fl., U.S. | I2 | 112 |
| Woodville, Ms., U.S. | K5 | 114 |
| Woodville, N.Z. | D5 | 72 |
| Woodville, Oh., U.S. | F3 | 108 |
| Woodville, Tx., U.S. | L2 | 114 |
| Woodward, Ia., U.S. | I2 | 110 |
| Woodward, Ok., U.S. | C7 | 116 |
| Woody, stm., Can. | F14 | 104 |
| Woody Head, c., Austl. | H4 | 110 |
| Woody Island, Ak., U.S. | H18 | 100 |
| Woolgoolga, Austl. | H10 | 70 |
| Woolmarket, Ms., U.S. | L8 | 114 |
| Woomera, Austl. | H2 | 70 |
| Woonsocket, R.I., U.S. | E15 | 108 |
| Woonsocket, S.D., U.S. | G9 | 118 |
| Wooramel, stm., Austl. | E2 | 66 |
| Wooramel, stm., Austl. | E3 | 66 |
| Wooster, Oh., U.S. | G5 | 108 |
| Worb, Switz. | E8 | 13 |
| Worcester, Eng., U.K. | I11 | 8 |
| Worcester, Ma., U.S. | E15 | 108 |
| Worcester, S. Afr. | I4 | 66 |
| Worden, Mt., U.S. | E17 | 122 |

| Wugang, China | F9 | 30 |
| Wugong Shan, mts., China | H2 | 34 |
| Wuhan, China | E3 | 32 |
| Wuhu, China | D7 | 34 |
| Wuhua, China | L4 | 34 |
| Wujiang, China | D9 | 34 |
| Wuji, China | E2 | 32 |
| Wukari, Nig. | H14 | 64 |
| Wum, Cam. | H15 | 64 |
| Wunnummin Lake, l., On., Can. | F15 | 96 |
| Wun Rog, Sudan | M5 | 60 |
| Wunstorf, Ger. | C9 | 10 |
| Wuppertal, Ger. | D7 | 10 |
| Wuppertal, S. Afr. | I4 | 66 |
| Würenlingen, Switz. | C9 | 13 |
| Würzburg, Ger. | F9 | 10 |
| Wurzen, Ger. | D12 | 10 |
| Wushan, China | E8 | 30 |
| Wusheng, China | F8 | 34 |
| Wushenqi, China | I7 | 118 |
| Wusong, China | D10 | 34 |
| Wutai, China | D9 | 30 |
| Wutai Shan, mtn., China | D1 | 32 |
| Wutangjie, China | F11 | 34 |
| Wutongqiao, China | F7 | 30 |
| Wuustwezel, Bel. | F6 | 12 |
| Wuvulu Island, i., Pap. N. Gui. | F11 | 38 |
| Wuwei, China | D7 | 30 |
| Wuwei, China | D6 | 30 |
| Wuxi (Wuhsi), China | D9 | 34 |
| Wuyi Shan, mts., China | I5 | 34 |
| Wuyuan, China | C8 | 30 |
| Wuzhi Shan, mtn., China | E10 | 40 |
| Wuzhong, China | D6 | 30 |
| Wuzhou (Wuchow), China | C11 | 40 |
| Wyaconda, Mo., U.S. | B5 | 114 |
| Wyaconda, stm., Mo., U.S. | B5 | 114 |
| Wyalusing, Pa., U.S. | F10 | 108 |
| Wyandotte, Mi., U.S. | H12 | 110 |
| Wyandra, Austl. | F6 | 70 |
| Wyangala, Lake, res., Austl. | I8 | 70 |
| Wyatt, Mo., U.S. | F7 | 114 |
| Wycheproof, Austl. | K5 | 70 |
| Wye, stm., U.K. | J11 | 8 |
| Wyeville, Wi., U.S. | F5 | 110 |
| Wykoff, Mn., U.S. | G3 | 110 |
| Wylie, Tx., U.S. | F10 | 116 |
| Wylie, Lake, res., U.S. | D5 | 112 |
| Wymark, Sk., Can. | H7 | 104 |
| Wymore, Ne., U.S. | K11 | 118 |
| Wyndham, Austl. | C5 | 68 |
| Wyndmere, N.D., U.S. | E10 | 118 |
| Wynne, Ar., U.S. | G6 | 114 |
| Wynnewood, Ok., U.S. | D9 | 116 |
| Wynniatt Bay, b., N.T., Can. | B10 | 96 |
| Wynona, Ok., U.S. | C10 | 116 |
| Wynot, Ne., U.S. | I10 | 118 |
| Wynyard, Austl. | M6 | 70 |
| Wynyard, Sk., Can. | G10 | 104 |
| Wyocena, Wi., U.S. | G6 | 110 |
| Wyodak, Wy., U.S. | G2 | 118 |
| Wyoming, Il., U.S. | I6 | 110 |
| Wyoming, Mi., U.S. | H10 | 110 |
| Wyoming, On., Can. | H13 | 110 |
| Wyoming, state, U.S. | E5 | 98 |
| Wyong, Austl. | I9 | 70 |
| Wysokie Mazowieckie, Pol. | C22 | 10 |
| Wyszków, Pol. | C21 | 10 |
| Wytheville, Va., U.S. | C5 | 112 |

**X**

| Xaafuun, Raas, c., Som. | F11 | 56 |
| Xacilbal, stm., N.A. | B3 | 92 |
| Xaidulla, China | B8 | 44 |
| Xainza, China | E4 | 30 |
| Xai-Xai, Moz. | E11 | 66 |
| Xalapa, Mex. | H11 | 90 |
| Xam (Chu), stm., Asia | E8 | 40 |
| Xambrê, stm., Braz. | G2 | 79 |
| Xam Nua, Laos | D8 | 40 |
| Xan (San), stm., Asia | G9 | 40 |
| Xangongo, Ang. | E3 | 58 |
| Xankändi (Stepanakert), Azer. | J7 | 26 |
| Xánthi, Grc. | H8 | 20 |
| Xanxerê, Braz. | D12 | 79 |
| Xapuri, Braz. | D7 | 82 |
| Xapuri, stm., Braz. | D7 | 82 |
| Xar Moron, stm., China | C10 | 30 |
| Xau, Lake, pl., Bots. | C7 | 66 |
| Xavantina, Braz. | D12 | 79 |
| Xaxim, Braz. | D12 | 80 |
| Xcalak, Mex. | H16 | 90 |
| X-Can, Mex. | G16 | 90 |
| Xenia, Il., U.S. | D8 | 114 |
| Xenia, Oh., U.S. | H3 | 108 |
| Xertigny, Fr. | D13 | 14 |
| Xeruã, stm., Braz. | B7 | 82 |
| Xhumo, Bots. | C7 | 66 |
| Xi, stm., China | G9 | 30 |
| Xiagaixin, China | C5 | 40 |
| Xiagezhuang, China | D7 | 32 |
| Xiahe, China | D7 | 30 |
| Xiamen (Amoy), China | K7 | 34 |
| Xiamen Gang, b., Asia | K7 | 34 |
| Xi'an (Sian), China | E8 | 30 |
| Xianfeng, China | F9 | 30 |
| Xiang, stm., China | B2 | 34 |
| Xiangcheng, China | B2 | 34 |
| Xiangcheng, China | E9 | 30 |
| Xianggang, prov., China | G9 | 30 |
| Xianggongshi, China | A2 | 34 |
| Xiangkhoang, Laos | E7 | 40 |
| Xiangkhoang, Plateau de, plat., Laos | E7 | 40 |
| Xiangride, China | D6 | 30 |
| Xianglu, China | H1 | 34 |
| Xianglu, China | G1 | 34 |
| Xianglu, China | D7 | 34 |
| Xianning, China | F3 | 34 |
| Xianxi, China | J7 | 34 |
| Xianyou, China | I7 | 34 |
| Xiaogan, China | E2 | 34 |
| Xiaogushan, China | D11 | 32 |
| Xiao Hinggan Ling, mts., China | B12 | 30 |
| Xiaoji, China | C8 | 34 |
| Xiaojiang, China | M2 | 34 |
| Xiaolan, China | M2 | 34 |
| Xiaoshan, China | E9 | 34 |
| Xiaoshan, China | H5 | 34 |
| Xiaoshixiang, China | E5 | 34 |
| Xiaoxi, China | I9 | 34 |
| Xiapu, China | H5 | 34 |
| Xiaying, China | F7 | 32 |
| Xibu, China | I1 | 34 |
| Xichang, China | F7 | 30 |

| Xicoténcatl, Mex. | F10 | 90 |
| Xié, stm., Braz. | G9 | 84 |
| Xieliouke, China | E10 | 44 |
| Xigeotun, China | C10 | 32 |
| Xigazê, China | F13 | 44 |
| Xihua, China | B3 | 34 |
| Xijielong, China | C7 | 40 |
| Xikouxu, China | J6 | 34 |
| Xiliao, stm., China | C11 | 30 |
| Ximiao, China | C7 | 30 |
| Xinavane, Moz. | E11 | 66 |
| Xinba, China | I7 | 32 |
| Xincheng, China | J3 | 34 |
| Xindian, China | F2 | 32 |
| Xindukou, China | B6 | 40 |
| Xing'an, China | F9 | 30 |
| Xingcheng, China | C8 | 32 |
| Xinghua, China | C8 | 34 |
| Xingkai Hu (ozero Chanka), l., Asia | B13 | 30 |
| Xinglong, China | C5 | 32 |
| Xingtai, China | F2 | 32 |
| Xingu, stm., Braz. | D8 | 76 |
| Xinhe, China | B7 | 34 |
| Xinhua, China | F3 | 32 |
| Xinhui, China | M2 | 34 |
| Xining, China | D7 | 30 |
| Xinjieji, China | G4 | 32 |
| Xinjiang, China | D9 | 30 |
| Xinjiang Uygur Zizhiqu (Sinkiang), prov., China | M3 | 34 |
| Xinjiulong (New Kowloon), China | E2 | 32 |
| Xinle (Dongchangshou), China | A10 | 32 |
| Xinmin, China | E9 | 34 |
| Xinshi, China | H5 | 32 |
| Xinwen (Suncun), China | D3 | 34 |
| Xinxian, China | H1 | 32 |
| Xinxiang, China | M1 | 34 |
| Xinxing, China | C3 | 34 |
| Xinyang, China | L2 | 34 |
| Xinzao, China | C5 | 32 |
| Xinzhangzi, China | A8 | 40 |
| Xiongjiachang, China | D5 | 34 |
| Xipamanu (Chipamanu), stm., S.A. | D7 | 82 |
| Xiping, China | B3 | 34 |
| Xique-Xique, Braz. | F10 | 76 |
| Xirdalan, Azer. | I7 | 26 |
| Xishu, China | G1 | 32 |
| Xitole, Gui.-B. | F2 | 64 |
| Xiuyan, China | C11 | 32 |
| Xixian, China | C3 | 34 |
| Xiyou, China | F7 | 32 |
| Xizang Zizhiqu (Tibet), prov., China | E3 | 30 |
| Xochicalco, hist., Mex. | H10 | 90 |
| Xochistlahuaca, Mex. | I10 | 90 |
| Xuancheng, China | E7 | 34 |
| Xuanhua, China | C3 | 32 |
| Xuchang, China | F10 | 34 |
| Xueao, China | F10 | 34 |
| Xuecheng, China | I5 | 32 |
| Xuji, China | D5 | 34 |
| Xun, stm., China | G9 | 30 |
| Xushui, China | D3 | 32 |
| Xuwen, China | D11 | 40 |
| Xuyong, China | F8 | 30 |
| Xuzhou (Süchow), China | A6 | 34 |

**Y**

| Yaan, China | E7 | 30 |
| Yablis, Nic. | C11 | 92 |
| Yablonovy Range see Jablonovyj chrebet, mts., Russia | G14 | 28 |
| Yabluniv, Ukr. | A8 | 20 |
| Yacambu, Parque Nacional, Ven. | C8 | 84 |
| Yacaré Norte, Riacho, stm., Para. | B9 | 80 |
| Yaco, Bol. | G8 | 82 |
| Yaco (Iaco), stm., S.A. | C6 | 82 |
| Yacuiba, Bol. | J10 | 82 |
| Yacyretá, Isla, i., Para. | D10 | 80 |
| Yādgīr, India | D4 | 46 |
| Yadkin, stm., N.C., U.S. | D6 | 112 |
| Yadkinville, N.C., U.S. | C6 | 112 |
| Yad Mordekhay, Isr. | E3 | 50 |
| Yadong, China | F4 | 30 |
| Yafran, Libya | B3 | 56 |
| Yağcılar, Tur. | J12 | 20 |
| Yagoua, Cam. | F10 | 54 |
| Yagradagzê Shan, mtn., China | C16 | 44 |
| Yaguachi Nuevo, Ec. | I3 | 84 |
| Yaguajay, Cuba | C5 | 94 |
| Yaguala, stm., Hond. | B8 | 92 |
| Yaguaraparo, Ven. | B11 | 84 |
| Yaguarón (Jaguarão), stm., S.A. | G12 | 80 |
| Yaguas, stm., Peru | I7 | 84 |
| Yahara, stm., Wi., U.S. | H6 | 110 |
| Yahk, B.C., Can. | H18 | 102 |
| Yahualica, Mex. | G8 | 90 |
| Yai, Khao, mtn., Asia | H5 | 40 |
| Yainax Butte, mtn., Or., U.S. | H4 | 122 |
| Yaizu, Japan | M13 | 36 |
| Yakima, Wa., U.S. | D5 | 122 |
| Yakima, stm., Wa., U.S. | D6 | 122 |
| Yako, Burkina | E8 | 64 |
| Yakobi Island, i., Ak., U.S. | G26 | 100 |
| Yakoma, D.R.C. | H5 | 56 |
| Yaku-shima, i., Japan | q5 | 37b |
| Yakutat, Ak., U.S. | G25 | 100 |
| Yakutat see Jakutija, state, Russia | D18 | 28 |
| Yakutsk see Jakutsk, Russia | E17 | 28 |
| Yala, Thai. | K6 | 40 |
| Yalahau, Laguna, b., Mex. | G16 | 90 |
| Yale, B.C., Can. | H13 | 102 |
| Yale, Mi., U.S. | G13 | 110 |
| Yale, Ok., U.S. | C10 | 116 |
| Yale, Mount, mtn., Co., U.S. | F10 | 120 |
| Yalgoo, Austl. | E3 | 68 |
| Yalinga, C.A.R. | N2 | 60 |
| Yalleroi, Austl. | E6 | 70 |
| Yalobusha, stm., Ms., U.S. | I7 | 114 |
| Yalong, stm., China | E6 | 30 |
| Yalova, Tur. | I13 | 20 |
| Yalta, Ukr. | I4 | 26 |
| Yalu (Amnok-kang), stm., Asia | C12 | 30 |
| Yamagata, Japan | I15 | 36 |
| Yamaguchi, Japan | M6 | 36 |
| Yamba, Austl. | H5 | 70 |
| Yambio, Sudan | H6 | 56 |

| Yambrasbamba, Peru | A3 | 82 |
| Yamdena, Pulau, i., Indon. | G9 | 38 |
| Yamethin, Myan. | D4 | 40 |
| Yamia, Niger | E15 | 64 |
| Yamma Yamma, Lake, l., Austl. | F4 | 70 |
| Yamoussoukro, C. Iv. | H7 | 64 |
| Yampa, Co., U.S. | D10 | 120 |
| Yampa, stm., Co., U.S. | D8 | 120 |
| Yamparaez, Bol. | H9 | 82 |
| Yampil', Ukr. | A12 | 20 |
| Yamsay Mountain, mtn., Or., U.S. | H4 | 122 |
| Yamuna, stm., India | H9 | 44 |
| Yamzho Yumco, l., China | F14 | 44 |
| Yanac, Austl. | K4 | 70 |
| Yanacachi, Bol. | G8 | 82 |
| Yanagawa, Japan | N5 | 36 |
| Yanahuara, Peru | G6 | 82 |
| Yanai, Japan | N7 | 36 |
| Yan'an, China | D8 | 30 |
| Yanaoca, Peru | F6 | 82 |
| Yanbu' al-Bahr, Sau. Ar. | I5 | 48 |
| Yanbutou, China | F4 | 34 |
| Yanceyville, N.C., U.S. | C7 | 112 |
| Yancheng, China | B9 | 34 |
| Yancheng, China | B3 | 34 |
| Yanchi, China | D8 | 30 |
| Yanco, Austl. | J7 | 70 |
| Yandev, Nig. | H14 | 64 |
| Yandoon, Myan. | F3 | 40 |
| Yanfolila, Mali | F5 | 64 |
| Yangcun, China | L3 | 34 |
| Yangguanpu, China | C4 | 34 |
| Yangjia, China | I7 | 32 |
| Yangjiang, China | G9 | 30 |
| Yangkoushi, China | G7 | 34 |
| Yangluo, China | B9 | 34 |
| Yangling, China | D5 | 32 |
| Yanglousi, China | F2 | 34 |
| Yangon (Rangoon), Myan. | B2 | 40 |
| Yangp'yŏng, S. Kor. | F15 | 32 |
| Yangquan, China | F1 | 32 |
| Yangsan, S. Kor. | H17 | 32 |
| Yangshuling, China | B6 | 32 |
| Yangtze see Chang, stm., China | E10 | 30 |
| Yangxiaodian, China | D5 | 34 |
| Yangyang, S. Kor. | E16 | 32 |
| Yangzhou, China | C8 | 34 |
| Yanheying, China | C7 | 32 |
| Yankdŏk, N. Kor. | D14 | 32 |
| Yankeetown, Fl., U.S. | J4 | 112 |
| Yankton, S.D., U.S. | I10 | 118 |
| Yankumiao, China | C5 | 34 |
| Yanqi, China | C4 | 30 |
| Yanqing, China | C3 | 32 |
| Yanque, Peru | F6 | 82 |
| Yantā, Leb. | A5 | 50 |
| Yantabulla, Austl. | G6 | 70 |
| Yantai (Chefoo), China | F9 | 32 |
| Yantian, China | H3 | 34 |
| Yanzhou, China | H4 | 32 |
| Yao, Japan | M10 | 36 |
| Yaopi, China | C8 | 34 |
| Yaoundé, Cam. | H9 | 54 |
| Yaoya, stm., Nic. | D10 | 92 |
| Yapacaní, Bol. | G9 | 82 |
| Yapacani, stm., Bol. | G9 | 82 |
| Yapen, Pulau, i., Indon. | F10 | 38 |
| Yapeyú, Arg. | E10 | 80 |
| Yappar, stm., Austl. | B4 | 70 |
| Ya'qūb, Sudan | K3 | 60 |
| Yaque del Norte, stm., Dom. Rep. | E9 | 94 |
| Yaqui, stm., Mex. | C5 | 90 |
| Yaracuy, state, Ven. | B8 | 84 |
| Yaraka, Austl. | E5 | 70 |
| Yarbasan, Tur. | K12 | 20 |
| Yardea, Austl. | I1 | 70 |
| Yaremcha, Ukr. | A8 | 20 |
| Yari, stm., Col. | H6 | 84 |
| Yarīm, Yemen | G4 | 47 |
| Yaring, Thai. | K6 | 40 |
| Yaritagua, Ven. | B8 | 84 |
| Yarkand see Shache, China | A7 | 44 |
| Yarkant (Yarkand), stm., Para. | D2 | 30 |
| Yarlung see Brahmaputra, stm., Asia | G15 | 44 |
| Yarmouth, Me., U.S. | D16 | 108 |
| Yarmouth, N.S., Can. | I7 | 106 |
| Yarram, Austl. | L7 | 70 |
| Yarraman, Austl. | F9 | 70 |
| Yarrawonga, Austl. | K7 | 70 |
| Yarumal, Col. | D5 | 84 |
| Yashiro-jima, i., Japan | N7 | 36 |
| Yasinya, Ukr. | A7 | 20 |
| Yasothon, Thai. | G8 | 40 |
| Yass, Austl. | J8 | 70 |
| Yasuni, stm., Ec. | H5 | 84 |
| Yata, Bol. | E8 | 82 |
| Yata, stm., Bol. | D9 | 82 |
| Yatakala, Niger | D10 | 64 |
| Yatesboro, Pa., U.S. | G7 | 108 |
| Yates Center, Ks., U.S. | N12 | 118 |
| Yates City, Il., U.S. | J5 | 110 |
| Yathkyed Lake, l., N.T., Can. | D13 | 96 |
| Yatsushiro, Japan | O5 | 36 |
| Yattah, W.B. | F4 | 50 |
| Yauca, Peru | G4 | 82 |
| Yauco, P.R. | E11 | 94 |
| Yauli, Peru | D3 | 82 |
| Yauri, Ec. | I4 | 84 |
| Yauri, Peru | F6 | 82 |
| Yautepec, Mex. | H10 | 90 |
| Yauyos, Peru | E4 | 82 |
| Yavarí (Javari), stm., S.A. | D4 | 76 |
| Yavarí Mirim, stm., Peru | J6 | 84 |
| Yaviza, Pan. | C4 | 84 |
| Yavne, Isr. | E3 | 50 |
| Yavoriv, Ukr. | F9 | 84 |
| Yawatahama, Japan | N7 | 36 |
| Yaxchilán, hist., Mex. | E10 | 90 |
| Yayao, China | B14 | 32 |
| Yazd, Iran | F13 | 48 |
| Yazmān, Pak. | F4 | 44 |
| Yazoo, stm., Ms., U.S. | J6 | 114 |
| Yazoo City, Ms., U.S. | J6 | 114 |
| Ybbs an der Donau, Aus. | G15 | 10 |
| Ybycuí, Para. | D10 | 80 |
| Ye, Myan. | G4 | 40 |
| Yecheng, China | B7 | 44 |
| Yech'ŏn, S. Kor. | G16 | 32 |
| Yecla, Spain | G10 | 16 |
| Yécora, Mex. | C5 | 90 |
| Yedseram, stm., Nig. | J1 | 70 |
| Yegros, Para. | D9 | 80 |
| Yehud, Isr. | D3 | 50 |
| Yei, stm., Sudan | N6 | 60 |
| Yekaterinburg see Jekaterinburg, Russia | F10 | 26 |
| Yela Island, i., Pap. N. Gui. | B10 | 68 |

| Name | Map Ref. | Page |
|---|---|---|
| Yelarbon, Austl. | G9 | 70 |
| Yele, S.L. | G4 | 64 |
| Yélimané, Mali | D4 | 64 |
| Yellow see Huang, stm., China | D10 | 30 |
| Yellow, stm., Ia., U.S. | G4 | 110 |
| Yellow, stm., In., U.S. | A10 | 114 |
| Yellow, stm., U.S. | L10 | 114 |
| Yellow, stm., Wi., U.S. | E3 | 110 |
| Yellow Grass, Sk., Can. | I10 | 104 |
| Yellowhead Pass, Can. | E16 | 102 |
| Yellowknife, N.T., Can. | D10 | 96 |
| Yellowknife, stm., N.T., Can. | D10 | 96 |
| Yellow Medicine, stm., Mn., U.S. | G12 | 118 |
| Yellow Sea (Huang Hai), Asia | B11 | 34 |
| Yellowstone, stm., U.S. | F15 | 122 |
| Yellowstone Falls, wtfl, Wy., U.S. | F15 | 122 |
| Yellowstone Lake, l., Wy., U.S. | F15 | 122 |
| Yellowstone National Park, Wy., U.S. | F15 | 122 |
| Yellowstone National Park, U.S. | F15 | 122 |
| Yellville, Ar., U.S. | F4 | 114 |
| Yelvertoft, Austl. | C3 | 70 |
| Yelwa, Nig. | F12 | 64 |
| Yemaotai, China | A10 | 32 |
| Yemassee, S.C., U.S. | G6 | 112 |
| Yemen (Al-Yaman), ctry., Asia | F3 | 42 |
| Yenangyaung, Myan. | D3 | 40 |
| Yen Bai, Viet. | D8 | 40 |
| Yenda, Austl. | J7 | 70 |
| Yende Millimou, Gui. | G4 | 64 |
| Yendéré, Burkina | F7 | 64 |
| Yendi, Ghana | G9 | 64 |
| Yengisar, China | D2 | 30 |
| Yeniköy, Tur. | J12 | 20 |
| Yenisei see Jenisej, stm., Russia | D15 | 26 |
| Yenshuichen, Tai. | L9 | 34 |
| Yeola, India | B3 | 46 |
| Yeoval, Austl. | I8 | 70 |
| Yeppoon, Austl. | D9 | 70 |
| Yerba Buena, Montaña, mtn., Hond. | C7 | 92 |
| Yerevan see Jerevan, Arm. | I6 | 26 |
| Yerington, Nv., U.S. | F6 | 124 |
| Yermasóyia, Cyp. | D2 | 48 |
| Yermo, Ca., U.S. | J9 | 124 |
| Yerupaja, Nevado, mtn., Peru | D3 | 82 |
| Yerushalayim (Al-Quds) (Jerusalem), Isr. | E4 | 50 |
| Yesa, Embalse de, res., Spain | C10 | 16 |
| Yesan, S. Kor. | G14 | 32 |
| Yeşilhisar, Tur. | B3 | 48 |
| Yeso, N.M., U.S. | E2 | 116 |
| Yeste, Spain | G9 | 16 |
| Yetman, Austl. | G9 | 70 |
| Yetti, reg., Afr. | G7 | 62 |
| Ye-u, Myan. | C3 | 40 |
| Yeu, Île d', i., Fr. | F4 | 14 |
| Yevlax, Azer. | I7 | 26 |
| Yevpatoriya, Ukr. | H4 | 26 |
| Yexian, China | B2 | 34 |
| Ygatimí, Para. | C11 | 80 |
| Yguazú, stm., Para. | C11 | 80 |
| Yhú, Para. | C11 | 80 |
| Yi, stm., Ur. | G10 | 80 |
| Yi'an, China | B12 | 30 |
| Yiannitsá, Grc. | I6 | 20 |
| Yibin, China | F7 | 30 |
| Yicheng, China | C9 | 34 |
| Yichang, China | E9 | 30 |
| Yichun, China | B12 | 30 |
| Yichun, China | F9 | 30 |
| Yidu, China | G6 | 32 |
| Yifug, Eth. | K9 | 60 |
| Yijianzhen, China | E7 | 34 |
| Yilan, China | B12 | 30 |
| Yiliang, China | B7 | 40 |
| Yinchuan, China | D8 | 30 |
| Ying, stm., China | C5 | 34 |
| Yingcheng, China | E2 | 34 |
| Yingde, China | K2 | 34 |
| Yingkou, China | C10 | 32 |
| Yingtan, China | G6 | 34 |
| Yingtian, China | G1 | 34 |
| Yining, China | C3 | 30 |
| Yinzhan'ao, China | L2 | 34 |
| Yirba Muda, Eth. | N10 | 60 |
| Yirga Alem, Eth. | N10 | 60 |
| Yirol, Sudan | N6 | 60 |
| Yirwa, Sudan | N4 | 60 |
| Yishan, China | B10 | 40 |
| Yishui, China | H6 | 32 |
| Yíthion, Grc. | M6 | 20 |
| Yitulihe, China | A11 | 30 |
| Yiwu, China | F9 | 34 |
| Yiyang, China | F9 | 30 |
| Ylivieska, Fin. | I19 | 6 |
| Ymir, B.C., Can. | H17 | 102 |
| Yoakum, Tx., U.S. | J9 | 116 |
| Yockanookany, stm., Ms., U.S. | J7 | 114 |
| Yoco, Ven. | B11 | 84 |
| Yocona, stm., Ms., U.S. | H7 | 114 |
| Yogyakarta, Indon. | j15 | 39a |
| Yoho National Park, B.C., Can. | F18 | 102 |
| Yoichi, Japan | d15 | 36a |
| Yojoa, Lago de l., Hond. | C7 | 92 |
| Yōju, S. Kor. | F15 | 32 |
| Yokkaichi, Japan | M11 | 36 |
| Yokohama, Japan | L14 | 36 |
| Yokosuka, Japan | L14 | 36 |
| Yokote, Japan | H15 | 36 |
| Yola, Nig. | G9 | 54 |
| Yolaina, Serranías de, mts., Nic. | F10 | 92 |
| Yolombó, Col. | D5 | 84 |
| Yom, stm., Thai. | F6 | 40 |
| Yonago, Japan | L8 | 36 |
| Yŏnan, N. Kor. | F14 | 32 |
| Yoncalla, Or., U.S. | G2 | 122 |
| Yonezawa, Japan | J15 | 36 |
| Yŏngam, S. Kor. | I14 | 32 |
| Yongamp'o, N. Kor. | D12 | 32 |
| Yong'an, China | J6 | 34 |
| Yŏngan, N. Kor. | B17 | 32 |
| Yongchang, China | F8 | 34 |
| Yŏngch'ŏn, S. Kor. | E15 | 32 |
| Yŏngch'ŏn, S. Kor. | H16 | 32 |
| Yongdeng, China | D7 | 30 |
| Yongding, China | K5 | 34 |
| Yongding, China | K5 | 34 |
| Yŏngdŏk, S. Kor. | G17 | 32 |
| Yŏngdong, S. Kor. | G15 | 32 |
| Yongfeng, China | H4 | 34 |
| Yonghŭng, N. Kor. | D15 | 32 |
| Yŏngju, S. Kor. | G16 | 32 |
| Yongkang, China | G9 | 34 |
| Yŏngmi-dong, N. Kor. | D13 | 32 |
| Yongsan'o, S. Kor. | F7 | 30 |
| Yongsan, S. Kor. | I14 | 32 |
| Yongsan, China | F7 | 30 |
| Yŏngwŏl, S. Kor. | F16 | 32 |
| Yongxin, China | I3 | 34 |
| Yŏngyn, N. Kor. | D13 | 32 |
| Yonkers, N.Y., U.S. | G13 | 108 |
| Yonne, dept., Fr. | E10 | 14 |
| Yopal, Col. | E6 | 84 |
| York, Al., U.S. | J8 | 114 |
| York, Austl. | F3 | 68 |
| York, Eng., U.K. | H12 | 8 |
| York, N.D., U.S. | C8 | 118 |
| York, Ne., U.S. | K10 | 118 |
| York, Pa., U.S. | H10 | 108 |
| York, S.C., U.S. | E5 | 112 |
| York, stm., Va., U.S. | B10 | 112 |
| York, Cape, c., Austl. | B8 | 68 |
| York, Kap, c., Grnld. | B13 | 86 |
| Yorke Peninsula, pen., Austl. | J2 | 70 |
| York Factory, Mb., Can. | A22 | 104 |
| York Sound, strt., Austl. | B5 | 68 |
| Yorkton, Sk., Can. | G12 | 104 |
| Yorktown, Tx., U.S. | K9 | 116 |
| Yorktown, Va., U.S. | B10 | 112 |
| Yorkville, Il., U.S. | I7 | 110 |
| Yorkville, N.Y., U.S. | D11 | 108 |
| Yoro, Hond. | B7 | 92 |
| Yoro, Mali | D8 | 64 |
| Yoro, dept., Hond. | B7 | 92 |
| Yoron-jima, i., Japan | t3 | 37b |
| Yosemite National Park, Ca., U.S. | G6 | 124 |
| Yos Sudarso, Pulau, i., Indon. | G10 | 38 |
| Yŏsu, S. Kor. | I15 | 32 |
| Yotausito, Bol. | G10 | 82 |
| Yotvata, Isr. | I4 | 50 |
| Youbou, B.C., Can. | H10 | 102 |
| Youghal, Ire. | J5 | 8 |
| Young, Austl. | J8 | 70 |
| Young, Az., U.S. | J6 | 120 |
| Young, Sk., Can. | G9 | 104 |
| Young, Ur. | G10 | 80 |
| Younghusband Peninsula, pen., Austl. | K3 | 70 |
| Youngstown, Ab., Can. | F23 | 102 |
| Youngstown, Fl., U.S. | I1 | 112 |
| Youngstown, N.Y., U.S. | D7 | 108 |
| Youngstown, Oh., U.S. | F6 | 108 |
| Youngsville, La., U.S. | L5 | 114 |
| Youngsville, N.C., U.S. | C8 | 112 |
| Youngsville, Pa., U.S. | F7 | 108 |
| Yountville, Ca., U.S. | F3 | 124 |
| Youssoufia, Mor. | D6 | 62 |
| Youxi, China | I7 | 34 |
| Youyang, China | F8 | 30 |
| Yozgat, Tur. | B3 | 48 |
| Ypacaraí, Para. | C10 | 80 |
| Yparé, stm., Para. | B10 | 80 |
| Ypé Jhú, Para. | B11 | 80 |
| Ypres (Ieper), Bel. | G2 | 12 |
| Ypsilanti, Mi., U.S. | H12 | 110 |
| Yreka, Ca., U.S. | C3 | 124 |
| Ystad, Swe. | N13 | 6 |
| Ytambey, stm., Para. | C11 | 80 |
| Yu, stm., China | C10 | 40 |
| Yu'alliq, Jabal, mtn., Egypt | F2 | 48 |
| Yuan, China | F9 | 30 |
| Yüanlin, Tai. | L9 | 34 |
| Yuanling, China | F9 | 30 |
| Yuanmou, China | B6 | 40 |
| Yuba, stm., Ca., U.S. | E4 | 124 |
| Yuba City, Ca., U.S. | E4 | 124 |
| Yūbari, Japan | d16 | 36a |
| Yubdo, Eth. | N6 | 60 |
| Yucaipa, Ca., U.S. | J8 | 124 |
| Yucatán, state, Mex. | G15 | 90 |
| Yucatán, Canal de, strt., N.A. | D2 | 94 |
| Yucatan Peninsula (Península de Yucatán), pen., N.A. | H15 | 90 |
| Yucca, Az., U.S. | J2 | 120 |
| Yucca Mountain, mtn., Nv., U.S. | H9 | 124 |
| Yucca Valley, Ca., U.S. | J9 | 124 |
| Yuci, China | D9 | 30 |
| Yuecheng, China | C3 | 34 |
| Yueyang, China | F2 | 34 |
| Yugoslavia (Jugoslavija), ctry., Eur. | G11 | 4 |
| Yukanbey, stm., China | J11 | 20 |
| Yukon, Ok., U.S. | D9 | 116 |
| Yukon, prov., Can. | D5 | 96 |
| Yukon, stm., N.A. | E14 | 100 |
| Yukon Flats, sw., Ak., U.S. | C21 | 100 |
| Yukou, China | C5 | 32 |
| Yŭli, Tai. | L10 | 34 |
| Yulin, China | D8 | 30 |
| Yulin, China | C11 | 40 |
| Yuma, Az., U.S. | L2 | 120 |
| Yuma, Co., U.S. | K5 | 118 |
| Yuma, Bahía de b., Dom. Rep. | E10 | 94 |
| Yumare, Ven. | B8 | 84 |
| Yumbel, Chile | I2 | 80 |
| Yumbo, Col. | F4 | 84 |
| Yumen, China | D6 | 30 |
| Yuncheng, China | D9 | 30 |
| Yungas, reg., Bol. | F8 | 82 |
| Yungay, Chile | I2 | 80 |
| Yungay, Peru | C3 | 82 |
| Yunhe, China | G8 | 34 |
| Yunnan, prov., China | F7 | 30 |
| Yunta, Austl. | I3 | 70 |
| Yunxian, China | E9 | 30 |
| Yura, Peru | G6 | 82 |
| Yurimaguas, Peru | A3 | 82 |
| Yuriria, Mex. | G9 | 90 |
| Yuriria, Laguna de l., Mex. | G9 | 90 |
| Yuruarí, stm., Ven. | D12 | 84 |
| Yurubi, Parque Nacional, Ven. | B8 | 84 |
| Yurumanguí, stm., Col. | F4 | 84 |
| Yusala, Laguna, l., Bol. | F8 | 82 |
| Yuscarán, Hond. | D8 | 92 |
| Yushan, China | B2 | 34 |
| Yü Shan, mtn., Tai. | L9 | 34 |
| Yushu, China | E6 | 30 |
| Yutian, China | B9 | 44 |
| Yuty, Para. | D10 | 80 |
| Yuwangcheng, China | D3 | 34 |
| Yuxian, China | A2 | 34 |
| Yuyao, China | E10 | 34 |
| Yvelines, dept., Fr. | D8 | 14 |
| Yverdon, Switz. | E6 | 13 |
| Yvetot, Fr. | C7 | 14 |

## Z

| Name | Map Ref. | Page |
|---|---|---|
| Zabajkal'sk, Russia | H15 | 28 |
| Žabari, Yugo. | E5 | 20 |
| Zabarjad, Jazīrat, i., Egypt | G3 | 47 |
| Zabīd, Yemen | G3 | 42 |
| Zabinka, Bela. | I7 | 22 |
| Ząbkowice Śląskie, Pol. | E16 | 10 |
| Žabljak, Yugo. | F3 | 20 |
| Zābol, Iran | F16 | 48 |
| Zābolī, Iran | H16 | 48 |
| Zabolotiv, Ukr. | A9 | 20 |
| Zabory, Russia | F15 | 22 |
| Zabré, Burkina | F9 | 64 |
| Zabrze (Hindenburg), Pol. | E18 | 10 |
| Zacapa, Guat. | C5 | 92 |
| Zacapa, dept., Guat. | B5 | 92 |
| Zacapu, Mex. | H8 | 90 |
| Zacatecas, Mex. | F8 | 90 |
| Zacatecas, state, Mex. | F8 | 90 |
| Zacatecoluca, El Sal. | D6 | 92 |
| Zacatlán, Mex. | H11 | 90 |
| Zacharovo, Russia | G22 | 22 |
| Zachary, La., U.S. | L5 | 114 |
| Zachmet, Turk. | C17 | 48 |
| Zacoalco de Torres, Mex. | G8 | 90 |
| Zacualpa, Guat. | B4 | 92 |
| Zacualtipán, Mex. | G10 | 90 |
| Zaculeu, hist., Guat. | B3 | 92 |
| Zadar, Cro. | E10 | 18 |
| Zadetkyi Kyun, i., Myan. | J5 | 40 |
| Zadoi, China | E5 | 30 |
| Zadonsk, Russia | I21 | 22 |
| Zafer Burnu, c., N. Cyp. | D3 | 48 |
| Zafir, U.A.E. | C8 | 47 |
| Zafra, Spain | G5 | 16 |
| Žagań, Pol. | D15 | 10 |
| Žagare, Lith. | E6 | 22 |
| Zaghouan, Tun. | M5 | 18 |
| Zagnanado, Benin | H11 | 64 |
| Zagora, Mor. | E8 | 62 |
| Zagreb, Cro. | D10 | 18 |
| Zāgros, Kūhhā-ye, mts., Iran | E9 | 48 |
| Žagubica, Yugo. | E5 | 20 |
| Zagyva, stm., Hung. | H20 | 10 |
| Zahana, Alg. | J11 | 16 |
| Záhedān, Iran | G16 | 48 |
| Zahlah, Leb. | A5 | 50 |
| Zahnitkiv, Ukr. | A12 | 20 |
| Zahodnjaja Dzvina (Daugava), stm., Eur. | F10 | 22 |
| Záhony, Hung. | G22 | 10 |
| Zahrān, Sau. Ar. | F3 | 47 |
| Zăicani, Mol. | B11 | 20 |
| Zaire see Congo, Democratic Republic of the, ctry., Afr. | B4 | 58 |
| Zaire see Congo, stm., Afr. | C2 | 58 |
| Zaječar, Yugo. | F6 | 20 |
| Zajsan, Kaz. | H14 | 26 |
| Zajsan, ozero, l., Kaz. | H14 | 26 |
| Zakamensk, Russia | G12 | 28 |
| Zákinthos, Grc. | L4 | 20 |
| Zákinthos, i., Grc. | L4 | 20 |
| Zakīyah, Syria | B6 | 50 |
| Zakopane, Pol. | F19 | 10 |
| Zala, Eth. | N9 | 60 |
| Zala, co., Hung. | I16 | 10 |
| Zalaegerszeg, Hung. | I16 | 10 |
| Zalalövö, Hung. | I16 | 10 |
| Zalanga, Nig. | F15 | 64 |
| Zalaszentgrót, Hung. | I17 | 10 |
| Zalău, Rom. | B7 | 20 |
| Zalegošč', Russia | I19 | 22 |
| Zalesje, Russia | C19 | 22 |
| Zalim, Sau. Ar. | D3 | 47 |
| Zalingei, Sudan | K2 | 60 |
| Zalishchyky, Ukr. | A9 | 20 |
| Zaltbommel, Neth. | E7 | 12 |
| Zaludok, Bela. | H7 | 22 |
| Zama, Ms., U.S. | J7 | 114 |
| Zamakh, Yemen | F5 | 47 |
| Zambezi (Zambeze), stm., Afr. | E6 | 58 |
| Zambia, ctry., Afr. | D5 | 58 |
| Zamboanga, Phil. | D7 | 38 |
| Zamboanga Peninsula, pen., Phil. | D7 | 38 |
| Zambrano, Col. | C5 | 84 |
| Zambrów, Pol. | B22 | 10 |
| Zambyl, Kaz. | I12 | 26 |
| Zamfara, stm., Nig. | E12 | 64 |
| Zamora, Ec. | J3 | 84 |
| Zamora, Spain | D6 | 16 |
| Zamora, stm., Ec. | I3 | 84 |
| Zamora-Chinchipe, prov., Ec. | J3 | 84 |
| Zamora de Hidalgo, Mex. | H8 | 90 |
| Zamuro, Punta, c., Ven. | B8 | 84 |
| Zana, hist., Alg. | C14 | 62 |
| Zanaga, Congo | B2 | 58 |
| Zandvoort, Neth. | D6 | 12 |
| Zandvoort, Circuit Autorace, Neth. | D6 | 12 |
| Zanesville, Oh., U.S. | H4 | 108 |
| Zangasso, Mali | E7 | 64 |
| Zanggezhuang, China | F8 | 32 |
| Zanjān, Iran | C10 | 48 |
| Zanjón, Arg. | D6 | 80 |
| Zanjón, stm., Arg. | F4 | 80 |
| Žannetty, ostrov, i., Russia | B23 | 28 |
| Zanthus, Austl. | F4 | 68 |
| Zanzibar, Tan. | C7 | 58 |
| Zanzibar, i., Tan. | C7 | 58 |
| Zaokskij, Russia | G20 | 22 |
| Zaostrovje, Russia | A16 | 22 |
| Zaouiet Azmour, Tun. | M6 | 18 |
| Zaouiet el Mgaïz, Tun. | M5 | 18 |
| Zaoxi, China | E8 | 34 |
| Zaozhuang, China | I5 | 32 |
| Zapadnaja Dvina, Russia | E15 | 22 |
| Zapadno-Sibirskaja ravnina, pl., Russia | E13 | 26 |
| Zapadnyj Sajan, mts., Russia | G10 | 28 |
| Zapala, Arg. | J3 | 80 |
| Zapata, Tx., U.S. | M7 | 116 |
| Zapata, Península de, pen., Cuba | C4 | 94 |
| Zapatera, Isla, i., Nic. | F9 | 92 |
| Zapatoca, Col. | D6 | 84 |
| Zapatosa, Ciénaga de l., Col. | C6 | 84 |
| Zapl'usje, Russia | C12 | 22 |
| Zapol'arnyj, Russia | G22 | 6 |
| Zapolje, Russia | C12 | 22 |
| Zapopan, Mex. | G8 | 90 |
| Zaporizhzhya, Ukr. | H5 | 26 |
| Zapotillo, Ec. | J2 | 84 |
| Zaprudn'a, Russia | E20 | 22 |
| Zara, Tur. | B4 | 48 |
| Zaragoza, Arg. | H9 | 80 |
| Zaragoza, Mex. | D5 | 90 |
| Zaragoza, Mex. | B6 | 90 |
| Zaragoza, Mex. | F10 | 90 |
| Zaragoza, Spain | D11 | 16 |
| Zarajsk, Russia | F21 | 22 |
| Zarand, Iran | F14 | 48 |
| Zárasai, Lith. | F9 | 22 |
| Zárate, Arg. | H9 | 80 |
| Zarautz, Spain | B9 | 16 |
| Zaraza, Ven. | C10 | 84 |
| Zarcero, C.R. | G10 | 92 |
| Zard Kūh, mtn., Iran | E11 | 48 |
| Zarečnyj, Russia | I23 | 22 |
| Zarembo Island, i., Ak., U.S. | H28 | 100 |
| Zarghūn Shahr, Afg. | D3 | 44 |
| Zaria, Nig. | F13 | 64 |
| Žarkovskij, Russia | F15 | 22 |
| Žarma, Kaz. | H14 | 26 |
| Zarqā', Nahr az-, stm., Jord. | D5 | 50 |
| Zarrīn Shahr, Iran | E11 | 48 |
| Zarubino, Russia | C16 | 22 |
| Zaruma, Ec. | I3 | 84 |
| Zarumilla, Peru | I2 | 84 |
| Žary (Sorau), Pol. | D15 | 10 |
| Žaryn', Russia | H16 | 22 |
| Zarzaïtine, Alg. | F15 | 62 |
| Zarzal, Col. | E4 | 84 |
| Zarzis, Tun. | D16 | 62 |
| Žáskär Mountains, mts., Asia | D7 | 44 |
| Zaslaue, Bela. | G10 | 22 |
| Zastavna, Ukr. | A9 | 20 |
| Zastron, S. Afr. | H8 | 66 |
| Zatyshshya, Ukr. | B13 | 20 |
| Zavalla, Tx., U.S. | K2 | 114 |
| Zavallya, Ukr. | A14 | 20 |
| Zavidovići, Bos. | E2 | 20 |
| Zavitinsk, Russia | G17 | 28 |
| Zavodovski Island, i., S. Geor. | J12 | 74 |
| Zavolžje, Russia | E26 | 22 |
| Zavolžsk, Russia | D25 | 22 |
| Zavoronežskoje, Russia | I23 | 22 |
| Zawiercie, Pol. | E19 | 10 |
| Zawiyat Shammās, Egypt | B4 | 60 |
| Zaza, stm., Cuba | D5 | 94 |
| Zaza, Presa, res., Cuba | C3 | 94 |
| Zazafotsy, Madag. | s22 | 67b |
| Zbiroh, Czech Rep. | F13 | 10 |
| Zduńska Wola, Pol. | D18 | 10 |
| Zealandia, Sk., Can. | G7 | 104 |
| Zearing, Ia., U.S. | H2 | 110 |
| Zeballos, B.C., Can. | G8 | 102 |
| Zebdani, Syria | A6 | 50 |
| Zebila, Ghana | F9 | 64 |
| Zebulon, Ga., U.S. | F2 | 112 |
| Zebulon, N.C., U.S. | C8 | 112 |
| Zeebrugge, Bel. | F3 | 12 |
| Zeehan, Austl. | M6 | 70 |
| Zeeland, Mi., U.S. | H9 | 110 |
| Zeeland, N.D., U.S. | F8 | 118 |
| Zeeland, prov., Neth. | F4 | 12 |
| Zeerust, S. Afr. | E8 | 66 |
| Zefat (Safad), Isr. | C5 | 50 |
| Zege, Eth. | L9 | 60 |
| Zehdenick, Ger. | C13 | 10 |
| Zeigler, Il., U.S. | E7 | 114 |
| Zeil, Mount, mtn., Austl. | D6 | 68 |
| Zeist, Neth. | D7 | 12 |
| Zeitz, Ger. | D12 | 10 |
| Zeja, Russia | G17 | 28 |
| Zeja, stm., Russia | G17 | 28 |
| Zejskoje vodochranilišče, res., Russia | G17 | 28 |
| Zelaya, dept., Nic. | E10 | 92 |
| Zele, Bel. | F5 | 12 |
| Želechów, Pol. | D21 | 10 |
| Zelenoborskij, Russia | H23 | 6 |
| Zelenogorsk, Russia | A12 | 22 |
| Zelenograd, Russia | E20 | 22 |
| Zelenogradsk, Russia | G3 | 22 |
| Zelenodol'sk, Russia | G4 | 22 |
| Železnodorožnyj, Russia | G4 | 22 |
| Železnodorožnyj, Russia | E8 | 26 |
| Železnogorsk, Russia | I18 | 22 |
| Železnogorsk-Ilimskij, Russia | F12 | 28 |
| Zelienople, Pa., U.S. | G6 | 108 |
| Zella-Mehlis, Ger. | E10 | 10 |
| Zell, Ger. | E7 | 10 |
| Zell am See, Aus. | H12 | 10 |
| Zel'onodol'sk, Russia | F7 | 26 |
| Zelów, Pol. | D19 | 10 |
| Zel'va, Bela. | H7 | 22 |
| Zelzate, Bel. | F4 | 12 |
| Zemcy, Russia | E15 | 22 |
| Zemetčino, Russia | H25 | 22 |
| Zémio, C.A.R. | G6 | 56 |
| Zemmour, reg., Afr. | H4 | 62 |
| Zempoala, hist., Mex. | H11 | 90 |
| Zemst, Bel. | G5 | 12 |
| Zendeh Jān, Afg. | D16 | 48 |
| Zeneta, Sk., Can. | H12 | 104 |
| Zenica, Bos. | E1 | 20 |
| Zenon Park, Sk., Can. | E11 | 104 |
| Zephyr, Tx., U.S. | H8 | 116 |
| Zephyrhills, Fl., U.S. | K4 | 112 |
| Zeravšan, stm., Asia | J11 | 26 |
| Zerbst, Ger. | D12 | 10 |
| Žerdevka, Russia | J24 | 22 |
| Zermatt, Switz. | F8 | 13 |
| Zernez, Switz. | E13 | 13 |
| Zernograd, Russia | H6 | 26 |
| Zeulenroda, Ger. | E11 | 10 |
| Zeven, Ger. | B9 | 10 |
| Zevenaar, Neth. | E9 | 12 |
| Zevenbergen, Neth. | E6 | 12 |
| Zeytindağ, Tur. | K11 | 20 |
| Žezkazgan, Kaz. | H11 | 26 |
| Zgierz, Pol. | D19 | 10 |
| Zhagenasongduo, China | D16 | 44 |
| Zhanggezhuang, China | G7 | 32 |
| Zhangjiakou (Kalgan), China | C2 | 32 |
| Zhangjinhe, China | E1 | 34 |
| Zhangmutou, China | M3 | 34 |
| Zhangping, China | J6 | 34 |
| Zhangtaizi, China | B11 | 32 |
| Zhangye, China | D7 | 30 |
| Zhangzhou (Longxi), China | K6 | 34 |
| Zhanjiang, China | D11 | 40 |
| Zhanjiaqiao, China | F2 | 34 |
| Zhao'an, China | L9 | 34 |
| Zhaoqing, China | L2 | 34 |
| Zhaotong, China | F7 | 30 |
| Zhaoyuan, China | F8 | 32 |
| Zhapu, China | E10 | 34 |
| Zhaxigang, China | D8 | 44 |
| Zhdanov see Mariupol', Ukr. | H5 | 26 |
| Zhegu, China | F14 | 44 |
| Zhejiang (Chekiang), prov., China | F11 | 30 |
| Zhengding, China | E2 | 32 |
| Zhengguo, China | L2 | 34 |
| Zhengjiaozhuang, China | C5 | 34 |
| Zhengzhou, China | E9 | 30 |
| Zhenjiang, China | C8 | 34 |
| Zhenping, China | E9 | 30 |
| Zhentoushi, China | A12 | 34 |
| Zhenyuan, China | F8 | 30 |
| Zhierling, China | C2 | 32 |
| Zhixia, China | F8 | 34 |
| Zhob, Pak. | E3 | 44 |
| Zhob, stm., Pak. | E3 | 44 |
| Zhongba, China | F3 | 30 |
| Zhongba, China | G6 | 34 |
| Zhongdian, China | A5 | 40 |
| Zhongheying, China | C7 | 40 |
| Zhongning, China | D5 | 34 |
| Zhongqing, China | D8 | 30 |
| Zhongsha, China | I5 | 34 |
| Zhongshan (Shiqishen), China | M2 | 34 |
| Zhongxiang, China | D1 | 34 |
| Zhoucun, China | G5 | 32 |
| Zhouning, China | H8 | 34 |
| Zhoushan Qundao, is., China | E11 | 34 |
| Zhoushuizi, China | E9 | 32 |
| Zhovten', Ukr. | B14 | 20 |
| Zhovti Vody, Ukr. | H4 | 26 |
| Zhuge, China | G6 | 32 |
| Zhuguozhen, China | C9 | 34 |
| Zhuhai, China | M2 | 34 |
| Zhujiang Kou, est., Asia | M2 | 34 |
| Zhulanbu, China | J4 | 34 |
| Zhuotian, China | J5 | 34 |
| Zhuoxian, China | D1 | 32 |
| Zhushan, China | E8 | 34 |
| Zhutian, China | G6 | 34 |
| Zhuya, China | H2 | 34 |
| Zhuzhou (Chuchow), China | H2 | 34 |
| Zhytomyr, Ukr. | G3 | 26 |
| Zi, stm., China | F9 | 30 |
| Žiar nad Hronom, Slvk. | G18 | 10 |
| Zibo (Zhangdian), China | G6 | 32 |
| Zicavo, Fr. | m24 | 15a |
| Ziegenhain, Ger. | E9 | 10 |
| Zigalovo, Russia | G13 | 28 |
| Ziguinchor, Sen. | E1 | 64 |
| Zihuatanejo, Mex. | I9 | 90 |
| Zikejevo, Russia | H17 | 22 |
| Zikhron Ya'aqov, Isr. | C3 | 50 |
| Žilina, Slvk. | F18 | 10 |
| Žilino, Russia | G4 | 22 |
| Zillah, Libya | C4 | 56 |
| Zillah, Wa., U.S. | D5 | 122 |
| Zillertaler Alpen, mts., Eur. | I11 | 10 |
| Žil'ovo, Russia | G21 | 22 |
| Zilupe, Lat. | E11 | 22 |
| Zilwaukee, Mi., U.S. | G12 | 110 |
| Zima, Russia | G12 | 28 |
| Zimapán, Mex. | G10 | 90 |
| Zimbabwe, ctry., Afr. | E5 | 58 |
| Zimnicea, Rom. | F9 | 20 |
| Zinal, Switz. | F8 | 13 |
| Zinder, Niger | E14 | 64 |
| Zingwanda, Sudan | N4 | 60 |
| Zion, Il., U.S. | H8 | 110 |
| Zion National Park, Ut., U.S. | G3 | 120 |
| Zionsville, In., U.S. | C10 | 114 |
| Zionz Lake, l., On., Can. | G23 | 104 |
| Zipaquirá, Col. | E5 | 84 |
| Ziqlāb, Wādī, val., Jord. | C5 | 50 |
| Žitkovo, Russia | A12 | 22 |
| Zittau, Ger. | E14 | 10 |
| Zitundo, Moz. | F11 | 66 |
| Ziway, Lake, l., Eth. | M10 | 60 |
| Ziwuji, China | C4 | 34 |
| Ziyun, China | F8 | 30 |
| Zizdra, Russia | H17 | 22 |
| Zizhong, China | F7 | 30 |
| Žižica, Russia | E14 | 22 |
| Zlatar, Cro. | C11 | 18 |
| Zlatoust, Russia | F9 | 26 |
| Zlín, Czech Rep. | F17 | 10 |
| Žlitan, Libya | B3 | 56 |
| Žlobin, Bela. | I13 | 22 |
| Złotoryja, Pol. | D15 | 10 |
| Złotów, Pol. | B17 | 10 |
| Zlynka, Russia | I14 | 22 |
| Zmeinogorsk, Russia | G14 | 26 |
| Zmí'ovka, Russia | I19 | 22 |
| Znamensk, Russia | G4 | 22 |
| Znamenskoje, Russia | F12 | 26 |
| Znam'yanka, Ukr. | H4 | 26 |
| Znob-Novhorods'ke, Ukr. | I16 | 22 |
| Znojmo, Czech Rep. | G16 | 10 |
| Żodzina, Bela. | G11 | 22 |
| Zofingen, Switz. | D4 | 13 |
| Zogno, Italy | D4 | 18 |
| Zollikofen, Switz. | D7 | 13 |
| Zollikon, Switz. | D10 | 13 |
| Zolotkovo, Russia | F24 | 22 |
| Zolotuchino, Russia | I19 | 22 |
| Žolymbet, Kaz. | G12 | 26 |
| Zomba, Mwi. | E7 | 58 |
| Zonguldak, Tur. | G14 | 4 |
| Zonza, Fr. | m24 | 15a |
| Zorgo, Burkina | F9 | 64 |
| Zorita, Spain | F6 | 16 |
| Zorkül', ozero, l., Asia | B5 | 44 |
| Zorritos, Peru | I2 | 84 |
| Zouar, Chad | D4 | 56 |
| Zouérat, Maur. | I4 | 62 |
| Zouping, China | G5 | 32 |
| Zourma, Burkina | F9 | 64 |
| Zrenjanin, Yugo. | D4 | 20 |
| Zriba, Tun. | M5 | 18 |
| Zuata, stm., Ven. | C10 | 84 |
| Zubcov, Russia | E17 | 22 |
| Zubova Pol'ana, Russia | G25 | 22 |
| Zuénoula, C. Iv. | H6 | 64 |
| Zuera, Spain | D11 | 16 |
| Zufār, reg., Oman | F9 | 47 |
| Zug, Switz. | D10 | 13 |
| Zug, state, Switz. | D10 | 13 |
| Zugdidi, Geor. | I6 | 26 |
| Zugersee, l., Switz. | D10 | 13 |
| Zugspitze, mtn., Eur. | H10 | 10 |
| Zuiderzee see IJsselmeer, Neth. | C7 | 12 |
| Zuid-Holland, prov., Neth. | D6 | 12 |
| Zujevka, Russia | F8 | 26 |
| Žukovka, Russia | H16 | 22 |
| Žukovskij, Russia | F21 | 22 |
| Zulia, state, Ven. | B6 | 84 |
| Zulia, stm., S.A. | C6 | 84 |
| Zulueta, Cuba | C5 | 94 |
| Zululand, hist. reg., S. Afr. | F10 | 66 |
| Zumba, Ec. | J3 | 84 |
| Zumbo, Moz. | E6 | 58 |
| Zumbro, stm., Mn., U.S. | F3 | 110 |
| Zumbrota, Mn., U.S. | F3 | 110 |
| Zungeru, Nig. | G13 | 64 |
| Zungur, Nig. | G14 | 64 |
| Zuni, N.M., U.S. | I8 | 120 |
| Zuni, stm., U.S. | J7 | 120 |
| Zunyi, China | F8 | 30 |
| Zuodeng, China | C9 | 40 |
| Zuoz, Switz. | E12 | 13 |
| Zūq Muṣbiḥ, Leb. | A5 | 50 |
| Zürayghat, Sau. Ar. | H6 | 48 |
| Zurich, On., Can. | G14 | 110 |
| Zürich, Switz. | D10 | 13 |
| Zürich, state, Switz. | D10 | 13 |
| Zürichsee, l., Switz. | D10 | 13 |
| Zuru, Nig. | F12 | 64 |
| Zutphen, Neth. | D9 | 12 |
| Zuwārah, Libya | B3 | 56 |
| Zuwayzā, Jord. | E5 | 50 |
| Zvenigorod, Russia | F19 | 22 |
| Zvishavane, Zimb. | C10 | 66 |
| Zvolen, Slvk. | G19 | 10 |
| Zvornik, Bos. | E3 | 20 |
| Zwedru, Lib. | G5 | 54 |
| Zweibrücken, Ger. | F7 | 10 |
| Zweisimmen, Switz. | E8 | 13 |
| Zwettl, Aus. | G15 | 10 |
| Zwickau, Ger. | E12 | 10 |
| Zwiesel, Ger. | F13 | 10 |
| Zwijndrecht, Neth. | E6 | 12 |
| Zwolle, La., U.S. | K3 | 114 |
| Zwolle, Neth. | C9 | 12 |
| Zymoetz, stm., B.C., Can. | C6 | 102 |
| Zyr'anovsk, Kaz. | H8 | 28 |
| Żyrardów, Pol. | C20 | 10 |
| Žytkavičy, Bela. | I10 | 22 |
| Żywiec, Pol. | F19 | 10 |